Standards-Based Reform and Students with Disabilities: Creating True Access to the General Education Curriculum

Margaret McLaughlin, Ph.D., Associate Director, Institute for the Study of Exceptional Children and Youth, University of Maryland; Principal Investigator, Educational Policy Reform Research Institute

Dr. McLaughlin discussed policies that encompass standards-driven reform and some of the challenges/tensions in implementing this reform, specifically in the area of access to the general education curriculum.

McLaughlin began by reiterating the statement made by Dr. Danielson regarding the confusion surrounding the meaning of "access to the general education curriculum," particularly when the different educational needs of various students are considered. According to McLaughlin, many educators find this term ambiguous, and policy clarification is needed. McLaughlin remarked that reform that is bringing curriculum access to students with disabilities is driven by a need and a desire to increase the achievement of all students, including these students.

Curriculum content and performance standards are the core of the standards-based reform initiative. Questions regarding what to teach and what levels of mastery to expect are central to standards-based reform. These questions are reflected in the various assessments that have been developed and the accountability measures that states and districts are implementing. Until recently, school governance has not been a major part of standards-driven reform in terms of "who decides what gets taught to whom under what conditions." However, the issue of *who* decides what happens in school is central to implementation of standards-based reform. Determining the content has been both a political and consensus process, with little research to support either what is included in the standards, or the rationale for setting particular criteria.

"Even today, there are some who say, 'This too will pass. We are going to get sick of this in few years.' If you still believe that in 2002, we are in serious trouble," McLaughlin said, indicating that it is important to look at the broader context. Putting the standards-based reform movement in historical context, McLaughlin described three "eras" of educational reform in America: (1) *public* education, (2) *access* to public education, and (3) *adequate* public education for all. The most significant of these eras was the public education era, during which the concept of universal public education emerged. During that era, though, access to public education was limited and often segregated. Next, educators attempted to create equal access for everyone. In the latter part of 20th century, discussion has turned to the importance of an adequate education for all students. The focus on standards emerged from this emphasis on an adequate education.

To understand the impact of the standards-based reform movement on students with disabilities, it is useful to first consider the intent to this movement. McLaughlin indicated that:

- Standards are at the core of educational reform and are the chief strategy for achieving equity.
- Standards are intended to change what and how teachers teach. Many teachers are frustrated because they can no longer teach what they believe needs to be taught.
- Assessments and accountability are the strategies for achieving standards.

- There is a critical need to distinguish between content standards and performance standards. Content standards are the "what" and performance standards are the "how well." Content standards have been created through a process of consensus, often through political committees that may or may not have adequate representation from educators.

Special educators, like other educators, may have concerns about content standards—why they have to teach that content. These concerns may result from the teacher's lack of knowledge about student capabilities and/or effective instructional strategies. Unfortunately, when teachers are unclear about effective instructional strategies or when they hold low expectations of students, students may not have opportunities to demonstrate their abilities. However, given the opportunity to learn content, many students can learn it. This is a key challenge that manifests itself through the IEP.

McLaughlin noted that the curriculum that many students with disabilities access is very focused on academic subject manner (reading, math, and science), in part because of the demands of standards testing. However, in an effort to do "macho standards setting" with higher expectations for student achievement, the content in particular subject areas has increased dramatically and the pace of instruction has increased to cover the subject matter. Often teachers feel as if they are on a treadmill with no time for activities such as reinforcement and reteaching. This affects students with disabilities and other students as well. Educators still need to reexamine the curriculum standards and gain a better understanding of the role of non-academic standards that relate to needed "life" skills.

The interdisciplinary content that is a part of standards-based reform requires greater collaboration. Science, math, and other content specialists must collaborate more with special educators to take advantage of the knowledge and strengths of each professional. At the elementary level, where the content knowledge is more general, this is not particularly problematic. However, at the secondary level, where advanced knowledge is required in chemistry and algebra, for example, this often breaks down. We need to examine expectations of teachers and preservice training to see if teachers are given adequate preparation in light of this emerging need.

When planning how to assist students in meeting the higher standards that are required, educators need to understand the distinction between accommodations and modifications. Accommodations are supports or services provided to help a student access the curriculum, whereas modifications change the content and performance expectations. In the past, the emphasis has been on modifying the curriculum (e.g., by reducing the amount of content or changing the level of the books used), which can result in denying the student access to the general education curriculum.

To assist students in meeting the expectations of the general education curriculum, McLaughlin suggested aligning the students' special education needs with a curriculum continuum (Figure 2). Most students should be expected to access the general education curriculum with no accommodations or modifications. Some students will need accommodations to master curriculum content. And a smaller number of students will need curriculum modifications that might include expanded or differential instruction and curriculum goals. The goal should be to move an increasing number of students out of the modified curriculum and into the general education end of the continuum by offering accommodations. Success in access should be measured by the number of students who participate in the general education curriculum.

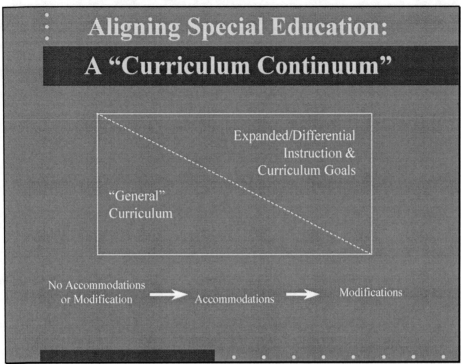

Figure 2. Aligning Special Education: "A Curriculum Continuum"

Despite the flaws inherent in the standards-based reform movement, McLaughlin views standards as a vehicle for defining an "appropriate" education for each child. However, the concept of "appropriate" must be driven by a standard that the student can be expected to master. Another strength of this movement is that standards create a consistency in the curriculum and further a shared language among all educators.

As standards are implemented, several policy and practice challenges must be addressed, including:
- Aligning the concepts of common content and performance standards, assessments, and accountability with the legal mandate for "individualized" education.
- Aligning standards, curricula, and IEPs.
- Building professional capacity—there is an incredible need to build teachers' and administrators' understanding of what access means, as well as when accommodations versus modifications in the curriculum are being made.

McLaughlin closed by saying that access to the general education curriculum is probably the most significant provision of the 1997 IDEA amendments. It will lead to a new understanding of what the term "appropriate" means and of the role of special education.

State Policies That Impact Access to the General Curriculum

Martha Minow, Ed.M., J.D., Professor, Harvard Law School; Co-Director on Policy, NCAC

Professor Minow described results from a NCAC policy study of curriculum access that was conducted in nine states.

Professor Minow presented key findings from a two-year state policy study on access to the general education curriculum for children with disabilities. The study examined the ways in which state and district policies affect actual practice. She acknowledged that although there are problems with the defining "appropriate," the IDEA legislation as defined in 1997 does state that "free appropriate education" for students with disabilities involves:

- Individualized services based on unique needs, not disability category. This represents a change in idea but not in practice.
- High expectations and meaningful access to the general education curriculum for every student. High expectations are a crucial ingredient in student performance.

The 1997 IDEA amendments include the vision of the "least restrictive environment," which requires: (1) teacher training and (2) related services, such as speech assistance, psychological services, physical therapy, and simple medical services. Under the IDEA amendments, a child with a disability is to be removed from the regular education environment when "the nature or severity of the disability is such that education in regular classes with the use of supplementary aids and services cannot be achieved satisfactorily." The amendments tilted access toward the mainstream classroom and represent a direct change in policy, although it is unclear how much practice has changed since the amendments were passed by Congress.

The amendments also sought "to ensure access of the child to the general curriculum so that he or she can meet the educational standards within the jurisdiction . . . that apply to all children." In addition, the amendments' vision includes non-discriminatory procedures to identify and place students with disabilities (although this vision is not the reality), and parental participation.

The NCAC study focused on nine states: California, Connecticut, Florida, Kentucky, Massachusetts, Minnesota, New Jersey, New York, and Texas. Its major finding was that little is known about the implementation of the law. The study revealed four general concerns across the states:

- Categorical placement of students;
- Frequent inclusion of students in mainstream classrooms without necessary supports, teacher training, or related services;
- Racial and gender disproportion in identification and placement of students (differences between minorities versus whites and boys versus girls); and
- Inadequate notification of parents (i.e., parents are not informed of their rights and role).

Among the conclusions reached from this policy study were that changes in policies and procedures in these areas could greatly enhance the achievement of students with disabilities.

Including Students with Special Needs

A Practical Guide for Classroom Teachers

Marilyn Friend
William D. Bursuck

Custom Edition

Taken from:
Including Students with Special Needs: A Practical Guide for Classroom Teachers, Fifth Edition
by Marilyn Friend and William D. Bursuck

Custom Publishing

New York   Boston   San Francisco
London   Toronto   Sydney   Tokyo   Singapore   Madrid
Mexico City   Munich   Paris   Cape Town   Hong Kong   Montreal

Cover Art: Courtesy of PhotoDisc/Getty Images.

Taken from:

Including Students with Special Needs: A Practical Guide for Classroom Teachers, Fifth Edition
by Marilyn Friend and William D. Bursuck
Copyright © 2009, 2006, 2002, 1999, 1996 by Pearson Education, Inc.
Published by Prentice Hall
Upper Saddle River, New Jersey 07458

This special edition published in cooperation with Pearson Custom Publishing.

Printed in the United States of America

14 15 16 V092 16 15 14 13 12

2009220040

DC

Pearson
Custom Publishing
is a division of

PEARSON

www.pearsonhighered.com

ISBN 10: 0-558-20745-6
ISBN 13: 978-0-558-20745-8

To Beth and Bruce

*our spouses and often unacknowledged collaborators—
for their support of our work, understanding of
our unkept promises ("just a couple more hours
and this chapter will be finished—promise"),
and patience with our need to try out new ideas
or express our frustration by sharing it with
someone else, who usually ends up being you.*

About the Authors

Marilyn Friend has worked in the field of education in a variety of roles for over 30 years. In addition to teaching in both special education and general education, she has worked as a teacher educator and staff developer and currently is a professor in the Department of Specialized Education Services at the University of North Carolina at Greensboro. Her particular areas of expertise—the focus of her research, teaching, writing, and work in the field—include inclusive schooling, co-teaching and other collaborative school practices, and family–school partnerships.

William Bursuck began his career as a general education teacher, and as a special education teacher and university teacher educator he has maintained an active interest in inclusive practices, publishing numerous research articles, successfully obtaining grants to conduct research, and publishing two books. Dr. Bursuck takes particular pleasure in providing classroom and future teachers with practical, evidence-based strategies to improve educational outcomes for students with special needs in this age of teacher accountability. He is a professor in the Department of Specialized Education Services at the University of North Carolina at Greensboro.

Brief Contents

Contents

CHAPTER 4   Assessing Student Needs   114

CHAPTER 5

Planning Instruction by Analyzing Classroom and Student Needs   150

CHAPTER 6

Students with Low-Incidence Disabilities   194

Students with High-Incidence Disabilities   240

CHAPTER **Students with Special Needs
Other Than Disabilities**   **272**

CHAPTER **Differentiating Instruction**   **316**

CHAPTER *10* Strategies for Independent Learning 364

CHAPTER *11*

Evaluating Student Learning   404

CHAPTER 12 Responding to Student Behavior 438

Features at a Glance

Features at a Glance (*continued*)

Preface

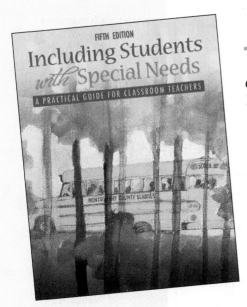

The early part of the twenty-first century has been a tumultuous time for public schools. Several years have now passed since the passage of the No Child Left Behind Act (NCLB) and the reauthorizaton of the Individuals with Disabilities Education Improvement Act (IDEA), both crucial pieces of legislation that have changed the direction of education. The goal of providing access to nearly all students, including those with disabilities and other special needs, to a single curriculum and usually in the general education setting still is viewed as challenging, complex, and controversial. Like all students, those who struggle to learn because of intellectual, physical, sensory, emotional, communication, or learning disabilities or other special needs are to be taught using research-based practices, and they are expected to reach the same high standards as all students. Importantly, teachers, administrators, and other professionals are more accountable than ever for ensuring that these lofty goals are accomplished.

In many ways, these legislative educational mandates are an extension of the beliefs that have provided the foundation for *Including Students with Special Needs: A Practical Guide for Classroom Teachers* since its first edition. In the fifth edition, we have had the opportunity more than ever before to integrate today's expectations for students with our own continued strong commitment to inclusive practices, a commitment tempered by our knowledge and experience of the realities of day-to-day teaching. We know that teachers cannot do the job themselves; they must also have strong and sustained administrative support and the resources required to transform ideas from thoughts to effective actions. We wish we could guarantee that all the pieces would be in place to accomplish the goals, but that is beyond our abilities. What we can do is provide for the general education teachers and others who have increasing responsibility for instructing students with disabilities or other special needs a firm grounding in special education practices, an understanding of the professionals who support these students and the procedures followed to ensure their rights are upheld, and a wealth of research-based strategies and interventions that can foster their success.

We have brought to this project our own backgrounds as teachers in the field and as teacher educators, researchers, and staff developers. We also bring our own diversity: Marilyn with expertise in elementary and secondary education, especially in urban settings, and in collaboration, inclusive practices, and co-teaching; Bill with expertise in secondary education, literacy, instructional strategies, assessment, and grading practices. The organization of the book and the amount of space devoted to various topics and subtopics reflect our priorities for preparing general education teachers to instruct effectively all the students they will encounter. These priorities are based on our research, our analysis of the research and scholarly literature on instruction and teacher preparation and professional development, and our experiences in teaching undergraduate and graduate educators as well as teacher educators. Our understanding, though, always has as its base our many conversations with general education and special education teachers who are diligently working, often in difficult circumstances and in spite of public criticism, to make a true difference in the lives of their students. We hope that we have managed to "get it right" and that our book has the right blend of being reader friendly while being informative and research-based. Above all, we hope this fifth edition is responsive to the many issues confronting teachers as they attempt to help all their students succeed.

New to the Fifth Edition

- Chapter 1 includes updated information on the **No Child Left Behind Act** and **IDEA 2004** as well as a revised discussion of inclusive practices framed in the context of current school reform initiatives.

- Chapter 2 introduces the concept of **response to intervention** as an alternative to traditional approaches for determining whether students have learning disabilities. It places increased emphasis on **parents' rights in making decisions** regarding their children who may have disabilities.

- Chapter 3 includes updated examples that illustrate the **increasing importance of professional collaboration** in the delivery of special education services. It now directly addresses the complexity of collaboration when disagreements occur, especially those between school professionals and parents.

- Chapter 4 includes fully updated information about the **participation of students with disabilities in high-stakes tests.** Response to intervention information is picked up here from Chapter 2 and more in-depth attention is devoted to it in this chapter.

- Chapter 5 presents updated information about the concepts of **differentiated instruction** and **universal design** and how they apply to including students with special needs. It also continues the discussion of RTI as an option for determining the presence of learning disability.

- Chapter 6 contains an increased focus on the topic of **autism spectrum disorders.** Another chapter revision is updated information concerning the use of technology to meet the needs of students with disabilities.

- Chapter 7 includes **updates to the definitions of learning disabilities and emotional disturbance** as well as to the popular Professional Edge features on controversial therapies and dyslexia.

- Chapter 8 includes updated coverage of **attention deficit–hyperactivity disorder** and the best ways to accommodate students with ADHD in the general education classroom. It also includes extensive updated statistics about the many **students who are at risk for school failure.**

- Chapter 9 has been retitled "Differentiating Instruction," and many practical examples of **differentiating instruction** for students in elementary, middle, and high schools are included.

- The topic of **writing,** introduced in Chapter 9, receives additional attention in Chapter 10, a revision designed to address professionals' increased concern and the evolving emphasis placed on writing in today's assessments.

- The already comprehensive section on **grading** in Chapter 11 has been thoroughly updated—important because grading is a common concern among general educators in inclusive schools.

- In addition to many updated references and readings, Chapter 12 is now based on **positive behavior supports.** It includes a checklist to guide readers through the steps of developing an **effective behavior intervention plan.**

- Chapter 13 has been updated with several new features. One of these is a set of websites that can assist teachers in **addressing student social skills.** Another is **advice from middle school students on enhancing the social integration** of students with disabilities in inclusive classrooms.
- The **margin notes** provide extensive updated research, websites, and data about students with disabilities and other special needs.
- Many of the **additional readings** at the end of each chapter have been revised so that they are as up to date as possible.

*O*rganization of the Book

The textbook is divided into four main sections. The first section provides fundamental background knowledge about the field of special education as well as current information on how students with disabilities are served within inclusive school environments. **Chapter 1** outlines key concepts for understanding special education, including provisions of the current reauthorization of IDEA. **Chapter 2** introduces the people who specialize in working with students with disabilities and the procedures through which students may be identified to receive special education services. **Chapter 3** discusses the principles of collaboration and the school situations in which professionals are most likely to collaborate to meet the needs of students with disabilities.

The second section of the book provides a framework for thinking about effective instructional practices for students who struggle to learn. **Chapter 4** explores both formal and informal assessment strategies that help teachers contribute to the decision-making process for students with disabilities. **Chapter 5** introduces INCLUDE, a step-by-step strategy for making instructional adjustments that helps teachers accommodate students with special needs in a more deliberate way. Reminders about using the INCLUDE strategy appear in all the remaining chapters of the book. This chapter also addresses the dimensions along which accommodations can occur.

The third section of the book introduces readers to students with specific disabilities and other special needs. **Chapters 6 and 7** address the various federally established categories of exceptionality and provide information about them essential for general education teachers in today's schools. **Chapter 8** considers students who may not receive special education but who nonetheless are at risk for school failure. However, the overall approach taken in these chapters (and in the text as a whole) is noncategorical. Even though students with disabilities or other special needs are unique, they share many physical, psychological, learning, and behavior characteristics, and they often benefit from similar instructional approaches.

The material in the fourth section of the text represents the heart of any course on inclusive practices: instructional approaches that emphasize teaching students effectively both in academic and in social and behavior areas, regardless of disability or special need. **Chapter 9** provides strategies for differentiating instruction for both basic skills and content-area instruction. The emphasis is on feasible approaches to differentiation. **Chapter 10** focuses on ways to help students with and without special needs become more independent learners by teaching them specific strategies. **Chapter 11** explores ways to evaluate classroom performance while ensuring that information gathered for diverse learners is accurate and helpful in guiding instruction. In **Chapter 12,** readers learn approaches for using positive approaches to address both minor and significant behavior challenges sometimes displayed by students. These strategies are applicable to a wide range of learners, not just those with disabilities. Finally, **Chapter 13** explores several approaches for building positive relations among students with and without special needs.

Features in This Edition

Every chapter of this text includes features designed to help readers learn more effectively, as well as to add to the general discussion in-depth information about topics such as teaching strategies, cultural diversity, and technology:

- **Learning Objectives** are listed at the start of each chapter as an organizational and study tool for readers.

- **Chapter-opening vignettes** serve as introductory cases to help readers think about how the content of chapters relates to teachers and students. They conclude with critical-thinking questions. These cases serve as examples throughout the chapters and are revisited in the Back to the Cases feature at the end of each chapter. The opening vignettes have been designed to introduce novice educators to the very real and sometimes complex needs of students.

- **Professional Edge** features provide numerous research-validated, practical teaching applications related to each chapter's topics. For example, Chapter 1 includes a checklist that educators can use to reflect on their level of cultural competence for working with their diverse learners.

- **Case in Practice** features clarify key principles by providing brief case studies related to chapter concepts and teaching scripts as models. Chapter 11, for example, has a new case about the fairness of differentiated grading, a much-discussed topic in the field.

- **Technology Notes** features illustrate the application of many types of technology available to support students with disabilities in inclusive schools. In Chapter 9, research on the effectiveness of the latest computer software on improving the writing skills of students with disabilities provides teachers with the most current information.

  - **Special Emphasis On . . .** features highlight topics related to nonacademic areas (for example, the arts, physical education, and counseling) that are frequently overlooked in other texts. These features also provide up-to-date information on addressing the needs of students from diverse backgrounds and English-language learners. Chapter 1, for example, includes ideas for physical educators working with students with disabilities.

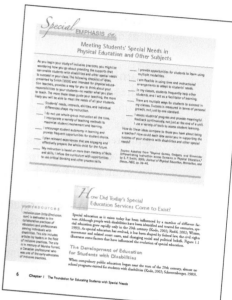

- **Working Together** features present cases in which professional and family collaboration is needed and provide tips for optimizing collaborative efforts. The Chapter 12 Working Together includes an example of what may occur when parents and professionals disagree.

  - **Marginal annotations** are designed to stimulate higher-level thinking and provide additional information on cultural and linguistic diversity, research, and useful websites. They provide readers access to the most current research related to teaching students with disabilities.
  - **Chapter summaries** review key information covered in each chapter for easy synthesis and reference.
  - **Back to the Cases** features revisit the chapter-opening vignettes within the context of relevant INTASC Principles and CEC Content Standards to illustrate the application of those principles and standards. Questions and activities help provide context for understanding the standards.

- **Applications in Teaching Practice** cases and activities at the end of each chapter are designed to encourage students to apply the chapter contents to real-life classroom situations.

- **Key Terms and Concepts** are listed at the end of each chapter and are high-lighted throughout the text with boldface type. They are explained with easy-to-understand definitions provided both in context and in a glossary at the back of the book.

- **Further Readings** offer students the opportunity to delve more deeply into some of the topics addressed in each chapter. In Chapter 8, for example, contemporary readings are included to extend learning on ADHD, poverty, and the expectations teachers set for all their students.

Supplements

The following supplements provide an outstanding array of resources that facilitate learning about students with disabilities and their families. For more information, ask your local Pearson Higher Education Sales Representative or contact the Allyn & Bacon Merrill Faculty Field Support Department at 1-800-526-0485.

For troubleshooting or compatibility questions on our technology products, please contact technical support directly at 1-800-677-6337 or http://247.pearsoned.com.

Resources for Instructors

- **Instructor's Resource Manual.** The Instructor's Resource Manual includes a wealth of interesting ideas and activities designed to help instructors teach the course. Each chapter includes a chapter-at-a-glance grid, instructor's overview and outline, activities and discussion questions, Internet resources, suggested readings, Internet assignments, handouts, and appendices. (Please request this item from your local Pearson Education sales representative; also available for download from the Instructor Resource Center at www.pearsonhighered.com/irc.)

- **Test Bank.** The Test Bank includes almost 900 questions, including multiple choice, true/false, matching, and essay questions. Page references to the main text, suggested answers, and skill types as well as correlations to Praxis principles and CEC Standards have been added to each question to help instructors create and evaluate student tests. (Please request this item from your local Pearson Education sales representative; also available for download from the Instructor Resource Center at www.pearsonhighered.com/irc.)

- **Computerized Test Bank.** The printed Test Bank is also available electronically through the Allyn & Bacon computerized testing system, TestGen. Instructors can use TestGen to create exams in just minutes by selecting from the existing database of questions, editing questions, and/or writing original questions. (Please request this item from your local Pearson Education sales representative; also available for download from the Instructor Resource Center at www.pearsonhighered.com/irc.)

- **PowerPoint™ Presentation.** Ideal for lecture presentations or student handouts, the PowerPoint™ Presentation created for this text provides dozens of ready-to-use graphic and text images. (Available for download from the Instructor Resource Center at www.pearsonhighered.com/irc.)

- **Allyn & Bacon Transparencies for Special Education, 2008.** A set of 100 acetate transparencies related to topics in the text. (Please request this item from your local Pearson Education sales representative; also available for download from the Instructor Resource Center at www.pearsonhighered.com/irc.)

- **Videotapes for Lecture Presentation.** These videos provide a way to bring video into your course for maximized learning.

  Snapshots: Inclusion Video (22 minutes in length) profiles three students of differing ages with various levels of disability in inclusive class settings. In each case, parents, classroom teachers, special education teachers, and school administrators talk about the steps they have taken to help the students succeed in inclusive settings.

  Snapshots II: Learning Disabilities, Mental Retardation, Emotional or Behavioral Disorders and *Snapshots II: Hearing Impairment, Visual Impairment, Traumatic Brain Injury* (20–25 minutes in length) is a two-video set of six segments designed specifically for use in college classrooms. Each segment profiles three individuals and their families, teachers, and experiences. These programs are of high interest to students. Instructors who have used the tapes in their courses have found that they help in disabusing students of stereotypical viewpoints and put a "human face" on the course material.

  Professionals in Action Videotape: Teaching Students with Special Needs (120 minutes in length) consists of five 15–30 minute modules presenting viewpoints and approaches to teaching students with various disabilities in general education classrooms, separate education settings, and various combinations of the two. Each module explores its topic via actual classroom footage and interviews with general and special education teachers, parents, and students themselves.

Resources for Students

PEARSON
myeducationlab
Where the Classroom Comes to Life

Your Class. Your Career. Everyone's Future.

MyEducationLab (www.myeducationlab.com) is a research-based learning tool that brings teaching to life. Through authentic in-class video footage, interactive simulations, rich case studies, examples of authentic teacher and student work, and more, MyEducationLab prepares you for your teaching career by showing what quality instruction looks like.

MyEducationLab is easy to use! In the textbook, look for the MyEducationLab logo in the margins and follow the simple link instructions to access the multimedia **"Homework & Exercises"** and **"Building Teaching Skills"** assignments in MyEducationLab that correspond with the chapter content. Homework & Exercises offer opportunities to understand content more deeply and to practice applying content. Building Teaching Skills assignments help you practice and strengthen skills that are essential to quality teaching through your analysis and response to student and teacher instructional encounters and artifacts.

The rich, thoughtful, and interactive elements you will encounter throughout MyEducationLab include:

- **Individualized Study Plan.** You have the opportunity to take tests before and after reading each chapter of the text. The test results automatically generate a personalized study plan for you, identifying areas of the chapter that you should reread to fully understand chapter concepts. You are also presented with interactive multimedia exercises to help ensure your learning. The study plan is designed to help you perform well on exams and to promote deep understanding of chapter content.
- **Video.** The authentic classroom videos in MyEducationLab show how real teachers handle actual classroom situations.
- **Case Studies.** A diverse set of robust cases illustrate the realities of teaching and offer valuable perspectives on common issues and challenges in education.
- **Simulations.** Created by the IRIS Center at Vanderbilt University, these interactive simulations give you hands-on practice at adapting instruction for a full spectrum of learners.
- **Readings.** Specially selected, topically relevant articles from ASCD's renowned *Educational Leadership* journal expand and enrich your perspectives on key issues and topics.
- **Student & Teacher Artifacts.** Authentic preK–12 student and teacher classroom artifacts are tied to course topics and offer you practice in working with the actual types of materials you will encounter daily as teachers.
- **Lesson & Portfolio Builders.** With this effective and easy-to-use tool, you can create, update, and share standards-based lesson plans and portfolios.

Acknowledgments

We know that we are very fortunate to be surrounded by people who are committed to helping us in our work. We are grateful to the many individuals who helped us during the preparation of the fifth edition of *Including Students with Special Needs.* Without their assistance and encouragement the project undoubtedly would have stalled. First and most important, we express our gratitude to our families. They have listened to us worry about how to meet the deadlines that sometimes seemed impossibly near, agonize over which new material to add and which existing material to delete, and obsess about the material to include in the book as well as that which must be relegated to the "maybe next time" file. They helped us sort through the conundrums, offered suggestions with the perspective of outsiders who deeply cared, and tolerated our need to hide in our offices as we wrote and rewrote. We cannot possibly say thank you in enough ways for their support.

We also thank the individuals who helped us with all the details that are necessary in writing a textbook. Graduate assistants DeAnna Hurley-Chamberlain, Cynthia Shamberger, and Megan Mimms confidently said "I can do that" when asked to find obscure bits of information, proofread, and check references. Sonia Martin, department administrative assistant at University of North Carolina at Greensboro, assisted in checking the manuscript for accuracy, including making sure all the references were included and any typos corrected. We especially thank her for lending a sympathetic ear as we worked through many moments of deadline stress. Through it all, she kept the essential ingredient of humor in the mix of our work.

The professionals at Allyn & Bacon also have supported this effort with both words and actions. Executive Editor Virginia Lanigan has steered this fifth edition through the many steps of its creation, offering guidance and encouragement with just the right touch of patience. Developmental Editor Alicia Reilly was, as always, meticulous in her efforts to keep the book clear, responsive to the needs of the field, and on target with the correct number of pages—and she demonstrated once again that nagging about deadlines and tasks still awaiting attention can be accomplished in a way that is neither overly intrusive nor offensive. Thanks, Alicia.

Special thanks go to the reviewers for this edition: Melina Alexander, Weber State University; Janetta Fleming Bradley, University of Tennessee at Chattanooga; Jeanne M. Burns, Buffalo State College; Laura B. Carpenter, Auburn University, Montgomery; Martha A. Cocchiarella, Arizona State University; Laurel M. Garrick Duhaney, SUNY New Platz; Joanne Eichinger, University of Rhode Island; J. Jeffrey Grill, Ohio Dominican University; Lisa C. Hanlon, Purdue University; Genevieve Howe Hay, College of Charleston; Gary Meers, University of Nebraska; Jackie Paxton, Arkansas Tech University; Barbara Ray, University of Tennessee at Chattanooga; and Qaisar Sultana, Eastern Kentucky University. We were impressed with the care with which they reviewed the manuscript and the insightful suggestions they made. They definitely helped us create a better textbook.

Finally, we continue to be grateful to all of our colleagues and students who influence our thinking about educating students with special needs in general education classrooms. Their questions about best practices, their challenges to our thinking, and their ideas for better communicating our message have been invaluable. We especially are appreciative of the individuals who have taken the time to correspond with us to share their impressions of the book, their concerns, and their ideas for what we might do the next time to improve our outcomes. We hope they see their influence in the current edition, and they can know with certainty that we continue to welcome their—and all readers'—input.

Including Students
with Special Needs

1

The Foundation for Educating Students with Special Needs

LEARNING *Objectives*

After you read this chapter, you will be able to

1. Explain key terms and concepts that describe special education.
2. Trace the historical events that have shaped contemporary special education services.
3. Outline the laws that govern current practices for educating students with disabilities.
4. Analyze your beliefs related to inclusive practices, taking into account contemporary knowledge and expectations about effective instruction and educational access, as well as parent perspectives.
5. Describe the categories of disabilities addressed in federal law, and identify other special needs your students may have.

Thomas is one of those students who makes his presence known very quickly. He announced on the first day in his seventh-grade social studies class that the color of the walls was *xantho* (yellow). For several days later that fall, he came to school wearing only socks on his feet, because as his mother explained, he had completely outgrown his old shoes but would not wear new, better-fitting ones because he said they "had knots in the toes." In all his classes, Thomas tends to keep to himself, and when group projects are assigned, he has difficulty knowing how to talk to his classmates about anything except the subjects he enjoys—French words commonly used in the English language and Alfred Hitchcock movies. When Thomas began elementary school, he was enrolled in a special education class for students with autism. However, most of his classmates had significant intellectual disabilities, and the teacher and Thomas's parents quickly realized that he needed to be challenged academically in a way that could not happen in that class. Since second grade, he has spent most of his time in general education classrooms. In some situations, a special education teacher worked in his classroom with the general education teacher or a paraprofessional was present to assist the teacher and all the students. Now such support generally is not necessary. Thomas meets with his special education teacher, Ms. Meyer, once each day with several other students who have learning and behavior disabilities to learn strategies related to their schoolwork. If an issue arises in a general education class, Ms. Meyer problem solves with the teacher to address it. Thomas would like to be a linguist when he grows up.

What is autism? Why is it so important for Thomas to access the same curriculum as his peers? What provisions in current laws ensure that Thomas has the right to be educated in general education as much as possible?

Angela is a second-grade student who loves school, has a wide circle of friends, and sometimes displays a stubborn streak. Even before she was born, she was identified as having Down syndrome, a genetic disorder usually accompanied by distinctive physical characteristics (for example, short stature, eyes that slant, heart problems) and a moderate intellectual disability. Angela has always remained in general education for at least part of the day. In kindergarten and first grade, she spent about half the day with other kindergarteners while receiving additional support in a special education classroom. This year, she is enrolled in an innovative language arts program: She receives reading skill instruction in the special education classroom, but she participates in the literature program in the general education classroom. Angela is thrilled to be "reading" the same books as her second-grade classmates. Angela's guardian is her grandmother, Ms. Costas; her mother was 19 years old when Angela was born and left a note soon after saying that she just couldn't face raising a baby with special needs by herself. Ms. Costas is a deeply religious woman and believes Angela was born in order to positively affect the lives of those around her. Ms. Costas is grateful for the support school professionals have provided to Angela, and she works closely with them to continue Angela's school success.

How likely are you to teach a student like Angela? What is an intellectual disability? What factors have led students like Angela to be educated in typical classrooms instead of special education classrooms?

Aaron has a learning disability that was identified when he was in second grade. He also takes medication for attention deficit–hyperactivity disorder (ADHD). Now in eleventh grade, Aaron is continuing to learn how to compensate for the academic difficulties he experiences. Although he is a bright and personable young man, he reads at about a seventh-grade level, and his writing is much like that of a student in second grade. He doesn't like to talk about his learning disabilities (LD); he doesn't want other students to make fun of him or treat him differently because he's LD. He is even more sensitive when asked to talk about why he takes medication. Even though his doctor has cautioned him to take the medication exactly as prescribed, he sometimes secretly skips taking it to see if he can get along without it. In his U.S. history class, Aaron is most successful on tests when he answers questions orally; he understands the concepts even if he sometimes cannot write his thoughts. Because he doesn't like to be singled out, however, he sometimes refuses to take tests or get additional assistance during study period, so his grades are lower than they could be. Aaron is an excellent athlete, and on the basketball court, he feels equal to his friends. However, his parents are concerned that his interest in sports is distracting him from schoolwork.

■ *How often will you meet students like Aaron? What is a learning disability? What types of supports and services do Aaron and other students with LD need to succeed in school?*

www.**r**esources

A website devoted to individuals with disabilities is Special Education Resources on the Internet (SERI) at www.seriweb .com. Topics to explore on the site include legal resources, parent resources, medical resources, and specific disability categories.

Students like Thomas, Angela, and Aaron are not unusual. They are among the 5.9 million school-age students in the United States who have disabilities that make them eligible for special education (U.S. Department of Education, 2004b). But their disabilities do not tell you who they are: They are children or young adults and students first. Like all students, they have positive characteristics and negative ones, they have great days and not-so-great days, and they have likes and dislikes about school and learning.

As a teacher, you probably will instruct students like Thomas, Angela, and Aaron along with other students with disabilities or other special needs. The purpose of this book is to help you understand these students and learn strategies for addressing their needs. You can be the teacher who makes a profound positive difference in a student's life. With the knowledge and skills you learn for teaching learners with exceptional needs, you will be prepared for both the challenges and the rewards of helping them achieve their potential.

What Key Terms and Concepts Define Special Education?

When professionals talk about students like Thomas, Angela, and Aaron, they may use several key terms. For example, when teachers refer to students with *disabilities,* they mean students who are eligible to receive special education services according to federal and state guidelines. **Special education** is the specially designed instruction provided by the school district or other local education agency that meets the unique needs of students identified as disabled according to federal and state eligibility criteria. Special education may include instruction in a general education or special education classroom, education in the community for students who need to learn life and work skills, and specialized assistance in areas such as physical education and vocational preparation. Students with disabilities also may receive **related services,** that is, assistance required to enable students to benefit from special education. Examples of related services include speech/language therapy, transportation to and from school in a specialized van or school bus, and physical therapy. Additionally, students with disabilities are entitled to **supplementary aids and services.** In other words, they must receive supports such as preferential seating, access to computer technology, and instructional adjustments that enable them to be educated with their peers who do not have disabilities. All special education, related services, and supplementary aids and services are provided to students by public schools at no cost to parents.

Reading Homework Exercise

Go to the Homework and Exercises section in Chapter 1 of MyEducationLab and look at the booklet "What Every Teacher Should Know about IDEA 2004 and Regulations" to find definitions of key terms used in special education.

Least Restrictive Environment

As you read this textbook and complete the activities designed for your course, you will learn many important facts and skills related to working with students with disabilities. However, one of the most important concepts for you to understand as a general educator is **least restrictive environment (LRE),** a provision in the federal laws that have governed special education for more than three decades. The LRE provision guarantees a student's right to be educated in the setting most like that for peers without disabilities in which the student can be successful with appropriate supports provided (Burstein, Sears, Wilcoxen, Cabello, & Spagna, 2004; Karger, 2004; Palley, 2006). For many students, the least restrictive environment is full-time or nearly full-time participation in a general education classroom. In fact, in 2002–2003, approximately 48.2 percent of all school-age students with disabilities received 79 percent or more of their education in general education classrooms (U.S. Department of Education, 2004b). This is true

> The LRE provision guarantees a student's right to be educated in the setting most like that for peers without disabilities in which the student can be successful with appropriate supports provided.

for Thomas, Angela, and Aaron, who were introduced at the beginning of this chapter. Thomas and Angela also receive instruction in a special education classroom each day. Aaron, who can succeed in social studies class when he gives test answers aloud, may leave his classroom for that purpose only. His LRE is a general education classroom; the test procedure is a supplementary service.

For some students—for example, some who have emotional or behavioral disabilities or autism—being in a general education classroom nearly all day may be academically and emotionally inappropriate. For these students, the LRE may be a general education classroom for part of the day and a special education classroom, sometimes called a *resource room,* for the remainder of the day. Yet other students' LRE may be a special education setting for most of the day, sometimes referred to as a *self-contained class.* Students with significant behavior problems and students who require intensive supports may be educated in this way. Finally, just a few students with disabilities attend separate or residential schools or learn in a home or hospital setting. These very restrictive options usually are necessary only for students with the most significant or complex disabilities.

Identifying an LRE other than a general education setting is a serious decision that usually is made by a team of professionals and a student's parents only after intensive supports have been provided in the general education classroom without success. These supports can include alternative materials or curriculum, assistance from a paraprofessional (that is, a teaching assistant) or a special education teacher, adaptive equipment such as a computer, or consultative assistance from a psychologist or counselor. Alternatively, a few students' needs are so great that a setting outside general education is the only one considered. Chapter 2 presents more detail about the range of LRE settings

DIMENSIONS OF

diversity

Issues related to race and culture continue to exist in special education. Even after more than 30 years of study, litigation, and other attention, African American students, when considered in terms of their representation among all students, are still overrepresented in special education, especially in the categories of learning disabilities and intellectual disabilities.

The concept of inclusive practices implies that students are more alike than different and that all students are welcomed members of their learning communities.

considered for students with disabilities. Here, the points to remember are that the LRE for most students with disabilities is general education and that you, as a professional educator, have a crucial role to play in these students' education.

Mainstreaming

When the LRE concept became part of special education laws during the 1970s, the LRE for most students with disabilities was a part-time or full-time special education class. When such students were permitted to participate in general education, it was called mainstreaming. **Mainstreaming** involves placing students with disabilities in general education settings only when they can meet traditional academic expectations with minimal assistance or when those expectations are not relevant (for example, participation only in recess or school assemblies for access to social interactions with peers). In most locales, *mainstreaming* now is considered a dated term and has been replaced with the phrase *inclusive practices,* which is explained in the next section. However, as you participate in field experiences and speak to experienced educators, you may find that in some schools, the vocabulary of inclusion is used, but the practices implemented seem more like mainstreaming. That is, teachers may say that their school is inclusive but then explain that students like Aaron, featured in the beginning of the chapter, need to be in separate classes because of their below-grade reading levels. This practice is actually mainstreaming.

Inclusive Practices

Over the past two decades, the entire structure of special education services has undergone significant change. Although federal law continues to stipulate that a range of settings must be made available to meet the needs of students with disabilities, many educators now seriously question the assumption that students who need more intensive services should routinely receive them in a restrictive setting such as a special education classroom

Analyze
and Reflect

Mainstreaming was an early interpretation of LRE. Schools today emphasize inclusive practices. How are these two concepts different? How might inclusive practices change the structure of schools and the roles of teachers, administrators, and even students and their families?

(for example, Connor & Ferri, 2007; Downing & Eichinger, 2003; Fitch, 2003; Simpson, deBoer-Ott, & Smith-Myles, 2003). These educators stress that in the past, many students with disabilities were only temporary guests in general education classrooms and that few efforts were made to provide assistance so they could be successfully educated with their nondisabled peers (for example, Artiles, Harris-Murri, & Rostenberg, 2006). These educators also contend that all or most supports for students with disabilities can be provided effectively in general education classrooms when teachers are prepared to work with such students and related concerns are addressed (McLeskey & Waldron, 2007a; Wolf & Hall, 2003). They further maintain that if students cannot meet traditional academic expectations, the expectations should be changed, not the setting. These educators reject the mainstreaming assumption that the setting dictates the type and intensity of services, and they support instead the concept of inclusive practices (Roach & Salisbury, 2006). The concept **inclusive practices** is founded on the belief or philosophy that students with disabilities should be fully integrated into their school learning communities, usually in general education classrooms, and that their instruction should be based on their abilities, not their disabilities. Inclusive practices have three dimensions:

> The concept of inclusive practices implies that all learners are welcomed at their schools and that they are seen as the responsibility of all educators.

1. *Physical integration:* Placing students in the same classroom as nondisabled peers should be a strong priority, and removing them from that setting should be done only when absolutely necessary.

2. *Social integration:* Relationships should be nurtured between students with disabilities and their classmates and peers as well as adults.

3. *Instructional integration:* Most students should be taught in the same curriculum used for students without disabilities and helped to succeed by adjusting how teaching and learning are designed and measured. For some students with significant intellectual disabilities, instructional integration means anchoring instruction in the standard general curriculum but appropriately adjusting expectations.

Ultimately, the concept of inclusive practices implies that all learners are welcomed at their schools and that they are seen as the responsibility of all educators (Frattura & Capper, 2006; Turnbull, Turnbull, Wehmeyer, & Park, 2003). The Special Emphasis On . . . illustrates how your thinking as a teacher can turn inclusive practices from an abstract concept into a reality, no matter who your students are.

Throughout this text, the phrase *inclusive practices* will refer to the belief that students with disabilities are full members of their school and classroom learning communities and that educators' strong preference is for them to be educated with their peers without disabilities. We generally agree that this approach to education maximizes the potential of all students and protects their rights. We prefer the phrase *inclusive practices* to the term *inclusion* because the latter can imply that there is a single model or program that can serve all students' needs, while the former more accurately conveys that inclusiveness is made up of many strategies and options. Later in this chapter, we address in more detail how inclusive practices increasingly form the basis for contemporary education practices.

You may find that teachers in your locale use words such as *LRE, mainstreaming,* and *inclusion* interchangeably, or they might have yet different terms to describe special education services. They may refer to *integrated classes* or *collaborative classes* when describing the general education classes in which students with disabilities participate. To assist you with the vocabulary of special education programs and instructional approaches, a glossary is provided at the back of this textbook. Keep in mind, though, that knowing the terms used in special education is not nearly as important as learning about your students, developing skills for addressing their needs, and celebrating your role in enabling them to achieve success.

Meeting Students' Special Needs in Physical Education and Other Subjects

As you begin your study of inclusive practices, you might be wondering how you go about providing the supports that can enable students with disabilities and other special needs to succeed in your class. The following checklist of ideas, presented by Smith (2005) and intended for physical education teachers, provides a way for you to think about your responsibilities to your students—no matter what you plan to teach. The more these ideas guide your teaching, the more likely you will be able to meet the needs of all your students.

_____ Students' needs, interests, abilities, and individual differences shape my instruction.

_____ I do not use whole-group instruction all the time. I incorporate a variety of teaching methods to maximize student involvement and learning.

_____ I encourage student autonomy in learning and provide frequent opportunities for student choice.

_____ I plan relevant experiences that are engaging and effectively prepare the whole child for the future.

_____ My instruction is based on more than mastery of facts and skills. I infuse the curriculum with opportunities to use critical thinking and other process skills.

_____ I provide opportunities for students to learn using multiple modalities.

_____ I am flexible in using time and instructional arrangements to adapt to students' needs.

_____ In my classes, students frequently help other students, and I act as a facilitator of learning.

_____ There are multiple ways for students to succeed in my classes. Success is measured in terms of personal growth, not just by one standard.

_____ I assess students' progress and provide meaningful feedback continuously, not just at the end of a unit. I use a variety of tools to assess student learning.

How do these ideas compare to those you have about being a teacher? How could each idea assist you in supporting the success of your students with disabilities and other special needs?

Source: Adapted from "Beyond Games, Gadgets, and Gimmicks: Differentiating Instruction across Domains in Physical Education," by S. P. Smith, 2005, _Journal of Physical Education, Recreation, and Dance, 76_(8), pp. 38–45.

How Did Today's Special Education Services Come to Exist?

Special education as it exists today has been influenced by a number of different factors. Although people with disabilities have been identified and treated for centuries, special education grew rapidly only in the 20th century (Kode, 2002; Rudd, 2002; Winzer, 1993). As special education has evolved, it has been shaped by federal law, the civil rights movement and related court cases, and changing social and political beliefs. Figure 1.1 illustrates some factors that have influenced the evolution of special education.

The Development of Education for Students with Disabilities

When compulsory public education began near the turn of the 20th century, almost no school programs existed for students with disabilities (Kode, 2002; Scheerenberger, 1983).

FIGURE *1.1* **Influences on Current Special Education Practices**

Students with disabilities that were relatively mild—that is, learning or behavior problems or minor physical impairments—were educated along with other students because their needs were not considered extraordinary. Many children with significant intellectual or physical disabilities did not attend school at all, and others were educated by private agencies or lived in institutions. In fact, for the first half of the 20th century, many states explicitly legislated permission for school districts to prohibit some students with disabilities from attending (Yell, Rogers, & Rogers, 1998).

Special classes in public schools that began as compulsory education became widespread during the 1920s and 1930s. Schools were expected to be like efficient assembly lines, with each class of students moving from grade to grade and eventually graduating from high school as productive citizens prepared to enter the workforce (Patton, Payne, & Beirne-Smith, 1986; Scheerenberger, 1983). Special classes were developed as a place for students who could not keep up with their classmates. Because many students with disabilities still were not in school, most of the students sent to special classes probably had mild or moderate learning or intellectual disabilities. Educators at the time believed that such students would learn better in a protected setting and that the efficiency of the overall educational system would be preserved (Bennett, 1932; Pertsch, 1936).

By the 1950s, special education programs were available in many school districts, but some undesirable outcomes were becoming apparent. For example, students in special

Reading Homework Exercise

Go to the Homework and Exercises section in Chapter 1 of MyEducationLab to view an interactive timeline that depicts the development of special education.

classes often were considered incapable of learning academic skills. They spent their school time practicing what were called "manual skills" such as weaving and bead stringing. Researchers began questioning this practice and conducted studies to explore the efficacy of special education. When they compared students with disabilities who were in special education classes to similar students who had remained in general education, they found the latter group often had learned more than the former (Blatt, 1958; Goldstein, Moss, & Jordan, 1965). Parents at this time also became active advocates for better educational opportunities for their children (Blatt, 1987). By the late 1960s, many authorities in the field agreed that segregated special classes were not the most appropriate educational setting for many students with disabilities (Blatt, 1958; Christopolos & Renz, 1969; Dunn, 1968; Hobbs, 1975; Lilly, 1971).

The Impact of the Civil Rights Movement on Special Education

During the 1950s and 1960s, another force began contributing to the development of new approaches for special education. The civil rights movement, although initially focused on the rights of African Americans, expanded and began to influence thinking

FIGURE *1.2* **Court Cases Affecting Special Education**

Matters relating to students with disabilities are addressed in federal and state laws. Issues concerning the interpretation of those laws often must be resolved through the courts. Since 1954, hundreds of legal decisions have clarified the rights of students with disabilities and the responsibilities of schools for educating them. The following cases have had a significant impact on special education.

Brown v. Board of Education (347 U.S. 483) (1954)

This U.S. Supreme Court case established the principle that school segregation denies students equal educational opportunity. Although the decision referred primarily to racial segregation, it has since become the cornerstone for ensuring equal rights for students with disabilities as well.

Pennsylvania Association for Retarded Children v. Commonwealth of Pennsylvania (343 F. Supp. 279) (1972)

In this suit, the U.S. District Court of the Eastern District of Pennsylvania ruled that schools may not refuse to educate students with mental retardation. The court ordered that a free public education was to be provided to *all* students.

Larry P. v. Wilson Riles (793 F.2d 969) (1986)

The U.S. District Court for the Northern District of California ruled that intelligence (IQ) tests could not be used to determine whether African American students had mental retardation because of the tests' racial and cultural bias. In 1986, the ruling was expanded to include IQ testing of these students for any disability.

Board of Education of Hendrick Hudson School District v. Rowley (632 F.2d 945) (1982)

The U.S. Supreme Court ruled that special education services must provide an appropriate education but that students with disabilities may not be entitled to optimum services. The parents of a student with a hearing loss were denied an interpreter for their child in school because the child was achieving at grade level.

Daniel R. R. v. State Board of Education (874 F.2d 1036) (1989)

This decision from the U.S. Court of Appeals for the Fifth Circuit established that the appropriate placement for students with disabilities depends on whether (1) a student can be satisfactorily educated in the general education setting with supplementary supports provided and (2) the student is mainstreamed to the maximum extent appropriate in cases in which the general education setting is not successful. For Daniel, a student with Down syndrome, the court ruled that the school district had not violated his rights when he was moved from general education after an unsuccessful attempt to include him.

Oberti v. Board of Education of Clementon School District (995 F.2d 204) (1993)

In this case, the U.S. Court of Appeals for the Third Circuit upheld a district court ruling that school districts must make available a full range of supports and services in the general education setting to accommodate students with disabilities, including the student with Down syndrome involved in the about people with disabilities (Chaffin, 1975; Fleischer & Zames, 2001). In the ***Brown v. Board of Education*** decision in 1954, the U.S. Supreme Court ruled that it was unlawful under the Fourteenth Amendment to discriminate arbitrarily against any group of people. The Court then applied this concept to the education of children, ruling that the state-mandated separate education for African American students could not be an equal education. This court decision introduced the concept of *integration* into public education, the notion that the only way to protect students' constitutional right to equal opportunity was to ensure that diverse student groups learned together. Soon people with disabilities were recognized as another group whose rights often had been violated because of arbitrary discrimination. For children, the discrimination occurred when they were denied access to schools because of their disabilities. Beginning in the late 1960s and continuing through today, parents and others have used the court system to ensure that the civil and educational rights of children with disabilities are preserved (Blanchett, Brantlinger, & Shealey, 2005). Figure 1.2 summarizes several influential court cases that have helped shape special education concepts and services.

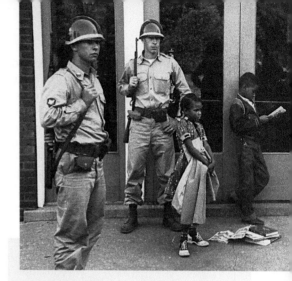

How did the civil rights movement of the 1950s and 1960s also result in rights for people with disabilities? How are these groups similar in terms of education?

suit. The court further stipulated that just because a student learns differently from other students does not necessarily warrant exclusion from general education.

Doe v. Withers (20 IDELR 422, 426–427) (1993)

As Douglas Doe's history teacher, Michael Withers was responsible for making the oral testing accommodations needed by this student with learning disabilities. Although he was also a state legislator, Withers refused to provide the oral testing and Douglas failed this class, thus becoming athletically ineligible. The West Virginia Circuit Court awarded the family $5,000 in compensatory damages and $30,000 in punitive damages. This case illustrates the extent of general education teachers' responsibility to make a good-faith effort to provide required accommodations for students with disabilities.

Schaffer v. Weast (126 S. Ct. 528) (2005)

In this dispute between the Schaffer family and the Montgomery County (Maryland) Public Schools, the U.S. Supreme Court ruled that the burden of proof in any disagreement about a student's individualized education plan

lies with the party bringing suit—in this case, the Schaffers. In many locales, it had to this point been assumed that a school district had to prove that its position in a suit was correct, even if the district had not filed the suit.

Winkelman v. Parma City School District (2007 U.S. LEXIS 5902; 75 U.S.L.W. 4329) (2007)

The Winkelmans sought to sue the Parma City School District because of a disagreement over the educational services for their son Jacob, who has autism. Although the lower court decided that the Winkelmans could not represent their son in court, the U.S. Supreme Court ruled that parents of children with disabilities themselves have rights through IDEA and thus are entitled to represent themselves (and hence their children) in court. That is, parents are not obligated to hire an attorney, as a lower court had decided.

Sources: Adapted from "Reflections on the 25th Anniversary of the Individuals with Disabilities Education Act," by A. Katisyannis, M. L. Yell, and R. Bradley, 2001, *Remedial and Special Education, 22,* pp. 324–334; "Medical Services: The Disrupted Related Service," by L. Bartlett, 2000, *Journal of Special Education, 33,* pp. 215–223; *Legal Issues in Special Educations,* by A. G. Osborne, 1996, Boston: Allyn & Bacon; "Adequate Access or Equal Treatment: Looking beyond the IDEA to Section 504 in a Post-Schaffer Public School," by C. J. Walker, 2006, *Stanford Law Review, 58,* pp. 1563–1622; and *Winkelman v. Parma City School District,* 2007, U.S. LEXIS 5902, 75 U.S.L.W. 4329.

The Council for Exceptional Children (CEC), founded in 1922 by Elizabeth Farrell, is a professional organization for teachers, administrators, parents, and other advocates for the rights of students with disabilities.

● **Section 504** One of the outcomes of the civil rights movement was legislation designed to prevent discrimination against individuals with disabilities, whether children in schools or adults in the workforce. **Section 504** of the Vocational Rehabilitation Act of 1973 is a civil rights law that prevents discrimination against all individuals with disabilities in programs that receive federal funds, as do all public schools. For children of school age, Section 504 ensures equal opportunity for participation in the full range of school activities (Walker, 2006). Through Section 504, some students not eligible for services through special education may be entitled to receive specific types of assistance to help them succeed in school.

For example, Sondra is a student with a severe attention problem. She cannot follow a lesson for more than a few minutes at a time; she is distracted by every noise in the hallway and every car that goes by her classroom window. Her teacher describes her as a student who "acts first and thinks later." Sondra does not have a disability as established in special education law, but she does need extra assistance and is considered disabled according to Section 504 because her significant attention problem negatively affects her ability to function in school. The professionals at her school are required to create and carry out a plan to help Sondra access education. Special education teachers may assist because they know techniques that will help Sondra, but Sondra does not receive special education services, and responsibility for the plan lies with the principal and teachers. Some of the other students who might receive assistance through Section 504 include those with health problems such as asthma and extreme allergies and those with physical disabilities who do not need special education. More detail on Section 504 is addressed in Chapter 8.

● **Americans with Disabilities Act** In July 1990, President George H. Bush signed into law the **Americans with Disabilities Act (ADA).** This civil rights law was based on the Rehabilitation Act of 1973, but it further extended the rights of individuals with disabilities. This law is the most significant disability legislation ever passed (National Council on Disability, 2006). It protects all individuals with disabilities from discrimination, and it requires most employers to make reasonable accommodations for them. Although ADA does not deal directly with the education of students with disabilities, it does clarify the civil rights of all individuals with disabilities and thus has an impact on special education. This law also ensures that transportation, buildings, and many places open to the public are accessible to people with disabilities. If you are a teacher with a disability, you might be influenced by ADA in the same way that it affects you in other situations. For example, if your school is not accessible to wheelchairs and undergoes renovation, then ramps, elevators, and wide entries with automatic doors probably will have to be installed. If you have a disability, this law also protects you from discrimination when you look for a teaching position.

Analyze and Reflect

Section 504 and ADA are civil rights laws, not education laws. What impact do they have on students, teachers, and schools?

The Legislative Basis for Contemporary Special Education

Influenced by researchers' growing doubts about the effectiveness of special education classes and by civil rights court cases, by the early 1970s many states had begun to address special education issues by passing laws to guarantee that students with disabilities would receive an appropriate education. Federal law soon mirrored this trend and continues to do so today.

In 1975, Congress passed Public Law (P.L.) 94-142, the Education for All Handicapped Children Act (EHCA), thereby setting federal guidelines for special education.

● **The First Federal Special Education Legislation** In 1975, Congress passed **Public Law (P.L.) 94-142,** the Education for All Handicapped Children Act (EHCA), thereby setting federal guidelines for special education and laying the foundation on which current special education practice rests. It took into account many of the early court decisions that established the civil rights of students with disabilities, and it mandated the concept of least

Professional EDGE

Special Education for Young Children with Disabilities

One of the provisions of P.L. 99-457 focuses special education services for young children on the entire family.

Although this textbook emphasizes the education of school-age students with disabilities and other special needs, young children with disabilities also are protected by special education law. Beginning in 1986 with P.L. 99-457, services have been guaranteed to children from birth through 5 years of age. These are some of the characteristics of early childhood special education:

- The focus for services is on the family, not just the child.

- Instead of an IEP, a young child has an individualized family service plan (IFSP) that spells out assistance needed by the child and family.

- Parents usually do most of the direct teaching of their babies and toddlers so that they take advantage of natural learning opportunities. Professionals who are sometimes called *early interventionists* may model ways for parents to work with their young children.

- Children ages 3 to 5 may receive special education services in their homes, at centers providing services just to children with disabilities, or in inclusive settings such as private or public preschools.

- As is true for school-age students, inclusive practices are the current dominant philosophy for educating young children with disabilities. By interacting with peers without disabilities, young children encounter strong language and behavior models and participate in age-appropriate activities. Inclusive practices for young children are preparation for inclusive practices during K–12 schooling.

During the 2002–2003 school year, a total of 265,145 children ages birth to 2 and 638,700 children ages 3 to 5 received services through IDEA (U.S. Department of Education, 2004b).

restrictive environment (LRE). This law also specifically described categories of disabilities that make students eligible to receive special education and clarified the related services to which students might be entitled. In addition, it established procedures for identifying a student as needing special education and outlined the rights of parents who disapprove of the educational services offered to their children.

● **Revisions and Refinements to Special Education Legislation** Since 1975, P.L. 94-142 has been reauthorized several times. As each reconsideration of the law has occurred, its core principles have been upheld. At the same time, the law has been extended and its provisions clarified. For example, in 1990 the name of the law was changed to the Individuals with Disabilities Education Act (IDEA) to reflect more contemporary person-first language. In addition, the term *handicapped* was removed from the law and the preferred term *disability* was substituted. This law also added significantly to the provisions for children from birth to age 5 with disabilities who had first been included in the law in 1986, the topic of the Professional Edge. It also bolstered provisions for supporting students with disabilities preparing to transition from school to work, postsecondary education, and other postschool options. One other important 1990 change in this law was the addition of two new categories of disability: autism and traumatic brain injury.

IDEA was revised again in 1997. Perhaps most important for general education teachers, this law recognized that most students with disabilities spend all or most of their school time in general education settings, and so it included a provision that the general education teacher usually should be a member of the team that writes the student's educational plan. Another important change occurred regarding assessment. Acknowledging that students with

DIMENSIONS OF diversity

As you prepare to be an educator, you will learn about the importance of developing *cultural competence*. Doing so involves valuing diversity, assessing your own views of diversity, being aware of the dynamics of intercultural interactions, developing cultural knowledge, and adjusting your teaching and other professional activities based on that knowledge (King, Sims, & Osher, 2007).

disabilities were often excluded from local and state assessments, the law added a requirement that students with disabilities be assessed like other students, using either the same assessment instrument employed with typical learners or some type of alternative instrument.

● **Current Special Education Legislation** On December 3, 2004, President George W. Bush signed into law P.L. 108-446, the most recent reauthorization of IDEA. Given the title the **Individuals with Disabilities Education Improvement Act** (and still referred to as IDEA, the term used in this book), this legislation mandated yet further refinements in special education. For example, this legislation streamlined some procedures and paperwork, and it also specified that all students with disabilities must participate in all assessment conducted by local school districts with needed supports provided (Hyatt, 2007). The law

---

FIGURE *1.3* **Provisions of the Individuals with Disabilities Education Improvement Act (IDEA)**

Core Principles

- *Free appropriate public education (FAPE).* Students with disabilities are entitled to attend public schools and receive the educational services they need. This education is provided at no cost to parents.

- *Least restrictive environment (LRE).* Students with disabilities must be educated in the least restrictive environment in which they can succeed with appropriate supports provided. For most students, this environment is the general education classroom.

- *Individualized education.* The instructional services and other assistance for a student with disabilities must be tailored to meet his needs according to a prepared individualized education program (IEP) that is reviewed and updated annually. IEPs are discussed in detail in Chapter 2.

- *Nondiscriminatory evaluation.* Students must be assessed using instruments that do not discriminate on the basis of race, culture, or disability. In considering eligibility for special education services, a student must be assessed by a multidisciplinary team in her native language using tests that are relevant to the area of concern. Eligibility cannot be decided on the basis of only one test.

- *Due process.* If a disagreement occurs concerning a student's eligibility for special education placement or services, no changes can be made until the issue has been resolved by an impartial hearing and, if necessary, the appropriate court, a procedure referred to as *due process*. Likewise, if schools disagree with parents' requests for services for their children, they may also use due process procedures to resolve the disputes.

- *Zero reject–child find.* No student may be excluded from public education because of a disability. Further,

each state must take action to locate children who may be entitled to special education services.

Additional Major Provisions

- *Transition services.* Transition services that prepare students for leaving school (for higher education, vocational training, or a job) must be addressed in IEPs for students beginning at age 16. These service needs must include strategies to improve academic and functional achievement that will foster student success and must be based on student strengths. Transition plans must be updated annually, and they must be written to include measurable goals for the postsecondary years.

- *General education teacher roles and responsibilities.* At least one general education teacher must participate as a member of the team that writes a student's IEP, unless school professionals and parents agree for some reason that this would not be beneficial to the student. In addition, the IEP must directly address student participation in general education and justify any placement that is not in general education.

- *Highly qualified special education teachers.* Special education teachers who teach core academic subjects must obtain two types of credentials. First, they must have a special education teaching credential. In addition, they must have an elementary or a secondary credential. In secondary schools, unless special education teachers work only with students with significant intellectual disabilities, they must be documented as being highly qualified in every core subject area in which they teach. However, in most states, if they work in general education classrooms, ensuring that students with disabilities receive their needed supports there, they also established that special education teachers must be **highly qualified** if they teach core academic content to students with disabilities. A provision that might be of particular interest to teachers is this: IDEA now permits school districts to use some of the funds allotted to special education to design strategies for prevention. That is, by providing intensive teaching, behavior interventions, and other supports, it may be possible to prevent some students from needing special education at all. The original principles of federal special education law and additional details on the provisions of P.L. 108-466 are summarized in Figure 1.3, and they are discussed further in Chapter 2.

● **No Child Left Behind Act of 2001**   The **No Child Left Behind Act of 2001 (NCLB)** (P.L. 107-110) was signed by President George W. Bush in January 2002. This

are not obligated to have the highly qualified status in those academic areas.

■ *Parent participation.* Parents must be part of the decision-making team for determining eligibility for special education services as well as for determining the appropriate educational placement for their children. Furthermore, schools now must report to parents on the progress of their children with disabilities at least as often as they report progress for students without disabilities.

■ *Evaluation and eligibility.* School districts generally have 60 days from the time a parent agrees that their child can be evaluated until a decision must be reached about the child's eligibility for special education. Students are not eligible for special education simply because of poor math or reading instruction or because of language differences. For some students, the requirement that a complete reassessment be completed every three years can be modified. That is, for older students already existing information can be used in lieu of repeatedly administering standardized tests.

■ *Disproportionate representation.* School districts must take specific steps to ensure that students from minority groups are not overidentified as being eligible for special education services. If disproportionate representation exists, districts must take steps to correct this problem.

■ *Assessment of students.* States are required to measure the academic progress of students who have disabilities, either by including them in the standardized assessments other students take or, for students with

significant intellectual disabilities, by using an alternate assessment process (requirements clarified in the No Child Left Behind Act). Students are entitled to appropriate accommodations (for example, extended time, large-print materials) during assessment.

■ *Discipline.* As needed, strategies for addressing a student's behavior must be included as part of the IEP. If a student is suspended or placed in an alternative interim placement, a behavior plan must be developed. In some cases (for example, when students bring weapons or drugs to school), schools may place students with disabilities in alternative interim placements for up to 45 days, pending a meeting to determine the next steps. Students must continue to receive special education services during this time.

■ *Paraprofessionals.* Paraprofessionals, teaching assistants, and other similar personnel must be trained for their jobs and appropriately supervised.

■ *Procedural safeguards.* States must make mediation available to parents as an early and informal strategy for resolving disagreements about the identification of, placement of, or provision of services for students with disabilities. The cost of mediation is borne by the state. Parents are not obligated to mediate, and mediation may not delay a possible hearing. Unless waived with parent approval, the school district also must convene a dispute resolution session prior to a formal hearing regarding disagreements related to special education.

In addition to these essential provisions of IDEA, you will learn more about other requirements of the law as they arise related to the topics addressed throughout this textbook.

Source: From Friend, Marilyn, *Special Education: Contemporary Perspectives for School Professionals,* 2/e. Published by Allyn & Bacon, Boston, MA. Copyright © 2006 by Pearson Education. Adapted by permission of the publisher.

law, considered by some the most sweeping federal education legislation ever enacted (for example, Yell, Katisyannis, & Shiner, 2006), is having a profound effect on the education of all students. The most central requirements of NCLB relate to accountability and raising academic expectations, the topic of the Professional Edge. That is, the law requires the achievement of students to be closely monitored. The goal is for all students, including those with disabilities, to be achieving at grade level in reading and math by the end of the 2013–2014 school year. The yearly benchmarks set toward achieving this goal are referred to as **adequate yearly progress (AYP),** and the law mandates that the scores of students with disabilities, as well as those of other students who might be considered at risk of learning failure, be included in AYP calculation. That is, if students with disabilities at a particular school are not improving in terms of achievement, that school cannot be considered to be making AYP and risks sanctions for failing to do so.

Professional EDGE

Accountability Requirements of the No Child Left Behind Act of 2001

The No Child Left Behind Act of 2001 (NCLB) brought sweeping changes to public education in the area of accountability, especially for students with disabilities. Here is a summary of those changes:

■ All states are required to administer assessments to all students attending public schools.

■ Students must be assessed in every grade from 3 through 8 in the areas of reading and mathematics. Students also must be assessed at least once across grades 10, 11, and 12.

■ Students must be assessed in the area of science at least once within each of these grade spans: 3–5, 6–9, and 10–12.

■ Assessment results must be reported in terms of proficiency levels, not just percentiles. Each state has developed a method for reporting proficiency, often using cutoff scores that rate students as having reached mastery or not.

■ Assessments must measure higher-order thinking skills.

■ Assessments must include the reporting of individual student scores so that parents can be informed of their children's achievement.

■ Students whose first language is not English must be assessed using tests written in English after they have received three consecutive years of instruction in U.S. schools. A few students are entitled to an additional two years of instruction before this requirement is implemented.

■ Each state must make adequate yearly progress (AYP) toward the goal of achievement at grade level for all students by 2014. Each state has set a baseline score for student achievement and has filed a plan for reaching this goal.

■ The assessment scores of students with disabilities, those whose first language is not English, and other student subgroups must be disaggregated (that is, reported separately) from overall student achievement scores. Students in these subgroups also must show AYP.

■ Schools in high-poverty areas (Title I schools) that fail for two years in a row to make AYP are subject to sanctions, including filing a plan for improvement and accepting technical assistance from the state. If student achievement does not improve after four years, students may be entitled to transfer to other schools and additional sanctions may occur.

What influence do you think these accountability requirements are having on students with disabilities and the professionals who educate them? How might they affect you as a teacher of students with disabilities in an inclusive school?

Source: From *Major Changes to ESEA in the No Child Left Behind Act,* by the Learning First Alliance, January 2003, Washington, DC: Author. Retrieved July 20, 2003, from www.nea.org/esea/images/ESEAsummary.pdf. Reprinted with permission.

NCLB also establishes that all students must be taught core academic content by teachers who are highly qualified in the content areas in which they teach. This provision has helped to ensure that students with disabilities, especially those in middle school and high school, have more access to general education settings and the teachers there who generally have more extensive knowledge about the core academic subjects than some special education teachers. This component of NCLB further strengthens the least restrictive environment provision of IDEA.

A third NCLB provision affecting students with disabilities is the expectation that teaching strategies, particularly those in reading and math, be based on rigorous research. That is, the law specifies that any programs, techniques, or strategies used to teach students should have a strong basis in studies that demonstrate their positive impact on student learning. Consistent with this provision of the law, you will find as you read this textbook that the strategies presented for improving student achievement are grounded in research.

Special education has evolved on the basis of many factors. When special education began, essentially no services were offered in public schools. Today comprehensive services in a wide variety of settings are supplied, and both very young children and young adults, as well as students in elementary and secondary schools, benefit from them. As the rights and needs of students with disabilities have been better understood and federal legislation has set higher standards for their education, general education teachers have become increasingly involved in their education, a trend that surely will continue.

www.resources

The website www.ed.gov/nclb/landing.jhtml?src=pb is the main page for information from the federal government on the No Child Left Behind Act. This site discusses proposed changes to the law, its accomplishments, and strategies for teachers to enhance student learning.

Why Are Inclusive Practices Essential in Today's Schools?

Now that you have learned about the key concepts that define special education, the development of the field, and the litigation and legislation that have shaped special education services, it is important to return one more time to the topic of inclusion. The purpose is to briefly explore why, as a result of all these factors, inclusive practices currently are receiving more attention than ever before among education professionals and parents. As you read the following discussion, remember that your goal should be to become an informed professional who recognizes the importance of inclusive practices while acknowledging the challenges sometimes encountered in implementing them.

Improving Student Outcomes

Any discussion of inclusive practices must first consider the effect on student achievement (Yell et al., 2006). That is, if students with disabilities in inclusive settings do not adequately progress in their learning, then inclusion is not in their best interests. At the same time, inclusive practices should not interfere with the achievement of other students. Generally, academic outcomes have been found to be positive for all students (Idol, 2006). For example, in a statewide study, researchers found that students with disabilities who spent more time in general education passed the eighth-grade assessment at a higher rate than similar students with disabilities who were educated in special education settings. Students educated in general education settings also graduated at a higher rate from high school with a standard diploma (Luster & Durrett, 2003). Another study found that students with mild mental retardation who were educated in general education classrooms generally made greater academic gains than their comparable peers in special education settings (Cole, Waldron, & Majd, 2004).

Reading Homework Exercise

Go to the Homework and Exercises section in Chapter 1 of MyEducationLab and access a linked article to learn what schools should be doing to include students with disabilities in the general education class.

Analyze and Reflect

Teaching students with disabilities has changed dramatically over the years. How have IDEA and NCLB altered the expectations of students with disabilities? As an educator, what are your responsibilities for addressing the provisions of these two laws as you work with all your students?

Yet other researchers have found positive effects of inclusive practices on mathematics achievement (Kunsch, Jitendra, & Sood, 2007), language development (Rafferty, Piscitelli, & Boettcher, 2003), problem-solving skills (Agran, Blanchard, Wehmeyer, & Hughes, 2002), and discipline referrals (Cawley, Hayden, Cade, & Baker-Kroczynski, 2002). Although only a few studies have been reported on the impact of inclusive practices on typical students, they suggest that these students' achievement is not hindered (for example, McDonnell et al., 2003).

Over the next several years, a much clearer picture of the achievement of students with disabilities in inclusive schools will likely emerge because of the AYP reporting requirement in NCLB. In the interim, teachers should gather their own data to document student achievement and use those data to make instructional decisions to maximize student learning.

Respecting Parent and Student Rights and Views

Parents generally are positive about special education services, and they usually prefer that their children be educated with peers in general education classrooms (J. Johnson & Duffett, 2002; Purcell, Turnbull, & Jackson, 2006). They believe that inclusive practices are beneficial for academic achievement, but probably even more so than educators, they also strongly believe that their children learn critical social skills when they spend most or all of the school day with their typical peers (Salend, 2006; Williams & Reisberg, 2003). One parent commented that when her fourth-grade son with autism was integrated into a general education classroom for most of the day, his behavior improved both at school and at home. She also noted that the other students in the class were clearly kind to her son, and she was grateful that they sought him out on the playground and chose him as a lunch partner.

When parents are uneasy about inclusive practices, their concerns usually relate to problems they have experienced or anticipate (for example, Hanline & Daley, 2002). For example, parents of children with physical disabilities have found that many teachers are poorly prepared to work with students with special needs and that these educators have not prepared students to have a classmate with a disability (Pivik, McComas, & Laflamme, 2002). Some parents find that their children seem more comfortable in a special education classroom that has fewer students and more structure (Johnson & Duffett, 2002). For all parents, perceptions of inclusive practices are more positive when they participate in collaborative decision making concerning their children's educational services (Matuszny, Banda, & Coleman, 2007).

Although few studies of students' perceptions of inclusive education have been reported, those available generally indicate that students prefer to receive their education with their peers. For example, Connor (2006) reported on the experience of a student named Michael who was identified as being learning disabled and also lived in poverty. Michael discussed extensively the stigma of being labeled as disabled and receiving services in the special education classroom. He strongly preferred remaining in general education.

Considering the Complexities of Inclusive Practices

Any discussion of inclusive practices also should acknowledge and explore the fact that complexities can occur when a strong commitment is made to educating students with disabilities with their peers. Some of the issues likely to arise in such discussions are confusion about the meaning of the term *inclusion*, perspectives of teachers and administrators, and implementation barriers.

● **A Problem of Understanding**   Although it is a bit surprising after so many years of discussion, one dilemma related to inclusion concerns its definition. Too often, research on inclusive practices and essays on their relative merits and drawbacks focus on where students are seated, that is, the amount of time they spend in general education classrooms (Idol, 2006; McGrath, Johns, & Mathur, 2004; Mock & Kauffman, 2002). As a result, some professionals argue that students with disabilities sometimes need a small-group, highly structured environment that is difficult to create in the general education classroom (Kavale, 2002), and they conclude that inclusion—sometimes using the phrase *full inclusion*—is not sound educational practice.

Alternatively, in many school districts and among some authors (for example, Handler, 2003; McLeskey & Waldron, 2007), inclusive practices are conceptualized as a belief system that emphasizes welcoming all students in a school learning community (Frattura & Capper, 2006). Just as important, inclusiveness is not judged solely on the location of a student's education. In these schools, factors such as those in the inclusive practices checklist in the Professional Edge on page 18 are stressed. As you have learned, this broader view is the one taken in this textbook. In highly inclusive schools, professionals and parents sometimes realize that instruction must occur in a separate setting. However, their goal is to return the student to instruction with peers as soon as possible and for as much time as possible. Further, they judge the effectiveness of inclusive practices on a student-by-student basis, monitoring student progress regardless of whether that progress looks similar to that of other students (for example, Brigham, Morocco, Clay, & Zigmond, 2006).

● **Perspectives of Professionals**   The perceptions of teachers and administrators regarding inclusive practices can be represented along a continuum (for example, DeSimone & Parmar, 2006; Pavri & Monda-Amaya, 2001; Rea, McLaughlin, & Walther-Thomas, 2002). In some studies, general education teachers in elementary, middle, and high schools are found to believe strongly in inclusive practices based on high standards for students (King & Youngs, 2003; McLeskey et al., 2001). Teachers who support inclusive practices report making instructional accommodations to facilitate student learning

www.resources

The National Dissemination Center for Children with Disabilities (whose acronym NICHCY is a holdover from the organization's previous name) provides extensive information on disabilities and disability-related issues for families, teachers, and others at www.nichcy.org. The website includes fact sheets and research briefs on specific disabilities as well as special education law. Most pages are available in Spanish as well as English.

Why are principals so important in the implementation of inclusive practices?

Checklist of Inclusive Practices

What types of activities do schools engage in to foster and sustain inclusive practices? The following are some of the key questions school professionals ask when analyzing their schools' inclusiveness. The more positive the responses educators make, the more likely it is that successful inclusive practices will be implemented.

- Does your school have a mission statement that expresses the belief that the professionals and other staff strive to meet the needs of all students? Is this mission statement discussed by staff and used to guide instructional practices?

- Have teachers and other staff members recognized that working toward an inclusive environment continues each year—that the process does not end?

- Have teachers had opportunities to discuss their concerns about student needs, and have steps been taken to address these concerns?

- Has planning to meet all students' needs included classroom teachers, special education teachers, other support staff, administrators, parents, and students?

- Have you clarified the expectations for students with special needs who are to be integrated into classrooms?

- Has shared planning time as well as possibly shared instructional time been arranged for teams of teachers?

- Have staff members received adequate professional development on pertinent topics (for example, collaboration, behavior supports, and curricular adaptations)?

- Have staff members become comfortable with working collaboratively?

- Has the plan for your inclusive school truly addressed the needs of *all* students?

- Have resources been allocated for increasing and sustaining inclusive practices?

- Have steps been taken to ensure that teachers will be rewarded for experimentation and innovation, even if their efforts sometimes are not successful?

- Have all teachers, even those who may not at first participate in teaching students who are more challenging learners, learned that they are integral to a schoolwide belief system?

- Have students had opportunities to learn about people representing all types of diversity, including individuals with disabilities?

- Have parents and families of students with and without disabilities been involved in the development, implementation, and evaluation of the school's inclusive services?

- Has a plan been developed for carefully monitoring the impact of approaches for meeting student diversity? Does this plan include strategies for revision?

- Have teachers and other staff identified benchmarks, including student outcome data, so that they have attainable goals to celebrate after one year? Two years? Three years?

Source: From Friend, Marilyn, *Special Education: Contemporary Perspectives for School Professionals,* 2/e. Published by Allyn & Bacon, Boston, MA. Copyright © 2006 by Pearson Education. Adapted by permission of the publisher.

and feeling positive about their work with students with disabilities (for example, Clayton, Burdge, Denham, Kleinert, & Kearns, 2006).

At the same time, some teachers' perceptions of inclusive practices are more ambivalent (Martin, Johnson, Ireland, & Claxton, 2003). They recognize the value of inclusive practices but are uncertain about implementation. In one study of mathematics teachers (DeSimone & Parmar, 2006), the teachers indicated that they had not learned enough about students with disabilities in their professional preparation programs and were uncertain about students' needs and how to address them. As you think about teaching students with disabilities and other special needs, what knowledge and skills do you anticipate needing? Among the items frequently mentioned are a commitment to inclusive practices and knowledge of effective instructional strategies (Stanovich & Jordan, 2002).

In addition to the views of teachers, principals' support of inclusive practices is essential, since principals are responsible for keeping the vision focused, fostering among staff an understanding of inclusion, and nurturing the development of the skills and practices needed to implement these practices (Salisbury & McGregor, 2002). Generally, principals report positive attitudes toward inclusive practices (for example, Praisner, 2003). Like teachers, though, they express concern that general education teachers may not have the skills to instruct students with disabilities in their classrooms (Cook, Semmel, & Gerber, 1999).

● **Implementation Dilemmas**   The challenges to inclusive practices seldom relate directly to instruction. Instead they often relate to practical matters and other pressures that exist in schools (Sindelar, Shearer, Yendol-Hoppey, & Liebert, 2006). These are common concerns:

■ *Time for shared planning.* General and special education teachers note that they need time to meet so they can design instructional strategies and discuss student learning and behavior. Nearly every study of inclusive practices includes mention of planning time as a barrier to implementation.

■ *Adequate and consistent personnel.* Because inclusive schooling relies so heavily on the strong collaborative relationships among school staff members, in schools where teacher turnover is high, it is difficult to sustain efforts to support students with disabilities in general education classrooms.

■ *Pressure related to high-stakes testing.* NCLB has resulted in tremendous pressure for all students to reach achievement goals. In some schools, teachers fear that having students with disabilities in their classes may lower their average class scores.

Have you heard teachers discuss any other challenges to inclusive practices? Issues such as the ones listed here are understandable, but they are not an excuse for denying students the education to which they are entitled.

Research Note

Technology can improve outcomes for students with disabilities. Myles, Ferguson, and Hagiwara (2007) found that when they taught an adolescent with Asperger syndrome to use a personal digital assistant (PDA), he was motivated by the use of technology and significantly increased the number of times he independently recorded homework assignments.

Putting the Pieces Together

In some ways, the various dimensions of inclusive practices are like puzzle pieces. However, in today's schools some of the pieces may be missing and others difficult to fit into place. Even in your own course, classmates may have a wide range of opinions about inclusive practices, and they may come across studies that present contradictory results. In your field experiences, you are likely to discover that in some schools inclusive practices are the norm, while in others very traditional approaches are still in place. You may find yourself struggling to reconcile all these views.

One way that you can put the puzzle together is to learn to teach in a way that is responsive to a wide range of student needs (Sobel & Taylor, 2006; Villa, Thousand, Nevin, & Liston, 2005) and to use collaboration with colleagues and parents, as described in the Working Together feature, as a means for extending your expertise. As you will learn later in this text, much is known about effective ways to instruct students with disabilities, and many of those strategies will help other students learn as well (for example, Abell, Bauder, & Simmons, 2005; McGuire, Scott, & Shaw, 2006; Pisha & Stahl, 2005). By welcoming all your students and making these strategies an integral part of your instruction, your part of the inclusive practices puzzle will fit right into place.

Finally, as you read about inclusive practices, keep in mind that the results researchers obtain and the viewpoints authors present are influenced by many variables, including the abilities and disabilities, ages, and cultural backgrounds of students; the attitudes,

> Much is known about effective ways to instruct students with disabilities, and many of those strategies will help other students learn as well.

The Importance of Collaboration for Meeting Student Needs

As you read this textbook and learn about your responsibilities in educating students with disabilities, you will find that *collaboration*—working together with others—is one of the keys to successful inclusive practices. Here are just a few examples of how you will collaborate on behalf of students:

- *Meeting with special education teachers.* You will meet frequently with special education teachers, both formally and informally. A special educator may contact you to see how a student is doing in your class, or you may contact a special educator to ask for new ideas for responding to a student's behavior. You and the special educator may share responsibility for meeting with parents during open houses or parent conferences.

- *Co-teaching.* Depending on local programs and services, you may co-teach with a special education teacher or related services professional such as a speech/language pathologist. In co-teaching, you share teaching responsibilities, with both educators working with all students. This topic is addressed in detail in Chapter 3.

- *Working with paraprofessionals.* If your class includes a student with a significant disability or several students

who need support, the student may be accompanied by a paraprofessional. You will guide the work of that individual in your class and collaborate to ensure that student support is appropriately provided.

- *Meeting on teams.* In today's schools, many teams support inclusive practices. Your grade-level or middle or high school department team will likely spend part of its time discussing students with disabilities and problem solving to address their needs. You also may be part of a team that tries to address student learning and behavior problems prior to any consideration of the need for special education. Further, if a student in your class is being assessed to determine whether special education is needed, you will be part of that team. The latter two teams are discussed in Chapter 2.

- *Interacting with parents.* Perhaps the most important part of collaborating on behalf of students with disabilities is working with parents. You may communicate with parents through notes sent home and through e-mail; meet with them occasionally as they express concerns about their children; confer with them at formal team meetings; and work with them as they volunteer at school, help with field trips, and participate in other school activities and initiatives.

---

knowledge, and skills of general and special education teachers; the commitment and participation of parents; the degree of support for inclusion from administrators, school policies, and school procedures; the type of outcomes measured; and even the predisposition of researchers and authors toward particular opinions about inclusive practices. As you develop your own understanding of inclusive practices, keep all these factors in mind to help you make sense of what you read. In this way, you will learn to be inclusive in your thinking but flexible in your approach to educating students with disabilities.

Who Receives Special Education and Other Special Services?

Throughout this chapter, we have used the phrase *students with disabilities*. At this point, we will introduce you to the specific types of disabilities that may entitle students to receive special education services, as well as other special needs that may require specialized assistance. As you read the following definitions, remember that a disability label can only provide general guidelines about a student. Labels are a form of shorthand that professionals use. However, no label can accurately describe a student. Your responsibility is to understand your students with disabilities in ways that extend beyond what any label communicates so you can help them reach their potential.

Categories of Disability in Federal Law

When we say that students have disabilities, we are referring to the specific categories of exceptionality prescribed by federal law. Each state has additional laws that clarify special education practices and procedures, and the terms used to refer to disabilities in state laws may differ from those found in federal law. For example, although federal law specifies the label *emotional disturbance* for some students, in some states, the term *behavior disorder* or *behavioral and emotional disability* is used. Similarly, although IDEA uses the term *mental retardation*, some states use the alternative *cognitive disability* or *intellectual disability*. Check with your instructor for the terms used in your state. According to IDEA, students with one or more of the following thirteen disabilities that negatively affect their educational performance are eligible for special education services. These disabilities also are summarized in the Professional Edge on the next page.

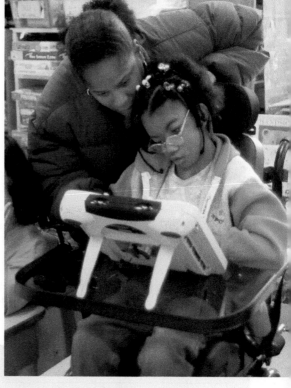

What are the responsibilities of general education teachers for educating students with significant disabilities? Why is it important to ensure that these students are welcomed at their schools?

- **Learning Disabilities** Students with *learning disabilities (LD)* have dysfunctions in processing information typically found in language-based activities. They have average or above-average intelligence, but they often encounter significant problems learning how to read, write, and compute. They may not see letters and words in the way others do; they may not be able to pick out important features in a picture they are looking at; and they may take longer to process a question or comment directed to them. They also may have difficulty following directions, attending to tasks, organizing assignments, and managing time. Sometimes these students appear to be unmotivated or lazy when in fact they are trying to the best of their ability. Aaron, described at the beginning of this chapter, has one type of learning disability, but many other types also exist, and no single description characterizes all students with LD. Learning disabilities are by far the most common special need: Slightly less than 50 percent of all students receiving special education services in public schools in 2002–2003 had a learning disability (U.S. Department of Education, 2004b).

- **Speech or Language Impairments** When a student has extraordinary difficulties communicating with others for reasons other than maturation, a *speech or language impairment* is involved. Students with this disability may have trouble with *articulation*, or the production of speech sounds. They may omit words or mispronounce common words when they speak. They also may experience difficulty in *fluency*, such as a significant stuttering problem. Some students have far-reaching speech or language disorders, in which they have significant problems receiving and producing language. They may communicate through pictures or sign language. Some students' primary disability is a speech or language disorder, and they may receive services for this. For other students with disabilities, speech/language services supplement their educational services. For example, a student with a learning disability also might receive speech/language services, as might a student with autism or traumatic brain injury. In these instances, speech/language services are often considered a related service, as defined earlier in this chapter.

- **Mental Retardation** Students with *mental retardation (MR)* have significant limitations in intellectual ability and adaptive behaviors. They learn at a slower pace than do

*R*esearch Note

Dunn, Chambers, and Rabren (2004) found that students with learning disabilities are less likely to drop out of school if they perceive that (1) a connection exists between what they are learning and life after high school, (2) someone in school is trying to help them, and (3) at least one class in high school is helpful to them.

IDEA Disability Categories

Discussions about students with disabilities sometimes seem to be contradictory. As you read this textbook and learn from your instructor and classmates, you will hear again and again that the specific disability labels students carry are not particularly important and that understanding students as unique individuals is what will help you be successful in teaching them. At the same time, students are labeled according to the 13 federal disability categories.

The former perspective is very true, but the latter is important, too. Federal special education currently provides funding for the costs of educating students with disabilities based on their identification within the 13 categories. Using disability labels also ensures that students' civil rights will be protected—rights that can extend throughout their lifetimes. So although you should not rely on labels to guide your perceptions of and decisions about students, labels currently have a function. Perhaps in the future, the benefits they provide will be made available and their often stigmatizing effects avoided. The categories of disabilities students must have in order to receive special education are summarized in the chart below.

Categories of Disability in Federal Special Education Law

Federal Disability Term	Alternative Terms	Brief Description
Learning disability (LD)	Specific learning disability	A disorder related to processing information that leads to difficulties in reading, writing, and computing; the most common disability, accounting for half of all students receiving special education.
Speech or language impairment	Communication disorder (CD)	A disorder related to accurately producing the sounds of language or meaningfully using language to communicate.
Mental retardation (MR)	Intellectual disability, cognitive impairment	Significant limitations in intellectual ability and adaptive behavior; this disability occurs in a range of severity.
Emotional disturbance (ED)	Behavior disorder (BD), emotional disability	Significant problems in the social-emotional area to a degree that learning is negatively affected.
Autism	Autism spectrum disorder (ASD)	A disorder characterized by extraordinary difficulty in social responsiveness; this disability occurs in many different forms and may be mild or significant.
Hearing impairment	Deaf, hard of hearing (DHH)	A partial or complete loss of hearing.
Visual impairment	Low vision, blind	A partial or complete loss of vision.
Deaf-blindness	—	A simultaneous significant hearing loss and significant vision loss.
Orthopedic impairment (OI)	Physical disability	A significant physical limitation that impairs the ability to move or complete motor activities.
Traumatic brain injury (TBI)	—	A medical condition denoting a serious brain injury that occurs as a result of accident or injury; the impact of this disability varies widely but may affect learning, behavior, social skills, and language.
Other health impairment (OHI)	—	A disease or health disorder so significant that it negatively affects learning; examples include cancer, sickle-cell anemia, and diabetes.
Multiple disabilities	—	The simultaneous presence of two or more disabilities such that none can be identified as the primary disability; the most common example is the occurrence of mental retardation and physical disabilities.
Developmental delay (DD)	—	A nonspecific disability category that states may choose to use as an alternative to specific disability labels for identifying students up to age 9 needing special education.

Note: More complete definitions of each category of disability in federal special education law are presented in Chapters 6 and 7.

other students, and they may reach a point at which their learning levels off. Although the federal listing of disability categories does not distinguish between students with mild mental retardation and those with more significant intellectual disabilities, many state listings do. Most individuals with this disability can lead independent or semi-independent lives as adults and can hold appropriate jobs. Because the term *mental retardation* can be very stigmatizing, the alternative term *intellectual disability* is becoming more common. In this text, the two terms are used interchangeably. Angela, one of the students you met in the introduction to this chapter, has an intellectual disability.

● **Emotional Disturbance**   When a student has significant difficulty in the social-emotional domain—serious enough to interfere with the student's learning—an *emotional disturbance (ED),* also sometimes called an *emotional and behavior disorder (EBD),* exists. Students with this disability may have difficulty with interpersonal relationships and may respond inappropriately in emotional situations. That is, they may have trouble making and keeping friends; they may get extremely angry when peers tease or play jokes on them; and they may show little or no emotion when it is expected, such as when a family pet dies. Some students with ED are depressed; others are aggressive. Students with ED display these impairments over a long period of time, across different settings, and to a degree significantly different from their peers. Students with emotional disabilities are not just students whose behavior in a classroom is challenging to address; rather, they have chronic and extremely serious emotional or behavioral problems.

● **Autism**   Students with *autism,* sometimes referred to as *autism spectrum disorder* because of its many variations, usually lack appropriate social responsiveness from a very early age. They generally avoid physical contact (for example, cuddling and holding), and they may not make eye contact. Problems with social interactions persist as these children grow; they appear unaware of others' feelings and may not seek interactions with peers or adults. They may have unusual language patterns, speaking without inflection, repeating what others say, or repeating something heard on television over and over. To feel comfortable, they may need highly routinized behavior, such as a formalized procedure for putting on their clothes or eating their meals. Some students with autism

> Some students with autism have above-average intelligence; others have intellectual disabilities.

have above-average intelligence; others have intellectual disabilities. The causes of autism are not well understood, and the best approaches for working with students with autism are still emerging.

Asperger syndrome, usually considered a type of autism, is receiving increased attention among professionals. Individuals with this disorder usually experience difficulty in social interactions and communication, and they often have a very narrow range of interests. However, with appropriate supports and teacher understanding, students with Asperger syndrome can be highly successful in school.

Thomas, one of the students you met at the beginning of the chapter, is identified as having autism. You can learn a little more about autism by reading the Case in Practice in which teachers meet to problem solve regarding another student with this disability.

● **Hearing Impairments**   Disabilities that concern inability or limited ability to receive auditory signals are called *hearing impairments (HI).* When students are *hard of hearing,* they have a significant hearing loss but are able to capitalize on residual hearing by using hearing aids and other amplifying systems. Students who are *deaf* have little or no residual hearing and therefore do not benefit from traditional devices that aid hearing. Some students with hearing loss may be assisted through the use of advanced technology such as a cochlear implant, a small, complex electronic device implanted

Video Homework Exercise

Go to the Homework and Exercises section in Chapter 1 of MyEducationLab to watch a video that illustrates the diversity of persons with disabilities.

fyi

A *primary disability* is one that most adversely affects a student's educational performance. A *secondary disability* is an additional disability that also affects a student's education but to a lesser degree. For example, a student identified with a learning disability as a primary disability could have an emotional disability or health impairment as a secondary disability.

Problem Solving in Inclusive Schools: The Classroom Teacher's Role

At Highland Elementary School, staff members are meeting to discuss David, a third-grader with autism. Ms. Dowley is David's teacher, and Ms. Jackson is the special educator who provides needed support. Ms. Janes, the school psychologist, also is present.

Ms. Dowley: David is really a puzzle and a challenge. He is behaving much better in class than he was at the beginning of the year, but he still disrupts the entire class when he has a bad day. One of the parents called yesterday to complain about David taking time away from her daughter and the rest of the class. I'm starting to feel the same way. I hope we can come up with some ideas to improve the whole situation.

Ms. Jackson: What kinds of things seem to trigger the problems?

Ms. Dowley: That's part of my concern. I'm still pretty new at teaching, and I have my hands full with the whole class. I don't even have time to think carefully about what's happening with David. I just deal with him when he does something inappropriate—bothering another student, refusing to come with the group—without really thinking about how it happened or how to avoid it, if that's possible.

Ms. Janes: You've mentioned problem behavior as one issue. Before we start addressing that, are there any other issues we should be discussing too?

Ms. Dowley: No. Right now, it's the behavior—and I want to be clear that I really can see all the other gains David has made. I *want* this to work for David, and I know his parents do too. They've been very helpful and always carry through with their part. I know David can be successful in my class—but it'll be much less stressful for all of us if we can work on his behavior.

Ms. Janes: It seems as though we need more information. One question I have is this: What happens with you and the other students when David does something inappropriate—talking in a loud voice, pushing books off the desk?

Ms. Dowley: Well, I try to ignore him, but that usually makes it worse. A few of the other students laugh, and that's not helping either.

Ms. Jackson: Maybe we should focus for a minute or two on when David doesn't have difficulty in class. What are the times of the day or the activities David does without having behavior problems?

Ms. Dowley: Let's see . . . He's usually fine and makes a good contribution when we're talking about science concepts. He loves science. When math is activity based, he's fine there, too.

Ms. Janes: Our meeting time is nearly up. I'd be happy to make time in my schedule to observe David, and perhaps Ms. Jackson could too. I know you need answers right away, but I hope we can get a clearer sense of the pattern of David's behavior so we can find the right strategy for addressing it. If we can get in to observe this week, could we meet next Tuesday to try to generate some strategies?

Ms. Dowley: Sure. That would be great. Let's just work out the details on observing.

REFLECTIONS

Why was this meeting a positive example of teachers addressing a student problem in an inclusive school? What did they do that has set them up for success? If you were trying to understand David better, what other questions would you ask about him? What would you like others to observe in the classroom in relation to him? In relation to you as the teacher? What do you think will happen at the next meeting? On the basis of this case, how would you describe the role of classroom teachers in addressing the challenges of inclusion?

---

near the ear that can provide a sense of sound. Depending on the extent of the disability, students with hearing impairments may use sign language, speech reading, or other ways to help them communicate.

● **Visual Impairments** Disabilities that concern the inability or limited ability to receive information visually are called *visual impairments (VI)*. Some students have *partial sight* and can learn successfully using magnification devices and other adaptive materials;

students who are *blind* do not use vision as a means of learning and instead rely primarily on touch and hearing. Depending on need, students with visual impairments may use braille, specialized computers, and other aids to assist in learning. Some students need specialized training to help them learn to move around successfully in their environment.

●   **Deaf-Blindness**   Students who have both significant vision and hearing impairments sometimes are eligible for services as *deaf-blind.* These students are categorized separately because of the unique learning needs they have, particularly in the domain of communication, and because of the highly specialized services they require. The degree of the vision and hearing loss may vary from moderate to severe and may be accompanied by other disabilities. Students in this category are likely to receive special education services beginning at birth or very soon thereafter.

●   **Orthopedic Impairments**   Students with *orthopedic impairments (OI)* have physical conditions that seriously impair their ability to move about or complete motor activities. Students who have cerebral palsy are included in this group, as are those with other diseases that affect the skeleton or muscles. Students with physical limitations resulting from accidents also may be orthopedically impaired. Students with orthopedic impairments are difficult to describe as a group because their strengths and needs vary tremendously. For example, some students with this disability are unable to move about without a wheelchair and may need special transportation to get to school and a ramp to enter the school building. Others may lack the fine motor skills needed to write and may require extra time or adapted equipment to complete assignments.

●   **Traumatic Brain Injury**   Students with *traumatic brain injury (TBI)* have a wide range of characteristics and special needs, including limited strength or alertness, developmental delays, short-term memory problems, hearing or vision losses that may be temporary, irritability, and sudden mood swings. Their characteristics and needs depend on the specific injuries they experienced, and their needs often change over time. Because TBI is a medical condition that affects education, diagnosis by a physician is required along with assessment of learning and adaptive behavior. Students who experience serious head trauma from automobile accidents, falls, and sports injuries are among those who might be eligible for services as TBI.

●   **Other Health Impairments**   Some students have a disease or disorder so significant that it affects their ability to learn in school. The category of disability addressing their needs is called *other health impairments (OHI).* Students who have chronic heart conditions necessitating frequent and prolonged absences from school might be eligible for special education in this category, as might those with severe and chronic asthma. Students with diseases such as acquired immune deficiency syndrome (AIDS), sickle-cell anemia, and diabetes also may be categorized as having other health impairments, depending on the impact of their illnesses on learning. Some students with attention deficit–hyperactivity disorder (ADHD) also receive special education services in this category.

●   **Multiple Disabilities**   The category used when students have two or more disabilities is called *multiple disabilities.* Students in this group often have an intellectual disability as well as a physical disability, but this category also may be used to describe any student with two or more disability types. However, this classification is used only when the student's disabilities are so serious and interrelated that none can be identified as a primary disability. Students with multiple disabilities often benefit from *assistive technology,* that is, simple or complex devices that facilitate their learning, as explained in the Technology Notes.

Analyze
and Reflect

Why is it important for teachers to think of students in terms of their strengths and abilities instead of the labels that describe their disabilities?

The Opportunities of Assistive Technology

Technology assists students with disabilities in many ways. Whether the students you teach have mild or significant disabilities, they can use technology to help them to communicate, complete assignments, and fully participate in school and community. *Assistive technology* is defined in a federal law that ensures that children and adults needing such assistance have access to it. The term refers to any device (that is, piece of equipment, product, or other item) that is used to increase, maintain, or improve the functional capabilities of an individual with disabilities.

Assistive technology sometimes is categorized according to its complexity. Here are examples of the levels of assistive technology students might use

No Technology or Low Technology

No technology (no-tech) or *low technology (low-tech)* refers to items that do not include any type of electronics. These are examples of low-tech devices:

- A rubber pencil grip that enables a student with a disability to better grasp a pencil or pen
- A nonslip placemat on a student's desk that makes it easier for her to pick up items because it stops them from sliding
- A study carrel that helps a student pay closer attention to the schoolwork at hand

Mid–Technology

Devices in the *mid-technology (mid-tech)* category use simple electronics. Examples include the following:

- A tape recorder that a student uses to record lectures
- A calculator that assists a student in completing math computations
- A timer that lets a student know it is time to change from one activity to another

Electronic communication boards are an example of high-tech assistive technology that benefits students with communication disorders.

High Technology

The third level of assistive technology is referred to as *high technology (high-tech)*. Items in this category use complex technology and often are expensive compared to no-tech and mid-tech items. Examples include these:

- Voice-recognition software that allows a student to dictate information that then appears in print on the computer
- Electronic communication boards on which a student can touch a picture and a prerecorded voice communicates for him. For example, a student touches a picture of himself and a voice says "Hello. My name is Danny. What is your name?"

Technology that used to be considered sophisticated (for example, talking watches and calculators, personal digital assistants) now is readily available and provides educational access for students with disabilities. As advances in technology continue, even more opportunities will become possible. As an educator, you should anticipate that assistive technology will be part of many students' tools for learning.

● **Developmental Delays** The category *developmental delays (DD)* is somewhat different than the other disabilities recognized in IDEA. It is an option that states may use for children ages 3 through 9. This category includes youngsters who have significant delays in physical, cognitive, communication, social-emotional, or adaptive development, but it is applied instead of one of the more specific disability categories. This option has two advantages: First, it avoids the use of more stigmatizing labels for young children, and second, it acknowledges the difficulty of determining the nature of a specific disability in young children. Not all states use this term. Is it used in your state?

Cross-Categorical Approaches to Special Education

Student Artifact Building Teaching Skills Exercise

Go to the Building Teaching Skills section in Chapter 1 of MyEducationLab for an activity about getting to know your students.

Federal and state education agencies and local school districts use the categories of disability described in the previous sections for counting the number of students receiving special education services and allocating money to educate them. When you prepare to teach a student, however, you probably will find that the specific category of disability does not guide you in discovering that student's strengths and devising appropriate teaching strategies. Further, students in different categories often benefit from the same instructional adaptations. Therefore, throughout this book, students are sometimes discussed in terms of only two categories:

1. **High-incidence disabilities** are those that are most common, including learning disabilities, speech or language impairments, mild intellectual disabilities, and emotional disturbance. Together these disabilities account for approximately 80 percent of the disabilities reported in 2002–2003 (U.S. Department of Education, 2004b).

2. **Low-incidence disabilities** are those that are less common and include all the other categories: moderate to severe mental retardation, multiple disabilities, hearing impairments, orthopedic impairments, other health impairments, visual impairments, deaf-blindness, autism, traumatic brain injury, and developmental delays.

Consistent with a **cross-categorical approach,** characteristics of students with disabilities are discussed in more detail in Chapters 6 and 7, where more attention is paid to students' learning needs than to their labels. In addition, although some strategies specific to categorical groups are outlined in those chapters (for example, the use of large-print books for students with visual impairments), most of the strategies presented throughout the text can be adapted for most students. If you adopt a cross-categorical approach in your own thinking about teaching students with disabilities, you will see that many options are available for helping all students succeed.

Why does the cross-categorical approach encourage teachers to identify strengths in all students? How does this help foster inclusive practices?

Other Students with Special Needs

Not all students who have special learning and behavior needs are addressed in special education laws. Many other students, described in the following sections, can benefit from the ideas presented throughout this book.

● **Students Who Are Gifted or Talented**   Students who demonstrate ability far above average in one or several areas—including overall intellectual ability, leadership, specific academic subjects, creativity, athletics, and the visual or performing arts—are considered *gifted* or *talented*. Erin is included in this group; she seems to learn without effort, and she also is eager to learn about almost everything. Evan is considered talented; still in elementary school, he has participated in state and national piano recitals, and his parents have requested that he have access to the music room during recess so he can practice. Students who are gifted or talented are not addressed in federal special education law, but many states have separate laws that provide guidelines for identifying and educating students with special talents. Adequate funds are not always provided to implement these laws, however, and so the availability and scope of services for students with particular talents vary across the country and even within a particular state.

● **Students Protected by Section 504**   Some students not eligible to receive special education services are entitled to protection through Section 504 and receive specialized assistance because of their functional disabilities, as described previously in this chapter. Among those likely to be included in this group are some students with attention deficit–hyperactivity disorder (ADHD). These students have a medical condition often characterized by an inability to attend to complex tasks for long periods of time, excessive motor activity, and/or impulsivity. The impact of this disorder on students' schoolwork can be significant. Students with ADHD may take medication, such as Ritalin or Strattera, that helps them focus their attention. Many students with learning disabilities or emotional disturbance also have ADHD, but these students receive assistance through IDEA, as do students with ADHD whose disorder is so significant that they are determined to be eligible for special education. Other students who may be protected by Section 504 include those with asthma, severe allergies, or epilepsy.

● **Students at Risk**   Often, the general term *at risk* refers to students whose characteristics, environment, or experiences make them more likely than others to fail in school (and they also may have disabilities). Students whose primary language is not English—sometimes referred to as *English-language learners (ELLs)*—sometimes are considered at risk, and they may need assistance in school learning. They may attend bilingual education programs or classes for English as a second language (ESL) to have opportunities to learn English while also learning the standard curriculum, or they may receive assistance in their general education classrooms. Some ELLs also have disabilities; when this is the case, both English-language instruction and special education are provided. By reviewing the checklist presented in the Professional Edge, you can analyze your readiness to work with students and families from diverse backgrounds, including those who are English-language learners.

A second group of at-risk students includes *slow learners,* whose educational progress is below average but who do not have a disability. These students are learning to the best of their ability, but they often cannot keep pace with the instruction in most general education classrooms without assistance. They are sometimes described as "falling between the cracks" of the educational system because while most professionals agree they need special assistance, they are not eligible for special education. They do sometimes receive assistance in remedial reading or math or tutorial programs.

Other students who might be considered at risk include those who are homeless; those who live in poverty or move frequently; those who are born to mothers abusing drugs or alcohol or who abuse drugs or alcohol themselves; and those who are victims

Promoting Cultural Competence: A Self-Assessment

Cultural competence refers to your understanding of and responses to diversity. Here is a tool designed to help you reflect on your awareness of a variety of factors that contribute to cultural competence.

_____ For students who speak a language or dialect other than English, I attempt to learn and use key words in their language so I am better able to communicate with them.

_____ I use visual aids, gestures, and physical prompts in my interactions with students who have limited English proficiency.

_____ When interacting with parents and other family members who have limited English proficiency, I always keep in mind the following:

     _____ Their limited English proficiency is in no way a reflection of their level of intellectual functioning.

     _____ Their limited ability to speak the language of the dominant culture has no bearing on their ability to communicate effectively in their language of origin.

     _____ They may be literate neither in their language of origin nor in English.

_____ I understand that it may be necessary to use alternatives to written communication for some families, as word of mouth may be a preferred method of receiving information.

_____ I encourage and invite parents or family members to volunteer and assist regardless of their ability to speak English.

_____ I use alternative formats and varied approaches to communicate with students and their family members who have disabilities.

_____ I recognize and accept that there often are differences between the language used at school and in the home setting.

_____ I avoid imposing values that may conflict with or be inconsistent with those of cultures or ethnic groups other than my own.

_____ I discourage students from using racial and ethnic slurs by helping them understand that certain words can hurt others.

_____ I screen books, movies, and other media resources for negative cultural, ethnic, or racial stereotypes before sharing them with students or parents.

_____ I understand and accept that *family* is defined differently by different cultures (e.g., extended family members, godparents).

_____ I recognize and accept that individuals from culturally diverse backgrounds may desire varying degrees of acculturation into the dominant culture.

_____ I recognize, accept, and respect that male–female roles in families may vary significantly among different cultures (e.g., who makes major decisions).

_____ I understand that age and life-cycle factors must be considered in interactions with individuals and families (e.g., a high value is placed on decisions of elders in many societies).

_____ I accept that religion and other beliefs may influence how families respond to illnesses, disease, disability, and death.

_____ I recognize and accept that folk and religious beliefs may influence a family's reaction and approach to a child with a disability.

_____ I understand that traditional approaches to disciplining children are influenced by culture.

_____ I understand that families from different cultures will have different expectations of their children for acquiring self-help skills.

_____ I accept and respect that customs and beliefs about food, its value, preparation, and use are different from culture to culture.

Source: Adapted from Goode, T. D. (2004). Promoting cultural competence and cultural diversity in early intervention and early childhood settings. Washington, DC: Georgetown University Center for Child and Human Development. Retrieved June 1, 2007, from www11.georgetown.edu/research/gucchd/nccc/documents/ Checklist.EIEC.doc.pdf.

of physical or psychological abuse. Students in these groups are at risk for school failure because of the environment or circumstances in which they live.

You may find it particularly challenging to seek assistance for students with special needs who do not have disabilities according to special education laws, because no single group of professionals is responsible for educating them. As students with disabilities spend increasing amounts of time in general education classes, special education teachers and other special services providers often informally assist teachers in planning and adapting educational activities for them. Thus, other students with special needs often benefit from the trend toward inclusive education for students with disabilities.

Summary

Special education refers to the specialized instruction received by the millions of students in the United States who have disabilities and is guided by the concept of the least restrictive environment (LRE). Current special education practices have evolved from a combination of historical factors, including the inception of compulsory public education early in the 20th century, research questioning instructional practices for students with disabilities, the civil rights movement and related court cases, and a series of federal civil rights and education laws, including Section 504, P.L. 94-142, ADA, IDEA, and NCLB.

Inclusive practices today have been shaped by the historical, legislative, and litigative dimensions of special education. Its primary goals are to improve student outcomes and respond to student and parent rights and perspectives. However, the implementation of inclusive practices can be complicated by uncertainty about their meaning;

professional understanding, attitude, and skill; and practical dilemmas related to funding and other resources.

Federal law identifies 13 categories of disability that may entitle students to special education services: learning disabilities, speech or language impairments, mental retardation (also called *intellectual disabilities*), emotional disturbance, autism, hearing impairments, visual impairments, deaf-blindness, orthopedic impairments, traumatic brain injury, other health impairments, multiple disabilities, and developmental delays. Many other students have special needs not addressed through special education, including those who are gifted or talented; who have ADHD; who are at risk, including English-language learners and slow learners; and whose life situations comprise high risk for school failure. Nearly all public school teachers are responsible for instructing students with disabilities and other special needs.

Back to the Cases

This section provides opportunities for you to apply the knowledge gained in this chapter to the cases described at the beginning of this chapter. The questions and activities that follow demonstrate how these standards and principles, along with other concepts that you have learned about in this chapter, connect to the everyday activities of all teachers.

Thomas, as you may remember from the beginning of the chapter, is a student with autism. If you believe that inclusion has been successful for Thomas, explain what factors led you to that conclusion and may contribute to successful inclusion with typically achieving peers.

(INTASC Principles 1.03 and 1.05 and CEC Standards 1 and 10.) If you believe that inclusion is problematic for Thomas, his teachers, or classmates, explain what factors led you to that conclusion and may prevent successful inclusion with typically achieving peers.

Angela underwent an interesting placement process. After you have read the description of her experiences at the beginning of the chapter, review the court cases provided in Figure 1.2. Each had an impact on inclusive practices in public schools across the United States. Which cases support the practices found in Angela's case? (INTASC Principles 1.05 and 9.02 and CEC Standard 1.) Offer specific examples to support your answer.

Aaron, as you may recall, is troubled by his learning disability. Several of the assistive technologies mentioned in the Technology Notes on page 26 could provide support for Aaron's problems with attention and written tests. Select two or three technologies that you would recommend to Aaron. (INTASC Principle 1.03 and CEC Standard 10.) Remembering that Aaron does not want to stand out or be treated differently, what would you say to him that would help him accept these assistive supports?

Key Terms and Concepts

Adequate yearly progress (AYP) (p. 14)

Americans with Disabilities Act (ADA) (p. 10)

Brown v. Board of Education (p. 9)

Cross-categorical approach (p. 27)

High-incidence disabilities (p. 27)

Highly qualified teacher (p. 13)

Inclusive practices (p. 5)

Individuals with Disabilities Education Improvement Act (IDEA) (p. 12)

Least restrictive environment (LRE) (p. 3)

Low-incidence disabilities (p. 27)

Mainstreaming (p. 4)

No Child Left Behind Act of 2001 (NCLB) (p. 13)

Public Law (P.L.) 94-142 (p. 10)

Related services (p. 3)

Section 504 (p. 10)

Special education (p. 3)

Supplementary aids and services (p. 3)

PEARSON
myeducationlab
Where the Classroom Comes to Life

Now go to the Friend and Bursuck, Fifth Edition, MyEducationLab course at www.myeducationlab.com to

- take a pretest to assess your initial comprehension of the chapter content
- study chapter content with your individualized study plan
- take a posttest to assess your understanding of chapter content
- engage in multimedia exercises to help you build a deeper and more applied understanding of chapter content

Applications in **Teaching Practice**

Understanding Contemporary Special Education

It is a new school year—your first as a teacher in the Danville School District. You are excited about your new job but worried about following the district curriculum and making sure your students succeed on high-stakes tests. Then you learn that you will be responsible for the following students, and you find that you need all the skills for reaching diverse groups of students that you learned in your professional preparation program:

■ Cassie is a bright young woman who has a visual impairment. To read, she uses a computer that greatly magnifies the materials. She also needs to work in bright light, and she gets fatigued from the effort required to use what little vision she has.

■ Ramon is a young man identified as having a learning disability. His reading ability is significantly below grade level. He also seems disorganized. He often forgets to bring materials and assignments to class, and he frequently asks for help immediately after directions for an assignment have been given.

■ Tory lives in a foster home. He was removed from his mother's care because of several incidents of abuse. Tory is an angry child. He often refuses to work, he sometimes loses his temper and throws a book or crumples a paper, and he misses school frequently.

Questions

1. What are the possible strengths that Cassie, Ramon, and Tory might bring to your classroom? How can you emphasize their possible strengths instead of their difficulties? What is the rationale for assigning these students to a general education classroom like yours? How do the provisions of IDEA and NCLB affect these students' educational rights and responsibilities? What are appropriate goals you as a teacher should have as you begin to instruct them? Discuss with your classmates how Cassie, Ramon, and Tory's special needs might be demonstrated in an elementary school, middle school, or high school classroom.

2. What are some of the benefits and opportunities of educating these students in your classroom? What positive outcomes should you expect? How can you ensure these positive outcomes?

3. What are some of the risks and concerns related to educating these students in your classroom? What types of systemic supports could prevent or significantly reduce these risks and concerns? How might your own beliefs be either a benefit or a risk for these students?

4. If you spoke with the parents of Cassie, Ramon, and Tory, what might you expect them to say? What unique views might each student's parents have? How might their views be influenced by their family cultures and experiences? What could you do to encourage parent participation for your students?

5. What are your concerns and questions when you think about your responsibilities for educating students with disabilities and other special needs in your classroom—whether in the elementary grades, middle school, or high school? In what ways do you think you can make a contribution to your students' education? What types of support might you need? If you write your responses to these questions, keep them with your text and use them as a basis for discussion as you learn more in later chapters.

Further Readings

Klein, S., & Kemp, J. (2004). *Reflections from a different journey: What adults with disabilities wish all parents knew.* New York: McGraw-Hill.

This book is a set of essays and stories told by individuals with disabilities about what it was like growing up. Although the primary audience is parents, the book contains much information about understanding students with disabilities that will be valuable to teachers and other educators.

O'Brien, R., & Smith, R. M. (2003). *Voices from the edge: Narratives about the Americans with Disabilities Act.* New York: Oxford University Press.

This book is a collection of stories about individuals with disabilities and their experiences in U.S. society. The book aims to demonstrate that in spite of federal legislation, people with disabilities still face many challenges in going about their daily lives.

Smith, J. D. (2003). *In search of better angels: Stories of disability in the human family.* Thousand Oaks, CA: Corwin.

> This book, based largely on the author's experience as a special educator for more than three decades, is a series of stories intended to help readers to understand individuals with disabilities in terms of their strengths, to care about these individuals' experiences, and to recognize the shared responsibility of all people to embrace diversity.

Wright, P. W. D., & Wright, P. D. (2007). *Wrightslaw: Special education law* (2nd ed.). Hartfield, VA: Harbor House Law Press.

> If you are interested in learning more about the laws that govern special education, this book provides the text of IDEA and its regulations as well as other laws related to the education of students with disabilities. Because this book is intended primarily for parents of children with disabilities, it is written in a straightforward and concise manner. It contains a wealth of information that could assist you as an educator.

2 Special Education Procedures and Services

LEARNING *Objectives*

After you read this chapter, you will be able to

1. Explain the roles and responsibilities of the individuals who may participate in educating students with disabilities.

2. Describe the process through which a student may become eligible to receive special education services.

3. Name the components of individualized education programs (IEPs) and provide examples of them.

4. Describe the types of services that students with disabilities may receive and the settings in which they may receive them.

5. Discuss how parents participate in special education decision making and what occurs when parents and school district representatives disagree.

6. Outline the role of general education teachers in the procedures and services of special education, reflecting on their critical contributions to positive outcomes for students with disabilities.

Mr. Rodriguez is preparing for a meeting with his school's academic and behavioral intervention team (ABIT). As a fifth-grade teacher, he continues to be concerned about Lauren. Lauren came to this school near the end of the past school year, and the records of her educational history are incomplete. Lauren is reading at a beginning third-grade level, and her academic struggles seem to contribute to emerging behavior problems. It is clear that an intensive intervention is needed to address Lauren's reading needs. Mr. Rodriguez knows that the others who will attend the meeting include the school psychologist, the principal, and two other teachers. He is prepared to share with them the data he has been gathering regarding Lauren's reading and writing skills as well as the information about her that he learned in speaking with her mother. A likely outcome of the meeting is that Lauren will be provided with what is referred to as *tier 2 intervention*, which includes 100 minutes per week of additional reading instruction provided by the school's reading specialist. If after 12 weeks of this intervention Lauren is not progressing, she may be a candidate for *tier 3*, which includes 45 minutes of daily intensive reading instruction in addition to the instruction offered by Mr. Rodriguez. If none of these efforts is successful, the team may decide her difficulties could be a disability and ask that she be considered for special education services.

■ *What steps do Mr. Rodriguez and other teachers take when their students are struggling? How are decisions made regarding whether Lauren's (and other students') difficulties are serious enough to consider assessing her for special education?*

Ms. Lee, a high school English teacher, has just pulled from her mailbox something titled "IEP at a Glance." As she reads through it, she realizes that it is a summary of the individualized education program (IEP) for Jennifer, one of her students. The summary includes a list of test accommodations Jennifer should receive, and it mentions steps being taken to help Jennifer prepare for a vocational program she will attend after high school. Ms. Lee notes that the speech/language therapist, the transition specialist, and the social worker are mentioned, but the special education teacher is listed as the person to contact to answer questions.

■ *What roles do classroom teachers play in the writing of and implementation of IEPs? How are they responsible for ensuring that IEP accommodations are available in the classroom? Who are the other service providers teachers may work with as they educate students with disabilities?*

Ms. Turner teaches science to seventh-graders. Toward the end of the last school year, she was invited to become a member of her school's inclusive practices team. At a summer professional development seminar, she learned that many of the students in her school leave general education classes for a significant part of each day to receive special education services and that some students attend a different school. She worked with her colleagues to develop a plan to examine whether the options available to students at her school encourage inclusive practices, to reconsider the types of services students should receive, and to enlist the assistance of administrators, parents, and teachers in refining the school's services.

■ *What is meant by the phrase* a continuum of placement options? *How does it affect students with disabilities? How does it affect general education teachers and other school staff? How are decisions about placement made?*

R egardless of the ages of the students you plan to teach, you will find that some of them struggle to learn. Some may appear to do everything they can *not* to learn. Others may try their best but still not be successful. You might even have students who you suspect have a vision or hearing problem so serious that it prevents them from learning. You may find yourself wondering whether some of these students should be receiving special education services and who will provide them.

This chapter introduces you to people who specialize in working with students with disabilities and procedures for deciding whether a student is eligible for special education services. You also will learn how students' individualized education programs (IEPs) are designed and monitored and which services students with disabilities use. You will discover that parents play a crucial role in special education procedures and that when they or students disagree with school professionals about special services, procedures exist to help them resolve these differences. Most important, you will learn about your role in working with other professionals and parents to determine student eligibility for special education, carrying out students' educational programs, and monitoring student learning.

> This chapter introduces you to people who specialize in working with students with disabilities and procedures for deciding whether a student is eligible for special education services.

*W*ho Are the Professionals in Special Education?

Students with disabilities are entitled to a wide range of supports and services. Not surprisingly, many different individuals can be involved in the delivery of these services. You probably will interact with some of these professionals, such as special education teachers, almost every day. Others you might work with only occasionally. Some of these professionals serve students indirectly or work only with the few students who have the most challenging disabilities. Together, however, these educators create, implement, and evaluate the special education that students with disabilities receive.

General Education Teachers

As the *general education teacher,* you are the first professional discussed in this section because for many students with suspected or documented disabilities, you are the person who has the most detailed knowledge of their day-to-day needs in your classroom. Your responsibilities span several areas. You are the person most likely to bring to the attention of other professionals a student whom you suspect may have a disability (Egyed & Short, 2006). That is, you may encounter a student who is reading significantly below grade level, a student whose behavior is so different from that of other students that you suspect an emotional disorder, or a student who has extraordinary difficulty focusing on learning.

When you suspect a disability, you document the student's characteristics and behaviors that led to your concern by gathering samples of the student's work, compiling descriptions of his behavior, and keeping notes of how you have attempted to address the problem (Lane, Mahdavi, & Borthwick-Duffy, 2003). You work with special education colleagues and other professionals to systematically implement interventions in your classroom to clarify whether the student's problems need further exploration (Buck, Polloway, Smith-Thomas, & Cook, 2003; Fuchs & Fuchs, 2006). If the student is referred

Video Homework Exercise

Go to the Homework and Exercises section in Chapter 2 of MyEducationLab to meet two teachers: one special educator and one general educator.

for assessment for special education, you contribute information about his academic and social functioning in your classroom and help identify the student's strengths, needs, and educational program components. For example, you might help others understand the curricular expectations in your classroom and the types of accommodations that may be necessary for the student to succeed there. If special education services are deemed necessary, you participate in deciding appropriate goals and, for some students, objectives. You also might assist special services staff members in updating parents on their child's quarterly and yearly progress. Most important, you are expected to work with special services staff to provide appropriate instruction within your classroom (Abell, Bauder, & Simmons, 2005; Burstein, Sears, Wilcoxen, Cabello, & Spagna, 2004). Several of the key responsibilities of a general education teacher are summarized in Figure 2.1.

FIGURE 2.1 **General Education Teacher Responsibilities Related to Implementing IDEA**

Identify students with special needs serious enough to seek input from colleagues.

Contribute to discussions of students as a member of an intervention assistance team.

Implement strategies and activities as part of a response to intervention (RtI) procedure.

Communicate with colleagues regarding students with disabilities.

Provide day-to-day instruction.

Collaborate with parents regarding student strengths and needs.

Participate in writing IEPs as a member of the multidisciplinary team.

When all your responsibilities are listed, your role in planning and providing special services to students may seem overwhelming. However, studies of general education teachers typically indicate that they are willing and able to contribute to the education of students with disabilities as long as some conditions are met. The most important conditions include having administrative leadership and staff preparation, sufficient time for teacher planning, and adequate funding and other resources for program support (Burstein et al., 2004; Elhoweris & Alsheikh, 2006; Idol, 2006).

Special Education Teachers

Special education teachers are the professionals with whom you are most likely to have ongoing contact in teaching students with disabilities. They are responsible for managing and coordinating the services a student receives, including writing and implementing the individualized education program (IEP). They also typically provide direct and indirect instruction to students who are assigned to them (Murray, 2004; Wasburn-Moses, 2005). In addition, they may consult with you regarding a student suspected of having a disability and work with you to determine whether a referral for assessment for possible special education is warranted, a process explained later in this chapter.

> Special education teachers are the professionals with whom you are most likely to have ongoing contact in teaching students with disabilities.

Depending on the state in which you teach and the disabilities of the students in your classroom, you may work with different types of special education teachers. Sometimes special education teachers are assigned to work with any of the students with disabilities in your class. For example, a special education teacher may support a student with learning disabilities and also a student with a moderate intellectual disability or a speech or language impairment. That professional works indirectly with other special education professionals to ensure that each student's educational plan is being implemented and monitored. In some locales, special education teachers work only with specific categories of students. Your school may have a specific teacher for students with learning disabilities or emotional disabilities. Likewise, a teacher for students with visual or hearing impairments may be available if needed. In states that do not use categorical labels for students, some teachers work with students with high-incidence disabilities or low-incidence disabilities.

www.**r**esources

Explore career options related to working with students with disabilities at the website for the National Clearinghouse for Professions in Special Education (www.special-ed-careers.org).

In other situations, special education teachers may be designated by the type of services they provide. For example, for some students with high-incidence disabilities in your class, you may work with a *consulting teacher* (Friend & Cook, 2007). This professional might meet with you regularly to monitor students' progress and address your concerns about students but might not directly teach them. You also might work with a *resource teacher* who divides time among directly instructing students, working with teachers regarding student needs, and co-teaching, a topic addressed in Chapter 3 (Knackendoffel, 2005). In some high schools, special education teachers now are assigned to work with a particular department, attending department meetings and providing supports for all students with disabilities enrolled in that department's courses.

Yet another type of special education teacher designated by type of services is an *inclusion specialist* or *support facilitator* (for example, Klinger & Vaughn, 2002). In inclusive schools, inclusion specialists are responsible for providing some student instruction, problem solving with teachers, and coordinating the services a student receives. Often they focus on ensuring that the needs of students with moderate, severe, or multiple disabilities are being met.

For some groups of students, the special educator with whom you interact might be an *itinerant teacher*. Itinerant teachers often have roles like the professionals just described, but they travel between two or more school sites to provide services to students (Correa-Torres & Howell, 2004). Teachers for students with vision or hearing disabilities often are itinerant. However, if you work in a school district where each school has only a few students with disabilities, even the special educator for students with high-incidence disabilities may deliver services this way.

One other type of special education teacher is a *transition specialist.* This professional typically works in a high school setting and helps prepare students to leave school for vocational training, employment, or postsecondary education (Council for Exceptional Children, 2000; Field, Sarver, & Shaw, 2003). No matter what subject you teach in high school, you might work very closely with a transition specialist, but this is especially likely in business education, consumer sciences, industrial and other vocational arts, and similar areas. This professional also spends time working directly with students to assess their skills and interests related to life after school. A transition specialist works with community businesses to arrange student job sites and resolve problems related to student workers (Leucking, 2004). This professional also may serve as a *job coach,* accompanying a student to a job site and helping her master the skills needed to do the job successfully.

As the nature of special education services changes, so do the job responsibilities and titles of special educators. For example, you might find that the professionals in your school who used to be called *special education teachers* are now referred to as *special services teachers (SSTs)* or *intervention specialists (ISs).* This change in title represents an effort to de-label teachers and parallels the effort to de-emphasize students' labels—that is, to focus on student needs rather than the language of disability. Regardless of the type of special education teachers with whom you work, you will find that they are important instructional partners who are no longer relegated to teaching just in the special education classroom. They support students by creating adapted materials, teaching with you in the general education classroom, working directly and separately with students who have disabilities, and often serving as coordinators for all the services any single student may receive.

Who are the professionals who support students with disabilities and their classroom teachers? What is the general education teacher's role in identifying students with disabilities and providing their instruction?

Other Specialists and Related Service Providers

In addition to working with special education teachers, you will have contact with a variety of other service providers (Downing, 2004). They, too, play important roles in educating students with disabilities.

● **School Psychologists** *School psychologists* offer at least two types of expertise related to educating students with disabilities. First, school psychologists often have a major responsibility for determining a student's intellectual, academic, social, emotional, and/or behavioral functioning. They typically contribute a detailed written analysis of the student's strengths and areas of need; in many school districts, this document is referred to as a "psych report" (that is, a psychological report). In a related role, school psychologists sometimes chair the multidisciplinary team that meets to decide whether a student has a disability and if so what types of services are needed (Arivett, Rust, Brissie, & Dansby, 2007).

A second major task for school psychologists is designing strategies to address students' academic and social or behavior problems (National Association of School Psychologists, 2002). Sometimes school psychologists serve as behavior consultants. Occasionally, they assist a teacher by working with an entire class group on social skills. They also might provide individual assistance to students with emotional or behavioral problems who are not eligible for special education. Unfortunately, many school districts can employ only

> In addition to working with special education teachers, you will have contact with a variety of other service providers. They, too, play important roles in educating students with disabilities.

Info Sheet Homework Exercise

Go to the Homework and Exercises section in Chapter 2 of MyEducationLab to learn how related services can be provided in inclusive classrooms.

enough school psychologists to complete required assessment duties; when this occurs, school psychologists may not be available to assist students or teachers directly.

● **Counselors**   Although *counselors* most often advise high school students and assist students with disabilities as they transition from school to postschool options (Milsom & Hartley, 2005), they also work at other school levels and contribute to the education of students with disabilities (Frye, 2005; National Clearinghouse for Professions in Special Education, 2003). For example, counselors in some school districts assess students' social and emotional functioning, including areas such as self-concept; motivation; attitude toward school, peers, and teachers; and social skills. Counselors also can provide services to both teachers and students. For teachers, they might suggest ways to draw out a student who is excessively shy, to incorporate activities designed to enhance students' self-concept into day-to-day classroom instruction, or to create an emotionally safe classroom environment. For students, counselors might provide individual assistance to a student struggling to understand a parent's death or unexplained departure from the family or other stressful events, arrange group sessions with several students who share specific needs, or work with an entire class on how to interact with a peer who has a disability.

Video Homework Exercise

Go to the Homework and Exercises section in Chapter 2 of MyEducationLab to see an assessment of a student's speech and language skills.

● **Speech/Language Therapists**   Many students with disabilities have communication needs. Some have mild problems in pronouncing words or speaking clearly. Others have an extremely limited vocabulary. Yet others rely on alternative means of communication, such as communication boards. The professionals who specialize in meeting students' communication needs are *speech/language therapists* (Hartas, 2004), and they have a tremendously diverse range of school responsibilities. At the early elementary level, they might work with an entire class on language development or with an individual student on pronouncing sounds. At the intermediate elementary level, they might work on vocabulary with a group of students and might also help a student with a moderate cognitive disability pronounce some words more clearly or combine words into sentences. At the middle or high school level, they often focus on functional vocabulary and work mostly with students with low-incidence disabilities. For example, they might help a student with an intellectual disability learn to read common signs and complete tasks such as ordering in a restaurant or asking for assistance.

● **Social Workers**   *Social workers'* expertise is similar to that of counselors in terms of being able to help teachers and students address social and emotional issues (Massat, 2006). Thus, social workers may serve as consultants to teachers and also may provide individual or group assistance to students. However, social workers have additional expertise. They often are liaisons between schools and families. For example, they can create a family history by interviewing parents and visiting a student's home; this information may be critical in determining whether a student needs special education services. Similarly, they may help other school professionals work with families on matters such as gaining access to community health services. The school social worker often follows up on teacher reports about the suspected abuse or neglect of students.

fyi

The term *gross motor skills* refers to students' ability to use their large muscles effectively for walking, hopping, running, skipping, and the like. The term *fine motor skills* refers to students' proficiency using their small muscles for tasks such as writing, buttoning, and grasping.

● **Physical Therapists and Occupational Therapists**   For some students to benefit from education, they require assistance for problems with gross and fine motor skills, such as skipping or tying shoelaces. Physical and occupational therapists are the professionals who have expertise in these areas (Neal, Bigby, & Nicholson, 2004).

Physical therapists assess students' needs and provide interventions related to gross motor skills. For example, they might provide direct training in large muscle movement and control for a student with a very awkward gait. They also might monitor how students should be physically positioned, whether in a wheelchair, standing with assistance, or on the floor; how their physical needs are affecting their educational needs; and how classroom settings can be adapted to accommodate their needs.

Occupational therapists are concerned with fine motor skills; they often have the responsibility of assessing students' use of their hands and fingers and developing and implementing plans for improving related motor skills. For example, an occupational therapist may assess whether a student with a severe learning disability can appropriately grip and use a pencil. This professional might help younger students or those with more severe disabilities learn skills for feeding or dressing themselves. Occupational therapists work increasingly with teachers to incorporate fine motor skills training into classroom routines.

● **Adaptive Physical Educators**   When students have significant gross or fine motor problems, typical physical education programs in schools may not meet their needs. *Adaptive physical educators* assess students' motor needs and address them by working with teachers, physical educators, and others or directly with students (Winnick, 2005). These professionals are experts in adapting traditional physical education activities for students with disabilities. For example, they might create a simplified form of a basketball drill so that a student who has difficulty running can participate in the activity. They also might create activities that help students develop such skills as balancing, skipping, running, and throwing as well as find ways for them to participate in organized sports programs.

> Adaptive physical educators assess students' motor needs and meet them by working with teachers, physical educators, and others or directly with students.

● **Nurses**   The link between students' medical and educational needs is provided by *nurses* (Selekman, 2006). They develop student medical histories as needed, and they may screen students for vision and hearing problems. They also provide the multidisciplinary team with information about specific medical conditions a student might have and the impact the student's medication could have on educational performance. Further, nurses assist other professionals in deciding whether a student's learning or behavior problem could have a medical basis and discussing such matters with parents. Nurses most often are responsible for ensuring day to day that students with disabilities take required medication and for providing first aid and other emergency treatment. They also work with teachers and families to monitor student medical needs (for example, whether a change in medication is causing drowsiness or hyperactivity).

● **Administrators**   The school principal, assistant principal, and sometimes a department chairperson or team leader are the *administrators* most likely to participate actively in the education of students with disabilities (Lasky & Karge, 2006; Wakeman, Browder, & Flowers, 2006). Their role is to offer knowledge about the entire school community and provide perspective on school district policies regarding special education and also to help address parents' concerns. Every team that determines whether a student is eligible for special education must have administrative representation. In one school, the mother of Marisha, a student with severe language delays, requested that her daughter receive speech/language therapy for 40 minutes daily. School professionals were in agreement that this amount of therapy was not appropriate. Dr. Wade, the principal, worked with the team and the parent to negotiate the amount of speech therapy needed to accomplish Marisha's goals.

In some locales, especially large urban and suburban districts where it is difficult to ensure that all required special education procedures are followed, a *special education coordinator* or *supervisor* is part of the district's administration. This professional specializes in understanding the sometimes complex procedures of special education. Coordinators help alleviate the pressure on principals and assistant principals to accurately interpret and follow guidelines. They also explain services and options to parents, problem solve with teachers when issues arise, and assist in monitoring to ensure that students with disabilities receive needed supports.

● **Paraprofessionals**   Individuals who assist teachers and others in the provision of services to students with disabilities are *paraprofessionals* (Riggs, 2004). These individuals usually have a certificate based on completing a community college or similar training program; some are even licensed teachers. Regardless, these service providers generally complete their work under the direction of teachers and other professional staff members. Paraprofessionals also might be called *paraeducators, instructional assistants, aides,* or other titles, depending on local practices.

School districts use paraprofessionals in many different ways (Trautman, 2004), but two roles are especially common. Some paraprofessionals are assigned to specific students who need ongoing individual assistance. For example, a student with no ability to move his arms may have a paraprofessional who takes notes for him and completes other tasks such as feeding. A few students have medical conditions requiring that a specially trained paraprofessional be present to monitor their status. Paraprofessionals in this role may be referred to as *personal assistants* or *one-to-one assistants.*

A second and more common role for paraprofessionals is to assist in the delivery of special services for many students. These paraprofessionals often work in both inclusive classrooms and special education classrooms as well as on the playground, at assemblies,

Working with Paraprofessionals

No matter what grade level you teach, you will likely find yourself at some point working closely with paraprofessionals, also called *paraeducators*. These individuals are employed by school districts to provide support to students with disabilities either by working with particular students one to one or by working in general or special education classrooms with several students.

Although paraprofessionals have been part of special education services and supports for many years, only in the past decade has much attention been paid to their preparation for their roles and responsibilities for students. Paraprofessionals do not have sole responsibility for any aspect of a student's educational program. Rather, they share responsibilities with teachers and other multidisciplinary team members, and they work under the direction of a special education teacher or another professional. If a paraprofessional is assigned to your classroom in order to support students with disabilities, you probably will be expected to direct her day-to-day activities there.

These are some of the responsibilities paraprofessionals may carry out:

- Locate, arrange, or construct instructional materials.
- Assist students with eating, dressing, personal care, and bathroom use.

- Help prepare the classroom for students and keep work areas neat.
- Instruct special education students individually, in small or large groups, and/or with typical peers, supervised by licensed educators, and as specified in students' IEPs or by professionals on the service delivery team.
- Collect student data to contribute to professional team members regarding student progress toward goals.
- Score tests and certain papers using a key.
- Maintain files or records about students.
- Supervise playgrounds, halls, lunchrooms, buses, and loading zones.
- Address students' specific health needs (for example, suction tracheotomy tubes as assigned and trained by a school nurse).
- Assist and facilitate appropriate peer interactions.
- Assist students using adaptive equipment or devices (for example, a communication board).
- Support student behavior and social needs according to plans.

and during bus duty. These paraprofessionals' primary responsibility is to work with students with disabilities, but they sometimes also help other students and the teacher as the need arises and time permits. The Professional Edge contains more information about working with paraprofessionals.

● **Other Specialists** Depending on student needs and state and local practices, other professionals also may participate in the education of students with disabilities. Some school districts have *consultants* who are used only when needs exist in their specific areas of expertise (such as significant behavior problems, autism, or traumatic brain injury). If you work in a school district in which many students are non-native English speakers, you also may work with *bilingual teachers* or *bilingual special education teachers*. Bilingual teachers are not special educators, but they sometimes help in decision making related to students with disabilities who have limited English skills. Bilingual special education teachers are professionally trained both in special education and bilingual education.

Two other types of specialists may provide services to your students with disabilities. One is a *mobility specialist* whose job is to help students with visual impairments learn how to become familiar with their environments and how to travel from place to place

---

- Participate positively in evaluative or feedback sessions for improvement of their skills.

- Participate in training and coaching sessions to improve their skills associated with all duties and tasks assigned.

- Communicate with professionals about their work and students' progress on assigned tasks.

- Move or accompany students from one place to another, assisting students with mobility and transition.

- Contribute to the effectiveness of the special education team by using appropriate communication, problem-solving, and conflict management strategies.

From the Research

As the list suggests, paraprofessionals offer many valuable services to students and teachers in support of students. In an interesting study of how parents perceive the work of paraprofessionals, Werts, Harris, Tillery, and Roark (2004) gathered data in classrooms about the activities of paraprofessionals. They then shared their data with 16 parents of students with disabilities. Parents generally were satisfied with the activities of paraprofessionals, and they noted that their children often referred to the paraprofessionals at home. However, parents also recommended that paraprofessionals receive more training for their jobs, that they

communicate more with parents since they have more contact with the students than any of the professionals, and that they implement more instructional modifications for the students.

This research suggests topics for educators to consider regarding how to involve paraprofessionals as partners in the education of students with disabilities, especially in inclusive schools. It also raises some questions related to how teachers should direct the work of paraprofessionals and what types of communication teachers versus paraprofessionals should have with parents.

Sources: "Managing Paraeducators in Your School: How to Hire, Train, and Supervise Non-Certified Staff," by N. K. French, 2003, Thousand Oaks, CA: Corwin; "Preparing and Managing Paraprofessionals," by M. L. Trautman, 2004, *Intervention in School and Clinic, 39*, pp. 131–138; "What Parents Tell Us about Paraeducators," by M. G. Werts, S. Harris, C. Y. Tillery, and R. Roark, 2004, *Remedial and Special Education, 25*, pp. 232–239.

safely. These specialists consult with classroom teachers regarding students with visual impairments. The other type of service provider is a *sign-language interpreter*. Interpreters are the communication link for students with significant hearing loss (National Clearinghouse for Professions in Special Education, 2003). Interpreters listen to the instruction in a classroom and relay it using sign language to students who are deaf or hard of hearing. An interpreter might accompany a student all day or might be needed only in specific academic subjects, such as language arts.

Professionals from agencies outside the school also are part of the specialist group. If a student has been receiving services through a hospital or residential program, a physician, nurse, social worker, or other representative from that facility may work with school personnel to ensure that the student has a smooth transition back to school. Individuals from the medical community also might be involved when students are being assessed for attentional problems or when they have been injured or ill. Similarly, professionals from outside agencies might be involved when a student is receiving assistance from a community service organization or has contact with the juvenile justice system. In these instances, caseworkers may serve as liaisons to the school. Students who are transitioning from school to adult services may need support from a professional in vocational rehabilitation. Finally, parents may obtain an expert opinion from a specialist not associated with the school, and this individual can attend multidisciplinary team meetings or submit written reports for team consideration.

Parents, Students, and Advocates

When decisions are being made concerning a student with a suspected or documented disability, the best interests of the student and her family must be represented. The parents—or a person serving in the role of a parent, such as a guardian or foster parent—have the right to participate in virtually all aspects of their child's educational program

Some professionals, like sign-language interpreters, provide highly specialized services to specific groups of students.

(Al-Hassan & Gardner, 2002; Dabkowski, 2004; L. G. L. Nelson, Summers, & Turnbull, 2004), a topic addressed in more detail later in this chapter.

Often parents are strong allies for general education teachers. They can assist teachers by reviewing at home what is taught in school, rewarding their child for school accomplishments, and working with school professionals to resolve behavior and academic problems.

Whenever appropriate, students with disabilities also should be active participants in decision making about their own education. Increasingly, educators are involving students so they can directly state their needs and goals and learn to advocate for themselves, a concept referred to as **self-determination** (Chambers, Wehmeyer, Saito, Lida, Lee, & Singh, 2007; Test, Mason, Hughes, Konrad, Neale, & Wood, 2004). The extent of student participation on the team depends on the age of the student, the type and impact of the disability, and the professionals' and parents' commitment. In general, the older the student, the greater her ability to contribute, and the higher the value placed on her contribution, the greater the participation. Thus, first-grade students with disabilities usually are not expected to participate in very many decisions about their education. However, high school students with disabilities usually attend and participate in their team meetings, and their priorities and preferences are central to decision making (Arndt, Konrad, & Test, 2006). These students often have strong opinions about what they would like to do after high school, and they also take on more responsibility for monitoring their progress in reaching their goals (Gringel, Neubert, Moon, & Graham, 2003; Martin, Marshall, & Sale, 2004). You can learn more about student participation on teams in the Professional Edge on page 46.

A final team member is an *advocate*. Sometimes parents sense that they do not know enough about the policies and procedures that govern special education to represent themselves. In other instances, they are not sure school district personnel are acting in the best interests of their children. In yet other situations, parents may be uncomfortable interacting with school personnel because of language or cultural differences or for other reasons. Parents have the right to bring an advocate to team and other school meetings concerning their children. This person serves as their advisor and sometimes their spokesperson. Advocates sometimes are professionals who are compensated by parents for their services. Alternatively, they may be volunteers provided through a professional organization or parent support group or by friends or relatives.

> Whenever appropriate, students with disabilities also should be active participants in decision making about their own education.

*H*ow Can You Decide Whether a Student Need Might Be a Disability?

You will play a key role in deciding whether a student in your class should be evaluated for the presence of a disability. Although youngsters with obvious intellectual, sensory, and physical impairments usually are identified when they are infants or toddlers, learning, language, attentional, and behavioral disabilities—such as those displayed by Lauren, introduced at the beginning of the chapter—often are not diagnosed until children experience difficulty in school. Because you are the professional in daily contact with the student, you are the person most likely to notice an unmet need. It is your judgment that often initiates the special education decision-making process.

> You will play a key role in deciding whether a student in your class should be evaluated for the presence of a disability.

Self-Determination for Students with Disabilities

Think how you would react if other people constantly controlled your life, deciding what you should wear, where you should go, what career you should pursue, and what type of housing and roommates you should have. Beginning at a very young age, children typically begin to express their wishes, and they learn that they have a right to act on those wishes. (For example, have you ever tried to convince a 3-year-old that the two articles of clothing she selected to wear do not match?) But despite good intentions by professionals and parents, many students and adults with disabilities have been denied opportunities to make their own life decisions. Reversing this situation has become a goal for the field (for example, Martin, Van Dycke, Christensen, Greene, Gardner, & Lovett, 2006; Wehymeyer, 2007). One way self-determination can occur is for students to actively participate in or lead their IEP meetings and other planning activities.

Student-Led IEPs

When students lead their IEP meetings, they learn to think and advocate for themselves (Mason, McGahee-Kovac, & Johnson, 2004). They can learn to do this beginning at a very early age. For example, elementary students might have the role of introducing their parents to the team and describing to team members what they have been learning in school. Students in middle school might explain their disabilities and the impact of those disabilities, share their strengths, and discuss accommodations needed. In high school, students might lead the entire conference, working to ensure that the IEP and transition plan reflect their preferences and plans for the future. Specific student roles can vary, and students should be prepared for participating so they know the process and ways they contribute to it. Further, general education teachers find that students who actively participate in their IEP meetings have better skills for interacting with adults, better understanding of their special needs, greater awareness of resources available to help them, and more willingness to accept responsibility for themselves (Test et al., 2004).

Person-Centered Planning

Another method of self-determination called *person-centered planning* was developed by professionals from both the United States and Canada and usually is related to IEP planning. It emphasizes these dimensions:

■ *Community presence.* Identify the community settings that the student uses and the ones that would benefit him. The intent is to incorporate these settings into the educational planning process.

■ *Choice.* Identify decisions made *by* the student and decisions made *for* the student. The goal of person-centered planning is to transfer as many choices to the student as possible.

■ *Competence.* Identify the skills that will best assist the student to participate fully in the school and community and the strategies that will be most effective for teaching those skills.

■ *Respect.* Clarify roles the student has in the school and local community. The goal is to strengthen and expand those roles and decrease or eliminate personal characteristics that might cause the student to be perceived by others in a stereotypical way.

■ *Community participation.* Specify people with whom the student spends time at school and in other settings. The goal is to identify individuals who can advocate for the student and to foster friendships with age-appropriate peers.

A number of person-centered planning approaches have been developed, and you may find that one of these is used in your school district. They include Making Action Plans (MAPs), Planning Alternative Tomorrows with Hope (PATH), and Circle of Friends.

Sources: Adapted from "How to Help Students Lead Their IEP Meetings," by C. Y. Mason, M. McGahee-Kovac, and L. Johnson, 2004, *Teaching Exceptional Children, 36*(3), pp. 18–25; and *Person-Centered Practices: Building Personalized Supports That Respect the Dreams of People with Disabilities,* by REACH of Louisville, n.d., retrieved September 15, 2004, from www.reachoflouisville.com/person-centered/Default.htm. Reprinted with permission.

Analyze Unmet Needs

As you teach, you sometimes will discover that you have a nagging concern about a student. This concern might begin early in the school year, or it might take several months to emerge. For example, when you review a student's records and consider your own impressions and concerns, you may decide that the student's achievement is not within the typical range, given the standards of your school district, community expectations, and state achievement standards. Should you ask other professionals to assess the student for eligibility for special education? Perhaps. But first, you need to ask yourself some questions.

● **What Are Specific Examples of Unmet Needs?** Having a vague worry about a student is far different from specifically stating a concern. For example, sensing that a student is unmotivated is not a clear concern. What does the student do that leads you to conclude that motivation is a problem? Is it that the student doesn't make eye contact when speaking to you or that the rewards and consequences that affect other students seem to have no effect, positive or negative, on this student? Vague concerns and hunches must be supported by specific information. Phrases such as "slow in learning," "poor attitude toward school," "doesn't pay attention," and "never gets work completed" might have very different meanings to different professionals. To prepare to share your concern with others, your first step is to ask yourself "When I say the student . . . , what examples clarify what I mean?"

● **Is There a Chronic Pattern Negatively Affecting Learning?** Nearly all students go through periods when they struggle to learn, behave inappropriately, or otherwise cause you concern. Sometimes a situation outside school affects a student. For example, parents divorcing, the family being evicted from its apartment, elderly grandparents moving in with the family, or a family member being injured or arrested might negatively affect student learning or behavior. However, the impact of these traumatic events should not be permanent, and the student should gradually return to previous levels of functioning.

Students with disabilities also may be affected by specific situations and events, but their learning and behavior needs form a chronic pattern. In other words, they struggle over a long period of time regardless of the circumstances. For example, Betsy, who has a learning disability, has difficulty remembering sight words no matter what level they are or how creatively they are introduced. Jared, a high school student with an emotional disability, is withdrawn whether sitting in a large class or interacting in a small group. Julianna, an eighth-grader who had a severe head injury last year, usually seems to grasp abstract concepts as they are taught, but she struggles to describe or apply them after instruction.

● **Are the Unmet Needs Becoming More Serious as Time Passes?** Sometimes a student's needs appear to become greater over time. For example, Ben, who seemed to see well at the beginning of the school year, now holds books closer and closer to his face, squints when he tries to read, and complains about headaches. Karen, who began the school year reluctant but willing to complete assignments, refuses to do any work during class by November. Indications that a student's needs are increasing are a signal to ask for input from others.

● **Is the Student's Learning or Behavior Significantly Different from That of Classmates?** As you think about your concerns about a student, ask yourself how he compares to other students. For example, it has been demonstrated that students at risk for special education referral achieve at a significantly lower level than other students and are more likely to have significant behavior problems (Hosp & Reschly, 2003). However, if you have eight students who are all struggling, the reason might be that the information or skills are beyond the reach of the entire group or that your teaching approach is not

Analyze and Reflect

What might be the effect—on the student and your perception of the student—of deciding prematurely that he should be referred as possibly having a disability? What strategies could you use to avoid making this error, particularly for students from diverse backgrounds?

accomplishing what you had planned. Even though self-reflection is sometimes difficult, when many students are experiencing problems, it is important to analyze how the curriculum or teaching might be contributing to the situation. In such instances, you should make changes in those two areas before seeking other assistance.

Keep in mind that many students have needs that *do* signal the presence of disabilities. Perhaps you are an elementary teacher who cannot seem to find enough books at the right level for one student in your fourth-grade class who is almost a nonreader. Perhaps you are an eighth-grade social studies teacher who is worried about two students' apparent inability to read the textbook or understand the themes of history integral to your curriculum. Maybe you are an algebra teacher who finds that one student seems to lack many prerequisite skills for succeeding in the course. Students with disabilities have needs that are significantly different from those of most other students.

● **Do You Discover That You Cannot Find a Pattern?** In some instances, the absence of a pattern in students' learning or behavior is as much an indicator that you should request assistance as is a distinct pattern. Perhaps Curtis has tremendous mood swings, and you arrive at school each day wondering whether he will have a good day or a bad day. However, you cannot find a way to predict which it will be. Or consider Becka, who learns science with ease but is failing English, according to a colleague on your seventh-grade team. You are not sure why her learning is so different in the two subjects. In a third example, in physical education, Tyrone seems to have average motor skills on some days but on other days frequently stumbles and cannot participate fully in the learning stations you have created.

Communicate Your Observations and Try Your Own Interventions

Your analysis of your students' unmet needs is the basis for further action. Although ultimately, you may decide to formally seek assistance for one of your students, part of your responsibility in attempting to help the student is gathering other information and trying to resolve the problem first.

● **Contact the Parents** One of your first strategies should be to contact the student's family (Hughes & Greenhough, 2006). Parents or other family members often can inform you about changes in the student's life that could be affecting school performance. Family members also can help you understand how the student's activities outside school might influence schoolwork, including clubs, gang involvement, employment, and responsibilities at home. Further, by contacting the family, you might learn that what you perceive as a problem is mostly a reflection of a cultural difference. For example, a student whose family emigrated from Thailand is extremely quiet because silence signals respect in her native culture, not because she is unable to participate.

Parents also are your partners in working to resolve some student learning problems (e.g., Benner & Mistry, 2007; Hughes & Kwok, 2007). They can assist you in monitoring whether homework is completed and returned to school, whether behavior problems are occurring on the walk home, or whether a physician is concerned about a child's medical condition. If you have students whose homes do not have a telephone or e-mail access and whose parents do not have transportation to come to school, your social worker or principal can help you make needed contact.

● **Contact Colleagues** Especially as a new teacher, you will want to informally discuss your concerns with other professionals to gain additional perspectives on the student's needs. In many schools, a special education teacher, assistant principal, department

Especially as a new teacher, you will want to informally discuss your concerns with other professionals to gain additional perspectives on the student's needs.

chairperson, or another professional can arrange to observe the student in your class and then discuss the observation. If your school psychologist is available, you might ask for consultation assistance. In schools where grade-level teams or other types of teams or departments meet, you can raise your concerns in that context. One hallmark of today's schools is an array of professionals with expertise in many areas. With a little exploration, you will likely find that your school has an in-house resource you can access to check your perceptions against a broader perspective.

Reading Homework Exercise

Go to the Homework and Exercises section in Chapter 2 of MyEducationLab to read about how one state is providing a system-wide intervention plan.

● **Try Simple Interventions**   Part of your responsibility as a teacher is to create a classroom where students can succeed. To cultivate such a setting, you can make simple changes as part of your efforts to address a student's unmet needs. Here are some examples:

- Have you tried moving the student's seat?
- Have you incorporated teaching strategies that help the student actively participate in lessons (for example, using choral responding, in which all students together repeat answers aloud)?
- Have you thought about ways to make your tests easier for the student to follow (for example, using more white space between items or sections)?
- Have you given the student only part of an assignment at one time to prevent him from becoming overwhelmed?
- Have you observed the student closely to determine whether helping her work one problem is enough to get her to work on the rest?

These are just a few alterations that many teachers make; many others are presented throughout this textbook. Sometimes these small accommodations are sufficient to help a student learn. In any case, you should try common interventions before deciding a student might need the far more intense service of special education.

● **Document the Unmet Need**   If you anticipate requesting assistance for a student, you need to demonstrate the seriousness of your concern and your systematic attempts to help meet the student's needs. If you have implemented a plan to improve student behavior, keep a record of how effective it has been. If you have contacted parents several times, keep a log of your conversations. If you have tried to decrease the number of times the student misses your first-hour class, summarize your attendance data. Strategies to document student needs serve two main purposes. First, they help you do a reality check on whether the problem is as serious as you think it is. If you gather data from other students as a comparison, you can judge whether the unmet needs of one student are significantly different from those of typical students. Second, the information you collect will help you communicate with other professionals. Special service providers cannot possibly meet every need in every classroom. Their work is reserved in large part for extraordinary student needs, and your documentation will help in decision making about providing the assistance you seek.

How Do Students Obtain Special Services?

The majority of students who receive special education have high-incidence disabilities (such as learning disabilities) that you may be the first to recognize. If you teach at the elementary level, you probably will have students nearly every year whom you refer for possible special services. If you teach in middle school, junior high, or high school, you will find that many students with disabilities already have been identified before they reach

Reading Homework Exercise

Go to the Homework and Exercises section in Chapter 2 of MyEducationLab to read about what you can do to gather information for the assessment process.

Building Teaching Skills Simulation Exercise

Go to the Building Teaching Skills section in Chapter 2 of MyEducationLab to learn how general education teachers participate in the prereferral process.

www.r e s o u r c e s

At Intervention Central (www.interventioncentral.org) you can find a wide array of tools for implementing response to intervention procedures. Among the many resources included on the site are templates for gathering student data and a bullying prevention booklet.

your classes. However, there are exceptions; students may be found eligible for special education at any time during their school years. As a teacher, you always have the option of asking a team of professionals to consider whether one of your students needs special education services.

Having a serious and documented concern about a student is only the first step in considering whether a disability may be present. Your concern brings the student to the attention of other school professionals so that further information can be gathered and decisions made. The specific, formal procedures that must be followed to determine student eligibility for special education services are designed to ensure that only students who truly need these services receive them. These procedures are described in the following sections and summarized in Figure 2.2, which illustrates the flow of the procedures from beginning to end.

Initial Consideration of Student Problems

General education teachers, principals, special services personnel, parents, physicians, and social service agency personnel all may initiate the process of obtaining special education for a student. Most often, however, a general education teacher notices a pattern of academic underachievement, inconsistent learning, serious behavior problems, difficulties in social skills, or a persistent physical or sensory problem. When such problems occur, the teacher brings the student to the attention of others who help decide whether special education services are warranted.

Depending on the policies of your state and local district, there are two ways that the process of formally addressing student learning and behavior concerns can begin: (1) via an intervention assistance team or (2) using response-to-intervention procedures, an option available since implementation of the 2004 reauthorization of the Individuals with Disabilities Education Improvement Act (IDEA).

● **Intervention Assistance Team**   One way to begin the process of helping a student suspected of having a disability is to bring the problem to the attention of a team (Friend & Cook, 2007). This team, often called an **intervention assistance team,** usually includes general education teachers, special services personnel, and an administrator. Teachers who want to "bring a student to the team" complete a referral form, on which they describe the student's strengths and problems and describe efforts they have made to assist the student. The teacher then meets with the team to discuss the written information, consider alternative strategies for assisting the student, and determine whether the student should have a detailed assessment for potential special education services (Lane et al., 2003). The unifying characteristic of this type of team is an emphasis on problem solving among all members.

● **Response to Intervention**   A relatively new procedure for analyzing students' learning problems is called **response to intervention (RtI).** Currently authorized just for students who may have learning disabilities, response to intervention calls for the systematic use of increasingly intensive, research-based interventions as a means for deciding whether a learning disability exists (Fuchs & Deshler, 2007). It is based on the presumption that approximately 75 to 80 percent of students will be able to learn if they receive high-quality instruction, that approximately 15 to 20 percent will benefit from moderately intensive instruction, and that the remaining 5 to 10 percent will need highly intensive instruction and possibly special education services. For example, Ms. Petersen is a first-grade teacher. She uses a district-adopted reading program in her class that has been demonstrated through research to be effective with students. This is called a *tier 1 intervention.* The most recent screening assessment showed that one of Ms. Petersen's students, Jorgé, has not made much progress in reading; his skills are still at a kindergarten level. A team agreed that Jorgé's problems are significant and decided that he should participate in a supplemental reading program in a small group led by the

FIGURE 2.2 The Decision-Making Process for Special Education

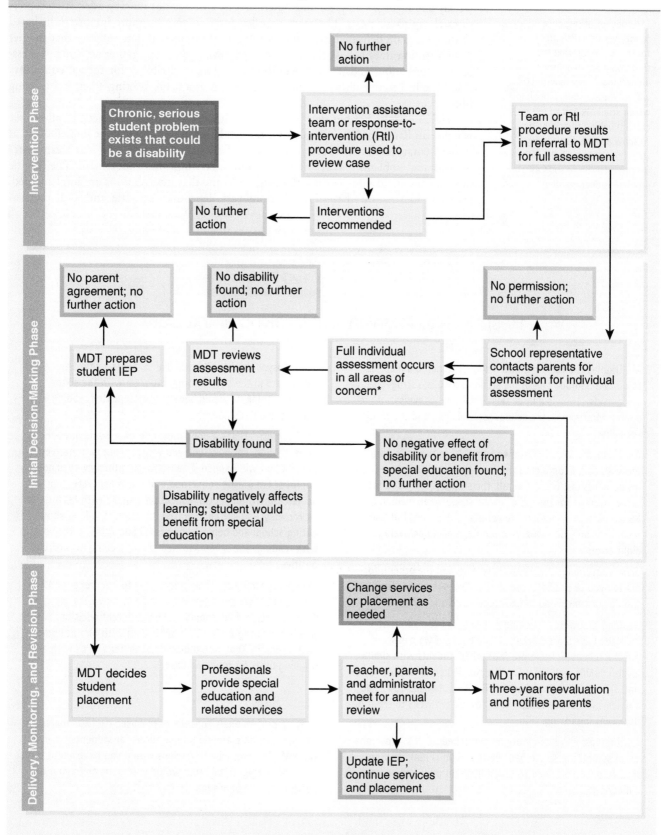

* Federal law permits the identification of students as having learning disabilities on the basis of RtI procedures. When this option is used, the full assessment activities may be significantly reduced.

The concept of response to intervention (RtI) arose from recognition that the traditional approach for identifying students with LD was a "wait-to-fail" model, in which students had to fall far enough behind in achievement to show a large discrepancy with their potential. RtI calls for intervention as soon as a problem is documented.

school's reading specialist. This service occurred four times each week for 30 minutes and was considered a tier 2 intervention. After 12 weeks, the team reviewed the data gathered weekly about Jorgé's progress and noted that he still was not making adequate progress to catch up to his peers. The team enrolled Jorgé in an even more intense skills-based reading program delivered five days a week for 50 minutes. If data indicate that the tier 3 intervention does not work, the team may review the data, gather additional assessment information, and make a decision about Jorgé's eligibility for special education. The Case in Practice illustrates what might occur at a team meeting when RtI is being implemented.

IDEA permits RtI but does not mandate it, and so you should check locally to see whether an RtI procedure is in place. Although RtI is mostly likely to be implemented at the elementary level, it can occur whenever professionals determine a student is experiencing learning problems that are significant and interfering with achievement. The specific number of tiers of intervention, the length of time that interventions are implemented, and the exact nature of the interventions vary depending on state and local policies.

Case in Practice

Response to Intervention: Looking at the Data

Mr. Thomas is a fourth-grade teacher attending a meeting to discuss Samuel, one of his students who is a struggling reader. Here is a brief segment of the conversation among Mr. Thomas, the school psychologist, and the reading specialist:

Mr. Thomas: With assistance from Ms. Jefferson (a paraprofessional), I completed the reading fluency measure for all my students last week. Overall, the students are just a little below average for this point in the school year, reading at 85 words per minute with fewer than five errors. But Sam is reading at only 50 words per minute, making an average of eight errors.

School psychologist: With these data and the other information you've provided, we should discuss whether Sam should start receiving more intensive instruction.

Reading specialist: Looking at his data, I can add that I already have a group that he could join, if we can work out the schedule. There are four other students with similar levels of skills, and I'm using the supplemental fluency materials from our reading program. But I would need you to do a quick curriculum-based check twice each week to see if his fluency is improving.

Mr. Thomas: We can work on the schedule. It's important to do something so we can see that Sam is making progress. And we just need to talk a little bit about the data collection.

School psychologist: I'd also like to suggest that Sam participate in the peer tutoring program with the sixth-graders. I think he would benefit from repeated reading with one of the older students.

Mr. Thomas: That's a good idea. I do have some questions, though. For how long will we try these two interventions? What will happen if Sam's reading fluency does not improve? I'm a little concerned that we should refer him for an assessment for special education. I spoke with his mother on Monday, and she commented that Sam is talking about hating school and being embarrassed about his problems with reading. She is very worried about keeping his attitude positive.

School psychologist: The guideline is to intervene for 12 weeks, but if we don't see any change in six weeks, we can meet to decide if we should make a different decision. Will Sam's mother agree to assist by reading with him at home each evening? That would provide both her and us with an ongoing basis for touching base.

REFLECTIONS

Why do professionals consider data-based decision making so important in planning interventions for students? If you were Mr. Thomas, what questions would you have about the planned intervention? What would you focus on in your conversations with Sam's mother?

However, one element of RtI is consistent: Even though it is included in federal special education law, it is largely the responsibility of general educators to carry it out (Fuchs & Fuchs, 2006). That is, as a general education teacher, you may be asked to work with a small group of students in your grade level during scheduled reading and language arts time, or you may be asked to assist in gathering data concerning student skill acquisition. Ultimately, the goal of RtI is to prevent some students from ever needing special education. At the same time, following RtI procedures will help ensure that students who need specialized instruction will receive it as soon as a problem is noticed.

Note that whether an intervention assistance team or RtI procedure is initiated, a parent is not legally required to be involved in the process. However, educators should notify parents of their concerns and enlist parental assistance in trying to solve the problem. In some schools, parents are invited to team meetings. Parents should never be surprised when the possibility of providing special education is raised. They should be made aware of the existence of any serious problem as soon as it is noticed.

Research Note

Slonski-Fowler and Truscott (2004) found that when general education teachers believe their input is valued, ideas for intervention are innovative instead of routine. Moreover, when the team provides follow-up, they are satisfied with the prereferral process. When these matters are not addressed carefully, general education teachers' perceptions are negative.

The Special Education Referral, Assessment, Eligibility, Planning, and Placement Process

If a student does not respond to increasingly intensive interventions or the intervention assistance team believes the student's needs are serious enough to consider special education as an option, the student's parents are formally contacted and the assessment process begins. At this point, a **multidisciplinary team (MDT)**—consisting of parents, educators, and others as appropriate—assumes responsibility for making educational decisions regarding the student. No student may receive special education unless the steps discussed in the upcoming sections are followed.

● **Parents' Rights** Before any discussion of how a student comes to receive special education services can proceed, it is essential that you understand how central parents are in all aspects of the referral, assessment, eligibility, planning, and placement process. As summarized in Figure 2.3, parents are key participants in all decision making related to their child's suspected or documented disability. They must be informed of their rights in their own language and in a manner they can understand (Fitzgerald & Watkins, 2006). If you teach older students, you also should know that beginning at least one year before reaching 18 years of age, students also must be informed directly of their rights, and at age 18, most students assume the rights that parents have held for them (National Center on Secondary Education Transition, 2002).

The very first application of parents' rights comes before any assessment process begins. That is, parents must give written permission for their child to be individually assessed. Although it is not common for parents to deny permission, if they do, the process must stop unless the school district asks for a hearing to compel parents to comply. As you read about the rest of the procedures related to special education, you will notice many references to the rights parents have.

● **Components of Assessment** Although the specific requirements regarding the types of data gathered vary somewhat by state and by the type of initial intervention processes used, assessment generally involves gathering information about a student's strengths and needs in all areas of concern. Typically, if the student has not had a vision and hearing screening and you have reason to suspect a sensory impairment, these tests precede other assessments. If sensory screening raises concerns, the parents are notified of the need for a more complete assessment by a physician or appropriate specialist.

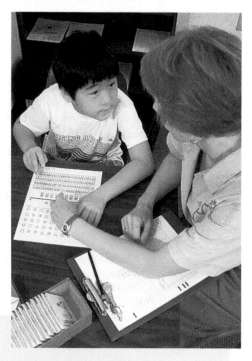

What areas of individual assessment are involved when a team is deciding whether a student is eligible for special education services? How is the information from these assessments used in decision making?

FIGURE *2.3* Parents' Rights in Special Education

IDEA stipulates procedural safeguards to ensure protection of parents' right to be active participants in their child's education. The following are some of the major safeguards provided to parents:

1. Parents are entitled to be members of any group that makes decisions about the educational placement of their child.

2. Parents are to be given written notice before the school initiates, changes, or refuses to initiate or change the identification or educational placement of their child.

3. Parents can participate directly in the determination of their child's eligibility for special education and the development of the individualized educational program (IEP) and its periodic review, generally at least annually (but in some cases, every three years).

4. The school must obtain written, informed parental consent before conducting a formal evaluation and assessment and before initially placing a student in a program providing special education and related services. (*Note:* Written parental consent is required for initial evaluation and initial placement. Subsequent formal evaluation and placement actions require written notice but not permission, as described in item 1.)

5. Parents can inspect and review any educational records maintained by the school district or other agency providing services under IDEA. Access to educational records will be granted to parents without unnecessary delay and before any meeting regarding an IEP or before any hearing relating to identification, evaluation, or placement of the child. In no case should access be delayed more than 45 days after the request has been made.

6. Parents may request and the school district must provide information on where an independent educational evaluation may be obtained. Parents may have the right to an independent educational evaluation at public expense in some instances. The results of an independent evaluation obtained by the parents at private expense will be considered by the local school district in any decision about provision of a free appropriate public education to the child. Such results also may be presented as evidence at a due process hearing.

7. Parents have the right to request mediation as a means to resolving conflict with the school district concerning their child with a disability. Mediation must be available to parents prior to a due process hearing, but it may not delay a hearing. The district, not the parents, bears the cost of mediation.

8. Parents have the right to request a hearing before an impartial hearing officer in cases in which they disagree with school district decisions regarding their child's education. The hearing may relate to any aspect of special education. If the parents fail to win a due process hearing at the local level, they may appeal the results at the state department of education. After this step, if parents still are dissatisfied with the outcome of the hearing, they may initiate court action. Note, though, that if parents' legal actions are judged to be frivolous, the school district may seek to recover the funds spent in defending the district.

9. Parents must be fully informed of their rights and the procedural safeguards related to special education. These rights must be communicated in writing and in a form parents readily can understand.

Sources: Adapted from "Questions and Answers about IDEA," *NICHCY NewsDigest, 21* (2nd ed.), January 2000, Washington, DC: National Information Center for Handicapped Children and Youth, retrieved September 15, 2004, from http://nichcy.org/pubs/newsdig/nd21txt.htm; and "Parental Rights in Special Education," April 2004, Trenton: New Jersey Department of Education, retrieved September 15, 2004, from www.state.nj.us.njded/parights/prise.pdf.

Assessments completed by school professionals may address any aspect of a student's educational functioning (Yell, 2005). Often, for example, the student's intellectual ability is assessed. An individual intelligence test (often referred to as an *IQ test*) is administered and scored by a school psychologist or another qualified school professional. Academic achievement usually is assessed too. The student completes an individual achievement test administered by a psychologist, special education teacher, educational diagnostician, or other professional. A third area often evaluated is social and behavior skills. This evaluation might involve a checklist that you and parents complete concerning a student's behavior, a test given by the school psychologist, or a series of questions asked of the student.

Another domain for assessment is the student's social and developmental history. A school social worker may meet with the parents to learn about the student's family life and major events in her development that could be affecting education. For example, parents might be asked about their child's friends and favorite out-of-school activities, their expectations for their child as an adult, and their child's strengths. Parents also might be asked whether their child has had any serious physical injuries, medical problems, or recurring social or behavior problems.

As another assessment component, a psychologist, counselor, or special education teacher often observes the student in the classroom and other settings to learn how he responds to teachers and peers in various school settings. For example, a psychologist may observe Chris, who usually plays with younger students during recess and gets confused when playground games are too complex. Chris also watches other students carefully and often seems to take cues for how to act from how they are acting. Similarly, a special educator may observe D. J., a sixth-grade student, in the cafeteria to try to understand what is triggering his many behavior incidents there. Such observations are helpful for understanding students' social strengths and needs.

If a potential need exists for speech, occupational, or physical therapy, another component is added to the assessment. The professionals in those areas complete assessments in their respective areas of expertise. A speech/language therapist might use a screening instrument that includes having the student use certain words, tell stories, and identify objects. The therapist also might check for atypical use of the muscles of the mouth, tongue, and throat that permit speech and for unusual speech habits such as breathiness in speaking or noticeable voice strain. Similarly, an occupational or physical therapist might assess a student's gait, strength and agility, range of motion, or ability to perform fine motor tasks such as buttoning and lacing.

Throughout the entire assessment process, IDEA specifically gives parents the right to provide information to be used as part of the evaluation. In addition, as the general education teacher, you can provide details on the student's performance in class, patterns of behavior, and discrepancies between expectations and achievement. Your informal and formal observations play an important role in assessment.

● **Assessment Procedures**   The exact procedures for assessing a student's needs vary according to the areas of concern that initiated the assessment process. The assessment must be completed by individuals trained to administer the tests and other assessment tools used; the instruments must be free of cultural bias; the student's performance must be evaluated in a way that takes into account the potential disability; and the assessment must provide data that are useful for deciding an appropriate education for the student. School professionals are responsible for ensuring that these obligations are met.

Decision Making for Special Services

After a comprehensive assessment of the student has been completed, the multidisciplinary team (MDT) meets to discuss its results and make several decisions (Dabkowski, 2004; Huefner, 2000; Miles-Bonart, 2002). The first decision the MDT must make is whether the student is eligible under the law to be categorized as having a disability. If team members decide that a disability exists, they then determine whether the disability is affecting the student's education and from they that decide whether the student is eligible to receive services through special education. In most school districts, these decisions are made at a single meeting, and parents must agree with the decisions being made or the student

DIMENSIONS OF
diversity

Hosp and Reschly (2003, 2004) reviewed studies on student referrals for interventions or assessment. They found that African American and Hispanic students were referred significantly more often than Caucasian students but that only African American students were found eligible for special education services significantly more often than Caucasian students.

Analyze
and Reflect

Think about yourself as a teacher, regardless of the level at which you plan to teach or the subject in which you are specializing. What unique contributions can you make to a team considering whether a student has a disability? Try to identify at least 10 contributions.

cannot receive special education services. Most school districts have specific guidelines to direct team decision making about the presence of a disability and the need for special education servives. However, the decisions ultimately belong to the team, and members may decide that the guidelines or descriptions do not exactly fit a particular case. For example, most states specify that students identified as having a mild intellectual disability should have an IQ less than 70 as measured on an individual intelligence test and should have serious limitations in adaptive behaviors. However, if a student's score is slightly above 70 and her adaptive skills are particularly limited, a team can still decide that she has a mild intellectual disability. Likewise, if a student has a measured IQ lower than 70 but seems to have many adaptive skills, the team might decide that she does not have an intellectual disability.

If the MDT determines the student has a disability affecting her education and is eligible for services according to federal, state, and local guidelines, the stage is set for detailed planning of the student's education and related services. This planning is recorded in the student's **individualized education program,** or **IEP.** The IEP is the document that outlines all the special education services the student is to receive. Specific guidelines must be followed in developing an IEP; more details about IEPs and their preparation are provided later in this chapter.

The final decision made by the MDT concerns the student's placement. *Placement* refers to the location of the student's education. For most students, the placement is the general education classroom, often with some type of support offered, either there or part-time in a special education setting. According to IDEA, when a placement is a location other than general education, justification must be provided for that decision. However, for a few students, the appropriate primary placement is a special education setting. Later in this chapter, special education services are discussed and placement options are outlined in more detail.

In your school district, the essentials of the procedures outlined in the preceding sections must be followed, but the timelines used and the names for the different parts of the process may vary. Nonetheless, all school district procedures are designed to ensure that students with disabilities are systematically assessed and that a deliberate and careful process is followed to provide for their education needs. Further, you are a critical participant in the entire process. A description of your rights as they relate to special education and students with disabilities is included in Figure 2.4.

Monitoring Special Education Services

In addition to specifying the procedures that must be followed to identify a student as needing special education services, federal and state laws also establish guidelines for monitoring student progress. The monitoring process is necessary to ensure that a student's educational program remains appropriate and that procedures exist for resolving disputes between school district personnel and parents.

● **Annual Reviews** The first strategy for monitoring special services is the **annual review.** At least once each year, a student's progress toward his annual goals must be reviewed and the IEP changed or updated as needed. The purpose of this annual review is to see that the student's best interests are being protected. Not all multidisciplinary team members who participated in the initial decisions about the student's disability and educational needs are required to participate in the annual review. However, a teacher instructing the student and an administrator or other professional representing the school district must meet with the student's parents to discuss whether goals and objectives (as required) have been met and what the next steps in the student's education should be. In practical terms, if your school district completes all annual reviews during a given month, you will find that the special education staff members with whom you

For many students, the general education teacher is most knowledgeable about their day-to-day functioning.

FIGURE 2.4   General Education Teachers' Rights in Special Education

As a general education teacher, you play a crucial role in the design and delivery of special education services. The following is a set of rights that attorney and disability advocate Reed Martin has compiled to clarify what you can expect as you work with students with disabilities and other special needs:

- *The right to seek assistance for a student in a classroom who is not receiving benefit.* It is illegal under federal special education law to leave a student to fend for himself in a classroom designed for others. The student has a right to be referred for necessary assistance, and the teacher has a concomitant right to make the referral when assistance is needed. This is not a right to remove that student from the classroom but rather a right to bring additional information or assistance into the classroom.

- *The right to recognize the teacher as an advocate.* The Americans with Disabilities Act recognizes teachers as advocates and outlaws retaliation or reprisals against and intimidation of teachers who advocate for their students.

- *The right to have a student fully evaluated.* The student has a right to be evaluated in every area that might adversely affect educational performance, and the teacher has a right to know everything educationally relevant to that student.

- *The right to receive any training needed.* As part of supplementary aids and services, if the key to serving a student appropriately is teacher training, then the teacher has a right to receive that training.

- *The right to participate in the IEP that develops the plan for a student in the teacher's class.* A general education teacher who works with the student is a participant in the IEP meeting unless agreement is reached that such participation is not needed. All the questions a classroom teacher has must be asked and answered. If the school's practice is simply to have a so-called representative of instruction at the meeting but that person does not represent the interests of the general education teacher, then the teacher should ask to have the IEP meeting reconvened to ask and answer questions that have not been addressed. If the teacher advocates in this way, she will be protected from reprisals of school administrators.

- *The right to receive the related services that should honestly be on the IEP.* If needed supplementary aids and services are not discussed at the IEP meeting, then the IEP violates the teacher's, student's, and parents' rights. If services are decided on at the meeting but are not provided in the classroom, the teacher's, student's, and parents' rights likewise are violated.

- *The right to be recognized as an advocate for all the students in the classroom.* A general education teacher has a duty to all the students in the classroom. This duty is not antagonistic to a student with special needs. The court cases on placing students in the least restrictive environment recognize that the interests of other students, and the ability of the teacher to teach the classroom, are balanced with the right of a student with special needs to be in that general education classroom.

- *The right to participate in assessing the effectiveness of the program.* When the multidisciplinary team leaves the meeting, it must have an IEP that is reasonably calculated to benefit the student. Once the IEP is begun, the teacher must have a role in assessing whether the IEP is working. During the year and at the next IEP meeting, the teacher's view is vital to determining whether the program and placement were appropriate.

- *The right to be treated as a professional.* Teachers are not just subordinate employees expected to carry out orders without questions. Rather, they are professionals with rights to ask for referral, for evaluation, for reevaluation, for an IEP meeting, and for further refinements of an IEP. However, teachers do not have the right to refuse to work with students with disabilities in their classrooms.

Source: From "Regular Teachers' Rights in Special Education," by R. Martin (n.d.). Retrieved September 5, 2004, from www.reedmartin.com/teacherrights.htm. This information is educational and not intended to be legal advice. Reprinted with permission.

work are unavailable because of their other responsibilities, such as meeting with parents. Depending on local practices, you will likely be asked to attend annual reviews for some students. For many students, the general education teacher is most knowledgeable about their day-to-day functioning. This concept was highlighted with the mandate in IDEA that a general education teacher participate in the development of each student's IEP, not necessarily by writing it but by contributing a classroom perspective.

The most recent reauthorization of IDEA included a new provision related to reviewing a student's educational program. In some states, an IEP may be reviewed once every three years instead of every year. If a state has this option, the IEP must be reviewed at natural transition points for the student (e.g., moving from middle school to high school), and parents have the right to request that an annual review be completed.

● **Three-Year Reevaluations**   A second monitoring procedure required by law is the **three-year reevaluation.** At least every three years, and more often if deemed necessary by the MDT, students receiving special education services must be reassessed to determine whether their needs have changed. This safeguard is designed to prevent students with disabilities from remaining in services or programs that may no longer be appropriate for them. In some cases, the reevaluation includes administering all the tests and other instruments that were used initially to identify the student as needing special education. However, IDEA permits existing information to be used for reevaluation instead of requiring new assessments. In fact, with parent and team agreement, the reevaluation may not involve any new assessment at all (Yell, 2005). On the basis of the three-year reevaluation, the MDT meets again to develop an appropriate IEP.

According to current law, parents are informed when it is time for a three-year reevaluation, but school districts are not required to obtain written permission for this monitoring procedure. This practice enables school districts to continue providing high-quality services to students without interruptions that could be caused if new permission had to be obtained.

● **Additional Reviews**   In addition to annual reviews and three-year reevaluations, IDEA specifically stipulates that an IEP must be revised whenever a lack of expected progress toward achieving goals is noted, reevaluation information is gathered, or parents

Why is it so important that the rights of students with disabilities and their parents be clearly articulated in the law and interpreted through the courts?

bring to the attention of the MDT information that affects the IEP. This suggests that an IEP may need to be revised more frequently than the once per year mandated by the basic requirements of the law. In some cases, necessary changes can be made with parent approval and without reconvening the team.

Parents have one more formal mechanism for obtaining information about their child's learning. IDEA specifies that the parents of students with disabilities have the right to receive progress reports about their children as often as do parents of typical learners. In many school districts, this means that formal communication about student learning progress now occurs every six or nine weeks during the school year, that is, at the end of each grading period.

● **Due Process**   Yet another strategy for monitoring students receiving special education services is **due process,** the set of procedures outlined in the law for resolving disagreements between school district personnel and parents regarding students with disabilities (Getty & Summy, 2004). Due process rights begin when a student is first brought to the attention of a team as potentially having a disability. Both the school district and parents are entitled to protection through due process, but parents typically exercise their due process rights when they fear the school district is not acting in the best interests of their child (Wright & Wright, 2006). For example, if parents have their child independently evaluated because they believe the assessment for special education did not accurately portray his needs and if the school district does not agree with the findings of the independent evaluator, the parents may request a due process hearing. Parents also may request a hearing if they disagree with the goals and objectives listed on the IEP and with the way services are being provided to meet those goals and objectives.

Due process hearings seldom address blatant errors on the part of the school or parents regarding special education; most often, they reflect the fact that many decisions made about students with disabilities are judgment calls in which a best course of action is not always clear. For example, Mr. and Mrs. Schubat filed a due process complaint against their daughter's school district because they did not believe the programs offered were addressing their daughter Judy's needs. They wanted Judy to be more actively involved in general education activities despite her multiple disabilities. School district personnel contended that the complexity of Judy's needs prevented her from being reasonably accommodated in a classroom. They also indicated that she was part of a reverse tutoring program, in which students without disabilities came to work in the special education setting. How do you think a hearing officer would decide this case? What information might be crucial for reaching an appropriate decision?

In practice, most school districts and parents want to avoid due process hearings, which tend to be adversarial and can damage the parent–school working relationship to the detriment of the student. To foster a positive working relationship, IDEA requires that all states have a system in place to offer **mediation** to parents at no cost as an initial means for resolving conflicts with schools (Wright & Wright, 2006). In mediation, a neutral professional skilled in conflict resolution meets with both parties to help them resolve their differences informally. Mediation, however, is not allowed to cause delay in the parents' right to a due process hearing. A hearing is preceded by mediation—a less formal dispute resolution strategy—unless parents decline this option.

Whether or not mediation occurs, IDEA also mandates a dispute resolution session, a sort of last chance for reaching agreement (Hyatt, 2007). If neither mediation nor a dispute resolution session is successful, a hearing is conducted by an independent and objective third party selected from a list provided by the state, but the school district bears the expense (D'Angelo, Lutz, & Zirkel, 2004). If either party disagrees with the outcome of a due process hearing, the decision can be appealed to a state-level review hearing officer. If disagreement still exists, either party can then take the matter to court.

Although school districts work closely with parents to avoid due process hearings, if one occurs concerning a student you teach, you may be called to testify. In such a case, you would be asked to describe the student's level of functioning in your classroom, the supports you provided, and your efforts with other special service providers to ensure the student was successful. An administrator and an attorney might help you prepare for the hearing, and they would answer any questions you might have about your role.

What Is an Individualized Education Program?

As mentioned earlier, the document that the multidisciplinary team uses to decide the best placement for a student with an identified disability and that serves as a blueprint for a student's education is called an *individualized education program.* The IEP addresses all areas of student need, including accommodations to be made in the general education setting and the services and supports to be provided there. The IEP also is the means through which student progress is documented (Etscheidt, 2006). Classroom teachers generally are

Reading Homework Exercise

Go to the Homework and Exercises section in Chapter 2 of MyEducationLab to learn how students can become active participants in their IEPs.

Reading Homework Exercise

Go to the Homework and Exercises section in Chapter 2 of MyEducationLab to access a checklist for collaborating with other professionals and families to develop IEPs.

Analyze
and Reflect

How might the IEP goals for a student with a significant disability (for example, a student in middle school who reads at a second-grade level or a student with multiple disabilities) be implemented in a general education class? What factors might lead the MDT to decide that services should not be delivered there? What are the costs and benefits of such a decision?

involved as team participants in preparing an IEP if a student has any participation in the general education setting (Gartin & Murdick, 2005; Turnbull, Huerta, & Stowe, 2006). Whether or not you are the teacher who serves in this role for particular students, if you have students with disabilities in your classroom, you will have opportunities to examine their IEPs or to meet with special educators to review highlights of these important plans, just as Ms. Lee, introduced at the beginning of the chapter, learned.

Accessing IEPs and learning about your state's requirements for them has been made more efficient with the increasing use of technology. The Technology Notes explains some of the electronic options related to IEPs and the procedures for developing them.

TECHNOLOGY NOTES

Using Technology for IEPs

Although IEPs are still written by hand in some locales, these essential documents increasingly can be created on a computer using commercially available software or templates created at the state level. In addition, there are banks of goals and objectives (as needed) that align with state curriculum standards, and these can be inserted into IEPs, thus streamlining the IEP-writing process. A few of the options that exist are outlined here.

Computerized IEPs

A number of companies have produced IEP software that enables educators to write an IEP electronically, sometimes even incorporating information from a district database so that basic demographic information already stored does not have to be entered separately. Examples of computerized IEP programs include IEPWriter (www.iepwriter.com), Special Education Automation Software (www.computerautomation.com), Easy IEP, and e-IEP PRO (www.e-ieppro.com). These programs enable multiple educators to access IEPs from their computers and help professionals generate the reports needed to report student progress.

Computerized IEPs reflect a contemporary use of technology in special education.

State and Local IEP Policies and Forms

Every state and many school districts now make available online their policies and procedures related to special education, and many include the forms needed for intervention assistance teams, response to intervention, special education referrals, IEPs, and other special education activities. A website for the state of Michigan is an example of how state information and forms are made available (www.michigan.gov/mde/0,1607,7-140-6530_6598-,00.html). You can generally find this type of information for your state by using an Internet search engine, searching for the state's department of education or the school district, finding the home page for the office of special education, and then scanning to find policies and procedural information.

Information on Specific Issues Related to IEPs

When you are asked to attend an IEP meeting, you may have questions about particular aspects of a student's disability. Throughout this textbook, many websites that are mentioned fall into the category of specific information on special education issues, services, and disability types. One site that provides many links to information you may find useful is Special Education Resources on the Internet (http://seriweb.com).

Required Components of an IEP

The essential components of the IEP were established by P.L. 94-142 in 1975, and they have been updated through the years. Although specific state requirements for IEPs vary somewhat, the federally required elements of IEPs are described in the following sections.

● **Present Level of Performance** Information about a student's current level of academic achievement, social skills, behavior, communication skills, and other areas of concern must be included on an IEP. This information serves as a baseline and makes it possible to judge student progress from year to year. Often, highlights of the information collected from the individual assessment of the student or response to intervention data are recorded on the IEP to partially meet this requirement. Individual achievement test scores, teacher ratings, and summary assessments by specialists such as speech therapists and occupational therapists can be used to report the present level of performance. Another component of this assessment is information about how the student's disabilities affect involvement in the general education curriculum.

● **Annual Goals and Short-Term Objectives** *Annual goals* are the MDT's estimate of what a student should be able to accomplish within a year, related to meeting his measured needs resulting from the disability. For some students, annual goals may refer primarily to academic areas and may include growth in reading, math problem solving, and other curricular areas. Specifically, a student with a learning disability might have an annual goal to read and comprehend books at a particular grade level or demonstrate skills for finding and keeping a job. For other students, annual goals address desired changes in classroom behavior, social skills, or other adaptive skills. An annual goal for a student with a moderate intellectual disability, for example, may be to order a meal at a fast-food restaurant. A student with autism might have participating in conversation as a goal. Annual goals also may encompass speech therapy, occupational and physical therapy, and other areas in which a student has specialized needs. There is no right number of annual goals. Some students have as few as two or three, and others as many as eight or ten. However, IDEA specifies that annual goals must be measurable, and increased emphasis is placed on annual goals that enable a student to progress in the general education curriculum.

Short-term objectives are descriptions of the steps needed to achieve an annual goal, and they may or may not be required for all students, depending on state policies. Federal law requires that short-term objectives be written only for the IEPs of students with significant intellectual disabilities. For example, for a student with multiple disabilities whose annual goal is to feed herself, short-term objectives might include grasping a spoon, picking up food with the spoon, and using the spoon to transport food from plate to mouth. The number of short-term objectives for each annual goal relates to the type and severity of the disability, its impact on student learning, and the complexity of the goal. For some students, only a few short-term objectives may be needed; for others, each annual goal may be divided into several smaller steps. Examples of IEP goals and objectives are included in the Professional Edge on the next page.

● **Extent of Participation in General Education** In keeping with the trend toward inclusive practices, the IEP must include a clear statement of justification for placing a student anywhere but in a general education classroom for all or part of the school day. Even for extracurricular and other nonacademic activities, if the team excludes the student from the general class, a specific, evidence-based explanation of why that student cannot participate in such activities must be part of the IEP.

● **Services and Modifications Needed** The IEP contains a complete outline of the specialized services the student needs; that is, the document includes all the special

Research Note

General education teachers report that when they participate in IEP meetings, they talk more and include more discussion of student strengths and needs, feel they have a better idea about what to do next, and view meetings positively (Martin et al., 2004).

Video Homework Exercise

Go to the Homework and Exercises section in Chapter 2 of MyEducationLab to view a discussion about a student by her team of professionals.

> The IEP must include a clear statement of justification for placing a student anywhere but in a general education classroom for all or part of the school day.

Sample IEP Goals and Objectives

The goals and objectives on IEPs are related to assessed student needs, and they are written in specific ways (Bateman & Linden, 2006). For example, they must be aligned with the curriculum for the grade level of the course in which the student is enrolled, regardless of the severity of the student's disability. In addition, they must be measurable and specify the conditions under which the student should be able to carry out an activity (such as the reading level of print material or the people with whom a student should communicate). They also should indicate the level of mastery needed (such as a level of accuracy in an assignment).

Goals outline the progress expected for approximately one school year, although three-year IEPs are being introduced in some states. For all students with significant intellectual disabilities who take alternate assessments and, in some states, for all students with disabilities, goals are supplemented by short-term objectives or benchmarks that measure progress toward achieving the annual goal. The following are sample IEP goals and objectives:

Students with Mild/Moderate Disabilities

- ■ *Goal:* When assigned to write an essay of three paragraphs, Jerome will use complete sentences, capital letters, and punctuation with 80 percent accuracy.

- ● *Objective:* When assigned to write one paragraph, Jerome will use periods, commas, question marks, and exclamation points with 90 percent accuracy.

- ■ *Goal:* Susan will complete at least 80 percent of her homework assignments in English, algebra, and U.S. history.

- ● *Objective:* Susan will write down homework assignments 90 percent of the time with 90 percent accuracy.

Students with Significant Intellectual Disabilities

- ■ *Goal:* Maria will make eye contact when communicating with adults in school in at least five out of six trials.

- ● *Objective:* Maria will make eye contact with the speech/language therapist during individual sessions in five out of six interactions initiated by the therapist.

- ● *Objective:* Maria will make eye contact when the special education teacher calls her name and looks at her in at least five out of six interactions.

- ● *Objective:* Maria will make eye contact when a classroom teacher calls her name and looks at her in at least five out of six interactions.

---

fyi

When students who have IEPs transfer from district to district or even from state to state, IDEA requires the new school district to provide services similar to those provided by the previous school district until records can be reviewed and adopted, amended, or dropped.

education instruction to be provided and any other related services needed to ensure instructional success. Thus, a student receiving adaptive physical education has an IEP indicating that such a service is needed. A student's need for special transportation is noted on the IEP, too. A student who is entitled to transition or vocational assistance has an IEP that clarifies these services. Perhaps most important, the statement of services must include information about the supplementary aids and services, described in Chapter 1, to be provided so that the student can access and progress in the general education curriculum.

One additional element of this IEP component concerns assessment. IDEA stipulates that if a student needs accommodations (for example, extended time) on district or state assessments, including high-stakes assessments, these should be specified on the IEP and implemented throughout the school year, not just for high-stakes tests. If a student is to be exempt from such assessments, the team must ensure the student will complete an alternate assessment that takes into account her functioning levels and needs. The No Child Left Behind Act set specific limits on which students are exempt from high-stakes testing and eligible for alternate assessments, and these limits were confirmed and clarified in IDEA. Most of the students with disabilities whom you teach will be required to complete mandated assessments, and their scores must be considered for measuring adequate yearly progress (AYP).

Part of identifying services is indicating who is responsible for providing them. Any of the professionals introduced earlier in this chapter could be listed on the IEP to deliver special services. As a general education teacher, you may be included, too. For some students, you will be the teacher who completes most of the required instruction; for others, you will assist but not be primarily responsible. For example, a student with a mild intellectual or learning disability probably will be able to complete many class tasks with minor accommodations that you can make. However, if your student has significant intellectual and physical disabilities, other professionals undoubtedly will help develop the materials and activities you will use when the student is in your classroom.

● **Behavior Intervention Plan**   A critical aspect of current regulations for educating students with disabilities concerns discipline and the need to respond to inappropriate behavior. Every student with significant behavior problems, not just those students labeled as having emotional disabilities, must have as part of the IEP an intervention plan based on a functional assessment of the student's behavior. This requirement reflects the increasing pressure for students to be supported in general education settings and the acknowledged difficulty of accomplishing that goal without fostering appropriate student behavior.

● **Date of Initiation and Frequency and Duration of Service and Anticipated Modifications**   Each IEP must include specific dates when services begin, the frequency of the services, the types of accommodations and modifications that are part of the services, and the period of time during which services are offered. Because the law generally requires that student progress in special education be monitored at least once each year (or alternatively, three years), the most typical duration for a service is a maximum of one year. If during the year an MDT member sees a need to reconsider the student's educational plan, additional IEP meetings can be convened or amendments made by phone with parent approval.

● **Strategies for Evaluation**   When a team develops an IEP, the members must clarify how to measure student progress toward achieving the annual goals and how to regularly inform parents about this progress (Etscheidt, 2006). For example, when short-term objectives are written, the team indicates the criteria and procedures to be used to judge whether each objective has been met. For the student learning to move around the school without assistance, the criteria might include specific point-to-point independent movement, and a checklist might be used to judge student progress toward reaching the goal. As with all aspects of special education, the evaluation criteria and procedures are individualized; they are as general or specific as needed to accomplish the student's educational goals.

● **Transition Plan**   For each student who is 16 years of age or older, part of the IEP is a description of strategies and services for ensuring that the student will be prepared to leave school for adult life. This part of the IEP is called a **transition plan.** Students with disabilities who are college bound might have a transition plan that includes improvement of study skills, exploration of different universities and their services for students with disabilities, and completion of high school course requirements necessary to obtain admission to a university. For students who plan to work immediately after graduation, the transition plan might include developing skills such as reading employment ads and filling out job applications, as well as developing important job skills such as punctuality, pleasant manners, and respect toward people in authority and customers. As with an IEP, there is no single correct way to write a transition plan. However, this plan must be tailored to match the assessed strengths and needs of the particular student. It is updated annually, with participation by professionals from agencies outside the school typically increasing as the student nears graduation or school departure at age 21 or 22.

In addition to the basic components, IEPs have several other requirements. For example, they are signed by the individuals who participate in their development, including the

Research Note

Response to intervention is being used to address behavior concerns as well as academic concerns. Fairbanks, Sugai, Guardino, and Lathrop (2007) found that an intervention more intensive than overall classroom management strategies was effective in addressing the behavior problems of half the students studied; the other half responded to an even more intensive intervention.

fyi

Both elementary and secondary students can benefit from student-led IEP meetings. Young children learn age-appropriate skills such as introducing their parents and stating their preferences. Middle and high school students identify their strengths and weaknesses, explain their need for accommodations, and discuss their plans for postschool education or employment (Barrie & McDonald, 2002).

Building Teaching Skills Research Article Exercise

Go to the Building Teaching Skills section in Chapter 2 of MyEducationLab to read case studies related to developing effective IEPs.

student's parent or guardian. They also list a justification for the placement recommended. For example, a decision that the student should receive some services in a pullout program might be justified on the basis of the student's need for one-to-one or small-group intensive instruction in a highly structured environment to succeed. In addition, if a student has specific types of needs, they must be addressed in the IEP. Examples of such needs are behavior, communication, braille (unless specifically excluded on the IEP), and assistive technology. In such cases, appropriate supports, services, and strategies must be specified (Drasgow, Yell, & Robinson, 2001).

The Value of IEPs

To some educators, IEPs represent paperwork that mostly consumes time and energy (Carlson, Chen, Schroll, & Klein, 2002). This is unfortunate because IEPs guide the education of students with disabilities. An IEP helps you clarify your expectations for a student and provides a means for you to understand the student's educational needs. The document also informs you about the types of services the student receives and when the student's educational plan will next be reviewed.

Your job is to make a good-faith effort to accomplish the goals and/or short-term objectives on the IEP as they relate to your instruction. If you do that, you will have carried out your responsibility; if you do not do that, you could be held accountable. For example, suppose an IEP indicates that a student should learn the concept of freedom of speech. You can demonstrate that you are helping the student learn this by providing class discussion, role-play activities, and access to appropriate resources on the Internet, even if the student does not master this concept. If you state that the student is expected merely to read about the concept in the textbook chapter and you refuse to create opportunities for supported learning in this area, you may be violating the IEP.

Do you have additional questions about your role in the prereferral, referral, or IEP process? Additional considerations are presented in the Working Together feature.

What Services Do Students with Disabilities Receive?

The services that a student with disabilities can receive are comprehensive, limited only by the stipulation that they must be necessary as part of that student's education. These services are provided in a variety of placements. Both the services and placements are determined by the multidisciplinary team.

Special Education and Related Services

As noted in Chapter 1, the types of services students receive can be grouped into three categories: special education, related services, and supplementary aids and services. *Special education* refers to the specially designed instructional services students receive. These services may include a curriculum aligned with the standard curriculum but significantly simplified, access to a special education teacher qualified to teach students with a particular disability, and individualized instruction using specialized approaches. When a student's special education teacher comes to the classroom and teaches with the general education teacher, that is special education. When a student leaves a classroom for 30 minutes three times each week for intensive tutoring, that is special education. When a middle school or high school offers a life skills class for students with disabilities, that is special education, too.

TOGETHER

Understanding the Intervention, Assessment, and Decision-Making Process

Even experienced teachers sometimes have questions about their roles and responsibilities related to intervention assistance teams, response to intervention procedures, the eligibility process, and the design of special education services. Here are a few common questions and their answers:

■ I work in a high school, and most students already have been identified by the time they get to this level. Do high schools still need to have intervention assistance teams and procedures in place to determine response to intervention?

Federal law requires that across all levels of schools, a system must be in place to identify students who might need special education. In one study of high school intervention assistance teams in an urban school district, researchers found that classroom teacher involvement on teams was essential for their success (Rubinson, 2002).

■ Do all the teachers on the middle school team need to attend the intervention assistance, response to intervention, and/or IEP team meetings for their students who have been referred or assessed?

In most cases, it is not reasonable to expect all the teachers on the middle school team to attend a meeting about a student with a suspected or identified disability. The composition of the prereferral team is a school's decision. In some cases, the middle school team might actually serve as the intervention assistance team. In others, a representative from the team might work with the team monitoring a student's response to intervention. When an initial IEP is written, in nearly all cases, one general education teacher can provide a representative perspective for the team.

■ Are general education teachers responsible for writing parts of the IEP?

Federal law requires participation of general education teachers in most IEP meetings because they bring an important viewpoint to them. However, those teachers generally do not write sections of the IEP. No matter what your role (for example, elementary, middle school, or high school teacher; related arts teacher; technology specialist), you are obligated to carry out any IEP provisions that pertain to you, including participating in services offered in the general education classroom and making adjustments to assignments and strategies as noted in the IEP.

Related services refer to all the supports students may need in order to benefit from special education. Examples of related services are speech therapy, transportation, physical and occupational therapy, adapted physical education, rehabilitation counseling, psychological services, and social work. A student's need to ride a special bus equipped with a wheelchair lift is a related service need, as is a student's need for assistance with personal care such as toileting.

Supplementary aids and services are all means used to enable students to succeed in a general education setting. They include materials that are written at a different level or reformatted to make them easier for students to read, peer or paraprofessional support, assistive and other technology, and even special professional development for general education teachers so they know how to address students' instructional needs.

As you might guess, the range of possibilities for special education, related services, and supplementary aids and services is immense. Some students, particularly those with high-incidence disabilities, receive a limited number of special education services and perhaps no related services at all. For example, Lucas, a high school student with a learning disability in math, attends a geometry class in which a special education teacher teams with a math teacher. Lucas's assignments are sometimes shortened, and he is allowed extra time to complete tests. He already is looking into colleges that are known to support

Video Homework Exercise

Go to the Homework and Exercises section in Chapter 2 of MyEducationLab to watch a paraprofessional work with a student.

students with his special needs. Students with more complex or severe disabilities may have a more highly specialized special education as well as numerous related services. For example, Charmon, a student with physical and intellectual disabilities, receives the services of a physical and occupational therapist, speech/language therapist, and inclusion specialist, as well as a special education teacher.

Student Placement and Educational Environments

Until recently, any discussion of special education services typically began with a discussion of the least restrictive environment (LRE) and rapidly moved to a detailed discussion of the place in which the services would occur. This was because many students spent some, most, or all of the school day in a special education classroom, where it was believed appropriate instruction could best be delivered. Now views about placement are changing (for example, Idol, 2006). Most school districts still use special education classrooms, even for students with relatively mild disabilities, and these are sometimes an appropriate LRE. However, the high standards and accountability provisions of NCLB and the requirement of IDEA that students with disabilities be taught by highly qualified teachers are leading to schools becoming more inclusive (U.S. Department of Education, 2004b). As in Ms. Turner's school, which you read about at the beginning of the chapter, school professionals are considering how to support students more effectively in general education settings. Figure 2.5 shows the continuum of placements, now referred to as *educational environments,* that must exist for students with disabilities and recent data on the percentage of students with disabilities in each of those placements.

As discussed earlier, the decision about placement is made by the MDT and reviewed along with the IEP at least annually (or in some states and for some students, every three years). Placement can be changed as often as appropriate, with parental permission. Generally, if the parents and school district representatives disagree about placement, the student remains in the current placement until the disagreement is resolved. Exceptions to this occur when discipline issues arise. Administrators may unilaterally change a student's placement (for example, through suspension) for up to 10 days, provided such methods are used with other students, too. If students with disabilities bring a weapon or drugs to school, they can be placed in an alternative educational setting for up to 45 school days while a decision is made concerning long-term placement (Yell, 2005).

● **Regular (General Education) Classes** Nearly half of students with disabilities spend 79 percent or more of the day in a general education setting (U.S. Department of Education, 2004b). A kindergartener with a communication disorder might be served by a speech/language therapist who comes to the classroom and teaches language lessons with the general education teacher. For a middle school student with intellectual and physical disabilities, an inclusion specialist might adapt a lesson on fractions by helping the student learn how to cut simple shapes into halves. For a high school student with a learning disability, a paraprofessional might provide assistance in biology class in carrying out lab directions and recording and completing assignments. This student also might have one class period covering study skills and strategies assistance in a special education classroom.

● **Resource Programs** Another group of students with disabilities attends school mostly in general education settings but also receives assistance in a special education classroom, often called a **resource room,** for 21 to 60 percent of the day (U.S. Department of Education, 2004b) in what is called a *resource program.* In elementary schools, resource programs sometimes are organized by the skills being taught. For instance, from 10:00 A.M. until 10:45 A.M., basic math skills may be taught, and all the second- and

www.resources

Many statistics about students with disabilities and how they receive education services come from the federally compiled annual reports to Congress on the implementation of IDEA. You can find copies of the reports from the past several years at www.ed.gov/about/reports/annual/osep/index.html.

fyi

Students with disabilities who are enrolled in faith-based private schools are entitled to some benefits from IDEA. Although these students must be identified by the public school district in that locale, they may receive only limited services that do not have to be available at the private school. They may be available only at the public school (Eigenbrood, 2004).

FIGURE *2.5* **IDEA Continuum of Educational Placements for Students with Disabilities**

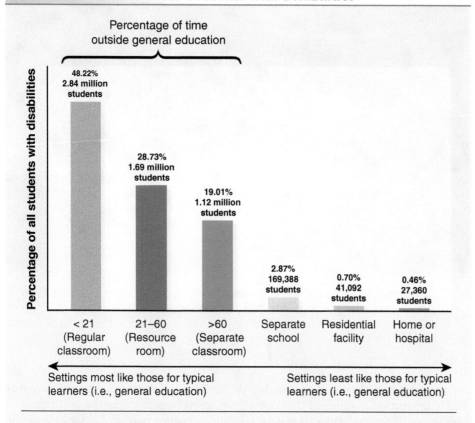

Source: From *26th Annual Report to Congress on the Implementation of the Individuals with Disabilities Education Act,* 2004, Washington, DC: U.S. Department of Education.

third-grade students needing math assistance may come to the resource room at that time. Alternatively, some resource rooms are arranged by same-age groups. For example, in these programs, all fifth-graders with disabilities in resource room programs may go to the resource room together. In another approach, special education teachers negotiate with general education teachers about specific times students will attend.

In middle schools and high schools, students are scheduled to have resource classes in the same way the rest of their classes are scheduled. For example, a student may attend a resource class that provides study strategies or reviews the curriculum being taught in general education classes. In some instances, core academic instruction is taught in the resource room by a special educator highly qualified in the academic area. How a resource program is organized depends on many factors, including the number of students to be served and their ages, the nature and intensity of their needs, and state and local policies.

● **Separate Classes** Some students with disabilities attend *separate classes* for more than 60 percent of the school day (U.S. Department of Education, 2004b). In this placement, a special education teacher has the primary instructional responsibility for the students who receive grades from the highly qualified special educator for the subjects taught there. However, a separate class placement does not mean that students

In the past, many students with disabilities attended separate classes or schools. Today they are educated in settings with their peers and access the same curriculum.

remain in a single classroom or that they do not interact with typical peers. They may receive instruction in different classrooms from several special educators, particularly in high school. They may attend a general education class for part of the day or a certain class period, and they also may participate with peers in related arts, assemblies, and other school activities.

Although Kurt is in a separate class most of the day at his high school, he takes a horticulture class with students without disabilities. A paraprofessional accompanies him because he has limited ability to understand directions and needs close guidance from an adult to participate appropriately. At Kyle's elementary school, 30 minutes each day is called *community time*, during which students read and write together, share important events from their lives, and learn about their neighborhood and community. For community time, Kyle goes to Mr. Ballinger's fifth-grade class. The students are about Kyle's age and assist him with the community activities and learning. Kyle's special education teacher helps Mr. Ballinger plan appropriate activities for him during that time.

If you teach in one of the related fields—for example, art, music, physical education, or drama—you will likely instruct students with disabilities regardless of their specific placement. More information about resources that can help you with this responsibility are included in the Special Emphasis On . . . feature.

● **Separate Schools**   A small number of students with disabilities attend public or private *separate schools* (U.S. Department of Education, 2004b). Some separate schools exist for students with moderate or severe intellectual and physical disabilities, although such schools are, for the most part, becoming obsolete. Other separate schools serve students with multiple disabilities who need high levels of specialized services. For example, in a small community near Chicago, approximately 25 students are educated at a separate school. These students all need the services of a physical and occupational therapist; most have complex medical problems that must be closely monitored; and most cannot move unless someone assists them. These students have opportunities for contact with typical

The Arts

If you are an art, music, dance, or drama teacher, you might wonder what role you play in the education of students with disabilities. In fact, in many school districts, you are the professional most likely to work with most if not all of the students with disabilities attending your school. In many cases, these students come to your class along with typical peers. In a few cases, a separate class has been arranged for them. Teachers in the arts often express the concern that little attention is paid to the support needs of students with disabilities in their classes, and few materials are available to prepare teachers in the arts for working with students with disabilities.

VSA provides resources for teachers of the arts for working with students with disabilities.

One organization that you will find particularly helpful is VSA Arts (formerly Very Special Arts), at www.vsarts.org. Founded in 1974 by Jean Kennedy Smith, VSA Arts is an international organization that creates learning opportunities through the arts for children and adults with disabilities. The organization has affiliates across the United States and in 60 other countries. Here are some of the resources they offer to teachers:

- Let Your Style Take Shape at www.vsarts.org/x1132.xml This free guide for teachers, with a downloadable poster, provides ideas for creating inclusive environments for students with disabilities, including lessons that integrate national standards for math with the visual arts.

- Living Research International Database (LRI) at http://livingresearch.vsarts.org/admin/index.cfm This site allows professionals and others to post information about the educational impact of the arts. After you register (at no cost), you can find summaries of studies, read others' research efforts in this area, and correspond with others concerning the arts for education.

- Start with the Arts at www.vsarts.org/x577.xml This program is designed to foster literacy skills for young children in inclusive settings. It stresses developing students' creativity; engaging them in expressing concepts, thoughts, and feelings; and helping them understand personal relationships in the world around them.

- Express Diversity! at www.vsarts.org/x594.xml This resource is a set of five modules with art activities designed for fifth-graders but adaptable for students in grades 1 through 7. The intent of the modules is to demonstrate that students with a wide range of abilities and disabilities can share in the joy of arts. The modules include one simulation activity (with cautions about the shortcomings of this approach for trying to understand individuals with disabilities), a creative writing exercise, an art mural activity, a performance arts activity, and a visual arts activity. The package of materials also includes letters (in Spanish as well as English) that can be sent home to explain the program to parents, bulletin board items, video biography cards about people with disabilities, and other support materials.

Source: Adapted from "Publications and Resources for Educators and Parents," by VSA Arts, 2003. Retrieved June 29, 2007, from www.vsarts.org/x572.xml. Express Diversity was developed under a grant from the U.S. Department of Education. However, the contents do not necessarily represent the policy of the U.S. Department of Education, and endorsement by the Federal Government should not be assumed. Reprinted with permission.

Zigmond (2003) suggests that questions about *where* students with disabilities should be educated are misguided and that the more important questions concern *how* best to help each student learn. What are the implications of this thinking for teachers? What impact could this thinking have on the continuum-of-placements model?

peers who are brought to the school through a special program to function as "learning buddies." Some students with serious emotional disabilities also attend separate schools. These students might harm themselves or others. They might not be able to cope with the complexity and social stress of a typical school, and so the least restrictive environment for them is a school where their highly specialized needs, including therapeutic supports, can be addressed.

● **Residential Facilities**   A few students have needs that cannot be met at a school that is in session only during the day. If students in separate settings have even greater needs, they might attend school as well as live in a public or private *residential facility*. Few students with disabilities are educated in this manner (U.S. Department of Education, 2004b). The students for whom this placement is the LRE often are those with severe emotional problems or severe and multiple intellectual, sensory, and physical disabilities. In some states, students who are blind or deaf also might receive their instruction in a residential facility, an approach that is supported by some professionals and parents and opposed by others.

A somewhat different group of students also can be considered under the residential placement option. According to IDEA, children and young adults with disabilities who are incarcerated in the juvenile justice system must receive special education services. Further, children and young adults who are convicted of crimes and incarcerated as adults also may be entitled to special education services, unless the IEP team determines there is a compelling reason to discontinue services. Why is it essential that the requirement for providing special education services to incarcerated youth be included in IDEA?

● **Home and Hospital Settings**   A very small number of students with disabilities receive their education in a home or hospital setting (U.S. Department of Education, 2004b). This placement often is used for students who are medically fragile, who are undergoing surgery or another medical treatment, or who have experienced an emotional crisis. For a few students with limited stamina, school comes to their homes because they do not have the strength to come to school. That is, a special education teacher comes to the home for a specified amount of time each week to deliver instruction. Home instruction also might be used for a student with serious behavior problems or for a student for whom there is disagreement about the appropriate school placement, pending resolution of the dispute.

> The appropriate and required educational setting for most students with disabilities is the same classroom they would attend if they did not have a disability.

One more point should be made about placement. For some students, the team may decide that their learning will suffer significantly if schooling stops during the summer. For these students, any of the services in any of the placements just described can be extended into school breaks and summer vacations through extended school year (ESY) programs.

Because of NCLB and IDEA, placements in separate classes and schools are far less preferred than those that support the education of students with disabilities in general education classrooms and schools. When placement includes a specialized setting, it often is appropriate for a specific skill or service and for a specific and limited period of time. The appropriate and required educational setting for most students with disabilities is the same classroom they would attend if they did not have a disability. As a general education teacher, you play a major role in the education of students with disabilities, so it is important for you to understand the kinds of special services your students receive.

Summary

Many individuals work to ensure that students with disabilities receive an appropriate education. These people include general education teachers; special education teachers; related service providers such as school psychologists, counselors, speech/language therapists, social workers, physical and occupational therapists, adaptive physical educators, nurses, administrators, paraprofessionals, and other specialists; and parents, students, and advocates. Depending on need, a student with a disability may receive instruction from just one or two of these professionals or from several of them.

To determine whether special services are needed, general education teachers usually begin a process of deciding whether to request that a student be assessed for the presence of a disability. They carry out this process by analyzing the nature and extent of the student's unmet needs; clarifying those needs by describing them through examples; determining that the needs are chronic and possibly worsening over time; comparing the student's needs to those of others in the class; possibly recognizing that no pattern seems to exist for the student's performance; and intervening to address the unmet needs and documenting those efforts.

Based on these early strategies, the student's needs may be assessed by an intervention assistance team (IAT). Alternatively, a set of procedures referred to as *response to intervention (RtI)* may be implemented as a means of finding ways to accelerate student learning. If the IAT decides that the interventions are not successful, a multidisciplinary team (MDT) follows federally established special education referral and assessment steps. This process includes completing an individualized assessment with parental permission, making decisions about the need for special education, developing an individualized education program (IEP), and monitoring special education services. If parents and school district personnel disagree on any aspect of a student's special education program or services and if the disagreement cannot be resolved informally, due process procedures, including mediation and dispute resolution sessions, are used to ensure that the student receives the appropriate education.

When an IEP is developed, it includes the student's present level of functioning, goals (and sometimes objectives), justification for any placement outside general education, needed services, the person(s) responsible for the services, beginning and ending dates for service delivery, and criteria for evaluation. The IEP also may include a behavior intervention plan and a transition plan. The IEP generally must be reviewed at least annually (in a few states, every three years), and the student must be reevaluated at least every three years. The services a student may receive, as outlined by the IEP, include special education and related services and a designation of placement: a general education classroom, resource program, or separate special education setting.

General education teachers play an integral role in the education of students with disabilities. They are involved in the early identification of students who appear to have special needs, contribute during the assessment and identification process, and implement IEP goals and possibly objectives, as outlined by the multidisciplinary team.

Back to the Cases

This section provides opportunities for you to apply the knowledge gained in this chapter to the cases described at the beginning of this chapter. The questions and activities that follow demonstrate how these standards and principles, along with other concepts that you have learned about in this chapter, connect to the everyday activities of all teachers.

Mr. Rodriguez will most likely include information about the "tier I" interventions he has used with Lauren at the meeting with the ABIT. While some school districts have selected research-based "tier I" interventions, other school districts may not have adopted specific programs. To help you understand RtI and the tiers of intervention, conduct a Google search using the key words "Response to intervention for reading disabilities" (or search for mathematics, writing, or another basic skill). Review at least three sources provided, noting the primary features of interventions described and decide which you would consider for your own teaching. Share this information with two peers from your class and, as a group, determine which intervention you would recommend to the entire class. (INTASC Principles 9.01 and 9.03.)

Ms. Lee is looking forward to working with the speech/language therapist, but she is unsure of what to expect. Does she need to tell the therapist what to do? Should she be keeping records of Jennifer's language difficulties? (INTASC Principle 1.04 and CEC Standard 8.) Using information from the chapter and the American Speech-Language-Hearing Association website (www.asha.org), outline how a speech/language therapist works with teachers and IEP teams. Then, explain what Ms. Lee should expect to happen in her classroom.

Ms. Turner, as you may remember, works with her school's inclusive practices team. As time passes, she becomes concerned that students' right to an inclusive education may create unrealistic expectations for a general educator's ability to work with those who have exceptional learning needs. She has other concerns about the amount of paperwork and time required to meet the IDEA requirement that general education teachers participate in IEP meetings. (INTASC Principles 1.04 and 10.02.) How would you assure Ms. Turner that she is a necessary participant in the process and address her concerns? In your answer, specifically address both Ms. Turner's responsibilities and personal concerns.

Key Terms and Concepts

Annual review (p. 56)
Due process (p. 58)
Individualized education program (IEP) (p. 56)
Intervention assistance team (p. 50)
Mediation (p. 59)
Multidisciplinary team (MDT) (p. 53)

Resource room (p. 66)
Response to intervention (RtI) (p. 50)
Self-determination (p. 45)
Three-year reevaluation (p. 58)
Transition plan (p. 63)

myeducationlab
Where the Classroom Comes to Life

Now go to the Friend and Bursuck, Fifth Edition, MyEducationLab course at www.myeducationlab.com to

- take a pretest to assess your initial comprehension of the chapter content
- study chapter content with your individualized study plan
- take a posttest to assess your understanding of chapter content
- engage in multimedia exercises to help you build a deeper and more applied understanding of chapter content

Applications in Teaching Practice

A Visit to an MDT Meeting

Ms. Richards teaches science to sixth-graders. Beginning in the fall, she and her team members will be working with Natasha, a student newly identified as having a learning disability. Natasha enjoys many friends and extracurricular activities, but she has extraordinary difficulties with reading fluency, comprehension, and written expression. She also has significant problems organizing her work and remembering to complete and turn in assignments. To help set appropriate goals for the coming year, Ms. Richards is participating in an MDT meeting to create an IEP for Natasha. Although it would be ideal for all the sixth-grade team members to attend the meeting, that is not feasible, and so Ms. Richards is representing her colleagues as well.

General education (sixth-grade) science teacher: Ms. Richards
General education (fifth-grade) teacher: Mr. Tucker
Special education middle school teacher: Ms. Hill
Principal: Ms. Hubbert
Psychologist: Ms. Freund
Speech/language therapist: Mr. Colt
Parent: Ms. Wright

Ms. Hubbert: Our next task is to develop goals for Natasha. I'd like to suggest that we discuss academics first, then social, and wrap up with related services needed. Let's look at Natasha's strengths first—in all those areas.

Mr. Colt: Natasha has a very strong speaking vocabulary. She is considerably above average in that realm.

Ms. Freund: Along with that, Natasha's general knowledge is very good. She also is near grade level in basic math skills, according to the most recent achievement test data.

Mr. Tucker: It's not really academics, but one strength I see that Natasha has is her willingness to help classmates. She really wants to help everyone in class learn even when she herself is struggling. She also was very active in extracurricular activities this year. She participated in the service learning program, volunteered to read to the kindergarten class, and competed in the after-school sports program.

Ms. Hill: As we write academic goals, then, we need to remember that Natasha has strong vocabulary skills and general knowledge and that she does not need help in math. Perhaps we can use her social skills and other interests to help in the academic arena. Ms. Wright, what strengths do you see in Natasha?

Ms. Wright: Hmmm. She minds me, that's for sure. And she helps out around the house with chores. She likes to help me watch her baby brother.

Ms. Hill: Helping really seems to be Natasha's thing—let's keep that in mind.

Ms. Hubbert: Let's focus for a minute on academic areas of need.

Ms. Freund: Reading comprehension and written expression are by far the areas that need the most work. Natasha's comprehension is just at a beginning third-grade level, and her written expression is below that.

Ms. Wright: She says she doesn't like reading because the other kids make fun of her when she can't read the words, and they tease her when Mr. Tucker gives her a baby book.

Ms. Richards: In middle school, that could be even more of a problem. We need to be sure that she uses the same textbooks as the other students next year. I'm sure we can also arrange to get some supplemental materials for her to use at home. Let's be sure that before we finish today, we talk about that some more.

Ms. Freund: Ms. Richards and Ms. Hill, given what you know and have heard about Natasha, what might be priorities for next year?

Ms. Hill: I agree that comprehension is the key. I think a goal should be for her to improve her comprehension to a fourth-grade level on reading tasks that include stories, textbooks, and other materials such as children's magazines.

Ms. Hubbert: Ms. Wright, how does that sound to you? [*Ms. Wright nods.*]

The conversation continues.

Before the meeting ends, the MDT has generated the following additional goals in reading comprehension using materials at her instructional level:

- Natasha will identify with 90 percent accuracy the main characters and the problem and solution in literature that she reads at a third-grade level.
- Natasha will comprehend 80 percent of both narrative and expository material she reads aloud (third- to fourth-grade level) and 80 percent on material she reads to herself.

Questions

1. What are the responsibilities of the professionals represented at the MDT meeting? Which of the professionals are required to attend? How would your responses be different if this were an annual review?

2. What role does Ms. Richards take at the meeting? Why is her presence helpful in creating an educational program for Natasha? How else might she contribute during this meeting?

3. What is the purpose of having both the fifth-grade teacher and a sixth-grade teacher attend the meeting? How might this improve the quality of the IEP? What problems might it cause?

4. What steps likely were completed prior to this meeting? How did the general education teacher prepare? What other team responsibilities were met?

5. What part of the IEP is the team addressing? What other parts have to be completed before the meeting ends? What must occur for the IEP to be valid?

6. What would happen if Natasha's mother asked the school district for a separate class as Natasha's placement and the school district disagreed with this?

Further Readings

French, N. K. (Ed.). (2004). Connecting schools and communities: The vital role of paraeducators [special issue]. *Remedial and Special Education, 25,* 200–264.

This special journal issue addresses many essential topics related to the roles and responsibilities of paraprofessionals in public schools. It includes discussion of the strategies school districts use to find and keep paraprofessionals, parent perceptions of the work of paraprofessionals, and the ways paraprofessionals work with students with significant disabilities.

Ulrich, M. E., & Bauer, A. M. (2003). Levels of awareness: A closer look at communication between parents and professionals. *Teaching Exceptional Children, 35*(6), 20–25.

This teacher-friendly article outlines types of reactions and stages parents may go through when they learn that their child has a disability. The article can help teachers better understand and respond appropriately to the parents of their students.

Wright, P. W. D., & Wright, P. D. (2006). *IDEA 2004*. Hartfield, VA: Harbor House Law Press.

This book, written primarily for parents, outlines the key provisions of the 2004 reauthorization of IDEA, including the procedures related to identifying students as eligible to receive special education, the requirements of IEPs, and the steps taken when a disagreement occurs. The book's friendly style makes it a useful reference for teachers looking for core information about federal special education law.

Zhang, D., & Benz, M. R. (2006). Enhancing self-determination of culturally diverse students with disabilities: Current status and future directions. *Focus on Exceptional Children, 38*(9), 1–13.

This journal article presents the idea of self-determination as it pertains to youth from diverse backgrounds preparing to transition from school to postschool options. It addresses the instructional strategies teachers can use to foster students' ability to advocate for themselves, including the importance of their active participation in IEP meetings.

3 Building Partnerships through Collaboration

LEARNING *Objectives*

After you read this chapter, you will be able to

1. Explain what the term *collaboration* means, and describe how collaboration is part of providing services to students with disabilities.

2. Clarify how an emphasis on collaboration in schools shapes the roles and responsibilities that you have as a general education teacher.

3. Describe services for students with disabilities and other special needs in which collaboration is integral, including shared problem solving, co-teaching, teaming, and consulting.

4. Identify ways you can work effectively with parents to successfully educate students with special needs.

5. Outline your responsibilities in working with paraprofessionals, and describe ways you can enhance collaboration with them.

Ms. Godina has 5 students in her biology class of 36 who have individualized education programs (IEPs). Natalie, who has a mild learning disability, does not need assistance in the course. James and Tyler, who both receive services for emotional disabilities, are capable of completing the work but need a great deal of structure and support. Carl, a student with an intellectual disability, does part of the course work, but he is not expected to master the extensive vocabulary or to write lengthy lab reports. Janet, who has a physical disability and limited stamina, requiring her to use a motorized wheelchair, often needs encouragement to keep up with the work. Four days a week, Ms. Godina is joined by Mr. MacLean, a special education teacher. During these class periods, the two teachers share teaching responsibilities and group the students for instruction in a variety of ways—by skill needs, interest, and random assignment, among others. On the day that Mr. MacLean is not in class, Ms. Hugo, a teaching assistant, is available to help Ms. Godina and individual students.

■ *What happens when two teachers share instructional responsibilities in a classroom? What topics might Ms. Godina and Mr. MacLean need to discuss to ensure that their shared teaching is effective?*

Ms. Swanson, a fourth-grade teacher, is meeting with Ms. O'Brien, a consultant on autism with whom the school district contracts for assistance when challenging situations arise and a different and knowledgeable perspective might help to address it. They are discussing Brittany, a student who is spending more and more time in general education. Last year, the maximum amount of time was about an hour, and that occurred during the highly structured math time, a subject in which Brittany excels. This year, one of the goals on her IEP is for her also to receive reading and writing instruction in the general education classroom. Ms. Swanson comments on the strides Brittany has made in managing the bustling atmosphere of the class, but she is concerned that Brittany is having more and more difficulty transitioning from one activity to another, even though she has a picture schedule that shows her, with times and drawings of activities, each segment of the day. In fact, this meeting was convened when Brittany refused to come with her class to the media center, where the students were to meet a local children's author. Ms. O'Brien listens to the details of what happened, asks Ms. Swanson for her analysis of the situation, offers to observe in the classroom later that day, and plans to meet to decide what strategies might alleviate the behavior challenges.

■ *What options do general education teachers have when one of their students with disabilities is experiencing extraordinary challenges? Why is it important to find solutions to such challenges, instead of quickly deciding that the student should be placed in a special education setting? What is the place of consultation in services for students with disabilities?*

Ms. MacDougal, the middle school inclusion facilitator, and Mr. Saunders, the seventh-grade team leader, are meeting with Chris's parents, Mr. and Mrs. Werner, for an after-school meeting. Mrs. Werner begins by declaring that the school is discriminating against Chris because of her learning disability. Mr. Werner asserts that Chris should not be singled out in any way because of her special needs and that he was unhappy to learn that she has been receiving tutoring during a lunch period study hall. He stresses that the family already provides tutoring for Chris so this type of discrimination will not occur at school. Further, Mr. and Mrs. Werner show the teachers Chris's modified assignment sheets, another example of discrimination. When Mr. Saunders starts to explain that he is modifying Chris's work so she can learn more in his class, Mr. Werner cuts him off, stating that a teacher's poor instructional practice is no excuse to destroy a child's self-concept through public humiliation.

If you were Mr. Saunders, what type of assistance would you want from Ms. MacDougal during this difficult interaction? How can you prevent miscommunication in your work with parents of students with disabilities?

In the past, becoming a teacher—whether in general education or in special education—meant entering a profession frequently characterized by isolation and sometimes loneliness (Little, 1993; Lortie, 1975). Teachers typically spent most of the day alone in a classroom with students. They learned that they were expected to have all the skills to manage student learning and discipline issues, and they rarely had opportunities to discuss their questions, concerns, and misgivings with anyone, especially their colleagues at school.

Over the past several years, that atmosphere of isolation has changed (Barth, 2006; Winn & Blanton, 2005). Elementary school teachers are meeting on grade-level teams to share ideas and problem solve, and middle school and high school teachers are creating interdisciplinary teams to redesign curriculum and share instructional responsibility for smaller groups of students. School reform efforts also are characterized by partnerships. For example, professional development schools, in which teacher trainees work with experienced educators and university instructors, emphasize team approaches (Paese, 2003). Likewise, entire schools are stressing the need to build collaborative professional learning communities to meet the current expectations of accountability for student learning and address the challenges of 21st-century schooling (DuFour, DuFour, Eaker, & Many, 2006).

As the scenes that open this chapter illustrate, these emerging partnerships extend to special education and other support staff as well. Particularly as schools increase inclusive practices, the working relationships among all the adults involved in the education of students with disabilities become critical. For example, as a general education teacher, you may find that your grade level or department team periodically meets to discuss the progress of students with disabilities. The goal is to share ideas and concerns in order to collectively ensure that these students are reaching their academic potential. Similarly, you might find that some of your students cannot complete the grade-level work you are accustomed to assigning. To assist you, a special education teacher might meet with you to design the necessary modifications.

At first glance, these interactions seem like logical, straightforward approaches to optimizing education. However, because of the strong education tradition of professionals

Video Homework Exercise

Go to the Homework and Exercises section in Chapter 3 of MyEducationLab to see general and special educators working collaboratively to provide support for students with disabilities.

working alone and the still-limited opportunities many teachers have had in preparing to work effectively with other adults, problems sometimes occur (Friend & Cook, 2007). In some instances, support personnel are reluctant to make suggestions for fear they will sound as if they are interfering with a classroom teacher's instruction. In other cases, a classroom teacher insists that no change in classroom activities is possible, even though a special education teacher is available for co-teaching. And often, when professionals in schools disagree, they are uncomfortable discussing the issues directly and struggle to find shared solutions.

Professionals in inclusive schools usually assert that collaboration is the key to their success in meeting the needs of all students (Brownell, Adams, Sindelar, & Waldron, 2006; Friend & Cook, 2007; Knackendoffel, 2005). Although research related to the outcomes of collaboration is just emerging (for example, Gable, Mostert, & Tonelson, 2004), it is clear that school professionals are banding together to better serve their students. The purpose of this chapter is to introduce you to the principles of collaboration and the school situations in which professionals are most likely to collaborate to meet the needs of students with disabilities. You also will learn how to develop strong working relationships with parents, an essential part of every teacher's responsibilities and an especially important one when educating students with special needs. The special partnerships that are formed when teachers work with paraprofessionals also are considered. Finally, you will find out how to respond when disagreements arise during collaboration.

www.resources

The Families and Advocates Partnership for Education (FAPE) project (www.fape.org) fosters collaboration among parents, advocates, and others to ensure that students with disabilities receive appropriate services. At FAPE's website, you can find many additional links as well as many materials in languages other than English (for example, Spanish and Vietnamese).

What Are the Basics of Collaboration?

As a teacher, you will hear colleagues refer to many of their activities as **collaboration.** Sometimes they will be referring to a team meeting to propose ideas to help a student; sometimes they will mean sharing a classroom to teach a particular subject; and sometimes they will even use the term as a synonym for inclusive practices. How can all these things be collaboration? Actually, they are not. Collaboration is how people work together, not what they do. As Friend and Cook (2007) have stated, collaboration is a *style* professionals choose to accomplish a goal they share. Professionals often use the term *collaboration* to describe any activity in which they work with someone else. But just the fact of working in the same room with another person does not ensure that collaboration occurs. For example, in some team meetings, one or two members tend to monopolize the conversation and subtly insist that others agree with their points of view. Although the team is seated together at a table, it is not collaborative.

True collaboration exists only on teams when all members feel their contributions are valued and the goal is clear, when they share decision making, and when they sense they are respected. The same can be said of other activities that bring professionals into proximity: Merely being together is not collaboration. It is how individuals work with each other that defines whether collaboration is occurring, a fact illustrated in the Professional Edge on page 80, which describes collaboration between general and special education teachers in secondary schools.

Reading Homework Exercise

Go to the Homework and Exercises section in Chapter 3 of MyEducationLab to read about how administrators, teachers, and staff used collaboration to improve their school.

Collaboration is how people work together, not what they do.

Characteristics of Collaboration

Collaboration in schools has a number of defining characteristics that clarify its requirements. Friend and Cook (2007) have outlined these key attributes.

● **Collaboration Is Voluntary** Teachers may be assigned to work in close proximity, but they cannot be forced to collaborate. They must make a personal choice to use this

Secondary Teachers and Collaboration

Middle and high school teachers in urban settings were asked to identify their expectations of their special education colleagues when they worked together in general education classrooms and to identify areas in which they themselves needed to improve. They mentioned the following items:

General Expectations for Special Educators

- Understand that students with disabilities are the priority but not the only responsibility.
- Get to know all of the students.
- If possible, provide a schedule of times in the classroom.

Planning Expectations for Special Educators

- Meet for planning at least two times per month.
- Discuss strategies for working with diverse learners.
- Provide some type of background information on each student in the class with an IEP.
- Look at long-range lesson plans and provide suggestions for how these plans can be carried out to benefit students with disabilities.
- Give suggestions for modifying tests and collaborating on grading decisions.

Expectations for Special Educators in Delivering Instruction

- If possible, share teaching responsibilities and presenting lessons.
- During class, walk around the room and provide assistance to students, monitor student work, and provide feedback regarding student performance.
- Provide more intensive support to students who need it.

Expectations for Special Educators in Classroom Management

- Consistently and actively reinforce standards for positive behavior.
- Take an active role in developing and implementing classroom routines.

- Consistently praise students.
- Feel free to intervene when behavioral problems arise during class.
- During conflict situations, either take over the class or leave the class with the students involved in the conflict.

Things General Educators Say They Need to Work On

- Provide the special educator with resources related to content.
- Open avenues of communication by being receptive and taking risks.
- Try to prepare instruction at least two weeks in advance.
- Offer a time to meet to discuss activities.
- Create opportunities for the special educator to lead instruction.
- Share responsibility and power in the classroom.
- Make it clear to students that the teachers in the class are equals.
- Ask for and use the special educator's ideas, opinions, and creativity.
- Try to remember the importance and value of different perspectives.
- Create a workspace in the classroom for the special education teacher.

Source: Adapted from "Clarifying Collaborative Roles in Urban High Schools: General Educators' Perspectives," by C. Murray, *Teaching Exceptional Children, 36*(5), 2004, pp. 44–51. Copyright 2004 by The Council for Exceptional Children. Reprinted with permission.

Working TOGETHER

Collaborating with Related Services Personnel

Although the professionals with whom you most often collaborate probably will be special education teachers, you also may work closely with related services personnel. The following are some points to keep in mind when working with speech/language therapists, physical therapists, adaptive physical educators, and other related services providers:

■ Related services professionals often serve students in several schools and may have difficulty adhering to schedules. Be respectful of their time by preparing your questions and concerns prior to a meeting and trying to keep within the timeframe for the session.

■ If a related services professional observes in your classroom, try to arrange a short meeting afterward. Face-to-face communication often can be more effective and efficient than follow-up via e-mail or other written communication.

■ Some related services professionals may not have a complete grasp of the expectations you have for students in your general education classroom. Help these professionals understand what types of activities your students complete, whether students with disabilities are experiencing difficulty, and how they can assist you.

■ In some schools, related services personnel co-teach. If you are assigned to co-teach with a related services professional, remember that the concepts and suggestions made in this chapter apply to them, too.

■ If one of your students receives related services outside the classroom, ask for updates so you can provide follow-up in the classroom and report any difficulties you notice.

■ In some situations, related services professionals who travel from school to school don't feel they are truly members of any school team. Help them feel welcome in your classroom and school.

style. For example, your principal may tell you and another teacher that you are expected to be part of an intervention assistance team. You can choose to keep your ideas to yourself instead of readily participating. Or you can conclude that even though you did not plan on volunteering for this activity, as long as you are a team member, you will contribute. Your principal assigned the activity; you decided to collaborate. Because collaboration is voluntary, teachers often form close but informal collaborative partnerships with colleagues regardless of whether collaboration is a schoolwide ethic.

● **Collaboration Is Based on Parity** Teachers who collaborate must believe that all individual contributions are equally valued. The number and nature of particular professionals' contributions may vary greatly, but all participants need to recognize that what they offer is integral to the collaborative effort. If you are at a meeting concerning a student's highly complex needs, you might feel you have nothing to offer. However, you have important information about how the student responds in your class and the progress he has made in developing peer relationships. The technical discussion of the student's disabilities is not your area of expertise, nor should it be; your ideas are valued because of your knowledge and skills related to teaching in your classroom. As you read Working Together, think of how the concept of *parity* applies to your interactions with related services personnel such as speech/language therapists and physical therapists.

Analyze and Reflect

Think about cultural differences. How might these differences enhance or constrain collaboration? What can you do to ensure that multicultural collaboration is successful?

● **Collaboration Requires a Shared Goal** Teachers truly collaborate only when they share a goal. For example, if a fifth-grade teacher and a special educator want to design a behavior intervention to help support a student with an emotional disability, their goal is clear. They can pool their knowledge and resources and jointly plan the intervention. However, if one teacher wants the student to spend more time in a special education setting and the other opposes that solution, they are unlikely to work collaboratively on this issue. The teachers might even think at the outset that they share a goal—assisting the student—but that broad statement does not capture their differing views of how the student can best be assisted. They need to resolve this difference for collaboration to occur.

● **Collaboration Includes Shared Responsibility for Key Decisions**   Although teachers may divide the work necessary to complete a collaborative teaching or teaming project, they should share as equal partners the fundamental decision making about the activities they are undertaking. This shared responsibility reinforces the sense of parity that exists among the teachers. In the behavior intervention example, the teachers share decisions about what the key problems are, what strategies might work, how long to try an intervention, and how the intervention may affect the student. However, if they assign many tasks to just one person, they are not collaborating. Instead, one may ask the school psychologists for ideas, review a book of behavior intervention ideas, and talk to last year's teacher. The other may call the parents to seek their input, interview the student, and prepare any needed materials, such as a behavior chart.

● **Collaboration Includes Shared Accountability for Outcomes**   This characteristic of collaboration follows directly from shared responsibility; that is, if teachers share key decisions, they also must share accountability for the results of the decisions, whether those results are positive or negative. If both teachers carry out their assigned tasks, the behavior intervention they design will have a high probability of success. If one fails to carry out a responsibility, valuable time will be lost and their shared effort will be less successful. If something happens that is wonderful (for example, the student's behavior changes dramatically in a positive direction), the teachers will share the success. If something happens that is not so wonderful (for example, the intervention appears to have no impact on the behaviors of concern), they will share the need to change their plans.

● **Collaboration Is Based on Shared Resources**   Each teacher participating in a collaborative effort contributes some type of resource. This contribution increases commitment and reinforces each professional's sense of parity. Resources may include time, expertise, space, equipment, and other assets. The teachers working on the behavior intervention contribute the time needed to make necessary plans, but they also pool their knowledge of working with students with behavior difficulties, share information about other professionals who might assist them, and contribute student access to the computer and other rewards they design.

● **Collaboration Is Emergent**   Collaboration is based on a belief in the value of shared decision making, trust, and respect among participants. Yet, although these qualities are needed to some degree at the outset of collaborative activities, they are not well developed in a new collaborative relationship. As teachers become more experienced at collaboration, their interactions become characterized by the trust and respect that grow within successful collaborative relationships. If the teachers described throughout this section have worked together for several years, they may share freely, including offering constructive criticism to each other. If this is their first collaborative effort, they will be much more likely to be a bit guarded and polite, because each will be unsure how the other person will respond.

> Collaboration is based on a belief in the value of shared decision making, trust, and respect among participants.

● **Prerequisites for Collaboration**   Creating collaborative relationships requires effort on everyone's part. Most professionals who have close collaborative working relationships note that it is hard work to collaborate—but worth every minute of the effort. They also emphasize that collaboration gets better with experience. When colleagues are novices at co-teaching or working on teams, their work seems to take longer and everyone has to be especially careful to respect others' points of view. However, with additional

www.resources

The Center for Effective Collaboration and Practice (http://cecp.air.org) is a federally funded organization designed to promote effective educational practices for students with emotional and behavior problems. This site includes links for parents, teachers, and other professionals on topics related to working together on behalf of these students.

collaboration, everyone's comfort level increases, honesty and trust grow, and a sense of community develops. The next sections discuss some essential ingredients that foster the growth of collaboration.

● **Reflecting On Your Personal Belief System**   The first ingredient for collaboration is your personal beliefs. How much do you value sharing ideas with others? Would you prefer to work with someone to complete a project, even if it takes more time that way, or do you prefer to work alone? If your professor in this course offered the option of a small-group exam, would you be willing to receive a shared grade with your classmates? If your responses to these questions suggest that you prefer working with others, you probably will find professional collaboration exciting and rewarding. If your responses are just the opposite, you might find collaboration somewhat frustrating. For collaboration to occur, all the people participating need to feel that their shared effort will result in an outcome that is better than could be accomplished by any one participant, even if the outcome is somewhat different from what each person envisioned at the outset (Friend, 2000; McLaughlin, 2002).

Part of examining your belief system also concerns your understanding of and respect for others' belief systems. This tolerance is especially important for your collaborative efforts with special educators in inclusive programs. For example, what are your beliefs about changing your teaching practices so that a student with disabilities can achieve the standards for your curriculum? At first, you might say that changing your teaching practices is no problem, but when you reflect on the consequence of that belief, you might have second thoughts. For example, changing your practices means that you must give alternative assignments to students who need them, that you must deliberately change the way you present information and the way you expect students to learn that information, and that you must grade students with disabilities differently than other students, if needed.

The special educators with whom you work are likely to believe strongly not only that alternative teaching practices are helpful in inclusive settings but that they are a requirement. How will you respond when you meet a colleague with this belief? If some general education teachers at your school oppose making accommodations for students with disabilities, will you feel pressured to compromise your beliefs and agree with them? Teachers everywhere have faced these issues. However, as collaboration becomes more integral to public schools, in part because of inclusive practices, it becomes more and more essential to learn to value others' opinions and respectfully disagree while maintaining a positive working relationship.

● **Refining Your Interaction Skills**   The second ingredient you can contribute to school collaboration is effective skills for interacting. In many ways, interaction skills are the fundamental building blocks on which collaboration is based, because collaboration occurs through interactions with others (Friend & Cook, 2004).

There are two major types of interaction skills: communication skills and steps to productive interactions. You already may have learned about the first type, communication skills, in a public speaking or communication course. These skills include listening, attending to nonverbal signals, and asking questions and making statements in clear and nonthreatening ways (DeVito, 2005, 2006). They also include paralanguage, such as your tone of voice and your use of comments like "uh-huh" and "ok." Additional information about communication skills is included in the Professional Edge on the next page.

What makes an interaction collaborative? Why has collaboration become so important for today's schools?

DIMENSIONS OF
diversity

Remember that nonverbal communication varies among cultures. The meaning of eye contact (or lack of eye contact) and appropriate distance during interactions are just two examples of nonverbal factors to consider in working with parents from cultures other than your own.

Barriers to Effective Communication

Effective communication is essential for professional collaboration. Here are some barriers to communication that teachers and administrators must overcome. Which might apply to you?

■ *Advice.* When you offer unsolicited advice to a colleague or parent, that person may be confused by your intent, may reject the advice and form an unfavorable opinion of you, or may feel obligated to follow the advice even if it seems inappropriate. In general, you should offer advice only when it is sought.

■ *False reassurances.* If you offer parents or colleagues false reassurances about student achievement, behavior issues, or social skills, you will damage your own credibility and set the stage for future issues. Being truthful is the best strategy, even if you are concerned that a difficult situation may result.

■ *Wandering interaction.* When another person communicates with you, it is sometimes easy to drift to peripheral topics that waste valuable time. For example, discussing a student's participation in varsity athletics when the concern is academic performance is a distraction that may reflect avoidance of the key issues.

■ *Interruptions.* When you interact with others, they are entitled to your full attention. Responding to a colleague who comes to your classroom door or asking another person to wait while you make a phone call harms the interaction. During an interaction, it also is important to avoid interrupting others. Especially when the person speaking has a language pattern that is slower than yours, you may have to make a concerted effort to wait until the person finishes speaking before adding your contribution.

■ *Being judgmental.* If you tend to speak in absolutes (for example, "The only way to resolve this is to . . ." or "I don't see any way for him to complete the work . . ."), you may be perceived as a professional who sees only one right answer. This may lead to others minimizing their conversation with you because they view it as futile.

■ *One-way communication.* Communication is most effective when it involves all participants. If one person monopolizes the interaction, the others' points of view are not represented and any decisions made will likely be questioned later.

■ *Fatigue.* If you are so tired that you cannot accurately follow the thread of a conversation, your communication will be impaired and you may misspeak or misunderstand others' messages. In such a case, it may be best to request rescheduling the interaction.

■ *"Hot" words and phrases.* In some communities and in some schools, certain words are "hot" and prompt emotional responses. For example, even the word *inclusion* sometimes is considered controversial. For productive interactions, such words (or even suspected words and phrases) are best avoided.

Do any of these barriers sound familiar? What examples of each can you and your classmates provide relating to your own communication experiences in internships or field experiences? What can you do to decrease the likelihood that these barriers will occur in your interactions with colleagues and parents?

Source: Adapted from "Communication in Interprofessional Collaboration" (Chap. 6, pp. 91–115), by M. P. Mostert, 1998, in *Interprofessional Collaboration in Schools,* Boston: Allyn & Bacon. Copyright 1998 by Allyn & Bacon. Adapted by permission.

The other type of interaction skill comprises the steps that make interactions productive. Have you ever been in a meeting and thought the same topic was being discussed repeatedly? Perhaps you wished someone would say, "I think we've covered this; let's move on." Or have you ever tried to problem solve with classmates or friends, only to realize that every time someone generated an idea, someone else began explaining why the idea could not work? In both instances, the frustration occurred because of a problem in the interaction process, that is, the steps that characterize an interaction. The most needed interaction process for you as a teacher is shared problem solving (Knotek, 2003; Wallace, Anderson, & Bartholomay, 2002), a topic addressed later in this chapter. Other interaction process skills include conducting effective meetings, responding to resistance, resolving conflict, and persuading others.

You need both types of interaction skills to collaborate. If you are highly skilled in communicating effectively but cannot contribute to get an interaction from its beginning to its end, others will be frustrated. Likewise, even though you may know the steps in shared problem solving, if you speak to others as though you know all the answers, they will withdraw from the interaction.

● **Contributing to a Supportive Environment** The third ingredient for successful collaboration is a supportive environment (Pugach & Johnson, 2002). As a teacher, you will contribute to this atmosphere through your personal belief system and interaction skills, but this environment includes other items as well. For example, most professionals working in schools that value collaboration comment on the importance of administrative support. Principals play an important role in fostering collaboration (Raforth & Foriska, 2006; Rea, 2005). They can raise staff awareness of collaboration by making it a school goal and distributing information about it to staff. They can reward teachers for their collaborative efforts. They can urge teachers who are uncomfortable with collaboration to learn more about it and experiment in small-scale collaborative projects, and they can include collaboration as part of staff evaluation procedures. When principals do not actively nurture collaboration among staff, collaborative activities are more limited, more informal, and less a part of the school culture. If you work in this type of school, you may find that you collaborate with specific teachers but that your efforts are not rewarded or otherwise fostered.

> Principals play an important role in fostering collaboration.

Another component of a supportive environment is having time available for collaboration (Johnston, Knight, & Miller, 2007; Sever & Bowgren, 2007). It is not enough that each teacher has a preparation period; shared planning time also needs to be arranged. In many middle schools, shared planning occurs as part of the middle school team planning period. In other schools, substitute teachers are employed periodically so that classroom teachers and special services staff can meet. In some school districts, early-release or late-arrival days are used; once each week or month, students are dismissed in the early afternoon or arrive later in the morning. Teachers use the time created to plan instructional units, confer about student problems, and attend professional development activities.

fyi

In our fieldwork with thousands of experienced teachers each year, lack of time is consistently noted as the most serious obstacle to collaboration.

As a teacher, you will find that time is an important issue (Khorsheed, 2007). The number of tasks you need to complete during available preparation time will be greater than the number of minutes available. The time before and after school will be filled with faculty meetings, meetings with parents, preparation, bus duty, and other assignments. You can help yourself maximize time for collaboration if you keep several things in mind. First, it may be tempting to spend the beginning of a shared planning time discussing the day's events or comparing notes on some school activity. But if you engage in lengthy social conversation, you will be taking time away from your planning. A trick discovered by teachers in collaborative schools is to finish the business at hand first and then to chat about personal and school events if time is left. Second, because you never truly have enough time to accomplish all that you would like to as a teacher, you must learn to prioritize. You have to choose whether collaborating about a certain student or teaching a certain lesson is justified based on the needs of students and the time available. Not everything can be collaborative, but when collaboration seems appropriate, time should be allocated for it.

What challenges can occur when school professionals collaborate with each other and with parents?

What Collaborative Services in Schools Foster Inclusion?

The basic principles of collaboration should be your guide to many types of partnerships in schools. These partnerships may involve other classroom teachers, special education teachers, support staff such as speech therapists and counselors, paraprofessionals, parents, and others. Four of the most common collaborative activities concerning students with disabilities are shared problem solving, co-teaching, teaming, and consultation. As you read about these activities, keep in mind that the face-to-face interactions that characterize them can be extended using electronic collaboration using technology now readily available. This is the topic of the Technology Notes.

Shared Problem Solving

**Case Study
Homework Exercise**

Go to the Homework and
Exercises section in Chapter 3
of MyEducationLab to see two
teachers meet to discuss a student
who is struggling in the general
education setting.

Shared problem solving is the basis for many of the collaborative activities that school professionals undertake on behalf of students with disabilities (Bahr & Kovaleski, 2006; Rubinson, 2002). Although shared problem solving sometimes occurs informally when a classroom teacher and a special education teacher meet to decide on appropriate accommodations or other interventions for a student, it also occurs in many other contexts. For example, as you read the applications that follow, you will find that some variation of shared problem solving exists in each. This happens because one way of thinking about co-teaching, teaming, and consultation is as specialized problem-solving approaches.

> When professionals share a problem-solving process, it is much more complex than when educators problem solve alone.

You might be wondering why problem solving is such a critical topic for professional partnerships. In fact, you may consider yourself already adept at problem solving, because it is an ongoing responsibility of educators. However, as many authors have noted (for example, Friend & Cook, 2007), when professionals share a problem-solving process, it is much more complex than when educators problem solve alone, because the needs, expectations, and ideas of all the participants must be blended into shared understandings and mutually agreed-on solutions. Successful shared problem solving requires skilled participants.

● **Discover a Shared Need**   The starting point for problem solving is discovering a shared need, which demonstrates the complexity of shared problem solving. If you face a problem that concerns only you, you try to resolve it by yourself. When you problem solve with colleagues and parents, all the participants need to perceive that a problem exists. Furthermore, it is important that all participants believe they can have an impact on the problem, that they feel accountable for the results of problem solving, and that they can contribute constructively to resolving the problem. When these conditions exist, shared problem solving results in a high level of commitment, as might be the case when you collaborate with your school's library media specialist to find appropriate learning materials and activities for one of your students with disabilities, a topic discussed in the Special Emphasis On . . . feature. When these conditions do not exist, shared problem solving is not shared at all and may appear one sided, with some participants trying to convince others to contribute. For example, many teachers report they have been unable to enlist parents' help in resolving discipline problems. They then go on to describe meetings with parents in which school personnel describe the problem and the parents respond that they do not see such behavior occurring at home. Too often, instead of all parties working to come to a shared understanding of

TECHNOLOGY NOTES

Electronic Collaboration

Collaboration traditionally has been thought of as the way in which professionals interact when they are face to face or perhaps on the phone. However, more and more collaboration is occurring through electronic means. It cannot always adequately replace face-to-face interactions, but it can enhance your other collaborative efforts and provide opportunities for you to learn from and about other professionals you might never have met. Here are examples of electronic collaboration options:

■ Would you like to correspond with educators in Canada? At Special Needs Opportunity Windows (SNOW) (http://snow.utoronto.ca), you can participate in a discussion forum on how teachers foster inclusive practices in their classrooms. The site also offers several other discussion options.

■ Are you interested in finding out what your colleagues around the United States are saying about working with students with disabilities? At A to Z Teacher Stuff (http://forums.atozteacherstuff.com), you can join any of several discussion forums concerning students with special needs or issues related to them. For example, recent postings include advice on managing time, responding to the needs of students with autism, and dealing with Back to School night. This website also includes a discussion forum for classroom discipline problems.

■ Are you seeking an international connection with colleagues? At the U.S. Department of Education's website (www.ed.gov/teachers/how/tech/international/index.html), you can find an extensive set of resources to help you meet and work with educators throughout the world.

■ Were you thinking of starting your own Web log or discussion board related to inclusive practices? Many options now exist. For example, you can follow the simple directions at Google Groups (http://groups.google.com) to set up your own group on a topic of interest, inviting others to correspond with you concerning students with disabilities and other topics.

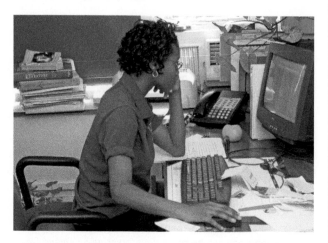

Technology offers new ways to enhance collaboration with colleagues and parents.

Of course, you should take all appropriate precautions to protect yourself when using the Internet and to protect your students' confidentiality.

■ Would you like basic information about electronic collaboration? Electronic Collaboration: A Practical Guide for Educators (www.alliance.brown.edu/pubs/collab/elec-collab.pdf) was developed by the Northeast and Islands Regional Educational Laboratory at Brown University (LAB), the National School Network, and the Teacher Enhancement Electronic Community Hall. Although now several years old, the site contains valuable information for beginners at electronic collaboration and a road map for even experienced electronic collaborators.

If you explore the Internet, you undoubtedly will find other sites that focus on electronic collaboration. These sites can give you fresh ideas, basic knowledge, and a broader understanding of how you and others can make a profound difference in the lives of students with disabilities. These sites also can help you to connect with colleagues from across the country and around the world who have similar interests and questions.

the problem behavior, this type of meeting ends with the parents superficially agreeing to assist in a problem they do not believe exists and the school professionals perceiving the parents as only marginally supportive. The dilemma can be avoided if more effort is made to identify a shared need to problem solve (Blue-Banning, Summers, Frankland, Nelson, & Beegle, 2004).

What Collaborative Services in Schools Foster Inclusion?   **87**

Collaboration between School Library Media Specialists and Teachers

If you are a preservice teacher, you will sometimes be looking for new ideas for reaching students with disabilities and other special needs. If you are studying to be a school library media specialist, you may be thinking, "That's exactly what I can help to accomplish!" In fact, the collaboration that occurs between teachers and school library media specialists often results in both more appropriate materials and resources for all students and better student outcomes. Media specialists can use the following suggestions to foster collaboration with teachers:

- Begin by establishing a relationship with just one teacher and developing effective collaborative projects. Successful examples of library media specialist–teacher collaboration can be contagious, creating a demand for other such experiences throughout the school. Success breeds success.

- Be open and friendly with teachers. Seek them out. They may not come looking for you. Having a proactive library media specialist is a prerequisite to successful collaboration.

- Volunteer to conduct staff development workshops on technology. Doing so will help to establish your credibility as an instructor and your expertise in a valuable area for potential collaboration.

- Develop administrator support for flexible scheduling and collaborative planning. Having administrator support can make a big difference in how hard or easy it is to create cooperative relationships with teachers.

- Sit in on team or grade-level meetings and other planning sessions.

- Study classroom and hallway bulletin boards; find out what is happening, and think of ways you might collaborate.

- Offer to be in class the day a teacher assigns a research project to give a pep talk about the use of various sources of information available.

How might each of these suggestions help teachers to educate all the students in their classrooms, including those with disabilities and other special needs? If you have the opportunity, ask a media specialist about collaborating in an inclusive school.

Source: Adapted from "Developing a Collaborative Culture," by R. V. Small, 2004. Retrieved September 30, 2004, from www.ala.org/ala/aasl/aaslpubsandjournals/slmrb/editorschoiceb/bestoferic/besteric.htm. Used by permission of Ruth V. Small, Syracuse University.

● **Identify the Problem** The most critical step in the problem-solving process is problem identification. However, when educators meet to share problem solving, they often feel pressured because of time constraints; hence, they may rush through this essential stage. Problem identification includes gathering information, compiling it, analyzing it, and reaching consensus about the nature of a student's problem.

In a shared problem-solving situation, you can help emphasize the importance of problem identification by asking whether everyone has agreed on the problem, by asking someone else to restate the problem to check your understanding of it, and by encouraging participants who have not spoken to share their opinions.

Consider the following situation, which shows what can happen when problem identification is not done correctly: A teacher in a shared problem-solving session says to the parent of a student whose attendance is irregular and who consistently comes to school without assignments or basic supplies, "We really need your help in making sure Demitrious gets up when his alarm goes off so he can catch the bus. And we'd like to establish a system in which you sign off on his written assignments." The parent replies, "It's so hard. I work until midnight, and I don't get up when it's time for the kids to go to school. I don't think he sees any point in the homework he's getting—that's why he doesn't bring it back." In this situation, the educator has identified the problem before the meeting has even started: Demitrious needs to assume responsibility, and his parents need to provide more guidance for school activities. Furthermore, the teacher is proposing a solution to the problem and not exploring the problem itself. The parent's response suggests that she does not see the same problem; in fact, the parent is implying that perhaps the problem belongs not to Demitrious at all but to the school staff.

Consider how this interaction could have been handled alternatively: The teacher says to the parent, "Ms. Trenton, thanks so much for taking time off work to meet with us. We appreciate your concern for Demitrious. Lately, we've seen a problem with his attendance. We asked you to come to school so we can learn about your perspective on this situation and to let Demitrious know that we're working together to help him." When the parent replies with the comment about her working hours and Demitrious's perception of the homework, the teacher replies, "That's important information for us. We're hoping we can find ways to motivate Demitrious to come to school—and that includes assigning homework that he sees as valuable." In this situation, the school professionals are working with the parent to identify the problem, not presenting the problem to her.

● **Propose Solutions**   Once a problem has been clearly identified, the next step is to create a wide range of options for solving the problem. One of the most common ways to come up with solutions is to brainstorm.

Brainstorming is based on two important principles. First, judgment is deferred; that is, to free the mind to be creative, people must suspend their predisposition to judge ideas. Second, quantity leads to quality; the more ideas that are generated for solving a problem, the more likely it is that novel and effective solutions can be found. Brainstorming requires openness and creativity. The fourth-grade team you read about at the beginning of this chapter was engaged in proposing solutions. What other solutions might they have generated if they had stressed brainstorming principles?

● **Evaluate Ideas**   With a list of ideas, the next step in shared problem solving is to evaluate the ideas by considering whether they seem likely to resolve the problem and are feasible. One way to evaluate ideas is to use a decision sheet like that illustrated in Figure 3.1. On this decision sheet, the participants stated the problem—to find ways of encouraging Angela to work independently on classroom tasks—and generated ideas for achieving this goal. They then selected criteria by which to judge the merits of each idea. They considered the following:

■ how well the idea would work for increasing the amount of time Angela spends on her independent assignments
■ the extent to which the idea has a reasonable time cost
■ the extent to which the idea preserves classroom routines

Ideas that were not seriously considered were crossed out, and the criteria for decision making were applied to those remaining, with each idea being rated against each criterion. In Figure 3.1, the two ideas with the highest ratings were assigning a study buddy and using picture directions.

● **Plan Specifics**   Once one or two ideas have been chosen using a process such as the one just described, more detailed planning needs to occur. For example, suppose you and others have decided you would like to try having a high school service club provide volunteer tutoring in an after-school program. Some of the tasks to assign include asking club members about their interests, arranging a place for the program, ensuring that needed supplies are available, obtaining permission to operate the program, establishing a schedule for students, determining who will provide adult supervision and scheduling it, advertising the program, and creating and conducting training sessions for the tutors.

Typically, at this step of shared problem solving, not only do participants list the major tasks that need to be completed to implement the solution, but they also decide

Research Note

A recent study of parents' perceptions found that parents valued both the quantity and quality of communication from educators; a sense of educators' commitment to the welfare of their children as students; and a feeling of equality in power, trust, and respect (Blue-Banning et al., 2004).

Case Study
Homework Exercise

Go to the Homework and Exercises section in Chapter 3 of MyEducationLab and consider whether poor collaboration is the cause for a student's failure.

FIGURE 3.1 A Sample Decision-Making Sheet for Problem Solving

Problem Statement: How can we encourage Angela to work independently on assigned classroom tasks?

Ideas:

Decision Making: (3 = high, 2 = medium, 1 = low)

Tape-record instructions	Don't give independent work
Have an assigned "study buddy"	Let her choose the assignment
Make the work easier	Make her stay in from recess to complete work
Use pictures for directions	Give her frequent breaks
Ask a parent volunteer to help	

Decision Making: (3 = high, 2 = medium, 1 = low)

Idea	Criteria			Total	Rank
	Time commitment is reasonable for teacher	Idea does not disrupt class routine	Angela will work for at least 5 minutes		
1. Audiotaped instructions	3	1	2	6	
2. Study buddy	3	3	3	9	1
3. Easier work	2	2	2	6	
4. Picture directions	3	2	3	8	2
5. Parent volunteer	1	3	2	6	
6. Choose assignment	1	2	1	4	
7. Frequent breaks	2	2	2	6	

who will take responsibility for each task. In addition, they specify a timeline for completing all the tasks and usually decide how long to implement the solution before meeting to evaluate its effectiveness.

● **Implement the Solution** If all the steps in the shared problem-solving process have been carefully followed, then implementing the selected idea(s) may be the most straightforward part of the process. When problem solving occurs concerning a student with a disability in an inclusive school, each team member may have some responsibility for implementing the solution. Occasionally, you will have much of the immediate responsibility. In other cases, parents will have a major role to play. Each person involved must do his part for the solution to have a high probability of success. During implementation, it is helpful to keep some type of record documenting your efforts and how the intervention affects the student.

● **Evaluate Outcomes** After a period of time—anywhere from just a few days to two or more weeks—the professionals who are implementing the solution meet to evaluate its effectiveness. At this time, three possibilities exist:

1. If the solution has been especially effective, it may be judged a success. It then will be continued to maintain the results, discontinued if no longer needed, or gradually phased out.

2. If the solution seems to be having a positive effect but is not ideal for some other reason, it may be modified. For example, suppose a behavior management plan is helping a student attend class rather than skip it, but the classroom teacher notes that the system is too time consuming. The problem-solving group may then try to streamline the plan to make it more feasible.

3. Even when the steps in problem solving are carefully completed, a solution occasionally is judged ineffective. The team then must decide what to do next: select a different solution, find additional solutions, or possibly reconsider whether the problem has been accurately identified. The team needs to consider all these possibilities before proceeding with additional problem solving.

> Professionals who regularly employ the strategies of shared problem solving are quick to acknowledge that the steps do not automatically lead to a simple solution.

Professionals who regularly employ the strategies of shared problem solving are quick to acknowledge that the steps do not automatically lead to a simple solution that always works. However, they report that when they problem solve in this fashion, they perceive that their professional time is well spent and that the problem-solving process is truly a collaborative endeavor.

Co-Teaching

Co-teaching occurs when two or more educators—one a general education teacher and the other a special education teacher or other specialist—share the instruction for a single group of students, typically in a single classroom setting (Friend & Cook, 2007). Although any two teachers can teach together (and this sometimes occurs at elementary, middle, and high schools), we focus here on the unique arrangement of two professionals with potentially very different points of view working together on behalf of all the students in a class, the type of arrangement that Ms. Godina and Mr. MacLean, introduced at the beginning of the chapter, have in their classroom.

Co-teaching is becoming a very popular service delivery option in inclusive schools (Bouck, 2007; Friend, 2008). In a classroom with several students with disabilities, combining the strengths of the general education teacher and a special educator can create options for all students (Friend & Cook, 2007). Co-teaching typically occurs for a set period of time either every day (for example, every morning from 9:30 until 10:15) or on certain days of the week (for example, on Mondays and Wednesdays during third period or second block). Occasionally, especially in middle and high schools, a group of students with disabilities who used to attend a separate class for a specific subject might join a general education class permanently. In such cases, the special education teacher may be available every day. For example, if a school used to have a general science class for students with disabilities, the group of six students from that class and their teacher might become members of a general education biology class of 22 students.

As effective as co-teaching is when carefully implemented, it is not the answer for every student with a disability or for every classroom in an inclusive school. Co-teaching is only one option for meeting the needs of students (Friend & Cook, 2004). It should be implemented when the number of students with disabilities in a class and the nature of their needs justify the presence of two teachers or the class is one in which all students with disabilities must enroll (for example, a high school U.S. history class).

Co-teaching provides true access to the general curriculum for students with disabilities. What opportunities and dilemmas may occur in co-teaching?

$\mathcal{R}$esearch Note

Co-teaching has been found to contribute significantly to raising the achievement scores of students with disabilities on mandated high-stakes achievement tests (Samuels, 2007).

Many approaches are available to teachers who decide to co-teach (Mastropieri, Scruggs, Graetz, Norland, Gardizi, & McDuffie, 2005). Friend (2008) has outlined some of the common ones, and they are depicted in Figure 3.2.

● **One Teach, One Observe** In this approach, one teacher leads the lesson and the other gathers data on students to understand them better and make instructional decisions. For example, while Ms. Tran, the general education teacher, leads a lesson in which students work in cooperative groups to answer questions about a map, Ms. Firestone, the special education teacher, may systematically observe three students who are known to struggle with social skills. Ms. Firestone may note on a chart the number of times those students initiate interactions with peers, as well as how often other students direct comments or questions to them. How can this information be helpful to the teachers? Teachers can observe students' ability to pay attention, work independently, make productive use of spare time, and seek assistance when they have questions. However this approach is used, it is essential that each educator sometimes take the primary teaching role in the class while the other observes. In this way, both teachers have the opportunity to watch the class in action, and both have credibility with students as a result of leading instruction.

● **Station Teaching** In *station teaching*, curricular content is divided into two parts. One teacher teaches half the content to half the students, while the other teaches the other half to the rest. The groups then switch, and each teacher repeats her part of the lesson. With classes of students who are able to work independently, a third group may be formed, in which students work alone or with learning partners who tutor each other

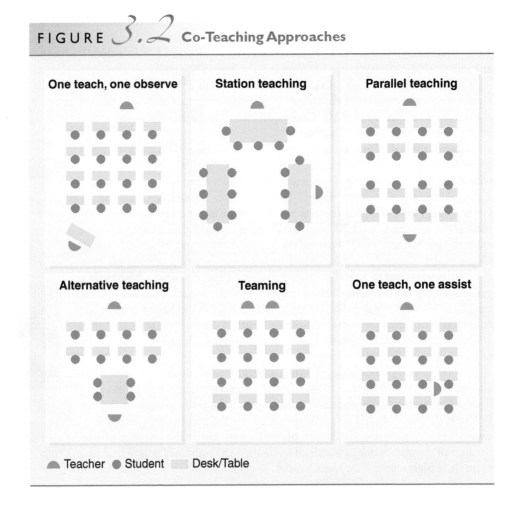

FIGURE 3.2 Co-Teaching Approaches

One teach, one observe

Station teaching

Parallel teaching

Alternative teaching

Teaming

One teach, one assist

▲ Teacher   ● Student   ▢ Desk/Table

on a review assignment. Alternatively, a parent, student teacher, intern, or volunteer may direct an activity at a third station. In an elementary school, an entire lesson based on stations may be completed in a single day; in a secondary school, a station may take an entire class period or more. For example, in a ninth-grade math class, some of the students are working with the general education teacher to learn one method for solving quadratic equations. A second group is meeting with the special education teacher to learn an alternative method. A third group of students is working in pairs on an assignment. Each station lasts an entire class period.

● **Parallel Teaching** Sometimes when two teachers are present, they find it advantageous simply to divide a heterogeneous class group and have each teacher instruct half the class. In this format, called *parallel teaching,* every student has twice as many opportunities to participate in a discussion or respond to teacher questions. A teacher particularly skilled in presenting information through pictures can use this approach while the other teacher emphasizes learning through listening. Students who prefer one method to the other can be placed with the appropriate teacher. In an elementary classroom, this approach may be used to enable students to read different books based on their interests or possibly skill levels. In a secondary classroom, this approach may give students more opportunities to respond during a discussion of a current events topic or for teachers to present different points of view on a topic, which students then can present to each other when the large group comes back together.

● **Alternative Teaching** In many classrooms, having one teacher work with most of the class in one large group while the other teacher focuses attention on a small group is sometimes appropriate. This co-teaching option is referred to as *alternative teaching.* Traditionally, the small group has been used for remediation, but many other options are recommended. For example, some students may benefit from preteaching. In *preteaching,* one teacher works with a small group of students who may struggle to learn (whether or not they have IEPs), who are shy, or who are just learning to speak English. Information to be presented the next day or later in the same day or class is taught to these students so that when questions are asked or vocabulary is introduced, the students have a jump start on learning.

Enrichment also works well in small groups. For example, as a unit of instruction on space exploration is concluding, several students may have a strong interest in the topic. As the other students review and complete assigned tasks, this group may meet to discuss career opportunities related to the space industry, write letters to obtain more information on the current U.S. space effort, or explore websites on related topics. The members in this group could include high-achieving students, students who have average academic achievement but strong interest in space topics, a student with a behavior disorder who would benefit more from this activity than from the assigned work, and a student with a moderate intellectual disability for whom the written task is not appropriate.

Grouping students for remediation is appropriate, but only when it is one of many grouping options and is used only occasionally. Otherwise, such an arrangement becomes the equivalent of running a special education program in the back of a general education classroom—an arrangement that completely undermines the purpose and principles of inclusive schooling.

● **Teaming** In the co-teaching option of *teaming,* the teachers share leadership in the classroom; both are equally engaged in the instructional activities. For example, one teacher may begin a lesson by introducing vocabulary while the other provides examples to place the words in context. Two teachers may role-play an important event from history or demonstrate how to complete a lab activity. Two teachers may model how to address conflict by staging a debate about a current event. One

www.resources

At the website coteach.com, you can find resources related to co-teaching and answers to common questions concerning this increasingly popular service delivery option for students with disabilities and other special needs.

Analyze and Reflect

Co-teaching is an energizing but complex way of providing services to students in general education classrooms. As you think about yourself as a professional, what aspects of co-teaching will likely be easy for you? Which might be challenging? What is your responsibility to work out differences with colleagues so that co-teaching is a success?

Effective teams can be found throughout society. How are teams such as this one similar to teams of school professionals?

teacher may lecture while the other models note-taking strategies on the chalkboard. You reach the limits of teaming only when you run out of exciting ideas for creating instruction with two teachers instead of one. Co-teachers who use this approach find it the most energizing of all the co-teaching options, but you should also be aware that you and a co-teacher might not be compatible enough in terms of teaching style to use it. If that is the case, using the other approaches might be more effective.

● **One Teach, One Assist** Occasionally during instruction, one teacher can be appropriately leading the lesson while the other is quietly assisting individual students. For example, while the special education teacher leads a lesson on a test review, the classroom teacher helps students individually as they have questions about the vocabulary. Alternatively, while the classroom teacher leads a lesson on the causes of World War II, the special education teacher helps keep students on task, checks written work as it is being completed, and responds quietly to student questions. The key to using this approach successfully is to make it only one out of many approaches you use. With overuse, one of the teachers, often the special educator, may perceive that she has no legitimate role in the class and functions mostly like a teaching assistant. In addition, if this approach to co-teaching is used too frequently, students may become overdependent on the extra help that always seems to be available.

● **Co-Teaching Pragmatics** As you consider these co-teaching approaches, you might notice that several other factors need to be taken into account in addition to how the teachers arrange themselves and the students (Friend, 2008; Keefe, Moore, & Duff, 2004). First, in a co-taught class, students are heterogeneously grouped so that those with disabilities are integrated appropriately with their peers without disabilities. Thus, in a station teaching arrangement, students with special needs are likely to be in each of the three station groups, and when alternative teaching occurs, the smaller group may or may not contain students with disabilities. Second, both teachers take on teaching and supportive roles. It is critical for students to view both teachers as credible; the special education teacher should not be seen as a helper who does not have teacher status. Third, the best approach to use depends on student needs, the subject being taught, the teachers' experience, and practical considerations such as space and time for planning. Novice co-teachers may prefer station teaching or parallel teaching over teaming, especially in a class that includes several students with attention problems who would benefit from a smaller group structure. We make this recommendation because the former approaches require less minute-to-minute coordination with another teacher. Finally, the type of curriculum sometimes dictates the approach. For example, a topic that is sequential obviously cannot be taught in stations; it may be presented best in a format of one teach, one assist, followed by parallel-taught study groups.

> In a co-taught class, students are heterogeneously grouped so that those with disabilities are integrated appropriately with their peers without disabilities.

www.resources

The Center for Collaborative Organizations at the University of North Texas (www .workteams.unt.edu) provides a glimpse into the importance of teams in a wide variety of professions. At this website, you can link to exercises for team building, assessments of your qualities for working on a team, and information on teams operating in specialized contexts. How do these items relate to your profession?

Working on a Team

In Chapter 2, you learned that you have responsibility as a member of an intervention assistance team or response to intervention (RtI) team to problem solve about students before they are considered for special education (Bahr & Kovaleski, 2006; Lee-Tarver, 2006; Slonski-Fowler & Truscott, 2004). You also learned you may be a member of the multidisciplinary team (MDT) that determines whether a student is eligible to receive special education services and then writes the student's IEP (Lytle & Bordin, 2001). These teams rely on collaboration among members, and it is important that you understand the concepts and procedures they and other school teams have that make them effective.

When you think about highly successful teams, what comes to mind? Your favorite athletic team? A surgical team? An orchestra? What is it about these teams that makes them successful? **Teams** are formal work groups that have certain characteristics. They have clear goals, active and committed members, and leaders; they practice to achieve their results; and they do not let personal issues interfere with accomplishment of their goals. Can you think of other characteristics of effective teams?

The teams you will be part of at school have many of the same characteristics as other kinds of teams (Fleming & Monda-Amaya, 2001). Their success depends on the commitment of every member and the clarity of their goals (Fratture & Capper, 2007; Hunt, Soto, Maier, & Doering, 2003). On effective school teams, members keep in mind why they are a team, setting aside personal differences to reach a goal that often is to design the best educational strategies possible for students with disabilities or other special needs.

● **Team Participant Roles**   As a team member, you must assume multiple roles. First, you have a professional role. In your role as a classroom teacher, you bring a particular perspective to a team interaction, as do the special education teacher, counselor, adaptive physical educator, principal, and other team members (Shapiro & Sayers, 2003). You contribute an understanding of what students without disabilities are accomplishing in your grade or course, knowledge of the curriculum and its pace, and a sense of the prerequisites of what you are teaching and the expectations for students likely to follow the next segment of instruction.

The second contribution you make is through your personal role. The characteristics that define you as a person shape this role. For example, are you an eternal optimist, a person who sees the positive aspects of almost any situation? If so, you will probably be the person who keeps up the team's morale. Are you a detail-oriented person who is skilled at organizing? If so, you will probably be the team member who ensures that all the tasks get completed and all the paperwork is filed.

Third, you have a team role to fulfill as well. You may be the individual who makes sure the agenda is being followed or who watches the time so team meetings do not last too long. Or you may have the role of summarizing and clarifying others' comments or suggesting ways to combine what seem to be contradictory points of view into integrated solutions to student problems. As an effective member, you will recognize your strengths and use them to enhance the team; you also will be vigilant so your weaknesses do not interfere with the team's accomplishing its tasks. Common formal team roles include team facilitator, recorder, and timekeeper. These roles might rotate so that every team member has the opportunity to experience each one. Informal team roles include being a compromiser, information seeker, and reality checker. These informal roles are not usually assigned, but team members ensure that they are fulfilled as the need arises.

● **Team Goals**   One of the keys to effective teams is attention to goals (Friend & Cook, 2007). Being clear and explicit about goals is particularly important in educational settings because team goals are often assumed or too limited. For example, on some intervention assistance teams, teachers perceive the team goal to be to document interventions so that the special education assessment and identification procedures can begin. Others believe the team functions to help teachers problem solve so the entire referral process can be avoided. Note how crucial this difference is. In the former case, a team may function as a sort of confirmation-hearing process for students with learning and behavior problems. In the latter case, it may be a resource and idea support group. Without clear and specific goals, teams often flounder.

Another aspect of team goals is especially important. The goals just discussed are commonly referred to as *task goals;* that is, they are the business of the team. But teams have another set of goals as well called *maintenance goals.* Maintenance goals refer to the team's status and functioning as a team. Maintenance goals may include beginning and ending meetings on time, finishing all agenda items during a single meeting, taking time to check on team members' perceptions of team effectiveness, and improving team communication both during meetings and outside them. These and other maintenance goals enable effective teams to accomplish the task goals they set.

*R*esearch Note

Each team member plays a crucial role. Knotek (2003) found that decisions about students referred to intervention assistance teams were influenced by the social status of team members, the comments made about students by high-status members, and the way they stated their comments.

Without clear and specific goals, teams often flounder.

Building Teaching Skills Simulation Exercise

Go to the Building Teaching Skills section in Chapter 3 of MyEducationLab for a simulation exercise that follows a teacher as she prepares to work with other professionals in her classroom.

The following example from an elementary school problem-solving meeting shows how each team member plays a vital role. The team included the principal, two general education teachers, a special education teacher, a speech/language therapist, a reading teacher, and a social worker. The reading teacher often spoke a great deal more than other team members, talking until others simply nodded their heads in agreement with whatever she wanted. At one team meeting, the reading teacher left early, just after the team had decided to assess a student for possible special education services. No sooner had the teacher left than the team members confronted the principal, explaining that they did not believe the data for the student justified a referral for assessment and asking the principal to make the reading teacher stop pushing through ideas other team members did not want. The principal made a wise reply. He said, "Wait a minute. If there's a problem, it's a team problem. If a poor decision was made, it was a team decision. It's not 'What am I going to do?' It's 'What are we going to do?'"

In the conversation that followed, team members recognized that all of them had a responsibility to speak out when they disagreed with an idea that was presented. They also acknowledged that they were uncomfortable confronting the reading teacher about her interactions during team meetings. However, with the help of the principal, the team spent part of the next meeting talking about each team member's verbal contributions and establishing procedures for checking all team members' perceptions prior to making a decision. Although taking these actions did not completely change the reading teacher's style, it did bring the team closer together and dramatically increased its effectiveness.

Consultation

fyi

Although special education teachers sometimes act as consultants, this role is more often filled by school psychologists, counselors, and specialists in areas such as student behavior management.

In some cases, you may find that you do not have direct support for a student in your classroom. Perhaps the student does not have an identified disability, or perhaps the student's needs can be met with occasional supports. For example, you might have an outgoing student who suddenly begins acting very withdrawn. Or you may learn that for the next school year, you will have a student who has a significant hearing loss; you would like to know how to assist the student and whether you should enroll in a sign-language class. As illustrated in the chapter-opening story about Brittany, if you have a student with autism in your class, you might find that both you and the special education teacher need assistance from someone else to help the student learn the best ways to transition from activity to activity. These are examples of situations in which you might seek support through consultation (Dole, 2004; Dover, 2005).

Consultation is a specialized problem-solving process in which one professional who has particular expertise assists another professional (or parent) who needs the benefit of that expertise (Dettmer, Thurston, & Dyck, 2005). For example, you may contact a behavior consultant for assistance when a student in your class is aggressive. You might meet with a vision or hearing consultant when a student with one of those disabilities is included in your class. If you have a student who has received medical or other services outside school, you may consult with someone from the agency that has been providing those services.

Although consultation is most effective when it is based on the principles of collaboration presented earlier in this chapter, it has a different purpose than collaboration (Schulte & Osborne, 2003). The consultant working with you may learn from you and benefit from the interaction, but the goal of the interaction is to help you resolve a problem or deal with a concern, not to foster shared problem solving in which both or all participants share the problem. In consulting, the assumption is that you are experiencing a problem and that the consultant's expertise will enable you to solve the problem more effectively.

The process of consulting generally begins when you as the teacher complete a request form or otherwise indicate you have a concern about a student (Kampwirth, 2005). The consultant then contacts you to arrange an initial meeting. At that meeting, the problem is further clarified, your expectations are discussed, and often arrangements are made for

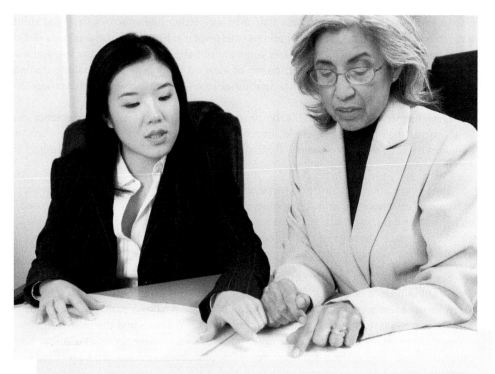

What is the role of a consultant in assisting you to educate your students with disabilities?

the consultant to observe in your room. Once the observation phase has been completed, the consultant and you meet again to finalize your understanding of the problem, generate and select options for addressing it, and plan how to implement whatever strategies seem needed. A timeline for putting the strategies into effect is also established. Typically, you then carry out the strategies. Following this phase, the consultant and you meet once again to determine whether the problem has been resolved. If it has, the strategy is either continued to maintain the success or eliminated as no longer needed. If the problem continues to exist, the consultant may suggest that you begin a new consulting process, or together you may decide that some other action is needed. When appropriate, the consultant closes the case.

For consulting to be effective, both the consultant and the consultee (that is, you as the teacher) need to participate responsibly. Your role includes preparing for meetings, being open to the consultant's suggestions, using the consultant's strategies systematically, and documenting the effectiveness of ideas you try.

The Complexity of Professional Collaboration

As you have read the information about collaborative services for students with disabilities, you probably have realized that they are based on caring and committed professionals who believe in the power of shared efforts and are open to the ideas of colleagues. However, even when all the conditions essential for collaboration are in place, disagreements can occur. And occasionally, you may find yourself working with a colleague or group of colleagues with whom you have deep disagreements. What happens then? Is collaboration possible?

Although most professionals would prefer that all interactions be pleasant and based on agreements, that of course is not a real-world expectation. You may find that you believe that the special educator who reads tests to the students with disabilities in your

**Building Teaching Skills
Internet Exercise**

Go to the Building Teaching
Skills section in Chapter 3
of MyEducationLab to learn
about different ways to implement
collaboration.

class is providing so much assistance that they are getting higher scores than you think accurately represents their learning. Perhaps your principal has said that she expects you to co-teach next year, and you are not sure you want to participate. Or perhaps you and one team member tend to have different points of view on everything from making changes in grading policies for students with disabilities to classroom behavior expectations for them.

Disagreement is an inevitable by-product of collaboration. Disagreements can be minor or major, and the people involved can be committed to resolving them or maintaining their own viewpoints. Regardless, here are a few ideas for responding to disagreements:

■ Try to view the situation from the perspective of the other person, using the concept of **frame of reference**—that is, the totality of the other person's viewpoint that is based on her background, experiences, education, and even work history in schools. Using a frame of reference can help you see things as the other individual sees them, a valuable first step in reaching agreement.

■ See if you can get agreement by trying a solution that can be re-evaluated at a later time. For example, if you think the special educator is providing too much assistance to students, as just mentioned, perhaps the test could be read by a paraprofessional, or perhaps you could read the test while the special educator supervised the other students taking it. After trying one of these (or other options) two or three times, you and your colleague should review them for effectiveness. Sometimes a solution can be reached if everyone knows it can be changed later as needed.

■ Examine your own part in the disagreement. If you tend to be a person for whom every issue is a big issue, a straightforward way to address disagreement is to work diligently to reflect on your behavior. If you tend to insist on your solution, you might want to deliberately work to acquiesce to others' preferences. For honest input on this difficult possibility, you might want to seek input from a colleague, mentor, or administrator.

Perhaps the most important message related to disagreements with colleagues is this: Disagreements provide opportunities to create new and better options for students. Disagreements may be stressful, but you can turn them into solutions by thinking carefully about your views and the basis for them, engaging in constructive conversations with other professionals, and keeping in mind that any resolution ultimately has as its goal helping students with disabilities.

How Can You Work Effectively with Parents?

The partnerships presented thus far in this chapter have focused primarily on your interactions with special education teachers and other professionals who will support you in meeting the needs of students with disabilities in your classroom. In this section, we emphasize your working relationship with parents.

Having quality interactions with the parents of all your students is important, but it is vital with the parents of students with disabilities (Summers, Hoffman, Marquis, Turnbull, Poston, & Nelson, 2005). Parents may be able to help you better understand the strengths and needs of their child in your classroom. They also act as advocates for their child, so they can help you ensure that adequate supports are provided for the child's needs. Parents often see their child's experiences in your classroom in a way that you cannot; when they share this information, it will help both you and the student achieve more success. Finally, parents are your allies in educating students (Whitbread, Bruder, Fleming, & Park, 2007). When you enlist their assistance to practice skills at home, to reward their child for accomplishments at school, and to communicate to their child messages consistent with yours, then you and the parents will be multiplying the student's educational opportunities and providing a consistency that is essential to maximize student learning.

Info Sheet Homework Exercise

Go to the Homework and Exercises section in Chapter 3 of MyEducationLab to learn how to prepare for a parent conference.

Understanding the Perspective of Family Members

You might be tempted to assume that because you work with a student with a disability in your classroom on a daily basis, you understand what it would be like to be the student's parent. This assumption could not be further from the truth. The parent of a high school student with a moderate intellectual disability as well as multiple physical disorders made this comment at a meeting of parents and teachers:

> You see my child in a wheelchair and worry about getting her around the building and keeping her changed. But remember, before you ever see her in the morning, I have gotten her out of bed, bathed her, brushed her teeth, washed her hair and fixed it, fed her, and dressed her. I have made sure that extra clothes are packed in case she has an accident, and I have written notes to teachers about her upcoming surgery. When she's at school, I worry about whether she is safe, about whether kids fighting in the hall will care for her or injure her, and whether they are kind. And when she comes home, I clean up the soiled clothes, work with her on all the skills she is still learning, make sure that she has companionship and things to do, and then help her get ready for bed. And I wonder what will be the best option for her when she graduates in 3 years. You can't possibly know what it's like to be the parent of a child like my daughter.

As a teacher, you need to realize what this parent so eloquently demonstrated: that you do not understand what it is like to be the parent of a child with a disability unless you too are the parent of such a child. This means you should strive to recognize that the range of interactions you have with parents is influenced in part by the stresses they are experiencing, their prior dealings with school personnel, and their own beliefs about their child and her future.

Apply this concept to Chris's parents, Mr. and Mrs. Werner, who were introduced at the beginning of the chapter. What factors might be influencing their interactions with school professionals? How would knowing about their reluctance to have Chris identified as needing special education and their concerns about the stigma of the learning disability label help the teachers respond appropriately to them?

Parents' Reactions to Their Child's Disability

Parents of children with disabilities have many reactions to their children's special needs, and these reactions may focus on positive or negative factors (Ferguson, 2002). Some parents go through several emotions roughly in a sequence; others may experience only one or several discrete reactions. For some, the reactions may be minor and their approach pragmatic. For others, their child's disability might affect their entire family structure and life. Part of your work with parents includes recognizing that the way they respond to you may be influenced by any of the following responses to their children's disabilities (Ferguson, 2002):

> Parents of children with disabilities have many reactions to their children's special needs, and these reactions may focus on positive or negative factors.

1. *Grief.* Some parents feel grief about their child's disability. Sometimes this is a sorrow for the pain or discomfort their child may have to experience; sometimes it is

sadness for themselves because of the added stress on the family when a child has a disability; and sometimes it is a sense of loss for what the child may not become. Grief may be temporary or it may be chronic, a realization nearly every day of how their lives are different from those of families with children who do not have disabilities. Parents have a right to grieve about their child—a right educators should respect.

2. *Ambivalence.* Another reaction parents may have toward their child is ambivalence. This feeling may occur as parents attempt to confirm that the child's disability is not temporary or fixable, as they try to determine what the best educational options are for their child, and as they ponder how their child will live as an adult. The decisions that parents of children with disabilities have to make are often difficult, and they continue throughout childhood and adolescence and sometimes through adulthood. Parents often attend meetings with school personnel at which tremendous amounts of information are shared with little time for explanation, and they often meet with representatives from many different disciplines. It is no wonder they may feel ambivalent.

3. *Optimism.* A college student was once interviewing the parent of a student with a mild intellectual disability. When asked what it was like having a child with an intellectual disability in the family, the parent replied, "Mary is my child. Just like any other child, I love her as my child. She is sometimes funny and sometimes clever and sometimes naughty. She can really get into trouble. She's just like my other children, except she's Mary." For this parent, her child's special needs are just part of the configuration of needs that any child in any family might have. In this family, the emphasis is on the person, not the disability. There are many families like this one. In these families, the special needs of the child are met without an extraordinary reaction. Parents may work diligently to optimize their child's education, and they are hopeful about their child's future. They work closely with educators and others to ensure that the child's life, whatever it may be, is the best one possible.

Analyze and Reflect

What is your own culture and background? How might your beliefs and experiences affect your interactions with parents and other family members from diverse groups? What steps should you take to ensure that you are *culturally competent,* that is, that you recognize your own perspective and accept others' perspectives?

How parents respond when they have a child with a disability depends on many factors. One is the intensity and complexity of the disability. The reaction of parents whose child is diagnosed with a learning disability in third grade will likely be somewhat different from that of parents who learned two months after their child was born that she could not see.

Another factor affecting the way parents respond is how the information about the disability is shared with them. When such information is presented in a coldly clinical manner, without adequate sensitivity to the parents' emotions, their response can be quite negative. This is true even for mild disabilities. When one parent was told about her son's learning disability, she said, "Wait a minute. Stop and let me think. Do you realize what you've just said? You've just unraveled my whole way of thinking about my son. What do you mean a *learning disability?* What does that mean? Will it ever change? How can you sit there and keep talking as though it's no big thing?" A father related how he learned about his daughter's moderate intellectual disability. A physician simply said, "She's retarded. There's nothing we can do." The father left the office crying, partly because of the information and partly because of the insensitive way it had been communicated.

Yet another factor influencing a family's response to having a child with a disability is culture (Harry, 2002; Klinger & Harry, 2006; Obiakor, 2007). In some cultures, disability is a spiritual phenomenon that may reflect a loss of the soul or evidence of transgressions in a previous life. In other families, a child with a disability is considered a reflection on the entire family. In some families, a disability is accepted as just part of who the child is. In others, it is believed that a cure should be sought. It is important to listen to family members as they discuss their child to better understand their perspective on him as well as their response to ideas and suggestions that you and the rest of the team make.

One other factor that affects the parents' response concerns resources, including financial support (Lott, 2003). When parents have the resources necessary to provide what

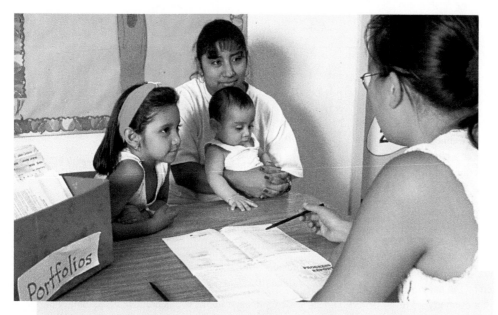

When professionals interact with parents, they should follow the principles of family-centered practices. What does this mean? Why is it especially important for interactions with parents from nondominant cultures?

they believe is the best set of support services for their child, they are less likely to experience negative emotions. However, when parents know that their child would benefit from some intervention, such as surgery, a piece of computer equipment, or tutoring, they are invariably frustrated if they cannot provide that needed support and have difficulty accessing it from school and community resources. Another important resource is personal. In large families, families with many supportive relatives living in the same community, or families with a strong network of neighbors and friends, the stresses of having a child with a disability are greatly reduced. When parents are isolated or when friends and family are uncomfortable with the child, the parents will likely experience far more difficulties.

● **Family-Centered Practices**   The recommended approach for working with families of students with disabilities is referred to as family-centered practices (Dunst, 2002). **Family-centered practices** are based on the notion that outcomes are best for students when their families' perspectives are respected, their families' input is sincerely sought, and school professionals view their job as helping families get the information they need to make the best decisions for their children. Do you agree with this approach? Most professionals do, but implementing it means setting aside preconceived notions about parents and families and sometimes respecting the fact that a family's goals for their child may not be the ones you would choose.

One of the most important factors that influences whether you can develop strong working relationships with parents and families is your sensitivity to the parents' point of view (Nelson, Summers, & Turnbull, 2004; Starr, Foy, Cramer, & Singh, 2006). Some parents find school an unpleasant or intimidating place. They may have had negative experiences when they were students, or if they are from another country, they may be unfamiliar with the expectations for parental involvement in U.S. public schools. If parents' primary language is not English, they may be uncomfortable because of the need for an interpreter, or they may misunderstand information communicated by school personnel, whether in face-to-face interactions or in writing. If parents are from a culture that views teachers as experts, they may wonder why you keep asking for their input. Some ideas for reflecting on and responding to parents from diverse cultures are included in the Professional Edge on page 102.

Individualized family service plans (IFSPs) are the documents that guide services for young children with disabilities. Strongly based on collaboration, IFSPs set the expectation that professionals and families are partners in the education of students with disabilities.

Involving Immigrant Parents of Students with Disabilities

Nearly all teachers and parents believe that they should form productive partnerships to best educate children. However, they also find that collaboration can be a challenge, especially if parents have only recently come to the United States. Here are some suggestions for fostering a positive working relationship:

- Try to understand the language needs of the family. If parents need information in a language other than English, they are entitled to receive it. If a translator is needed in meetings, this service should be provided. The translator often can be chosen by the parents or can be another parent of a child with a disability.

- Check to see whether English classes are offered to parents by your school district. In a large district, a welcome center or parent center also may operate. If so, share this information with parents.

- Use icons (for example, happy faces and sad faces) to convey information. If you need to send essential information to the family, ask about having it translated.

- Avoid jargon. Provide specific examples to illustrate the information you are communicating.

- Verify with parents that your communication has been understood. Be aware that some parents may consider it rude to ask you to repeat information, so you should be alert to the possible need to restate what you have said.

- Develop your own key vocabulary list in the parents' language (for example, special education terms, greeting words, and action words) so you can participate

directly in some small way in communicating with them.

- Read about the family's culture. Ask parents who are bilingual to describe the education system in their native country.

- Welcome parents to your classroom and be respectful of cultural differences in the willingness to share information.

- Include cultural and religious holidays on school calendars.

- Visit families at home, if this practice is customary in your school district. However, remember that some families will prefer to meet you at a neutral location such as a library rather than in their home.

- Encourage family members to become involved in their child's education. Try to connect immigrant families with other families from their native country.

- Remember that confusion and misunderstanding are common when language and cultural differences exist. Be quick to seek further understanding and slow to lay blame. The dilemma may be related to language or culture.

Source: Adapted from "Involving Immigrant Parents of Students with Disabilities in the Educational Process," by S. Al-Ahssan and R. Gardner, *Teaching Exceptional Children, 34*(5), 2002, pp. 52–58. Copyright 2002 by The Council for Exceptional Children. Reprinted with permission.

Some parents may not be visibly involved in their children's education because of pragmatic barriers. Parents who work at jobs that are far from school may not be able to take time off to participate in activities at school and may not be able to afford the lost work time. For some parents, involvement is largely a matter of economics: The costs of child care and transportation may prevent them from being able to work with you. These parents, however, may be involved through their work with their child at home.

In general, your attitude toward parents and their perceptions of their children greatly affect how you interact with them. If you telegraph through your choice of words, your question-asking skills, and your body posture that parents should see their children as you do and accept your input without question, then you are violating the principles of family-centered practice, and you probably will find that parents will not communicate with you readily. However, if you make parents feel welcome in your classroom or by phone or e-mail, listen carefully to their perceptions and concerns, treat them as important, and work with them to address student needs, then many benefits will ensue for the student, the family, and you (Ulrich & Bauer, 2003).

Collaborating with Parents

As a school professional, you can make family-centered practices a reality when you find ways to effectively collaborate with parents. Some examples of positive ways to partner with parents include home–school communication, parent conferences, parent education, and direct parent involvement in volunteer programs and similar activities.

● **Home–School Communication**   One simple way to build a positive working relationship with parents is by using informal and formal home–school communication strategies. For example, at the beginning of the school year, you can send home a letter to parents that introduces you and explains your classroom goals for the year. You can follow this up with a positive phone call to parents sometime during the first few weeks of the school year. A positive call is particularly important for parents of students with disabilities because they often hear from educators only when a problem exists.

You can continue a system of communication with parents throughout the school year. For example, some teachers send home weekly updates or newsletters to the parents of all their students (e.g., Dardig, 2005). For a student who is struggling, you might exchange a notebook in which you briefly list accomplishments of the day and a parent writes back with information from home (Davern, 2004). A time-saving alternative is to have a checklist that describes the positive behaviors expected of your student (for example, "Raises hand to ask a question"; "Comes to class with all needed materials"). You can then check the items that were successfully completed for that day. For a student with severe disabilities in your class, a paraprofessional might assist by preparing under your direction daily communication to parents (Chopra, Sandoval-Lucero, Aragon, Bernal, De Balderas, & Carroll, 2004). Whenever you use a daily communication system, you should encourage parents to respond so you are aware of their perspectives and concerns.

Some teachers are finding that electronic communication can be a useful tool. If the families of your students have access to e-mail, you can send a group communication or electronic newsletter on a weekly basis, and you can send information about a specific student more frequently as needed. Some teachers also use e-mail to ensure that communication about homework is clear (Salend, Duhaney, Anderson, & Gottschalk, 2004). Remember, though, that some families cannot readily access a computer, so you need to use an alternative means of communication with them.

Finally, remember that your strategies for home–school communication may be influenced by culture. With some families, indirect communication through print or electronic media will not be effective. In such cases, your responsibility is to ensure that you reach out to the parents through a phone call or an invitation for them to come to school to meet. Depending on local policy and parent preference, you might even suggest meeting the parents at a local library or another setting that might be perceived as more parent-friendly than school. In general, you should remember that if your goal is to enhance collaboration with parents, the communication approaches you select should clearly help you achieve that purpose.

● **Parent Conferences**   In addition to the informal, day-to-day communication in which you engage with parents, you also can collaborate with them through conferences. Preparing for, conducting, and following up on parent conferences helps ensure that this communication vehicle is valuable for the parents of all your students, including those with disabilities.

Before a conference, you should clarify the purpose of the meeting. Is it to speak to a group of parents about your overall goals for the year? Is it to meet individually with parents to discuss their child's progress? You can help parents prepare for the latter type of meeting by sending home in advance of the conference a list of questions and suggestions.

Case Study Homework Exercise

Go to the Homework and Exercises section in Chapter 3 of MyEducationLab to read what a teacher says has helped him connect to student families for over 30 years.

DIMENSIONS OF
diversity

Many parents, especially those from minority groups, can find school an intimidating place. You can promote participation by encouraging parents to come to school meetings with a friend or another family member and by asking them positive questions early during meetings (for example, "What does your child say about school at home?").

A sample of such a conference-preparation flyer is presented in Figure 3.3. As you prepare questions for parents, you also should think about the questions you wish to address with them and make a list. Finally, you will communicate more effectively if you have samples of student work, your grade and plan books, and other pertinent student records easily available.

During the conference, your goal is to create a two-way exchange of information. Whether meeting with parents by yourself or with a special educator, you can accomplish this goal when you greet parents positively, arrange to meet with them at a table instead of at your desk, set a purpose for the conference, and actively involve them in discussion. In addition, you should use language respectful of the parents, their child, and their culture. Avoid using jargon (for example, acronyms such as AYP and MDT). In addition, you should work to understand that parents might interpret the meaning of disability and educators' response to it in ways that differ from educators. For example, some African American parents may distrust school professionals and the decisions made about their children because of past segregation and discriminatory special education practices (Salend & Duhaney, 2005).

After a parent conference, you should complete several tasks. First, you should write a few notes to remind yourself of the important points discussed. These notes will help you improve the accuracy of your recollections. Second, if you made any major decisions regarding strategies that you and the parents will implement, you should write a brief note to the parents to confirm the decisions you made. Third, if you agreed to any action (for example, sending information to parents or asking a counselor to call parents), it is best to carry it out as soon as possible. Finally, if the special education teacher did not attend the conference, he may appreciate receiving a brief note from you with an update on the conference outcomes.

FIGURE *3.3* **Sample Set of Questions to Help Parents Prepare for Conferences**

1. What are your priorities for your child's education this year?

2. What information would you like me to know that would help me better understand and instruct your child? What are your child's learning strengths? Unique needs?

3. What are the best ways to communicate with you? Phone or voice mail? E-mail or text message? Face to face? Written notes?

4. What questions do you have about your child's education?

5. How could we at school help make this the most successful year ever for your child?

6. Are there any topics you want to discuss at the conference for which I might need to prepare? If so, please let me know.

7. Would you like other individuals to participate in the conference? If so, please give me a list of their names so I can invite them.

8. Would you like me to have particular school information available? If so, please let me know.

Remember to let parents know how to contact you prior to a conference. Also keep in mind that special educators usually participate with you in conferences regarding students with disabilities. They are invaluable in helping to respond to parent questions and concerns.

● **Parent Education**   Another type of communication with parents can be accomplished through a variety of parent education activities. Although you probably would not undertake this type of activity without your colleagues, you may find parent programs helpful for informing parents and giving them an opportunity to discuss important matters concerning their children. For example, if your school decides to emphasize inclusive practices, an information session for the parents of all students might be very helpful. One school invited the parent of a student with disabilities to present on this topic to other parents at the beginning of the school year; the result was increased understanding and a positive start. Some schools offer parent programs related to understanding children's behavior, preparing for transitions from one school level to the next, and other topics of common interest, including ADHD.

● **Parent Involvement**   One additional type of collaboration with parents occurs through their involvement in their children's schools. Some parents, especially at the elementary level, make time to volunteer at school, tutoring students, assisting with clerical chores, and helping to supervise students on field trips. Other parents cannot make such commitments, but they might be willing to help design a newsletter by working at their convenience or to come to school on a Saturday to help set up for a special event. Alternatively, some schools help parents get involved by making school facilities more available. For example, some schools regularly hold evening sessions during which parents can bring their children to school to work on computers, read, or participate in discussion groups. Some schools find space in the building to set up a parent center, a comfortable gathering place designed for and operated by parents where books can be borrowed and important school district and community information is available.

● **The Complexity of Parent Collaboration**   Just as with your interactions with colleagues, your interactions with parents sometimes will be successful and satisfying and sometimes will be challenging and perplexing. The notion of frame of reference applies as well. The more you can understand what is behind a parent's thinking, the better prepared you will be to try to work for a solution. Keep in mind that some parents of students with disabilities feel they have had to fight to get for their children the services to which they are entitled, and so they may come across as aggressive, even if you approach an interaction with the intent of collaboration. Occasionally, a parent will ask you for something that truly is not reasonable, and in such a case, you should enlist the assistance of the special education teacher and possibly an administrator in responding.

If a disagreement with a parent occurs, avoid making unilateral statements such as "We don't offer any services in a special education classroom" or "I won't permit that type of assistance in my classroom." Remember that because students with disabilities have special rights, you run the risk of speaking in error and causing further difficulties. One strategy that usually is recommended is to let the parent know that you will be back in touch after checking on options. This provides you with the time needed to seek additional information, enlist assistance, and formulate options for resolving the matter. You can read about an example of a meeting in which a parent and professionals disagree in the Case in Practice.

How Can You Work Effectively with Paraprofessionals?

Throughout this chapter, the assumption has been made that all the individuals involved in forming school partnerships have equal status; that is, a general education teacher has approximately the same level of authority and equivalent responsibilities as a special

Video Homework Exercise

Go to the Homework and Exercises section in Chapter 3 of MyEducationLab to learn how information provided by families can be a valuable resource for professionals who work with students with disabilities.

fyi

Vocabulary related to paraprofessionals can be confusing. Accepted terms for these school staff members include *paraeducator* and *teaching assistant*. In large districts, specially trained paraprofessionals might have a title related to their training, such as *behavior technician* or *personal* or *one-to-one assistant*. The term *aide* is considered out of date for these individuals.

Case in Practice

A Problem-Solving Meeting

Mitchell has been experiencing a variety of difficulties in his eighth-grade classes. The greatest concern expressed by his teachers is that he refuses to use any of the materials that have been specially prepared for him by the special educator, Ms. Antovich. This definitely is affecting his grades. His teachers believe he is quite capable of learning the material and have asked Mitchell's parents to come to school to discuss what to do. Along with Ms. Cox, Mitchell's mother, the meeting is being attended by Ms. Antovich; Mr. Graf, the team's math teacher; and Mr. Crain, the assistant principal. The school professionals have explained their concerns, and they are ready to seek Ms. Cox's assistance.

Mr. Crain: Given what we've described, Ms. Cox, I'm wondering what your reaction is.

Ms. Cox: I didn't realize letting Mitchell receive special education meant he was going to be singled out in class. No wonder he won't use the things Ms. Antovich is preparing. I'm sure he's embarrassed. He said something at home about that the other day, and I wasn't sure what he was referring to. Now I know. Just stop singling him out!

Ms. Antovich: I should clarify the types of adapted materials I've been providing, Ms. Cox. My goal is to make anything that is used in class as much like the other kids' materials as possible. Most of the time, several students are using them. I'm not sure it's the materials themselves that are the issue. I think Mitchell has decided that he doesn't want any type of assistance in class.

Mr. Graf: That is the impression I have. For example, it really helps Mitchell to use a calculator for computation, and calculators are available for all the students who want to use them. But Mitchell refuses. As a result, he makes avoidable errors and hurts his scores.

Ms. Cox: How many other kids use calculators?

Mr. Graf: Several do. It's just an accepted part of my class.

Ms. Cox: All I know is that he feels stupid in his classes. He's proud, just like his father. He doesn't want anyone to know that school is so hard for him, and I know he doesn't want people helping him.

Mr. Crain: You've added the information that Mitchell is embarrassed by any assistance received in the classroom, and that's helpful. We still have to address two key issues. First, Mitchell is unlikely to succeed in his classes without supports. With supports, he seems to do well, and so there is no justification for even thinking about pulling him out of his classes to a special education setting. Second, he is seeing supports as embarrassing. Perhaps we should focus on how to integrate supports better into the instruction so they are not seen by Mitchell as embarrassing.

Ms. Graf: I'm open to any ideas we can come up with. This is such a critical year in math instruction, and I know the other teachers feel the same way about their subjects.

Ms. Antovich: Ms. Cox, how would it be if I had a private conversation with Mitchell to raise the issue of embarrassment with him? I could then give you a call to discuss options we might try. But I'll really need your assistance in convincing Mitchell to do whatever we plan.

The meeting continued for another few minutes while details of the plan were outlined.

REFLECTIONS

What parts of a problem-solving process did this meeting include? How effective were the professionals in exploring Ms. Cox's perspective on her son's problem? What was the role of each professional attending the meeting? Could any of them have been excused? Should others have been invited? What did the professionals say that might have lessened Ms. Cox's concern? That could have increased it? Mitchell was not present at this particular meeting. Why not? How could Mitchell's input be included anyway? How might the meeting have been different with him present? What are your responsibilities as a professional educator when parents disagree with your perceptions of their child with a disability? What types of assistance might you seek to help address the matter?

education teacher, speech/language therapist, school psychologist, reading teacher, and so on. In many school districts, individuals in these types of positions are referred to as *certified staff* or *professional staff*.

One other partnership you may form involves another type of staff. As mentioned in Chapter 2, **paraprofessionals,** or paraeducators, are school personnel employed to assist certified staff in carrying out educational programs and otherwise helping in the instruction of students with disabilities. (Although some school districts also employ other types of paraprofessionals, for this discussion, we refer only to paraprofessionals who are part of special education services.) Paraprofessionals usually have completed two years of college or have passed an examination related to their responsibilities, but they generally are not required to have a college degree. When students with disabilities are members of your class, a special educator may not have adequate time or opportunity to assist them frequently, or the students might not need the direct services of that professional. Instead, a paraprofessional might be assigned to you for a class period or subject or, depending on the intensity of student needs, for much of the school day (Giangreco, Edelman, & Broer, 2003; Trautman, 2004).

Understanding Your Working Relationship with Paraprofessionals

The partnerships you form with paraprofessionals are slightly different from those you form with certified staff because you have some supervisory responsibility for a paraprofessional's work, a situation that would not exist in your work with other colleagues (French, 2003). For example, you may be expected to prepare materials for the paraprofessional to use in working with a group of students, you may have the responsibility of assigning tasks to this person on a daily basis, and you may need to provide informal training to the paraprofessional regarding your classroom expectations.

Many classroom teachers have never been supervisors, and they worry about what types of tasks to assign to a paraprofessional and how to set expectations (Giangreco & Broer, 2005; Riggs, 2004). Adding to the complexity of the situation is the fact that some paraprofessionals have extensive professional preparation, a teaching license, and years of classroom experience, which makes them prepared to do nearly everything you do; others meet only the minimum requirements and have little experience working with students. In Chapter 2 you learned about the types of responsibilities paraprofessionals may have in your classroom. If you will be working with a paraprofessional, you probably will receive a written description of that person's job responsibilities, specifying the activities that individual is to complete. Also you can arrange to meet with the special education teacher or other professional who has overall responsibility for the paraprofessional's job performance.

Two general guidelines for working effectively with paraprofessionals are these: First, paraprofessionals generally enjoy working with students and want to participate actively in that process, and they should have the opportunity to do so. However, they also are expected to help teachers accomplish some of the chores of teaching, such as record keeping and instructional preparation tasks. Second, paraprofessionals always complete their instructional assignments under the direction of a teacher who either has already taught the information or has decided what basic work needs to be completed; that is, paraprofessionals should not engage in initial teaching, nor should they make instructional decisions without input from a certified staff member.

You have a key role in setting expectations for a paraprofessional who may work in your classroom, for ensuring that you and the paraprofessional are satisfied with your working relationship, and for resolving any problems that arise. At the beginning of the school year, you can orient the paraprofessional to your classroom by providing a place for him to keep personal belongings and instructional materials, explaining essential rules and policies for your classroom, clarifying where in the classroom you want him to work, and asking him to voice questions and concerns (French, 2003). It is particularly important to touch base with the paraprofessional frequently early in the school year to be certain that expectations are clear. The paraprofessional may be working in several classrooms and trying to remember several sets of directions from different teachers, all with

You have a key role in setting expectations for a paraprofessional who may work in your classroom.

Info Sheet Homework Exercise

Go to the Homework and Exercises section in Chapter 3 of MyEducationLab for information about how you and your paraprofessional can work collaboratively and effectively.

Research Note

In a study of paraprofessional turnover and retention in inclusive schools, Ghere and York-Barr (2007) found that keeping these essential personnel required providing appropriate training, increasing salaries, matching paraprofessionals' preferences to their assignments, and creating a collaborative culture.

their own styles. You might even find that discussing these topics is best accomplished in a meeting that includes the special education teacher, you, any other general education teachers involved, and the paraprofessional. Figure 3.4 outlines some questions you might need to ask concerning your work with paraprofessionals to ensure your experience is positive for you and your students as well as the paraprofessional.

To continue nurturing the working relationship you have with a paraprofessional, you should communicate clearly and directly all activities you would like him to complete. Some paraprofessionals report that they enter a classroom only to find that the teacher is already working with students and expects the paraprofessional to know what lesson to review with the students with special needs, assuming that the special education teacher has provided this direction. Meanwhile, the special educator is assuming that the general education teacher is guiding the paraprofessional. Unfortunately, in this situation the paraprofessional may be left wondering how to proceed.

Collaborating with Paraprofessionals

An often-asked teacher question regarding paraprofessionals is this: Given the supervisory nature of teacher–paraprofessional work, is it possible to collaborate with this group of staff members? The answer is yes. Paraprofessionals can collaboratively participate in shared problem solving about student needs, planning field trip details, and making decisions regarding how best to adapt information for a specific student (French, 2003; Riggs, 2004). Your responsibility as a teacher is to encourage this type of collaboration. At the same time, you should clearly inform the paraprofessional when a matter being discussed is not one in which the principles of collaboration are appropriate. It also is important that you tell paraprofessionals when they are meeting your expectations and that you

---

FIGURE 3.4 Questions for General Educators to Ask Concerning Working with Paraprofessionals

- Is the paraprofessional in my class provided as a general support, or is she assigned on behalf of a particular student?
- What range of activities should I expect the paraprofessional to complete related to academic instruction? Behavior? Student social interactions? Physical assistance?
- Are there specific activities the paraprofessional must carry out? Should not carry out?
- To what extent am I responsible for assigning the paraprofessional specific tasks and activities in the classroom?
- What strategies will be used to ensure that communication among the special education teacher, paraprofessional, and me is clear and consistent? How will we meet on a regular basis to discuss student progress, problems, and paraprofessional responsibilities in the classroom?
- Should the paraprofessional communicate directly with the parents?
- Should we discuss any issues related to confidentiality?
- What training has the paraprofessional had for working in my classroom? For working with students with disabilities? What preparation has the paraprofessional had related to the curriculum for which I am responsible?
- What should I do if I am uncomfortable with something the paraprofessional is doing or reporting or if other problems occur?
- What should I do on days that I don't have anything in particular for the paraprofessional to do?

---

promptly address any issues of concern as soon as you become aware of them. For example, Ms. Fulton is a paraprofessional in the seventh-grade math class. At a recent brief meeting, the math teacher thanked her for quietly answering students' questions about directions and providing assistance in reading items in the textbook. However, he also directed Ms. Fulton to avoid assisting students in answering the problems being worked. His judgment is that her help is approaching the level of providing students with answers. He illustrates his point by talking through with her an example of how to help a student who asks for help. His directions to Ms. Fulton were direct and clear but also respectful of her many years of experience in working with students with disabilities.

The Complexity of Collaborating with Paraprofessionals

Most of your interactions with paraprofessionals will be positive, and you will realize how valuable these school personnel are in inclusive classrooms. Although most paraprofessionals work diligently, have a tremendous commitment to working with students with disabilities, and manage their roles superbly, problems occasionally arise. If you teach older students, you might find that the paraprofessional does not have enough knowledge of the information being presented to reinforce student learning. A few paraprofessionals violate principles of confidentiality by discussing classroom or student matters away from school. Some paraprofessionals are disruptive in classrooms—for example, their speech is too loud or their movements are too noticeable. If problems such as these occur and cannot be resolved directly between you and the paraprofessional, you should ask the special educator with whom you work to meet with you and the paraprofessional to problem solve. If further action is needed, an administrator such as a principal or special education coordinator can assist. Ultimately, you are directing the day-to-day work of the paraprofessionals in your class. If problems arise, it is your responsibility to follow up until they are resolved and students' support is being provided appropriately.

An entirely different type of problem can occur, but it is equally serious. Some paraprofessionals tend to hover over students with disabilities, preventing them from establishing social relationships with peers and fostering dependence instead of independence (Giangreco & Doyle, 2002). You should discuss this well-intentioned but inappropriate activity with such paraprofessionals and give clear, alternative directions for their interactions with students. By offering encouragement and addressing concerns, you can establish an environment that will make your collaboration with paraprofessionals invaluable.

Video Homework Exercise

Go to the Homework and Exercises section in Chapter 3 of MyEducationLab for a snapshot of how classroom aides/paraprofessionals can support student learning in general education classes.

fyi

Some paraprofessionals are highly trained to work with students with specific disabilities. For example, a paraprofessional working with students who are deaf probably will know sign language. A paraprofessional working with a student with autism probably has been prepared to respond to the student's behaviors using specific strategies known to be effective.

Summary

Collaboration has become an important job responsibility for all educators and is especially important in educating students with special needs. Collaboration is a style professionals use in interacting with others, and it involves key characteristics such as voluntary participation, parity, shared goals, shared responsibility for key decisions, shared accountability for outcomes, shared resources, and the emergence of trust, respect, and a collaborative belief system. You can help make your school's collaborative efforts more successful by identifying and clarifying your personal beliefs about collaboration, refining your interaction skills, and contributing to a supportive environment.

Collaboration can occur in many programs and services, but for students with special needs, the most common ones are shared problem solving, co-teaching, working in teams, and consulting. Each of these applications has its own set of guidelines and own use in educating students, but each sometimes leads to disagreements that all professionals have a role in resolving.

Another collaborative responsibility teachers have relates to parents. You need to understand parents' perspectives on having a child with a disability; work collaboratively with them on the basis of your respect for their perspective; communicate effectively with them in conferences and in other ways; and respond professionally to them in team meetings, annual reviews, and other interactions at which you and they are present. Collectively, this approach to working with parents is referred to as *family-centered practice*. You may occasionally experience difficult interactions with parents; in these instances, using principles for effective communication and asking for assistance are essential.

A final group with whom general education teachers collaborate is paraprofessionals. Understanding your roles and responsibilities and those of the paraprofessionals, and basing your collaboration on them, leads to positive working relationships, particularly if you understand how to address problems that occur as they work with you on behalf of the students with disabilities in your classroom.

Back to the Cases

This section provides opportunities for you to apply the knowledge gained in this chapter to the cases described at the beginning of this chapter. The questions and activities that follow demonstrate how these standards and principles, along with other concepts that you have learned about in this chapter, connect to the everyday activities of all teachers.

Ms. Godina and Mr. MacLean ask for your advice on co-teaching. Briefly outline or describe two styles of co-teaching you might recommend to them. Assume that you have chosen to teach this grade level and subject area. (INTASC Principle 10.01 and CEC Standard 5.) For each of these two co-teaching styles, answer the following questions:

- Why would you select this style to teach this particular content?
- How does this style meet the needs of each student with special needs in the class?

Ms. Swanson and Ms. O'Brien began their professional relationship to consult about Brittany's difficulty transitioning to the media center. However, they discovered other areas where they wanted to work together to improve Brittany's learning experiences as well. They agreed to become more collaborative in their working arrangement. Where do you think they might encounter some difficulty as they make a shift in the relationship? What suggestions would you give them so that in the end their partnership is successful?

Ms. MacDougal listens to the exchange between the Werners and Mr. Sanders. As they discussed concerns, she determines that the meeting is not going to come to a productive end. She quickly decides to suggest that the participants enter into a shared problem-solving activity. (INTASC Principle 10.04 and CEC Standard 10.) Is this an appropriate strategy for this meeting? Provide reasons for your thinking.

Key Terms and Concepts

Collaboration (p. 79)

Consultation (p. 96)

Co-teaching (p. 91)

Family-centered practices (p. 101)

Frame of reference (p. 98)

Paraprofessionals (p. 106)

Shared problem solving (p. 86)

Teams (p. 94)

myeducationlab

Where the Classroom Comes to Life

Now go to the Friend and Bursuck, Fifth Edition, MyEducationLab course at www.myeducationlab.com to

- take a pretest to assess your initial comprehension of the chapter content
- study chapter content with your individualized study plan
- take a posttest to assess your understanding of chapter content
- engage in multimedia exercises to help you build a deeper and more applied understanding of chapter content

Applications in **Teaching Practice**

Collaboration in the Washington School District

Although the administrators in the Washington School District would tell you that staff members have always worked together well, when increasing inclusive practices was made part of the district's strategic plan, it became clear that collaboration also needed to be a priority. Each principal was asked to work with staff members to incorporate collaboration into the school's improvement plan. Each school created a committee to study collaboration and its application in inclusive schools, set priorities, and plan staff development. Committee members also created a plan for evaluating the impact of increased collaboration on student outcomes.

In every elementary, middle, and high school, the teachers reviewed their school mission statement as a starting point for discussions of their beliefs about how students learn, how teachers teach, and how schools can be learning communities. In most of the schools, the teachers quickly realized that their mission statement did not explicitly say that teachers in the school were expected to work together to meet the needs of all their students. During after-school meetings, the mission statements were revised.

Next teachers began to discuss various forms their collaboration might take. In one elementary school, Carole, a first-grade teacher anticipating a class group with many special needs, argued strongly for co-teaching. She stated that she needed someone to help her for at least a couple of hours each day. Peggy, another teacher, reminded her that with only two special education teachers and one paraprofessional available for everyone from kindergarten through fifth grade, she was asking for far too much, especially because these professionals also had other responsibilities. Jim, the special education teacher who works with students with moderate and severe disabilities, agreed. He noted that he had to reserve time to work individually with some of his students in a special education setting.

Co-teaching was a popular topic in other schools too. In the middle school, one special education teacher was assigned to each team, and the teachers learned that they had the responsibility for deciding how to co-teach while making sure that students' IEP goals were addressed. Most teams decided that co-teaching should occur mostly in English and math classes. In the high school, the teachers approached their investigations with caution. First, they decided that special education teachers should be assigned to academic departments. Then they decided that co-teaching would occur only in English for the first year. Other services would remain the same while everyone became accustomed to working together. These teachers also decided that they wanted to learn more about collaboration skills, and they arranged with a local consultant for professional development as well as for observations of and feedback related to their interactions during meetings.

Principals made planning time a priority. They ensured that co-teaching teams could meet every week, but they also required that lesson plans be submitted after those meetings. Principals also decided to survey teachers, paraprofessionals, and parents at the halfway point of the school year and again at the end of the year in order to gauge perceptions of these efforts to enhance collaboration.

With much excitement and some anxiety, the district's administrators and teachers finished their detailed planning. They were a little concerned about new teachers who might be hired during the summer and how to help them become oriented quickly to the collaborative initiative. They also were concerned about whether they could demonstrate that working more closely improved student achievement, the ultimate goal. However, they felt they had worked closely to develop the plan and were eager to implement it.

Questions

1. Which characteristics of collaboration can you identify in the teachers' interactions and plans? Which are not evident?

2. How were the teachers working to ensure their collaborative efforts would be successful? What is the role of the principal in fostering collaboration?

3. How would you respond to Carole? What do you recommend she do? What do you recommend her colleagues do in their interactions with her?

4. Why would it be important to incorporate a statement about collaboration into a school mission statement? Check the websites of your local schools. Are their mission statements posted? If so, do they address collaboration, either directly or indirectly?

5. How could the teachers communicate with parents about their plans? What reactions might they expect from parents? Why? How could they involve parents in their programs?

6. How might collaboration among professionals be similar and different in the elementary schools, middle schools, and high schools? What opportunities and constraints might exist for each group?

Further Readings

Friend, M., & Cook, L. (2007). *Interactions: Collaboration skills for school professionals* (5th ed.). Boston: Allyn & Bacon.

This book is designed to help all the professionals who work in schools to enhance their collaboration skills, including their communication, the collaborative services they provide to students, and their ability to address difficult or controversial situations.

Hanson, M. J., & Lynch, E. W. (2003). *Understanding families: Approaches to diversity, disability, and risk.* Baltimore: Brookes.

This book examines the impact of disability on families, combining information from recent research as well as practical ideas for working effectively with families, including families of young children with disabilities.

Harry, B., & Klingner, J. K. (2006). *Why are so many minority students in special education? Understanding race and disability in schools.* New York: Teachers College Press.

This book is intended to provide education professionals with an understanding of the disproportionate representation of African American and Hispanic students in some special education categories. The book explores families' interactions with school professionals, teachers' biases, and strategies for fostering better understanding and more equitable education for all students.

Peck, A. F., & Scarpati, S. (Eds.). (2004). Communication and collaboration [special issue]. *Teaching Exceptional Children, 36*(5), 1–80.

In this journal, teachers are invited to learn about a variety of topics related to collaboration—from co-teaching to home–school communication to working with paraprofessionals and physical therapists.

Assessing Student Needs

LEARNING Objectives

After you read this chapter, you will be able to

1. Explain how general education teachers can contribute significantly to the assessment process.
2. Describe the uses of high-stakes, standardized achievement, and psychological tests in making educational decisions for students with special needs.
3. Describe how alternate assessments for students with significant cognitive disabilities can be developed and scored.
4. Define curriculum-based assessment and explain how it can help general education teachers.
5. Construct and use probes of basic academic skills, prerequisite skills and knowledge in content areas, and independent learning skills.
6. Use curriculum-based assessment to make special education decisions.

Ms. Lyons is concerned that Rob, a student in her second-grade class, is not keeping up with the rest of the class in math. She knows that he will be taking the state math test in third grade, and she is afraid that if he continues to fall behind, he won't meet state standards. Mr. Blair, the special education teacher, suggests that Ms. Lyons do some informal assessment herself before referring Rob for special education or other services.

What kinds of assessments can Ms. Lyons use to clarify Rob's problems in math? How might these assessments help her make changes in Rob's math instruction? Under what circumstances should she refer Rob for special education or other services?

Mr. Blount teaches a high school U.S. history class. He has learned that three students with disabilities will be in his class this fall. Mr. Blount was told that these students have some reading problems and may have trouble reading the textbook. He decides to make up a test to give at the beginning of the year to see how well all of his students are able to use the textbook. Using a section of a chapter from the text, he writes questions to test how well students can figure out the meanings of key vocabulary words, use parts of the book (for example, the table of contents, glossary, and index), read maps, and read for information (for example, note main ideas and draw conclusions). When Mr. Blount gives the test, he finds that the three identified students have trouble reading the text, but many other students also have difficulty.

How might Mr. Blount use the information from this assessment to differentiate instruction for his students?

Roberto is a student with moderate to severe disabilities who is in Ms. Benis's sixth-grade social studies class. As a result of Roberto's cerebral palsy, he has significant cognitive, language, and motor deficits. Roberto can read his name, as well as some high-frequency sight words. He uses a wheelchair, and he has trouble with fine motor movements such as cutting and handwriting. Roberto speaks with the aid of a communication board.

How can Roberto meet state standards for sixth grade in social studies? What kinds of assessments can Ms. Benis use to determine whether Roberto is meeting standards in social studies?

As more and more students with disabilities are being served in general education classes, teachers need to make many important decisions that can greatly affect these students' success. This is particularly important in view of federal requirements in the Individuals with Disabilities Education Act (IDEA) that all students with disabilities participate in district testing programs and in No Child Left Behind, which requires that all students make adequate yearly progress as measured by high-stakes tests. For example, in the preceding vignettes, Ms. Lyons wanted to help Rob before he failed the state math test in grade 3. Mr. Blount wanted to find out whether his students could read the textbook for his history class to help him decide which students would benefit from adapting the book. Ms. Benis needed to include Roberto, who had moderate to severe disabilities, in her social studies class but had to figure out how he would meet the state standards. To respond effectively in situations such as these, teachers need accurate, relevant information. Thus, they need to develop informal measures to help them make a number of instructional decisions as well as to participate in special education decision making. This chapter explores assessment strategies that help general education teachers contribute to the process of decision making for students with special needs. This involves determining matters such as whether a student needs special education services; when a student is ready to learn in inclusive settings; when an alternative to state testing is required; and what classroom accommodations and modifications to try, continue to use, or change.

How Do Your Student Assessments Contribute to Special Education Decisions?

Reading Homework Exercise

Go to the Homework and Exercises section in Chapter 4 of MyEducationLab to read about the informal methods for assessment that will give general education teachers information to share with other professionals.

As a classroom teacher, you make an important contribution to the process of identifying and meeting the needs of students with special needs. A major part of that contribution involves assessing student needs. **Assessment** has been defined as the process of gathering information to monitor progress and to make educational decisions when necessary (Overton, 2005). The two most common ways of collecting information are through standardized, commercially produced tests and through informal tests devised by the teacher. Much of the information in this chapter is about ways in which these measures can be used to make decisions about students with special needs. General education teachers contribute assessment information in six important decision-making areas for students with special needs: screening, diagnosis, program placement, curriculum placement, instructional evaluation, and program evaluation.

Screening

Analyze and Reflect

What questions are involved in making a screening decision? Under what circumstances might it be difficult to screen for a disability?

In Chapter 2 you learned that **screening** involves the decision about whether a student's performance differs enough from that of his or her peers to merit further, more in-depth assessments to determine the presence of a disability. For example, to clarify Rob's problems in math, Ms. Lyons from the chapter-opening vignette examined the most recent group achievement test scores for her class in math and found that Rob's total math score was one to two years below grade level. Ms. Lyons then gave Rob and his classmates some minitests on various math computation skills she had taught to see whether Rob was behind his peers in these skills. Using this information, Ms. Lyons found that a number of students were performing similarly to Rob. She therefore decided not to refer Rob for

Students' needs can be identified, addressed, and monitored through assessment based on observation, screening, diagnostic testing, program placement and evaluation, curriculum placement, and instructional evaluation. What role do general education teachers play in assessing students' special needs?

a more comprehensive evaluation until she first tried making some changes in the classroom with Rob and several other students.

Diagnosis

The major decision related to **diagnosis** concerns eligibility for special education services, a decision you first learned about in Chapter 2. Does a student meet established federal guidelines for being classified as having a disability? If so, what are the nature and extent of the student's disability? For example, Paula was a student in Ms. Clark's class. In September, when Paula appeared to be struggling to keep up with the class in reading, Ms. Clark paired her up with a classmate for 15 minutes before reading each day to go over key words and vocabulary. When Paula's reading accuracy and fluency problems persisted even after four weeks of this extra help, Ms. Clark arranged for her to have 30 minutes more practice later in the day with the reading teacher. After a month of this extra help, Paula still showed no improvement. Ms. Clark suspected she had a learning disability and referred her for a case study evaluation. The school psychologist gave Paula a test on cognitive functioning—including a test of memory, attention, and organization—and an individual achievement test. She found that Paula was slow in processing visual information (that is, letters, numbers, and shapes) and that her achievement in reading was significantly lower than that of other students her age. However, her achievement in math was at grade level. Ms. Clark evaluated Paula's classroom reading performance by having her and five average students read orally and answer questions from a grade-level trade book that was part of the classroom literature program. Paula's oral reading fluency was below that of her peers, and she was able to answer only 40 percent of the comprehension questions. In the end, Paula was declared eligible to receive services for learning disabilities, because she did not respond favorably to two levels of extra classroom help; she showed problems processing visual information

Analyze and Reflect

What questions are involved in diagnosing a student? What role can you, as a general education teacher, play in answering these questions?

Case Study Homework Exercise

Go to the Homework and Exercises section in Chapter 4 of MyEducationLab to hear a teacher share her concerns about a student who is having difficulties and does not like school.

quickly enough; and her achievement differed significantly from that of her classmates, as measured by both a standardized achievement test and informal classroom reading tests. Working Together highlights effective ways to communicate results of diagnostic tests, as well as resulting decisions about placement, to parents.

Program Placement

Analyze
and Reflect

What questions are involved in making a program placement? How do issues of least restrictive environment and free appropriate education enter into answering these questions?

The major **program placement** decision involves the setting in which a student's special education services take place (for example, in a general education classroom, resource room, or full-time special education classroom). The individualized education program (IEP) team must make this decision carefully. In the past, the tendency was to pull students out of general education classrooms without considering whether they could be supported within the general education program instead. In today's schools, the emphasis is on doing all that can be done within the general education class first. This approach is consistent with guidelines for accessing the general education curriculum outlined in IDEA and the response to intervention (RtI) approach in which students with learning disabilities are identified by monitoring how they respond to instruction. RtI was discussed in Chapter 2 as part of IDEA. Still, students have different needs, and some may require instruction in a specific area at a level of intensity that cannot be delivered in the general education classroom. That is why it is important to make placement decisions based on measures that accurately reflect student performance in class. For example, Carlos was eligible to receive services for learning disabilities in math. His IEP team needed to decide whether his learning needs could be accommodated by adapting the math methods and materials in the general education classroom or whether he should be provided more intensive math instruction in a resource room setting. Carlos's classroom teacher gave Carlos and his classmates a series of informal math tests. She found that Carlos was significantly behind his peers on some but not all of the tests; his math problem solving was very deficient compared to that of his classmates, but his math computational skills were fine. The IEP team decided to keep Carlos in his general education class and to support his instruction in problem solving by providing him extra teacher-guided practice whenever a new problem-solving skill was introduced. The team also decided to carefully monitor Carlos's problem-solving skills; if those skills showed little improvement, they would consider other options.

fyi

Program placement decisions for students with moderate to severe cognitive disabilities should be based on the supports needed to meet the curricular goals outlined in their IEPs.

Curriculum Placement

Analyze
and Reflect

How might questions dealing with curriculum placement help address IDEA's concerns about access to the general education curriculum?

Curriculum placement involves deciding at what level to begin instruction for students. For an elementary school teacher, such a decision may mean choosing which reading or math book a student should use. For example, Ms. Tolhurst has her students read orally and answer questions to find the appropriate trade books for them to read. That is, she determines the level of difficulty at which the books in her classroom reading program are neither too easy nor too hard for them. At the secondary level, curriculum placement decisions are likely to determine which class in a sequence of classes a student should take. For example, Mr. Nowicki, the guidance counselor, was trying to decide whether to place Scott in Algebra 1. He asked the math department to identify basic math skills that all students entering algebra should have. The department constructed a test based on those skills and gave it to Scott as well as other incoming ninth-graders.

Of course, information about curriculum placement also provides teachers with a good measure of the extent to which students with disabilities are accessing the general education curriculum, an explicit goal of IDEA. In the examples just mentioned, a student with a disability in Ms. Tolhurst's class who can read only books that are two levels below grade level could be seen as having great difficulty accessing the general education reading curriculum. In contrast, a student who enters Mr. Nowicki's algebra class with all of the necessary prerequisite skills is fully accessing the district math curriculum.

Working TOGETHER

Communicating Effectively with Parents

Mrs. Perez has just attended a multidisciplinary committee meeting for her son Jorge and is distraught. First, being in the same room with all those professionals made Mrs. Perez nervous; she felt like an outsider who was there because she had done something wrong. Second, she was embarrassed that her English wasn't very good, so she was afraid to say anything. She had hoped the meeting would result in Jorge's getting extra help, but that was not what happened at all.

The school psychologist, Mr. Tanner, talked too fast and used a lot of technical language Mrs. Perez didn't understand, such as "performance-based," "verbal IQ," and "age and grade-level expectations." He said Jorge was in the slow-learner range. Mrs. Perez was afraid that he meant her Jorge was stupid. She thought that Jorge was unable to understand tests because his English skills weren't very good, but she was afraid to say so.

When the special education teacher said that Jorge was two to three years below grade level in reading and writing and about one year below level in math, Mr. Tanner nodded, saying that that was about what could be expected for someone with Jorge's ability. Mrs. Perez wondered whether that meant there was no hope for Jorge. His teacher said that Jorge was having trouble keeping up in class and that last year he had failed to pass the state tests in reading and writing. Mrs. Perez wanted to hear more about what the class was doing and how Jorge was coping with the material, but she was afraid she would offend Jorge's teacher. Mr. Tanner finished by saying that Jorge was behind in his skills but achieving as expected given his scores on the IQ test. He said that Jorge wasn't eligible for special education services and asked Mrs. Perez if she had any questions.

Mrs. Perez knew that Jorge's English skills were holding him back, but now the committee members were telling her he couldn't get any extra help. Having a million questions but not knowing how to ask them, she nodded her head and left the meeting, afraid that there was no hope for her Jorge in school.

Addressing the Dilemma

Chapter 3 presented communication barriers that can exist between parents and teachers. Here are some ideas that this team could have implemented to remove some of those barriers and improve communication with Mrs. Perez:

- It appears that few attempts were made to make Mrs. Perez feel comfortable. Taking time at the beginning of the meeting to introduce everyone present and to break the ice usually helps. Making sure that parents are not seated apart from the rest of the team will also make them feel more a part of the group.

- Mrs. Perez has difficulty speaking English. The team should have predetermined the extent of her English skills and provided supports such as a translator if needed. Even suggesting that Mrs. Perez bring an advocate with better English skills would have greatly facilitated the communication process.

- The team needed to explain the testing and eligibility process using nontechnical language that Mrs. Perez understood. Such communication should have started when parental consent for a case study evaluation was first attained. Clearly, Mrs. Perez had expectations that the process would lead to extra help for Jorge. The team needed to explain more carefully the criteria that eligibility is based on and the fact that providing services is not an automatic process.

- The standardized tests needed to be more carefully explained. Mrs. Perez appears to have had serious reservations about their validity.

- Given that persons from some other cultures often have difficulty asserting themselves with authority figures from the majority culture, more care needed to be taken to obtain Mrs. Perez's consent to the committee's decision. Simply asking whether she had any questions was not enough. Explaining the decision in concrete terms also would have helped—for example, "This means Jorge will not get extra help in special education. Do you understand that? Do you agree with this decision by the committee?"

- The team neglected Mrs. Perez's primary need: to get help for her son. Even if Jorge was not eligible for special education, the team should have described other options for help in the school, such as Title I reading programs or supports for English-language learners.

Instructional Evaluation

Decisions in **instructional evaluation** involve whether to continue or change instructional procedures that have been initiated with students. For example, Ms. Bridgewater is starting a peer tutoring program to help Cecily, a student with severe cognitive disabilities, read her name and the names of her family members. Each week, Ms. Bridgewater tests Cecily to see how many of the names she has learned. She uses the results of the tests to find out whether the peer-tutoring program is helping Cecily make progress. In another example, Mr. Jackson decides to accompany each of his history lectures with a graphic organizer of the material. He gives weekly quizzes to find out whether the graphic organizer is helping his students better learn the material.

Program Evaluation

Analyze and Reflect

What questions are involved in evaluating the program of a student with special needs? Under what circumstances might a student with disabilities require more special education services? Require fewer services? Be ready to exit special education?

Program evaluation decisions involve whether a student's special education program should be terminated, continued as is, or modified. One consideration is whether or not the student is meeting standards, as evidenced by reaching goals or attaining benchmark levels on assessments. For example, when Addie, a student with a reading disability, attained benchmark levels in reading fluency and comprehension for her grade level, her program was changed. She was integrated into the general education reading program, and her performance was carefully monitored to ensure that her gains were maintained.

Another way to evaluate the success of special education programming is by monitoring the attainment of IEP goals. For example, Amanda is receiving social work services twice per week. Her IEP goal is to decrease the number of times she has a verbal confrontation with Mr. Alvarez, her teacher. Mr. Alvarez is keeping track of the number of times daily that Amanda refuses to comply with his requests to see whether sessions with the social worker are improving Amanda's behavior.

What Information Sources Are Used in Programming for Students with Special Needs?

www.resources

The use of high-stakes testing is a controversial issue in today's schools. The website of the American Psychological Association (www.apa.org) is a good place to learn about all kinds of assessment, including high-stakes testing.

A number of information sources are used in programming for students with special needs. The use of multiple assessment sources is consistent with the principle of nondiscriminatory testing, discussed in Chapter 2, which says that no single measure should be used to establish eligibility for special education services. The measures described in this section include high-stakes achievement tests, standardized achievement tests, psychological tests, alternate assessments, and curriculum-based assessments.

High-Stakes Achievement Tests

Analyze and Reflect

On what are high-stakes tests based? Are all students with disabilities required to take them? To what testing accommodations are students with disabilities entitled? Do testing accommodations give students with disabilities an unfair advantage?

A key requirement of IDEA is that students with disabilities have maximum access to the general education curriculum. Unlike in the past, however, access today is defined not as spending a certain amount of time in general education but as making meaningful progress toward meeting general curriculum goals (Nolet & McLaughlin, 2005). In general education today, that means meeting educational standards. Standards, which are set by individual states, comprise what students should be able to know or do as a result of their public education. For the past three decades, general dissatisfaction with public education has dramatically raised learning standards and has led to increased accountability for schools as they teach students to attain those standards.

As you learned in Chapter 1, **high-stakes tests** are assessments designed to measure whether students have attained learning standards. These tests are a type of assessment referred to as *criterion referenced* because they involve comparing student performance to a specific level of performance, or benchmark, rather than to a norm, or average, as with traditional standardized achievement tests. Most states have created their own high-stakes tests based on an agreed-on set of learning outcomes. For each identified outcome, standards or benchmarks are set that represent an acceptable level of knowledge or competence. Schools are then evaluated on the basis of the percentage of students meeting standards on each of the learning outcomes identified. For example, State A wanted all its fifth-graders to be able to comprehend the key elements of short stories, such as character, setting, problem identification, problem resolution, and moral. Reading experts were chosen by the state to create an item that would test student competence in comprehending short stories. The experts chose a short story written at the fifth-grade level and developed a series of multiple-choice questions about the story elements. They then tried out the test on a diverse sample of students and through careful analysis determined that students who could answer at least 90 percent of the story-element questions were competent at identifying story elements. State A then tested all its fifth-grade students on this item to determine the percentage that could identify key elements in short stories.

How do high-stakes tests relate to students meeting educational standards? What are the implications for students with special needs?

IDEA requires that most students with disabilities take their states' high-stakes tests. This is how districts can show the degree of access to the general education curriculum attained by students with disabilities. These IDEA requirements were reinforced by the No Child Left Behind Act (NCLB), which requires that all children in each of grades 3–8 and at least once in grades 10 through 12 take high-stakes tests to show whether they are meeting state standards or making adequate progress toward them. NCLB requires that at least 95 percent of students with disabilities take high-stakes tests. Both IDEA and NCLB require that the results for students with disabilities be aggregated with the results of the other students and reported publicly. Results for students with disabilities must also be disaggregated and reported separately; students with disabilities who are tested are held to the same standards and levels of adequate yearly progress as their classmates without disabilities.

To ensure that the scores obtained are accurate, students with disabilities are entitled to a range of accommodations while taking high-stakes tests. Common accommodations include changing the setting of the test (for example, allowing students to take tests in special education classrooms), changing the timing of the test (for example, providing extended time or more frequent breaks), changing the response format (for example, allowing students to mark responses in test books rather than on Scantron sheets), and changing the presentation format (for example, using a braille edition of a test or giving directions in sign language) (Roeber, 2002; Thurlow, Elliott, & Ysseldyke, 2003). A more complete description of the accommodations available and a process for finding the right accommodations for individual students is provided in the Professional Edge on page 122. Up to 3 percent of students with significant intellectual disabilities are entitled to take alternate assessments geared to their individual needs as specified on their IEPs. Alternate assessments are described in more detail later in the chapter.

Why is the issue of high-stakes testing and students with disabilities important for you? The answer is that students with disabilities who are included in your classroom (except for those with significant intellectual disabilities) are expected to meet the same standards as everyone else. And under NCLB, consequences are involved when students fail to meet expectations. The names of failing schools are posted publicly, children in failing schools are allowed to transfer to higher-performing schools, and failing schools can be required to provide extra tutoring for all students not making adequate yearly progress. Furthermore, in as many as 23 states, students need to pass an exam to receive a high school diploma, and at least 6 states require that students pass a test to be promoted to a certain grade (Thompson

Reading Homework Exercise

Go to the Homework and Exercises section in Chapter 4 of MyEducationLab to find an article that outlines ways to determine whether students who are ELL may need to be referred for special education evaluation.

fyi

Rose (2000) suggests that traditional assessments are limited in accuracy because they involve only one questioning medium, print; allow limited means of expression, usually using fine motor skills; and involve a limited means of engagement (test taking) that is stressful and undermines performance. He proposes a system of *universally designed assessments* that, through the use of the latest technology, allow for greater testing accuracy through multiple means of engagement, expression, and representation of information. For more information, see www.cast.org.

Professional EDGE

Accommodations for Students with Disabilities on Standardized Tests

Under guidelines from IDEA and NCLB, most students with disabilities are required to take district and state standardized tests, including state high-stakes tests. A list of standard accommodations provided is shown here. Keep in mind that research on effective strategies for determining which students get which accommodations is still being done. Given the range of abilities within all disability groups, it is recommended that teachers avoid using students' labels to make these decisions and instead base them on individual student characteristics.

Research Note

Elliott and Roach (2002) have conducted a series of studies about the impact of providing testing accommodations to students with disabilities. While Elliott and Roach emphasize that much more research is needed, they were able to draw the following conclusions from their work:

- Students with disabilities participate in large-scale assessments more often when testing accommodations are available.

- Packages of individual accommodations are more effective than individual accommodations alone.

- Approximately 50 to 70 percent of students with disabilities produce higher test scores when they receive accommodations.

- Approximately 15 to 20 percent of students without disabilities also produce higher test scores when they receive accommodations.

- Reading aloud is not a valid accommodation for students taking reading tests.

Edgeman, Jablonski, and Lloyd (2006) have described a process for IEP teams to use when deciding on testing accommodations for individual students. A more general process for linking students with the appropriate accommodations is described in the Professional Edge on page 415 in Chapter 11.

Types of Testing Accommodations

Setting	Presentation
• Provide special lighting. • Provide adaptive or special furniture. • Provide special acoustics. • Administer the test to a small group in a separate location. • Administer the test individually in a separate location. • Administer the test in a location with minimal distractions.	• Provide the test on audiotape. • Increase spacing between items or reduce number of items per page or line. • Increase size of answer spaces. • Provide reading passages with one complete sentence per line. • Highlight key words or phrases in directions. • Provide cues (for example, arrows and stop signs) on answer forms. • Secure papers to work area with tape or magnets.
Timing	**Responding**
• Allow a flexible schedule. • Extend the time allotted to complete the test. • Allow frequent breaks during testing. • Provide frequent breaks on one subtest but not another.	• Allow marking of answers in booklet. • Tape-record responses for later verbatim transcription. • Allow the use of a scribe. • Provide copying assistance between drafts.
Scheduling	**Other**
• Administer the test in several sessions, specifying the duration of each session. • Administer the test over several days, specifying the duration of each day's session. • Allow subtests to be taken in a different order. • Administer the test at a different time of the day.	• Make special test preparations. • Provide on-task/focusing prompts. • Make any accommodation that a student needs that does not fit under the existing categories. • Conduct an alternate assessment.

Source: Testing Students with Disabilities: Practical Strategies for Complying with District and State Requirements (2nd ed.), by M. L. Thurlow, J. L. Elliott, and J. F. Ysseldyke, 2003. Thousand Oaks, CA: Corwin. Reprinted with permission.

& Thurlow, 2003). Therefore, it is critical for you to carefully monitor the progress of your students with disabilities and, if needed, to provide extra supports or resources to ensure that the standards are met. Effective monitoring requires paying close attention to the results of high-stakes tests. More important, it requires you to keep track of student performance on a daily basis using assessments such as the ones described in this chapter.

Standardized Achievement Tests

Another common source of information for making educational decisions is **standardized achievement tests.** These tests are designed to measure academic progress, or what students have retained from the curriculum. Unlike the high-stakes tests just described, standardized achievement tests are *norm referenced.* In a norm-referenced test, the performance of one student is compared to the average performance of other students in the country who are the same age or grade level. Student performance is often summarized using grade equivalents and/or percentile ranks.

● **Group-Administered Tests** Two major types of standardized achievement tests are group-administered and individually administered diagnostic tests. As the name implies, *group-administered standardized achievement tests* are completed by large groups of students at one time; this usually means that the general education teacher gives the test to the entire class. These tests assess skills across many areas of the curriculum, none in much depth. For this reason, they are intended to be used solely as screening measures. Nonetheless, caution is advised in using these scores, even if only for screening. As with any test, the general education teacher should be sure that students with disabilities receive appropriate accommodations when taking the test. Otherwise, the resulting score may be a measure more of the disability than of the ability. For example, Alicia has a learning disability in reading and has problems comprehending written directions. When Alicia obtained a low score on a social studies test, it was hard to determine whether her low score was due to a lack of knowledge or her inability to follow the directions.

Another potential problem with group-administered standardized achievement tests is that the norms used to interpret scores are of little use when evaluating students with disabilities; these students are often excluded from the norming group because they have taken the test with accommodations. Also, all students may be affected by the fact that the content of the test might not match what is taught in a particular classroom (Deno, 1985, 2003; Marston, 1989). For example, one teacher stressed problem solving in his science class, whereas the standardized achievement test given in his district stressed the memorization of facts. Therefore, the teacher had to give his own tests to determine whether students were learning the material.

Finally, standardized achievement tests might be culturally biased and have led to the overrepresentation of minorities in special education classes (Banks & Banks, 2007; Skiba et al., 2006; deValenzuela et al., 2006). For example, Bill comes from a single-parent home in the city. When he read a story on a standardized achievement test about an affluent two-parent family in the suburbs, he had difficulty predicting the outcome.

Whereas in the past, group-administered standardized achievement tests were used to make administrative and policy decisions on a school district or even national level, it appears that today, high-stakes tests are being used more often for these purposes. Given the time and effort it takes to test an entire school, as well as the value of instructional time to children's learning, many schools have found it more prudent to use only their state's high-stakes test.

● **Individually Administered Tests** A special education teacher or the school psychologist usually gives **individually administered diagnostic tests** as part of a student's case study evaluation. Although these tests may screen student performance in several curricular areas, they tend to be more diagnostic in nature. For example, an individually administered diagnostic reading test may include test components in the areas of letter identification, word recognition, oral reading, comprehension, and phonetic skills; a diagnostic test in

fyi

In order to make adequate yearly progress (AYP), schools must have (1) at least 95 percent of enrolled students participate in the testing program; (2) all students and all subgroups, including students with disabilities, score at least proficient at the state's AYP targets for that year; and (3) all students and all subgroups meet AYP targets for graduation or attendance (Yell, Katsiyannas, & Shiner, 2006).

www.resources

For more information on the topic of state and national testing policies, access the website of the National Center on Educational Outcomes (NCEO) at http://education.umn .edu/nceo.

DIMENSIONS OF
diversity

Poverty often is mentioned as a key factor underlying the overrepresentation of ethnic minorities in special education. Skiba et al. (2005) studied the impact of poverty on representation in special education and found that its contribution was weaker than previously thought and inconsistent. While poverty in U.S. society needs to be addressed, discriminatory practices within the schools need to be addressed as well.

math might include math computation, fractions, geometry, word problems, measurement, and time. Because individually administered diagnostic tests provide information on a range of specific skills, they can be useful as an information source in making educational decisions. For example, Tamara scored two years below grade level on the comprehension subtest of an individually administered diagnostic test in reading. Yet in an oral reading sample taken from her fourth-grade reader, she read both fluently and accurately. On the basis of these two findings, her teacher placed her in a literature-based reading program that stressed skills in reading comprehension.

Although individually administered diagnostic tests may be more helpful than group-administered achievement tests, they are still subject to many of the same problems. Again, you should always verify findings from these tests using more informal measures based on the content you teach.

Psychological Tests

Psychological tests are used as part of the process of evaluating students with special needs, particularly to determine whether a student has cognitive or learning disabilities. Reports of the results of these tests are often written by school psychologists and consist of a summary of the findings and the implications for instruction. **Psychological tests** can include intelligence tests and tests related to learning disabilities (Overton, 2005; Salvia & Ysseldyke, 2007).

The overall purpose of psychological tests is to measure abilities that affect how efficiently students learn in an instructional situation. These abilities are inferred based on student responses to items that the test author believes represent that particular ability. For example, comprehension, an important learning ability, is often assessed on psychological tests (Salvia & Ysseldyke, 2007). To test their comprehension, students may be asked to read and answer questions about a series of directions or other tasks described in printed material. Student scores are then compared to a norm group of other same-age students, with an average score being 100. Other abilities commonly assessed by psychological tests include generalization (the ability to recognize similarities across objects, events, or vocabulary), general or background information, vocabulary, induction (the ability to figure out a rule or principle based on a series of situations), abstract reasoning, and memory (Salvia & Ysseldyke, 2007).

Psychological tests can be helpful if they clarify why students may not be learning in class and lead to effective changes in instruction. For example, the results of Tiffany's test showed that she had difficulty with visual memory. Her teacher, Ms. Fasbacher, felt that this was related to her poor performance in spelling. As a result, Ms. Fasbacher provided Tiffany with extra practice on her weekly spelling lists. Interpreting the results of psychological reports seems less daunting if you follow these five general guidelines:

1. Do not be intimidated by the sometimes generous quantity of technical terms and jargon. You have the right to expect that reports be translated into instructionally relevant language.

2. In the event of discrepancies between psychological reports and your experience, do not automatically discount your experience. The results of psychological tests are most valid when corroborated by classroom experience. Keep in mind that your impressions are the result of many more hours of classroom observation than are psychological evaluations, which are based on fewer samples of student behavior and on samples that represent behavior that takes place outside the classroom.

3. Be sure to check the technical adequacy of the psychological tests included in your report. You may be surprised to find that many of these tests are not acceptable. The recent emphasis in RtI of using students' responses to instruction to identify learning disabilities further reinforces the importance of not relying solely on standardized tests.

4. Be sure to check for possible cultural bias. Psychological tests may discriminate against students from culturally diverse or disadvantaged backgrounds. The various

fyi

Psychological tests may be better measures of expressive language skill, memory, fine motor abilities, and factual knowledge than they are measures of potential or reasoning ability (Marston et al., 2003). They are also time consuming to give and only indirectly related to daily classroom instruction.

DIMENSIONS OF

diversity

Psychological tests can be biased against students from diverse backgrounds. Use them only in conjunction with other formal and informal measures.

www.resources

The home page for the National Council on Measurement in Education (NCME), www.ncme.org, provides information on the organization and links to other relevant measurement-related websites.

Strategies for Fair Assessment of Diverse Students

Although today's teachers are much more knowledgeable about the presence of bias in assessing poor students and students from culturally diverse backgrounds (Grossman, 1995), bias and discrimination continue to exist. The following two lists identify areas that can be problematic when assessing diverse students and provide strategies for assessing and interpreting their performance more accurately, respectively.

Problem

1. Students may exhibit test anxiety due to lack of familiarity with the assessment process.

2. Students may lack motivation to perform well on tests because of differing cultural expectations.

3. Students may not respond to traditional motivators.

4. Students' test scores may be depressed because the assessor is unfamiliar or speaks a different language.

5. Students may have different communication styles; for example, they may not feel comfortable asking for help with directions or may respond using fewer words.

6. Students may be unwilling to take risks; for example, they may be reluctant to guess on a test even though it is to their benefit.

7. Students may be accustomed to working at a slower pace.

8. Students may lack exposure to test content.

9. Students may not be proficient in the language used for a test.

10. Students may speak with a dialect that differs from that of the assessor.

Recommendation

1. Give students practice tests. Teach test-taking skills.

2. Qualify test performance with class performance.

3. Individualize reinforcers; use individualistic, competitive, and cooperative goal structures.

4. Allow more time to establish rapport and gain trust.

5. Check for understanding of directions; avoid automatically penalizing students for not saying enough or not giving details.

6. Teach students strategies for when and how to make a best guess on a test.

7. Extend test-taking time to accommodate students' pace.

8. Eliminate unfamiliar content or don't give the test.

9. Assess students using both English and students' native language.

10. Do not count dialectical differences as errors; examine your attitudes about nonstandard dialects for potential bias.

Research Note

Abedi, Hofstetter, and Lord (2004) reviewed the research literature on the effectiveness of testing accommodations for English-language learners in the content areas of math, science, and social studies. The accommodations studied included assessing in the students' native language, modifying the level of English in questions, providing extra time, providing dictionaries and glossaries, and oral administration. In general, the researchers found evidence for the effectiveness of only two accommodations: (1) modifying the language (but not the content) of the test items by reducing low-frequency vocabulary and complex language structures and (2) providing students with definitions or simple paraphrases of potentially unfamiliar or difficult words on the test. Not surprisingly, the authors found that these accommodations helped all students, not just English-language learners. Research shows that curriculum-based assessment also works well with English-language learners, whether the assessment is in their native language or not (Deno, 2003).

ways in which psychological and other tests can be biased, along with suggestions for making them more fair, are presented in the Special Emphasis On . . . feature.

5. Keep in mind that the primary purpose of psychological tests is to establish possible explanations for particular learning, behavioral, or social and emotional problems. Such explanations should be springboards for helping students overcome these problems, not excuses for students' lack of achievement.

fyi

The NCEO offers these recommendations for developing alternate assessment systems: (a) define the purpose of the alternate assessment system, and identify who is qualified to participate in it; (b) identify the common core of learning, for example, what students need to know and be able to do; (c) develop participation guidelines; (d) determine how results will be organized and summarized; and (e) integrate these results with those from the general assessment.

Reading Homework Exercise

Go to the Homework and Exercises section in Chapter 4 of MyEducationLab for an overview of the commonly used intelligence tests used to determine academic potential.

Alternate Assessments

As you have learned, IDEA and NCLB require states to include students with disabilities in statewide and districtwide educational assessments. Although most students with disabilities are able to participate when given appropriate accommodations, a small percentage of students are entitled to alternate assessments. The most common group of students taking **alternate assessments** are those who typically work on a more individualized curriculum and do not have to meet the same requirements as those students graduating with a standard diploma. In other words, they are required to meet the same broad standards as your other students, but they meet them in different, more basic ways.

For example, one of the standards in Ms. Barber's state is that students develop an appreciation for literature. One of the ways that Darrell, a student with a significant intellectual disability, meets that standard is by watching a video of *Oliver Twist* and answering questions using his communication board. School districts may provide this option to up to 1 percent of their students.

Although districts in some states such as Kentucky and Vermont began using them earlier, most school districts began using alternate assessments in 2002, the year required for implementation by IDEA. This means that guidelines for conducting alternate assessments are still evolving. Alternate assessment information can be collected in a number of ways including (1) a portfolio or collection of student work gathered to demonstrate student performance on specific skills and knowledge; (2) an IEP-linked body of evidence or collection of work, similar to a portfolio, demonstrating student performance on standards-based IEP goals and objectives; (3) a performance assessment or direct measures of a student's skill, usually in a one-on-one assessment; (4) a checklist of skills reviewed by persons familiar with the student; and (5) a traditional test requiring student responses, typically with a correct and incorrect forced-choice answer format (Browder, Wakeman, & Flowers, 2006; Gong & Marion, 2006; Quenemoen, Rigney, & Thurlow, 2002).

Students with more severe disabilities participate in alternate assessments that stress authentic skills and experiences in real-life environments. What skills do you think are being assessed here?

The system of alternate assessment used by the state of Kentucky is a good example of a portfolio system (Kleinert & Kearns, 2001). In Kentucky, all students, regardless of disability, are required to meet standards in a range of areas, including using patterns to understand past and present events and to predict future events; using technology effectively; demonstrating knowledge, skills, and values that have lifetime implications for involvement in physical activity; and completing a postsecondary opportunities search (Kearns, Kleinert, Clayton, Burdge, & Williams, 1998). Although the portfolios reflect the same set of outcomes for all students, students with significant intellectual disabilities meet them in different ways. For example, Damon met the standard of completing a search for postsecondary opportunities by compiling a list of his work preferences and specific jobs aligned with his preferences. Sibilie demonstrated her effective use of technology by using an augmentative communication device across a range of school and community settings. Carolyn, a student with multiple disabilities, demonstrated achievement in skills and values related to physical activity by participating in a volleyball game in physical education class. Linus demonstrated his ability to use patterns to understand events by recognizing that on days when his paraprofessional wasn't in school he had less time to get ready for recess. A sample electronic portfolio used for an alternate assessment is shown in the Technology Notes on pages 433–434.

Here are eight questions to consider about alternate assessments when you have a student in your classroom with severe disabilities:

1. *What are the district's eligibility requirements for alternate assessments?* Keep in mind that only a small number of students have disabilities so severe that they are eligible. The decision to give an alternate assessment should not be based on whether the student is expected to do poorly on the general education assessment.

2. *Is the focus of the assessment on authentic skills and on assessing experiences in community or real-life environments?* For a younger child the community might mean the school, playground, or home; for a high school senior the community might mean the store, bank, or other commercial or public sites.

3. *Is the assessment aligned with state standards?* The skills assessed should have a meaningful relationship to content areas covered by the standards, such as reading and math. For example, one of Clifford's IEP goals in language is to communicate by pointing to pictures on a communication board. Chatrice is learning to give correct coins to the bus driver as a way to meet the math standards. As the general education teacher who is responsible for students' meeting the regular state standards, you may be in the best position to answer this question of standards alignment.

4. *Is the assessment tied to ongoing classroom instruction and data collection?* If alternate assessments are truly to help students with significant intellectual disabilities meet state standards, then they must help a teacher guide instruction on a daily basis, as opposed to relying on a checklist of skills or a one-time observation of performance. For instance, Everett's teacher took weekly video clips of Everett eating lunch and had another teacher rate his competence in feeding himself. These weekly clips were used by Everett's teacher to gradually reduce the level of teacher assistance given to him while working toward his goal of completely feeding himself.

5. *Is the assessment closely linked to the IEP so that expectations between home and school are consistent?* Tying alternate assessments to the IEP ensures appropriate parent and student involvement in the assessment/teaching process. Studies show that parent and student involvement in the alternate assessment process is positively related to student outcomes on alternate assessments (Kampfer, Horvath, Kleinert, & Kearns, 2001).

6. *Are the measured skills integrated across many areas?* Personal and social skills, for example, should be assessed right along with academic and literacy skills, rather

fyi

The results of alternate assessments are included when determining whether a district makes adequate yearly progress (AYP) as part of the No Child Left Behind Act (NCLB).

Building Teaching Skills Simulation Exercise

Go to the Building Teaching Skills section in Chapter 4 of MyEducationLab for an activity about accountability.

www.resources

Learn about the National Assessment of Educational Progress (NAEP), the only ongoing national test of academic progress, at www.nagb.org.

What Information Sources Are Used in Programming for Students with Special Needs?   127

Some states have been using
out-of-level tests for students
whose achievement lags behind
that of their peers but do not
have significant cognitive
disabilities (NCEO, 2007). For
example, a sixth-grade student
reading at the second-grade
level would be given the
second-grade high-stakes
test. Out-of-level testing is
not allowed in federal NCLB
regulations. The government
recommends that states use
the alternate assessment with
the modified standards option
discussed in this section.

**Info Sheet Homework
Exercise**

Go to the Homework and
Exercises section in Chapter 4 of
MyEducationLab to find information
about a variety of problems that
students may exhibit in your
classroom.

Curriculum-based measurement
(CBM) is a particular kind of
curriculum-based assessment.
CBM is characterized by a
research base establishing its
technical adequacy, as well
as standardized measurement
tasks and scoring procedures
that are brief and fluency
based (Deno, 2003). The DIBELS
measures described in the
Professional Edge on page 132
are examples of CBM.

than separately. For example, Ms. Halpern assesses Thomas's literacy *and* social skills when he is ordering food at a fast-food restaurant.

7. *Are there clear scoring guidelines, and have staff been adequately trained to consistently apply these guidelines when evaluating student performance?* Recent studies (for example, see Johnson & Arnold, 2004) show that this issue can be a problem when evaluating student portfolios. In some cases, scoring problems have actually prevented states from releasing results to students and parents. Check the scoring guidelines for your students performing alternate assessments. When possible, get involved in the assessment training. Although you will usually not be responsible for scoring your students' alternate assessments, becoming familiar with them will ensure that the help you provide will be focused and relevant to your students' IEP goals.

8. *Are scores on the assessment used to continually monitor the extent to which it leads to better outcomes for students?* Alternate assessments should inform the need for services, which in turn should lead to more productive, independent lives for students with severe disabilities in school and the community. For example, Eduardo's teacher, Ms. Bland, noticed that Eduardo was able to ask for help more effectively in class than in the community. She decided to observe the two settings and look for differences. She noticed that Eduardo was receiving too much help from his paraprofessional in class and that this was discouraging Eduardo's independence when he was out of class. Ms. Bland's observation led to more careful monitoring of Eduardo's paraprofessional to ensure that the level of support she was providing was eventually reduced.

Up to 2 percent of students with disabilities can take alternate assessments based on modified academic achievement standards (U.S. Department of Education, 2007). This alternate assessment option is intended for students whose disabilities have prevented them from achieving grade-level proficiency and who are not likely to reach grade-level achievement within the same timeframe as their classmates without disabilities. Before this provision was added, these students either had to take the grade-level assessment, which often was too difficult, or an alternate assessment intended for students with severe intellectual disabilities, which was too easy.

When the modified academic achievement standards option is used, curricular goals are aligned with grade-level content standards, but the level of achievement expected may be simplified. For example, Josh needs to demonstrate meeting the seventh-grade language arts standard of analyzing how literary elements affect the meaning of text, such as the influence of setting on the conflict and its resolution. Josh does so by reading an easier version of *Swiss Family Robinson* and answering comprehension questions that have lower cognitive demand. It is the responsibility of the IEP team to determine eligibility for this alternate assessment option.

Curriculum-Based Assessments

Because of the limited utility of standardized achievement tests and psychological reports for making day-to-day instructional decisions, you need other tools in order to be a partner in the evaluation process. **Curriculum-based assessment (CBA)** is an effective option that in many instances can be an alternative to standardized tests. CBA has been defined as a method of measuring students' level of achievement in terms of what they are taught in the classroom (for example, Deno, 2003; Hosp & Hosp, 2003; Tucker, 1985). In CBA, student performance also is measured repeatedly over time, and the results are used to guide instruction (Hosp & Hosp, 2003; Tucker, 1985). CBA has a number of attractive features. When using CBA, you select the skills that are assessed based on what you teach in class, thus ensuring a match between what is taught and what is tested. This match makes CBA measures accurate indicators of student access to the general education curriculum and ideal for use in prereferral or response to intervention RtI systems.

In the chapter-opening vignette, before referring Rob to special education, Ms. Lyons gave him some curriculum-based assessments in math to determine the specific kinds of problems he was having. She then implemented a peer-tutoring program and used these same tests to measure its effectiveness. Mr. Blount used an informal reading assessment based on his U.S. history textbook to see how well his students were able to read the text.

Research shows that when teachers use CBA to evaluate student progress and adjust their instruction accordingly, student achievement increases significantly (Deno, 2003; Fuchs, Fuchs, Hamlett, & Stecker, 1991; Shinn, Collins, & Gallagher, 1998).

*W*hat Kinds of Curriculum-Based Assessments Can You Create for Your Students?

Analyze
and Reflect

Why is it harder to design probes for higher-level thinking skills such as math problem solving? What can teachers do to make sure that probes of higher-level skills provide useful, accurate information?

Two major kinds of CBAs are commonly used: probes of basic academic skills (for example, reading, math, and writing) and probes of content-area knowledge and learning strategies (for example, vocabulary knowledge, prerequisite skills, textbook reading, and note taking). Although probes of basic academic skills relate more directly to elementary school teachers and probes of content-area knowledge and learning strategies to middle and high school teachers, each of these measures is relevant for both groups. For example, high school students need to perform basic skills fluently if they are to have ready access to curriculum content; elementary school students need early training in learning strategies to make the difficult transition to middle and high school instruction easier.

Building Teaching Skills Simulation Exercise

Go to the Building Teaching Skills section in Chapter 4 of MyEducationLab for an activity about accessing the general education curriculum.

Probes of Basic Academic Skills

Probes are quick and easy measures of student performance in the basic skill areas of reading, math, and written expression. They consist of timed samples of academic behaviors

These teachers are using information from assessment probes to make decisions about their students with special needs. How can you use assessment probes to make decisions in your area of teaching?

and are designed to assess skill accuracy and fluency. Probes can sample a range of skills in a particular area, as in a mixed probe of fifth-grade math computation problems in addition, subtraction, multiplication, and division; or they can sample one skill area, such as letter identification or writing lowercase manuscript letters.

Typically, students work on probe sheets for one minute. The teacher then records the rate of correct and incorrect responses as well as any error patterns. Student performance rates have been shown to be useful for making many of the important evaluation decisions described earlier in the chapter: screening, diagnosis, program placement, curriculum placement, instructional evaluation, and program evaluation (Deno, 2003; Shinn et al., 1998; Tindal & Marston, 1990). The Professional Edge describes the importance of considering both student accuracy and student fluency when assessing basic academic skills.

Probes are classified according to how students take in task information (for example, seeing or hearing) and how they respond (for example, writing or speaking). They include four major types: see-say, see-write, hear-write, and think-write. For example, when reading orally from a textbook, students *see* the text and *say* the words. Hence, oral reading is referred to as a see-say probe. Similarly, in a spelling probe, students *hear* the teacher dictate words and *write* the words as they are dictated. This is a hear-write probe.

As you develop CBA, keep in mind the following three suggestions:

1. Identify academic skills that are essential in your particular room or grade. In the elementary grades, include skills in handwriting, spelling, written expression, reading (for example, letter identification, letter sounds, oral reading accuracy, and comprehension), and math (for example, number identification, computation, problem solving, time, and money).

2. Select skills representing a *sample* of skills that are taught, not necessarily every skill. Performance on these skills then acts as a checkpoint for identifying students in trouble or measuring student progress. For example, in assessing reading performance, having students read a passage aloud from their reading or literature book and then answer comprehension questions may not represent all the reading skills you have taught (such as words in isolation), but it will include a representative sample of many of these skills.

3. Even though CBA is considered informal assessment, its utility in helping to make instructional decisions depends on the teacher's keeping the difficulty level of the assessment items, as well as the administration and scoring procedures, consistent over time (Deno, 2003). For example, Ms. Solomon was monitoring the progress of three of her students with special needs in oral reading fluency. Every two weeks, she conducted one-minute timings using passages from their third-grade reading book. To make sure the information she was getting was accurate, she conducted her timings the same way each time and made sure that the passages selected for the timings were roughly equivalent in difficulty.

4. Remember, curriculum-based assessment has been used successfully by teachers for many years. Therefore, assessments as well as norms or benchmarks may already exist for many of the skills you are teaching. See the WWW Resources marginal notation on page 129 for potential sources.

● **Probes of Reading Skills**   The critical reading skills in the elementary years include phonemic awareness, letter sounds, word recognition, vocabulary, and comprehension. Phonemic awareness can be measured using a hear-say probe. See the Professional Edge on page 132 for specific examples of how to assess phonemic awareness. Student ability to identify letter names and sounds can be assessed using a see-say probe. Word recognition and comprehension can be assessed using a see-say oral passage reading probe, such as the one in Figure 4.1.

*R*esearch Note

Tindal et al. (2003) developed a series of curriculum-based measures in reading and math for use in alternate assessment programs. Their research showed that effective measures were brief and easy to give and provided information of potential use to teachers.

*R*esearch Note

Good (2002) studied the relationship between the oral reading performance of third-grade students and their performance on the Oregon Statewide Assessment Test (OSAT), Oregon's high-stakes test. He found that of 91 students who met benchmark levels of 110 words correct per minute in oral reading fluency in May of grade 3, 90 students, or 90 percent, met standards on the OSAT. Of the 23 students scoring below the benchmark of 70 words per minute, only four students, or 17 percent, met state standards.

Assessing Student Rates on Basic Academic Skills

When basic skills or other academic content is assessed informally in the classroom, *student accuracy* is usually stressed. For example, we say that Jill formed 85 percent of her cursive letters correctly, John was 90 percent accurate on his addition facts, or Al identified key pieces of lab equipment with 100 percent accuracy. Although accuracy is important, because it tells us whether a student has acquired a skill or section of content, accuracy is not the only useful index of pupil performance. *Student fluency*, or how quickly a student is able to perform a skill or recall academic material, is also relevant. Before you consider the reasons for assessing student fluency provided here, consider this: If your car needed service and you had your choice between two mechanics, both of whom did accurate work and charged $35 an hour but one of whom worked twice as fast as the other, which mechanic would you choose?

The Rate Rationale

1. Students who are proficient in a skill are more likely to remember the skill, even if they do not need to use it very often. If they forget the skill, they need less time to relearn it.

2. Students who are proficient in a basic skill are better able to master more advanced skills. For example, students who can perform addition problems fluently often acquire advanced multiplication skills more easily.

3. Performance of basic skills at an automatic level frees students to perform higher level skills more readily. For example, students who can read fluently with understanding are more likely to be successful in high school classes that require reading lengthy textbook assignments in little time. Students who know their math facts without counting on their fingers can solve word problems more efficiently.

4. Students with special needs are often so labeled because they work more slowly than their peers. Fluency scores allow teachers to compare these students directly with their classmates on this important dimension of speed; they also provide a useful index of student progress, including, for some students, readiness for inclusion in general education classes.

Using the Research

If you are interested in learning how your students' oral reading rates compare to national norms, Hasbrouck and Tindal (2006) have compiled national norms based on student oral reading fluency scores from multiple school districts across the country. These norms are shown in the accompanying table. Notice that separate norms are presented for fall, winter, and spring to account for student growth during the year. So if Simone is reading 80 words correct per minute in February of second grade, she is reading above the 50th percentile for winter of grade 2.

Oral Reading Fluency Norms, Grades 1–8

Grade	Percentile	Fall WCPM	Winter WCPM	Spring WCPM
1	75		47	82
	50		23	53
	25		12	28
2	75	79	100	117
	50	51	72	89
	25	25	42	61
3	75	99	120	137
	50	71	92	107
	25	44	62	78
4	75	119	139	152
	50	94	112	123
	25	68	87	98
5	75	139	156	168
	50	110	127	139
	25	85	99	109
6	75	153	167	177
	50	127	140	150
	25	98	111	122
7	75	156	165	177
	50	128	136	150
	25	102	109	123
8	75	161	173	177
	50	133	146	151
	25	106	115	124

WCPM: Words correct per minute
SD: Standard deviation
Count: Number of student scores
Source: From "Oral reading fluency norms: A valuable assessment tool for reading teachers," by Jan Hasbrouck and Gerald Tindal, *The Reading Teacher, 59*(7), 636–644. Copyright 2006 by the International Reading Association. Reprinted with permission of the International Reading Association (www.reading.org) via Copyright Clearance Center.

Using DIBELS Probes to Identify Children at Risk for Reading Problems

The problem with identifying children who are experiencing reading difficulties is that by the time they are identified, they are already so far behind that catching up is often a losing proposition. That is why the current emphasis in reading instruction is on preventing reading problems before they become insurmountable. To do this, children who are at risk of having reading problems need to be identified early.

Fortunately, more than three decades of research show that two early language skills are highly predictive of reading success in school: letter-naming fluency and phonemic segmentation (Good, Gruba, & Kaminski, 2002). Good and his colleagues at the University of Oregon have developed a series of measures that can be used to measure these and other early literacy skills called the Dynamic Indicators of Basic Early Literacy Skills, or DIBELS (frequently referred to as "dibbles") (Kaminski & Good, 1996). A hallmark of the DIBELS assessments is efficiency, with each measure taking less than five minutes to give. DIBELS measures are also well

researched; benchmarks helpful in identifying children at risk have been identified for each of the measures. The DIBELS measures of phonemic segmentation and rapid letter naming have been used successfully to identify children at risk from the middle of kindergarten to the middle of grade 1.

The ability to identify or retrieve from memory letters of the alphabet already learned is a good early indicator of reading fluency. Ultimately, children who can read accurately and fluently are much more likely to understand what they are reading (Fuchs & Fuchs, 2001). The DIBELS Letter Naming Fluency measure gives students a one-minute see-say letter-naming probe using guidelines discussed in this chapter. Shown below are benchmarks that can be used to identify children who are at risk in kindergarten. As not all kindergarteners come to school knowing their letters, some schools delay giving this measure until the middle or even the end of kindergarten. Note that DIBELS assessments measure fluency, so benchmarks reflect the number of letters identified correctly per minute.

Benchmarks for DIBELS Letter Naming Fluency Assessment

	Beginning of Kindergarten	Middle of Kindergarten	End of Kindergarten	Beginning of Grade 1
At Risk	Less than 2	Less than 15	Less than 29	Less than 25
Some Risk	2–7	15–26	29–39	25–36
Low Risk	8 or more	27 or more	40 or more	37 or more

Phonemic segmentation involves the understanding that speech is composed of individual sounds (Bursuck & Damer, 2006; Chard & Dickson, 1999). Phonemic segmentation is the ability to say the individual sounds in words that are presented orally. In giving the DIBELS Phoneme Segmentation Fluency measure, the teacher presents a series of words orally and the student says the sounds in each

word. For example, the teacher says *sad,* and the student says *ssss . . . aaaa . . . dddd.* The teacher continues to present words for one minute, and then the total number of phonemes or sounds identified correctly in a minute is scored. Shown below are benchmarks for the DIBELS Phoneme Segmentation Fluency measure from the middle of kindergarten through the middle of grade 1.

Benchmarks for DIBELS Phoneme Segmentation Fluency Assessment

	Middle of Kindergarten		End of Kindergarten–Middle of Grade 1
At Risk	Less than 7	*Deficit*	Less than 10
Some Risk	7–17	*Emerging*	10–34
Low Risk	18 or more	*Established*	35 or more

All of the DIBELS measures, including videos of persons administering them, are available free of charge at the DIBELS website: http://dibels.uoregon.edu. For more information on how to teach phonemic awareness, including phonemic segmentation, see Bursuck and Damer (2006) and Carnine, Silbert, Kameenui, and Tarver (2004).

Source: Summary of Decision Rules for Intensive, Strategic, and Benchmark Instruction Recommendations in Kindergarten through Third Grade (Technical Report No. 11), by R. H. Good, D. Simmons, E. A. Kame'enui, and J. Wallin, 2002, Eugene: University of Oregon, Department of School Psychology.

FIGURE *4.1* See-Say Probe: Oral Passage Reading

Time	1 minute
Materials	*Student*—Stimulus passage
	Examiner—Duplicate copy of stimulus passage, pencil, timer
Directions to Student	"When I say 'Please begin,' read this story out loud to me. Start here [examiner points] and read as quickly and carefully as you can. Try to say each word. Ready? Please begin."
Scoring	As the student reads, place a mark (/) on your copy over any errors (mispronunciations, words skipped, and words given). (If student hesitates for three seconds, give him the word and mark it as an error.) If student inserts words, self-corrects, sounds out, or repeats, do not count as errors. When the student has read for one minute, place a bracket (]) on your copy to indicate how far the student read in one minute. (It is usually good practice to let students finish the paragraph or page they are reading rather than stopping them immediately when one minute is over.) Count the total number of words read during the one minute sample. Tally the total number of errors (words mispronounced, words skipped, and words given) made during the sample. Subtract the total number of errors from the total words covered to get number correct (total words – errors = correct words per minute).

If students complete the passage before the minute is up, compute student rate using this formula:

$$\frac{\text{\# Correct words}}{\text{Seconds}} \times \frac{60}{1} = \text{Correct words per minute}$$

Note	Probe is administered individually. If you use the optional comprehension questions, be sure to have students finish the passage first.

Billy decided to go down by the river and	(9)
demonstrate his fishing ability. He always could deceive	(17)
the fish with his special secret lure. He had his best	(28)
luck in his own place, a wooded shady spot downstream	(38)
that no one knew about. Today he was going to try	(49)
to catch a catfish all the boys called Old Gray. Old Gray	(61)
was a legend in this town, because even though many boys	(72)
had hooked him, he always managed to get away.	(81)
This time Billy knew that if he sat long enough, he could	(93)
catch his dream fish!	(97)

1. Who is the main character in this story?
2. Where does the story take place?
3. What problem is Billy trying to solve?
4. How is Billy going to try to solve the problem?
5. What do you think is going to happen?

Source: From *Curriculum-Based Assessment and Instructional Design,* by E. Lessen, M. Sommers, and W. D. Bursuck, 1987, DeKalb, IL: DeKalb County Special Education Association. Used with permission.

Although the easiest method for assessing comprehension is to use the questions that accompany most classroom reading series, if you are having your students read trade books, you may need to design your own questions, which can be a difficult task. Carnine, Silbert, Kameenui, and Tarver (2004) have suggested one practical model for designing comprehension questions, based on story grammar. *Story grammar* is simply the description of the typical elements found frequently in stories. These include theme, setting, character, initiating events, conflict, attempts at resolution, resolution, and reactions. These elements can be used to create comprehension questions that may be more appropriate than traditional main idea and detail questions, because story grammar describes the organization of most stories that elementary school students are likely to read. The Case in Practice shows how a teacher uses story grammar with one of her second-grade students.

At times, you might not wish to ask questions about a story. Specific questions can give students clues to the answers, and they especially help students identify the information you think is important to remember or the way you organize this information. One

Case in Practice

Using Story Grammars

Ms. Padilla's second-grade students have just read the story *The Funny Farola*, by Ann Miranda and Maria Guerrero. The story is about a girl and her family participating in an ethnic festival in their city. The girl, Dora, makes a *farola*, which is a type of lantern people carry while marching in a parade. Dora's family laughs at her farola, because it is in the shape of a frog. However, her unusual farola saves the day when it helps Dora and her parents find Dora's lost brother and sister.

Ms. Padilla is assessing Chantille's comprehension of the story using the story grammar retelling format.

Ms. Padilla: Chantille, you have just read *The Funny Farola*. Would you tell me in your own words what the story is about?

Chantille: The story is about a girl named Dora who made this funny frog that she carried in a parade. You see, her brother and sister got lost at the parade 'cause they were having such a good time, but they got found again 'cause they could see Dora's frog.

Ms. Padilla: Chantille, where does this story take place?

Chantille: It took place in a city and the people were having a big festival. That's why they were having the parade.

Ms. Padilla: Chantille, what was the problem with Dora's frog?

Chantille: Well, it was called a *farola*, which is a kind of lantern. Everyone was making them for the parade. Dora's family laughed at her farola 'cause they had never seen a frog farola before.

Ms. Padilla: You said that Dora's sister and brother got lost. What did they do to solve that problem?

Chantille: Well, they saw Dora's frog, so they knew where to find them.

Ms. Padilla: How did you feel at the end of the story?

Chantille: I felt happy.

Ms. Padilla: Why did you feel happy?

Chantille: Well, 'cause Dora's brother and sister found their mom and dad.

Ms. Padilla: Chantille, what lesson do you think this story teaches us?

Chantille: Not to get lost from your mom and dad.

A score sheet that Ms. Padilla completed for Chantille is shown in the accompanying figure. A plus (+) means that Chantille responded accurately to that element without any prompting or questioning; a check mark (✓) means that Chantille mentioned the element after she was questioned or prompted; a minus (–) means that she failed to refer to the element even after questioning or prompts.

Look at Chantille's scores. As you can see, she had a good idea of who the main characters were and received a + for this component (Characters). Chantille named two problems in the story: Dora making a farola that her family laughed at and Dora's brother and sister getting lost. Chantille identified the problem of the lost kids without being prompted, and the problem of the funny farola with prompts; thus, a + and a ✓ were scored for Goal/Problem.

way to solve this problem is to have students retell stories after they read them. Students themselves then must organize the information they think is important, and you can evaluate the completeness of their recall. Such a situation has two requirements for effective evaluation to occur: a standard set of criteria to evaluate the completeness of the retelling and the opportunity to evaluate each student's retelling individually. The Professional Edge on page 132 offers additional means of assessing students' reading skills. The Case in Practice on pages 144–145 shows how curriculum-based probes can be used in a multitiered, RtI model to monitor students' responses to instruction and make eligibility decisions for special education.

- **Probes of Written Expression**   Written expression can be assessed using a think-write probe. In this probe, the teacher reads the students a story starter. The students then have one minute to plan a story and three minutes to write it. This probe is scored according to the number of intelligible words the student is able to write per minute (total words

Research Note

Allinder, Bolling, Oats, and Gagnon (2000) found that students of teachers who regularly asked themselves the following questions when giving curriculum-based measures made more academic progress in math computation: On what skills has the student done well during the last two weeks? What skills should be targeted for the next two weeks? How will I attempt to improve student performance on the targeted skills?

Story Grammar Retelling Checklist

Student Name	Story Elements Evaluated													
	Theme		Setting		Characters		Goal/Problem		Attempts		Resolution		Reactions	
Chantille	–		✓		+		+	✓	–		+	–	+	

+   Responded correctly without prompting
✓   Responded correctly after prompting
–   Did not identify relevant story component

It was unclear from Chantille's response exactly how the characters tried to solve their problem, so she received a – for Attempts. Chantille did say the problem was solved when Dora's brother and sister saw the frog; she received a + for this element of Resolution. However, she did not say how this resolved the problem of her family laughing at the farola, so she received a –. Chantille's reaction to the story was appropriate, so a + was scored. For Setting, Chantille received a ✓; she identified the setting after Ms. Padilla prompted her. Finally, Chantille received a – for Theme. This response was lacking, even after prompting.

Notice that Ms. Padilla's prompts included explicit references to the various story grammar components.

For example, she asked, "You said that Dora's sister and brother got lost. What did they do to solve that problem?" as opposed to asking a more general question, such as "What happened to Dora's sister and brother?" This use of specific language makes the story grammar components more clear, a necessary structure for younger, more naïve learners.

REFLECTIONS

How could story retellings be incorporated into a classroom literature-based program? How do you think these results will be helpful to Ms. Padilla?

Simulation Homework Exercise

Go to the Homework and Exercises section in Chapter 4 of MyEducationLab to learn how to create and use curriculum-based assessments.

fyi

King-Sears, Burgess, and Lawson (1999) suggest using the following steps, abbreviated as the mnemonic APPLY, when using CBA in your classroom: Analyze the curriculum, prepare items to meet curriculum objectives, probe frequently, load data using a graph format, and yield to results for making revisions and decisions.

written, or TWW). Intelligible words are those that make sense in the story. This way of scoring is useful for screening students for serious writing difficulty (Shinn & Hubbard, 1992). Norms for written expression probes are available at this website: www.aimsweb.com/measures/written/norms.php. If you are interested in other diagnostic information, such as grammar usage, spelling, handwriting, punctuation, vocabulary, or ideas, you can score this probe differently or give another probe designed to measure these areas specifically (see Choate, Enright, Miller, Poteet, & Rakes, 1995; Ellis & Colvert, 1996; Howell & Morehead, 1993; and Mercer & Mercer, 2005, for sample informal assessments in these areas).

● **Probes of Math Skills**   Teachers in the primary grades need to measure student identification of numbers, coins, and geometric figures. This assessment can be done as a see-say probe using numbers and symbols. Computation and problem-solving skills can be assessed using see-write probes (for example, see Howell & Morehead, 1993, as well as the WWW Resources on page 141).

Content-Area Assessments

Although content-area teachers can use CBA probes to test student knowledge of subject matter (see Figure 4.2), they may need to take a somewhat different approach to student assessment. Content-area classrooms are characterized by increased curricular demands with fewer opportunities for individualization; students are expected to learn more material and to take responsibility for learning much of it on their own. While IDEA and NCLB clearly state that the curricular expectations for most students with disabilities are the same as for their classmates without disabilities, students who enter a class significantly behind their classmates either in background knowledge or independent learning skills are likely to struggle. Thus, it is important to identify these students early so that they can be better prepared when they enter a content-area class. For example, at the beginning of this chapter, Mr. Blount assessed his history students' ability to read the class textbook independently because students in his class were expected to read much of the material on their own.

● **Probes of Prerequisite Skills**   The decision to place a particular student in a given middle school or high school class depends on identifying which skills or content is prerequisite. For example, the English department at a high school developed a test of prerequisite skills for ninth-grade English. Clarise, a student with a learning disability, was

FIGURE 4.2   **Using Curriculum-Based Assessment (CBA) Probes in Content Areas**

Content Area	CBA Probe Examples
Geography	Identify each state's location on a map by writing the correct state abbreviation.
	Match the terrain of an area to corresponding industries and products.
	Compare and contrast regions so that two similarities and two differences are provided.
Science	Given science terms to define, write the correct definitions.
	Identify steps in the scientific process, and describe how to apply each step to a given hypothesis.
	Describe the human body systems so that each system's function and relationship to other systems is stated.

Source: From "Applying Curriculum-Based Assessment in Inclusive Settings," by M. King-Sears, M. Burgess, and T. Lawson, *Teaching Exceptional Children, 32*(1), 1999, pp. 30–38. Copyright 1999 by The Council for Exceptional Children. Reprinted with permission.

given this test at the end of eighth grade to find out whether this class was appropriate for her. For skills-oriented classes such as math and English, prerequisite skills are those covered in elementary school or previously taught courses, such as computation skills for algebra and sentence writing for English. For classes that stress content rather than basic skills (for example, science), having the necessary background information to understand the new material is also vital.

Unfortunately, the process of determining whether students have necessary prerequisite skills can be problematic. A key problem involves identifying these skills. Teachers' choices of prerequisite skills often include skills that a student can bypass while still retaining access to course content, such as reading in a history class (which can be bypassed by using an oral text) or written expression in a science class (which can be bypassed by using oral tests and reports). When testing for prerequisite skills, you must be careful not to inadvertently exclude students with special needs, many of whom are capable of passing content classes despite their problems in certain basic skills areas.

Such problems suggest the need for a fair way of making placement decisions for students with special needs at the high school level. A potentially useful method is for teachers to develop probes to evaluate student performance on critical prerequisite skills. The probe-development process, which is similar to the process of developing curriculum-based assessment described previously in this chapter, consists of the following six steps:

1. Identify critical content learning or skills for your class.
2. Identify entry-level content or skills needed. Be certain these are not skills for which a bypass strategy is possible.
3. Develop a probe to measure the identified skills.
4. Administer the probe to current classes to make sure that students passing the class are able to pass the probe.
5. Set a minimum score necessary for student course entry based on the results of the preceding step. You may want to use an acceptable range rather than a single score, particularly during the initial stages of this process.
6. As with all educational decisions, no one score should be the sole basis for a decision. Other factors, such as student motivation and level of supportive assistance, need to be considered.

● **Measures of Independent Learning Skills** When students enter high school, they find an environment often not as supportive as the smaller elementary and junior high or middle school environments they left. The student body is often larger and more diverse. Daily routines change and curriculum is more difficult (Sabornie & deBettencourt, 2004). High schools also demand a much higher level of student independence through the application of a range of independent learning skills. These skills, often referred to as *learning strategies,* include note taking, textbook reading, test taking, written expression, and time management. A student's ability to perform these various skills independently can make the difference between passing or failing a class. For example, at the beginning of the chapter, Mr. Blount decided to assess textbook-reading skills because these were important for success in his class. A sample instrument to measure textbook-reading skills, which was originally developed by Voix (1968) and later adapted by Lessen, Sommers, and Bursuck (1987), is shown in Figure 4.3. Notice that the reading tasks for this measure are taken directly from the students' history and science textbooks. Doing this ensures that the results will be relevant for the particular classroom situation. Note also that this textbook-reading assessment can be given to the entire classroom at once, enabling the assessment of many students who have trouble reading their textbooks, not just students with special needs.

As with the basic and prerequisite skills mentioned previously, probes can be developed to assess independent learning. A key consideration is that the tasks used for assessment should parallel the tasks students are faced with in your classroom: If you are evaluating textbook reading, the reading task should come from the textbook you are using in class; if

The maze (Shin, Deno, & Espin, 2000) is a curriculum-based measure for assessing reading comprehension that can be given either in groups or using a computer. To give the maze, select a passage at the student's grade or instructional level; then delete every seventh word. In place of each deleted word, insert three choices. One of the choices is the correct choice, and the other two are distracters. Students read the passage silently and circle the answers they think are correct. Unlike most CBMs, the maze is not timed. The number or percentage of correct responses is scored. Research has shown that the maze is an effective, time-saving way to measure regularly student growth in reading comprehension (Shin et al., 2000).

FIGURE *4.3* Evaluating Content-Area Textbook-Reading Skills

Suggestions for specific types of questions are included here. The information in parentheses explains or offers additional information about a particular item.

Using Parts of the Book

1. On what page would you find the chapter called _____?
   (Tests ability to use table of contents.)

2. Of what value to you are the questions listed at the end of each chapter?
   (Tests understanding of a specific study aid.)

3. How are the chapters arranged or grouped? (Tests knowledge of text organization.)

4. What part of the book would you use to find the page reference for the topic _____? (Tests knowledge of index.)

5. On what page would you find the answer to each of the following questions?
   (Tests ability to use index.)

Using Source Materials

1. What library aid tells you the library number of a book so that you are able to find the book on the shelves? (Tests knowledge of functions of cataloging systems.)

2. What is a biography? (Tests knowledge of a type of reference book.)

3. Explain the difference between science fiction and factual science materials.
   (Tests knowledge of important types of science materials.)

Comprehension

These questions would be based on a three- or four-page selection from the textbook.

Vocabulary

1. Turn to page _____. How does the author define the word _____? (Tests ability to use context clues and the aids the author uses to convey the meaning of a word.)

2. Define _____.

3. What is a _____?

4. *Vocabulary in context:* From the paragraph on page 584 beginning "In Poland, the Soviet Union . . . ," write an appropriate and brief definition of each of the following words: _____, _____, and _____.

Noting Main Ideas

These questions would ask for main points of information, such as the main ideas of longer, important paragraphs of a chapter or the summary of an experiment. (*Examples:* What are atoms composed of? What reason was given for the conservation of human resources? What is the result of the photosynthetic process?)

Noting Details

These questions should ask for specific bits of information, such as an aspect of a process, the application of a law, the principal steps in an experiment, a life cycle, or incidents in the life of a scientist. (*Examples:* Describe the photosynthetic process. What are the different stages in the cycle of precipitation and evaporation? List the major incidents in the life of Marie Curie.)

Drawing Conclusions

Ask questions about the significance or value of a finding, the implication of a description of some species or natural phenomenon, causes and effect, or a comparison of two or more types of organisms. The questions should call for answers that are not stated in the text. (*Examples:* Illustrate the term *balance of life.* What conclusion can you draw from the importance of the photosynthetic process? What is the principal difference between mitosis and meiosis?)

Applying Theoretical Information

These questions would ask for examples of practical uses of scientific law and principles. (*Examples:* Explain the relationship of photosynthesis to the conservation of plant life. Explain the idea that air confined in a small area exerts pressure in all directions in relation to the action of air in a football.)

Following Directions

These questions would ask learners to show the sequence of steps or ideas for solving a problem or performing an experiment or the sequence of a chain of events. (*Examples:* What is the second step of the experiment? What should you do after you have placed the flask over the burner?)

Understanding Formulas and Symbols

These questions test student understanding of how symbols and formulas are used with scientific data. (*Examples:* What does the H refer to in the symbol H_2O? What does 40# mean?)

Maps and Graphs

Use questions that require knowledge of map and graph symbols and how to use them. (*Examples:* Use the graph on page 602 to answer these questions: By 1925, how many millions of people inhabited Earth? How many times over will the world population have increased from 2000 to 2050? Use the map on page 174 to answer these questions: Who ruled Gascony in the 12th century? Who governed the major portion of Flanders after 1550?)

Study Reading

Directions: Read pages 584–586. Take notes. Then, close your book and keep it closed. However, you may use the notes you made to help you answer the following questions. (Have questions on a separate sheet for distribution after notes have been made.) *Note:* Ask detail, main idea, and inference questions.

Source: Adapted from *Evaluating Reading and Study Skills in the Secondary Classroom: A Guide for Content Teachers,* by R. G. Voix, 1968, Newark, DE: International Reading Association. Copyright 1968 by the International Reading Association. Reprinted with permission.

---

you are measuring a student's ability to take lecture notes, the task should involve elements similar to a typical lecture delivered in your class.

Once the task has been selected, next decide what kind of measure to use. Three possible choices are direct observation checklists, analysis of student products, and student self-evaluation. With *direct observation checklists,* the teacher develops a list of observable steps necessary to perform a given strategy. Next, the teacher has a student perform a classroom task that requires her to use the strategy and records on the checklist which behaviors the student performed.

Although direct observation of student behavior can provide much more useful information, it is time consuming, particularly when you are a high school teacher who teaches many students each day. For most students, you can use analysis of student products or

When students enter high school, they are likely to face demands for a higher level of independence and responsibility for their own learning.

student self-evaluations. Nonetheless, if you have the luxury of a free moment with an individual student, such as before or after school or during a study hall, the time spent directly observing a student perform a task is very worthwhile.

Analysis of student products involves looking at student notebooks, tests, papers, and other assignments or written activities to find evidence of effective or ineffective strategy performance. In most cases, you can evaluate your whole classroom at once, and you do not have to score the products while you are teaching.

In *student self-evaluations,* students perform a task such as taking a test, are given a checklist of strategy steps, and are then asked to tell which of these steps they used (Mercer & Mercer, 2001; S. P. Miller, 1996). Student self-reports are useful for several reasons. They can provide information about strategy behaviors that cannot be directly observed. Student evaluations also stimulate student self-monitoring, a behavior critical for independent learning. Self-report measures can also include interview questions that further clarify strategy usage. For example, one teacher asked, "What was the first thing you did when you received your test?" As with all measures, student self-evaluations need to be corroborated by information from other sources (for example, direct observation checklists and student products). Such corroboration may be particularly important for students with special needs, many of whom have difficulty evaluating their own behavior.

How Are Curriculum-Based Probes Used to Make Special Education Decisions?

Academic probes can help teachers make many of the assessment decisions discussed previously in this chapter. Several examples are discussed in the following sections.

Peer Comparison in Screening

The key question involved in screening is whether a student is different enough from his peers on important skills in a given academic area (or areas) to indicate that some form of classroom accommodation is necessary. If the difference between a student and his peers continues or worsens despite repeated attempts in the classroom to remediate, a referral to special education and a more comprehensive assessment may be necessary.

When screening, first select probes in the area(s) of suspected difficulty. Next, give the assessment to the student in question and compare his or her performance to benchmark or norm levels to find out the extent of the achievement gap. Benchmarks or norms are available for probes in most basic skill areas (see WWW Resources on this page). You might also want to assess your entire class to identify other students at risk and obtain valuable feedback about the overall effectiveness of your teaching.

Note the results of an oral reading fluency probe given by a third-grade teacher to his entire class in April, shown in Figure 4.4. Each score represents the number of correct words read orally per minute from a grade-level passage in the classroom reading program. The teacher was particularly interested in the performance of the student who ended up scoring 50 words correct per minute. According to the norms shown on page 131, this student is well below the 25th percentile score for this time of year of 78 words correct per minute, a definite sign of being at risk. Although this student may need extra support from the classroom teacher or even a referral to special education, other factors should also be considered, including how he performs across other academic skills assessed and whether other students in the class are having similar problems. This low score did prompt the teacher to seek prereferral consultation to get ideas for improving the student's reading performance. The teacher also planned to regularly monitor the student's progress in oral reading fluency to help guide future decision making about his program.

Note that three other students in the class scored 10 or more words below 97, the 50th percentile. According to Hasbrouck and Tindal (see page 131), this puts them at some risk in reading. The teacher decided to monitor the progress of these students more regularly while also providing them with a peer-tutoring program to give them extra practice in reading fluency. Finally, the teacher learned from this experience that 19 of his 23 students were achieving at acceptable levels on an important indicator of reading ability.

If benchmarks don't exist for the assessment selected, compare the performance of the student in question to half the median of the entire class or a subsample of the class (for example, five average performers). The median, or middlemost score, is used to summarize the scores because it is affected less by extreme scores than the mean, or average, which could over- or underestimate the performance of the group as a whole. The teacher in Figure 4.4 used a score equal to one-half the median as a cutoff for identifying students who are having trouble with that particular skill (Shinn & Hubbard, 1992). Such a cutoff point typically identifies 6 to 12 percent of a class or grade level that may be experiencing difficulty with a particular skill (Bursuck & Lessen, 1987; Marston, Tindal, & Deno, 1984). As shown, the class scores range from a high of 190 words read correctly per minute to a low of 50 words read correctly per minute. The median, or middlemost, score for the class is 123 words read correctly per minute. A score of 61.5 words read correctly per minute is half the median. Our student in question was the only student scoring below this point. Deno and colleagues (2002) have shown that using the bottom 20 percent of a class can also be helpful in identifying students who are at risk.

The Technology Notes illustrates a way to use software to evaluate your students.

Fluency and Accuracy in Diagnosis

CBA probes also can help teachers diagnose specific skills deficits. For example, a student who performs poorly on a math facts probe may not know the math facts or may simply be unable to write numbers fast enough. You can figure out which situation exists by examining the student's rate, or *fluency*, of think-write number writing. Likewise, keeping track of the number of errors per minute, or *accuracy*, in oral reading can help you detect a particular student's reading problem. Figure 4.5 shows the results of an oral reading probe for two third-grade students. The correct reading rate for both students is 53. However, Student 1 seems to have a problem with reading fluency. What she reads, she reads accurately; the problem is that 53 words correct per minute is slow for a third-grade student. Student 2, moreover, is less accurate in her reading than Student 1; she is making many word identification errors and needs to be further assessed to ascertain whether these errors are part of a pattern or are due to carelessness. The Case in Practice on pages 144–145 shows how CBA can be used to monitor student progress within an RtI, multitiered problem-solving model of instruction.

FIGURE 4.4   Classroom Performance on Academic Skill Probe in Reading

Grade 3, Reading Orally in Context, April 2006

Number of correct words per minute read orally

190	136	103
189	128	99
172	125	97
160	123	86
159	120	84
151	119	80
139	119	50*
136	117	

Median   123
Median/2 61.5

*Denotes score of median/2 or lower

*www.*resources

The Center for Innovations at the University of Missouri (www.cise.missouri.edu/links/research-cbm-links.html) provides teachers with a wealth of resources to help implement research-based practices related to curriculum-based measurement.

Analyze and Reflect

What kinds of diagnostic information can you learn by checking both student fluency and accuracy that you would be unable to learn from checking accuracy alone?

Computerized Curriculum-Based Measurement

You may be wondering how you are going to assess your students systematically and still have time to prepare and teach your lessons. Researchers have developed a product that may help you (Fuchs, Hamlett, & Fuchs, 1998). They have developed software that makes scoring and interpreting curriculum-based measures in math much easier. In the Fuchs et al. system, students take a weekly probe test that measures required math operations for a given grade level. Students then are taught to enter their own data into a computer program that scores their test and summarizes the results.

The software program summarizes student performance using a display like the one shown in the accompanying figure. The graph shows the student's rate and accuracy on weekly math tests over time. This student (Sheila Hemmer) went from a score of 10 digits correct per minute at the beginning of October to a score of more than 30 digits correct per minute in March. The skills profile chart shows which skills (A1 = first skill in addition; S2 = second skill in subtraction) have been mastered and which may require more instruction.

Individual Student Performance

FIGURE 4.5 Reading Fluency Information for Two Students

Student 1		Student 2	
Number of words correct per minute	Number of words incorrect per minute	Number of words correct per minute	Number of words incorrect per minute
53	2	53	16

Summary of Class Performance

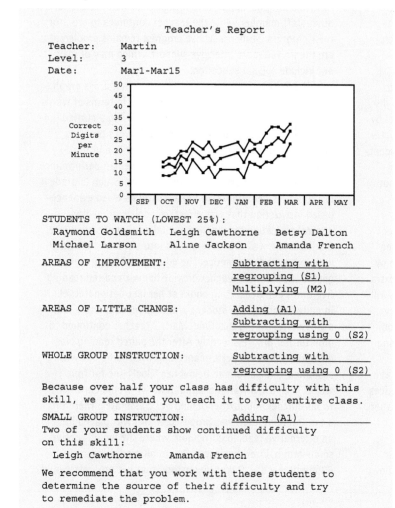

Teacher's Report

Teacher: Martin
Level: 3
Date: Mar1-Mar15

STUDENTS TO WATCH (LOWEST 25%):

Raymond Goldsmith   Leigh Cawthorne   Betsy Dalton
Michael Larson   Aline Jackson   Amanda French

AREAS OF IMPROVEMENT: Subtracting with
                         regrouping (S1)
                         Multiplying (M2)

AREAS OF LITTLE CHANGE: Adding (A1)
                         Subtracting with
                         regrouping using 0 (S2)

WHOLE GROUP INSTRUCTION: Subtracting with
                         regrouping using 0 (S2)

Because over half your class has difficulty with this
skill, we recommend you teach it to your entire class.

SMALL GROUP INSTRUCTION: Adding (A1)
Two of your students show continued difficulty
on this skill:

Leigh Cawthorne   Amanda French

We recommend that you work with these students to
determine the source of their difficulty and try
to remediate the problem.

Teachers also receive a display like the one shown here. The graph shows the teacher, Mr. Martin, how his students progressed from October through March. The top line indicates scores at the 75th percentile; the middle line, scores at the 50th percentile; and the bottom line, scores at the 25th percentile. The lists below the graph provide information about which students should be monitored; areas in which the class has improved or not changed; and recommendations for skills that could be covered in whole-group instruction (most of the class needs instruction) or small-group instruction (only one or two students).

Similar software programs for math concepts and problem solving (Fuchs, Hamlett, and Fuchs, 1999) and reading (Fuchs, Hamlett, and Fuchs, 1997) are also available.

Source: Figures from "Classwide Curriculum-Based Measurement: Helping General Educators Meet the Challenge of Student Diversity," by Fuchs, Fuchs, Hamlett, Philips, and Bentz, 1994, *Exceptional Children 60*(6), 518–537. Reprinted with permission.

The fact that CBA probes measure fluency as well as accuracy adds an important diagnostic dimension. For example, if the reading performance of the two students in Figure 4.5 were reported solely as a percentage of accuracy, the results would look like those shown in Figure 4.6. Using percentages alone, Student 1 does not appear to have a problem at all. However, as previously shown, she is reading much more slowly than Student 2.

Skill Mastery and Curriculum Placement

Inclusive education involves the use of a variety of instructional grouping arrangements. Sometimes students are grouped based on their skill levels; other times a broader range of student skills is desired in a group. Students with special needs benefit from both types

Case in Practice

Using a Classroom-Based Problem-Solving Model

IDEA 2004 allowed school districts to use an alternative way of identifying students with learning disabilities that relies on the use of curriculum-based assessment, rather than traditional achievement and intelligence tests. In this approach, students with learning disabilities are identified based on how they respond to instruction of various levels of intensity, often referred to as *tiers*. This approach is called *response to intervention (RtI)*. RtI has been offered as an alternative to discrepancy formulas, which try to identify learning disabilities by eliminating low intellectual ability (IQ) as a reason for achievement problems. Using a discrepancy formula approach, students are declared learning disabled if their intelligence is within the normal range yet their level of achievement clearly is not. Typically, a standard of difference is declared beyond which a student can be identified as having a learning disability.

The process of using the discrepancy between student achievement and ability to identify students with learning disabilities has come under attack, in large part because by the time students are discrepant enough to qualify for extra support, they are already so far behind that catching up will be difficult, if not unlikely. This problem with discrepancy formulas has led some researchers to refer to this method of identification as the "wait to fail" method of identifying learning disabilities.

The RtI process begins with effective instruction in the general education classroom using evidence-based practices (National Association of State Directors of Special Education, 2006). Students who are at risk are identified, and their progress in the evidence-based curriculum is monitored regularly using curriculum-based assessment. Often their progress is monitored using a graph similar to the one shown for Marni. Students whose progress is less than desired receive additional support from their classroom teacher or other staff member while the teacher continues to monitor their progress. Students whose progress remains problematic are then given more intensive support, which may or may not include special education.

The RtI approach clearly can be seen in Marni's graph. Her progress in reading is being monitored in terms of words read correctly and incorrectly per minute using a curriculum-based oral reading fluency assessment. Marni's progress graph is divided into three parts: tier 1, tier 2, and tier 3. Note that an aim line is drawn from her median performance in tier 1 to benchmark performance in May, which in grade 4 is 120 words per minute. In tier 1, Marni received evidence-based instruction that was effectively delivered by her general education teacher, yet she failed to make adequate progress. She was therefore moved into tier 2 and provided with extra reading practice. The educational team suggested that Marni's teacher provide her with paired reading five times per week using books at her instructional level. In paired reading, the student practices reading orally with a classmate. During this time, Marni's teacher continued to monitor her progress weekly. After the paired reading was introduced, Marni's performance improved some but wasn't sustained; she performed below her "Goal" line for four weeks in a row, a warning signal that she would continue to fall further and further behind her classmates. Therefore, a tier 3 intervention was proposed. Marni was placed in an alternative reading curriculum where she would receive small-group, intensive instruction in all reading areas for 60 minutes a day. It was understood that her progress would

FIGURE *4.6* **Percentage of Accuracy in Passage Reading for Two Students**

Student 1	Student 2
Percentage of accuracy	Percentage of accuracy
96	70

of instructional arrangements. You can use CBA probes to group your students by rank ordering and then visually inspecting your students' probe scores. For example, Mr. Glass wanted to form cooperative groups in math. He used scores on a problem-solving task probe, picking one lower performer, two middle performers, and one higher performer

Response to Intervention (RtI), Classroom-Based Program Graph: Marni

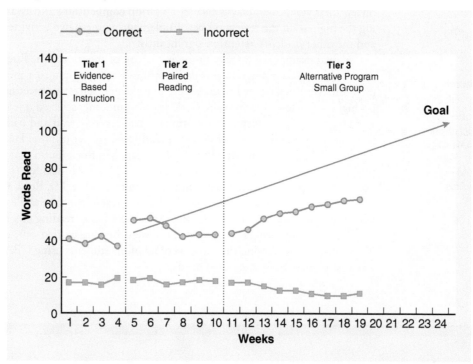

continue to be monitored and that she would be referred to special education if her progress continued to stall. Note that while still below benchmark, Marni began to make steady progress. Therefore, her team decided to keep her in tier 3 but without being referred to special education. The team further decided that Marni would remain in tier 3 until she reached benchmark levels in oral reading fluency and reading comprehension.

for each group. Ms. Robins, in contrast, found that three of her students were having difficulty with capitalization but the rest of the class were not. She formed a small group of those having difficulty to review capitalization rules.

Monitoring Student Progress and Instructional Evaluation

Although education has come a long way in terms of researching what constitutes effective teaching, predicting whether a given technique will work for a given student in a particular situation is still difficult. It is thus important that you carefully monitor the results of your teaching. This monitoring is particularly relevant for students with special needs who by definition are less likely to respond favorably to commonly used instructional methods.

Analyze
and Reflect

How could the information from student progress-monitoring probes be used to establish eligibility for special education services?

www.resources

For the latest research on student testing, curriculum, and achievement, go to the website of the National Institute on Student Achievement, Curriculum, and Assessment at www.ed.gov/offices/OERI/SAI/index.html.

Simulation Homework Exercise

Go to the Homework and Exercises section in Chapter 4 of MyEducationLab to learn how to get started using curriculum-based assessments and how to communicate your findings.

CBA probes, because they are time efficient, easy to give, and match what is taught in the classroom, are ideal for monitoring student progress in class. For example, Mr. Harris was interested in whether Maria, a student with learning disabilities, was retaining any of the words featured on weekly spelling lists. She had scored 90 and above on her weekly tests, but Mr. Harris was unsure whether she was remembering the words from week to week. He developed a spelling probe using words from previous spelling lists. He gave the probe to his entire class and found that Maria and 10 other students were retaining only 20 percent of the words. As a result, he started a peer-tutoring program to help students review their words. Mr. Harris also set up group competitions and awards for groups scoring the highest on the review probes. Implementing these two activities improved Maria's and the other students' retention significantly.

A final example of a CBA probe is worthy of mention. Mr. Rock's school recently switched its reading program from a literature-based program to a more structured basal program. Mr. Rock wanted to make sure that the new series was meeting the needs of both his higher- and lower-performing students. He randomly selected one representative 300-word passage from a story that the students had recently read and had each student read it orally, recording the number of words read correctly per minute. He also asked the students several questions about what they had read. Mr. Rock found that one of his students read at a rate much slower than his classmates. Mr. Rock decided to provide him with extra reading practice with a peer tutor three times a week. Mr. Rock also found that two other students read much more fluently than the rest of the class while still understanding what they had read. He decided to place them in a group reading at a higher grade level.

Teaching approaches, no matter how well they are carried out, can affect students differently. By monitoring the progress of all of his students using CBA probes, Mr. Rock was able to meet their individual needs.

Summary

General education teachers can make assessments that contribute to six decision-making areas of special education: screening, diagnosis, program placement, curriculum placement, instructional evaluation, and program evaluation. General education teachers can go to a number of information sources to make these decisions for students with special needs.

High-stakes tests and group-administered standardized achievement tests can be used to screen students having difficulty, but they have serious drawbacks for making other types of decisions. Individually administered diagnostic tests provide more specific information but are susceptible to many of the same problems as group-administered tests. Psychological tests, such as tests of intelligence and tests related to learning disabilities, measure abilities that affect how efficiently students learn in an instructional situation.

A small percentage of students who are typically working on a more individualized curriculum do not have to meet the same requirements as those students graduating with a standard diploma. These students are eligible for alternate assessments. Curriculum-based assessment (CBA) measures student achievement in terms of what they are taught in the classroom. There are two major kinds of CBA: probes of basic academic skills and probes of content-area knowledge and strategies. CBA is helpful in making a range of special education decisions, particularly those involving day-to-day instruction. CBA norms and peer comparison methods can help screen students who are having academic difficulty. Probes can also be used to help teachers diagnose specific skill deficits to help form instructional groups and allow teachers to monitor the progress of students in class by measuring student performance over time. Finally, curriculum-based measures comprise an important part of response to intervention (RtI), a way of identifying learning disabilities based on students' response to instruction.

Back to the Cases

This section provides opportunities for you to apply the knowledge gained in this chapter to the cases described at the beginning of this chapter. The questions and activities that follow demonstrate how these standards and principles, along with other concepts that you have learned about in this chapter, connect to the everyday activities of all teachers.

Ms. Lyons has determined that Rob's needs should be discussed with the school's instructional assistance team. In addition to presenting information outlining Rob's specific problem areas in mathematics, Ms. Lyons will need to describe what teaching methods, strategies, and/or accommodations she has used to support his learning and how he has responded to them. This is an assessment strategy often referred to as *response to intervention* (RtI). (INTASC Principle 8.03 and CEC Standard 8.) How might Ms. Lyons document the instructional strategies she has tried with Rob and the results they have provided? Provide a rationale for your choices.

Mr. Blount has been proactive in assessing how well his students can use the assigned text in his class and has used the data from those assessments to teach the prerequisite skills needed to learn from the text. However, he is aware that if his special education students have difficulty reading textbooks, they may also have difficulty

reading the texts of high-stakes, end-of-grade tests required in his school system. He wants to use appropriate accommodations during these tests. (INTASC Principles 8.01 and 8.05 and CEC Standard 8.) How should Mr. Blount determine which accommodations to use? Further, how might he prepare his students to use these accommodations?

Roberto will most likely have difficulty participating in the standardized assessments given in his state. Ms. Benis and Roberto's special education teacher met after school yesterday to discuss what assessment methods they will use to demonstrate Roberto's progress toward meeting state standards. At this meeting, the two teachers reviewed the full range of options available and prepared a list of pros and cons for each option. (INTASC Principles 4.05, 8.02, 8.03, and 8.05; and CEC Standard 8.) What would be on your list of options? As you prepare your list, include the pros and cons of each option based on what you know about Roberto.

Key Terms and Concepts

Alternate assessments (p. 126)

Assessment (p. 116)

Curriculum-based assessment (CBA) (p. 128)

Curriculum placement (p. 118)

Diagnosis (p. 117)

High-stakes tests (p. 120)

Individually administered diagnostic tests (p. 123)

Instructional evaluation (p. 120)

Program evaluation (p. 120)

Program placement (p. 118)

Psychological tests (p. 124)

Screening (p. 116)

Standardized achievement tests (p. 123)

PEARSON
myeducationlab
Where the Classroom Comes to Life

Now go to the Friend and Bursuck, Fifth Edition, MyEducationLab course at www.myeducationlab.com to

- take a pretest to assess your initial comprehension of the chapter content
- study chapter content with your individualized study plan
- take a posttest to assess your understanding of chapter content
- engage in multimedia exercises to help you build a deeper and more applied understanding of chapter content

Applications in Teaching Practice

Collecting and Using Assessment Information

It is October 1, and you are concerned about two students in your reading program. The students' parents have commented that they have not seen improvement in their children's reading at home. You have also noticed that both of these students pick books during independent reading that are too hard for them and repeatedly guess at words without approaching them systematically. You wonder whether you should make some changes in their reading program.

Questions

1. What areas of reading do you want to assess here? Why?

2. How will you assess each area using the curriculum-based assessment procedures described in this chapter? What probes will you give? What will your probes look like? How will you score them?

3. What additional assessment information (for example, standardized tests, psychological tests) will you collect?

4. How will you use the information you obtained in Questions 2 and 3? Under what circumstances will you decide to accommodate the students in the current program? To use an alternative program? To advocate for intensive instruction from a special education teacher?

5. What will you do to evaluate the changes suggested in Question 4? What measures will you give? How often? What kinds of decisions will you be making?

6. How might these students be served within an RtI system of instruction and assessment?

Yolanda is a student with a learning disability in your class who has been receiving indirect support or consultation in one area. You are interested in knowing how she is doing relative to the rest of the class. Select the subject area in which Yolanda has been receiving indirect support (reading, math, or written expression). Then select a particular skill in that subject matter that you have been working on in your class (for example, in reading: sight-word reading, passage reading, comprehension, letter or letter–sound identification; in math: any math computation skill, word problems, money, geometry; in written expression: writing mechanics, writing productivity, quality of ideas). Next, describe a curriculum-based assessment strategy you would use to judge how well Yolanda is doing on that skill as compared with her classmates. Respond to the following questions in your description.

Questions

1. How will you use curriculum-based norms to measure the extent of Yolanda's problem?

2. What additional information will you collect to clarify Yolanda's problem?

3. How will you use probe information to measure the effectiveness of classroom supports for Yolanda?

4. How will you use probe information to help you instruct the rest of the class?

The high school resource room teacher has suggested that Antoine, who has a learning disability, be included in your second semester class. The teacher has asked you to help collect some information to assist him in deciding what support service (if any) Antoine should receive. Assuming you are a math teacher, describe a strategy for determining whether Antoine has the prerequisite skills for your class. Your strategy should respond to the following questions.

Questions

1. What skills will you include on your probe and why?

2. Are all these skills essential, or could some of them be bypassed?

3. How will you design, administer, and score your probe?

4. How will you determine whether Antoine is experiencing academic difficulty?

5. How will you use the information collected to determine needed support services for Antoine?

6. How might the information collected help you in teaching the rest of the class?

If you are teaching a class for which the ability to read the textbook is an important skill, select a sample textbook from your content area. Then develop a probe of content-area reading skills using the model shown in Figure 4.3.

Questions

1. How did you select the skills to be included on your probe?

2. How could you use the information collected to determine the nature and extent of classroom support needed for students with disabilities? For the rest of the class?

Design a one- or two-day lesson in the content area of your choice, describing briefly all the instructional activities involved. Be sure to specify objectives for as many of the following student outcome areas as possible: using patterns to understand past and present events and to predict future events, using technology effectively, demonstrating skills and values for physical activity, and completing a postsecondary opportunities search. Tell how you would use an alternate assessment to measure the progress of Darrell, a student with a severe intellectual disability who is in your class.

Questions

1. What outcomes would you expect for your students without disabilities?

2. What outcomes would you expect for Darrell?

3. Describe how you would assess the outcomes for Darrell using alternate assessment devices. Include evaluation criteria for each of the assessments described.

Further Readings

Espin, C. A., Shin, J., & Busch, T. W. (2005). Curriculum-based measurement in the content areas: Vocabulary matching as an indicator of progress in social studies learning. *Journal of Learning Disabilities, 38*(4), 353–363.

> While examples of curriculum-based measures in basic skill areas are readily available, curriculum-based measures in subject-matter areas, such as science and social studies, are much harder to find. This article describes the development of a promising way of monitoring student progress in social studies using a student-read vocabulary measure. The authors provide a practical example at the end of the article about using the measure to monitor the progress of students with disabilities included in general education social studies classes.

Garcia, S., & Ortiz, A. (2006). Preventing disproportionate representation: Culturally and linguistically responsive prereferral interventions [electronic version]. *Teaching Exceptional Children, 38*(4), 64–68.

> This article is full of practical ways for schools to avoid the chronic problem of overrepresentation of English-language learners in special education programs.

Hosp, M. K., & Hosp, J. L. (2003). Curriculum-based measurement for reading, spelling, and math: How to do it and why. *Preventing School Failure, 48*(1), 10–17.

> The authors present clear, nontechnical guidelines for monitoring student progress using curriculum-based measurements in reading, spelling, and math.

Kleinert, H., Green, P., Hurte, M., Clayton, J., & Oetinger, C. (2002). Creating and using meaningful alternate assessments. *Teaching Exceptional Children, 34*(4), 40–47.

> This very practical article contains a wealth of examples of alternate assessments for students with significant intellectual disabilities.

Salvia, J., & Ysseldyke, J. E. (2007). *Assessment in special and inclusive education* (10th ed.). Boston: Houghton Mifflin.

> A classic text that is an excellent reference for learning about standardized tests used in special education.

5 Planning Instruction by Analyzing Classroom and Student Needs

LEARNING Objectives

After you read this chapter, you will be able to

1. Explain what it means to make reasonable accommodations for students with special needs.
2. Describe the steps of the INCLUDE decision-making process for accommodating students with special needs in your classroom.
3. Identify and describe the key elements of a classroom environment.
4. Describe the major components of classroom organization, and explain how they can be adapted for students with special needs.
5. Explain various ways students can be grouped for instruction in an inclusive classroom.
6. Explain how the use of effective classroom materials and instructional methods can benefit students with special needs.

Mr. Rodriguez teaches world history at a large urban high school. When he introduces new content to his students, he teaches to the whole class at once. First, he reviews material that has already been covered, pointing out how that material relates to the new content being presented. Next, he provides any additional background information that he thinks will help students understand the new material better. Before Mr. Rodriguez actually presents new material, he hands out a partially completed outline of the major points he will make. This outline helps students identify the most important information. Every 10 minutes or so, he stops his lecture and allows students to discuss and modify the outline and ask questions. When Mr. Rodriguez completes his lecture, he organizes students into cooperative learning groups of four to answer a series of questions on the lecture. Manuel is a student with a learning disability in Mr. Rodriguez's class. He has a history of difficulty staying on task during lectures and figuring out what information to write down. He also has trouble remembering information from one day to the next. Mr. Rodriguez has noticed that Manuel has a particular interest in soccer and loves to perform for his classmates.

How well do you think Manuel will perform in Mr. Rodriguez's class? What changes in the classroom environment might help Manuel succeed? How might Mr. Rodriguez capitalize on Manuel's interests and strengths?

Josh has cerebral palsy. He is in the normal range in ability; in fact, he excels in math. However, he has a lot of trouble with muscle movements, has little use of his lower body and legs, and also has problems with fine muscle coordination. As a result, Josh uses a wheelchair, has trouble with his speech (he speaks haltingly and is difficult to understand), and struggles to write letters and numbers correctly. Josh is included in Ms. Stewart's second-grade class.

How can Ms. Stewart set up her classroom to make it easier for Josh to perform? What aspects of the classroom environment will Ms. Stewart need to adapt for Josh? How can she use technology to facilitate Josh's inclusion? Why will math be an important subject for Josh in Ms. Stewart's class?

Disabilities and other special needs arise when characteristics of individual students and various features of students' home and school environments interact. Effective teachers analyze the classroom environment in relation to students' academic and social needs and make accommodations and modifications to ensure students' success in the classroom. For example, Manuel has difficulty staying on task and retaining new information. However, features of Mr. Rodriguez's class make it easier for Manuel to function. The partially completed lecture outlines help Manuel focus his attention on specific information as he tries to listen and stay on task; the pauses help him catch any lecture information he might have missed. The review sessions are intended to help Manuel retain information by giving him a mechanism for rehearsing newly learned material. In another case, Josh has some serious motor problems, but he may be able to function quite independently if Ms. Stewart makes her classroom accessible to a wheelchair and works with special educators to use assistive technology to meet Josh's needs in handwriting and oral communication.

This chapter introduces you to a systematic approach to helping all students with special needs gain access to the general education curriculum, a requirement of the Individuals with Disabilities Education Act (IDEA). Part of that approach is for you to be the best teacher you can be so that fewer of your students require individualized instruction in the first place. Despite your best efforts, however, there will always be students who require a more individualized approach. The **INCLUDE** strategy is provided for these students. Although there are other ways to differentiate instruction for students with special needs, INCLUDE gives teachers a systematic process for accommodating students based on their individual needs and the classroom demands on or expectations of the teacher.

INCLUDE gives teachers a systematic process for accommodating students based on their individual needs and the classroom demands on or expectations of the teacher.

The rest of the text expands and elaborates on this approach. Later chapters also present a more in-depth look at the relationship between your classroom environment and the diverse needs of learners. An important assumption throughout the text is that the more effective your classroom structure is, the greater the diversity you will be able to accommodate and the fewer individualized classroom changes you will need to make.

*H*ow Can the INCLUDE Strategy Help You Make Reasonable Accommodations for Students with Special Needs?

At a recent conference presentation that included both classroom teachers and special education teachers, one of the authors of this text asked the audience how many of those present worked with students with disabilities. A music teacher at the back of the room called out, "Everyone in schools works with students with disabilities!" He is right. As you have learned in the previous chapters, IDEA entitles students with disabilities to "access," "participation," and "progress" in the general education curriculum. These entitlements were reinforced by the No Child Left Behind Act of 2001 (NCLB), which requires that most students with disabilities meet the same standards as their classmates without disabilities. Therefore, although the professionals who specialize in meeting the needs of students with disabilities are valuable and provide critical instructional and support systems for students, ultimately you and your peers will be the primary teachers for many students with disabilities and other special needs, and you will form partnerships with special educators to meet the needs of others. That makes it critical for you to feel comfortable making accommodations and modifications for students in order for them to have fair access to your curriculum.

The INCLUDE strategy is based on two key assumptions. First, student performance in school is the result of an interaction between the student and the instructional environment (Broderick, Mehta-Parekh, & Reid, 2005; Pisha & Coyne, 2001; Smith, 2004). Consequently, what happens in a classroom can either minimize the impact of students' special needs on their learning or magnify it, making accommodations necessary. In the first chapter-opening example, Mr. Rodriguez engaged in a number of teaching practices that minimized the impact of Manuel's learning disability, such as starting each class with a review of material covered the day before, providing the students with lecture outlines to help them identify important ideas, and engaging his students in regular discussions of the material presented. Nevertheless, if part of Manuel's learning disability is in reading and the classroom text used in Mr. Rodriguez's class is too difficult for Manuel to read independently, Mr. Rodriguez will need to accommodate Manuel's problems in reading. This aspect of the INCLUDE approach is consistent with the idea behind response to intervention (RtI). If all students receive effectively delivered, evidence-based instruction, then fewer will be identified as needing more supports. Further, those eventually identified for special education—the most intensive level of support—will be only those truly in need.

The second key assumption of INCLUDE is that by carefully analyzing students' learning needs and the specific demands of the classroom environment, teachers can reasonably accommodate most students with special needs in their classrooms. You can maximize student success without taking a disproportionate amount of teacher time or diminishing the education of the other students in the class. For example, with the help of the special education teacher, Mr. Rodriguez provided Manuel with a digital text with a built-in speech-to-print component and study guide. Soon Mr. Rodriguez discovered that other students in the class could also benefit from using the digital text and made it available to them. In this way, reasonable accommodations often assist many students in the class.

The INCLUDE strategy contains elements of both universal design and differentiated instruction, two widely recognized approaches to addressing classroom diversity in general and inclusion in particular. The idea of **universal design** originated in the field of architecture, where it was learned that designing buildings for persons with diverse needs from the beginning makes them more accessible and saves money spent on costly retrofits of ramps and automatic doors. As applied to classrooms, the idea is that instructional materials, methods, and assessments designed with built-in supports are more likely to be compatible with learners with special needs than those without such supports (Curry, 2003; Hitchcock, Meyer, Rose, & Jackson, 2002; Pisha & Stahl, 2005), and they minimize the need for labor-intensive accommodations later on. For example, print alternatives such as graphics, video, and digital text allow students with reading problems to more readily access subject content. The use of templates with partially filled-in sections and links to more information can help students construct a better essay.

The idea behind **differentiated instruction** is that a variety of teaching and learning strategies are necessary to meet the range of needs evident in any given classroom. Students' diverse needs are met by differentiating the content being taught, the process by which it is taught, and the ways students demonstrate what they have learned and their level of knowledge through varied products (Anderson, 2007; Broderick, Mehta-Parekh, & Reid, 2005). Differentiation is achieved by providing materials and tasks at varied levels of difficulty and with varying levels of instructional support, through the use of multiple grouping arrangements, student choice, and varied evaluation strategies (Tomlinson, 2000).

Differentiated instruction is consistent with the approach taken in this text for accommodating students with special needs. In fact, the INCLUDE process of determining

www.@resources

For more information on universal design, go to the Teaching Every Student page of the Center for Applied Special Technology (CAST) website: www.cast.org/tes.

INCLUDE Homework Exercise

Go to the Homework and Exercises section in Chapter 5 of MyEducationLab to practice using INCLUDE with worksheets and case studies.

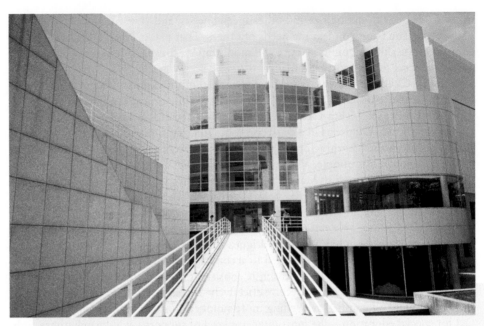

How does the concept of universal design relate from architecture to teaching? How does this concept simplify the job of a general education teacher?

student supports based on student needs and classroom demands is an ideal vehicle for implementing differentiated instruction in your classroom. The way differentiated instruction is addressed in INCLUDE also is consistent with the RtI principle that when it comes to providing effective instruction, one size doesn't fit all.

The INCLUDE strategy for differentiating instruction for students with special needs in the general education classroom follows seven steps:

INCLUDE

Step 1 Identify classroom demands.
Step 2 Note student learning strengths and needs.
Step 3 Check for potential areas of student success.
Step 4 Look for potential problem areas.
Step 5 Use information to brainstorm ways to differentiate instruction.
Step 6 Differentiate instruction.
Step 7 Evaluate student progress.

These steps are designed to apply to a broad range of special needs and classroom environments. Throughout this text, this icon will denote suggestions for differentiating instruction according to this strategy, with an emphasis on the appropriate step.

INCLUDE Step 1: Identify Classroom Demands

Because the classroom environment significantly influences what students learn, identifying and analyzing classroom requirements allows teachers to anticipate or explain problems a given student might experience. Then by modifying the environment, teachers can solve or reduce the impact of these learning problems. Common classroom demands relate to classroom management, classroom grouping, instructional materials, and instructional methods.

● **Classroom Management** The ways in which a teacher promotes order and engages students in learning in a classroom are referred to as *classroom management* (Doyle, 1986; Miller & Hall, 2005). Classroom management includes a number of factors:

- *Physical organization,* such as the use of wall and floor space and lighting
- *Classroom routines* for academic and nonacademic activities
- *Classroom climate,* or attitudes toward individual differences
- *Behavior management,* such as classroom rules and monitoring
- *The use of time* for instructional and noninstructional activities

Classroom management strategies can have real benefits for students with special needs. For example, LaVerna is a student who needs adaptations in physical organization; she uses a wheelchair and requires wide aisles in the classroom and a ramp for the step leading to her classroom. Shawn has behavioral difficulties and thus would benefit from a behavior management system; he might go to his next class prior to the end of each period to eliminate potential opportunities to fight with classmates. He would also benefit from an efficient use of time; minimizing transition times or the amount of time between activities would eliminate further opportunities for inappropriate interactions with his classmates.

● **Classroom Grouping** Teachers use a variety of *classroom grouping* arrangements. Sometimes they teach the whole class at once, as when they lecture in a content area such as social studies. Other times teachers may employ small-group or one-to-one instruction. For example, they may teach a small group of students who have similar instructional needs, such as a group of students who all require extra help on multiplication facts or an individual student who needs extra help with an English assignment. Teachers may also group students of differing interests and abilities in an effort to foster cooperative problem solving and/or peer tutoring. Students respond differently to these types of groupings. For example, Mike needs accommodations in classroom grouping in order to succeed; he might do better in a small group in which other students read assignments aloud so that he can participate in responding to them. Using a variety of grouping strategies based on student need is sometimes referred to as *flexible grouping,* an essential part of differentiated instruction (Anderson, 2007).

● **Instructional Materials** The types of *instructional materials* teachers use can have a major impact on the academic success of students with special needs. Although many teachers are choosing to develop or collect their own materials, published textbooks are most commonly used. Published textbooks include basic skills texts called *basals,* often used in reading and mathematics, and texts that stress subject-matter content in areas such as history and science. Other materials commonly used by teachers include concrete representational items such as manipulatives and technological devices, including audiovisual aids, telecommunication systems, and computers. Roberta's use of large-print materials to assist her in seeing her work and Carmen's use of a study guide to help her identify important information in her history text are both examples of differentiating instruction by making changes in instructional materials.

> The types of instructional materials teachers use can have a major impact on the academic success of students with special needs.

● **Instructional Methods** The ways in which teachers present content or skills to students and evaluate whether learning has occurred are the essence of teaching and are crucial for accommodating students with special needs. These are their *instructional methods.* Teachers use a number of different approaches to teach content and skills. Sometimes they teach skills directly, whereas other times they assume the role of a facilitator and encourage students to learn on their own, providing support only as needed. Instructional methods also involve student practice that occurs either in class, through independent seatwork activities or learning centers, or out of class through homework. Ms. Correli's decision to use a PowerPoint presentation in class and then give Lon a copy of the slides to help his learning is an example of an accommodation in presenting subject matter. Using a paraprofessional to write a student's words is an example of an accommodation in student practice.

Student evaluation, or determining the extent to which students have mastered academic skills or instructional content, is an important aspect of instructional methods. Grades are frequently used to communicate student evaluation. For some students, grading is an appropriate evaluation strategy. But for others, such as Anita, a fifth-grade student who has a moderate intellectual disability and is learning to recognize her name, a narrative report might be a better evaluation tool.

When evaluating students with disabilities, teachers must focus on measuring what a student knows rather than the extent of his disability. For example, Alex, who has a severe learning disability in writing, may need to answer test questions orally to convey all he knows; if he gives written answers, only his writing disability may be measured.

INCLUDE

Step 2: Note Student Learning Strengths and Needs

Once instructional demands are specified, the *N* step of INCLUDE calls for noting student strengths and needs. Remember that students with disabilities are a very heterogeneous group; a disability label cannot communicate a student's complete learning profile. For example, some students with intellectual disabilities can learn many life skills and live independently, whereas others will continually need daily assistance. Also keep in mind that students with disabilities are more like their peers without disabilities than different from them. Like their nondisabled peers, they have patterns of learning strengths and weaknesses. Focusing on strengths is essential (Epstein, 2004; Epstein, Rudolph, & Epstein, 2000; Shaywitz, 2003). Teachers who see the strengths in students teach positively, helping students to see themselves and others positively, to see learning positively, and to overcome their weaknesses (Tomlinson & Jarvis, 2006).

Three areas describe student learning strengths and needs: academics, social-emotional development, and physical development. Problems in any one of these areas may prevent students from meeting classroom requirements, resulting in a need for differentiated instruction. Strengths in any of these areas can help students overcome these problems. For example, a student with good listening skills may be able to compensate for her reading problem by using a digital recording of her history textbook.

● **Academics**   The first part of academics is *basic skills,* including reading, math, and oral and written language. Although these skills might sometimes be bypassed (for example, through the use of a calculator in math), their importance in both elementary and secondary education suggests teachers should consider them carefully. For example, a student with a severe reading problem is likely to have trouble in any subject area that requires reading, including math, social studies, and science and on any assignment with written directions.

Cognitive and learning strategies make up the second part of academics. These strategies involve "learning how to learn" skills, such as memorization, textbook reading, note taking, test taking, and general problem solving. Such skills give students independence that helps them in adult life. Students with problems in these areas experience increasing difficulty as they proceed through the grades. For example, students who have difficulty memorizing basic facts likely will have trouble learning to multiply fractions, and students who cannot take notes may fall behind in a history course based on a lecture format.

Survival skills, the third area of academics, are skills practiced by successful students, such as attending school regularly, being organized, completing tasks in and out of school, being independent, taking an interest in school, and displaying positive interpersonal skills (Brown, Kerr, Zigmond, & Harris, 1984; Kerr & Nelson, 2006). Students lacking in these areas usually have difficulty at school. For example, disorganized students are not likely to have work done on time, nor are they likely to deliver parent permission forms for field trips to their parents or return them to school. Survival skills also help some students compensate for their other problems. For example, given two students with identical reading problems, teachers sometimes offer more help to the student who has good attendance and tries hard.

● **Social-Emotional Development** Students' social-emotional development involves classroom conduct, interpersonal skills, and personal-psychological adjustment. Classroom conduct problems include a number of aggressive and disruptive behaviors, such as hitting, fighting, teasing, hyperactivity, yelling, refusing to comply with requests, crying, and destructiveness. Although most of these behaviors may be exhibited by all children at one time or another, students with special needs may engage in them more frequently and with greater intensity.

Conduct problems seriously interfere with student learning and can lead to problems in interpersonal relations and personal-psychological adjustment. For example, students who are disruptive in class are less likely to learn academic skills and content. Their outbursts also may be resented by their peers and may lead to peer rejection, social isolation, and a poor self-image.

Interpersonal skills include but are not limited to initiating and carrying on conversations, coping with conflict, and establishing and maintaining friendships. Although these skills are not ordinarily part of the explicit school curriculum, their overall impact on school adjustment makes them important. For example, students lacking in peer support may have difficulty completing group projects (an example of student practice) or finding someone to help with a difficult assignment (an example of homework).

> Conduct problems seriously interfere with student learning and can lead to problems in interpersonal relations and personal-psychological adjustment.

Personal-psychological adjustment involves the key motivational areas of self-image, frustration tolerance, and proactive learning. For example, students with a poor self-image and low tolerance for frustration may do poorly on tests (an example of student evaluation); students who are inactive learners may have difficulty pursuing an independent science project (an example of student practice).

● **Physical Development** Physical development includes vision and hearing levels, motor skills, and neurological functioning. Students with vision problems need adapted educational materials. Students with poor fine motor skills may need a computer to do their homework, an accommodation in student practice. Finally, students with attention deficits may need a wider range of approaches for instruction, including lecture, discussion, small-group work, and independent work.

Step 3: Check for Potential Areas of Student Success

The next INCLUDE step is *C*, analyzing student strengths in view of the instructional demands identified in Step 1 and checking for activities or tasks students can do successfully. Success enhances student self-image and motivation. Look for strengths in both academic and social-emotional areas. Reading the "Current Levels of Performance" section of the IEP is a good way to begin identifying a student's strengths. For example, Jerry doesn't read but can draw skillfully. In social studies, his teacher asks him to be the class cartographer, drawing maps for each region of the world as it is studied. Kareem has a moderate intellectual disability and learns very slowly, but he always comes to school on time. His second-grade teacher appoints him attendance monitor. Dwayne has attention deficit–hyperactivity disorder (ADHD), is failing all his classes in school, and is beginning to become difficult to handle at home. His parents and teachers have noticed, however, that he is able to identify personal strengths, has a good sense of humor, and can enjoy a hobby. They support Dwayne's positive interests by enrolling him in the school band.

Step 4: Look for Potential Problem Areas

In the *L* step of the INCLUDE strategy, student learning needs are reviewed within a particular instructional context, and potential mismatches are identified. For example, Susan has a learning need in the area of expressive writing; she is unable to identify spelling errors in her work. This is an academic learning need. When evaluating students' work her history teacher, who believes that writing skills should be reinforced in every class, deducts one letter grade from papers that contain one or more spelling errors. Susan also cannot read the history text accurately and fluently enough to understand it. For Susan to succeed in history class, these mismatches need to be addressed. Similarly, Sam has a severe problem that prevents him from speaking fluently. This physical problem creates a learning need. His fourth-grade teacher requires that students present book reports to the class. Again, a potential mismatch exists that could prevent Sam from succeeding. Mismatches such as those experienced by Susan and Sam are resolved by differentiating instruction, the topic of the next two INCLUDE steps.

Step 5: Use Information to Brainstorm Ways to Differentiate Instruction

Once potential mismatches have been identified, the *U* step of INCLUDE is to use this information to identify possible ways to eliminate or minimize their effects. IDEA stipulates two ways to differentiate for students with disabilities: accommodations and modifications.

● **Accommodations**   **Instructional accommodations** are typically defined as services or supports provided to help students gain full access to class content and instruction, and to demonstrate accurately what they know (Nolet & McLaughlin, 2005). It is important to remember that with accommodations, school expectations that students meet learning standards remain unchanged. This means that students with disabilities receiving accommodations are expected to learn everything their classmates without disabilities are supposed to learn (Nolet & McLaughlin, 2005). Examples of accommodations include bypassing students' learning needs by allowing them to employ compensatory learning strategies, making an adjustment in classroom teaching materials, using group organization, and teaching students basic or independent learning skills.

Bypass or *compensatory strategies* allow students to gain access to or demonstrate mastery of the school curriculum in alternative ways. For example, Susan, the student with problems in spelling and reading, could benefit from several bypass strategies. For spelling, having a computerized spell checker could help. Alternatively, she could enlist the help of a peer to proofread her work. To help Susan access content in her history text, she could use an electronic reader. She also could be allowed to have her exams read to her so she could demonstrate her knowledge of history without her reading disability being an obstacle. Bypassing cannot be used in a primary area of instruction, however. For instance, Susan cannot spell check her spelling test, but she can spell check her history homework. Similarly, she cannot have a reading test read to her, but it would be appropriate to have a history test read to her. Also, bypassing a skill does not necessarily mean that the skill should not be remediated. Susan may need both spelling and reading instruction, either as part of her English class or in a more intensive pullout type of setting. Finally, bypass strategies should encourage student independence. For example, Susan might be better off learning to use a spell checker rather than rely on a peer proofreader.

Teachers can also provide accommodations in their *instructional methods, materials, grouping, and classroom management* to help students succeed. For example, if Ramos has attention problems, he might be seated near the front of the room, and he might benefit from a special system of rewards and consequences as well as a classroom from which "busy" bulletin board displays are removed. All these are classroom management accommodations. A change in classroom instruction would be to call on Ramos frequently during class discussions and to allow him to earn points toward his grade for appropriate participation. Ramos might pay better attention in a small group—a grouping change—and he might be better able to comprehend his textbooks if the key ideas are highlighted—a materials accommodation.

A third option for accommodating students with special needs is to provide *intensive instruction on basic skills and learning strategies*. Often a special education teacher carries out this instruction in a resource room. This approach assumes that basic skills and learning strategies are prerequisites for successful general education experiences. It also assumes that some children require instruction delivered with a greater degree of intensity than can reasonably be provided by a general educator responsible for 20–30 students (Bursuck, Smith, Munk, Damer, Mehlig, & Perry, 2004).

What classroom demands might this student have difficulty meeting? What bypass strategies or adaptations might help him demonstrate that he has learned his assignment as well as his classmates have?

Unfortunately, the results of research on whether skills taught in pullout programs transfer to the general education class are mixed (Kavale & Forness, 2000). Some studies show positive results (Freeman & Alkin, 2000; Marston, 1996; Snider, 1997), whereas others show minimal effects (Baker & Zigmond, 1995; Wang, Reynolds, & Walberg, 1988). Studies do suggest that teachers play an important role in determining whether skills taught in a separate setting transfer to their classrooms (Ellis & Lenz, 1996; Sabornie & de Bettencourt, 2004). For example, Ms. Henry had Jamie in her English literature class; Jamie was receiving pullout services on taking effective lecture notes. First, Ms. Henry found out from the special education teacher what strategy for note taking Jamie was learning. Then she reminded Jamie to perform the strategy before she delivered a lecture and sometimes even during a lecture. Finally, Ms. Henry collected Jamie's notes on a weekly basis to see whether she was performing the strategy correctly, giving specific feedback to her as needed and reporting her progress to the special education teacher.

An alternative is for the general education teacher to provide this type of instruction. This option is feasible when many students have similar instructional needs and when the teacher can easily monitor skill development. For example, Mr. Higgins, a seventh-grade science teacher, lectures frequently. As a result, students need to be proficient note takers. At the beginning of the school year, Mr. Higgins noticed during a routine check of student notebooks that many students were not taking adequate notes. With assistance from the special education teacher, he taught note taking as part of science. Three students for whom note taking was especially difficult handed in their notes each day so Mr. Higgins could monitor their progress. Working Together discusses a co-teaching situation in which the general education teacher is developing a strategy to provide accommodations in her classroom with the help of the special educator.

fyi

In the multitier approach described in the Professional Edge on pages 326–327 in Chapter 9, students can receive intensive instruction without having to be referred for special education.

● **Modifications** Instructional or curricular **modifications** are made when the content expectations are altered and the performance outcomes expected of students change (Giangreco, 2007; Nolet & McLaughlin, 2005). Typically, students who receive modifications have behavioral and/or intellectual disabilities that are so severe that the curricular expectations in general education are inappropriate. These are usually the same students described in Chapter 4 as being eligible for alternate assessments. Instructional modifications are generally of two types: teaching less content and

> Students who receive modifications have behavioral and/or intellectual disabilities that are so severe that the curricular expectations in general education are inappropriate.

The Reluctant Co-Teacher

Juanita Kirk, a math teacher, initially was excited about co-teaching with Susan Harris, the special educator assigned to the seventh-grade team. Now, though, she is disillusioned. Although Susan was offered paid planning time during the summer, she declined to participate, explaining that she had made her family the focus of her summers and that she would not make professional commitments during that time. Juanita could understand that, but then, at their first meeting in the fall, Susan explained to Juanita that she had always disliked math and had not studied it since she was in high school. She said that she would be most comfortable adjusting to co-teaching by spending the first semester taking notes for students, learning the curriculum, and then helping individual students after instruction had occurred. She stated clearly that she did not have much time for preparing outside class given all her other responsibilities, and she also made it clear that she did not consider it her responsibility to grade student work.

Juanita was surprised. This was not at all what she expected co-teaching to be. She envisioned a partnership in which she and her colleague not only could make instruction more intensive but also could energize math instruction by using various grouping arrangements and brainstorming new ways to reach their students. Now six weeks into the school year, she is beginning to think that co-teaching is more like having an assistant in the classroom—an assistant who is highly paid for not doing very much work. She wonders if this is how co-teaching looks in English, the other seventh-grade course to which Susan is assigned. If you were Juanita, how would you address this situation?

Addressing the Dilemma

These are some ideas Juanita could use to make the co-teaching situation with Susan more productive:

- Juanita should find a quiet time and a private place to discuss the situation with Susan. She should directly relate to Susan that she is disappointed in how co-teaching has occurred thus far and then wait to see what Susan has to say.

- If Juanita suspects that Susan lacks confidence in her ability to teach math, she might try to broach this topic using a comment such as this: "You've mentioned that you haven't had math since high school. What a change it must be to be assigned to this class! I think we need to talk about topics we're teaching this year that are most familiar to you so that I don't inadvertently ask you to lead instruction in an area you haven't even thought about for years." This type of statement might prompt Susan to describe more fully what she could do in the classroom.

- As an alternative, Juanita might try being more proactive. For example, she might plan a co-taught set of lessons that call for students to be in three groups, one group having the purpose of reviewing previously taught information (for example, basic problem solving, fractions). She could explain to Susan that after more than a month of adjusting to having a two-teacher classroom, she was ready to try something new and then describe the plan, offering Susan the review group to lead. If Susan expressed reluctance, Juanita could request that they try this for one week and then review the plan's success.

---

teaching different content (Nolet & McLaughlin, 2005). For example, in order to meet district grade-level science standards, Ms. Lamb's class was learning to label the parts of the human digestive system and state the purpose for each. Manny, a student with a severe intellectual disability included in Ms. Lamb's class, met the same learning standard by pointing to his stomach when asked where food goes when it is eaten. This is an example of teaching less content. In contrast, teaching different content means that the curricular outcomes are different from those of the rest of the class. For example, an instructional goal for Tony, a student with autism, is to remain calm when there is a change in the classroom schedule.

It is important to reserve instructional modifications for students with only the most significant disabilities. Otherwise, instructional modifications reduce a student's opportunity to learn critical knowledge, skills, and concepts in a given subject, leaving gaps in learning that can interfere with meeting school standards and that can be a disadvantage in later school years and beyond. For example, when one class was learning four reasons for the worldwide spread of AIDS, Steven, a student with a learning disability, was required to learn only two reasons, because he had difficulty remembering information. However, when Steven was required to take the state high-stakes science test, he was held responsible for learning the same information about AIDS as everyone else. It would have been more effective for the school to help Steven better remember science content by using mnemonic devices rather than reducing the amount of information. In short, reducing or simplifying content inappropriately can lead to watering down the curriculum.

Step 6: Differentiate Instruction

After you have brainstormed possible accommodations or modifications, you can implement the *D* step in INCLUDE, which involves selecting strategies to try. A number of guidelines are suggested here to help you decide which strategies to select.

- **Select Age-Appropriate Strategies**   Students' accommodations and modifications should match their age. For example, using a third-grade book as a supplement for an eighth-grade science student who reads at the third-grade level would embarrass the student. In such a situation, a bypass strategy such as an audiotaped textbook would be preferable if the student has the necessary background and intellectual skills to listen to the book with understanding. A good rule of thumb is to remember that no students, whether in first or twelfth grade and regardless of their special needs, want to use what they perceive as "baby" books or materials.

- **Select the Easiest Approach First**   Accommodations need to be feasible for the general education teacher. Although making accommodations and modifications often means some additional work for you, it should not require so much time and effort that it interferes with teaching the entire class. For instance, it is easier to circle the 6 out of 12 math problems you want Maria to complete than to create a separate worksheet just for her.

- **Select Accommodations and Modifications You Agree With**   You are more likely to implement an approach successfully if you believe in it (Polloway, Bursuck, Jayanthi, Epstein, & Nelson, 1996), especially in the area of behavior management. For example, in selecting rewards for good behavior, if you are uncomfortable with giving candy, try giving time for desirable activities such as time on the computer. However, accommodations and modifications should not be considered only in light of teacher beliefs. IDEA is clear that the unique needs of students take precedence over the convenience of schools. With imagination and some input from special educators, you will undoubtedly find strategies that match your teaching approach while maximizing your students' learning.

- **Determine Whether You Are Dealing With a "Can't" or a "Won't" Problem**   Blankenship and Lilly (1981) describe a "can't" problem as one in which the student, no matter how highly motivated, is unable to do what is expected. A "won't" problem is one in which the student could do what is expected but is not motivated to do so. Each type of problem may require a different accommodation. A student unable to do what is expected might need a bypass strategy; a student unwilling to do the work might need a behavior management strategy. Making this distinction can also save you time. For example, if a student fails a test because she doesn't feel like working on the day of the test, then a teacher's attempt to provide extra tutorial assistance will likely be wasted effort. "Can't" and "won't" problems are particularly relevant for adolescents, who are often less likely than younger students to work to please their teachers.

- **Give Students Choices**   Adding the element of choice challenges students to make decisions, encourages them to be more responsible for their own learning, and allows them to more readily demonstrate what they know by tapping into their strengths and interests (Anderson, 2007; Carolan & Guinn, 2007).

● **Select Strategies with Demonstrated Effectiveness**   Over the past 30 years, a massive body of professional literature on effective teaching practices has accumulated. Being familiar with this research can help you avoid fads and other unvalidated practices. The strategies suggested throughout this text are based on research and form a starting point for your understanding of validated practices. Such an understanding has always been important, but it is particularly important in view of the recent emphasis placed on evidence-based practices in NCLB. An important way to stay professionally current is to read relevant professional journals.

Step 7: Evaluate Student Progress

Although there are many effective teaching practices, it is difficult to predict which will be effective for a given student. As a result, once an accommodation or modification is implemented, the *E* step of INCLUDE is essential: Evaluate strategy effectiveness. You can track effectiveness through grades; observations; analysis of student work; portfolios; performance assessments; and teacher, parent, and student ratings. Evaluating this information will help you decide whether to continue, change, or discontinue an intervention. In an RtI model, this evaluation information can be used to assign students to more intensive instructional tiers, including special education. For more information on this approach, see the Professional Edge in Chapter 9 on page 326.

In the next section, the relationship between your classroom and the diverse needs of learners is examined. As you have read, the use of effective practices allows teachers to accommodate more diversity in their classrooms while at the same time reducing the need for making more individualized adaptations. The key aspects of classroom environments are shown in Figure 5.1. These features include classroom management, classroom grouping, instructional materials, and instructional methods.

INCLUDE

Analyze
and Reflect

What impact would the use of universal design have on teacher implementation of the INCLUDE strategy?

Analyze
and Reflect

What are the similarities and differences between INCLUDE and differentiated instruction?

fyi

The rest of this chapter aims to help you answer two questions: How can I teach my whole class so that students' individual difficulties are minimized? What changes in instructional environment might I still need to make to meet individual students' special needs?

How Is an Inclusive Classroom Managed?

Classroom management comprises all of the things teachers do to organize students, space, time, and materials to maximize effective teaching and student learning (Wong & Wong, 1998). As described here, classroom management involves physical organization, routines for classroom business, classroom climate, behavior management, and use of time. The classroom management strategies described in the following sections are part of a larger body of strategies for promoting positive student behavior called *positive behavior supports (PBS)*. PBS is described in greater depth in Chapter 12. You also may need to use the INCLUDE strategy to make reasonable accommodations for students with special needs in all of these areas.

Physical Organization

The way a classroom is physically organized can affect student learning and behavior in a number of areas (Kerr & Nelson, 2006). Carefully arranged classrooms can decrease noise and disruption, improve the level and quality of student interactions, and increase the percentage of time that students spend on academic tasks (Paine, Radicchi, Rosellini, Deutchman, & Darch, 1983). The physical organization of a classroom influences learning conditions for all students, as well as the accessibility of instructional presentations and materials for students with sensory and physical disabilities. Physical organization includes

FIGURE *5.1*   **Overview of Classroom Environments**

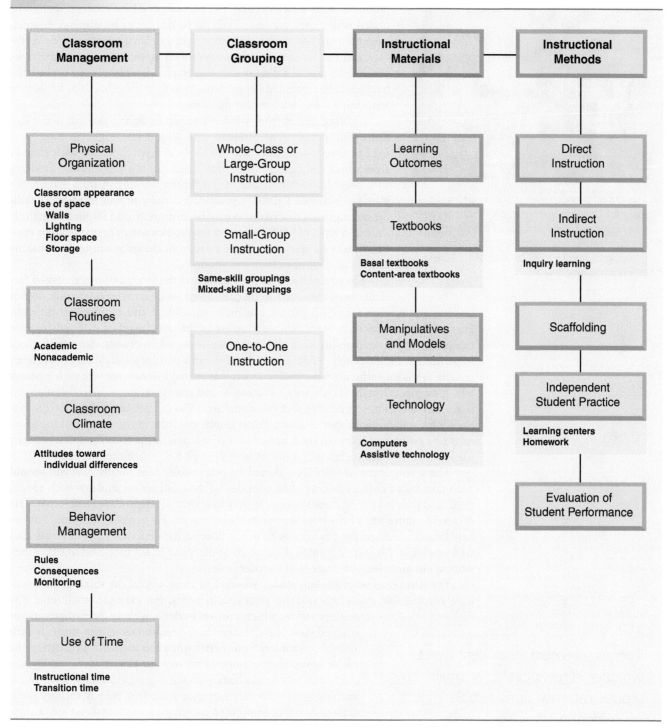

the appearance of the classroom and the use of space, including wall areas, lighting, floor space, and storage.

Wall areas can be used for decorating, posting rules, displaying student work, and reinforcing class content, sometimes through the use of bulletin boards. For example, one teacher taught a note-taking strategy and posted the steps on a bulletin board to help her

This is a teacher-centered grouping arrangement for large-group instruction. What are some advantages and disadvantages of this strategy for students with special needs? What other ways of grouping students should be part of a teacher's instructional repertoire?

students remember them. In using wall space, keep in mind two possible problems. First, wall displays may divert students with attention problems from concentrating on instruction. These students should be placed where they are least likely to be distracted by displays. Second, students may not notice that important information appears on a display, and teachers may need to direct their attention to it. For example, Ms. Huerta posted a display showing graphic representations of the basic fractions. She reminded her students to look at these fractions while they were doing their independent math work.

Lighting, either from windows or ceiling lights, also can affect students with special needs. Students with hearing loss might need adequate light to speech-read; they also are likely to have problems with glare in areas where the light source comes from behind the speaker. Students with visual impairments also have difficulty working in areas that are not glare free and well lighted. Occasionally, students with learning disabilities or emotional disturbances may be sensitive to and respond negatively to certain types of light. In most cases, problems with lighting can be remedied easily by seating students away from the glare caused by sunshine coming through the classroom windows.

The organization of floor space and the kinds and placement of furniture used also need to be considered. For example, floors that do not have a nonslip surface can make wheelchair and other travel difficult. Furniture that is placed in lanes can block access to the chalkboard or materials such as computers and make mobility difficult for students in wheelchairs or students with visual impairments. Tables, pencil sharpeners, and chalkboards that are too high may prove inaccessible to students who use wheelchairs. Desks that are too low can interfere with students who have prostheses (artificial limbs). Placement and configuration of special equipment in science labs, computer centers, and vocational areas also can present difficulties in accessibility for students with special needs. For example, the lathe in the woodworking room might be positioned too high for a person in a wheelchair to operate; the space between work areas in the science lab might not be wide enough for a wheelchair to pass.

The arrangement of your class should be predictable. This means that you should not make major changes without first considering their impact on students with special needs and then informing these students so they have time to adapt. For example, Mr. Tate decided to move one of the bookshelves in his classroom. He noticed, however, that the new location blocked the passageway from the door to the desk of a student in his class who was blind. Mr. Tate informed the student of the move in advance, and together they worked out an alternative route to the student's desk.

The arrangement of student desks, whether in rows, circles, or small groups, can have considerable impact on students with special needs. For example, traditional row configurations, which provide students with an immediate, unobstructed view of the teacher, have been shown to help students with attention disorders focus better when the teacher is instructing the whole group at one time. However, the placement of desks into clusters of four works better when using mixed-ability, cooperative learning groups to help integrate a student who is socially withdrawn. Another important consideration about floor space concerns student monitoring: Teachers should be able to see all parts of the classroom at all times, whether they are teaching large or small groups or are working at their desks. Designing such visual access means that all specially designated areas in the classroom, such as learning/interest centers, computer stations, small-group instructional areas, and study carrels, need to be positioned so they can be monitored.

An additional area of physical organization is storage. For example, students with visual disabilities may need to store equipment such as tape recorders, large-print books,

The arrangement of student desks, whether in rows, circles, or small groups, can have considerable impact on students with special needs.

braille books, and magnifying devices. For students with severe disabilities, space might be needed to store book holders, paper holders, page turners, braces, crutches, and communication boards.

Routines for Classroom Business

Video Homework Exercise

Go to the Homework and Exercises section in Chapter 5 of MyEducationLab to see two teachers co-teaching in a general education classroom and discussing their teaching methods with a mentor.

Establishing clear routines in both academic and nonacademic areas is important for two reasons. First, routines that are carefully structured (that is, clear to students and used consistently) reduce nonacademic time and increase learning time. Second, you can prevent many discipline problems by having predictable classroom routines.

Most students, especially those with special needs, find stability in knowing that classroom activities will be similar each day. In the absence of this stability, misbehavior often follows. Many examples of misbehavior can be related to breaks in school routines. On the day of a field trip, elementary school students are more likely to hit or push, to delay beginning assignments, and to do poor work. In middle schools and high schools, teachers often dread shortened schedules for assemblies and other school programs because of increased student behavior problems.

You can create daily classroom routines that help students learn. For example, you might expect fourth-graders to enter your classroom each morning, begin their morning work, and read quietly if they finish before instruction begins. Having routines for sharing time, setting up science experiments, preparing to go to physical education, moving to the computer lab, and so on helps students meet your expectations. Routines are especially helpful to students who need a strong sense of structure in classroom life. In secondary schools, routines might include having specific lab procedures, starting each class with a five-minute review, or scheduling a particular activity on the same day every week. For example, in a geometry class, students who complete their assignments might choose to begin the day's homework, complete a Math Challenger worksheet from the activity file, or work on research papers or other long-term projects.

Classroom Climate

A number of authors have noted that classroom climate contributes significantly to the number and seriousness of classroom behavior problems (Jones & Jones, 1990; Marzano & Marzano, 2003) as well as student achievement (Stipek, 2006). The classroom climate concerns the overall atmosphere in the classroom—whether it is friendly or unfriendly, pleasant or unpleasant, and so on. Climate is influenced by the attitudes of the teacher and students toward individual differences. For instance, is the classroom characterized by a cooperative or a competitive atmosphere? Is the classroom a safe place for all students to take risks? Are skills for interacting positively with children and adults actively supported in the classroom?

DIMENSIONS OF diversity

Kleinfeld (cited in Gay, 2002), in her 1974/1975 research on Athabascan Inuit and American Indian children, found that the most effective teachers demonstrated personal caring and concern for students while at the same time demanding and facilitating high academic performance. Foster (1995, 1997) and Ladson-Billings (1994) observed similar traits among effective teachers of African American students.

Teachers who communicate respect and trust to their students are more successful in creating a positive classroom environment in which fewer behavior problems occur (Arends, 2004; Marzano, 2003). For example, Mr. Elliott reprimanded a student who talked out of turn by saying, "I know you have a question about your work, and I'm glad you care enough to ask for help; but I need to have you raise your hand because I can only help people one at a time." Mr. Elliott showed respect for the student and built the student's trust by not putting her down. Yet Mr. Elliott stuck to his rule about not speaking before being called on and explained why it was important. Similarly, Ms. Belson asked Harriet to define the word *diffident*. Harriet gave an incorrect definition, saying it meant "being bored." Ms. Belson said, "Harriet, I can see how you might think the meaning is 'bored' because *diffident* looks a lot like *indifferent*. The word actually means 'lacking in confidence.'"

You can build the overall quality of your communication with your students in many small ways. For example, finding the time each week to speak privately with students lets them know that you care about them as individuals. Asking older students sincere questions about their friends, out-of-school activities, or part-time jobs also conveys your interest in them. Taking the time to write positive comments on papers lets students know that you appreciate their strengths and do not focus only on their needs. When you encourage each student to achieve his or her own potential without continually comparing students to one another, you are communicating the idea that each class member has a valuable contribution to make. Teachers who fail to take these small steps toward positive communication with students or who publicly embarrass a student or punish a group because of the behavior of a few soon may create a negative classroom climate that thwarts appropriate and effective learning.

Behavior Management

Behavior management refers to teacher activities that directly promote positive student behavior. It includes establishing classroom rules, providing consistent consequences, and monitoring student behavior.

Rules help create a sense of order and expectations for a classroom, and they form a significant first step in setting up a learning environment based on preventive classroom management. Teachers who are effective classroom managers have well-defined rules for their classrooms (for example, Olson, Platt, & Dieker, 2007; Ornstein & Lasley, 2004).

Effective classroom rules share three key characteristics: They are brief and specific, positively worded, and clearly understood by students (Alberto & Trautman, 2005; Doyle, 1990) and accommodate students from different cultures (Grossman, 1995).

Be sure to explain rules carefully to your students so that they are understood. Post rules during the first weeks of school, explain and discuss them, and model them for students. Early attention to setting your classroom expectations has a yearlong payoff. By rehearsing and focusing student attention on rules, you make them part of students' understanding of their classroom interactions. If you do not take this time to teach the rules, too often they become merely a bulletin board display, ignored by teachers and students alike.

Also, be sure that your rules accommodate students from different cultures. For example, rules about respecting other students' property may be puzzling for Latino students, for whom sharing one's belongings is a highly valued activity. Similarly, rules related to aggressive behavior may need to be enforced with care for students whose parents expect them to stand up for themselves, especially when someone says something derogatory about a student's family (Grossman, 1995). It is important to note that taking cultural differences into account does not necessarily mean that the rules need to be changed, only that the rules may need to be more carefully explained and enforced.

In addition to having clear expectations, teachers also need to tie their expectations to a set of consistent *consequences*. This means demonstrating that the same consequences apply to everyone and on a consistent basis. For example, Ms. DuBois has a rule that students are to raise their hands before speaking in class. She has also established the consequence that students receive one point for each class period they go without a single talk-out. Points earned figure into each student's grades for the class. Ms. DuBois is careful only to give points to students who meet the criterion of no talk-outs per day, regardless of who is involved or what the circumstances are, because she knows that enforcing rules arbitrarily greatly diminishes their effectiveness. Ms. DuBois also is sure to provide specific verbal praise along with the points to increase students' future chances of behaving appropriately without receiving points. Of course, Ms. DuBois realizes that sometimes rules need to be individualized, as in the case of Justin, a student with Tourette's syndrome, who is allowed one talk-out per class as specified on the behavior intervention plan (BIP) included in his individualized education program (IEP).

Finally, teachers need to *monitor* student classroom behaviors frequently. For example, you should scan the room to check that students are following the rules. To do this, you always need to have a clear view of the entire class, regardless of the activity in which you or the class are engaged. When student behavior is not carefully monitored, students

Research Note

Research suggests that the most effective classroom rules are ones that students develop themselves and express with teacher guidance (Bullara, 1993).

DIMENSIONS OF

diversity

If your classroom includes students who are not native English speakers, you need to make sure that they understand classroom expectations. You may need to explain in concrete terms in a one-to-one situation what you expect, with the possible help of a translator, a student's parents, or both.

choose not to follow the rules consistently. For example, Charmaine was a student in Ms. Patrick's fifth-grade class who had behavior problems. Ms. Patrick had a rule that students needed to complete all their independent work before they could go to the computer station to play a problem-solving game. Ms. Patrick did not have time to monitor Charmaine's behavior. One day, she saw Charmaine at the computer station and asked her whether she had completed her assignments. Not only had Charmaine not completed her assignments on that day, but she hadn't done any work for the past three days. Thereafter, Ms. Patrick was careful to monitor the work progress of all her students.

Use of Time

The way teachers use time in the classroom is one of the most important aspects of classroom organization. Effectively using instructional time and managing transition time constitute two particularly important tasks.

● **Using Instructional Time**   The amount of time that students are meaningfully and successfully engaged in academic activities in school is referred to as **academic learning time** (Arends, 2004). Research has shown that more academic learning time in a classroom results in increased student learning (Berliner, 1990). Time usage is particularly important for students with special needs, who may need more time to learn than their peers.

Paine and colleagues (1983) suggest several ways in which teachers can maximize academic learning time. One way is to minimize the time spent on organizational activities such as lunch counts, opening activities, getting drinks, sharpening pencils, cleaning out desks, and going to the bathroom. For example, teach students how to perform organizational tasks efficiently and how to hold them to a firm time schedule when carrying them out. Another way is to select activities that have the greatest teaching potential and that contribute most to students' achieving the core school curriculum. Although learning activities can be fun, they should ultimately be selected for the purpose of teaching students something important. Finally, the strategies described in this chapter and throughout this book for managing your classroom, grouping your students, and adapting your methods and materials also help ensure the productive use of your students' time. One specific technique to increase the academic learning time of your students is described in the Professional Edge on pages 168–169.

● **Managing Transition Time**   Just as important as the amount of time spent in activities is the management of transition time. **Transition time** is the time it takes to change from one activity to another. Transition time occurs when students remain at their seats and change from one subject to another, move from their seats to an activity in another part of the classroom, move from somewhere else in the classroom back to their seats, leave the classroom to go outside or to another part of the school building, or come back into the classroom from outside or from another part of the building (Paine et al., 1983).

Research studies show that teachers sometimes waste academic learning time by not managing transitions carefully (Ornstein & Lasley, 2004). Paine and colleagues (1983, p. 85) suggest that you have rules devoted specifically to transitions and that you teach these rules directly to students. As with all rules, those for transitions need to be consistently monitored and reinforced.

The way you organize classroom materials also can affect the management of transitions. For example, you need to have all materials ready for each subject and activity. In addition, materials should be organized so that they are easily accessible. No matter how well organized your transitions are, you still may need to adapt them for some students with special needs. Students with physical disabilities may need more time to take out or put away their books. Students with physical and visual disabilities may have mobility

Info Sheet Homework Exercise

Go to the Homework and Exercises section in Chapter 5 of MyEducationLab for a list of websites dedicated to inclusion of students with low-incidence disabilities.

DIMENSIONS OF

diversity

For ideas about designing lesson plans for English-language learners, go to http://coe.sdsu.edu/people/imora/Mora Modules/ELDInstruction.htm.

Teacher Artifacts Homework Exercise

Go to the Homework and Exercises section in Chapter 5 of MyEducationLab to learn about the kinds of rules teachers use.

Using "Sponges" to Increase Academic Learning Time

You almost always have times during the day when you have a minute or two before a scheduled academic activity or before the class goes to lunch, an assembly, or recess. You can fill that extra time with productive activities by using "sponges." Sponges are activities that fit into brief periods of time and give students practice or review on skills and content you have already covered in class. The following lists of sponges can help you "soak up" that extra classroom time.

Lower-Grade Sponges

1. Tell children to be ready to state one playground rule.

2. Tell children to be ready to list the names of children in the class that begin with *J* or *M* and so on.

3. Tell children to be ready to draw something that is drawn only with circles.

4. Tell children to be ready to think of a good health habit.

5. Flash fingers—have children tell how many fingers you hold up.

6. Say numbers, days of the week, and months and have children tell what comes next.

7. Ask what number comes between two numbers: for example, 31 and 33, 45 and 47.

8. Ask children what number comes before or after 46, 52, 13, and so on.

9. Write a word on the board. Have children make a list of words that rhyme with it.

10. Count to 100 by 2s, 5s, 10s, and so on, either orally or in writing.

11. Think of animals that live on a farm, in the jungle, in water, and so forth.

12. Name fruits, vegetables, meats, and the like.

13. List things you can touch, things you can smell, and so on.

Dismissal Sponges

1. "I Spy"—ask children to find something in the room that starts with *M, P,* and so on.

2. Ask children to find something in the room that has the sound of short *a,* long *a,* and so forth.

3. Number rows or tables. Signal the number of the table with fingers, and allow children to leave accordingly.

4. Count in order or by 2s, 5s, and so on.

5. Say the days of the week, the months of the year, and so on.

---

problems that cause them to take more time with such transitional activities as getting into instructional groups or moving from room to room. Furthermore, you may need an individualized system of rewards or other consequences to guide students with ADHD or behavior disorders through transition times.

How Can You Group All Your Students for Instruction in Inclusive Classrooms?

Students with special needs benefit from a variety of classroom grouping arrangements, including large- and small-group instruction, one-to-one instruction, and mixed- and same-skill groupings. The flexible use of classroom grouping arrangements is an important part of differentiated instruction (Broderick, Mehta-Parekh, & Reid, 2005). Remember that the particular arrangement you choose depends on your instructional objectives as well as your students' particular needs.

6. Ask what day it is, what month it is, what date it is, what year it is. Ask how many months are in a year, how many days are in a week, and so on.

7. Use reward activities:

"We have had a good day! Who helped it to be a good day for all of us? Betty, you brought flowers to brighten our room. You may leave. John, you remembered to rinse your hands, good for you. You may leave. Ellen showed us that she could be quiet coming into the room today. You may leave, Ellen. Bob remembered his library book all by himself. Dawn walked all the way to the playground—she remembered our safety rules. Lori brought things to share with us. Tom surprised us with a perfect paper—he must have practiced. . . ."

Students' good deeds can be grouped together to speed up dismissal. The teacher can finish with, "You're all learning to be very thoughtful. I'm very proud of all of you and you should be very proud of yourselves."

8. Use flashcards. A first correct answer earns dismissal.

9. Review the four basic shapes. Each child names an object in the room in the shape of a triangle, circle, square, or rectangle.

Upper–Grade Sponges

1. List the continents.

2. Name as many gems or precious stones as you can.

3. List as many states as you can.

4. Write an abbreviation, a roman numeral, a trademark, a proper name (biological), or a proper name (geographical).

5. Name as many countries and their capitals as you can.

6. List the names of five parts of the body above the neck that are spelled with three letters.

7. List one manufactured item for each letter of the alphabet.

8. List as many nouns in the room as you can.

9. List one proper noun for each letter of the alphabet.

10. Name as many parts of a car as you can.

11. List as many kinds of trees as you can.

12. List as many personal pronouns as you can.

13. Name as many politicians as you can.

How many sponges can you think of for your grade or subject area? Additional ideas for sponges can be found at the Busy Teachers' Web Site K–12: www.ceismc. gatech .edu/busyt.

Source: From "Effective Teaching for Higher Achievement," by D. Sparks and G. M. Sparks, 1984, *Educational Leadership, 49*(7).

Whole-Class or Large-Group Instruction

Students with special needs benefit from both whole-class (or large-group) and small-group instruction. One advantage of whole-class instruction is that students spend the entire time with the teacher. In small-group instruction, students spend part of the time with the teacher and also spend time working independently while the teacher works with other small groups. Research shows that the more time students spend with the teacher, the more likely they are to be engaged (Rimm-Kaufman, La Paro, Downer, & Pianta, 2005) and the more they learn (Rosenshine, 1997; Rosenshine & Stevens, 1986). This increase in learning may be because students are more likely to go off task when they are working on their own, particularly when they have learning or behavior problems. Whatever grouping arrangements you use, try to make sure that students spend as much time as possible working with you.

Another advantage of whole-group instruction is that it does not single out students with special needs as being different from their peers. However, you may need to make accommodations within whole-group instruction for students with special needs. For example, students in Mr. Nichols's fourth-grade class were reading *Charlotte's Web* as a large-group instructional activity. Simone read more slowly than the rest of the class. To help her

Info Sheet Homework Exercise

Go to the Homework and Exercises section in Chapter 5 of MyEducationLab to learn about ways to effectively use peer partners in inclusive classrooms.

keep up, Mr. Nichols provided the book on tape. He also gave Simone more time to answer comprehension questions about the story in class because it took her longer to look up some of the answers. In another example, before his lectures, a high school science teacher identified technical words he was going to use and then worked before school with a small group of students with vocabulary problems to help them learn the words.

Small-Group Instruction

You may encounter situations in which small-group instruction is more appropriate for students with special needs. You can use same-skill groupings and mixed-skill groupings in setting up your groups.

Same-skill groupings, often referred to as *homogeneous groupings,* are helpful when some but not all students are having trouble mastering a particular skill and need more instruction and practice. For example, Ms. Rodgers was showing her students how to divide fractions that have a common denominator. She gave her class a quiz to see who had learned how to do the problems. She found that all but five students had mastered the skill. The next day, Ms. Rodgers worked with these five students while the rest of the class did an application activity. Small-group instruction is not only for special education or remedial students; most students benefit from extra help in a small group at one time or another. In fact, many times students with special needs do not need extra instruction.

Small same-skill groups have also proven effective in basic skill areas when students are performing well below most of the class (Bursuck et al., 2004; Mosteller, Light, & Sachs, 1996). For example, Lori is in Ms. Hubbard's fourth-grade class and is reading at the second-grade level. Lori is learning decoding and vocabulary skills in a small group with other students who read at her level. Because the group is small and homogeneous, Ms. Hubbard is able to proceed in small steps, present many examples, and allow students to master skills before they move on. Lori is making progress and feels good about herself because she is becoming a better reader.

Clearly, some students do require instruction that is more individualized and intensive than can be provided in the large group (Bursuck et al., 2004). However, small same-skill groups should be used only when attempts to make accommodations in the large group have been unsuccessful. Same-skill groups tend to become permanent and take on a life of their own. Thus, the ultimate goal of any small group should be its eventual dissolution. Also, on many days students can benefit from instruction with the rest of the class. For example, Lori's group participates in large-group reading when the teacher is reading a story and the class is working on listening comprehension. Another potential problem in using same-skill groupings is the danger that students in a low-achieving group in one area will be placed in low-achieving groups in other areas even though their skill levels do not justify it. For example, just because Lori is in the lowest-level reading group does not automatically mean she needs to be in low-achieving groups in other areas such as math.

The major advantage of **mixed-skill groupings,** or *heterogeneous groupings,* is that they provide students with special needs a range of positive models for both academic and social behavior. In mixed-skill groupings, students often help each other so such groups can also be a vehicle for providing direct instruction to individual students, something for which classroom teachers often do not have the time. In addition, mixed-skill groups, like large groups, tend not to single out students with special needs.

One-to-One Instruction

Providing **one-to-one instruction** for students with special needs can be very effective under some circumstances. In this grouping arrangement, students work with a teacher, a paraprofessional, or a computer on well-sequenced, self-paced materials that are geared to their specific level. For example, Waldo is having trouble with addition and subtraction facts. For 15 minutes each day, he works at the classroom computer station on an individualized drill-and-practice program. Right now he is working on addition facts through 10. When he masters these, the software will automatically provide more difficult problems. Shamika, a student with a moderate to severe intellectual disability, works with a paraprofessional on selecting food items for a balanced lunch while the rest of the class listens to a presentation on the process of performing a nutritional analysis.

Although one-to-one instruction may be appropriate in some circumstances, it is not necessarily the grouping arrangement of choice in either general or special education. First, it is inefficient; when it is carried out by the classroom teacher the extensive use of one-to-one instruction will result in less instructional time for everyone. Second, the logistics of one-to-one instruction sometimes require that students complete much independent work while the teacher moves from student to student. This can lead to high levels of off-task behavior, a problem many students with special needs experience (Hardman, Drew, & Egan, 2005; Mercer & Pullen, 2005). Third, the lack of peer models in one-to-one instruction makes it more difficult to motivate students, a problem particularly relevant at the high school level (Ellis & Sabornie, 1990). Sometimes, habitual use of one-to-one instruction can exclude students from critical social interactions. Finally, when a student requires this type of instruction for extended periods of time, further analysis is required of her needs and instructional setting.

How Can You Evaluate Instructional Materials for Inclusive Classrooms?

Learning Outcomes

Instructional materials are designed to cover a range of *learning outcomes*. These outcomes reflect Bloom's revised taxonomy related to levels of thought. The six levels of thought, from lowest to highest, include remembering, understanding, applying, analyzing, evaluating, and creating (Anderson & Krathwohl, 2001, pp. 67–68):

1. *Remembering* involves retrieving, recognizing, and recalling relevant knowledge from long-term memory. For example, Ms. Lopez's American history class was studying the Revolutionary War. One of her remembering outcomes was for students to recall two major colonial leaders.

2. *Understanding* involves constructing meaning from oral, written, and graphic messages through interpreting, giving examples, classifying, summarizing, inferring, comparing, and explaining. For understanding, Ms. Lopez's students compared the family backgrounds of two colonial leaders.

3. *Applying* involves using information to solve a problem or produce some result. For this level of outcome, Ms. Lopez's students constructed a theory as to why colonial leaders refused to abolish slavery.

4. *Analyzing* is breaking up material into its parts and determining how the parts relate to one another and to an overall structure or purpose through differentiating, organizing, and attributing. For analyzing, Ms. Lopez's students differentiated how the colonists reacted to each British provocation leading up to the start of the Revolutionary War.

5. *Evaluating* involves making judgments based on criteria and standards through checking and critiquing. For this level of thought, students critiqued the colonial leaders as to their qualifications to lead the country as president.

6. *Creating,* the highest level of thought, involves putting together elements to form a coherent whole or reorganizing elements into a new pattern or structure through

Research Note

Vaughn and colleagues (2003) compared the effectiveness of three group sizes for providing supplemental instruction to struggling readers: 1:1 (1 teacher with 1 student); 1:3 (1 teacher with 3 students); and 1:10 (1 teacher with 10 students). Both the 1:1 and 1:3 grouping sizes were highly effective and significantly more effective in improving reading comprehension than the 1:10 grouping size.

Research Note

Elbaum, Moody, and Schumm (1999) asked third-grade students what they thought of mixed-skill grouping in reading. Students said that small-group work was often noisy, encouraged disruptive students, and made it harder to get help from the teacher. Children with reading problems were anxious when working in small mixed-skill groups, because the grouping made their problems more obvious. Some children who were high achieving felt that working with struggling readers hindered their progress.

generating, planning, and producing. For creating, some of Ms. Lopez's students composed a song about the colonial leaders.

Keep in mind several important points when selecting the levels of thought required by your students' learning outcomes. First, in general, select outcomes reflecting a range of levels of thought, even if a range is not represented in the textbooks you are using. Textbooks and teachers tend to stress remembering at the expense of other levels of thought. Second, base your selection of outcomes on your students' strengths and needs, not their labels. Teachers tend to choose outcomes requiring lower levels of thought for students with special needs, regardless of their learning profiles. Use the INCLUDE strategy to choose the appropriate level of learning for all of your students.

The nature of the instructional materials you use is another very important consideration in accommodating students with special needs in your classroom. Consider the learning outcomes you desire as you select instructional materials that include textbooks, manipulatives and models, and technology.

Textbooks

Basal textbooks (often called *basals*) are books used for instruction in any subject area that contain all the key components of the curriculum being taught for that subject. The careful evaluation of basals is vital because the selection of well-designed textbooks that require few accommodations for students with special needs can save you much time and energy. For example, a math basal that contains plenty of practice activities does not need to be adapted for students who require lots of practice to master a skill. Similarly, a history textbook that highlights critical vocabulary and includes clear context cues to help students figure out the words on their own may make it unnecessary for teachers to prepare extensive vocabulary study guides.

Fortunately, over the past 20 years, guidelines have been developed for distinguishing well-designed texts (Armbruster & Anderson, 1988; Coyne, Kame'enui, & Carnine, 2007; King-Sears, 2001). A set of questions to help you evaluate basals and other basic skills materials is included in the Professional Edge on pages 174–175. Carefully evaluating basals helps alert you to any accommodations you may need to make. For example, a spelling basal with little provision for review can be troublesome for students who have problems retaining information; you may want to develop review activities for every three lessons rather than every five, as is done in a given book.

Many teachers are choosing to develop or collect their own materials rather than depend on published basal series. For example, some teachers have their students read trade books instead of traditional reading books; others have their students engage in the actual writing process rather than or in addition to answering questions in a book. Still others involve their students in real-life math-problem solving rather than use basal math books. Even if your school does not use basals, the guidelines discussed here for teaching basic skills apply.

Content-area textbooks, which are books used for instruction in subject areas such as science and social studies, also need to be evaluated. In secondary schools, students are often expected to read their textbooks to access curriculum content (Sabornie & deBettencourt, 2004; Mercer & Pullen, 2005). Because students are required to read and understand their texts, often without previous instruction, the texts should be written at a level at which students can easily understand them. Armbruster and Anderson (1988) refer to readable textbooks as "considerate." Considerate textbooks are easier for students to use independently and require fewer teacher adaptations. The following guidelines refer to aspects of considerate textbooks involving content, organization, and quality of writing.

● **Check the Content Covered in the Text to See Whether It Stresses "Big Ideas" Rather Than Facts in Isolation** "Big ideas" are important principles that enable learners to understand the connections among facts and concepts they learn

(Coyne et al., 2007). For example, in a text that stressed facts in isolation, students learned that Rosa Parks was an important figure because she led the Montgomery bus boycott in 1955. In a text that stressed big ideas, students learned that the bus boycott, led by Rosa Parks in 1955, was carried out in response to the problem of segregation in the South in the early 1950s and that the boycott was the first in a series of civil rights protests eventually leading to the Civil Rights Act of 1965.

● **Check to See Whether Support Is Provided for Student Comprehension**
Support for student comprehension can be detected in the following three ways:

1. *Check the organization of the headings and subheadings.* Make an outline of the headings and subheadings in a few chapters. How reasonable is the structure revealed? Is it consistent with your knowledge of the subject matter?

2. *Check the consistency of organization in discussions of similar topics.* For example, in a science chapter on vertebrates, information about the different groups of vertebrates should be similarly organized; that is, if the section on amphibians discusses structure, body covering, subgroups, and reproduction, the section on reptiles should discuss the same topics, in the same order.

3. *Look for clear signaling of the structure.* A well-designed text includes information headings and subheadings. The most helpful headings are those that are the most specific about the content in the upcoming section. For example, the heading "Chemical Weathering" is a more helpful content clue than the heading "Another Kind of Weathering." A well-signaled text also includes format clues to organization. Page layouts, paragraphing, marginal notations, graphic aids, and the use of boldface, italics, and/or underlining can all serve to highlight or reinforce the structure. For example, a discussion of the four stages in the life cycle of butterflies could be signaled by using a separate, numbered paragraph for each state (that is, 1. Egg; 2. Larva; 3. Pupa; 4. Adult) and by including a picture for each stage. Finally, look for signal words and phrases that designate particular patterns of organization. For example, the phrases *in contrast* and *on the other hand* signal a compare-and-contrast organization, whereas the words *first, second,* and *third* indicate an enumeration or list pattern.

● **Check to See That Important Background Knowledge Is Activated**
Despite the importance of background knowledge for comprehension (Beck & McKeown, 2002; Marzano, 2004), many textbooks assume unrealistic levels of students' background knowledge (Gersten, Fuchs, Williams, & Baker, 2001). A failure to activate important background knowledge may be especially problematic for students with special needs, who are more likely to lack this information (Hallahan et al., 2005; Lerner, 2006). A number of textbook features indicate adequate attention to background knowledge. For example, social studies texts often activate background knowledge by providing definitions for important vocabulary content, displaying geographical information on maps, and featuring timelines delineating when key events took place (Coyne et al., 2007).

● **Check for Quality of Writing** The quality and clarity of writing can also affect student comprehension. Quality of writing can be evaluated in five ways:

1. *Look for explicit or obvious connectives, or conjunctions.* The absence of connectives can be particularly troublesome when the connective is a causal one (for example, *because, since, therefore*), which is frequently the case in content-area textbooks. Therefore, look especially for causal connectives. For example, the sentence *Because the guard cells relax, the openings close* is a better explanation than the sentences *The guard cells relax. The openings close.*

*R*esearch Note

Harniss, Caros, and Gersten (2007) found that students with special needs learned more history content, were more actively engaged in instruction, and answered more questions correctly when using a text that linked content information into "big ideas," supported and guided students in their use of the information, and provided extensive practice and review. The comparison group was instructed using a traditional nationally distributed text.

fyi

Taped textbooks can be helpful for students with reading problems. Ellis (1996) suggests that you tape only key sections of texts and that you highlight the main points in the text to help students focus on the most critical information. The Technology Notes feature for Chapter 10 describes a strategic reader that has many technological supports for students to make reading their textbooks easier.

Guidelines for Evaluating Basals and Other Basic Skills Curricula

Before evaluating any material, read the evaluative questions below and place an asterisk next to each that is critical for the type of material you are examining. Answer each question with yes or no. Examine all your responses in a single area, paying special attention to the questions you designated as critical. Rate each area inadequate (1), adequate (2), or excellent (3). If the area is inadequate, designate whether the features can be easily modified (M).

Rating Scale:	Inadequate	Adequate	Excellent	Easily modified
	1	2	3	M

1 2 3 M   Effectiveness of Material

Yes No   Is information provided that indicates successful field testing or class testing of the material?
Yes No   Has the material been successfully field tested with students similar to the target population?
Yes No   Are testimonials and publisher claims clearly differentiated from research findings?

1 2 3 M   Prerequisite Skills

Yes No   Are the prerequisite student skills and abilities needed to work with ease in the material specified?
Yes No   Are the prerequisite student skills and abilities compatible with the objectives of the material?
Yes No   Are the prerequisite student skills and abilities compatible with the target population?

1 2 3 M   Content

Yes No   Are students provided with specific strategies rather than a series of isolated skills?
Yes No   Does the selection of subject matter, facts, and skills adequately represent the content area?
Yes No   Is the content consistent with the stated objectives?
Yes No   Is the information presented in the material accurate?
Yes No   Is the information presented in the material current?
Yes No   Are various points of view—including treatment of cultural diversity, individuals with disabilities, ideologies, social values, gender roles, and socioeconomic status—represented objectively?
Yes No   Are the content and the topic of the material relevant to the needs of students with disabilities?

1 2 3 M   Sequence of Instruction

Yes No   Is the scope and sequence of the material clearly specified?
Yes No   Are facts, concepts, and skills ordered logically?
Yes No   Does the sequence of instruction proceed from simple to complex?
Yes No   Does the sequence proceed in small, easily attainable steps?

2. *Check for clear references.* Another problem to watch for is confusing pronoun references when more than one noun is used. For example, consider the following: *Both the stem of the plant and the leaf produce chloroform, but in different ways. For one, the sun hits it, and then . . .* Here, the pronouns *one* and *it* could be referring to either the stem or the leaf. Also, look out for vague quantifiers, those that do not modify the noun being quantified (for example, *some, many, few*). For example, the sentence *Some whales have become extinct* is clearer than *Some have become extinct.* In addition,

Rating Scale:

Inadequate	Adequate	Excellent	Easily modified
1	2	3	M

1 2 3 M   Behavioral Objectives

Yes No   Are objectives or outcomes for the material clearly stated?
Yes No   Are the objectives or outcomes consistent with the goals for the target population?
Yes No   Are the objectives or outcomes stated in behavioral terms, including the desired behavior, the conditions for measurement of the behavior, and the desired standard of performance?

1 2 3 M   Initial Assessment and Placement

Yes No   Does the material provide a method to determine initial student placement in the curriculum?
Yes No   Does the initial assessment for placement contain enough items to place the learner accurately?

1 2 3 M   Ongoing Assessment and Evaluation

Yes No   Does the material provide evaluation procedures for measuring progress and mastery of objectives?
Yes No   Are there enough evaluative items to measure learner progress accurately?
Yes No   Are procedures and/or materials for ongoing record keeping provided?

1 2 3 M   Instructional Input (Teaching Procedures)

Yes No   Are instructional procedures for each lesson either clearly specified or self-evident?
Yes No   Does the instruction provide for active student involvement and responses?
Yes No   Are the lessons adaptable to small-group and individualized instruction?
Yes No   Are a variety of cueing and prompting techniques used to gain correct student responses?
Yes No   When using verbal instruction, does the instruction proceed clearly and logically?
Yes No   Does the material use teacher modeling and demonstration when appropriate to the skills being taught?
Yes No   Does the material specify correction and feedback procedures for use during instruction?

1 2 3 M   Practice and Review

Yes No   Does the material contain appropriate practice activities that contribute to mastery of the skills and concepts?
Yes No   Do practice activities relate directly to the desired outcome behaviors?
Yes No   Does the material provide enough practice for students with learning problems?
Yes No   Are skills systematically and cumulatively reviewed throughout the curriculum?

Source: From *Instructional Materials for the Mildly Handicapped: Selection, Utilization, and Modification,* by A. Archer, 1977, Eugene: University of Oregon, Northwest Learning Resources System. Used by permission of the author.

check for definite pronouns without a clear referent (for example, *She saw him,* where the identity of *him* is not specified).

3. *Look for transition statements.* Transitions help the reader move easily from idea to idea. Given that a text covers many topics, make sure that the topic shifts are smooth. For example, in a biology chapter on the respiratory system, the text signals the transition from naming the parts of the respiratory system to describing the

In this information age, informational literacy is central to success and even to survival. However, Duke (2000), in a study of 20 first-grade classrooms, found a scarcity of informational texts present, and only 3.6 minutes of class time per day involved activities with information texts. This scarcity was particularly dramatic in schools in lower socioeconomic areas, where half the classrooms observed spent no time at all with informational texts. Why do you think this is so? Why is this problem particularly detrimental for children from lower socioeconomic areas? What can you do as a teacher to bring more information into your classroom?

actual respiratory process by stating *Next, the role each of these parts of the body plays in the respiratory process will be described.*

4. *Make sure chronological sequences are easy to follow.* In a discussion of a sequence of events, the order of presentation in the text should generally proceed from first to last; any alteration of the order could cause confusion if not clearly signaled.

5. *Make sure graphic aids are clearly related to the text.* Graphic aids should contribute to understanding the material rather than simply provide decoration or fill space, should be easy to read and interpret, and should be clearly titled and labeled and referenced in the text so the reader knows when to look at them.

No matter how well designed conventional basal and content-area texts may be, they are still largely print based and fixed and uniform in format. As a result, conventional materials are likely to present barriers for students with disabilities (Pisha, 2003). For example, students who are blind will need a print alternative, such as braille; students with physical challenges may be unable to turn the pages in a text; students with attention and organizational problems may be unable to identify main ideas; and students with reading disabilities may not be able to read material accurately and quickly enough to comprehend it. Unfortunately, teachers may lack both the time and expertise to adapt these materials.

Modern digital texts can present the same content as conventional printed books but in a format that is more flexible and accessible (Pisha & Stahl, 2005). Digital versions of texts can be easily converted to braille, virtual pages can be turned with the slight press of a switch, and any words in the text can be read aloud. An example of a textbook made more accessible through technology is described in the Technology Notes in Chapter 10 on page 381.

Manipulatives and Models

Manipulatives and models can help students make connections between the abstractions often presented in school and the real-life products and situations these abstractions represent. *Manipulatives* are concrete objects or representational items, such as blocks and counters (for example, base-10 blocks for math), used as part of instruction. *Models* are also tangible objects; they provide a physical representation of an abstraction (for example, a scale model of the solar system). Strategies to help students make these connections have great potential benefit for students with special needs, who may lack the background knowledge and reasoning skills to understand abstractions (Cass, Cates, Smith, & Jackson, 2003; Smith, 2004). Still, manipulatives and models should be used carefully, because their use with students with special needs has not been heavily researched (Cass et al., 2003; Stein, Kinder, Silbert, & Carnine, 2005). When using these tools, consider the following seven guidelines (Marzola, 1987; Ross & Kurtz, 1993):

www.resources

Acquiring digital texts can be difficult. That's why IDEA established the National Instructional Materials Accessibility Standard (NIMAS). NIMAS sets a standard for file formats used in producing textbooks so they can be more easily converted into accessible formats such as braille and large-print using digital text. For more information about NIMAS, go to www.NIMAS.org.

1. *Select materials that suit the concept and developmental stage of the students.* When you are first introducing a concept, materials should be easy to comprehend. Generally, the order in which you introduce materials should follow the same order as students' understanding: from the concrete to the pictorial to the abstract. However, not all students need to start at the same level. For example, in a biology lesson on the heart, many students benefit from viewing a three-dimensional model of a human heart, whereas other students are able to understand how a heart works just by seeing a picture of one.

2. *Use a variety of materials.* Students with special needs may have trouble transferring their understanding of a concept from one form to another. For example, Curtis's teacher always demonstrated place value using base-10 blocks. When Curtis was given a place-value problem using coffee stirrers, he was unable to do it. Curtis's teacher could have prevented this problem in the first place by demonstrating place

The use of manipulatives and models in this biology class makes learning more concrete. What are ways manipulatives and models can be used to make subject matter content in other areas more concrete?

value using a range of manipulative materials, such as coffee stirrers, paper clips, and so on.

3. *Use verbal explanations whenever possible to accompany object manipulation.* Models and manipulative demonstrations should be preceded and accompanied by verbal explanations of the concept or skill being demonstrated. Verbal explanations are valuable because students may not be able to identify the important features of the model on their own. For example, Ms. Balou put a model of a two-digit-by-two-digit multiplication problem on the board. She verbally explained to her students all the steps in computing the problem and wrote each step on the chalkboard as it was completed.

4. *Encourage active interaction.* It is not enough just to have the teacher demonstrate with manipulatives or models as students observe. Students need to interact actively with models and manipulatives. Hands-on experience helps them construct their own meaning from the materials.

5. *Elicit student explanations of their manipulations or use of models.* Encourage your students to verbalize what they are doing as they work with models and manipulatives. This is a good way for you to assess whether they really understand the concept or skill. For example, Ms. Conway had her students name the main parts of the human heart using a model. Mr. Abeles had his students explain out loud how they would subtract 43 from 52 using base-10 blocks. Although explanations can help you evaluate how your students process information, students with special needs may not be able to articulate concepts right away because of language problems or a lack of reasoning skills. These students may require frequent demonstrations of how to articulate what they are doing.

6. *Present clear guidelines for handling manipulatives to prevent management problems.* Although manipulatives can be helpful instructional tools, they also can create

DIMENSIONS OF
diversity

Fennema and colleagues (1998) and Carr and Jessup (1997) found that girls in grades 1–3 tended to use concrete strategies and boys tended to use abstract strategies when solving multidigit addition and subtraction problems. Ambrose (2002) makes these suggestions for encouraging girls to use mental math: (a) let them know that efforts to do math "in their heads" are valued; (b) create a spirit of risk taking by encouraging students to try new things, and send the message to students that they don't have to be perfect; (c) give students easy problems when they have no access to manipulatives, to foster the habit of trying mental math; and (d) keep a close eye on girls so that you can catch them in the act of using mental math, and celebrate these attempts. Give students opportunities to verbalize and reflect on their attempts.

Research Note

Moreno and Duran (2004) taught addition and subtraction skills to fifth- and sixth-grade students using virtual manipulatives. One group was taught using virtual manipulatives alone, while the other group received verbal guidance from a teacher along with the manipulatives. The results favored the group that received verbal guidance along with the virtual manipulatives.

www.resources

The National Center to Improve Practice in Special Education through Technology, Media and Materials has gathered and synthesized information about technology, disabilities, and instructional practices through a broad range of resources. This site also provides opportunities for teachers to exchange information, build knowledge, and practice through collaborative dialogue: www2.edc.org/ncip.

management problems, particularly in larger groups when your physical access to students is limited. For example, Ms. Leifheit wanted her students to manipulate blocks to show the sounds in words. Each child received three blocks. When the children heard a word such as *man,* they were to move a block as they said each sound: *m-a-n.* Ms. Leifheit had trouble getting students' attention at the beginning of the lesson because they were busy handling the blocks. She also found that students were not listening to her say the words, again because they were playing with the blocks. Ms. Leifheit decided to break the class into smaller groups so she could more carefully monitor student use of the blocks. She also established a simple rule: When the teacher is talking, students are not to touch their blocks.

7. *Move your students beyond the concrete level when they are ready.* Some students with special needs may have trouble moving from one learning stage to another. One effective way to help students make the transition from the concrete to the abstract is to pair concrete tasks with paper-and-pencil tasks. For example, Ms. Conway had her students label a picture of a human heart after they had observed and discussed a physical model. Mr. Abeles had his second-graders solve subtraction problems using manipulatives and then record their answers on a traditional worksheet. However, Marsh and Cooke (1996) found that students with learning disabilities who were taught to solve story problems using manipulatives were able to solve similar problems at an abstract level without having to go through the representational stage.

Technology

Teachers today have available to them a broad array of technologies to enhance the presentation of material to their students. As mentioned in Chapter 1, technologies range from low- to high-tech options. One common use of computers in inclusive classrooms is to provide instruction to students through drill-and-practice programs, tutorials, and simulations. In general, *drill-and-practice programs* are used most often with students with special needs. Such programs have been shown to be effective for students with special needs largely because they allow students to learn in small steps, provide systematic feedback, and allow for lots of practice to mastery. Still, not all drill-and-practice programs are created equal (Arends, 2004; Okolo, 2000). Look for programs that

- Directly relate student responding to the instructional objective
- Have animation or graphics that support the skill being practiced
- Provide feedback that helps students locate and correct their mistakes
- Store information about student performance or progress that can be accessed later by the teacher
- Have options for controlling features such as speed of problem presentation, type of feedback, problem difficulty, and amount of practice

Computers can also provide initial, sequenced instruction for students, using tutorials in problem solving, decision making, and risk taking and using simulations. Each of these forms of computer-assisted instruction has potential advantages and disadvantages (Roblyer, Edwards, & Havriluk, 2004). For example, *tutorials* can present instruction to mastery in small, sequential steps, an instructional approach shown to be effective with students with special needs. Tutorials can also provide one-to-one instruction at varying levels of difficulty, something teachers usually do not have time to do. Still, you need to check to be sure that students have the necessary prerequisite skills to benefit from the tutorials. In addition, tutorials may not provide sufficient review for students, and students may not be motivated enough to work through them independently (Roblyer et al., 2004). *Simulations* are of great potential benefit in teaching students to be active learners by confronting real-life situations. However, simulations may be difficult to integrate with academic curriculum, may require much teacher assistance, and can be time consuming (Roblyer et al., 2004).

Assistive technology (AT) is an important part of an inclusive classroom. An assistive-technology device is any piece of equipment that is used to increase, maintain, or improve the functional capabilities of a child with a disability. An assistive-technology service is any service that directly assists a child in the selection, acquisition, or use of an assistive-technology device, according to the Technology-Related Assistance for Individuals with Disabilities Act of 1998. As you have already learned, a range of high- to low-tech AT is available to enable students with disabilities to communicate or to access information by allowing them to bypass their disability. Ways to use INCLUDE to determine the AT needs of students with disabilities are described in the Technology Notes.

How Can You Analyze Instructional Methods in Relation to Student Needs?

Teachers use a number of instructional methods in class, including direct instruction, indirect methods of instruction, scaffolding, independent student practice, and evaluation of student performance. Each of these methods should be analyzed in relation to student needs and then used and/or adapted as needed.

Elements of Direct Instruction

Several decades of research in teaching effectiveness have shown that many students learn skills and subject matter more readily when it is presented explicitly in what is often referred to as **direct instruction** (Rosenshine & Stevens, 1986; Stronge, 2002). Direct instruction consists of six key elements:

1. *Review and check the previous day's work (and reteach if necessary).* This aspect of direct instruction may include establishing routines for checking homework and reviewing relevant past learning and prerequisite skills. These procedures are important because students with special needs might not retain past learning and/or know how to apply it to new material. For example, on Thursday Ms. Guzik taught her students how to round to the nearest whole number. On Friday she gave her class a story problem to solve that required rounding. Before the students solved the problem, she pointed to a chart in the front of the room that displayed a model of how to round numbers and suggested that they refer to this chart as they solved the problem.

2. *Present new content or skills.* When content or skills are presented, teachers begin the lesson with a short statement of the objectives and a brief overview of what they are going to present and why. Material is presented in small steps, using careful demonstrations that incorporate illustrations and concrete examples to highlight key points. Included within the demonstrations are periodic questions to check for understanding.

3. *Provide guided student practice (and check for understanding).* At first student practice takes place under the direct guidance of the teacher, who frequently questions all students on material directly related to the new content or skill. You can involve all students in questioning by using unison oral responses or by having students answer questions by holding up answer cards, raising their hands when they think an answer is correct, or holding up a number to show which answer they think is right. For example, when asking a yes-or-no question, tell your students to hold up a 1 when they think the answer is yes and a 2 when they think the answer is no.

Research Note

Research shows that students are usually more attentive to varied, fast-paced presentations than to other kinds (Darch & Gersten, 1985). The key to providing a fast-paced presentation is to begin the directions for the next question (or for correction of the current question) immediately after the students make a response to the first question. It also helps to limit your own talk to give your students as many opportunities to respond as possible.

fyi

Whole language represents an indirect, constructivistic approach.

*www.*resources

For more information about direct instruction, consult the Association for Direct Instruction at www.adihome.org.

Using INCLUDE to Determine Assistive-Technology Needs

According to IDEA, the IEP team must consider whether a child needs assistive-technology (AT) devices and services as part of his or her plan for an appropriate education. This decision is further complicated by the fact that more than 29,000 AT devices exist for individuals with disabilities and aging adults (Baush & Hasselbring, 2004). The INCLUDE strategy can assist greatly in helping the team make this decision. What follows is a series of questions related to AT that teams may want to incorporate into the INCLUDE process. These questions were adapted from ones originally suggested by Beigel (2000), Marino, Marino, and Shaw (2006), and Pedrotty-Bryant, Bryant, and Raskind (1998).

Identify Classroom Demands

1. How do you present information? For example, teachers who use a lot of classroom discussions place a particular demand on children's speaking abilities; teachers who lecture frequently place a strain on students' writing and organizational skills.

2. What types of grouping arrangements do you use? An emphasis on cooperative learning places a burden on student communication skills.

3. What types of assignments do you make? For example, a project-driven class requires students to find and organize resource materials and then present them to the class in a clear, orderly way.

4. What are the primary ways you assess and evaluate your students? Oral assessments can place a strain on student verbal communication skills; written assessments place demands on written language skills such as handwriting, spelling, and sentence and paragraph construction.

5. How comfortable are you with having a learner who uses AT in the classroom? Your role in this process is very important. Without your support for learning to use AT and then continuing its use, a student may abandon her device.

6. What is the physical structure of your classroom and school? Issues such as whether there are adequate electrical outlets or tables large enough to accommodate a computer and various peripherals need to be considered.

Note Learner Strengths and Needs and Check for Potential Success and Problem Areas

1. What purposeful motoric movement does the student have? A purposeful movement is one that the learner controls in a conscious, consistent manner (Beigel, 2000, p. 240). Examples of purposeful motoric movement include raising an eyebrow, moving the fingers of one hand in a motion similar to that of typing, and using a pen or pencil to write or draw.

2. How willing is the student to try new activities or tasks? Using AT requires a willingness to change on the part of the student. Your knowledge of the student in this area can help determine the nature of the equipment selected (for example, easy to use or hard to use) as well as the amount of time needed to achieve independent usage.

3. What does the student desire from the use of AT? The personal goals of the learner can greatly influence AT usage. Relevance of the material is an important factor in learning to perform any skill. For example, Tamra had an expressed desire to write poetry and was quite receptive to learning to use a laptop with a large keyboard especially designed for her.

4. What emotional and psychological supports does the student need when learning to use the device? Some students may require considerable emotional and psychological support as they learn to use an AT device. You or other staff working with the student should provide such support when it is needed, as students who become frustrated or disinterested will not likely use the device. It is important to remember that students cannot be forced to use AT; they can only be encouraged and supported whenever using the device.

5. What level of training do the student and others who interact with the student need? You, the student, and

other staff working with the student need to be given the opportunity to see how the various devices work and to see who needs training and in what areas.

6. What impact if any do the student's socioeconomic status and cultural background have on the use of AT? Students who live in poverty, as well as their parents, are less likely to have previous experience with technology and may need more extensive training. There is also the question of the impact of culture on the acceptance of AT by students and their families.

Brainstorm and Differentiate Instruction

You need to consider the features of the technical devices as well as the extent to which they help students meet identified IEP goals:

1. How durable is the device? All devices that are used in schools should be able to withstand minimal bumps and jars common in schools.

2. What setup and maintenance issues must be addressed? How easy is the device to update and repair? Do compatibility issues with other technology already in the classroom need to be addressed? Devices that are difficult to maintain, take a long time to repair, are not easily upgraded, or are incompatible with other technology should be avoided, because eventually they will be abandoned.

3. How willing is the vendor of the device to provide a trial or loaner period of use for the student? You often need to try several devices in the school environment before a final AT decision can be made.

4. What is the reputation of the company in terms of construction, service, training, and reliability? These questions can be answered by consulting publications that deal with AT (*Team Rehab, TAM Connector*), contacting organizations (Council for Exceptional Children, Center for Applied Special Technology), and asking others who use AT.

5. Does the student have the psychomotor skills needed to use the device in a functional manner? This question should be answered during student assessment. Many devices can be adapted for students with limited motoric control; if a device can't be adapted, then it is unrealistic to expect that it will be used.

6. Is the device aesthetically acceptable to the student? Some students may prefer a certain color or type of mouse; others may prefer a brightly colored exterior as opposed to the typical colors of blue, black, and beige; still others may want to decorate their equipment (as long as this doesn't interfere with its function). If students' aesthetic needs are not addressed, they may feel the device doesn't fit into their social milieu and will not likely use it.

7. Does the device meet the student's needs in a way that is easily understood by others? Students should be able to use their devices without causing a distraction. In addition, the device should not be so complex that only the vendor is able to program the device or explain how it can be used.

8. How portable is the device? For AT to be useful, the student or support person must be able to move the device from one class to another—from an elementary classroom to a special class such as art or physical education or between various academic classes in a middle or high school environment.

Evaluate Student Progress

The ultimate goal of AT is to enable students to more readily meet their IEP goals. Pedrotty-Bryant et al. (1998, p. 55) suggest that teachers ask the following questions when determining whether the assistive technology selected is an appropriate match for the student.

- To what extent does the AT assist the student in compensating for the disability?
- To what degree does the technology promote student independence?
- What is the student's opinion of the technology adaptation?
- What is the family's opinion of the AT?
- Is the AT efficient and easy for the student to use?
- Does the device promote meeting IEP goals and objectives in the least restrictive environment?

Building Teaching Skills
Case Studies Exercise

Go to the Building Teaching
Skills section in Chapter 5
of MyEducationLab to learn about
planning classroom arrangements
for inclusion.

This approach can be used with spelling too. Have your students spell words on an index card and then hold up their answers. Unison responses not only give students more practice but also allow you to monitor student learning more readily. Prompts and additional explanations or demonstrations are provided during guided practice when appropriate. Effective guided practice continues until students meet the lesson objective. For example, Mr. Hayes was teaching his students how to add *es* to words that end in *y*. After modeling two examples at the board, he did several more examples with the students, guiding them as they applied the rule to change the *y* to *i* before they added *es*. Next, Mr. Hayes had students do a word on their own. Students wrote their answers on whiteboards and held up the boards when directed by Mr. Hayes. Mr. Hayes noticed that five students did not apply the rule correctly. He called these students up to his desk for additional instruction and had the rest of the students work independently, adding *es* to a list of words on a worksheet.

4. *Provide feedback and correction (and reteach when necessary).* When students answer quickly and confidently, the teacher asks another question or provides a short acknowledgment of correctness (for example, "That's right"). Hesitant but correct responses might be followed by process feedback (for example, "Yes, Yolanda, that's right because . . ."). When students respond incorrectly, the teacher uses corrections to draw out an improved student response. Corrections can include sustaining feedback (that is, simplifying the question, giving clues), explaining or reviewing steps, giving process feedback ("The reason we need to regroup in this subtraction problem is that the top number is smaller than the bottom number"), or reteaching last steps ("Remember, at the end of this experiment you need to tell whether the hypothesis was accepted or rejected. Let me show you what I mean"). Corrections continue until students have met the lesson objective, with praise used in moderation. Specific praise ("I'm impressed by how you drew a picture of that story problem!") is more effective than general praise ("Good boy, Leon").

5. *Provide independent student practice.* Students practice independently on tasks directly related to the skills taught until they achieve a high correct rate. Practice activities are actively supervised and students are held accountable for their work.

6. *Review frequently.* Systematic review of previously learned material is provided, including the incorporation of review into homework and tests. Material missed in homework or tests is retaught (Rosenshine & Stevens, 1986).

It is important to note that for older students or for those who have more subject-matter knowledge or skills, these six steps can be modified, such as by presenting more material at one time or spending less time on guided practice. For example, when a second-grade teacher presented a unit on nutrition, she spent a whole week defining and showing examples of complex carbohydrates, fats, sugar, and protein. In an eighth-grade health class, this material was covered in one day, largely because students already had much background information on this topic. Moreover, each of the direct instruction steps is not required for every lesson you teach, although they are particularly helpful to students with learning and behavior problems, who have been shown to benefit greatly from a high level of classroom structure (Hallahan et al., 2005; Mercer & Pullen, 2005; Swanson & Deshler, 2003). The Case in Practice presents an example of a direct instruction lesson.

Indirect Methods of Instruction

Indirect instruction is based on the belief that children are naturally active learners and that given the appropriate instructional environment, they actively construct knowledge and solve problems in developmentally appropriate ways (Knight, 2002). This type of teaching is often referred to as *constructivistic* because of the belief that students are capable of constructing meaning on their own, in most cases without explicit instruction from the

Case in Practice

A Direct Instruction Lesson

This direct instruction lesson is designed to help students use pronouns clearly. Notice that Mr. Francisco first reviews the preskill of what a pronoun is. Then he guides students through the skill of substituting pronouns for nouns.

Mr. Francisco: Remember, yesterday we said that for every noun, there's a more general word called a *pronoun*. So, for the word *boys*, the pronoun is *they*. For the word *car*, the pronoun is *it*. What's the pronoun for the word *James?*

Students: He.

Mr. Francisco: Right. You're going to rewrite sentences so they have no nouns, only pronouns. Here's the first sentence: *Elephants eat grass.* What's the noun in the subject?

Students: Elephants.

Mr. Francisco: What's the pronoun that replaces *elephants?*

Students: They.

Mr. Francisco: What's the noun in the predicate?

Students: Grass.

Mr. Francisco: What's the pronoun that replaces *grass?*

Students: It.

Mr. Francisco: What is the entire sentence with pronouns?

Students: They eat it.

Mr. Francisco: Right. Look at the pronouns written on the board: *he, she, it, they, him, her, them.* You're going to use

these words to rewrite sentences so they won't have any nouns, just pronouns. Here's Sentence 1: *George is watching birds.* What noun is the subject?

Students: George.

Mr. Francisco: What's the noun in the predicate?

Students: Birds.

Mr. Francisco: What's the sentence with pronouns in place?

Students: He is watching them.

Mr. Francisco: Good. Look at the next sentence: *Fred and Carlos build houses.* You are going to write it with pronouns in place of the nouns. [Teacher observes students and gives feedback.]

Mr. Francisco: Here's the sentence you should have: *They build them.*

[Teacher repeats with two more examples.]

REFLECTIONS

What direct instruction steps did Mr. Francisco use here? Why is direct instruction particularly effective for students with learning and behavior needs? In what situations would you *not* want to use direct instruction? Why?

Source: Adapted from *Reasoning and Writing: A Direct Instruction Program,* by S. Engelmann and B. Grossen, 2001, Columbus, OH: SRA/McGraw-Hill.

---

teacher (Hallahan et al., 2005; Knight, 2002). Indirect instruction is used by classroom teachers for both basic skills and content areas.

A common indirect method is called **inquiry learning,** or *discovery learning* (Jarolimek, Foster, & Kellough, 2004; Maroney, Finson, Beaver, & Jensen, 2003; National Research Council, 1999). Unlike direct instruction, which is very teacher centered, in the inquiry approach the teacher's role is that of a facilitator who guides learners' inquiry by helping them identify questions and problems. (Jarolimek et al., 2004; Knight, 2002). The learners therefore are placed in situations that require considerable initiative and background knowledge in finding things out for themselves. In this way, students are actively involved in their own learning (Jarolimek et al., 2004).

You can see these elements of inquiry learning in a social studies lesson on Inuit or native Alaskan people developed by Lindquist (1995). The goal of the lesson was for students to "realize that there are many different groups of Inuit people, each having unique customs and traditions, but whose culture has been shaped by the Far North" (Lindquist, 1995, p. 54). First, the teacher gave the students five minutes to list everything they knew about the Inuit people. The teacher then had some students share their lists with the class.

Student sharing of their background knowledge was followed by a short film on the Inuit people. After the film, the students were asked to cross out anything on their lists that the film caused them to change their minds about. When the children had revised their lists, the teacher divided the class into pairs; each pair was asked to research a different Inuit tribe. They were to gather information about food, shelter, clothing, and language. Each pair of students recorded information about their particular tribe on a data sheet and reported their information to the class. As each group reported, the teacher synthesized the information on an overhead chart, creating a graphic display for comparing and contrasting similarities and differences among the various tribes.

Maroney and colleagues (2003) recently compiled a list of skills required for success in an inquiry-based approach to teaching science. A range of competencies was listed in the areas of classroom behavior skills, social skills, group coping skills, basic academic skills, science process skills, and inquiry skills (see Table 5.1).

As you can see in the table, the sheer number of skills listed is daunting when applied to all children, let alone to children who are likely to have problems in many of these areas. Clearly, for an inquiry approach to be effective for students with special needs, you will need to provide them with extensive supports such as the use of scaffolds described in the next section (Rapp, 2005).

Scaffolding

Scaffolding is an approach that has been used successfully to support students as they develop problem-solving skills (Larkin, 2001; Olson et al., 2007). Scaffolds are "forms of support provided by the teacher (or another student) to help students bridge the gap between their current abilities and the intended goal" (Rosenshine & Meister, 1992, p. 26).

Before using scaffolding, you need to find out whether students have the necessary background ability to learn a cognitive strategy (Rosenshine & Meister, 1992). For example, a strategy for helping a student read a physics textbook is not useful if the student

fyi

Scaffolding is a helpful strategy for teaching basic skills in addition to problem-solving skills.

With appropriate support, nondirect instruction can be effective for students with special needs. What steps should this teacher take to ensure effective instruction using scaffolding?

TABLE 5.1

Student Skills Required for Success in Inquiry-Based Learning

Classroom Behavior Skills

- Listens quietly to directions and instruction
- Follows classroom rules
- Follows directions accurately
- Is prepared with needed materials
- Begins work promptly
- Works quietly
- Asks for help when needed
- Completes assignments on time
- Completes work at acceptable level of accuracy
- Accepts criticism and corrections

Basic Academic Skills

- Can read and comprehend required materials
- Has necessary writing skills
- Can understand information presented
- Has required math and measurement skills
- Knows basic necessary science concepts
- Understands necessary vocabulary
- Can use equipment and materials
- Has skills needed to succeed in a given activity

Social Skills

- Interacts appropriately with others
- Has acceptable conversation skills
- Thinks before acting
- Shows a friendly attitude
- Uses language appropriately

Science Process Skills

- Gathers information through observation
- Communicates observations and findings
- Makes an educated guess/hypothesis
- Uses experimentation to solve a problem
- Uses measurement to record results
- Uses graphs and diagrams effectively
- Uses classification skills
- Forms generalizations
- Makes reasonable predictions based on data

Group Coping Skills

- Works cooperatively in a group
- Contributes to group work
- Expresses opinions
- Disagrees politely
- Listens to others
- Negotiates and compromises
- Accepts criticism

Inquiry Skills

- Understands the problem
- Generates simple questions
- Generates complex questions
- Uses previously learned information to solve problems
- Is motivated by inquiry
- Can accept more than one answer
- Displays confidence in own ideas

Source: Adapted from "Preparing for Successful Inquiry in Inclusive Science Classrooms," by S. A. Maroney, K. D. Finson, J. B. Beaver, and M. M. Jensen, *Teaching Exceptional Children, 36*(1), 2003, 18–25. Copyright 2003 by The Council for Exceptional Children. Reprinted with permission.

lacks basic knowledge of mathematics and physical properties. Similarly, teaching a strategy for solving math word problems cannot succeed if the student does not have basic math computation skills. Using scaffolding to teach higher-order cognitive strategies consists of six stages:

1. *Present the new cognitive strategy.* In this stage, the teacher introduces the strategy concretely, using a list of strategy steps. The teacher then models the strategy, including all "thinking" and "doing" steps. For example, Mr. Bridges is teaching his history class how geographic features and natural resources affect the growth and location of cities. First, he introduces the problem-solving strategy to his students: (a) define the problem, (b) propose hypotheses to explain the problem, (c) collect data to evaluate your hypotheses, (d) evaluate the evidence, and (e) make a conclusion. These steps are posted on the chalkboard for easy reference. Mr. Bridges then models the strategy by showing students a map of the state of Illinois and thinking out loud as he applies the steps. For example, he explains how he would sort through many pieces of information in determining which factors led to the development of Chicago (for example, being on Lake Michigan) and which did not (for example, cold climate).

2. *Regulate difficulty during guided practice.* At this stage, students begin practicing the new strategy using simplified materials so they can concentrate on learning the strategy. First, the strategy is introduced one step at a time. Students are guided carefully through the steps, with the teacher anticipating particularly difficult steps and completing these difficult parts of the task as necessary. Before tackling difficult problems, such as the geography of Chicago, Mr. Bridges has his students use the problem-solving steps to solve simpler problems on topics familiar to them. For example, he has them solve problems such as why the cookies someone made were dry, why a hypothetical student is late for school every day, or why the school lunches taste awful. He also helps students brainstorm ideas for how to collect data, a step that can be difficult. Mr. Bridges does this by compiling an initial list of data collection procedures for each problem. For the problem of why the cookies were dry, Mr. Bridges gives his students a list of possible data collection procedures, such as identifying the ingredients, finding out how long the cookies were baked, and figuring out how old the cookies were.

3. *Provide varying contexts for student practice.* Students practice the strategy on actual classroom tasks under the teacher's direction. The teacher starts out leading the practice, but the students eventually carry out the practice sessions in small cooperative groups. In Mr. Bridges's class, students practice the problem-solving strategy using examples from their history textbooks.

4. *Provide feedback.* The teacher provides corrective feedback to students using evaluative checklists based on models of expert problem solving carefully explained to the students. Students are encouraged to evaluate their performance using these checklists. For example, each time Mr. Bridges's students use the problem-solving strategy, they evaluate their performance by asking themselves questions such as these: Did we clearly state the problem? Did we state a complete list of hypotheses? How thorough were our data collection procedures? Were we able to evaluate all the hypotheses using the information collected? Did we interpret the results accurately? Were our conclusions consistent with our results?

Student independence is encouraged by removing elements of the scaffold.

5. *Increase student responsibility.* Next the teacher begins to require students to practice putting all the steps together on their own. Student independence is encouraged by removing elements of the scaffold. For example, prompts and models are diminished, the complexity and difficulty of the materials are increased, and peer support

is decreased. The teacher checks for student mastery before going to the last step, independent practice.

6. *Provide independent practice.* Finally, the teacher provides the students with extensive practice and helps them apply what they have learned to new situations. For example, Mr. Bridges shows his students how problem solving can be used in other subjects, such as science.

Independent Student Practice

The major purpose of practice is to help students refine or strengthen their skills in various areas. Consider the following seven guidelines for using practice activities effectively in your classroom:

1. *Students should practice only skills or content they have already learned.* This guideline is particularly important in order for students to be able to perform practice activities independently. Tasks that are too difficult can lead to high levels of off-task behavior.

2. *Practice is more effective when students have a desire to learn what they are practicing.* Whenever possible, point out to students situations in which they can use the skill in other phases of learning. For example, you may explain to your students that if they learn to read more quickly, they will be able to finish their homework in less time.

3. *Practice should be individualized.* Exercises should be organized so that each student can work independently.

4. *Practice should be specific and systematic.* Practice should be directly related to skills and objectives you are working on in class. This guideline is particularly important for students with special needs, who require more practice to master academic skills.

5. *Students should have much practice on a few skills rather than little practice on many skills.* Focusing on one or two skills at a time is less confusing and gives students more practice on each skill.

6. *Practice should be organized so that students achieve high levels of success.* Correct answers reinforce students and encourage them to do more. Most students need at least 90 percent accuracy when doing practice activities, though higher-achieving students can tolerate a 70 percent rate as long as the teacher is present to assist them (Good & Brophy, 1986).

7. *Practice should be organized so that the students and teacher have immediate feedback.* You need to know how students are progressing so you can decide whether to move to the next skill. Students need to know how they are doing so they can make meaningful corrections to their work (Ornstein & Lasley, 2004).

For students with special needs, consider these additional questions: What are the response demands of the activity? Do students have to answer orally or in writing? How extensive a response is required? Do the students have enough time to finish the activity? Response demands are important because students who are unable to meet them will not be able to do the practice activity independently. For example, Mr. Edwards is having his class practice weekly vocabulary words by orally stating their definitions. Ross stutters and is unable to answer out loud. Mr. Edwards allows Ross to submit a written list of definitions. Ms. Osborne is having her students complete short-answer questions in their history books. Clarice has a physical disability and is unable to write her answers independently. She uses an adapted classroom computer to prepare her answers. Mr. Nusbaum has asked his students to write a paragraph summarizing the reasons for the stock market crash of 1929. Maurice cannot write a coherent paragraph

DIMENSIONS OF
diversity

Love and Kruger (2005) studied the beliefs of successful teachers of African American students in six urban schools. The teachers endorsed beliefs about a communal learning environment, success for all students, teaching as giving back to the community, and the importance of students' ethnicity. Moreover, the teachers viewed their role to be disseminators of knowledge, and they believed in the usefulness of drill and practice.

Content-area instruction requires teaching new vocabulary words, many of which can be technical. Gersten, Baker, and Marks (1998) suggest the following research-based strategies when teaching vocabulary to English-language learners who have learning difficulties.

Focus Vocabulary Instruction on a Small Number of Critical Words

Providing extensive drill on lengthy word lists is ineffective for students with learning difficulties. Instead, focus on several critical words at a time and emphasize these for several days. Enhance understanding of vocabulary by showing how the words are used in a variety of contexts, including below-grade-level books in the same subject area, texts in different content areas, and personal writing projects.

Provide Multiple Exposures

Expose students to the word in a variety of contexts before they begin to develop a deeper understanding of its meaning and use it as part of their expressive vocabulary. Multiple exposures can include how the word is used in below-grade-level books in the same subject area, texts in different content areas, and personal writing projects.

Introduce New Words before They Are Encountered in Reading

The introduction of vocabulary should be done explicitly during a short segment of class time, usually around five minutes (Echevarria, 1998). During these five minutes, say the vocabulary word, write it on the board, ask students to say and write it, and then define the word using pictures, demonstrations, and examples familiar to students. (See "Modeling Examples and Using Synonyms and Definitions" in Chapter 9.)

Practice with New Words

Give students many opportunities to practice the new words they are learning. Gersten and colleagues (1998) report an example of teaching the word *audience* in *Mr. Popper's Penguins*. After teaching the definition of *audience*, the teacher discussed other kinds of audiences with the class, such as an audience at a Roots concert, an audience at a *Harry Potter* movie, an audience at a football game, and an audience with the pope. It is critical that English-language learners have lots of practice so they can go from a basic understanding of a word to actually being able to use the word in classroom conversation.

Focus on Idioms

Idioms may be hard for English-language learners to understand, because their overall meaning can be quite different from their individual parts. Still, idioms can be used effectively to focus students' attention on important differences between standard and contextual definitions of words, as well as to increase student comprehension. For example, in a history class devoted to the rise of labor unions, a union

but can answer orally into a tape recorder. Amanda writes very slowly, so Mr. Nusbaum gives her more time to complete the activity. Ways in which direct instruction and scaffolding can be used to teach vocabulary to English-language learners are discussed in the Special Emphasis On . . . feature.

● **Learning Centers**   One common way of providing practice for students is through *learning centers,* classroom areas where students work alone or in groups as they engage in a variety of activities, often without the assistance of the classroom teacher (Opitz, 2007). Learning centers are called by a variety of names, including "interest centers, learning stations, activity areas, free choice areas, booths, and enrichment centers" (Patillo & Vaughn, leader was quoted as using the idiom "Hit them in the pocketbook where it hurts." The teacher explained carefully that this expression was not to be taken literally and that it simply meant the unions wanted to hurt managers by causing them to lose money.

Develop Word Banks

A *word bank* is a place where key vocabulary is stored and posted for students' reference throughout a teaching unit or beyond. Selection of words for word banks should be based on their relevance for understanding key concepts, high frequency of use, and relevance to students' lives. For example, in a unit on the topic of the greenhouse effect, explaining what the ozone layer is would be more important than presenting the definition of fluorocarbons. Word banks can be created by groups of students or by students individually. They can also be visually displayed. For example, as a word is introduced, its meaning and key attributes can be written on chart paper and posted in the room. The displays can then become reference points for students, help them remember definitions and relationships among words, and provide guides for correct spelling. Word banks can also be dynamic; as students learn more about words, this new information can be added to existing definitions. For example, the class that was learning the word *audience* came across the term *audience share* in an article students read about a current television show. The class added this use of *audience* to its visual display.

Use Visual Organizers

Visual organizers can help students access and understand vocabulary that they could not understand if presented only verbally. Examples of using visual or graphic organizers to teach vocabulary are described in Chapter 9.

From the Research

Carlo et al. (2004) used similar strategies when teaching vocabulary to 94 fifth-grade English-language learners (ELLs) and 75 English-only learners (EOs). The researchers taught students new vocabulary words in meaningful texts, allowing them access to Spanish versions of the texts; taught words in varying contexts; and used word analysis strategies that included spelling, pronunciation, meaningful word parts (morphology), and word order (syntax) as well as depth of meaning. The students showed greater growth than a comparison group on depth of vocabulary knowledge, understanding multiple meanings, and reading comprehension. The effects were large for both the ELLs and EOs, although ELLs scored lower on both the pretest and posttest measures.

1992, p. 12). Well-designed learning centers can provide students with special needs opportunities to be more actively engaged in learning, practice new skills, increase proficiency in skills acquired, and apply knowledge and skills to novel situations (King-Sears, 2007, p. 138). Learning centers can provide teachers with ways to provide differentiated instruction.

The key to effective use of learning centers is to design activities that are meaningful and can be accomplished independently. To do that, you must have a clear idea of what you want your students to learn ("Where are we going?"), how your students can practice information taught ("Who needs to practice what?"), and what your students' learning levels are ("What kinds of activities allow students to meaningfully practice and/or apply information learned?") (King-Sears, 2007, p. 138). Use the INCLUDE strategy to make adaptations for individual students as necessary.

- ● **Homework** Another common form of practice used by teachers is *homework*. Research shows that homework can have a positive effect on student achievement when it is properly assigned (Cooper, 1989).

Homework is often a challenge for students with special needs. For example, most teachers expect homework to be completed independently, and students must have the sensory, academic, and organizational skills to do so. A student with a severe reading disability might be unable to read a chapter in a history book and answer the questions without some form of accommodation such as a peer reader or taped text. Similarly, a student with fine motor difficulties might be unable to answer the questions unless allowed to do so orally or with an adapted word processor. In addition, you may need to provide this same student more time or to assign fewer questions. Therefore, it is important that you carefully examine your own particular homework requirements and modify them to ensure full participation by all your students.

Evaluation of Student Performance

The major purpose of student evaluation is to determine the extent to which students have mastered academic skills or instructional content. Chapter 4 discussed formal and informal assessments that can be used to evaluate student progress. Student evaluations are also communicated through grades, which are determined in a number of ways, including classroom tests and assignments. Because student evaluation is so important, you need to consider how classroom tests and assignments may interact with student learning needs. Most critical is that the method of evaluation measures skill or content mastery, not a student's disability. For example, Carson, a student who has an attention deficit, should be given tests in small segments to ensure that the tests measure his knowledge, not his attention span. Similarly, Riesa, a student with a severe learning disability in writing, needs to take an oral essay test in history if the test is to be a valid measure of her history knowledge rather than her writing disability. The type of report-card grade used, as well as the system used to arrive at that grade, might also need to be modified for some students. For example, Hal was discouraged about always getting a C in English, no matter how hard he tried. His teacher decided to supplement his grade with an A for effort to encourage Hal to keep trying. Mr. Henning encouraged his students to come to class on time by giving them credit for punctuality.

Summary

Various aspects of classroom environments can affect the learning of all students, including those with special needs. Fewer individualized accommodations for students with special needs are required in classrooms that are well structured and organized. However, even in the best situations, some accommodations are needed.

The INCLUDE strategy is a decision-making process to help teachers make reasonable accommodations for students with special needs. Reasonable accommodations are those that maximize student access to the general education curriculum without taking a disproportionate amount of time or diminishing the education of the other students in the class. The INCLUDE process is much like that used for providing differentiated instruction. The steps in INCLUDE are as follow: identify classroom demands; note student learning strengths and needs; check for potential areas of student success; look for potential problem areas; use information to brainstorm ways to differentiate instruction; differentiate instruction; and evaluate student progress.

An important part of the INCLUDE strategy is analyzing classroom demands. Demands covering four major areas should be analyzed: classroom management, classroom grouping, instructional materials, and instructional methods. Classroom organization includes physical organization, classroom routines, classroom climate, behavior management (including classroom rules, consequences, and monitoring), and use of time. Key aspects of classroom grouping involve the use of whole-class and small instructional groups, same-skill and mixed-skill groups, and one-to-one instruction. Instructional materials that need to be considered are basal textbooks, content-area textbooks, manipulatives and models, and instructional and assistive technology. With regard to teaching demands, two common instructional models used in schools are direct and indirect instruction.

Sometimes students with special needs require support in the form of scaffolds when participating in indirect teaching. Also consider the demands of your student practice and learning center activities, and follow guidelines for using them effectively. Finally take into account how student learning needs may interact with your classroom evaluation system, including tests and grading.

Back to the Cases

This section provides opportunities for you to apply the knowledge gained in this chapter to the cases described at the beginning of this chapter. The questions and activities that follow demonstrate how these standards and principles, along with other concepts that you have learned about in this chapter, connect to the everyday activities of all teachers.

Mr. Rodriguez has provided a digital copy of the text and a daily review of previously presented content, outlines of lectures, and small-group discussions to support Manuel's learning of content. Step 7 of the INCLUDE strategy asks teachers to evaluate student progress. (INTASC Principles 1.03 and 4.04.) Using information in this chapter and Chapter 4, suggest two assessment methods that Mr. Rodriguez might use to assess Manuel's progress. Explain why you selected these two methods.

Josh may face peers who have difficulty adjusting to his speech. As a result, they may shy from interactions with him. Based on information provided in this chapter, describe two ways Ms. Stewart can use classroom management, grouping, instructional materials, or specific teaching methods to support Josh's interactions with peers. (INTASC Principles 5.01 and 5.03 and CEC Standard 5.) Explain why you think these methods would be helpful for Josh.

Key Terms and Concepts

Academic learning time (p. 167)

Assistive technology (AT) (p. 179)

Differentiated instruction (p. 153)

Direct instruction (p. 179)

INCLUDE (p. 152)

Indirect instruction (p. 182)

Inquiry learning (p. 183)

Instructional accommodations (p. 158)

Instructional modifications (p. 159)

Mixed-skill groupings (p. 170)

One-to-one instruction (p. 170)

Same-skill groupings (p. 170)

Scaffolding (p. 184)

Transition time (p. 167)

Universal design (p. 153)

Where the Classroom Comes to Life

Now go to the Friend and Bursuck, Fifth Edition, MyEducationLab course at www.myeducationlab.com to

- take a pretest to assess your initial comprehension of the chapter content
- study chapter content with your individualized study plan
- take a posttest to assess your understanding of chapter content
- engage in multimedia exercises to help you build a deeper and more applied understanding of chapter content

Applications in Teaching Practice

Planning Accommodations in the Instructional Environment

Consider the following two scenarios:

- Verna is a student with a learning disability in Ms. Chang's fourth-grade class. Ms. Chang uses whole-group instruction in math. This method is sometimes hard for Verna, who is behind her peers in math. Verna is slow to answer math facts, has trouble keeping numbers straight in columns, and sometimes forgets a step or two when she is computing a problem that requires several steps.
- Mr. Howard wants to teach the following textbook-reading strategy to his ninth-grade history students (Bartelt, Marchio, & Reynolds, 1994):
  R *Review* headings and subheadings.
  E *Examine* boldface words.
  A *Ask* "What do I expect to learn?"
  D *Do* it: Read!
  S *Summarize* in your own words.

Questions

1. Identify the demands in Ms. Chang's class that are likely to be challenging for Verna.

2. How can Ms. Chang use the remaining steps in the INCLUDE strategy to help Verna succeed in the large group?

3. How can Ms. Chang use direct instruction to teach students to round numbers to the nearest 10? Design such a lesson.

4. With what demands will Mr. Howard's students have to contend when learning the READS strategy?

5. How can Mr. Howard use scaffolding to teach the READS strategy?

6. Find a drill-and-practice computer program for elementary or high school students and evaluate it. Does it meet the criteria discussed in this chapter?

Further Readings

Arends, R. I. (2004). *Learning to teach* (6th ed.). New York: McGraw-Hill.

This book is an invaluable resource for teachers that provides models and strategies for teaching all subject areas at all levels.

Kameenui, E. J., & Darch, C. (2003). *Instructional classroom management: A proactive approach to behavior management* (2nd ed.). White Plains, NY: Longmont.

A wealth of practical strategies are described for preventing behavioral problems through carefully planned instruction.

Marchand-Martella, N. E., Slocum, T. A., & Martella, R. C. (2004). *Introduction to direct instruction.* Boston: Allyn & Bacon.

This guide to published direct instruction programs is an indispensable resource.

Marino, M. T., Marino, E. C., & Shaw, S. F. (2006). Making informed assistive technology decisions for students with high-incidence disabilities. *Teaching Exceptional Children, 38*(6), 18–25.

A brief history of legislation in the area of assistive technology (AT) is provided, along with many practical suggestions for setting up a process in your school district to meet the AT needs of students with disabilities.

Pisha, B., & Stahl, S. (2005). The promise of new learning environments for students with disabilities. *Intervention in School and Clinic, 41*(2), 67–75.

This article provides an excellent overview of applications for instructional design to all aspects of the classroom.

Reys, B. R., & Reys, R. E. (2006). The development and publication of elementary mathematics textbooks: Let the buyer beware. *Phi Delta Kappan, 87*(5), 377–383.

Selecting the right textbook for your students can be difficult, and as these authors note, the quality of the text should be the standard, not the quantity of ancillary materials provided. This article provides critical questions for teachers to consider when looking for a quality math textbook.

6 Students with Low-Incidence Disabilities

LEARNING *Objectives*

After you read this chapter, you will be able to

1. Describe what it means to say that a student has a low-incidence disability, and apply the INCLUDE strategy to effectively instruct these students in your classroom.
2. Outline the characteristics of students with autism spectrum disorder and the accommodations general educators can make for them.
3. Describe the characteristics of students with moderate, severe, and multiple disabilities, including intellectual disabilities and deaf-blindness, and the accommodations general educators can make for them.
4. Explain the characteristics of students with sensory impairments (that is, vision or hearing loss) and the accommodations general educators can make for them.
5. Explain the characteristics of students with physical, medical, and health impairments and the accommodations general educators can make for them.
6. Critically analyze your own beliefs about and skills for implementing inclusive practices for students with low-incidence disabilities.

Kylie is a first-grade student with a moderate intellectual disability. She is described by her teachers and her mother as a "bundle of energy," and she is enthusiastic about school and all the activities that occur in her classroom. Although Kylie is just learning to recognize colors and identify shapes and is a prereader, she receives nearly all her instruction in the first-grade classroom. Because Ms. Wilson often uses cutouts, puppets, and other concrete strategies to illustrate the literature being read, Kylie follows along without much difficulty. When other students work on writing or editing, Kylie works with a computer program, either practicing shapes and colors or learning to recognize her name.

What are the learning characteristics and needs of students like Kylie? What are appropriate expectations for Kylie's teacher to have for her this year? What accommodations does Kylie need to succeed in first grade? If Ms. Wilson has a question about Kylie, how can she find an answer?

Sean is a twelfth-grade student identified as having Asperger syndrome, a type of autism spectrum disorder (ASD). Although he spent much of the day in a special education classroom when he was in elementary school, he now receives all his core academic instruction in general education classes. His special education teacher, Ms. Morrow, is working with him one period a day to ensure that he understands assignments, completes the school's learning and study skills curriculum, and prepares to attend community college next year. Sean generally has done very well in high school. One of his greatest supports has been his friend Jonas, who explains when Sean does not understand a classmate's joke and inconspicuously guides Sean when he seems unsure of himself in social situations. As Sean looks forward to college, he is not worried about the academic requirements; he is a very bright young man who grasps most concepts easily. His greatest concerns are dealing with large classes, being surrounded by strangers who may not understand his special needs, and advocating for himself by going to the Office of Disability Services.

What is autism spectrum disorder? What should Sean's teachers do to help him learn? What accommodations might Sean need now, in high school, and later in community college?

Alyssa is a senior this year. She plans to become a special education teacher someday, and she is studying hard to improve her chances of succeeding in college. As the result of a very high fever, Alyssa has had a profound hearing loss since she was 3 months old. Alyssa did not learn a lot of sign language until she began high school. She now prefers signing to oral language as a communication approach, and she has an interpreter who accompanies her to core academic classes. Alyssa's most difficult subject is English. She has problems writing down her ideas logically and elaborating on them.

How does a hearing loss or deafness affect learning for students like Alyssa? What are Alyssa's responsibilities for self-advocacy? What can her teachers do to help her prepare for college?

Students like Kylie, Sean, and Alyssa have the same right as other students to be part of a classroom community with nondisabled peers. For Kylie and other young children with significant disabilities, attending first grade with peers prepares them for the demands of school and also creates the expectation that they can fully participate in a typical educational environment and live as valued and contributing members of communities after their school years. For Sean and Alyssa, being successful in college depends on receiving the strong academic background available in general education classes. However, because of their disabilities these and other students in inclusive schools might need specialized instruction, equipment, and other assistance in order to be successful.

In this chapter, you will learn about the characteristics and needs of students with **low-incidence disabilities,** which include autism; moderate, severe, and multiple disabilities; sensory impairments; and physical, medical, and health disabilities. The federal terms for these disabilities and the number of students with these disabilities served through the Individuals with Disabilities Education Act (IDEA) are summarized in Table 6.1. You also will explore accommodations specific to the unique needs of these students that general education teachers and other professionals can make to enable them to learn.

What Are Low-Incidence Disabilities?

When you work with students with low-incidence disabilities, you will notice immediately the diversity of their abilities and needs, the range of educational services they access, and the variety of specialists who ensure they receive an appropriate education. The following points can help you keep in perspective these students' uniqueness and your role in their education:

> Students with low-incidence disabilities together make up less than 20 percent of all the students with disabilities in schools.

1. Students with low-incidence disabilities together make up less than 20 percent of all the students with disabilities in schools. That means that you are unlikely to teach these students every year unless your school has a program that brings together students with these disabilities from across your school district, sometimes referred to as a *cluster program* or *district class.* Otherwise, you may encounter students with low-incidence disabilities only a few times in your career.

2. Students with low-incidence disabilities often have received some type of special education service since birth or shortly thereafter. They might come to kindergarten already having attended an infant program and preschool program in a day-care, inclusive preschool, or special education setting in which their special needs were addressed. You also may find that many supports and extensive technical assistance are available for your students with low-incidence disabilities.

3. Students with low-incidence disabilities need the same type of attention from you that other students do. If you are unsure about a student's needs, it is nearly always best to rely on the same professional judgment you use in working with other students. If you encounter difficulty, you can access the technical support that special education professionals offer. Students with certain disabilities, especially significant or complex ones, often are accompanied by paraprofessionals or personal assistants,

TABLE *6.1*

School-Age Students with Low-Incidence Disabilities
Receiving Special Education Services in 2002–2003[a]

Federal Disability Category	Defining Characteristics	Total Number of Students	Percentage of All Students Receiving IDEA Services	Percentage of All Students Ages 6–21
Mental retardation	Significant below-average general intellectual functioning with deficits in adaptive behavior	580,375	9.85[b]	.88
	Identified between birth and 18 years of age			
	Adversely affects educational performance			
Multiple disabilities	Two or more disabilities so interwoven that none can be identified as the primary disability	130,443	2.21	.20
	Adversely affect educational performance			
Hearing impairments	Hearing loss is permanent or fluctuating, mild to profound in nature, in one or both ears	71,112	1.21	.11
	Loss may be referred to as *hard of hearing* or *deaf*			
	Adversely affect educational performance			
Orthopedic impairments	Physically disabling conditions that affect locomotion or motor functions	73,617	1.25	.11
	May be the result of a congenital anomaly, disease, accident, or other cause			
	Adversely affect educational performance			
Other health impairments	Conditions resulting in limited strength, vitality, or alertness and caused by chronic or acute health problems	390,295	6.62	.59
	Adversely affect educational performance			
Visual impairments	Vision loss in which the student cannot successfully use vision as a primary channel for learning or has such reduced acuity or visual field that processing information visually is significantly inhibited and specialized materials or modifications are needed	25,520	0.43	.04
	Adversely affect educational performance			
Autism	Developmental disability characterized by impairments in communication, learning, and reciprocal social interactions	118,092	2.00	.18
	Usually identified in infancy or early childhood			
	Adversely affects educational performance			
Deaf-blindness	Presence of both a vision loss and hearing disability that causes severe communication and related problems	1,536	0.00	.00
	Adversely affects educational performance			

continued

What Are Low-Incidence Disabilities?   197

TABLE *6.1*

Continued

Federal Disability Category	Defining Characteristics	Total Number of Students	Percentage of All Students Receiving IDEA Services	Percentage of All Students Ages 6–21
Traumatic brain injury	Impairment manifested by limited strength, vitality, alertness, or other impaired development resulting from a traumatic brain injury Adversely affects educational performance	21,384	0.36	.02
Developmental delay	Significant delay in one or more of these areas: physical development, cognitive development, communication development, social or emotional development, or adaptive development Needs special education and related services Applicable for children ages 3–9	58,075	.99	.09

[a] Students ages 6–21 receiving services through IDEA, Part B (U.S. Department of Education, 2004). Note that the disability category developmental delay does not distinguish among children with mild versus significant disabilities; not all children in this category may have low-incidence disabilities.
[b] Because federal categories of disability do not distinguish among students with various degrees of mental retardation, it is difficult to provide a precise estimate of the number of students with moderate or severe intellectual disabilities. However, approximately one-third of the students in this category have moderate or severe intellectual disabilities.

Source: From *Twenty-Sixth Annual Report to Congress on the Implementation of the Individuals with Disabilities Education Act,* 2004, Washington, DC: U.S. Department of Education.

who might work with them for several years. Such an individual may be able to offer insight about responding to a given student, but the responsibility for ensuring the student's educational success is yours.

You may have some concerns about meeting the needs of a student with a low-incidence disability in your classroom. The Professional Edge suggests questions you can ask to prepare for teaching a student with a low-incidence disability. The questions address the student's strengths and potential, learning and social needs, and physical or health needs. They also cover domains in which accommodations might be needed, including the physical arrangement of the classroom. What other questions would you add?

If you look ahead in this textbook, you will find that both this chapter and Chapter 7, on high-incidence disabilities, address students with intellectual disabilities, also called *mental retardation.* This dual consideration occurs because the federal category of mental retardation is used for all students with intellectual disabilities, whether mild, moderate, or severe. This chapter addresses only students with moderate or severe intellectual disabilities. Students with mild intellectual disabilities have characteristics and needs similar to those of students with learning and behavior disabilities, and they are discussed with those groups in Chapter 7.

You also should be aware that some of the students discussed in this chapter, as well as some of those in Chapter 7, may be identified as having a **developmental delay.** This term, allowed in IDEA for children ages 3 through 9, indicates the presence of a significant physical, intellectual, communication, or social or emotional delay without specifying a specific disability category.

Simulation Homework Exercise

Go to the Homework and Exercises section in Chapter 6 of MyEducationLab to consider the question, "What do you see when you see a person with a disability?"

Questions to Ask When Working with Students with Low-Incidence Disabilities

When you teach a student with a low-incidence disability, you probably will have concerns about the student's needs and your responsibilities for helping her succeed. In your conversations with special educators, related services personnel, and administrators, you might ask questions such as these about the student:

Student Strengths and Needs

1. What are the student's greatest strengths?

2. What activities and rewards does the student most enjoy?

3. What are the student's needs in these domains: academic? social? emotional? behavioral? other?

4. Does the student have physical or health needs that require my attention? For example, does the student need to take medication? Is the student likely to have a reaction to medication? Does the student tire easily? Does the student need assistance in moving from place to place?

5. What else should I know about this student's strengths and needs?

Student Goals

1. What are the three or four most important instructional goals for this student in my class? What are the academic, social, behavioral, emotional, and other goals?

2. What are the goals for this student in each subject (for elementary teachers)? How do the goals for this student interface with the instructional goals of this course (for

secondary teachers)? Overall, how do the goals for this student align with the general curriculum?

3. What are the goals that this student is working on throughout the day? Which goals are emphasized during different periods of the day?

Student Supports and Accommodations

1. If I have a question about the student, whom should I talk to? What other professionals may be in contact with me about this student or come to my classroom?

2. Does the student have a paraprofessional or interpreter? If a paraprofessional is assigned, what responsibilities should that person carry out? For what activities should the student, not the paraprofessional, be responsible? To what extent can the paraprofessional help other students in the class?

3. What other services (for example, speech/language services) will the student access? How often? Who will be in touch to help arrange these services? Will they be delivered in the classroom or in another location?

4. Do I need to adjust the physical environment for this student? If so, how?

5. Do I need to adjust my expectations for this student because of physical or health needs? If so, how? Are there restrictions on this student's participation in any class activities? If so, what?

6. How can I best adjust my teaching to accommodate the student's needs?

What Accommodations Can You Make for Students with Autism Spectrum Disorders?

Autism was first identified as a disorder in 1943 by Dr. Leo Kanner. Since then, it has been the source of much research and ongoing professional debate. At various times, autism has been viewed as either a type of emotional disability or as a special form of intellectual disability. However, professionals now recognize that autism is a unique disorder that occurs in many forms, and they usually refer to this group of disabilities as **autism spectrum disorders (ASD)** to convey its diverse nature. The prevalence of autism spectrum disorders

Info Sheet Homework Exercise

Go to the Homework and Exercises section in Chapter 6 of MyEducationLab for a description of strategies for teaching and including students with ASD.

has been rising steadily over the past decade, partly due to better diagnosis (Fighting Autism, 2004; Fombonne, 2003; National Institute of Mental Health, 2007). ASD is believed to occur in some form in anywhere from 1 in 500 to 1 in 150 children. This disability affects boys more than girls in a ratio of approximately 3:1 to 4:1, and it often occurs with other disorders, including intellectual disabilities and attentional and communication disorders. What is important to remember is that, contrary to traditional understanding, many individuals with autism spectrum disorders do not have intellectual disabilities and may be gifted or talented (Nash & Bonesteel, 2002). If you teach a student with autism spectrum disorder, you will find that it is both rewarding and challenging—that sometimes the student is a frustrating enigma and other times the student's progress in learning and contributions to the school community are exciting.

Characteristics of Students with Autism Spectrum Disorders

Although autism is like most of the other low-incidence disabilities in that it can exist in many variations, from mild to severe, and cannot be treated as a single disorder with a single set of adaptations, it does have specific characteristics.

www.resources

The website of the Autism Society of America, at www.autism-society.org/site/PageServer, provides a variety of information about ASD and links to resources helpful for teachers.

● **Social Relationships**   Significant difficulty with social relationships is an essential characteristic of individuals with autism. Many students with autism resist human contact and social interactions from a very early age and have difficulty learning the subtleties of social interaction (Denning, 2007). These students often do not make eye contact with others, and they can seem uninterested in developing social relationships. For example, typical young children often ask the teacher to watch them do something ("Look at me!"), and they bring interesting items to share with their teacher and classmates. A young child with autism, however, may not seek out such opportunities for social interactions. Albert, a 13-year-old with autism, discussed his problems in the social domain. He maintained that others viewed him as extremely ugly, but he did not understand why he did not have friends. When an interviewer asked him what he talked about with others, the two topics he mentioned were wind and smells in the environment (Cesaroni & Garber, 1991). He did not take on the perspective of others, and he did not understand that talking about others' interests, so different from his own, also were part of social interaction.

● **Communication**   A key reason students with autism spectrum disorder experience difficulty in social relationships is the challenges they face in using and responding to traditional verbal and nonverbal communication (e.g., Ingersoll, Dvortcsak, Whalen, & Sikora, 2005; Toth, Munson, Meltzoff, & Dawson, 2006). These students often have significantly delayed language development, and if they have language skills, they struggle to maintain conversation with another person. In writing about her experiences of being autistic, Temple Grandin, one of the most famous individuals with ASD and a university professor who has designed livestock facilities, provides clear examples of her communication problems (Grandin, 2002). She explains that when she was young she simply did not have the words to communicate and so frequently resorted to screaming. She also comments that as she grew up, she observed others but did not understand how to fit in. Unlike Grandin, many students with autism spectrum disorders cannot write or otherwise easily communicate about their experiences, and they may use behaviors instead of words to convey many needs. Unless they are taught alternative behaviors, they might hit a peer as a way of saying hello or run from the classroom instead of saying they do not like the assignment just given. Some students with autism have *echolalic speech;* they repeat what others have said instead of producing original communication. Working to ensure productive communication is a central part of working with students with ASD.

- **Student Interests**   Another characteristic of students with autism is a narrow range of interests. For example, one student may be fascinated with radios to the exclusion of nearly everything else; another might focus on a single period in history and have an expert's understanding of that era. When students with autism have such interests, they can spend literally hours absorbed in a private world of exploration. They might act bored with every topic and every activity unless it relates to their special interest. This behavior sometimes has a negative impact on social relationships with peers and adults, because individuals with ASD do not discern that others are not as interested in their preferred topic as they are. However, researchers now are exploring how students' focused interests can be used as a tool for fostering the development of social and communication skills (Winter-Messiers et al., 2007).

- **Student Stress**   Students with autism have a low threshold for and difficulty in dealing with stress (Myles & Adreon, 2001). A change in classroom seating assignments could be difficult for a student with autism, as could the introduction of a new route from the classroom to the bus or an alternative order for the day's activities. Particular noises or odors or a noisy environment also can be stressful. Many students with autism respond to stress with stereotypic behaviors. They complete the same action or motion again and again. For example, they may rock rapidly in the chair, spin an object repeatedly, or twirl their arms. In other situations, students might develop a ritual to complete a task. They might need 10 minutes to prepare to complete an assignment because they need to arrange paper and pencil on the desk in a precise pattern, check that all the books in the desk are also stored in a specific order, and make sure the desk is aligned precisely at the intersection of tiles on the classroom floor. In your classroom, you should be aware of potentially stressful situations for a student with autism. You can allow time for the student to prepare for the situation, talk about the situation well in advance, assign a peer partner to assist the student, and enlist the assistance of a special educator or paraprofessional. If a student's response to stress is demonstrated with aggressive or disruptive behavior, you should work closely with a special educator, behavior consultant, or other specialist to address the problem. In some instances, the student might need to spend part of the school day in a more structured, less stressful environment, such as the school library or learning center.

*R*esearch Note

Although some individuals contend that autism can be linked to the MMR (measles–mumps–rubella) vaccine, the Centers for Disease Control and Prevention (2002) reports that no published scientific evidence supports this claim.

> In your classroom, you should be aware of potentially stressful situations for a student with autism.

Students with Asperger Syndrome

One group of students with autism spectrum disorder that should be highlighted comprises those with Asperger syndrome (Verte, Guerts, & Roeyers, 2006). A wide range of students may be identified with this disability. Students with **Asperger syndrome** have extraordinary difficulty in social interactions, such as making eye contact, using facial expressions appropriately and understanding those of others, and seeking out peers and other people, even though their language and intellectual development are typical. They also may have difficulty in using language correctly, confusing whether to use first-person (*I*), second-person (*you*), or third-person (*she* or *he*) pronouns. These students also may insist on specific routines in the classroom and at home, and as noted earlier, they may have extraordinary interest in a specific topic (for example, models of aircraft, countries in Asia) to the extent that they do not realize that others may not share their interest. Many students with Asperger syndrome have very high intellectual ability, and they appropriately spend the school day with peers in general education classrooms and continue on to college (Adreon & Durocher, 2007). However, because of their difficulty with social interaction, they may struggle to make friends. Sean, the student you met at the beginning of this chapter, has Asperger syndrome.

Accommodations for Students with Autism Spectrum Disorders

Although it is impossible to provide a comprehensive list of strategies for helping students with ASD to succeed in your classroom, the following suggestions illustrate how your efforts can make a significant difference in these students' lives.

● **Responding to Behavior**   Students with autism spectrum disorders often have behaviors that are unusual and can be disturbing to teachers and students who do not understand them. These behaviors also can interfere with learning. However, many of the behaviors can be corrected with highly structured behavior support programs. Others have relatively simple solutions, and some can be ignored. For example, if a student with autism withdraws from classroom activities and begins rocking every day at about 11:00 A.M., it could be a signal that he is too hungry to work until an 11:45 A.M. lunchtime. Providing a snack in a quiet corner of the classroom could reduce the problem. Many students with autism spectrum disorders can receive some or all of their education in a general education classroom, provided that needed supports are in place (Myles, 2005).

Generally, the accommodations that help to reduce behavior problems involve creating a structured and predictable environment and encouraging appropriate social interactions (Grandin, 2002; Kluth, 2003). To create a positive learning environment, establish clear procedures and routines for classroom tasks and follow them consistently. For example, in an elementary classroom, you can create procedures for students to retrieve their coats at lunchtime or begin each day with the same activities in the same order. For secondary students, you can set a clear pattern in your instruction by beginning each class with a 3-minute review followed by a 20-minute lecture followed by a 15-minute individual or small-group work session. Instead of relying on words to prompt students about these procedures, work with a special educator to create picture cards that depict the procedures. Students with autism spectrum disorder often respond better to pictures than words. Several specific strategies for working with students with autism spectrum disorder are summarized in the Professional Edge on pages 204–205.

In addition to structure, students with autism spectrum disorder may need opportunities during the day to work alone and be alone (Myles & Adreon, 2001). This time serves as a break from the stresses of the classroom and the social and communication demands of that setting. A special education teacher probably can advise you about whether this is necessary for a particular student and can assist in making arrangements for a quiet place, sometimes referred to as *home base,* for the student to work.

● **Fostering Social Interactions**   To help a student with social interactions with peers and adults, you can observe the student's behavior to understand its purpose from her perspective (Denning, 2007). If a student has been working in a small group but suddenly leaves the group and runs out the door, it could be a signal that she has misunderstood a comment made by another student. Other social areas in which general education teachers can work with special educators to accommodate students with autism spectrum disorders include teaching them to wait, to take turns, to stop an activity before it is complete, to negotiate, to change topics, to finish an activity, to be more flexible, to be quiet, and to monitor their own behavior.

● **Communicating with Students**   Communication with students with autism is accomplished through a wide variety of strategies (Grandin, 2007; Toth et al., 2006). Some students with autism can communicate adequately with speech, especially when they do not feel pressured. With young children, this sort of communication sometimes can be prompted by interrupting a child during a favorite activity (for example, playing

> To create a positive learning environment, establish clear procedures and routines for classroom tasks and follow them consistently.

with a toy) and then permitting the child to resume the activity after communicating with you (Sigafoos & Littlewood, 1999). Other students learn to communicate through sign language, just as many students who are deaf or hard of hearing do. For some students, the motor activity of signing seems to help them successfully convey their needs and preferences. For yet other students, communication boards are useful tools. By simply touching pictures, students can communicate with others even when they cannot speak the appropriate words. Other communication devices that help students who have limited speech, including those with autism, are described later in this chapter.

In general, when you learn that you will teach a student with autism, you should ask to meet with a special educator who can share with you the student's strengths and needs and help you plan for the school year. Few single descriptors are adequate to describe these students, and their diversity and complexity will sometimes frustrate you and at other times make you proud to be a professional educator.

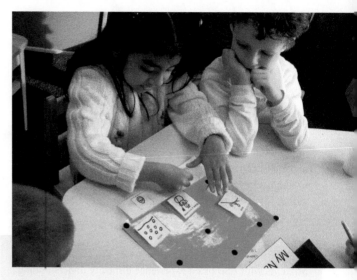

Why is it so important for teachers to assist students with autism in learning social skills for interacting with their peers as well as teachers and other adults at school?

What Accommodations Can You Make for Students with Moderate, Severe, or Multiple Disabilities?

Students with moderate, severe, or multiple disabilities include those whose intellectual impairments and adaptive behavior deficits are so significant and pervasive that considerable support is needed for them to learn. This group also includes students with multiple disabilities, that is, students who have two or more disabilities that significantly affect their learning. Both groups of students typically have activities and assignments that differ somewhat from those of other students in your class, but their work still should be aligned with the general curriculum for which you are responsible. These students also can benefit from social interactions with classmates who do not have disabilities.

Students with Moderate to Severe Intellectual Disabilities

Students with moderate to severe intellectual disabilities have ongoing needs for support during their school years and into adult life. Some students are able to learn the academic, social, and vocational skills that enable them to live independently or semi-independently as productive adults. Others' learning will be more limited, and they may need intensive services throughout their lives. In many school districts, students with moderate or severe disabilities are integrated into general education classrooms, most often at the elementary school level but sometimes at the middle school and high school levels as well. One class in which these and many other students with disabilities commonly participate is physical education, the topic of the Special Emphasis On . . . feature.

Most states use scores on intelligence tests and adaptive behavior scales to determine the presence of an intellectual disability. Although intelligence tests must be interpreted carefully and are not helpful in designing instruction for students, an overall IQ score of less than 70 with significant difficulty in the area of adaptive behaviors (for example, ordering a meal in a restaurant) leads to eligibility for special education in the category of

Video Homework Exercise

Go to the Homework and Exercises section in Chapter 6 of MyEducationLab to see how Carlyn, a student with an intellectual disability, interacts with her peers in preschool.

Teaching Students with Autism Spectrum Disorder

Specialized techniques can be used to teach students with autism spectrum disorder (ASD). These approaches are designed to draw on students' strengths, focus their attention, and address their unique needs. Three examples of approaches proven effective with these students are social stories, the picture exchange communication system (PECS), and visual schedules.

Social Stories

Students with ASD often experience difficulty understanding social expectations, especially when those expectations vary across situations. An example situation concerns when it is OK to run at school. This social story might assist a student with autism:

Running

> I like to run. It is fun to go fast.
> It's OK to run when I am playing outside.

I can run when I am on the playground.
I can run during P.E.
It is not OK to run when I am inside, especially at school.
Running in the hallways is not safe.
Teachers worry that someone may get hurt if I run into them.
When people are inside, they walk.
I will try to walk in the hallways and run only when I am outside on the playground.

After preparing this type of story, the teacher reads it several times with the student, preferably just before the situation in which running is an issue. As the student learns to follow the advice in the story, the teacher gradually reduces repetition of the story until it is no longer needed.

Social stories can be used in many situations. Try writing a social story for each of these situations:

- a high school student who is using profanity when speaking with adults at school

FIGURE 6.1

Examples of PECS Pictures

soccer

school bus

line up

mental retardation. Students with moderate or severe intellectual disabilities generally have IQ scores of approximately 55 or below. Leaders in the field argue that a more appropriate strategy for identifying individuals with intellectual disabilities is to define the disability by adding other key factors, including social participation, health, and individual functioning within the broader context of school, home, and community (American Association on Mental Retardation, 2002). Kylie, whom you learned about at the beginning of the chapter, is a student with a moderate intellectual disability. As you read the following sections, think about how she might learn in your classroom.

FIGURE *6.2*

Examples of Visual Schedules

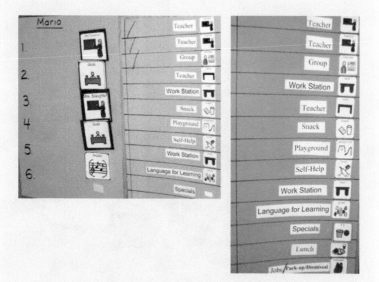

As students learn the system, they begin to initiate communication by bringing a picture to another individual to obtain the pictured item or make a need known. Eventually, students use this system to form sentences and answer questions. Research has demonstrated the effectiveness of this system (Magiati & Howland, 2003). If you teach students with autism, you might interact with them using PECS.

a crayon, a basketball) for the actual item when the student points to it or picks it up (see Figure 6.1). No words are used.

Visual Schedules

Most students with ASD benefit when they have a clear and consistent schedule that is explained ahead of time. Working with a special educator, you can develop visual schedules that use pictures only, pictures and words, or words only (see Figure 6.2). Visual schedules can be displayed in the classroom, placed on the student's desk, or kept in an assignment notebook.

■ a middle school student who talks only about one topic

■ an elementary student who takes her shoes off when in the cafeteria

Picture Exchange Communication System

The picture exchange communication system (PECS) is a strategy for teaching individuals with ASD to initiate communication with peers and others. PECS is taught to students in a highly structured series of steps. Initially, the teacher or another person working with the student exchanges a picture of a desired item (for example,

Sources: From *Social Stories,* by the Center for Autism and Related Disabilities, University of Florida, n.d., retrieved November 23, 2004, from http://card.ufl.edu/handouts/socialstories.html; *Visual Schedule Systems,* by L. Kamp and T. McElean, 2000, Vancouver, BC: Special Education Technology—British Columbia, retrieved November 23, 2004, from http://www.setbc.org/projects/vss/default.html; *Beyond Autism PECS Pictures/Icon Pages* (p. 15), n.d., retrieved November 23, 2004, from the Beyond Autism website, http://trainland.tripod.com/pecs15.htm; and "A Pilot Evaluation Study of the Picture Exchange Communication System" (electronic version), by I. Magiati and P. Howland, 2003, *Autism: The International Journal of Research and Practice, 7,* pp. 297–320.

● **Learning Needs and Rate** Generally, students with moderate or severe intellectual disabilities have several noticeable characteristics. First, the amount of information they can learn may be limited, and second, the rate at which they learn may be slow. These two factors suggest that considerable repetition of skills essential for adult functioning is needed. For example, Destiny, a middle school student with a severe intellectual disability, is learning to communicate her needs to others. She has a communication device that enables her to indicate that she needs a drink of water, that she needs to use the bathroom, and that she is hungry. Her paraprofessional sometimes works with

Special EMPHASIS on

Physical Education

In many schools, physical education teachers work with all students, both those with and without disabilities, and evidence supports inclusive approaches. For example, Lorenzi, Horvat, and Pellegrini (2000) studied typical elementary students and those with intellectual disabilities as they shared unsupervised recess time. The authors found that for both groups, boys tended to have a higher level of activity and to raise their heart rate more than girls. However, they also found that both boys and girls with intellectual disabilities raised their heart rate more than their classmates. The authors concluded that inclusive recess settings fostered healthy habits for students with disabilities.

Strategies and Approaches

The key to successfully including students with low-incidence disabilities in physical education classes is careful planning with the students' IEP teams using the INCLUDE strategy. Here are some guidelines for accommodating students:

- Whenever possible, allow time for students to gain independence in the activities.

Evidence shows that inclusive approaches in physical education are successful for students with low-incidence disabilities.

- Focus on student abilities, not disabilities. Use student and parent information to give yourself greater understanding of what students are capable of learning and doing.

DIMENSIONS OF

diversity

Rogers-Adkinson, Ochoa, and Delgado (2003) provide reminders for working with families of students with significant disabilities from nondominant cultures: Namely, the technical terms related to students with disabilities may be unfamiliar to these parents, the traditions in their homes may seem contradictory to the goals of American schooling, and their religious beliefs may affect how they respond to the child.

her on this skill, but her classmates also ask her questions related to these needs. Jordan, an elementary student with a moderate intellectual disability, is learning a variety of preacademic skills within his general education classroom, including telling a story from a picture book, recognizing his name and address, and understanding directional prepositions such as *up, down, inside,* and *outside.* He rehearses these as opportunities arise during general instruction, and when other students are completing individual assignments that are beyond his capability, he works on his skills on the computer, sometimes with a peer assistant.

Students with moderate or severe intellectual disabilities usually also need to learn many other essential skills that go beyond academics. One example is social skills. Several IEP goals and objectives may relate to participating in one-to-one or small-group interactions with peers, responding to questions asked by others, and sharing toys, games, or materials. These students also may need to learn how to participate appropriately in nonacademic and extracurricular activities, such as field trips and after-school programs (Wagner, Cadwallader, Garza, & Cameto, 2004). Without direct assistance from teachers implementing inclusive practices, these students may have difficulty making friends throughout their school careers (Doré, Dion, Wagner, & Brunet, 2002; Geisthardt, Brotherson, & Cook, 2002).

- Take into account students' social and emotional readiness for activities, not just their physical readiness.

- Encourage students to choose and adapt activities.

- Maintain activity integrity, but make enough changes so that students can participate successfully.

- Emphasize cooperative games. One example is a relay race in which the objective is to "beat the clock," that is, to improve personal performance.

- Avoid elimination games. Students who most need to participate often are the first eliminated.

- Use stations as a means to provide student with a wide variety of activities at various skill levels.

- Maintain students' right to take risks. Be careful about assuming that certain activities are not suitable for certain students.

- When introducing activities, keep explanations simple, demonstrate, use multisensory approaches, check for understanding, break instruction into small pieces, and ensure students understand any safety issues.

- Check the physical environment to be sure it is appropriate—for example, ensure the space is large enough to accommodate wheelchairs, shortened distances for students with stamina problems, and consistency for students with visual impairments.

- Adapt equipment as needed—for example, change the weight, color, or size of balls or targets.

- Modify student roles when appropriate, for example, by having students stay on base while another student runs, by simplifying the type of movement required, or by changing scoring to foster student success.

- Modify rules to enhance successful participation, for example, by adapting time given for an activity.

- Arrange activities that encourage all students to learn real-world social skills through their peer interactions during physical education.

- Use peers without disabilities to assist students with disabilities by having them share roles, tutor or coach, or assist students during class activities.

Source: Adapted from "Beyond Games, Gadgets, and Gimmicks: Differentiating Instruction across Domains in Physical Education," by S. P. Smith, 2005, *Journal of Physical Education, Recreation, and Dance, 76*(8), pp. 38–45; and "Inclusion of a Diverse Population" (electronic version), by S. L. Sutherland and S. R. Hodge, 2001, *Teaching Elementary Physical Education, 12*(2), p. 16. © 2001 by Human Kinetics. Adapted with permission from Human Kinetics (Champaign, IL).

● **Maintenance of Learned Skills**   A second characteristic of individuals with moderate or severe intellectual disabilities is that they may have difficulty maintaining their skills; without ongoing practice, they are likely to forget what they have learned. In the classroom, you may find this means that it is not necessary to provide new activities each day. For example, Jordan, the student mentioned previously who is learning to recognize his name and address, will need computer practice on that skill for many days. In addition, once he has identified the information, he should practice printing it on cards, writing it on the chalkboard, and saying it aloud. Extensive practice on a single skill using many approaches is usually appropriate.

● **Generalization of Learning**   A third characteristic of students in this group is that they may have difficulty generalizing skills learned in one setting or situation to another. It is thus critical that they learn as many skills as possible in context. For example, rather than have these students practice buttoning and unbuttoning out of context, as part of a segregated classroom exercise, they can apply this skill in the morning and afternoon as they enter and leave school wearing coats or sweaters. Older students need to learn how to greet classmates and teachers appropriately, for example, with a handshake or by just saying hello instead of shouting or tightly hugging them. This skill is most easily taught as students meet and greet people throughout the school, not in a special education classroom.

Video Homework Exercise

Go to the Homework and Exercises section in Chapter 6 of MyEducationLab to watch a teacher deliver a lesson incorporating academics into a functional curriculum.

● **Skill Combination**   One additional characteristic of students with moderate to severe intellectual disabilities is difficulty combining a series of small skills into a larger one. For example, a student may be taught each step involved in making a sandwich, but unless the steps are taught in an integrated way, the student probably is going to have difficulty carrying them out in a logical sequence. Some older students can learn to use personal digital assistants (PDAs) to help them remember sequences of skills (Davies, Stock, & Wehmeyer, 2002). How might this student characteristic affect your instruction of them?

Crystal is a young woman with **Down syndrome,** a genetic disorder that often includes a moderate intellectual disability. Her story is typical for such a student in a school district committed to inclusive education. She attended elementary school with her peers even though she did not always learn the same things they were learning. Her teachers expected her to behave appropriately, and her peers helped her when she got confused by the teacher's directions or otherwise needed support in the classroom. As Crystal moved to middle school, she participated with peers in co-taught science and social studies classes and elective classes such as foods and computers, and she received some of her reading and math instruction in a special education classroom. In high school, she took several classes, including choir, U.S. history, home economics, career exploration, and family living. She also entered a vocational preparation program so she would be ready to get a job after high school. At 21, Crystal graduated from high school. She now works in a local medical office. Her job includes duplicating medical records, doing simple filing, running errands, and helping get mail ready to send. Crystal's success as an adult is in large part a result of learning many skills while in inclusive schools.

● **Accommodations for Students with Moderate to Severe Intellectual Disabilities**   Are you a bit surprised at the implication in this chapter that students with significant intellectual disabilities should participate in general education? Had you assumed that they would receive specialized instruction in a special education classroom?

The latter perception is unfortunately still common (Agran, Cavin, Wehmeyer, & Palmer, 2006), but it is out of date. Research indicates that students with moderate or severe intellectual disabilities benefit from attending school as members of general education classrooms (e.g., Browder, Wakeman, Spooner, Ahlgrin-Delzell, & Algozzine, 2006). In one review of 36 studies on including students with intellectual disabilities in general education settings, the authors found that students did better both academically and socially than comparable students in self-contained special education classrooms (Freeman & Alkin, 2000). In fact, many of the adaptations and general school conditions needed by students with moderate and severe disabilities are the same ones that make learning more successful for all students. Added to those are a few unique strategies designed for the abilities and special needs of each individual student (Clayton, Burdge, Denham, Kleinert, & Kearns, 2006) and instructional principles, such as those described next.

● **Match Expectations to Instruction**   Both the No Child Left Behind Act of 2001 (NCLB) and IDEA set the expectation that the goals and objectives for all students, including those with significant intellectual disabilities, refer to the same general curriculum. This does not mean that these students are expected to learn all the same information as other students, but it does imply that the goals and objectives on their IEPs should be related to the grade-level or course competencies. In this regard, the INCLUDE strategy can help you, working with colleagues, effectively teach students with moderate or severe intellectual disabilities. For example, in a social studies class, the goal for most students might be to understand detailed topographical maps. At the same time, a student with a moderate intellectual disability might work to locate on a map states where relatives live, and a student with severe mental retardation might work to identify photos of businesses in the community. Your plan should be to use the principles of universal design for learning (UDL) that were introduced in Chapter 5 to ensure that assignments appropriate for a student draw from the standard curriculum or are as close to it as possible (Wehmeyer, Lattin, Lapp-Rincker, & Agran, 2003). Table 6.2 provides additional examples of how the skills that might appear on a student's IEP can be mapped onto the general curriculum.

TABLE 6.2

Sample Skills from an IEP Mapped onto Fifth-Grade School Subjects

IEP Objectives	Activities/Subjects				
	Social Studies	Math	Reading	Physical Education	Lunch
To recognize pictures for expressive communication purposes	Use daily schedule to get out book Match pictures related to social studies	Determine story problem for peers by matching same pictures	Answer questions by pointing to pictures Sequence three pictures in order to retell story	Choose equipment using photographs Choose partner using school photographs	Use pictures to request type of milk from cafeteria person Point to pictures to converse with peers
To follow directions quickly	Watch peers get out materials and follow their lead Sequence pictorial cards in order Put away materials and get ready for next subject	Watch peers get out materials and follow their lead Work on math skills as instructed Change activity when directed	Watch peers get out materials and follow their lead Find appropriate page in book Answer questions by pointing Put away materials and get ready for next subject	Line up for PE Move to area on floor by PE teacher Follow teacher and group	Line up for lunch with class Go to lunch room Stay at table until dismissed
To interact with peers in a positive way	Sit with classmate Do not destroy peer's work Pass out materials	Sit with classmate Do not destroy peer's work Pass out materials Respond to three offers of help	Sit with classmate Choose book to read from peers Respond to peers's questions	Respond to peers when they initiate Share equipment Clap for peers when they do well	Respond to peers when they initiate Initiate topics using schedule and magazine Respond to peer's questions
To make decisions	Decide who will read to her Request help when needed Pick appropriate pictures from three pictures based on question	Decide which math activities to do Decide which manipulatives to use: first, second, third	Choose book to read Choose peer to read with Choose place to read	Decide which two of three exercises to do and in what order	Choose milk Choose person to sit next to Choose where to go when finished eating and with whom
To work independently	Stay on task without adult nearby for 10 minutes Raise hand to get help	Stay on task without adult nearby for 10 minutes Raise hand to get help	Stay on task without adult nearby for 10 minutes Raise hand to get help	Stay on task without adult nearby for 10 minutes Start each exercise/ activity on own Raise hand to get help	Stay on task without adult nearby for 10 minutes Obtain milk with peer support Eat meal with no prompts

Source: Adapted from "First Steps: Determining Individual Abilities and How Best to Support Students" (pp. 37–70), by M. A. Demchak and J. E. Downing, 2002, in *Including Students with Severe and Multiple Disabilities in Typical Classrooms: Practical Strategies for Teachers* (2nd ed.), Baltimore: Paul H. Brookes Publishing Co. Reprinted with permission.

Why do instructional adaptations and strategies for including students with moderate to severe cognitive disabilities benefit all students in a classroom? What does this indicate about focusing on student similarities, rather than their differences?

● **Identify Optimal Times for Specialized Instruction**   Students with moderate or severe disabilities sometimes need to learn skills that will not likely arise as part of the traditional school curriculum, but these activities should nevertheless be integrated into instruction. For example, students might complete activities such as gathering homework, handing out materials, working on key vocabulary related to the topic being studied, and helping the teacher to call on students. How could each of these activities relate to a student's IEP goals and objectives? Why might activities such as these represent appropriate instruction for some students?

● **Enlist Natural Support Systems**   Peers, older students, parent volunteers, student teachers, interns, and other individuals at school all can assist a student with a moderate or severe disability (Carter & Kennedy, 2006; Ryndak & Alper, 2003). Peers often can answer simple questions or respond to basic requests without adult intervention. They sometimes also can make needed adjustments in equipment, retrieve dropped articles, and get needed instructional materials for the student. Older students can serve as peer tutors or special buddies, both for instruction and for the development of appropriate social skills. Parents, student teachers, interns, and others all can assume part of the responsibility for supporting students. For example, an administrative intern who reads a story to the class releases the classroom teacher to observe or work with a student with a moderate or severe intellectual disability. A student teacher can work with a small instructional group that includes both typical learners and a student with an intellectual disability.

● **Create a Collaborative Effort with Families**   As with your other students, when you teach a student with a moderate or severe disability, you should communicate regularly with the student's parents. Families know their children better than school professionals do, and parents can provide valuable information about teaching them. Parents

Analyze
and Reflect

What strategies implemented in meeting the needs of students with moderate or severe disabilities also are beneficial to students without disabilities? That is, how are these two groups of students more alike than different?

Collaborating to Support Students with Significant Disabilities

Collaboration is essential for students with low-incidence disabilities to have opportunities to participate in general education settings. One approach that has been useful for students, parents, and school professionals is called the McGill Action Planning System (MAPS). Developed in Canada by experts in inclusive practices for students with significant disabilities, MAPS is based on a set of questions focusing on strengths that parents, other family members, professionals, students, and peers answer in one or more meetings intended to ensure that a student has positive learning experiences. Here are the questions that guide this process:

- *What is this student's history?* This question is answered by family members so that others have a better understanding of the student.

- *What is your dream for the child?* As participants answer this question, they are encouraged to think about what they want for the student and what they think the student wants. This is a question of vision, not present-day realities. The team members should dream some here and verbalize those dreams.

- *What is your nightmare?* Parents sometimes find this question particularly hard to answer because it requires thinking of their child facing difficulties. But if participants can verbalize their nightmares and fears, they will have taken an important step in becoming committed to making sure this nightmare never occurs.

- *Who is the student?* Take turns describing the student. Participants continue taking turns until no one has anything else to add. When the list is completed, particular

people in the group, such as family members, are asked to identify what they believe are three especially important descriptors.

- *What are the student's gifts?* The individuals collaborating to plan for the student might look back on the ways they have described the student in answering the previous question. They focus on what they believe the student can do, instead of what the student cannot do.

- *What are the student's needs?* The parents' answers to this question might vary considerably from those of the student's peers or teachers. When the list has been completed, the group decides which needs are top priority, demanding immediate attention.

- *What would an ideal day at school be like for the student?* Some MAPS groups answer this question by outlining a typical school day for students without disabilities who are the student's age. The team might think about how the needs outlined in answering the previous question could be met at school. After that, the team could think about the kinds of help a student needs to truly achieve inclusion at school.

Consider the various people involved in the MAPS process. Why is it critical to include general education teachers? What unique contribution might a student's peers make? How does MAPS represent a model for collaboration that also could be useful in thinking about working together on behalf of other students?

Source: From *The MAPS Process: Seven Questions,* by the Circle of Inclusion Project, University of Kansas, 2002. Retrieved November 22, 2004, from www.circleofinclusion.org/english/guidelines/modulesix/a.html.

---

also might have questions about how to reinforce at home the skills learned at school. One strategy for drawing on parent, family, and peer knowledge about a student with a low-incidence disability to plan an effective education is included in the Working Together. Occasionally, you may encounter a family that does not want to be actively involved in the education of their child. In such a case, it is your responsibility to accept their decision without judging it.

Like all parents, the parents of students with moderate or severe disabilities respond to their children based on many factors, including their culture. For example, in some Puerto Rican, Mexican, and Colombian families, the mother or both parents are blamed for having a child with significant disabilities, and raising this child is seen as penance for past sins (Rogers-Adkinson, Ochoa, & Delgado, 2003). These parents' degree of acceptance of a child at a low level of functioning may frustrate teachers trying to help the student to learn

Video Homework
Exercise

Go to the Homework and
Exercises section in Chapter 6
of MyEducationLab to see how
adapted keyboards and word
prediction software help many
students complete academic work.

Info Sheet Homework
Exercise

Go to the Homework and
Exercises section in Chapter 6
of MyEducationLab to see how
assistive technology devices make
the daily activities of schooling
possible for students with physical
disabilities.

skills and relying on parents to practice the skills at home. For students who are bilingual, issues may arise as educators try to teach English survival words (for example, *stop, danger*) at school when only the native language is spoken in the home.

● **Take Advantage of Assistive Technology**   Both high- and low-technology options help students learn. Some students experience success when you provide them with pictures that remind them of key concepts, and with the widespread availability of digital cameras, infinite opportunities exist to take photos of signs, locations, people, and other items that can be used as tools for contextual learning. Many students who cannot use language to communicate use various forms of **augmentative and alternative communication (AAC),** that is, various communication forms—unaided (for example, gestures) or aided (for example, computer software)—that enable students to convey their messages. These are addressed in the Technology Notes. Other students use technology to aid movement.

Students with Multiple Disabilities

Because students with multiple disabilities often have extraordinary needs, they are considered a distinct group in IDEA. Most students with multiple disabilities have an intellectual disability and a physical or sensory impairment. The needs of these students and the accommodations that help them succeed can be similar to those for students with moderate and severe intellectual disabilities, the differences being mostly a matter of degree and complexity.

> Most students with multiple disabilities have an intellectual disability and a physical or sensory impairment.

However, a few issues may arise more often that particularly concern these students. You may find that the number of special service providers who come to the classroom to work with students with multiple special needs (for example, a special educator, a paraprofessional, a speech/language therapist, or an occupational therapist) is high and occasionally a distraction in the classroom. Also care must be taken that a wheelchair, computer equipment, other therapeutic equipment, and specialized materials (for example, large books in three-ring binders made with many pictures) for a student with multiple disabilities are seamlessly integrated into classroom practices so as not to interfere with traffic patterns, safety, and storage.

Because many students with multiple disabilities have limited speech and do not easily convey their preferences and needs, communicating with them can be a challenge. One strategy for communication is using alternative and augmentative communication (AAC) systems, which are sometimes used by students with moderate or severe intellectual disabilities (and other disabilities affecting communication), as described in the previous section.

Analyze
and Reflect

What are the reasons that
the curriculum for students
with significant disabilities
now is aligned with that for
all students? What are the
implications of this requirement
for general education teachers?

As a teacher, you can expect most but probably not all students with multiple disabilities to participate in general education activities in your school. They will likely receive considerable support from a special education teacher or a paraprofessional. Thus, co-teaching and other classwide integration activities are likely (Giangreco & Doyle, 2002). These professionals and other members of the multidisciplinary team can assist you in setting expectations for students, planning appropriate educational experiences, monitoring their performance, and problem solving when concerns arise (Downing, 2002). In an elementary school, a student with multiple disabilities might attend your class for morning activities, remain in the room for part of language arts instruction (Browder et al., 2006; Downing, 2005), and participate in art and music with other students. That student also might receive some services in other building locations (for example, the library, gym, learning center, or special education classroom). In a secondary school, a student with multiple disabilities might attend some core classes with peers, some classes with a vocational emphasis (for example, consumer math or a school food service/restaurant program), and some special classes for learning other functional and job-specific skills.

Augmentative and Alternative Communication

Augmentative and alternative communication (AAC) is the term for an individual's use of ways other than speech to send a message to another individual. AAC includes nonaided communication, such as sign language and gestures and facial expressions, and it also includes aided communication, such as using computers and other simple or complex devices as tools. You might be familiar with a children's story about AAC: E. B. White's *The Trumpet of the Swan,* in which Louis, a swan who cannot make the same sounds as other swans, learns to use a trumpet as his voice.

Many students with low-incidence disabilities use AAC devices either as their primary means of communication or as supplements to traditional speech. To facilitate a student's use of such devices, a team that includes the student and family members, the speech/language pathologist, teachers, and others evaluates the communication needs and abilities of the student; explores options, sometimes by having the student try out different devices for a specific period of time; teaches the student to use the selected device; and monitors its effectiveness. These are some examples of AAC devices that your students might use:

- *Communication boards.* Many students with significant disabilities use communication boards. These boards may be as simple as a set of pictures that depict common tasks or needs. The student points to the appropriate picture using a finger, fist, elbow, eyes, or alternative means such as a head pointer. More complex communication boards are electronic. Pointing at pictures may activate prerecorded messages, such as "I need to be excused to the restroom" and "Hello. My name is Jorge. What is your name?" For middle and high school students, communication boards can be designed to include necessary key vocabulary terms.

- *Switches and scanning devices.* Some students cannot push a button or point at a picture. However, they might be able to indicate a choice using a switch. Thus, when a scanning device is used, a series of options is presented (for example, "I am hungry," "I am thirsty," or "I am tired"), and the student chooses the one that communicates the intended message. The switch is the means for making the choice. The student may have the motor control to slap a large button switch to stop items being shown on a computer screen, or she may make a slight head movement that activates a switch with an electronic voice that responds.

Information about augmentative and alternative communication is available on many websites and from many organizations, including these:

Communication boards can be simple or complex and tailored to meet the needs of the student and the learning situation.

The Discover Switch is designed for students who write using computers but operate them with a switch. This device includes picture and word banks, as well as other helpful tools.

- Augmentative and Alternative Communication Connecting Young Kids (YAACK), a website with basic information and links to many other resources (http://aac.unl.edu)

- International Society for Augmentative and Alternative Communication (ISAAC) (www.isaac-online.org)

Source: Adapted from *Introduction to Augmentative and Alternative Communication,* by American Speech-Language-Hearing Association, 2004, Rockville, MD: Author. Retrieved November 22, 2004, from www.asha.org/public/speech/disorders/Augmentative-and-Alternative.htm.

Deaf-Blindness

Although students with dual sensory impairments, or *deaf-blindness,* typically are not totally blind or deaf, they do have extraordinary needs related to staying in touch with the environment, making sense of events that most teachers and students take for granted, and learning with a limited ability to see and hear (Byrnes & Majors, 2004). These students sometimes have average or above-average intelligence (as did Helen Keller), but they often have intellectual or other disabilities. They typically need a wide array of special services throughout their school careers and into adulthood (Nelson, 2005).

How a student with deaf-blindness is educated in any particular school varies considerably. In some schools, professionals, paraprofessionals, and parents judge that students who are deaf and blind can be successful in an inclusive environment with extensive supports (Bruce, 2007), but they disagree somewhat on the types of and approaches to service delivery. In addition to instructional support in a general education setting, these students often need extensive training to learn to communicate through sign language, signals and gestures, touch cues, and other means (Bruce, Godbold, & Naponelli-Gold, 2004). In addition, students who are deaf-blind need assistance in social interactions with their peers. Teachers can facilitate interactions by doing the following (Goetz & O'Farrell, 1999):

- Arrange the classroom to promote the active participation of students who are deaf-blind.
- Prompt students with special needs and typical learners to interact with each other.
- Interpret for typical students the behaviors of students who are deaf-blind. For example, pushing and shoving may be an indication that the student is excited about playing with the other students.

In other schools, a student who is deaf-blind may be a member of your class, accompanied by a special education teacher or paraprofessional, only on some field trips, at assemblies, in selected class activities, or for particular school programs. The specialists working with the student can prepare both you and other students in the class, letting you know how to approach and greet the student, telling you what to expect in terms of behavior, and explaining why inclusive activities are important for the student and what learning or social objectives are being addressed.

What Accommodations Can You Make for Students with Sensory Impairments?

Students with *sensory impairments* have either vision loss or hearing loss so significant that their education is affected. Their specialized needs can range from slight to complex. Because school learning relies heavily on seeing and hearing, students with these disabilities often experience academic problems and need both teacher accommodations and adaptive equipment. What challenges might these students encounter with the content you plan to teach?

In some cases, a vision or hearing problem is identified by professionals in the school setting. If you notice any of the symptoms described in the Professional Edge, you should alert your school nurse or health technician as well as the student's parents.

Students with Visual Impairments

Students with **visual impairments** cannot see well enough to use vision as a primary channel for learning without significant assistance. Some students are considered *legally blind,* which means that the vision in the best eye, with correction, is 20/200 or lower, or the

Warning Signs That Students May Have Vision or Hearing Loss

As a school professional, you sometimes will be in a unique position to judge whether a student may be experiencing a vision or hearing loss. If you observe any of these warning signs, you should alert your school nurse and follow district guidelines for seeking other assistance for the student.

Signs of Possible Vision Loss

- Frequent rubbing or blinking of the eyes
- Short attention span or daydreaming
- Poor reading
- Avoiding close work
- Frequent headaches
- A drop in scholastic or sports performance
- Covering one eye
- Tilting the head when reading
- Squinting one or both eyes
- Placing head close to book or desk when reading or writing
- Difficulty remembering, identifying, and reproducing basic geometric forms
- Poor eye–hand coordination skills

Signs of Possible Hearing Loss

- Failure to pay attention to casual conversation
- Giving wrong, inappropriate, or strange responses to simple questions

- Apparently functioning below cognitive potential
- Frequent and recurring ear infections
- Complaints of ringing in the ears, "head noises," and/or dizziness
- Complaints of pain in the ears or discharge
- Withdrawing from interactions with peers
- Frustration or other unexplained behavior problems
- Limited speech or vocabulary
- Frequent mispronunciation of words
- Placing head close to book or desk when reading or writing
- Watching a speaker intently to hear
- Failure to hear someone who is speaking from behind
- Turning up the volume on the television or when using the computer
- Difficulty hearing when using the phone

Sources: Adapted from *Warning Signs of Vision Problems,* by Eye Care Council, 1998, retrieved November 22, 2004, from www .seetolearn.com/warning.html; *An Educator's Guide to Hearing Impairment,* by N. Crowe, November 2002, retrieved November 22, 2004, from www.nsac.ns.ca/envsci/staff/ncr/hearing.pdf; and *Teaching Students Who Are Hard of Hearing,* by Northeast Technical Assistance Center, n.d., Rochester, NY: Author, retrieved November 22, 2004, from www.netac.rit.edu/publication/tipsheet/teaching.html.

visual field is 20 degrees or less. In other words, what a person with normal vision can see at 200 feet, someone with this level of vision can see at a maximum of only 20 feet. Those students legally blind because of a limited visual field can see just a 20 percent or smaller slice of what a person with normal vision can see within his range of vision.

Although the concept of legal blindness is an important one that helps students access special services throughout their lives, a different set of terms is used in schools. For educators, the term *blind* generally is reserved to describe the few students who have little or no useful vision. They use touch and hearing for most learning. Most students with visual impairments are *partially sighted,* meaning that they have some useful vision. Their vision is between 20/70 and 20/200, or they have another vision problem that has a serious negative effect on their learning.

Accommodations for Students with Visual Impairments

fyi

Although a few students have guide dogs, adults are more likely to use them because of the care they need, the training involved in obtaining them, and the expense of maintaining them.

Info Sheet Homework Exercise

Go to the Homework and Exercises section in Chapter 6 of MyEducationLab to learn about ways in which students with visual impairments may need extra support.

Students with visual impairments have the same range of intellectual ability as other students, but they typically have had fewer opportunities to acquire information usually learned visually (Pogrund & Fazzi, 2002). For example, students generally learn about maps by looking at them. Although students who are blind can learn by feeling a raised map, this method is not as efficient as seeing it. The same problem can occur with academics. Students with visual impairments often experience learning difficulties simply because they cannot easily use vision to process information. Think about how you read this text: You probably scan the pages, focus on words and phrases in boldface print, and visually jump between reading the type and looking at figures, features, and photos. If you only could read this book by magnifying it 15 times, by listening to it on audiotape, or by reading it in braille, you would find it much more tedious to scan, select important words and phrases, and go back and forth between components. If you multiply this dilemma across all the visual learning tasks students face, then you can begin to understand the challenges of learning with a visual impairment.

As is true for all individuals, students with visual impairments vary in their social and emotional development. Some students encounter little difficulty making friends, interacting appropriately with peers and adults, and developing a positive self-concept. Other students need support in these areas (Bishop, 2004). For example, it is important to teach some students who cannot see to adhere to social norms, such as facing a person when talking, taking turns, and keeping an appropriate social distance. Conversely, teachers should keep in mind that some students might miss another student's or a teacher's puzzled expression about something they had said and continue to interact as if they were understood. Teachers also should help other students to understand that a student with a visual impairment cannot help a wiggling eye or that such a student stands a little too close during interactions because she has difficulty judging distance.

Planning Instruction for Students with Visual Impairments

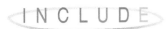

Accommodations needed by students with visual impairments depend on many factors, and the INCLUDE strategy can guide your planning. First, take into account the student's overall ability level, use of learning strategies and other learning skills, and attentional and motivational levels, just as you would for any other student. Then, working with a special educator, make accommodations relative to the amount of the student's residual vision and the nature of her vision problems. Be sure to keep in mind that these students have many essential life skills to master that other students take for granted (for example, proper eating manners, maintaining appropriate social distance during interactions, keyboarding, signature writing, and proficiency in using adaptive technology). These skills sometimes are referred to as the *expanded core curriculum,* because they are as essential to these students as are the skills of the traditional curriculum (Lohmeier, 2005). Time must be made in their school careers to teach these skills (Ferrell, 2005). Some specific accommodations you can make and unique needs you must consider for students with visual impairments are covered in the following sections.

> Accommodations needed by students with visual impairments depend on many factors, and the INCLUDE strategy can guide your planning.

● **Orientation and Mobility** One important area of need for students with visual impairments is orientation and mobility, that is, the sense of where they are in relation to other objects and people in the environment and the ability to move about within a space. For example, students with visual impairments need to understand where furniture, doorways, bookshelves, and the teacher's desk are in the classroom in relation to their own location. In addition, they need to be able to move from the classroom to the auditorium to the cafeteria and out to the bus in a timely manner. Your first task in preparing for a student with a visual impairment might be to arrange your classroom carefully, leaving adequate space for all students to move about. Depending on the amount of sight the student has, you might need to keep furniture and supplies in consistent places and make sure the student has an opportunity to learn where everything is. If you decide to rearrange the room or move your supplies, alert the student with a visual impairment to the changes and allow opportunities to adapt to them. Another orientation and mobility issue is safety. Half-open doors and trash cans inadvertently left in aisles can be serious hazards for students with visual impairments. For fire drills and emergencies, pair all students with buddies to assist each other so as to avoid singling out an individual with a visual impairment.

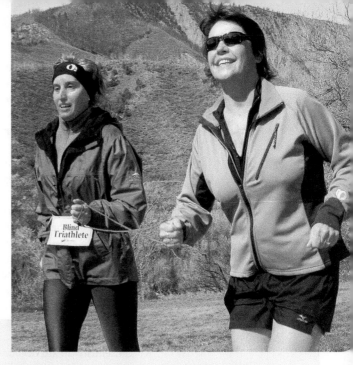

In all your work with students with disabilities, your ultimate goal is to enable them to lead full and productive lives after they finish school.

● **Teaching Students with Visual Impairments** You might be asked to modify your teaching slightly to accommodate a student with a visual impairment. For example, you might need to identify the novels you plan to use in class prior to the start of the school year so they can be ordered in braille, large-print, or audiotape format. For visual clarity, you might need to use a whiteboard with a black felt-tipped marker instead of a traditional chalkboard, or you might need to provide the student with paper that has heavy black lines instead of the traditional light blue ones. In addition, you should be sure to recite what is written on the board; call students by name so the student with a visual impairment can learn the sounds of classmate's voices and where they are seated; allow the student to move close to demonstrations and displays; give specific directions instead of using general words such as *here* and *there;* and seat the student to optimize visual learning (for example, away from bright light or near the front of the room). Usually, an itinerant vision specialist or another special educator will alert you to these types of accommodations and arrange for any classroom modification.

Some general adjustments in your classroom also can help a student with a visual impairment. Meet with the itinerant vision specialist or other special educators to discuss the student's needs and extent of assistance required, including the important matter of problems related to storing the student's specialized equipment. Based on this information, some or many accommodations might be appropriate. Assign a buddy to assist a new student at the beginning of the school year, especially in dealing with the cafeteria, moving from room to room, and locating supplies. This assistance might be discontinued later in the school year to avoid creating unneeded dependence.

Some students with visual impairments need additional time to complete assignments, whether during class or as homework. Monitor the student closely to ensure he is not spending too much time on a single task; this might be a signal that the task needs to be shortened or otherwise modified. Be alert for a student's need for a change-of-pace activity. A student who is fidgeting or refusing to work might be fatigued; this is a common problem for students who have to make extraordinary efforts to learn using vision. Letting the student take a break or substituting an alternative activity both helps the student and prevents discipline problems. Also keep in mind how to plan alternative learning opportunities for students. If you are talking about history and using a timeline, for example, use white glue or some other means of marking points on the timeline so a student with a visual impairment can participate meaningfully in the discussion by touching the points and feeling the distance between them. A vision specialist can help you develop such alternative learning opportunities. Finally, teachers sometimes worry about how the

Video Homework Exercise

Go to the Homework and Exercises section in Chapter 6 of MyEducationLab to see that students with visual impairments can be active, contributing members of the school community.

*R*esearch Note

Like other students with disabilities, students with visual impairments are concerned with self-determination. In one study, 54 students with visual impairments, ages 8 to 23, reported that they had few opportunities to make choices at home, at school, with friends, for health care, and in physical education classes (Robinson & Lieberman, 2004).

use of words and phrases such as "Do you see my point?" and "That's quite a sight!" will affect a student with a visual impairment. Generally, you should just use the vocabulary you normally would; avoiding words related to seeing is not necessary.

● **Learning Tools for Students with Visual Impairments**   Students with visual impairments use a wide variety of devices or equipment to facilitate their learning. If they have some residual vision, they can use devices to help them acquire information visually. Some use simple devices such as magnifying lenses and bright lights to read or do other schoolwork. Others hold their books close to their eyes or at a specific angle to see the print. Many students with visual impairments use computers. For example, if students use a speech synthesizer or text enlarger with a standard word-processing program, they may be able to type their assignments exactly as their peers do. For students who read braille, assignments can be printed on a braille printer as well as a standard printer so both teacher and student can read them. A further sample of the learning tools available for students with visual impairments is included in the Technology Notes on pages 220–221.

Students with Hearing Loss

Students who are deaf or hard of hearing, referred to in IDEA as having **hearing impairments,** cannot hear well enough to use hearing as a primary channel for learning without significant assistance. Because a huge proportion of both formal and incidental learning occurs through casual conversations, presentations by teachers and others, and overheard information and thus relies on understanding language, many professionals consider deafness and other hearing loss to be primarily language or communication impairments (for example, Luckner & Muir, 2001). A small number of students with hearing impairments are *deaf;* they cannot process linguistic information through hearing, either with or without hearing aids. Most of these students, however, are *hard of hearing,* meaning that they have some residual hearing that lets them process linguistic information through hearing, usually by using hearing aids or other assistive devices.

To determine the severity of a hearing loss, professionals check the loudness of sounds, as measured in decibels (dB), and the pitch or tone of sounds, as measured in hertz (Hz). Normal speech is usually in the 55 to 60 dB range at 500 to 2,000 Hz. In contrast, a whisper is about 15 to 25 dB, and a rock band plays at about 110 dB. Students with a hearing loss of 25 to 40 dB are considered to have a mild loss; they might not hear every word in a conversation or might not distinguish between words with similar sounds (such as *breathing* and *breeding*). Those with a loss of 40 to 60 dB have a moderate loss; they typically cannot hear enough of a conversation to follow it auditorily. Those with a loss of 60 to 80 dB have a severe loss, and those with a loss of more than 80 dB have a profound loss. Alyssa, whose story you read at the beginning of the chapter, has a profound hearing loss. Students with severe and profound hearing losses typically cannot process speech, even when amplification is used. They rely on sight as an alternative means of learning.

Another factor professionals consider in judging the seriousness of a student's hearing loss is the age when the loss occurred. Students who have been deaf or hard of hearing since birth are often at a disadvantage for language learning because they did not go through the natural process of acquiring it. These students can speak, but because they learned to talk without hearing how they sounded, their speech may be difficult to understand. They might prefer sign language and an interpreter for communicating with you and others. Students who lose their hearing after they learn language, that is, after about age 5, sometimes experience fewer language and speech difficulties.

Accommodations for Students Who Are Deaf or Hard of Hearing

Students with hearing losses have the same range of intellectual ability as other students. However, if intelligence is assessed using a test based on language, students with hearing loss might have lower scores. Academically, many students struggle because their hearing loss affects their ability to understand language, which in turn affects their learning. Alyssa, the student with a profound hearing loss introduced at the beginning of the chapter, finds this problem especially frustrating. Evidence suggests that students who are deaf or hard of hearing and are educated in general education settings usually read better than their peers who are educated in special education classrooms (Easterbrooks, 1999). However, these students might have difficulty learning vocabulary and as a result understanding the materials they read and the lessons you present (Marschark, Convertino, & LaRock, 2006). For example, students with hearing losses often miss subtle meanings of words, which can affect both their learning and their social interactions. One simple example can illustrate the complexity of learning language. Think of all the meanings you know for the word *can*. As a noun, it refers to a container made of metal for storing food—for example, *a can of peas*. But it also means a container with a lid, as in the type of can that tennis balls are packaged in. *Can* also has slang meanings as a synonym for both *bathroom* and *prison*. As a verb, it means "to be physically able," as in *I can lift that box*. It also refers to preserving produce from the garden, as in *I plan to can green beans this year*; to losing a job, as in *I just got canned*; and to the state of being likely, as in *Can that be true?* If you think about all the words in the English language that have multiple and sometimes contradictory meanings, it becomes easier to understand the difficulties faced by students who are deaf or hard of hearing, who may not informally learn these meanings.

Socially and emotionally, students who are deaf or hard of hearing are sometimes immature (Punch, Hyde, & Creed, 2004). This lack of maturity occurs for two reasons. First, much of the etiquette children acquire comes from listening to others and modeling what they say and do. This learning is not available to many students who are deaf or hard of hearing. Second, these students can become confused in interactions that involve many people and multiple conversations. Because these types of situations often are uncomfortable for them, students with hearing impairments sometimes avoid them and fail to develop the social skills needed in group interactions. For example, Jim is a seventh-grade student with a moderate hearing loss. When students work in lab groups in Mr. George's science class, Jim tends to withdraw because he cannot follow what everyone is saying. Sometimes he tries to participate in the activity, but he often does so by making an exaggerated face or drawing a cartoon to show others. He does this even when the other students are working intently, and they become annoyed with his antics. When Jim realizes his attempts to participate are not being successful, he pulls away from the group and becomes passive. Mr. George and the special education teacher are working to address this problem. Mr. George makes sure that he monitors the groups' work, and he sometimes intervenes by asking Jim a question that helps him participate in his group. Mr. George reminds his students that unless every group member understands a science experiment, the group is not finished. Jim also receives help on his social interactions in a support group led by a social worker, which he attends with several other students twice each week.

● **Teaching Students Who Are Deaf or Hard of Hearing** Accommodations for students who are deaf or hard of hearing emphasize helping them use whatever residual hearing they may have and accessing language to promote formal and informal learning. Although the specific types of accommodations needed by a student you teach will be determined by the multidisciplinary team that writes the student's IEP, the following are some common ones.

Many students who are deaf or hard of hearing get some information through *speech reading*, or watching others' lips, mouth, and expressions. Given this, the teacher should always face the class when presenting information and stand where no glare or shadow makes it difficult for students to see. Using an overhead projector instead of writing on the chalkboard also is a good idea. A teacher also should stand in one location instead of

> Academically, many students struggle because their hearing loss affects their ability to understand language, which in turn affects their learning.

fyi

Even the best speech readers get only about 25 percent of a spoken communication. Most individuals receive only 5 to 10 percent of spoken communication using this strategy.

Video Homework Exercise

Go to the Homework and Exercises section in Chapter 6 of MyEducationLab to watch a teacher, paraprofessional, and student with a hearing loss discuss how inclusion works for them.

Assistive Technology for Students with Visual Impairments

The electronic braillewriter is a device with six keys that the student simultaneously presses down in various combinations to produce the special system of raised dots that can be read through touch.

Large-print books are low-tech options for students with visual impairments.

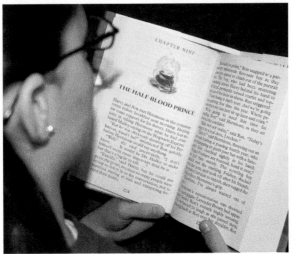

Harry Potter and the Half-Blood Prince
© J. K. Rowling, 2005

A portable notetaker is equipped with six keys and a spacebar, as well as a speech synthesizer.

The slate and stylus is a simplified device for producing braille.

moving around the room, and the student should sit near the teacher. These adjustments facilitate speech reading but also are necessary if an interpreter is present. Teachers should avoid exaggerating sounds or words; doing this makes it more difficult for the student, not easier. Because some students with hearing losses do not use speech reading and because even those who do get only part of the message that way, teachers should use as many visual aids as possible. Important directions can be written on the chalkboard, using either words or, for younger students, pictures. For older students, major points in a lecture can be written on an overhead projector or on the chalkboard. With an overhead projector, the teacher can face students while writing, thus enabling students with hearing impairments to speech read.

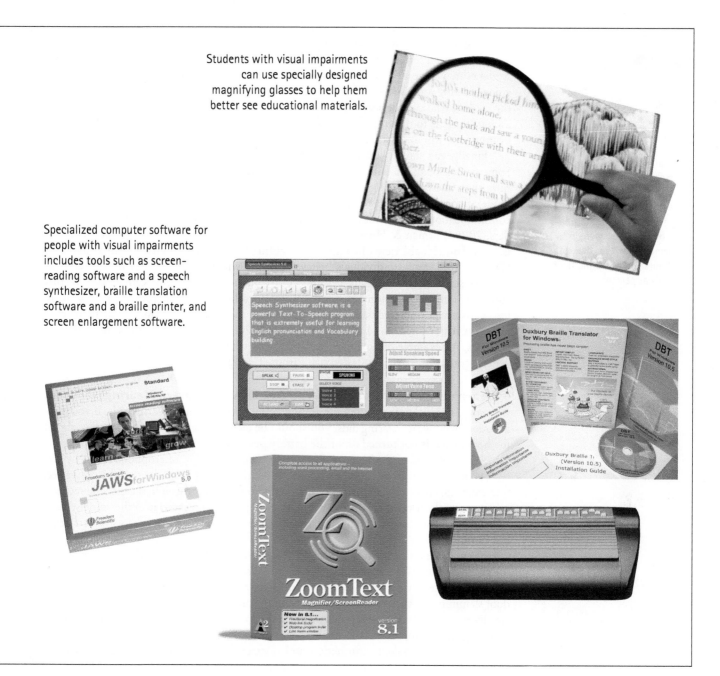

Students with visual impairments can use specially designed magnifying glasses to help them better see educational materials.

Specialized computer software for people with visual impairments includes tools such as screen-reading software and a speech synthesizer, braille translation software and a braille printer, and screen enlargement software.

If a student who is deaf or hard of hearing speaks to you and you do not understand what she has said, ask her to repeat the information. If you still do not understand or the student becomes frustrated, switching to paper and pencil is sometimes appropriate. When a student appears confused following directions or answering a question you ask, the difficulty might be vocabulary. Try substituting a simpler word or offering a word you think the student might be trying to convey. Above all else, be patient when communicating with students who are deaf or hard of hearing.

As with students who have visual impairments, safety also must be kept in mind for students with hearing impairments. Assigning a buddy to assist such a student during a fire, tornado, or earthquake drill is a simple strategy for addressing this issue. For other specific adaptations regarding safety, a special educator with expertise in working with these students can assist you.

If a student who is deaf or hard of hearing uses sign language, you might consider enrolling in a sign class yourself and, especially in elementary and middle school, inviting a deaf education teacher to your class to teach some signs to the entire group. High school students may have an option for learning sign language as a course. Students generally enjoy learning some signs, and both you and they will be better able to communicate with the student who cannot hear. For example, you might use the sign for "line up" instead of asking students to do this. When you use the sign, everyone, including the student with hearing loss, will understand.

Finally, you should be aware that the field of deaf education is facing complex issues. Some professionals, parents, and community members believe that students should maximize their use of oral language; others argue that sign language should be the primary mode of communication. Yet others favor teaching students both sign language and oral communication skills (National Institute on Deafness and Other Communication Disorders, 2006; Pittman & Huefner, 2001). Controversy exists too about Deaf culture, that is, some individuals' view of deafness as a cultural phenomenon rather than a disability (Davis, 2007). Some individuals believe students who are deaf should be educated in separate schools with specially designed curricula and experiences. Others believe this approach leads to isolation for students. If your school includes students with hearing losses, you may hear discussion concerning these topics, and knowing about them may help you better understand the range of perspectives among professionals, parents, and students. An example of how to include students who are deaf or hard of hearing in the general education classroom is described in the Case in Practice.

- **Learning Tools for Students Who Are Deaf or Hard of Hearing** Students with some residual hearing often use amplification devices such as hearing aids. If you have a student who wears hearing aids, you should be alert for signs of inattention that signal the hearing aid is not turned on or the battery needs to be replaced.

A second type of device is an FM system consisting of a microphone worn by the teacher and a receiver worn by the student. When the teacher talks, the sound is converted into electrical energy and carried on a specific radio frequency through the air. The receiver converts the electrical energy back to sound, amplifies it, and sends it to the student's ear. Alternatively, with this system the classroom may be equipped with speakers so all students can more clearly hear the teacher's voice.

Keep in mind that hearing aids and FM systems both amplify sounds, but they do not discriminate the teacher's voice from other sounds. Thus, a student wearing hearing aids can be distracted by the amplified noise of someone typing on the computer keyboard, a door slamming, or chairs scraping on the floor. A student using an FM device also hears the amplified sound of a teacher's jewelry hitting the microphone or the static from a teacher's fingering the microphone. Any of these extraneous noises can interfere with a student's understanding of spoken information and distract from learning. Amplification clearly assists some students who have hearing impairments, but it has limits.

A third type of device also is becoming more common. Cochlear implants and related technology are creating options for some students to hear electronically. These sophisticated devices are being used even with young children, and it is likely that you will teach a student who has a cochlear implant. These devices enable students to perceive sound, but they are not a cure for a hearing loss. Students using them usually continue to need speech-language therapy and other supports (Preisler & Tvingstedt, 2005).

Students who have a severe or profound hearing loss often use sign language. Sometimes they use *American Sign Language (ASL)*, a distinct language that is not based on standard English grammar and structures. Learning ASL is like learning any other second language. Other students use a manually coded English (MCE) system, such as *signed exact English (SEE)*, that is, spoken English converted to a set of signs. With either method, students sometimes also use *finger spelling*, in which every letter of a word is

Blue-Banning, Turnbull, and Pereira (2002) found that Hispanic parents whose children with disabilities were making the transition from school to postschool activities expressed a wide range of hopes and expectations about future living, employment, and free-time options. They were in agreement, however, about the importance of accepting their children as persons.

Including Students Who Are Deaf or Hard of Hearing

Ms. Skinner is a fifth-grade teacher at Lunar Elementary School. This year in her class of 31, she has two students with hearing loss. The girls, who are twins, have profound hearing loss that has been present since birth. Because they use sign language as their primary means of communication, they are accompanied by Ms. Mohammed, an interpreter.

Ms. Skinner discusses what it is like to teach in this class:

> When I first heard I was going to get Jenna and Janice this year, I was worried. I knew they'd been in fourth grade and done well, but there's so much more curriculum at this level. I didn't know how I was going to teach everything and also do all the work necessary for Jenna and Janice and at the same time deal with end-of-grade testing and all that pressure.
>
> As it turns out, it hasn't been much of an adjustment at all. Ms. Mohammed interprets for the girls, and she adds explanations if they need it. The hardest part for me was learning to stay in one place when I talk. For a teacher like me, who is constantly moving around the room, that has been very difficult. Ms. Mohammed has taught all of us some basic signs—that puts us all in touch. Jenna and Janice have some

serious academic problems, mostly related to vocabulary, but the other kids just think of them as classmates. I've learned a lot this year. I'm a lot more confident that I really can teach any student who comes through my door!

REFLECTIONS

Why might teachers be worried about having students like Jenna and Janice in their classrooms? What is the best way to get over this worry? How would having these students in a middle school social studies class or high school civics class differ in terms of expectations and accommodations compared to those in an elementary class? What aspects of teaching might be particularly challenging for you if you had students like Jenna and Janice in your classroom? How would you help these students compensate for their difficulty in vocabulary? What do you imagine is the impact of having an interpreter in the classroom most of the time? What type of assistance might you ask from the twins' parents to help them master the subjects you will be teaching?

---

spelled out. Finger spelling may be needed for names or technical terms for which no signs exist.

Especially in secondary schools, students who use sign language sometimes are accompanied by interpreters who translate your words and those of classmates into sign language (Yarger, 2001). An interpreter needs to sit facing the student and near you so the student can both watch you and follow the interpreter. Some older students also use a note taker (who could be a classmate) because they cannot both watch an interpreter and teacher and take notes. However, even if a student uses an interpreter, you should speak directly to the student when asking questions, giving directions, or otherwise conversing. Do not speak to the interpreter instead of the student. The interpreter will make sure the student understands what you say. For example, you should say to Paige, a student with a profound hearing loss, "Do the first five examples on the page." You should *not* direct your remarks to the interpreter by saying "Tell Paige to do the first five examples on the page." Also keep in mind that interpreters need breaks. You might be asked to make small changes in your instructional pattern to ensure that the interpreter can take a break without negatively affecting the student's learning.

Some high school students may use another communication option called *C-print.* Using a computer, the captionist types what is being said in class using a standard set of abbreviations. The student, usually using a second computer connected wirelessly to the computer of the captionist, reads what is being said with only a three-second delay. Some research suggests that this communication approach is preferable to traditional interpreting, partly because a transcript can be produced, which of course can facilitate learning (Elliot, Stinson, McKee, Everhart, & Francis, 2001). You can learn about other examples of technologies that support students with a hearing loss in the Technology Notes on pages 224–225.

Assistive Technology for Students Who Are Deaf or Hard of Hearing

Hearing aids are common assistive technology for people with hearing impairments.

A sound field system is similar to an FM system but uses speakers so the teacher's voice is amplified for the entire class.

Cochlear implants are devices that electronically transmit sound to the brain, bypassing the ear itself.

What Accommodations Can You Make for Students with Physical, Medical, or Health Disabilities?

Some students receive special education and related services because they have physical disorders, chronic or acute medical problems, or health impairments that interfere with their learning. In IDEA, three categories of disabilities can be loosely grouped in this

This is an FM system, in which the teacher wears a microphone and the student wears a receiver.

C-print is a system in which a typist enters a teacher lecture and student comments into a laptop computer for simultaneous display on a second computer used by the student.

Closed captioning, words printed at the bottom of the screen, enables students with hearing loss to watch videos and television.

OF THE POST OFFICE'S "CELEBRATE THE CENTURY" SERIES. WHICH WILL HAVE A SET OF 15 STAMPS FOR EACH

area: orthopedic impairments, other health impairments, and traumatic brain injury. **Orthopedic impairments (OI)** are diseases or disorders related to the bones, joints, and muscles. **Other health impairments (OHI)** include medical and health conditions such as AIDS, seizure disorders, cancer, juvenile diabetes, and asthma. **Traumatic brain injury (TBI)** is any insult to the brain caused by an external force, including injuries sustained in auto accidents and during play. Students with these kinds of disabilities, which are caused by a wide variety of physical and health problems, differ greatly in their levels of ability and academic achievement and in their needs, which can range from modest to extensive. The following sections provide examples of the specific conditions that fall into these disability categories.

Orthopedic Impairments

Students with orthopedic impairments, often referred to as *physical disabilities,* are those with significant physical needs. The types of special needs these students may have include the following.

www.@resources

Information about the causes, classification, prognosis, treatment, and psychological aspects of cerebral palsy can be found at the website for United Cerebral Palsy, at www.ucp.org.

● **Students with Cerebral Palsy** In public schools, the largest group of students with orthopedic impairments comprises those who have *cerebral palsy (CP).* Some 9,750 infants and preschoolers are diagnosed each year as having this condition (United Cerebral Palsy, n.d.), a 25 percent increase over the past decade. Cerebral palsy occurs because of injury to the brain before, during, or after birth and results in poor motor coordination and abnormal motor patterns. These problems can occur in just the arms or legs, in both the arms and legs, or in a combination of limbs and with varying degrees of severity. For some students, CP also affects other muscle groups, such as those controlling the head and neck. Thus, some students with cerebral palsy walk on their toes with their knees close together. Their arms may be positioned with their elbows bent and their hands positioned near shoulder height. Other students with CP need braces or a walker to move about. Yet others use wheelchairs. For some students, head supports prevent the head from lolling side to side. Intellectually and academically, students with CP can be gifted, average, or below average, or they might have intellectual disabilities.

Don is a student with cerebral palsy. His arms and hands are drawn up close to his body, and he does not control their movement. He moves around school in a motorized wheelchair, and Mike, his personal assistant, helps with personal care (for example, going to the bathroom, eating) and tasks such as writing. Don's intellectual ability is average but his physical disabilities sometimes cause others to think he has an intellectual disability as well, especially because his speech is difficult to understand. Don's teachers have learned to engage him in class activities by asking yes-or-no questions to which he can respond fairly easily. If they ask a question requiring a longer answer, they give Don time to form the words needed and do not let other students speak for him.

Video Homework Exercise

Go to the Homework and Exercises section in Chapter 6 of MyEducationLab to watch as two special education teachers discuss a student's educational plan.

● **Students with Muscular Dystrophy** Another orthopedic impairment is *muscular dystrophy (MD),* a group of diseases that weakens the muscles. Students with this disorder have increasing difficulty walking and otherwise actively moving about. Gradually, they lose their ability to stand and require a wheelchair. They also tire more and more easily. Students with muscular dystrophy may have a normal lifespan, but some die as children or young adults (National Institute of Neurological Disorders and Stroke, 2007). Frank was a student with MD. When he began elementary school, he seemed no different from any other student. However, when he began middle school, he started using a wheelchair when he became tired. By the end of that year, he was using the wheelchair all the time. By late in his sophomore year, Frank was too weak to attend school and received instruction from an itinerant teacher at his home. He died in late September of his junior year of high school.

fyi

Spina bifida is a physical disability in which the spinal cord protrudes from an opening in the spine, and it may lead to paralysis and mental retardation. The incidence of this disability has been dropping rapidly since 1997, when the Food and Drug Administration (FDA) strongly recommended that some foods, such as bread, be fortified with folic acid, a nutrient known to prevent spina bifida.

● **Students with Spinal Cord Injuries** A third orthopedic impairment is *spinal cord injury.* As the term implies, this injury occurs when the spinal cord is severely damaged or severed, usually resulting in partial or extensive paralysis (National Spinal Cord Injury Association, 2004). Spinal cord injuries most often are the result of an automobile or other vehicle accident. The characteristics and needs of students with this type of injury often are similar to those of students with cerebral palsy. Judy suffered a spinal cord injury in a car accident. She was hospitalized for nearly half the school year, and at the time she returned to school, she could not walk and had the use of only one arm. She is as bright and articulate as ever and still gets in trouble when she challenges teachers' authority. What has changed is how she moves from place to place.

Cerebral palsy, muscular dystrophy, and spinal cord injuries are just a sample of the range of orthopedic impairments students can have. You also may teach students who have physical disabilities caused by amputations or birth defects that result in the absence of all or part of a limb. Likewise, you might have a student with juvenile rheumatoid arthritis, a chronic swelling of the joints usually accompanied by soreness and limited mobility. Whatever orthopedic impairment a student has, your responsibility is to learn about the student's needs and work with special education professionals to ensure those needs are met through various adaptations.

Teaching Students with Orthopedic Impairments

The adaptations you make for students with physical disabilities will depend on the nature and severity of the disabilities and on the students' physical status. For example, you need to be alert to changes you might need to make in the physical environment so that students can comfortably move into, out of, and around the classroom. Such changes include rearranging classroom furniture and adding supports such as handrails. Other physical accommodations, such as creating adapted workspaces with large tables and lowering chalkboards, can facilitate student learning. Of course, students with orthopedic impairments also may use assistive technology, a topic you have learned about earlier in this chapter and in other chapters. Ideas to help you think about the best uses of such technology are presented in the Technology Notes on the following page.

What adjustments might you need to make in your classroom arrangement and procedures to accommodate the needs of a student with a physical disability?

A second area of accommodation to consider for students with orthopedic impairments involves their personal needs (Friend, 2008). Many students become fatigued and might have difficulty attending to learning activities late in the school day. A few take naps or otherwise rest. Other students need to stop during the school day to take medication. Some students need assistance with personal care, such as using the bathroom and eating. Students who use wheelchairs might need to reposition themselves or be repositioned by an adult because of circulation problems. This repositioning can be done readily for young children, who can be moved to sit or lie on the classroom floor during stories and other activities. Paraprofessionals typically assume personal-care responsibilities and those related to moving students. If you have questions about these areas, a special educator can assist, or the student's parent can explain what is needed.

It is not possible to generalize about students' academic and social needs. Some students with orthopedic impairments enjoy school and excel in traditional academic areas. Some students with cerebral palsy are gifted. Other students with these disabilities experience problems in learning. Some are charming and gregarious students who are class leaders; others have a low self-concept and have problems interacting with peers. If you think about a student like Judy, the student introduced previously who has a spinal cord injury, you can imagine that her reaction to her accident and need to use a wheelchair are influenced by many factors, including her family support system, her self-concept, and her peers' reactions. The suggestions throughout this text for working with students to help them learn and succeed socially are as applicable to this group of students as to any other.

Other Health Impairments

Students with health impairments often are not immediately recognizable to a casual observer. However, their disabilities may be significant.

● **Students with Seizure Disorders**   One group of health impairments is seizure disorders, or *epilepsy,* a physical condition in which the brain experiences sudden but

TECHNOLOGY NOTES

Making Sense of Assistive Technology

Teachers in inclusive classrooms can be overwhelmed by the number and variety of technological options their students may have. As you consider the use of assistive technology for your students with disabilities, as well as for other students, keep these points in mind:

- When you are providing input related to the technology use, opt for open-ended devices whenever possible, ones that permit customizing for both student and tasks. For example, software that may be used by several students is preferable to programs designed for just one student.

- Try the lowest technology solution before assuming that high technology is needed. A larger mouse may adequately accommodate a student; an entirely different keyboard or computer may not be needed.

- Collaborate with others. Keeping abreast of all new developments is an impossible task for one person to accomplish. If you learn how to use a program or device, share your knowledge with others, and they can do the same for you. Also work closely with other professionals, such as assistive-technology specialists who might be employed in your school district.

- Collaborate with parents to be sure that technology devices that go home are used for the purpose intended and returned to school for use there.

- Ensure that devices used by students are age- and gender-appropriate. For example, a high school student using a talking word processor should use the adult voice option, not the child voice. Software, even if presenting very basic skills, should appear appropriate for a student's age.

- Avoid the belief that you have to understand completely a piece of assistive technology before you can use it and help your students use it. In many cases, "jumping in," even when you are uncertain, is the strategy of choice.

- Check on your school district policy concerning equipment use (home versus school), maintenance, and repairs. Although you are not responsible for these areas, being knowledgeable can help you and parents avoid problems.

- Ask for training on equipment or devices that your students will use. Given that you are teaching the student, you should not rely on the special educator to provide all expertise.

- Experiment with assistive technology. You may discover an option that will help some of your students or identify problems that should be addressed.

Source: Adapted from "Using Assistive Technology in the Inclusive Classroom," by J. B. Merbler, A. Hadadian, and J. Ulman, 1999, *Preventing School Failure, 43,* pp. 113–117. Reprinted with permission of the Helen Dwight Reid Educational Foundation. Published by Heldref Publications, 1319 Eighteenth St., N.W., Washington, DC 20036-1802. Copyright © 1999.

DIMENSIONS OF

diversity

The parents of students in your class might have disabilities, including orthopedic impairments, vision or hearing loss, and intellectual disabilities. What special factors do you need to consider to interact effectively with parents who have disabilities?

brief changes in functioning. The result often is a lapse of attention or consciousness and uncontrolled motor movements. A single seizure is not considered a symptom of epilepsy, but if several seizures occur, the disorder is diagnosed. About 200,000 new cases of epilepsy are counted each year, with 45,000 of them occurring among children under the age of 15. Most cases have no specific cause determined (Epilpesy Foundation, n.d.).

Epilepsy can produce different types of seizures. *Generalized tonic-clonic seizures* (previously called *grand mal seizures*) involve the entire body. A student experiencing a generalized tonic-clonic seizure falls to the ground unconscious; the body stiffens and then begins jerking. Breathing may become shallow, and the student might lose bladder or bowel control. After a minute or two, the movements stop and the student regains consciousness. The steps you should take when a student has a generalized tonic-clonic seizure are summarized in the Professional Edge.

Other seizures do not involve the entire body. *Absence seizures* (previously called *petit mal seizures*) occur when students appear to blank out for just a few seconds. If they are walking or running, they might stumble because of their momentary lapse of awareness. When you observe a student with these symptoms, alert the school nurse or another professional who can further assess the student. It is not unheard of for students to attend

What to Do When a Student Has a Seizure

As an educator in an inclusive school, and as a responsible citizen, you should know how to respond when someone has a seizure. The Epilepsy Foundation recommends these steps for responding to generalized tonic-clonic seizures:

1. Keep calm and reassure other people who may be nearby.

2. Clear the area around the person of anything hard or sharp.

3. Loosen ties, scarves, jewelry, or anything else around the person's neck that may make breathing difficult.

4. Put something flat and soft, like a folded jacket, under the person's head.

5. Turn the individual gently onto his side. This will help keep the airway clear. Do not try to force his mouth open with any hard implement or with your fingers. It is not true that a person having a seizure can swallow his tongue, and efforts to hold the tongue down can injure the teeth or jaw.

6. Do not hold the person down or try to stop his movements.

7. Do not attempt artificial respiration except in the unlikely event that an individual does not start breathing again after the seizure has stopped.

8. Stay with the person until the seizure ends naturally.

9. Be friendly and reassuring as the person regains consciousness.

10. Follow whatever procedures have been established for notifying parents that a seizure has occurred.

11. Call for medical assistance in these situations:

   ■ The seizure lasts more than five minutes.

   ■ The person is not wearing an epilepsy/seizure disorder ID.

   ■ The person is pregnant or carrying other medical ID.

   ■ The person has a slow recovery, a second seizure, or difficult breathing afterward.

   ■ Signs of injury are apparent.

Further information about what to do in the case of seizures and more information about this disorder are available from the Epilepsy Foundation at www.epilepsyfoundation.org/answerplace.

Sources: From *First Aid for Generalized Tonic Clonic (Grand Mal) Seizures and First Aid Steps for Convulsions,* by the Epilepsy Foundation, 2003. Retrieved November 22, 2004, from, respectively www.epilepsyfoundation.org/answerplace/Medical/firstaid/firstaidkeys.cfm and www.epilepsyfoundation.org/answerplace/Medical/firstaid/seizurefachart.cfm. Copyright 2008, Epilepsy Foundation of America, Inc. Reprinted with permission.

school for several years before someone realizes that their inability to pay attention actually is the result of a seizure disorder.

Most students who have seizures take medication to control their disorder. If necessary, you should monitor the consistency with which the medication is taken because that greatly affects its effectiveness. If the medication is carefully monitored and a student's size and status are not changing, you might not even be aware of the student's disability. However, when children are growing rapidly and gaining weight and when they approach puberty and undergo many physical and hormonal changes, seizures may occur as their bodies change.

Although no relationship exists between seizure disorders and academic performance, you may find that a student with this disability is reluctant to engage in interactions with peers out of fear of their reaction to the seizures (Mittan, 2005). Students also may experience low self-esteem. If a student will likely have recurring seizures, you may want (with student and parent support) to explain epilepsy to your class or ask a specialist to do that. What is important is that typical learners understand that, although somewhat frightening, epilepsy is not dangerous, is not controlled by the student who has the disorder, and is not contagious.

● **Students with Sickle-Cell Disease**   Another health impairment is *sickle-cell disease.* This disorder is inherited and occurs most often in African American individuals, with an incidence of 1 in 500. Out of every 12 African Americans, 1 carries the gene for the disorder. The disease also is occasionally found in other groups, including Greeks and Italians (Operation Sickle Cell, 2007). Sickle-cell disease occurs when normally round blood cells are abnormally shaped liked sickles. This makes the blood thicker and prevents it from efficiently carrying oxygen to tissues. The effect on individuals who have this disorder is fatigue and reduced stamina, as well as mild to severe chronic pain in the chest, joints, back, or abdomen; swollen hands and feet; jaundice; repeated infections, particularly pneumonia; and sometimes kidney failure (Operation Sickle Cell, 2007). No reliable treatments currently are available for individuals who have this disease. In children, sickle-cell disease can affect growth. Students with this disorder experience crises in which their symptoms are acute and include high fevers, joint swelling, and extreme fatigue; they are likely to miss school during these times. A student with this health impairment often needs assistance in making up for missed instruction and encouragement for dealing with the pain and discomfort.

● **Students with AIDS**   A third health impairment is **acquired immune deficiency syndrome (AIDS).** AIDS results when students are infected with the *human immuno-deficiency virus (HIV)* and their bodies lose the ability to fight off infection (DePaepe, Garrison-Kane, & Doelling, 2002). At the end of 2005, approximately 1,411 children under the age of 13 were living with AIDS (AVERT, 2007). This figure is considered a significant underestimate of the incidence of this disease, however, because several states, including some with a high incidence of reported AIDS infections, do not release HIV statistics to the Centers for Disease Control. Students with AIDS often can attend school with little assistance until their illness progresses to the point that they lack the stamina to complete schoolwork or that the risk of catching an infection or illness from a classmate becomes too great. No medical cure currently exists for AIDS; however, advances in treatment are extending life expectancy. Studies of the impact of AIDS on children are just beginning.

● **Students with Asthma**   A fourth example of a health impairment is *asthma.* Children with asthma comprise the largest group of chronically ill children in the United States. Approximately 5 million youngsters have this illness, and at any single time, most educators have two students in their classrooms who have asthma (Asthma and Allergy Foundation of America, 2007). This disease of the lungs is characterized by episodes of extreme breathing difficulty (Gabe, Bury, & Ramsay, 2002). It can be triggered by allergens such as pollen, dust, and animal dander, but often it can be controlled with medication.

Although only students with moderate or severe asthma will likely receive special education services, any student with asthma may need special consideration in your classroom. For example, these students probably are absent more than other students and need assistance in mastering missed concepts. When in school, they sometimes feel tired or generally unwell, and they may need to be excused from some activities (Madden, 2000). Some students use an inhaler to treat their condition; you should monitor that they carry this medication as needed.

● **Students with Cancer**   Yet another health impairment is *cancer,* an uncontrolled division of abnormal cells. Childhood cancer is fairly rare, with just 9,510 cases diagnosed in 2005 and a predicted survival rate of 79 percent, a dramatic improvement over the 50 percent rate of just 30 years ago (American Cancer Society, 2007). The most common forms of cancer among children are leukemia (that is, blood cell cancer) and brain tumors. Students with cancer may miss significant amounts of school because of hospitalization and other treatments; in some cases, their cognitive functioning may be affected by radiation therapy or chemotherapy. Sometimes students first identified as having a health impairment because of cancer are identified after treatment as having one or more learning disabilities. At the beginning of the chapter, you were introduced to Julian, a fifth-grade student who has this disease.

● **Additional Disorders and Conditions That May Affect Students**   Students may have many other health impairments. For example, you may have a student who has been badly burned and is undergoing medical treatment and physical or occupational therapy to restore range of movement in affected limbs. Other health impairments your students might have include hemophilia, a genetically transmitted disease in which blood does not coagulate properly; juvenile diabetes, a condition in which the body does not produce enough insulin to process the carbohydrates eaten; and cystic fibrosis, a genetically transmitted disease in which the body produces excessive mucus that eventually damages the lungs and causes heart failure. Keep in mind that some students with health impairments are not eligible for special education because their conditions do not negatively affect their educational performance. These students are likely to receive support through Section 504 plans, a topic introduced in Chapter 2 and discussed further in Chapter 8.

● **Teaching Students with Health Impairments**   As noted throughout this discussion, the accommodations you make for students with health impairments often relate to helping them make up for work missed because of absence or hospitalization and to recognizing and responding to their social and emotional needs. In one study of parents' and educators' perceptions of problems faced by children with chronic illness, parents reported that their children's most frequent problems were "feeling different," undergoing constant medical procedures, experiencing pain, and facing death. Educators listed absences, falling behind in school, lack of interaction with peers, the school's inability to meet the student's needs, and social adjustment as the most serious problems (Shepard & Mahon, 2002).

General strategies for working with students with health impairments include these:

1. Find out the students' most difficult problems, and help them work through them. Strategies include having students write or draw about their concerns and referring students to the school counselor or social worker as you see a need.

Tourette syndrome (TS), a tic disorder that includes involuntary body movements (mild or severe), occurs in about 10 out of every 10,000 school-age children. The symptom most commonly associated with TS is uncontrolled shouted obscenities, but this actually occurs in only about 15 percent of cases (Centers for Disease Control and Prevention, 2004).

Even when students are hospitalized for serious illnesses, they may continue their education. How can you assist these students in the transition back to school?

2. Provide materials for the students about others who have a similar disease or disorder. Books, videotapes, websites, movies, and other informational materials can help students with health impairments understand how others have successfully coped with their illnesses. These materials also can be useful for explaining the needs of these students to peers without disabilities.

3. Consider including death education in your curriculum if you have a student with a life-threatening condition, such as cancer. A special educator, counselor, or social worker probably can prepare a unit and help you present it. Alternatively, prepare yourself for responding to the potential death of a student and helping classmates cope with this loss.

4. Work closely with families. Parents often can be the most valuable source of information concerning their children's status and needs. In addition, they can alert you to upcoming changes in medications and emotional problems occurring at home, and they can help their children work on missed school assignments (Shepard & Mahon, 2002).

In terms of academic and curricular adaptations, you should respond to students who have health impairments as you would to students with disabilities. Using the INCLUDE strategy, you can identify their needs. If modifications in the environment, curriculum, or instruction are needed, you can carry them out using the suggestions made throughout the remainder of this text.

Traumatic Brain Injury

Traumatic brain injury (TBI), sometimes called *acquired brain injury*, occurs when a student experiences a trauma to the head from an external physical force that results in an injury to the brain, often including a temporary loss of consciousness. TBI is the leading cause of disability and death among children, and it has many causes, including falls, bicycle and motor vehicle accidents, sporting accidents, accidents on playground equipment, child abuse, and gunshot wounds (Brain Injury Association of America, 2004; Youse, Le, Cannizzaro, & Coelho, 2002). More than 1 million children and adolescents sustain a TBI each year. Although most of these injuries are mild, some 30,000 youngsters have a lifelong disability as a result of TBI (National Dissemination Center for Children with Disabilities, 2006). Whether TBI is the result of a severe injury or a mild one, it can have a pervasive and significant impact on a student's educational performance. Recovery from a TBI can take months or even years, and some students with severe TBI spend time in rehabilitation after their hospitalization and before returning to school. Other students with mild or moderate injuries are likely to go directly from the hospital back to their homes and schools (Bullock, Gable, & Mohr, 2005; Hooper, 2006). Students with TBI often return to school at some point during the recovery process, but predicting their abilities and the point at which they will reach their best outcomes is impossible given various lengths of recovery time and alternative patterns for treatment (Deidrick & Farmer, 2005).

> TBI is the leading cause of disability and death among children.

www.resources

The Brain Injury Association of America website, at www.biausa.org, includes information about causes, cost, prevention, and treatment of TBI. It even has a kids' corner.

One of the most perplexing aspects of teaching students with TBI is that they can appear just as they did prior to their injuries yet have significant learning and social problems. They also can seem back to normal one day, only to seem lethargic and incapable of learning the next. Because of the extreme variability in needs of students with TBI, the information presented in this section should be considered illustrative. If you teach a student with TBI, seek input from a specialist.

● **Characteristics of Students with Traumatic Brain Injury** Intellectually, students with TBI might have the same abilities they had before, or they might experience a loss of capacity. For example, after an automobile accident, Michael, a high school honor student who used to be a class leader, was left struggling to remaster basic math facts. His injury affected his school learning. Students might experience difficulty initiating and organizing their learning tasks, remembering what they have learned, and reasoning or problem solving. They also might have difficulty processing verbal information and producing spoken and written language.

Students with TBI also have physical needs. Depending on the severity of the injury and extent of recovery, some students have limited use of their arms and legs. Others have problems in fine motor movements, such as those needed to grasp a pencil or turn the pages of a book. Yet others have limited strength and stamina. Students with these needs sometimes attend school only part of the day.

Socially and emotionally, students with TBI experience many difficulties. Sometimes they have changes in their personalities; they are not who they used to be. Many of these students remember what they were able to do prior to their injuries and sometimes become depressed as they recognize their current limitations (National Dissemination Center for Children with Disabilities, 2006). Because these individuals often need a high degree of structure and do not respond well to change, they can display behavior problems when a sudden disruption in schedule occurs, as when an assembly interrupts an accustomed routine. Some students lose their ability to interpret and respond appropriately to social cues. As a result, they might laugh at inappropriate times, speak loudly when everyone else has realized a whisper is needed, or wander off when distracted by something. Their behaviors can be puzzling or frustrating unless you understand how to respond to them. Some of the most common challenges for students with TBI, along with potential responses teachers can make, are described in Table 6.3.

● **Families and Traumatic Brain Injury**   It is especially important to mention families as one of the considerations about TBI (Wade, Stancin, & Taylor, 2004). Often parents and siblings have witnessed a student in a totally unresponsive state, and they have psychologically prepared for the possibility of his death. They might be tremendously relieved that the student survived but at the same time traumatized by the amount of physical care he needs and the drain the injury has had on the family's financial and psychological resources. Depending on the amount of uncertainty about the extent to which the student eventually can recover, the impact of the TBI on the student's intellect and personality, and the family's ability to provide for the student's needs, the family can experience a range of emotions, including shock, denial, sorrow, and anger (Carnes & Quinn, 2005). Eventually, many families adapt. Regardless, you need to be sensitive to the family's stress and their changing capacity to follow up on homework as well as schoolwork to support your efforts.

● **Teaching Students with Traumatic Brain Injury**   If you teach a student with TBI, you might attend at least one planning meeting to discuss the details of the student's abilities and needs and to prepare for helping the student in the classroom. This transition planning typically occurs when a student is moving from the hospital or rehabilitation center back to school and usually involves personnel from both settings. Planning is essential to ensure that appropriate expectations are set for the student, procedures are established for responding to changes in the student's condition, and all services are coordinated (Bowen, 2005; Lemanek, 2004).

In your classroom, accommodations relate to physical needs, instructional and organizational routines, academic content, and the social environment. Because students with TBI need structure and routine, you should follow a consistent pattern in classroom activities, expect consistent types of student responses, and keep supplies and materials in consistent places in the classroom. If a break in routine is necessary, you can prepare the student by alerting him, assigning a buddy, and staying in close proximity.

Case Study Homework Exercise

Go to the Homework and Exercises section in Chapter 6 of MyEducationLab to meet a student with TBI and follow along as her teachers plan for her.

fyi

For professionals to make proper decisions regarding the most appropriate educational setting for a student with TBI, they consider information such as neuropsychological functioning, prior school records, current academic ability, observations from teachers and family members, and student self-reports.

> If you teach a student with TBI, you might attend at least one planning meeting to discuss the details of the student's abilities and needs and to prepare for helping the student in the classroom.

TABLE 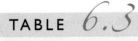6.3

Classroom Accommodations for Students with Traumatic Brain Injury

Post–TBI Cognitive Challenges	Macroenvironment	Microenvironment	Structure and Pacing	Teaching Style
Attention/ Concentration	Seat student near teacher. Minimize distractions. Use FM unit and earplugs to minimize external noise. Provide out-of-classroom activities in low-stimulation environments.	Use peer note takers. Use tape recorders. Provide assignments and activities in writing. Use large-print books with low density on the page.	Use small groups for teaching. Alternate instruction, activity, and rest. Schedule classes to capitalize on periods of highest attention.	Refocus student with verbal and/or nonverbal cues. Plan frequent breaks.
Information-processing speed		Use peer note takers and tape recorders. Review taped materials/ peer notes to identify missed critical information.	Slow the pace of classroom instruction. Allow extra time for completion of in-class tests/assignments/ homework. Reduce homework load. Allow more time for student to respond.	Do not rush or challenge the student. Provide anticipatory cuing to prepare responses in advance. Frequently repeat information to enhance processing abilities.
Memory	Provide written materials to back up classroom instruction.	Use tape recorder to review critical information. Use an organizer as an external memory aid. Test using multiple-choice format. Use fact cards and cue sheets to aid recall. Use highlighters to focus attention to information.	Utilize the student's best learning modality (e.g., visual, auditory). Encourage tape-recording new class content. Encourage writing down class assignments in daily organizer.	Provide adequate repetition for mastery. Encourage student to repeat information to ensure comprehension.
Executing functioning	Designate a specific location to return homework. Display classroom schedule.	Develop a system to indicate that homework has been handed in. Use a binder with subject sections and pockets for homework. Color-code sections of binder and book covers by subject. Create maps to aid between-class travel; do in-school travel training.	Review daily routines to reorient student. Cue student to record homework assignments. Encourage outlining oral and written assignments.	Encourage student to use organizer daily. Break large projects or tasks into component parts or steps. Prepare student before the topic shifts.

Source: Adapted from *Students with Traumatic Brain Injury: Identification, Assessment, and Classroom Accommodations,* by M. Hibbard, W. A. Gordon, T. Martin, B. Raskin, and M. Brown, 2001, New York: Research and Training Center on Community Integration of Individuals with Traumatic Brain Injury, Mount Sinai School of Medicine. Retrieved November 22, 2004, from http://mssm.edu/tbinet/alt/pubs/tbikids.pdf.

You may need to make changes in the academic expectations for a student with TBI. Because students might know information one day but forget it the next or learn with ease sometimes but struggle to learn at other times, the need for flexibility is ongoing. Students also are likely to become frustrated with their inability to learn the way they did in the past, so your patience in reteaching information, providing additional examples and exercises, and using strategies to help them focus attention is essential.

Socially, emotionally, and behaviorally, students with TBI rely on you to set clear expectations but also to be supportive of and responsive to their changing needs. One student, Gary, had been in a coma but gradually regained enough ability to function that he returned to his middle school—at first for only an hour or two each day and eventually for the entire day. However, he continued to forget common words and grew increasingly frustrated when he could not convey messages. His teachers began providing the words he needed. Because many students with TBI seem unable to form a realistic picture of how they are functioning, you might need to confront them gently about socially inappropriate behavior. Frustrated with his language skills, Gary yelled at friends, yet his sentences remained unclear. Teachers intervened to help him learn to manage his anger and to assist friends to understand him. Students with TBI also might overestimate their abilities. Informally, you can assist in this area by discussing realistic options for the near future and, with older students, for career choices.

In general, many of the accommodations needed by students with TBI are largely the same as those needed by students with physical or health disabilities, learning disabilities, and emotional disabilities. The uniqueness of students with TBI and the reason they are grouped as a separate category in IDEA is that their needs are difficult to predict, change either slowly or rapidly, and vary in intensity. Teachers who are patient and willing to meet students wherever they are and work forward from there can help students with TBI achieve school success.

Video Homework Exercise

Go to the Homework and Exercises section in Chapter 6 of MyEducationLab to see Oscar, a student who is physically disabled and cannot use his arms or hands, working in a high school math class.

Summary

Students with low-incidence disabilities comprise less than 20 percent of all students with disabilities. However, they account for eight of the federal categories of disability (that is, orthopedic impairments, other health impairments, traumatic brain injury, hearing impairments, visual impairments, deaf-blind, multiple disabilities, and autism) and part of the mental retardation and developmental delay categories. Together, these students have tremendously diverse abilities, challenges, and needs. Many of them can succeed in your classroom if you take into account that you will teach only one or two students with these disabilities at any single time and that they are students first and have disabilities second. Many of the teaching strategies you already have learned are effective in teaching these students, and other professionals and parents are available to assist you in creating successful learning experiences for them.

One growing group of students with low-incidence disabilities is composed of those with autism spectrum disorder (ASD), referred to as *autism* in federal special education law. Students with autism spectrum disorder have a wide range of intellectual and other abilities, and they have impairments in social relationships, communication, range of interests, and capacity to respond to stressful events. They need a highly structured learning environment with clear procedures and routines. Recently, more attention has been paid to students with one type of ASD, Asperger syndrome.

Moderate or severe intellectual disabilities, multiple disabilities, and deaf-blindness also are considered low-incidence disability categories. These students learn slowly, and they usually need assistance to maintain and generalize their skills and to combine skills to complete complex activities. They may not learn as much as other students or in the same ways, but their goals and objectives are aligned with the general curriculum. In a general education setting, these students need appropriate supports and teachers who have made a commitment to effective teaching and learning practices, such as instruction tailored to student skill levels, heterogeneous student groupings, natural support systems, and development of partnerships with families.

Students with sensory impairments are those with significant limitations for processing information using visual or auditory channels. The impact of these students' disabilities on their education can be slight or significant. They often have needs related to academic learning, social and emotional skills, and skills for living in their environments.

They also use adaptive equipment or materials to help them learn.

Some students have orthopedic impairments (that is, physical disabilities), other health impairments (that is, serious medical or health conditions), and traumatic brain injury (that is, trauma to the head from an accident or other injury). Their special supports and services are determined by their needs. Students in these groups often have medical problems that directly or indirectly affect their learning. Their intellectual levels can vary widely. Most students in this group have social and emotional challenges because of their illnesses, and accommodations in these areas will likely be necessary.

Back to the Cases

This section provides opportunities for you to apply the knowledge gained in this chapter to the cases described at the beginning of this chapter: Kylie, Sean, and Alyssa. The questions and activities that follow demonstrate how these standards and principles, along with other concepts that you have learned about in this chapter, connect to the everyday activities of all teachers.

Kylie appears to be learning successfully in her first-grade year. Her teachers have made the necessary accommodations and modifications to support her learning needs. However, Kylie's mother is beginning to question whether Kylie should continue to be fully integrated into the general education classroom as she progresses into upper-elementary grades. She has requested a meeting with several of the upper grade teachers. You have been invited to this meeting, which will be held tomorrow afternoon. (See INTASC Principles 2.02, 4.04, and 9.02; and CEC Standards 3, 9, and 10.) In preparation for the meeting, the principal has given each of you a list of questions to answer:

1. Why is it important for Kylie to continue her education with same-age peers in the general education classroom?

2. What can you do to support Kylie's learning needs?

3. What life skills are essential for Kylie to learn that can best be taught in the general education classroom?

Sean, as you may recall, has autism spectrum disorder. Given what you know about him and this disorder, explain how you would establish and maintain

your classroom to provide a supportive environment for a student like him. (INTASC Principles 2.02, 4.04, and 4.07, and CEC Standards 2 and 3.) Remember what you learned in Chapter 5 about using the INCLUDE strategy to guide your teaching of students with exceptional learning needs. Step 1 of the strategy requires teachers to consider their classroom demands. Your answer should include topics such as physical classroom organization, routines, and learning groups, as well as any other areas that you consider important for Sean's welfare.

Alyssa has the most difficult time with English, particularly developing ideas logically and elaborating on them. Recall what you may have learned elsewhere about typical language development in children, and compare it to what you have learned in this text about problems experienced by students with hearing loss. Then consider how general educators might support Alyssa's language development. (INTASC Principles 4.04, 4.07, and 4.08; and CEC Standards 2 and 3.) What would you do to help Alyssa learn to develop ideas along with the vocabulary needed for elaboration that will help her prepare for college level academics?

Key Terms and Concepts

Acquired immune deficiency syndrome (AIDS) (p. 230)

Asperger syndrome (p. 201)

Augmentative and alternative communication (AAC) (p. 212)

Autism (p. 199)

Autism spectrum disorder (ASD) (p. 199)

Developmental delay (p. 198)

Down syndrome (p. 208)

Hearing impairments (p. 218)

Low-incidence disabilities (p. 196)

Orthopedic impairments (OI) (p. 225)

Other health impairments (OHI) (p. 225)

Traumatic brain injury (TBI) (p. 225)

Visual impairments (p. 214)

PEARSON
myeducationlab
Where the Classroom Comes to Life

Now go to the Friend and Bursuck, Fifth Edition, MyEducationLab course at www.myeducationlab.com to

- take a pretest to assess your initial comprehension of the chapter content
- study chapter content with your individualized study plan
- take a posttest to assess your understanding of chapter content
- engage in multimedia exercises to help you build a deeper and more applied understanding of chapter content

Applications in **Teaching Practice**

Planning for Students with Low-Incidence Disabilities

Mr. Walker teaches English to ninth-graders. This year he will have several students with learning disabilities and emotional disabilities in his class, but his primary concern is Terrell, a young man who has cerebral palsy and limited vision. Mr. Walker has been told that Terrell has average intelligence and is quite capable of following the standard course of study for English but that he needs several accommodations. Mr. Walker is meeting with Ms. Bickel from the special education department to ask questions about Terrell.

Mr. Walker: I need more information about Terrell. Can he really do the work? How much can he see? How is he going to take tests? What is his assistant supposed to be doing? Am I accountable if Terrell has a medical problem during class? Is it likely that will happen? I hear that Terrell has all sorts of computer equipment and a motorized wheelchair. I have 34 other students in that class period, and I'm concerned about just fitting everyone in the door!

Ms. Bickel: It sounds like you haven't gotten the information I thought you had. Let me try to clarify. Terrell is quite a good student. He usually gets A's and B's in his core academic classes, and he is highly motivated to learn. He has every intention of going to college, and right now he hopes to be an editor. Because he can't use his voice, he talks using his communication board. I'll be working with you to be sure the board includes all the key words you want it to contain. All Terrell has to do is point his head toward the answer he wants and the laser pointer will activate the board, which says the answer out loud. One accommodation Terrell probably will need is extra time to answer; he really wants to participate but might need a moment to get the laser beam focused on the answer he wants to give. His equipment is all adapted to take into account his limited vision.

Mr. Walker: I'll have to see how that works. What does his assistant do?

Ms. Bickel: Mr. Owen is responsible for Terrell's personal care and making sure he gets from class to class. He also takes notes for Terrell and records answers Terrell gives on his communication board. He can help you out in class if there's a chance, but Terrell needs his attention much of the time.

Mr. Walker: Oh, I wasn't trying to get more help. I just need an idea of what this will be like. I need an extra place for Mr. Owen in class, don't I?

Ms. Bickel: Yes, he'll need to sit next to Terrell most of the time.

The teachers continue talking for another 45 minutes, problem solving about the space issue and trying to ensure that Terrell will experience success and that Mr. Walker understands Terrell's needs. In the first week of school, Ms. Bickel asks Mr. Walker how it is going with Terrell. Mr. Walker comments that he is surprised how smoothly things are going. Terrell spoke via the communication board in class on the first day, and the other students asked a few questions about the equipment. Most of them already knew Terrell, however, and were accustomed to interacting with him. Mr. Walker asks whether Ms. Bickel can help him deal with two other students who already seem to have behavior problems.

Questions

1. What type of disability does Terrell have? Why is he included in Mr. Walker's English class?

2. What accommodations should Mr. Walker make in his classroom and his instruction to address Terrell's special needs?

3. If you were meeting with Ms. Bickel, what additional questions would you ask about Terrell? About needed accommodations?

4. What assistance would you need from Ms. Bickel to feel comfortable teaching Terrell?

5. What would your expectation be for working with Terrell's parents? What might you learn from them that would help you be more effective in teaching Terrell? What expectations might you have of them in working with you?

6. Review the entire chapter and all the information about students with low-incidence disabilities presented in it. What are the benefits of inclusive practices related to students in this group? What concerns and questions do you have for working with students with low-incidence disabilities? Which of your personal and professional beliefs will be most challenged when you work with students with low-incidence disabilities? Why?

Further Readings

Browder, D. M., & Spooner, F. (Eds.). (2006). *Teaching language arts, math, and science to students with significant cognitive disabilities.* Baltimore, MD: Brookes.

With the expectations set by NCLB and IDEA for all students to access the general curriculum, individuals who work with students with significant intellectual disabilities are charged with finding ways to match the goals and objectives these students may have with the curriculum for all students. This textbook is designed to teach the process of curriculum alignment for language arts, math, and science, drawing on the expertise of many researchers in the field to present core concepts and strategies for real-world practice.

Bullock, L. M. (Ed.). (2005). Traumatic brain injury [special issue]. *Preventing School Failure, 49*(4), 4–64.

This special journal issue provides important information about students with traumatic brain injury and strategies for understanding and working with them. Among the topics included are educational accommodations, school reentry, strategies for addressing behavioral challenges, perspectives from education professionals, and resources on TBI.

Myles, B. S. (2005). *Children and youth with Asperger syndrome: Strategies for success in inclusive settings.* Thousand Oaks, CA: Corwin.

This teacher-friendly book, written by a well-known expert in the field of autism spectrum disorders, provides many strategies for working with students with Asperger syndrome in inclusive settings, including classroom environment modifications; accommodations using technology; and strategies to support students emotionally, behaviorally, socially, and organizationally. The book demonstrates that knowing effective techniques to use with students with Asperger syndrome can help ensure that they will have appropriate access to the general curriculum.

Watson, S., & Johnston, L. (2007). Assistive technology in the inclusive science classroom. *Science Teacher, 74*(3), 34–38.

This article illustrates the uses of assistive technology (AT) in a general education classroom, specifically in the area of science. The authors describe no-tech, lite-tech, and high-tech options for students and examine AT applications in seven key instructional areas: organization, note taking, writing assistance, productivity, access to reference materials, cognitive assistance, and materials modification.

7 Students with High-Incidence Disabilities

After you read this chapter, you will be able to

1. Explain what is meant by *high-incidence disabilities*, and describe their prevalence and the key elements of the federal definitions for each of the high-incidence categories.
2. Describe the characteristics and needs of students with communication disorders, and explain how you can differentiate classroom instruction for them using the INCLUDE strategy.
3. Describe the characteristics and needs of students with learning and behavioral disabilities and how you can differentiate instruction for them using the INCLUDE strategy.

Will is a fourth-grade student at LaForb Elementary School. Most people who know him outside school would never guess that he has a learning disability. He converses easily with children and adults, has a great sense of humor, and is renowned among his peers for his "street smarts." Unfortunately, things don't go as well for Will in school. While he passed his third-grade end-of-grade test in math, the tests in reading and written language were another story altogether. Will reads slowly, struggling with each word, and as a result he often cannot tell his teacher what he has read. His written language is also a problem. When he does attempt a written assignment, it takes him an extremely long time to write even a few sentences. The sentences contain many misspelled words, are poorly constructed and illegible, and convey little meaning. As a fourth-grader, Will has been more disengaged from his classes. He is spending longer periods of time in the hall or the principal's office, usually for refusing to do his classwork and homework. Recently, Will's frustration has been growing as the pressure mounts to get ready for his end-of-grade tests and middle school.

What disability does Will seem to have? What factors may be contributing to his academic problems? What kinds of differentiated instruction should Will's teacher provide to help him progress in the general education curriculum? What other kinds of support do Will and his teacher need? Why do students like Will often become discipline problems?

ReNaye is nearly 15 and is usually in some kind of trouble in school and out. According to her grandmother, she has always been a strong-willed child, but she seems to have become more aggressive after losing her mother in a car wreck when she was in the third grade. ReNaye's grades have been going down consistently since then. She does well in English, but her math grades have been getting lower each year. Last year, she failed the end-of-grade test in math for the first time. She also frequently refuses to work in her history and science classes. In class, ReNaye gets upset easily and resorts to bullying and teasing her classmates. She has had several discipline referrals, and the principal keeps threatening to suspend her for her actions but has yet to follow through. Her attendance has been sporadic at best, and her teachers and grandmother don't know what to do to help her.

What is ReNaye's likely disability? How can her general education teachers accommodate her behavior? What kinds of support do ReNaye and her teachers need?

Analyze and Reflect

Compare Table 7.1 with Table 6.1 on pages 197–198. How do these tables support the concept of high-incidence and low-incidence disabilities? How do the concepts of mild, moderate, and severe disabilities also contribute to a cross-categorical view of students with special needs?

Students like Will and ReNaye have high-incidence disabilities. These students' disabilities affect their language, learning, and behavior. You probably will teach students with high-incidence disabilities in your classroom. The expectation in the Individuals with Disabilities Education Act (IDEA) is that students with high-incidence disabilities will spend most of their time in general education, while meeting the same curricular standards as their classmates without disabilities. In order to meet the goals set forth in IDEA, students with high-incidence disabilities require support from general and special education professionals. Usually this support is in the form of instructional accommodations rather than modifications. For instance, Will is learning word-processing skills to help him overcome his problems with spelling and handwriting. He is also using texts on CD-ROM in his science and social studies classes, which are sometimes co-taught. ReNaye and her teachers have developed an individualized behavior contract in which she is allowed extra access to the computer lab for attending class and complying with teachers' requests. This chapter covers characteristics and needs of students with high-incidence disabilities and differentiated instruction that enable these students to gain better access to the general education curriculum.

What Are High-Incidence Disabilities?

Students with **high-incidence disabilities** have speech or language disabilities, learning disabilities, emotional disturbance, or mild intellectual disabilities. These students make up over 80 percent of all students who have disabilities (U.S. Department of Education, 2004a). The federal terms for high-incidence disabilities and the proportion of students with these disabilities served through IDEA are summarized in Table 7.1. Students with high-incidence disabilities share three important characteristics:

1. They are often hard to distinguish from peers without disabilities, particularly in nonschool settings.

2. They often exhibit a combination of behavioral, social, and academic problems.

3. They benefit from systematic, explicit, highly structured instructional interventions such as those discussed in Chapter 5, this chapter, and throughout the remainder of this book. Having these interventions in place will help them meet the same standards as their classmates without disabilities.

What Accommodations Can You Make for Students with Communication Disorders?

Reading Homework Exercise

Go to the Homework and Exercises section in Chapter 7 of MyEducationLab to watch educators consider the strengths of students who process information atypically.

Communication is the exchange of ideas, opinions, or facts between people. Effective communication requires a sender to send a message that a receiver can decipher and understand. Students with communication disorders have problems with speech and/or language that interfere with communication. They need accommodations that help them better understand and express oral language.

Proportion of Students with High-Incidence Disabilities
Receiving Special Education Services in 2002–2003[a]

Federal Disability Category	Defining Characteristics	Total Number of Students	Percentage of All Students Receiving IDEA Services
Learning disabilities[b]	A heterogeneous group of disorders resulting in significant difficulties in the acquisition and use of listening, speaking, reading, writing, reasoning, and mathematical skills.	2,839,311	48.18%
	Disorders are intrinsic to individuals and presumed to be due to central nervous system dysfunction.		
	Disorders are *not* primarily due to (a) sensory or motor disorders; (b) intellectual or developmental disabilities; (c) emotional disturbance; or (d) environmental, cultural, or economic disadvantage.		
Emotional disturbance[c]	Behavioral or emotional responses in school programs that are so different from appropriate age, cultural, and ethnic norms that they adversely affect academic performance.	480,187	8.1%
	More than a temporary, expected response to stressful events in the environment.		
	Consistently exhibited in two different settings, at least one of which is school related.		
	Persists despite individualized interventions within the educational program.		
Speech[d] or language[e] impairments	Speech is disordered when it deviates so far from the speech of other people that it calls attention to itself, interferes with communication, or causes the speaker or listeners distress.	1,103,091	18.7%
	Three kinds of speech disorders are articulation (abnormal production of speech sounds), voice (absence of or abnormal production of voice quality, pitch, loudness, resonance, and/or duration), and fluency (impaired rate and rhythm of speech, for example, stuttering).		
	Language is disordered when comprehension and/or use of a spoken, written, and/or other symbol system is impaired or does not develop normally.		
	Language disorders may involve form (word order, word parts, word usage), content (word meaning), or function (words that communicate meaningfully).		

[a] Students ages 6–21 receiving services through IDEA, Part B (U.S. Department of Education, 2004). Additional students receive services under Part H of the same law, and under Chapter 1.
[b] Adapted from National Joint Committee on Learning Disabilities, definition of learning disabilities as cited in Hammill, 1990, p. 77.
[c] Adapted from Forness and Knitzer (1992).
[d] From definitions developed by Van Riper and Emerick (1996).
[e] From definitions developed by the American Speech-Language-Hearing Association (1993).

Source: From *Twenty-Sixth Annual Report to Congress on the Implementation of the Individuals with Disabilities Education Act,* 2004, Washington, DC: U.S. Department of Education.

fyi

Stuttering is the most common kind of speech problem involving fluency. Stuttering is a speech impairment in which an individual involuntarily repeats a sound or word, resulting in a loss of speech fluency.

www.resources

For more information about stuttering, visit the website of the National Center for Stuttering at www.stuttering.com.

Understanding Speech Problems

Speech is the behavior of forming and sequencing the sounds of oral language (Hallahan & Kauffman, 2005). One common speech problem is with **speech articulation,** resulting in the inability to pronounce sounds correctly at and after the developmentally appropriate age. For example, Stacey is in second grade but cannot pronounce the *s* sound, a sound most students master by age 5. Other speech difficulties involve voice and fluency. Examples of these speech problems are shown in Figure 7.1.

Because communication is social, students with speech disorders, such as **stuttering,** often experience social problems. Students who can clearly communicate draw positive attention from peer relationships, but students who cannot are often avoided by their peers and sometimes ridiculed. The experience of peer rejection can be devastating, leading to a lack of confidence, a poor self-image, social withdrawal, and emotional problems later in life (Cowen, Pederson, Babijian, Izzo, & Trost, 1973). For example, after years of being ridiculed by peers, Jeffrey, a high school ninth-grader who stutters, speaks infrequently and has no friends. He would like to ask a girl in his math class out but is petrified he will not be able to do so without stuttering.

Understanding Language Problems

Language is a system of symbols that we use to communicate feelings, thoughts, desires, and actions. Language is the message contained in speech. Language can exist without speech,

---

FIGURE *7.1* **Speech Problems**

Articulation

1. Has difficulty pronouncing sounds correctly (at and after the developmentally appropriate age). Frequent articulation errors include *f, v, k, g, r, l, s, z, sh, ch,* and *j.* Sounds may be distorted or omitted, or one sound may be inappropriately substituted for another.

2. Speech may be slurred.

Voice

1. Speech is excessively hoarse.

2. May use excessive volume or too little volume.

3. Speech has too much nasality.

4. Speech lacks inflection.

Fluency

1. Stutters when speaking.

2. May have excessively slow rate of speech.

3. May exhibit uneven, jerky rate of speech.

Sources: Adapting Instruction in General Education for Students with Communication Disorders, by D. Barad, 1985, unpublished manuscript, De Kalb: Northern Illinois University; and *Introduction to Communication Disorders* (3rd ed.), by R. Owens, D. Metz, and A. Haas, 2007, Boston: Allyn & Bacon.

such as sign language for people who are deaf, and speech without language, such as birds that are trained to talk (Hardman et al., 2005). Students who have language problems have trouble with either or both of two key parts of language: receptive language and expressive language. **Receptive language** involves understanding what people mean when they speak to you. **Expressive language** concerns speaking in such a way that others understand you. Receptive language problems occur when students are unable to understand what their teachers and peers are saying. For example, students with receptive language difficulties may not understand questions, may have trouble following directions, and may not be able to retain information presented verbally. Students with expressive language problems are unable to communicate clearly; their spoken language may include incorrect grammar, a limited use of vocabulary, and frequent hesitations. Some common receptive and expressive language problems are listed in Figure 7.2.

Students with language problems may also have difficulty using language in social situations. For example, they may be unable to vary their conversation to match the person with whom they are talking or the context in which it is occurring. Students with language problems may also have difficulty taking turns while speaking during a conversation, recognizing when a listener is not understanding the message and taking action to clarify, and in general being a considerate speaker and listener (Bos & Vaughn, 2005). As with problems in communicating clearly, problems in using language appropriately can seriously impede students' social development and peer relationships. General education teachers can intervene in the classroom to help such students socially.

Early language development forms the underpinning for much of the academic learning that comes when students go to school. It is not surprising then that students with speech and language disorders are likely to have trouble with academics as well (Catts & Kamhi, 2005). Problems with sounds can result in students' having difficulties acquiring word analysis and spelling skills. Receptive language problems can make comprehension very difficult and can result in trouble understanding mathematical terms such as *minus, regroup,* and *addend* and confusion in sorting out words with multiple meanings, such as *carry* and *times* (Mercer & Pullen, 2005). Furthermore, language disabilities can seriously impede the content-area learning stressed in middle, junior high, and high school. In these settings, much information is provided orally using lecture formats, the vocabulary and concepts covered are much more abstract, and students are expected to learn with less support from the teacher. These demands are difficult for students with language disorders.

Another part of learning independently is solving problems. Students with language disorders may have difficulty verbalizing the steps to solve a problem. For example, when Veronica, a language-proficient student, solves story problems, she talks to herself as follows: "First I need to read the whole problem. Then I need to decide what the problem is asking for and whether I need to add, subtract, multiply, or divide. Okay, the problem is asking how much Alex weighs. It says that Alex is 3 pounds heavier than Dominique and that Dominique weighs 125 pounds. So if Alex weighs 3 pounds more, his weight will be a bigger number than Dominique's, so I need to add." A student with language problems cannot talk herself through such problems.

Accommodations for Students with Communication Disorders

As discussed in Chapter 5, the INCLUDE strategy suggests that before you differentiate instruction, you should carefully consider potential student problems in view of your instructional demands. For students with speech and language problems, note especially any areas in which students are required to understand oral language (for example, listening to a lecture or a set of verbal directions) or to communicate orally (for example, responding to teacher questions or interacting with classmates when working in cooperative groups). The following discussion highlights specific suggestions for working with students with speech and language disorders.

fyi

In remembering the distinction between *receptive* and *expressive* communication disorders, think of the root words *receive* and *express*.

DIMENSIONS OF

diversity

It is incorrect to view students as having communication disorders when they use ethnic or regional dialects, speak a form of nonstandard English learned at home, or are native speakers of languages other than English and have limited English proficiency.

Info Sheet Homework Exercise

Go to the Homework and Exercises section in Chapter 7 of MyEducationLab to document appropriate strategies and methods to support students with speech and language disorders.

INCLUDE

FIGURE *7.2* Language Problems

Receptive Language Problems

1. Does not respond to questions appropriately

2. Cannot think abstractly or comprehend abstractions as idioms ("mind sharp as a tack"; "eyes dancing in the dark")

3. Cannot retain information presented verbally

4. Has difficulty following oral directions

5. Cannot detect breakdowns in communication

6. Misses parts of material presented verbally, particularly less concrete words such as articles (*the* book; *a* book) and auxiliary verbs and tense markers ("He *was* going"; "She *is* going")

7. Cannot recall sequences of ideas presented orally

8. May confuse the sounds of letters that are similar (*b, d; m, n*) or reverse the order of sounds and syllables in words (*was, saw*)

9. Has difficulty understanding humor or figurative language

10. Has difficulty comprehending concepts showing quantity, function, comparative size, and temporal and spatial relationships

11. Has difficulty comprehending compound and complex sentences

Expressive Language Problems

1. Uses incorrect grammar or syntax ("They walk down together the hill"; "I go not to school")

2. Lacks specificity ("It's over there by the place over there")

3. Frequently hesitates ("You know, um, I would, um, well, er, like a, er, soda")

4. Jumps from topic to topic ("What are feathers? Well, I like to go hunting with my uncle")

5. Has limited use of vocabulary

6. Has trouble finding the right word to communicate meaning (word finding)

7. Uses social language poorly (inability to change communication style to fit specific situations, to repair communication breakdowns, and to maintain the topic during a conversation)

8. Is afraid to ask questions, does not know what questions to ask, or does not know how to ask a question

9. Repeats same information again and again in a conversation

10. Has difficulty discussing abstract, temporal, or spatial concepts

11. Often does not provide enough information to the listener (saying, "*We* had a big fight with *them*," when *we* and *them* are not explained)

Sources: Adapting Instruction in General Education for Students with Communication Disorders, by D. Barad, 1985, unpublished manuscript, De Kalb: Northern Illinois University; and *Strategies for Teaching Students with Learning and Behavior Problems* (6th ed.), by C. S. Bos and S. Vaughn, 2005. Copyright © 2005 by Allyn & Bacon. Reprinted by permission.

● **Create an Atmosphere of Acceptance**   Help students who have difficulty expressing themselves believe they can communicate without worrying about making mistakes. You can foster this nonjudgmental atmosphere in several ways. First, when a student makes an error, model the correct form instead of correcting the student's mistakes directly:

Teacher: Kareem, what did Jules do with the frog?

Kareem: Put pocket.

Teacher: Oh. He put it in his pocket?

Kareem: Yes.

Second, try to allow students who stutter or have other fluency problems more time to speak, and do not interrupt them or supply words that are difficult for them to pronounce. Offering praise or other reinforcement for successful efforts to communicate, as you would for your other students, is also helpful. Sometimes, you should praise even an attempt:

Teacher: Anthony, what did you do when you went home yesterday?

Anthony: Television.

Teacher: Great, you told me one thing you did. You watched television.

Finally, try to minimize peer pressure. One effective way to do this is to model and reinforce tolerance of individual differences in your classroom.

● **Encourage Listening and Teach Listening Skills**   Even though students spend more time listening than doing any other school activity, very little time is devoted to teaching listening skills (Lerner, 2006). Stressing listening is particularly important for students with receptive language disorders. Take the following four steps to stress listening:

1. Listen carefully yourself and praise listening among your students. For example, when Ms. Hernandez listens to a student speak, she leans forward and nods. Many of her students copy these listening behaviors.

2. Be sure to engage your students' attention before you begin speaking by increasing your proximity to the listeners, by giving direct instruction (such as, "Listen to what I'm going to say"), and by reducing competing stimuli (have only one activity going on at one time, or have only one person speak at a time). You can also use verbal, pictorial, and written advance organizers to cue students when to listen (for example, "When we get to number 3 on this list, I want you to listen extra carefully for an error I am going to make") (Sabornie & deBettencourt, 2004).

3. Make oral material easier to understand and remember by simplifying vocabulary, simplifying sentence structure using high-frequency words, repeating important information, giving information in short segments using visual aids for emphasis, having students rehearse and summarize information, and using cues that signal when you are going to say something important (Mandlebaum & Wilson, 1989).

4. Teach listening skills directly. Provide practice on skills such as predicting what might be heard, following directions, appreciating language, identifying main ideas and supporting details, drawing inferences, differentiating fact from fiction, and analyzing information critically.

When you speak, you can also enhance your students' listening skills by stressing words that are important to meaning. For example, say "He *hit* the *ball*" or "*He* hit the

*R*esearch Note

Saunders, Foorman, and Carlson (2006) observed 85 kindergarten classrooms. In some of these classes, English-language development (ELD) for English-language learners (ELLs) was taught as a separate block; in others, ELD was included as part of the regular language arts block. The researchers found that ELLs in classrooms with separate ELD blocks had modest but significantly higher English oral language and literacy scores than students who were part of the regular language arts block, as measured by a common standardized language test. Why do you think this is so?

Even though students spend more time listening than doing any other school activity, very little time is devoted to teaching listening skills.

ball," depending on what you want to emphasize. Stressing inflectional patterns, such as using an upward inflection when asking a question, also helps students better understand what you are saying.

DIMENSIONS OF

diversity

Carlo and colleagues (2004) improved the reading vocabulary of mixed groups of Anglo and Latino fifth-graders using two strategies. They allowed native Spanish speakers access to the text's meaning in Spanish. They also presented vocabulary words in meaningful contexts and reinforced word meanings through activities that stressed spelling, pronunciation, meaningful word parts, syntax, and depth of meaning.

● **Use Modeling to Expand Students' Language**   You can expand the language of students with expressive language problems by adding relevant information to student statements:

Student: John is nice.

Teacher: Yes, he is very nice and polite too.

You can also expand language by broadening a minimal statement:

Student: My shoe.

Teacher: Your shoe is pretty.

Modeling to expand students' language is most effective when it is done as an ongoing part of your everyday communications. Students can also learn to model behavior for themselves. The Technology Notes feature explains a high-tech method of self-modeling using video.

● **Provide Many Meaningful Contexts for Practicing Speech and Language Skills**   The goal of successful language programs is to teach students to use appropriate language in a variety of social and academic situations, both in and out of school. You can help students with all types of speech and language problems meet that goal by providing as many opportunities as possible to practice language skills within meaningful contexts (Hardman et al., 2005). Practice helps students refine language skills and make them more natural and automatic. When students practice in many different contexts, they can apply what they learn more readily. For example, Ms. Crum just taught her class the meaning of the word *ironic.* During health class, the students discussed the irony of the government's warning people against fat consumption and then funding school lunches that are high in fat. During a trip to the museum, Ms. Crum pointed out the irony of the guard's telling them to be quiet when he was wearing shoes that squeaked loudly when he walked.

It is also helpful to encourage students with communication disorders to talk about events and experiences in their environment, describing them in as much detail as possible (Hardman et al., 2005). For example, Ms. Cusak, a first-grade teacher, starts every Monday by having two students tell about something they did over the weekend. Mr. Drake, a sixth-grade teacher, uses a *Saturday Night Live* format whereby students in his class act out something funny that happened to them over the weekend.

Finally, whenever possible, instruction should be embedded in the context of functional areas. For example, in Ms. Taylor's consumer math class, she has students go out to appliance stores, talk to salespeople about service contracts, and then describe and compare the various service contracts that are available. In Ms. Ellen's second-grade class, students invite and converse with classroom visitors.

Info Sheet Homework Exercise

Go to the Homework and Exercises section in Chapter 7 of MyEducationLab to find suggestions for students with severe communication disorders.

What Are the Academic Needs of Students with Learning and Behavioral Disabilities?

Students with learning and behavioral disabilities have learning disabilities, mild intellectual disabilities, and emotional disturbance. These are the students who are most likely to be included in your classroom. Students with **learning disabilities** are students who achieve

TECHNOLOGY NOTES

Changing Behavior Using Video Self-Modeling

One of the time-tested truths of education is that students learn by example. According to social learning theory, one important way students learn new behaviors is by watching other students perform or model them. Given that modeling is most effective when the person doing the modeling is similar to the observer, what would happen if the modeling were done by the person herself? There is a method of instruction that does just that. It is called *video self-modeling*. The idea is that seeing themselves perform successfully provides students with clear information on how to best execute skills while at the same time strengthening their beliefs in their own capabilities (Bandura, 1969).

Video self-modeling has been used to help students of all ages perform a variety of behaviors successfully in school settings, including on-task behavior, fluent speech, following teacher directions, talking with adults, reading fluently, raising hands, and answering teacher questions (Dowrick, Kim-Rupnow, & Power, 2006; Hitchcock, Dowrick, & Prater, 2003). Furthermore, this technique can provide a motivational boost for students with learning, behavior, and communication problems, who often see themselves as incapable of doing the right thing.

Video self-modeling is most helpful when students engage in a behavior at some times but not others. For example, Cedric stutters in class but not when he is with the speech teacher. Ronald is able to resolve conflicts with other students while in the classroom but not on the playground. Delaney can read fluently in her small reading group but not when she reads the same material in front of the entire class.

To implement video self-modeling, you first need to produce a video of the student engaging in the target behavior. Select a setting for modeling that is the same as or similar to the setting where you eventually want the student to engage in the behavior. For example, modeling hand-raising would take place during a real class; a demonstration of self-control when there is a conflict during play could take place on the playground. Next make sure that the student is able to engage in the behavior required. For example, for reading fluency, students should be modeling using books at their reading level. For question answering, students must have answered questions in class before, and the questions must be ones to which they know the answers. Finally, create a situation in which students receive positive consequences for engaging in the behavior. For example, Floyd could earn points every time he raised his

Video self-modeling can be used to help students of all ages perform a variety of behaviors successfully in school settings.

hand in the modeling session and then was able to cash the points in for minutes on the computer. Carmella was told she would earn a special sticker for solving a conflict with a classmate during free play. For situations when you will be doing the teaching, enlist the help of school support staff to shoot the video. Be sure to obtain parent permission prior to taping.

Once you have shot your video, edit it so that it shows only a sample of exemplary behavior. The tape needs to be long enough to completely show the behavior in question, but it should be only as long as it needs to be; often that is five minutes or less. Don't worry if your school doesn't have sophisticated editing equipment. The rudimentary equipment available in most schools should work fine. When your video is edited, you are ready to show it to the student. For maximum effect, show the video once per day, over a period of days, on an every-other-day basis. Be sure to specify the settings where you want the student to perform the behavior as well as the general expectation that you want her to do the behavior more often.

Research Note

Hitchcock and colleagues (2003) reviewed the research literature for studies looking at the effectiveness of video self-modeling in school-based settings. They found 18 studies consistently showing that video self-modeling was effective for strengthening academic skills and classroom behavior. The review also showed that video self-modeling helps students maintain appropriate behaviors and apply them in new settings.

INCLUDE

less than typical students academically because they have trouble with processing, organizing, and applying academic information. Students with learning disabilities are of normal intelligence, have presumably received adequate instruction, and have not been shown to be sensory impaired, emotionally disturbed, or environmentally disadvantaged. Students with **mild intellectual disabilities** are students who have some difficulty meeting the academic and social demands of general education classrooms, in large part because of below-average intellectual functioning (that is, scoring 55–70 on an IQ test). Students with mild intellectual disabilities can meet at least some of the academic and social demands of general education classrooms. Students with **emotional disturbance** are of average intelligence but have problems learning primarily because of external (acting out, poor interpersonal skills) and/or internal (anxiety, depression) behavioral adjustment problems.

Students with learning disabilities, mild intellectual disabilities, and emotional disturbance differ in a number of ways (Hallahan & Kauffman, 2005; Sabornie, Evans, & Cullinan, 2006). The behavior problems of students with emotional disturbance are more severe, and students with mild intellectual disabilities have lower levels of measured intelligence. Students with learning disabilities may have more pronounced learning strengths and weaknesses than students with mild intellectual disabilities, who are likely to show lower performance in all areas. Still, the academic and social characteristics of students with these disabilities overlap considerably. All three groups may experience significant problems in academic achievement, classroom behavior, and peer relations (Stichter, Conroy, & Kauffman, 2007).

Although scientists have developed sophisticated computerized imaging techniques to detect neurological differences in children with learning and behavioral disabilities, the precise causes of these disabilities in individual children are largely unknown because learning and behavior result from a complex interaction between students' individual characteristics, the various settings in which they learn, and the tasks or other demands they face in those settings (Hallahan et al., 2005; Smith, 2004; Ysseldyke, Algozzine, & Thurlow, 2000). It is often difficult to identify the primary cause of a learning or behavior problem. For example, Thomas is lagging behind his classmates in acquiring a sight-word vocabulary in reading. Learning disabilities tend to run in his family, but Thomas's school district also changed reading series last year. In addition, Thomas's parents separated in the middle of the school year and divorced several months later. Why is Thomas behind in reading? Is it heredity? Is it the new reading program? Is it his parents' marital problems? All these factors may have contributed to Thomas's problem.

The most important reason students with high-incidence disabilities are grouped for discussion is that whatever behaviors they exhibit and whatever the possible causes of these behaviors, these students benefit from the same instructional practices (Algozzine, Ysseldyke, & Campbell, 1994; Bateman, 2004; Kame'enui et al., 2002). These practices are introduced in this chapter and covered in considerable depth throughout the rest of this book. For example, Raeanna has a mild intellectual disability. She has difficulty reading her classmates' social cues. As a result, she does not recognize when she is acting too aggressively with her classmates and often is rejected. Del is a student with learning disabilities. He also has trouble reading the social cues of his peers. Although Raeanna and Del may learn new social skills at different rates, both can benefit from social skills training that provides considerable guided practice and feedback on how to read social cues. The point to remember is that categorical labels are not particularly useful in describing specific students or developing instructional programs for them (Hardman et al., 2005). For example, both Damon and Aretha have learning disabilities, yet their areas of difficulty differ. Damon has a severe reading problem but excels in mathematics and various computer applications. Aretha, on the other hand, is reading at grade level but has significant problems with math. Though both students are categorized as having learning disabilities, they have very different needs. You must analyze each individual student's needs and differentiate instruction, as necessary. This individualization is at the heart of the INCLUDE strategy, introduced in Chapter 5.

Students with learning and behavioral disabilities have many academic needs. They have difficulty acquiring basic skills in the areas of reading, written language, and math.

They also may lack skills necessary for efficient learning, such as attending to task, memory, organizing and interpreting information, reasoning, motor coordination, independent learning skills, and academic survival skills.

Reading Skills

Students with learning and behavioral disabilities have two major types of reading problems: decoding and comprehension. Decoding problems involve the skills of identifying words accurately and fluently. Accuracy problems are most readily observed when students read orally, mispronouncing words, substituting one word for another, or omitting words (Lerner, 2006). Students with reading fluency problems can read words accurately but do not recognize them quickly enough. They read slowly, in a word-by-word fashion, without grouping words together meaningfully (Hallahan et al., 2005; Lerner, 2006). Many of these reading decoding problems are exemplified in the following oral reading sample by a student with a learning disability:

> Then Ford had, uh, other i . . . a better idea. Take the worrrk to the men. He deee. . . . A long rope was hooked onto the car . . . wheels. . . . There's no rope on there. The rope pulled the car . . . auto . . . the white wheels along . . . pulled the car all along the way. Men stood still. Putting on car parts. Everybody man . . . put on, on, a few parts. Down the assembly line went the car. The assembly line saved . . . time. Cars costed still less to buh . . . bull . . . d . . . build. Ford cuts their prices on the Model T again. (Hallahan et al., 2005, p. 370)

Here is the passage the student tried to read:

> Then Ford had another idea. Take the work to the men, he decided. A long rope was hooked onto a car axle and wheels. The rope pulled the axle and wheels along. All along the way, men stood still putting on car parts. Down the assembly line went the car. The assembly line saved more time. Cars cost still less to build. Ford cut the price on the Model T again. (Hallahan et al., 2005, p. 370)

Students who have serious difficulties decoding written words are sometimes referred to as having *dyslexia*. The Professional Edge on pages 252–253 discusses the meaning of this term and suggests instructional approaches.

Students with learning and behavioral disabilities often have problems comprehending stories in the elementary grades and content-area textbooks and advanced literature in the upper grades (Bursuck & Damer, 2007). Although these difficulties result in part from poor decoding skills, they may also occur because these students lack background and vocabulary knowledge as well as strategies for identifying the key elements of stories and content-area texts. For example, after Connor's grandmother talked to him about her homeland of Vietnam, he was able to understand a well-written expository text about the Vietnam War. Todd's teacher asked him questions about a book he had just read as part of his classroom literature program. Todd was unable to tell her where the story took place (setting) or the lesson of the story (moral) because the answers to these questions were not directly stated in the story and Todd lacked the necessary inference strategies to figure them out. In another instance, Patsy was unable to answer a study question comparing the causes of World Wars I and II because she could not locate key words, such as *differences* and *similarities*. In addition, students with these disabilities may not be able to adjust their reading rate to allow for skimming a section of text for key information or for reading more slowly and intensively to answer specific questions. For example, Dennis takes a lot of time to locate key dates in his history book because he thinks he needs to read every word in the chapter while he is looking for the dates.

Written Language Skills

The written language difficulties of students with learning and behavioral disabilities include handwriting, spelling, and written expression. Handwriting problems can be caused by a lack of fine motor coordination, failure to attend to task, inability to perceive

Understanding Dyslexia

The term *dyslexia* is used a lot these days. You hear that a friend's child has dyslexia, or you see a person who is dyslexic on television, or you read that Albert Einstein and Thomas Edison had dyslexia. The word *dyslexia*, which means "developmental word blindness," has a medical sound to it, but until recently there was little convincing evidence to show that it was medically based. Thanks to the development of computerized imaging techniques, such as functional magnetic resonance imaging (fMRI) and positron-emission tomography (PET scan), as well as recent studies of twins (Olson, 2006), evidence of an organic, genetic basis for dyslexia is beginning to accumulate.

Recent studies using computerized imaging show that the brain activity of students with dyslexia differs from that of students who are good readers (Shaywitz, 2003; Shaywitz & Shaywitz, 2007; Simos et al., 2007). For example, from an early age and often into adulthood, dyslexics show a pattern of underactivation in a region in the back of the brain that enables first accurate and then automatic reading. This pattern of underactivity appears to be present in dyslexics regardless of their age, sex, or culture (Shaywitz, 2003). That is why dyslexics have problems initially "cracking the code" and then problems later on developing reading fluency.

Studies of twins, sibling analysis, and family pedigree analysis have confirmed a genetic basis for learning disabilities (Fiedorowicz, 2005; Olson, 2006). Twin studies have shown that if one twin has a reading disability, the probability of the other twin having a reading disability is 68 percent for identical twins and 40 percent for fraternal twins. Studies also have shown that if there is a family history of dyslexia, the probability of an offspring having a reading disability is significantly increased (Fiedorowicz, 2005). While specific chromosomal links have been hypothesized, no definite conclusions about the genetic transmission of reading disabilities have been reached.

Knowing the cause of severe reading problems is one thing; knowing what to do to help students who have these problems is another altogether. Put very simply, students with dyslexia have serious problems learning to read despite normal intelligence, normal opportunities to learn to read, and an adequate home environment. Although the precise organic cause of dyslexia continues to be researched, considerable evidence suggests that reading problems associated with dyslexia are phonologically based (Blachman, 1997; Foorman, 2003; Stanovich & Siegel, 1994). Students with dyslexia have difficulty developing *phonemic awareness*, the understanding that spoken words are made up of sounds. Phonemic awareness problems make it hard for these students to link speech sounds to letters, ultimately leading to slow, labored reading characterized by frequent starts and stops and multiple mispronunciations. Students with dyslexia also have comprehension problems largely because their struggle to identify words leaves little energy for understanding what they read.

Students with dyslexia also have trouble with the basic elements of written language, such as spelling and sentence and paragraph construction. Finally, students with dyslexia may have difficulty understanding representational systems,

Studies of reading performance in other cultures and countries, such as Italy, where there is more sound–spelling regularity in the written language, show that there are still some individuals who have trouble learning to read words (Paulesu et al., 2001, as cited in Hallahan et al., 2005).

and/or remember visual images accurately, and inadequate handwriting instruction in the classroom (Mercer & Pullen, 2005). Students may have problems in the areas of letter formation (is the letter recognizable?), size, alignment, slant, line quality (heaviness or lightness of lines), straightness, and spacing (too little or too much between letters, words, and lines).

Students with learning and behavioral disabilities also have trouble with spelling (Wanzek et al., 2006). The English language consists largely of three types of words: those that can be spelled phonetically, those that can be spelled by following certain linguistic rules, and those that are irregular. For example, the words *cats, construction,* and *retell* can be spelled correctly by applying phonics generalizations related to consonants, consonant blends (*str*), vowels, root words (*tell*), prefixes (*re*), and suffixes (*ion, s*). The word *babies* can be spelled by applying the linguistic rule of changing *y* to *i* and adding *es*. Words such as *said, where,* and *through* are irregular and can be spelled only by such as telling time, directions, and seasons (Bryan & Bryan, 1986). Dyslexia commonly is considered a type of learning disability, and students with dyslexia are served under the learning disability classification of IDEA.

It is important to identify students with dyslexia and other severe reading disabilities early, before they fall far behind their peers in word-recognition reading skills. Early identification is particularly urgent given recent studies showing that effective language instruction appears to generate repair in underactivated sections of the brain (Shaywitz, 2003; Simos et al., 2007). The recent movement toward identifying reading disabilities based on children's response to intervention (RtI) will likely help schools to identify children earlier than the traditional approach of establishing a discrepancy between children's ability and reading achievement. This is because schools using a discrepancy model often have to wait for children to get older to have a large enough discrepancy between achievement and ability to be eligible for special education services. In this way, students who appear to be learning letter names, sounds, and sight words at a significantly slower rate than their classmates can receive intensive support as early as kindergarten. See the Professional Edge in Chapter 4 on page 132 for specific assessment strategies to identify children at risk for reading failure early.

From the Research

A large body of research (Blachman, 2000; Foorman, 2003; McCardle & Chhabra, 2004; Moats, 2007; National Reading Panel, 2000; Oakland, Black, Stanford, Nussbaum, & Balise, 1998; Snow, Burns, & Griffin, 1998; Swanson, 2000) shows that many students with severe reading disabilities benefit from a beginning reading program that includes the following five elements:

1. *Direct instruction in language analysis.* For example, students need to be taught skills in sound segmentation by orally breaking down words into their component sounds.

2. *A highly structured phonics program.* This program should teach the alphabetic code directly and systematically by using a simple-to-complex sequence of skills, teaching regularity before irregularity, and discouraging guessing.

3. *Writing and reading instruction in combination.* Students need to be writing the words they are reading.

4. *Intensive instruction.* Reading instruction for at-risk students should include large amounts of practice in materials that contain words they are able to decode.

5. *Teaching for automaticity.* Students must be given enough practice that they are able to read both accurately and fluently.

For students who are dyslexic, visit the website Dyslexia: The Gift at www.dyslexia.com. Curriculum aids, a bookstore, discussion board, and links to further information are provided.

remembering what they look like. Students with learning and behavioral disabilities may have trouble with all three types of words.

Students with learning and behavioral disabilities have two major types of written expression problems: product problems and process problems (Isaacson, 2001; Mercer & Pullen, 2005). Their written products are often verb–object sentences, characterized by few words, incomplete sentences, overuse of simple subject–verb constructions, repetitious use of high-frequency words, a disregard for audience, poor organization and structure, and many mechanical errors, such as misspellings, incorrect use of punctuation and capital letters, and faulty subject–verb agreements and choice of pronouns (Mercer & Pullen, 2005).

These students also have trouble with the overall process of written communication. Their approach to writing shows little systematic planning, great difficulty putting ideas on paper because of a preoccupation with mechanics, failure to monitor writing, and little

Teachers often mistake natural stages of child and adolescent development for signs of the presence of learning disabilities or emotional problems. Reversing letters or confusing *b* and *d*, for example, is common among children first learning to write.

Research Note

In a study of manuscript writing, Graham, Weintraub, and Berninger (2001, as cited in Mercer & Pullen, 2005) found that five letters (q, z, u, j, and k) accounted for 43 percent of all illegible letters written. Newland (1932, as cited in Mercer & Pullen, 2005) found that for cursive writing, the letters a, e, r, and t accounted for about 50 percent of all illegible letters written. It is likely that your students with handwriting problems will have trouble forming these and other letters.

FIGURE 7.3 Written Expression Sample of a 14-Year-Old Student with a Learning Disability

www.resources

IEPs for most students with learning and behavioral disabilities include goals and supports in the academic areas of reading, math, and writing. The IEP page of the website LDOnLine at www.ldonline.org/ld_indepth/iep/iep.html provides many links to help parents and teachers develop IEPs in academic areas.

fyi

Ways to increase accessibility of materials and formats for math instruction include keeping models on the board; providing graph paper to align problems; and using visual cues, such as color-coded or boldfaced signs and arrows, as reminders of direction and frames to set off problems and answers.

useful revision (Mercer & Pullen, 2005). A writing sample from a student who has a disability is shown in Figure 7.3. What types of product problems do you see in this sample? What process problems do you think might have led to these problems?

Math Skills

Math also can be problematic for students with learning and behavioral disabilities (Cawley, Parmar, Foley, Salmon, & Roy, 2001; Miller & Hudson, 2007; Strang & Rourke, 1985; Swanson & Jerman, 2006). Common problems include the following:

1. *Problems with spatial organization.* Students may be unable to align numbers in columns, may reverse numbers (write a 9 backward, read 52 as 25), or may subtract the top number from the bottom number in a subtraction problem:

$$\begin{array}{r} 75 \\ -39 \\ \hline 44 \end{array}$$

2. *Lack of alertness to visual detail.* Students misread mathematical signs or forget to use dollar signs and decimals when necessary.

3. *Procedural errors.* Students miss a step in solving a problem. For example, they may forget to add a carried number in an addition problem or to subtract from the regrouped number in a subtraction problem:

$$\begin{array}{r} 29 \\ +53 \\ \hline 72 \end{array} \qquad \begin{array}{r} 41 \\ -28 \\ \hline 23 \end{array}$$

4. *Failure to shift mindset from one problem type to another.* Students solve problems of one type, but when required to solve problems of another type, they solve them in the way they did those of the first type. For example, Kristy has just completed several word problems that required addition. The next problem requires subtraction, but she continues to use addition.

5. *Difficulty forming numbers correctly.* Students' numbers are too large or are poorly formed, which makes solving computational problems awkward, particularly when the students are unable to read their own numbers.

6. *Difficulty with memory.* Students are frequently unable to recall basic math facts or use their working memory when solving problems involving multiple steps.

7. *Problems with mathematical judgment and reasoning.* Students are unaware when their responses are unreasonable. For example, they do not see the obvious errors in 9 − 6 = 15 or 4 + 3 = 43. They may also have trouble solving word problems. For example, they may be unable to decide whether to add or subtract in a word problem, focusing on cue words such as *less, more,* or *times* rather than comprehending accurately the situation described in the problem. This difficulty is shown in the following problem: "A boy has three times as many apples as a girl. The boy has 6. How many does the girl have?" Students with disabilities are likely to answer 18 instead of 2 because they think the presence of the word *times* in the problem means they need to multiply (Cawley et al., 2001, p. 325).

8. *Problems with mathematical language.* Students may have difficulty with the meanings of key mathematical terms, such as *regroup, place value,* and *minus* (Lerner, 2006; Mercer & Pullen, 2005). They may also have trouble participating in oral drills (Lerner, 2006) or verbalizing the steps in solving word or computational problems (Cawley, Miller, & School, 1987).

Students from culturally and linguistically diverse backgrounds may have additional problems learning math skills. Some potential trouble spots and strategies for dealing with these trouble spots are shown in the Special Emphasis On . . . feature.

Learning Skills

Students with learning and behavioral disabilities have difficulty performing skills that could help them learn more readily. One such skill is *attention.* Students may have difficulty coming to attention or understanding task requirements (Hallahan et al., 2005). For example, Janice frequently fails essay tests; she is unable to focus on key words in the questions to help her organize a response. As a result, she loses valuable writing time just staring at the question and not knowing how to begin. Benito misses important information at the beginning of science lectures because he takes five minutes to attend to the teacher's presentation.

Students may also have trouble focusing on the important aspects of tasks. For example, Anita can tell you the color of her teacher's tie or the kind of belt he is wearing but nothing about the information he is presenting. When Arman tries to solve word problems in math, he is unable to tell the difference between information that is needed and not needed to solve the problem.

Finally, students with learning and behavioral disabilities may have trouble sticking to a task once they have started it. This lack of task persistence is largely due to a lack of confidence resulting from a history of school failure. The emotional repercussions of school failure are covered later in this chapter in the discussion of the personal and psychological adjustment of students with learning and behavioral disabilities.

Memory problems may also make learning difficult for students (Hallahan et al., 2005; Lerner, 2006). Some problems occur when information is first learned. For example, Carla cannot remember information when it is presented just once. Sal has practiced math facts many times but still cannot remember some of them. Students may also have trouble with working memory. For example, Denise adds a column of numbers such as 6, 8, 4, and 5. When it is time to add in the 5, she forgets that the total up to that point was 18. Finally, students may also fail to retain what they learn. For example, Abby learned her addition facts but could not recall them when solving more complex problems.

Research Note

Gersten, Jordan, and Flojo (2005) found that kindergarten students who could perform the following skills were less at risk for having math disabilities: knows which digit in a pair is larger, has sophisticated counting strategies, recognizes numbers fluently, and has a good working memory for numbers.

Research Note

Many educators claim that students have certain learning preferences or styles and that teaching to accommodate these styles enhances instruction, particularly in reading. In a review of more than 40 research studies on learning styles, Kavale, Hirshoren, and Forness (1998) found no evidence for teaching based on learning styles. Our advice is to meet individual needs by always teaching to as many senses as possible.

Analyze and Reflect

What learning needs might students with learning and behavioral disabilities share? How might their needs be different? How might you modify instruction for basic academic skills for these students?

Accommodating Learners in Math
Who Are Linguistically and Culturally Diverse

Math can be a challenging subject for all students, including students with learning and behavioral difficulties. Students from linguistically and culturally diverse backgrounds may face additional challenges when learning math. In the fol-lowing table, Scott and Raborn (1996) present some potential trouble spots and suggested strategies for teaching math to students from linguistically and culturally diverse backgrounds.

Trouble Spot	Recommendation
Learning a new language	▪ Determine the student's level of proficiency in both English and the native language.
	▪ Assess math abilities in both languages.
	▪ If a student is stronger in math than in English, provide math instruction in the primary language.
	▪ Listen to the words you most frequently use in teaching math. Work together with the ESL teacher to help the student learn these words or to help you learn them in the student's language.
	▪ Use a variety of ways to communicate such as gesturing, drawing sketches, writing basic vocabulary and procedures, rewording, and providing more details.
	▪ Provide time and activities that will allow students to practice the English language and the language of math.
Cultural differences	▪ Use story problem situations that are relevant to the student's personal cultural identity (e.g., ethnicity, gender, geographical region, age).
	▪ Share examples of the mathematical heritage of the student's culture (e.g., folk art, African and Native American probability games, measurement systems).
	▪ Involve family and community members in multicultural math.
Tricky vocabulary	▪ Use concrete activities to teach new vocabulary and the language of math.
	▪ Use only as many technical words as are necessary to ensure understanding.
	▪ Give more information in a variety of ways to help students understand new vocabulary.
	▪ Develop a picture file; purchase or have students make a picture dictionary of math terms and frequently used vocabulary.
Symbolic language	▪ Allow students to draw pictures, diagrams, or graphic organizers to represent story problems.
	▪ Make clear the meanings and function of symbols.
	▪ Point out the interchangeable nature of operations.
	▪ In algebra, teach students to translate phrases to mathematical expressions.
Level of abstraction and memory	▪ Allow students to develop mathematical relationships using concrete representations accompanied by verbal descriptions.
	▪ Develop mathematical understanding from concrete to abstract form.
	▪ Use visual and kinesthetic cues to strengthen memory.
	▪ Keep distractions to a minimum.

Research Note

Grossen (2002) implemented a math curriculum with middle school English-language learners that stressed the use of scaffolding to teach students explicit problem-solving strategies. After a year, the percentage of students at grade level significantly increased; the number of children significantly below grade level dropped considerably.

Source: From "Realizing the Gifts of Diversity among Students with Learning Disabilities," by P. Scott and D. Raborn, 1996, *LD Forum, 21*(2), pp. 10–18. Reprinted by permission of the Council of Learning Disabilities.

Students with learning and behavioral disabilities may have trouble *organizing and interpreting* oral and visual information despite adequate hearing and visual skills (Lerner, 2006). For example, Rodney is a student with a learning disability who has trouble with visual tasks. He frequently loses his place while reading and copying; has trouble reading and copying from the chalkboard; does not notice details on pictures, maps, and photographs; is confused by worksheets containing a great deal of visual information; and often cannot remember what he has seen. LaTonya has trouble with auditory tasks. She has difficulty following oral directions, differentiating between fine differences in sounds (*e/i*, *bean/been*), taking notes during lectures, and remembering what she has heard.

Students also may lack the *reasoning* skills necessary for success in school. Important reasoning skills include reading comprehension, generalization (the ability to recognize similarities across objects, events, or vocabulary), adequate background and vocabulary knowledge, induction (figuring out a rule or principle based on a series of situations), and sequencing (detecting relationships among stimuli) (Salvia & Ysseldyke, 2007). For example, Stu has difficulty understanding a lecture on the civil rights movement because he lacks necessary background information; he is unsure what a *civil right* is. Tamara has trouble recognizing a relationship on her own, even after repeated examples; her teacher presented five examples of how to add *s* to words that end in *y,* but Tamara still could not figure out the rule.

Some students with learning and behavioral disabilities may have *motor coordination and fine motor impairments* (Lerner, 2006). For example, Denise is a first-grade student who has some fine motor and coordination problems. She has trouble using scissors, coloring within the lines, tying her shoes, and printing letters and numbers. Cal is in third grade. His handwriting is often illegible and messy. He is also uncoordinated at sports, which has limited his opportunities for social interaction on the playground because he is never selected to play on a team.

Independent learning also can be a challenge for students with learning and behavioral disabilities. They have been referred to as *passive learners,* meaning that they do not believe in their own abilities; have limited knowledge of problem-solving strategies; and even when they know a strategy, cannot tell when it is supposed to be used (Hallahan et al., 2005; Lerner, 2006). Being a passive learner is particularly problematic in the upper grades, where more student independence is expected. For example, when Laverne reads her science textbook, she does not realize when she comes across information that she does not understand. So instead of employing a strategy to solve this problem, such as rereading, checking the chapter summary, or asking for help, she never learns the information. As a result she is doing poorly in the class. When Darrell studies for tests, he reads quickly through his text and notes but does not use strategies for remembering information, such as asking himself questions, saying the information to himself, or grouping into meaningful pieces the information he needs to learn.

Students with learning and behavioral disabilities may also have problems in the area of **academic survival skills,** such as attending school regularly, being organized, completing tasks in and out of school, being independent, taking an interest in school, and displaying positive interpersonal skills with peers and adults (Brown et al., 1984; Kerr & Nelson, 2006). For example, Duane is failing in school because he rarely shows up for class; when he does attend class, he sits in the back of the room and displays an obvious lack of interest. Nicole is always late for class and never completes her homework; her teachers think she does not care about school at all.

As you can see, students with learning and behavioral disabilities have problems in a number of academic and learning areas. Some parents and teachers have tried unproven interventions in search of quick fixes for students with learning and behavioral disabilities. The issue of using unproven, controversial therapies is discussed in the Professional Edge.

Video Homework Exercise

Go to the Homework and Exercises section in Chapter 7 of MyEducationLab to watch teachers and a parent discuss the impact of a student's behavior on his educational progress and find a solution to his problem.

> Being a passive learner is particularly problematic in the upper grades, where more student independence is expected.

fyi

Estimates of the percentage of students with learning disabilities who are at risk for social problems range from 38 to 75 percent (Bryan, 2005).

Controversial Therapies in Learning and Behavioral Disabilities: What Does the Research Say?

Being the parent or teacher of a student with learning disabilities is not easy. Students with learning and behavioral disabilities often do not respond favorably to the first approach tried—or for that matter, to the first several. Failure and frustration can lead to the search for miracle cures. This problem is compounded by the fact that journals that publish research about the effectiveness of various treatments are not normally read by parents and teachers. Unfortunately, this void is readily filled by a steady stream of information, much of it not substantiated by research, from popular books, lay magazines, television talk shows (Silver, 2006), and now the Internet. Sinha and Efron (2005) recently surveyed Australian parents of children with ADHD and found that 68 percent of them had used or were currently using controversial therapies.

As a teacher, you need to be well informed about these therapies so you can give parents reliable, up-to-date information when they come to you for advice. The best way to get this information is to read professional journals. Any treatment may work for a few students, but this is not the same as demonstrating effectiveness in a controlled research study. If you or a student's parents decide to use a controversial therapy, you must monitor its effectiveness carefully and discontinue it if necessary. Several controversial therapies are summarized here, including the latest research findings for their effectiveness.

Neurophysiological Retraining

In this group of approaches, learning difficulties are seen as the result of dysfunctions in the central nervous system that can be remediated by having students engage in specific sensory or motor activities. One common example of this approach is *patterning* (Doman & Delacato, 1968), in which students are taken back through earlier stages of development (creeping and crawling). Another approach is *optometric visual training*, in which students do eye exercises designed to improve their visual perception and hence their reading skills. A third approach, *vestibular training*, takes children through tasks involving spatial orientation, eye movements, and balance, with the goal of improving their academic performance, especially in reading. A fourth neurophysiological approach is *applied kinesiology*. According to this chiropractic theory, learning disabilities are caused when "two specific bones of the skull shift out of position and cause pressure on the brain" (Silver, 2006, p. 393). The treatment, which consists of manipulating the bones of the skull as well as other bones and muscles, can be quite painful for the child (Silver, 2006).

A fifth approach is *auditory processing training*. This theory attributes learning disabilities to the failure of the body to organize incoming auditory stimuli into meaningful patterns, despite normal hearing. Training involves filtering out sounds believed to be interfering with the child's auditory perception, the eventual goal being to teach the ear to do this filtering on its own. Examples of auditory processing training include Bernard's auditory training integration and the Tomatis method.

A final neurophysiological approach is the so-called brain gym (Hyatt, 2007). The brain gym consists of a series of movements that are claimed to activate the brain, promote neurological repatterning, and facilitate whole-brain learning (Dennison & Dennison, 1994). The brain gym approach is based on the theory that learning problems are caused when sections of the brain and body don't work together, thereby blocking a child's ability to learn (Dennison & Dennison, 1994). The prescribed movements are intended to improve the integration of mind–body movements and in so doing enhance learning.

No research evidence suggests that any of these methods improves students' cognitive functioning or reading ability (American Academy of Pediatrics, 1999; Hallahan et al., 2005; Silver, 2006).

Diet Control Therapies

A number of therapies involve using diet to control hyperactivity and other learning disorders. One of these (Feingold, 1975) claimed to decrease student hyperactivity by eliminating various artificial flavors, colors, and preservatives from the student's diet. Most research studies have shown that the Feingold diet is not effective in controlling hyperactivity (Bateman, Warner, Hutchinson, et al., 2004; Smith, 2004). Others have suggested that refined sugars in the diet lead to hyperactivity. Again, these claims have not been proven by research (Barkley, 1995; Rojas & Chan, 2005).

Another diet therapy for learning disorders involves using megavitamins to treat emotional or cognitive disorders (Cott, 1977, 1985). This therapy has not been verified by research (Smith, 2004). One theory purports that deficiencies in trace elements such as copper, zinc, magnesium, manganese, and chromium along with the more common elements of calcium, sodium, and iron cause learning disorders, but these claims remain unsubstantiated (Silver, 2006). Still another theory claims hypoglycemia (low blood-sugar levels) causes learning disabilities. Clinical studies on this theory have been inconclusive (Rappaport, 1982/1983; Smith, 2004).

Finally, combinations of herbs, spices, and other ingredients have been recommended in recent years as a treatment for ADHD, as well as for learning disabilities. The effectiveness of these alternative medicines has yet to be validated by research (Silver, 2006).

Scotopic Sensitivity Syndrome

This syndrome has been defined as a difficulty in efficiently processing light, which causes a reading disorder (Irlen, 1991; Lerner, 2006). Symptoms include abnormal sensitivity to light, blinking and squinting, red and watery eyes, frequent headaches, word blurriness, print instability, slow reading, skipping and rereading lines, and difficulty reading at length because of general eye strain and fatigue (Irlen, 1991). Following a screening test, students identified as having scotopic sensitivity are treated with plastic overlays or colored lenses, which can be expensive. Although many people treated with tinted lenses claim that the lenses eliminate their symptoms and help them read better, research shows that the effects of the lenses are mixed (Silver, 2006). Caution is advised.

Allergies

Although there seems to be a relationship between allergies and brain functioning, a clear cause-and-effect relationship has yet to be established (Silver, 2006). Two persons who have written a lot about the relationship between allergies and learning disabilities and ADHD are Dr. Doris Rapp and Dr. William Crook. Dr. Rapp suggests the elimination of certain foods from the diet, such as milk, chocolate, eggs, wheat, corn, peanuts, pork, and sugar. She performs an "under-the-tongue" test (not validated) that she claims determines whether a child is allergic to any or all of these foods. Dr. Crook's recent work has focused on child reactions to a specific yeast and the development of specific behaviors following a yeast infection. According to Silver (2006) and Smith (2004), neither Crook nor Rapp supports these findings with research. In addition, the established profession of pediatric allergies does not accept either of these treatments (Silver, 2006).

Emerging Therapies

Rojas and Chan (2005) have reported on a number of therapies being recommended more often to treat learning and behavior difficulties often associated with ADHD. These therapies include fatty acid supplementation, homeopathy, yoga, massage, and green outdoor settings. Rojas and Chan conclude that the overall body of evidence does not support the use of any of these therapies either by itself or in concert with treatments of established effectiveness, such as medication and behavior therapy.

Controversial Therapies and the Internet

As the number of Internet sites created for specific disabilities and related health issues increases, so too does information about controversial therapies. Because information on the Internet is not reviewed for quality, Ira (2000) suggests that you do the following to determine the credibility of the various websites you visit:

1. Click on the About Us or Contact Us links or buttons at a website. These links may inform you of who is on the team of people running a particular website. Many sites, particularly those that want to prove their credibility, feature a page describing their background, history, and affiliations (the About Us section) and mailing and e-mail addresses and phone numbers (the Contact Us section).

2. Try to establish links with other sites. Sites with reliably usable information may have endorsements from prominent special needs organizations or may have links to other websites with more information on the subject. Look for links to other associations or educational or even government-supported institutions related to the subject. The more independent sites that validate a recommendation, the more credible it is. The following are specific sites that may address doubts about the credibility of a particular controversial therapy:

www.interdys.org	International Dyslexia Society
www.ldanatl.org	Learning Disabilities Association of America
www.ncld.org	National Center for Learning Disabilities
www.cldinternational.org	Council for Learning Disabilities

3. Ask friends and special needs associations to recommend websites that are informative. You can also e-mail people you think can offer advice on the credibility of a particular site.

4. Examine the content of the site for typographical and grammatical errors. As with books, magazines, and journals, credibility is often reflected in editorial excellence.

5. Check to see how often the site is updated. A site that is updated regularly with new research findings is most likely to be run by people interested in learning the truth rather than perpetuating their own point of view.

6. Check to be sure that a given finding has been validated by a credible, refereed research publication. Many of these publications are available on the Web.

What Are the Social and Emotional Needs of Students with Learning and Behavioral Disabilities?

Info Sheet Homework Exercise

Go to the Homework and Exercises section in Chapter 7 of MyEducationLab to document appropriate strategies and methods to support students with social and emotional needs.

Considering students' social needs is crucial, because students who have social adjustment problems in school are at risk for academic problems (Anderson, Kutash, & Duchnowski, 2001; Coleman & Webber, 2002; Lane, Wehby, & Barton-Arwood, 2005), as well as serious adjustment problems when they leave school (Carter & Wehby, 2003; Kauffman, 2005). Students with learning and behavioral disabilities may have needs in several social areas, including classroom conduct, interpersonal skills, and personal and psychological adjustment.

Students with learning and behavioral disabilities may engage in a number of aggressive or disruptive behaviors in class, including hitting, fighting, teasing, hyperactivity, yelling, refusing to comply with requests, crying, destructiveness, vandalism, and extortion (Deitz & Ormsby, 1992; Friend, 2008; Hallahan & Kauffman, 2005). Although many of these behaviors may be exhibited by all children at one time or another, the classroom conduct of students with behavioral disorders is viewed by teachers as abnormal, and their behavior has a negative impact on the other students in class (Cullinan, Epstein, & Lloyd, 1983; Hallahan & Kauffman, 2005).

For example, Kenneth is an adolescent with learning and behavior problems. His father died last year, and his mother has been working two jobs just to make ends meet. Kenneth has begun to hang out with a rough crowd and has been getting into fights in school. He has also been talking back to his teachers frequently and refusing to comply with their demands. Kenneth's behavior has gotten so bad that other students and their

Students who are experiencing emotional problems might be withdrawn, anxious, or depressed. What can you do to help these students in your classroom?

Working TOGETHER

Learning from Others

Marcia Lamb is beginning her first year of teaching third grade at a large urban elementary school. She has 25 students in her class. Three students have IEPs: One student has behavior disorders, and two have learning disabilities. After the first full week of school, Marcia is clearly struggling to get control of her class. During large-group instruction, many children are off task. Even when students are paying attention, they call out answers without raising their hands. Transitioning from one subject to the next seems to take forever because few students do as they are told. There is constant complaining that the work is too hard. Although some of the problems involve her students with disabilities, Marcia is having problems with most of the students at one time or another.

Marcia doesn't know what to do. She was assigned a faculty mentor, but every time she sees her in the hall, she seems so busy that Marcia is reluctant to ask her anything. The special education teacher also seems busy and is still in the process of setting up her schedule. Marcia is afraid to tell the principal she is having problems. What should Marcia do?

■ An important part of working together is recognizing that problem solving works best when it is done in teams. Seeking help from an individual or team is not a sign of weakness but an effective strategy that

also sends the message that you recognize you have a problem and want to do something about it. Marcia needs to set up an appointment with her mentor right away to discuss the problems she is having with her class. The mentor can share her experiences with Marcia and give her ideas for structuring her class to prevent many of her current problems from recurring.

■ Another key part of working together is recognizing the strengths of your colleagues and accessing their particular areas of expertise as needed. Marcia needs to make an appointment with the special education teacher to discuss her efforts with the three students with disabilities included in her class. These students may require a more individualized effort, and special education teachers specialize in making such accommodations for students with disabilities. Marcia may also be able to set up a co-teaching arrangement whereby she and another teacher teach together sometime during the day. Co-teaching is a powerful way for new teachers to acquire expertise from their more experienced colleagues.

■ As for contacting her principal, although there is no need to directly involve the principal at this time, Marcia should not feel reluctant to let her know she has been working with her colleagues to help her be a more effective teacher. No doubt they value the act of self-improvement as an important quality in a new teacher.

---

parents are complaining about it to the teacher. Guidelines for disciplining students like Kenneth are described in Chapter 12. Ways to get support from colleagues in solving academic and behavior problems in your classroom are described in Working Together.

Interpersonal Skills

Students with learning and behavioral disabilities are likely to have difficulty in social relations with their peers. Evidence for these problems comes from more than 20 years of research showing that these students have fewer friends, are more likely to be rejected or neglected by their peers (Bryan, 2005), and are frequently rated as socially troubled by their teachers and parents (Smith, 2004). Many of these problems can be traced to the failure of students to engage in socially appropriate behaviors or social skills in areas such as making friends, carrying on conversations, and dealing with conflict.

There are a number of explanations for why students have social skills problems. Some students may simply not know what to do in social situations. They may lack knowledge because they do not learn from naturally occurring models of social behavior at home or

> **DIMENSIONS OF diversity**
>
> Social skills are learned in cultural contexts. Teach your students about the variance in social behaviors within all cultures and emphasize the notion that families and individuals experience their cultures in personal ways.

Reading Homework Exercise

Go to the Homework and Exercises section in Chapter 7 of MyEducationLab to learn about characteristics of and interventions for helping students with nonverbal learning disabilities.

in school. Students also may have trouble reading social cues and may misinterpret the feelings of others (Bryan, 2005; Lerner, 2006; Silver, 2006). For example, a story was told recently about five boys sitting on the floor of the principal's office, waiting to be disciplined. Four of the boys were discussing failing or near-failing grades and the trouble they were going to be in when the fifth boy, a student with a learning disability, chimed in to say that his grandparents were coming to visit the next week.

Other students may know what to do—but not do it. For example, some students with learning and behavioral disabilities are impulsive; they act before they think. In Del's sessions with the school social worker, he is able to explain how he would act in various social situations, but in an actual social setting, he gets nervous and acts without thinking.

Some students may choose not to act on their previous knowledge because their attempts at socially appropriate behavior may have gone unrecognized and they would rather have negative recognition than no recognition at all. For example, James was rebuffed by one group of students so often that he began to say nasty things to them just to provoke them. He also began to hang out with other students who chronically misbehaved because, according to James, "At least they appreciate me!"

Finally, some students may know what to do socially but lack the confidence to act on their knowledge in social situations, particularly if they have a history of social rejection or lack opportunities for social interactions. Consider Holly, a student who is socially withdrawn. Holly worked for a year with her school counselor to learn how to initiate a social activity with a friend but is afraid to try it out for fear of being rejected.

Personal and Psychological Adjustment

Students with little success at academics and/or social relationships may have personal and psychological problems as well (Kerschner, 1990; Torgesen, 1991; Vaughn & Haager, 1994). One common personal problem is self-image. Students with learning and behavioral disabilities often have a poor self-concept; they have little confidence in their own abilities (Lerner, 2006; Licht, Kistner, Ozkaragoz, Shapiro, & Clausen, 1985; Silver, 2006). Poor self-image can in turn lead to **learned helplessness.** Students with learned helplessness see little relationship between their efforts and school or social success. When these students succeed, they attribute their success to luck; when they fail, they blame their failure on a lack of ability. When confronted with difficult situations, students who have learned helplessness are likely to say or think, "What's the use? I never do anything right anyway."

Not surprisingly, low self-esteem and learned helplessness often result in actions likely to be interpreted as a lack of motivation. For example, Denny is a 15-year-old sophomore in high school. He has been in special education since the second grade. He has never received a grade better than a C and has received quite a few D's and F's. Last quarter, Denny started to skip classes because he felt that even when he went to class, he did not do well. Denny is looking forward to dropping out of school on his 16th birthday and going to work for a fast-food chain, where, he reasons, at least he will be able to do the work.

Students with learning and behavior problems may also have severe anxiety or depression (Cullinan, 2007; Maag & Reid, 2006). Depressed or anxious students may refuse to speak up when in class, may be pessimistic or uninterested in key aspects of their lives, may be visibly nervous when given an assignment, may become ill when it is time to go to school, or may show a lack of self-confidence when performing common school and social tasks. For example, Barrett is a 9-year-old boy with a consistent history of school failure. He is sick just about every morning before he goes to school. At first his mother let him stay home, but now she makes him go anyway. When at school, Barrett is very withdrawn. He has few friends and rarely speaks in class. Barrett's teachers tend not to notice him because he is quiet and does not cause problems. If you have a student in your class who you think may be depressed, consult the Diagnostic Criteria for Major Depression (American Psychiatric Association, 2000).

It is important to keep in mind that while students with learning and behavioral disorders are at risk for having personal and psychological adjustment problems, not

Info Sheet Homework Exercise

Go to the Homework and Exercises section in Chapter 7 of MyEducationLab to see why students with learning and behavioral problems often have difficulties solving problems; read about a strategy for teaching problem solving.

all of these students have these problems. In one study, Nunez et al. (2005) found that just under half of the students with learning disabilities did not differ in self-concept and learned helplessness from their classmates without disabilities. Using INCLUDE to find the individual needs and strengths of your students will help ensure that you will make accommodations for them based on their unique needs.

What Accommodations Can You Make for Students with Learning and Behavioral Disabilities?

As you have just read, students with learning and behavioral disabilities have a range of learning and social-emotional needs. Although these needs may make learning and socializing difficult for them, students with learning and behavioral disabilities can succeed in your classroom if given support. Some initial ideas about how you can accommodate students with learning and behavioral disabilities in your classroom are discussed next. A more in-depth treatment of such accommodations can be found in Chapters 8–13.

Addressing Academic Needs

As we have already discussed, you can discern whether students with learning and behavioral disabilities need differentiated instruction by using the INCLUDE strategy to analyze their academic needs and the particular demands of your classroom. In most cases, students with learning and behavioral disabilities are expected to meet the same curricular

www.resources

LDOnLine is an interactive guide to learning disabilities for parents, students, and teachers. This website offers newsletters, teaching tips, and more: www.ldonline.org.

Info Sheet Homework Exercise

Go to the Homework and Exercises section in Chapter 7 of MyEducationLab to learn about behavior problems that can occur when students lack social skills.

INCLUDE

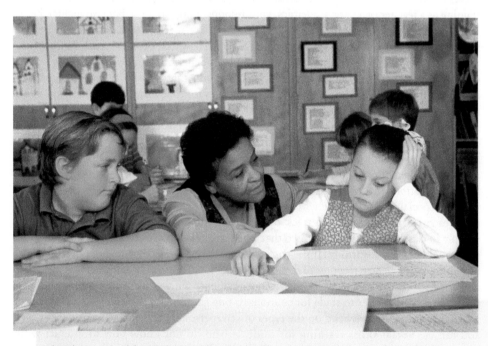

In what ways might students with cognitive, emotional, and behavioral disorders have difficulty learning? How can teachers address each of these areas of difficulty?

Analyze and Reflect

What social-emotional needs might students with learning and behavioral disabilities share? To what extent are students' social-emotional problems related to their academic problems? Why is it important to address students' social and emotional needs?

Info Sheet Homework Exercise

Go to the Homework and Exercises section in Chapter 7 of MyEducationLab for a list of research-based strategies for you to use when teaching.

expectations as their classmates without disabilities. Therefore, when differentiating their instruction, provide them with instructional accommodations rather than modifications. Try the three types of accommodations described in Chapter 5: bypassing a student's need by allowing the student to employ compensatory learning strategies; making an accommodation in classroom management, grouping, materials, and methods; and providing the student with direct instruction on basic or independent learning skills. For example, Jessica, who has learning disabilities, has enrolled in Mr. Gresh's high school general science class. Mr. Gresh uses a teaching format in which the students first read the text, then hear a lecture, and finally conduct and write up a lab activity (demands). Jessica has severe reading and writing problems. She is reading at about a sixth-grade level and has difficulty writing a legible, coherent paragraph (student learning needs). However, she does have good listening skills and is an adequate note taker (student strength). In Mr. Gresh's class, Jessica will have difficulty reading the textbook and meeting the lab-writing requirements independently (problem). She will be able to get the lecture information she needs because of her good listening skills (success). Mr. Gresh, with help from Jessica's special education teacher, brainstorms a number of possible accommodations for Jessica and then agrees to implement three of them. He develops a study guide to help Jessica identify key points in the text (materials and methods). He also sets up small groups in class to review the study guides (grouping) and assigns Jessica a buddy to help her with the writing demands of the lab activity (bypass). Finally, Mr. Gresh and the special education teacher set up a schedule to monitor Jessica's progress in writing lab reports and reading the textbook (evaluation). Several more examples of how the INCLUDE strategy can be used to differentiate instruction are provided in Table 7.2.

Addressing Social and Emotional Needs

One of the most important reasons given for inclusive education is the social benefit for students with and without disabilities (Freeman & Alkin, 2000; Stainback & Stainback, 1988). Unfortunately, experience shows that many students with learning and behavior problems do not acquire important social skills just from their physical presence in general education classes (Hallahan et al., 2005; Sale & Carey, 1995). Although much of the emphasis in your training as a teacher concerns academics, your responsibilities as a teacher also include helping all students develop socially, whether or not they have special needs. As with academics, the support students need depends largely on the specific social problems each student has.

Students who have significant conduct problems benefit from a classroom with a clear, consistent behavior management system. In classrooms that are effectively managed, the rules are communicated clearly and the consequences for following or not following those rules are clearly stated and consistently applied. Conduct problems can also be minimized if students are engaged in meaningful academic tasks that can be completed successfully. Still, conduct problems may be so significant that they require a more intensive, individualized approach. For example, ReNaye, whom you read about at the beginning of this chapter, repeatedly talked out and loudly refused to carry out any requests her teachers made of her. Her school attendance was also spotty. ReNaye's general education teachers got together with her special education teacher to develop a **behavior contract.** According to the contract, each teacher was to keep track of ReNaye's attendance, talk-outs, and refusals to comply in class. The contract specified that when she talked out or refused to comply once, she would be given a warning. If she engaged in either of these behaviors again, she would be required to serve five minutes of detention for each violation. The contract also specified that for each class ReNaye attended without incident, she would receive points that her parents would allow her to trade for coupons to buy gasoline for her car.

Accommodations depend on the types of interpersonal problems your students have. You can use **social skills training** for students who do not know how to interact with peers and adults (Lane et al., 2005; McGinnis & Goldstein, 2005; Stichter et al., 2007; Walker & Rankin, 1983). For example, Tammy is very withdrawn and has few friends. One day her teacher took her aside and suggested that she ask one of the other girls in class

TABLE 7.2

Differentiating Instruction for Students with Learning and
Behavioral Disabilities Using Steps in the INCLUDE Strategy

Identify Classroom Demands	Note Student Strengths and Needs	Check for Potential Successes, Look for Potential Problems	Differentiate Instruction
Student desks in clusters of four	*Strengths* Good vocabulary skills *Needs* Difficulty attending to task	*Success* Student understands instruction if on task *Problem* Student off task—does not face instructor as she teaches	Change seating so student faces instructor
Small-group work with peers	*Strengths* Good handwriting *Needs* Oral expressive language— problem with word finding	*Success* Student acts as secretary for cooperative group *Problem* Student has difficulty expressing self in peer-learning groups	Assign as secretary of group Place into compatible small group Develop social skills instruction for all students
Expectation for students to attend class and be on time	*Strengths* Good drawing skills *Needs* Poor time management	*Success* Student uses artistic talent in class *Problem* Student is late for class and frequently does not attend at all	Use individualized student contract for attendance and punctuality—if goals are met, give student artistic responsibility in class
Textbook difficult to read	*Strengths* Good oral communication skills *Needs* Poor reading accuracy Lacks systematic strategy for reading text	*Success* Student participates well in class Good candidate for class dramatizations *Problem* Student is unable to read text for information	Provide audiotaped textbook Highlight student text
Lecture on women's suffrage movement to whole class	*Strengths* Very motivated and interested in class *Needs* Lack of background knowledge	*Success* Student earns points for class attendance and effort *Problem* Student lacks background knowledge to understand important information in lecture	Give student choice of video to view or leveled book to read before lecture Build points for attendance and working hard into grading system
Whole-class instruction on telling time to the quarter hour	*Strengths* Good coloring skills *Needs* Cannot identify numbers 7–12 Cannot count by 5s	*Success* Student is able to color clock faces used in instruction *Problem* Student is unable to acquire time-telling skills	Provide extra instruction on number identification and counting by 5s

continued

TABLE *7.2*

Continued

Identify Classroom Demands	Note Student Strengths and Needs	Check for Potential Successes, Look for Potential Problems	Differentiate Instruction
Math test involving solving word problems using addition	*Strengths* Good reasoning skills *Needs* Problems mastering math facts, sums of 10–18	*Success* Student is good at solving problems *Problem* Student misses problems due to math fact errors	Allow use of calculator
Multiple-choice and fill-in-the-blanks test	*Strengths* Good memory for details *Needs* Cannot identify key words in test questions Weak comprehension skills	*Success* Student does well on fill-in-the-blank questions that require memorization *Problem* Student is doing poorly on multiple-choice parts of history tests	Use bold type for key words in multiple-choice questions Teach strategy for taking multiple-choice tests Give student choice of alternatives to show knowledge other than multiple-choice items

home some day after school. Tammy told her that she would never do that because she just would not know what to say. Tammy's teacher decided to spend several social studies classes working with the class on that skill and other skills such as carrying on a conversation and using the correct words and demeanor when asking another student whether he or she would like to play a game. She felt that many of the students in class besides Tammy would benefit from these lessons. First, Tammy's teacher posted the steps involved in performing these skills on a chart in front of the classroom. Then she and several students in the class demonstrated the social skills for the class. She next divided the class into small groups, and each group role-played the various skills and was given feedback by classmates and peers. To make sure that Tammy felt comfortable, the teacher put her in a group of students who had a positive attitude and liked Tammy. An example of how to carry out social skills training is presented in the Case in Practice.

For students who know what to do in social situations but lack the self-control to behave appropriately, **self-control training** can be used (Henley, 2003; Kauffman, 2005). Self-control training teaches students to redirect their actions by talking to themselves. For example, Dominic did not handle conflict very well. When his friends teased him, he was quick to lose his temper and to verbally lash out at them. His outbursts only encouraged the students, and they continued teasing and taunting him any chance they got. Dominic's teacher taught him a self-control strategy to help him ignore his friends' teasing. Whenever he was teased, Dominic first counted to 5 to himself to get beyond his initial anger. He then told himself that what they were saying wasn't true and that the best way to get them to stop was to ignore them and walk away. Whenever he walked away, Dominic told himself he did a good job and later reported his efforts to his teacher.

Some students may know what to do socially but lack opportunities for using their social skills. For example, students who are newly included in your classroom and/or new to the school need opportunities to interact with classmates to get to know them better. One way to create opportunities for social interaction is to allow students to work in small groups with a shared learning goal. For example, Thomas is a student with a mild

Building Teaching Skills Simulation Exercise

Go to the Building Teaching Skills section in Chapter 7 of MyEducationLab to learn about providing instructional supports that facilitate the mastery of new skills.

Case in Practice

A Social Skills Training Session

Ms. Perez and her fourth-grade class are working on a unit on social skills in social studies. They are learning the skill of listening to someone who is talking by doing the following:

1. Look at the person who is talking.

2. Remember to sit quietly.

3. Think about what is being said.

4. Say yes or nod your head.

5. Ask a question about the topic to find out more.

Jeanine, a student in the class, has just practiced these listening skills in front of the class by role-playing the part of a student who is talking to her teacher about an assignment. In the role-play, Ms. Perez played herself. The class is now giving Jeanine feedback on her performance.

Ms. Perez: Let's start with the first step. Did Jeanine look at me when I was talking? Before you answer, can someone tell me why it's important to look at the person who is talking?

Lorna: You don't want the other person to think you're not listening even though you are. So you really have to *show* them you are listening.

Ms. Perez: That's right, Lorna. Well, how did Jeanine do on this one?

Charles: Well, she looked at you at first, but while you were explaining the assignment she looked down at her feet. It kind of looked like she wasn't listening.

Jeanine: I was listening, but I guess I should have kept good eye contact all the way through.

Ms. Perez: Yes, Jeanine. To be honest, if I didn't know you better, I would have thought that you didn't care about what I was saying. You need to work on that step. The next step is to remember to sit quietly. How did Jeanine do with this one?

Milton: I think she did well. She remembered not to laugh, fidget, or play with anything while you were talking.

Ms. Perez: I agree, Milton. Nice work, Jeanine. Now, can someone tell me what the next listening step is?

Kyrie: It's to think about what the person is saying.

Ms. Perez: Right, Kyrie. Let's let Jeanine evaluate herself on this one.

Jeanine: Well, I tried to think about what you were saying. Once I felt my mind start to wander, but I followed your suggestion and started thinking about a question that I could ask you.

Ms. Perez: Good, Jeanine. Trying to think of a question to ask can be very helpful. How did you think you did on the next step? Did you nod your head or say yes to show you were following me?

Jeanine: I think I did.

Ms. Perez: What do the rest of you think? Did Jeanine nod her head or say yes?

Tara: Well, I saw her nod a little, but it was hard to tell. Maybe she needs to nod more clearly.

Ms. Perez: Jeanine, you need to nod more strongly or the teacher won't realize you are doing it.

REFLECTIONS

What teaching procedures is Ms. Perez using to teach her students listening skills? Do you think they are effective? What could she do to make sure that her students use this skill in their classes? For what settings outside school would these and other social skills be important?

---

intellectual disability who is included in Mr. Jeffreys's sixth-grade class. This is Thomas's first year in general education; until this year, he was in a self-contained special education classroom. Mr. Jeffreys has decided to use peer-learning groups in science because he thinks they will be a good way for Thomas to get to know his classmates and make some friends. Every two weeks, Thomas has the opportunity to complete various lab activities with a different group of his choice.

Students who exhibit learned helplessness can benefit from **attribution retraining** (Ellis, Lenz, & Sabornie, 1987b; Fulk, 1996; Mercer & Pullen, 2005). The idea behind attribution retraining is that if you can convince students that their failures are due to lack of effort rather than ability, they will be more persistent and improve their performance

fyi

Motivation is an important factor in the achievement of students with learning and behavior problems (Sideridis & Scanlon, 2006). Passive learning, learned helplessness, and a low self-image all play an important part in student motivation.

A small proportion of the high school students with disabilities with whom you will come in contact will be lesbian, gay, bisexual, or transgender (LGBT) persons. Their numbers are hard to substantiate because they usually do not self-identify. These students frequently need counseling because they are likely to be confronted with hostile attitudes while identifying or coming to terms with their sexuality (Harley et al., 2002). LGBT students with disabilities may also need support to address socially appropriate behaviors and strategies for interpreting the messages they may receive, whether positive or negative. Finally, school staff need to monitor the quality and character of the school climate to ensure that all students are treated fairly and that discrimination based on sexual orientation is not tolerated.

in the face of difficulty (Hallahan et al., 2005; Schunk, 1989). You can enhance student self-image by using the following strategies (Mercer & Pullen, 2005):

1. *Set reasonable goals.* When setting goals for students, make sure they are not too easy or too hard. Self-worth is improved when students reach their goals through considerable effort. Goals that are too ambitious perpetuate failure. Goals that are too easy can give students the idea that you think they are not capable of doing anything difficult.

2. *Provide specific feedback contingent on student behavior.* Feedback should be largely positive, but it should also be contingent on completion of tasks. Otherwise, students are likely to perceive your feedback as patronizing and just another indication that you think they are unable to do real academic work. Do not be afraid to correct students when they are wrong. Providing corrective feedback communicates to students that you think they can succeed if they keep trying and that you care about them.

3. *Give students responsibility.* Assigning a responsibility demonstrates to students that you trust them and believe they can act maturely. Some examples include taking the class pet home on weekends, taking the lunch count, being a line leader, taking messages to the office, and taking attendance.

4. *Teach students to reinforce themselves.* Students with a poor self-image say negative things about themselves. You can help students by reminding them of their strengths, encouraging them to make more positive statements about themselves, and then reinforcing them for making these statements.

5. *Give students a chance to show their strengths.* Part of the INCLUDE strategy is to identify student strengths and then help students achieve success by finding or creating classroom situations in which they can employ their strengths. For example, Cara cannot read very well but has an excellent speaking voice. After her group wrote a report on the 1960 presidential election, Cara was given the task of presenting the report to the whole class.

Summary

Students with high-incidence disabilities are those who have speech and language disabilities, learning disabilities, emotional disturbance, or mild intellectual disabilities. These students make up over 80 percent of all students who have disabilities. They are often hard to distinguish from their peers; exhibit a combination of behavior, social, and academic problems; and benefit from systematic, highly structured interventions.

Students with communication disorders have a number of learning, social, and emotional needs. Their language problems can affect their performance in academic and social areas. The academic and social performances of stu-

dents with speech and language problems can be enhanced through a number of accommodations, including creating an atmosphere of acceptance, actively encouraging and teaching listening skills, using modeling to expand students' language, and teaching within contexts that are meaningful for students.

Students with learning and behavioral disabilities receive special education services within the categories of learning disabilities, mild intellectual disabilities, and emotional disturbance. Students with learning and behavioral disabilities have many academic needs. They may also lack skills necessary for efficient learning, such as attending to task, memory, organizing and interpreting information, reasoning, motor coordination, independent learning skills, and academic survival skills. You can make accommodations for these students in academic areas using the INCLUDE strategy.

Students with learning and behavioral disabilities have social and emotional difficulties in classroom conduct, interpersonal skills, and personal and psychological adjustment. Accommodations for students with learning and behavioral disabilities in social areas include individualized behavior management, social skills training, self-control training, and attribution retraining.

Back to the Cases

This section provides opportunities for you to apply the knowledge gained in this chapter to the cases described at the beginning of this chapter? The questions and activities that follow demonstrate how these standards and principles, along with other concepts that you have learned about in this chapter, connect to the everyday activities of all teachers.

Will has difficulty with two important basic skills: reading and writing. His teachers need more information about methods for supporting Will's reading and writing so that he can learn the content needed to pass his end-of-grade tests and make a smooth transition to middle school (INTASC Principles 2.02, 4.04, and 9.02; and CEC Standards 3 and 4). There are two popular websites that offer information specifically for and about persons with learning disabilities: Schwab Learning (http://schwablearning.org) and LD Online (http://ldonline.org). Your task is to visit those websites and find information that you think would help teachers meet the learning needs of students with problems similar to Will's. Complete an annotated list of articles, videos, and links to additional information from those websites that you might share with Will's teacher and the peers in your class.

ReNaye, as you may remember, demonstrated aggressive and noncompliant behaviors. Her behavior was addressed with a behavior contract.

However, over the years she has missed opportunities to learn due to her frequent absences and discipline referrals, resulting in lower grades and a failed end-of-grade test in ninth-grade mathematics. Most likely she lacks some basic skills and knowledge that she will need to successfully progress. Now her team is meeting to discuss how they can help her make up the missed work and successfully pass the math test. The text notes that students with learning and behavior problems are often grouped together because they benefit from the same instructional practices. Using the information from the text, as well as from your search for solutions to Will's difficulties, describe two or three teaching strategies or accommodations that you think would help ReNaye's teachers support her (INTASC Principles 2.02, 4.04, and 9.02; and CEC Standards 2, 3, 4, and 10). Provide a rationale for your answer.

Key Terms and Concepts

Academic survival skills (p. 257)

Attribution retraining (p. 267)

Behavior contract (p. 264)

Emotional disturbance (p. 250)

Expressive language (p. 245)

High-incidence disabilities (p. 242)

Learned helplessness (p. 262)

Learning disabilities (p. 248)

Mild intellectual disabilities (p. 250)

Receptive language (p. 245)

Self-control training (p. 266)

Social skills training (p. 264)

Speech articulation (p. 244)

Stuttering (p. 244)

Now go to the Friend and Bursuck, Fifth Edition, MyEducationLab course at www.myeducationlab.com to

- take a pretest to assess your initial comprehension of the chapter content
- study chapter content with your individualized study plan
- take a posttest to assess your understanding of chapter content
- engage in multimedia exercises to help you build a deeper and more applied understanding of chapter content

Applications in Teaching Practice

Using the INCLUDE Strategy with Students with High-Incidence Disabilities

Answer the following questions to show how you would apply the INCLUDE strategy to differentiate instruction for the students described in the vignettes at the beginning of this chapter. To help you with this application, refer to Table 7.2 and to the section on the INCLUDE strategy in Chapter 5.

Questions

1. What communication, academic, behavioral, and social and emotional needs does each student have?

2. Keeping in mind the major aspects of the classroom environment, including classroom management, classroom grouping, instructional materials, and instructional methods, what kinds of problems are these students likely to have?

3. How would you differentiate instruction for each of these students?

4. Are the accommodations you would make reasonable in terms of teacher time and ease of implementation? What support (if any) would you need to carry them out?

5. How can you monitor the effectiveness of your differentiated instruction? What can you do next if your first attempt is ineffective?

Further Readings

Forness, S. R., Walker, H. M., & Kavale, K. A. (2003). Psychiatric disorders and treatments: A primer for teachers. *Teaching Exceptional Children, 36*(2), 42–49.

   This article provides essential information for teachers on the diagnosis and treatment of child psychiatric disorders, including oppositional, defiant, and conduct disorders; attention deficit–hyperactivity disorders; depression; anxiety; schizophrenia; and autism spectrum disorder.

Ganz, J. B., Cook, K., & Earles-Vollrath, T. L. (2007). A grab bag of strategies for children with mild communication deficits. *Intervention in School and Clinic, 42*(3), 179–187.

   The authors present a variety of research-based teaching strategies that address communication or social skills, require few materials or resources that would not already be present in the school and home, and require minimal training to be implemented.

Rhode, G., Jensen, W. R., & Morgan, D. P. (2003). *The tough kid new teacher kit: Practical classroom management survival strategies for the new teacher.* Longmont, CO: Sopris West.

The authors describe a variety of practical classroom management strategies and ideas that can be readily carried out by classroom teachers. The book also suggests a number of resources to help teachers in the area of behavioral, social, and academic assessments for challenging students.

Shaywitz, S. (2003). *Overcoming dyslexia: A new and complete science-based program for reading problems at any level.* New York: Knopf.

Shaywitz has written an excellent introductory book for parents and teachers on the causes of and treatments for severe reading problems. She takes the latest scientific research on reading disabilities and translates it into a very readable, practical book.

Silver, L. B. (2006). *The misunderstood child: Understanding and coping with your child's learning disabilities* (4th ed.). New York: Times Books.

This is another very readable book on the topic of learning disabilities: what they are and how to treat them.

8 Students with Special Needs Other Than Disabilities

LEARNING Objectives

After you read this chapter, you will be able to

1. Describe students protected through Section 504 and the accommodations general education teachers can make for them.

2. Explain accommodations general education teachers can make to address the special needs of students with attention deficit–hyperactivity disorder (ADHD).

3. Outline the adaptations that students who are gifted and talented may need in general education classrooms.

4. Explain how cultural diversity influences education, critically analyzing your own response to students from cultures other than your own and your skills for addressing their needs.

5. Describe how general education teachers can accommodate students at risk for school failure, including students affected by poverty, abuse or neglect, substance abuse, and other factors.

Maria is an eighth-grade student whose family immigrated to the United States from Mexico three years ago. At first, Maria attended a bilingual program in which she learned some core content in Spanish while working on her English skills. For the past year, though, she has not received any special educational support. Maria is bilingual—a speaker of both Spanish, the language spoken in her home, and English, the language she usually speaks at school. However, she still sometimes misunderstands what her teachers mean and struggles with some of the material being taught. Her language skills are not yet advanced enough to easily grasp abstract concepts. Maria likes school; she wants to go to college but is not sure this is a realistic goal. Her parents both work, but she has three sisters and a brother, and there is no extra money for higher education. Her oldest sister attends the community college, working a full-time job to earn the money she needs to contribute to the family and pay tuition, and Maria is eager to be old enough to earn money too. Maria's teachers are already encouraging her to become an educator; they recommended her for a special summer program designed to recruit future teachers who will work in their communities. Maria is thrilled to have this opportunity.

■ *What special needs might students like Maria have? What is your responsibility for finding ways to help all your diverse students succeed in school? How can you develop a better understanding of students and families from diverse cultures?*

José is a student in Mr. Lee's seventh-grade math class. Mr. Lee comments that José never is completely still in class: He drums his pencil, plays with his calculator, or tears paper into thin strips. Mr. Lee also has noticed that José's attention is drawn to nearly anything that goes on in class—or outside. He watches as another student looks for something in her backpack, stares at a student sharpening a pencil, and stops working when the fan comes on in a computer at the side of the classroom. Instead of raising his hand during class discussions, José just blurts out what is on his mind, and he is as likely to make a comment about his latest adventure in his neighborhood as he is to contribute a comment relevant to the topic at hand. José frequently is written up for misbehavior; the principal keeps reminding him that if he would *think* before he *acts,* he would avoid most of the problems. José's grandmother reports that he is "all boy," much like his father was.

■ *Does José have a disability? What are José's special needs? What is the responsibility of school personnel for meeting those needs?*

Lydia is a fourth-grade student who is gifted and talented. She has been reading since age three, and she frequently borrows her sister's high school literature anthology as a source of reading material. She knew most of the math concepts introduced in fourth grade before the school year began. She has a strong interest in learning French and playing flute and piano, and she volunteers to read to residents of a local nursing home. Lydia's idea of a perfect afternoon is to have a quiet place to hide, a couple of wonderful books, and no one to bother her. Lydia's teacher, Mr. Judd, enjoys having her in class because she is so enthusiastic about learning, but he admits that Lydia's abilities are a little intimidating. He also has noticed that Lydia doesn't seem to have much in common with other students in class. She is a class leader but does not appear to have any close friends, as other students do.

■ *Is Lydia entitled to receive special services because of her giftedness? Is Lydia typical of students who are gifted or talented? What can Mr. Judd do to help Lydia reach her full potential? What social problems do students like Lydia encounter?*

Tam is a junior in high school, but he doubts that he will finish the school year. He describes school as "pointless," and he continues to come only because he would hate to hurt his mother's feelings by dropping out. He is absent often, especially from his first-block U.S. history class, and he usually does not bother to do homework or read assignments. Tam does not belong to any clubs at school or participate in any athletics. After school, Tam hangs out with his friends, often congregating in the alley behind an electronics store and not returning home until well after midnight. He is considering an offer to run drugs that recently was made by Michael, a 21-year-old dropout whom Tam admires. Tam has a juvenile record; he is on probation for stealing a car. Michael told him, though, that the risks of prison are minimal until he turns 18 and that his records will be expunged at that time even if he gets arrested again. Tam's logic is that he knows many people who make money this way. Tam's teachers describe him as "unmotivated," a student who has vastly more potential than they see him using.

■ *How common are students like Tam? What other characteristics and behaviors might Tam display in school? If Tam were your student, how would you try to reach him? What are your responsibilities to students like Tam?*

DIMENSIONS OF

diversity

Equity pedagogy is the term to describe the use of instructional strategies that address the learning characteristics and cognitive styles of diverse populations. If you complete an Internet search using this term, you can find research and teaching resources for effectively working with all your students.

Most educators agree that many students who are not eligible to receive special education have needs as great as or greater than those of students protected by the Individuals with Disabilities Education Act (IDEA). For example, Maria has made great progress in learning English, but she still experiences difficulties with the technical language of academic content. Even though José has a significant attention problem, he does not qualify for special education. Lydia's teacher is concerned that he cannot possibly make time to provide the advanced instruction that would benefit her, but his school district does not offer any programs for students who are gifted or talented until middle school. Tam's teachers worry about his future and are frustrated that they cannot make his life better and help him reach his potential. They feel powerless to influence students like Tam, who have so many difficulties in their young lives, and they question how traditional academic standards and activities can be made relevant for those students.

This chapter is about students who are not necessarily eligible for special education but whose learning is at risk and whose success often depends on the quality of the instruction they receive and the care provided by general education teachers. Did you attend school with students with extraordinary needs such as these? Were you one of those students? If either is the case, you bring to your teacher-preparation program an understanding and empathy that other teacher candidates may not have, and you may have a perspective on student diversity that you can draw on in addressing student needs. The students examined in this chapter fall into one or more of these groups: those who have functional disabilities protected by Section 504, the civil rights law introduced in Chapter 1, but not protected by IDEA, including those with attention deficit–hyperactivity disorder; those who are gifted and talented; those whose native language is not English and whose cultures differ significantly from that of most of their classmates; and those who are at risk because of life circumstances, including poverty, child abuse, drug abuse, transience (for example, migrant families), and other factors.

The rationale for discussing Maria, José, Lydia, Tam, and other students like them in this text has four parts:

1. Students with these types of needs often benefit greatly from the same strategies that are successful for students with disabilities. Thus, one purpose is to remind you that the techniques explained throughout this text are applicable to many of your students, not just those who have individualized education programs (IEPs).

2. You should recognize that you will teach many students with a tremendous diversity of needs resulting from many different causes, disability being just one potential factor. Creating appropriate educational opportunities for all your students is your responsibility.

3. Students with special needs often are referred for special education services because caring teachers recognize that they need help. It is essential that you realize that special education is much more than help and is reserved for just the specific groups of students already described in Chapters 5 and 6.

4. Although many special educators are committed to helping you meet the needs of all your students, including those at risk, they cannot take primary responsibility for teaching students like Maria, José, Lydia, and Tam. These are not students who "should be" in special education. Rather, they represent the increasingly diverse range of students that all teachers now instruct. As such, they highlight the importance of creating classrooms that respect this diversity and foster learning regardless of students' unique needs, backgrounds, and experiences.

This chapter also highlights how complex student needs have become (Bennett, 2003; Frattura & Capper, 2006; Ginsberg, 2005). For example, you probably realize that students with disabilities also can have the special needs described here. For example, a student with a physical disability also might be academically gifted. A student with an intellectual disability also might live in poverty. A student with a learning disability might speak a language other than English at home. You probably recognize, too, that the student groups emphasized in this chapter are not necessarily distinct, even though it is convenient to discuss them as if they were. Students who live in poverty can also be gifted and members of a cultural minority. An abused student can be at risk because of drug abuse.

Keep in mind as you read this chapter that your responsibility as a teacher for all students—regardless of their disabilities and other special needs—is to use the principles of the INCLUDE strategy to identify strengths and needs, arrange a supportive instructional environment, provide high-quality instruction, and foster student independence. When students have multiple needs, these tasks can be especially challenging, and you should seek assistance from colleagues, parents, and other professional resources.

Which Students Are Protected by Section 504?

In Chapter 1, you learned that some students with special needs who do not meet the eligibility criteria for receiving services through IDEA are considered functionally disabled, as defined by **Section 504** of the Vocational Rehabilitation Act of 1973. The primary goal of this law is to prevent discrimination against these individuals. Students with functional disabilities are entitled to receive reasonable accommodations that help them benefit from school. These accommodations can include some of the same types of services and supports received by students eligible through IDEA, but there are crucial differences between the two statutes as well (Richards, Brown, & Forde, 2007).

Understanding Section 504

First, the definition of a disability in Section 504 is considerably broader than it is in IDEA. In Section 504, any condition that substantially limits a major life activity, such as the ability to learn in school, is defined as a *disability*. This definition means that students with a wide range of needs that do not fall within the 13 federal disability categories for education are eligible for assistance through Section 504. For example, a student who is photophobic (that is, highly sensitive to bright light) might receive services through Section 504 and so also might students with significant attention problems, drug addiction, chronic health problems, communicable diseases, temporary disabilities resulting from accidents or injury, environmental illnesses, and alcoholism (U.S. Department of Health and Human Services, Office of Civil Rights, 2006).

Second, unlike IDEA, Section 504 does not provide funds to school districts to carry out its requirements (deBettencourt, 2002). The expectation is that schools should take whatever steps are necessary, even if additional funds are required, to eliminate discrimination as defined through this statute. Third, the responsibility for making accommodations for students who qualify as disabled through Section 504 belongs to general education personnel, not special education personnel. Special educators might provide some informal assistance, but their aid is not mandated as it is in IDEA. The types of accommodations required vary based on student needs but could include alterations in the physical environment, such as providing a quiet workspace or a room with specialized lighting; modifications in instruction, such as decreasing the number of items in an assignment, allotting additional time to complete it, or providing a notetaker; organizational assistance, such as checking a student's backpack to ensure that all materials for homework are there; and making changes in a student's schedule, such as allowing a rest period. Table 8.1 summarizes the differences between these important laws.

The regulations governing Section 504 are similar to those for IDEA. That is, for students to receive assistance through Section 504, their needs must be assessed and a decision made concerning their eligibility (Richards et al., 2007). School districts are obligated to use a child-find procedure, that is, to actively seek students who should receive Section 504 support. They also must screen students (typically using some type of prereferral process), convene a team and obtain parent permission to evaluate student needs (although formal testing, as typical for IDEA, is not necessarily required), determine eligibility for services, and create a plan to implement services in the general education classroom. Although Section 504 services sometimes are considered when a student is not found eligible for special education, school districts usually should assess some students for Section 504 assistance who would not be assessed at all for special education services.

When students are determined eligible and have Section 504 plans, those plans cover their instructional programs as well as after-school programs, field trips, summer programs, and other extracurricular activities (T. E. C. Smith, 2002). The plans outline the accommodations needed, who is to implement them, and how they will be monitored. A sample of the types of accommodations that may be incorporated into a Section 504 plan is presented in the Professional Edge on page 278.

www.resources

You can find a wide variety of presentation materials and papers related to Section 504 at the website of the Council of Educators for Students with Disabilities (www.504idea .org/504resources.html).

When students are determined eligible and have Section 504 plans, those plans cover their instructional programs as well as after-school programs, field trips, summer programs, and other extracurricular activities.

TABLE 8.1

Examples of Differences between IDEA and Section 504

Component	IDEA	Section 504
Purpose	To provide federal financial assistance to state and local education agencies to assist them in educating children with disabilities	To eliminate discrimination on the basis of disability in all programs and activities receiving federal financial assistance
Individuals protected	All school-age children who fall within 1 or more of 13 specific categories of disability and who, because of such disability, need special education and related services	All school-age children who have a physical or mental impairment that substantially limits a major life activity, have a record of such an impairment, or are regarded as having such an impairment (major life activities include walking, seeing, hearing, speaking, breathing, learning, working, caring for oneself, and performing manual tasks)
Free and appropriate public education (FAPE)	Requires that FAPE be provided only to those protected students who, because of disability, need special education or related services Defines FAPE as special education and related services; a student can receive related services under IDEA if and only if the student is provided special education and needs related services to benefit from special education Requires a written IEP and a required number of specific participants at the IEP meeting.	Requires that FAPE be provided only to those protected students who, because of disability, need regular education accommodations, special education, or related services. Defines FAPE as regular or special education and related aids and services; a student can receive related services under Section 504 even if the student is in regular education full time and is not provided any special education Does not require a written IEP document but does require a plan prepared by a group of persons knowledgeable about the student
Funding	Provides additional funding for protected students	Does not provide additional funds; IDEA funds may not be used to serve students protected only under Section 504
Evaluation	Requires reevaluation to be conducted at least every three years Does not require a reevaluation before a change of placement but evaluation data, including progress toward goals and objectives, should be considered	Requires periodic reevaluation; the IDEA schedule for reevaluation can suffice Requires reevaluation before a significant change in placement
Placement procedures	An IEP meeting is required before any change in placement	A reevaluation meeting is required before any "significant change" in placement
Grievance procedures	Does not require a grievance procedure or a compliance officer	Requires districts with more than 15 employees to (1) designate an employee to be responsible for assuring district compliance with Section 504 and (2) provide a grievance procedure for parents, students, and employees
Due process	Contains detailed hearing rights and requirements	Requires notice, the right to inspect records, the right to participate in a hearing and to be represented by counsel, and a review procedure
Exhaustion	Requires the parent or guardian to pursue an administrative hearing before seeking redress in the courts	Does not require an administrative hearing prior to Office for Civil Rights involvement or court action; compensatory damages possible
Enforcement	Enforced by the U.S. Office of Special Education Programs (OSEP); compliance monitored by state department of education and OSEP	Enforced by the U.S. Office for Civil Rights

Source: From *Meeting the Needs of All Students,* by the Parent Advocacy Coalition for Educational Rights, 2004, Minneapolis, MN: Author. Retrieved July 26, 2007, from www.pacer.org/parent/504.html#IDEA504. Reprinted with permission from PACER Center, 952-838-9000.

Section 504 Accommodations

Many types of accommodations can be written into a Section 504 plan. The only guidelines are that the adjustments should be (1) individualized to meet students' needs and (2) reasonable, or designed to "level the playing field" for these students. These accommodations should go beyond those typically offered to all students (for example, allowing students to choose from among several projects). Here are some examples of accommodations you might find in a Section 504 plan:

■ Seat the student nearest to where the teacher does most instruction.

■ Provide clues such as clock faces indicating beginning and ending times for instruction or assignments.

■ Establish a home–school communication system for monitoring behavior.

■ Fold assignments in half so the student is not overwhelmed by the quantity of work.

■ Make directions telegraphic—that is, concise and clear.

■ Tape record lessons so the student can listen to them again.

■ Use multisensory presentation techniques, including peer tutors, experiments, games, and cooperative groups.

■ Provide practice tests that are very similar in structure and appearance to actual tests.

■ Mark right answers instead of wrong answers.

■ Send a set of textbooks to be left at home so the student does not have to remember to bring books to and from school.

■ Provide books on tape so the student can listen to assignments instead of reading them.

Remember that Section 504 accommodations may vary greatly depending on a student's special needs, such as a medical condition or physical problem, drug or alcohol abuse, ADHD, or others.

Sources: Adapted from *Ideas for an IEP or Section 504 Plan,* by D. Simms, 2000, retrieved on September 13, 2000, from www .angelfire.com/ny/Debsimms/education.html; and *Sevier County (TN) School System Section 504 Examples of Program Accommodations and Adjustments,* retrieved December 3, 2004, from www.slc.sevier.org/ 504ana.htm. Adapted by permission of the Sevier County Department of Special Education.

Students Eligible for Services under Section 504

Although many students can qualify for assistance through Section 504, three groups are addressed in this chapter: students with medical or health needs, students with learning problems, and students with attention deficit–hyperactivity disorder (ADHD). The first two groups are discussed here; students with ADHD are covered in more depth in the subsequent section.

● **Students with Chronic Health or Medical Problems** Students with chronic health or medical problems—for example, those with communicable or chronic diseases—who are not eligible for IDEA services according to established criteria and as determined by a multidisciplinary team, comprise one of the major groups that can qualify for assistance through Section 504. For example, a student who has asthma not serious enough to be considered a disability under IDEA might have a Section 504 plan. The plan could address accommodations related to the student's need for occasional rest periods, opportunities to take medication, exemption from certain physical activities, and provisions to make up assignments and tests after absences. Similarly, a student with severe allergies might have a Section 504 plan that specifies materials in school that cannot be used (for example, paints, chalk, peanut products), guidelines for participation in physical education, and requirements for providing assignments that can be completed at home if necessary.

The increasing rate of childhood obesity has led to yet another group who might receive accommodations: students who have diabetes. The student who is diabetic might have a plan that addresses permission to use the restroom whenever requested; permission to keep a bottle of water present even during class; permission to test blood glucose whenever necessary, including in the classroom; and postponement of high-stakes testing without penalty if blood glucose is too high or too low.

● **Students with Learning Problems**   A second group of students who may receive support under Section 504 comprises those who experience significant learning problems but who are not determined to have a learning disability (Brady, 2004). For example, Carson is a student who experiences extraordinary difficulty in reading. Although his school district does not recognize the term *dyslexia,* a local clinic has diagnosed him with that disorder. A recent evaluation led to a conclusion that he is not eligible for special education services as learning disabled. However, the team decided that he should have the protection of a Section 504 plan because his reading skills are poor and thus affect his school success. Carson receives remedial reading instruction, but his Section 504 plan includes testing in a separate, quiet location with some tests read aloud and access to text-to-speech software for classwork.

As you can tell, some of the responsibility for implementing Section 504 plans belongs to administrators, who authorize physical modifications to classrooms and make arrangements for students to have rest periods or take medications. Your responsibility is to implement instructional accommodations outlined in the plan, such as providing assignments in advance and allowing extra time for work completion. Your interactions with students protected by Section 504 differ from your interactions with other students only in your responsibility to make the required accommodations. You also may find that some students with Section 504 plans have learning and behavior problems that seem very similar to those of students with disabilities. These students will benefit from the many strategies presented in this text.

*H*ow Can You Accommodate Students with Attention Deficit–Hyperactivity Disorder?

Students with attention problems have been a concern of teachers for many years. In fact, labels such as *hyperkinesis* and *minimal brain dysfunction* have been applied to these students since the 1940s (Barkley, 2006), and the first medication to help them was developed in the 1950s (Eli Lilly, 2003). The challenges that these students present for teachers, parents, and peers have raised awareness that they have a disorder, prompted research about their characteristics and needs, and fostered the development of new interventions for assisting them in school and everyday life. Some students with significant attention problems as described in this section are eligible for services through IDEA, but many receive assistance through Section 504 (Mattox & Harder, 2007).

The term for significant attention problems is **attention deficit–hyperactivity disorder (ADHD),** a condition defined in the *Diagnostic and Statistical Manual of Mental Disorders (DSM–IV–TR)* (American Psychiatric Association, 2000). ADHD is diagnosed when an individual has chronic and serious inattentiveness, hyperactivity, and/or impulsivity that is more severe and occurs more frequently than in peers. You also might hear the term *attention deficit disorder (ADD)* being used to label the condition. *ADD* is an earlier

www.*r*esources

Access the website for Children and Adults with Attention-Deficit/Hyperactivity Disorder (CHADD) at www.chadd.org. CHADD is a nonprofit organization dedicated to bettering the lives of those with ADHD and their families.

Article Homework Exercise

Go to the Homework and Exercises section in Chapter 8 of MyEducationLab to read about some new insights into ADHD.

term for describing attention problems, and some professionals use the terms *ADHD* and *ADD* interchangeably.

Students with ADHD generally have symptoms that fall into one of these three categories (American Psychiatric Association, 2000):

1. *ADHD—predominantly inattentive type.* Students in this group often appear to daydream. They may not hear teacher directions, sometimes skip parts of an assignment they do not notice, and frequently lose things. However, they do not move around more than their peers.

2. *ADHD—predominantly hyperactive–impulsive type.* Students in this group are hyperactive—that is, they move around far more than their peers—and they tend to be impulsive, acting before thinking. They squirm in their seats, tap pencils or fingers, and blurt out answers during instruction.

3. *ADHD—combined type.* Students in this group display the characteristics of both of the other types of ADHD. They experience extraordinary difficulty both in focusing their attention and in restricting their movement.

Think about José, the student you met at the beginning of the chapter. Which type of ADHD seems to best characterize him?

Estimates of the prevalence of ADHD suggest that 3 to 5 percent of all individuals, children and adults, have this disorder (NIMH, 2006) and that it occurs in boys as opposed to girls at a rate of two or three to one (Neuman et al., 2005). Experts seem to agree that it affects approximately 3 to 7 percent of students (Salend & Rohena, 2003), making it one of the most commonly diagnosed childhood psychiatric disorders. Estimating prevalence is difficult because no single official census of these students is gathered and research results vary depending on the sample of students studied (American Academy of Pediatrics [AAP], 2000). ADHD also occurs frequently with other disabilities. Specifically, approximately 26 percent of students with learning disabilities and 43 percent of students with behavioral or emotional disabilities also have ADHD (Forness & Kavale, 2001).

The causes of ADHD are not clear. Researchers have found that one important factor is heredity (Levy, Hay, & Bennett, 2006). Students who have ADHD are likely to have a family pattern of this disorder. In fact, 25 percent of the relatives of individuals with ADHD also have ADHD, compared with 5 percent in the typical population (NIMH, 2006). Researchers also have found that the brains of individuals with ADHD are different from those of others: The amount of electrical activity is unusually low in the parts of the brain regulating attention, and the chemicals in the brain that transmit information may not function properly (Barkley, 2006). The environment also may play a role in causing ADHD. Children prone to have this disorder who live in very unstructured homes are more likely to develop it. A few authors have suggested that ADHD is caused by food additives or food allergies, inner ear problems, vitamin deficiencies, or bacterial infections, but none of these causes has been demonstrated to be valid (NIMH, 2003).

Usually, a diagnosis of ADHD is the result of individualized testing for intellectual ability and achievement, a medical screening completed by a doctor, and behavior ratings completed by family members and school professionals (AAP, 2000). Based on that information, a school team decides whether the student's disorder meets the criteria of other health impairment under IDEA, whether a Section 504 plan is needed, or whether no specific intervention is warranted.

fyi

Behavior rating scales frequently are used to determine whether a student has ADHD. Commonly used rating scales include the Achenbach Behavior Checklist for Parents, the Connors Rating Scale, and the Behavior Problems Checklist.

Characteristics and Needs of Students with Attention Deficit–Hyperactivity Disorder

The characteristics and needs of students with attention deficit–hyperactivity disorder can vary considerably. Although all students might occasionally demonstrate some symptoms of ADHD, students diagnosed with this disorder display many of them prior to 7 years of age. Further, their symptoms are chronic and extraordinary. Consider this account from Mr. Mitchell, a high school social studies teacher, about Benjamin, one of his students:

> I keep Ben seated right in the front of the room, next to where I'm most likely to stand while I'm teaching the large group. When I ask the class a question, Ben is likely to jump out of his seat and wave his hand in my face or jump up and down to get me to call on him. Sometimes I try to make eye contact with him to get him to sit down, but it usually works better if I just put my hand on his shoulder and push a little. When my students are working on their own, I may turn around to notice that Ben is "sitting" by balancing on the top of the back of his seat. If I make a general comment to the class about settling down, everyone does—except Ben. I try very hard not to correct him publicly, since he really doesn't seem to know what he is doing. Having Ben certainly has taught me a new kind of patience.

Intellectually, students with ADHD can function at any level, although the disorder usually is diagnosed in students who do not have intellectual disabilities. Students who are below average in ability and achievement, who are average learners, and who are gifted and talented all can have ADHD (Antshel et al., 2007). Their shared characteristics relate to how their brains function. That is, ADHD is not really about inattention; rather, it is the inability to *regulate* attention. The disorder develops when students fail to develop *executive functions*, that is, the ability to carry out the mental activities that help most people regulate their behavior (Barkley, 2006; Brown, 2007). Executive functions include these four activities:

1. *Working memory*—the ability to remember what tasks are supposed to be done and how much time there is to do them

2. *Self-directed speech*—the silent self-talk that most people use to manage complex tasks

3. *Control of emotions and motivation*—the ability to talk oneself into calming down when faced with a difficult or frustrating task

4. *Reconstitution*—the ability to combine skills learned across a variety of settings in order to carry out a new task, such as a student's knowledge that the rule for speaking in a low voice applies not only in the classroom but also in the hallways, lunchroom, and office

Think about friends from high school who were diagnosed with ADHD or students with whom you now work who have this disorder. How do they display these problems in executive functions in school? At home? In other settings?

Academically, students with ADHD may have difficulty in reading, especially long passages for which comprehension demands are high; in spelling, which requires careful attention to detail; in listening, especially when a large amount of highly detailed information is presented; and in math, which often requires faster computational skills than students with ADHD can handle (DuPaul et al., 2006; Reid, Trout, & Schartz, 2005). All these learning problems can be related to students' problems in executive functions.

Socially and emotionally, students with ADHD are at risk for a variety of problems (Harpin, 2005). For example, they are more likely to be depressed or to have extremely low self-confidence or self-esteem. Likewise, they are likely to have conflicts with parents, teachers, and other authority figures. These students often are unpopular with peers, frequently are rejected by them, and have difficulty making friends. Students with ADHD may feel demoralized, but they also may be bossy and obstinate.

The frequency of behavior problems of students with ADHD varies (Duhaney, 2003). Students whose disorder is inattention might not act out in class, but they may be disruptive when they try to find a lost item or constantly ask classmates for assistance in finding their place in a book or carrying out directions. Students with hyperactive–impulsive

Worksheet Homework Exercise

Go to the Homework and Exercises section in Chapter 8 of MyEducationLab for help with aligning teaching strategies with areas of potential difficulty for students with ADHD.

fyi

Determining whether a student has ADHD is a decision that can be made only by a pediatrician or family physician. Educators should never offer a diagnosis to parents but may encourage parents to contact their child's doctor to discuss their concerns.

Case Study Homework Exercise

Go to the Homework and Exercises section in Chapter 8 of MyEducationLab to review a case study of a student with ADHD.

disorder often come to teachers' attention immediately because they have so many behavior problems. Their constant motion, refusal to work, and other behaviors can be problematic even in the most tolerant environment. Examples of the behaviors displayed by students with ADHD are included in Figure 8.1.

FIGURE 8.1 **Behavior Characteristics of Students with Attention Deficit–Hyperactivity Disorder**

Inattention

- making careless mistakes
- having difficulty sustaining attention
- seeming not to listen
- failing to give close attention to details in schoolwork and related activities
- failing to finish tasks
- having difficulty organizing
- avoiding tasks that require sustained attention
- losing things
- becoming easily distracted
- being forgetful

Hyperactivity

- fidgeting
- being unable to stay seated
- moving excessively (restlessness), including climbing on furniture and other items
- having difficulty making and keeping friends
- being "on the go"
- talking excessively
- being prone to temper tantrums
- acting in a bossy way
- being defiant

Impulsivity

- blurting out answers before questions have been completely asked
- having difficulty awaiting a turn
- interrupting conversations/intruding upon others
- acting before thinking
- being viewed as immature by teenage peers
- failing to read directions

Sources: Adapted from "Arranging the Classroom with an Eye (and Ear) to Students with ADHD," 2001, *Teaching Exceptional Children, 34*(2), pp. 72–81; and "Psychiatric Disorders and Treatment: A Primer for Teachers," by S. R. Forness, H. M. Walker, and K. A. Kavale, 2003, *Teaching Exceptional Children, 36*(2), pp. 42–49.

Interventions for Students with Attention Deficit–Hyperactivity Disorder

As a result of recent studies (Miranda, Jarque, & Tárraga, 2006; MTA Cooperative Group, 2004), professionals now recommend that five types of interventions be used for students with ADHD: environmental supports, academic interventions, behavior interventions, parent education, and medication.

● **Environmental Supports**   The way you arrange your classroom can either foster learning for students with ADHD or impede it. To help students, your classroom should be free from distracting items, such as mobiles hung from the ceiling that twirl in air currents and piles of extra books or art supplies. Some students might benefit if you let them work using a *desk carrel,* a three-sided cardboard divider that blocks visual distractions. You also can provide a classroom environment conducive to learning for these students by having very clear classroom rules and routines. Further, if a change in the normal pattern of classroom activities is necessary, you can alert all students and make sure to support those with ADHD by assigning peer partners to assist them or by quietly letting them know what activity is next. Finally, you can consciously pace your instruction to mix tedious or repetitive classroom activities with those that permit students more variety and activity.

How can you arrange your classroom to improve learning for students with ADHD? What are other interventions you can try for these students?

● **Academic Interventions**   Students with ADHD typically struggle with academic achievement, although the extent of their learning problems can vary considerably (DuPaul & Stoner, 2003; Gehrling, 2006). To assist students with ADHD academically, use the INCLUDE model as a strategy to design lessons and effectively teach these students. As you implement the steps of INCLUDE, keep these ideas in mind for teaching students with ADHD:

I N C L U D E

1. Try to emphasize only essential information. For example, keep oral instructions as brief as possible. Rather than giving directions, providing multiple examples, and then recapping what you have said, instead list directions by number using very clear language—for example, "First, put your name on the paper. Second, write a one-sentence response for each question. Third, put your paper in the basket on the counter by the door."

2. When reading for comprehension, students with ADHD tend to perform better on short passages than on long ones. Thus, rather than have a student with ADHD read an entire story or chapter, have him read just a small part of a long story or expository passage and check comprehension at that point; then have him read another part and so on. Similarly, when older students have lengthy assignments, it is better to break them into smaller parts, assigning each component individually and checking progress.

3. In math, give students extended periods of time to complete computational work because their attentional problems interfere with their efficiency in this type of task.

4. In all large-group instruction, keep the pace rapid and provide many opportunities for students to participate, such as trading answers to questions with a partner, working with manipulatives, and repeating answers as a class after one student has responded.

Analyze and Reflect

What are some of the cognitive, academic, social, emotional, and behavior characteristics common in students with ADHD? Which of these characteristics are displayed by José, the student you met at the beginning of the chapter? How might these characteristics affect the other students in the classroom? Your teaching practices?

Additional suggestions for teaching students with ADHD are presented in Figure 8.2.

In addition to the types of interventions just outlined, most recommendations for helping students with ADHD academically are similar to those for students with learning and emotional disabilities and other students who need highly structured and especially

FIGURE *8.2* Strategies for Teaching Students with ADHD

- Give clear and complete directions for all in-class assignments and homework, including the amount of time allotted and evaluation criteria.

- Provide a rationale to students for each assignment they are asked to complete.

- Check students' understanding of assignments by having them repeat back the directions.

- Break long assignments into several shorter assignments.

- Schedule time while students work in class for them to obtain teacher feedback about their progress.

- Use the Internet to remind students about homework assignments.

- Motivate students by commenting on their strengths and accomplishments.

- Ensure that instruction is fast paced.

- Use high levels of student participation and movement during instruction.

- Tailor questions to students' knowledge and skill levels.

- Use visual organizers (for example, graphic organizers, semantic webs).

- Help students remember important instructional tasks by using learning strategies (see Chapter 10).

- Draw on students' interests during instruction (for example, their culture and experiences).

- Have students work with peer partners.

Source: Adapted from "Educational Interventions for Students with ADD," by S. J. Salend, H. Elhoweris, and D. vanGarderen, 2003, *Intervention in School and Clinic, 38,* pp. 280–288.

clear instruction. Later chapters in this book feature many additional instructional approaches that meet the needs of students with ADHD. The Technology Notes provides an example of a strategy for assisting students with ADHD to use the Internet effectively as a tool for learning.

● **Behavior Interventions** For responding to behavior of students with ADHD, professionals generally recommend interventions that emphasize structure and rewards, such as specific verbal praise ("Martin, you began your work as soon as I gave the assignment"), stickers and other symbols of appropriate behavior ("Tamatha, you will earn a sticker for each five math problems you complete"), and games that emphasize rewards for positive classroom behaviors (Duhaney, 2003; Gehrling, 2006). Reprimands and consequences may be needed at times, but these should be mild and used less often than rewards.

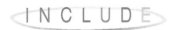

As the INCLUDE strategy outlines, you should first consider environmental demands and address these as a means of preventing behavior problems. For example, students with ADHD exhibit less acting-out behavior when they sit near the front of the room, and, as noted earlier, they often benefit from working in an area with few visual or auditory distractions (for example, away from posters and bulletin board displays and computers signaling with tones and music). Likewise, allowing a student to move from one desk to another in the classroom and permitting her to stand while working are examples of simple environmental support strategies that may help prevent serious behavior problems.

Technology and Students with ADHD

As teachers continue to integrate technology with instruction, they should keep in mind the unique needs of students with ADHD. For example, students with ADHD may have difficulty focusing on the most relevant information on a webpage. They also may need assistance in reading webpages effectively. The acronym RUD PC and its accompanying steps form a strategy to help students with ADHD use the Internet as a learning resource.

Read the title and headings.

- Read the title and headings.
- See how the page is organized. Some pages have boxes or circles containing information; some have information presented in book form. If there are boxes, pay special attention to the bigger boxes, which usually have more information.

Use the cursor to skim the page.

- Do not read everything on the page carefully.
- Read quickly to find what is included on the website.

Decide if the page is worth reading completely.

- If you need the information for an assignment, then read it carefully. If there are a lot of boxes and circles on the page, then figure out a system for reading all of them. It may help to start with the biggest box and then go to each of the smaller ones, or it may help to start at the left and move to the right.

- If you find that the information is not important to you because it is not related to your assignment, then keep surfing.

Print the page.

- If you decide that you need to read the information in more detail, then print the page or bookmark the site and read the page again later.
- Sometimes it is easier to read printed copies of pages because the print is bigger and there may be fewer distractions working away from the computer.

Collect bibliographic information.

- Copy the website address and URL so you can cite it for any research you are doing.
- Find the author and title (if available).
- Find the date of publication (if available).

In Chapter 10, you will learn more about learning strategies and their use with students with learning difficulties. Remember that such strategies can assist students in a wide variety of academic tasks, including completing research and assignments that require use of the Internet.

Source: From *Academic Success Strategies for Adolescents with Learning Disabilities and ADHD* (pp. 180–181), by E. Minskoff and D. Allsopp, 2003, Baltimore: Paul H. Brookes.

If a student needs to be corrected, provide a clear and direct but calm reprimand. If you say "Tamatha, I know you are trying hard, but please try to remember to raise your hand before speaking," Tamatha might not even realize that you are correcting her. A preferred response would be to say quietly to her "Tamatha, do not call out answers. Raise your hand." This message is much clearer.

● **Parent Education** Yet another dimension of working successfully with students with ADHD involves parent education and collaboration (Mathur & Smith, 2003; Mattox & Harder, 2007). Although offering parent education generally is not the sole responsibility of a new teacher, you can contribute in this area by suggesting that parents of students with ADHD be invited to sessions to learn strategies for responding to their children's behavior, ways to create a discipline system that includes both rewards and consequences, tips for helping these children to make friends, and skills for working with school professionals to ensure academic success. Parents of students in middle school and high school also benefit from learning about their children's rights and responsibilities as they graduate from school and enter a college or work setting (Wolraich et al., 2005). Parents from some cultural groups may be less comfortable than other parents in seeking or participating in parent education programs, and you may be able to assist them by explaining the offered training and encouraging them to attend (Mattox & Harder, 2007). Parent education by itself is not sufficient to address the needs of students with ADHD, but it can help to maximize the benefits of other interventions.

● **Medication** The most common intervention for students with ADHD demonstrated by researchers to have the most benefit (MTA, 2004) is medication. Prescribing medication is a decision that is made by parents with their physicians; educators may not tell parents that a child needs this intervention. Approximately 2.5 million students take medication for ADHD (Centers for Disease Control and Prevention, 2005), and this represents approximately 2.9 percent of students under the age of 19. Medication is most commonly taken by students ages 6 to 12. It is effective for 70 to 80 percent of the students for whom it is prescribed, especially if combined with other interventions (that is, environmental supports, academic and behavior interventions, and parent education) (MTA, 2004).

The most common type of medication prescribed for students with ADHD is a group of stimulants, including Ritalin, Cylert, Adderall, and Focalin. However, students may take other medications, including antidepressants such as Norpramin, Tofranil, and Zoloft; antihypertensives such as Clonidine and Tenex; and Strattera, a relatively new medication developed specifically for this disorder. More information about the medications prescribed for ADHD is described in Table 8.2.

> The most common type of medication prescribed for students with ADHD is a group of stimulants.

Despite the apparent effectiveness of medications in treating ADHD, their use remains somewhat controversial (Barkley, 2006). Teachers encounter the problem of students not consistently taking their medication or of sharing their medication. This situation can not only result in a loss of learning, but it can even endanger other students. Another issue concerns the proper dosage. Some researchers contend that a dosage high enough to cause an improvement in behavior can negatively affect a student's academic learning and performance (Forness & Kavale, 2001). A third area of concern pertains to side effects. Some parents and professionals believe that medication may suppress weight and height gain, even though research indicates that this side effect is temporary (DuPaul et al., 2006; Kollins, Barkely, & DuPaul, 2001). Yet other parents are concerned that taking medication may predispose their children to future drug use and problems in adulthood, another perception that has not been supported by research (Barkley, 2004; National Resource Center on ADHD, 2004).

As a teacher, your responsibilities related to medication are indirect. You should know about the medications commonly prescribed, alert your school nurse and parents if you suspect that a change in student learning or behavior might be related to medication, and be prepared to respond to parental and medical inquiries regarding the effects of medication on particular students.

Families of Children with Attention Deficit–Hyperactivity Disorder

Just like families of other students with disabilities and special needs, families of students with ADHD cannot be described using a single set of characteristics. However, it is fair to say that for many families, having a child with ADHD affects every area of family functioning and adds significant stress for parents and siblings both at home and in interactions with school personnel (Harpin, 2005). For example, Tate is a student with ADHD. Nearly every day at school, he has some sort of negative experience because of either inattention during instruction or a behavior disruption during lunch or passing periods. As a result, Tate's parents receive quite a few late-afternoon phone calls from school personnel. In trying to respond to the teachers and keep clear their expectations

TABLE *8.2*

Overview of Medications Commonly Used for ADHD

Brand Name [Generic Name]	Type of Medication	Advantages	Disadvantages	Comments
Concerta [Methylphenidate]	Psychostimulant	Works quickly Lasts up to 12 hours	Not recommended for children in families with a history of tic disorders	First true once-a-day ADHD medication approved by the FDA
Ritalin [Methylphenidate]	Psychostimulant	Excellent safety record Easy to use and evaluate Works in 15–20 minutes	Lasts only 4 hours Must be administered frequently	Most frequently prescribed medication Watch for tics or Tourette's syndrome
Ritalin SR (sustained release) [Methylphenidate]	Psychostimulant	Excellent safety record Easy to use and evaluate Long lasting (6–8 hours)	Does not work as well as regular Ritalin	Can be used along with regular Ritalin
Focalin [Dextromethylphenidate]	Psychostimulant	Works quickly Only half the dose of Ritalin is needed	Lasts only 4–5 hours Must be administered frequently	Refined form of Ritalin
Dexedrine [Dextroamphetamine]	Psychostimulant	Excellent safety record Rapid onset (20–30 minutes)	Lasts only 4 hours Must be administered frequently	Some students have fewer side effects than when on Ritalin
Dexedrine (sustained release) [Dextroamphetamine]	Psychostimulant	Excellent safety record Long lasting (6–8 hours)	Slower onset (1–2 hours)	Can be used along with standard Dexedrine, which permits once-daily dosing
Adderall [Single-entity amphetamine product]	Psychostimulant	Works quickly May last somewhat longer than other standard stimulants (3–6 hours)	High potential for abuse	May help students for whom Ritalin has not been effective
Adderall XR [Single-entity amphetamine product]	Psychostimulant	Works quickly Lasts about 12 hours	High potential for abuse	Not recommended for long-term use
Tofranil and Norpramin [Imipramine and desipramine]	Antidepressant	Long lasting (12–24 hours) Can be administered at night Often works when stimulants do not	Has possible side effects May take 1–3 weeks for full effects Should not be started and stopped abruptly	High doses may improve depression symptoms and mood swings

continued

TABLE 8.2

Continued

Brand Name [Generic Name]	Type of Medication	Advantages	Disadvantages	Comments
Catapress [Clonidine]	Antihypertensive	Can be used with students with Tourette's syndrome	Tablets are short lasting (4 hours) Patches are expensive	Often has positive effect on defiant behavior
Strattera [Atomoxetine hydrochloride]	Norepinephrine reuptake inhibitor	Lasts about 8–10 hours Noncontrolled prescription medication	Relatively new medication Long-term effects on children are not known	First nonstimulant ADHD medication approved by the FDA

Sources: From *Special Education: Contemporary Perspectives for School Professionals* (p. 231), by M. Friend, 2005, Boston: Allyn & Bacon; and "Medication Chart to Treat Attention Deficit Disorders," by H. C. Parker, 2003. Retrieved December 2, 2004, from www.ldonline.org/ld_indepth/add_adhd/add_medication_chart.html. Reprinted by permission of Harvey C. Parker.

for Tate's school performance, they often punish him by taking away computer time or some other privilege. Tate dislikes school, dreads the phone ringing when he gets home, and feels like all his parents ever do is criticize him. His parents are very concerned that they are having an increasingly difficult time getting through to Tate about his behavior. What seems to be developing is a negative cycle of teacher–parent–child interaction that will likely lead to frustration and ineffective intervention (LeFever, Villers, Morrow, & Vaughn, 2002).

When working with families like Tate's, your job as a teacher is to try to build positive relationships by encouraging parents to reward their children for being successful and by helping them see their children's strengths (Mathur & Smith, 2003). Some parents struggle with their own role in their child's disorder, particularly when they believe that a child is "just like his father." Teachers have to be careful not to blame parents for their children's ADHD but at the same time not to condone inappropriate student behavior that a parent might excuse by saying that the child can't help it.

Families face additional concerns as their children with ADHD reach adolescence and adulthood. Although professionals used to think that children outgrew ADHD as they approached adolescence, it is now clear that for most individuals, ADHD is a lifetime disorder (Barkley, 2006; Minskoff & Allsopp, 2003). Adolescents with ADHD may have more negative moods than other teens. They also may spend more time with friends and less time with family, and they may be prone to tobacco and alcohol abuse (Whalen, Jamner, Henker, Delfino, & Lozano, 2002). Parents and family members are faced with responding to these children's emotions and potentially harmful behaviors (McCleary, 2002; Wolraich et al., 2005).

> Although professionals used to think that children outgrew ADHD as they approached adolescence, it is now clear that for most individuals, ADHD is a lifetime disorder.

Finally, teachers should understand the varied family responses to ADHD diagnosis and treatment based on cultural differences (Mattox & Harder, 2007). For example, in one study researchers investigated the perceptions of Mexican, Mexican American, and Puerto Rican mothers toward the behavior of their children with ADHD (Schmitz & Velez, 2003). The researchers found that across these three Latino subgroups, the mothers who were the least acculturated were the least tolerant of their children's hyperactive behavior. In another study, parents from Caucasian, African American, and Hispanic groups in one community were queried about ADHD. Although children from the three groups were identified as having ADHD in approximately the same proportion, African American parents were less likely than Caucasian parents to agree to medication as an intervention, and Hispanic parents were the least likely to agree (Rowland, Umback, Stallone, Naftel, Bohlig, & Sandler, 2002).

How Can You Accommodate Students Who Are Gifted and Talented?

In addition to students who cannot meet typical curricular expectations, you also will have in your classroom students who have extraordinary abilities and skills. The term used to describe these students is **gifted and talented.** *Giftedness* traditionally has referred to students with extraordinary abilities across many academic areas and *talent* to students with extraordinary abilities in a specific area. Now, however, the terms often are used interchangeably. The federal definition for this group of students is stated in the 1988 Jacob Javits Gifted and Talented Students Education Act (Javits Act, P.L. 100-297), which identifies children and youth who possess demonstrated or potential high-performance capability in intellectual, creative, specific academic and leadership areas or the performing and visual arts. The federal definition further clarifies that these students need services in school that other students do not. However, unlike the services offered through IDEA, federal legislation does not require specific services for gifted and talented students, and so the extent to which programs exist is determined largely by state and local policies (Zirkel, 2004). In fact, the Javits Act is not a funding mechanism for programs for students who are gifted and talented. Its purpose is to provide a means of coordinating efforts to enhance schools' ability to serve these students, and its emphasis is on identifying and educating students who are traditionally represented in programs for students who are gifted and talented.

An ongoing discussion in defining giftedness and serving these students concerns prevalence. As is true of prevalence figures for other groups of students with special needs, the reported prevalence of giftedness varies considerably from location to location, depending largely on the definitions adopted by states and school districts, funding, and identification procedures. In today's schools, approximately 12 percent of students are served as gifted and talented (Council of State Directors of Programs for the Gifted, 2001). This is slightly more than the percentage of students receiving services for having disabilities.

The reported prevalence of giftedness and talent also is greatly affected by two other factors. First, over the past several years, researchers and writers have offered alternative definitions of giftedness and questioned traditional criteria for identification that rely on intelligence measures (that is, IQ tests). For example, Tomlinson (2001) notes that intelligence is not static and that schools should create opportunities in supportive environments to maximize the potential of all students, instead of limiting services to just a selected few.

Another conceptualization of giftedness is one that you already may have studied. Gardner (1993) conceptualizes intelligence as being multifaceted. He argues that measured IQ is far too narrow a concept of intelligence and that a person's ability to problem solve, especially in new situations, is a more useful way of thinking about intelligence. Gardner (1993) has proposed that *multiple intelligences* describe the broad array of talents that students possess, and he describes these eight intelligences:

1. verbal/linguistic

2. visual/spatial

3. logical/mathematical

www.*r*esources

At the website for the University of Connecticut's Neag Center for Gifted Education and Talent Development (www.gifted .uconn.edu), you can read about current trends in the field, programs for students who are gifted and talented, and resources to help teachers address these students' needs.

4. bodily/kinesthetic

5. musical

6. intrapersonal (that is, self-understanding)

7. interpersonal

8. naturalist

9. existentialist

Notice the wide range of abilities captured in this notion of intelligence. The impact of using these broader definitions is that 20 percent or more of students may be identified as being gifted or talented, according to some estimates (Callahan, 2005). How might applying these broader definitions of giftedness affect services for students who are gifted and talented? What does this information imply for you as a school professional?

The second factor that affects the number of students identified as gifted and talented is the notion of potential. Although some students who are gifted and talented easily can be identified because they use their special abilities and are willing to be recognized for them, others go unnoticed. These students mask their skills from peers and teachers because low expectations have been set for them or their unique needs have not been nurtured. Groups at risk for being underidentified include young boys, adolescent girls, students who are so highly gifted and talented as to be considered geniuses, students from racially and culturally diverse groups, and students with disabilities (Birdsall & Correa, 2007; Moore, Ford, & Milner, 2005). In many school districts, focused attention has been placed on these groups to ensure students are identified.

> Although some students who are gifted and talented easily can be identified because they use their special abilities and are willing to be recognized for them, others go unnoticed.

Characteristics and Needs of Students Who Are Gifted and Talented

Students who are gifted and talented have a wide range of characteristics, and any one student considered gifted and talented can have just a few or many of these characteristics. Although early studies presented a limited number of descriptors, the studies frequently were conducted with high-achievers from privileged backgrounds and did not take into account the diverse nature of today's society (Terman, 1925). More recently, deciding whom to identify as gifted and talented and how to describe them has become complex, especially with the increasingly recognized need to address giftedness and talent among the entire population, including students from diverse groups (Bonner, 2003). Professionals now recommend that identification procedures include both traditional and nontraditional measures (Bracken & Brown, 2006). *Traditional measures* include intelligence and achievement tests, grades, and teacher recommendations. *Nontraditional measures* include nonverbal ability tests, creativity tests, student portfolios, performance-based measures (for example, giving a presentation or performing a dance), and parent and peer recommendations. The following information about student characteristics is intended to provide an overview of students who are gifted and talented and should be viewed as a sample of what is known, not a comprehensive summary.

fyi

Students who have disabilities but also are gifted and talented are referred to as *twice exceptional*. These students are entitled to special education services because of their disabilities, and they also access programs designed to nurture their talents.

● **Intellectual Abilities and Academic Skills**   The area of intellectual functioning and academic skills is the most delineated aspect of gifted education. Students who are gifted and talented generally have an extraordinary amount of knowledge because of their insatiable curiosity, keen memory, unusual ability to concentrate, wide variety of interests, high levels of language development and verbal ability, and ability to generate original ideas. They also have an advanced ability to comprehend information using accelerated and flexible thought processes, a heightened ability to recognize relationships between diverse ideas, and a strong capacity to form and use conceptual frameworks. These students tend to be skilled problem solvers because of their extraordinary ability to pick out relevant information and their tendency to monitor their problem-solving efforts (Steiner, 2006).

The intellectual abilities of students who are gifted and talented sometimes lead them to high academic achievement but not always. Consider these three students who are gifted and talented:

■ Belinda was identified as gifted and talented in second grade. She has been reading since age 3, seems as comfortable interacting with adults as with peers, and invariably becomes the leader of the groups of children with whom she plays, even when they are older. She enjoys school immensely and wants to be a university professor when she grows up. Belinda is similar to Lydia, whom you read about at the beginning of this chapter.

■ Tomas also is identified as gifted and talented. He has been taking violin and piano lessons since age 5, and now in the seventh grade he is a veteran pianist. He already plans to major in music theory when he goes to college, and he offers his own interpretations of both classical and contemporary music. In his academic studies, however, Tomas is slightly below average in achievement. He also is somewhat shy; he appears more comfortable with his musical instruments than with his peers.

■ Charles is a sophomore in high school. He lives in a neighborhood where education is not valued and getting high grades is viewed as showing off. As a result, the nearly straight A's that used to define Charles's report cards have dropped over the past year, and now he is earning mostly C's and D's.

How might the needs of these students differ? How could you encourage each student to reach his or her potential?

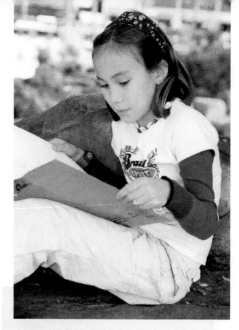

Students who are gifted and talented are often difficult to identify and challenging to teach. What kinds of intelligence might you recognize in your students? Within your inclusive classroom, how might you address the academic and social-emotional needs of students who are gifted and talented?

● **Social and Emotional Needs**   Socially and emotionally, gifted and talented students can be well liked and emotionally healthy, or they can be unpopular and at risk for serious emotional problems. Affectively, they tend to have unusual sensitivity to others' feelings as well as highly developed emotional depth and intensity, a keen sense of humor that can be either supportive or hostile, and a sense of justice (Schuler, 2002). They often have a sense of obligation to help others and may become involved in community service activities. Teachers sometimes assign these students to help other students, an acceptable practice unless done so often that it interferes with advanced learning opportunities. These students often set high expectations for themselves and others, which can lead to frustration when those expectations are not met.

Because some gifted students have a superior ability to recognize and respond to others' feelings, they can be extremely popular with classmates and often sought as helpmates. However, if they tend to show off their talents or repeatedly challenge adult authority, they may be perceived negatively by peers and teachers and have problems developing appropriate social relationships (Colangelo & Davis, 2003). For example, Ms. Ogden is concerned about eighth-grader Esteban. On some days, he seems to have just a four-word vocabulary: "I already know that." He says this to his teachers, his peers, and his parents about nearly any topic under discussion. Although it is often true that Esteban does know about the subject being discussed, Ms. Ogden finds herself becoming annoyed at his style of interacting, and she knows the other students do not want to be grouped with Esteban because of it.

Students' emotional status is one factor that contributes to their social skills. Some gifted and talented students are self-confident, have a strongly positive self-concept, and are generally happy (Colangelo, 2002). Others, however, feel isolated or alienated and can experience depression, low self-concept, and other emotional problems, especially as they

Article Homework Exercise

Go to the Homework and Exercises section in Chapter 8 of MyEducationLab to learn strategies for challenging the abilities of students who are gifted.

move from childhood to adolescence. Some research suggests that students who are gifted and talented are at risk for bullying (Peterson & Ray, 2006). If these students find school boring and have difficulty forming friendships, they also can have poor attitudes toward learning and school activities in general. These students are at risk for dropping out of school (Renzulli & Park, 2002).

● **Behavior Patterns**   Students who are gifted and talented display the entire range of behaviors that other students do. They can be model students who participate and seldom cause problems, often serving as class leaders. In this capacity, students are sensitive to others' feelings and moderate their behavior based on others' needs (Colangelo, 2002). However, because students who are gifted and talented often have an above-average capacity to understand people and situations, their negative behavior can sometimes be magnified compared with that of other students. This behavior can be displayed through an intense interest in a topic and refusal to change topics when requested by a teacher. Other behavior problems displayed by some students who are gifted and talented include being bossy in group situations, purposefully failing, and valuing and participating in counterculture activities (Colangelo, 2002).

Interventions for Students Who Are Gifted and Talented

Although some school districts operate separate classes and programs for students who are gifted and talented, you likely will be responsible for teaching these students in your classroom. The general concept used to think about meeting the needs of students who are gifted and talented is *differentiation* (Renzulli, 2005; Tomlinson, 2005), the same concept of meeting diverse student needs suggested for thinking about the instruction of students with academic and behavior problems.

Four specific strategies often used to challenge gifted and talented students are curriculum compacting, acceleration and enrichment, specific differentiation strategies during instruction, and individualized interventions (VanTassel-Baska, 2003). As you read the following descriptions of these strategies and the examples of their implementation, think about how the INCLUDE strategy could guide you in implementing them. In the Case in Practice, you can see an application of instruction for a student who is gifted and has a learning disability.

● **Curriculum Compacting**   Some gifted and talented students already have mastered much of the traditional curriculum content of the public schools, and they may be bored when asked to listen to a lecture or complete an assignment that does not challenge them (Reis & Renzulli, 2004). In *curriculum compacting,* teachers assess students' achievement of instructional goals and then eliminate instruction on goals already met. The time gained is used to pursue special interests, work with a mentor, or study the same topic at a more advanced level. How could you use curriculum compacting in your planned teaching?

● **Acceleration and Enrichment**   In some school districts, you may learn that *acceleration* is part of the programming available for students who are gifted and talented. That is, these students may skip a grade or complete the standards for two grades in a single year. In high school, acceleration may relate to a specific subject. For example, a student with extraordinary math skills might enroll in advanced coursework in that area while following the traditional curriculum for English and social studies. Acceleration also is seen in high schools that offer the College Board's Advanced Placement (AP) program. Students have the option of completing college credit for one or more advanced courses taken in high school. Are you aware of other acceleration options offered to high school students?

INCLUDE

Analyze and Reflect

What are your beliefs about professionals' responsibilities for providing special instruction and programs for students who are gifted and talented? How should you balance these responsibilities with those for teaching average students? Those at risk for school failure? Those who have disabilities?

Case in Practice

Meeting the Needs of a Twice-Exceptional Student

Ms. Davis is taking a few minutes to reflect on the meeting she and her seventh-grade team had yesterday with their school psychologist, the facilitator for their school's program for students who are gifted and talented, and the special education teacher. The meeting was called because of the teachers' concerns about Isaac, a student whom the teachers characterize as a student of "contradictions." Here are examples of what they mean:

- For a multimedia project in English, Isaac produced original music and directed several classmates to produce a performance he recorded expertly using video equipment he borrowed from a teacher at the high school. The day the project was due, however, he forgot to bring it to school and told his teacher that it wasn't very good anyway.

- In social studies, Isaac can explain in detail not just the events of world history but also the societal forces that influenced them. His mother attributes this knowledge to his love of the documentaries and other programming on history available on television.

- In math, Isaac struggles. He often disrupts class by making jokes ("I know what algebra is—it's underwear for a mermaid (algae-bra)." "Did you hear what happened in the other class? Mr. Somers asked John to solve the problem 'What is $2q + 8q$?' When John said '$10q$,' Mr. Somers said, 'You're welcome!'").

The other professionals at the meeting spent some time explaining that Isaac is *twice exceptional;* that is, he is gifted and also has a learning disability. This is why he has a learning-strategies class as one of his electives and is in the co-taught English class.

In reviewing information about Isaac and discussing how to help him reach his potential (and reduce disruptions in class), the professionals talked about how to help him use his significant intellectual abilities in a constructive way. The psychologist advised the teachers that Isaac sometimes misbehaves to avoid tasks he is afraid he may not do well. The special educator mentioned that she is concerned about Isaac's self-esteem. Suggestions for working with Isaac included giving him as many choices as possible regarding assignments, offering ways other than reading for him to acquire information, and arranging peer tutoring in math, the one in which Isaac struggles the most.

REFLECTIONS

What does it mean for a student to be *twice exceptional?* Why might students who are twice exceptional have low self-esteem? How can you help these students succeed? Should a student like Isaac be enrolled in a program for students who are gifted? Why or why not?

Enrichment is an instructional approach that provides students with information, materials, and assignments that enable them to elaborate on concepts being presented as part of the regular curriculum and that usually require high levels of thinking (Reis, 2007). This common classroom option requires you to find related information, prepare it for the students who need it, and create curriculum-relevant alternative activities for them. For enrichment to be effective, you need to ensure that students have opportunities to complete assignments designed to encourage advanced thinking and product development, that they do such assignments in lieu of other work instead of as additional work, and that many learning resources are available to them both in and out of the classroom (K. Smith & Weitz, 2003).

● **Differentiation** Perhaps one of the most practical approaches you can use for working with students in your class who are gifted and talented is to systematically plan lessons based on *differentiation,* the same approach introduced for your work with students who have disabilities. Recall that differentiation is based on the understanding that students should have multiple ways to reach their potential (Tomlinson, 2004a). As a teacher, you can use the INCLUDE strategy to think about the specific strengths and needs of these students; identify problem areas in critical thinking, analysis, and

Info Sheet Homework Exercise

Go to the Homework and Exercises section in Chapter 8 of MyEducationLab for a description of strategies for teaching and including students who are gifted and talented.

INCLUDE

other advanced skills; and decide how to address these problem areas through activities integrated into instruction.

● **Individualized Interventions**   All of the previously described approaches may be effective for students who are gifted and talented, but students who have special circumstances—those who live in poverty, who are from nondominant cultures, or who also have disabilities—may need even further special attention. For example, some students may downplay their abilities because academic achievement is not valued in their immediate community and they fear being rejected (Moore, Ford, & Milner, 2005). For these students, you may want to find mentors from similar backgrounds so students see that drawing on their talents can lead to positive outcomes. For some students, interacting with peers from a similar background can be helpful, especially if they are given tasks that foster critical-thinking skills. In addition, students in this group may benefit when technology is integral to instruction, either as a resource for learning or a tool for accessing learning, as might be the case for students with disabilities. The Professional Edge provides a checklist that can be useful for recognizing students who might be gifted underachievers.

> Some students may downplay their abilities because academic achievement is not valued in their immediate community and they fear being rejected.

Some professionals contend that strategies for instructing students who are gifted and talented are appropriate for most students (Gubbins, 2002; Tomlinson, 2005). They suggest that your job as a general education teacher is to design effective instruction for all students and that this instruction should also meet the needs of students who are gifted and talented. To reach all your students, you need to offer activities that address several ability levels at one time, accommodate a variety of interest areas, and enable students to integrate their learning and maximize their potential.

What Are the Needs of Students from Culturally Diverse Backgrounds?

The racial, cultural, and linguistic diversity of U.S. classrooms has been increasing for decades, and all indications are that it will continue to do so. For example, in 1972, just 22 percent of students enrolled in grades 1 through 12 were members of minority groups; in 2004, the number had risen to 43 percent (Daltom, Sable, & Hoffman, 2006). In the largest 100 school districts in the United States—the districts that account for 23 percent of all the school-age students in the country—the number was 70 percent. During the same school year, 11 percent of all students, approximately 3.8 million of them, received services as English-language learners (ELLs).

However, trying to accurately capture the diversity of today's students is a complex matter. Consider the following facts: If you live in an area near a large city, the diversity of your student population will likely increase dramatically over the next decade. If you teach in an inner-city area or rural district, you may find little change in diversity but decreasing student enrollment. The Harvard Civil Rights Project has published data suggesting that, despite the now 50-year-old *Brown v. Board of Education* court decision ending segregated schooling, U.S. public schools are gradually resegregating (Orfield & Lee, 2004). In particular, African American and Latino students are more likely now than they were in the 1980s to be educated in a school with few Caucasian students. But diversity itself is being redefined. In the 2000 U.S. Census, individuals could indicate that they were members of more than one race. The result is that traditional approaches to calculating racial diversity in schools are losing meaning.

Reading Homework Exercise

Go to the Homework and Exercises section in Chapter 8 of MyEducationLab to read what every teacher should know about English-language learners.

Gifted Underachievers

One of the challenges you will face as an educator is maximizing the potential of all your students. One group that can be difficult to reach is students who are gifted and talented yet underachievers. Your gifted underachievers may be students who do poorly on tests, do not turn in daily work, or achieve below grade level. At the same time, you may notice that they learn quickly when interested, are highly creative, and value projects they they choose themselves. The following strategies are designed to help you to think about how your instruction can better match the needs of these students.

Provide more flexibility to foster peer and social relationships among students

- Allow students to do more teaching of others.
- Organize multiage groups across grade levels.

Assist students with successful transitions

- Develop adoption program of younger students by older students.
- Offer transition survival courses when students change grade levels/schools.
- Provide parent education programs about transitions.

Promote empowerment and autonomy for students

- Solicit student input for teacher planning of learning activities.
- Include some self-paced/mastery learning opportunities.

- Promote recognition and awards for achievement and effort.
- Provide leadership training and school opportunities for students to demonstrate leadership skills.
- Involve students in evaluating the school and providing solutions for improvement.

Improve the learning environment for students

- Expand learning beyond the classroom and into the community.
- Allow students to participate in governance.
- Use flexible instructional groups based on needs.
- Promote alternative grading systems that encourage students to continue to try.
- Encourage positive confrontation and conflict resolution.

Consider how you could take each of these ideas and apply it in a real teaching situation. Why do you think strategies such as these are beneficial for gifted underachievers?

Source: "Gifted and Talented Students at Risk," by K. Seeley, 2004, *Focus on Exceptional Children, 37*(4), pp. 1–9.

Evidence suggests that students from cultures other than Anglo-European ones sometimes experience extraordinarily high failure rates in school. For example, in 2005, approximately 9.4 percent of all young adults in the United States ages 16 through 24 did not have a high school diploma and were not enrolled in school. However, this number included 22.4 percent of Hispanic young adults and 10.4 percent of African American young adults but only 6.0 percent of non-Hispanic white individuals (National Center for Education Statistics [NCES], 2007). Although some of these students may later return to complete school in a GED program, many will not.

The reasons for these students' failure to complete school are complex and interrelated but involve several identifiable factors. First, students from racial and ethnic minority groups often lack role models because most teachers are from the majority Anglo-European culture (Wiggins, Folo, & Eberly, 2007). In addition, instructional practices can negatively affect students. In particular, textbooks with cultural biases can promote stereotypes and

Analyze and Reflect

Why are students with culturally and linguistically diverse backgrounds given special attention in a textbook about students with special needs? How could practices in general education classrooms inadvertently cause African American students or others to be identified inappropriately as eligible for special education services?

Video Homework Exercise

Go to the Homework and Exercises section in Chapter 8 of MyEducationLab for a snapshot of a bilingual classroom.

www.resources

The National Center for Education Statistics' Common Core of Data (http://nces.ed .gov/ccd) can inform you about diversity in schools nationwide, in your state, or in a specific district. This website also has information designed to help students understand their schools.

omit culturally important information. Teaching practices that do not allow opportunities for student-centered learning also can put students from different cultures at a disadvantage because students' background and experience may lead them to learn more effectively from small-group peer interactions (Bennett, 2003; Nieto, 2002/2003). A mix of teaching approaches is needed. Finally, school policies and programs can penalize students. For example, few schools operate mentor programs specifically designed to connect students from diverse cultures with leaders in business, industry, and education. These contacts can be essential for helping students succeed.

Diversity and Special Education

The relationship among school failure, special education, and diverse student needs is not a comfortable one (Hosp & Reschly, 2004). Historically, students from racial and cultural minorities sometimes were inappropriately placed in special education programs based on discriminatory assessment practices. Evidence suggests that this unfortunate bias is still an issue today (Salend & Duhaney, 2005), particularly for African American students and English-language learners (Artiles, Rueda, Salazar, & Higareda, 2005). The reasons for this bias continue to be studied. Some researchers maintain that the issue concerns poverty more than race or ethnicity, a topic addressed later in this chapter. But it also includes bias in curriculum and instruction, teacher attitudes, and the special education referral process (Skiba, Poloni-Staudinger, Simmons, Feggins-Assiz, & Chung, 2005).

Cultural Awareness

Understanding the characteristics of students who are members of racially and culturally diverse groups involves recognizing that learning and behavior problems can be created by the contradictions between some of these students' home and community experiences and the expectations placed on them at school (Banks, 2001). It also includes

How are students from culturally diverse backgrounds at risk for school failure? How can you promote student acceptance of cultural differences in your classroom?

acknowledging that teachers sometimes misunderstand students and their parents, which can lead to miscommunication, distrust, and negative school experiences.

If you live in an area in which many different cultures are represented in a single classroom, the thought of learning about all of them can be intimidating. It is probably not possible, nor is it necessary, to learn many details about all the cultures of your students (Trumbull & Pacheco, 2005). However, it is your responsibility to learn the fundamental characteristics students might have because of their backgrounds. For example, some students might hesitate to ask questions because of concern about interacting with the teacher, who is perceived as an authority figure. If you understand this reticence, then you can make a special effort to initiate interactions with these students. Further, when a student displays troublesome behavior, you should determine whether a cultural reason may have prompted the behavior before responding to it or assuming that it represents misbehavior. Of course, you also should keep in mind that not all students from diverse backgrounds encounter these problems, nor do all families from racial or ethnic minority groups use discipline practices different from those schools use.

The INCLUDE strategy can be a valuable tool for making decisions about instruction for students from culturally and linguistically diverse groups. First, you should consider the demands of the classroom setting and identify the strengths and interests students bring to the learning environment. Next, you should look for potential problem areas throughout your entire instructional program. Use that information to brainstorm ideas for resolving the problems and select those with the most potential for success. As you go through this process, it is essential to monitor student progress and make adjustments as needed. An example of strategies related to teaching reading to students who are English-language learners is included in the following Professional Edge.

The impact of cultural and linguistic diversity in educational settings can be examined from three perspectives: how cultural factors affect student behavior, how teaching approaches can be tailored to culturally diverse groups, and how communication with non-native English speakers can be enhanced. We will examine each perspective briefly.

- **Cultural Factors and Student Behavior** Various cultural values can affect students' behaviors and how educators interpret these behaviors. For example, for some Native American and immigrant students, time is a fluid concept not necessarily bound by clocks (Hodgkinson, 2000/2001). A student might come to school late by Anglo-European cultural standards that measure time precisely but on time according to events happening at the student's home. Another example of the differences between Anglo-European standards and some students' cultures concerns school participation. Hispanic students sometimes are more likely to participate when they have established close relationships with their teachers and peers (Banks, 2001). Contrast this fact with the common high school structure, in which one teacher sees as many as 180 students each day and often uses an instructional format that minimizes interaction. In such a setting, some Hispanic students—especially those who have only recently come to the United States—can be at a great disadvantage. If these opportunities are not offered in the classroom, some students will be denied an essential learning tool.

- **Informed Instructional Decision Making** Effective decisions about teaching strategies are made by matching the needs of students from culturally diverse backgrounds to instructional approaches (Richards et al., 2007). For example, many African American students, as well as many Hispanic American and Asian American students, respond well to cooperative rather than competitive teaching and learning environments (Bennett, 2003). Likewise, because traditional Native American students sometimes dislike responding individually and out loud in a large-group situation, you may need to create

INCLUDE

Effective decisions about teaching strategies are made by matching the needs of students from culturally diverse backgrounds to instructional approaches.

English–Language Learners and Reading

Although English-language learners (ELLs) often have trouble learning to read (Kindler, 2002), they can be successful if the appropriate accommodations are made for them. Here are ways you can make your reading instruction more meaningful for ELLs while also building their oral language skills.

Teach Segmenting and Blending

When students *segment* words, they break words apart into their individual phonemes (fish = /f/-/i/-/sh/). When they *blend*, they say a spoken word when the sounds are said slowly (/f/-/i/-/sh/ = fish).

■ Give ELLs more opportunities to use new English vocabulary by having them blend or segment these new words before using them in complete sentences.

■ Have ELLs segment and blend using words from their first language. For example, have them blend a name such as *Jorgé* or clap the sounds in holidays such as Navidad or Cinco de Mayo.

■ Make reference to cultural dress while engaging students in rhyming using oral rhymes such as these: "The sari is green, worn by the teen; The babushka is black and tied in the back" (McCollin & O'Shea, 2005, p. 41).

■ During storytime, while building student vocabulary and listening comprehension skills, ask students to segment and blend words taken from a picture book about their culture.

Teach Associations between Written Letters and Sounds

Home, school, and community interests can be used to teach ELLs the associations between written letters and sounds, or *phonics.*

■ For Spanish-speaking students have students sound out decodable Spanish words appearing on signs, community newspapers, and in books written in Spanish. Then have students use the English equivalents of these words in complete sentences orally, in writing, or both.

■ If you are not sure whether students know words being sounded out, show them pictures of the words after they have sounded them out. Showing pictures after students have read the words will ensure they are using phonics to figure out the words while also building their English vocabulary. Showing pictures also provides additional opportunities for the students and teacher to engage in dialogue about the word—again, building oral language skills.

■ Distinguish between errors and articulation differences. For example, José read the word *meet* as /mit/. In Spanish, a long *e* is often pronounced as a short *i*; therefore, *meet* could be identified correctly but pronounced as /mit/. To find out what the problem was, José's teacher asked him to use the word in a sentence. This allowed the teacher to check José's word reading skills while also reinforcing his vocabulary and syntactical knowledge by having him use the word in a sentence. See Bursuck and Damer (2007, p. 119) for an entire list of possible English pronunciation problems for native speakers of Spanish.

Build Students' Reading Fluency

Reading fluency is the ability to read connected text accurately, quickly, and with expression and is an important bridge between word recognition and comprehension. It also requires the reader to use intonation and stress to convey meaning. Understanding the importance of reading

opportunities for individual contact and quiet participation. Such instructional thinking and approaches, referred to as *equity pedagogy,* should become integral to your teaching (Richards et al., 2007).

● **Cross-Cultural Communication**   For students who do not speak English as their native language, going to school can be a frustrating experience, resulting in some common problems. First, students who do not use English proficiently can easily be discriminated against when they are assessed. For example, the No Child Left Behind Act of 2001 (NCLB) requires that students be assessed in the standard way after a limited period of exemption because of language differences. However, some students may not be ready with expression is difficult for ELLs since languages such as Spanish convey differences in meaning by changing word order.

- Read a section of text related to cultural themes, mores, values, traditions, history, or customs to students, modeling appropriate stress and intonation. Then have students read the same section back to you, provide them with feedback, and have them repeat as needed.

- For independent practice, provide taped models of orally read text. Have students try to read like the tape, and then evaluate their performance. Of course, the stories also can be used as a vehicle for building listening comprehension, or expressive language, and writing skills.

Teach Vocabulary, Including Idioms

As you learned in Chapter 5, ELLs may learn basic vocabulary but struggle to learn the meaning of English-language idioms, such as "up the creek."

- Have students practice reading idioms like these with the appropriate rhythm and stress in connected speech (Celce-Murcia, 2000, p. 170):

All talk and no action	Talk shop
Talk is cheap	Talk through your hat
Talk a blue streak	Talk someone's head off

- Say each phrase and then have students repeat it, imitating your tone and inflection; discuss the meaning of each idiom (Bursuck & Damer, 2007). Also have students use each idiom in a sentence and write stories or draw pictures of idioms they choose.

Enhance Oral Language

The key to reading comprehension for ELLs is knowledge of oral language (Yang, 2002). Oral language can be enhanced through student reading or by reading to students.

- Select material relevant to students' experiences and backgrounds.

- Encourage students to summarize passages using familiar words after reading or listening.

- Keep a balance between expository (informational) and narrative (storytelling) material. Schools with higher proportions of students at risk tend to stress stories despite the fact that these students have major gaps in background knowledge.

- Because ELLs may be reluctant to volunteer to answer questions, call on nonvolunteers to answer in class while helping students to elaborate as they respond using modeling and guided practice.

- When you read aloud, talk slowly to give students the time needed to process what you are saying.

- When reading a long section of text, ask questions periodically rather than just at the end. This approach provides more direct support for comprehension and holds students' attention while modeling a question-asking strategy students eventually should use themselves.

- Have students write about the text they are reading or listening to improve their reading comprehension skills.

to participate in high-stakes assessments, so their scores may underestimate their actual achievement. Second, students with limited English skills sometimes are perceived by teachers and classmates as deficient. Teachers might have difficulty understanding students and assume they have limited ability, and peers may exclude them from social activities because of language differences (Oakes & Lipton, 2003). Third, language-related issues sometimes lead to the belief that when English is not students' primary language, they must be segregated from other students to learn. If you understand your students' levels of language proficiency as summarized in the Professional Edge on page 300, you can ensure that your instruction takes language into account and avoid or reduce some of the challenges non-native English speakers face.

Levels of Language Proficiency

When you teach students who are English-language learners, you will find that you must understand their level of language proficiency in order to design effective instruction. Further, you will need to keep in mind that language proficiency for any single student could vary significantly depending on whether the task at hand involves speaking, listening, reading, writing, or a combination of them. The following chart provides a continuum of the five levels of language proficiency, including the performance definition and some of the ways students function for each.

At the given level of English-language proficiency, English-language learners will process, understand, produce, or use:

5: Bridging	<ul><li>The technical language of the content areas</li><li>A variety of sentence lengths of varying linguistic complexity in extended oral or written discourse, including stories, essays, and reports</li></ul> ▶ Oral or written language approaching comparability to that of English-proficient peers when presented with grade-level material
4: Expanding	<ul><li>Specific and some technical language of the content areas</li><li>A variety of sentence lengths of varying linguistic complexity in oral discourse or multiple related paragraphs</li></ul> ▶ Oral or written language with minimal phonological, syntactic, or semantic errors that do not impede the overall meaning of the communication when presented with oral or written connected discourse with occasional visual and graphic support
3: Developing	<ul><li>General and some specific language of the content areas</li><li>Expanded sentences in oral interaction or written paragraphs</li></ul> ▶ Oral or written language with phonological, syntactic, or semantic errors that may impede the communication but retain much of its meaning when presented with oral or written narrative or expository descriptions with occasional visual and graphic support
2: Beginning	<ul><li>General language related to the content area</li><li>Phrases and short sentences</li></ul> ▶ Oral or written language with phonological, syntactic, or semantic errors that often impede the meaning of the communication when presented with one- to multiple-step commands, directions, or questions or a series of statements with visual and graphic support
1: Entering	<ul><li>Pictorial or graphic representation of the language of the content areas</li><li>Words, phrases, or chunks of language when presented with one-step commands or directions</li></ul> ▶ *WH*-questions (that is questions beginning with the words *who, what, where, when, why,* and *how*) or statements with visual and graphic support

Source: From English Language Proficiency Standards for English Language Learners in Kindergarten through Grade 12: Frameworks for Large-Scale State and Classroom Assessment, by M. Gottlieb, 2004, Madison, WI: WIDA Consortium. Retrieved December 1, 2004, from www.doe.state.de.us/DPIServices/Desk_Ref/ELP_StandardsOV.pdf. Reprinted with permission.

For students from culturally and linguistically diverse backgrounds, home–school communication is critical. You might have difficulty even in basic communication, however, because of language differences and the lack of availability of an interpreter. A second problem you may face concerns cultural values and parent responses to school personnel (Green, 2005; Obiakor, Utley, Smith, & Harris-Obiakor, 2002). For example, in a traditional Asian family, pride and shame often are emphasized and indirectness is valued. Imagine a parent conference in which an insensitive teacher describes in detail the academic and learning problems an Asian child is having and directly asks the parents whether they can assist in carrying out a home–school behavior change program. If they follow traditional Asian values, the parents might be humiliated by the public accounting of their child's failures and embarrassed at the teacher's direct and unnecessary request for their assistance.

A third example of the importance of communication relates to parents' perceptions of school and how they should interact with school personnel contrasted to school staff expectations for parent involvement. For example, the parents of some students may find school foreign and intimidating and believe that their role is to listen passively to what school personnel say. For students from diverse cultural backgrounds who have disabilities, it is particularly important to ensure that adequate information is communicated to parents about students' instructional programs and the procedures used in special education (Zhang & Bennett, 2003). You share this responsibility with special education professionals.

Families and Diversity

Many teachers find that not only do they have to put focused effort into understanding students and family members because of language barriers and global cultural differences, but also that they simply do not grasp the day-to-day realities of their students' and students' families' lives. Probably the single best strategy for improving understanding is to set aside all the books, lesson plans, and ideas about diversity and multiculturalism and simply *listen* to families (Trumbull & Pacheco, 2005). In addition to being willing to make the time to learn about families, Sánchez (1999, pp. 354–357) recommends the following:

1. Be willing to step outside your comfort zone by going into the community to learn about your students' and similar families.

2. Adopt the unequivocal view that all families are involved in and significant to their children's education and that schooling is only one source of education.

3. Be willing to examine your own story more deeply.

4. Be willing to challenge stereotypes and reduce prejudice.

5. Be willing to explore the sociocultural context in the lives of families and teachers.

6. Be willing to examine your own teaching practices from a family perspective.

7. Be willing to distribute power.

You can respond with respect and sensitivity to your students, as well as their families, by carefully listening to them and recognizing that the most important factor about working with others is that unless you have been in their situation, you cannot completely understand it. Working Together provides some suggestions for fostering collaboration with families by focusing on making them feel welcomed and valuable in their children's education.

Multicultural and Bilingual Education

Creating a classroom in which students' cultures are acknowledged and valued is a fundamental characteristic of **multicultural education,** that is, curriculum and instruction that reflect the diversity of society. Multicultural education begins with examining how you decorate your classroom and how you select learning materials. Do your bulletin boards display the work of students from ethnic and cultural minority groups? When you portray

Info Sheet Homework Exercise

Go to the Homework and Exercises section in Chapter 8 of MyEducationLab to learn about strategies for teaching and including students who are culturally and linguistically different.

Video Homework Exercise

Go to the Homework and Exercises section in Chapter 8 of MyEducationLab to watch teachers discuss techniques they use to meet student needs.

www.resources

The National Association for Bilingual Education is an organization concerned with the quality of education received by students whose native language is not English. You can learn more about this organization by visiting its website at www.nabe.org.

TOGETHER

Creating a School Environment for Collaborating with Parents

Collaboration between school professionals and parents and families is less about creating a set of activities than it is about forming a mindset based on "want to" rather than "ought to." This is especially important when working with families from diverse racial and cultural groups. To foster this positive approach toward working with parents and families, try these ideas:

■ Survey the parents of your students to find out what information they need. Arrange to have your survey translated into the languages spoken in the homes of your students.

■ Call to invite uninvolved parents to come to a school event or activity.

■ Work with other professionals at your school to contact parents' places of worship for ideas on how to foster positive relationships with parents and the community.

■ Let parents know a specific time and/or day of the week they can reach you by telephone or in person at school.

■ Ask parents to volunteer in your classroom, either tutoring students or teaching mini-lessons about their hobbies, interests, or jobs.

■ Call parents to praise their child—and do this more than once.

■ Develop home-learning activity packets that are related to your learning objectives. However, be sure they are family friendly—that is, that only basic supplies are needed to complete them.

■ With parent permission, connect an uninvolved parent with a parent who is involved.

■ Keep a list of community resources at your fingertips. Although your school social worker or other professionals also might have this information, you may be able to offer informal assistance in a way that is respectful and low key.

■ Have your students create a newsletter to send home. In it, describe important activities. Have secondary students keep a journal for their parents, outlining what they are studying.

■ Ask for parents' input regarding what works best with their child, especially regarding discipline and rewards.

Source: Adapted from *Home-School Collaboration: Building Effective Parent-School Partnerships*, by S. L. Christenson, 2002, Minneapolis: Children, Youth, and Family Consortium, University of Minnesota. Retrieved December 5, 2004, from www.cyfc.umn.edu/schoolage/resources/home.html. Reprinted by permission.

historical events, do you include information about members of several cultural groups? Does your classroom contain stories or literature about successful individuals from a variety of cultures? Is respect for diversity infused throughout your curriculum?

Two points are especially noteworthy regarding multicultural education. First, professionals agree that multicultural education should not be an event that occurs for one week of the school year. Rather, it should be addressed through integration of multicultural information in students' educational activities. Second, multicultural education is not a topic that is confined to social studies, as some educators believe. It should pervade all subject areas, being reflected in the stories or literature addressed in language arts or English, in the assignments given in science and math classes, and in the community contacts students make in vocational classes.

If the school in which you teach has a very diverse student population, programs for supporting **English-language learners (ELLs)** also will be important. For example, **bilingual education programs** are based on the assumption that students need to learn English by being immersed in the language environment, but until a level of proficiency in English is achieved, many students do not learn concepts and skills from English-language instruction (Bennett, 2003). In bilingual programs, students spend part of the school day receiving instruction in core academic areas in their native language and the

Strategy Homework Exercise

Go to the Homework and Exercises section in Chapter 8 of MyEducationLab to read about how a teacher differentiates instruction for students who are ELLs.

remainder of the day with English-speaking students. For students receiving special education services, a bilingual special education program staffed by a bilingual special education teacher may be provided in which students receive individualized services designed to strengthen their learning and drawing on their language and culture. Yet other students learn through English as a second language (ESL) programs in which instruction occurs primarily in English although separate from general education and no specific attempt is made to preserve students' native language. In a few elementary schools, English-language learners participate in the typical classroom, with a bilingual teacher joining the class for all or part of the day (Bahamonde & Friend, 1999; Reeves, 2006).

If you develop curiosity about your students' cultures and languages, you can be sensitive to their learning needs and responsive to them. If you consider yourself as much a learner as a teacher in interacting with these students, you will become culturally competent and help them effectively access the curriculum and succeed in school.

Case Study Homework Exercise

Go to the Homework and Exercises section in Chapter 8 of MyEducationLab to review a case study of an ELL who is placed in a special education program.

How Can You Meet the Needs of Students Who Are at Risk?

In addition to all the other special needs you find among students, you will likely encounter one that is found in virtually every public school classroom in the country. That special need is being at risk for school failure. Students who are *at risk* are those who have been exposed to some condition or situation that negatively affects their learning. Most teachers include in this description students who were prenatally exposed to drugs, including alcohol; students who use drugs or whose family members are drug users; students who are homeless; and students who have been neglected. Others include students who are bullies and those who are victims, as well as those who have recently experienced the death of someone close to them. Students who are school phobic are at risk, as are those who are considered suicidal, physically unattractive or obese, socially underdeveloped, and slow or marginal learners. It is difficult to understand the range of problems students face and the tremendous impact these problems have on their lives. One school district committee, formed to identify the district's at-risk learners and create options for helping them succeed, became overwhelmed at the enormity of their task. One teacher finally suggested that at-risk students were all students who were not achieving in the way teachers thought they could for any reason that prevented their learning.

You might be wondering why students who are at risk are discussed in a text about students with disabilities. Three reasons are central:

1. With a well-designed education, many students who are at risk for school failure succeed in school. The strategies for accommodating the needs of students with disabilities are usually effective for students at risk; these strategies are discussed throughout this text. By using the INCLUDE strategy, you can identify ways to help these students reach their potential.

2. Effective early school experiences for students who are at risk can establish a pattern of success in school learning that carries through high school (Gersti-Pepin, 2006). Without such experiences, students at risk are more likely to be identified as having learning or emotional disabilities.

3. Many students with disabilities also are students at risk. Many students with disabilities have been abused, some live in poverty, and others use illegal drugs.

Increasing your understanding of risk factors and approaches for working with students at risk benefits all students at risk for school failure, whether they have disabilities or not.

Analyze and Reflect

Students at risk may live in difficult situations over which they have no control, and their learning may be adversely affected. Should educators adjust their instruction and grading practices for these students? Justify your opinion.

INCLUDE

Characteristics and Needs of Students at Risk

Intellectually, socially, emotionally, behaviorally, and physically, students considered at risk are as diverse as students in the general school population. What distinguishes them from other students is the high likelihood that they will drop out of school prior to earning a high school diploma and that they will experience difficulty throughout their lives. Some students at risk also share other characteristics and needs, including a tendency to be noncompliant, problems in monitoring their own learning and behavior, language delays, difficulties with social relationships, and problems understanding the consequences of their behaviors (Severson, Walker, & Hope-Doolittle, 2007). To illustrate further the needs these students have, three representative groups of at-risk students are briefly discussed in the following sections: (1) students who live in poverty, including those who are homeless; (2) students who have been abused or neglected; and (3) students who live in homes in which substance abuse occurs or who themselves are substance abusers. Keep in mind that even though this discussion treats each group as distinct for the sake of clarity, any single student could be in all four groups.

> Intellectually, socially, emotionally, behaviorally, and physically, students considered at risk are as diverse as students in the general school population.

● **Students Who Live in Poverty**   Approximately 39 percent (that is, 28.4 million) of U.S. children under 18 years of age live in low-income families—that is, in families whose income is up to double the level considered poverty, or $20,000 for a family of four (National Center for Children in Poverty, 2006). A total of 18 percent of children live in poverty. These children live in all parts of the country, but most are in the South (11.2 million children in poverty) and West (7.2 million children in poverty). Moreover, 55 percent of these children (that is, 15.6 million) have at least one parent who works full-time year-round; just 19 percent do not have an employed parent. Approximately 21 percent of children in low-income families moved during a one-year period, compared to 10 percent of children in other families.

Students who live in poverty have many problems that affect their learning. These children score significantly lower on academic assessments than students who do not live in poverty, and they are more likely to have been retained at least once (Children's Defense Fund, 2003). They also might not have nutritious meals to eat, a safe and warm place to play and sleep, or needed supplies to complete homework. These students are sometimes worried about their families' circumstances, and older students might be expected to work evenings and weekends to help support the family or to miss school to babysit younger siblings. Students living in poverty also are more likely than advantaged students to experience parental neglect, witness violence, and change schools and residences frequently.

Some poor families are homeless. It is now estimated that 1.35 million children are homeless each year, with an average age of 6 years (National Coalition for the Homeless, 2006). In addition to families who are homeless, many are in temporary living arrangements with relatives or friends. Homelessness results in many educational problems. Students sometimes leave their neighborhood school or transfer from school to school when they move to a shelter or stay with family or friends. This can leave gaps in their learning. Some students are placed in foster care when the family is homeless, and this arrangement affects their social and emotional adjustment. In addition to learning problems, students who live in poverty or who are homeless sometimes (although not always) display acting-out, restless, or aggressive behaviors; anxiety; depression; and regressive behaviors (Popp, Stronge, & Hindman, 2003).

● **Students Who Are Abused or Neglected**   A second group of students at risk includes those who are physically abused, sexually abused, psychologically abused, or neglected each year (U.S. Department of Health and Human Services, 2006). Nearly 1,500 children die each year as a result of abuse or neglect. Although the precise meaning of the term **child abuse** varies from state to state, it generally refers to situations in which a parent or other caregiver inflicts or allows others to inflict injury on a child or permits a substantial risk of injury to exist. **Child neglect** is used to describe situations in which a parent or other caregiver fails to provide the necessary supports for a child's well-being, such as basic food and shelter, education, medical care, and other items. Figure 8.3 summarizes the demographic characteristics of students who are abused and the individuals who abuse them.

Some students who have been abused or neglected show visible signs, such as bruises, burns, and other untreated physical problems. They also might complain of hunger. The following student characteristics might signal to school professionals the presence of abuse or neglect (United Federation of Teachers, 2007):

fyi

Homeless children have to make many educational and personal adjustments as a result of four conditions in their lives: constant moving, frequent change of schools, overcrowded living quarters, and lack of basic resources such as clothing and transportation.

unexplained bruises and welts	begging or stealing food
unexplained fractures	constant fatigue, listlessness, or falling asleep in class
unexplained lacerations or abrasions	extended stays at school
wariness of adult contacts	pregnancy
apprehensiveness when other children cry	sexually transmitted disease
fear of parents or going home	difficulty walking or sitting
unexplained absences	torn, stained, or bloody underclothing
behavioral extremes such as aggression and withdrawal	pain or itching in the genital area
unattended physical problems and medical needs	unwillingness to change for gym
constant lack of supervision	withdrawal to infantile behavior
hunger	bizarre, sophisticated, or unusual sexual behavior or knowledge
poor hygiene	
inappropriate dress	poor peer relationships

You should be aware that as a teacher, you have a legal and ethical obligation to report suspected child abuse among your students. Although the specific reporting requirements for teachers vary from state to state, federal law requires that every state maintain a hotline and other systems for reporting abuse, and every state has statutes that define abuse and neglect and establish reporting procedures. If you suspect that one of your students is being abused, you should follow your school district's procedures for reporting it. If you are unsure about those procedures, you should notify your principal, school social worker, or school nurse.

www.resources

At the Child Abuse website of the National Institutes of Health (www.nlm.nih.gov/medlineplus/childabuse.html), you can find information about the symptoms of child abuse and your responsibilities as an educator for reporting it.

● Students Who Live with Substance Abuse or Are Substance Abusers

A third group of students at risk for school failure comprises those involved in substance abuse. Some students' parents have abused drugs and alcohol. The impact on students can begin before they are born and often affects them throughout their lives.

Babies born to mothers who drink alcohol heavily during pregnancy may have a medical condition called **fetal alcohol syndrome (FAS)** or a milder form known as **fetal alcohol effects (FAE).** Babies with FAS or FAE are smaller than expected, may have facial and other slight physical abnormalities, and often experience learning and behavior problems when they go to school. The prevalence estimate for these disorders is 1 in every 100 live births, or some 40,000 infants each year. Some researchers estimate that as many as 1 in 8 children in the United States has some type of permanent brain damage related to the mother's alcohol use during pregnancy (National Organization on Fetal Alcohol Syndrome, 2004), and FAS and FAE together are considered the leading preventable cause of

FIGURE *8.3* Child Abuse: A National Profile

In 2004, more than 5.5 million children were reported to child protective services because of suspected abuse or neglect. Some 872,000 of these cases were substantiated. This was a decrease (11.9 cases per 1,000 children versus 12.3 cases per 1,000 children) from 2002.

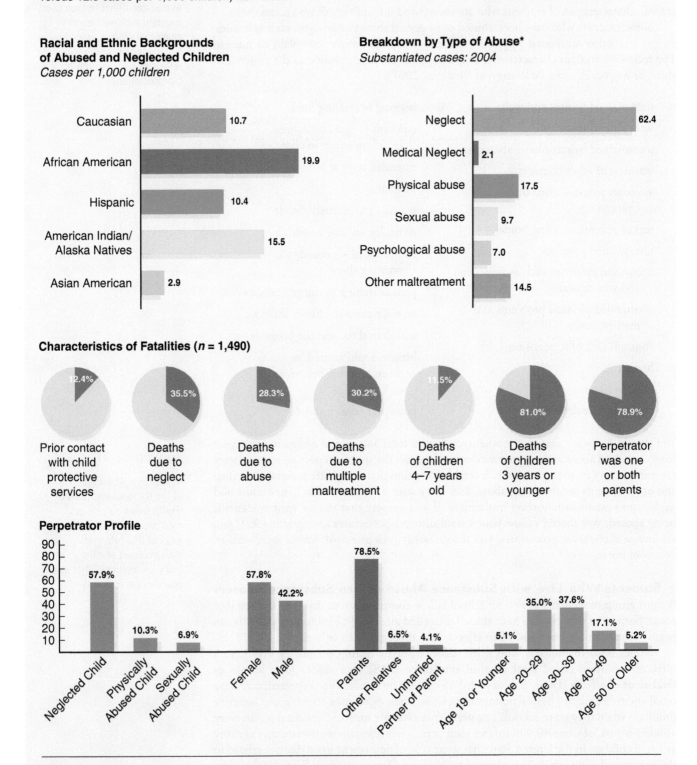

Racial and Ethnic Backgrounds of Abused and Neglected Children
Cases per 1,000 children

Caucasian 10.7
African American 19.9
Hispanic 10.4
American Indian/Alaska Natives 15.5
Asian American 2.9

Breakdown by Type of Abuse*
Substantiated cases: 2004

Neglect 62.4
Medical Neglect 2.1
Physical abuse 17.5
Sexual abuse 9.7
Psychological abuse 7.0
Other maltreatment 14.5

Characteristics of Fatalities (n = 1,490)

Prior contact with child protective services 12.4%
Deaths due to neglect 35.5%
Deaths due to abuse 28.3%
Deaths due to multiple maltreatment 30.2%
Deaths of children 4–7 years old 11.5%
Deaths of children 3 years or younger 81.0%
Perpetrator was one or both parents 78.9%

Perpetrator Profile

Neglected Child 57.9%
Physically Abused Child 10.3%
Sexually Abused Child 6.9%
Female 57.8%
Male 42.2%
Parents 78.5%
Other Relatives 6.5%
Unmarried Partner of Parent 4.1%
Age 19 or Younger 5.1%
Age 20–29 35.0%
Age 30–39 37.6%
Age 40–49 17.1%
Age 50 or Older 5.2%

*Total is more than 100 percent because some children were reported for multiple types of abuse.
Source: Adapted from *Child Maltreatment 2004*, Washington, DC: Department of Health and Human Services.
Retrieved July 31, 2007, from www.acf.hhs.gov/programs/cb/pubs/cm04/index.htm.

childhood intellectual impairment. Students with FAS or FAE tend to use poor judgment, leaving a situation when things do not go as planned or failing to predict the consequences of their behavior.

Babies born to mothers who have been abusing drugs often are low in weight. They also are likely to become overstimulated, which leads to an array of behaviors associated with irritability. When these children reach school age, they are likely to experience a wide variety of learning and behavior problems. Some are low-achievers, and others may become eligible for special education services. These children may be inattentive, hyperactive, and impulsive (Conners et al., 2004).

Researchers estimate that nearly 1 in 4 children grows up in a home in which alcohol or drugs are abused. These children are at risk because of a number of factors. For example, they are at risk for being neglected or abused. In homes in which drugs are abused, children may be passive recipients of drugs that can be inhaled, or they may accidentally ingest other drugs. Students who live in homes in which alcohol or drugs are abused often display at least several of the following characteristics at school (Germinario, Cervalli, & Ogden, 1992, p. 106):

- poor or erratic attendance
- frequent physical complaints and visits to the nurse
- morning tardiness, especially on Mondays
- inappropriate fear about the possibility of their parents being contacted
- tendency to equate any drinking with being drunk or being alcoholic
- perfectionistic and/or compulsive behavior
- difficulty concentrating, hyperactivity
- sudden emotional outbursts, crying, temper tantrums
- regression (for example, thumbsucking)
- friendlessness, isolation, withdrawn behavior
- passivity during routine activities but being active or focused during drug and alcohol awareness lessons
- lingering after drug and alcohol awareness lessons to ask unrelated questions
- signs of abuse or neglect

A third group of students affected by substance abuse includes those who themselves abuse drugs or alcohol. In 2005, 9.9 percent of youths ages 12 through 17 reported currently using illicit drugs (U.S. Department of Health and Human Services, 2007). Although overall illicit drug use has fallen among eighth-, tenth-, and twelfth-graders over the past decade (National Institute on Drug Abuse, 2006), abuse of the prescription pain killer OxyContin has doubled among eighth-graders (from 1.3 to 2.6 percent). Other areas of concern relate to eighth-graders' decreased disapproval of drugs such as Ecstasy and hallucinogens such as LSD (National Institute on Drug Abuse, 2006). In 2001, 10.1 million youths ages 12 through 20 indicated they were current drinkers, with nearly half of those classified as binge drinkers (U.S. Department of Health and Human Services, 2007). Among youths ages 12 through 17, 14.9 percent were current cigarette smokers.

Students with emotional disabilities are at particularly high risk for alcohol and drug abuse. Students who are substance abusers often have poor diets and sleep disturbances, feel a great deal of stress, and are at risk for depression and suicide. In school, they typically recall only information taught while they are sober, interact poorly with peers and teachers, and display excessive risk-taking behaviors.

As you can see, students who live in poverty, who are abused or neglected, and who live with substance abuse, as well as other at-risk students, collectively have many characteristics and needs that affect their learning. Although some of these students are resilient and do not suffer long-term consequences from their stressful lives (Jaffee, Caspi, & Moffit, 2007; Jones, 2007), the majority do not thrive without the support of an understanding school system and knowledgeable and committed teachers.

fyi

By age 18, 48 percent of young men and 45 percent of young women have had sexual intercourse. Among those adolescents, 1 in 4 develops a sexually transmitted disease (Centers for Disease Control and Prevention, 2006).

DIMENSIONS OF

diversity

Students who are mobile account for approximately 1 percent of all learners (Titus, 2007). Examples of mobile students include those displaced by catastrophes such as Hurricane Katrina and children of migrant workers.

Interventions for Students at Risk

As a teacher, you sometimes will be faced with the frustrating situation of not being able to take away from your students the stresses that often prevent them from learning to their potential. However, as explained in the Special Emphasis On . . . feature, your school counselor may be able to help address some of these needs. You can offer these students a safe environment by providing clear expectations and instructional support, making school an important place in their lives.

Generally, recommendations for intervening to teach students at risk include four goals, none of which is completely unique to these students: set high but realistic expectations, establish peers as teaching partners, collaborate with other professionals, and support family and community involvement. Each recommendation is discussed briefly here.

● **Set High but Realistic Expectations** When you are teaching students who are at risk, it is tempting to make assumptions about how much they are capable of learning. For example, you might think that a student who does not have books at home and whose parents are either unable or unwilling to read with her cannot be a successful learner. The result of such thinking often is creating inappropriately low expectations that students might "live down" to (Janisch & Johnson, 2003). Having low expectations also can lead to overusing teaching strategies that emphasize drilling students on lower-level academic

fyi

In 2005, the most recent year for which data are available, 13.1 percent of high school students were considered overweight and 45.6 percent reported trying to lose weight (Centers for Disease Control and Prevention, 2006).

Special EMPHASIS on

Counselors and Students at Risk

If you plan to become a school counselor, you will have an essential role to play in helping all the staff members of a school work effectively with students at risk and their families. For example, many students at risk are socially isolated. This increases the likelihood that they will be the victims or perpetrators of bullying; that they will experience physical, sexual, or psychological abuse by adults; and that they will become depressed and at risk for suicide. These are some of the strategies counselors can use to help students who are socially isolated:

■ Develop personal relationships with students. Doing so helps to break the notion some students have that there is no one to help them.

■ Help students increase their social contacts and relationships with peers. Options include teaching social skills through role-playing, arranging small-group interactions based on the needs of a targeted student, and encouraging the student to participate in clubs, organizations, and activities that are primarily social.

■ Arrange activities that bring together several families. When the social contacts of the adults in a student's life are expanded, the student will likely benefit. One example is a school-based family night at which computers are available, the media center is open, and informal parent education is offered.

Not surprisingly, many of the strategies for helping students also involve helping families. If family members feel marginalized (that is, they do not feel comfortable and welcome at school), then counselors also face the task of overcoming this barrier. They may do this by arranging for family members to meet with school staff members at a site other than school, involving church or other trusted community leaders in developing family advocacy programs, and working with teachers to find friendly ways to invite family members to participate in their children's education.

Teachers can consider which of these ideas they can take responsibility for implementing. As a teacher, what questions do you have about the role of counselors in fostering success for students who are at risk? How could you work with a counselor to facilitate positive interactions among school professionals and parents of students at risk for school failure? What other ideas do you have for working effectively with at-risk students and their families.

skills. Although drill activities have a place in educating at-risk students, they must be balanced with other approaches. Students need to learn thinking processes along with basic skills, and they need to learn to construct their own knowledge along with receiving it from you. This approach is illustrated in the description of Wesley Elementary School (Pollard-Durodola, 2003), an inner-city school with a surprising record of academic success for students that is attributed to creating a safe and structured school environment, high expectations for students and teachers, a curriculum designed to directly address student needs, plans to prevent problems, and strong instructional leadership. This project demonstrates that when school professionals collaborate, they can reach the wide range of needs their students may have.

One other strategy for setting high expectations should be mentioned. Many professionals understand that the still-common practice of *tracking*—that is, grouping students for instruction by perceived ability—can discriminate against students at risk. For example, a recent longitudinal study of student achievement in mathematics found that when students were heterogeneously grouped in middle school math classes, they took more math classes in high school and did better in whatever classes they took than did students who had been homogeneously grouped for math in middle school (Burris, Heubert, & Levin, 2006).

Grouping students heterogeneously generally does not place high-achieving students at a disadvantage, and it may help raise the achievement of at-risk learners. Although teachers appropriately group students by their needs for instruction in specific skills as part of their overall instructional plan and some secondary schools offer advanced classes that result in a limited amount of tracking, you should be aware of the potential negative effects of tracking. As a teacher, you can ensure that you do not overuse this type of grouping in your classroom, and you can work with your colleagues to create a school in which students of many different abilities learn together.

One word of caution about setting standards is necessary: Some students who are at risk live in such high-stress situations outside school that they might not have much support from their parents and other family members for completing school assignments and homework. Two examples from teachers help to illustrate this point. One talked about a student who was not returning homework. The teacher was penalizing the student by giving her lower grades and making her complete the work during recess. The teacher later found out that the student's family was quite poor and had a single lightbulb in their tiny apartment. When the bulb burned out, there was no light after sunset, and doing homework became impossible. Another teacher described a high school student who always slept in class. In-school suspension did not help, nor did attempts to contact the student's parents. The teacher later learned that this student left school each day, cooked dinner for her younger siblings, and then worked at a fast-food restaurant until midnight. Having high expectations is important, but they need to be tempered with understanding of the circumstances in students' lives outside school.

Effective instruction for students at risk includes the same strategies you would use for other students, with particular attention to the physical and social-emotional challenges these students often face. Students at risk need a structured learning environment, systematic instruction in basic skill areas, and strategies for learning independence. The Technology Notes on page 310 provides one example of a tool to enhance the learning of at-risk students.

● **Establish Peers as Teaching Partners** Peers learning from one another is a strategy that was recommended earlier for students from diverse cultural and linguistic backgrounds; it is also useful for at-risk students. For example, in the Success for All (SFA) Program (Munoz, Dossett, & Judy-Gullans, 2003), an intensive early reading program designed to help at-risk learners acquire foundational learning that helps them throughout

High expectations contribute to the greater academic success of some students at risk. In your classroom, how can you identify students who are at risk? What other interventions and instructional strategies can you use to help them succeed in school?

Case Study Homework Exercise

Go to the Homework and Exercises section in Chapter 8 of MyEducationLab to read how one teacher supports her students who are at risk.

A Little Technology with a Big Impact on Student Learning

Advances in digital technology have created more and more options for enhancing student learning. The key is to integrate the technology into daily classroom use and match it to students' needs.

Mini-Me Recorder

The Mini-Me recorder is a small, round device that permits the teacher to record a 10- to 20-second message, which the student then can play back by pushing a button. This is the same technology used in the musical and prerecorded greeting cards now available to consumers. This small device can provide support to many learners who struggle, enabling them to experience more independence and confidence. Some examples of its use include these:

- Flashcards of key sight words are prepared by the teacher using foamboard (because it is thick enough to insert the Mini-Me device). The teacher records one of the words on each Mini-Me device and attaches it to the appropriate flashcard. When using the flashcards, the student first attempts to say the word and then pushes the button to check for the correct answer.

- Using cards similar to those just described, all students can participate in peer tutoring. For example, in a kindergarten or first-grade class, students can show each other their word cards and then check their answers by pushing the playback button on the Mini-Me.

Mini-Me Recording Device

- For a student with ADHD, a brief recorded message might be prepared each day with a reminder of the day's homework or items to bring to school the next day (library books, permission form for the field trip). For this purpose, the Mini-Me could be placed in a student's pencil case or a special pocket in her backpack.

What other uses can you think of for this recording device? For elementary age students? For middle school and high school students? How might such a device facilitate student learning in English or language arts? Math? Science? Social studies?

Source: Adapted from "Using Assistive Technology to Include Low-Performing Students in Peer Tutoring: A Little Help from Mini-Me," by R. R. Van Norman, 2007, *Journal of Special Education Technology,* 22(1), pp. 53–57.

---

their school careers, a key component is a cooperative learning approach. Students work with each other in structured groups to learn vocabulary, writing, comprehension, and other reading skills. This program appears to have great potential for helping students achieve school success.

Case Study Homework Exercise

Go to the Homework and Exercises section in Chapter 8 of MyEducationLab to read how a fourth-grade teacher manages her classroom to support her students who are at risk.

● **Collaborate with Other Professionals** A third strategy for teaching at-risk students involves increasing your problem-solving capability by adding the skills and resources of your colleagues. Problem solving with your colleagues about at-risk students allows you to check your own perspectives against theirs, gain access to their expertise, and coordinate your efforts. For example, if you are teaching Shaneal, a student whom you suspect has been abused, you can first ask the counselor or social worker whether there is any past documentation of abuse and you can request that one of these professionals speak with the student. If you are teaching Jack, a student who is missing quite a few school days and increasingly refuses to complete assignments, you might want to consult with colleagues about the causes of Jack's behavior and how to address them.

- **Support Family and Community Involvement**   It is essential that you maintain positive contact with parents and other caregivers of your at-risk students, just as you would with other students. However, the level of participation you can expect will vary considerably. Some parents will be anxious to ensure that their children have all the advantages an education can give them, and they will do all they can to assist you in teaching. Parents who are not functioning well themselves, however, probably cannot be expected to participate actively in their children's education. To involve families and communities in their children's education, you might try several ideas. Sometimes it might be more appropriate to require a student to bring to school something personally important from home and to base an assignment on that, rather than to assign more traditional homework. It also can be helpful to assist parents in connecting with community resources such as health clinics and social service agencies. One school district that was struggling because of the rapidly increasing number of at-risk students worked with local church leaders to connect families with resources and improve the communication between school personnel and families.

When you think about the diversity of students you may teach, it is easy to become overwhelmed by the challenge of meeting all students' instructional needs. Classrooms structured to celebrate diversity, rather than treat it as a deficiency or an exception, are classrooms that blend structure and flexibility and provide many options for learning.

Building Teaching Skills Case Study Exercise

Go to the Building Teaching Skills Exercises section in Chapter 8 of MyEducationLab to learn about fostering student accountability for classroom work.

Building Teaching Skills Case Study Exercise

Go to the Building Teaching Skills Exercises section in Chapter 8 of MyEducationLab to learn about teaching exceptional learners and students at risk.

Summary

In addition to students with disabilities, you will teach many other students who have extraordinary learning needs. Some students receive specialized services through Section 504, federal legislation requiring that accommodations be provided by general educators to students who have functional disabilities that might limit their access to an education. Many of the students protected through Section 504 have physical conditions, medical problems, and significant learning needs, and their plans outline the academic, behavioral, and physical or medical accommodations required to provide them with appropriate educational access.

One specific group of students who receive Section 504 assistance comprises those with attention deficit–hyperactivity disorder (ADHD), a medically diagnosed disorder characterized by chronic and severe inattention and/or hyperactivity–impulsivity. Students with ADHD may receive a variety of environmental, academic, and behavior interventions; training to assist their parents in understanding and responding to their needs; and medication.

Students who are gifted and talented form a second group of students with special needs. Students who are gifted and talented include those with generally high intellectual ability as well as those with talents in specific areas such as music. The interventions used most often to help them achieve school success are curriculum compacting, enrichment and acceleration, differentiation, and individualized interventions.

A third group of students with special needs includes those from culturally and linguistically diverse backgrounds. These students and their families sometimes have values that differ from those of schools. Teachers need to learn about students' cultures, teach in a manner that is responsive to those cultures, and acknowledge and value diverse cultures in the classroom to teach students from these backgrounds effectively.

Finally, students at risk for school failure because of environmental influences such as poverty, child abuse, and drug addiction also have special needs. Because students at risk often live in unpredictable and stressful environments, strategies for teaching them include setting appropriate expectations, establishing peers as teaching partners, collaborating with other professionals, and working closely with families and community members.

Back to the Cases

This section provides opportunities for you to apply the knowledge gained in this chapter to the cases described at the beginning of this chapter. The questions and activities that follow demonstrate how these standards and principles, along with other concepts that you have learned about in this chapter, connect to the everyday activities of all teachers.

Maria and her teachers have set a goal for Maria to become a teacher and are hopeful that she will be able to attend a summer program where she can learn more about teaching. You are concerned that her English-language skills may hamper her experience—particularly her difficulties with abstract concepts. Review what you have learned about teaching students who experience language processing difficulties and consult the Professional Edge on page 300. Suggest strategies, technologies, or instructional supports that will help Maria prepare for the new challenge and support her learning experience during the summer program. Explain why you believe your suggestions may benefit Maria. (INTASC Principles 3.04 and 6.03; and CEC Content Standards 3, 5, and 6.)

José, as you may recall, needs special attention. Mr. Lee has come to the student assistant teacher for help with José, because nothing he has tried has worked. After hearing his concerns, the team decides to write a Section 504 plan; as a member of the team, you will help select appropriate accommodations for José. After reviewing this chapter, the Professional Edge on page 278, and Figure 8.2, share the accommodations you would recommend. (See INTASC Principles 3.03 and 7.01; and CEC Content Standards 2 and 3.) List each accommodation, and explain why you believe it is appropriate for José.

Lydia, as you may remember, has special talents and academic ability. However, her family is very concerned that she is not getting appropriate opportunities to use her talents and academic ability. You have invited family members to a conference tomorrow afternoon in which you will address their concerns with a proposal for future accommodations. (INTASC Principle 7.01 and CEC Content Standard 4.) In preparation, you ask a peer to work with you to do the following:

- Develop a matrix of pros and cons for the instructional strategies commonly used with students who are gifted and talented
- Write a rationale for using or not using each strategy for Lydia
- Create a proposal to present to the family that includes a combination of strategies you believe will be most appropriate

Tam, as you may recall, is a student at risk and needs help. His first-block history teacher sat at your table during lunch today. During a general conversation about working with at-risk students, the teacher shared Tam's story. Based on the interventions you read about in this chapter for students who are at risk, what strategies might you suggest your colleague employ to help Tam? (INTASC Principle 9.04 and CEC Content Standards 3 and 5.)

Key Terms and Concepts

Attention deficit–hyperactivity disorder (ADHD) (p. 279)
Bilingual education programs (p. 302)
Child abuse (p. 305)
Child neglect (p. 305)
English-language learners (ELLs) (p. 302)

Fetal alcohol effects (FAE) (p. 305)
Fetal alcohol syndrome (FAS) (p. 305)
Gifted and talented (p. 289)
Multicultural education (p. 301)
Section 504 (p. 275)

Now go to the Friend and Bursuck, Fifth Edition, MyEducationLab course at www.myeducationlab.com to

- take a pretest to assess your initial comprehension of the chapter content
- study chapter content with your individualized study plan
- take a posttest to assess your understanding of chapter content
- engage in multimedia exercises to help you build a deeper and more applied understanding of chapter content

Applications in Teaching Practice

Diversity in a High School Class

Ivan Robinson is a first-year high school teacher in a large urban school district. Although it is only the fourth week of school, he is concerned. Although he is confident of his knowledge of history and civics, as well as his teaching skills, and he feels he has a strong commitment to teaching all the students assigned to him, he is worried that he won't be able to meet the vast array of student needs represented in his second-block class this year. Mr. Robinson is well aware that his students' needs are diverse, particularly in this section. For example, Thuan, who just immigrated to the United States from Vietnam, speaks very little English and seems overwhelmed by nearly everything at school. Mr. Robinson can't recall ever seeing Thuan smile. As Mr. Robinson discusses U.S. history, he knows that much of the information is beyond Thuan's understanding because of language differences and that Thuan does not have the context for grasping the themes in U.S. history.

Then there is Sonny. Sonny is supposed to be taking medication for ADHD, but it doesn't seem to be having the intended effect on him. At an after-school meeting, Mr. Robinson, the school psychologist, the counselor, and the assistant principal discussed the matter with Sonny, and it was noted that Sonny recently had decided he had outgrown the need for medication and sometimes was not taking it. Sonny did say, though, that a few times he decided to catch up by taking a double dose. The counselor is supposed to follow up on this unhealthy and potentially dangerous thinking about medication and keep Mr. Robinson informed. In the meantime, Sonny is in his class and, as Mr. Robinson puts it, is either "bouncing off the walls or zoned out."

Jenny is a concern as well. She and her twin sister, Jenna, are struggling academically despite receiving a lot of individual attention and having supportive parents. Neither girl is reading well enough to complete the chapters in the history text. Both girls have been referred in the past for special education services, but neither is eligible to receive them. Mr. Robinson knows that the twins' father has been out of work for nearly a year, that the girls both work after school and have little time for homework or tutoring assistance, and that the family is barely getting by on donations from friends and their church. Mr. Robinson heard last week that one of the grandparents had also come to live with the family. He wonders how much of the twins' learning problems are related to their home situation.

Mr. Robinson also teaches Kimberly, who just moved into the district and is so far ahead of the other students that Mr. Robinson wishes she were taking his course through the local community college. Two other students, Lisa and Paul, are from families that have very little; they come to school without supplies and seem reluctant to interact with the other children.

As he reflects on his class, Mr. Robinson realizes that at least half the students have a special need of one kind or another, and he suspects that he only knows a fraction of their life stories. He wants to reach them all to share his love of history, but he is not sure he can accomplish his goal.

Questions

1. How typical is the type of class Mr. Robinson has? What other types of diverse needs might you expect to be represented in a class you will teach?

2. What general strategies might Mr. Robinson use in his class that would benefit many students with special needs and harm none?

3. For each student with special needs Mr. Robinson has identified, consider how the INCLUDE strategy could be used. Fill in the following chart, perhaps working with a classmate to generate ideas for information not specifically outlined in the preceding student descriptions. Be sure to address academic, social-emotional, behavioral, and medical-physical needs.

INCLUDE

	Thuan	Jenny and Jenna	Kimberly	Sonny	Lisa and Paul
Identify					
Note					
Check					
Look					
Use					
Decide					
Evaluate					

4. Twelve special education teachers are assigned to Mr. Robinson's school, and he works extensively with Mr. Settle. What is Mr. Settle's role in assisting Mr. Robinson and other teachers in the school to meet the diverse needs of students, including those who do not have IEPs? Who else might assist Mr. Robinson as he designs instruction and plans how to help his students succeed?

5. How might Mr. Robinson work with the parents of his students to help ensure their needs are addressed? What barriers might he encounter? How should he address these barriers? What inadvertent biases could he have toward his students' families? How could these biases relate to your own views as a novice educator?

6. What realistic expectations can Mr. Robinson set for himself as a teacher for this school year?

Further Readings

Barkley, R. A. (2006). *Attention-deficit hyperactivity disorder* (3rd ed.). New York: Guilford Press.

If you are interested in in-depth learning about ADHD, this book presents a contemporary and comprehensive overview of the topic. It includes chapters on the history of ADHD, problems that often accompany this disorder, ways that professionals can assess children to determine if they have ADHD, and treatments. One chapter focuses on school-based interventions.

Nieto, S. (Ed.). (2005). *Why we teach*. New York: Teachers College Press.

Have you thought about why you want to be a teacher? Perhaps you want to reach the diverse students described in this chapter. This book is a collection of essays by real teachers, professionals who may not make headlines, but who can inspire and challenge you to create similar classrooms that have as a goal the highest standards for all students.

Payne, R. (2005). *A framework for understanding poverty* (4th ed.). Highlands, TX: Aha Process.

Payne offers to educators and other professionals a fresh perspective on understanding poverty and working with students who live in poverty. She defines poverty as far more than a lack of financial resources and presents concrete strategies teachers should implement to better reach these students.

Popp, P. A., Stronge, J. H., & Hindman, J. L. (2003). *Students on the move: Reaching and teaching highly mobile children and youth* (Urban Diversity Series). Washington, DC: National Center for Homeless Education and ERIC Clearinghouse on Urban Education (ERIC Document Reproduction Service no. ED482661).

This handbook, available without charge through the ERIC system, is designed to help teachers and other professionals learn about students who move frequently (for example, children of migrant workers, children living in deep poverty, children of military families). The handbook blends research summaries with case studies and includes a checklist of interventions to support these students as well as a list of related children's literature and activities.

9 Differentiating Instruction

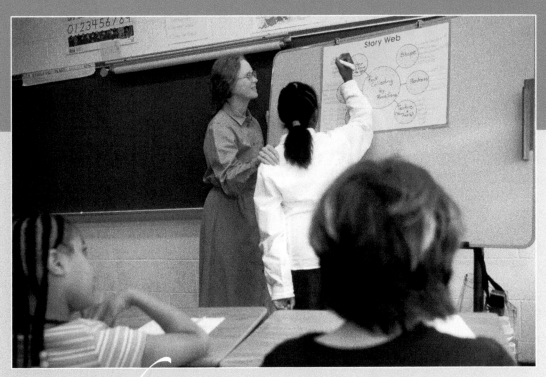

LEARNING Objectives

After you read this chapter, you will be able to

1. Describe accommodations you can make for students who do not have the preskills necessary to learn new skills.

2. Select and sequence instructional examples to help students access basic skills instruction.

3. Accommodate individual learners by providing the direct instruction, practice, and review needed to help them acquire basic skills.

4. Describe accommodations you can make when activating background knowledge, organizing content, and teaching terms and concepts.

5. Make lessons accessible for students with special needs by improving the clarity of your written and oral communication.

6. Describe strategies for involving parents in teaching their children.

7. Adapt independent practice activities for students.

8. Describe how you can make modifications in your classroom materials and activities for students with moderate to severe disabilities.

Ms. Diaz was teaching her fourth-grade class how to write percentages for fractions using this example from her math book:

Write a percent for $\frac{7}{8}$.

$\frac{7}{8}$ means $7 \div 8$.

$$0.87\frac{4}{8} = 0.87\frac{1}{2} = 87\frac{1}{2}\%$$

$$8\overline{)7.00}$$
$$\underline{64}$$
$$60$$
$$\underline{56}$$
$$4$$

Divide until the answer is in hundredths. Give the remainder as a fraction.

$$\frac{7}{8} = 87\frac{1}{2}\%, \text{ or } 87.5\%$$

To show her students how to do this problem, Ms. Diaz wrote the example on the board, pointing out that the fraction 7/8 means 7 divided by 8. She then explained that they would have to divide until the answer was in hundredths and would have to give the remainder as a fraction. Following this instruction, Ms. Diaz assigned the students 15 similar problems to do independently. Abdul, who is a student in this class, has a learning disability. Abdul has experienced some difficulties with math skills since he entered the second grade. He has difficulty learning new skills unless he is given many opportunities for instruction and practice. Abdul answered none of the 15 problems correctly. He missed converting the fractions to percentages, because he forgot that it means 7 divided by 8; Abdul divided 8 by 7 instead.

■ *How can Ms. Diaz differentiate instruction to prevent Abdul from having this misunderstanding? How could this lesson have been taught to Abdul to prevent this misunderstanding?*

Cecily is a student with a hearing loss who is in Ms. Boyd's U.S. history class. Cecily has failed every test so far, because the tests are based mainly on the textbook, which she has difficulty reading. Cecily can read most of the words in the text, but she reads very slowly. Because of this, she is unable to pick out main ideas in the text. Cecily also has trouble figuring out the meanings of key vocabulary words in context, even though they are highlighted in the text, and she doesn't know how to use the glossary. Last week, Cecily was assigned a chapter to read for homework. She spent almost two hours reading 15 pages, and when she was done, she cried in frustration because she could not remember anything she had read. Until recently, Cecily has enjoyed a small group of friends who teach her popular phrases while she teaches them sign language for their favorite topics—clothes, movies, and boys. However, their friendship has been strained because Cecily is spending so much time on her assignments.

■ *What can Ms. Boyd do to help Cecily read and remember key ideas in her textbook? What can she do to help Cecily understand new vocabulary words?*

Albert has attention deficit–hyperactivity disorder (ADHD) and is included in Ms. Olivieri's second-grade class. Albert has trouble following written directions and doing independent practice assignments that have more than one part. He also complains that his seatwork assignments are too hard for him. During seatwork, Albert is frequently out of his chair, either getting help from or bothering other students in the class. Ms. Olivieri feels that she is already spending too much time helping Albert.

■ *What should Ms. Olivieri do to make seatwork a more successful experience for Albert and give herself more time to work with other students?*

INCLUDE

As you have already learned, the curriculum methods and materials teachers use have a strong influence on how readily students learn in the classroom. In fact, the better the materials and the teaching, the fewer the individual accommodations required for students with special needs. However, for a variety of reasons, you may not have control over the materials used in your school. Furthermore, despite your best teaching efforts, some students will still need individual accommodations or modifications to gain access to important skills and content. For example, in the chapter-opening cases just described, merely showing Abdul how to do one problem is not enough. He will need guidance through a number of examples before he will be ready to do problems independently. In addition, you can help Cecily focus on important information in her textbook by giving her a study guide that has questions pertaining to the most important content in each chapter. You can also have Cecily identify words she does not know and ask a classmate to help her with the meanings before she reads. For Albert, you can make sure all directions are clearly written using words he can identify; you can also give the directions orally and guide students through several practice examples before they are required to work independently. Of course, you also want to be sure that Albert has the necessary academic skills to complete assignments independently.

The purpose of this chapter is to provide you with strategies for making accommodations and modifications in curriculum materials, teacher instruction, and student practice activities that are reasonable to carry out and increase the likelihood of success for students with special needs. Remember, most students with disabilities included in your classroom are expected to meet the same curricular goals as their classmates without disabilities. Therefore, most of the strategies for differentiating instruction covered in this chapter fall into the category of accommodations, which we learned in Chapter 5 are supports that allow students to more readily access the general education curriculum.

It is also important to note that the instructional accommodations described in this chapter can at times be carried out with your entire class. At other times, they might be presented with individual students or as a part of small groups. The way you choose to accommodate your students with special needs depends on classroom demands, the characteristics of individual students, and the overall level of functioning of your class. For example, in the case of Abdul, if he has many other classmates who are struggling to write percentages for fractions and if he can attend to a task in a large group, then Ms. Diaz can accommodate him by building more guided practice into her large-group instruction. If only Abdul and a few of his classmates are having trouble learning percents and/or if Abdul has trouble paying attention in a large group, then Ms. Diaz would be better off accommodating Abdul either one to one or in a small group. You can use the INCLUDE strategy to help you make decisions about the best way to make accommodations for your students with special needs.

Instructional modifications, as we learned in Chapter 5, are used for students who have more severe disabilities and who have alternative curriculums specified on their individualized education programs (IEPs). Strategies for making appropriate instructional modifications are covered at the end of this chapter, as well as in Chapter 6.

How Can You Make Accommodations for Students with Special Needs in Basic Skills Instruction?

Basic skills instruction means primarily instruction in the academic skills of reading, writing, and math. However, you may also apply effective principles for differentiating basic skills instruction to content areas such as science. Four aspects of basic skills instruction for which you may need to make accommodations for students with special needs are preskills; the selection and sequencing of examples; the rate of introduction of new skills; and direct instruction, practice, and review.

Teaching Preskills

Darrell is in Ms. Rayburn's second-grade class. In language arts, he is experiencing a problem common to many students with special needs. On Tuesday, Darrell was at his desk reading a book on his favorite topic: magic. However, when Ms. Rayburn asked Darrell specific questions about the book, he was unable to answer them. It turned out that Darrell was unable to identify most of the words in the book and was just pretending to read. Another student, Tamika, is in Mr. Thomas's Algebra 1 class. She is having difficulty solving basic equations with one unknown because she has yet to master basic math computational skills.

Preskills are basic skills necessary for performing more complex skills. Prior to teaching a skill, you should assess students on the relevant preskills and if necessary teach these skills. Darrell was unable to comprehend the book about magic because he lacked the word identification skills needed to read the words. He may need instruction in word attack skills; he may also need to be encouraged to read trade books at his reading level. Tamika will need additional instruction and practice on her computational skills if she is going to be successful in Algebra 1. Because textbooks do not generally list preskills, you need to ask yourself continually what preskills are required, and you need to be on the lookout for students who lack them. Looking at the instructional demands in this way is a key part of applying the INCLUDE strategy. Determining the potential impact of student preskills on instruction may mean informally assessing such skills. For example, before Ms. Tompkins taught her kindergarteners to tell time, she checked to see whether they could identify the numbers 1–12 and count by 5s to 60. Before teaching students to look up words in a dictionary, Mr. Thurman checked to see whether his students could say the letters in the alphabet, could alphabetize words to the third letter, and knew whether to turn to the front, middle, or end of the dictionary when looking up a certain word. Mr. Thomas began his Algebra 1 class by assessing his class on basic computational skills.

If you are teaching a skill and find that most of your students lack the necessary preskills, teach these preskills directly before teaching the more complex skill. If only one or two students lack preskills, you can accommodate them with extra practice and instruction through a peer or parent volunteer or with the help of a special service provider. For example, Ms. Cooper was preparing a lesson on how to find the area of a rectangle. Before beginning the lesson, she gave her students a multiplication probe and found that almost half the class was still having problems with their multiplication facts. Ms. Cooper set up a peer tutoring program in which students who knew their facts were paired with students who did not; the pairs practiced facts for 10 minutes each day for a week. Students who preferred to work alone practiced their math facts using a drill-and-practice computer-based program. Ms. Cooper still introduced finding the area of rectangles as scheduled, but she allowed students to use calculators until they had mastered their facts.

Selecting and Sequencing Examples

The way you select and sequence instructional examples can affect how easily your students learn. For example, Alex's practice activities for a week in Mr. Huang's third-grade math class are shown in Figure 9.1. Mr. Huang has been covering two-digit subtraction with regrouping. On Monday through Thursday, Alex was given five of these problems and got them all right. On Friday, he was asked to do a mixture of problems, some requiring regrouping and some not. Alex got only three of the problems correct because he was unable to discriminate between subtraction problems that required regrouping and those that did not. He was unable to differentiate these two types of problems in part because his daily practice pages had included only one problem type. Carefully preparing the **example**

FIGURE 9.1   Alex's Math Work

Monday's Seatwork

²₍₁₎ 35 −17 18	³₍₁₎ 42 −15 27	²₍₁₎ 38 −19 19	³₍₁₎ 41 −22 19	⁶₍₁₎ 74 −49 25

$$\begin{array}{ccccc}
\overset{2\ 1}{35} & \overset{3\ 1}{42} & \overset{2\ 1}{38} & \overset{3\ 1}{41} & \overset{6\ 1}{74} \\
-17 & -15 & -19 & -22 & -49 \\
\hline
18 & 27 & 19 & 19 & 25
\end{array}$$

Tuesday's Seatwork

$$\begin{array}{ccccc}
\overset{5\ 1}{64} & \overset{6\ 1}{70} & \overset{8\ 1}{91} & \overset{5\ 1}{68} & \overset{7\ 1}{82} \\
-38 & -32 & -58 & -39 & -28 \\
\hline
26 & 38 & 33 & 29 & 54
\end{array}$$

Wednesday's Seatwork

$$\begin{array}{ccccc}
\overset{8\ 1}{94} & \overset{5\ 1}{61} & \overset{2\ 1}{33} & \overset{6\ 1}{76} & \overset{7\ 1}{81} \\
-57 & -45 & -19 & -38 & -47 \\
\hline
37 & 16 & 14 & 38 & 34
\end{array}$$

Thursday's Seatwork

$$\begin{array}{ccccc}
\overset{4\ 1}{55} & \overset{2\ 1}{30} & \overset{8\ 1}{72} & \overset{8\ 1}{96} & \overset{8\ 1}{83} \\
-29 & -18 & -28 & -59 & -38 \\
\hline
26 & 12 & 44 & 37 & 45
\end{array}$$

Friday's Seatwork

$$\begin{array}{ccccc}
\overset{8\ 1}{96} & \overset{3\ 1}{43} & \overset{7\ 1}{89} & \overset{5\ 1}{67} & \overset{6\ 1}{75} \\
-53 & -18 & -33 & -28 & -57 \\
\hline
313 & 25 & 416 & 39 & 18
\end{array}$$

selection you use for instruction and student practice can help students learn to differentiate among problem types.

You can help students make key discriminations between current and previous problem types by using examples that at first require the application of only one particular skill (Carnine, Silbert, Kame'enui, & Tarver, 2004). When students can perform these problems without error, add examples of skills previously taught to help students discriminate between the different problem types. Doing this also provides students with needed review. An easy accommodation for Alex would have been to add several problems that did not require regrouping to each daily teaching and practice session once he had shown that he could compute the regrouping problems accurately when they were presented alone.

Ms. Owens ran into a different example-related problem when teaching her students word problems in math. In her examples, when a word problem included the word *more*, getting the correct answer always involved subtracting, such as in the following problem:

> Alicia had 22 pennies. Juanita had 13. How many more pennies does Alicia have than Juanita?

However, on her test, Ms. Owens included the following problem:

> Mark read 3 books in March. He read 4 more books in April. How many books did Mark read?

www.**resources**

High-interest, low-reading-level material is essential for teachers to have for older students with reading problems, but it is always at a premium. *The Key New Readers Newspaper Project* provides stories on all different topics at beginning, middle, and advanced reading levels. Go to www.keynews.org.

Several students with special needs in Ms. Owens's class subtracted 3 from 4 because they thought the presence of the word *more* signaled subtraction. Ms. Owens needed to include problems of this latter type in her teaching to prevent such misconceptions.

Consider this example: When Mr. Yoshida taught his students how to add *ed* to a word ending in *y,* he demonstrated on the board as follows:

carry + ed = carried   hurry + ed = hurried

Next, Mr. Yoshida had his students add *ed* to five words ending in *y.* Finally, he assigned students 10 practice problems in their English books that looked like this:

Write the past tense of *marry.*

A number of students were unable to answer the questions in the book, even though they knew how to add *ed* to words ending in *y,* because the practice examples in the book required students to know what the meaning of past tense and how to form the *past tense* was by adding *ed.* The book's practice activity was very different from the instructional examples Mr. Yoshida used, which only required students to add *ed* to words ending in *y.*

Both Ms. Owens's and Mr. Yoshida's examples demonstrate an important aspect of selecting instructional examples: The range of your instructional examples should match the range of the problem types used when you assess student learning. Ms. Owens could have prevented problems in her class by expanding her range of examples to include word problems that contained the word *more* but that were not solved by subtracting. Mr. Yoshida could have better prepared his students for the practice activities in the English book by using examples that referred directly to forming the past tense by adding *ed.* Note that some students with special needs may still struggle even when the instructional examples used are appropriate. These students may require an individual accommodation that could be as simple as a reminder that the word *more* can have more than one meaning or that the past tense is formed when adding *ed* to a verb. Or the accommodation could be as involved as providing additional instruction using concrete representations of the different meanings of *more* or verbs ending in *ed.*

The following shows a different example selection problem. Tawana's class was covering several high-frequency sight words that appeared in their classroom reading program. On Wednesday, Tawana learned the word *man,* but on Thursday, after the word *men* was presented, she was unable to read *man* correctly. Tawana's word identification problem illustrates another example selection problem, namely, **example sequencing.** The visual and auditory similarities of *man* and *men* make learning these words difficult for many students who are at risk and students with learning disabilities, who may have trouble differentiating words that look and/or sound the same. One way to prevent this problem is to separate the introduction of *man* and *men* with the introduction of other dissimilar high-frequency words, such as *dog, house,* and *cat.* Students with special needs may also need an individual accommodation such as more practice learning the words, color coding the vowels *a* and *e,* and spelling the two words using letter blocks.

This same sequencing idea can be applied to teaching letter sounds. For example, when deciding on the order in which to teach the sounds, consider separating letters that look and sound the same, such as *b* and *d, m* and *n,* and *p* and *b.* The careful sequencing of instruction can also be applied to teaching higher level content. For example, when Mr. Roosevelt, a high school chemistry teacher, taught the chemical elements, he separated those symbols that look and/or sound similar, such as bromine (Br) and rubidium (Rb), and silicon (Si) and strontium (Sr). Knowledge of how sequencing can affect learning can help you recognize the need to differentiate instruction. For example, Ms. Mann, unlike Mr. Roosevelt, was unable to change the order in which she taught the chemical elements without drastically modifying her chemistry text. When she noticed that bromine and rubidium were taught closely together, she allowed more time for students to practice in their study groups before introducing a new element.

fyi

Student errors and misconceptions also stem from the over- or undergeneralization of concepts. Careful selection and sequencing of a range of examples can help prevent these kinds of errors.

DIMENSIONS OF
diversity

Listening is the weakest academic language skill for English-language learners. Khisty (2002, p. 34) suggests the following strategies when teaching math to Latino students: (1) write words on an overhead projector or on the board as they are spoken or point to words in a prepared written text as they are delivered; (2) always contextualize instruction through the use of models, real objects, drawings, and other visual aids; and (3) have students act out problems or concepts.

INCLUDE

www.resources

The ProQuest K–12 website, at www.proquestk12.com, provides lesson plans that include modifications for students with special needs.

Article Homework Exercise

Go to the Homework and Exercises section in Chapter 9 of MyEducationLab to learn about strategies for students who struggle with math word problems

Deciding the Rate of Introduction of New Skills

Students sometimes have difficulty learning skills when they are introduced at too fast a rate. For example, Mr. Henry was teaching his ninth-grade English students how to proofread rough drafts of their writing for errors in using capital letters and punctuation marks. He reviewed the rules for using capital letters, periods, commas, question marks, and exclamation points. Next, he had students take out their most recent writing samples from their portfolios to look for capitalization and punctuation errors. Carmine found that he had left out capital letters at the beginning of two sentences, but he did not find any of the punctuation errors he had made. He missed them because Mr. Henry had taught his students to proofread their papers for capital letters and punctuation marks simultaneously. A better pace would have been first to work on proofreading for capitalization errors and then to add one punctuation mark at a time (first periods, then commas, followed by question marks, and then exclamation points).

In another example of the **rate of skill introduction,** Ms. Stevens was working on reading comprehension with her students. She introduced three new comprehension strategies at once: detecting the sequence, determining cause and effect, and making predictions. However, when applying the INCLUDE strategy, she recognized that Carlos, a student with a mild intellectual disability, learned best when he was taught one strategy at a time. Ms. Stevens accommodated Carlos by forming a group with three other students who, like Carlos, would benefit from learning these comprehension strategies one by one before being asked to carry them out simultaneously. As an additional accommodation, she temporarily removed cause-and-effect and prediction questions from these students' written comprehension exercises until they had been taught these strategies directly in their small group. When Mr. Wallace, the special education teacher, came to co-teach, he worked with these students on detecting the story sequence. Learn more about working with special education teachers in the Working Together.

These examples demonstrate an important principle about introducing new skills to students with special needs: New skills should be introduced in small steps and at a rate slow enough to ensure mastery prior to the introduction of more new skills. Furthermore, you may want to prioritize skills and even postpone some, as Ms. Stevens did. Many commercially produced materials introduce skills at a rate that is too fast for students with special needs. As just illustrated, a common accommodation is to slow down the rate of skill introduction and provide more practice. Other students in the class, including those with no formally identified special needs, often benefit from such accommodations as well. If a student happens to be the only one having a problem, you can seek additional support from special needs staff, paraprofessionals, peers, and/or parent volunteers.

Given the current atmosphere of accountability in U.S. schools, it is often hard for teachers to slow down the rate at which they introduce new information for fear they will be unable to cover all the material that will appear on high-stakes tests. Although covering content efficiently is an important consideration, learning is usually best served when teachers carefully construct a foundation of skills and concepts based on student performance, rather than the school calendar.

Slowing down the rate of skills introduced is an accommodation in the way curriculum is presented, but it is not the same thing as reducing the amount of curriculum to be learned. You need to be careful not to reduce the expectations for your students with special needs who are expected to meet the goals of the general education curriculum. Otherwise, they will have difficulty meeting state standards. However, for your students with moderate to severe intellectual disabilities, it may be appropriate to make an instructional modification by decreasing the amount of curriculum. For example, Ms. Evers modified Robin's curriculum by shortening her spelling lists from 15 to 3 words and selecting only high-frequency words specified on her IEP.

Working TOGETHER

Asking for Help

Ms. Gabriel is starting her first year as a high school history teacher. She just found out that she will have four students with learning disabilities included in her fifth-period U.S. history class. The special education teacher, Mr. Colbert, left the students' IEPs in her mailbox with a brief note asking her to look them over to see what kinds of accommodations she is required to make in her teaching. The IEPs state that she is supposed to give students their tests orally, modify their homework assignments, and adapt the textbook.

Ms. Gabriel is confused. In the first place, she is unsure exactly what an *accommodation* is. Second, how is she supposed to give tests orally to these students and still give the rest of the students written tests? Also, she doesn't know what the IEP means by *modifying* homework and *adapting* the text. She's particularly worried about homework because she knows students won't like it if they know that other students are doing less homework. Ms. Gabriel feels that Mr. Colbert should have met with her to explain more clearly what she needed to do. Still, she is new to the school and is afraid to admit she doesn't know what to do. Mr. Colbert is also the wrestling coach, and Ms. Gabriel doesn't feel very comfortable communicating with him.

If you were Ms. Gabriel, what would you do?

- Including students with special needs is a team effort. In order for the team to be effective, all of the team members need to be clear about student goals and faculty responsibility for helping meet those goals. Ms. Gabriel is correct that a meeting needs to be called to clarify what she needs to do with the students.

- In calling the meeting, Ms. Gabriel should set a positive tone for problem solving. Rather than complain that a meeting should have been called, Ms. Gabriel should write a note to Mr. Colbert explaining that she is excited about the challenge of working with these students in her class, has some questions as to how she can best meet their needs, and would like to meet briefly with him about it.

- At the meeting, Ms. Gabriel must be careful to not put Mr. Colbert on the defensive. One way to put him at ease right away would be to establish empathy. Ms. Gabriel can do that by recognizing how busy he is and thanking him for taking the time to meet with her.

- Even though Ms. Gabriel may not feel comfortable interacting with a coach, she needs to be careful to react to his ideas, not his personality. She needs to realize that good ideas can come from persons whose personalities don't match hers.

- Ms. Gabriel can further establish good communication with Mr. Colbert by explaining her questions using non-evaluative language. For example, rather than address the subject by saying that she doesn't see how she can give tests two different ways or modify homework without being unfair to the other students, she should ask Mr. Colbert for his ideas about how to carry out these accommodations. For example, for the problem with homework, she could ask "What specific homework accommodations do these students need? Do the other students ever complain when you make homework accommodations for students with disabilities? What do you say to them?"

- The need to keep her interaction with Mr. Colbert positive and productive should not compromise the equally important need for Ms. Gabriel to attain the appropriate supports for her included students with special needs. An effective team player is assertive yet also treats colleagues with respect.

Providing Direct Instruction and Opportunities for Practice and Review

Students with special needs may require more direct instruction and review if they are to acquire basic academic skills. Consider the following example. Youn is in Ms. Howard's spelling class. On Monday, Ms. Howard gave students a pretest on the 15 new words for the week. On Tuesday, the students were required to use each word in a sentence. On Wednesday, the teacher scrambled up the letters in all the words and had the students put them in the correct order. On Thursday, students answered 15 fill-in-the-blank questions,

Video Homework Exercise

Go to the Homework and Exercises section in Chapter 9 of MyEducationLab to watch a teacher and students engaged in direct instruction.

Direct instruction may help Abdul, whom you read about at the beginning of the chapter. His teacher, Ms. Diaz, could teach the skill of writing percentages for fractions directly by listing the steps in solving such problems on the board; having students say all the steps; solving several sample problems for students by following the listed steps; leading students through solving similar problems using the steps until they are able to do them independently; and assigning problems for students to do independently, reminding them to follow the steps listed on the board.

*R*esearch Note

Research shows that many students with learning disabilities need direct instruction in letter sounds in order to eventually learn to identify words systematically (Ehri, 2004).

each of which required one of the new spelling words. On Friday, Youn failed her spelling test even though she had successfully completed all the spelling activities for that week. Youn did poorly on her spelling test because the daily spelling activities did not provide her with enough direct instruction and practice on the spelling words. Although activities such as using spelling words in sentences are valuable in the right context, they do not provide practice on the primary objective of this particular lesson, which is spelling all 15 words correctly from dictation. One way to accommodate Youn individually would be to have a peer tutor give her a daily dictation test on all 15 words; have Youn write each missed word three times, saying each letter in the word as she writes; and then retest her on all 15 words again.

This example demonstrates another problem that students with special needs have when learning basic skills: retention. Melissa had mastered addition facts to 10 as measured by a probe test in October, but when she was given the same test in January, she got only half of the facts correct. Similarly, Thomas, in his world history class, could state the major causes of World War I in November, but he could not remember them when asked to compare them to the causes of World War II in February. A common way to differentiate instruction for such students is to schedule more review for them. This review should be more frequent following your initial presentation of the material and then can become less frequent as learning is established. For example, instead of waiting until January to review addition facts, Melissa's teacher could first provide review weekly, then every other week, and then every month. Thomas's history teacher could periodically review key concepts and information that Thomas may need to apply later, either through homework, a learning center activity, an instructional game or contest, or an activity in a co-taught class. If Thomas and Melissa were the only ones in their classes in need of review, their teachers could accommodate them individually by giving them extra help before school or while the rest of the class was working independently.

A related concern is that indirect instructional approaches may be appropriate for some students but may need to be supplemented for others. For example, Felix and Bill were learning to read in Ms. Farrell's class. Neither boy had mastered the *ch* sound (as in *chin*). On Monday, Felix came across the word *chair* in a trade book he was reading. His teacher pronounced the word and stated, "When *c* and *h* are together in a word, they usually say *ch*." The next day, Felix came to the word *chip* in his book, and he figured it out, remembering what Ms. Farrell had told him the day before. For Felix, one example in

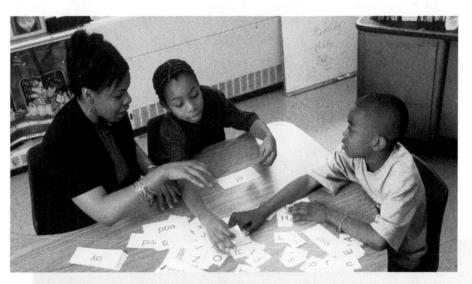

Some students need additional instruction and practice when they are learning new skills. What prerequisite concepts and skills might you teach for this reading assignment? What kinds of additional practice might you provide?

his book and a brief teacher explanation were enough for learning to occur. On Monday, Bill also came across a *ch* word, and he too was told what the word was and what sound *c* and *h* make when they come together in a word. Unlike Felix, however, when Bill came across another *ch* word the next day, he could not remember the sound of these letters. Having the teacher tell him just once the sound *ch* made was not enough. Bill required more direct instruction and practice than Felix, such as that provided in the activity shown in Table 9.1.

This discussion of Felix and Bill raises an important issue: General education teachers need to know more than one approach to meet the needs of individual students. Felix can learn sounds with minimal instruction while reading books; Bill cannot. Bill's teacher may need to accommodate Bill and maybe other students in the class by providing them with some direct instruction on letter–sound correspondence. This direct instruction can involve having students both say and write their sounds. Learn more about how to provide differentiated instruction in reading in the following Professional Edge.

Another example reinforces the idea that some of your students with special needs may need more direct instruction and practice. Mr. Diaz was teaching his high school

DIMENSIONS OF

diversity

In Native American cultures, children learn new skills by first observing them and then doing them. Native American students can benefit from direct teaching approaches that first stress modeling or demonstrating skills. You can make demonstrations particularly effective for your Native American students by showing them what the final product looks like before the demonstration (Sparks, 2000).

Analyze and Reflect

Under what circumstances would you accommodate individual students by changing how you teach the entire class? When would accommodating students be more appropriately carried out individually or in small groups?

Video Homework Exercise

Go to the Homework and Exercises section in Chapter 9 of MyEducationLab to watch a teacher explain how she prepares and supports her students as they plan and write a biography.

TABLE 9.1

Direct Instruction of *ch* Sound

Teacher	Student
I. Teach directly the *ch* sound in isolation.	
Teacher writes on the board: *ch, or, ee, ch, th, sh, ch,* and *ing.*	
1. Teacher models by saying the sound of the new letter combination and tests by having the students pronounce it. Teacher points to *ch.* "These letters usually say *ch.* What sound?"	"*ch*"
2. Teacher alternates between the new combination and other combinations. Teacher points to a letter combination, pauses 2 seconds, and asks, "What sound?"	Say the combination sound
3. Teacher calls on several individual students to identify one or more letter combinations.	
II. Teach directly the *ch* sound in words.	
Teacher writes on the board: *chin, chair, chip, boot, beam, chomp, stain, chum, moon,* and *chat.*	
1. a. Students identify the sound of the letter combination in *chin,* then read the word. Teacher points under the combination letters and asks, "What sound?"	"*ch*"
b. Teacher points to left of word. "What word?"	"*chin*"
c. Teacher repeats step 1(a–b) with remaining words.	
2. a. Students reread the list without first identifying the sound of the letter combination. Teacher points to *chin,* pauses 2 seconds, and asks, "What word?"	"*chin*"
b. Teacher repeats step 2(a) with remaining words.	
3. Teacher calls on individual students to read one or more words.	

Source: Adapted from *Direct Instruction Reading* (4th ed.), by D. Carnine, J. Silbert, and E. J. Kame'enui, and S. G. Tarver, 2004, Upper Saddle River, NJ: Merrill/Prentice Hall. Copyright © 2004. Reprinted with the permission of Prentice-Hall, Inc., Upper Saddle River, NJ.

Providing Differentiated Instruction in Reading Using a Multitiered Model

The idea behind differentiated instruction is that a variety of teaching and learning strategies are necessary to meet the range of needs evident in any given classroom. Nowhere is the need for differentiated instruction more evident than in beginning reading. Research tells us that while about 20 to 30 percent of students acquire reading skills readily without the need for extra support, another 20 to 30 percent require some additional support, and about 30 percent require intensive support if they are to learn to read (Lyon, 1998).

Bursuck and colleagues (2004) implemented a multitiered model of differentiated beginning reading instruction in grades K–3 in three low-performing urban schools. The model had originally been implemented successfully in two rural schools (Dickson & Bursuck, 1999, 2003). The purpose of the multitiered model was to provide varying levels of student support depending on student need. The model is shown in Figure 9.2.

Tier 1 was the standard general education reading program but with some teaching strategies added because of the high percentage of students in the three schools who were struggling to learn to read. These enhancements included many of the teaching methods described in this chapter such as careful example selection, a gradual rate of introducing new skills, direct teacher instruction, and the provision of many opportunities for practice and review. The general education reading program was also adapted to make the teaching of phonics more explicit and systematic, a key recommendation by the National Reading Panel (2000).

The performance of students in Tier 1 was continually monitored using curriculum-based measures of key literacy skills such as phonemic awareness, letter sounds, word identification, passage-reading fluency, and reading comprehension. Students who were not acquiring key literacy skills according to the assessments continued to receive instruction in Tier 1 but were provided with Tier 2 instruction as well. It consisted of extra daily practice and fluency building

on skills covered in the classroom reading series using small, same-skill groups of 2–8 students and delivered by the classroom teacher or a trained paraprofessional. The progress of Tier 2 students continued to be regularly monitored. If these students continued to show problems acquiring beginning reading skills, they moved to more intensive instruction in Tier 3.

Tier 3 was an intensive alternative reading program designed for at-risk readers called *Reading Mastery* (Engelmann & Bruner, 2003). The *Reading Mastery* curriculum is characterized by a carefully designed instructional sequence as well as the extensive use of scaffolding to support student learning. Tier 3 instruction was carried out in small groups by either a Chapter I or special education teacher and was conducted when the rest of the students were involved in word-reading activities that were too difficult for them. Tier 3 students still participated in many of the general education reading activities, but care was taken to coordinate those activities with the students' Tier 3 reading program.

Similar to other research (O'Connor, 2000; Torgesen, 2000), this study found that approximately 5 percent of the students continued to struggle to acquire beginning reading skills, even with Tier 3 instruction. These students moved to Tier 4.

Tier 4 instruction was provided by a special education teacher and was characterized by smaller instructional groups (no more than three students per group), a slower rate of skill introduction, and more extensive scaffolds or supports, such as in-depth auditory discrimination training (Lindamood & Lindamood, 1998).

The results showed that the overall performance of the three schools on the state reading test in grade 3 exceeded levels of performance in the same schools before the model was implemented (Bursuck, Damer, & Dickson, 2005). Also of interest was that children receiving help in Tiers 2 and 3 had

Article Homework Exercise

Go to the Homework and Exercises section in Chapter 9 of MyEducationLab to learn how to help older students who struggle because they may lack basic reading skills.

English students how to write a persuasive essay, including how to develop a thesis, add supporting details, reject counterarguments, and end with a conclusion. He described the steps in writing a persuasive essay while showing students an example of a well-written persuasive essay. He then asked the students to write a one-page persuasive essay for homework. Brenda handed in her essay the next day; although her paper showed some potential, her thesis lacked clarity, her details were sketchy, and she forgot to reject possible counterarguments. Brenda needed more instruction and guided attitudes toward reading that were as positive as their Tier 1 classmates, minorities were not overrepresented in Tiers 2 and 3, and referrals to special education decreased in all three schools (Bursuck & Damer, 2007). (For an example of multitiered instruction in math, see Fuchs et al., 2006.)

Multitiered instruction is being used in many schools to implement the response to intervention (RtI) model of identifying students with learning disabilities that you have read about in previous chapters. Why do you think this is so?

FIGURE *9.2*

Multitiered Model of Differentiated Reading Instruction

Tier 1
Grade-Level Instruction with Added Strategies

Tier 2
Boosters for Poor Responders to Tier 1

Tier 3
Intensive Alternative Program for Poor Responders to Tiers 1 and 2

Tier 4
Special Education

practice on how to write a persuasive essay than Mr. Diaz had provided. He could have applied the INCLUDE strategy, anticipated Brenda's problems, and provided guided practice by writing essays with the class until even the lower performers such as Brenda seemed comfortable performing the task. He could also have had the students write a persuasive essay independently in class so that he could monitor their performance and accommodate individual students using corrective feedback and more instruction if necessary.

Finally, it is important to remember that practice is most effective when it *follows* direct instruction; practice is never an adequate substitute for direct instruction. For example, Mr. Hanesworth designed a board game in which students get to move ahead if they can answer a division fact problem. The problem is that five students in his class still do not understand the concept of division. For them, the board game practice activity is likely to result in failure. Mr. Hanesworth can accommodate these learners in a small group by providing additional instruction on division for them while allowing the rest of the class to play the board game independently. Of course, later on, Mr. Hanesworth can reward the hard work of the small group by allowing them to practice a skill they know using a game-like format.

Clearly, you may need to differentiate instruction to enable students with special needs to acquire basic skills. An example of how to differentiate basic skills instruction using INCLUDE is presented in the Case in Practice. In addition, the Technology Notes introduces ways to use technology to assist students with special needs with their writing. Students may also need accommodations when subject-area content is presented, the primary teaching focus as students move into the upper grades.

Case in Practice   INCLUDE

Applying INCLUDE to a Basic Skills Lesson

Ms. Dettman loves to look on the Internet for what she calls "teacher-tested" lesson plans. She found a lesson yesterday on the topic of math story problems (Bowen, n.d.), an area in which her students often struggle and in which she is always looking for something different to do. The teacher who used this technique claimed that it had had a positive impact on her class's performance last year on the state's high-stakes test in math. Ms. Dettman decided to try it.

In this lesson, the teacher posts a daily story problem on tagboard. The skill targeted (for example, division, fractions) varies from day to day. The problem is read aloud first thing in the morning and students have until lunchtime to solve it. The children keep a special file folder containing an answer sheet for the week's problems. Children are required to show their work. After lunch, three or four students go to the board to solve the problem. They talk aloud about how they solved the problem. Each child has an incentive chart posted in class. Every day, two students collect and score papers and a sticker is awarded for correct answers. Students receive a prize when they reach five stickers, and then a new chart is posted.

Ms. Dettman has a group of four students in class who have trouble in math; three of these students have learning disabilities in both reading and math. Because the curricular goals for these students are the same as those of everyone

else in the class, instructional modifications are not required. Ms. Dettman reviewed the demands of this activity to see whether any accommodations were needed. She identified the following seven demands:

1. Read the problem.
2. Identify the operation needed to solve the problem (for example, add, subtract).
3. Write a number sentence.
4. Convert the number sentence to a computation problem.
5. Solve the computation problem.
6. Label the answer.
7. Check work.

Next, Ms. Dettman thought about areas where she might need to make accommodations. She considered the students' preskills. Three of the students have reading problems, but the fact that the story problems would be read out loud eliminated the need for an accommodation such as a bypass strategy. However, Ms. Dettman thought the students would have trouble translating the story problems into a sentence; they all have reading comprehension problems and had previously struggled to pick the correct operation when they solved story

How Can You Make Accommodations for Students with Special Needs When Teaching Subject-Area Content?

The instruction of academic content includes areas such as history and science. This instruction mainly involves the use of textbooks and lecture–discussion formats, but it also can include other activities, such as videos, films, hands-on activities, and cooperative learning. Although content-area instruction generally is associated with instruction in secondary schools, the information presented here is relevant for elementary teachers as well.

In this section, you learn how you can differentiate instruction to help students with special needs learn subject-area content. Strategies for making accommodations are stressed for activating background knowledge, organizing content, and teaching terms and concepts. As with basic skills, you can provide accommodations for students with special

Info Sheet Homework Exercise

Go to the Homework and Exercises section in Chapter 9 of MyEducationLab to learn how technology can help struggling readers learn subject-area content.

problems in class. The four students also don't know their math facts, and their computational accuracy is inconsistent, even though they understand the concepts behind the four basic operations. Computation could be a definite problem as well. None of the students struggle with handwriting, so the writing demands of solving the word problem would not be problematic. In addition, one student is artistically inclined, a strength that Ms. Dettman planned to build on.

Ms. Dettman was concerned about the fact that different types of story problems were selected for the activity each day in the lesson plan. She thought that this variety might confuse the four students who seem to work best when new problem types are added gradually as others are learned. Ms. Dettman was also concerned that student modeling of problem solving at the board by thinking out loud was a great idea, but she felt the students with problems in math might not benefit from it without more careful structuring.

Ms. Dettman decided to make the following accommodations for the four students. Although she would continue to work with them on improving the accuracy of their math computation skills, for this activity she would allow them to bypass their current difficulties in this area by letting them use calculators.

Ms. Dettman also decided to provide the students with a visual diagram to guide them through the problem-solving steps, along with small-group guided practice to ensure they used the strategy appropriately. Part of that small-group guided practice would include teacher and student think-alouds to make the problem-solving steps more conspicuous for the students. Also, when students came to the board to solve problems out loud in the large group, bonus points would be awarded to those students paying careful attention, particularly to the think-aloud part. Ms. Dettman would use only story problems that the students were capable of solving independently. That way, they would get needed independent practice as well as a realistic opportunity to earn stickers and cash them in for a prize at the end of the week.

Finally, Ms. Dettman would appoint the student with artistic talent to be the class artist. She would come to the board and draw a picture representing the problem.

REFLECTIONS

Why do you think Ms. Dettman made instructional *accommodations* for the four struggling students rather than instructional *modifications?* How did Ms. Dettman use the INCLUDE strategy to come up with instructional accommodations for those students? How effective and feasible are these accommodations? What would you do differently if you were the teacher?

Relating subject-area content to students' background knowledge makes material more relevant for students. It also motivates students to draw on their own background knowledge when they encounter new information, thereby helping them assume responsibility for their own learning (Gersten, Baker, & Marks, 1998).

needs by changing how you teach the entire class or by making individualized accommodations either one to one or in small groups. Strategies for teaching science to English-language learners (ELLs) are described in the Special Emphasis On . . . .

Activating Background Knowledge

The amount of background knowledge students have can greatly influence whether they can read subject matter with understanding. To illustrate, read this list of words:

are	making	between
only	consists	often
continuously	vary	corresponding
one	curve	points
draws	relation	variation
set	graph	table
if	values	isolated
variables	known	

TECHNOLOGY NOTES

Using Web-Based Programs to Improve Student Writing Performance

As you learned in Chapter 7, students with disabilities face many challenges with writing (Graham, 2006). Tele-Web (Technology-Enhanced Learning Environments on the Web) is an Internet-based software program that can help students with disabilities overcome these problems. Tele-Web helps students write expository text that is well organized; contains an introduction, body paragraphs, and a conclusion; and meets the knowledge demands of the reader (Englert, Zhao, Dunsmore, Collings, & Wolberg, 2007). Tele-Web uses two devices to support student writing. First, mapping tools are used to help students generate ideas and details for their papers. An example of one of these mapping tools, the *concept map*, is shown in Figure 9.3 (page 332). Note how in this example, the concept map prompts students to organize their ideas for a paper about pets around six major topics, including what kind of pet it is, what it looks like, what it eats, what it does, how to care for it, and why it makes a good pet. Students are taught to move their ideas, or supporting details, to their respective boxed categories using a click-and-drag feature that is also part of Tele-Web.

The second device is a template known as the *supported report*. The supported report guides students through the writing process using a series of prompts. An example supported report is shown in Figure 9.4 (page 333). First, a printed reminder of the teacher's oral instructions

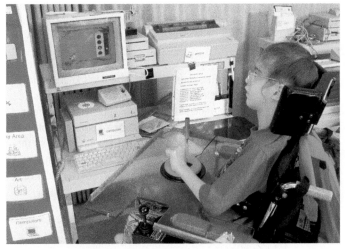

How might speech-synthesis and word-prediction programs help this student with her journal entries? What other types of assistive technology might help her with her writing?

appears at the top of the screen. To help students stage their ideas, *Title* and *Introduction to Paper* boxes appear. Next, a *Topic Sentence Box* prompts students to generate a topic sentence for their first paragraph. Immediately following the topic sentence box is a *Supporting Details Box* used to cue students to choose details that support their topic sentence. Each time students click to add a paragraph, new topic sentence and paragraph boxes appear. Finally, a *Concluding Sentence Box* is provided near the bottom of the computer screen prompting students to conclude their papers.

Were you able to read all of them? Do you know the meanings of all these words? Now read the following passage:

> If the known relation between the variables consists of a table of corresponding values, the graph consists only of the corresponding set of isolated points. If the variables are known to vary continuously, one often draws a curve to show the variation. (From Michaelson, 1945, as cited in Lavoie, 1991)

Chances are, if you were asked to summarize what you just read, you would be unable to do so despite the fact that you probably answered yes when asked whether you could read and understand all the words individually. You may lack the background knowledge necessary to understand this very technical paragraph. The knowledge students bring to a content-area lesson is often as important for understanding as the quality of the textbook or instructional presentation (Marzano, 2004; Pressley, 2000). For students to understand content material, they need to relate it to information they already know.

Unfortunately, teachers often fail to consider background information. Students with disabilities and students who are at risk may have two problems with background

Research Note

Studies of English-language learners show that making connections with students' culture, background, and experiences can lead to high levels of student engagement in instruction (Foorman et al., 2004).

In addition to these features, TELE-Web uses a pop-up window to prompt students to evaluate their writing through a series of self-questions, as shown in Figure 9.4. Example questions include Did I tell what the pet looks like? Did I use a topic sentence? Did I use concluding sentences? The questions disappear when students return to composing their papers, fostering independence by providing only temporary support.

TELE-Web has three additional features that allow students to access online support: (1) a spell checker that matches words in the paper against an online dictionary; (2) a text-to-speech function that allows the computer to read back student texts; and (3) an online submission feature through which teachers provide feedback and students revise and publish their papers.

Englert et al. (2007) tested TELE-Web against a paper-and-pencil approach to teaching writing that offered similar supports but without the use of computers. The papers of students with disabilities who used TELE-Web had a greater range of information about their writing topics and were better organized, showing a clear relationship among the introduction, body, and conclusion.

Shown below is a list of other Internet sources for software that can help students with writing assignments (Gillette, 2006):

Software Programs That Can Read Digitized Text

Write OutLoud (Don Johnston Incorporated)
www.donjohnston.com
Read OutLoud (Don Johnston Incorporated)
www.donjohnston.com
Kurzweil 3000 (Kurzweil Educational Systems)
www.kurzweiledu.com

Read & Write Gold
www.texthelp.com

Software Programs That Assist Students with Planning Compositions

Draft Builder (Don Johnston Incorporated)
www.donjohnston.com
Inspiration (Inspiration)
www.inspiration.com/store/main/index.cfm

Talking Word Processors

IntelliTalk III (IntelliTools) Intellitools
www.intellitools.com
Word 2003 (Microsoft)
www.microsoft.com/office/word/produinfo/default.mspx

Voice Recognition Software

Scansoft Dragon Naturally Speaking
www.nuance.com/naturallyspeaking/standard
Word 2003 (Microsoft)
www.microsoft.com/office/word/prodinfo/default.mspx

Word Prediction Software

Co:Writer (Don Johnston Incorporated)
www.donjohnston.com
Read & Write Gold
www.texthelp.com

FIGURE 9.3
TELE-Web Concept Map

"Concept Map 03/05/2004 "

Instructions: Many people own pets, but some people do not have a pet. Pick an animal and map out information for someone who does not know anything about that pet. Think about what you know. Include details under each category. Then add more ideas until you write everything you know about the pet.

Read Instructions

What is the pet | What it looks like | What it eats

How to care for the pet | Why it makes a good pet

Add Idea | Save | Preview

Clear all Ideas

HAND-IN

Prompts

- Did I tell : [Read]
- 1. What is the pet [Read]
- 2. What it looks like [Read]
- 3. What it eats [Read]
- 4. What it does [Read]
- 5. How to care for the pet [Read]
- 6. Why it makes a good pet [Read]

Source: From "Scaffolding the writing of students with disabilities through procedural facilitation: Using an Internet-based technology to improve performance," by C. S. Englort, Z. Yang, K. Dunsmore, N. Collings, and K. Wolberg, 2007, *Learning Disability Quarterly*, 30(1), pp. 9–29.

FIGURE 9.4

TELE-Web Supported Writing

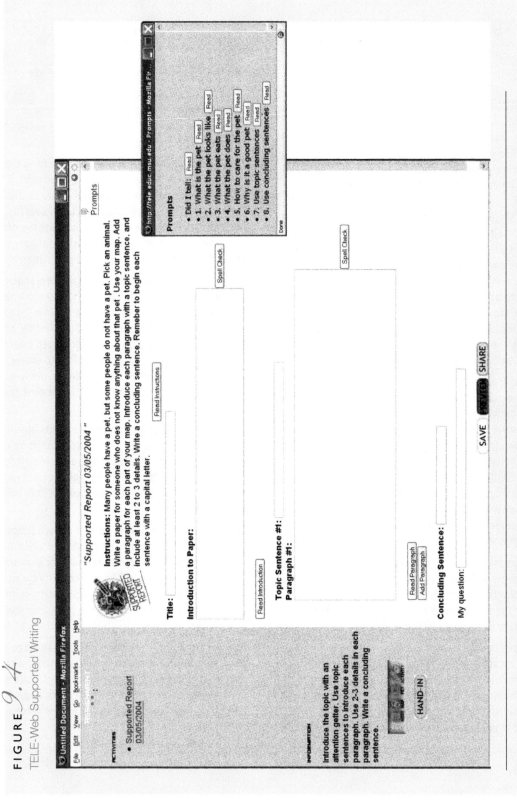

Source: From "Scaffolding the writing of students with disabilities through procedural facilitation: Using an Internet-based technology to improve performance," by C. S. Englort, Z. Yang, K. Dunsmore, N. Collings, and K. Wolberg, 2007, *Learning Disability Quarterly, 30*(1), pp. 9–29.

Strategies for Teaching Science to English-Language Learners

You learned in Chapter 8 that the racial, cultural, and linguistic diversity of U.S. classrooms has been increasing and will continue to do so. English-language learners (ELLs), or students for whom English is not their primary language, are an increasingly large proportion of this group. Unfortunately, ELLs struggle in school (Snow & Biancarosa, 2003). Nowhere is this fact more evident than in science, where information about teaching ELLs can be hard to find (Watson, 2004).

While ELLs share the characteristic of having limited English proficiency, it is important to realize that they are a diverse group. ELLs come to your science classroom with different levels of background knowledge, literacy in their native language, family involvement in their education, intellectual ability, and motivation to do well in school, to name a few areas. All of these factors, in addition to English proficiency, should be considered when differentiating ELLs' science instruction using these strategies (Short & Echevarria, 2004/2005; Watson, 2004):

- For students in your class who speak little or no English, label parts of your classroom and lab equipment with both English names and names from the students' native language. Using Spanish, for example, the labels would be *science book/ciencia libro*. Besides helping to initiate communication with your ELLs, labeling in English and another language also demonstrates to English-speaking students the difficulties students face when learning a new language. Requiring all of your students to learn both names effectively reinforces this idea.

- Place less emphasis on the traditional approach of having students read the textbook prior to engaging in a laboratory activity. Instead, start with the laboratory experience. The concreteness of laboratory experiences makes the text more comprehensible.

- Whenever possible, show objects, draw pictures, or act out the meanings of key terms. For example, when teaching the concept of *scientific classification*, one teacher demonstrated the concept by having students take off their left shoes and put them in a pile in the front of the room. The students classified the shoes

in different ways, such as shoes that lace, slip on, and buckle.

- Repeat instructions, actions, and demonstrations as needed, speaking slowly and using simple sentence structure whenever possible.

- Demonstrate procedures and provide clarifying diagrams and illustrations before students begin lab work. For example, before students begin a lab exercise, provide them with a written procedural guide, go over key terms by placing them on the board, demonstrate the procedures, and actively monitor students' performance by circulating among them as they are completing the lab.

- Assign lab partners to ELLs. The lab partners should be strong in science and willing to work with students who are ELLs. Placing two ELLs together in a group along with one English speaker is also effective, particularly if one of the ELLs is more advanced than the other in English skills. Encouraging ELLs to express their thoughts to a partner before reporting to the whole class promotes language learning and the confidence to speak out in class.

- If appropriate, enlist the support of parents in building students' background knowledge about topics before they are introduced in class. Background knowledge provided in students' native language allows them to better follow what is discussed, even if they don't know every word.

- Schedule time for review at the end of each lesson, pointing out key concepts and vocabulary while making connections to lesson objectives and state standards. This is essential, because ELLs may concentrate so intently on processing language during instruction that they are unable to identify the most important information expressed.

- Give feedback to your students on their language use in class. For example, model for your students how scientists talk about their experimental findings. Have students try to use the language of scientists when orally presenting their lab reports, and give them feedback on their performance.

knowledge: They may simply lack the necessary knowledge, or they may know the information but be unable to recall it or relate it to the new information being presented.

● **Using the Prep Strategy**   One teaching strategy for determining how much knowledge students already have about a topic so that you can decide how much background information to present in class prior to a reading assignment is called the **PReP (PreReading Plan) strategy** (Langer, 1984). The PReP strategy has three major steps:

1. *Preview the text or lesson, and choose two to three important concepts.* For example, for a science lesson, Mr. Amin chose the concept of photosynthesis and the keywords *cycle* and *oxygen.*

2. *Conduct a brainstorming session with students.* This process involves three phases. In Phase 1, students tell you what comes to mind when they hear the concept. This gives you a first glance at how much they already know about the topic. In Phase 2, students tell you what made them think of their responses in Phase 1. This information can help you judge the depth of and/or basis for their responses, and it also provides a springboard for students to refine their responses in Phase 3. In Mr. Amin's class, he discovered in Phases 1 and 2 that two of the students mistakenly thought that photosynthesis had to do with photography because of the presence of *photo* in the word. This error provided an opportunity to build on students' knowledge. Mr. Amin explained that *photo* means light and that in photography, a camera takes in light and combines it with certain chemicals on film to make pictures. He then said that plants take in light too, and when the light combines with chemicals in the plant, carbohydrates and oxygen are made. This process is called *photosynthesis.* In this way, Mr. Amin used what the students already knew to teach them a concept they did not know. In Phase 3, students can add to their responses based on the discussion in Phase 2.

3. *Evaluate student responses to determine the depth of their prior knowledge of the topic.* During this step, you can decide whether students are ready to read the text and/or listen to a lecture on photosynthesis or whether they first need more information. Determining the needs of your students with respect to the demands of your instruction is an important part of INCLUDE. In Mr. Amin's class, two students continued to have trouble understanding that photosynthesis was something plants did with light to make carbohydrates and oxygen. They needed more information before they were ready to read the chapter. Mr. Amin accommodated these students by showing them a video illustration of photosynthesis including concrete examples that weren't necessary to use with the rest of the class.

● **Preparing Anticipation Guides**   Anticipation guides can help you activate student knowledge about a particular topic and construct bridges to new information by encouraging students to make predictions (Readence, Moore, & Rickelman, 2000; Vacca & Vacca, 2004). **Anticipation guides** consist of a series of statements, some of which may not be true, related to the material that students are about to read (Burns, Roe, & Ross, 2001). Before teaching, students read these statements that either challenge or support ideas they may already have about the subject. This process catches their interest and gives them a reason for listening and reading. Providing questions or statements prior to reading also aids comprehension for all students, including those with special needs.

For example, Ms. Henry constructed an anticipation guide prior to teaching a unit on the nervous system. Her anticipation guide included the following statements:

■ A person cannot function without the nervous system.
■ The nervous system helps us study and learn about new things.
■ There are gaps between the nerve cells in our bodies.
■ Nerve cells do different jobs in the body.
■ The central nervous system is only one part of the nervous system.

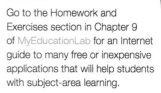

www.**resources**

Education World, at www .education-world.com, provides a searchable database of more than 50,000 sites related to curriculum ideas. Many of the resources are geared especially to students with exceptionalities.

Info Sheet Homework Exercise

Go to the Homework and Exercises section in Chapter 9 of MyEducationLab for an Internet guide to many free or inexpensive applications that will help students with subject-area learning.

INCLUDE

Article Homework
Exercise

Go to the Homework and
Exercises section in Chapter 9
of MyEducationLab to read about
strategies that can be incorporated
into content teaching that will help
struggling readers.

- Our brains do not control our reflexes.
- Persons cannot hold their breath until they die.
- Some people can swim without thinking about it.

When using the anticipation guide, Ms. Henry needed to make an accommodation for several of her students with reading problems. After distributing the guide, she met with these students in a small group and read each item out loud, clarifying terms such as *central nervous system, reflexes,* and *nerve cells.* Ms. Henry also accommodated students with reading problems by highlighting important ideas from the selection, dividing the text into smaller sections, having these students complete the anticipation guide with peer buddies, and giving students a chance to read the text at home before discussing it in school (Kozen, Murray, & Windell, 2006).

● **Providing Planning Think Sheets** Activating background information and building bridges to current knowledge is also of concern to teachers when asking students to write. Some researchers recommend **planning think sheets** to help writers focus on background information as well as on the audience and purpose of a paper (Englert et al., 1988). For audience, students are asked to consider who will read the paper. For purpose, students clarify why they are writing the paper (for example, to tell a story, to convey information, or to persuade someone). Finally, students activate background knowledge and organize that knowledge by asking themselves questions such as What do I know about the topic? and How can I group or label my facts? (Englert et al., 1988). A planning think sheet for a paper assignment might contain write-on lines for students to answer the following questions (Raphael, Kirschner, & Englert, 1986):

- What is my topic?
- Why do I want to write on this topic?
- What are two things I already know that will make it easy to write this paper?
- Who will read my paper?
- Why will the reader be interested in this topic?

Students with special needs may need more teacher modeling and guided practice before being able to complete think sheets independently. You can deliver these accommodations using a small teacher-led group. You can further differentiate instruction and motivate students by providing a range of paper topics that students can choose from. Students can also be permitted to respond orally to the questions.

Organizing Content

Research shows that many students, including students with special needs, have difficulty understanding important ideas and their interrelationships in content areas such as social studies and science (Kame'enui, Carnine, Dixon, Simmons, & Coyne, 2002; Lawton, 1995). These students can benefit from the use of supports or scaffolds that help them identify and understand important information. As we discussed in Chapter 5, one form of support is to organize the curriculum according to big ideas rather than facts in isolation. Another form of support is to make these big ideas more evident to students through the use of advance organizers, cue words for organizational patterns, study guides, and graphic organizers.

● **Using Advance Organizers** **Advance organizers** include information presented verbally and/or visually that makes content more understandable by putting it within a more general framework. They are particularly effective for students with special needs who may have limited background knowledge and reading and listening comprehension skills (Swanson & Deshler, 2003). Examples of advance organizers include the following (Lenz, 1983):

- identifying major topics and activities
- presenting an outline of content
- providing background information

fyi

Advance organizers help
activate prior learning,
keep students on task, and
provide reference points for
remembering tasks that need to
be completed.

- stating concepts and ideas to be learned in the lesson
- motivating students to learn by showing the relevance of the activity
- stating the objectives or outcomes of the lesson

While a well-constructed advance organizer presented to the entire class will meet the needs of most students, those with special needs may benefit from a more individualized approach. For example, Mr. Serano motivated Zak by tying an advance organizer for a lesson about weather to Zak's interest in aviation. Ms. Williams explained to Rinaldo that his lesson objective was to identify and write numbers from 10 to 100. The rest of the class was learning to add two-digit numbers. Ms. Hardy used an individualized advance organizer to communicate to Carlos, who struggles with writing, that he could demonstrate what he learned in the unit on explorers by designing a map showing the countries the major explorers came from. The rest of the class wrote two-page papers about the countries involved in exploration, including the major explorers from each country.

- **Employing Cue Words for Organizational Patterns** Big ideas are often the central focus of an **organizational pattern** of information. The most common patterns of information include the descriptive list and the sequence of events in time, comparison/contrast, cause/effect, and problem/solution (Baxendell, 2003; Ellis, 1996). Each of these patterns of information can be made more conspicuous for students through the use of cue words. For example, cue words for a list, description, or sequence might include *first, second,* and *third;* cue words for comparison/contrast would be *similar, different, on the one hand,* and *on the other hand;* cue words for cause/effect might be *causes, effects, because,* and *so that;* and cue words for problem/solution would be *problem, solution,* and *resolve.* Cue words are important for students with special needs, many of whom have difficulty telling the difference between important and unimportant information (Hallahan et al., 2005; Kame'enui et al., 2002).

Text that does not contain clear cue words requires students to make a number of inferences, which may be difficult for students with special needs. Rewriting the book is obviously not a reasonable way to differentiate instruction. Instead, you can accommodate students by helping to make the key concepts more explicit using teaching strategies described in this text, such as study guides and graphic organizers. Or you can use alternative means of presenting the same information, such as videos or books that are more clearly written.

- **Constructing Study Guides** The general term **study guide** refers to outlines, abstracts, or questions that emphasize important information in texts (Mercer & Mercer, 2001). Study guides are helpful in improving comprehension for students with special needs in content-area classrooms (Lovitt, Rudsit, Jenkins, Pious, & Benedetti, 1985). For example, at the beginning of this chapter, Cecily was having trouble picking out key ideas in her U.S. history text, a common problem for students at all educational levels. She might benefit from a study guide that cues students to important information by asking them questions about it. Procedures for constructing study guides are shown in the next Professional Edge. A sample study guide for a section of a social studies text on Truman's Fair Deal is shown in Figure 9.5.

> You can accommodate students by helping to make the key concepts more explicit using teaching strategies described in this text, such as study guides and graphic organizers.

Study guides can be used with the entire class or as an accommodation for individuals or small groups of students. Horton (1987) suggests the following ways to differentiate instruction using study guides:

1. Allow 2 or 3 inches of margin space in the study guide in which students can take notes. Draw a vertical line to indicate the margin clearly. For example, in the study guide in Figure 9.5, the answer to the first vocabulary question is "*Consumables* are products that cannot be used over again." You may want to have students write this vocabulary word along with its complete definition in the margin. Some students with special needs find a new word easier to understand if you first use the overhead

Video Homework Exercise

Go to the Homework and Exercises section in Chapter 9 of MyEducationLab to learn about how teachers can use multilevel assignments to support learning.

How to Develop Study Guides

Study guides help improve the comprehension of all students, especially those with special needs who are included in content-area classrooms. Follow these steps to develop a study guide from a content-area textbook:

1. Go through the entire book and mark the chapters you want to cover for the term and those you do not.

2. Indicate the sequence in which you will assign the chapters; that is, note the one that comes first, second, and so forth.

3. Read the material in the first chapter carefully. Mark the important vocabulary, facts, and concepts that you expect students to learn. Cross out any material you do not intend to cover.

4. Divide the chapter into logical sections of 1,000- to 1,500-word passages. (The length will depend, of course, on how detailed the material is and how much of it you deem important.)

5. Write brief sentences that explain the main ideas or emphasize the vocabulary, facts, or concepts in the passage. Write 15 sentences per passage.

6. Place these sentences in order so the material in one leads to the next and so forth.

7. To create questions, either leave out a few words in each sentence or change each sentence into a question.

For example, the following statement was identified as important in a chapter on natural disasters:

A 2 percent sales tax was passed to pay for relief efforts after the massive floods of 1993.

This statement could be turned into a question by leaving out several words:

_____ was passed to pay for relief efforts after the massive floods of 1993.

You could also change the statement into a question:

How did the people pay for the relief efforts after the massive floods of 1993?

8. Make a transparency of sentences and/or questions using large type.

9. Prepare sheets for the students, using regular type.

10. Prepare an answer sheet for the teacher.

11. Develop a multiple-choice test to cover the material in the study guide. The test should have 10–15 items, with four possible choices for each question.

Source: From *Study Guides: A Paper on Curriculum Modification,* by S. V. Horton, 1987, Seattle: University of Washington.

---

to discuss the definition along with a series of positive and negative examples. Specific strategies for presenting new vocabulary are presented later in the chapter.

www.resources

The Education Development Center's webpage for the National Center to Improve Practice in Special Education through Technology, Media, and Materials, at www2.edc.org/ncip, provides many ideas on how to implement research-based teaching practices with students with special needs.

2. Print page numbers next to the sentences in the study guide to show where to find missing words in the textbook.

3. Print the missing words at the bottom of the page to serve as cues.

4. Leave out several words for more advanced students and fewer for students with special needs. For example, in Figure 9.5, the *effect* part of the big idea could be simplified as "The *effect* of strikes such as the railroad strike was that the stability of the American economy was threatened and _____."

5. Arrange for peer-teaching situations; pair students and have them take turns being the teacher and the student.

6. Use the study guide for homework assignments. Assign students a passage in the text and give them accompanying study guides (either with or without the pages marked for easy reference). Have them complete the guides and study the material for homework.

FIGURE *9.5* **Sample Study Guide for Truman's Fair Deal**

Vocabulary

Consumables are products that _____.

Some positive examples of consumables are _____, _____,

and _____. A negative example of a consumable is _____.

Big Ideas

The **problem** was that after World War II, price controls were lifted and the cost of

_____, _____, and other consumer goods

went _____.

The **solution** was for workers to _____.

The **effect** was that _____ and _____.

7. Ask students to keep and organize their study guides from a number of passages and to study them as they review for unit or end-of-semester tests.

8. Place reading passages, study guides, and tests on a computer. Use print-to-speech software for students who have difficulty with word reading.

9. Whenever possible, write the study guide at a reading level that fits most of your students. Students with reading and writing problems may need to have the study guide read to them or respond to the questions orally.

10. Use INCLUDE to decide whether to put related but more basic information in the guide. For students with more significant challenges, make an instructional modification by changing the content load so it remains related to the topic at hand but is more basic. For example, Ms. Hall required that Al, a student with a mild intellectual disability in her fourth-grade class, identify fruits and vegetables that were high in fiber, while the rest of the class responded to questions about the biochemical processes involved when the body digests fiber. When the students were tested on the content covered in the guide, Al was held responsible for answering his more basic questions, which covered content that had been previously specified on his IEP.

Of course, study guides are not a substitute for direct instruction. The amount of direct instruction necessary varies with the difficulty of the material. In general, students need more help completing study guides for texts that assume high levels of student background knowledge and in which key information needs to be inferred as opposed to being explicitly presented. The INCLUDE strategy can help you determine whether more direct instruction is needed and whether it needs to be delivered as part of large- or small-group instruction.

● **Creating Graphic Organizers** Another way teachers can help students organize content is to use **graphic organizers.** This strategy gives students a visual format to organize their thoughts while looking for main ideas (Baxendell, 2003). Archer and Gleason (2004) suggest the following five guidelines for constructing graphic organizers:

1. Determine the critical content (for example, vocabulary, concepts, ideas, generalizations, events, details, facts) that you wish to teach your students. Helping students

**Building Teaching Skills
Case Study Exercise**

Go to the Building Teaching Skills Exercises section in Chapter 9 of MyEducationLab for a series of content area exercises designed for specific grade levels.

INCLUDE

fyi

Teachers successfully use graphic organizers at all phases of instruction, from advance organizers to review. Graphic organizers, sometimes called *concept maps* or *semantic webs,* can make your lessons multisensory and are helpful for students with special needs.

www.resources

These two sites provide collections of many ready-to-use graphic organizers: www.teachervision.fen .com/graphic-organizers/ printable/6293.html and www.graphic.org.

focus on the most critical information is important for several reasons. First, students with special needs may have trouble identifying the most important information in an oral lesson or textbook chapter. In most cases this will be content stressed in your state's standards. Second, it is easier for students to remember several main ideas than to remember many isolated details. Third, putting too much information on a graphic organizer can make it so visually complex that students may have trouble interpreting it.

2. Organize concepts into a **concept map,** a type of graphic organizer or visual representation that reflects the structure of the content, such as stories, hierarchies (top-down and bottom-up), feature analysis, diagrams, compare/contrast, and timelines. Because the purpose of a graphic organizer is to clarify interrelationships among ideas and information, you should keep it as simple as possible. Figure 9.6 shows a completed comparison/contrast concept map.

3. Design a completed concept map. Completing the map before you teach with it will ensure that the information is clear and accurate and can be presented to your students in a timely manner.

4. Create a partially completed concept map to be completed by students during instruction. Having students fill out the map as you present your lesson is an excellent way to keep them on task. Also, many students with special needs benefit from a multisensory approach; seeing the information on the graphic, hearing it from the teacher, and writing it on the map helps them better retain the information presented.

5. Create a blank concept map for students to use as a postreading or review exercise. This structure for review is easy for students to use.

Once you have constructed graphic organizers, you can use them as follows (Carnine et al., 2004):

1. Distribute partially completed concept maps to your students.

2. Project the map on a screen using PowerPoint or an overhead projector, displaying only those portions you wish students to attend to. Limiting the amount of information you present at one time will help students with attention problems who have trouble focusing on more than one piece of information at a time.

3. Introduce the information on the concept map proceeding in a logical order; stress the relationships among the vocabulary, concepts, events, details, facts, and so on.

FIGURE 9.6 Comparison/Contrast Concept Map

Attribute	Native Americans	Settlers
Land	Shared Lived close to it without changing it Respected it	Owned Cleared it Used it

Summary

Native Americans and settlers had different ideas about land. Native Americans shared the land whereas the settlers owned individual pieces of it. Native Americans lived close to the land; they respected it and did not change it. Settlers used the land for their own gain.

4. At natural junctures, review the concepts you have introduced. You can do this by placing the blank map on the overhead and asking students questions about the content. This review is essential for students who have difficulty learning large amounts of information at one time.

5. At the end of the lesson, review the critical content again using the blank concept map. You can also have students complete the blank maps for homework. These maps will help students organize their studying and also help you find out what they have learned.

Video Homework Exercise

Go to the Homework and Exercises section in Chapter 9 of MyEducationLab to watch a teacher using handheld whiteboards for formative assessment.

In most cases, using graphic organizers will be helpful for your entire class. Students with attention or listening problems may benefit from the additional accommodations of having a completed graphic explained to them prior to instruction for use as an advance organizer and then completing a blank organizer after instruction with the teacher or a peer for extra practice and review.

Students with gaps in background knowledge may benefit from additional work with graphic organizers that summarize background information. This can be provided as part of small-group or one-to-one instruction. For example, to prepare some of her students with special needs to complete the graphic organizer shown in Figure 9.6, Mr. Jackson read sections of two stories: one about the settlers in Ohio in the 1700s and another about the Delaware tribe, who also lived in Ohio at the time. He also provided additional ways for students to demonstrate their knowledge of this and other differences between settlers and Native Americans by having students write short stories or produce their own picture books. The Case in Practice on page 342 illustrates how one teacher uses a graphic organizer called a *story map* to help her students better comprehend a particular story.

Teaching Terms and Concepts

Content-area instruction is often characterized by a large number of new and/or technical vocabulary words and concepts. Students who have special needs or who are at risk are likely to have difficulty with the vocabulary and concept demands of many content-area texts and presentations. For example, consider the following passage from a general science text:

> Thousands of years ago, Scandinavia was covered by a thick ice sheet. The mass of the ice forced the crust deeper into the denser mantle. Then the ice melted. The mantle has been slowly pushing the land upward since then. This motion will continue until a state of balance between the crust and mantle is reached again. This state of balance is called *isostasy* (ie-soss-tuh-see). (Ramsey, Gabriel, McGuirk, Phillips, & Watenpaugh, 1983)

Although the term *isostasy* is italicized for emphasis, other technical terms and concepts, such as *crust* and *mass,* also may pose a problem for students and require special attention. These words may be particularly difficult because students are likely to be familiar with their nonscientific meanings, which are quite different from their technical meanings (for example, *mass* as in church; *crust* as in bread). You need to check student understanding and teach vocabulary directly, if necessary, using one of the strategies covered in this section.

● **Modeling Examples and Using Synonyms and Definitions** Carnine and colleagues (2004) propose an approach to teaching terms and concepts that entails three related ways of teaching new vocabulary to students: modeling examples, synonyms, and definitions. Although there is some variation from method to method, all three use the following five steps:

1. Pick a range of both positive and negative examples to teach your new word. Example selection is most important. A range of positive examples is used to make sure students can apply the word to a variety of contexts or forms. For example, if you are teaching your students the word *rectangle,* you want them to identify a rectangle

Case in Practice

Teaching with Story Maps

Story maps are graphic organizers that provide students with a visual guide to understanding and retelling stories. They have been shown to help students with special needs read with better comprehension (Carnine et al., 2004; Pearson & Fielding, 1991). In the account that follows, Ms. Barrows, a second-grade teacher, is using the story map in Figure 9.7 to teach her students the story *The Funny Farola* (Miranda & Guerrero, 1986). She has demonstrated using the maps for a week now, so her students are familiar with the format. Today, she is providing guided practice for her students on how to use the maps.

Ms. Barrows: Boys and girls, today we're going to read a story entitled *The Funny Farola*. A *farola* is a lantern used to give light. What do you think the story is going to be about?

Juliane: Maybe it's going to be about a lantern that looks funny.

Lee: Maybe it's about something funny happening to someone who has a farola.

Ms. Barrows: Well, before we read and find out, who can tell me what a story map is?

Darwain: Well, it's a map that guides us through a story kind of like a regular map tells us where we're going when we're driving a car.

Ms. Barrows: That's right, Darwain. Now let's read the first page and find out who the main characters in this story are and where the story takes place. When you find out, we'll fill them in on our story maps. [She distributes a blank story map to each student.]

FIGURE 9.7
Story Map

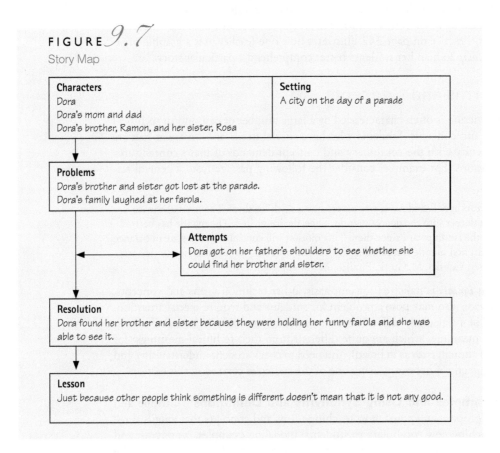

Characters	Setting
Dora Dora's mom and dad Dora's brother, Ramon, and her sister, Rosa	A city on the day of a parade

Problems
Dora's brother and sister got lost at the parade.
Dora's family laughed at her farola.

Attempts
Dora got on her father's shoulders to see whether she could find her brother and sister.

Resolution
Dora found her brother and sister because they were holding her funny farola and she was able to see it.

Lesson
Just because other people think something is different doesn't mean that it is not any good.

Harley: I know, the story is about Dora Rivers, her sister Rosa, her brother Ramon, and her mom and dad. I think Dora is the main character.

Ms. Barrows: That's right, Harley. Let's all fill in the main characters on our maps.

Ms. Barrows: Where do you think the story takes place? It's hard to tell, because the writers don't come right out and say it.

Lovell: I think it takes place in a city.

Ms. Barrows: Why do you think so, Lovell?

Lovell: Because it sounds like it's a big parade, and cities have big parades.

Ms. Barrows: Good thinking, Lovell. When stories don't come out and say things, we have to figure it out by thinking hard, and that's what you did. Let's all fill in the setting on our maps. [They do.] Remember, we said last week that all stories have a problem that needs to be solved. Read the next four pages and find out what the problem is here. [The students read the passage.] What's the problem?

Harley: Well, Dora's little brother and sister got lost at the parade.

Ms. Barrows: Right. That's one problem. Write it on your maps. Now, does anyone see another problem?

Eliseo: I know. Dora made a farola that looked like a frog and everybody laughed at her.

Ms. Barrows: Eliseo, what's wrong with a farola that looks like a frog? I thought it looked cute.

Eliseo: Well, I think it was because Dora's was different from everyone else's. In the pictures in the story, there were no farolas that looked like animals.

Ms. Barrows: That's right, Eliseo. Let's all put this problem on our maps. [They do.] Let's read the next page and find out what Dora and her mom and dad attempted to do to try to find her brother and sister.

Lovell: Dora got up on her father's shoulders to see whether she could see her brother and sister.

Ms. Barrows: Do you think this will help Dora find her brother and sister?

Lesa: I don't think so. There are so many people there.

Ms. Barrows: Well, let's all finish the story and find out. [They finish reading the story.] So, did Dora find her brother and sister?

Juliane: Yes. She found them because they were carrying her funny farola and it really made them stand out in the crowd.

Ms. Barrows: That's right. Let's fill in how Dora solved the problem on our story maps. [They do.] What about Dora's other problem? Was it solved too?

Juliane: Yes. They didn't think Dora's farola was so funny anymore, because it helped them find Dora's brother and sister.

Ms. Barrows: That's right. How do you think Dora felt at the end?

Lovell: I think she felt happy.

Ms. Barrows: Why do you think that, Lovell?

Lovell: Well, because she found her brother and sister and no one thought her farola was stupid anymore.

Ms. Barrows: Good thinking, Lovell. I'd like the rest of you to put how *you* think Dora felt, and why, on your maps. Remember, we said a part of stories is a lesson that they teach us. What lesson do you think this story teaches?

Harley: Well, just because something is different doesn't mean it's no good.

Ms. Barrows: Good thinking, Harley. Let's all put down the lesson of this story on our maps.

REFLECTIONS

How did Ms. Barrows use the story map to help her students comprehend the story? Which students do you think would benefit most from this approach? What should Ms. Barrows do to get her students ready for completing story maps on their own? Under what circumstances might Ms. Barrows have to differentiate her instruction to accommodate students with special needs?

This teacher is modeling positive and negative examples to clarify the meaning of a new concept. How can using both examples and nonexamples help make the meaning of new terms and concepts clear?

whether it is big, small, empty, or shaded. Therefore, when showing students examples of rectangles, show them big rectangles, small rectangles, empty rectangles, and shaded rectangles. If you are teaching your students the word *vehicle,* you want them to recognize a vehicle whether it is a car, boat, or bicycle. Whereas positive examples help students learn the range of a word, negative examples help them discriminate the new word from other words that may be similar. For example, for teaching *rectangle,* use figures such as triangles, circles, and trapezoids as negative examples. For teaching *vehicle,* use a chair, a house, and even an exercise bike as negative examples. Generally, you should use at least six examples to teach a new word and include among them at least two negative examples.

2. If you are teaching a word using a synonym, students must already know the synonym. For example, when teaching the word *gigantic* using the synonym *huge,* first make sure students know what *huge* means. If you are teaching a word using a definition, the definition should be stated simply and clearly and should contain only words for which students know the meaning. Consider the following definition of *vehicle* for third grade:

   Vehicle: A method of transportation that takes a person from one location to another

   This definition uses a number of words that third-graders might not know. Instead, consider a simpler definition that younger students can understand:

   Vehicle: An object that takes you from place to place

3. Tell students the meaning of the words either through modeling positive and negative examples or by presenting positive and negative examples using a synonym or a definition. For example, if you were teaching *rectangle* by modeling positive and negative examples, you might say the following as you pointed to your examples:

   This is a rectangle. . . . This is a rectangle. . . . This is *not* a rectangle. . . . This is a rectangle.

If you were teaching *vehicle* using a definition, you might say the following:

A vehicle is an object that takes you from place to place. What is a vehicle? [Point to a picture of a car.] This is a car. It is an object that takes you from place to place. It is a vehicle. . . . This is a boat. It is an object that takes you from place to place. A boat is a vehicle. . . . This is a chair. A chair is an object, but it doesn't take you from place to place. It is *not* a vehicle.

Finally, if you were teaching the word *gigantic* using the synonym *huge,* you might say this:

Today we're going to learn the meaning of the word *gigantic.* What's the word? *Gigantic* means huge. [Point to a picture of an elephant.] An elephant is a gigantic animal. It is huge. [Point to a picture of a redwood tree.] This is a redwood tree. It is gigantic. It is huge. [Point to a smallish dog.] This is a dog. The dog is *not* gigantic. The dog is *not* huge.

4. Ask students a series of questions to ascertain whether they can discriminate positive examples from negative examples. For example, ask "Is this a rectangle or is this *not* a rectangle?" Have students answer in a complete sentence, saying "Yes, this is a rectangle" or "No, this is not a rectangle." If students know the other figure, they can respond "No, this is not a rectangle. It is a triangle." Note that requiring students to answer in complete sentences using the new word, instead of having them answer with only a yes or no, forces them to use the word. The more times students use a new word, the greater the likelihood they will learn it. Responding in complete sentences reinforces important expressive language skills that are often problematic for students with special needs. If students have been taught a word using a definition or synonym, follow your question with "How do you know?" Their reasons for answering yes or no will reveal whether they are correctly using the definition or just guessing. For example, to test whether students know what a vehicle is, you might say the following:

What is this? (It is a car.) Is a car a vehicle or is a car not a vehicle? (A car is a vehicle.) Why do you say that? (A car is a vehicle because it is an object that takes you from place to place.) What is this? (It is a chair.) Is a chair a vehicle or is it not a vehicle? (A chair is not a vehicle.) Why do you say that? (A chair is not a vehicle because it doesn't take you from place to place.)

5. The purpose of this step is to discover whether students can discriminate the new word from words they learned previously. This step is carried out through a series of open-ended questions. For example, in teaching *rectangle,* the teacher points to a rectangle along with other figures already taught and asks "What is this?"

Teaching vocabulary by modeling examples or by using synonyms and definitions can benefit all your students. Use modeling examples when students may not understand words that explain the meaning of the new word (for example, teaching students what a *herringbone* design is). Use synonyms when students already know another word with a meaning similar to the new word; for example, you could teach the word *bow* (of a ship) using the synonym *front.* Use definitions when a longer explanation is needed to define a word and students already understand the words that make up the explanation. Regardless of which procedure you use, be sure to monitor the performance of your students with special needs carefully using periodic questioning as you teach and differentiating your vocabulary instruction as needed. For example, English-language learners and other learners with special needs cannot rely solely on linguistic information to learn and retain vocabulary. For these students, accommodations can include bringing in real objects and visuals, such as photographs; matching your actions with your words by conducting demonstrations; allowing students

> Teaching vocabulary by modeling examples or by using synonyms and definitions can benefit all your students.

FIGURE *9.8* Concept Diagram

| Concept Name: | Nonviolent resistance |
| Definition: | Protesting in a peaceful way |

Always	Sometimes	Never
Peaceful	Done in a group	Violent
	Done individually	

Positive Examples	Negative Examples
Picketing	Shouting match
Boycott	Physical attack
Sit-in	Revolutionary war
Hunger strike	Riot

to hear and see vocabulary by using films, DVDs, and books on tape; and having students engage in hands-on activities by performing pantomime and drawing pictures (Hill & Flynn, 2006). Students can also be motivated by personalizing the questions in your vocabulary instruction. For example, when Ms. Hendrix taught her students the meaning of *vehicle,* she included in her presentation photos of the family cars of her hard-to-motivate students. She further engaged Rinaldo by giving him the job of holding up the photos in front of the class during the presentation.

● **Making Concept Diagrams** Constructing **concept diagrams** is a method that combines graphic organizers with the methods just described using definitions, synonyms, and positive and negative examples (Bulgren, Schumaker, & Deshler, 1988). A sample concept diagram for the concept of nonviolent resistance is shown in Figure 9.8. First, the teacher selects a keyword from a story or lecture. Next, she constructs a diagram that features the definition of the word; the characteristics that are always present, sometimes present, and never present; and positive and negative examples that can be used to model the word. Finally, the teacher presents the concept diagram to students as follows (Carnine et al., 2004):

1. Present the word and its definition.

2. Discuss which characteristics are always, sometimes, and never present.

3. Discuss one of the positive examples and one of the negative examples in relation to the characteristics.

4. Check other positive and negative examples to discover whether they match the characteristics.

How Can You Improve Clarity in Written and Oral Communication?

In effective instruction, ideas are clearly tied together, which enables students to understand them more easily. The need for instructional clarity applies to both written communication and oral communication. Written communication, in many school situations, involves the use of textbooks and other printed materials, such as handouts, homework, and written tests. Oral communication can include instructional behaviors such as giving directions, asking questions, and delivering lectures.

When a textbook is not written clearly or a lecture is not presented clearly, students have to make critical connections between ideas on their own, a skill that many students who are at risk may not have. Students with special needs may not be able to recognize that they do not understand the material, or they may not be aware of strategies to try when instruction is difficult to understand. For example, when reading a text, they may not know how to use keywords and headings or how to look at the end-of-chapter questions to get main ideas. During oral presentations, students may not feel comfortable asking questions to clarify the information presented because often they are not sure what to ask and are afraid of looking stupid. Finally, students with special needs may lack the background knowledge necessary to construct meaning on their own. If you communicate clearly and use materials that do so as well, students with special needs can be more successful and the need for differentiated instruction will be reduced.

Clarity in Written Communication

The importance of clearly written communication is illustrated by these two textbook passages about western migration in the United States:

> Many of the farmers who moved in from New England were independent farmers. Land cost about a dollar an acre. Most men could afford to set up their own farms. Livestock farming was quite common on the frontier. Hogs could be fed in the forests. The cost of raising hogs was low. (Senesh, 1973, as cited in Armbruster, 1984)

> Most of the farmers who moved in from New England were independent farmers. Being an independent farmer means that the farmer can afford to own his own farm. Around 1815, most men could afford their own farms because lands were cheap—it cost only about a dollar an acre. Many of these independent farms were livestock farms. For example, many frontier farmers raised hogs. Hog farming was common because hogs were inexpensive to keep. The cost of raising hogs was low because the farmer did not have to buy special feed for the hogs. The hogs did not need special feed because they could eat plants that grew in the surrounding forests. (Armbruster, 1984)

The second passage is much easier to understand; it requires fewer inferences by the reader and fewer accommodations by the teacher. It also defines *independent farmer* for the reader. If students were reading the first passage, you might have to provide this definition—which you could do orally or in a study guide. The reason farmers turned to raising livestock can be inferred from the first paragraph, but it is stated directly in the second. For students reading the first paragraph, teachers may need to make the accommodation of posing questions prior to reading to establish an understanding of this relationship: for example, "Why did the farmers turn to raising livestock?"

Obviously, teaching every paragraph like this is not feasible. But this example underscores the need for adopting structurally and organizationally coherent textbooks. Accommodations may still be needed for individual learners, but they should be made only for sections containing the most important information.

Another aspect of written language that can make comprehension more difficult is the use of pronouns. A general rule of thumb is that the closer a pronoun is to its referent, the easier it is to translate. Consider the following section of text:

> Now life began to change. The Eskimo hunters could see that these tools were useful. So they became traders, too. They trapped more furs than their families needed.
> Then they brought the furs to the trading posts. There they could trade the furs for supplies they had never had before. Because the new tools helped Eskimo hunters get along better, they became part of the Eskimo environment. (Brandwein & Bauer, 1980)

Analyze
and Reflect
Stahl and Shiel estimate that teachers can realistically teach 300 words per year, which translates to about 8–10 per week (as cited in Armbruster, Lehr, & Osborn, 2001). This means that there will never be enough time to teach all of the words students are unlikely to know. If you were teaching a new unit in a subject area, what criteria would you use for word selection? What would you do with words that you were unable to select?

www.resources
Get practical ideas about specific teaching problems from actual teachers in the field from Teachers Helping Teachers, at www.pacificnet.net/~mandel.

Another aspect of written language that can make comprehension more difficult is the use of pronouns. A general rule of thumb is that the closer a pronoun is to its referent, the easier it is to translate.

Many readers may have trouble figuring out whom *they* refers to in this passage. Although the placement of most pronouns is not this problematic, understanding pronouns can be difficult for students with special needs. However, students can be taught to make sense of pronouns (Carnine et al., 2004). Before students read, identify unclear pronouns. Have students underline the pronouns in a passage. Then show them how to find the pronouns' referents by asking questions. Study the following example:

Passage

Curtis and Dorva skipped school. They were grounded for a week. He was sorry. She got mad.

Student Questioning

Teacher: "Curtis and Dorva skipped school." Who skipped school?

Students: Curtis and Dorva.

Teacher: "They were grounded for a week." Was Curtis grounded?

Students: Yes.

Teacher: Was Dorva grounded?

Students: Yes.

Teacher: "He was sorry." Was Curtis sorry?

Students: Yes.

Teacher: Was Dorva sorry?

Students: No.

Teacher: "She got mad." Did Dorva get mad?

Students: Yes.

Depending on the level of sophistication of your class, this instruction could be done with the entire class or performed as an accommodation for individual students who struggle to understand sentences containing pronouns.

Clarity in Oral Communication

Just as the quality of textbook writing affects student learning, so too does the quality of teachers' oral language. Three particularly important areas of oral language are giving directions, asking questions, and presenting subject matter (such as in a lecture).

● **Giving Directions**   Giving oral directions is the most common way that teachers tell their students what they want them to do. When directions are not clear and have to be repeated, valuable instructional time is wasted. Consider this set of directions given by a middle school teacher at the beginning of a social studies lesson:

Unclear Instruction

All right, everyone, let's settle down and get quiet. I want you all to get ready for social studies. Shh. . . . Let's get ready. Alice and Tim, I want you to put those worksheets away. We need our books and notebooks. (Evertson et al., 1983, p. 143)

How clear is the teacher about what she wants her students to do? Now read this alternative set of directions:

Clearer Instruction

All right, everyone, I want all of you in your seats facing me for social studies. [Teacher pauses.] Now, I want you to get out three things: your social studies book, your spiral notebook, and a pencil. Put everything else away so that you have just those three things—the social studies book, the spiral notebook, and the pencil—out on your desk. [As students get out their materials, the teacher writes "Social Studies, page 55, Chapter 7 on Italy" on the chalkboard. She waits until students have their supplies ready and are listening before she begins talking.] (Evertson et al., 1983, p. 143)

In the first example, the teacher does not get the students' attention before giving them directions. She is also unclear in communicating what she wants her students to do. For example, the words *settle down* and *get ready* are not defined for the students. In the second example, the teacher first gets her students' attention and then very specifically states all the things they need to do.

Lavoie (1989) has suggested four guidelines for giving directions that are helpful either for your entire class or as accommodations for individual students with special needs:

1. State commands specifically, using concrete terms. In the Clearer Instruction example, the teacher was very specific about what the students needed to do to get ready for social studies. They had to get out three things: their books, notebooks, and pencils. The first teacher told them only to "get ready."

2. Give "bite-size" directions; avoid a long series of directions. The second teacher first had her students sit down and face her; then she had them take out their materials; finally, she had them turn to the chapter they were going to read that day.

3. Whenever possible, accompany explanations with a demonstration. For example, Mr. Gaswami asked his students to take out their science books, turn to the beginning of the chapter, identify five keywords, and define them using the glossary. Mr. Gaswami showed his students what he wanted them to do by opening his book to the chapter, pointing out that the keywords were italicized, and then defining several keywords to demonstrate how to find and paraphrase the meanings using the glossary in the back of the book. He also displayed pictorial images of these directions on the board, to help students read and remember all the steps.

4. Use cuing words such as "Look up here" and "Listen, please" before giving directions. Gestures such as a raised hand are also effective in getting students' attention.

● **Asking Questions**   Asking students questions is a vital part of instructional clarity. The way you question your students is important for several reasons. Questioning is a quick way of assessing what your students have learned. In addition, questioning through the use of follow-up probes can help you analyze your students' errors. For example, Ms. Dilworth's third-grade class was given the following math problem:

Three-fourths of the crayons in Bob's box of a dozen crayons are broken. How many unbroken crayons are there?

Ms. Dilworth asked Kareem what the answer was, and Kareem answered that there were four unbroken crayons left. Ms. Dilworth asked Kareem to explain how he got that answer. Kareem said, "Because three-fourths means three groups of four, and because there is only one group left, that group has four in it." By asking a question, Ms. Dilworth found out that Kareem did not know the concept of three-fourths. Questions can also be used to redirect students to the correct answer when they make mistakes. For example, Ms. Dilworth might have asked Kareem a number of follow-up questions: "How many crayons did you start with? How many is a dozen? What fraction of the crayons was broken? What does *three-fourths* mean? What would one-fourth of 12 be?"

Last and perhaps most important, it is through effective questioning that your students can learn thinking skills. Well-constructed questions provide students with a model for effective thinking; in time, students learn to ask themselves these same questions as they solve problems. For example, Ms. Collins wanted her students to ask themselves key questions while they read stories to help improve their comprehension. At first she asked them questions while they read, such as, "What is the story about? What is the problem?

Another use of cuing is to let a student know that he or she can expect to be called on to respond orally when you present a particular cue that only the student knows. This way the student can attend to a lesson with less anxiety about speaking in class.

Research Note

Okolo, Ferretti, and MacArthur (2007) analyzed discussions in four middle school history classes that included students with special needs. They found that the teacher who had the most student participation and highest state test scores responded to students' ideas and understanding on an individual basis, made extensive use of repetition, and made frequent attempts to personalize history and link it to students' thoughts and experiences.

What is the solution? What's going to happen next? Is your prediction still good? Do you need to change your prediction? What makes you think so?" In time, she taught the students to ask themselves these questions as they read independently.

Although asking questions can be a very potent teaching strategy, to achieve maximum benefit, questioning needs to be carried out correctly. Wilen, Ishler, Hutchinson, and Kindsvatter (1999) suggest the following guidelines for using questions in your classroom:

1. *Phrase questions clearly to ensure that students know how to respond.* For example, a vague question such as "What about the Great Depression?" forces students to guess rather than to consider carefully a direct response to the question. Better wording would be "What were the two primary causes of the Great Depression?"

2. *Provide a balance between higher- and lower-level questions.* The important point to keep in mind is that both kinds of questions are important. Lower-level, or convergent, questions help you find out whether students have the basic understanding necessary for higher-level thought. Further, critical and creative thinking can be developed by using convergent and evaluative questions. Although incorporating more higher-level skills into the curriculum is positive, it is important to realize that lower-level knowledge is still important, particularly for students with special needs. Students with special needs may not readily acquire lower-level knowledge. Failing to help them acquire this understanding can prevent them from ever developing higher-level understanding. Also, lower-level questions can give students an opportunity to succeed in class. Finally, research suggests that lower-level questions may be most appropriate in teaching basic skills to students who are at risk (Berliner, 1984; Emmer, Evertson, Sanford, Clements, & Worsham, 1983).

3. *Adapt questions to the language and skill level of the class, including individual students in the class.* Your questions should accommodate a range of needs, from lower-performing students to gifted students. For example, a question for a lower-performing student might be, "From what you have just read, how does the demand for a product affect its supply?" For students with more skills, the question might become, "Going beyond the article a little, how does price affect supply and demand and at what point is market equilibrium reached?"

4. *Vary the wait time depending on the nature of the question asked.* If the question covers review material or material of little difficulty, the wait time—or time you allow your students to think about the answer—is brief. However, if a question covers material that is new and/or difficult for your students, give them more time to think before responding.

5. *Involve all students in classroom questioning by calling on nonvolunteers as well as volunteers.* Calling on all students also allows you to monitor student learning efficiently. In addition, calling on nonvolunteers (who frequently are students with special needs) demonstrates that you hold them accountable for listening and leads to higher levels of on-task behavior. However, as mentioned before, you should match questions with student ability to maximize the likelihood of student success. Finally, for lower-level questions, consider using unison responding, or having all students respond at once together. Unison responding allows more student opportunities for practice and recitation and can lead to higher levels of correct responses and on-task behavior (Carnine, 1981).

Use the INCLUDE strategy to ensure that the questions you ask in class match the instructional levels of your students. For example, as part of a curriculum modification stated on her IEP, Melissa was learning to identify numbers from 100 to 999; the rest of the class was learning long division. During a class presentation on how to solve three-digit division problems, Mr. Henry called on Melissa to identify the hundreds-place number that was being divided. Sam, another student in the class, was expected to learn the same long division problems as everyone else, but he was clearly having trouble doing so, as judged by his homework and

fyi

Wait time gives students a chance to think and respond orally to teachers' questions. The duration of wait times should reflect the types of questions: one or two seconds for lower-level questions and three to five seconds for higher-level questions.

DIMENSIONS OF

diversity

For students with limited English proficiency, pause three to five seconds for lower- and higher-level questions.

in-class performance. Mr. Henry questioned him in a different way by asking him to explain the first step in solving the problem after it had already been solved at the board.

● **Presenting Subject Matter**   Communicating clearly to your students when you are presenting subject-area content orally, such as in a lecture, also is important. The following section of a lecture was delivered during a geography lesson on Italy:

Teacher 1

Italy is in southern Europe, down by France and the Mediterranean Sea. It's a peninsula in the Mediterranean. There are a lot of beautiful islands in the Mediterranean off of Italy and Greece as well. Sardinia and Sicily are islands that are part of Italy. Corsica, Capri, and some other islands like Crete and Cyprus are in the same part of the world, but they don't belong to, although they may be close to, Italy. You could turn to the map of Europe that's in your text to see where Italy is. (Evertson et al., 1983, pp. 143–144)

The language used by this teacher lacks clarity. For example, he presents information about a number of islands but is unclear in explaining how these islands relate to the main topic, which seems to be the location of Italy. The teacher is also vague when he says, "[The islands] don't belong to, although they may be close to, Italy." In addition, the teacher uses the word *peninsula* but does not define it. Finally, this explanation needs the visual display of a map to bring clarity to it, but the teacher refers to a map only at the end of the explanation, almost as an afterthought. Then, rather than require students to refer to it, he leaves them with the impression that its use is voluntary. The only students who will know where Italy is after this lecture are those who already knew before the lecture. Many students with special needs will likely be left behind. An example of another lecture on the same topic is much clearer:

Analyze
and Reflect

Part of being an effective teacher is recognizing when you are communicating content clearly to your students and when you are not. What are some ways that you can monitor the quality of your oral and written communication with your students?

Teacher 2

Now, I want all eyes on me. [The teacher then gestures to the world map next to her. The continent of Europe is highlighted.] The continent we have been studying the past month is highlighted here on this map of the world. What continent is it? [The teacher calls on a nonvolunteer who is also a struggling student to identify the continent. The teacher then shows a map of Europe with the countries they have already studied highlighted: France, Switzerland, and Austria.] What are the names of these countries that we have already studied? [The teacher has the class respond in unison and then shows the map of Europe with Italy highlighted.] This is the new country we are studying today. It is called *Italy.* [The teacher writes the word *Italy* on the board as she says it.] What is this country called? [The teacher has the class respond in unison.] Italy is a large peninsula shaped like a boot that extends into the Mediterranean Sea. [The teacher writes *peninsula* on the board, sounding out the syllables as she writes.] What's the word everyone? [Because students have studied the word once before, the teacher calls on a nonvolunteer to define it.] Corrine, what is a *peninsula?*

While this teacher's presentation is much more clear, she may still need to differentiate instruction for her students. For example, Juan, a student with attention problems, may respond better to a film than a teacher lecture. Carmen, who has a learning disability, has trouble organizing information presented orally and may benefit from using a graphic organizer of the key geographical features of Italy. Damon, a struggling student who has difficulty retaining information, may benefit from completing a blank copy of the graphic organizer as part of a student study team.

How Can You Involve Parents in Teaching Their Children?

Teachers are always looking for ways to find extra help for students who take more time to learn new content or skills. That is why we often hear teachers say, "If only his parents would work with him more at home." Although we know parents can promote

Video Homework
Exercise

Go to the Homework and
Exercises section in Chapter 9
of MyEducationLab to see how
including and collaborating with
parents of your diverse students
can unearth hidden funds of
knowledge.

learning by showing affection for their children, by displaying interest in their children's schoolwork, and by expecting academic success, the effectiveness of parents tutoring their children at home is less clear. The results of research on the effectiveness of parent teaching are mixed; some experts say it is effective whereas others question it (Erion, 2006, Mercer & Pullen, 2005). When determining whether to involve parents in tutoring their children, Mercer and Pullen (2005) suggest taking the following factors into account:

1. Are there reasons for deciding against tutoring (for example, mother–father disagreement over the necessity of tutoring, health problems, financial problems, marital problems, or a large family with extensive demands on parental authority)?

2. Do parents have the resources of a professional (for example, a teacher) to assist them? The success of home tutoring may depend on cooperative efforts.

3. Can the sessions be arranged at a time when there is no interruption from siblings, callers, or other demands? These children need sustained attention in order to learn.

4. Will the child become overwhelmed with academic instruction and resent the home sessions or feel overly pressured?

5. Do the parents become frustrated, tense, disappointed, or impatient during the tutorial sessions? These parents may spend their time better with the child in activities that are mutually enjoyable.

6. Do the tutorial sessions create tensions among family members? For instance, do the siblings view the sessions as preferential treatment?

7. Does the parent resent tutoring the child or feel guilty every time a session is shortened or missed? Are the sessions usually enjoyable and rewarding?

Of course, if you decide to have parents tutor their child, the same strategies for teaching skills and content to students with special needs covered earlier in this chapter still apply. For example, only skills or content at a student's level should be presented, and the progression of skills or content should be gradual and based on student mastery. In addition, parents should be carefully trained to present new information or skills clearly and enthusiastically and to provide appropriate corrections and encouragement as needed. Parents should also limit the length of the tutoring sessions to 15 minutes for children up to grade 6 and 30 minutes for older students and should begin and end each session with an activity that is fun and that the child is successful at (Cummings & Maddux, 1985, as cited in Mercer & Pullen, 2005). Also, care must be taken to select the most appropriate time to tutor and to select a place that does not restrict the activities of other family members and is not too distracting. Finally, tutoring should be held at the same time and place to establish a clear routine (Mercer & Pullen, 2005, p. 125).

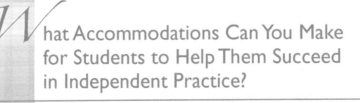

What Accommodations Can You Make for Students to Help Them Succeed in Independent Practice?

As discussed in Chapter 5, the main purpose of practice activities is to provide students with opportunities to refine skills or solidify content that they have already learned and to allow you to monitor their performance. To achieve these purposes, students should be able to complete practice activities such as seatwork, those included as part of learning centers, and homework assignments independently.

Even under ideal circumstances and with the best intentions, it is difficult to design practice activities that meet the needs of all students in your class. Problems arise because of individual characteristics, and individual accommodations need to be made using INCLUDE. For example, students with severe reading problems may have difficulty reading directions that are clear to everyone else. Students with attention problems may have trouble answering questions that have multiple steps. Students with physical disabilities may be unable to perform the writing requirements of their assignments. In the case of students with severe intellectual disabilities, practice activities may need to be modified totally so they are consistent with the students' skill levels and the goals and objectives on their IEPs.

I N C L U D E

Differentiating Seatwork Assignments

One problem with seatwork is that the practice activities may not contain enough items for the student to achieve mastery. This limitation is important, because students with disabilities often require more practice to master skills and content. For example, Ms. Jennings has just taught her students to solve two-step story problems in math that require first adding and then subtracting. She demonstrated three problems in front of the class and then guided her students through three more. Ms. Jennings then had students independently complete five problems in the math book. She found that only half the students answered all the problems correctly and that the rest of the class needed more practice. Many math books have extra problems for students who need more practice, but some do not. You may need to either make up your own items or to find similar items from other books.

Another common problem with seatwork is that the directions are too difficult. Complicated or confusing directions can prevent students from completing their seatwork successfully. For example, some directions are excessively wordy: "Use the words letters stand for and the sense of the other words to find out what the new word in heavy black print is" (Center for the Study of Reading, 1988, p. 14). This is just a convoluted way of saying "Read." Other directions have too many steps: "Read the first sentence, and fill in the missing word. Read the second sentence. Find the word from the first sentence that makes sense in the second sentence and print it where it belongs. Then, do what the last sentence says. Repeat for all the other sentences" (Center for the Study of Reading, 1988, p. 14).

Affleck, Lowenbraun, and Archer (1980) have suggested five accommodations you can make to directions to ensure that students with special needs know what to do prior to working independently. Use INCLUDE to figure out whether these accommodations need to be done with your entire class or only with one or a small group of students:

1. **Verbally present the tasks.** This strategy can be applied to the whole class, particularly when many students are having problems with the directions. You can accommodate the needs of individual students by pairing a worksheet with an auditory tape that explains the directions.

2. **Add practice examples** that you can do with the whole class or a small group of students who are having particular difficulty.

3. **Write alternative sets of directions.** You can project these onto a screen using an overhead projector or PowerPoint, or you can distribute individual copies to students.

4. **Highlight the important words** in the directions.

5. **Have students help each other** when the directions are difficult.

fyi

Pincus (2005, p. 76) suggests asking yourself these questions when deciding whether to use a particular worksheet with your students: (1) Does the worksheet aim at a research-based goal? (2) Does the worksheet employ effective and efficient means to reach that goal? (3) How can the worksheet best be used: for instructional modeling? for guided practice? or as a pre- or posttest? (and if so, what does the teacher learn)?

I N C L U D E

Video Homework Exercise

Go to the Homework and Exercises section in Chapter 9 of MyEducationLab to listen as a teacher gives editing instructions to peer partners.

FIGURE *9.9* Seatwork Activity

Name _____

The Sound of Short *i*

A. Say each word. Circle the words that have the vowel sound you hear in *hit*.

lick	milk	cane	time
might	away	drink	gone
rabbit	house	sing	girl
this	come	five	fish

B. Make new words by changing the first letter or letters.

pick   _____   _____   _____

wing   _____   _____   _____

slip   _____   _____   _____

C. Fill in each blank with one of the words that you circled above to complete the sentences.

1. The boys and girls will _____ a song in school.

2. My father and I went to the river and caught a big _____.

3. _____ is not the book I want to read.

4. The fluffy little _____ ran across the road.

5. My mother gave me a glass of _____.

---

fyi

Before starting independent practice, complete sample items for the students. Talk through each step, modeling your thought process and decision making. Use questioning to check that students understand directions.

Students may also have trouble when single pages of seatwork contain a number of different tasks. This combination of tasks can cause problems for students with special needs, who often have difficulty making the transition from one task to another. Consider the example shown in Figure 9.9. This worksheet has three different tasks. Students need to make a number of transitions within one worksheet to complete the activity successfully. Also, students are required to use words circled in Part A as answers to Part C. Using answers from one part of a worksheet as answers to questions on another part is confusing and assumes that students will answer the first part correctly. You could modify this worksheet by visually cuing the change of task on the page (for example, draw a line between tasks) and by correcting Part A before the students do Part C.

Differentiating Learning Center Activities

As you learned in Chapter 5, another way to provide extra practice for students is in classroom learning centers. Examples of how to differentiate activities in learning centers are shown in Figure 9.10.

Differentiating Homework Assignments

As they do with in-class practice activities, students with special needs may have difficulty completing traditional homework assignments. A major reason for student failure to

Video Homework Exercise

Go to the Homework and Exercises section in Chapter 9 of MyEducationLab to watch first graders use a digital activity to practice counting back.

FIGURE *9.10* Examples of Differentiated Learning Center Activities

OUTCOME:
Students read or listen to information and then write or type responses to questions about the information.

MATERIALS:
Books, books-on-tape, computer software for typing, worksheets with varied levels of questions about the information.

DIFFERENTIATION:
- Some students complete fill-in-the-blank responses.
- Some students respond to a prompt and write an essay response.
- Some students complete an outline as they are listening.

Source: Adapted from "Designing and Delivering Learning Center Instruction," by M. E. King-Sears, 2007, *Intervention in School and Clinic, 42*(3), pp. 137–147.

complete homework assignments independently, successfully, and without undue stress is that the assignments are too difficult to begin with. Before you give your students an assignment, ask yourself the following questions:

1. What skill (for example, reading, written expression, or math) demands does the assignment make on the students? Are the students capable of meeting these skill demands?

2. What background knowledge (for example, vocabulary or concepts) does the assignment demand of the students? Are the students capable of meeting the demand for background knowledge?

3. Is the purpose of the assignment clear to students?

4. If the assignment involves skill practice, does it include a lot of practice on a few skills rather than a little practice on a lot of skills?

5. Are clear, written directions provided for how to complete the assignment?

6. Is enough time allotted to complete the assignment?

Even if you answered yes to all these questions, students with special needs may require additional accommodations. For example, students with reading problems may need extra assistance with homework directions. Students with physical disabilities may need assignments shortened, or they may need to respond orally rather than in writing. Remember to use the INCLUDE strategy to make adaptations that fit your assignments and the individual characteristics of your students with special needs. A survey of general education teachers (Polloway, Epstein, Bursuck, Jayanthi, & Cumblad, 1994) showed that teachers favored the following homework accommodations: adjusting the length

www.*r e s o u r c e s*

For homework help, students can go to these two sites—www.infoplease.com/homework and www.highschoolhub.org/hub/hub.cfm—and be linked instantly to information on the academic subject of their choice, including math, English, literature, social studies, and science. Students can also be linked to tutorials in a wide range of subject areas.

Video Homework Exercise

Go to the Homework and Exercises section in Chapter 9 of MyEducationLab where a teacher explains how she provides support for homework assignments using technology.

INCLUDE

All students can benefit from homework and other independent practice activities. What are some strategies you can use to make homework and other assignments more effective for students with special needs?

of assignments; providing extra teacher help; providing a peer tutor for assistance; setting up student study groups; providing auxiliary learning aids (for example, computers and calculators); checking more frequently with students about assignments (for example, clarifying when they are due and what is required); and allowing alternative response formats (for example, oral or written).

Successful homework also depends on individual student skills. Not only do students need to be proficient in basic academic skills, but they also need to be able to learn independently. For example, they need to recognize their homework problems and seek help when necessary. They also need to manage their time effectively. Strategies for teaching these and other independent learning skills are covered in more depth in Chapter 10.

Finally, the success of homework also depends on the involvement of parents. Parent involvement is particularly important for students with special needs because they are more likely to struggle with homework (Bursuck et al., 1999). Parents play two key roles: overseeing the homework process while their children are at home and communicating with the school regularly about homework. Parents can oversee the homework process by having daily discussions about homework with their children, creating an environment at home that is conducive to getting homework done, supervising homework activities periodically during the time set for homework, and providing support and encouragement for homework completion (Bursuck et al., 1999).

Despite the importance of homework, home–school communication about it is likely to be a problem (Harniss, Epstein, Bursuck, Nelson, & Jayanthi, 2001; Munk et al., 2001). Parents of students with special needs want much more communication with teachers about homework and feel that teachers should make more of an effort to initiate such communication (Munk et al., 2001). Likewise, teachers feel that parents do not initiate communication about homework often enough, take homework seriously enough, and follow through with commitments they make about helping their children with homework (Epstein et al., 1997).

Contacts with parents about homework can be increased by conducting parent–teacher meetings in the evening for working parents and by taking advantage of the ever-increasing use of e-mail, a great potential time-saver (Harniss et al., 2001). Another strategy for increasing communication is to establish a homework hotline that can be accessed by phone or a website that provides certain types of homework assistance. You can also involve parents in the homework process at the beginning of the school year and on an ongoing basis thereafter using checklists, newsletters, informed notes, phone calls, and parent discussion groups (Margolis, 2005). For example, at the open house at the beginning of the school year, Ms. Ordonez gives parents information about course assignments for the semester, homework support available in the classroom, and policies on missed homework and extra-credit assignments. She then sends home school progress updates every four weeks; the progress reports include a section on homework completion.

Teachers can also ask parents whether they want to have homework information sent home daily, to sign that they reviewed their children's homework, and to note their children's efforts and describe their difficulties. By signing assignments and indicating their children's effort or difficulty in completing them, parents communicate to their children that they and the teacher are working together and care about homework being completed (Margolis, 2005). It is also important to understand that homework may be a lower priority for families when compared to other home issues. For example, Mr. Gentry knew

Analyze
and Reflect

Select a commercially prepared student practice activity in the subject area and grade level you plan to teach. Critique the activity in light of the guidelines for assigning homework. How might you adapt this worksheet for a student with special needs?

www.resources

Webmath, at www.webmath .com, is a website designed to help students with specific math problems they encounter in class or in homework. Answers to problems are generated and produced in real time, at the moment Web users type in their math problems and click on Solve.

that Dominique's family had recently been evicted from their apartment and were living in their car. Until Dominique's family was able to find another place to live, Mr. Gentry arranged for him to complete his homework before or after school. Ultimately, the most effective way of warming parents to the homework process is to only send home work that students can complete successfully and independently.

Making Instructional Modifications for Students with Moderate to Severe Disabilities

Students with moderate to severe disabilities often cannot perform some or all of the steps in tasks carried out every day by students without disabilities. In the past, this inability to perform tasks in the same way as other students was interpreted to mean that these students could not benefit from these activities. Today, the emphasis is on making modifications for students with moderate to severe disabilities so that they can meet curricular standards in a more functional way, as guided by their IEPs (Lowell-York, Doyle, & Kronberg, 1995; Nolet & McLaughlin, 2005).

One way to modify materials and activities for students with moderate to severe disabilities is to conduct an **environmental inventory.** The purpose of an environmental inventory is to find out what modifications are needed to increase the participation of these students in the classroom as well as in community environments (Vandercook, York, & Forest, 1989) and to help them meet more functional curricular objectives specified on their IEPs. The environmental inventory process involves asking yourself four questions:

1. What does a person who does not have a disability do in this environment?

2. What does a person who has a disability do in this environment? What is the discrepancy?

3. What types of supports and/or accommodations can be put in place to increase the participation level or independence of the student with special needs?

4. What functional outcomes can the student meet as a result of this participation?

An example of how this process is used in a classroom environment is shown in Figure 9.11. This example involves Roberto, a student with moderate to severe disabilities whom you read about at the beginning of Chapter 4. Roberto is in Ms. Benis's sixth-grade social studies class. The class is working in small groups on depicting the steps in the recycling process for paper, metal, and plastic. Each group is studying a different recycled material. Roberto lacks the motor and cognitive skills necessary to participate like everyone else.

Ms. Benis decides to accommodate instruction for Roberto. She assigns him to the group that his friend Seth is in. She also decides to use different materials with Roberto. Ms. Benis has a paraprofessional help Roberto find pictures of recycled products; Seth helps Roberto paste these pictures onto the group's diagram. Mr. Howard, Roberto's special education teacher, helps Roberto identify recycled products in grocery stores and restaurants. Roberto's parents help him sort the recycling at home.

All of these activities help Roberto meet his IEP goal of participating in community recycling efforts. Examples of making instructional modifications using INCLUDE are described in the Case in Practice on page 359.

Research Note

J. S. Nelson and colleagues (1998) surveyed middle school students of varying achievement levels about their preferences for homework accommodations. The most preferred accommodations were completing assignments entirely at school, working on assignments in small groups, beginning homework in class with the teacher checking understanding, and allowing extra-credit assignments. The least preferred accommodations were making changes to assignments for individual students and using assignment notebooks.

www.resources

Do you want to post your own homework assignments on the Internet without a website of your own? Go to Ed Gate's SchoolNotes webpage, at www.schoolnotes.com.

Analyze and Reflect

Students with special needs often require more practice when learning a new skill or content. Logistically, how can you provide more practice for some students while at the same time meeting the needs of your students who are ready to move to new material?

FIGURE *9.11* **Environmental Inventory Process**

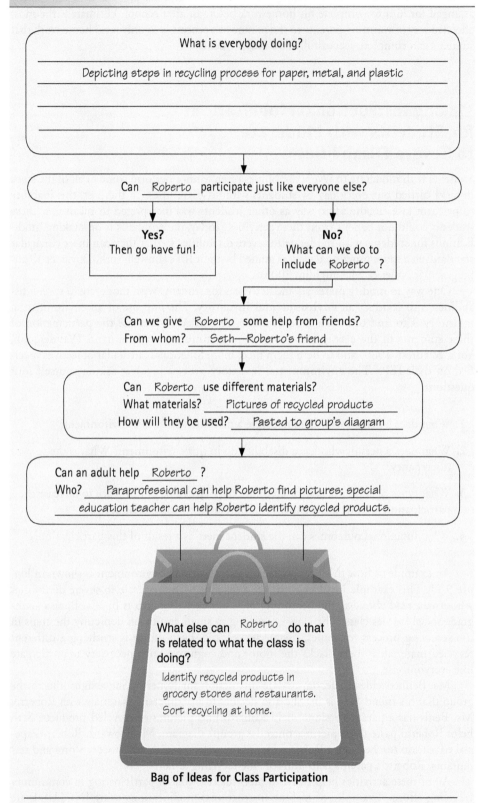

What is everybody doing?

Depicting steps in recycling process for paper, metal, and plastic

Can ___Roberto___ participate just like everyone else?

Yes?
Then go have fun!

No?
What can we do to include ___Roberto___?

Can we give ___Roberto___ some help from friends?
From whom? ___Seth—Roberto's friend___

Can ___Roberto___ use different materials?
What materials? ___Pictures of recycled products___
How will they be used? ___Pasted to group's diagram___

Can an adult help ___Roberto___?
Who? ___Paraprofessional can help Roberto find pictures; special education teacher can help Roberto identify recycled products.___

What else can ___Roberto___ do that is related to what the class is doing?

Identify recycled products in grocery stores and restaurants.
Sort recycling at home.

Bag of Ideas for Class Participation

Source: From "The McGill Action Planning System (MAPS): A Strategy for Building the Vision," by T. Vandercook, J. York, and M. Forest, 1989, *Journal of the Association for Persons with Severe Handicaps, 14*(3), pp. 205–218.

Making Instructional Modifications in a Middle School Consumer and Food Science Class

Mr. Gagliano teaches a middle school consumer and food science class. He recently taught a unit on cooking and nutrition, including how to shop for food. The targeted state standards for the unit were as follows:

1. Students demonstrate the knowledge and skills needed to remain physically healthy.

2. Students evaluate consumer products and services and make effective consumer decisions.

One part of the unit covered vegetarianism. The goal was for the students to plan, shop for, and cook a vegetarian meal. After defining *vegetarianism* and providing a brief history of vegetarianism in the United States, Mr. Gagliano planned to show a video on the Food and Drug Administration (FDA) nutritional guidelines, including how to decipher nutritional information on a food product label. Mr. Gagliano then planned to break the class into four groups and assign each group the task of designing a vegetarian meal meeting FDA nutritional guidelines.

Ramone is a student with moderate intellectual disabilities who is included in Mr. Gagliano's class. Ramone can do basic math at about the second-grade level and reads below the first-grade level. Although his oral language skills are adequate to carry on a conversation, his ability to interact with others in a small group is limited. Ramone's IEP objectives include the following:

1. Prepare three basic meals independently.

2. Use a calculator to budget money while shopping.

3. Make purchases with the "next-dollar" strategy (for example, paying $6.00 and "one more dollar for cents" for an item that costs $6.62).

4. Increase functional sight-word vocabulary to 200 words.

5. Work appropriately in small groups for up to 50 minutes.

Mr. Gagliano and Ms. Henning, Ramone's special education teacher, met to decide how Ramone's instruction during this unit could be modified. They agreed that the curricular demands for the rest of the class were not appropriate for Ramone, and they planned the following instructional modifications based on Ramone's IEP:

1. Ramone will record the possible choices for the menu (for example, main dishes, dessert, drink). He will actively participate in the making of the final choices. A classmate will help him with spelling as needed.

2. Ramone will record the choices for the grocery list. He will also be assigned the job of checking the kitchen to make sure that items on the list are not already there.

3. Ramone will practice reading the words from the grocery list with the help of his group.

4. Ramone will assist with the shopping, using his calculator to budget the group's money, making purchases using the "next-dollar" strategy, and reading his grocery words to find his items. Ramone will be assisted by his group as needed.

5. Ramone will assist the group in cooking the meal.

Following the activity, Ramone, with assistance from Mr. Gagliano and Ms. Henning, evaluated his performance using checklists based on his related IEP objectives. The evaluations were placed in Ramone's alternate assessment portfolio.

REFLECTIONS

Do you think it was appropriate for the teachers to plan instructional modifications for Ramone rather than instructional accommodations? How were the expectations for Ramone different from those of his classmates? How were they similar? Should students such as Ramone get credit for meeting state standards when their instruction is modified? How useful is the INCLUDE strategy in planning instructional modifications for students with moderate to severe disabilities?

Source: Adapted from "Creating and Using Meaningful Alternate Assessments," by H. Kleinert, P. Green, M. Hurte, J. Clayton, and C. Oetinger, 2002, *Teaching Exceptional Children, 34*(4), pp. 40–47. Copyright 2002 by the Council for Exceptional Children. Reprinted with permission.

Summary

Teachers who communicate clearly through the curriculum materials they use and the information they present orally in class can meet the needs of a broad range of students without having to make accommodations. Nonetheless, despite your best efforts, you will still need to differentiate your instruction by making some accommodations for students who are at risk or have other special needs. Sometimes accommodations are delivered while teaching the entire class, while others are made with individual students or as part of small groups.

You may need to differentiate your basic skill instruction in the areas of preskills; selecting and sequencing examples; the rate of introduction of new skills; and the amount of direct instruction, practice, and review.

In teaching subject-area content to students with special needs, accommodations may have to be made in activating background knowledge, organizing content, and teaching terms and concepts. Your written and oral communication with students must be clear.

Including parents in teaching their children can be helpful. You may also need to make accommodations for students in independent practice activities such as seatwork, those found in learning centers, and homework.

Students with moderate to severe disabilities often cannot perform some or all of the steps in everyday tasks. These students require instructional modifications based on an alternative curriculum set forth on their IEPs. You can use an environmental inventory as well as the INCLUDE strategy to modify your classroom activities for these students.

Back to the Cases

This section provides opportunities for you to apply the knowledge gained in this chapter to the cases described at the beginning of this chapter. The questions and activities that follow demonstrate how these standards and principles, along with other concepts that you have learned about in this chapter, connect to the everyday activities of all teachers.

Ms. Diaz notes that lately Abdul has been showing signs of losing the motivation to try new math skills. She has increased the number of examples and practice opportunities each time she introduces a new skill and provides oral and written directions for all seatwork activities. Another teacher has suggested that she use an advance organizer whenever she introduces a new skill. Develop an advance organizer for the lesson in the case study for teaching conversion of fractions into percentages. (INTASC Principles 1.03, 4.03, and 7.02; and CEC Standard 4.) After you have completed that task, explain why using advance organizers might help increase Abdul's motivation to learn new skills, especially math skills.

Cecily, as you may remember, struggles with reading comprehension. At the end of this case, we ask how Ms. Boyd might help her read and remember content in her history text. Later in the chapter, we suggest that a study guide might be a useful tool for Cecily. Developing effective study guides that move beyond the knowledge (recall) level of Bloom's taxonomy is a skill that requires practice. (INTASC Principles 1.03, 7.02, and 7.04; and CEC Standard 3.) Construct a study guide that would effectively support and extend Cecily's learning as she reads the history text, using the following instructions.

Ask one to three classmates to form a work group. Select a portion of a chapter from this text and individually develop a study guide for that portion (see the Professional Edge "How to Develop Study Guides"). Once everyone in the group has completed a study guide, compare your guides using these questions:

- Do you and your peers agree on the important or key topics? Do you agree on the important vocabulary words to be included? Note and discuss differences.
- Do the study guides match the objectives listed at the beginning of the chapter?
- Are your questions written to help Cecily understand the material at the higher levels of Bloom's taxonomy (applying, analyzing, evaluating, and creating)? Are they also written to help her with knowledge and comprehension of specific facts?
- Collaborate with your peers to incorporate everyone's ideas into a single study guide that will meet Cecily's needs.

Albert, as you may remember, struggles to complete seatwork. Ms. Olivieri has taken several steps to improve Albert's ability to complete seatwork independently. First, she starts lessons in which she will introduce a new skill by reviewing the skills previously learned that apply to the new skill. Next, as she teaches the new skill, she regularly offers numerous examples of work she expects students to complete during independent practice. Finally, she provides clear, step-by-step directions in both oral and written formats. She has noted that Albert's ability to do correct work has improved. However, he still has difficulty completing the same quantity of work that his peers are able to complete. Once he has completed some portion of the work, he is out of his seat to sharpen a pencil, throw away scrap paper, or chat with a friend. Since Ms. Olivieri has experienced some success with Albert, she is encouraged to continue working to help him become independent in completing his seatwork. What might she try next? (INTASC Principles 1.03, 4.04, and 7.02; and CEC Standards 3 and 4.) Explain why you selected these strategies or interventions.

Key Terms and Concepts

Advance organizers (p. 336)
Anticipation guides (p. 335)
Concept diagrams (p. 346)
Concept map (p. 340)
Environmental inventory (p. 357)
Example selection (p. 319)
Example sequencing (p. 321)

Graphic organizers (p. 339)
Organizational pattern (p. 337)
Planning think sheets (p. 336)
PReP (PreReading Plan) strategy (p. 335)
Preskills (p. 319)
Rate of skill introduction (p. 322)
Study guide (p. 337)

Now go to the Friend and Bursuck, Fifth Edition, MyEducationLab course at www.myeducationlab.com to

- take a pretest to assess your initial comprehension of the chapter content
- study chapter content with your individualized study plan
- take a posttest to assess your understanding of chapter content
- engage in multimedia exercises to help you build a deeper and more applied understanding of chapter content

Applications in Teaching Practice

Developing a Repertoire of Instructional Accommodations

You want to teach a group of at-risk students to spell the following contractions: *can't, aren't, couldn't, shouldn't, wouldn't, don't, won't,* and *isn't.*

Questions

1. How can you evaluate whether your students have learned the contractions?

2. What preskills should you be concerned with, how can you assess them, and what can you do with students who do not know them?

3. How can you sequence instruction? Why did you choose this particular sequence?

4. How can you provide direct instruction, practice, and review for your students?

5. At what rate should you introduce the contractions?

Design a study guide for a section of Chapter 2 of this text.

Questions

1. What steps did you go through in constructing your study guide?

2. How did you select the vocabulary and concepts that you included?

3. How would you use the study guide to teach students who are at risk or other students with special needs?

Develop a graphic organizer for a major concept in Chapter 1 of this text.

Questions

1. How did you select the concept? Is it a big idea?

2. How would you use the graphic organizer to teach students who are at risk or other students with special needs?

Design a lesson to teach the concept of *reasonable accommodations* using a definition.

Questions

1. Is your definition stated clearly, simply, and concisely?

2. What positive and negative examples did you use?

3. How can you find out whether your students know the meaning of the concept?

4. How can you find out whether your students can differentiate this concept from other concepts presented in the text?

5. How would you teach the concept using a concept diagram format?

You are teaching a lesson on the respiratory system. First you describe the respiratory process (for example, diaphragm contracts; air rushes into nose and/or mouth; air travels down trachea; air enters lungs through bronchial tubes; and so forth) using a chart showing the key parts of the respiratory system (for example, nose, throat and trachea, bronchial tubes, lungs). Next you plan to have students work in small, heterogeneous groups on labeling a model of the respiratory system and describing all the key steps in the respiratory process.

Questions

1. Based on this lesson, complete an environmental inventory for a student with a moderate to severe intellectual disability.

2. Using INCLUDE, what other modifications might you make for this student?

Further Readings

Beck, I. L., McKeown, M. G., & Kucan, L. (2002). *Bringing words to life: Robust vocabulary instruction.* New York: Guilford.

> Rarely do the terms *practical* and *research-based* merge as they do in this indispensable little book on teaching vocabulary to all learners.

Clayton, J., Burdge, M., Denham, A., Kleinert, H. I., & Kearns, J. (2006). A four-step process for accessing the general education curriculum for students with significant cognitive disabilities. *Teaching Exceptional Children, 38*(5), 20–27.

Cushing, L. S., Clark, N. M., Carter, E. W., & Kennedy, C. H. (2005). Access to the general education curriculum for students with significant cognitive disabilities. *Teaching Exceptional Children, 38*(2), 6–13.

Giangreco, M. F. (2007). Extending inclusive opportunities. *Educational Leadership, 64*(5), 34–37.

> These articles provide practical ideas about making curriculum modifications for students with significant intellectual disabilities.

Fahsl, A. J. (2007). Mathematics accommodations for all students. *Intervention in School and Clinic, 42*(4), 198–203.

Miller, S. P., & Hudson, P. J. (2006). Helping students with disabilities understand what mathematics means. *Teaching Exceptional Children, 39*(1), 28–35.

> These articles provide many useful ideas for making accommodations for students with special needs in math.

Rammell, C., Wedgeworth, L., Brown, C., Combley, R., Hewitt, C., Raybould, H., Todd, J., & Williams, J. (2003). *Collins COBUILD learners' dictionary: Concise edition.* London: HarperCollins.

> The explanations written in full, natural English in this dictionary make it an ideal resource for English-language learners.

Thorndike, E. L., & Barnhart, C. L. (1998). *Thorndike Barnhart children's dictionary: Medallion edition.* Chicago: Scott Foresman–Addison Wesley.

> Clear definitions are essential for student understanding of new vocabulary. The definitions in this are among the best we have seen in children's dictionaries.

10 Strategies for Independent Learning

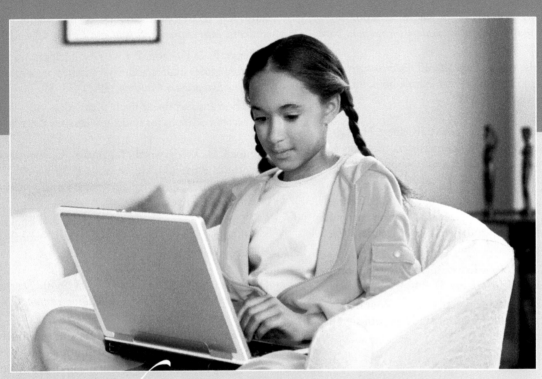

LEARNING *Objectives*

After you read this chapter, you will be able to

1. State ways that teachers can encourage student self-awareness and self-advocacy.
2. Describe ways that independent learning strategies can be developed and taught.
3. List and describe successful learning strategies in the areas of reading and reading comprehension, listening and note taking, written expression, math problem solving, and time and resource management.
4. Describe ways that students can learn to use learning strategies independently.

Gerald is a student with learning disabilities in Mr. McCrae's ninth-grade English class. Gerald has had problems in the area of written expression throughout his school years, consistently failing to meet standards on the state high-stakes assessment. It is not that he does not have good ideas. When Gerald talks about what he is going to write, it sounds great. However, when he tries to get his ideas on paper, he becomes very frustrated. Writing is difficult for Gerald. One problem is that his papers lack organization. They rarely have a good introduction and conclusion, and the body is usually out of sequence. Gerald also makes a lot of mechanical errors; his papers are full of misspellings, and he frequently leaves out punctuation marks and capital letters. When asked by Mr. McCrae why he does not proofread his papers, Gerald responded that he does.

■ *What can Mr. McCrae do to help Gerald learn to organize his papers better? How can he help Gerald proofread his papers better for mechanical errors?*

Traci is a student in Ms. Cord's third-grade class. Traci has yet to meet standards on the state high-stakes assessment in math, but her scores have never been low enough to make her eligible for special education services. Traci has trouble solving story problems in math because she does not have a systematic way of working on them.

When she starts a problem, she looks for the numbers right away rather than first reading the problem carefully. For example, one day she saw the numbers 23 and 46 in a problem and automatically added them to get a sum of 69. The problem called for subtraction, but Traci did not know that, because she had not read the problem.

■ *What can Ms. Cord do to help Traci solve math word problems more successfully? How can Ms. Cord help Traci become a more independent problem solver?*

Ron is a twelfth-grade student with a moderate intellectual disability who has problems with organization. He is often late for school, because, according to his parents, he rarely plans ahead and is always getting his materials ready for school at the last minute. Ron is usually late for class as well. He says that he cannot keep track of what he needs to bring to each class, so he is constantly going back to his locker, which makes him late. His locker is a complete mess. In the afternoons, Ron has a part-time job helping to clean copying and fax machines as part of a work-study program. His supervisor has expressed concern that Ron has been late for work several times and frequently misses his bus, causing his co-workers to have to drive him home.

■ *What can Ron's teachers do to help him become better organized?*

All these students share a common problem: They are unable to meet the academic and organizational demands of school independently. Being able to work independently is a skill that has become increasingly important as more and more students are expected to meet state and federal standards. Gerald needs to be able to organize his papers better, not just in English but in all areas, because teachers often judge quality on the basis of organization, neatness, and the number of spelling or punctuation errors. Traci needs to solve problems more systematically, not just in math but in other classes and outside of school as well. Ron needs a strategy for managing his time: Being punctual and having the necessary supplies or materials are essential for success on his alternate assessments as well as eventually in the world of work. The fact is, as students move through the grades and on to careers or postsecondary education, more and more independence is expected and necessary for success.

Strategy Homework Exercise

Go to the Homework and Exercises section in Chapter 10 of MyEducationLab to learn how teaching students to use self-reporting can improve self-awareness.

Students need to perform independently in five key areas: gaining information, storing and retrieving information, expressing information, self-advocating, and managing time (Ellis & Lenz, 1996). Gaining information involves skills in listening to directions during lessons and on the job and in reading and interpreting textbooks, source books, and other media. Storing information consists of strategies for taking notes and preparing for tests or other evaluations. Students also need to retrieve information when needed. For example, they need to remember how to carry out a task such as cleaning and clearing a table or how to follow safety procedures during science lab. Expressing information includes the tasks of taking tests and writing papers. It also involves employment tasks such as developing a printed menu for a fast-food restaurant. Self-advocacy skills help students set realistic school or life goals and develop and carry out a plan to meet those goals. Finally, students need to have the time management skills to organize their time and efforts toward meeting their goals.

Although all these skills become more important as students progress through school, independence should be stressed at all levels of instruction. Unfortunately, many students, including those who are at risk or have other special needs, lack basic independent learning skills. Traditionally, when students needed learning-strategy instruction, they were referred to special education classes, remedial reading or math programs, or special study-skills courses. But in inclusive classrooms, learning strategies can be taught to students with special needs in several ways. Moreover, often learning strategies can be covered in class so that all students can benefit. For example, when Mr. Cooper discovered that many of his students in U.S. history were having trouble taking notes, he presented a note-taking strategy to his whole class. Similarly, Ms. Carpenter taught her biology class a strategy for taking multiple-choice tests because her students were scoring low as a group on these kinds of questions.

> Being able to work independently is a skill that has become increasingly important as more and more students are expected to meet state and federal standards.

Sometimes when students have more intensive skill needs, more individualized strategy instruction might take place outside the classroom. For example, some students with special needs may need to have a strategy broken down into small steps, view multiple demonstrations of a strategy, and practice the strategy many times before they learn it. If the collaborative support of other education professionals is lacking, this level of instruction may be difficult to deliver within the time and curricular constraints of the general education classroom. Ron, from the chapter-opening case, has just such extraordinary needs. He needs a strategy designed specifically for his organizational problems; a plan for getting to his afternoon job on time would not be relevant for the rest of his classmates. In cases such as these—in which a special educator teaches a strategy to individual students—your job is to encourage and monitor student use of the strategy in your class and to provide students with feedback on their performance. However, in most cases, you can teach many of these skills in your class while still covering the required academic content. In fact, teaching learning strategies to students allows you to cover more material because your students become able to learn on their own.

You should do all you can to encourage and teach independent learning strategies to your students. This chapter focuses on ways you can build student independence in learning by encouraging student self-awareness and self-advocacy skills, developing and teaching independent learning strategies directly in class, and teaching students to use specific strategies on their own. Keep in mind that the strategies discussed apply most directly to students with high-incidence or sensory disabilities and to students who are at risk for learning problems.

How Can You Encourage Student Self-Awareness and Self-Advocacy?

As we have said, as students move through elementary, middle, and high school and on to postsecondary education or the world of work, the level of independence expected by those around them increases. Teachers expect students to come to class on time, master content through reading and lectures, keep track of assignments, organize study and homework time, set realistic career goals, and participate in curricular and extracurricular activities to meet these career goals. Students also are expected to recognize when they have a problem and to know where to go for help. Clearly, students need to look out for themselves, to become self-advocates. **Self-advocacy** is an important part of self-determination, or the ability to make decisions and direct behavior so that the desired goals are achieved (Holverstott, 2005). While the goal of becoming self-determined is important for all students, it is particularly important for students with special needs, who, as you learned in Chapter 7, are at risk for learned helplessness and low self-esteem.

Adjusting to changing expectations can be difficult for all students, but especially for those with disabilities. Many students with special needs are not aware of their strengths and weaknesses (Brinckerhoff, 1994; Scanlon & Mellard, 2002) and lack self-advocacy skills (Durlak, Rose, & Bursuck, 1994; Janiga & Costenbader, 2002). Self-advocacy skills can be taught to students of all ages and disabilities (Test, Fowler, Brewer, & Wood, 2005).

In effective student self-advocacy training, students learn their strengths and weaknesses, the potential impact of these strengths and weaknesses on their performance, the support they need to succeed, and the skills required to communicate their needs positively and assertively. Generally speaking, special educators have much of the responsibility for teaching self-advocacy directly. However, general education teachers are in a good position to teach all students about the opportunities and expectations of the adult world related to self-awareness and self-advocacy. For example, in applying the steps in INCLUDE, when Ms. Gay observed that Meredith was getting F's on her independent work in class, Ms. Gay surmised that Meredith's problem was at least in part due to her being afraid to ask for help. Ms. Gay decided to spend five minutes with the whole class to talk about knowing when and how to ask for help. She felt this discussion would help Meredith and other students in the class be more assertive when they had a problem. In another situation, Cecil, a student with a vision impairment who was in Mr. Jordan's algebra class, sat in the front row but was still unable to see the problems on the board, because Mr. Jordan formed his numbers too small. However, Cecil did not feel comfortable asking Mr. Jordan to write larger. With his special education teacher, Cecil practiced asking Mr. Jordan for help. Cecil then asked Mr. Jordan directly, who responded that it would be no problem to write bigger. Mr. Jordan also gave Cecil some additional pointers

Info Sheet Homework Exercise

Go to the Homework and Exercises section in Chapter 10 of MyEducationLab for information about a metacognitive strategy for problem solving and self-advocacy.

INCLUDE

Info Sheet Homework Exercise

Go to the Homework and Exercises section in Chapter 10 of MyEducationLab to learn about teaching self-determination skills.

TOGETHER

Fostering Team Communication and Self-Advocacy

Avery was a student in Mr. Katz's sophomore biology class. In about the third week of school, Avery approached Mr. Katz after class. Avery said he had a learning disability and that his special education teacher said he had a legal right to receive more time to take his classroom tests. Mr. Katz was concerned. He felt that it wasn't fair to let Avery have extra time when he couldn't do that for the rest of the class. Mr. Katz also knew that new state tests in science were going into effect soon and that getting more time to take classroom tests was not a good way to prepare Avery for them. In Mr. Katz's eyes, if Avery failed to meet standards in science, he, Avery's teacher, would be accountable. Furthermore, Mr. Katz was furious that no one had told him about this issue. He knew Avery had learning disabilities and that he might need extra help, but no one had said anything about changing how he took tests. Mr. Katz remembered that he had been unable to attend Avery's individualized education program (IEP) meeting due to a scheduling conflict, but shouldn't someone have told him about something as important as this?

What has gone wrong here? What should Mr. Katz do?

- Even though Avery has a legal right to testing accommodations, Mr. Katz seems to have little knowledge of what this right involves and how eligibility for testing accommodations is determined by the IEP team. The proper time to have addressed Mr. Katz's concerns about

testing accommodations was before the plan was put in place, not after. At the high school level, it is common for some teachers not to attend IEP meetings. However, even if a teacher is not at the IEP meeting, it is the responsibility of the team to inform all relevant staff members about what has been decided.

- The more basic problem here is that Avery's IEP team has not been operating as such. In effective teaming, the group's goals, as well the means toward attaining those goals, need to be clear to all team members. While Avery's special education teacher might be doing the right thing in teaching Avery to advocate for himself, the success of this effort depends on all of the team members' understanding the goal and working together to help the student attain it.

- Unfortunately, communication problems such as this one can happen in this era of teacher shortages and school regulation. What should Mr. Katz do? An understandable response would be to play the victim and complain bitterly to whomever would listen. However, this response would undermine Mr. Katz's obligations as a member of Avery's IEP team, the purpose of which is to work together for the betterment of Avery's education. A more proactive approach would be to view the situation as a team communication problem in need of a solution. Mr. Katz should request a meeting, express his concerns about Avery's accommodations, and work to reach a team consensus consistent with Avery's unique needs.

---

on how to describe his disability and how to ask his teachers for accommodations. The Working Together stresses the importance of teachers working together as a team when helping students acquire self-advocacy skills.

How Can You Effectively Teach Independent Learning Strategies in Class?

In addition to teaching students to advocate for their own educational needs, another way you can help your students become more independent is to teach them strategies for learning how to learn (Lenz, 2006). These methods are collectively referred to as learning strategies. **Learning strategies** are techniques, principles, and rules that enable a student to learn to solve problems and complete tasks independently (Lenz, Ellis, & Scanlon, 1996;

Schumaker, Deshler, & Denton, 1984). Learning strategies, which are similar to study skills, not only emphasize the steps needed to perform a strategy (for example, steps to follow in reading a textbook) but also stress why and when to use that strategy as well as how to monitor its usage. For example, when Ms. Blankenship taught her students a strategy for reading their textbook, she pointed out that the strategy would save them time yet improve their test scores. She also taught them to judge how well they were using the strategy by filling out a simple checklist as they read. The Case in Practice shows how the INCLUDE strategy can be used to select the appropriate learning strategies for your students.

INCLUDE

An important component of teaching learning strategies effectively is to present well-designed strategies. As you recall from the discussions of effective materials in Chapters 5 and 9, the better your materials are designed, the greater the chance that they will work for your

Case in Practice   INCLUDE

Using INCLUDE to Guide Instruction in Learning Strategies

Mr. Devereau taught social studies at Martin Luther King Jr. Middle School. He had a reputation for expecting a lot from his students; throughout the year, he expected them to be able to learn an increasing amount of subject matter independently.

Prior to the first day of school, Mr. Devereau was informed that his first-period class included eight students with learning disabilities and two with behavior disorders. He was also told that a special education teacher, Ms. Finch, was assigned to the class as a co-teacher. Mr. Devereau had never had this many students with disabilities at one time before; he also had never worked with a co-teacher. Still, he was hopeful that Ms. Finch would be able to help him, so he set up an appointment to meet with her.

Ms. Finch: What demands do students have to meet to be successful in your class?

Mr. Devereau: I expect students to begin to learn on their own. That is what is expected when they get to high school. I assign most of the reading of the text to be done outside of class, and I require students to take notes from class lectures and DVDs that I show. With my lectures, I use mainly PowerPoint slides. I distribute copies of the slides to students before class.

Ms. Finch: How does your grading system work?

Mr. Devereau: Grades are based on student performance on two multiple-choice tests and a five-page report on a famous person in pre–Civil War America.

Ms. Finch: Based on how your class is structured, my concern is that the students' IEPs show that they all are likely to have problems finding main ideas in both the textbook and the class lectures. But I know of some learning strategies that would help them be more successful in these areas.

Mr. Devereau: That sounds good. It's likely that other students in the class would benefit from these strategies as well.

Mr. Devereau and Ms. Finch decided to each take a strategy. Mr. Devereau would teach the note-taking strategy while he was lecturing in class. Ms. Finch would assist by modeling note taking at the board and/or monitoring student note-taking performance and providing corrective feedback as necessary. Ms. Finch was to teach the students two textbook-reading strategies: one for scanning a text and another for summarizing the big ideas in the text. She was to work on these strategies daily during the last 15 minutes of class until the students were able to perform them independently. While Ms. Finch and Mr. Devereau thought that the students with special needs would also have trouble with the multiple-choice tests and the five-page report, they decided that covering these strategies at the same time would be too much. However, they agreed to show the students how the strategies they were learning for note taking and textbook reading could also help them with their tests and research paper.

REFLECTIONS

How did Mr. Devereau and Ms. Finch use INCLUDE to help their students? Was it appropriate for them to teach the strategies to the entire class? Why? Under what circumstances might it have been more appropriate to teach the learning strategies to smaller groups? Which strategies described in this chapter might be appropriate for Mr. Devereau and Ms. Finch to use? What might they do to tie the strategies the students are learning to their needs in test taking and report writing?

students with special needs without requiring you to make major accommodations. Some effective guidelines for designing learning strategies are presented in the Professional Edge.

For students to use learning strategies independently, they must first learn to perform them accurately and fluently. Research shows that most students benefit when the teacher directly explains how learning strategies can help them complete academic tasks (Lenz, 2006). However, students vary in the amount of structure they need to acquire learning strategies (Lenz, 2006). Some students can construct successful strategies on their own from repeatedly completing tasks in their classes (Pressley & Hilden, 2006). Other students may need simple prompts and models to develop strategies. This level of structure can usually be delivered by the general education teacher in a large-group setting. Still other students may require more intensive instruction, often in a small group, that includes explicit describing and modeling of the strategy as well as extensive practice and feedback about how to apply the strategy to their course demands (Swanson, 2001). The following steps have proven effective for teaching learning strategies (Deshler et al., 1996):

1. Assess current strategy use.

2. Clarify expectations.

Professional EDGE

Developing Your Own Learning Strategies

You can use the guidelines here either to create your own learning strategies or to evaluate ones that are commercially produced. By following these suggestions, you will not always need to depend on commercial publishers for your learning materials. Rather, you can develop learning strategies to fit the students in your class.

1. Identify skill areas that are problematic for most of your students, such as taking multiple-choice tests or writing lecture notes.

2. For each skill area, specify student outcomes, such as scoring at least 10 percent higher on multiple-choice tests or writing down key main ideas and details from a lecture.

3. List a set of specific steps students need to follow to reach the identified outcomes. You may want to ask other students who have good test-taking and note-taking skills what they do. Presented here is a sample reading comprehension strategy called *RAP* (Ellis & Lenz, 1987):

   R   *Read* a paragraph.

   A   *Ask* yourself what were the main idea and two details.

   P   *Put* the main idea and details in your own words.

4. Your strategy should contain no more than eight steps. Having more steps makes the strategy difficult to remember.

5. Your steps should be brief; each should begin with a verb that directly relates to the strategy.

6. To help students remember the steps, encase the strategy in a mnemonic device (for example, the acronym RAP for the reading strategy just presented).

7. The strategy should cue students to perform behaviors for thinking (remembering), for doing (reading), and for self-evaluation (surveying or checking their work).

8. A textbook-reading strategy that was developed by teachers (Bartelt, Marchio, & Reynolds, 1994) and that meets the guidelines for developing an effective learning strategy follows:

   R   *Review* headings and subheadings.

   E   *Examine* boldface words.

   A   *Ask*, "What do I expect to learn?"

   D   *Do* it—Read!

   S   *Summarize* in your own words.

Source: Adapted from "Generalization and Adaptation of Learning Strategies to Natural Environments: Part 2. Research into Practice," by E. Ellis, K. Lenz, and E. Sabornie, 1987, *Remedial and Special Education, 8*(2), pp. 6–23. Copyright © 1987 by Hammill Institute on Disability. Reprinted with permission.

3. Demonstrate strategy use.

4. Encourage students to memorize strategy steps.

5. Provide guided and independent practice.

6. Administer posttests.

These steps include many of the effective teaching practices described in Chapters 5 and 9. Use the INCLUDE strategy to help you determine the level of structure you need to provide to students as you deliver each step.

Assess Current Strategy Use

Students often are receptive to instruction when they can clearly see what problems they are having and how the strategy you are teaching can help them overcome these problems. Therefore, learning-strategy instruction begins with an assessment of how well your students can currently perform a skill, a part of the N and C steps of INCLUDE. As you learned in Chapter 4, specific learning strategies can be assessed using direct observation checklists, analyses of student products, and student self-evaluations.

You also need to assess whether your students have the preskills necessary to perform the strategy. For example, on the one hand, students who can discriminate between main ideas and details in a lecture are ideal candidates for learning a note-taking strategy; students who can read all the words on a test and understand the class content will benefit most from a test-taking strategy. On the other hand, students who cannot identify most of the words in their texts are not logical candidates for learning a textbook-reading strategy; students whose seatwork activities are too hard for them will not benefit from a strategy to help them organize their independent practice activities.

As you have learned, students with special needs often lack critical preskills. Before you decide to teach a particular strategy, you should identify its preskills and assess them separately. If most students lack the preskills, they can be taught as part of your everyday instruction. If only a few have problems with preskills, these students need to receive additional instruction in class, with a peer or adult tutor, through co-taught lessons, or in a learning center or special education setting.

Clarify Expectations

Learning strategies have the potential of empowering your students because they enable them to learn and succeed in and out of school on their own, without undue help from others. When you introduce learning strategies to students, you need to point out their potential benefits clearly and specifically. Carefully explained expected outcomes can be motivating, particularly as students get older and teacher encouragement alone may no longer be enough to keep them interested.

The first step in getting and keeping students motivated to learn is to provide a strong rationale for why learning the strategy is important. This rationale should be directly tied to current student performance as well as to the demands of your class, two essential pieces of information derived from the INCLUDE process. For example, when introducing a new note-taking strategy, Mr. Washington pointed out that the class was able to identify on average only half of the main ideas presented on a note-taking pretest. He also told his class that half of the material on his tests would come from information presented during his lectures. Finally, Mr. Washington explained that taking good notes can help students outside of school as well; in many job situations, employers give directions that need to be written down.

The next step in clarifying expectations is to explain specifically what students should be able to accomplish when they have learned the skill. For example, Ms. Thompson told her class that after learning a textbook-reading strategy, they would be able to do their homework faster. Also, give students an idea of how long it will take them to learn the

INCLUDE

INCLUDE

Simulation Homework Exercise

Go to the Homework and Exercises section in Chapter 10 of MyEducationLab and walk through the steps for teaching learning strategies.

INCLUDE

strategy. For example, you could make a chart showing the instructional activities to be covered each day and the approximate number of days it will take to learn the strategy. The advantage of presenting the information on a chart is that steps can be crossed out or checked off as completed. The act of checking off completed activities can be very motivating for students. It is also a way of demonstrating self-monitoring, an effective independent learning skill that we discuss later in this chapter.

Demonstrate Strategy Use

In demonstrating strategies, keep in mind three important points. First, remember that the process one goes through in performing a task or solving a problem should be carefully explained. For example, demonstrate both thinking and doing behaviors. Talking aloud to yourself while performing the skill is particularly important for many students with special needs, who often do not develop spontaneously organized thinking patterns.

Second, present both positive and negative examples of appropriate strategy use, carefully explaining why they are positive or negative. This explanation can help students tell the difference between doing a strategy the right way and doing it incorrectly, a distinction that can be difficult for students with special needs to make without direct instruction. For example, Mr. Washington demonstrated effective and ineffective note-taking strategies using the overhead projector. As a student listened to a short videotaped lecture, he took notes systematically, writing down key ideas and details. Next, using the same lecture, he demonstrated ineffective note taking by trying to write down every word.

Third, after you demonstrate, ask frequent questions to test student understanding. Frequent questioning can help you monitor student understanding and determine whether more demonstration is needed. Keep in mind that for many students, including those with disabilities, one demonstration may not be enough.

www.resources

The following websites can provide information about helping students make the transition from school to work:

LD OnLine: www.ldonline.org/ld_indepth/transition/transition.html

All Means All School-to-Work Project: http://ici.umn.edu/all

Vocational and Educational Services for Individuals with Disabilities: www.vesid.nysed.gov/do/transition.htm

Demonstrating the use of a learning strategy involves explaining both the thinking and the doing parts of a process, showing examples and nonexamples of effective strategy use, and checking learners' understanding. How do these steps help students with special needs acquire learning strategies?

Encourage Students to Memorize Strategy Steps

The purpose of having students memorize the steps in the strategy is to make it easier for them to recall the strategy when they need to use it. To help students learn the steps, you can post them prominently in your classroom at first so that you and your students can refer to them throughout the class or day. Students may also need to be drilled on saying the strategy steps. To practice, students could pair off and quiz each other; or you could ask students the strategy steps before and after class. For example, each day during the last several minutes of class, Ms. Henry quizzed four of her social studies students on the steps of the KWL reading strategy.

Even though memorizing a strategy can help students recall it, you may not want to spend too much time on this step, particularly for some of your students with special needs, who may have memory problems. For these students, you might include the steps to all the strategies they are learning in a special section of their assignment notebooks. For strategies used most often, cue cards listing strategy steps can be taped to the inside cover of textbooks or notebooks.

Provide Guided and Independent Practice

As we have already stated, students must learn how to perform strategies accurately and fluently before they can attempt them independently. Such proficiency requires considerable practice. Five ways of providing practice on learning strategies are suggested. One way is to have students practice with controlled materials when they are first learning a strategy. **Controlled materials** are generally materials at the student's reading level, of high interest, and relatively free of complex vocabulary and concepts. Because controlled materials remove many content demands on the learner, they allow students to focus all their energy on learning the strategy. Controlled materials also allow for initial success, which is important for motivation. For example, Mr. Bernard was teaching his students a strategy for taking essay tests in current events. At first, he had his students practice this strategy on simply worded, one-part essay questions about material familiar to the students, such as people and events in the areas of rock music, movies, television, and sports. As students became better at using the strategy, Mr. Bernard gradually introduced more complex questions on less familiar topics, such as the AIDS epidemic in Africa and the economic conditions in Mexico. Finally, he used sample test questions.

A second way to provide students with practice is first to guide them and then to allow them to perform independently. By *guided practice,* we mean giving students verbal cues when they are first attempting a skill. For example, before and while her students were practicing a strategy, Ms. Waters asked them questions such as, "What will you do first?" "Why did you do that?" "What should you do after you are done with the strategy steps?" "Which key words are you going to look for in the questions?" "How will you know which are the main ideas?" and "Was the sentence I just read a main idea? Why?" Once most students seem able to answer your reminder questions, you can gradually stop asking them so that students are eventually performing independently. Some students may need little guided practice or none at all. These students can be allowed to work independently right away.

A third practice technique is to give feedback that is specific and encourages students to evaluate themselves (Lenz, 2006; Lenz et al., 1996). For example, Dominique has just performed the steps of a proofreading strategy in front of the class. Her teacher says, "Good job, Dominique! I knew you could do it." Denise performed the same strategy in front of her class and her teacher asked, "How do you think you did? What do you need to focus on most the next time?" The feedback Dominique received does not clearly tell her what she did right, nor does it encourage self-evaluation. The feedback given to Denise encourages self-evaluation, a critical part of independent learning. Of course, if Denise cannot evaluate her own performance at first, the key parts of good performance have to be pointed out to her and practice on self-evaluation provided.

Research Note

Reeve (2006) reports that teachers can be structured but still be supportive of student independence by (1) being attuned to students' wants and needs; (2) establishing a sense of relatedness or warmth, affection, and approval for students; (3) affirming students' capacity for self-direction while accepting them for who they are; and (4) exerting gentle discipline by guiding and explaining why one way of thinking or behaving is right and another is wrong, as opposed to merely insisting on compliance.

A fourth aspect of practicing learning strategies is to praise students only when they have produced work that is praiseworthy. Praise that is not tied to student performance or is exaggerated, often for the purpose of enhancing student self-image, may only reinforce student inadequacy. For example, because of a history of failure in learning situations, students with special needs often see little relationship between their efforts and classroom success. When you give nonspecific praise to these students, it is easier for them to attribute your praise to something other than competence, such as sympathy ("I'm so bad at this, she has to pretend I did well").

Encourage students to reinforce themselves and to take responsibility for both their successes and their failures.

Fifth, encourage students to reinforce themselves and to take responsibility for both their successes and their failures. For example, after doing well on a note-taking strategy, Alicia was encouraged by her teacher to say, "I did a good job. This time I paid attention and wrote down all the main ideas. I need to do the same the next time." Alicia's teacher was showing her how to attribute her success to factors under her control. This approach can help her become a more active, independent learner.

Administer Posttests

fyi

Knowing which strategies to teach your students is an important outcome of using the INCLUDE strategy.

When it appears from your practice sessions that most students have acquired the strategy, give them the pretest again, this time as a posttest, to test their mastery. If according to your posttest, students have not acquired the strategy, then identify where the breakdown occurred and then provide additional instruction and/or practice. If more than 20 percent of the students need extra practice or instruction, they can receive additional help in a large or small group. If fewer than 20 percent of the students require more assistance, those needing more individualized practice can be provided with peer tutors or support staff.

What Are Some Examples of Successful Learning Strategies?

There is a growing research base of learning strategies that work for students who are at risk or who have special needs. These strategies cover many areas, including reading and reading comprehension, listening and note taking, written expression, math-problem solving, and time and resource management. An array of strategies that incorporate many of these effective practices are summarized in the following sections. Many of these strategies can be used with students at all levels—elementary, middle, and secondary.

www.resources

The Instructional Strategies Online Database (ISOD) (Hodges et al., 2007) provides a wealth of learning strategies for students. ISOD is designed to be searched by content area, grade level, and other key information about strategies, such as rationale, material needs, procedures, corresponding standards, and adaptations. ISOD is found on the Internet at http://edhd.bgsu .edu/isod. The database opens at a home page where the user can click on "Search the database" to begin a search.

Word-Identification and Reading Fluency Strategies

Students cannot always depend on the teacher to help them figure out difficult words. They also need to read fluently enough so that they can understand what they are reading and finish assignments in a timely manner. The next two strategies are designed to help students help themselves in the important areas of word identification and reading fluency.

● **Identifying Words in Textbook Reading** Middle and high school students are likely to encounter technical words in their content-area textbooks that have multiple syllables, making them difficult for students to identify. A strategy designed to help students with special needs identify difficult words in their textbook reading is described here

(Archer, Gleason, & Vachon, 2003, p. 95). The strategy helps students break apart words and then put them back together again. First, teach your students to break words apart on paper by having them do the following:

Info Sheet Homework Exercise

Go to the Homework and Exercises section in Chapter 10 of MyEducationLab for a list of research-based cognitive learning strategies.

1. Circle the word parts at the beginning of the word (prefixes).
2. Circle the word parts at the end of the word (suffixes).
3. Underline the letters representing vowel sounds in the rest of the word.
4. Say the parts of the word.
5. Say the parts fast.
6. Make it a real word.

Here is an example of this strategy:

(r e)(c o n)s t r u c(t i o n)

Once your students can perform all of these steps on paper, they are gradually encouraged to perform the steps in their heads, as follows (Archer et al., 2003, p. 95):

1. Look for word parts at the beginning and end of the word, and vowel sounds in the rest of the word.
2. Say the parts of the word.
3. Say the parts fast.
4. Make it a real word.

To be successful with this strategy, students need to be able to perform two critical preskills. They need to know sounds the vowels make, and they need to be able to pronounce prefixes and suffixes. Students lacking in these preskills need to be taught them prior to strategy instruction. For words that have parts that are hard to decode, encourage students to say the parts they know and then use the strategy described next for using the context to figure out the word. Of course, it is fair to get help from a classmate or the teacher if all of these strategies have been tried and students are still unable to figure out the word.

● **WARF** To be successful understanding content-area textbooks, students need to read quickly enough so that they can think about word meaning rather than squander their energy on word identification. Students may also have to adjust their rate of reading, depending on their purpose for reading (Mercer & Pullen, 2005). Minskoff and Allsopp (2003) suggest a strategy to help students who can read accurately at least at the third-grade level but need to increase and/or adjust their reading speed. It is called *WARF:*

W   *Widen* your eye span.
A   *Avoid* skip-backs.
R   *Read* silently.
F   *Flex* your reading rate.

Case Study Homework Exercise

Go to the Homework and Exercises section in Chapter 10 of MyEducationLab to see how strategies can be used in specific content areas.

Students are first taught to widen their eye span and not read word by word. They are taught to group words, not reading the articles (for example, *the* or *a*) or auxiliary words (for example, *is* or *are*), so they can focus on words that give meaning. As part of this **W** step, they are also taught to try to group words meaningfully (for example, for the words *a sunny day*, focus on *sunny* and *day*). In the **A** step, avoiding skip-backs, students are taught to keep reading if they don't understand something, using context clues to gain understanding. They are told to go back only if this is unsuccessful. In the **R** step, students are taught to read silently, avoiding reading aloud in a whisper by pressing their lips together. In the final step, **F,** students learn to change their reading rate depending on the difficulty and/or familiarity of the material. For example, when students are looking for information, they need to know to read quickly as they search for key words on the page. When students read important information they need to understand or memorize, they need to be aware to read more slowly. Conversely, if students are reading information they know well, they can adjust their rate and read faster.

> Teachers have the time to teach only about two vocabulary words per day at the most. Therefore, students need strategies to help them figure out the meanings of words independently.

Vocabulary Strategies

In addition to being able to identify technical vocabulary, students must also know what words mean if they are to understand what they read. Strategies for using direct instruction to teach new vocabulary were covered in Chapter 9. Realistically, however, teachers have the time to teach only about two vocabulary words per day at the most (Armbruster, Lehr, & Osborn, 2001).

A strategy that your students can use to help them figure out the meaning of words independently is shown in Figures 10.1 and 10.2. To perform this strategy, students must first learn the meaning of common morphemes.

Reading Comprehension Strategies

Reading comprehension strategies are intended to help students meet the independent reading demands of content-area classes successfully, particularly in the middle and upper grades. Although reading primarily involves textbooks, students must be able to read and understand a variety of source books as well. The following are examples of proven reading comprehension strategies for students of all grade levels.

● **SCROL**   One example of a reading comprehension strategy is *SCROL* (Grant, 1993). The SCROL strategy enables students to take notes when they are reading, an important

---

FIGURE *10.1*   **Word-Part Clues**

1. Look for the *root word*, which is a single word that cannot be broken into smaller words or word parts. See if you know what the root word means.

2. Look for a *prefix*, which is a word part added to the beginning of a word that changes its meaning. See if you know what the prefix means.

3. Look for a *suffix*, which is a word part added to the end of a word that changes its meaning. See if you know what the suffix means.

4. Put the meaning of the *root word* and any prefix or suffix together and see if you can build the meaning of the word.

Source: Teaching Children to Read and Write: Becoming an Influential Teacher (2nd ed.), by R. B. Ruddell, 1999, Boston, MA: Allyn & Bacon. Copyright © 2006 by Pearson Education. Adapted by permission of the publisher.

FIGURE *10.2* **Vocabulary Clues**

When you come to a word and you don't know what it means, use these clues:

1. *Context clues:* Read the sentences around the word to see if there are clues to its meaning.

2. *Word-part clues:* See if you can break the word into a root word, prefix, or suffix to help figure out its meaning.

3. *Context clues:* Read the sentences around the word again to see if you have figured out its meaning.

Source: Teaching Children to Read and Write: Becoming an Influential Teacher (2nd ed.), by R. B. Ruddell, 1999, Boston, MA: Allyn & Bacon. Copyright © 2006 by Pearson Education. Adapted by permission of the publisher.

study strategy, and to use text headings to aid their comprehension and help them find and remember important information. The SCROL strategy has five steps:

S   *Survey* the headings. In the assigned text selection, read each heading and subheading. For each heading and subheading, try to answer the following questions: What do I already know about this topic? What information might the writer present?

C   *Connect.* Ask yourself, How do the headings relate to one another? Write down key words from the headings that might provide connections between them.

R   *Read* the text. As you read, look for words and phrases that express important information about the headings. Mark the text to point out important ideas and details. Stop to make sure that you understand the major ideas and supporting details. If you do not understand, reread.

O   *Outline.* Using indentations to reflect structure, outline the major ideas and supporting details in the heading segment. Write the heading and then try to outline each heading segment without looking back at the text.

L   *Look* back. Now look back at the text and check the accuracy of the major ideas and details you wrote. Correct any inaccurate information in your outline. If you marked the text as you read, use this information to help you verify the accuracy of your outline.

Advise students to follow steps 3–5 (**R–L**) every time they encounter a section with headings in the text they are reading. Taking notes using SCROL improves student comprehension while also providing students with a product that can help them study more effectively for tests.

● **PARS**   *PARS* is a simplified textbook-reading strategy that is good for younger students and students without much experience using textbook-reading strategies (Cheek & Cheek, 1983). The four steps of PARS follow:

P   *Preview* the material by scanning the chapter and surveying the introductory statement, headings, graphic aids, and chapter summary to identify main ideas.

A   *Ask* questions that relate to the main ideas discovered when surveying the chapter.

R   *Read* the chapter to answer the questions developed.

S   *Summarize* the main ideas in the chapter.

*R*esearch Note

Mason et al. (2006) found that instruction in reading strategies was more effective when it was combined with instruction in written expression. In their study, students were taught a strategy for reading expository text called *TWA* (**T**hink before reading; think **W**hile reading; think **A**fter reading). After students learned TWA, they were taught a writing strategy to summarize material they had just read. The strategy was called *PLANS:* **P**ick goals; **L**ist ways to meet goals; **A**nd make **N**otes and **S**equence notes. The combined use of TWA and PLANS led to student gains in reading comprehension and writing.

Remember that just telling students the steps of a learning strategy is not enough. Letting students watch you perform the strategy and then carefully guiding students as they learn to perform it are essential if students are to learn to use PARS to gain access to the content of their textbooks more independently.

● **CAPS**   You have learned that students who can comprehend stories are able to identify key parts of stories called story grammars (see the Case in Practice in Chapter 4). *CAPS* is a self-questioning strategy that guides students as they look for these important story elements (Leinhardt & Zigmond, 1988). The strategy is composed of the following steps:

C	Who are the *characters?*
A	What is the *aim* of the story?
P	What *problem* happens?
S	How is the problem *solved?*

CAPS is particularly effective for students in elementary school, where key reading demands involve understanding stories.

● **SLiCK**   A common accommodation for students with reading disabilities is the bypass strategy of providing them with an oral text. However, some students still struggle to understand a text, even when they no longer have to read it. *SLiCK* (Boyle et al., 2002) is a strategy designed to help students comprehend textbooks prerecorded on CD-ROM. It involves the following steps:

S	*Set* it up.
L	*Look* ahead through the chapter.
C	*Comprehend.*
K	*Keep* it together.

In the **S** step, the student sets it up by opening the textbook to the start of the assigned section; readying a worksheet containing the SLiCK strategy steps at the top, with spaces to record key information such as headings, subheadings, and key vocabulary words; and putting the CD in the CD player. In the **L** step, the student looks ahead through the chapter using the CD book, player, and print textbook. The student notes keywords, headings, and subheadings and records them on the worksheet. In the comprehend, or **C**, step, the student reads along with the CD, pausing to record important details under the headings and subheadings previously identified. The student is encouraged to think of big ideas by writing minisummaries as he or she reads. In the final step, **K**, the student combines all of the minisummaries to get the big picture about what the section of text means.

Boyle and colleagues (2002) report that students acquire the **S** and **L** steps quickly, while the **C** and **K** steps require considerable teacher modeling and practice before they are learned.

● **RUDPC**   You have learned that successful comprehension requires an understanding of how information in stories and expository text is organized and that students with learning disabilities and attention deficit–hyperactivity disorder (ADHD) often have trouble identifying organizational patterns. While we typically think of organizational patterns as applying to written text, information presented on computer screens has an organizational scheme as well (Minskoff & Allsopp, 2003). Research assignments in school routinely require students to access information on the Internet. Research shows that students need to learn how to navigate the different parts of a website to acquire efficiently the information they need (Kuiper, Volman, & Terwel, 2005). Often this involves ignoring the many distractions that can appear on the computer screen.

Minskoff and Allsopp (2003) developed the *RUDPC* strategy for helping students derive important information from a webpage. The steps are as follows:

R   *Read* the title and headings.

U   *Use* the cursor to skim the page.

D   *Decide* whether you need the page.

P   *Print* the page.

C   *Copy* the bibliographic information.

When reading a website, students need to make quick decisions about whether a given section of a webpage provides information they are looking for. Reading everything on the screen is inefficient. Students with special needs may need explicit instruction on the **D** step in order to learn to make these judgments. Minskoff and Allsopp (2003) also suggest that for some students, printing pages prevents them from being distracted by graphics or frustrated by small fonts.

● **POSSE**   Another reading comprehension strategy is *POSSE* (Englert & Mariage, 1991). This strategy includes many reading practices that have been shown to aid reading comprehension, such as graphic organizers, text structures, stimulation of student background knowledge, and self-monitoring. The steps in this strategy are as follows:

P   *Predict* ideas.

O   *Organize* the ideas.

S   *Search* for the structure.

S   *Summarize* the main ideas.

E   *Evaluate* your understanding.

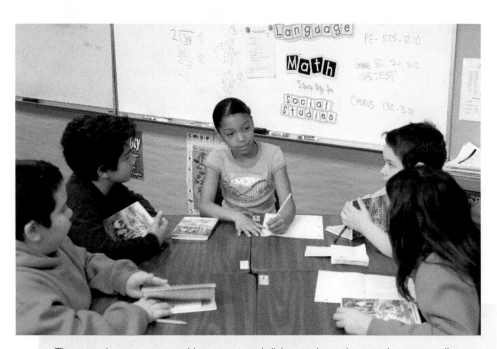

These students are engaged in a structured dialogue about the text they are reading, a peer-mediated comprehension strategy called reciprocal teaching. What strategies must students be taught before they can practice reciprocal teaching?

Analyze
and Reflect

What makes reciprocal teaching
a powerful technique for
teaching reading comprehension
to students who are at risk or
who have special needs? In what
other areas could reciprocal
teaching be used?

*R*esearch Note

Kim et al. (2006) improved the
reading comprehension skills
of middle school students with
disabilities using reciprocal
teaching adapted for use in a
computer-based instructional
format.

When students are predicting, they can be given a sentence starter such as *I predict that . . .* For this step, students are taught to use signals from a variety of sources, including title, headings in bold, pictures, keywords, and so on. Brainstorming is very important in this step.

A technique used for teaching the POSSE strategy steps is a process called reciprocal teaching. **Reciprocal teaching** is a way to teach students to comprehend reading material by providing them with teacher and peer models of thinking behavior and then allowing them to practice these thinking behaviors with their peers (Palincsar & Brown, 1988). At first, the teacher leads the dialogue, demonstrating how the strategies can be used during reading. As instruction goes on, the teacher gives the students more and more responsibility for maintaining the dialogue. Eventually, students are largely responsible for the dialogue, though the teacher still provides help as necessary. Research shows that the most important part of the technique is the teacher's releasing control and turning the dialogue over to the students (Englert & Mariage, 1991).

A sample dialogue for reciprocal teaching is presented in the Case in Practice. After reading the Case in Practice, think of the reasons reciprocal teaching is such a powerful technique for teaching reading comprehension to students who are at risk or who have special needs. In what other areas could reciprocal teaching be used? The Technology Notes feature describes computer software that teaches students key reading comprehension strategies geared to their individual reading levels.

Case in Practice

Teaching Script for Demonstrating POSSE

The students in this class have just read a section of text that focuses on Loch Ness. They are now applying the search, summarize, and evaluate steps of POSSE.

Teacher: What is the main topic the text is talking about?

Peg: The Loch Ness monster.

Teacher: What was this section about? What was the main idea?

Peg: Oh, the lake. I have two questions: "What is a lake?" and "What lives in it?"

Teacher: Do you mean this particular lake or any lake?

Peg: This lake. Joe?

Joe: It's foggy, it's deep, and it's long and narrow.

Peg: Don?

Don: The land beside the lake, you don't know if it is real soft and you could fall through it.

Teacher: So it could be soft and swampy.

Ann: I think the Loch Ness monster lives there.

Teacher: Is Ann answering your question, Peg?

Peg: No.

Teacher: What was your question?

Peg: I had two: "What is a lake?" and "What lives in the lake?"

Joe: But the book never answered that. I have a question about the main idea. Aren't we supposed to do a question about the main idea?

Teacher: Just about what we read.

Joe: Yes, but Peg asked us, "What lives in the lake?" but it doesn't really mention that in the book.

Teacher: That's true. The major idea has to do with Loch Ness and what it looks like. A minor idea that we really inferred rather than directly read in the article was that the Loch Ness monster lives in the lake.

Peg: Are there any clarifications?

Students: [No response.]

Teacher: I have a clarification. You had trouble reading some of these words and I wondered if you know what some of them mean. What does *ancestors* mean?

[The teacher continues discussing vocabulary.]

Source: From "Making Students Partners in the Comprehension Process: Organizing the Reading 'POSSE,'" by C. S. Englert and T. V. Mariage, 1991, *Learning Disability Quarterly, 14,* pp. 133–134. Used by permission of Council for Learning Disabilities.

Thinking Reader: The Textbook of the Future

Textbooks are the most common method of delivering subject-area information to students of all grades but particularly to those who are in middle school or high school. Yet many students with and without special needs experience problems comprehending their textbooks. Whereas some of these problems are due to reading slowly and/or inaccurately, students also lack strategies for locating and retaining important information in their texts. Unfortunately, standard textbooks provide teachers and students with little support in teaching and learning important comprehension strategies. Enter the Thinking Reader.

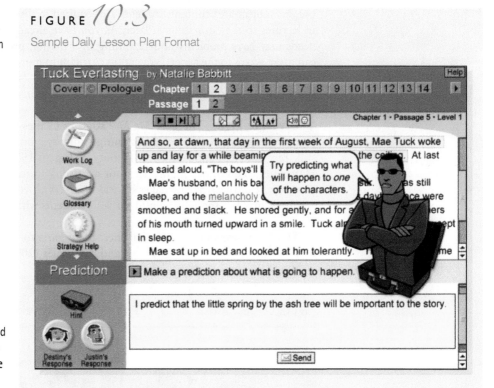

FIGURE *10.3*

Sample Daily Lesson Plan Format

The Thinking Reader incorporates a variety of supports into electronic text in order to teach research-based reading comprehension strategies such as summarizing, questioning, clarifying, predicting, and visualizing. The supports can be customized to accommodate individual student reading abilities by systematically reducing the level of structure as students become more proficient in the reading comprehension strategies. The goal is for students to select independently the strategy that best fits their comprehension needs.

The specific supports in the program include a human voice feature that reads the text while highlighting it and natural intonation to support the finding of main ideas and the development of fluency. Comprehension is supported through a series of strategy prompts that guide students as they practice the comprehension strategies. For example, at the end of each passage, students might be asked to predict what will happen in the story, clarify something that they find confusing, summarize the passage, or visualize what is happening. Students respond to the prompts in three formats: open-ended, fill-in-the-blank, and oral response. There are also supports for vocabulary development including

a contextual glossary with Spanish translations for English-language learners.

Perhaps the most helpful aspect of the Thinking Reader is the availability of supports to help students think about the passage. The program employs an *agent* who provides hints for each strategy (for example, "Try predicting what will happen to one of the characters") or think-alouds (for example, "I remembered that both Winnie's grandmother and the stranger are very interested in music. She is excited to hear the music again, and he seems to find it meaningful that she has heard it before. So I predict that the music will be important in some way"). A sample screen display is shown in Figure 10.3.

Note: The Thinking Reader was developed by Dr. David Rose and Dr. Bridget Dalton at the Center for Applied Special Technology (CAST). The program is based on research cited in this text, including a report of the National Reading Panel (2000), principles of universal design (Dalton & Pisha, 2001), and reciprocal teaching (Palincsar & Brown, 1988). The Thinking Reader has been used successfully to teach comprehension strategies to students with learning disabilities (Dalton & Pisha, 2001).

Listening and Note-Taking Strategies

Students in all grades need to be able to understand information presented orally by their teachers. In elementary school, students are required to follow many oral directions and listen when the teacher is reading aloud or presenting information orally. In middle school, junior high, and high school, where lecturing is a common way for teachers to present subject-area content, students are required to discern and record key information in lectures so they can study it later. As you have already learned, students with special needs may have problems understanding information presented orally. These problems can make access to the general education curriculum more difficult for them. The listening and note-taking strategies described in the next section were designed to help all students learn more successfully from their teachers' presentations.

● **Give Me Five**   The *Give Me Five* strategy focuses students' attention on five body parts in order to improve their listening skills: *eyes* on the speaker, *mouth* quiet, *body* still, *ears* listening, and *hands* free (Prouty & Fagan, 1997, as cited in Swain, Friehe, & Harrington, 2004). See Figure 10.4 for a helpful illustration of this strategy. The concrete nature of this strategy makes it ideal for use with younger students. Its multisensory emphasis may be especially helpful for your students with disabilities.

● **TALS**   Once students marshal their body parts to help them pay careful attention to what the teacher is saying, Swain and colleagues (2004) suggest introducing another

FIGURE *10.4* **The Give Me Five Listening Strategy**

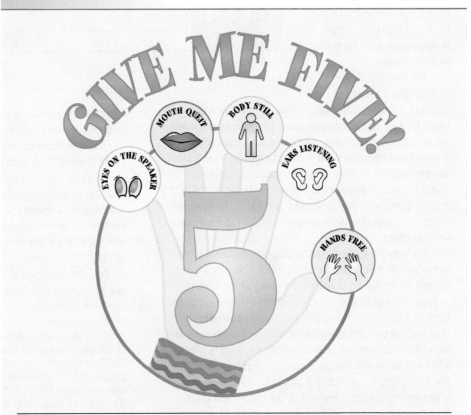

Source: From *Language Strategies for Children*, by V. Prouty and M. Fagan, 1997, Eau Claire, WI: Thinking Publications (800-225-4769). Copyright 1997 Thinking Publications. Reprinted with permission.

strategy, *TALS,* to help them prepare for the material to come and sift through all they hear for the most important information. Identifying important ideas in a lecture is expected of all students as early as middle school. This means that students need to learn this important skill early, and TALS is designed specifically for younger children. The steps in TALS are as follow:

T   *Think.*

A   *Ask* why.

L   *Listen* for what?

S   *Say* to self.

Mr. Lewis's students used the TALS strategy when learning the key parts of stories using story maps. When reading stories out loud, he instructed the students, "Think about the story parts, ask why a story map is important, listen for the different parts of a story map, and say to yourself the parts of the story."

● **TASSELL**   As students move into the upper grades, they are required to take notes for longer periods of time. Longer lectures require sustained attention, a skill that is often problematic for students with special needs (Smith, 2004). The *TASSELL* strategy is recommended for students who have trouble maintaining their level of attention (Minskoff & Allsopp, 2003). It includes the following steps:

T   *Try* not to doodle.

A   *Arrive* at class prepared.

S   *Sit* near the front.

S   *Sit* away from friends.

E   *End* daydreaming.

L   *Look* at the teacher.

For the **E** step, encourage students to monitor their attention. When they find they are daydreaming, they should immediately change their position, sit forward, and make eye contact with the teacher. Then they should write down whatever the teacher is saying, regardless of its importance (Minskoff & Allsopp, 2003). For the **L** step, encourage students to keep their eyes on the teacher when they are not taking notes or looking at the chalkboard, overhead, PowerPoint presentation, or computer screen (Minskoff & Allsopp, 2003).

Another self-monitoring strategy for helping students sustain attention is addressed in the Special Emphasis On . . . feature.

● **CALL UP**   *CALL UP* is a research-based strategy for taking lecture notes. It has the following steps (Czarnecki, Rosko, & Fine, 1998):

C   *Copy* from the board or transparency.

A   *Add* details.

L   *Listen* and write the question.

L   *Listen* and write the answer.

U   *Utilize* the text.

P   *Put* in your own words.

When copying from the board, a transparency, or a PowerPoint slide, students listen and look for cue words and phrases that identify main ideas, copy them down in the margin, and underline them. Students also listen for details, writing them 1 inch from the margin with a dash (—) in front of each detail. Students listen for teacher or student questions that

*R*esearch Note

Boyle and Weishaar (2001) examined the effects of a strategic note-taking strategy on the recall and comprehension of students with learning and behavior disabilities. Students were taught to prompt themselves to tap into their background knowledge before the lecture and to identify and summarize main ideas and details during and after the lecture. The study found that students who were taught this strategy scored significantly higher on measures of immediate recall, long-term free recall, comprehension, and the volume of notes recorded than students in a control group who used conventional note taking.

Getting Students to Study in Study Hall

The idea behind study hall seems simple enough: Give students extra time during the day to study or do homework and they will get better grades in their classes. Unfortunately, the idea of study hall and its everyday reality can be very different. While the effectiveness of study hall depends on a number of factors, a key element is the ability of the students to study.

Studying requires that students remain on task for continuous periods of time, an ability that can be a problem for students with special needs. A program of self-monitoring, a skill for fostering student independence, can be used to increase the time on task in study hall for adolescents with learning disabilities (Dalton, Martella, & Marchand-Martella, 1999). This self-monitoring program consists of two parts: a self-monitoring form and a behavior checklist and rating form (see Figures 10.5 and 10.6).

FIGURE 10.5

Study Hall Self-Monitoring Form

| | Name _____ |
| | Date _____ |

Are you working?

9:05	❑ Yes	❑ No
9:10	❑ Yes	❑ No
9:15	❑ Yes	❑ No
9:20	❑ Yes	❑ No
9:25	❑ Yes	❑ No
9:30	❑ Yes	❑ No
9:35	❑ Yes	❑ No
9:40	❑ Yes	❑ No
9:45	❑ Yes	❑ No
9:50	❑ Yes	❑ No

Source: Adapted from "The Effects of a Self-Management Program in Reducing Off-Task Behavior," by T. Dalton, R. C. Martella, and N. E. Marchand-Martella, 1999, *Journal of Behavioral Education, 9*(3–4), pp. 157–176.

On the self-monitoring form, every five minutes the students circle yes if they are working or on task at the designated time or no if they are not working or are off task. On the behavior checklist, students check yes or no in answer to whether they engaged in certain behaviors before class, during class, and after class. Students also rate their overall behavior in class on a scale of 1 to 5, with 1 being *poor* and 5 being *great.*

FIGURE 10.6

Study Hall Behavior Checklist and Rating Form

Before Class

Did you get your homework done?	❑ Yes	❑ No
Did you find out what you'll be doing in class?	❑ Yes	❑ No
Did you get started on time?	❑ Yes	❑ No

During Class

| Did you self-monitor to stay on task? | ❑ Yes | ❑ No |

After Class

Did you follow the teacher's directions?	❑ Yes	❑ No
Did you work on the assignment for the entire time you were given?	❑ Yes	❑ No
Do you have homework tonight?	❑ Yes	❑ No

How Was Your Behavior?

Poor	Needs Improvement	Okay	Good	Great
(1)	(2)	(3)	(4)	(5)

Source: Adapted from "The Effects of a Self-Management Program in Reducing Off-Task Behavior," T. Dalton, R. C. Martella, and N. E. Marchand-Martella, 1999, *Journal of Behavioral Education, 9*(3–4), pp. 157–176.

If you are using this strategy with students in study hall, you need to be sure that they know what to do. First, they need to understand what on- and off-task behavior is. This can be easily covered by providing them with several examples and having them tell you whether they are on task or off task. Students also need to practice using the self-monitoring form with someone supervising to be sure they are completing it correctly. The difficult part is getting them to look up at the clock at the appropriate time. Students who struggle with this step can benefit from a tape or CD that signals at regular intervals when to look at the clock. Begin the strategy when the students show you that they know what to do.

In the research by Dalton and colleagues (1999) using this strategy, the rate of student off-task behavior in study hall was decreased. The students' study hall teacher also noted improved behavior when the self-monitoring program was being used.

they think can inform their understanding and write them, indented, under the appropriate main ideas. Students also record answers under the main ideas. The last two steps can be carried out at home or in study hall. Students first read about the main ideas in their textbooks and then paraphrase the information under each main idea in a space previously left blank. Students record relevant text pages in the margins so they can refer to the text at a later time if needed. Try posting the CALL UP steps prominently in your classroom. As you lecture, model the various steps while explicitly telling your students which steps you are performing and why. For example, Mr. Sauter was lecturing his class on the topic of the respiratory system. He wrote *respiratory system* on the board and directed his students to write down this main idea of the lecture. He then told them to add the details of the parts of the respiratory system (for example, *nose, lungs, mouth,* and *windpipe*) to their notes. Mr. Sauter posed important questions as he lectured such as "What is the purpose of the bronchial tubes?" He directed students to copy down these questions as he raised them. Finally, Mr. Sauter asked students to answer all questions raised for homework.

As we have said, to learn this or any other note-taking strategy, students need the preskill of being able to tell the difference between main ideas and details. Some students choose key words that represent main ideas, but others attempt to write down everything and need to be taught directly how to differentiate main ideas and details. For example, Mr. Abeles discovered that many students in his history class were unable to identify the main ideas in his lectures. First, he explained the difference between main ideas and details: A *main idea* is what a whole section or passage is about; a *detail* is what just one part of a section or passage is about. For several weeks he stopped after presenting a section of material and put three pieces of information on the board—one main idea and two details. He asked the students which was the main idea and why. When his students were doing well at these tasks, Mr. Abeles had them write their own main ideas for a section of a lecture, which were shared with the class, and then he provided corrective feedback as necessary.

Writing Strategies

Another area that requires student independence is writing and proofreading papers. Several research-based strategies are useful to help students in this area.

● **POWER** One strategy that helps students organize all the steps in the writing process is called *POWER* (Englert et al., 1988). The process involves the use of self-questioning, graphic organizers, and peer editing using the following steps:

P   Planning
O   Organizing
W   Writing
E   Editing
R   Revising

The POWER strategy teaches students four different organizational structures for writing papers: stories, comparison/contrast, explanations, and problem/solution (Englert et al., 1988). When writing stories, students use key story elements—Who? When? Where? What happened? How did it end?—to organize their papers. A comparison/contrast structure includes information on what subjects are being compared (for example, Native Americans and settlers), on what characteristic of those subjects is being compared (views about land), and on how the subjects are alike and/or different in relation to that characteristic (Native Americans shared land; settlers owned land). Explanations involve telling how to do something, such as explaining the steps in changing a tire. In a problem/solution structure, a problem is identified (for example, it took too long to travel from the East to the West in the early 1800s in the United States), the cause of the problem is explained (the only way to go from the East to the West was by stagecoach), and the solution is stated (the transcontinental railroad was built).

*R*esearch Note

Peverly et al. (2007) conducted research to answer this question: What accounts most for taking quality notes: how quickly students are able to produce written letters; the amount of material students can store, access, and use in working memory; or the ability to listen for main ideas? In two studies, the researchers found that how quickly students were able to produce written letters accounted most for quality note taking. This finding has two important implications. First, teachers need to spend more time teaching handwriting in the elementary years. Second, for students who struggle with handwriting, teachers should bypass strategies for note taking and make available laptop computers.

DIMENSIONS OF

diversity

When having students write, try to make a strong connection between writing assignments and their communities. For example, Trueba, Moll, and Diaz (1982, as cited in Reyes & Molner, 1991) had students conduct home and community interviews on topics of concern to the community, such as the value of bilingual education. Students were then required to write up their findings. The researchers found that students' writing and their attitudes toward writing improved significantly.

For the *planning* stage, students focus on the audience for the paper, the purpose, and the background knowledge that is necessary to write the paper. In the *organizing* step, students decide which organizational pattern fits their paper (for example, story, comparison/contrast) and then complete a pattern guide to help them organize their ideas. A **pattern guide** is a graphic organizer designed to help students organize their papers. A sample pattern guide for a comparison/contrast paper is shown in Figure 10.7. Notice that the words that are not in boxes—*Both same, In contrast to, Similarly,* and *However*—are key words that are used frequently when making comparisons. These words help students make the transition to writing sentences. For example, in Figure 10.7, two kinds of pizza are being compared and contrasted. The student might write, "The crusts of deep dish and regular pizza are the same in that they both are made of white flour. This is in contrast to their thickness; deep dish pizza crust is much thicker."

In the *writing* stage, the teacher demonstrates and thinks aloud to show students how to take the information gathered in the planning and organizing steps and produce a first draft. For example, you can compose an essay comparing two kinds of pizza using an overhead projector, thinking out loud as you write. You can involve students by asking questions such as, "What would a good topic sentence be? Is this a good example? How do you think I should end this? Why?" You could also have students write the paper along with you.

The *editing* step teaches students to critique their own writing and to identify areas in which they need clarification or assistance, an important self-evaluation skill. Editing is a two-step process involving student self-evaluation and peer editing. For self-evaluation, students reread and evaluate their drafts, starring sections of the paper they like best and putting question marks in the margins by passages they think may be unclear. Finally, students

FIGURE 10.7 **Pattern Guide for Comparison/Contrast Paper**

Compare/Contrast

What is being compared and contrasted?
Deep dish pizza and regular pizza

On what characteristics?
Crust

| Both same | Alike? White flour | Different? Deep dish is thicker | In contrast to |

On what characteristics?

| Similarly | Alike? | Different? | However |

Source: From "A Case for Writing Intervention: Strategies for Writing Informational Text," by C. S. Englert, T. E. Raphael, L. M. Anderson, H. M. Anthony, K. L. Fear, and S. L. Gregg, 1988, *Learning Disability Quarterly, 3*(2), p. 108. Reprinted with permission.

think of two questions to ask their peer editors. For example, Jorge asked his peer editor whether he had used capital letters and punctuation correctly. He was also concerned about whether his paper was long enough and asked for suggestions on how to add information.

For **peer editing,** several steps are followed. First, the writer reads the paper to a peer editor while the editor listens. The peer editor then summarizes the paper. Next, the editor evaluates the paper, sharing with the writer an analysis of salient features of the writing that might guide a revision or lead to improvement. For example, the peer editor might suggest that the writer add key words or reorganize the paper for clarity. Then the peer editor and the writer brainstorm ways to improve the paper.

A research-based strategy called *TAG* can also help students with the peer-editing process (Carlson & Henning, 1993; MacArthur & Stoddard, 1990). The TAG strategy involves three simple steps:

T   *Tell* what you like.

A   *Ask* questions.

G   *Give* suggestions.

As discussed previously, students need to be provided with models and guided practice for doing these steps prior to doing them independently.

In the *revising* step, students decide on changes to be made using their self-evaluation marks and peer feedback. Englert and colleagues (1988) suggest that the teacher model how to insert or change the order of information, all the while providing a rationale for any changes. All modifications are made directly on the first draft. Last, the teacher and student have a conference, and changes in writing mechanics are suggested. Following this conference, a final draft is composed on clean sheets of paper.

● **COPS**   When students have to proofread their papers independently, they might use a strategy called *COPS* (Alley, 1988). In the COPS strategy, students question themselves as follows:

C   Have I *capitalized* the first word and proper nouns?

O   How is the *overall appearance* of my paper? Have I made any handwriting, margin, or messy errors?

P   Have I used end *punctuation,* commas, and semicolons carefully?

S   Do words look like they are *spelled* right; can I sound them out or use the dictionary?

Although COPS has been shown to be effective, students need preskills to perform this strategy adequately. Before teaching COPS, consider the following questions: Can the students recognize misspelled words? Do the students know rules for using capital letters and punctuation? Can they apply these rules? Can the students use a dictionary? If the answer to any of these questions is no, teach these skills directly before teaching students the COPS strategy.

● **W-W-W What=2 How=2**   This strategy was developed and researched by Harris, Graham, and Mason (2003) to help elementary-age students write stories:

W   *Who* is the main character?

W   *When* does the story take place?

W   *Where* does the story take place?

W   *What* does the main character do or want to do? What do other characters do?

W   *What* happens then? What happens with other characters?

H   *How* does the story end?

H   *How* does the main character feel? How do the other characters feel?

www.resources

Inspiration is a software program designed to help students plan and organize research projects through outlines and concept maps. For more information on this program, go to www .inspiration.com.

Analyze **and Reflect**

How would you use INCLUDE to find out whether students needed to learn the COPS strategy? What assessment information would you collect to monitor student progress in learning COPS?

DIMENSIONS OF

diversity

Cohen and Riel (1989) conducted a study to explore the effects of writing using the Internet for authentic audiences of peers from different cultural backgrounds. They found that essays written for distant peers were superior to essays written to be graded by their teachers; essays for authentic peers were more explicit and detailed.

FIGURE *10.8* **Practice Cue Cards for W-W-W What=2 How=2**

Source: Adapted from "Self-Regulated Strategy Development in the Classroom: Part of a Balanced Approach to Writing Instruction for Students with Disabilities," by K. R. Harris, S. Graham, and L. H. Mason. *Focus on Exceptional Children, 35*(7), 1–17.

Students with weak writing skills and other language difficulties will require more support with the vocabulary and concepts. Their instruction can be differentiated by giving them more practice or by using a graphic organizer and picture cues, such as the one in Figure 10.8.

● **Report Writing**   Report writing is something many students would prefer to avoid, largely because they lack a systematic way of writing successfully. Graham, Harris, and MacArthur (2006) report success teaching students a six-step report-writing strategy originally developed by MacArthur et al. (1996). The steps in the strategy are as follow:

1. Choose a topic.

2. Brainstorm all you know and would like to know about the topic.

3. Organize your ideas by main points and details on a web-type graphic organizer, where main ideas and subordinate ideas are linked together through the use of lines and arrows.

4. Read to find new information and verify the accuracy of information already generated. (Add, delete, and modify items on the Web as necessary.)

5. Write your report using the information you organized on the Web, but continue planning as you write.

6. Check to be sure you used everything you wanted from the Web (p. 291).

In Graham et al. (2006), the report-writing strategy was co-taught by general and special educators using many of the suggestions for teaching a learning strategy described earlier in the chapter. First, they clarified expectations by carefully describing the qualities of a good report and showing the students actual examples of well-written reports. Next the teachers encouraged students to memorize the strategy, and then the special education teacher demonstrated how to use the strategy while holding a running dialogue with herself. For example, to show the students how to keep themselves focused, she asked herself, "What do I need to do?" To show the students how to keep themselves on task, the teacher said to herself, "Keep going." To demonstrate how to self-monitor, the teacher said, "Does this part make sense?" To show students how to cope with frustration, she said, "I can do this."

For guided practice, the teachers differentiated instruction. The special education teacher co-wrote reports with some of the students with special needs in a small group, while the general education teacher worked with the remainder of the class in a large group, providing reduced support. Once students were writing independently, the teachers required them to reflect on what they were doing in a daily journal. Students were also reminded to continue to manage the writing process by talking to themselves. In all, it took the students six weeks to master the report-writing strategy—time that the teachers felt was well spent, given the improvement in student reports that resulted.

● **Learning Spelling Words**   A study strategy can help students learn unknown spelling words (Graham & Freeman, 1986). Students are required to carry out the following five steps:

1. Say the word.

2. Write and say the word.

3. Check the word.

4. Trace and say the word.

5. Write the word from memory and check your spelling.

If students misspell the word in step 5, they need to repeat all five steps.

Strategies for Using Technology to Improve Student Writing

● **Using the Internet**   The Internet can enhance the writing process for all students, including those with special needs. Smith, Boone, and Higgins (1998) have described the different ways the Internet can expand the writing process, as shown in Figure 10.9.

● **Revising Essays**   This strategy uses a word processor for revising essays (Graham & Harris, 1987). Students instruct themselves using the following six steps:

1. Read your essay.

2. Find the sentence that tells you what you believe—is it clear?

3. Add two reasons why you believe it.

fyi

You can see a writing strategy co-taught in a videotape published by the Association of Supervision and Curriculum Development (Alexandria, Virginia) titled *Teaching Students with Learning Disabilities: Using Learning Strategies* (2002).

www.resources

The Write Site, at www .writesite.org, is designed for language arts students in middle school. The site allows students to take on the roles of journalists and editors to research, write, and publish their own newspaper. The site provides unit outlines, handouts, exercises, downloadable teaching material, information about how to write, and more.

FIGURE *10.9* The Internet-Expanded Writing Process

Writing Process Phases	Typical Activities	Internet Activities
Prewriting	Brainstorming	Keyword searching
	Outlining	Browsing
	Clustering	Downloading information
	Collecting information	
Writing	Writing series of drafts	
Revision	Peer responding	E-mailing drafts to other kids for response
	Teacher responding	
	Editing	E-mailing drafts to experts for response
	Revising	
Publishing	Final drafting	
	Binding into a book	
	Reading by others in class	
	Reading by parents	
WWW Revision		Final draft is reviewed for possible hypertext links to other WWW sites.
		Additional searches are made for possible links.
		Story is pasted into a WWW creation program.
		Hypertext links are added.
WWW Publishing		Story file is transferred to a classroom WWW site on a networked computer.
		URL address is established.
		The story WWW page is registered with search page Yahooligans! for international access.
		Uncle in Kathmadu can read it.

Source: From "Expanding the Writing Process to the Web," by S. Smith, R. Boone, and K. Higgins, 1998,
Teaching Exceptional Children, 30(5), pp. 22–26. Copyright 1998 by the Council for Exceptional Children.
Reprinted with permission.

4. SCAN each sentence:

   S   Does it make *sense?*

   C   Is it *connected* to your belief?

   A   Can you *add* more?

   N   *Note* errors.

5. Make changes on the computer.

6. Reread your essay and make final changes.

● **Using Spell Checkers Effectively** Spelling checkers can help students identify misspelled words and spell them correctly. However, one problem with spell checkers is that the correctly spelled version of a word that the student is attempting to write is not always presented as an alternative. This happens when the combination of letters that the student has typed does not approximate closely enough the intended word for the software to offer the needed choices. Because the correct word does not appear on the first attempt, students often click on "Go to Next Word" or "Skip Word" without making a change. The result is a paper with many misspelled words.

Ashton (1999) describes the *CHECK* strategy, a sequence of steps designed to help students use any spell checker more effectively. The sequence of steps in the strategy is as follows:

C *Check the beginning sounds.* Most spell checkers search for similar words beginning with the same letter as the word typed. Therefore, the correctly spelled version of the word is more likely to appear when at least the first letter is correct. For this step, students check the beginning sound of the word and ask themselves what other letter could make that beginning sound. For example, if the student is attempting to spell the word *elephant* but has begun the word with *ul,* teach him or her to ask what other letter(s) make that beginning sound.

H *Hunt for the correct consonants.* If trying a new beginning sound does not help, have students change other consonants in the word. Ashton (1999, p. 26) tells of a boy who was writing about Egypt and wanted to use the word *pyramid.* His first spelling attempt was *perament,* but the only suggested word was *per.* The boy continued to sound out the word and changed the spelling to *peramed.* This still did not produce the word he was looking for, so he changed his spelling again to *peramid. Pyramid* then appeared in the suggested word list, and the student recognized it as being the correct spelling.

E *Examine the vowels.* Selecting the correct vowel when spelling is especially difficult, because vowels make so many sounds. Spell checkers can help students figure out which sound to use for a particular vowel or vowel combination. For example, a student spelled the place where she ate lunch as *cafitirea.* After substituting other possible vowels in the word, she came close enough to the actual spelling to elicit the word *cafeteria* on the suggested list.

C *Changes in word lists give hints.* Sometimes students can use words in the suggested word list to find the correct spelling. For example, a student trying to spell the word *favorite* first tried *fovoriute.* When this spelling did not produce the correct alternative, she changed her original spelling to *foariute,* then *fovaritue,* then *favaritue.* After the last try, the word *favor* was given as a suggested spelling. Using that word, she typed *favoritue,* which brought *favorite* to the list—the correct spelling, which she recognized.

K *Keep repeating steps 1 through 4.* The most important aspect of using this strategy effectively is to give it repeated chances, trying as many different letter combinations as you can. However, at some point students may want to use another source, such as a dictionary, personalized word list (a continually updated list of words students have looked up before), classmate, teacher, or parent.

Strategies for Problem Solving in Math

Increasingly, teachers are focusing on problem solving as a major component of the math curriculum. This concentration is consistent with the math standards developed by the National Council of Teachers of Mathematics (2000), which also stress the importance of teaching problem solving. However, research indicates that if students with special needs are to become good problem solvers, they must be taught how to problem solve directly. A common (but by no means the only) way to introduce problem solving to students in a classroom context is through story or word problems. An effective technique for teaching word problems for students with special needs is presented in the next Professional Edge.

● **STAR** The *STAR* strategy has been used successfully to teach older students with disabilities to solve math problems, including algebra (Gagnon & Maccini, 2001, p. 10). It consists of the following steps:

*R*esearch Note

Hetzroni and Shrieber (2004) studied the use of a word processor for enhancing the written expression of junior high school students with learning disabilities. They found a clear difference in quality between handwritten and computer-produced writing. Using paper and pencil, students wrote papers that had more spelling mistakes and lower overall quality of organization and structure.

*R*esearch Note

DeLaPaz (1999) reviewed the research on dictation and speech-recognition systems and concluded that these systems can allow students with disabilities to circumvent handwriting, spelling, and punctuation problems, freeing them to focus on higher-level concerns, such as planning and generating content. DeLaPaz warns, though, that students need to be taught carefully how to use this technology and that students with disabilities still need to be taught skills for critical planning and content generation that many of them lack.

The Key Word Strategy for Solving Math Story Problems: Is There a Better Way?

The key word strategy is an example of an ineffective strategy that many students with special needs use or are taught to use in solving math story problems (Kelly & Carnine, 1996). In this approach, students associate key words such as *more, in all, gave away,* and *left over* with certain mathematical operations. The key word strategy is attractive to teachers and students because sometimes it works. For example, the word *more* is commonly associated with subtraction, as in the following problem:

Jose has 15 cents. Carmen has 10 cents. How much *more* money does Jose have?

Unfortunately, many times the word *more* appears in word problems that call for addition, as in the following problem:

Charmaine had 15 cents. Her mother gave her 10 *more* cents. How many cents does she have now?

Kelly and Carnine (1996) suggest teaching students with special needs a more effective strategy for solving math word problems using problem maps and math fact families. Their strategy for teaching single-operation addition and subtraction problems follows:

For any addition/subtraction situation, there are two "small" numbers and a "big" number (the sum).

An addition/subtraction number family is mapped this way:

$$\xrightarrow{\quad 7 \quad 9 \quad} 16$$

The preceding family represents the following addition/subtraction facts:

$7 + 9 = 16$	$16 - 9 = 7$
$9 + 7 = 16$	$16 - 7 = 9$

A missing *big* number implies addition:

$$\xrightarrow{\quad 8 \quad 22 \quad} \Box \qquad 8 + 22 = \Box$$

A missing *small* number implies subtraction:

$$\xrightarrow{\quad \Box \quad 22 \quad} 30 \qquad 30 - 22 = \Box$$

or

$$\xrightarrow{\quad 8 \quad \Box \quad} 30 \qquad 30 - 8 = \Box$$

These maps can then be applied to a variety of addition and subtraction word problems. Kelly and Carnine (1996, p. 6) give the following example involving comparison problems:

S   *Search* the word problem, reading the problem carefully and writing down knowns or facts.

T   *Translate* the word problem into an equation in picture form by choosing a variable, identifying the operation, and representing the problem through manipulatives or picture form.

A   *Answer* the problem.

R   *Review* the solution by rereading the problem and checking the reasonableness of the answer.

Examples of how STAR can be used to solve division problems with integers are shown in Figure 10.10.

Note how the teacher moves students beyond the concrete application phase and into semiconcrete and abstract phases. Moving students beyond concrete representations is important for students with special needs, because if they are to become independent learners, they must be able to work at an abstract level. While students with special needs benefit from working with manipulatives and other concrete representations, teachers must make sure to move students to more abstract levels as soon as they are able.

In comparison problems, the difference between two values being compared may be information given in a problem (for example, Marco sold 57 fewer subscriptions than Lui) or the unknown in a problem (for example, How much heavier was Mary?). Because of the words *sold fewer* in the following problem, many students with LD will subtract.

> Marco sold 57 fewer magazine subscriptions than Lui. Marco sold 112 subscriptions. How many subscriptions did Lui sell?

Students can use number families to avoid this confusion. The first step is to represent the problem using a number family; students must determine whether each of the two numbers given in the problem is a small number or the big number. The students are shown a simple way to do this:

They find the sentence that tells about the comparison and read it without the difference number. For example, students are taught to read the first sentence without the 57: "Marco sold fewer subscriptions than Lui." Because Marco sold fewer subscriptions, Marco is represented by a small number. By default, Lui is the big number. The students write M for Marco and L for Lui:

$$\xrightarrow{\quad M \quad} L$$

The word problem also gives a number for the difference between Marco and Lui. That number always has to be a small number. Marco sold 57 fewer, so 57 is the other small number:

$$\xrightarrow[\quad\quad]{57 \quad M} L$$

Next the students read the rest of the problem. The problem asks about Lui and gives a number for Marco, so the students draw a box around L and replace the M with 112:

$$\xrightarrow[\quad\quad]{57 \quad \overset{112}{\cancel{M}}} \boxed{L}$$

Because the problem gives both small numbers, the students write an addition problem.

$$\begin{array}{r} 57 \\ +112 \\ \hline \end{array}$$

The answer tells how many magazine subscriptions Lui sold.

See Stein, Silbert, and Carnine (1997) for similar word problem strategies as applied to multiplication, division, and multistep story problems.

Source: Excerpt from "The 'Key Word' Strategy for Solving Math Story Problems," by B. Kelly and D. Carnine, 1996, reprinted by permission of Council for Learning Disabilities.

● **LAMPS** The *LAMPS* strategy (Reetz & Rasmussen, 1988) can be used as an aid to help remember the steps in regrouping or carrying in addition:

L	*Line up* the numbers according to their decimal points.
A	*Add* the right column of numbers and ask . . .
M	"*More* than 9?" If so, continue to the next step.
P	*Put* the 1s below the column.
S	*Send* the 10s to the top of the next column.

● **SLOBS** To help with borrowing in subtraction, teach students to follow the steps in the *SLOBS* strategy (Reetz & Rasmussen, 1988):

S	*Smaller:* Follow steps.
L	*Larger:* Leap to subtract.
O	*Cross off* the number in the next column.
B	*Borrow* by taking one 10 and adding to the next column.
S	*Subtract.*

Sample problem: Suppose the temperature changed by an average of –2˚F per hour. The total temperature change was –16˚F. How many hours did it take for the temperature to change?

Phase of Instruction	Star Strategy

1. Concrete Application

Students use blocks to represent the problem. General guidelines: inverse operation of multiplication.

Algebra tiles: ▨ = 1 unit

Prompts students to:

Search problem (read carefully, ask questions, write down facts); translate the problem using blocks; answer the problem using the tiles; and review the solution (reread the problem, check reasonableness and calculations).

1)
Students begin with no tiles on the workmat.

2)

3)

a. Count the number of sets of –2 needed to obtain –16.

b. Students add 8 sets.

c. Students count the number of sets needed (8).

2. Semiconcrete Application

Students draw pictures of the representations.

Prompts students to:

Search problem (read carefully, ask questions, write down facts); translate (represent) the problem via drawings and write down the equation; answer the problem using drawings and write the answer; and review the solution (reread the problem, check reasonableness and calculations).

3. Abstract Application

Students first write numerical representations:

–16 ÷ 2 = x, apply the rule for dividing integers to obtain x = +8, and reread and check the answer.

Prompts students to:

Search problem (read carefully, ask questions, write down facts); translate the problem into an equation; answer the problem (apply the rule for division integers); and review the solution (reread the problem, check reasonableness and calculations).

Source: "Preparing Students with Disabilities for Algebra," by J. C. Gagnon and P. Maccini, 2001, *Teaching Exceptional Children, 34*(1), 8–15. Copyright 2001 by the Council for Exceptional Children. Reprinted with permission.

For the problem

$$\begin{array}{r} 72 \\ -\,46 \\ \hline \end{array}$$

students look at the top number on the right to see whether it is smaller or larger than the bottom right number. If it is smaller, the students follow the rest of the steps. They cross off the number in the next column to the left to borrow one unit from that column (reducing that number by one) and add it to the other column. In the problem shown, they borrow 10 from the left column and then subtract. If the number is larger, students proceed directly to the subtract step. They repeat the steps if more digits are to be subtracted.

● **FOIL** The *FOIL* strategy (Crawford, 1980) helps prevent algebra students from missing one of the four products needed to calculate multiplication of a binomial by another binomial. Students follow these four steps:

F   Multiply *first* terms.

O   Multiply *outermost* terms.

I   Multiply *innermost* terms.

L   Multiply *last* terms.

For example, the FOIL strategy can be applied to the following problem:

$(x + 4)(x + 3)$
A   B C D

In the **F** step, the student multiplies the first two factors in each binomial, $x \times x = x^2$, or using the letters, *AC*. Next, in the **O** step, the student multiplies the first factor in the first binomial and the second factor in the second binomial, $x \times 3 = 3x$, or *AD*. Then, in the **I** step, the student multiplies the second factor of the first binomial and the first factor of the second binomial, $4 \times x = 4x$, or *BC*. Finally, in the **L** step, the second factors of both binomials are multiplied: $4 \times 3 = 12$, or *BD*. This strategy applies only to the special case of multiplying two binomials.

Strategies for Managing Time and Resources

A lack of organization is a common characteristic of students with disabilities (Lerner, 2006; Silver, 2006). For example, Ron, one of the students introduced at the beginning of the chapter, has trouble organizing.

Organizing study materials involves having the appropriate school supplies, making sure these supplies are brought to class when they are needed, and having an organized notebook to ensure easy access to information. First, you can make sure that students obtain the appropriate school supplies by requiring that they tell their parents what materials they need, because you will not be able to call each of their parents individually each day to remind them what to bring. In many cases, teachers tell their students what to bring and assume that the students will do the rest on their own. However, this method may not be structured enough for some students who, like Ron, are likely to forget what you said, are not organized enough to write it down, or even when they do write it down, cannot find it when they get home.

Second, you can encourage students to write the information down rather than try to remember it. Having the information on the board or overhead helps ensure that their lists are accurate. You may also want to duplicate the list and distribute it to your students.

Finally, encourage your students to ask themselves the following or similar questions, which can help them remember school supplies as well as assignments throughout the school year:

■   What is due tomorrow in school?
■   What do I need to do to get it done tonight?
■   What materials or other things do I need to get the job done?
■   Whom can I ask for help in doing this?

These questions can at first be posted on the board to help students remember them and to prompt their use. You can help motivate students to bring needed materials by providing positive recognition for those who do bring their supplies to school. For example,

Research Note

Tournaki (2003) compared the effectiveness of two kinds of instruction to teach students two-digit addition facts $(2 + 3 = 5)$: strategy instruction and drill and practice. Strategy instruction consisted of teaching the students to start with the larger number and then count upward using the smaller number. For drill and practice, students memorized the answers to the facts. The results showed that the students with learning disabilities improved their performance only when they used the strategy. General education students performed equally well with both kinds of instruction, but on a transfer task requiring the addition of three digits (for example, $2 + 4 + 4 = 10$), the strategy groups performed better.

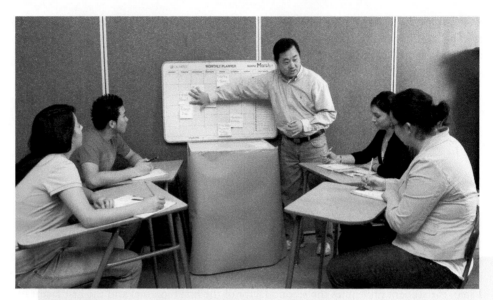

Strategies for managing time and organizing materials help provide the structured routines that many students need to succeed in school. What are the three steps in teaching students how to use weekly assignment calendars?

Mr. Gutierrez gave school pencils to students who had all their supplies in school. Ms. Habner put the names of her students on a "responsible students" list, from which she chose people for classroom jobs.

You may need to make accommodations for students with special needs. For example, students with physical disabilities may need a classmate or parent to bring their supplies into school. Students who live in poverty might be unable to afford supplies other than materials the school or teacher provides.

Besides having to organize their materials, students also need to organize their time, particularly as they get older and the demands made on their time increase. More schools are now teaching their students to use schedule books to help them arrange their time (Bryan, Burstein, & Bryan, 2001; Jenson, Sheridan, Olympia, & Andrews, 1994; Patton, 1994). You can teach your students to use a weekly schedule book in the following three ways:

1. *Teach students to differentiate between short- and long-term assignments.* Short-term assignments are those that can be completed in one or two days and that take one or two steps to complete, such as reading a chapter in the history textbook and answering the questions at the end of the chapter. Long-term assignments take more than two days to complete and take more than two steps to get done. Writing a five-page report on a current event is an example of a long-term assignment. The difference between short- and long-term assignments can be taught readily to the whole class at once by giving them the definitions and teaching them to apply these definitions to a series of examples.

2. *Teach students to task analyze long-term tasks.* Start by modeling the task-analysis process of breaking long-term tasks into component subtasks, estimating the amount of time it will take to perform each subtask, and then scheduling time to complete the subtasks in a schedule book. You can model this by distributing an already completed **task analysis** and timeline for your first several long-term assignments. Then have students begin to develop their own task analyses, first under your guidance and later independently.

DIMENSIONS OF

diversity

Teachers with a multicultural perspective take into account that students from different cultural backgrounds might have different routines as well as different resources for addressing, structuring, and completing projects.

www.resources

TimeLiner is a software program designed to help students organize information for research projects using a timeline. For more information, go to www.teachtsp.com.

3. *Show students how to record information in their schedule books.* Have students enter fixed activities or activities you do every week, occasional activities or activities that are different from week to week, and due dates for assignments. Students can also prioritize assignments; schedule time to work on assignments; and monitor assignment completion, including rescheduling or adding time to work on assignments.

Many schools have had success using schoolwide programs with a single system of keeping track of assignments in schedule books that students use in every class. The consistency and repetition that are naturally a part of such a system seem to benefit students, including those with disabilities, many of whom are more successful when teachers stick to a daily routine. Students with special needs may require additional accommodations, however, such as the classroom teacher's checking and/or initialing their schedule books before they leave class. This step is particularly important when students are first learning to use a schedule book.

How Can Students Learn to Use Strategies Independently?

Info Sheet Homework Exercise

Go to the Homework and Exercises section in Chapter 10 of MyEducationLab for an explanation of a metacognitive strategy that supports independent use of learning strategies.

Some students may have trouble using a learning strategy independently, even after they have learned how to do it. Their problem could be that they do not know when to use a strategy or how to keep track of how well they are using it and how to change their behavior if necessary.

Three strategies that can help students perform tasks more independently are self-instruction, self-monitoring, and self-questioning. Like all learning strategies, these "self" strategies may need to be carefully taught using the teaching practices described in this chapter.

> Some students may have trouble using a learning strategy independently, even after they have learned how to do it.

Self-Instruction

In **self-instruction,** learners are taught to use language to guide their performance. In essence, students are taught to talk themselves through a task. The idea is that if they can talk themselves through a task, they will not need help from anyone else. Self-instruction has been successfully used to teach students with disabilities strategies for math, test taking, reading comprehension, and writing (Uberti, Mastropieri, & Scruggs, 2004).

The first step to teach students self-instruction techniques is to explain that self-instruction involves giving oneself instructions on how to do a task. For example, self-instruction can be used to help get seatwork done or to remember to use a strategy for a multiple-choice test. Next ask students to identify a situation that requires the use of a specific skill, such as getting their seatwork done in reading or taking a 10-minute science quiz on Friday. Demonstrate how to write down the steps needed to perform that task. For example, to get seatwork done, the student first decides how much effort to put into this task. Next he or she decides what is supposed to be done. Finally, the student decides what the first step in completing the task should be, what the next step should be, and so forth, until the seatwork is done. When students are finished, they praise themselves for a job well done. Ask students to rehearse the steps through self-talk or peer review, going over all the steps involved in completing a seatwork task from beginning to end.

After you have demonstrated how to apply self-instruction, have the students practice in a role-play situation, and give them feedback. In the seatwork task, for example, you could put a sample reading task on the classroom screen using PowerPoint or the

Analyze and Reflect

Research suggests that once students learn a "self" strategy, they have trouble recognizing when it is appropriate to use it. Why do you think this is so? What can you do as a teacher to ensure that your students apply the strategies they are learning?

FIGURE 10.11 My Self Statements

W-W-W What=2 How=2

To think of good ideas:

_____

_____

_____

While I work:

_____

_____

_____

To check my work:

_____

_____

_____

_____

Source: From "Self-Regulated Strategy Development in the Classroom: Part of a Balanced Approach to Writing Instruction for Students with Disabilities," by K. R. Harris, S. Graham, and L. H. Mason. *Focus on Exceptional Children, 35*(7), 1–17.

overhead projector and demonstrate the steps by thinking out loud. The students could then practice in pairs and give each other feedback, with you monitoring and also giving feedback. To help guide their students who were taught the WWW What=2 How=2 writing strategy described earlier, Harris, Graham, and Mason (2003) had students record things they would say to themselves prior to, during, and after writing using the forms shown in Figure 10.11.

Self-Monitoring

In **self-monitoring,** students watch and check themselves to make sure they have performed targeted behaviors. Self-monitoring has been shown to be effective in making positive changes in the academic and social behavior of students with disabilities (Daly & Ranalli, 2003). It is a critical aspect of independent learning, because being independent often requires students to check their performance to see whether it is effective and make a change when a particular strategy is not working (Hallahan et al., 2005; Reid, 1996). Self-monitoring can also be a strong motivator for students by providing them concrete evidence of their progress.

In teaching self-monitoring to your students, first explain to them that self-monitoring is a way they can check their own behavior to make sure they are doing the right thing. Ask the students to identify a behavior or a learning strategy that they need to do in class. For example, students may select a behavior such as being on task or on time for classes, or they may choose a strategy such as the COPS proofreading strategy described earlier in the chapter.

The next step is to select a practical and expedient way for students to measure the behavior. One possibility is to have them count on a card or pocket counter the number of times the behavior occurs. For example, Yashika recorded on an index card the number of her talk-outs in reading class. Another possibility is to use a checklist to keep track of behaviors as they occur.

Teach students to use the measurement system through demonstration, practice, and feedback, and continue to encourage and reinforce the use of self-monitoring in your class. Self-monitoring can be applied to any learning strategy.

fyi

Brimijoin, Marquisse, and Tomlinson (2003) report a teacher using a car windshield metaphor to teach students to monitor their understanding. The teacher asked, "How many [of you] are clear as glass about how greatest common factor works? How many have bugs on your windshields? How many have windshields covered with mud?" (p. 70). The same teacher also supported self-evaluation by using a red–yellow–green cup system for students to communicate their need for assistance. If a student put a red cup on the desk, it meant, "I can't go on without help." A yellow cup meant that the student had questions but wasn't completely blocked; and a green cup meant that the student understood what he was doing.

Self-Questioning

Self-questioning is a form of self-instruction in which students guide their performance by asking themselves questions. The idea behind self-questioning is that if students can guide their own behavior by asking themselves questions, then they will not always need a teacher or other adult present to perform.

In teaching students self-questioning, have them first identify the behaviors, duties, or tasks that are required in class. For example, students can identify steps needed to proofread a written paper, such as checking the correct use of capital letters, punctuation, spelling, and appearance. Have students write these tasks in question form, asking, for example, "Have I capitalized all words correctly? Have I used the right punctuation marks in the right places? Have I spelled all the words correctly? Is my paper neat?"

As in self-monitoring, the next step is to select a practical and expedient way for students to measure the behavior, such as recording behaviors as they occur using a checklist. Students might practice self-questioning in pairs for feedback. Other practical measures include keeping task questions on index cards and putting them in a convenient place. For example, students might put the proofreading questions on an index card and tape it to the inside cover of their notebooks.

Montague, Warger, and Morgan (2000) taught students with disabilities to solve math word problems using a strategy that included elements of self-instruction, self-monitoring, and self-questioning. The strategy is shown in Figure 10.12. Also, applications of self-strategies to student behavior in study hall are shown in the Special Emphasis On . . . feature on page 384.

Research Note

Wehmeyer and colleagues (2003) studied the use of self-monitoring with students with developmental and intellectual disabilities. They found that the use of "self" strategies improved the students' class participation and decreased their rate of problem behaviors.

Building Teaching Skills Exercise

Go to the Building Teaching Skills section in Chapter 10 of MyEducationLab to explore some of the learning problems that underlie many of the academic difficulties experienced by students who are at risk.

FIGURE **Using Self-Instruction, Self-Monitoring, and Self-Questioning in a Math-Problem-Solving Strategy**

Math–Problem Solving

Read (for understanding)

Say:	Read the problem. If I don't understand, read it again.
Ask:	Have I read and understood the problem?
Check:	For understanding as I solve the problem.

Paraphrase (in your own words)

Say:	Underline the important information. Put the problem in my own words.
Ask:	Have I underlined the important information? What is the question? What am I looking for?
Check:	That the information goes with the question.

Visualize (a picture or a diagram)

Say:	Make a drawing or a diagram.
Ask:	Does the picture fit the problem?
Check:	The picture against the problem information.

Hypothesize (a plan to solve the problem)

Say:	Decide how many steps and operations are needed. Write the operations symbols (+, –, ×, ÷)
Ask:	If I do . . . , what will I get? If I do . . . , then what do I need to do next? How many steps are needed?
Check:	That the plan makes sense.

continued

FIGURE *10.12* Continued

Estimate (predict the answer)

Say:	Round the numbers, do the problem in my head, and write the estimate.
Ask:	Did I round up and down?
	Did I write the estimate?
Check:	That I use the important information.

Compute (do the arithmetic)

Say:	Do the operations in the right order.
Ask:	How does my answer compare with my estimate?
	Does my answer make sense?
	Are the decimals or money signs in the right places?
Check:	That all the operations are done in the right order.

Check (make sure everything is right)

Say:	Check the computation.
Ask:	Have I checked every step?
	Have I checked the computation?
	Is my answer right?
Check:	That everything is right. If not, go back.
	Then ask for help if I need it.

Source: From "Solve It! Strategy Instruction to Improve Mathematical Problem Solving," by M. Montague, C. Warger, and T. H. Morgan, 2000, *Learning Disabilities: Research and Practice, 15*(2), pp. 110–116. Reprinted by permission of Blackwell Publishing.

Summary

General education teachers can help all their students, including students with special needs, become independent learners. One way teachers can build student independence is to encourage student self-awareness and self-advocacy.

Another way to help your students become more independent is to design and teach effective learning strategies in class. Effective learning strategies can be developed by identifying skills that are problematic for most of your students, specifying relevant student outcomes, and listing a set of specific steps students need to follow to reach the identified outcomes. These steps should be brief, should number no more than eight, and should be encased in a mnemonic device. They should also cue students to perform thinking,

doing, and self-evaluating behaviors. Methods of teaching learning strategies to students include assessing current strategy use, clarifying expectations, demonstrating strategy use, encouraging students to memorize strategy steps, providing guided and independent practice, and administering posttests.

Many strategies that can help students become independent learners are available in the areas of reading and reading comprehension, listening and note taking, writing, problem solving in math, and managing time and resources. Three strategies that can help students learn to use these strategies independently are self-instruction, self-monitoring, and self-questioning.

Back to the Cases

This section provides opportunities for you to apply the knowledge gained in this chapter to the cases described at the beginning of this chapter. The questions and activities that follow demonstrate how these standards and principles, along with other concepts that you have learned about in this chapter, connect to the everyday activities of all teachers.

Gerald has problems in written expression including organization and mechanical errors. Mr. McCrae has determined that organization is most important, because the mechanical errors can be corrected after Gerald has produced an organized written product. Mr. McCrae has selected the POWER strategy to teach Gerald to use. You are interested in applying this strategy in your teaching, so you work with Mr. McCrae to develop a script for teaching it. (See the Case in Practice "Teaching Script for Demonstrating POSSE" on page 380 for a sample script.) In the planning portion of POWER, you may want to consider an editing strategy such as COPS and a graphic organizer from Chapter 9. After you have written your script, compare scripts with a peer partner from your class. (INTASC Principles 4.01, 4.07, and 5.04; and CEC Standards 5 and 7.)

Traci, as you may recall, struggled with solving word problems. After helping her with a strategy for solving such problems, Ms. McCord reflects on Traci's skills in other academic areas. Traci often cannot answer comprehension questions regarding details in short passages of text or storybooks. Ms. McCord wonders whether Traci's difficulties in reading might be similar to the ones she experienced in word problems. (INTASC Principle 4.01 and CEC Standard 5.) What do you think? Explain your thinking. Suppose that she does discover that the difficulties are similar. What strategies would you teach Traci that would be useful for reading word problems? Provide a reason for each of your choices.

Ron often came unprepared to class. However, after several weeks of his teachers working with Ron, he is now coming to class with all of the books and materials he needs. In fact, he completed his homework assignments every day this week. He is proud that he has been remembering to check his schedule book and the checklist in his locker. However, he still experiences difficulty getting to school and work on time, and on four days last week, he missed the bus that takes him home. After deciding that the next step is to teach Ron to use self-instruction and self-monitoring strategies for the home and work situations, you have learned about a website found at http://coe.jmu.edu/Learningtoolbox/index.html where you can find a strategy that will help Ron manage time when he is away from the school environment. Once you are at this website, enter as a teacher and select the "Strategy List" from the column on the left. (INTASC Principles 4.07 and 5.04; and CEC Standards 4 and 5.) Select two strategies that you think will work for Ron and share your choices with two peers. After all of you have shared your strategies and the reasons for your choices, select two you would present to Ron so that he can choose the one he wants to use.

Key Terms and Concepts

Controlled materials (p. 373)

Learning strategies (p. 368)

Pattern guide (p. 386)

Peer editing (p. 387)

Reciprocal teaching (p. 380)

Self-advocacy (p. 367)

Self-instruction (p. 397)

Self-monitoring (p. 398)

Self-questioning (p. 399)

Task analysis (p. 396)

PEARSON
myeducationlab
Where the Classroom Comes to Life

Now go to the Friend and Bursuck, Fifth Edition, MyEducationLab course at www.myeducationlab.com to

- take a pretest to assess your initial comprehension of the chapter content
- study chapter content with your individualized study plan
- take a posttest to assess your understanding of chapter content
- engage in multimedia exercises to help you build a deeper and more applied understanding of chapter content

Applications in **Teaching Practice**

Designing Strategies for Independence

Latasha is a student who has a moderate hearing loss. Although her hearing aid helps, she still has to depend a lot on speech reading to communicate. She also speaks slowly and has trouble saying high-frequency sounds such as *sh* and *t*. Latasha has a poor self-image and is reluctant to interact with her peers and teachers. Design a self-advocacy program for Latasha.

Questions

1. What skills would you teach Latasha to use for self-advocacy?

2. How would you get Latasha to use these skills in your class and in other in-school and out-of-school situations?

Cal is a student with organizational problems; he is chronically late for class and rarely finishes his homework. Design an organizational strategy for Cal using the guidelines for developing strategies covered in this chapter.

Questions

1. How would you teach the organizational strategy you have designed using the guidelines covered in this chapter for effectively teaching a learning strategy?

2. How would you teach Cal to apply the strategy independently using self-instruction? Self-monitoring? Self-questioning?

Evaluate the design of any one of the learning strategies in the chapter using the guidelines in the Professional Edge on page 370.

Questions

1. Is there anything you would change about the strategy? How would you teach the strategy using the six steps described in this chapter?

2. How would you help students apply the strategy independently using the three "self" strategies discussed in this chapter?

Further Readings

Daly, P. M., & Ranalli, P. (2003). Using countoons to teach self-monitoring skills. *Teaching Exceptional Children, 35*(5), 30–35.

> *Countoons* are cartoon versions of self-recording devices that students can use to keep track of their behaviors, even when they cannot read. This practical article describes how to use countoons to teach your students with special needs important self-management skills.

Holverstott, J. (2005). 20 ways to promote self-determination in students. *Intervention in School and Clinic, 41*(1), 39–41.

> Students who are independent have self-determination, or the ability to make decisions and direct their own behavior to reach desired goals. This article describes 20 practical ways to promote self-determination in all students.

Lancaster, P. E., Schumaker, J. B., & Deshler, D. D. (2002). The development and validation of an interactive hypermedia program for teaching a self-advocacy strategy to students with disabilities. *Learning Disability Quarterly, 25*(4), 277–302.

> Research showing the effectiveness of using an interactive hypermedia program (IHP) to teach high school students with high-incidence disabilities to advocate for themselves is reported here.

Minskoff, E., & Allsopp, D. (2003). *Academic success strategies for adolescents with learning disabilities and ADHD.* Baltimore: Brookes.

> A book full of practical learning strategies for organization, test taking, studying, note taking, reading, writing, mathematics, and advanced thinking.

Strichart, S. S., & Mangrum, C. T. (2001). *Teaching study skills and strategies to students with learning disabilities, attention deficit disorders, or special needs* (3rd ed.). Boston: Allyn & Bacon.

> Described here are 169 reproducible activities that provide opportunities for learning and student practice in study skills and learning strategies, selected because of their relevance for students with special needs.

11 Evaluating Student Learning

LEARNING Objectives

After you read this chapter, you will be able to

1. Identify and describe accommodations that can be made before, during, and after testing students with special needs.
2. Describe ways to grade students with special needs.
3. Explain how performance-based and portfolio assessments can be used for students with disabilities.

Staci is a student in Ms. Stevens's high school earth science class. Staci has a learning disability that causes her to have trouble reading textbooks. Staci also has difficulty figuring out multiple-choice test questions, the kind that Ms. Stevens uses on her exams and quizzes. Staci says that she knows the material but just needs more time to take the tests, because she reads slowly. During the past marking period, Ms. Stevens gave four multiple-choice tests, each worth 20 percent of the final grade. Scores on homework assignments counted for the remaining 20 percent. Staci earned a grade of B on her homework, but she had two D's, one C, and one F on the tests. Ms. Stevens assigned her a grade of D for the marking period. Ms. Stevens felt this was a fair grade because most of Staci's peers scored much higher on the tests. Ms. Stevens is also committed to keeping her reputation as a teacher with high standards. When Staci received her grade for the marking period, she asked her parents why she should work so hard when she couldn't seem to get good grades anyway. Staci's parents felt that she had improved during the last marking period but that her grade did not show it. They were afraid that Staci would stop trying and eventually drop out of school.

■ *What are the issues here? What could Ms. Stevens do to help Staci?*

Jennifer is in Ms. Robinson's third-grade class. She has a hearing loss and has some trouble in reading but is doing well in Ms. Robinson's classroom reading program.

Ms. Robinson is pleased with her progress and has given her A's in reading for the first two grading periods. Recently, Jennifer's parents became very upset when they learned that Jennifer was reading only at the first-grade level according to district standardized tests. They wondered how she could have done so poorly on the standardized tests when she has been bringing home A's on her report card.

■ *What would you tell Jennifer's parents if she were in your class? How could you change your grading procedures to prevent communication problems like this from occurring?*

Lucille is a student with a mild intellectual disability who is in Mr. Henry's fourth-grade math class. On the basis of her current performance in math, which is at the first-grade level, Lucille's individualized education program (IEP) team set math goals for her in the areas of basic addition and subtraction. The rest of the class is working on more difficult material based on the fourth-grade math curriculum. Lucille's IEP objective for the second marking period was to compute in writing within 20 minutes 20 two-digit by two-digit addition problems with regrouping with 80 percent accuracy. She received direct instruction on these problems from Mr. Brook, her special education teacher, who was co-teaching with Mr. Henry. As a result, she met her goal for the marking period.

■ *How should Mr. Henry grade Lucille? School policy mandates letter grades.*

One of a teacher's major jobs is to evaluate the educational progress of students. The information collected during evaluation activities can indicate whether teaching has been effective and can help teachers alter instruction as needed. Classroom evaluations also are helpful in giving students (and their parents) an idea of how well they are performing in school, and they can be used by principals and school boards to evaluate the effectiveness of their schools.

Even though evaluation activities are very important, the ways in which students are evaluated most frequently—testing and grading—can be problematic for students with disabilities, their teachers, and their parents. For example, Staci and her earth science teacher have a problem because Staci's test scores more often reflect her learning disability than her knowledge of earth science. Jennifer's teacher has a problem in communicating the meaning of Jennifer's grades to her parents. She graded Jennifer based on Jennifer's progress and effort in class. Jennifer's parents, however, thought she was being graded in comparison with her peers and therefore expected their daughter to be performing at or above grade level, not below. Lucille's teacher needs to give Lucille a grade even though she has different curricular goals than the other students in the class. Further complicating these problems is the current climate of accountability and the related expectation that most students with disabilities will meet standards. This expectation makes it imperative that accommodations in evaluation be done without compromising students' ability to meet standards on high-stakes tests. As you work with students with disabilities or special needs, you will experience these and other challenges in evaluating their learning. In this chapter, you learn a number of ways to solve these problems.

How Can Accommodations Be Made for Students with Special Needs When Giving Classroom Tests?

Although testing has always been a major part of U.S. education, the recent emphasis on school reform, with its dominant theme of raising educational standards, promises to make educators rely even more on tests in the future (Albrecht & Jones, 2003; Nolet & McLaughlin, 2005; Roeber, 2002). This increasing emphasis on test performance accompanies concerns about the test performance of students with disabilities. As described in the vignette about Staci at the beginning of this chapter, testing can be a very trying experience for many of these students and their families.

Most important in testing students with disabilities is ensuring that test results reflect their knowledge and skills, not their disabilities. Fortunately, classroom tests can be designed or modified in ways that help you test students with disabilities fairly and with a reasonable amount of accuracy. As shown in Table 11.1, accommodations for students with special needs can be made in three contexts: before the test, during the test administration, and after the test during grading procedures. Many of these accommodations can also benefit students who do not have disabilities.

Accommodations before the Test

You can do a number of things before a test to help students with disabilities. First, you can prepare a *study guide* that tells students what to study for the test. A study guide can help

TABLE *11.1*

Examples of Testing Accomodations

Before the Test	During the Test	After the Test
Study guide	Alternative forms of questions	Changed letter or number grades
Practice test	Alternative ways of administering tests	
Individual tutoring		Changed grading criteria
Teaching test-taking skills		Alternatives to letter and number grades
Modified test construction		

students avoid wasting valuable time studying everything indiscriminately and instead help them concentrate on the most important information. Study guides can also assist students with memory problems by focusing their efforts on only the most critical material. Second, you can give a *practice test*. This test can clarify your test expectations and also benefits the class by familiarizing students with the test format. Practice tests are also helpful to students who have trouble following directions and to those who are anxious about taking tests and often fail to cope immediately with an unfamiliar test format. Finally, many students with disabilities also benefit from *tutoring* before tests. Tutoring can be offered before or after school and may be carried out by peer tutors or paraprofessionals. Tutors can provide guidelines for what to study or help directly with particularly difficult content.

fyi

Planning your tests and test accommodations at the beginning of instruction helps you clarify what is essential to teach and achieve a good match between your tests and instruction.

Students can help each other prepare effectively for tests using directly taught study strategies. What strategies might these students be using to prepare for an upcoming test?

Ellis and Ryan (2003) found that a significant part of the cognitive differences between African American and Caucasian college students resulted from ineffective test preparation and test-taking skills on the part of the African American students.

Another option is to teach students *test-taking skills.* This option can help students take your classroom tests and state high-stakes tests as well. Students may need a number of test-taking skills, including ones for studying for tests, taking objective tests, and writing essay tests.

When studying for tests, students often are required to remember a lot of material. This can be difficult for students with learning or intellectual disabilities, who may have memory problems. Students can benefit from strategies that help them remember important content for tests. For example, Georgia uses a memorization technique called **chunking.** After she studies a chapter in her text, she tries to recall five to seven key ideas. These key thoughts help trigger her recall of more significant details. After reading a chapter about the life of Harriet Tubman, for example, she remembers information in chunks—Tubman's early years, her experiences with the underground railroad, and so on. These general ideas help her remember details such as when Harriet Tubman was born and how many slaves she helped to free.

Mnemonic devices also can help students remember information for tests. **Mnemonics** impose an order on information to be remembered using words, poems, rhymes, jingles, or images to aid memory. For example, Mr. Charles wants his class to remember the six methods of scientific investigation. He tells the students to think of the word *chrome* (Cermak, 1976). The following six steps make up the *CHROME* strategy:

C	Categorization
H	Hypothesis
R	Reasoning
O	Observation
M	Measurement
E	Experimentation

Another mnemonic device that can help students remember definitions and factual information is called the keyword method (Mastropieri, 1988; Uberti, Scruggs, & Mastropieri, 2003). The **keyword method** uses visual imagery to make material more meaningful to students and hence easier to remember. First, a vocabulary word or fact is changed into a word that sounds similar and is easy to picture. For example, to help remember that the explorer Hernando de Soto came from Spain, students might be shown the picture in Figure 11.1, a bull (to symbolize Spain) at a counter sipping a soda (the keyword for *de Soto*) (Carney, Levin, & Levin, 1993). When students are asked to name an explorer who came from Spain, they are told to think of the keyword for de Soto. Next, they are told to think back to the picture the keyword was in and remember what was happening in the picture. Finally, they are told to answer the question. (So who was an explorer from Spain?)

Many students do poorly on tests because they do not study for tests systematically. Teach students to organize their materials so that they avoid wasting time searching for such items as notes for a particular class or the answers to textbook exercises. Making random checks of students' notebooks is one way to find out how well organized they are. For example, Ms. Barber stresses note taking in her fifth-grade social studies class. Every Friday afternoon, she checks the notebooks of five students in her class. She gives students bonus points if they have notes for each day and if their notes are legible and include key information. Also teach students strategies for how to process material when they are studying. For example, Ms. Treacher shows her third graders a verbal **rehearsal strategy** for learning spelling words. She says the word, spells it out loud three times, covers the word, writes the word, and then compares her spelling to the correct spelling. Another effective rehearsal strategy is for students to ask themselves questions about the most important information to be learned.

Students, including those with special needs, may not test well because they lack strategies for actually taking the tests. For example, Sal rarely finishes tests in science because

The Study Guides and Strategies website (www.studygs.net) provides study guides as well as strategies for preparing for and taking tests. The site provides study skills resources including several links to study skills guides and interactive tutorials.

FIGURE 11.1 Keyword for de Soto

Source: From "Mnemonic Strategies: Instructional Techniques Worth Remembering," by R. N. Carney, M. E. Levin, and J. R. Levin, 1993, *Teaching Exceptional Children, 25*(4), p. 27. Reprinted by permission of the Council for Exceptional Children.

Strategy Homework Exercise

Go to the Homework and Exercises section in Chapter 11 of MyEducationLab to learn about three mnemonic devices that can help students improve memory of content.

*R*esearch Note

Robinson and colleagues (1998) found that students who studied for tests using graphic organizers and delayed reviewing their notes by two days performed better on tests than students using traditional outlines who studied their notes immediately after recording them.

he spends too much time on questions that he finds difficult. Laura has trouble with true–false questions because she does not pay attention to key words such as *always, never, usually,* and *sometimes.* Lewis's answers to essay questions contain much irrelevant information and do not focus on what the questions are asking. The Professional Edge on pages 410–411 offers suggestions for teaching students strategies for taking objective tests. These strategies work for taking high-stakes tests too.

Students also need strategies for taking essay tests. Performing well on essay tests requires that students know the content covered; can follow directions, including identifying and understanding key words; and can organize their ideas. All these areas can be problematic for students with disabilities. The following six suggestions might prove helpful to students taking essay tests:

1. Read over the entire exam before you begin. If you have memorized information related to specific questions, jot it down before you write your answer.

2. Look for key instructional words in the questions to help you determine how to structure your answer and determine what information to include. For example, you would include different information and use a different structure if you were asked to *list* the reasons for the American Revolution versus *discuss* them.

3. Organize your answers. A rule of thumb in answering essay questions is that you should spend at least one-fourth of your time planning what you are going to write.

4. Leave time to proofread your answers for clarity, legibility, spelling, and grammar.

DIMENSIONS OF

diversity

Research shows that improving students' test-taking skills, including those of African American, Hispanic, and Native American students and students who are poor, improves their scores on tests. From 5 to 14 hours of instruction spread over 5 to 7 weeks appears to be the range of time needed to improve students' so-called test wiseness (Grossman, 1995). Strategies for teaching test wiseness and other independent learning skills are covered in this chapter.

Professional EDGE

Teaching Test-Taking Strategies

Strategies for Taking Objective Tests

Many students flounder when taking tests because they do not approach tests in any organized way. You can help your students approach their objective tests more systematically by teaching them the strategies described here. The following six rules for responding to multiple-choice and true–false items are based on a comprehensive review of the research literature (Scruggs & Mustropieri, 1988):

1. **Respond to the test maker's intention.** Answers to test questions should take into account the way material is treated in class. For example, Rob had this item on his social studies test:

   > During the occupation of Boston, the British received their most severe losses at Bunker Hill.
   >
   > True
   > False

   Even though Rob had learned at a recent trip to the museum that the Battle of Bunker Hill was actually fought on Breed's Hill, his teacher had not brought up this point in class. Therefore, Rob responded by circling *true*.

2. **Anticipate the answer.** Before students attempt to answer the question, they should fully understand its meaning. Therefore, they should try to figure out the answer before they read the possible answers. For example, Armand was answering the following multiple-choice item:

   > What does an astronomer study?
   > a. plants
   > b. music
   > c. history
   > d. stars

   After he read the question, Armand thought about the word *astronomy* and what his teacher had talked about in class, such as the fact that astronomers use telescopes and that they look at stars and planets. He then read all the possible choices and circled *d, stars,* as the correct answer.

3. **Consider all alternatives.** Many students with special needs, such as students with learning disabilities, tend to answer too quickly, choosing the first available choice. Students should be encouraged to read all the choices before responding. Students can monitor their behavior by putting a check mark next to each choice after they have read it.

4. **Use logical reasoning strategies to eliminate unlikely answers.** Even if students do not know the answer to a question, they can improve their chances of getting it right by using what knowledge they do have to eliminate unlikely choices. For example, Dolores read the following item:

   > In which country would it be impossible to use a sled in the winter?
   > a. Guatemala
   > b. Canada
   > c. Zimbabwe
   > d. Norway

Analyze and Reflect

Rewrite or adapt the strategies for taking essay tests as an illustrated handout for younger students who are expected to write one or two complete paragraphs in response to a question. Which keywords would you teach younger students to help them answer appropriately?

5. When writing an answer, leave margins and do not write on the back of the paper. If your writing is large, write on every other line. Leaving some extra space makes the exam easier for the teacher to grade.

6. If you do not have time to write an answer, write your outline for the answer. Often teachers give you a substantial amount of credit if they can see that you knew the information and simply did not have time to write the answer.

All students benefit from tests that are written clearly and assess pertinent knowledge or skills. Thus, everything that you have learned about writing good tests in your teacher-education program applies here. Still, test items can be well written but constructed in a way that results in problems for students with special needs. When this situation occurs, *modified test construction* is necessary. For example, Carmen has difficulty reading tests that are visually cluttered. She might benefit from triple spacing between test items and extra

Dolores did not know the geographical locations of Guatemala or Zimbabwe, but she did know that Canada and Norway were countries where it snowed often. She then took a guess between *a* and *c* and chose *a*, the correct answer. By eliminating two of the items, she improved her chance of getting the question right by 25 percent.

5. *Use time wisely.* As already mentioned, a frequent test-taking problem is failing to budget time. Some students spend so much time on some items that they have little time left for others. While taking tests, students should check the time periodically to make sure they have enough time left to answer the remaining questions. You can assist students by writing the time remaining on the chalkboard several times during the testing period. Students also can be taught to estimate the amount of time they should spend on each question. For example, if students are taking a 100-item test in a 50-minute period, they should figure on spending no more than one-half minute per question. After 25 minutes, they can then check to see that they have completed at least 50 items. Finally, teach students to spend more time on items on which they have at least partial knowledge and less time on questions for which they have no knowledge.

6. *Guess, if all else fails.* Most tests do not have a penalty for guessing. On standardized tests especially, tell your students that if they do not answer a question, they have no chance of getting it right, but if they guess, they have a 50 percent chance of getting true-false questions right and a 25 percent chance of getting most multiple-choice questions right.

Strategies Using Think-Alouds

Teaching test-taking strategies explicitly and systematically can help ensure students will be able to apply the strategies in completing actual classroom tests. Once you have selected a strategy aligned with your tests, show your students how to use it. Be sure your demonstration includes thinking aloud about what the strategy is, why it is important, and when and where to use it. Provide students with both guided and independent practice using the strategy and offer systematic corrections, as needed. Notice how the teacher in this example uses a think-aloud to teach the strategy of *anticipating the answer* that you just read about:

> OK. The question is asking me what an astronomer studies. I'm going to try to figure out the answer before I even look at the choices, because that will make picking the right answer easier. This is helpful for Ms. Busey's tests, because she always tests us on things she's talked about in class. So, let's see. What has Ms. Busey said in class about astronomy? Well, she's been telling us about how astronomers use these powerful telescopes to look at stars and planets. So the answer probably will have something to do with stars and planets. In looking at the possible answers, the choices of plants, music, and history don't make sense, but choice *d* is stars. That must be the right answer.

space between lines. Juan scores poorly on tests because he is unable to read many of the words used in the items; the items contain complex sentences with many words that are above his reading level and that his teacher did not use while teaching.

Practical ways of constructing objective tests that allow you to measure student knowledge more accurately are shown in the Professional Edge on the next page. Strategies for constructing test items for English-language learners are shown in Special Emphasis On . . . .

Accommodations during the Test

If changes in test construction are intended for the whole class, they can be incorporated into the original master before duplicating. However, when changes are intended only for one or two students, you can make them as students take the test. For example, Ms. Minter's co-teacher, Ms. James, was working with Barry on his test-taking skills.

fyi

Another consideration in constructing tests is to arrange test items in chronological order to match the sequence of instruction.

Modifications in Test Construction for Students with Disabilities

All of your students will do better on clearly written tests that ask questions pertaining specifically to the material covered in class and in the textbook. But your students with disabilities especially require well-phrased and visually accessible tests if they are to succeed at test taking. The following modifications, although beneficial to all your students, can be crucial for your students with special needs:

1. Tests should be typewritten and photocopied.

2. Make tests visually uncluttered by leaving sufficient space between items (3 spaces) and between lines within items (1½ spaces). Do not crowd pages with items; keep wide margins.

3. Use symmetrical spacing. For multiple-choice tests, align possible responses vertically rather than horizontally, and type the question and possible responses on the same page. Permit students to circle the letter of the correct answer rather than write it in front of the item.

4. Provide additional spacing between different types of test questions. Provide separate directions and a sample item for each type of test question.

5. For completion, short-answer, and essay questions, leave sufficient space to write the answer. Students do not do as well when they must continue their answers on the back of the page or on the next page.

6. Leave space for students to answer on the test rather than using machine scoring or answer sheets. Some students have difficulty transferring answers from one page to another.

7. For students who have difficulty with multiple-choice questions, reduce the number of possible answers. Students might choose the correct answer from three, for example, rather than from four or five possible responses.

8. For students who read slowly and students who have organizational problems, avoid the following constructions in matching items: long matching lists—keep lists to five or six items and group by concepts; lengthy items; and drawing lines to the correct answer, which can be confusing for students with visual–motor problems (Wood, Miederhoff, & Ulschmid, 1989). Lists with 10 to 15 entries in the first column can be simplified by preselecting three to four choices from the second column for each item in the first column. Record these choices beside the item in the first column and have the student select the correct answer from the smaller pool.

Consider the following example:

Match the definition on the left with the word on the right by writing the letter for the word in the blank next to the definition.

1. in a sudden way _____   a. brightness
2. not able _____   b. visitor
3. to make bright _____   c. suddenly
4. one who visits _____   d. happiness
5. in a happy way _____   e. rearrange
6. to tell again _____   f. brighten
7. to arrange beforehand _____   g. retell
8. state of being happy _____   h. prearrange
9. to arrange again _____   i. unable
10. state of being bright _____   j. happily

These questions will be less confusing for your students with disabilities if you modify them using the guidelines just described:

1. in a sudden way _____   a. brightness
                                  b. visitor
                                  c. suddenly
                                  d. retell

2. to make bright _____   a. happily
                                  b. unable
                                  c. brighten

9. Change fill-in-the-blank items to a multiple-choice format, providing three or four choices for the blank. Students select the correct answer only from the choices given. This modification changes the task from one of recall (memory) to one of recognition.

10. For essay questions, review the questions, keywords, and tasks with students individually and help students develop answer outlines. Permit dictated or taped responses when appropriate.

11. Consider color-coding, underlining, enlarging, or highlighting key words and mathematical symbols.

Source: Adapted from *Accommodations for Secondary Learning Disabled/Mainstreamed Students on Teacher-Made Tests*, by J. N. Williams, 1986, unpublished manuscript, Wheaton, MD: Wheaton High School.

Special EMPHASIS on

Testing English-Language Learners in Math-Problem Solving

Recent research reveals two important findings about English-language learners (ELLs) and tests. The bad news is that the test scores of English-language learners in all subject areas, including math, are much lower than those of native English speakers (Abedi, Hofstetter, & Lord, 2004). The poorer test performance of ELLs in math occurs not because they know less about the math content but because they have a hard time understanding the language used in test items. In effect, the language demands of the test render the test invalid and unfair. However, the good news is that test scores for English-language learners can be improved by decreasing the complexity of the language (Abedi et al., 2004). In fact, simplifying the language of test items is more helpful to ELLs than translating the items into their native language (American Institutes for Research, 1999). Here are some examples of how you can simplify language when writing math problems for your students (Abedi et al., 2004):

- Change unfamiliar or infrequently used nonmath vocabulary. For example, the phrase "a certain business concern" is unfamiliar and difficult to understand; the substituted phrase "Acme Company" is more common and easier to understand.

- Change the voice of verbs from passive to active. For example, change "If a marble is taken from the bag" to "if you take a marble from the bag."

- Shorten the length of noun phrases. For example, the phrase "the pattern of the puppy's weight gain" can be changed to "the pattern above."

- Replace conditional clauses with separate sentences or change the order of the conditional and main clauses. For example, consider the sentence "If two batteries in the sample were found to be dead, then the workers had to inspect all of the batteries." This sentence

can be simplified by changing it into two sentences: "The workers found two dead batteries in the sample. Because of this, they had to inspect all of the batteries." You could also change the order of the clauses: "The workers had to inspect all of the batteries when they found that two batteries in the sample were dead."

- Remove or change relative clauses. For example, change "What is the total number of newspapers that Lee delivers in 5 days?" to "How many papers does Lee deliver in 5 days?"

- Change complex question phrases to simple question words. For example, change "which is the best approximation of the number . . . ?" to "approximately how many . . . ?"

- Make abstract wordings more concrete. For example, change "2,675 radios sold" to "2,675 radios that Mr. Jones sold."

Examine the following word problem from the Massachusetts Comprehensive Assessment System (at www.doe.mass.edu/mcas/2003/release):

Students in Mr. Jacob's English class were giving speeches. Each student's speech was 7–10 minutes long. Which of the following is the best estimate for the total number of student speeches that could be given in a 2-hour class?

a. 4 speeches

b. 8 speeches

c. 13 speeches

d. 19 speeches

What problems do you think an English-language learner might have with this question? How would you change the item to make it more understandable?

She was helping Barry consider each choice in multiple-choice questions carefully, rather than always picking the first choice. Ms. James began by using an alternative form of question for Barry. When using **alternative forms of questions,** the teacher changes the type of question asked (for example, multiple-choice instead of essay questions) or the construction of the question (for example, adding a word bank for fill-in-the-blank questions). Ms. James used an alternative form of question by decreasing the number of choices on Barry's test items from four to two to make it easier to apply the strategy; on Barry's tests, she blackened two of the four choices. Eventually, however, she added choices to be sure that Barry was able to take the same tests as his classmates. Ms. James used this

www.resources

Ways to apply principles of universal design to constructing tests can be found at the website for the National Center on Educational Outcomes (NCEO): www.education.umn.edu/nceo/OnlinePubs/Policy15.htm.

type of accommodation for another student with reading comprehension difficulties by underlining key words in each question. She gradually eliminated the underlining as the student showed he was able to identify the key words in questions without them.

The way that tests are given to students with disabilities can also affect the accuracy of the results. Students, like Staci from the chapter-opening case, who have reading comprehension problems, might do better on tests if given more time to finish them or if allowed to take them orally. Students with written expression problems might benefit from a dictionary or a handheld spell checker or by dictating their answers. Seating students with attention problems near you when they take a test might help them stay on task longer. These are all examples of **alternative ways of administering tests.** The alternative ways of giving tests that are shown in the Professional Edge are grouped according to students' areas of difficulty.

As the Professional Edge on page 415 indicates, students might also benefit from the use of an alternative test site. An **alternative test site** is a type of testing accommodation that involves changing the location where a student with a disability is tested to make sure the results of the test are accurate. For example, testing in the resource room might help students with attention problems (by allowing them to take their tests in a setting with fewer distractions) and students with written language problems (by permitting them to answer test questions orally). Changing the test site also protects students who are taking the test in a different way from being embarrassed. However, before sending a student out of class to take a test, you should first try other options.

For example, Ms. Edwards allows her students to choose whether to have a test read to them. Those who do not want the test read aloud can work independently while she reads the test to the rest of the students. She also gives the students to whom she reads the test more help with directions and the meanings of key vocabulary or difficult questions. Mr. Collins and Ms. Klein are co-teaching. Mr. Collins supervises students taking the test silently while Ms. Klein reads the test to another group of students. If you do find it necessary to send a student out to take a test, be sure to coordinate your plans in advance with the special education teacher to avoid scheduling problems.

Accommodations after the Test

You may also need to use alternative test-grading procedures for students. For example, because Matt has a learning disability, he has trouble remembering large amounts of information for tests. This memory problem has affected Matt's test scores, which so far include two F's and one D. Matt's teacher, in collaboration with the special education teacher and Matt's parents, identifies the most important information in the chapter and tells Matt to study that for the test. When Matt takes the test, he answers only the 15 questions that his teacher marked with an asterisk, which test the key information he was told to study. The rest of the class answers 30 questions—the 15 that Matt answers plus 15 more covering other material in the chapter. Out of his 15 questions, Matt gets 13 correct. In deciding how to grade Matt, the teacher considers three grading options: changing letter or number grades, changing the grading criteria, and using alternatives to traditional letters and numbers.

Changing letter or number grades by adding written comments or symbols or by giving multiple grades can help clarify what a grade means. In Matt's case, his teacher could give him a B on the test but with an asterisk, meaning that his test covered a different amount of content than that of the rest of the class. Giving multiple grades can be helpful on tests that require written responses. For example, on an English test, Jacinto is required to write an essay on the character Boo Radley in the novel *To Kill a Mockingbird*. When his teacher grades his essay, she assigns him one grade based on the quality of his analysis of the character and another grade for writing mechanics. Having *grading rubrics,* or guidelines, to follow when evaluating student performance helps students understand the criteria by which their work is judged. A strategy designed to help students use grading rubrics to improve their performance is described in the Professional Edge on page 416. A sample rubric designed for English-language learners to evaluate their effort is shown in Figure 11.3.

Accommodations in Administering Classroom Tests

Even a well-constructed test can fail to measure the knowledge of students with disabilities accurately if it is inappropriately administered. The accommodations you make in administering tests to students who have special needs depends on the students' area of difficulty. Use the following chart to help you decide which accommodations to try with students with disabilities included in your class.

| Accommodation | Area of Difficulty | | | | |
	Reading	Writing	Listening	Speaking	Organizing: Paying Attention
Oral explanation of directions	X				X
Repetition of directions; student repetition of directions	X		X		X
Oral, taped, or dictated test; oral clarification of written answers by student	X	X			X
Written test; written directions			X	X	
Extra time	X	X		X	
Time checks during the test					X
Segmented test with separate directions for each section	X		X		X
Peer or other assistance:					
to read directions	X				
to check comprehension	X				
to check spelling		X			
Technological aids:					
placemarks or markers	X				X
word processor		X			
tape recorder	X	X		X	
Visual aids and cues; verbal and visual prompts for word retrieval			X	X	
Use of outlines, diagrams, charts, tables, and webs to organize or answer	X	X			X
Permitted use of noncursive writing		X			
Use of previously prepared notes or rehearsed answers				X	
Alternative sites:					
to minimize noise/distraction			X		X
for alternative testing	X	X			
Seating proximity to teacher			X		X
Teacher paraphrase or summary of student answers in complete thoughts				X	
Checklist for materials needed and preparation					X
Allowing answering directly on test rather than answer sheet		X			

Source: Adapted from *Accommodations for Secondary Learning Disabled/Mainstreamed Students on Teacher-Made Tests,* by J. N. Williams, 1986, unpublished manuscript, Wheaton, MD: Wheaton High School.

Using Grading Rubrics with Students

The use of grading guidelines called *rubrics* benefits students in many ways. Rubrics help students do the following:

- better understand their teachers' expectations
- monitor their progress
- judge the quality of their work (Jackson & Larkin, 2002)

Steps for creating and using rubrics, developed by Goodrich (1996/97, as cited in Jackson & Larkin, 2002), are described in Table 11.2.

Jackson and Larkin (2002) created the *RUBRIC strategy* to help students use rubrics to assess the quality of their work. The steps of the RUBRIC strategy are shown in Figure 11.2.

Jackson and Larkin (2002) make suggestions for teaching students to carry out the RUBRIC strategy. Teach students what rubrics are by showing them some examples. Internet resources for finding rubrics include RubiStar, at http://rubistar.4teachers.org; the rubrics page of Teach-nology, at www.bestteachersites.com/web_tools/rubrics; Kathy Schrock's guide to assessment and rubric information, at http://school.discovery.com/schrockguide/assess .html#rubrics; and Project Based Learning, at http:// pblchecklist.4teachers.org.

Once students know what rubrics are, they are ready to learn to apply the RUBRIC strategy. In general, apply the same steps described in Chapter 10 for teaching learning strategies, including clarifying expectations, demonstrating strategy use, and providing guided and independent practice.

When students are performing the *R* step, encourage them to familiarize themselves with the criteria to be applied to each component of the task. Getting the "big picture" prevents students from diving into the task without thinking, a common problem for students with disabilities.

In the *U* step, students work individually and apply the rubric to one of their products, giving it a score. During this step, students are encouraged to ask questions about the clarity of the scoring guidelines as well as to verbalize their thought processes to someone else, receiving feedback as needed.

For the *B* step, students select a buddy to help them rate the product again. The student and the buddy then review the material together in the *R* step, forming a team to compare scores and ideas. They then present their scores to the larger group of students, explaining how they used the rubric and why they agreed or disagreed. Next, the group gives the team feedback on how they applied the rubric, which the team then uses to identify and award a new set of scores together in the *I* step. In the final step, *C*, students check their work.

TABLE 11.2

Steps for Creating and Using Rubrics

1. Look at models	Show students good and poor examples of student work for a particular task. Help students identify characteristics of each.
2. List criteria	Use the characteristics to generate a discussion about what is considered quality work.
3. Articulate gradations of quality	Describe best and worst levels of quality on a continuum, and then fill in the middle levels of quality.
4. Practice on models	Have students use the rubric created in Steps 2 and 3 to assess the examples of good and poor work in Step 1.
5. Use self-assessment and peer assessment	Stop students occasionally as they are working on a task to have them assess the work.
6. Revise	Encourage students to revise their work based on the feedback they receive in Step 5.
7. Use teacher assessment	Assess students' work by using the same rubric they have used to assess their own and their peers' work.

Source: Adapted from Goodrich, as cited in "Rubric: Teaching Students to Use Grading Rubrics," by C. W. Jackson and M. J. Larkin, 2002, *Teaching Exceptional Children, 35*(1), 40–45.

FIGURE 11.2

The Rubric Strategy

R	**Read** the rubric and the material to be graded
U	**Use** the rubric to give an initial score
B	**Bring** a buddy to help you rate again
R	**Review** the material together
I	**Identify** and award the scores together
C	**Check** the scores again

Source: "RUBRIC: Teaching Students to Use Grading Rubrics," by C. W. Jackson and M. J. Larkin, 2002, *Teaching Exceptional Children, 35*(1), pp. 40–45.

FIGURE *11.3*   **Effort Rubric Adapted for English-Language Learners**

4		I worked until I finished. I tried even when it was difficult. This lesson helped me learn more English.
3		I worked until I finished. I tried even when it was difficult.
2		I tried, but I stopped when it was too difficult.
1		I didn't try.

Source: From "Classroom Instruction That Works with English Language Learners," by J. D. Hall and K. M. Flynn, Alexandria, VA: ASCD.

A second option is to change the **grading criteria,** or the standards on which the grade is based. For example, Matt's teacher could give him a grade of B by basing his grade on a different standard: 15 questions rather than 30. You may instead want to base a student's grade on the percentage correct of the items tried instead of on the total number of questions. This alteration may help students who work accurately but slowly. Giving partial credit is another possible option. For example, when Ms. Jordan grades student answers to math story problems, she gives students points for underlining key words in the question and setting up the equation correctly. These extra points can motivate students who are improving but do not increase their test scores significantly. Students can also be allowed to retake tests. They can then be graded using their score on the retake or averaging their original score with their retake score.

A third grading option is using **alternatives to letter and number grades,** such as pass/fail grades and checklists of skill competencies. For example, Matt could be given a grade of P (pass), because he mastered 7 of 10 key concepts in the chapter, or he could be rated on a **competency checklist** showing which key concepts in the chapter he learned. While all of these test-grading accommodations allow students to be more successful, care

www.*r*esources

EdWeb: Exploring Technology and School Reform (http://edwebproject.org) is a website that includes education-focused discussion groups in which you can discuss testing, grading, and many other educational issues.

must be taken to assure that students are prepared to meet state standards. For example, Matt's teacher needs to be certain that the content for which Matt is held responsible reflects state standards and that reducing the content for which he is held responsible will not interfere with his attainment of state standards.

How Can Accommodations in Report-Card Grading Be Made for Students with Special Needs?

Report-card grading is perhaps the most prevalent and controversial evaluation option used in schools. The practice of grading by letters and percentages began in the early 20th century, a time of great faith in the ability of educational measures to assess students' current levels of learning accurately and also predict future levels of learning. High grades were seen as a sign of accomplishment, intended to spur students on to greater achievements. Those who received low grades were either placed in basic-level or special classes or were encouraged to join the workforce (Cohen, 1983).

Times certainly have changed. Laws have been passed guaranteeing that our evaluations do not discriminate on the basis of disability, race, or ethnicity. These laws also guarantee an appropriate education for all students, not just those who can succeed with minimal intervention. Furthermore, our ability to compete in the global economy depends on better educational outcomes for all our citizens, not just a privileged few. These changes have led to new demands that go beyond the relatively simple matter of identifying good and poor students. For example, how can evaluations be modified to ensure that they do not discriminate against students with disabilities? How can they be used to motivate students to stay in school, to communicate educational competence and progress to parents and students, and to guide our teaching as we strive to meet the needs of an increasingly diverse student body?

Although answers to these and other questions about grading are beginning to emerge, in large part we continue to use a grading system that was intended to fulfill a purpose much more narrow in scope. The use of traditional letter and number grades has caused problems for teachers, who must communicate with many audiences, including parents, students, administrators, and legislators. These audiences often are looking for information that is not readily communicated using a single number or letter (Guskey, 2006; Munk & Bursuck, 2001, 2003). For example, students may be interested in how much progress they have made, whereas their parents want to know how their children compare to their classmates as well as to children nationwide. Principals, on the other hand, may need to provide college admissions offices with indicators of student potential to do college work. Teachers also are increasingly left with many conflicting concerns about grading, including upholding the school's standards, maintaining integrity with other teachers, being honest with students, justifying grades with other students, motivating students for better future performance, communicating accurately to the students' next teachers, and avoiding the reputation of being an "easy" teacher (Munk & Bursuck, 2003).

Increased inclusion in schools has put even more burdens on grading systems. As illustrated in the vignettes at the beginning of the chapter, grading can present serious challenges for students with disabilities and their teachers. Staci was not a good test taker, yet 80 percent of her report-card grade in earth science was based on her test performance. She was concerned that her grade did not accurately reflect her effort or progress in class. Jennifer's parents were surprised to find that their daughter had received A's in reading all year but was reading below grade level on a recent standardized achievement test. Lucille was working on math skills that were more basic than those the rest of the class covered,

DIMENSIONS OF
diversity
What do grades mean in the United States? How are grades used and to what ends? How do values about grades in the national culture affect students with special needs? How do they affect students from other cultures?

DIMENSIONS OF
diversity
In what ways might grading systems be unfair? Which student groups are affected the most? What provisions do school districts make for evaluating students who are culturally different or whose first language is not English?

Report-card grades for students with disabilities and other students with special needs must be carefully explained to prevent misunderstandings. What grading accommodations or modifications might these people be discussing?

and her teacher was unsure how to grade her performance. Add to these problems the concern that grades need to relate to student performance on state high-stakes assessments used in conjunction with No Child Left Behind (NCLB).

Despite these problems, a number of reasons support the continued use of grades. First, many parents want to see how their children compare to other students and demand grades. In addition, grades are efficient and can make decision making easier, particularly for schools making decisions about promotion to the next grade level and for colleges and universities making admissions decisions (Munk & Bursuck, 2001). Despite their many limitations, grades are likely to be used by teachers and schools for many years to come. Teachers need to recognize the limitations of certain types of grades, however, and, when necessary, differentiate grading systems to ensure they are fair to all students.

The next section is divided into two topics. First, grading practices that benefit all students, including students with disabilities, will be described. Second, strategies for individualized grading will be covered. Individualized grading is only carried out with students with disabilities as expressed in their IEPs.

Grading Practices That Benefit All Students

Grading practices that benefit all of your students include using differentiated report cards, avoiding grades of zero, and reporting student progress frequently.

Differentiated report cards are report cards that have individualized provisions for students to clarify the meaning of their grades. Differentiated report cards can be used with most students in your class and are appropriate for students with disabilities (1) who are working toward the same learning standards as the rest of the class, (2) whose progress is being appropriately monitored, and (3) who are receiving accommodations that result in reasonable access to the general education curriculum (Munk, 2007). You can differentiate report-card grades for your students in several ways. Two of the most practical of these include making changes to letter and number grades and reporting separate grades.

Changes to letter and number grades clarify report-card grades by supplementing them with other ways of evaluating and reporting student progress, such as written or verbal comments, logs of student activities, and portfolios. Written or verbal comments can be used to clarify areas such as student ability levels as compared with peers and the extent of student effect. For example, Roberto's teacher gave him an O (outstanding) in reading, because he increased the number of trade books he read, but she also commented on his report card that the books he read were below grade level.

Comments about student ability levels can prevent misunderstandings, particularly when parents find their children are performing below standard on state tests. For instance, in the chapter-opening vignette, Jennifer's mother thought her daughter's high grade in reading meant that she was reading at grade level. An explanation on Jennifer's report card would have put her grade in context. Keep in mind, however, that students sometimes compare report cards with their classmates and might be embarrassed by comments that indicate they are working below grade level. To prevent this situation, you might use an alternative procedure, such as talking to parents or sending them a separate note of clarification. In addition, report-card comments should never state that the student is receiving special services; this would be a violation of student confidentiality.

Finally, the basis for arriving at number or letter grades on report cards is often not clear. For example, does the grade represent a student's performance in comparison with his or her classmates, or is it based on the student's progress toward meeting objectives on his or her IEP? Failure to clarify the basis for grades can lead to issues of fairness raised by students, as shown in the Case in Practice, as well as communication problems with parents, as shown in the Working Together.

Case in Practice

Fairness

Ms. Rodriguez had never questioned her decision to become a middle school science teacher—that is, not until last week. She has always had students with disabilities included in her class and felt comfortable being able to meet their individual needs while maintaining high standards. This year, she has three such students in her class: one with learning disabilities, another who has an emotional disturbance, and a third with a mild intellectual disability. All three students have testing or grading accommodations written into their IEPs. To complicate matters, this year, for the first time, her students without disabilities are complaining. Tricia wants to know why Tyrell is allowed extra time to take his tests. She feels she would do better too if given extra time. Monikee questions why Maya receives extra points for coming to class but she does not. Even Dayrone, who never complains about anything, wants to know why Garrett has to learn fewer vocabulary words than the rest of the class.

Ms. Rodriguez has always believed that fairness means everyone should receive what he or she needs, which is not necessarily the same thing. Still she has to think carefully about how best to respond to her students' concerns about fairness. She believes she can likely appeal to Tricia's independence and sense of right and wrong if she can get her to think more clearly about the situation. So Ms. Rodriguez

tells Tricia, "You don't think it's fair. Please write me a note about your feelings, and we'll talk about it later." Monikee will require a different approach. Because she thrives on Ms. Rodriguez's attention, Ms. Rodriguez concludes that she is complaining because she needs something special too. Ms. Rodriguez tells her, "Maya is getting extra points because she is working on something that is really hard for her. Do you want to work on something that is hard for you?" Ms. Rodriguez is concerned that students like Dayrone complain when they feel the teacher is unsure about a classroom policy. Ms. Rodriguez feels that in general, it is important to respond to complaints of unfairness consistently and without explanation. Therefore, she says to Dayrone, "I'm sorry. I can't make comments about anyone else's work. May I help you with your own?" (Welch, 2000, p. 37).

REFLECTIONS

What are the different ways Ms. Rodriguez responds to her students' complaints about fairness? Is each approach appropriate? Can you think of other ways she could have responded to her students' complaints? What could Ms. Rodriguez do in the future to prevent complaints about fairness?

Communicating with Parents about Grades

Mr. and Mrs. Washington's son Delarnes is in Mr. Campbell's junior English class. Delarnes received an F in English for the last marking period, and Mr. and Mrs. Washington are upset. They know Delarnes is working hard in the class because they are spending a lot of time helping him with his English homework at night. They schedule a meeting with Mr. Campbell to learn more about the problem.

When Mr. and Mrs. Washington arrive at the meeting, Mr. Campbell is seated at a table with the chairperson of the English department, Dr. West. The Washingtons hadn't expected someone else to be at the meeting and it makes them fear that Delarnes has done something terrible. After asking the Washingtons to sit down, Mr. Campbell introduces Dr. West, who talks for what seems like forever on the state English standards and on how the state "seems to be setting the bar higher every year."

The Washingtons aren't sure how the state standards affect Delarnes' English grade but are afraid to ask. Mr. Washington is beginning to grow impatient. He had expected the meeting to be about helping Delarnes. Next Mr. Campbell says that while Delarnes seems to be working hard, he has failed both of the grammar tests during the quarter, and his essay on Frederick Douglass has received a score of D–. Mrs. Washington helped Delarnes outline that paper but hasn't heard anything about it since. Delarnes hasn't told his parents about the grammar tests. When Mr. Campbell asks the Washingtons if they will help Delarnes more at home, Mr. Washington explodes, saying that they *have* been helping him at home, asking why they haven't been told about Delarnes's problem in English before, and demanding that the school do something to help him.

Why are Mr. and Mrs. Washington upset? What could Mr. Campbell have done to make the meeting more productive?

■ Mr. Campbell needs help on how to conduct a more effective parent conference. Even though the Washingtons initiated the meeting, Mr. Campbell could have set the stage for a more comfortable and productive meeting by telling Mr. and Mrs. Washington beforehand what Delarnes's problem was and explaining that the purpose of the meeting was to get their ideas about Delarnes's problem and to come up with a plan to help him improve. Parents are often unaware of the specifics of their child's performance in class. Telling the Washingtons in advance about Delarnes's performance in the class would have given them a chance to get over their shock and come to the meeting better able to help solve the problem. Also, by expressing his interest in the Washingtons' ideas, Mr. Campbell would have communicated to them that they had valuable information to offer—a critical precursor to a successful parent conference.

■ Mr. Campbell should have also explained to Mr. and Mrs. Washington in advance that Dr. West was going to attend and why. For example, if Mr. Campbell had said that he was going to invite Dr. West because she could be of great help, her presence would not have been as intimidating. Also Dr. West should have stuck to the topic at hand when addressing Mr. and Mrs. Washington, which was how to solve Delarnes's problem. Telling them about the difficulties of being an educator was irrelevant and served to further alienate them. Mr. Washington was correct in thinking that the focus of the meeting should be about his son.

■ Finally, Mr. Campbell should have invited someone to the meeting with whom the Washingtons felt comfortable, such as a special education teacher, guidance counselor, or social worker. Lacking that, he could have encouraged them to bring someone along for help and/or moral support.

In the end, the meeting failed to accomplish what should have been its purpose—namely, to help Delarnes learn more and get a better grade in English class. Mr. Campbell and Dr. West should have involved Mr. and Mrs. Washington in developing an improvement plan for Delarnes that included both parental and school responsibilities, as well as a way to monitor the plan's effectiveness. Had a plan with a realistic chance for success been put in place, Mr. Washington would have left the meeting with a handshake, rather than shaking his head.

Because report-card grades are primarily summaries of student performance, they provide few specifics about student performance over a period of time. You can use **daily activity logs** of student activities and achievement to provide ongoing information for students and their parents. Daily observations of students can be recorded in a notebook or journal, directly on a calendar, or on self-sticking notes.

Analyze and Reflect

How should students who are receiving instructional accommodations be graded? Is it fair to give them the same grade as everyone else? Think of a situation where it wouldn't be fair to grade a student with a disability like everyone else.

Strategy Homework Exercise

Go to the Homework and Exercises section in Chapter 11 of MyEducationLab to learn how teachers make decisions when assigning categorical grades.

Whatever type of daily activity log is used, entries should at least include the date, the student's name, the classroom activity, and a brief description of the observation. For example, Ms. Parks was concerned about the progress of one of her students, Carrie, in the area of word-identification skills. Each day during an hour-long literature class, Ms. Parks observed how Carrie approached the trade books she was reading. One day she recorded that Carrie spontaneously used the parts of a multisyllable word to figure out its pronunciation and meaning.

Information taken from the logs can be summarized periodically. These summaries can then be shared with parents as often as necessary to clarify student grades. For example, Leroy received a D in math for the marking period. His parents called his teacher to set up a conference to discuss the grade and find out how Leroy could improve. Leroy's teacher shared a log summary indicating that Leroy had not followed along while she was demonstrating solutions to math problems on the chalkboard. Leroy's teacher differentiated her instruction by collaborating with his parents and setting up a contract for Leroy that encouraged him to attend to such demonstrations. She also moved Leroy's seat so she could more readily monitor his behavior and arranged extra time for a peer tutor to go over the problems with Leroy on a one-to-one basis.

Another way to differentiate report-card grading is to report **separate grades,** each based on a different grading element and corresponding set of criteria (Guskey, 2006). Teachers become frustrated when they have to communicate multiple messages using a single grade. For example, Ms. Lsu wanted to tell her parents which standards her students had met by reporting on the quality of the products they had produced, such as tests, reports, and projects. However, she also wanted to tell parents about the processes involved in developing the products, such as the effort that went into creating them and the work habits her students had displayed. In addition, Ms. Lsu wanted to communicate how much her students had progressed. Fortunately Ms. Lsu's school had just adopted a personalized grade report format, such as the one shown in Figure 11.4 for Ms. Lsu's student Mander. Note that Ms. Lsu used a number grade to evaluate Mander's products for the marking period, thus providing a realistic assessment of his performance on state standards. Ms. Lsu was also able to communicate Mander's level of effort using the three-point scale of *Excellent, Satisfactory,* and *Needs Improvement.* Finally, Mander's progress was communicated by reporting his grades for the previous marking period.

Educators have voiced several concerns about differentiated report cards. The first is that factoring elements such as effort and progress into students' grades diminishes grades' accuracy as indicators of the mastery of standards (Wormeli, 2006). Moreover, this reduction in grading accuracy accounts for discrepancies between students' high school course grades and their performance on state high-stakes tests (Guskey, 2006). In our view, the strategies for differentiating report-card grades described here represent realistic ways for teachers to minimize this problem.

Some teachers also question whether students who receive instructional accommodations should be graded in the same manner as students who do not receive accommodations. It is important to remember that the curricular expectations for students receiving accommodations are the same as for all students. As you have learned, the purpose of accommodations is to maximize access to the general education curriculum by reducing or minimizing the interaction between a student's disability and classroom demands and by allowing for the valid assessment of learning that is not affected by disability. Thus, students' accommodations do not signify reduced expectations, and most students receiving accomodations do not require a different grading system (Munk, 2007).

Another effective grading practice for all of your students is to avoid giving zeroes for work not submitted or tests missed due to unexcused absences. Some teachers give zeroes for missing assignments on the grounds that it teaches students personal responsibility (Munk, 2007). The truth is that the practice of giving zeroes for work not submitted is full of problems.

First, a grade of zero distorts the final grade and diminishes its value as an indicator of what was learned (Wormeli, 2006). For example, Cherise had the following scores on six

FIGURE *11.4* Personalized Grade Report

In English 10, the class has just completed a unit on poetry that focused on the standard of developing an appreciation and understanding of this literary form. Students continue to use exploratory writing to respond to literature read in class. Mander failed to complete two assignments worth 25 percent collectively this term. This has significantly affected his overall mark. Mander can improve his performance by ensuring assignments are completed and handed in on time. He has yet to meet standards in this area.

Mark to Date	70%
Previous Mark	80%
Effort	
Excellent	
Satisfactory	✓
Needs Improvement	
Periods Absent since Beginning of Course	4
Periods Late since Beginning of Course	6

This term, Mander has worked toward meeting standards in algebra. In particular, he has studied units on the operations of polynomials, equation solving, and factoring polynomials. Class time is used wisely. He organizes work effectively. He aims for excellence. To date, he is on target to meet standards in all of these areas. Keep up the good work, Mander!

Mark to Date	90%
Previous Mark	75%
Effort	
Excellent	✓
Satisfactory	
Needs Improvement	
Periods Absent since Beginning of Course	None
Periods Late since Beginning of Course	None

Source: Adapted from "Reporting Achievement at the Secondary Level: What and How," by J. Bailey and J. McTighe, in *ASCD Yearbook: 1996, Communicating Student Learning* (pp. 119–140), edited by T. Guskey, Alexandria, VA: Association for Supervision and Curriculum Development.

classroom quizzes: 100, 100, 100, 95, 100, 0. She received a zero on quiz 6 because of an unexcused absence. Cherise's average score for the quizzes with a score of zero figured in was 83 percent. She received a grade of B– despite the fact that she earned an A on every quiz she took. Not only does giving Cherise a zero for the quiz she missed distort what she learned, but it could also undermine her motivation. Missing work and missed tests may also result from organizational problems related to a learner's disability or life circumstances beyond her control. For example, Cherise is involved in family child care. On the day of the quiz, she had to take her younger brother to the doctor because her mother was working.

Wormeli (2006) suggests giving a grade of 60 percent rather than zero as a way of lessening the impact of a missed assignment or test. While this practice would lessen the numerical impact of a zero (Cherise would have averaged 93 percent, rather than 83 percent), in our view, there are more proactive ways to solve the problem of giving zeroes. First, make sure all students understand your grading policies for late or missed work. Second, allow students to turn in late work for full or partial credit. Third, increase the level of communication regarding assignments, tests, and due dates. Finally, for students with disabilities, consider setting an IEP goal for improving time management, including the self-monitoring of work completion (Munk, 2007).

A final grading practice that can benefit all of your students is to report student progress more frequently. Report-card grades only come out four times a year. Students as well as parents need more frequent feedback than that. Of course, the frequency with which

Artifact Homework Exercise

Go to the Homework and Exercises section in Chapter 11 of MyEducationLab to see the goals and self-evaluation written by a upper elementary student.

you provide student progress reports will vary depending on the student as well as the time demands made on you as a teacher.

Using Individualized Grading with Students with Disabilities

Article Homework Exercise

Go to the Homework and Exercises section in Chapter 11 of MyEducationLab for research that can help teachers when assigning grades to students with disabilities.

Grading accommodations and modifications can be used to individualize your grading system for students with disabilities (Munk, 2003). Individualizing grading is legal for students with disabilities as long as the accommodations and modifications that compromise them appear on students' IEPs. However, individualized grading should not be used with students without IEPs unless it is available to all students in the class (Salend & Duhaney, 2002). All school districts have some grading policy, and you should check to see whether individualized grading is covered by your policy. See the Professional Edge for a discussion of the legalities of grading students with disabilities.

Broadening the factors considered in grading is helpful for students with disabilities, who as a group tend to receive low or inaccurate grades (Munk & Bursuck, 2005). While teachers are willing to make changes in how they grade students with disabilities (Bursuck et al., 1996), the accommodations and modifications they make can be unsystematic (Polloway et al., 1996). Informal and unsystematic decisions, even when made in a student's best interest, can lead to confusion and threaten the validity of the resulting grade (Silva, Munk, & Bursuck, 2005). The individualized grading described here involves making judgments but in a systematic way. Individualized grading is also done in conjunction with the student's IEP. That makes individualized grading legally binding and can prevent problems such as the ones described at the beginning of the chapter for Jennifer and Lucille.

Individualized grading includes accommodations that involve changing either the elements being graded (such as curriculum content, class participation, and homework) or the values or weights assigned to these elements. Individualized grading is called for when a learner has a moderate to severe disability and modified curricular expectations. Individualized grading is also called for when a learner has a high-incidence disability, receives a series of low or failing grades despite the delivery of appropriate classroom accommodations, and seemingly will benefit from increased access to the general education curriculum via individualized grading. Merely having an IEP, trying hard, failing because of missed work, or receiving poorly administered accommodations or modifications is not enough to qualify a student for individualized grading (Munk, 2007).

Researchers have identified two general types of individualized grading: (1) grading accommodations that involve changing the grading elements, or what counts toward earning a grade; and (2) grading accommodations that involve changing the value of the grading elements, or how much each element counts toward the final grade. Accommodations that involve changing the grading elements include basing all or part of the grade on progress on IEP objectives (Munk, 2003); basing all or part of the grade on performance on prioritized content and assignments (Guskey & Bailey, 2001; Munk, 2003); and emphasizing learning strategies and effort in a balanced grading system (Guskey & Bailey, 2001; Munk, 2003). Changing the value of the grading elements includes basing part of the grade on improvement over past performance and modifying grading weights and scales. All of these types of individualized grading are summarized and described in greater detail in the sections that follow.

● **Basing All or Part of the Grade on Progress on IEP Objectives** For this type of individualized grading, **progress on IEP objectives** is used as the basis for part or all of a student's report-card grade (Munk, 2003). Grading on the basis of progress on IEP objectives would have been appropriate for Lucille, the student in the opening vignettes whose math curriculum was modified on her IEP. Whereas the rest of the class was working on decimals, she was working on two-digit by two-digit addition problems with regrouping. Because her IEP objective was to score 80 percent or better when given 20 of these problems, her fourth-grade teacher and special education teacher agreed to give

The Legalities of Grading Students with Disabilities

Report-card grades are often used to make important educational decisions about students such as eligibility for honors awards, graduation, and admission to postsecondary education. Because of the importance of grades, teachers need to exert great care when modifying their grading systems for students with and without disabilities. While most schools have a written grading policy containing guidelines for giving and interpreting grades, many grading policies focus on the grading scale and the schedule for reporting grades to parents, not on judgments required for grading students with disabilities (Munk, 2003).

The following are some commonly asked questions and answers about grading students with disabilities (LRP Publications, 1997; Salend & Duhaney, 2002). As legal guidelines for grading are constantly being refined, you should consult your school policies and your building administrator prior to modifying your grading system. It is also important to document all grading accommodations and modifications for students with disabilities on their IEPs.

1. *Can I give modified grades to a student with a disability who is in my classroom and receiving accommodations?* Using alternative grading systems for students with disabilities is appropriate but only if you make the same ones available for your students without disabilities as well. However, you do not need to make grading modifications available to all students when they are specified on a student's IEP.

2. *If a student who is enrolled in my class has alternative curricular objectives specified on her IEP, can I exclude her from my regular grading system and evaluate her based on her IEP objectives?* In effect, students in an alternative, more basic curriculum are not considered to be officially enrolled in your class for credit. Therefore, you may grade them solely on the basis of their IEP objectives.

3. *Can I collaborate with an included student's special education teacher when assigning the student a grade?* Col-

laborating with a student's special education teacher is entirely appropriate (and desirable) as long as collaboration is specified on the student's IEP.

4. *If I want to communicate to parents and employers that a student in my class has a modified curriculum, can my school indicate on the student's transcript that the class was a special education class?* No. It is illegal to specify that a class is *special education*. However, there is general agreement that alternative terms can be used to communicate curricular differences, although as yet no terms have been officially sanctioned by the courts. Use a term such as *basic, level 1,* or *modified curriculum,* as long as this term is also used in courses besides special education such as classes within gifted and talented programs. Asterisks or other symbols can also be used to communicate a modified curriculum as long as courses for all students are handled in a similar way. Transcripts sent to postsecondary schools can contain courses designated as special education when families and students are informed and give their written consent (Salend, 2005).

5. *Can we include grades earned in special education classes or general education classes taken with support when we calculate districtwide GPAs and rank them for purposes of creating an honor role or assigning scholarships?* Grades earned by students in special education classes or general education classes taken with support cannot be arbitrarily or categorically dismissed by the district. However, districts can implement a system of weighted grades that assigns points to grades depending on the difficulty of the subject matter. Weighted systems are permissible as long as they are fair and simple to understand. Districts can also establish a list of core courses that must be completed to be eligible for honors, class rankings, or participation in certain activities. Again the important consideration is that all students are similarly affected, not just students with disabilities.

her an A if she met her objective, a B if she scored between 70 and 80 percent, a C if she scored between 60 and 70 percent, and so forth. To ensure that Lucille's mother had an accurate picture of Lucille's standing in relation to her peers, Lucille's teacher included a written comment on Lucille's report card indicating that her grade was based on different curricular objectives as agreed to on her IEP.

Basing grades on progress on IEP objectives can also be helpful for students who are in special education but do not have modified curricular expectations. For example, Manny

How might the strategy of
grading on the basis of
improvement help Staci and her
parents, whom you read about
at the beginning of the chapter?
What other grading methods
described in this chapter might
be helpful?

is a student with a learning disability who is included in Mr. Ottens's middle school science class. Manny receives pullout services in writing but is still expected to meet the same curriculum standards in science as his classmates. During Manny's IEP conference, it was decided that 10 percent of his science grade would be determined by progress on an IEP objective stating that "Manny will write complete sentences using correct spelling, grammar, and sentence structure." Mr. Ottens agreed to evaluate Manny's written work in science using these criteria. Mr. Ottens would give each assignment Manny submitted a writing grade along with a regular grade. Manny's average writing grade would count 10 percent toward his report-card grade in science.

Basing all or part of a student's daily work grade or report-card grade on IEP objectives, as was done for Lucille and Manny, is advantageous in several ways:

1. It allows the team to consider how and when IEP objectives can be addressed in the general education classroom.

2. It informs students, parents, and teachers which objectives are important and how supports can be provided.

3. It ensures that a student's grade reflects progress on skills that have been identified as most important for him by the team.

4. It eliminates the redundancy of reporting grades separately from progress on IEP objectives.

5. It improves communication among parents, students, and teachers about grading in the general education classroom.

Of course, basing grades or progress on IEP objectives carries the risk that students with disabilities will be evaluated using criteria unrelated to expectations in general education. When curricular objectives in general and special education are out of sync, student access to the general education curriculum is compromised. That is why, to the maximum extent possible, IEP objectives should be based on the general education curriculum.

● **Basing All or Part of the Grade on Performance on Prioritized Content and Assignments**   This type of individualized grading is basing all or part of a student's grade on his performance on prioritized curriculum content and assignments deemed most important by the teacher (Munk, 2003). **Prioritization of curriculum** benefits students for whom remembering, organizing, and accessing the content in the general education curriculum is a difficult and time-consuming process. Limiting the content load and assignments to the essentials for these students can make learning success more likely. Teachers can prioritize their content based on a number of sources including state learning standards, local curriculum guidelines, skills or content needed for future classes or postsecondary education, relevance to students' lives, or other criteria established by the IEP team (Munk, 2003). Basing priorities on standards is particularly important in the current climate of school accountability.

Claudia is included in Mr. Gonzales's middle school science class. She has learning disabilities; she has difficulty remembering factual material, reads quite slowly, and has problems organizing what she reads into main ideas. Claudia's IEP team decided that content prioritization would help her access the science curriculum more efficiently, particularly since the science textbook was hard to read and very content dense. Mr. Gonzales agreed to prioritize the content for the next grading period when he was covering the topic of cells. He identified the following content as most important based on state learning standards (Munk, 2003, p. 74):

1. Identify nine major parts of all cells.

2. Use a microscope to view cells of different organisms.

**Strategy Homework
Exercise**

Go to the Homework and
Exercises section in Chapter 11
of MyEducationLab for two
methods recommended for
assigning grades to students with
disabilities and two that are not
recommended.

3. Describe the stages in photosynthesis.

4. Describe the functions of cells.

5. Describe the similarities and differences between cells of animals and plants.

6. Identify parts of cells as viewed under a microscope.

Mr. Gonzales assured the team that this content reflected the major information in the state standards pertaining to cells. He explained that content ideas 1, 3, and 4 would be evaluated using short-answer tests and ideas 2, 5, and 6 would be evaluated based on Claudia's performance on submitted lab reports. The team decided that her labs and tests would be graded based on the percentage correct on all items pertaining to her prioritized content. The resulting number grade would be converted to a letter grade using the same grading scale used schoolwide. Mr. Gonzales said that Claudia would be encouraged to participate in all of the other class activities for the grading period, including answering end-of-chapter questions in the textbook, but that the activities related to her prioritized content would be emphasized in arriving at her grade.

Using prioritization for individualized grading has a number of advantages. It directs the team to focus the need for supports on the most important content and assignments. For example, Claudia needed the most support on completing lab reports related to her curricular objectives and preparing for short-answer tests. Less support was needed for end-of-chapter questions in the text and producing lab reports on other topics. Prioritization may also reduce the risk that students' performance on less important content and activities will pull down their grade. For example, end-of-chapter questions are difficult for Claudia because they take her so long. In the past, she never completed them, and her low grades on these activities reduced her overall grade for the marking period. Finally, the process of prioritizing content can help teachers identify the most important elements of the curriculum. Knowing and communicating what is most important about the curriculum benefits all students, not just those with disabilities.

A problem that could arise when using prioritization involves the choice of which content to stress and which to de-emphasize. This decision is best made collaboratively by the student, parents, and teachers as part of the IEP process and of course while keeping state standards clearly in mind.

● Emphasizing Learning Strategies and Effort in a Balanced Grading System

Traditionally, grading has focused on the evaluation of student products without taking into account the learning strategies and effort required to come up with the products. For example, in Mr. Kellogg's sophomore English class, students write a five-page persuasive essay and are graded on various qualities of the essay submitted, such as length, organization, mechanics, and the integration of elements essential to a persuasive essay. When grading his students, Mr. Kellogg does not consider the amount of effort students put into the paper or the extent to which the students employ learning strategies. Brad is a student included in Mr. Kellogg's class. He is receiving help from his special education teacher, Ms. Laslow, in writing, but he feels discouraged. His grades in Mr. Kellogg's class have remained at D−, despite all the hard work he has been doing with his special education teacher, Ms. Laslow, on learning strategies for writing such as outlining key essay elements, proofreading, self-monitoring, and using word processing. Mr. Kellogg has indicated that he has seen no changes in Brad's writing since the beginning of the year.

Brad's IEP team decided to use **balanced grading** that took into account Brad's learning-strategy performance and effort. The team decided to give Brad credit for performing the writing strategies that he was learning from Ms. Laslow. When Brad submitted the final draft of his paper, he also gave Mr. Kellogg a copy of his paper outline and

Analyze and Reflect

What are the advantages of making individualized grading a part of students' IEPs? Under what circumstances might you want to differentiate grading for your students without disabilities?

Prioritization directs the IEP team to focus the need for supports on the most important content and assignments.

www.resources

Find out about testing and grading policies being used around the country by visiting the website of the Council of Chief State School Officers (CCSSO), at www.ccsso.org.

a completed self-monitoring checklist of all of the writing steps he followed. The team agreed that the quality of the outline and checklist would count 25 percent toward Brad's final grade on the paper. As a way of recognizing Brad's effort, the team also agreed to give him bonus points for submitting his paper to Mr. Kellogg once early for feedback and for getting the final paper in on time.

Brad's individualized grade is an example of a grading type that attempts to balance an emphasis on the quality of the product with the effort and skill that went into producing it. Balanced grading has a number of advantages. First, as you have already learned, students with disabilities may have difficulty performing learning strategies that typical students complete effortlessly (Munk, 2003). These strategies include the basic reading, writing, math, and computer skills covered in Chapters 5 and 9, and the independent learning strategies described in Chapter 10. Often these are the skills on which students receive help from special educators but have difficulty applying in their general education classes. Including student performance on these academic learning skills in the grading process helps focus students' attention on applying them in their general education classes. Balanced grading also leads to greater collaboration and coordination between general education and special education teachers. Once Brad's individualized grading approach was agreed to, Mr. Kellogg took a greater interest in Brad in class. For example, he began to remind Brad to perform the skills present on his self-monitoring checklist. As a result, Brad was better able to apply what he had learned from Ms. Laslow to meeting the requirements in Mr. Kellogg's class.

While rewarding effort is a key part of balanced grading and a potentially effective way to sustain student motivation, it is a type of individualized grading that must be done with great care. First, effort is much more difficult to assess than academic progress (Gersten et al., 1996). Also, the relationship between effort and achievement is not always predictable; a student may work hard but master little of the content (Munk, 2003). Munk (2003) advises IEP teams to ask the following questions when considering incorporating effort into a student's grade:

- Do you have evidence that when the student tries harder, he performs better on assignments?
- Can the team agree on how to measure effort?
- Will the student perceive the accommodation as an incentive to keep working hard? (p. 90)

Analyze and Reflect

Educators such as Wormeli (2006) warn against counting effort as part of a student's grade. What are the drawbacks of including effort in grades? When might giving students credit for effort be beneficial?

In Brad's case, based on input from his mother, the committee felt that rewarding him for effort was necessary and would be effective. The team also agreed that they could measure his level of effort by noting whether he handed in an early draft of the paper to Mr. Kellogg for feedback and whether he submitted the final draft of the paper on time.

Finally, while learning processes and effort are important, ultimately it is the product or outcome that is most important. Placing too much emphasis in grading on process use or effort can send the message that the quality of the final product is not important—a message inconsistent with most grading policies.

● Basing Part of the Grade on Improvement over Past Performance

This type of individualized grading involves basing part of a grade on improvement. **Improvement grades** can be incorporated into a traditional grading system by assigning extra points for improvement or by moving students up a grade on the scale if they improve, particularly if they are on the border between grades. Consider the case of Aretha, whose average on spelling tests in her general education classroom for the last marking period was 77 percent, an improvement of more than 40 percentage points over the preceding marking period. Although her true grade for spelling was technically a C, Aretha's IEP team had agreed in advance that her teacher would raise her grade a letter if she were to bring her test average up to at least 75 percent. The team also agreed, however, that once she reached 75 percent, she would be graded using the same scale as the rest of the class for the remaining grading periods.

In another example, Roberto's IEP team agreed that if he read a minimum of five trade books during the grading period—an improvement of four over his performance for the previous grading period—he would receive a grade of O (outstanding) in reading, because he read so many more books than before. The team felt that even though other students in the class were reading more books at a more difficult level, Roberto deserved an O if he improved that much. His teacher did note on Roberto's report card, however, that the books he read were one to two years below grade level. The team also decided that Roberto would have to improve his performance by at least one book per marking period if he were to continue to receive a grade of O in reading.

Perhaps the greatest benefit of grading based on improvement is that it motivates students to try harder. In fact, basing part of students' report-card grades on improvement can motivate students to take better advantage of available supports or attempt more work than they would do ordinarily. In the preceding examples, Aretha worked more conscientiously during her instructional support time in the resource room because she thought it would improve her spelling grade in general education. Roberto read even more books than the minimum of five required in his IEP.

One potential drawback of grading on the basis of improvement is the risk that students will become dependent on special contingencies. For example, when Aretha finally reaches 75 percent on her spelling tests, will she balk when asked to perform better to receive a grade of B next time? Will Roberto expect that he will always be able to receive an O in reading by reading just five trade books? As was done for Aretha and Roberto, teachers need to continue to increase the criteria for successful performance until students are performing under the same conditions as their classmates without disabilities. Another problem can arise if students do not possess the skills needed to show improvement. For example, if Aretha's knowledge of sound–spelling relationships is well below that needed to spell her weekly spelling words correctly, no level of incentive will be enough to improve her performance. If there are no books in the classroom library that Roberto can read, he will be unable to reach his objective of reading five books and answering comprehension questions, regardless of the grading incentive. Teachers should select improvement as a grading accommodation only when the student's performance clearly demonstrates the presence of the prerequisite skills needed to meet the goal.

- **Modifying Grading Weights and Scales** This type of individualized grading involves changing the grading scale used to assign a specified letter grade or changing the weights assigned to different requirements when determining a report-card grade. In the case of Staci from the chapter-opening vignettes, for example, her teacher, Ms. Stevens, counted tests as 80 percent of the grade and homework as 20 percent. Staci's IEP team decided that they could help her become less discouraged by using **modified weights and scales** grading. The team decided to reduce the percentage Ms. Stevens counted for tests from 80 to 50 percent, while keeping homework at 20 percent. However, the team also added a new assignment: Staci would be required to make a taped summary of responses to a study guide at the end of each text chapter. This assignment would count for 20 percent of Staci's grade. The remaining 10 percent of her grade would comprise other accomplishments, such as being prepared, attempting all class activities, and participating in class. Ms. Stevens defined these other accomplishments as the percentage of school days for which Staci had her materials for class, completed in-class assignments, and asked at least one question in class. Because Staci's IEP team members were concerned that she would drop out of school, they also decided to make a temporary change in the grading scale for her. Staci's modified scale would be as follows: A = 90–100%; B = 80–89%; C = 70–79%; and so on. The regular school scale was this: A = 93–100%; B = 85–92%; C = 77–84%, and so on. Staci's IEP team planned to move her back to the school grading scale when her grades improved for two consecutive marking periods.

The benefit of changing the grading scale or weights is that doing so may motivate students to keep trying because they can earn a higher grade that seemed out of reach before. This was certainly the case for Staci, who was in need of a motivator because she had been trying hard but with little success to show for it. However, changing the grading scale and/or the weights for class requirements must be implemented cautiously because these accommodations do not require a change in the student's performance. This lack of increased performance expectations may send a message to students that they have no need to improve. Changing the weights and/or the grading scale may also be perceived by classmates and other teachers as unfair. Because of this we do not recommend changing the grading scale unless other instructional accommodations are used as well. In the case of Staci, a number of accommodations were used in conjunction with changing weights and the grading scale. While Staci's tests counted less toward her grade, she was still expected to learn key content by submitting an orally completed study guide for each chapter in the text. She was also expected to be prepared for class, attempt all class activities, and ask questions in class. Often changing weights is perceived to be fairer if weight is shifted to alternative ways to assess student learning, not simply away from a requirement that is particularly difficult for a student (Munk, 2003). Finally, the IEP team planned to reestablish the regular grading scale as soon as Staci showed signs of success in class.

How Can Performance-Based Assessment Benefit Students with Special Needs?

Article Homework Exercise

Go to the Homework and Exercises section in Chapter 11 of MyEducationLab to read about successful implementation of performance-based projects that allow teachers to assess authentic student learning.

DIMENSIONS OF
diversity

Because teachers' evaluations of lower-income and non-European students can be prejudiced, performance-based assessments can be subject to bias. However, anecdotal evidence shows that when teachers follow specific scoring procedures, performance-based assessment provides much useful information about non-European students and students with limited English proficiency (Heath, 1993).

Ms. Johnson is just completing a unit on persuasive writing and has her students write letters to the editor of a local newspaper, trying to persuade readers to support the building of a new county facility for elderly people. Mr. Repp is teaching drawing to scale as part of a map-reading unit and has his students make a map of the neighborhood that could be used by visitors from Japan. Ms. Overton's class is working on basic bookkeeping skills and has her students plan a budget for a fund-raiser to earn money to build a new jungle gym for the playground.

All these teachers are checking their students' progress with a method of evaluation called performance-based assessment. **Performance-based assessment** "provides students with opportunities to demonstrate their mastery of a skill or concept through performance of a task" (Haager & Klingner, 2005, p. 66). Performance-based assessment measures learning processes rather than focusing only on learning products. It frequently involves using **authentic learning tasks,** or tasks that are presented within real-world contexts and lead to real-world outcomes.

Mr. Repp could have asked his students to compute the mileage between several cities using a mileage key, a more traditional map-reading assignment. Instead, he has them create their own maps within a real context, because he wants to see how well they can apply what they have learned to an actual problem. Not only does Mr. Repp evaluate students' maps, but he also evaluates parts of the learning process, such as how well his students select and implement learning strategies and collaborate with their classmates during problem solving.

Using performance-based assessment can be very helpful for students with disabilities and other special needs who may be included in your classroom. Performance-based assessment can offer students options for demonstrating their knowledge that do not rely exclusively on reading and writing, areas that often impede the successful testing performance of students with disabilities. For example, Calvin, a student with reading problems who is in Mr. Repp's class, completed the map activity successfully but would have had trouble with a traditional paper-and-pencil test of the same material.

Performance-based tests also are not subject to the same time constraints as traditional tests. Time flexibility can benefit students who need more time, such as those with reading fluency problems, or students who need to work for shorter time periods, such as those with attention deficit–hyperactivity disorder. Again using the example of Mr. Repp's map-drawing activity, students had some time limits (they had to finish in one week) but did not have to do the entire project in one sitting.

Students with disabilities may also have particular difficulty making the connection between school tasks and tasks in the real world. Performance-based assessment can help them understand this connection, particularly if an assessment is followed up with instruction directly geared to skill applications. For example, Ms. Johnson, whose students were required to write letters to the editor, discovered that many of her students were unable to support their arguments directly with specific examples. She therefore spent some class time demonstrating to students how they could support their arguments and guiding them through several practice activities.

As you can see, using performance-based assessment has many potential benefits for students with special needs. Nonetheless, you may still need to make accommodations for students with disabilities when they participate in performance-based assessments. For example, Gregory is a student with cerebral palsy in Mr. Repp's social studies class. Gregory has very little control over fine motor movements in his hands. As a result, he is unable to write or draw. Gregory obviously needs to have the drawing-to-scale map task adapted. One possible accommodation would be to have Gregory make an audiotape to accompany the map that would provide the Japanese visitors with a self-guided tour. Or consider Rhonda, a student with a learning disability who has difficulty expressing herself in writing. Rhonda is included in Ms. Johnson's class. The class is writing letters to the editor as a way of practicing persuasive writing skills. As an accommodation, Ms. Johnson has Rhonda develop an oral editorial that is sent to the local public radio channel. In some cases then, accommodations for performance-based tests can be made just as readily as those made for traditional tests.

Some students with special needs may have problems with performance-based tests that are more difficult to accommodate. For instance, students might have difficulty making the connection between school tasks and real-world tasks. You need to teach these students directly how to make those connections. For example, Ms. Riley's class is learning to compute subtraction problems. As a performance-based test, Ms. Riley has her class compare prices of various brands of the same products in the grocery store and compute price differences using subtraction. Cleo, a student in the class who has a mild intellectual disability, is unable to perform the task because he has never used subtraction as it applies to money or products in the grocery store. The next day in class, Ms. Riley includes examples of subtracting amounts of money in her daily instruction. She also includes story problems dealing with the subtraction of money, some of which involve grocery store products. This accommodation helps Cleo make the connection between money and the supermarket.

Students with special needs also lack important preskills that are necessary for problem solving. You need either to teach these preskills or to allow such students to bypass the preskills altogether to carry out performance-based tasks. For example, Sam has a learning disability in math; he does not know basic math facts and as a result cannot get Ms. Riley's product comparisons correct. Ms. Riley allows him to perform the task with a calculator. She also requires that he spend five minutes per day using a computer-based math fact program until he learns basic math facts. Anna has visual disabilities; another student reads to her the prices of the brands and she writes them down.

For students with more severe disabilities, you may need to modify or scale down performance-based tasks by using the guidelines for developing alternate assessments described in Chapter 4 and the environmental inventory process described in Chapter 9. For example, Derek has severe intellectual disabilities and lacks basic math skills other than simple number identification. Ms. Riley has Derek participate in the same task as the other students but has him perform an easier step. She has Derek pick groups of products that students are to compare. This task is more consistent with Derek's IEP goal of being able to classify similar objects, such as three kinds of cola or two types of bread.

As an alternative to pencil-and-paper tests, performance-based tests allow students to demonstrate their knowledge and skills through application in real-world contexts. What are some ways to support students with special needs as they participate in performance-based assessment?

Video Homework Exercise

Go to the Homework and Exercises section in Chapter 11 of MyEducationLab to see a second-grade student and her teacher discussing her work products.

Article Homework Exercise

Go to the Homework and Exercises section in Chapter 11 of MyEducationLab to learn how schools are using digital portfolios to assess student learning and progress.

How can technology help teachers develop alternate assessments for students with moderate to severe disabilities?

Video Homework Exercise

Go to the Homework and Exercises section in Chapter 11 of MyEducationLab for suggestions by a teacher on using and constructing portfolios to assess student learning and progress.

DIMENSIONS OF

diversity

Barootchi and Keshavarz (2002) found that portfolio assessments increased Iranian English-language learners' achievement and feelings of responsibility toward monitoring their own academic progress.

Finally, students with special needs may have trouble meeting the problem-solving demands of performance-based tests. For example, Peter has attention deficits and approaches problems impulsively; he rushes to find an answer and fails to consider all the options. For Peter, performance-based tests are important because they give him the opportunity to learn critical problem-solving skills. Nonetheless, for students like Peter to succeed, performance-based tasks need to be modified and problem-solving skills need to be taught directly. For example, Mr. Kelsey's class is applying work they have done in computing areas and perimeters to the task of planning a garden. Before having students design their own gardens, Mr. Kelsey carefully demonstrates how he would design his. This demonstration is very helpful for students in the class such as Peter, who are not natural problem solvers and need a model to guide them. Mr. Kelsey also scales down Peter's assignment, asking him to design only one section of a smaller garden.

As you can see, the use of performance-based tests with students with disabilities can be helpful, but it can also be problematic. For this reason, use performance-based tests in conjunction with other classroom-based and standardized tests.

How Can Portfolio Assessment Benefit Students with Special Needs?

Portfolio assessment is a method of evaluation in which a purposeful collection of student work is used to determine student effort, progress, and achievement in one or more areas (Montgomery, 2001). A portfolio collection typically contains the observable evidence or products of performance assessment, evidence that may or may not reflect authentic tasks (Poteet, Choate, & Stewart, 1993). This evidence includes many different sources of information, such as anecdotal records, interviews, work samples, and scored samples such as curriculum-based assessment probes.

Portfolios can be very helpful for teachers working with students with disabilities. Portfolios can assist teachers in evaluating student progress toward IEP objectives and in guiding instruction. For example, Ms. Pohl is interested in finding out whether the extra math practice sheets she is sending home with Robert are improving his scores on weekly math computation tests. She consults Robert's portfolio and finds that his performance has improved quite a bit over the last two months. Ms. Pohl tells Robert's parents of his progress. They agree to continue the extra practice for at least another month.

Portfolios also emphasize student products rather than tests and test scores. This emphasis benefits students with special needs, many of whom are poor test takers. It may also highlight student strengths better than traditional tests, which tend to have a narrow academic focus. For example, Leshonn's teacher uses portfolios to evaluate her social studies students. Leshonn has problems in reading and writing but has good artistic ability and excellent oral language skills. During the last marking period, his class studied the growth of suburban areas after World War II, a content area included in the state standards. Leshonn designed a scale model of Levittown, one of the first planned communities. He also developed a tape-recorded explanation to go with the model that explained the key features of the community. His performance on these projects was excellent and enabled him to raise his overall grade for the class because his scores on the two tests given during the marking period were low.

Finally, a key component of portfolio assessments is student self-evaluation. Students with special needs, who are often described as not being involved in their own learning, can benefit greatly from self-evaluation. For example, students might complete a self-assessment after they have finished a unit of instruction. This evaluation can then become a part of the students' portfolios. The Technology Notes features the use of assistive technology in helping students with severe intellectual disabilities construct their own portfolios.

TECHNOLOGY NOTES

Conducting Alternative Assessments Using Electronic Portfolios

In Chapter 4, you learned that students with moderate to severe intellectual disabilities working on a more functional curriculum are not required to take state high-stakes tests but must show that they have met state standards in more basic ways using alternative assessments. You also learned how the state of Kentucky implements its alternate assessments using student portfolios. Denham and Lahm (2001) reported the efforts of four students who used assistive technology to make their portfolios. All four students had moderate to severe disabilities and were unable to use the standard computer keyboard effectively. They used the IntelliKeys keyboard as an adaptation.

IntelliKeys is an enlarged keyboard that enables users with physical, visual, or intellectual disabilities to easily type, enter numbers, navigate on-screen displays, and execute menu commands. IntelliKeys helps students produce artifacts for their portfolios related to their IEP objectives and can be customized for specific students using individually designed overlays. The overlay for Amanda, a student with severe intellectual disabilities, is shown in Figure 11.5.

Amanda's teacher constructed this overlay using Overlay Maker 3, a software program. The response keys were grouped according to color and were used to facilitate the making of correct choices. The overlay provided response choices that Amanda was to use to complete an activity sheet shown on the computer. Amanda's activity sheet is shown in Figure 11.6.

For Amanda, questions on the activity sheet were tied to her performance on activities related to her IEP goals, such as loading a soda machine, recycling cans, and shopping at the store. The activity sheet and overlay were designed to allow Amanda to read the text with text-reading software and construct a variety of sentences in response to the questions asked on the activity sheet using the overlay. By pressing a response choice on the overlay, Amanda caused the text programmed into that cell to be entered into the activity sheet. All answers were read back to Amanda, allowing her to confirm the correctness of her answers. Note that some of the questions required a yes or no response while others required a more open-ended answer. The complexity

FIGURE *11.5*
Amanda's IntelliKeys Overlay

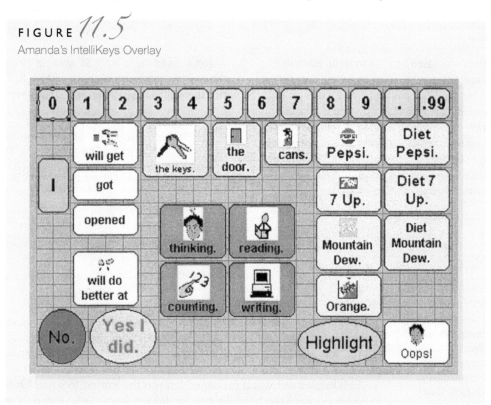

continued

FIGURE *11.6*

Amanda's Soda Machine Activity Sheet

Prompt	Response			
Did I use my schedule?				
Did I use my sheet so I know what to do next?				
Did I write what sodas were needed?				
How many cans did we need?				
Did I put the can in the right place?				
Did I do a good job?				
Next time I will do better at . . .				

of these questions was based on what Amanda was able to do. Amanda was assisted in her effort by a classroom peer without disabilities. The peer provided prompts and assistance when needed. When Amanda answered with assistance, her answer was shown in a different color, allowing her teacher to monitor her level of independent performance.

According to Denham and Lahm (2001, p. 13), "Before using the IntelliKeys, Amanda was limited to handwriting her responses, which was painstakingly slow. The IntelliKeys system allowed her to write 56 words in 20 minutes, a feat she could not have accomplished without it. Amanda's reaction to the IntelliKeys system was, 'This is neat.'"

Sources: "Using Technology to Construct Alternate Portfolios of Students with Moderate and Severe Disabilities," by A. Denham and E. Lahm, 2001, *Teaching Exceptional Children, 33*(5), pp. 10–17; and Overlay Maker (Version 3) (computer software), 2004, Petaluma, CA: IntelliTools.

Research Note

Johnson and Arnold (2004) examined the validity of one state's alternate assessment portfolio system using commonly accepted professional standards and found serious shortcomings. While portfolios are potentially valuable evaluation tools, they should supplement, not supplant, standardized achievement, psychological, and curriculum-based measures.

You may have to make accommodations when using portfolios with students with special needs, particularly in selecting and evaluating portfolio pieces. For example, Jerome was asked to select an example of his best work in written expression for his portfolio. However, he was uncertain what "best work" meant: Was it the paper that he tried his hardest on? Was it the paper that was the hardest to write? Or was it the one that he or his teacher liked best? Because he did not know, Jerome simply selected one paper at random. Similarly, when Thanh was asked to evaluate for his portfolio his efforts to solve a word problem in math, all he could come up with was whether he had the correct answer. You need to teach students such as Jerome and Thanh how to select and evaluate portfolio pieces.

Summary

As a teacher, you have a number of tools at your disposal for evaluating students' progress, including tests, report-card grades, performance-based assessments, and portfolios. Although each of these evaluation methods can also help you measure the progress of students with special needs included in your class, accommodations for students with special needs may need to be made when using any one of them to ensure that the evaluation information measures students' skill levels or content knowledge, not their disabilities or other special needs.

Testing accommodations can be made before testing, during testing, and after testing when tests are graded. Accommodations before the test include study guides, practice tests, tutoring, teaching test-taking skills and strategies, and modifying test construction. During the test, you can make alternative forms of questions and allow alternative ways of administering tests. Accommodations after the test involve grading tests and include changing letter or number grades, changing the criteria on which grades are based, and using alternatives to letter and number grades.

Practices in report-card grading that can benefit all students include using differentiated report cards, avoiding the use of zeroes, and reporting progress frequently. Individualized grading involves changing the grading elements and/or changing the value of the elements. Examples of individualized grading that change the elements include grading on the basis of IEP objectives, prioritizing educational content and assignments, and balanced grading. Examples of changing the value of grading elements include grading on the basis of improvement and using modified grading weights and scales.

Performance-based assessment measures learning processes rather than focusing exclusively on learning products and frequently involves authentic, or real-world, tasks. This type of assessment can be helpful in evaluating the performance of students with special needs because it does not rely exclusively on formats that create problems for students with disabilities. However, accommodations may need to be made for students with special needs by teaching directly the connection between school tasks and real-world tasks, allowing students to bypass preskills, scaling down the tasks, and teaching problem solving directly using performance-based tasks.

Portfolio assessment can also benefit students with special needs. Portfolios typically contain the observable evidence or products of performance assessment, such as anecdotal records, interviews, work samples, and scored samples. While portfolios can be helpful for teachers working with students with special needs, students with special needs may need to be taught how to select and evaluate their portfolio pieces.

Back to the Cases

This section provides opportunities for you to apply the knowledge gained in this chapter to the cases described at the beginning of this chapter: Staci, Jennifer, and Lucille. The questions and activities that follow demonstrate how these standards and principles, along with other concepts that you have learned about in this chapter, connect to the everyday activities of all teachers.

Staci, as you may recall, struggled during tests because of her reading problem. Her reading problem is a common one for students with learning disabilities. Many teachers face the same dilemma as Ms. Stevens: How can she provide Staci with an opportunity to demonstrate her learned knowledge and skills that will not be affected by her reading disability? Review the information in your text regarding accommodations that can be made before, during, and after a test. In addition, consider what you have learned throughout this text about technology. Develop plans for working with Staci to improve her test-taking skills as she prepares for an exam and takes the exam. (INTASC Principles 4.05, 8.03, and 8.05; and CEC Content Standards 8 and 10.) Share your plan with a peer to discuss its pros and cons.

Jennifer, as you may recall, reads at a lower level than her classmates but receives A's. Her parents have questions about her grade in reading, and so do some of her classmates. Jennifer shared her report card with a classmate, who then reported Jennifer's A to several other classmates. Three of those classmates are distressed because they did not earn A's and feel they are reading much harder books than Jennifer. The teacher overheard two of the students taunting Jennifer by calling her the "teacher's pet" and laughing about the "baby books" she read. When the teacher stopped the girls and asked them why they were being cruel to Jennifer, they complained about the unfairness of Ms. Robinson's grading system. What could the teacher have done to avoid situations such as this one? How might you have responded to the girls? (INTASC Principle 10.04 and CEC Content Standard 10.)

Lucille will be in your classroom this year. Her previous teachers used one of the five types of individualized grading accommodations identified by researchers: progress based on IEP objectives. You have thought carefully about the issue of adapting your grading procedures to reflect Lucille's learning and progress in your class. You are planning a conference with her guardians and the special education teacher to discuss a change in the grading procedures. You would like to use another of the five individualized grading accommodations that you feel would also be helpful for your grade and content area. To prepare for the conference, outline your plan for using one of the other grading accommodations in your content area, and list your reasons for selecting this alternative individualized grading procedure. (INTASC Principles 4.05, 8.03, and 10.04; and CEC Content Standards 8 and 10.)

Key Terms and Concepts

Alternative forms of questions (p. 413)

Alternative test site (p. 414)

Alternative ways of administering tests (p. 414)

Alternatives to letter and number grades (p. 417)

Authentic learning tasks (p. 430)

Balanced grading (p. 427)

Changing letter or number grades (p. 414)

Chunking (p. 408)

Competency checklist (p. 417)

Daily activity logs (p. 421)

Differentiated report cards (p. 419)

Grading criteria (p. 417)

Improvement grades (p. 428)

Individualized grading (p. 424)

Keyword method (p. 408)

Mnemonics (p. 408)

Modified weights and scales (p. 429)

Performance-based assessment (p. 430)

Portfolio assessment (p. 432)

Prioritization of curriculum (p. 426)

Progress on IEP objectives (p. 424)

Rehearsal strategy (p. 408)

Separate grades (p. 422)

PEARSON
myeducationlab
Where the Classroom Comes to Life

Now go to the Friend and Bursuck, Fifth Edition, MyEducationLab course at www.myeducationlab.com to

- take a pretest to assess your initial comprehension of the chapter content
- study chapter content with your individualized study plan
- take a posttest to assess your understanding of chapter content
- engage in multimedia exercises to help you build a deeper and more applied understanding of chapter content

Applications in Teaching Practice

Making Accommodations When Evaluating Students with Special Needs

Eugene, Tara, and Jamie are students in your fourth-grade class. Eugene has been identified as having a specific learning disability. He has good study skills, but his problems in reading and written expression place him at a disadvantage when he takes tests. Failure on tests has increased his test anxiety; he often misses items he knows because when he is anxious during a test he tends to get careless.

Tara has a learning disability and receives intensive reading instruction in the resource room. Her short-term objectives for this marking period include reading a first-grade literature book at a rate of 20 words correct per minute with four or fewer errors per minute and discerning who the main character of the story is, what the main problem in the story is, and how the problem is solved.

Jamie is a student with mild intellectual disabilities. You are about to start a unit on adding and subtracting fractions. The IEP objective for Jamie is to identify the fractions, ¼, ⅓, and ½.

Questions

1. What tests will you be giving in this class?

2. For one of these tests, what accommodations might you need to make for Eugene before testing? In constructing the test? In administering the test? In grading the test?

3. At the end of the marking period, should you give Tara a grade in reading? Why or why not? Assuming that Tara has met her short-term objectives in reading, what do you think her grade for the marking period should be? Should her grade be modified in any way?

4. Describe a performance-based test that you could use to measure Jamie's knowledge of her target fractions. How would you score this test? How could you use portfolio assessment to measure Jamie's progress on this unit?

Further Readings

Guskey, T. R., & Bailey, J. M. (2001). *Developing grading and reporting systems for student learning.* Thousand Oaks, CA: Corwin.

> This thoughtful book provides essential background knowledge on effective grading and reporting practices in education.

Layton, C. A., & Lock, R. H. (2007). 20 ways to use authentic assessment techniques to fulfill the promise of No Child Left Behind. *Intervention in School and Clinic, 42*(3), 169–173.

> These authors provide practical suggestions for incorporating authentic assessment into the classroom environment.

Munk, D. D. (2003). *Solving the grading puzzle for students with disabilities.* Whitefish Bay, WI: Knowledge by Design.

> A very practical book that includes a careful description of a research-based process that IEP teams can follow to grade students with disabilities. The book contains numerous case studies and many reproducible grading accommodation tools.

Popham, W. J. (2004). *Classroom assessment: What teachers need to know* (4th ed.). Boston: Allyn & Bacon.

> This readable text covers practical ways teachers can use and interpret assessments within an educational context of accountability, including No Child Left Behind.

Wormeli, R. (2006). *Fair isn't always equal: Assessing and grading in the differentiated classroom.* Portland, ME: Stenhouse.

> Wormeli provides numerous strategies for differentiating grading and assessment practices while remaining accountable for your students' performance on high-stakes tests.

12 Responding to Student Behavior

LEARNING Objectives

After you read this chapter, you will be able to

1. Outline strategies for promoting positive behavior and preventing misbehavior with groups of students, including students with special needs.
2. Explain simple techniques for responding to individual student misbehavior.
3. Describe the purpose of a functional behavior assessment and its steps for deciding how to respond to chronic, inappropriate individual student behavior.
4. Outline systematic approaches for increasing individual students' positive behaviors and decreasing their negative behaviors.
5. Idehtify how to help students manage their own behavior.
6. Articulate your own beliefs regarding your responsibilities for addressing student behavior in positive ways and describe how your beliefs may influence student actions.

Joseph, a high school junior with a learning disability and an emotional disability, comes late to his algebra class at least twice each week. He seldom participates in class discussions, and he does not ask questions. Unless Mrs. Akers repeatedly asks him not to, Joseph sits with his head down on his desk. When discussing Joseph with the special education teacher, Mrs. Akers describes his demeanor as "sullen." Mrs. Akers has been teaching high school math for many years, and she believes students have the responsibility to be interested in the subject, to attend class, and to participate. She knows Joseph is heading toward a failing grade for this grading period, even though she thinks he could do the work with a little more effort. She believes Joseph has given up on learning since he failed to pass the math section of the high school proficiency test and refused to enroll in after-school tutoring program that might have helped him to pass it when he takes it again.

■ *What is Joseph's responsibility for his learning? What is Mrs. Akers's responsibility for making instruction appealing to students like Joseph? What strategies could help Joseph meet Mrs. Akers's class expectations for him?*

Katie has a moderate intellectual disability. Every time she enters the classroom, she says loudly, "I'm ba-ack," even if she has been gone for only a moment. Although she is in sixth grade, she frequently sucks her thumb and rocks in her chair. When she sees a student in the hallway, she waves—and continues waving long after the student has passed by. If she needs assistance, she leaves her seat and goes to the teacher, no matter what activity is occurring in the class. Katie's social studies teacher, Mr. Lowell, is losing patience with her "babyish" behaviors. He believes Katie is learning many social skills through the small-group work the class does, and he knows Katie's paraprofessional, with direction from the special education teacher, is ensuring that Katie learns key concepts of the sixth-grade social studies curriculum. Mr. Lowell is most concerned about the impact of Katie's behaviors on the class. Despite class discussions about how best to respond to Katie's outbursts, several students continue to snicker when Katie calls out, which often leads to other behavior problems.

■ *How could Mr. Lowell address both Katie's inappropriate classroom behaviors and other students' responses to them?*

Ms. Wright was informed that her kindergarten class would include three students with disabilities. She was confident that her teacher preparation program had given her the skills for this responsibility, and she welcomed the opportunity to make a positive difference in the lives of these and all her students. But Ms. Wright did not envision a student like Jaden. Jaden came to kindergarten after receiving early childhood services in another elementary school in the district. Although the teacher from that program reported that Jaden had made tremendous progress both academically and socially, he is still quite different from other kindergarteners. Ms. Wright is not concerned about academic skills; she believes firmly that she can help Jaden take the next steps in his learning. It is his behavior that concerns her. Jaden gets frustrated easily and seems to express his frustration through his behavior. He has had several tantrums that included crying and kicking that lasted for longer than 15 minutes. He also sometimes runs from the class, a clear safety issue. In addition, Jaden has "shut down" while at school, crawling under a desk, hiding his face, and refusing to interact with teachers or peers. Ms. Wright is looking forward to the meeting about Jaden scheduled for this afternoon. She needs assistance in reaching Jaden when he is upset, preventing some of the situations that lead to his challenging behaviors, and creating a plan to help him learn behaviors that will enable him to succeed in school.

What purpose might Jaden's behavior be serving for him? How could Ms. Wright constructively respond to Jaden's behavior? What is a teacher's responsibility for making accommodations for a student like Jaden?

All teachers are responsible for the behavior of their students. Whether you teach 5-year-olds in a kindergarten class or 17-year-olds in eleventh-grade English, the environment you create in your classroom affects whether students' inappropriate behaviors escalate or improve, and your response to such behaviors significantly influences students' learning.

The public is concerned about student behavior too. Despite the fact that total incidents of school violence have decreased over the past 20 years (U.S. Department of Justice, 2005), disruptive behavior has increased (Centers for Disease Control and Prevention, 2007), and Americans still list lack of discipline and fighting, violence, and gangs among the top problems facing public schools (Rose & Gallup, 2006). The Professional Edge takes a brief look at school violence and related student warning signs.

To begin a discussion of discipline, we present some basic concepts to provide a context within which you should consider your responses to student behavior. First, it is essential to recognize that the root word of *discipline* is *disciple,* meaning "a follower of a teacher." Even though discipline often is associated with obedience, **discipline** mostly is about learning. It is a means of ensuring that students have the maximum opportunity to learn from their teachers. Discipline is never an end in and of itself. As you learn about approaches for ensuring classroom discipline in this chapter, you will be finding ways to enhance your students' learning.

Second, a few professionals characterize discipline and classroom management strategies as negative—as being about teacher control and power (for example, Kohn, 2006). This view fails to take into account the very real dilemma teachers face in attempting to keep a classroom full of students interested in learning in a way that is safe and respectful of all students. By using strategies that encourage appropriate behavior, you can create conditions that enable your students to reach their potential, rather than manage their behavior for your convenience or to command compliance (for example, Schoen & Nolen, 2004).

Third, teacher beliefs about discipline have a strong cultural basis, and some evidence suggests that a teacher is far more likely to refer students for discipline problems when they are from a culture other than the teacher's (Salend & Taylor, 2002; Skiba, Michael, Nardo, & Peterson, 2002). In addition, teachers may unintentionally vary their use of discipline techniques (for example, talking to the student versus taking away a privilege) depending on the student's culture or ethnicity (Jensen, 2004; Rausch & Skiba, 2006). All teachers have an obligation to monitor their behavior to ensure that their responses are not based on racial bias or cultural ignorance.

Addressing School Violence

As a school professional, you have a responsibility to be alert for students who are at high risk for committing acts of violence against themselves or others. Most of these students display early warning signs that should signal to you a need for help. As you review the warning signs listed here, which have been identified through research, keep in mind that your concern for a student should not lead you to jump to conclusions. Instead, if you have serious concerns about a student, you should ask for assistance from your colleagues, including school counselors, social workers, and administrators, and, with their support, you should work with parents and the student to address the issues at hand.

Early Warning Signs of Potential for Violence

- *Social withdrawal.* Some students gradually withdraw from social contact because of depression, rejection, or a lack of confidence.

- *Excessive feelings of isolation.* Although most students feel isolated occasionally, a sense of isolation sometimes is associated with aggression and violence.

- *Excessive feelings of rejection.* Some aggressive students who are rejected by peers seek out other aggressive students who in turn reinforce their aggressive tendencies.

- *Victimization by others.* Students who have been physically or sexually abused are at risk of becoming violent.

- *Feelings of being picked on and persecuted.* Students who believe they are teased, bullied, or humiliated at home or at school may vent their feelings through aggression or violence.

- *Low school interest and poor academic performance.* A drastic change in school performance or poor school achievement accompanied by frustration can be a warning sign for acting out.

- *Expression of violence in writings and drawings.* When violent themes are directed at specific individuals (for example, teachers, peers) over time, a student should be referred to a counselor or another professional for assistance.

- *Uncontrolled anger.* Getting angry is natural, but if a student is frequently and intensely angry in response to minor incidents, it may signal a potential for violence.

- *Patterns of impulsive and chronic hitting, intimidating, and bullying behavior.* If behaviors such as these are not addressed, they can escalate to violence.

- *History of discipline problems.* Chronic behavior problems sometimes signal underlying emotional needs that are unmet.

- *Past history of violent and aggressive behavior.* Unless a student with a history of aggressive and violent acts receives counseling, the behaviors are likely to continue and even escalate.

- *Intolerance for differences and prejudicial attitudes.* Intense prejudice (regarding, for example, race, ethnicity, religion, gender, or sexual orientation) may lead to violence against individuals perceived to belong to the targeted group.

- *Drug and alcohol use.* The use of drugs and alcohol tends to reduce self-control, thus increasing the chance of being either a perpetrator or victim of violence.

- *Affiliation with gangs.* Students who are members of gangs that support antisocial values may act on group beliefs.

- *Inappropriate access to, possession of, and use of firearms.* Students who have a history of aggression, impulsiveness, or other serious emotional problems should not have access to firearms and other weapons.

- *Serious threats of violence.* One of the most reliable indicators that a student is likely to commit a violent act is a specific and detailed threat.

Source: Adapted from *Early Warning, Time Response: A Guide to Safe Schools,* by U.S. Department of Education, Special Education and Rehabilitative Services, 1998, Washington, DC: Author. Retrieved August 10, 2007, from www.ed.gov/about/offices/list/osers/osep/gtss.html.

Article Homework Exercise

Go to the Homework and Exercises section in Chapter 12 of MyEducationLab to learn how teachers can establish positive classroom dynamics by using research-based strategies and building positive relationships with students.

Fourth, the strategies for addressing behavior can be informal or formal, with the latter requiring careful data collection and a plan for accomplishing specific goals. The first part of this chapter addresses informal approaches, ones that may assist many students. The latter part addresses the formal requirements for addressing serious behavior problems for students with disabilities.

Teachers who actively, carefully, and creatively apply approaches for classroom management and who monitor the success of their strategies, adapting them as needed, can have a positive influence on student learning (Babkie, 2006; Carr, 2007). Many issues are beyond a teacher's control—you do not have the power to increase the financial support available to schools, nor can you remove the public pressures that surround many curriculum, instruction, and school reform initiatives. However, you can affect and are ultimately accountable for the learning of your students, and your skills for addressing discipline can help you maximize the time available for instruction.

What Are Positive Behavioral Interventions and Supports?

Over the past several years, researchers from several universities have worked to identify strategies for preventing behavior challenges as well as techniques for addressing common and intensive behavior problems. This body of work has been integrated at the University of Oregon through the U.S. Office of Special Education Programs (OSEP) National Technical Assistance Center on Positive Behavioral Interventions and Supports (PBIS) (U.S. Department of Education, 2004a). **Positive behavioral interventions and supports (PBIS)** are based on these four elements:

1. clearly defined outcomes

2. behavioral and biomedical science

3. practices demonstrated effective through research

4. systemic approaches that enhance the learning environment and outcomes for all students

PBIS interventions are grouped by their intensity. The first level is called *primary prevention,* and it is designed to create schoolwide and classroom environments that address the needs of approximately 80 percent of students (Ervin, Schaughency, Matthews, Goodman, & McGlinchey, 2007; Freeman et al., 2006; Handler, Rey, Connell, Their, Feinberg, & Putman, 2007). The second level, *secondary prevention,* is designed to quickly and efficiently address student behavior problems in order to prevent them from becoming more serious, and it addresses an additional 15 percent of students (Filter, McKenna, Benedict, Horner, Todd, & Watson, 2007). The final level, *tertiary prevention,* includes intensive interventions for the 5 percent or so of students whose behavior problems are chronic or exceptionally serious.

The sections that follow present a wide array of procedures grounded in PBIS principles. Some aim for primary prevention of problems and some for fostering positive behavior in groups of students. Also addressed for the secondary and tertiary levels of intervention for students with disabilities is a specific and federally mandated way of problem solving about student behavior called *functional behavior assessment.* In addition, strategies are outlined for responding to these more serious individual student behaviors and creating positive behavior supports. Together, these techniques provide the foundation teachers need for effective classroom management.

www.resources

To learn more about PBIS, including explanations of primary, secondary, and tertiary interventions, visit the National Technical Assistance Center on Positive Behavioral Interventions and Supports, at http://pbis.org/main.htm.

How Can You Use Positive Behavior Supports to Prevent Discipline Problems?

Over the past several years, researchers have focused not just on the prevalence of behavior issues and violence in U.S. schools but also on the characteristics of students who are perpetrators and victims. For example, males are most often involved in incidents of school violence; bullying behavior is most common among upper-elementary students; African American students are victims of school violence slightly more often than other students; little difference is found in the rate of violence in urban, suburban, and nonmetropolitan schools; and overall student attitude is directly related to participation in violence (Furlong & Morrison, 2000; National Center for Education Statistics, 2004). Information such as this is helpful in addressing discipline and violence, but what it most clearly points out is that the starting point for intervention is *prevention.*

Thus, we begin by outlining ideas for preventing behavior problems (Ervin et al., 2007); these are the primary prevention strategies addressed in PBIS. In many cases, you can make the difference between having a classroom in which the stress level is high and "keeping control" is a constant struggle and having a classroom in which student learning is supported by the environment and behavior problems are rare. You can make this difference by creating a caring instructional environment conducive to learning and using effective communication to foster a positive classroom climate (DuPaul & Wyeandt, 2006).

Instructional Environments Conducive to Learning

In Chapter 5, you learned that many factors contribute to creating an instructional environment that fosters student learning. Many of these same factors also promote appropriate

Reading Homework Exercise

Go to the Homework and Exercises section in Chapter 12 of MyEducationLab to read about identifying and preventing behavior problems by creating a positive classroom climate.

Article Homework Exercise

Go to the Homework and Exercises section in Chapter 12 of MyEducationLab to read about the importance of establishing rapport with marginalized students.

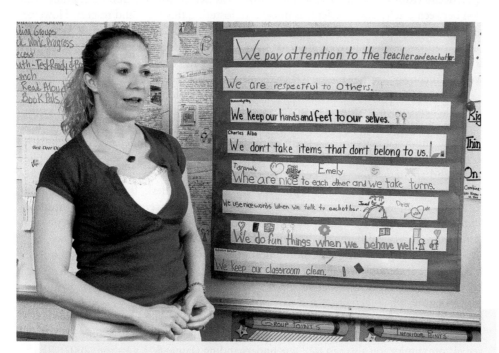

How do clear rules and discussions with students about expectations foster a classroom climate that encourages appropriate behavior?

classroom behavior. For example, teachers need to set clear expectations in their class-rooms through rules that students understand and follow (George, White, & Schlaffer, 2007; Lane, Wehby, & Cooley, 2006). You need only a few rules, but they should have the following characteristics:

1. Be specific and stated using positive wording

2. Be posted and discussed with students early in the school year

3. Be rehearsed while students learn them

4. Be enforced consistently

Rules also should be monitored and changed as needed. Table 12.1 contains sample rules and related student and teacher responsibilities that can be adapted for various grade levels.

Another key factor related to the instructional environment and discipline is establishing clear classroom routines. Routines should be established for beginning the school day or class period, transitioning from one activity to another, moving about in the classroom, and ending the school day or class period. Students who have routines are less likely to misbehave because they can meet classroom expectations for behavior. In classes such as art, music, drama, and physical education, in which students may be very active participants, routines are especially important. The Special Emphasis On . . . feature provides additional specific tips for addressing discipline in such classes.

> Students who have routines are less likely to misbehave because they can meet classroom expectations for behavior.

Effective Classroom Communication

Teachers who treat their students with respect and trust are more successful than other teachers in creating a positive classroom environment in which fewer behavior problems occur (Rimm-Kaufman & Chiu, 2007; Wheeler & Richey, 2005). Communication between teacher and students is integral to fostering this trust and respect. However, teacher–student communication is a complex matter, and problems often arise. For example, sometimes teachers provide students with too much information or information that is not clear, and students become confused. And sometimes teachers give one message with words but convey another message with their tone of voice or nonverbal behaviors.

Another dimension of teacher–student communication concerns language differences. When students struggle to understand English, their behaviors may at first appear to be challenging. For example, a first-grader is asked to complete several directions at one time and has a tantrum as a result of the frustration of not understanding. Similarly, a high school student apparently ignores a teacher's direction to put away project supplies and spend any remaining time beginning the homework assignment. When the teacher addresses this behavior, the student pushes everything off his desk. Is this a behavior problem or an example of misunderstanding and frustration? Teachers working with students who are not proficient English speakers should take care to distinguish problems that result from language differences from misbehavior.

The overall quality of your communication with your students is built in numerous small ways. For example, finding time each week to speak privately with students lets them know that you value them as individuals. Asking older students sincere questions about their friends, out-of-school activities, and part-time jobs also conveys that you care. Taking the time to write positive comments on papers shows students that you appreciate their strengths and are not focusing only on their needs. Using nonverbal signals instead of or in addition to verbal communication also can facilitate understanding (Jamie & Knowlton, 2007). Teachers who fail to take these small steps toward positive communication with students or who publicly embarrass students or punish a group for the behavior of a few soon create a negative instructional environment that thwarts appropriate behavior and effective learning.

Case Study Homework Exercise

Go to the Homework and Exercises section in Chapter 12 of MyEducationLab to learn about positive behavior management techniques that can be employed with students at varying grade levels, ranging from elementary to high school.

TABLE *12.1*

Recommended Rules and Responsibilities for Inclusive Classrooms

Recommended Rule	Student Expectations	Teacher Responsibilities
Enter the classroom quietly.	Walk in and speak softly. Put away belongings. Take assigned seat.	Stand at the door. Wait to share conversations with students. Establish areas for putting away coats, turning in assignments, and so on. Create a permanent seating arrangement. Recognize appropriate behaviors.
Begin work on time.	Listen to or read instructions carefully. Begin to work immediately.	Prepare practice assignments in advance. Expect students to begin work promptly. Monitor student behavior. Recognize appropriate behaviors.
Stay on task.	Ignore distractions from others. Continue to work without interruptions.	Assign developmentally appropriate tasks. Check for student understanding. Provide positive and corrective feedback. Monitor student behavior and assignment completion progress. Prevent or end distracting behaviors. Recognize appropriate behaviors.
Complete work on time.	Check assignment completion requirements. Ask questions to better understand. Set goals for assignment completion.	State complete assignment information, including grading criteria. Provide appropriate models and demonstrations. Teach goal setting. Allow sufficient class time to work. Recognize appropriate behaviors.
Follow directions at all times.	Listen carefully. Ask questions for understanding. Do as all teachers request.	Gain student attention. Give clear directions for particular situations. Check for student understanding. Provide examples and/or demonstrations. Monitor student behavior. Recognize appropriate behaviors.
Listen while others speak.	Maintain a positive body posture. Look at the person speaking. Note important information. Signal for more information.	Teach listening skills. Model good listening skills. Encourage verbal elaboration. Encourage "risk-free" active participation. Recognize appropriate behaviors.
Use appropriate language.	Avoid angry and foul words. Use kind words to tell how you feel.	Teach appropriate statements for avoiding conflicts. Teach techniques for self-control. Model respect toward students and peers. Recognize appropriate behaviors.
Keep hands, feet, and objects to self.	Avoid hitting, kicking, or throwing things.	Teach safety habits and procedures. Teach techniques for self-control. Recognize appropriate behaviors.

Source: From "How Do Your Classroom Rules Measure Up? Guidelines for Developing an Effective Rule Management Routine," by J. A. Rademacher, K. Callahan, and V. A. Pederson-Seelye, 1998, *Intervention in School and Clinic, 33*, pp. 284–289. Copyright © 1998 by the Hammill Institute on Disability. Reprinted with permission.

Discipline in Related Arts Classes

Classes such as art, music, physical education, drama, and others that go beyond the core academic curriculum often provide students with disabilities opportunities to demonstrate their unique talents. However, these classes also have a high risk for discipline problems unless principles such as those presented throughout this chapter are put in place. In addition, keep the following ideas in mind to ensure that these learning environments are designed to foster student learning:

- Carefully explain expectations for classroom behavior on the first day of school. Review these rules in subsequent classes. Ask students to explain the expectations.

- Reward students for following classroom expectations, particularly at the very beginning of the school year. Remember to always pair a reward with verbal praise.

- Be organized. Have specific places where materials and supplies are kept and specific procedures students are to follow in getting and returning them. Remember that whenever students have to wait, the likelihood of misbehavior will increase. Likewise, when procedures are not clear, behavior problems are more likely to occur.

- Be sure that your class is an appropriate blend of listening and doing. Students who participate in engaging activities are less likely to misbehave than those who are disinterested because of a lack of engagement.

- Related arts classes sometimes can become a bit noisy as students engage in their tasks. Have a nonverbal way of gaining student attention (for example, a chime or series of claps that students join in repeating). Teach students to respond to it, and reward them for doing so.

- Watch your timing. One problem that can occur in related arts classes is a rush at the end of the class period to wrap up the planned activity. When students rush, behavior problems may result.

- Ask your special education teacher if any students have behavior intervention plans. If so, find out what your role should be in ensuring their plans are implemented. For students without plans, ask for suggestions to foster positive behavior.

- If you find that a student is displaying challenging behavior, seek assistance immediately. It is far easier to address a small problem than to intervene in a well-established and serious problem.

- Use peers to improve behavior. You might find that assigning every student a peer buddy can address minor sources of misbehavior, such as being unsure of directions. Alternatively, have peer buddies only for students who are likely to struggle in your class.

Effective Teaching Methods

Another critical strategy for preventing behavior problems is to provide instruction that is relevant, interesting, individualized, and active (Hoover & Patton, 2005; Lingo, Slaton, & Jolivette, 2006; Reid & Green, 2006). Recall from Chapters 9 and 10 that learning is enhanced through the use of clear and systematic instructional approaches and strategies that actively engage students in learning. We remind you of this information because effective instruction plays a critical role in classroom behavior management. Students who are given boring or outdated materials, who are asked to complete dozens of worksheets with little instructional value, who have few opportunities to create their own learning through projects or activities, or who seldom see their own culture reflected in their learning tasks are likely to misbehave (Kohn, 2004).

Schoolwide Strategies

One additional prevention strategy goes beyond your classroom. PBIS supports the use of schoolwide prevention strategies that are developed in a systematic way (for example,

esearch Note

Elementary teachers viewed self-control and cooperation as essential social skills for students, while assertion was perceived as less important (Lane, Givner, & Pierson, 2004).

Hendley, 2007; Warren et al., 2006). To begin, a school identifies a leadership team to guide the PBIS development process. This team analyzes all available information concerning student discipline, obtains a commitment from each staff member for addressing identified problems, and manages the process of establishing schoolwide expectations based on input from teachers and other staff members. Once general expectations have been set and specific applications of these expectations have been created for classrooms and specific school areas, the leadership team monitors implementation and proposes revisions as needed. For example, a common schoolwide expectation is that students will be respectful of themselves, of others, and of property. In the lunchroom, the specific expectations might include these:

- Use a soft voice at all times.
- Ask for assistance if something spills or is dropped.
- Remove all trays and dispose of all trash when you are finished eating.

What might the specific applications be for a locker room? A classroom? On the bus?

Case Study Homework Exercise

Go to the Homework and Exercises section in Chapter 12 of MyEducationLab to find scenarios and strategies that focus on the establishment of classroom norms and expectations through the development of rules and procedures.

How Can You Promote Positive Group Behavior?

In effective classrooms, teachers and students respect each other and students are busily engaged in learning (Maag, 2004). Students attend to their work, interact with each other politely and without verbal or physical fighting, and ignore the occasional misbehavior of classmates instead of encouraging it. In many classrooms, you can promote positive behaviors such as these by using behavior management strategies designed specifically for the whole class (Lannie & McCurdy, 2007). For example, all students might participate in discussing classroom discipline issues, helping each other monitor their behavior, and earning privileges or rewards as individuals or as members of cooperative learning groups. The following sections describe effective whole-group strategies, such as token economies and other peer-mediated approaches to behavior management.

> Teachers can promote positive behaviors such as these by using behavior management strategies designed specifically for the whole class.

Token Economy

A long-respected group behavior management procedure that might be effective in your classroom is a **token economy** (Kazdin, 1977; Petscher & Bailey, 2006). This primary prevention strategy creates a system in which students earn "money" that they exchange for rewards. As in any economy, certain tasks have more or less value than others, and rewards have more or less cost. In one form of token economy, students receive imaginary money that they record in checkbooks. When they purchase a privilege, the cost of it is subtracted from the balance. Follow these steps to create a classroom token economy:

1. *Identify the behaviors for which students can earn credit.* You might select completing and turning in work, keeping hands to oneself, talking in a classroom voice, bringing to class all needed (and specified) learning supplies, returning homework, or exhibiting other behavior that can be clearly observed. A number of behaviors can be specified and posted in the classroom. Students can be involved in deciding what behaviors to include.

2. *Decide on the classroom currency.* You can use points, punches on a card, poker chips or other tokens, play money, or any other system. In choosing a currency, keep in mind that you will need to award it and monitor its use. In large classrooms, efficiency in issuing and exchanging the currency can become critical.

fyi

Suggested alternatives to zero-tolerance policies regarding serious behavior infractions include (1) in-school suspension, (2) school or community service in addition to academic work and tutoring, and (3) structured problem solving to state specifically what students need to do to address their behavior problems (Casella, 2003).

What responsibility do general education teachers have for creating systems to address minor behavior problems in their classrooms? How do such systems benefit all students, both typical learners and those with special needs?

Article Homework Exercise

Go to the Homework and Exercises section in Chapter 12 of MyEducationLab for an article that encourages teachers to be empathetic to their adolescent students.

3. *Assign a value to each target behavior.* Simple behaviors should have a lower value than more difficult behaviors. In a very simple system, you would assign the same value (for example, one point) for each target behavior on a daily basis.

4. *Decide on the privileges or rewards students can earn.* Having variety in the possible purchases students can make will help maintain interest in the system. For older students, the list of options might include a make-your-own-homework-assignment privilege or a homework pass; for younger students, tokens might be redeemed for lunch with the teacher. It is important to include on the reward list at least one item that costs the minimum amount of currency a student might earn (for example, one point). Doing so will ensure that all students have the opportunity to participate in the economy.

5. *Assign purchase prices to the privileges or rewards.* In general, if a reward is readily available and not limited in quantity, its purchase price should be lower. Items that are tangible (and perhaps literally cost more), limited in supply, high in perceived value, or time consuming to obtain should have a higher cost. One teacher had access to hundreds of sets of plastic beads; the beads became quite the rage in the classroom, but they were not very costly. However, lunch alone with the teacher was a high-priced privilege. For secondary students, a low-cost reward might be computer use; a high-cost reward might be a free pass on a homework assignment.

6. *Explain the economy to students.* As you probably have discerned, you can make an economy as simple or complex as you have the creativity to develop and your students have the ability to understand. It often is beneficial to demonstrate the economy with several examples to ensure that students understand it. With younger students, this might mean showing them chips that have been earned and then cashing them in for a prize. For older students, the system can be described briefly and, more importantly, the accounting system can be explained.

7. *Establish a systematic way for students to exchange their currency for privileges or rewards.* In most classrooms, it is effective to allow students to use their currency once a week or once every two weeks on a particular day. By having a consistent time and system for the exchange, you avoid a constant stream of student requests for privileges or rewards and the aggravation of the constant monitoring this would require.

How you establish your token economy depends partly on the age of your students. For younger students, you may need to use tangible currency (for example, tokens, beads, play money). Older students are more capable of using points and other symbolic currencies. Likewise, younger students need more opportunities to exchange their currency, whereas older students are more able to save their currency to earn more expensive privileges or rewards over a longer period of time.

> Teachers are tremendously creative in adapting token economies to their students' needs and their own teaching styles.

Teachers are tremendously creative in adapting token economies to their students' needs and their own teaching styles. For example, one teacher held an auction in her classroom every two weeks, offering items donated by local businesses or obtained at garage sales. Students bid on items using the currency they had earned. Another teacher wanted to encourage students to learn about real economies. She permitted students to borrow tokens from one another and to purchase items from one another using their currency. One student sold his designer pencils to classmates with tokens as the currency of exchange.

To work effectively, a token economy should be carefully planned and allow flexibility for adjustment as the need arises. For example, you might need to change the reward list or the amount of currency required to obtain particular rewards. You also should keep in mind that a token economy is best used when most or all students in a class or group need support for appropriate behaviors. Thus, you might use a token economy early in the school year, again right after the holiday break, and then not again until the last month of school. During other periods, less comprehensive strategies may be adequate.

Other Peer-Mediated Approaches

Many teachers create their own whole-class approaches for supporting positive behavior and reducing negative behavior (Rimm-Kaufman & Chiu, 2007; Sobel & Taylor, 2006). These approaches typically consider the relationships among students' background and experiences, the learning environment, the materials used in teaching, and the activities in which students engage. Strategies often include the use of class meetings with an emphasis on rewarding appropriate behavior and building a sense of community in the classroom. This type of approach is highly recommended as a strategy for promoting positive behavior for students from racially and culturally diverse backgrounds.

How you group students for instruction also can serve as a group behavior management technique (Maheady, Mallette, & Harper, 2006). For example, if you have students work with learning buddies or peer tutors, you probably can reduce the amount of misbehavior because students will become more actively engaged in their learning and have the added responsibility of serving as a "teacher." Similarly, if you have students work in small instructional groups and stipulate that no one can earn a reward unless the group completes the work, students will have a natural incentive for focusing on their learning and be less likely to misbehave. For a student like David, introduced at the beginning of this chapter, peer-mediated instructional approaches can foster appropriate social interactions because they create the need to interact positively within a small-group, structured environment.

What Are Positive Behavior Strategies for Responding to Minor Individual Behaviors?

For some students, including students with special needs, the steps you take to create a positive and productive learning environment may not be sufficient to eliminate behavior problems, nor do group behavior management strategies always work. These students may need much more specialized approaches—secondary prevention strategies—and you will find it helpful to follow the steps of the INCLUDE model outlined in Chapter 4 when planning and implementing these strategies. However, before you decide to use that approach, try a number of simpler strategies. Teachers long have relied on the principle of least intervention in addressing student behavior needs. The strategies described in the following sections include minimal interventions, such as "catch 'em being good," and techniques for managing students' surface behaviors.

Use Minimum Interventions

Teachers sometimes contribute unintentionally but significantly to student misbehavior. They do this by inadvertently bringing out negative student behaviors and responding too strongly to minor misbehaviors, actions that sometimes cause students to misbehave more. For example, when asked directly to begin work, a student might refuse. However, when given a choice regarding which assignment to do first, the student might comply.

Article Homework Exercise

Go to the Homework and Exercises section in Chapter 12 of MyEducationLab to learn how teacher–student dialogue can increase student acceptance and responsibility for their own behavior.

Article Homework Exercise

Go to the Homework and Exercises section in Chapter 12 of MyEducationLab to read how one teacher turned a serious situation into a learning experience.

*R*esearch Note

When Farmer, Goforth, Clemmer, and Thompson (2004) examined school discipline problems among African American middle school students in a rural community, they found that boys were referred for discipline problems far more than girls, that girls with major offenses had many school difficulties, and that aggression was a key determinant of whether boys were referred.

What individual strategies can you use in responding to individual behavior? How can teacher feedback strengthen positive behavior? How can you find out what types of rewards your students respond to?

DIMENSIONS OF

diversity

For students from diverse backgrounds, especially those with limited English proficiency, a private "catch" of good behavior can be more effective than a public one because you can better gauge the student's understanding of your message.

Info Sheet Homework Exercise

Go to the Homework and Exercises section in Chapter 12 of MyEducationLab to learn how reflective analysis of behavior incidents can help teachers to improve their classroom management skills.

Similarly, when reprimanded for using profanity in the classroom, some students will use the reprimand as a signal to continue the language to get further attention. Ignoring occasional inappropriate language might lessen the problem.

When working with students with special needs, it is essential to stay alert to how you might be contributing to a student's behaviors, either through your own responses to the behavior or through your classroom structure and lesson format (Kern & Clemens, 2007). Four examples of minimum interventions teachers use to address minor student misbehavior follow.

● **"Catch 'Em Being Good"**   A versatile and long-recognized strategy for reducing inappropriate student behavior and increasing appropriate behavior is called "catch 'em being good." In short, when a student is behaving according to expectations, you acknowledge and reward the behavior. For example, if third-grader Connor enters the room and immediately begins his work, you might say to him, "I like the way you went right to your desk, Connor. That's exactly what you're supposed to do!" This comment has the effect of rewarding Connor's behavior. At the same time, it clearly lets other students know that going directly to one's seat is a behavior they should do too. In a middle school or high school social studies class, a teacher might privately say to a student who is chronically late, "I noticed you were at your seat with materials ready when the bell rang. Nice going." Although the privacy of the comment eliminates its potential positive impact on other students, it has the benefit of preventing student embarrassment.

● **Make High-Probability Requests First**   Banda and Kubina (2006) describe a successful strategy for helping students with autism who have difficulty transitioning between activities in the classrooms, such as halting work on a language arts assignment to get ready to leave the classroom to go to physical education. With this approach, make several simple requests the student is likely to complete prior to making the targeted request. For example, if it is time for first-grader Angel to put away his crayons and join a group reading a story, first get Angel's attention by saying something like, "Angel, give me five." Follow this with asking Angel to tell you his address (or another appropriate piece of personal information that he is learning and likely to share). Next ask him to shake hands, another behavior he knows and usually readily does. Finally, request that Angel leave his coloring and join the reading group. Each request should be followed by verbal praise (for example, "Right" or "Good job"). How could this approach be used with an older student?

● **Use Grouping Strategies**   In many schools, students with disruptive behaviors tend to seek out others who misbehave as seatmates or groupmates. Using a very simple strategy may significantly reduce misbehavior in such situations. When a highly disruptive student is partnered with students who are not disruptive, inappropriate behavior will likely decrease (Tournaki & Criscitiello, 2003). This strategy should be part of any plan for addressing disruptive behavior. It also has potential for a student like Joseph, one of the students described at the beginning of the chapter. Because Joseph is extremely quiet, a teacher might decide to place him with a group of students who model positive social skills and are unlikely to make fun of him or encourage misbehavior.

Manage Students' Surface Behaviors

Another relatively simple strategy for responding to student behaviors is managing their **surface behaviors** (Maag, 2001; Redl, 2007). Long and Newman (1971) proposed long ago that a teacher's initial response to student behavior often determines whether a problem situation develops and how intense it is. If a teacher treats a minor misbehavior as a major infraction, the result might be a strong negative student response followed by a stronger teacher response and, ultimately, a serious behavior problem. For example, if a student mutters under her breath something negative about an assignment and the teacher responds by asking in a stern voice, "What did you say?" the incident will likely escalate. The student might reply, "Nothing," the teacher may repeat the request, and the student may eventually say something that requires a negative consequence.

Such interactions can be avoided if teachers are prepared to shift the focus of the interaction. Suggestions for heading off such problems include purposefully ignoring minor incidents and using humor to defuse tense classroom situations. Examples of initial response techniques are outlined in the following Professional Edge.

These initial response techniques are most suited to minor misbehaviors and unlikely to resolve serious discipline issues. Also, responding to students' surface behaviors sometimes can have the effect of increasing them. For example, if you use humor with a student and she responds by talking back, then your humor may be increasing rather than decreasing the inappropriate behavior. If this happens, switch to another approach or work with colleagues to examine the behavior more carefully and devise a more individualized response to it, as described in the remainder of this chapter.

Reading Homework Exercise

Go to the Homework and Exercises section in Chapter 12 of MyEducationLab for information about managing common misbehaviors and chronic misbehaviors, including those for a preschooler.

How Can Functional Behavior Assessment and Behavior Intervention Plans Help You Respond to Serious Individual Behaviors?

When students with disabilities have chronic and significant behavior problems, you are not expected to design and use tertiary prevention strategies by yourself. You will find that the Individuals with Disabilities Education Act (IDEA) contains many provisions that guide how teachers and other school personnel should respond to serious student behaviors (Etscheidt, 2006; Lo & Cartledge, 2006; Ryan, Katsiyannis, Peterson, & Chmelar, 2007; Zilz, 2006). These procedures, addressing everything from contacting parents to guidelines related to suspension and expulsion, are summarized in Figure 12.1.

In addition, you will work with a team of colleagues to complete a more detailed analysis of the behaviors of concern and to plan, carry out, and evaluate systematically the effectiveness of a range of interventions (Kamps, Wendland, & Culpepper, 2006). This legislatively mandated approach, referred to as **functional behavior assessment (FBA)**, is a problem-solving process implemented for any student with a disability who has chronic, serious behavior problems. Its basis is the ongoing conflict between protecting the rights of students with disabilities and respecting teachers' and school administrators' concerns about preventing school violence, maintaining safe schools, and disciplining students with disabilities.

FBA is a detailed and documented set of procedures designed to improve educators' understanding of exactly what a problem behavior looks like: where it occurs, when it occurs, and what function it serves for the student. FBA leads to ideas about how to change the behavior and a specific plan for doing so (Kamps et al., 2006; Scott & Caron, 2005). An FBA and *behavior intervention plan (BIP)* must be included as part of a student's individualized education program (IEP) whenever it is needed; these procedures are not only for students whose disability is emotional or based in behavior (Maag & Katisyannis, 2006). For example, a student with autism might need these procedures to address her difficulty in transitioning from one school activity to another.

In this section of the chapter, you will learn why FBA is important and how the process works. Later sections of this chapter outline examples of the strategies that might be included in FBA.

Research Note

Warren et al. (2006) reported that the use of PBIS strategies in an urban middle school had significant positive results in just one year, including a 20 percent decrease in office discipline referrals, 23 percent decrease in time-outs, and 57 percent decrease in out-of-school suspensions.

Strategies for Managing Students' Surface Behaviors

As an educator, you sometimes will be faced with the dilemma of how to respond to students' *surface behaviors*—that is, inappropriate behaviors that students display, such as refusing to work, sitting with head down, and calling out answers. In some cases, these and other behaviors may be symptoms of serious problems that need the careful attention of a functional behavior assessment (described later in this chapter). However, a first approach can be to use simple techniques with the intent of heading off a potentially tense classroom situation. The following strategies, most of which are suited for responding to minor misbehaviors, can help you deal with problem behaviors as soon as they occur:

1. *Planned ignoring.* If a student's behavior will not likely harm others or spread to others, you might decide to ignore it. For example, a student who repeatedly sighs loudly could be signaling a loss of interest; instead of responding to the sighing, recognize that the student needs to change activities soon. If you ignore inappropriate behavior, you should be sure to give the student attention for appropriate behavior.

2. *Signal interference.* Communicate with students about surface behaviors by using nonverbal signals, such as eye contact and gestures (for example, putting your finger to your lips to request silence). Reward students for responding to more direct signals (for example, "Take out your books"), and they will be more likely to carry out requests promptly.

3. *Proximity control.* Sometimes simply moving closer to a misbehaving student will resolve the problem. However, if the behavior continues, it may mean that your nearness actually is rewarding the student and a different technique should be used.

4. *Interest boosting.* If a student appears to be losing interest in a task or activity, refocus attention immediately by asking a specific question about her progress or otherwise paying specific attention to her work.

5. *Tension reduction through humor.* For some minor misbehavior, your best response might be humor. For example, suppose a student who was frustrated with an assignment tossed a textbook into the trash can. Instead of scolding or lecturing, the teacher exclaimed "Two points!" and then went on to assist the student with the assignment. Care must be taken, though, that the humor is not perceived as a way to embarrass or criticize the student.

6. *Hurdle help.* For some students, beginning an assignment can be overwhelming. As a result, they may refuse to start working or misbehave to avoid starting. You can help them begin and avoid a behavior issue by assisting with the first example, asking questions to facilitate their thinking, prompting them to follow steps, or literally cutting an assignment into parts and giving them one small part at a time.

7. *Support from routine.* Creating more structure in the classroom can avert discipline problems. For example, expecting all students to enter class, sit down, and begin the warm-up work by the time the bell rings may help some students avoid being disruptive. Displaying the schedule and using clear patterns for classroom activities also will help eliminate disruptions.

8. *Direct appeal to valued areas.* Students sometimes see their schoolwork as irrelevant. If you can identify a meaningful context for assigned work, students may be more likely to complete it. For example, work with decimals can be related to sports statistics.

9. *Removing seductive objects.* When students bring distracting items to school (for example, pens that light up, souvenirs from a recent trip, personal electronics), teachers usually should hold them for safekeeping. Other objects in the classroom environment also can become a focus for misbehavior and should be hidden. For example, if you have costumes at school for the play, keep them in a closet; if you set up an intriguing science lab, cover the materials until it is time to use them.

10. *Antiseptic bouncing.* When behavior is starting to become an issue or you see signals that a behavior problem is likely to occur (for example, a student seems to be angry as she comes into the classroom), consider giving the student the opportunity to move to a quiet corner of the classroom or to step outside the room to reduce tension. Doing so will help some students calm down and avoid trouble. Similarly, some students will benefit from being sent on a simple errand that takes them out of the classroom and provides them with a purposeful activity.

Source: Adapted from "Management of Surface Behavior: A New Look at an Old Approach" [electronic version], by J. W. Maag, 2001, *Counseling and Human Development, 33*(9), pp. 1–10.

FIGURE *12.1* IDEA Provisions Related to Discipline

IDEA includes a number of provisions for addressing issues that relate to students with disabilities and their behavior. The following list is a sampling of those provisions:

- Parents must be given an opportunity to participate in all meetings with respect to the identification, evaluation, and educational placement of the student and the provision of a free appropriate public education. This provision applies to behavior problems as well as academic problems.

- School personnel can consider on a case-by-case basis unique circumstances that may affect decisions about a change in placement for a student who violates a school's student conduct code.

- When a student's placement is changed because of her behavior, her education must continue so that progress can continue toward the accomplishment of IEP goals and, for some students, objectives. Access to the general curriculum must be assured, and any behavior intervention plan must continue.

- Within 10 school days of a decision to change the placement of a student because of a behavior code infraction, school officials must hold a special meeting to complete *manifestation determination,* that is, a decision about whether the behavior is related to the student's disability or poor implementation of the IEP. If the behavior is related to the disability, functional behavior assessment (FBA) must be completed and a behavior intervention plan (BIP) must be created and

implemented. (Details on these topics are included later in this chapter.)

- School officials can remove a student to an appropriate interim alternative educational setting or suspend him for not more than 10 days in the same year (to the extent that such alternatives are applied to students without disabilities) if he violates the school's student conduct code.

- Parents have to be notified of all procedural rights under IDEA, including expanded disciplinary rights, not later than the day on which the decision to take disciplinary action is made.

- School personnel may remove a student with disabilities to an interim alternative educational setting for up to 45 school days if the student has brought a weapon to school or a school function, knowingly possesses or uses illegal drugs or sells or solicits the sale of a controlled substance while at school or a school function, or causes serious bodily injury to another person. This action may be taken whether or not the behavior is found to be related to the student's disability, and it may extend beyond 45 days if that policy is in effect for other students and the student's behavior is not related to the disability.

- In the case of a student whose behavior impedes her learning or that of others, the IEP team must consider, when appropriate, strategies to address that behavior. FBA must look across contexts to include school, home, and community.

Sources: Adapted from *Highlights of New Legislation to Reauthorize the Individuals with Disabilities Education Act (IDEA), PL 108–466: The Individuals with Disabilities Education Improvement Act of 2004,* by J. West, L. Pinkus, and A. Singer, January 2005, Washington, DC: Washington Partners; and *What Every Teacher Should Know about IDEA 2004,* by M. Madlawitz, 2006, Boston: Allyn & Bacon.

Rationale for Functional Behavior Assessment

When a student displays behaviors that are especially aggravating or seem directed at purposely causing a classroom disruption, it is tempting to respond simply by trying to stop the behavior and get back to the business of educating the student. However, if you do not understand why the behavior is occurring and how to address that underlying cause, the behavior will likely recur.

In FBA, inappropriate behaviors are viewed as serving a function or purpose for the student. Understanding this function will help you identify the actual problem the student is experiencing and decide how to respond to it instead of the symptomatic behavior (Frey & Wilhite, 2005; Scott et al., 2004). Functions of behavior include avoiding something (for example, work, people) or obtaining something (for example, attention, help). Put simply, this conceptualization of student behaviors suggests that before you respond, you should ask Why is the student doing this? Table 12.2 describes in more detail some common student behaviors and their possible functions.

An example can help clarify the idea of identifying the function of behaviors. Daniel is in the sixth grade. When the sixth-grade teaching team meets to discuss student problems, Mr. Adams expresses concern that Daniel often swears in class. Ms. Jefferson adds that Daniel picks fights with other students several times each week. Dr. Hogue agrees that Daniel is having problems and recounts a recent incident in which he was sent to the office. As the teachers talk, they begin to look past Daniel's specific behaviors and focus instead on the function the behaviors are serving. They realize that in one class, Daniel was disruptive when a difficult assignment was being given; in another, the problem was occurring as quizzes were being returned; and in the third, the incident happened immediately before Daniel's turn to give an oral book report. The teachers agree that Daniel's intent has been to escape situations in which he fears he might fail.

Once you identify the function of a problem behavior, you can assist the student in changing the behavior. In Daniel's case, it would be easy for the teachers to decide on a reward system to get Daniel to swear less in Mr. Adams's class. However, that solution would have more to do with the teachers' need to have well-mannered students than with Daniel's need to avoid the possibility of failing. An alternative approach would be

TABLE 12.2

Possible Functions of Student Behaviors

Function	Goal	Example of Behavior
Power/control	Control an event or a situation	Acts to stay in the situation and keep control: "You can't make me!"
Protection/escape	Avoid a task or activity; escape a consequence; stop or leave a situation	Has a tantrum at the start of every math lesson; skips social studies class
Attention	Become the center of attention; focus attention on self	Puts self in the forefront of a situation or distinguishes self from others—for example, burps loudly during class instruction
Acceptance/ affiliation	Become wanted or chosen by others for mutual benefit	Hangs out with troublemakers; joins a clique or gang
Self-expression	Express feelings, needs, or preoccupations; demonstrate knowledge or skill	Produces inappropriate drawings—for example, of aerial bombings, body parts, occult symbols
Gratification	Feel good; have a pleasurable experience; reward oneself	Acts to get or maintain a self-determined reward—for example, hoards an object, indulges in self-gratifying behavior at others' expense
Justice/revenge	Settle a score; get or give restitution, apology, or punishment	Destroys others' work; meets after school to fight; commits acts of vandalism

Source: From "Our Five Basic Needs: Application for Understanding the Function of Behavior," by L. M. Frey and K. Wilhite, 2005, *Intervention in School and Clinic, 40,* pp. 156–160.

to permit Daniel to receive his quizzes before the start of class or perhaps to participate in the after-school homework club that includes a group that studies for quizzes. Another intervention strategy might be to permit Daniel to give his oral report to one peer or to audiotape it beforehand. Thus, the question of intervening to address Daniel's behavior has shifted from How can we get Daniel to be less disruptive in the classroom? to How can we help Daniel use more appropriate strategies to avoid situations in which he fears he will fail?

This approach to understanding student behavior is more complex than looking at the surface behavior the student displays and trying to stop it; it requires looking for patterns in a student's behavior and describing them clearly in concrete terms (Dieterich, Villani, & Bennett, 2003; Shippen, Simpson, & Crites, 2003). This approach takes more time and effort, but it greatly increases the likelihood that you and your colleagues will be able to design an effective intervention to assist the student. In addition, you should keep in mind that although many of the students involved in functional assessment and the development of a behavior plan have high-incidence disabilities, this method of addressing behavior was first used with individuals with significant intellectual disabilities, primarily to develop appropriate social and communication behavior. Certainly, this method can also be used appropriately to help students with those disabilities succeed in your classroom. The Case in Practice explores using functional assessment for such students.

The following sections present in more detail the process of completing FBAs. The procedure includes seven specific steps (Lee & Jamison, 2003; Ryan, Halsey, & Matthews, 2003):

1. verifying the seriousness of the problem

2. defining the problem behavior in concrete terms

3. collecting data to better understand the behavior

4. analyzing the data and forming hypotheses about function

5. developing a behavior intervention plan (BIP)

6. implementing the plan and gathering data on its impact on the behavior

7. monitoring intervention effectiveness and proceeding to appropriate next actions

Verifying the Seriousness of the Problem

As we have noted in this chapter, many classroom behavior problems can be eliminated or significantly reduced through the use of supportive classroom practices, group behavior management techniques, and low-key individual interventions. A first step in functional assessment is to determine whether these standard strategies already have been implemented. For example, if you have a student who is bullying others, a topic addressed on page 457's Professional Edge, your team might ask you to complete a questionnaire about the tactics you have used to address the student's behavior, and a psychologist, special education teacher, or other educator may observe and interview the student. In cases of acting-out behavior, other students may be observed. The latter approach is used to determine whether the student's behavior is typical or significantly different from that of classmates.

Defining the Problem Behavior

The second step of FBA is to ensure that the behaviors of concern are defined and described in a specific way. Teachers working with students with serious behavior problems often use a type of verbal shorthand to describe their concerns. They may refer to a student as "disruptive" or describe a student as being "always off task." They may comment that a student is "often up and wandering around the classroom" or express concern that a student is "sullen and unresponsive" or "unmotivated." Although these general statements

Analyze and Reflect

How would understanding the function of a student's behavior influence your response to it? How does this approach differ from traditional responses to student behavior? How could you use the notion of behavior functions to understand how students can find and press teachers' "hot buttons"?

Internet Homework Exercise

Go to the Homework and Exercises section in Chapter 12 of MyEducationLab and link up with information about and forms for functional behavior plans.

Case in Practice

Supporting a Student with Autism Using Functional Behavior Assessment

Mary Elizabeth, a student with autism, just moved to the area. At her previous school, she spent most of her day in the general education classroom with the support of an instructional assistant and a special educator. She was nearly at grade level in math and just a year or so behind in reading.

In her first week at John Glenn Elementary School, however, Mary Elizabeth repeatedly tried to bite and hit staff and students, had several noisy tantrums, and refused to attempt any academic tasks. On two different days, it took two adults to remove her from the general education classroom to the resource room. Ms. Lieberman, the third-grade teacher, was astonished at this disastrous beginning, especially because she had carefully prepared her other students for their new classmate and had done some quick reading about what to expect of a student with autism.

Within the week, Ms. Lieberman was at her wits' end and even more distraught when the instructional assistant quit. Mr. Poulos, the school psychologist, quickly called together the team, including Ms. Lieberman and himself as well as special

education teacher Ms. Daugherty, principal Dr. Cook, and Mary Elizabeth's parents, Mr. and Mrs. O'Toole. Mary Elizabeth refused to be part of the meeting, but Ms. Daugherty spoke with her individually about the problems and ideas to address them.

The team's task was to complete the FBA checklist included here. Although occasional incidents still occurred, the team was successful in addressing Mary Elizabeth's behavior problems and helping her adjust to her new school.

REFLECTIONS

Working with your classmates, complete as many items on the checklist as possible (for example, write a definition of the behavior, identify replacement behaviors, and so on). What aspects of the FBA and BIP process seem straightforward? Which seem challenging? If you were Ms. Lieberman, what types of assistance would you request during the transition time as the behavior plan was being implemented? What expectations would you have for all the other people at this meeting to participate in implementing an intervention?

Functional Behavior Assessment/Behavior Intervention Plan Checklist

Student _____   Date _____

Team leader _____   Grade _____

Behavior(s) of concern _____
_____

Yes	No	
		1. Is the student behavior of concern clearly defined?
		2. Have replacement behaviors that serve the same function (or result in the same outcome) for the student been identified, along with the circumstances under which they should occur?
		3. Are multiple sources of information available that have been collected from various individuals (e.g., teachers, parents, classmates, student)? At least two separate indirect measures and multiple direct measures (e.g., ABC charts, scatterplots) that capture multiple occurrences/nonoccurrences of the behavior (and its context) should be in agreement.
		4. Does the information gathered by the team indicate a consistent behavior pattern?
		5. Is the hypothesis statement written according to the three-term contingency (i.e., Under x conditions, the student does y in order to achieve z) so that an intervention plan can easily be produced?
		6. Is the plan aligned with student needs and assessment results?
		7. Does the plan address all aspects of the social/environmental contexts in which the behavior of concern has occurred?
		8. Is there a strategy to verify the accuracy of the hypothesis statement?
		9. Does the plan address both short-term and long-term aspects of student behavior (and its social/environmental context), including procedures to eliminate reliance on unacceptable behavior?
		10. Does the plan include practical ways to monitor both its implementation (e.g., checklist) and effectiveness as a behavior intervention plan?
		11. Does the plan include ways to promote the maintenance and generalization of positive behavior changes in student behavior?
		12. Is the plan consistent with systems of student behavior change and support available in the school?

Source: Adapted from *Functional Behavior Assessment/Behavior Intervention Plan Checklist,* Center for Effective Collaboration and Practice, 2000. Retrieved August 12, 2007, from http://cecp.air.org/fba/problembehavior3/appendixa.htm.

Bullying: The Problems and Some Interventions

Bullying is a serious problem. Approximately 30 percent of students report being a bully, being bullied, or both (Nansel et al., 2001). An extensive amount of information now is available concerning this behavior problem, including physical bullying, psychological bullying, and bullying in cyberspace (Berger, 2007). As a professional educator, you should be aware of what types of bullying occur, who is likely to be bullied, and what you can do to help.

What Is Bullying?

Bullies generally consider themselves bigger, stronger, more popular, or in some other way more powerful than their victims. Bullying can take several forms:

- physical violence
- verbal taunts, name-calling, put-downs
- threats and intimidation
- extortion or stealing money or possessions

Students who are bullied often are perceived as different for various reasons:

- appearance (for example, overweight, clothing, presence of a disability)
- intellect (too smart or not smart enough)
- racial or ethnic heritage
- socioeconomic background
- cultural or religious background
- sexual orientation

What Can Educators and Schools Do?

Teachers and other school professionals can help all students feel safe using strategies such as these:

- Ensure that students understand what bullying means, what behaviors it includes, and how it makes people feel.

- Develop and post class rules against bullying (for example, "Treat others as you would like to be treated").
- Establish appropriate consequences for bullying (for example, student pays for damaged belongings, apologizes).
- Encourage students to discuss bullying and positive ways to interact with others.
- Discuss the dangers of online and other electronic interactions and the seriousness of bullying using that type of communication.
- Take immediate action when bullying is witnessed or reported.
- Administer a bullying survey to students.
- Praise prosocial and helpful student behavior.
- Pay close attention for bullying during recess and other unstructured times.
- Take student reports of bullying seriously.
- Involve parents in terms of sharing information and enlisting their assistance.
- Interview bullies, victims, and witnesses separately.

Source: Adapted from "Bullying: What's New and What to Do" (electronic version), by J. Rosiak, 2004, *Be Safe & Sound, 1*(4), pp. 3–6. Copyright 2004 by the National Crime Prevention Council. Reprinted with permission.

---

may have specific meaning to the teachers making them, they are too vague and tend to be too subjective to be useful in addressing the student's behaviors. The alternative is to describe behaviors in specific and concrete terms. It sometimes is helpful to jot down vague descriptions of behaviors and then review them, focusing on the specific incidents and details characterizing the behaviors: "Yesterday during the first 30 minutes of language arts, Michael left his desk six times"; "When I ask Chenille a direct question, she looks away and does not answer"; "Juan talks out three to five times each class period—he does not raise his hand; "Hayden has been late coming to class an average of three times per week for the past month." If several behaviors are identified, it often is most helpful to prioritize the one that should be addressed first instead of trying to design interventions for several behaviors at one time.

Collecting Data to Better Understand the Behavior

www.resources

At the Wrightslaw website, on the Behavior Problems and Discipline page (www .wrightslaw.com/info/discipl .index.htm), you will find information related to legal perspectives on discipline, particularly for students with disabilities.

The third step in FBA requires systematically gathering information about a behavior's occurrence and the situation in which it occurs. By doing this, team members are able to judge more accurately whether the behavior follows a particular pattern, for example, occurring during certain types of activities or at certain times of the day. Identifying a pattern will assist team members in understanding the function and seriousness of the behavior in relation to teachers' classroom expectations. At the same time, by measuring the behavior when it becomes a concern and continuing to do so after a plan for addressing it has been implemented, team members can decide whether their efforts to change the behavior have been successful. Sometimes you may be able to observe and record student behavior yourself. However, if this is not feasible, a school psychologist, special education teacher, administrator, paraprofessional, or another professional may help to complete this task.

● **Anecdotal Recording** One useful strategy for measuring student behavior is to record specific incidents, including what happened immediately before the behavior (antecedents) and what happened as a result of the behavior (consequences). This approach is called an *antecedents–behaviors–consequences (ABC) analysis*. For example, whenever Ms. Carlisle directs the class to form cooperative groups (antecedent), Carlos gets up from his seat and heads for the pencil sharpener (behavior). Ms. Carlisle then tells Carlos to join his group (consequence). By observing Carlos and keeping an ongoing ABC log of Carlos's behaviors in the classroom, Ms. Carlisle has found out that whenever the class is transitioning from one activity to another, Carlos is likely to be off task. A sample ABC analysis is shown in Figure 12.2. Note that an ABC analysis should be completed for behaviors that occur only occasionally (for example, throwing a chair, having a tantrum); if you have a student who engages in this type of behavior, a special education teacher, counselor, or psychologist might interview you to complete the ABC analysis.

FIGURE *12.2* **Sample ABC Analysis**

Student Name: Denton R.   **Date:** 2/25/08
Location: Math—Mr. B   **Observer:** Mr. D
Start Time: 1:02   **Stop Time:** 1:15

Antecedents	Behaviors	Consequences
1:03 Students get out books and open to begin class.	D. pulls out his cap and puts it on.	Students around D. start laughing and saying "Hey."
1:05 Teacher notices D. and tells him to remove cap.	D. stands, slowly removes cap, and bows.	Students applaud.
1:14 Teacher asks D. a question.	D. says, "Man, I don't know."	Another student says "Yeah, you're stupid." Others laugh.

- **Event Recording**   One straightforward way to measure a behavior is to count how many times it occurs in a given period of time. This approach, called *event recording*, is appropriate when the behavior is discrete—that is, when it has a clear starting and stopping point. For example, it might be appropriate to use event recording to count the number of times John is late to class during a week or the number of times David blurts out an answer during a 30-minute large-group social studies lesson. Conversely, event recording probably will not be helpful in measuring Jane's tantrum or Jesse's delay in starting his assignment, because these behaviors have more to do with how long they last than with the number of times they occur.

> One straightforward way to measure a behavior is to count how many times it occurs in a given period of time.

Event recording is relatively easy. You can keep a tally on an index card taped to your desk or plan book or as a bookmark in one of your teacher's manuals. The key to event recording is to have an accurate total of the number of times a behavior occurred.

- **Permanent Product Recording**   If your concern about student behavior relates to academics, it may be simplest to keep samples of work as a means of measuring behavior, a strategy called *permanent product recording*. For example, if students in a U.S. history class regularly have to respond to 10 discussion questions during a single class session, you might keep Sam's completed work to document the percentage of questions he is attempting or the percentage of his responses that are correct.

- **Duration Recording**   For some behaviors, the concern is the length of time the behavior lasts. The strategy of *duration recording* might be used with a young student who cries each morning at the start of the school day, a middle school student who takes an extraordinary amount of time to locate all her learning materials, or a high school student who delays beginning assignments. Often, accurately recording the duration of a behavior will require that you have a stopwatch and be able to notice the moment the behavior begins and the moment it ends. However, duration recording also can measure how long students take to complete assignments. You could ask students to write on their papers the times they began and finished their work and reward them for recording the information accurately.

- **Interval Recording**   Sometimes you have concerns about a student's behavior, but none of the systems just described offer a way to record the occurrence of the behavior. For example, you might be concerned about how well a student is staying on task during an independent assignment or the extent to which a student plays with others during free-choice time. In these cases, *interval recording* may be the preferred measuring strategy. To use this approach, you specify a length of time for the observation and then divide the time into smaller intervals. For example, you might observe a 10-minute work or play period divided into 30-second intervals. As you observe the student throughout each 30-second interval, you indicate whether the behavior has been present for that entire interval by marking + or − on the recording form. Clearly, this type of recording requires that someone else, such as a co-teacher, lead the class while you gather data or that another individual, such as a school psychologist, conduct the observation.

- **Time Sampling**   Whereas interval recording requires observing a student continually, *time sampling*, a similar strategy, involves only periodic observation of the student. For example, if you wanted to observe whether Patricia interacted with classmates during a 20-minute group assignment, you could divide the time period into ten 2-minute observations. At the end of each 2-minute interval, you would glance to see whether Patricia was interacting at that moment and record your observation accordingly.

Time sampling is less demanding than interval recording, because you observe only momentarily instead of continuously. However, it does include the risk that the behaviors

Analyze
and Reflect
Which strategy—interval recording or time sampling— would be most appropriate for observing and recording the behavior of a seventh-grade student who is withdrawn and refuses to speak when he is asked to participate during instruction? Why?

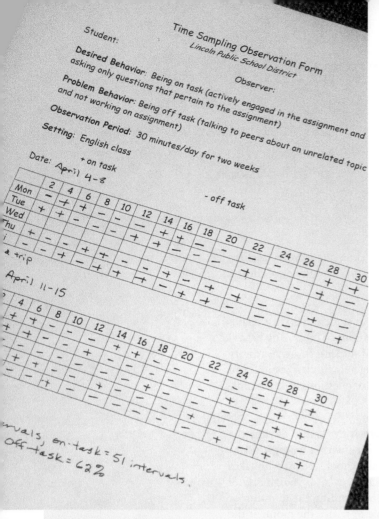

Time Sampling Observation Form
Lincoln Public School District

Student:

Observer:

Desired Behavior: Being on task (actively engaged in the assignment and asking only questions that pertain to the assignment)

Problem Behavior: Being off task (talking to peers about an unrelated topic and not working on assignment)

Observation Period: 30 minutes/day for two weeks

Setting: English class

+ on task

− off task

Date: April 4–8

	2	4	6	8	10	12	14	16	18	20	22	24	26	28	30
Mon	−	+	+												
Tue	+	+	−	−	−	−									
Wed	+	−	−	−	−	+	+	+							
Thu	−	−	+	−	+		+	−							
...trip	−	+	−	+	+	+	+	+		+	−	−	−		
						+	+		−	+		−	+	+	

April 11–15

	2	4	6	8	10	12	14	16	18	20	22	24	26	28	30
	−	+	+	−	−	−		+	+		−			+	+
	+	+	−	−	−	−									+
	−	−	−	−	+	+		+			−				
	+	+	−			−	+				−		+	+	
	−	−	−			+				−		−	+	+	
		+	−	+	+			+		−	−			+	+
								+				+		−	+
												+		−	+
														+	+

...vals, on-task = 51 intervals.

Off-task = 62%

How might a behavior chart help you collaborate with others to develop a plan for responding to a student's behavior? What other methods of recording behavior might you use to determine whether your behavior management plan is working?

you observe at each sampling are not typical of what has occurred until that moment. This system also can be expedient when your goal is to observe several students at one time: By glancing at three different students and immediately recording the behavior of each one, you can look at the behavior patterns of each student during a single observational period. Teachers who use time sampling often need a signal to alert them to observe and record the behavior. For example, they might wear an earphone that enables them to hear a prerecorded tone after each interval. Like interval recording, time sampling is most easily accomplished through collaboration with a colleague or teaching assistant.

● **Other Data Sources** Functional behavior assessment rarely consists of just classroom observations. Most likely, team members will ask questions about your perceptions of how the student's behavior has developed or changed and your attempts to contact the parents and otherwise address the behavior. Family members may be interviewed, and an analysis of the structure, length, and characteristics of the student's entire school day may be considered, as may the physical classroom environment and classroom climate. The student also is likely to be interviewed; her perspective can add important information to other data gathered (Kinch, Lewis-Palmer, Hagan-Burke, & Sugai, 2001). Any factor that might contribute to the behavior may be explored.

Professionals sometimes say that such precise behavior measurement and exhaustive consideration of the causes of the behavior are not realistic. It is true that you would not routinely have the time to use these strategies. However, when you are faced with a student whose behavior is particularly persistent and puzzling, the time you and the team take to analyze it systematically can give you a clearer picture of how to address the problem and effectively alleviate it (Newcomer & Lewis, 2004). Further, by using generic, multipurpose recording forms and sharing the observation and interviewing tasks with other professionals and paraprofessionals, you may find that this step in a functional assessment is not as burdensome as you might imagine.

Analyzing the Data and Forming Hypotheses

At the fourth step in FBA, all the pieces come together. Consider, for example, Kyle, whose middle school teachers had expressed concern about his frequent loud and profane outbursts during class. Conducting five 20-minute observation sessions revealed that Kyle spoke loudly using profanity an average of 2.2 times per session (event recording) during large-group instruction (classroom environment). An ABC analysis illustrated that the talking out occurred when the teacher asked the whole class group to read a paragraph in the book, review a chart or graph, or complete some other reading-related task (anecdotal recording). The other students looked at and laughed at Kyle after the talk-outs. The teacher nearly always corrected Kyle, and in just over half the instances, he challenged the teacher's reprimand, saying for example, "I did not," or pounding his fists on his desk and then putting his head down. In an interview, Kyle said that he got called on in class only when he did not know the answer, and he said he knew more than teachers gave him credit for.

In analyzing these data, Kyle's teacher and other team members hypothesized that his talking out served two functions: First, it was a means of avoiding being called on when the question required a reading task, an area of significant academic difficulty for Kyle. Second, it was a means of getting attention from both peers and the teacher.

This step in the process is something like detective work. With the data collected, team members try to identify patterns in the behavior, purposes it might serve for the student, and factors that might make the behavior better or worse. In Kyle's case, the teachers recognized that instead of responding to the profanity and outbursts, they needed to address his fear and need for positive attention.

Developing a Behavior Intervention Plan

Once hypotheses have been generated, team members can develop a **behavior intervention plan (BIP)** based on them. This fifth step in functional behavior assessment may include any number of interventions. For example, the BIP might include modifying the physical or instructional arrangement of the classroom (seating Kyle nearer to where the teacher usually stands or using more cooperative groups); changing antecedents (permitting students to ask each other for help while reading the material being discussed); altering consequences (the teacher ignoring at least some occurrences of the talking out); teaching alternative behaviors to the student (having Kyle record his own behaviors and reward himself for raising his hand); or modifying curricular materials (using fewer questions for which reading is required) (Gresham, Van, & Cook, 2006; Kauffman, Mostert, Trent, & Hallahan, 2002; Wheeler & Richey, 2005).

Different types of rewards and consequences that you might incorporate into a BIP are presented later in this chapter. Figure 12.3 contains an example of a behavior intervention plan.

Implementing the Plan

Once the BIP has been developed, you and the team, often including the student, reach the sixth step in functional behavior assessment: implementing your plan. Having a clear plan for implementation is important because the key to this approach is a systematic response to the behavior. This phase requires several actions. Teachers and other professionals implementing the BIP should monitor the consistency with which they implement the plan. In addition, if peers or family members have implementation responsibilities, every effort should be made to ensure that their roles are reasonable, that they understand and can carry out their parts of the plan, and that any concerns they have are addressed (Peck-Peterson, Derby, Berg, & Horner, 2002). Throughout implementation, data on the BIP's impact should be gathered so that monitoring, described next, will be facilitated.

Monitoring the Plan's Effectiveness

You began the process of FBA gathering information about the student's behavior prior to thinking about how to respond to it. The behavior records you keep as you implement the BIP enable you to determine whether the plan is working (Fairbanks, Sugai, Guarding, & Lathrop, 2007). To proceed with the seventh step, monitoring the plan, you and the team use the same recording strategies presented in the third step of FBA, and you can provide data-recording forms to your peers and others who were not initially involved in the process. Remember that behavior does not change rapidly; the team should be committed to following the plan for a specified period of time—perhaps two or three weeks or even more—before deciding whether it is effective.

As you monitor the plan, you may observe any of a number of effects. First, the inappropriate behavior may stop completely or the desired behavior may be displayed consistently. If this happens, you may decide to gradually withdraw the plan. For example, if you are intervening to eliminate a student's profane language use in class and no profane

FIGURE *12.3*   Sample Behavior Intervention Plan

Student: Tom Clark

Date Developed: 9/29/08

Grade: 7

School: Swift Creek Middle School

Date Implemented: 10/1/08

Baseline Data Results: Tom destroyed assignments on 5 out of 5 observation days.

Hypothesis Statement: Tom's behavior is related to frustration brought on by a discrepancy between his skill level and the skill level necessary to complete the assignments. Much of Tom's destructive behavior is related to his isolated seating from his peers in the classroom. Tom feels singled out because he sits at a table by himself.

Type of Intervention Plan: Educational _X_ Behavioral _____

Person(s) Responsible for Implementing Plan: Science teacher

DESCRIPTION OF THE BEHAVIOR

Behavior	Behavior Defined
Tom destroys his written assignments.	Tom wads up and tears up his assignment papers.

INTERVENTION GOAL:

To decrease the number of occurrences when Tom destroys his assignments to 0 per week

---

INTERVENTION PLAN:

1. Seat Tom with a peer who has good on-task behavior. The peer will review directions with Tom and assist him in getting started with assignments.

2. Provide Tom with a daily monitoring assignment checklist to improve the following areas of difficulty:

   Assignment Checklist

   _____ I understood teacher directions.   _____ I asked for help when I needed it.

   _____ I answered all questions.   _____ I understood the assignment.

   _____ I need more time.   _____ I turned in my assignment.

3. Provide Tom with academic modifications, including these:

   a. Extend time to complete and turn in assignments if needed.
   b. Provide outlines, study guides, and graphic organizers with textbook assignments to assist Tom in identifying important information.
   c. Provide Tom with a word/definition list to use when completing worksheet assignments.
   d. Provide peer assistance with some assignments.
   e. Provide additional instructional modifications as needed.

4. Provide directions to Tom in a variety of ways (verbal, written, through direct instruction, and through peer assistance).

5. Reinforce Tom's academic productivity and assignment completion.

---

language is occurring, then you can gradually increase the length of time without profanity required to earn a reward and then move to using just verbal praise. This is called *fading out* a reward system.

Second, the plan you are implementing may have value but need modification. Perhaps it requires too much time to implement or the rewards need adjustment. Such alterations are not unusual; simply modify the plan and continue to monitor its effectiveness. For example, if you created a point system for your sophomore keyboarding student that

<table>
<tr><td colspan="2">

WHEN AND WHERE THE PLAN WILL BE IMPLEMENTED:

The plan will be implemented in Tom's science class for 3 consecutive weeks beginning 10/1/08.

</td></tr>
</table>

INTERVENTION DATA COLLECTION SUMMARY:

Week 1. Decrease in behavior to 3 occurrences.

Week 2. Decrease in behavior to 2 occurrences.

Week 3. Decrease in behavior to 1 occurrence.

FOLLOW-UP AND REVIEW DATE(S):

Follow-up and review meeting 10/24/08

COMMENTS:

The intervention plan is successful with Tom.

The team agreed to write the interventions outlined in this plan in Tom's IEP.

The team will meet in 3 weeks for review.

TEAM MEETING PARTICIPANTS:

Name	Position
_____	_____
_____	_____
_____	_____
_____	_____

Source: From "Functional Assessment: A Systematic Process for Assessment and Intervention in General and Special Education Classrooms," by M. E. McConnell, P. B. Hilvitz, and C. J. Cox, 1998, *Intervention in School and Clinic, 34*(1), pp. 10–20. Copyright © 1998 by the Hammill Institute on Disability. Reprinted with permission.

includes earning points for being seated when the bell rings, turning homework in at the beginning of class, and having an assignment notebook and pen in class, you might discover that the system is too difficult to monitor. You might then eliminate the points for everything except homework for a student who chronically fails to come to class on time with assignments in hand.

Third, the plan may not be working. As you track the number and duration of tantrums for one of your students, you might learn that they are occurring more often and lasting longer. When a situation like this occurs, the team needs to analyze what is happening and create an alternative plan, again following the steps that have been outlined. If other options do not seem appropriate, a more significant change, such as a change in the student's placement, may need to be considered.

> You increase options for responding to student behavior by creating partnerships with parents.

Finally, it is imperative that you work closely with parents to resolve student behavior problems. Parents sometimes can clarify reasons a student suddenly is behaving in a particular way (for example, a death in the family, a divorce, an unusually exciting weekend trip, a cultural response to a school activity). In addition, they can reinforce school messages at home and help provide rewards at home earned by appropriate behavior during the school day. Parents are likely to be members of the team completing the functional behavior assessment and behavior intervention plan, and their contributions cannot be emphasized enough. You increase options for responding to student behavior by creating partnerships with parents, even when you may disagree with their perceptions, a topic addressed in the Working Together.

What Are Effective Strategies for Responding to Serious Individual Behaviors?

The FBA procedure provides educators with clear guidelines for assisting students with significant behavior problems. The strategies that are part of that process might include some of the simple approaches you read about earlier in this chapter, but they also will likely include interventions that are more long term and systematic to increase preferred behaviors and decrease undesirable behaviors. The principles for interventions are the same whether you use simple strategies or more intensive interventions, but the latter usually are carried out across time in a consistent and well-documented manner. They also may involve the use of contracts, in which the expectations for behavior are specified and rewards and consequences are clearly spelled out. The interventions covered in the following sections include increasing desirable behaviors, decreasing undesirable behaviors, and using behavior contracts.

Increasing Desirable Behaviors

All students, even the most challenging, have some appropriate behaviors you would like to increase. The primary strategy for increasing appropriate behavior is called *reinforcement*. Reinforcement is any response or consequence that increases a behavior (Jones & Jones, 2004; Safran & Oswald, 2003).

Case Study Homework Exercise

Go to the Homework and Exercises section in Chapter 12 of MyEducationLab for a case study that will allow you to apply what you have learned in this chapter.

It is important for you to keep in mind that reinforcement can increase negative as well as positive behaviors. For example, when a teacher puts a sticker on a student's chart because the student completed his assignment without calling out for unneeded help, the student will be more likely in the future to continue to work independently. When a teacher says to a student who is wandering around the classroom, "Sit down!" the student will be more likely in the future to be out of her seat again. In both instances, reinforcement was applied. In the first case, it rewarded a desirable behavior; in the second, it rewarded an undesirable behavior.

● **Positive and Negative Reinforcement** Anytime you respond to a behavior with a consequence that makes it more likely for the behavior to occur again, you are using **positive reinforcement** (Kauffman et al., 2002). When you reward a student for appropriate behavior and that behavior increases, positive reinforcement has occurred. For

Working TOGETHER

When Differences of Opinion Occur

Few people would disagree that collaboration is essential for working with students with disabilities, and most professionals enjoy their interactions with colleagues and parents. However, collaboration can be challenging when differences of opinion occur. Think about conflicts such as the one described here. Consider role-playing this interaction with your classmates to practice using the suggestions offered.

Ms. Bonnet requests a meeting with you. She is quite upset, accusing you of treating her daughter Taylor unfairly. She says Taylor has told her that other students are misbehaving more than she is but that you discipline only her. Ms. Bonnet wants you to stop.

- It is tempting in this type of interaction to become defensive, explaining that you have been fair and that Taylor is not telling the whole story. Instead, first be sure that Ms. Bonnet has relayed her story. When she finishes speaking, paraphrase what she has said, succinctly summarizing the information without making any judgments—for example, "Taylor has told you that other students misbehave but that I discipline only her." Notice that you are not necessarily agreeing with this perspective, only restating it.

- Try asking Ms. Bonnet for a specific example of what Taylor has described. That may help you to understand more about the situation.

- If Taylor is not present, it probably would be best to leave this matter unresolved and to arrange a meeting that includes her. That way, the situation can be more fully explored.

- As you discuss the situation with Taylor and her mother, ask Taylor what she thinks would make things more fair. You do not necessarily have to agree with her perspective, but it is important to know what she thinks should occur.

- Develop a strategy to address Taylor's concerns, and try it for a week. This might include touching base momentarily with Taylor each day or keeping a record of your interactions with her. Even if you believe that Taylor's accusations are wildly inaccurate, trying to verbally reinforce her appropriate behavior can help to ease the tension.

- Consider the possibility that Taylor may be accurate in her perception. Are you inadvertently noticing her because her voice tends to be louder than the voices of other students? Could you be responding to a cultural difference? Did Taylor do something earlier in the school year that has made you overly aware of her behavior? Are you especially watchful of her because you know that she has a behavior intervention plan?

Situations that involve conflict can be stressful, but with careful communication and a willingness to consider others' opinions, you can successfully address them.

---

instance, if you tell a student that she may use the classroom computer after she completes five math problems and she completes all the problems, you are positively reinforcing math problem completion through computer rewards.

Negative reinforcement operates somewhat differently. Suppose you set up a system with your ninth-grade English students whereby they must have their homework signed each night by their parents until they have brought it back to school on time at least 9 out of 10 times. Because students see having their homework signed by their parents as an undesirable consequence, they will increase their promptness in turning in homework to avoid the consequence. Any increase in behavior to avoid a consequence is the result of **negative reinforcement** (Wheeler & Richey, 2005).

Although negative reinforcement can be effective, positive reinforcement usually should be tried first because having students work toward a positive outcome is preferable to having them work under the threat or perceived threat of a negative consequence.

Some professionals object to using positive reinforcement with students, because they fear it teaches students they are entitled to a payoff for appropriate behavior. These professionals contend that students should complete their schoolwork and behave appropriately simply because these are the right things to do. This discussion often is addressed as one of external versus internal motivation (for example, Kohn, 2006). Although learning

fyi

Your colleagues and the students you teach often can give you a wealth of ideas for effective rewards. Keep in mind that simple, inexpensive reward systems are more likely to be feasible than ones requiring extensive record keeping or having a high cost.

and behaving appropriately because of internal motivation, rather than the expectation of external rewards, certainly is preferable, some students who struggle to learn and behave as expected are simply not able or likely to do so. These students may behave and respond appropriately in school because of internal motivation only when they are extremely interested in a subject or topic or experience repeated success over an extended period of time. Additional strategies, including reinforcement, provide the support they need to succeed in their learning.

> To ensure that positive reinforcement is successful for students with special needs, keep in mind that many different types of rewards can be used.

● **Types of Reinforcers**   To ensure that positive reinforcement is successful for students with special needs, keep in mind that many different types of rewards can be used. Four of these types include the following:

1. *Social reinforcers* are various types of positive interactions that a teacher, parent, or peer can give a student to reward appropriate behavior and increase it. These reinforcers might include a positive phone call home to parents, a pat on the back or hug, verbal praise, or selection as Citizen of the Month. Social reinforcers, especially clear and specific verbal praise, always should be tried before other positive reinforcers, because they are the most natural type of reward in a school environment. If you find it necessary to employ other types of rewards, you should use them only in conjunction with social reinforcers. Your long-term goal should always be to have students respond to rewards that occur naturally in their classroom environment.

2. *Activity reinforcers* involve activities such as playing games, having extra recess, helping a teacher in another class, and participating in other coveted individual or group pastimes. Generally, activities that directly relate to a student's educational goals (for example, practicing math skills on the computer) are preferable to those that are solely recreational (for example, playing a noneducational computer game).

3. *Tangible reinforcers* are prizes and other objects that students can earn as symbols of achievement and that students want to obtain. A student who is earning baseball cards for completing assignments is receiving a tangible reinforcer. Putting stickers on papers is another example of this type of reinforcer. Tangible rewards often can be naturally integrated into classroom activities. For example, a student can earn the rocket pieces and household chemicals needed to create a highly interesting science experiment that is not offered to other students but addresses concepts that are part of the curriculum. However, the amount of the tangible reinforcer must be appropriate for the amount of positive behavior required. Students earning the science materials just mentioned should be expected to display appropriate behaviors over a lengthy period of time, not just for an afternoon. If the tangible reinforcer is a scented sticker, perhaps an afternoon of appropriate behavior is the right amount for the reward being given.

4. *Primary reinforcers* are foods and other items related to human needs that a student finds rewarding. They are much more basic than secondary reinforcers, which comprise the three types just described: social reinforcers, activity reinforcers, and tangible reinforcers. Primary reinforcers used in schools often are edible and might include a piece of candy, a soft drink, or a piece of fruit. Although you might occasionally employ primary reinforcers as a special treat, generally you should use them only if a student is incapable of understanding more natural rewards or other types of rewards are not effective. This is important for two reasons. First, the potential negative impact of food reinforcers on student health is a concern, and second, food reinforcers are not a natural part of the school learning process. In school, students are expected to work to learn, to prepare for adulthood, and, more immediately for some, to earn teacher praise or a grade. Candy is not a routine part of the learning environment. If you plan to use primary reinforcers such as food, check with a

Analyze and Reflect

Which types of reinforcers might be most appropriate for each student described at the beginning of this chapter? How did you make these decisions?

school administrator to find out about local policies governing their use. Also check with parents, both for permission and about possible student food allergies. Keep in mind nutritional issues as well.

● **Effective Use of Positive Reinforcers**   In addition to understanding the different types of positive reinforcers, you need to know some principles for using them effectively (Walker, Shea, & Bauer, 2003). Three principles are key:

1. *Make sure that the positive reinforcers are clear and specific and that students understand the relationship between their behavior and rewards.* The rewards students earn need to be specific. For example, rewarding a student with time on the computer is not precise enough. If it is a reward, the amount of computer time for the specific behavior displayed should be clarified. Clarity and specificity are especially important when you use verbal praise. Saying to a student "Good job!" is far less effective than saying "Good job! You asked three other students for help before you asked me." The former praise is vague; the latter praise explicitly states what behavior is being rewarded.

2. *Vary how much and how often you reward students.* If a student displays very little positive behavior, you may reward it heavily at first just to increase it. As the student learns to use the appropriate behavior more readily, you should decrease the amount and intensity of the reward. For example, if at first you were rewarding a student with free-choice reading time for every two assignments completed, you might gradually change the reward so the student must complete four assignments—and get at least 90 percent on each—to earn the free-reading reward. Another way to vary rewards is to enlist parent assistance. For example, Donna's mother might agree to provide a privilege, such as access to a preferred video game, when the teacher sends a note home indicating that Donna completed her independent work within a specified time. The only caution in asking parents for their help is the uncertainty of knowing for sure whether they will provide and withhold the reward the way they are supposed to.

3. *Make sure a student desires the reward selected.* If you propose to make a positive phone call home when a student participates in group work but the student does not care what his parents think, then your reward is unlikely to work. Instead the student may be far more motivated to choose three homework problems *not* to do. You can determine your students' preferences for rewards by asking them what types of incentives they like or having them rank their preferences from a list of rewards you provide.

Related to the concept of reward desirability is that of *satiation.* Simply stated, a student who receives the same reward over a period of time eventually may no longer find it rewarding (Contrucci-Kuhn, Lerman, & Vondran, 2006). If five minutes of free time is given repeatedly, after a while the student may come to expect the free time and not work to receive it. When this happens, it is important to change the reward.

You often can avoid the problem of satiation by using a *reinforcement menu,* which is a list of rewards from which students may choose. The menu can be posted in the classroom, or students can keep individual lists. Some rewards might be reserved for extraordinary performance. Many websites provide ideas for rewards and other ways to increase student behavior. Some of these are outlined in the Technology Notes.

Decreasing Undesirable Behaviors

Many teachers find that some students with special needs have inappropriate classroom behaviors that need to be decreased. These might include aggressive behaviors such as calling classmates names and poking, pinching, and hitting others; verbal outbursts such

fyi

If your school has students with extraordinarily challenging behaviors, you may learn that they sometimes need to be physically restrained. Physical restraint is used only by staff members who have specific training so that students and adults remain safe, and most school districts have strict policies concerning its use.

Help on the Web for Responding to Student Behavior

The Internet is a valuable resource for information about responding to student behavior. You can find specific strategies for responding to common behavior problems, such as talking out, moving around the classroom without purpose, and failing to start or complete an assignment in class. You also can find checklists for deciding whether a behavior problem is serious, forms for recording behaviors, and templates for interventions such as student contracts. Here is a sampling of particularly valuable websites:

Dr. Mac's (McIntyre's) Amazing Behavior Management Advice Site   www.behavioradvisor.com

> This website lives up to its name. It offers basic information for new teachers related to setting up positive classroom behavior management systems, strategies for addressing common student behavior problems, examples and explanations of interventions such as contracts and token economies, and links to hundreds of additional websites. This site also provides a teacher bulletin board for posting problems and receiving assistance. Recent examples ranged from a 4-year-old who chronically bullies classmates to a high school student with Down syndrome who does not want to leave the gym after his physical education class ends.

Center for Effective Collaboration and Practice   http://cecp.air.org/fba/problembehavior/strategies.htm#techniques

> This organization is dedicated to improving the lives of students with emotional and behavior problems.

Of particular interest is the detailed but easy-to-read information on this page of its website about completing a functional behavior assessment and creating and implementing a behavior intervention plan. Moreover, this site contains many other types of valuable information regarding school violence, prevention of behavior problems, and related topics.

Kentucky Department of Education Behavior Home Page   www.state.ky.us/agencies/behave/interact/interaction.html

> This webpage is a portal to a variety of links about responding to student behavior. Information addresses the law and legal requirements, positive behavior supports, bullying, time-out, and safe schools. Also included are several forums/blogs about student behavior.

North Carolina Department of Juvenile Justice and Delinquency Prevention, Center for the Prevention of School Violence   www.ncdjjdp.org/cpsv

> This webpage provides information about making schools safe environments conducive to learning. It features specific sections for topics not frequently addressed, including ideas related to physical education and foreign language as well as specific locations in schools, such as restrooms.

---

as calling out answers, swearing, and making nonsense statements during large-group instruction; and other behaviors such as fleeing the classroom when feeling stressed, copying others' work, and refusing to work. Just as some strategies increase desirable behaviors, other strategies are designed to decrease undesirable behaviors.

Decreasing behavior generally is accomplished through one of these four strategies (Jones & Jones, 2004; Kauffman et al., 2002):

1. differential reinforcement of behaviors that are incompatible with the undesirable behavior

2. extinction, or ignoring the behavior until the student stops it

3. removing something desirable from the student

4. presenting a negative or aversive consequence

The latter two strategies—removing something desirable and presenting a negative or aversive consequence—are considered *punishment.* Punishment occurs when a consequence applied has the effect of decreasing a behavior. These strategies violate the principles of

PBIS and should be employed only when accompanied by strategies that increase desired behaviors. Each of the four strategies is explained in the following sections.

● **Differential Reinforcement of Incompatible and Other Behaviors**   Reinforcers can be used to decrease inappropriate behaviors by increasing related appropriate behaviors. Perhaps you have a student like Patrick in your classroom. Patrick has a severe learning disability. He tends to be very dependent on you for affirmation that he is doing his work correctly; he seems to be constantly at your elbow asking, "Is this right?" To change this behavior, you might want to try praising Patrick when you can catch him working independently at his desk. This technique is called **differential reinforcement of incompatible behaviors.** You are reinforcing a positive behavior—working independently at the student's own desk—that is incompatible with the negative behavior—being at your desk asking for affirmation (Conyers et al., 2003; Walker et al., 2003). Your goal in this case is to decrease Patrick's tendency to come to your desk (inappropriate behavior) by systematically rewarding him for staying at his desk (appropriate behavior), which prevents him from being at your desk. You also could decide to reward him for asking a classmate for assistance—that is, by reinforcing other behaviors.

● **Extinction**   Another approach to decreasing negative behavior is **extinction.** To extinguish a behavior, you stop reinforcing it; eventually, the behavior decreases (Walker et al., 2003; Wright-Gallo, Higbee, & Reagon, 2006). This strategy often is appropriate when a student has a minor but annoying undesirable behavior, such as tapping a pencil or rocking a chair, which you inadvertently have been reinforcing by calling attention to it or otherwise responding to it. However, extinction is appropriate only when the behavior is minor and does not threaten student well-being. Also, before an ignored behavior will decrease, it will likely increase; that is, at first the student might tap the pencil more loudly or rock more rapidly before stopping. If you respond to the behavior at this higher level (by telling the student to stop the noise or to keep still), you inadvertently reward the student for the exaggerated behavior through your response. If you think you cannot ignore a behavior while it increases, then extinction is not the strategy to use.

● **Removing Reinforcers**   In some instances, you can decrease inappropriate behavior by taking away from the student something desired, a strategy called **removal punishment.** One example of removal punishment is **response cost,** which involves taking away a privilege, points, or some other reward (Curtin, Pisecco, & Hamilton, 2006). An informal use of response cost occurs when a teacher takes away recess, a field trip, or attendance at an assembly because of misbehavior. More systematically, a student may lose a certain amount of free time each time he swears in class. Similarly, a student may lose the privilege of helping in the classroom because she refuses to begin assigned tasks.

If you are considering using response cost, keep in mind that it is effective only if the student currently has reinforcers you can remove. For example, denying a student access to a special school program will decrease his negative behavior only if he wants to attend the program. Also, response cost sometimes fails because the negative behavior is being reinforced so strongly that the response cost is not effective. In the example just described, if the student receives a lot of peer attention from acting out in class, the response cost of not attending the school program might be too weak to counteract the strong appeal of peer attention. Finally, because response cost teaches a student only what *not* to do, it is essential that you simultaneously teach the student desired behaviors—what she *should* do.

Another removal punishment strategy is **time-out,** which involves removing a student from opportunities for reward (Wolfgang, 2001). Many elementary school teachers use a simple form of time-out when they require students who are

Analyze
and Reflect

How could extinction be implemented in your classroom to decrease a student's undesirable behavior? What implications does using extinction have on the other students in the classroom? How would you decide that extinction is not an appropriate technique to try?

Because response cost teaches a student only what *not* to do, it is essential that you simultaneously teach the student desired behaviors—what she *should* do.

What strategies can you use to respond to a student whose behavior problems are serious and persistent? How should you balance the student's rights and needs with those of your other students?

misbehaving on the playground to spend a few minutes in a "penalty box." The reward from which students are removed is playtime with classmates. Time-out can be used in a number of ways depending on the age of the student, the nature of the inappropriate behaviors, and the student's response to isolation. For example, it may be sufficient in a kindergarten or first-grade classroom to have a time-out chair in a quiet corner of the classroom. When Heather pushes another child, she is told to sit in time-out, where she can observe other students in the reading circle but cannot interact with them. If this is not effective, then placing a carrel on the student's desk or using a screen (possibly made from a large box) around a chair might be the next step. For older students and for those with more challenging behaviors, the time-out may need to be in a location totally removed from the student's class. For example, when Louis swears at his teacher, he is sent to the time-out room, a small, undecorated room with just a desk and chair that adjoins the counselor's office. However, for Cherri, time-out means going to Ms. Eich's room across the hall, where she doesn't know the students.

The school district in which you work may have a policy concerning whether time-out is used, and if it is, how to implement it effectively. Also keep the following considerations in mind:

1. The length of the time-out should vary depending on the student's age, the type of challenging behavior, and the amount of time it takes for the time-out to achieve the result of decreasing an undesirable behavior. Younger students and those with limited intellectual ability often require shorter time-out periods than older students with learning and behavior problems.

2. When using time-out, be sure to give students a warning, let them know why they are being given the time-out, and deny them access to attractive activities during time-out. The warning provides students an opportunity to correct the behavior;

the explanation ensures they understand the reason for time-out; and the absence of attractions guarantees that time-out does not become a reward for the student.

3. Giving a student attention as part of a time-out process sabotages its effectiveness. Sometimes teachers who are using time-out accompany the student to the time-out area and explain the student's behavior on the way, arguing with the student about the time-out procedure and otherwise providing the student with a great deal of attention. This attention may reinforce the student's behavior and in effect negate the purpose of using time-out.

4. If a student refuses to go to a time-out location, you may need to ask for assistance with enforcing your decision. However, you also should keep in mind that if time-out becomes a power struggle between you and a student, it might not be the appropriate strategy to use.

5. Be aware that for some students, isolation is in itself rewarding. For time-out to be effective, the environment from which the student is removed must be rewarding. Some students are happy to be left completely alone for as long as possible. For students who prefer isolation, time-out clearly is not an appropriate strategy for reducing misbehavior.

6. Attend to the safety needs of students in time-out settings. It is highly unethical to send an upset student to an unsupervised time-out location. If time-out is used, it must include adult supervision, a safe location for the student, and monitoring for student comfort and safety.

● **Presenting Negative Consequences**   The final strategy for decreasing undesirable student behavior, **presentation punishment,** is the least preferable, because it involves presenting negative consequences to students (Rubin, 2005). For example, when a teacher verbally reprimands a student, the *reprimand* is a negative consequence intended to decrease student misbehavior. It is a mild punisher, one of the most common used in schools.

Another type of presentation punishment is *overcorrection,* in which a student is directed to restore a situation to its original condition or a better condition. This strategy is useful when a student has damaged classroom property or otherwise created a mess. For example, a student who scribbles on a chalkboard might be assigned to erase and wash all the boards in the room. A student who writes on a desktop might be required to stay after school to clean all the desktops in the classroom. A student who throws trash on the floor might be given the task of sweeping the classroom and adjoining hallway. This strategy can make clear the undesirable consequences of negative behaviors, but it is not without problems. First, the student must be willing to complete the overcorrection activity. In fact, it might be extremely difficult to compel this behavior. If a student refuses to complete the task, a confrontation might occur. In addition, the overcorrection requires close teacher supervision. A student should not be left alone to complete the assigned task, which could translate into a significant time commitment from the teacher.

Physical punishment is another traditional presentation punishment. Although corporal punishment, carried out within specific guidelines, still is permitted in schools in nearly half of the states, most educators strongly oppose its use (Cameron, 2006; Hinchey, 2003). Physical and other types of punishment have many potential negative effects, including the following (Straus, 2001):

1. Punishment often suppresses a student's undesirable behavior but does not change it. Once a student realizes or observes that physical punishment no longer follows a behavior, that behavior will likely recur. Thus, a student who is physically punished for stealing will likely steal again if he is relatively sure no one can discover the theft.

fyi

School districts that allow corporal punishment usually have clear guidelines, including obtaining advance parent permission, specifying how punishment is administered, and requiring the presence of a witness.

2. Although punishment might reduce or eliminate a particular behavior, other undesirable behaviors might be substituted. For example, a student who is strongly scolded for talking out might at the first opportunity deface a bulletin board as a way of getting even.

3. Punishment sometimes has an opposite effect on behavior, increasing instead of decreasing it. This is especially true when the student craves adult attention. For example, if you verbally correct a student for not working, she may enjoy your attention and attempt even less work to obtain your attention again. In this case, the intended punishment clearly has not served its purpose.

4. Through the teacher's modeling, students might learn that they too can control people by using punishment. For example, a student might imitate a teacher's scolding when tutoring a younger student. Likewise, the student might hit a classmate perceived as weaker if physical punishment is part of the school's disciplinary procedures. Similarly, students who are physically punished at home might use hitting at school with peers.

In general then the message for you as a teacher responding to student behaviors in class is this: Increasing positive behaviors through the use of reinforcers, especially when these desirable behaviors can substitute for undesirable behaviors, is the preferred approach to behavior management. If you find it necessary to decrease undesirable behaviors, the preferred strategies are reinforcing the positive incompatible behaviors and extinction. Removal or presentation punishment should be a last resort, used only as part of an ongoing behavior intervention plan and involving a team decision. If you do use punishment, keep in mind all the potential problems with it and monitor its use closely.

Using Behavior Contracts

Using behavior contracts is one straightforward way to apply the strategies for increasing and decreasing behavior. A **behavior contract** is an agreement between the teacher and student that clearly specifies the expectations for the student, the rewards for meeting those expectations, the consequences of not meeting them, and the timeframe for which the agreement is valid (Mruzek, Cohen, & Smith, 2007; Wright, 2007).

> Using behavior contracts is one straightforward way to apply the strategies for increasing and decreasing behavior.

Contracts are best used with students like Joseph and perhaps David from the chapter-opening vignettes, who are old enough to understand their content and whose disabilities either do not affect their cognitive functioning or affect it only marginally. However, simple contracts can be used with almost any student (Jones & Jones, 2004). As you review the sample contract in Figure 12.4, notice that it has more detail than some student contracts you may have seen. For students with special needs who have behavior challenges, contracts with less detail often are ineffective in changing behavior. The added components of the contract in Figure 12.4 significantly increase its impact on the student.

The original and still most comprehensive information on how to write student behavior contracts comes from Homme (1970). He stressed the following points:

1. The reward that goes with the contract should be immediate, that is, as close in time as possible to the performance of the desired behavior.

2. An initial contract should call for and reward small amounts of the desired behavior. For example, requiring a student to read an entire book to earn a reward probably would be too frustrating a task for a student with a reading problem. Instead, the student could be rewarded for each chapter (or even each chapter section or page) completed.

FIGURE *12.4* Sample Student Contract

For <u>Mia</u>   Class <u>History—Mr. Lee</u>

(Student name)

I agree to do these things (what, how much, how well, how often, how measured):

<u>Every day when the bell rings, I will be in my seat with my book, notebook, and a pen ready. During class, I will answer questions only when called on (2 warnings per class for calling out).</u>

For doing them I will receive (what, how much, how often, when):

<u>1 point/day for being prepared, 1 point/day for appropriate class participation. Every time I accumulate 8 points, I may earn 5 extra-credit points toward my course grade.</u>

Outstanding performance will be if I

Keep my contract 5 days in a row (10 points in a 5-day week)

My bonus for outstanding performance is

The option of skipping 1 homework assignment during the week after the bonus is earned

If I don't meet the terms of my contract, this is the consequence:

If fewer than 5 points are earned in a week, I forfeit participating in the History Jeopardy! competition the following Monday.

This contract will be renegotiated on

October 19, 2008

<u>Mia</u>   <u>Mr. Lee</u>

Student signature   **Teacher signature**

<u>September 15, 2008</u>   <u>September 15, 2008</u>

Date   **Date**

3. Rewards should be distributed frequently in small amounts. This approach has been proven more effective than using fewer but larger rewards.

4. A contract should call for and reward accomplishments, rather than obedience. That is, it should reward the completion of assigned work or appropriate behavior, rather than teacher-pleasing behaviors such as staying in one's seat.

5. The performance should be awarded only after it has occured. This rule seems obvious but is often overlooked. Students who are allowed privileges or rewards before or during assigned work are far less likely to complete it successfully than those who are rewarded after it.

6. The contract must be fair. The amount of work required of the student and the payoff for completing the work must be balanced.

7. The terms of the contract should be clear to the student. The contract should be put in writing and discussed with the student. Each component of the contract

should be expressed in language the student understands. If the student is not able to understand a contract, this strategy is probably not appropriate. Both the student and the teacher should sign the contract.

8. The contract must be honest. The teacher should be willing to carry out the terms of the contract as written and do so immediately. In practice, this means that you should be sure you can deliver on the promises you make.

9. The contract should be positive. It should specify student accomplishments and rewards, rather than restrictions and punishments.

10. The contract should be used systematically. If the contract is enforced only occasionally, the result may be worse (or at least very confusing) for the student than not using one at all.

How Can You Help Students Manage Their Own Behavior?

The strategies just outlined for increasing positive and decreasing negative student behavior rely on the teacher providing rewards or consequences to the student. Another set of strategies, far less teacher directed, involves having students take an active role in regulating their own behavior (Peterson, Young, Salzberg, West, & Hill, 2006). These strategies are preferred because they promote student independence by giving students skills they can use in many school settings and outside school as well (L. R. Johnson & C. E. Johnson, 1999). They have been used with very young children; with students who have learning disabilities, emotional disabilities, autism, and intellectual disabilities, as well as other special needs; and with a wide range of academic and social behaviors.

Cognitive Behavior Management Strategies

In **cognitive behavior management (CBM),** students are taught to monitor their own behavior, make judgments about its appropriateness, and change it as needed (for example, Gunter, Miller, Venn, Thomas, & House, 2002; Meichenbaum, 1977; Patton, Jolivette, & Ramsey, 2006). Many elements of CBM were introduced in Chapter 10 as a means of increasing student independence in academic learning and organization. In this chapter, they are applied to helping students manage their own classroom conduct and social behavior in a variety of situations. For example, Joseph, the student with a learning disability introduced at the beginning of this chapter, might be able to use CBM to manage his own classroom behavior. Two specific CBM strategies are commonly used to teach students how to manage their own behavior. These are self-monitoring and self-reinforcement.

> In cognitive behavior management (CBM), students are taught to monitor their own behavior, make judgments about its appropriateness, and change it as needed.

● **Self-Monitoring**   Students learn to monitor and record their own behavior in *self-monitoring*. For example, a student might keep a daily tally of the number of assignments completed or the number of times he waited until the teacher was between instructional groups to ask a question. A student might also use self-monitoring to monitor the rate at which she completes and turns in homework assignments or any other behavior (Daly & Ranalli, 2003; Toney, Kelley, & Lanclos, 2003). Students with more advanced skills could even wear headphones to listen to an audiotape with prerecorded signals and record whether they are on task at the sound of each tone. Students also can self-record their nonacademic behaviors. For instance, they can tally the number of times they leave their seat without permission or ask permission before leaving the classroom.

● **Self-Reinforcement**   Another CBM strategy, *self-reinforcement,* often is used in conjunction with self-monitoring. In this approach, students self-evaluate and then judge whether they have earned a reward. For example, Eric might award himself three points for a high self-monitoring score, two points for an average score, and no points for a low score. When he accumulates 20 points, he chooses a reward from his personal reinforcement menu. His favorite reward might be working on a timeline for critical events of the 20th century. The teacher periodically checks the accuracy of Eric's self-evaluation and self-reinforcement. He earns a bonus point for being accurate in his assessment of himself, even if that assessment is occasionally negative. If Eric has to give himself no points for a low score and his teacher checks his accuracy that day, he receives a bonus point because he accurately assessed his work.

Teaching Cognitive Behavior Management Strategies

Generally, teaching a CBM strategy to a student with special needs involves three main steps:

1. *Discuss the strategy with the student and present a rationale for its use.* If you cannot clarify for the student what the strategy is or how it works, he might not be a good candidate for CBM. To check understanding, ask the student to explain the approach back to you. You can even summarize the goal of the strategy and the rewards and consequences in a contract.

2. *Model for the student what you expect.* For example, you might use an old sample of the student's work and walk through the strategy you plan to use, such as showing the amount of completed work that represents a high score or a low score. Alternatively, you might use a brief role-play to demonstrate to the student how to self-monitor behavior and record it.

3. *Provide practice and feedback.* For this step, the teacher rewards the student for correctly using the strategy until the student is confident enough to use it without such support. If you are teaching a student to use CBM, use reinforcers with the student until she has mastered the strategy. Even after mastery, it is helpful to reward the student periodically for successfully self-managing behavior. This step can be enhanced by helping the student develop a personal reinforcement menu so rewards are meaningful. Parents and colleagues sometimes can assist in implementing this step.

Although CBM is not appropriate for every student behavior problem, it has the advantage of teaching a student to monitor and take responsibility for his own behavior. Because of increased student responsibility, cognitive behavior management is a far more effective long-term strategy for some students than are more traditional classroom rewards. Students can transfer self-management strategies to other classrooms and teachers and even into adult life. By collaborating with special education teachers and other school professionals, you can design a CBM program that truly makes a difference in a student's life.

Analyze and Reflect

How can the steps in the INCLUDE process guide your responses to questions regarding classroom management and student behavior issues?

Building Teaching Skills Simulation Exercise

Go to the Building Teaching Skills section in Chapter 12 of MyEducationLab for two simulations that will give you an overview of behavior management plans and take you step by step through developing the first three parts of a plan you can use.

Summary

Responding to student behavior begins with prevention: By setting clear expectations, fostering respect and communication, and establishing effective teaching methods, teachers can create a positive classroom learning environment that encourages appropriate behavior and discourages inappropriate behavior. Such basic techniques meet the needs of many students with and without disabilities. In addition, you can use simple group techniques, such as a token economy, to promote positive student behavior. One systematic approach for addressing prevention as well as the more intensive interventions needed by some students is called *positive behavioral interventions and supports (PBIS)*.

For students needing additional behavior supports, using low-intrusion strategies such as "catch 'em being good," grouping students, and managing surface behaviors can help prevent minor behavior problems from becoming serious ones. However, when such strategies are inadequate, you may find it necessary to participate in functional behavior assessment (FBA) with your team to prepare and follow a behavior intervention plan (BIP) tailored to the student's needs. Such a plan may be part of the IEP if the need arises for any student with a disability. A behavior intervention plan may include one or many strategies for increasing desirable student behavior (for example, reinforcement) or decreasing undesirable student behavior (for example, extinction, removal punishment). It also may be presented to the student in the form of a behavior contract. For some students, cognitive behavior management strategies such as self-monitoring and self-reinforcement also can be employed.

Back to the Cases

This section provides opportunities for you to apply the knowledge gained in this chapter to the cases described at the beginning of this chapter. The questions and activities that follow demonstrate how these standards and principles, along with other concepts that you have learned about in this chapter, connect to the everyday activities of all teachers.

Joseph, as you may remember, seems to have given up trying to learn. Mrs. Akers is sure that Joseph has the potential to be successful in her class. In addition, she is concerned that her attitude toward his behavior has limited her ability to support his needs. Based on her concern and desire to help him achieve, Mrs. Akers has spent several hours reading about behavior management techniques and discussing Joseph's individual needs with the special education teacher. She has decided that using a token economy will work best in her high school class, because she can reward all the students who do well. She requests your help. (INTASC Principles 5.04 and 5.05; and CEC Content Standards 5 and 9.) Her questions are these:

- What behaviors should I target with all students that would be most helpful with Joseph?
- What currency would be most appropriate for adolescents? (Make a list of those items that you think would be most motivational to adolescents.)
- How can I explain this to the students in a way that will motivate Joseph to participate?

Katie, as you may recall, frequently disrupts the class. Her behavior is hampering her successful inclusion in Mr. Lowell's sixth-grade class. Mr. Lowell will meet tomorrow with teachers from the sixth-grade team, the special education teacher, Katie's mother, her paraprofessional, and Katie. They will discuss a plan to use CBM to teach Katie more age-appropriate behaviors for school and to reinforce those behaviors at home. As a member of the team, you have been asked to come to the meeting with your written responses to the following concerns. (Of course, the team will want to hear your rationale for all of your answers.) (INTASC Principles 5.02, 5.04, and 5.05; and CEC Content Standards 5 and 8.)

- What behavior(s) will you target first? If you have identified more than one behavior, list the behaviors in order of priority.
- What schedule of reinforcement do you believe is most appropriate to begin this management plan?
- What reinforcer(s) do you suggest for Katie?
- How would you teach Katie to self-monitor this behavior?

Ms. Wright has discovered that Jaden's behavior is more difficult than she had imagined, but she cannot allow Jaden's behavior to continue, and action must be taken. She is aware that there are five simple and effective responses to student behavior, but she is not sure which to use. She has asked you to list the pros and cons for using each of the five responses with Jaden. (INTASC Principles 5.04 and 5.05; and CEC Content Standards 5 and 9.) In addition, she is particularly interested in which of the techniques for managing surface behaviors you would recommend. Include the rationales for all of your decisions.

Key Terms and Concepts

Behavior contract (p. 472)

Behavior intervention plan (BIP) (p. 461)

Cognitive behavior management (CBM) (p. 474)

Differential reinforcement of incompatible behaviors (p. 469)

Discipline (p. 440)

Extinction (p. 469)

Functional behavior assessment (FBA) (p. 451)

Negative reinforcement (p. 465)

Positive behavioral interventions and supports (PBIS) (p. 441)

Positive reinforcement (p. 464)

Presentation punishment (p. 471)

Removal punishment (p. 469)

Response cost (p. 469)

Surface behaviors (p. 450)

Time-out (p. 469)

Token economy (p. 447)

PEARSON myeducationlab
Where the Classroom Comes to Life

Now go to the Friend and Bursuck, Fifth Edition, MyEducationLab course at www.myeducationlab.com to

- take a pretest to assess your initial comprehension of the chapter content
- study chapter content with your individualized study plan
- take a posttest to assess your understanding of chapter content
- engage in multimedia exercises to help you build a deeper and more applied understanding of chapter content

Applications in Teaching Practice

Developing Strategies for Responding to Individual Student Behavior

Ms. Bind teaches eighth-grade English. One of her students is Russell, a student identified as having a learning disability and behavior problems. Russell tends to be the class clown. He makes flippant remarks that border on being disrespectful of other students and Ms. Bind. He often is reprimanded for chatting with other students instead of listening and then complaining that he doesn't know how to do the assignment that was just explained. The other students generally like Russell, and they sometimes urge him to engage in more classroom antics.

   Ms. Bind is not alone in her concern about Russell's behavior. His other teachers report a similar pattern. All are concerned about his slipping grades and worry that in high school it will be difficult for him to get the adult supervision that has helped him be more successful in middle school. Ms. Bind's tally of classroom incidents from the last week suggests that Russell is reprimanded at least six times per class period. The reprimands tend to occur when the class is transitioning from one activity to another—for example, from a large-group lecture to an individual assignment. Ms. Bind also has noted that Russell brags about his friends in a gang and threatens to "get" other students with these friends.

Ms. Bind, special education teacher Mr. Clark, counselor Ms. Lassaux, and parent Ms. Pinelli have been meeting about Russell. The first step in their functional behavior assessment was to think about whether any simple strategies have been effective and about the intent of Russell's behavior. They decide that the behaviors he has been displaying probably have to do with seeking attention from both peers and teachers, but they conclude that current interventions are inadequate. Using observational data from the classroom and interview information from other teachers, the lunchroom supervisor, and Russell himself, they spend considerable time discussing what sources of appropriate attention are available to Russell, and they weigh the pros and cons of various alternatives for responding to Russell's behavior. They also engage in a conversation about the impact other students are having on maintaining Russell's behavior when they encourage him. Ms. Bind is convinced that if Russell's audience were not so attentive, many of his problems might take care of themselves.

Questions

1. What strategies could Ms. Bind and the other teachers use to address the group response to Russell's behavior? What cautions would you have for them in trying these strategies?

2. What simple strategies outlined early in this chapter could Ms. Bind use to help Russell behave more appropriately in class? For each strategy, identify potential positive outcomes that could occur, as well as potential problems.

3. What information about Russell do you think the team gathered? How can this information be used to help them create a behavior intervention plan?

4. What types of reinforcement might work for Russell? How can Ms. Bind decide which reinforcers to use if reinforcement is the strategy selected? Which types of reinforcers would you avoid in this case?

5. How might Russell respond to strategies designed to decrease his negative behavior? For example, how might he react if he receives a detention each time he disrupts class? What type of negative consequence is detention?

6. Will Russell likely be able to use cognitive behavior management? Why or why not? If you decided to try a CBM strategy, how would you go about it?

7. Alone or with classmates, draft a sample behavior intervention plan (BIP) for Russell. Be prepared to defend the information you create for it and the interventions you plan to implement.

8. How should Russell and his mother be involved in the discussion about his behavior? What contributions could each make?

Further Readings

Axelman, M. J. (2006). African American youth speak out about the making of safe high schools. *Preventing School Failure, 50*(4), 37–44.

> Based on interviews with students and information from the professional literature, this article discusses how well-intentioned educators may misinterpret the behavior of African American youth, especially in urban settings, leading to confrontation and student disenfranchisement. This article provides a great opportunity for discussion about cultural expectations of schools and their impact on some students.

Cameron, M. (2006). Managing school discipline and implications for school social workers: A review of the literature. *Children and Schools, 28,* 219–227.

This article provides a brief overview of common school discipline policies, including those related to student codes of conduct and corporal punishment. The author critiques these negative approaches to discipline and outlines a rationale for eliminating them and focusing instead on strategies that emphasize rewards and other positive outcomes.

Peck, A., & Scarpati, S. (Eds.). (2004). Using positive behavior support strategies [special issue]. *Teaching Exceptional Children, 37*(1), 7–62.

This special issue of a journal designed for teachers includes eight articles related to using positive behavior supports. Topics range from evaluating the school climate to decreasing acting-out behavior to using peer mentoring with high school students. The articles describe specific cases and interventions and include checklists and forms you can adapt for your own use.

Sprick, R. S. (2002). *Discipline in the secondary classroom: A problem-by-problem survival guide* (2nd ed.). San Francisco: Jossey-Bass.

This book provides a wealth of practical information for secondary teachers for creating an effective classroom management system, addressing everything from setting classroom expectations to establishing fair grading systems to specific strategies for responding to common student behavior problems. The book includes specific ideas for resolving 42 common student behavior issues.

Building Social Relationships

Objectives

After you read this chapter, you will be able to

1. Describe how children with and without disabilities interact with one another and how you can promote positive interactions among them.

2. Use a variety of strategies to promote friendship and social support between students with and without disabilities or other special needs.

3. Describe the characteristics of peer tutoring programs in inclusive schools and outline how to establish and maintain those programs.

4. Explain how to use cooperative learning strategies as a means of facilitating inclusive education.

5. Describe social skills needs of students with disabilities and explain how you can help to ensure that students learn these skills.

6. Analyze your responsibility for fostering positive social relationships among students with disabilities and their typical peers.

Tyler is a student at Winding Creek Elementary School, and he has a moderate intellectual disability. Beginning when he was 4 years old and attending an inclusive preschool program, his teachers have stressed the development of social skills and the importance of friendship. In kindergarten, Tyler's best friend was Nicholas, another child from the neighborhood, who would quickly explain, arm often draped around Tyler's shoulder, to anyone who seemed curious about the friendship: "Tyler lives down the street from me. Me and Tyler play together all the time, and we get to do sleepovers!" Now in fourth grade, Nicholas is still quick to protect Tyler and include him in neighborhood and school activities. Tyler also participates in a community soccer program with Nicholas, and he is a Boy Scout. Tyler's parents are firmly committed to his participation in general education and typical activities. They comment, "While we appreciate all the efforts of special educators, there is no 'special education' after high school. We want Tyler to learn as much as possible from his peers so he can get further as an adult and feel comfortable living in the regular world."

■ *Why is it important for teachers to deliberately address the social interactions of students with disabilities? What strategies can teachers use to foster friendships between students with and without disabilities? What are the roles of parents and families in fostering the development of their children's social skills and relationships?*

Kathleen and her eighth-grade social studies class are studying the effect of civil war on the citizens and economies of developing countries. Mr. Geib announces at the beginning of class that the students should move into teams for a cooperative assignment that will take the entire class period. The 32 students move their desks into groups and gather their materials. After being reminded that this is not visiting time, the students settle into groups of five or six. Kathleen's group has five members of varying abilities and skills. Behavior stemming from Kathleen's emotional disability usually is not evident in this group. Her peers do not respond to her teasing and inappropriate comments, and over time episodes of such misbehavior have become infrequent. Classmates assist Kathleen to be a constructive group member to help the team get extra points and a possible free pass on a future assignment. The two other students in the class who have identified disabilities are in two other groups. Mr. Geib distributes materials to the students and gives directions. When everyone is working, he goes from group to group, answering questions and helping students stay focused on their assignment.

■ *What is the impact of this type of grouping arrangement on student outcomes in a diverse classroom? Is it more or less effective than traditional instruction? How can Mr. Geib ensure that students share the assigned work, instead of just one or two students completing the assignment for everyone in their group? What is the social benefit of this classroom grouping arrangement?*

Demetrius has several goals on his individualized education program (IEP) this year, pertaining to learning social skills. Furthermore, his teachers and other service providers are committed to helping him interact more successfully with his peers and teachers. For example, as a junior with

Asperger syndrome who academically is near grade level, Demetrius often forgets to take into account the expressions on people's faces when he is talking with them. The result is that he sometimes keeps talking about a topic long after his friends are showing through their expressions that they are bored or frustrated. The counselor is working with Demetrius on this skill so he can effectively "read" the nonverbal communication of his friends and other students and teachers with whom he interacts. Demetrius is planning to work in a local printing shop when he completes high school next year, and so social skills for the work environment also are being stressed, including speaking in an appropriate voice, asking for assistance when needed, listening politely to others, and greeting others promptly so as not to imply ignoring them.

Why do social skills need to be taught specifically to many students with disabilities? How can social skills instruction be integrated into an inclusive classroom? What is the role of the general education teacher in teaching social skills to students with disabilities?

Current school reform initiatives—with their emphasis on academic accountability for all students, including those with disabilities and other special needs—clearly are influencing the current trends in inclusive education. However, another important dimension of educating students with disabilities with their nondisabled peers is related to the development of social skills and opportunities for socialization with typical peers (Chadsey & Han, 2005; Copeland et al., 2004; Dyson, 2005; King, 2005).

Many educators understand that students with disabilities and other exceptional needs learn appropriate social behaviors and develop friendships, collectively referred to as **social skills,** only when they have opportunities to interact with their nondisabled peers. At the same time, students without special needs learn that individuals with disabilities are people, and they develop sensitivity to people who may not be exactly like themselves along with a sense of social responsibility to include individuals with special needs in the classroom community.

How do the social benefits of inclusive education occur? As you may guess, simply integrating students with disabilities into a classroom is not enough. Physically placing students together does not teach students with disabilities the skills they may need, nor does it prepare students without disabilities to be respectful of their classmates with special needs. Especially in this era of extraordinary pressure related to raising students' academic achievement, you must be proactive to ensure that social benefits accrue to all students. Furthermore, if challenges arise—for example, students tease or bully their classmates or students continue to have difficulties in their social interactions with peers and adults—you have the responsibility to address these problems, enlisting the assistance of special educators, counselors, and others as necessary. This chapter provides several strategies that you can implement to build positive social relationships for all students in your classroom.

As you begin to think about the social dimension of inclusive education, keep in mind several ideas. First, although academics are your primary concern, equally important is your attention to helping all students, regardless of whether they have special needs, learn social skills. The degree of success that any student can achieve in adulthood often is determined largely by his ability to effectively interact with others. Because social

www.resources

The Smithsonian historical exhibit on the history of the disability rights movement includes a wealth of information about disability and has a section written expressly for children. You can access this valuable resource at http://americanhistory.si.edu/disabilityrights/exhibit_menu.html.

skills are so important, attention to them should begin at a very early age and continue throughout students' school years (Brophy-Herb, Lee, Nievar, & Stollak, 2007; Macy & Bricker, 2007). Second, you do not need to teach students social skills apart from the curriculum for which you will be responsible (Organ & Gonzalez-DeHass, 2004; Welton, Vakil, & Carasea, 2004). As you read this chapter, you will realize that many skills related to developing positive social relationships can be incorporated into your daily instruction, as Mr. Geib was doing in Kathleen's class. Third, the issue of social relationships should be an integral part of your classroom expectations. Remember that for some students, the social component of their education is a primary classroom goal, even if academic goals are significantly adapted. For example, Tyler's IEP includes several goals related to peer interactions and the development of friendships; the purpose of his being in fourth grade has as much to do with learning important life social skills, such as talking to peers and participating in group activities, as it does with learning arithmetic skills. Kathleen is learning how to be a member of a group without being disruptive. For Demetrius, however, academic and social goals are equally important. One of your responsibilities as a teacher in an inclusive classroom is to clarify these expectations with special educators.

Finally, be aware that some students with disabilities may have goals on their IEPs related to social skills. These might include skills such as making eye contact, initiating conversations, asking questions, and using assistive technology to communicate with peers and teachers. Your responsibility is to help address such goals, not by stopping instruction to focus on them but to incorporate strategies into your classroom teaching and learning activities.

What Is Your Role in Promoting Positive Social Interactions among Students with and without Disabilities?

A beginning point for creating a classroom in which students understand, appreciate, support, and interact respectfully with each other is studying what is known about children's social interactions. This knowledge provides a basis for thinking about how to group students and supervise their interactions to accomplish the social goals of inclusion.

Research on social relationships and interactions among students with and without disabilities has been ongoing almost since special education programs began in public schools (Bennett, 1932). During the 1950s and 1960s, researchers studied the social adjustment and acceptance by peers of students with intellectual disabilities. Sometimes they found that students in special education classes had better social adjustment than similar students in general education classes (Cassidy & Stanton, 1959). Other times they found few differences (Blatt, 1958). More consistent were the findings on students' peer acceptance: Researchers found that students with intellectual disabilities were less often accepted and more often rejected by their peers than students without disabilities (Johnson & Kirk, 1950; R. V. Miller, 1956).

When mainstreaming became an important trend during the 1970s, additional studies were completed to help educators understand the social needs of students with disabilities in general education settings. What became clear was that placing students with disabilities, especially those with intellectual disabilities, in classrooms with nondisabled peers did not by itself ensure that positive social relationships would develop. In fact, the opposite was true. Students in classes with mainstreamed peers generally disliked the students with disabilities or did not accept them (Goodman, Gottlieb, & Harrison, 1972; Iano et al., 1974). In attempting to identify why these consistent negative findings occurred, many different characteristics of students with disabilities were examined, including academic potential, label, age, gender, behavior, and physical appearance. Also studied were the ways in which students received special education services, teachers' behaviors, the amount of time students spent in mainstream classrooms, and the types of interactions among students with and without disabilities. The picture that emerged was not clear. Many characteristics and other factors seemed to contribute to student social problems, but none was singularly important.

As students with disabilities in today's schools rightfully have come to spend more and more time in general education classrooms, attention has focused once again on the interactions between these students and their classmates without disabilities. Although some studies have continued to confirm earlier research suggesting that students with disabilities experience difficulty in being socially accepted by peers (for example, de Boo & Prins, 2007; Doré, Dion, Wagner, & Brunet, 2002; Fusell, Macias, & Saylor, 2005), other studies have suggested a more positive outlook. For instance, although Freeman and Alkin (2000) found that the social acceptance ratings for students with intellectual disabilities in general education settings were not as high as those for typical learners, they were higher than those for students with intellectual disabilities in separate special education classrooms. Yet other research has found a mixed picture. When Pavri and Monda-Amaya (2001) interviewed elementary students with learning disabilities and their general and special education teachers about school social interactions, they found that students felt they were part of the social network at school. However, the students also experienced loneliness at times. Further, the teachers tended to foster social interactions by using teacher-directed interventions, such as arranging peer tutoring (discussed later in this chapter), even though students preferred to try to address social situations on their own. This complex picture of students' social relationships suggests that simply mixing students with and without disabilities in single classrooms may not result in an integrated social system for them (Copeland et al., 2004; Odom, Zercher, Li, Marquart, Sandall, & Brown, 2006). Especially as students move from elementary school and into middle and high school, social interactions in school—with peers as well as teachers—may need to be nurtured. The Professional Edge provides the perspective of middle school students on this important topic.

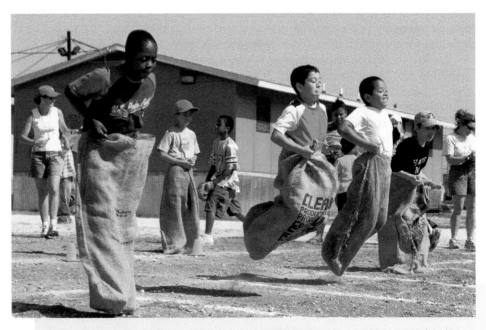

What is the teacher's role in creating opportunities for students' social interactions?

Middle School Students Speak Out about Friendship with Students with Disabilities

What strategies should teachers use to foster the social inclusion of students with disabilities? Chadsey and Han (2005) decided that the best way to answer that question was to ask students directly. The 33 middle school students who were interviewed offered these ideas:

- Segregation is unfair. Put students with disabilities in our classrooms more often. If they need extra help, provide them with extra help in our classes; don't put them in separate classes.

- Teachers should come into classes to give us more information about students with disabilities. Tell us why they might act differently or have trouble learning. Tell us how they are the same as us.

- Don't let students make fun of students with disabilities. Give us a reason to be nice to students with disabilities. Praise students with disabilities in the classroom so we know you think they are doing a good job.

- Create programs where both students with and without disabilities can hang out with each other. Don't always have us teach them; create programs that are fun for all of us.

- Use volunteer peer partners. Let us be buddies. Make sure only nice students are volunteers.

- Group students with disabilities into our social networks. It's better to include students with disabilities in our groups rather than pair them alone with us. Also include them in groups with popular kids.

- Have students with disabilities tell us about their disabilities. If we know more about a disability, from the student himself or herself, then we will likely feel more positive.

- Clubs and after-school activities should include kids with disabilities and should be of interest to everyone. Students with disabilities should be included in our extracurricular activities after school—not everything should occur during school hours.

- Let students with disabilities take the same bus as us. Some of our busses should be made accessible so all of us can attend after-school activities.

Source: From "Friendship-Facilitation Strategies: What Do Students in Middle School Tell Us?" by J. Chadsey and K. G. Han, 2005, *Teaching Exceptional Children, 38*(2), pp. 52–57. Copyright 2005 by the Council for Exceptional Children. Reprinted with permission.

The fact that student social relationships might not occur spontaneously does not mean that inclusive practices are unsuccessful. What it does mean is that teachers have a significant responsibility to ensure that peer relationships grow (for example, Harlacher, Roberts, & Merrell, 2006). Many professionals have been working to develop strategies to help accomplish this. Generally, these strategies can be grouped into three categories: creating opportunities for students with and without disabilities to have meaningful face-to-face interactions, nurturing support and friendship between students with and without disabilities, and providing positive role models.

Creating Opportunities for Social Interactions

The first component in promoting positive interactions among students with and without disabilities is to provide opportunities for them to interact. In both elementary and secondary classrooms and regardless of the academic content being addressed, this means structuring activities and assigning students to groups so that interacting becomes part of classroom instruction, as was accomplished in Mr. Geib's classroom described at the beginning of this chapter. Arranging service-learning activities in which students with and without disabilities all participate is another way to encourage interactions (Kleinert et al.,

Research Note

Although paraprofessionals have good intentions, they may actually cause harm when they hover around students with disabilities instead of fostering their social interactions with classmates (Cautson-Theoharis & Malmgrem, 2005). Teachers should monitor for this problem and directly address it.

2007; Scott, 2006). For instance, students might work together to pick up debris from a local park, visit a senior citizen center, or contact local government officials to support a new recycling initiative.

Creating special programs is another way to accomplish the goal of meaningful interactions. For example, in one high school, peer buddies were assigned to provide students with significant intellectual disabilities with more and better opportunities to participate in general education classes (Copeland et al., 2004). In this program, students without disabilities were partnered with students with disabilities to provide academic and social support. Data from group interviews of participating nondisabled students suggested that these students identified many ways that their classmates with disabilities were socially isolated in schools. They also learned that they could foster social interaction by advocating for their buddies, facilitating interactions with other students, and modeling appropriate social interactions.

Yet another way to encourage interaction among students is through nonacademic activities. For example, Kleinert, Miracle, and Sheppard-Jones (2006) surveyed teachers of students with significant disabilities and found that general education teachers often were mentioned as being significant in supporting student participation in activities such as youth organizations and other extracurricular activities, including those associated with faith-based organizations.

You may be able to identify many other strategies for fostering interactions between students with and without disabilities, interactions that build positive social relationships. How could you do this in an elementary classroom? A middle school class? A high school class? In a nonacademic setting? Even a small amount of attention on your part in arranging such interactions can have a significant benefit for all your students.

Nurturing Support and Friendship

Arranging student interactions is a start, but it is not enough. The second component in building social relationships is to nurture mutual support and friendship between students with and without disabilities. They following sections describe several examples of programs and strategies for accomplishing this goal.

● **Circle of Friends** One specific program with demonstrated effectiveness in promoting friendships is **Circle of Friends** (Demchak, n.d.; Forest, Pierpoint, & O'Brien, 1996). When a new student, especially one with many special needs, joins a class group, the students in the group learn to build a circle of friends around that student. As part of this process, each student reviews her own circle of friends by drawing four concentric circles around a figure representing herself. The first circle contains closest friends, such as family members. The second circle contains others close to the student, such as neighbors and family friends. The third circle contains acquaintances, such as members of the student's soccer team. The outer circle contains people paid to help, such as teachers and camp counselors. The purpose of this step in the activity is to help students understand how many people are part of their lives.

Students then are shown the circles of a person with only a few names inserted and are asked how they would feel and act if their circles had so few entries. Next a classmate with a disability is mentioned as possibly having few names in his circles. Students generate ideas of how they could become part of that classmate's circle of friends. Students who do become part of their classmate's circle meet regularly to discuss their friendship with that student. This structured friendship-building strategy has been demonstrated effective for fostering appropriate social interactions between students with and without disabilities, an effect that extends beyond the planned meetings to the entire school day (Kalyva & Avramidis, 2005; Miller, Cooke, Test, & White, 2003).

> Creating special programs is another way to accomplish the goal of meaningful interactions.

Article Homework Exercise

Go to the Homework and Exercises section in Chapter 13 of MyEducationLab for some facts and myths about bullying as well as a prevention program.

fyi

Although friendship is a naturally occurring part of life for most people, many students with disabilities find it difficult to make and keep friends (Dopp & Block, 2004).

486   **Chapter 13**   Building Social Relationships

● **General Friendship-Building Strategies**   Many general strategies can be used to nurture friendships among the students you teach. For example, teachers of elementary students might consider incorporating friendship skills into their instruction (Bovey & Strain, 2003). A teacher might discuss during morning circle time how to get a friend's attention or ask a friend for help. Enlisting the help of students who have these skills, the teacher can use role-playing to teach the skills to the class as a whole. As the day progresses, the teacher can point out students acting like friends in their interactions and reward the group for their positive behaviors. In particular, the teacher could direct Cami, a student with a learning disability, to ask Terri, a classmate with similar interests, for assistance with an assignment. This informal teaching and prompting can facilitate the development of positive interactions and friendships. By teaching students how to greet one another, express friendship, and resolve conflicts, teachers can foster positive peer relationships and provide students with a strong basis for lifelong interaction skills. You can learn more about teaching friendship skills to students in the following Professional Edge.

Another general strategy for fostering support and friendships is making slight changes in activities to encourage the participation of students with disabilities (Turnbull, Percira, & Blue-Banning, 2000). In Ms. Kerner's civics class, for example, students were asked to choose from among several civic organizations they might like to research. Instead of working independently, students who chose the same organizations were grouped and encouraged to use print, Internet, and other resources to complete the project. By intentionally placing students in groups, Ms. Kerner increased the participation of students with disabilities with classmates.

● **Resolving Support and Friendship Problems**   Sometimes you have to address problems related to student support and friendship, particularly for students whose IEPs contain significant accommodations and modifications. Some students (and some teachers too) express concern about the fairness of making these adjustments for students with special needs, including changing the consequences for misbehavior, altering the amount or type of work expected, grading on a more generous scale, and using rewards to which other students may not have access. The Professional Edge on page 490 offers advice about responding to issues of fairness.

● **Parents and Friendship**   As you work to foster positive social interactions and friendships between students with and without disabilities, keep in mind that parents play a key role in this part of their children's lives (Taub, 2006). For example, parents of students with disabilities can provide information about their children's communication strategies and make suggestions about including them in classroom activities. Parents also can be very effective in exposing their children with special needs to a wide variety of individuals who may become friends (Geisthardt, Brotherson, & Cook, 2002). You also may find that parents of students without disabilities may take active steps to foster friendships with classmates with special needs because of the importance they place on helping their children understand the value of each person's abilities. Parents also may contribute in small but meaningful ways by providing transportation to recreational activities after school hours, arranging birthday parties and other social functions for students at their homes, and volunteering to lead school activities that bring students together for social interactions (for example, clubs).

Keep in mind, though, that parents' perspectives on their children's friendships may be influenced by their cultures. For example, in one study of friendship between Hispanic children with disabilities and children without disabilities, the researchers found that although parents valued friendship development for their children with disabilities, the time parents spent facilitating those friendships sometimes was perceived as time taken away from highly valued extended-family interactions (Turnbull, Blue-Banning, & Pereira, 2000). Another finding was that children's friends often were their cousins or other relatives. You can review many of the suggestions presented throughout this textbook for working effectively with families in the Working Together.

Case Study Homework Exercise

Go to the Homework and Exercises section in Chapter 13 of MyEducationLab to learn about effectively monitoring discussions that take place during small group work.

esearch Note

Woods and Poulson (2006) successfully taught students with developmental delays to initiate interactions with peers by teaching them scripts of how to carry out this basic social skill.

Professional EDGE

Teaching Students How to Make Friends

As a teacher, you will use many informal strategies to nurture friendships among students. For a few students, you may collaborate with a special educator or counselor in using a formal instructional package that builds student social skills. However, a third option also exists. Particularly with elementary students, you may decide to teach friendship skills directly using these steps:

1. *Identify someone to whom you can introduce yourself.* Students should examine their surroundings and find someone with whom they would like to play or talk. Students should be given examples of how people look when they want to play or talk. To illustrate, the teacher can use pictures of students engaging in a variety of activities—for example, a student finishing a homework assignment, a student coloring alone, a student with a sad face, and a student with a happy face.

2. *Smile and approach the person.* The teacher should model walking up to someone with a smile on her face. Students should practice this while approaching a peer.

3. *Introduce yourself.* Students should say their names, ask the other person his name, and look at the person and smile. The teacher should continue modeling.

4. *Ask open-ended questions to get and give information.* Students can ask the other student what he is playing

with, what's happening, and so forth. Students need to know that *open-ended questions* have answers of more than two or three words. Students should remember to look at the person and smile. The teacher now can ask two students to model for the class, or the teacher can continue modeling. A list of questions can be provided for the students if they are able to read, or the teacher can provide questioning prompts. This step will depend on the level of the students.

5. *Suggest something to play or do together.* Students should find some activity or game to play on the playground, during free time, or during passing period. The teacher can prompt pairs to engage in an activity and provide ideas for students so their interaction will continue.

Once students have learned these skills, you can provide them with simple reminder cards with words and/or pictures so they can practice on their own. Teaching these steps will be even more effective if you use children's literature to illustrate how friends are made. Some books about making friends include the following:

Books for Students Preschool through Middle School

- Aliki, *We Are Best Friends*
- Anglund, J. W., *A Friend Is Someone Who Likes You*

Providing Positive Role Models

A third component of promoting positive peer relationships is offering positive role models. There are several ways to do this. First, as a teacher in an inclusive school, you might be the most influential model for students learning how to interact with a peer with a disability. If you are positive in your interactions and avoid responding to a student with a disability as a "guest" instead of a full classroom member, students will respond in kind. For example, if you talk to a student with a severe disability as though he were a very young child, even though you are teaching an eighth-grade class, other students probably will treat the student as a young child too. However, if you speak in an age-appropriate voice, so will your students. Similarly, if you expect a student with a learning disability to behave similarly to other students instead of making exceptions (provided that this expectation is appropriate), peers in the class will have the same expectations. Interacting with students with disabilities in the same way that you interact with everyone else provides the modeling that helps shape all student interactions.

Students without disabilities also need to see that students with disabilities and other special needs have many contributions to make. Pointing out contributions made by students with disabilities, giving them standard classroom responsibilities, and recognizing their best efforts regardless of whether they fit within traditional curriculum standards—all

- Barkin, J. C., & James, E., *Are We Still Best Friends?*

- Berenstain, S., & Berenstain, J., *The Berenstain Bears and the Trouble with Friends*

- Cohen, M., *Will I Have a Friend?*

- Crary, E., *I Want to Play*

- De Regniers, B. S., *May I Bring a Friend?*

- Holabird, K., *Angelina and Alice*

- Iwasaki, C., *Will You Be My Friend?*

- Lystad, M., *That New Boy*

- Moncure, J. B., *A New Boy in Kindergarten*

- Prather, R., *New Neighbors*

- Robinson, N. K., *Wendy and the Bullies*

- Stevenson, J., *Fast Friends: Two Stories*

- Viorst, J., *Rosie and Michael*

Books for Students Middle School through High School

- Arrick, F., *What You Don't Know Can Kill You*

- Bauer, J., *Thwonk!*

- Creech, S., *Absolutely Normal Chaos*

- Draper, S., *Tears of a Tiger*

- Kindl, P., *Owl in Love*

- Lester, J., *Othello*

- Lowry, L., *The Giver*

- Mahy, M., *The Catalogue of the Universe*

- McDaniel, L., *Now I Lay Me Down to Sleep*

- Myers, W. D., *Darnell Rock Reporting*

- Naylor, P. R., *Shiloh*

- Wiethorn, R. J., *Rock Finds a Friend*

- Wolff, V. E., *Make Lemonade*

- Woodson, J., *I Hadn't Meant to Tell You This*

- Zolotow, C., *The New Friend*

Sources: Adapted from Madison Public Library, "Friends Like These . . . Books for Young Teens about Friendship," retrieved March 15, 2005, from www.madisonpubliclibrary.org/youth/booklists/friends.html; and "Friendship and Stories: Using Children's Literature to Teach Friendship Skills to Children with Learning Disabilities" [electronic version], by K. L. DeGeorge, 1998, *Intervention in School and Clinic, 33,* pp. 157–162. Copyright © 1998 by the Hammill Institute on Disabilities. Reprinted with permission.

these actions lead peers to recognize that students with special needs are valuable classroom community members. Family, community, and national support groups also can be resources for providing positive role models.

Promoting positive peer relationships needs to be part of your automatic teaching behavior throughout the school year. Evidence suggests that a long-term approach for fostering peer interactions is most effective and that when teachers stop attending to students' social relationships, those relationships tend to deteriorate (Freeman & Alkin, 2000; Maag, 2005).

How Can You Provide Education about Individuals with Disabilities?

Besides promoting positive social interactions between students with and without disabilities, teachers play an important role in educating their students about all types of differences among individuals, including disabilities. Even during years in which you have few

On the Issue of Fairness

Many teachers struggle in deciding how to respond to students who claim that something in class is not fair—whether it is the fact that two students receive the same amount of credit for doing very different types of work; that several students take their tests in a small-group, separate setting with extra adult assistance available; or that one student's misbehavior results in a warning whereas another's results in a trip to the office. Although there are no easy solutions to these problems, Welch (2000) suggests the following strategies:

- Reflect back a student's feelings, perhaps by asking the student to write you a note about his or her perspective on the issue.

- Listen for other meanings in students' comments because their complaints may be disguised requests for increased teacher attention.

- Offer something special to young children for hard work. If one student is receiving stickers, also offer them to a complaining student, but only for "extra hard" work.

- Respond to students' fairness complaints consistently and without explanation. Legally and ethically, you may not discuss one student's work with another student; your response should convey this unambiguously: "You know I won't talk to you about anyone's work but your own. How can I help you to do your work?"

- Teach students about three types of fairness: equality (everyone gets the same thing), equity (reward is based on contribution), and need (reward is greatest to those with the greatest need).

- Establish a procedure such as class meetings by which students can discuss their concerns about fairness.

- Develop a caring, cooperative classroom community using strategies suggested throughout this textbook and especially in this chapter.

- Provide and enforce schoolwide procedures related to fairness so that a consistent approach is used on the playground and in the cafeteria, gym, hallways, and other locations where fairness may become an issue.

- Clarify within yourself your legal and moral obligation to make accommodations for students with disabilities.

- Occasionally, a student has a legitimate concern about fairness. It is just as important to know when and how to push a student with a disability to do more as it is to know when to make accommodations.

Ultimately, issues about fairness will be minimal if you make it clear in your classroom—whether you teach students who are 5 years old or 15 years old—that students learn at different rates and in different ways and that the job of the teacher is to help all students by adapting schoolwork to their needs.

Source: Adapted from "Responding to Student Concerns about Fairness," by A. Welch, 2000, *Teaching Exceptional Children, 33*(2), pp. 36–40. Reprinted with permission.

---

*R*esearch Note

Kolb and Hanley-Maxwell (2003) interviewed the parents of adolescents with disabilities. They learned that the parents believed that the teenage years are crucial for learning social skills and that getting along, including forming friendships and other relationships, is integral to their children's development.

or no students with disabilities in your class, you can positively affect student understanding and attitudes toward individuals with disabilities by incorporating information about them into your curriculum. This section describes three strategies for doing so: informing students through direct instruction, using video and print media, and demonstrating and using adaptive technology. The Case in Practice demonstrates the strong need for school-based disability awareness and sensitivity training to be embedded in a general program of fostering respect for diversity.

Informing through Direct Instruction

One of the most straightforward strategies for teaching students about individuals with disabilities is to provide them with relevant information. For example, you might invite guest speakers to your class to discuss what it is like to have a disability and how people with disabilities lead successful lives. Alternatively, you might arrange to have professionals who provide services to individuals with disabilities talk about their

Working TOGETHER

Collaborating with Families

Parents are your partners in fostering the development of students' social skills. Parents know their children in ways that educators cannot, and they have at heart their children's best interests. Whether you are addressing a social skills concern, an academic achievement matter, or any other topic related to any of your students, think about these questions as you prepare to interact with parents:

- Do I use effective communication strategies in my interactions with families?
- Do I take into account families' preferences based on their cultures?
- Do I avoid using jargon?
- Do I define unfamiliar terms?
- Do I use good listening skills, such as clarifying, paraphrasing, and summarizing?
- Do I attend to the nonverbal communication of parents and family members?
- Do I collaborate with families during IEP meetings?
- Do I seek verbal and written input from families regarding their children in my classroom?
- Do I inform the families of students with disabilities about student progress at least as often as the families of students without disabilities?
- Do I value the contributions of parents and family members?
- Do I base all interactions on the assumption that parents want what they believe is best for their children?

- Do I acknowledge the strengths and coping strategies families have developed for working with children with disabilities?
- Do I recognize the contributions of members of extended families?
- Do I provide opportunities for families to be involved in the classroom and school in meaningful ways?
- Do I try to develop collaborative relationships with families?
- Do I see the contributions of families as equal in value to the contributions of school staff?
- Do I try to identify goals that are shared between the school and families?
- Do I recognize that the school and families share responsibility for student outcomes?
- Do I demonstrate caring and concern for students and their families?
- Do I get to know my students with disabilities in ways unrelated to their disabilities?
- Do I schedule meetings at times that are convenient for families?
- Do I help families access additional resources in the community when needed?
- Do I treat family members as I would want to be treated?

Source: From "Collaborating with Families Checklist," by the Training and Technical Assistance Center, College of William and Mary, 2002. Retrieved February 11, 2005, from www.wm.edu/ttac/articles/family/collab2.html. Reprinted with permission.

---

careers. You also can find individuals to speak to your students through local disability advocacy groups or parent groups. A local college or university also might be a valuable resource.

In addition, you can educate students about disabilities by incorporating relevant topics into the curriculum. As you teach, you can mention famous individuals with disabilities who have contributed to various fields. For example, when studying the presidents, you can mention the fact that Franklin D. Roosevelt had polio and used a wheelchair. With older students, you can explore the reasons controversy arose about whether a statue of this president should depict him in a wheelchair. In science, you can explain Thomas Edison's hearing loss and Albert Einstein's alleged learning disability. In the fine arts, examples of individuals with disabilities include actor Christopher Reeve, singer Ray Charles, and composer Ludwig van Beethoven.

Case in Practice

Intervening to Promote Positive Social Interactions

Ms. Giano, a middle school teacher, is in a quandary. This afternoon she received a phone call from Ms. Perez concerning Jesse, her son. Ms. Perez related that Jesse had come home from school looking disheveled and with torn books and papers. At first he wouldn't tell his mother what had happened, but eventually he related the story. Jesse has albinism. He has very little pigment in his skin, hair, and eyes. His skin is very pale, and his hair seems almost white. In addition, Jesse has a serious vision problem related to his albinism, and he also has been identified as having a learning disability. He told his mother that several of his classmates had begun making fun of him on the walk to the bus and then continued on the bus. They had been doing this almost since the beginning of the school year, but things had been getting worse lately. Today, Jesse explained, he couldn't stand it anymore and he lunged at the boys. The bus driver intervened, but all the boys now were to be brought back to school by their parents for fighting.

Ms. Perez was upset. She also mentioned to Ms. Giano that Jesse had asked her not to call school, that he would deal with the situation and accept the discipline for fighting

on the bus. He was afraid that his classmates' teasing would become even worse if it was made an issue. Ms. Perez is not satisfied; she wants something done to stop the teasing and protect her son. She is concerned that Jesse is becoming discouraged and has read about the association between such teasing and depression, especially among middle and high school students.

REFLECTIONS

How does this story relate to the topic of bullying? If you were Ms. Giano, what would you say to Ms. Perez? What is the role of the general education teachers in ensuring that students are treated respectfully? How would you address this issue with Jesse? With the other boys? If you think they should have an additional consequence, what should it be? What might you try as an all-homeroom activity to foster better understanding among your diverse students? Would your response to the situation and interventions be significantly different if you plan to teach elementary students? High school students? How so?

Students' understanding of and respect for individuals with disabilities are fostered more through an ongoing education program than through occasional special events that highlight this topic. For example, if your school participates in an ongoing program to increase students' understanding of racial, cultural, religious, and other types of diversity, disability awareness should be included as another type of diversity.

Using Video and Print Media

Individuals with disabilities have been portrayed in print and other media for many years, but a shift gradually has occurred in the nature of that portrayal. Instead of being viewed as victims or objects of pity, people with disabilities now often are central characters, and having a disability is just one dimension of their roles. A trip to your local library or video store or a casual reading of a television program guide or newspaper can lead you to a wealth of information, as can a quick search about this topic on the Internet. You can identify media that relate to your instructional goals, find ways to incorporate them into your lessons, and arrange discussions so your students feel free to ask questions and share their insights.

www.resources

Recreation and leisure are an important part of everyone's life and a vehicle for social relationships. You can learn about one recreational opportunity for people with disabilities by visiting the website of Alpine Alternatives, at www.alpinealternatives.org.

Your school or district might have educational videos about students with disabilities that are designed specifically for school-age children. Many award-winning movies also address disability and are appropriate for older students. These films include *Radio, My Left Foot, Rain Man, As Good as It Gets, Mr. Holland's Opus, The Kid and I, Born on the Fourth of July, The Miracle Worker, If You Could See What I Hear, Mask, Children of a Lesser God, Forrest Gump,* and *Shine* (Disability Films, 2007). Television shows and made-for-TV movies (for example, *Wit, Suddenly*) also address disability topics.

Books are written by and for children about virtually every type of disability and other special need. Reading or assigning an appropriate book to your class can be an excellent strategy for introducing a new student and his special needs or for promoting awareness. A reading assignment also can help open up a discussion about interacting with and treating classmates respectfully. Consider these four criteria in selecting children's literature that addresses disability (Smith-Arrezzo, 2003):

1. The structural elements of the book should be well developed.

2. The book should be appealing to children, with the characters with disabilities portrayed in realistic ways.

3. The book should have a positive emotional tone.

4. The book should present information about special education accurately.

Newspapers carry stories about individuals with disabilities, requirements of the Americans with Disabilities Act, and trends toward inclusive education. National newspapers, such as *USA Today,* the *New York Times,* and the *Wall Street Journal,* are good sources of this type of information, but local newspapers also carry stories you can use. For example, when a major league baseball player had a seizure during a ball game, a local newspaper ran a story on what to do when someone is having a seizure. The high-interest article became a valuable teaching tool for sports-minded middle school students.

How do students without disabilities learn about their peers with disabilities? How can teachers promote friendships between students with and without exceptionalities?

Demonstrating and Using Adaptive Technology

Another means of educating students about individuals with disabilities is exploring technology resources (Behrmann & Jerome, 2002). For example, you can teach students about the powerful tools available to facilitate communication, including touch screens, talking word processors, customized computer keyboards, computer voice input, and word-prediction programs. You can demonstrate for students the capabilities of talking computers, calculators, and watches. You also can engage students in learning about low-tech devices such as talking watches and no-tech items such as pencil grips and study carrels. Students using assistive technology can demonstrate their equipment for classmates, thus educating peers but at the same time creating an opportunity for social interactions.

*H*ow Can You Develop and Support Peer Tutoring?

Students also learn about disabilities and other special needs through direct experience and structured interactions with classmates. **Peer tutoring** is a system of instruction in which pairs of students with relatively equal standing are given formal roles for promoting each other's achievement (Bond & Castagnera, 2006; Ryan, Reid, & Epstein, 2004). The tutor role most often is held by a peer in the same class, school, or school district as the tutee. *Tutees* are the students who receive the instruction from peer tutors. When peer tutoring is used with students with disabilities, the goal often is twofold: fostering social interactions and enhancing academic achievement (Anderson, 2007; Friedland & Truesdell, 2006; Mastropieri, Scruggs, & Berkeley, 2007).

The effectiveness of peer tutoring for enhancing student social interactions and academic achievement has been established through more than two decades of research. For example, Mastropieri, Scruggs, Spencer, and Fontana (2003) compared two approaches to teaching history to students with mild disabilities. Some of the students were taught a structured note-taking process, while others participated in a peer-tutoring program. When achievement data for the two groups were compared, the students who had participated in the tutoring program outperformed the other students. The teachers reported that students in the tutoring program spent more time on task, and the students expressed interest in using peer tutoring in other academic classes. Socially, the students reported that peer tutoring made time in class go by quickly and that they enjoyed interacting with their classmates in order to learn.

Peer-Assisted Learning Strategies (PALS) is another highly structured peer tutoring program that has been repeatedly demonstrated through research to be effective for students with disabilities (McMaster, Fuchs, & Fuchs, 2006) and English-language learners (Sáenz, L. M., Fuchs, L. S., & Fuchs, 2005). For example, a group of first-grade teachers implemented PALS for their students with and without disabilities (Baker, Gersten, Dimino, & Griffiths, 2004). Several years after the initial successful research study, the teachers were still using the peer-tutoring program effectively at least twice each week in math. Because the program includes a built-in data collection system, they also were able to report that the effect on student academic achievement was highly positive. The teachers reported that PALS had a positive impact on student social development as well. They noted that the program taught students to work effectively with many different peers, instead of just their friends, by helping them to learn how to say positive things to one another. This result carried far beyond the math instructional period.

Peer tutoring also has a positive impact on tutors, particularly when older tutors with marginal skills work with younger students (Topping, 2005). Studies have found that secondary students at very high risk for dropping out of school learned their academic content better and had a more positive attitude toward school and learning when they participated as tutors in a cross-age peer-tutoring program (Nazzal, 2002; Walker, 2006). Jennifer, one of the tutors in the study, commented that tutoring made her want to try to learn harder, because she realized that what she was doing was actually helping her younger tutee—that her efforts really made a difference.

Research on peer-tutoring programs has addressed factors such as the ages of the tutor and tutee, the amount of time allocated for tutoring, the content selected, students' characteristics, and the amount of program structure. All these factors can influence peer-tutoring outcomes but not in predictable ways. You may find that you need to experiment with several options to create the most successful experiences for your students.

Analyze
and Reflect

How might peer tutoring benefit students with and without disabilities? Those whose first language is not English? How would you go about deciding which type of peer-tutoring program to implement? How would you make a decision about its effectiveness?

Peer tutoring also has a positive impact on tutors, particularly when older tutors with marginal skills work with younger students.

Developing Peer-Tutoring Programs

Developing a peer-tutoring program can be as simple or complex as you want it to be. You can create your own system within your classroom, partner some or all of your students with another group of students, or help coordinate a schoolwide tutoring program. Established and researched programs also exist, such as the **Classwide Peer Tutoring (CWPT)** program (for example, Burks, 2004; Greenwood et al., 2001; Maheady, Mallette, & Harper, 2006; Ryan et al., 2004), in which all the students in a class take on the roles of tutor and tutee in turn and follow a set of clear steps for helping each other to learn. CWPT is described in Figure 13.1. Steps for setting up a peer-tutoring program of your own are described in the following sections.

● **Selecting Tutors** To create a **same-age tutoring** program in your classroom, consider pairing students who are both high-achievers rather than pairing a high-achiever with

FIGURE *13.1*   **Steps in Classwide Peer Tutoring**

1. Assign all students to tutoring pairs that change weekly or biweekly.

2. Assign each tutoring pair to one of two classroom teams.

3. Teach all students a specific series of steps for presenting and practicing content.

4. Teach all students specific strategies for correcting tutees and rewarding correct responses.

5. Provide tutoring pairs with daily assignments.

6. Instruct tutors to keep score: When a tutee answers a question correctly, a point is scored for the team.

7. Announce the winning team and post point totals.

8. Reward the winning team with a privilege or class applause.

9. Reverse the tutor/tutee arrangement each session, or have both students take the tutor role within each session.

a low-achiever. Then pair other students whose understanding of the topic at hand is fairly similar. This arrangement reduces the problem of high-achievers becoming impatient with low-achievers and the concern about high-achieving students missing their own opportunities for learning. However, same-age tutoring done in this way has two drawbacks: High-achieving students do not learn the skills for interacting with students with special learning needs, and low-achieving students lose learning role models. Another approach is to pair students randomly and use a **reciprocal tutoring** approach, in which both students alternate between the tutor and tutee roles.

In a **cross-age tutoring** approach, older students tutor younger ones. For example, if you teach in the primary grades, you might ask the fifth-grade teachers to provide tutors for your students. Teachers can collaborate to partner entire classes and institute regularly scheduled cross-class tutoring. If a middle school, junior high, or high school is located nearby, its students also could serve as tutors. If you teach in a middle school or high school, you might establish a peer-tutoring program for the school a level below yours so that high school students tutor in the middle school and middle school students tutor in the elementary school. At the secondary level, older students might serve as tutors and mentors for younger students (Dopp & Block, 2004). Seniors might be paired with freshmen or sophomores in this way.

As you decide how to establish a tutoring program, keep in mind students with disabilities and other special needs. Sometimes students with disabilities can serve as tutors to their classmates. An older student without a disability can be an ideal tutor for a younger student with a disability. Also an older student who has a learning or intellectual disability or who is at risk for school failure can be an effective tutor for a younger student with or without a disability. In other words, you can structure a tutoring program in many ways. What is important is making deliberate decisions about structure based on the strengths and needs of the students.

Depending on your goals, you might try a variation of peer tutoring by turning to adult tutors (Al Otaiba & Pappamihiel, 2005). In some school districts, the best available pool of tutors is college students or adult volunteers, such as students' parents and grandparents, recently retired teaching staff, and local business personnel. Adults can make better judgments about the content being taught and learned than student peers, and they might better be able to informally address student social skills. Tutees often look up

*R*esearch Note

Spencer and Balboni (2003) reviewed 35 studies of peer tutoring at the elementary level involving students with varying levels of intellectual disability. The students successfully served as both tutors and tutees in teaching and learning academic, social, and daily-living skills.

Info Sheet Homework Exercise

Go to the Homework and Exercises section in Chapter 13 of MyEducationLab to learn how using peer partners is an effective strategy for establishing a collaborative community in your class.

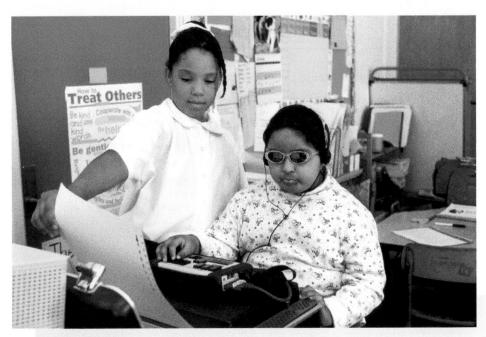

How can peer tutoring programs benefit students in your classroom? What combinations of tutors and tutees might work best for the grade level you plan to teach?

*R*esearch Note

In a study of the PALS approach to peer-mediated instruction, Calhoon (2005) found that it was more effective than traditional instruction in improving the letter–word identification, word attack, and passage comprehension skills of middle school students with learning disabilities enrolled in a remedial reading program.

to older tutors, who provide a special type of individual attention. Adults also have the maturity that eliminates the behavior problems that sometimes occur with peer partners. Of course, if your goals include helping students improve peer relations, some form of traditional peer tutoring is your best option.

● **Deciding How Much Tutoring Should Occur** The specific time allocated to peer tutoring depends on the needs of the students and the structure of the program. Although no specific guidelines can be given, in many cases tutoring in elementary schools occurs two to four times each week for 20 or 30 minutes and as often as daily for one class period in high schools (Baker et al., 2004; Calhoon & Fuchs, 2003; Mortweet et al., 1999). This amount of tutoring ensures continuity yet does not detract significantly from the rest of students' educational programs.

● **Providing Time for Peer Tutoring** Peer tutoring can occur as part of independent work time or as a periodic activity in which an entire class participates. Cross-age tutoring needs to occur on a schedule that accommodates both the tutor and the tutee. Optimal times can include the beginning of the school day as students arrive, the middle of the afternoon when both the tutor and the tutee need a change-of-pace activity, near the end of the school day, or after school. As much as possible, tutoring in a content area should occur within the content-area class.

Effective peer-tutoring programs provide practice on skills already taught by the teacher and use standard formats that help tutors know how to do their job.

In some middle schools and high schools, peer tutoring is a service-learning activity that is an elective course or a course for students hoping one day to be teachers. In such cases, tutoring occurs during the class period available for the tutor, and it might occur in the tutee's classroom, the library or media center, or a study hall or advisory classroom.

● **Selecting Content and Format for Tutoring** Effective peer-tutoring programs provide practice on skills already taught by the teacher and use standard formats that help tutors know how to do their job (Bond & Castagnera, 2006; Heron, Villareal, & Yao, 2006). For example, many elementary peer-tutoring programs have tutors and tutees working on basic math facts, spelling or vocabulary words, and comprehension questions on social studies and science materials already taught in class. In middle and high schools, peer tutoring may occur to review vocabulary, concepts, and skills or to provide assistance to a student in a core academic class (for example, algebra or biology) that the tutor has successfully completed.

Highly structured formats for tutoring sessions are best. For example, tutors might be instructed to begin a vocabulary session by reviewing all eight words from last time and then showing each new word, waiting for a response, and marking the response as correct or incorrect. The tutor praises correct responses, corrects errors, and asks the tutee to repeat the corrected responses. If the students finish their list, they review it until the end of the tutoring session. This example illustrates the need to have a clear set of procedures for tutors to follow, whatever format you use. Having well-defined procedures will help keep participants in tutoring sessions on task.

● **Training Tutors** Professionals generally agree that effective peer-tutoring programs carefully prepare tutors for their teaching roles. Tutor training should accomplish five main purposes (Barron & Foot, 1991):

1. Training should provide tutors with structures and procedures for tutoring, as just described.

2. Training should give tutors a systematic way of tracking the tutees' learning.

3. Training should help tutors develop positive interaction skills, including ways to praise tutees and correct their errors.

4. Training should develop tutors' problem-solving skills so they can generate ideas about how to proceed when procedures are not working or when tutees get confused or misbehave.

5. Training should add perceived value and credibility to the program and its participants.

Sample topics for a peer tutor training program are outlined in Figure 13.2.

Supporting Peer-Tutoring Programs

A training program for peer tutors should include follow-up and assessment. For example, in a cross-age tutoring program, it is important to bring tutors together periodically to discuss how they are doing and how they have resolved problems and to thank them for their work. When tutoring extends beyond your own class group, it is a nice touch to provide tutor appreciation certificates or other tokens of appreciation.

Several other factors go into the supports needed for a successful peer-tutoring program. These factors are discussed in the sections that follow.

● **Management and Supervision** Once your peer-tutoring program has been established, you should continue to supervise it. This ongoing supervision will enable you to praise tutor pairs having constructive work sessions, to identify potential problems when they are small and easily resolved, and to monitor student learning. If you have the assistance of a paraprofessional in your classroom, this person can help with day-to-day supervision responsibilities. As your tutoring program progresses, you might find it necessary to revise the format, regroup students, introduce "graduates," and devise new ways to thank tutors for their work.

● **Staff and Administrative Support** Unless you plan a peer-tutoring program that stays within the confines of your classroom, you will need the support of your colleagues

Students' interactions with others are determined partly by cultural expectations. Be sure to consider this fact as you work to positively influence how your students treat one another.

FIGURE 13.2 Topics for Training Peer Tutors

1. Sensitivity to others' feelings, need for acceptance, and fear of rejection

2. Ways to develop positive relationships with tutees, including using respectful language, giving positive reinforcement, showing personal interest, and offering constructive feedback

3. Effective communication and interaction skills: giving clear directions, making teaching interesting to the tutee, acting interested and being interested, explaining things in another way, correcting the tutee without criticism, praising correct responses, and admitting mistakes

4. Tutoring procedures and guidelines: having all needed materials prepared, beginning a session without teacher assistance, breaking big steps into smaller ones, showing how to do something if the tutee does not understand, giving the tutee time to think before responding, helping but not doing the work for the tutee, monitoring time to finish on schedule, and reviewing what has been taught

5. Procedures for gathering data on the tutee's learning, such as using a checklist or helping the tutee chart progress

6. Problem solving about issues that could come up during peer tutoring

7. The tutoring schedule and the need for commitment

and administrators. Other teachers might have ideas for how to pair students and arrange formats and opportunities for tutoring, and the special services staff might have creative ways of including students with special needs in the tutoring program. Administrators can provide support and assistance in arranging schedules, communicating with parents, and finding funds for the incidental supplies you might need.

● **Assistance from Volunteers** In addition to helping with tutoring, volunteers also might be willing to manage a peer-tutoring program, thus relieving you from many details of operation. For example, volunteers could establish the procedures for recruiting peer tutors, offer the tutors training, match tutors with tutees, monitor tutoring sessions, assess student learning, problem solve with tutors, and arrange a thank-you event for them. Education majors and teacher trainees in local colleges and universities can assist with these tasks at the elementary or secondary school level, as can members of a parent or community organization familiar with peer tutoring.

Video Homework Exercise

Go to the Homework and Exercises section in Chapter 13 of MyEducationLab to watch two boys demonstrate a peer tutoring situation.

● **Communication about Peer Tutoring** Support for peer-tutoring programs often depends on communication with parents and other community members. If you plan a peer-tutoring program for students, you should alert parents and explain your instructional approach and rationale. If you participate in a tutoring program that includes several classes, you might want to write a letter to parents announcing the availability of the program and providing its rationale.

Although most parents will readily agree to permit their children to participate as tutors or tutees, a few might have questions about tutors losing instructional time teaching others and the effectiveness of tutoring for students who have difficulty learning. Being prepared for questions such as these will help you answer them readily. Your administrator also can provide support in this area. As your tutoring program progresses, keep parents apprised of student activities through periodic notes or class newsletters or updates provided by your home–school hotline or district newsletter. In middle schools and high schools, where peer tutoring might be an elective course, information on the program can be added to the school website, possibly with a list of frequently asked questions and information for signing up as a tutor or tutee.

How Can You Use Cooperative Learning Strategies to Facilitate Social Inclusion?

Peer tutoring offers one structured alternative for promoting positive peer relationships while also enhancing academic achievement. Another option for accomplishing these goals is **cooperative learning.** Cooperative learning has its roots in the U.S. civil rights and school desegregation movements. Very soon after the 1954 *Brown v. Board of Education* U.S. Supreme Court decision established that separate schools cannot be equal, Allport (1954) wrote that simply putting students of different races in the same schools would not accomplish integration. He went on to clarify that integration would require opportunities for students to interact with one another in situations in which they had equal status. Further, he stated that school administrators would have to endorse the students' interactions. In practice, this meant that students needed opportunities to interact with one another in structured social situations not controlled by teachers but nevertheless strongly sanctioned by school authorities—situations free of unreasonable academic pressures that might inadvertently place some students in a lower status in terms of perceived competence.

Cooperative learning was developed as a means of creating these conditions during traditional classroom instruction (Sharan et al., 1984). For more than four decades, cooperative learning has been employed as a strategy for promoting positive student interactions in diverse classrooms (Gillies, 2007). It has been used as a strategy for achieving racial and cultural integration, assisting socially isolated learners, fostering inclusive education for students with disabilities and other special needs, and accommodating culture-based learning styles.

Research Note

Avcioğlu (2007) found that cooperative learning was an effective means of teaching social skills to elementary students with hearing loss.

The Rationale for Cooperative Learning

As you can see from the history of cooperative learning, its primary purpose is to increase students' ability to interact with each other in appropriate ways. Many studies over the past 25 years have addressed this topic. For example, Gillies and Ashman (2000) found that after three school terms, students who had worked in cooperative learning groups were more involved in group activities and provided more direction and assistance to other group members than students who had participated in loosely structured groups. Students in cooperative classrooms also are more likely to show affection toward other class members, invite others to join a group activity, and thank or praise each other. Although fewer studies on secondary students are available, the same trends exist (Mastropieri et al., 2006; McMaster & Fuchs, 2002).

For students with disabilities, the social benefits of cooperative learning appear to accrue in the same way they do for other students. One early review of nearly 100 studies of cooperative learning (Johnson, Johnson, & Maruyama, 1983) demonstrated positive social effects for students with disabilities as well as for those with other special needs, especially when students were given specific instruction in collaborative skills. Other more recent studies have found similar results (Jenkins, Antil, Wayne, & Vadasy, 2003). In fact, cooperative learning often is recommended as a fundamental component of inclusive classrooms (Fore, Riser, & Boon, 2006; Piercy, Wilton, & Townsend, 2002). Although the value of cooperative learning lies historically in its potential for creating positive peer interactions, it also can enhance learning and achievement (Hänze, & Berger, 2007;

Video Homework Exercise

Go to the Homework and Exercises section in Chapter 13 of MyEducationLab to watch students with and without disabilities complete a cooperative learning activity.

Ryan et al., 2004). For students without disabilities, cooperative learning has strongly and repeatedly been demonstrated an effective instructional approach for achievement in reading, math, science, physical education, and other areas (for example, Dyson, 2002; Emmer & Gerwels, 2002; Gillies, 2007; Jenkins et al., 2003; Maheady, Michielli-Pendl, Harper, & Mallette, 2006).

The academic outcomes of cooperative learning for students with disabilities vary and cannot always be assumed to be strong (McMaster & Fuchs, 2002). However, some evidence suggests that for students with high-incidence disabilities, cooperative learning is at least as effective as other instructional approaches (for example, Gillies, 2007; Mastropieri et al., 2006; Ryan et al., 2004). Even stronger results have been noted for other students with special needs, including students who are English-language learners (Slavin, 1999; U.S. Department of Education, 2007) and those at risk for school failure (Vaughan, 2002). For students with severe intellectual disabilities or multiple disabilities, the issue of academic achievement as traditionally measured is not usually a central concern.

Characteristics of Cooperative Learning Approaches

Cooperative learning generally has four fundamental and essential characteristics: positive interdependence, face-to-face interactions, individual accountability, and emphasis on interpersonal skills (Gillies, 2007). First, the students in the groups have *positive interdependence*. Either they reach their goal together, or no one is able to achieve it. For example, in Mr. Reilly's classroom, the students earn points when all the members in their cooperative groups get at least 70 percent on their weekly spelling test. Group members work very hard to help all members learn the spelling words.

Second, cooperative learning requires face-to-face interactions. In Mr. Sutter's class, students have opportunities to work directly with their group members to accomplish learning goals related to reviewing the use of advertising approaches in magazines.

Third, members of cooperative groups have individual accountability. On the weekly vocabulary test in Ms. Mather's chemistry class, students who have difficulty learning are not excused from taking the test, nor are high-achievers permitted to answer for all group members. Each member is required to make a contribution.

Finally, cooperative learning stresses student interpersonal skills, such as how to ask questions, how to praise classmates, and how to help another student learn. When Ms. Bolter notices positive interpersonal interactions among her seventh-grade English students, she gives them "Bolter Bucks" to spend on a variety of privileges and rewards.

These four characteristics of cooperative learning distinguish it from other approaches to learning common in schools. For example, much school learning is competitive, or based on winners and losers. Spelling matches and other instructional games in which only one student wins are competitive. Another example of school competition is found in many athletic programs. A second type of traditional learning approach is individualistic. In individualistic learning, student achievement is not dependent on how others achieve. For example, a teacher sets up a system in which each student who completes 90 percent of the homework, makes at least a B average on unit tests, and completes two projects by meeting criteria outlined in a rubric is assigned an A for the grading period. If all the students in the class meet these standards, then all will earn that grade. If only one student meets the standard, however, only that student will earn an A. All students can be winners; one student's achievement does not affect other students' chances of success. An individualistic approach is the basis for special education and most remedial programs.

All three approaches—cooperative, competitive, and individualistic—have a place in schools. However, the social and interactive components of cooperative learning are not possible in either of the other two approaches. That means that this approach especially needs to be incorporated into the school curriculum, particularly in inclusive schools striving to foster positive interactions between students with and without disabilities.

www.resources

If you would like to learn more about types of cooperative learning, the Success for All Foundation has made available an extensive summary. You can find this information at www.successforall.com.

Developing Cooperative Learning Programs

Given the many positive effects of cooperative learning for all students, you probably will find it an effective instructional approach in your classroom. You might decide to use cooperative groups three times each week for language arts activities, for instance, or once each week for test review. Regardless of how you incorporate cooperative learning into your classroom, you can achieve the best results by following some basic guidelines.

● **Form Cooperative Learning Groups** One of your first considerations in creating a cooperative learning program is deciding on the size and makeup of the groups. Regardless of the specific cooperative learning approach you choose, the age, abilities, and needs of your students will help determine group size. For example, if you teach second grade, you probably will use groups of three at the beginning of the school year and consider larger groups after students become accustomed to cooperative learning procedures. If you teach eighth grade, you might be able to begin the year with groups of five.

Factors besides age should be considered too. In a class with mature students, larger groups are possible; in a class with immature students, groups of three (or even teaming up in pairs and using peer tutoring for a time) might be best. Students with very limited ability might need a smaller group; more able students can succeed in a larger group. Notice that the range of group size is from two to five or six. Larger groups become difficult for students to participate in and for teachers to manage.

You should assign students to cooperative groups to create heterogeneous groupings; that is, if your class includes four students with disabilities, you should distribute them among the cooperative groups. Likewise, high-achievers and low-achievers should be assigned across groups. The success of cooperative learning is based on students learning to value and respect each person's contributions. Although skill grouping sometimes is appropriate, deciding to place students together in groups according to ability generally undermines the purpose of cooperative learning.

> You should assign students to cooperative groups to create heterogeneous groupings.

How can cooperative groups be used to teach both academic content and skills for working with peers? What skills do students need to work successfully?

Video Homework Exercise

Go to the Homework and Exercises section in Chapter 13 of MyEducationLab to watch a class as it breaks into collaborative groups.

Teachers sometimes ask how long cooperative groups should be kept intact. There is no single right answer to that question. If you change groups too frequently, students do not have enough opportunity to learn about each other and reach a high level of cooperative functioning. However, if you keep the same groups for too long, students do not have the chance to work with other classmates. A general guideline is to keep cooperative groups for at least a two- or three-week period but to change them at least at the end of each grading period. This recommendation, of course, is based on the presumption that the cooperative groups meet at least two or three times each week.

● **Prepare Students for Cooperative Learning** A high school English teacher participated in a university class on cooperative learning and decided that she and the special educator could use this strategy in their co-taught class. They carefully planned a series of cooperative activities, assigned students to groups, and waited for positive results. They quickly learned why teaching students to cooperate is such an important component in developing cooperative learning programs! The students bickered with each other and were impatient with students who did not immediately answer questions. Some decided to try to complete their work alone, even though it required input from others. Before students work together, it is essential to teach them cooperative skills (Cooper, 2002).

The skills for cooperative group members have been recognized for many years (Johnson, Johnson, Holubec, & Roy, 1984) and can be categorized under the headings of *forming, functioning, formulating,* and *fermenting*:

1. *Forming.* Students need forming skills to move into cooperative groups and carry out basic tasks with politeness and respect. These skills are the most rudimentary.

2. *Functioning.* Functioning skills are procedural, including monitoring time limits, asking for help, and clarifying fellow group members' statements. These skills help groups interact constructively and productively.

3. *Formulating.* Formulating skills are more advanced procedural skills and include asking other students to elaborate on their comments so everyone understands them better, devising strategies for remembering important information, and relating new information to information previously learned.

4. *Fermenting.* Fermenting skills are those students use to participate in their groups as critical thinkers and problem solvers. These skills include integrating members' ideas to form a new idea, questioning others about their ideas to analyze them further, attempting to provide multiple answers, and expressing or testing hypotheses.

Forming and functioning skills usually are introduced to students first and can be practiced in groups using games and simple instructional activities that have little academic demand. In addition to helping students learn how to get into their groups and how to speak to each other with respect, functioning skills also involve assigned student roles. All cooperative group members should have assigned roles that help the group function effectively. In some classrooms, group-member assignments include the encourager, the monitor, the leader, and the recorder, as shown in Figure 13.3. The *encourager* has the responsibility of making positive comments to other group members. The *monitor* helps keep the group on task and watches the time. The *leader* gets the group started on its task and facilitates its work. The *recorder* writes down any information the group is responsible for producing. Depending on students' ages and skills, additional responsibilities can be added. In some classrooms, group roles rotate so each student has an opportunity to try all the roles. If a student with a disability cannot carry out a role (for example, that of recorder), a classmate might help out or that student might not be assigned that role.

One other functioning skill is especially important: giving feedback. Students need to speak to each other respectfully and assist each other with this skill, particularly when one student has made an error. Consider one student providing appropriate feedback to another student: "Cecily, today in the group you told Mel he was dumb because he didn't know the answer. That's against group rules." Notice how this very brief example helps the group interaction. The student speaking does not tell Cecily that she is the dumb one, nor does the student tell Cecily what she should have said. Instead, the speaker points out the group expectation for being respectful.

In general, preparing students for cooperative groups includes identifying the skills they need to learn, planning how you will teach them, teaching the skills and allowing students opportunities to practice them, and gradually increasing your expectations for students' cooperative behavior. More ideas for teaching cooperative skills are included in the Professional Edge on page 504.

FIGURE 13.3 Student Roles in Cooperative Groups

- **Select Curricular Content**   Almost any subject matter you teach can be adapted for cooperative learning. In elementary schools, cooperative learning is used in language arts for reading and writing activities as well as in math, science, and social studies. In secondary schools, cooperative learning works well in English, math, science, social studies, fine arts, and other coursework. The key to selecting content is to be sure you already have provided initial instruction to the students so they are not expected to master new information without your guidance. Further, the content needs to be formatted clearly. It might be a chapter from a textbook, print materials you have duplicated, or a structure for preparing a report on the topic at hand. Students should be able to understand what the assignment is and how to go about completing it.

- **Choose a Cooperative Learning Program**   The number of approaches to cooperative learning seems to grow each year. For our discussion, three commonly used approaches are outlined: Jigsaw Classroom, Numbered Heads Together, and Cooperative Integrated Reading and Composition (CIRC).

In a **Jigsaw Classroom** (Aronson, 2005), students are assigned to heterogeneous work groups. Each member of the work group also is assigned to a separate expert group. Work groups meet and decide which member to assign to which expert group. For example, in a unit on the Midwest, experts might be assigned for four topics: geography, economy, culture, and cities. All team members then read the material, with each member focusing on his expert topic. After reading, team members join their respective expert groups, which are composed of all students in the room who share the same expert topic. The expert groups review their portion of the instructional material and then return to teach it to their work-group members. Group members ask each expert questions to help clarify the information being presented. After all the group members have taught their segments of the information and the groups have had an opportunity to review their learning, a quiz or other evaluation procedure is used, and each group member is graded individually on this assessment.

Since the original Jigsaw approach was created in the early 1970s, a number of variations have been published as Jigsaw II, Jigsaw III, and Jigsaw IV. In Jigsaw IV, the most recent version (Holliday, 2002), students are given a clearer overview of the learning unit than in earlier versions and the expert groups are given quizzes to check their knowledge before members return to their work groups. Further, work groups take a shared quiz as practice prior to being given an assessment in which each student is individually accountable.

In **Numbered Heads Together** (Kagan, 1990; Maheady, Michielli-Pendl, Harper, & Mallette, 2006), students are assigned to cooperative groups (usually four or five in a

Teaching Cooperative Skills

For cooperative learning to be successful, you should teach students the needed interpersonal and communication skills. Here is a five-step process for teaching cooperative skills (Johnson, Johnson, & Holubec, 1998):

1. *Make sure students understand the need for the teamwork skill.*

    ■ Ask students to develop a list of social skills needed to improve group work. From the skills they list, emphasize one or two.

    ■ Present a case to students so they can see it is better to know the skill than not know it. Compliment students who use the skills in the classroom.

    ■ Illustrate the need for the skill through a role-play that provides a nonexample in which the skill is obviously missing in a group.

2. *Make sure students understand what the cooperative learning skill is and how and when to use it.*

    ■ Define the skill in terms of verbal and nonverbal behaviors, and explain thoroughly what students have to do. After the skill is listed (for example, giving directions to the group's work), ask the class, "What does this skill look like?" (nonverbal behaviors) and "What does this skill sound like?" (verbal behaviors).

    ■ Demonstrate and model the skill in front of the students, and explain it step by step so students have a concrete idea of what the skill entails in terms of verbal and nonverbal behaviors.

    ■ Have students practice the skill twice in their groups before the lesson starts.

3. *Set up practice situations and encourage skill mastery.*

    ■ Assign a social skill either as a specific role for a certain student or as a general responsibility for all members of the group. Introduce skills gradually (for instance, one new skill every week) and repeat previously introduced skills until mastery occurs.

    ■ Observe each group and record who uses the skill, how frequently, and how effectively. You can begin

using a very simple observation form that measures only two or three skills. Student observers should be used as soon as possible.

    ■ Cue the use of skills periodically during a lesson by having a student demonstrate the skill in front of classmates.

    ■ Intervene in cooperative groups to explain the skills and show how to use them.

    ■ Coach students on how to improve the use of the skill.

4. *Give students feedback on their use of the skill.*

    ■ Help students reflect on how to engage in the skill more effectively in the future.

    ■ Have the observer in each group report to group members on the information gathered, and have group members in turn report their impressions about their behavior.

    ■ Have the observer provide positive feedback to all group members about their efforts to learn and help others learn. Provide your own feedback to the class as a whole.

5. *Make sure students practice the cooperative learning skill until it becomes automatic. Look for these four stages of skill development:*

    ■ awkward, the beginning stage, when there is awkwardness in engaging in the skill

    ■ phony, when students use the skill but feel inauthentic

    ■ mechanical

    ■ integrated, when the skill occurs naturally

Remember that students should be expected to learn cooperative skills gradually and that steps such as these will enable you to eventually teach students strategies that will help them in school and throughout their lives.

Source: From *Cooperation in the Classroom,* by D. Johnson, R. Johnson, and E. Holubec, 1998, Interaction Book Company. Retrieved February 11, 2005, from www.intime.uni.edu/coop_learning/ch5/teaching.htm.

group) and count off by number. The teacher then poses a question to the group and students are asked to "put their heads together" to be sure all group members know the answer. After a brief time, the teacher reassembles the whole class and calls out a number. All the students with that number stand and one student responds to the question, or they all write the answer on slates and hold them up for the teacher to see. Students responding correctly score points for their teams. This simple cooperative learning approach can be used for questions with single correct answers as well as for those with many responses.

Cooperative Integrated Reading and Composition (CIRC) is a cooperative learning program designed to help students in elementary and middle schools work on reading, writing, and other language arts (Calderon, 1999; Slavin, 1994; U.S. Department of Education, 2007). CIRC has three main components: activities related to the basal reading materials, direct instruction for reading comprehension, and integration of writing with language arts.

Although CIRC is a rather complex cooperative learning approach, generally it includes these activities: First, students are assigned to one of two or three reading groups based on their reading levels. (Alternatively, teachers may skip grouping and teach to the whole group.) In addition, students are teamed with one or two other students within the reading group, and then two teams consisting of students with different reading groups (that is, four or six students) are created. These secondary teams foster heterogeneous grouping in the class and encourage students to help each other. The heterogeneous teams receive points based on each team member's performance on book reports, tests, and other class work. All teams that average 90 percent on assigned work are awarded Superteam status; those reaching an average of 80 percent are called Greatteams. Other key activities for CIRC include partner reading with the assigned homogeneous and heterogeneous teammate(s), direct instruction by the teacher on reading comprehension skills, story-related writing, word learning, story retelling, and spelling. Teammates also preassess each other and help each other practice skills not mastered before final testing occurs.

Analyze
and Reflect

Think about peer-tutoring and cooperative learning programs. In what situations might each be most appropriate? To respond, take into account students' strengths and needs, your own teaching style, and the curricular content you would be addressing.

● **Monitor Program Effectiveness**   Much of the work in developing a cooperative learning program is deciding which approach to use, preparing materials, and helping students learn cooperative skills. However, once students are established in cooperative groups, your role becomes one of monitoring and managing your class (Cooper, 2002). For example, if you notice that a student is having difficulty in a group, you might decide to join that group briefly to judge whether students can resolve the problem themselves or need your assistance. If a student seems to be struggling because of the complexity of the lesson content, you can make an on-the-spot adaptation to help the student and the group. If a student is being disruptive, your proximity might be sufficient to settle that student. As you monitor, you also can observe students' use of cooperative skills and check the progress of their learning. For example, you might observe whether students are using the learning strategies described in Chapter 10 to help them succeed in the lesson. By observing, you can plan your next lessons and address any issues concerning cooperative skills.

> Once students are established in cooperative groups, your role becomes one of monitoring and managing your class.

By applying the INCLUDE strategy, you quickly can see that many of the teaching strategies presented in this text can be incorporated into cooperative learning experiences. For example, a student in a cooperative group can have adapted materials. The group can use a learning strategy to practice problem solving. You can use an entire array of instructional interventions and strategies for independence as part of your cooperative learning activities. Cooperative groups provide a constructive classroom structure, one that provides opportunities for adapting instruction for individual needs, building self-esteem and group spirit, addressing students' own goals, and promoting positive attitudes toward others. You have an almost limitless number of options for using this structure to accomplish your academic and social goals for students.

INCLUDE

*H*ow Can You Help Students with Disabilities Improve Their Social Skills?

For many students with disabilities and other special needs, your efforts to create a classroom learning environment that fosters positive peer relationships will enable them to be class members who are liked and valued by their peers. For some students, though, you will need to go further. Research has shown that some students with disabilities have persistent problems in their social interactions (Canney & Burn, 2006; de Boo & Prins, 2007; Lane, Pierson, & Givner, 2004) and that these students benefit from specific instruction to help them learn needed social skills (Denham, Hatfield, Smethurst, Tan, & Tribe, 2006; DeRosier & Marcus, 2005).

Social skills can be thought of as the behaviors that help students interact successfully with their peers, teachers, and others and that help students win social acceptance. They include accurately recognizing and responding to emotions expressed by others; identifying and effectively solving social problems, such as disagreements about who can play with a toy or decisions about sneaking out of school with a group of peers; expressing preferences in socially acceptable ways; and initiating kind or helpful acts. Social skills range from very simple to complex. For example, for a young student or a student with a moderate intellectual disability, social skills might include learning how to greet others by saying hi instead of hugging, how to take turns during games or large-group activities, and how to ask to join a group. For adolescents with learning or behavior problems—students like Kathleen and Demetrius, whom you read about at the beginning of this chapter—social skills might include expressing emotions appropriately, disagreeing with others (especially adults) in acceptable ways, and avoiding situations in which confrontation is likely to occur.

Although special educators play an active role in teaching social skills to students with especially strong needs, you also can address these skills. Many of the ideas presented in this chapter assist students to learn social skills, but in this section, additional specific strategies to bring social skills training to your classroom are outlined. These ways include using informal instruction, behavioral interventions, and formal social skills training. Additional resources for teaching social skills are presented in the Technology Notes.

Using Informal Instruction

As illustrated throughout this chapter in examples of teachers actively nurturing the development of positive peer social relationships in their classrooms, you will have many informal opportunities to help students develop the social skills they will need throughout their lives (Boaler, 2006). For example, if you are showing students an instructional video and appropriate student interactions occur as part of it, you might want to point out in a class discussion what made the interactions so positive. Then students practice the same skills. Similarly, classrooms can include social skills as part of classwide or schoolwide themes. For example, in one middle school, students illustrated stories that demonstrated how to respond when peers were pressuring them to make fun of other students. Finally, you can individually instruct students in social skills as appropriate situations occur. When Mr. Calles observed Charles, a sophomore with a mild intellectual disability, stick his tongue out at another student when the student laughed at him, he made it a point to speak with both boys about other ways to interact.

Even though you may consider your primary responsibility to be teaching specific curriculum competencies to your students, your awareness of the need to develop student social skills and your willingness to incorporate informal social skills instruction into your class activities can contribute significantly to a sense of classroom community (Barton-Arwood, Morrow, Lane, & Jolivette, 2005). And forming a positive classroom community is essential for inclusive schools. The Special Emphasis On . . . feature illustrates this approach to social skills training in a drama class.

fyi

For students with autism, social stories—brief vignettes that directly address situations encountered by students—can provide a basis for teaching social skills (Scattone, Tingstrom, & Wilczynski, 2006).

DIMENSIONS OF
diversity

Some students experience social pressure related to school. For example, in a case study of a tenth-grade, African American, middle-class student, Day-Vines, Patton, and Baytops (2003) reported that the student was chastised by her African American peers for succeeding academically, speaking standard English, and living in an affluent neighborhood while she simultaneously was teased by her white peers for her academic and social status. How could you, as a teacher, help in such a situation?

Using Behavioral Interventions

A specific strategy for teaching social skills to students is to use behavioral interventions such as the ones you learned about in Chapter 12. For example, you can reward your entire class for treating a new class member with respect and friendship. If you have a student whose social problems include teasing class members or talking out of turn, you can reward the class for not responding to the inappropriate behaviors. To use these types of behavioral interventions, you need to identify clearly the behaviors you want to foster, choose an appropriate reward structure, create a simple record-keeping system, explain the intervention to students, and systematically implement your plan. For example, in a high school civics class serving sophomores and juniors, a student whose first language was Spanish and who also had learning disabilities enrolled in October. Rosana, a quiet individual who was very self-conscious about her English skills, seldom volunteered answers in class. When she did speak, several classmates mocked her accent and started calling her "Roseanna-danna," after the still-famous *Saturday Night Live* character. The teacher created a citizenship scorecard for the class that rewarded students for being respectful. Classmates soon pressured the name-callers to stop, since their unkind words were penalizing the entire group.

Although inclusive education emphasizes students' access to general curriculum, it also provides a means for teaching all students the essential skills for living in a diverse world.

TECHNOLOGY NOTES

Using Technology to Teach Social Skills

Many teachers express concern about the social skills of all their students, including those with disabilities. At El Dorado Middle School in Concord, California, staff members were awarded funding to produce strategies for teaching social skills as outlined in California's curriculum standards. Developed by general education and special education teachers, a speech/language therapist, and others, including a number of volunteers, the resulting website includes more than 100 lessons, student activities, and other resources for teaching social skills. These materials, which are available to guests, are aligned with language arts curriculum and typical middle school literature (but many of the ideas are appropriate across grade levels). After two years of implementing many of the ideas provided on the website, discipline referrals at the diverse school have decreased dramatically.

Here are examples of the many tools and materials available at www.cccoe.net/social/opening.htm:

- *Literature* At a link titled "Stories and Social Skills Lessons," you can find separate lists of sixth-, seventh-, and eighth-grade literature with a list of specific social and related skills that can be addressed using each.

- *Assessment* At a link titled "Evaluating Progress," you can read about strategies for determining the effectiveness of your social skills teaching efforts. You also can link to the results of research completed by the authors of the website.

- *Record Keeping* The webpage by this title includes simple forms for tracking your attention to social skills. These forms are also cross-referenced to middle school literature.

- *Materials* The "Free Downloads" link opens up an extensive set of materials that teachers can use with students. The materials include a variety of activities related to topics such as idioms, fables, and pantomime. A number of teacher materials also are posted here.

- *Student Activities* The section of the site called "Student Activities" includes links to crossword puzzles and word search activities, all related to social skills development. Also available here are pretest and posttest assessments.

Source: Adapted from *Teaching Social Skills in the Language Arts Curriculum: A Guide for Middle School Educators.* Retrieved September 1, 2007, from www.cccoe.net/social/opening.htm.

Special EMPHASIS on

Fostering Social Skills in Drama Class

Although all teachers should recognize the importance of informally or formally teaching social skills to their students, teachers in related arts classes often have unique opportunities to address these essential life skills. One example is a drama class.

Elliot is a twelfth-grade student with physical and intellectual disabilities who is attending Roosevelt High School. He is learning vocational skills but also spends three periods each day in the same classes as his peers without disabilities. One of his classes this year is drama. This class was one that Elliot expressed an interest in taking, and the team responsible for his IEP agreed it would provide many opportunities for addressing his social skills goals.

Here are some examples of the skills and activities that Mr. McKinnon, the drama teacher, is incorporating into the class. These activities do not in any way disrupt the typical flow of instruction, and at the same time, they address Elliot's special needs:

1. *Following directions.* One important social skill is following directions given by others. In the drama class, students often are instructed to move their bodies in certain ways or to move to particular parts of the room.

2. *Expressing frustration.* To express frustration, you can say you are frustrated, show the emotion on your face, or let it out by hitting a wall or throwing an object.

For Elliot, learning to express frustration verbally is important, and so Mr. McKinnon has ensured that several of the scenes students must act out are related to expressing frustration.

3. *Interacting with peers.* Elliot tends to sit by himself instead of initiating interactions with peers. In the drama class, he regularly is asked to initiate interactions and is rewarded for doing so appropriately. He also works as the prop manager for the class. When classmates or the teacher ask for certain props, Elliot has opportunities for interactions.

4. *Speaking in an appropriate tone of voice.* When Elliot speaks, he often forgets whether to use an inside or an outside voice. In the drama class, students do exercises to practice using their voices to convey meaning. As part of the exercises, Elliot learns to attend to this basic social skill.

What other social skills might students with disabilities be able to work on within the context of a drama class? What about in other specialized classes, such as art and music?

Source: Based on "The High School Student" (pp. 143–167), by J. E. Downing, 2002, in *Including Students with Severe and Multiple Disabilities in Typical Classrooms: Practical Strategies for Teachers* (2nd ed.), Baltimore: Brookes.

Info Sheet Homework Exercise

Go to the Homework and Exercises section in Chapter 13 of MyEducationLab for an explanation of how using social autopsies can turn a social error into a learning experience.

Behavioral interventions also can be used to reinforce appropriate social skills. When teachers see students with social skills needs interacting appropriately, they should make positive comments to the students. In secondary schools, these comments usually are offered in private to avoid embarrassing students. For example, a student advisor overheard a conversation between a chemistry teacher and a student with an explosive temper. The teacher was chiding the student for failing to turn in assignments on time. The student replied, "Yeah, I know I haven't been doing too well on the homework." Later the advisor congratulated the student for acknowledging the teacher's feedback without becoming defensive or making a comment that might have led to detention. Think about the INCLUDE strategy that you have applied throughout this textbook. How could it be used to help you decide how to use behavioral approaches to teach and reinforce social skills?

Using Social Skills Training Programs

If you have several students who need social skills instruction, you might find useful one of the many prepackaged social skills training programs available to teachers. For example,

Think Aloud (Camp & Bash, 1985; Wehmeyer, 2002) is a problem-solving package that can be used very effectively to teach social skills to elementary school students. Students are taught to ask themselves a series of questions whenever they are faced with a problematic situation: What is the problem? What should I do? What is my plan? Am I following the plan? Teachers rehearse these steps with students and provide opportunities for students to practice the steps in structured situations. Teachers also remind students to look for the steps when they observe students behaving appropriately.

An example of a social skills package for adolescents is Skillstreaming the Adolescent (Goldstein, Sprafkin, Gershaw, & Klein, 1980; Seferian, 1999). This package includes structured procedures for teaching nearly 50 different social skills using modeling, role-playing, and feedback. Teachers can select and use only the skill lessons most pertinent to their class groups. For example, if a high school class is having problems because several students are extremely aggressive, the module on that topic might be helpful.

However you decide to help students develop social skills, keep in mind that several other professionals are available in your school who may have advanced training in teaching social skills and can assist you in this aspect of your curriculum. For example, if your school has a teacher for students with emotional disabilities, he might be able to co-teach social skills lessons with you. Similarly, a school counselor or social worker could help you build social skills lessons into your instructional program. For students with the most needs for social skills instruction, professionals such as these probably will take the lead role and ask you to follow up by reinforcing appropriate social skills in the general education setting (Johns, Crowley, & Guetzloe, 2005).

Final Thoughts about Inclusion and the INCLUDE Strategy

With your understanding of strategies and approaches for building student social relationships, you now have the final ingredient for making your classroom a place where students want to come and want to learn. You know about the foundations of special education and the procedures followed for identifying students with disabilities. You have a strategy—INCLUDE—for guiding your decisions about student needs and interventions. You know about the importance of having the support and assistance of colleagues and parents, whether for planning an instructional program for a student, teaching with you in the classroom, or problem solving when concerns arise. You also understand some of the most important characteristics and needs of students with disabilities and other special needs. You have learned many strategies for helping students succeed in your classroom, including creating a positive instructional environment, assessing student needs, making instructional interventions, helping students be independent, and evaluating their learning. And you have learned several approaches for responding to students' discipline and behavior needs and fostering positive social relationships among students.

What is most important, however, is the statement that appeared in the first chapter of this text: Students with disabilities and other special needs are children and youth first. If you keep that in mind and use the knowledge you have gained, you will positively touch the lives and learning of all the students who call you *teacher*.

In addition to fostering the academic growth of students in inclusive schools, teachers also work to ensure that their students with and without disabilities and other special needs build positive social relationships. Learning social skills is especially important because research over the past four decades has demonstrated that students with disabilities are more likely than other students to have a negative status in their classrooms.

DIMENSIONS OF

diversity

Olmeda and Trent (2003) reviewed studies of social skills training programs related to minority students. They found that these programs did not take into account students' cultural backgrounds, and they recommended that such programs would be more effective if they were more culturally responsive.

Video Homework Exercise

Go to the Homework and Exercises section in Chapter 13 of MyEducationLab to see how social skills can be taught in actual social situations.

INCLUDE

www.resources

The IRIS Center (http://iris .peabody.vanderbilt.edu/da/ chalcycle.htm) is a national organization that aims to provide high-quality resources for college and university faculty and professional development providers about students with disabilities. IRIS seeks to obtain this goal by providing free, online, interactive training enhancements that translate research about the education of students with disabilities into practice.

Summary

Teachers can help students develop positive peer relationships in inclusive classrooms by creating ways for students to have face-to-face interactions, nurturing the development of friendship and support among students, and providing positive role models. Another aspect of addressing the social curriculum in general education classrooms is educating students without special needs about individuals who have disabilities and other special needs. The direct presentation of information, use of print and video media, and demonstration of adaptive technology are approaches to introducing students to the characteristics and needs of students with disabilities.

One specific instructional approach that helps create positive student relationships is peer tutoring. Peer tutoring benefits both tutors and tutees, including students with disabilities. Teachers can create tutoring programs that are contained within their classrooms or that use several class

groups or even an entire school or multiple school levels. A second instructional approach recommended for inclusive classrooms is cooperative learning. To set up a cooperative learning program, teachers need to decide on the size and makeup of the groups; prepare students to work cooperatively; identify the instructional content to be used in the groups; select a cooperative learning approach, such as Jigsaw Classroom, Numbered Heads Together, or Cooperative Integrated Reading and Composition (CIRC); and monitor the effectiveness of the approach.

Sometimes students with disabilities need additional intensive instruction to learn social skills. This instruction can involve informal social skills instruction as part of the classroom curriculum, behavioral interventions, and formal social skills training programs, often taught in partnership with special services providers such as special education teachers.

Back to the Cases

This section provides opportunities for you to apply the knowledge gained in this chapter to the cases described at the beginning of this chapter. The questions and activities that follow demonstrate how these standards and principles, along with other concepts that you have learned about in this chapter, connect to the everyday activities of all teachers.

Tyler has been promoted to your class. Last year Tyler's teacher used several methods to address diversity and inclusion with the class. You want to support that work with additional activities. In previous years the teachers have used commercial storybooks about students with exceptional needs, including students who are English-language learners or are from other cultures. You think the students are old enough to read age-appropriate literature and view commercial videos. Select five books and five videos that you think are age- or content-appropriate that you might use in your classroom. To find books, you might visit your local library, bookstore, or search an online bookstore such as Amazon.com. To find appropriate videos, you can visit a local video rental store or use Google.com to search the words *movies* and *disabilities*. Other resources for videos can be found on the Internet at websites such as Bridges4Kids (www.bridges4kids .org/Reviews.html). Once you have found your materials,

outline an activity to incorporate one of them into your curriculum. (INTASC Principles 5.03 and 9.02; and CEC Content Standards 5 and 9.)

Kathleen experiences a very positive inclusion situation. Her team members do not respond to her teasing or inappropriate remarks and expect her to contribute to their efforts. Such positive interactions may not occur without some training or support from the teacher. Explain how you believe Mr. Geib created a classroom environment where students with disabilities are expected to participate fully and successfully in cooperative learning groups. Be specific about activities or actions he used and why you believe these selected actions were successful. (INTASC Principles 2.05, 5.03, 9.01, and 9.02; and CEC Content Standards 2, 5, and 9.)

Demetrius is making progress, with the counselor's help, in responding to nonverbal communications of others. However, he still has problems in the classroom. You think that he needs support from his peers for real-life experience in accepting feedback from others in social situations. Demetrius will need to be able to accept such responses from co-workers and customers at the print shop where he plans to work. As his classroom teacher, what would you do to teach his peers to provide positive, constructive feedback when Demetrius does not respond to nonverbal communication? (INTASC Principles 2.05, 5.03, 9.01, and 9.02; and CEC Content Standards 2, 5, and 9.) For example, how should his peers respond if Demetrius continues to talk when others have lost interest or speaks too loudly during small-group work sessions? Naturally, you will need to help Demetrius learn to accept their prompts and suggestions. The chapter provides several suggestions for appropriate activities; select one and explain why you chose it.

Key Terms and Concepts

Circle of Friends (p. 486)

Classwide Peer Tutoring (CWPT) (p. 494)

Cooperative Integrated Reading and Composition (CIRC) (p. 505)

Cooperative learning (p. 499)

Cross-age tutoring (p. 495)

Jigsaw Classroom (p. 503)

Numbered Heads Together (p. 503)

Peer-Assisted Learning Strategies (PALS) (p. 494)

Peer tutoring (p. 493)

Reciprocal tutoring (p. 495)

Same-age tutoring (p. 494)

Social skills (p. 482)

Now go to the Friend and Bursuck, Fifth Edition, MyEducationLab course at www.myeducationlab.com to

- take a pretest to assess your initial comprehension of the chapter content
- study chapter content with your individualized study plan
- take a posttest to assess your understanding of chapter content
- engage in multimedia exercises to help you build a deeper and more applied understanding of chapter content

Applications in Teaching Practice

Planning for Promoting Positive Peer Relations

Mr. Barkley is reviewing his class roster and his plans for the upcoming school year. He knows he will have four students with learning and behavior disabilities—Jay, Doug, Ray, and Jasmine—in his sixth-hour class. He also will have Theodore, a bright young man with cerebral palsy who uses a wheelchair and has a personal assistant. Theodore cannot write or type; he points to symbols on his communication board. Having talked to other teachers, Mr. Barkley is a little worried about this group because several of the other students in the class also have special needs, including Kusi, who has attention deficit–hyperactivity disorder, and Micki, who is gifted. Right now, the following items appear on his planning list:

1. Talk to Ms. M. [special education teacher]. What are reasonable expectations for the students with disabilities? Does Theodore need any extraordinary assistance? What is he going to be like in class? Do I need to know anything special about having his personal assistant in my classroom? How can I help Theodore connect with the other students in the class? How can I help Theodore participate in class discussions? What should my expectations be for Jay, Doug, Ray, and Jasmine? What should they be able to do in class—everything? 80 percent? What are the social goals for these students? Doug's IEP has several goals related to social skills—what is my responsibility for addressing them? Could we review the students' IEPs to clarify what I should stress with them?

2. Talk to the counselor. How feasible would it be to observe in the classroom and then perhaps facilitate some basic social skills lessons with the entire class during the first nine-week grading period? Twice each week for 20 minutes?

3. Set up cooperative learning groups for the first grading period and get all materials ready. Goal: two cooperative learning activities per week, with first two weeks spent on teaching social skills in groups. Group size? Maybe three, given class composition, with a move to four for the second grading period.

4. Check on the availability of an after-school tutoring program at the elementary school this year. Provide as a reward for some of the students? Other peer-tutoring options?

5. Request more information on Jasmine. See the note about her participation in a social work group on Thursdays during advisory period.

Mr. Barkley's planning list goes on along these lines for another page.

Questions

1. Why is Mr. Barkley concerned about the social interactions of his students? Why is this as much a part of his responsibility as teaching the academic subject matter? How can Mr. Barkley balance the pressure he feels to help his students reach high standards and prepare for high-stakes testing with his understanding that students also need to learn effective strategies for working with each other and adults?

2. What strategies could Mr. Barkley use to sensitize his students to Theodore's needs? What might he do if Jay, Doug, Ray, or Jasmine becomes the object of student complaints about fairness during the school year?

3. What approach to peer tutoring is Mr. Barkley considering? What options might he try to arrange? Who in his class might be the best candidates for each peer-tutoring approach?

4. What questions might Mr. Barkley have concerning the social needs of Kusi and Micki?

5. Mr. Barkley notes that he needs to spend the first two weeks of cooperative learning sessions on social skills. What skills might he teach? How might he teach them? If you were Mr. Barkley, which type of cooperative learning would you implement? How might this type of social skills instruction differ among elementary, middle, and high school students?

6. It appears that Mr. Barkley has one student who will receive social skills instruction in a separate group, and he is requesting that the counselor help him teach social skills during the first grading period. How could a special education teacher also help Mr. Barkley address the social needs of all his students?

Further Readings

Gordon, E. E. (2005). *Peer tutoring: A teacher's resource guide*. New York: Scarecrow Education Press.

This handbook is designed to provide classroom teachers with all the information they need to develop and implement a peer-tutoring program, from selecting a type of program to training tutors to judging program quality. Although not written specifically about students with special needs, it has a wealth of information.

Peck, A., & Scarpati, S. (Eds.). (2002). Social skills development [special issue]. *Teaching Exceptional Children, 35*(1), 8–67.

This special journal issue provides several examples of social skills interventions that span a range from young children to adolescents. The editors place these interventions in the context of inclusive schools.

Snell, M. E., & Janney, R. (2006). *Social relationships and peer support* (2nd ed.). Baltimore: Brookes.

This book, part of a series of publications intended to help educators who are creating and sustaining inclusive practices in their schools, begins by exploring the importance of social relationships in such schools. It also outlines effective strategies for facilitating social relationships and provides ideas for teaching social skills to students. Steps for starting and maintaining a social skills training program are included as well.

Utley, C. (Ed.). (2001). Peer-mediated instruction and interventions: Parts 1 and 2 [special issues]. *Remedial and Special Education, 22*(1–2).

In these two consecutive issues of RASE, you can review an in-depth analysis of a variety of peer-mediated learning approaches, including peer tutoring and cooperative learning, and their application in general education settings. The articles address students with a variety of special needs as well as academic and behavior interventions.

Appendix
CEC Content Standards and INTASC Core Principles

CEC Special Education Content Standards for All Beginning Special Education Teachers

Standard 1: *Foundations*

Special educators understand the field as an evolving and changing discipline based on philosophies, evidence-based principles and theories, relevant laws and policies, diverse historical points of view, and human issues that have historically influenced and continue to influence the field of special education and the education of and treatment of individuals with exceptional needs both in school and society. Special educators understand how these influence professional practice, including assessment, instructional planning, implementation, and program evaluation. Special educators understand how issues of human diversity can impact families, cultures, and schools, and how these complex human issues can interact with issues in the delivery of special education services. They understand the relationships of organizations of special education to the organization and functions of schools, school systems, and other agencies. Special educators use this knowledge as a ground upon which to construct their own personal understandings and philosophies of special education.

Beginning special educators demonstrate their mastery of this standard through the mastery of the CEC Common Core Knowledge and Skills, as well as through the appropriate CEC Specialty Area(s) Knowledge and Skills for which the program is preparing candidates.

Standard 2: *Development and Characteristics of Learners*

Special educators know and demonstrate respect for their students first as unique human beings. Special educators understand the similarities and differences in human development and the characteristics between and among individuals with and without exceptional learning needs (ELN). Moreover, special educators understand how exceptional conditions can interact with the domains of human development and they use this knowledge to respond to the varying abilities

INTASC Core Principles for General and Special Education Teachers

Principle 1

The teacher understands the central concepts, tools of inquiry, and structures of the discipline(s) he or she teaches and can create learning experiences that make these aspects of subject matter meaningful for students.

Implications for students with disabilities: Both general and special education teachers demonstrate an understanding of the primary concepts and ways of thinking and knowing in the content areas they teach as articulated in INTASC subject matter principles and other professional, state, and institutional standards. They understand the underlying values and implications of disability legislation and special education policies and procedures as they relate to their roles and responsibilities in supporting the educational needs of students with disabilities. All teachers provide equitable access to and participation in the general curriculum for students with disabilities.

Principle 2

The teacher understands how children learn and develop, and can provide learning opportunities that support the intellectual, social, and personal development of each learner.

Implications for students with disabilities: Both general and special education teachers understand that all children have similar patterns of learning and development that vary

515

and behaviors of individuals with ELN. Special educators understand how the experiences of individuals with ELN can impact families, as well as individuals' ability to learn, interact socially, and live as fulfilled contributing members of the community.

Beginning special educators demonstrate their mastery of this standard through the mastery of the CEC Common Core Knowledge and Skills, as well as through the appropriate CEC Specialty Area(s) Knowledge and Skills for which the program is preparing candidates.

Standard 3: *Individual Learning Differences*

Special educators understand the effects that an exceptional condition can have on an individual's learning in school and throughout life. Special educators understand that the beliefs, traditions, and values across and within cultures can affect relationships among and between students, their families, and the school community. Moreover, special educators are active and resourceful in seeking to understand how primary language, culture, and familial backgrounds interact with the individual's exceptional condition to impact the individual's academic and social abilities, attitudes, values, interests, and career options. The understanding of these learning differences and their possible interactions provide the foundation on which special educators individualize instruction to provide meaningful and challenging learning for individuals with ELN.

Beginning special educators demonstrate their mastery of this standard through the mastery of the CEC Common Core Knowledge and Skills, as well as through the appropriate CEC Specialty Area(s) Knowledge and Skills for which the program is preparing candidates.

Standard 4: *Individual Strategies*

Special educators possess a repertoire of evidence-based instructional strategies to individualize instruction for individuals with ELN. Special educators select, adapt, and use these instructional strategies to promote challenging learning results in general and special curricula and to appropriately modify learning environments for individuals with ELN. They enhance the learning of critical thinking, problem solving, and performance skills of individuals with ELN, and increase their self-awareness, self-management, self-control, self-reliance, and self-esteem. Moreover, special educators emphasize the development, maintenance, and generalization of knowledge and skills across environments, settings, and the life span.

individually within and across cognitive, social, emotional, and physical areas. They recognize that children with disabilities may exhibit greater individual variation in learning and development than students without disabilities, and that a disability often influences development and functioning in more than one area. Teachers use knowledge of the impact of disabilities on learning and development to optimize learning opportunities for each student.

Principle 3

The teacher understands how students differ in their approaches to learning and creates instructional opportunities that are adapted to diverse learners.

Implications for students with disabilities: Students with disabilities come from a variety of cultures, languages, classes, and ethnicities. Disability, like other aspects of diversity, may affect a student's approach to learning and a teacher's approach to teaching. Teachers understand students with disabilities within the broader context of their families, cultural backgrounds, socioeconomic classes, languages, communities, and peer/social groups.

Principle 4

The teacher understands and uses a variety of instructional strategies to encourage students' development of critical thinking, problem solving, and performance skills.

Implications for students with disabilities: Ensuring that students with disabilities can participate successfully in the general curriculum requires teachers to tailor their instructional strategies to the particular learning needs of individual students. General and special education teachers use a variety of instructional strategies and technologies and know how to modify and adapt the general curriculum to accommodate individual students' needs. Students with disabilities who have goals related to an expanded curriculum will also need specialized instruction to achieve those goals.

Beginning special educators demonstrate their mastery of this standard through the mastery of the CEC Common Core Knowledge and Skills, as well as through the appropriate CEC Specialty Area(s) Knowledge and Skills for which the program is preparing candidates.

Standard 5: *Learning Environments and Social Interactions*

Special educators actively create learning environments for individuals with ELN that foster cultural understanding, safety and emotional well being, positive social interactions, and active engagement of individuals with ELN. In addition, special educators foster environments in which diversity is valued and individuals are taught to live harmoniously and productively in a culturally diverse world. Special educators shape environments to encourage the independence, self-motivation, self-direction, personal empowerment, and self-advocacy of individuals with ELN. Special educators help their general education colleagues integrate individuals with ELN in regular environments and engage them in meaningful learning activities and interactions. Special educators use direct motivational and instructional interventions with individuals with ELN to teach them to respond effectively to current expectations. When necessary, special educators can safely intervene with individuals with ELN in crises. Special educators coordinate all these efforts and provide guidance and direction to paraeducators and others, such as classroom volunteers and tutors.

Beginning special educators demonstrate their mastery of this standard through the mastery of the CEC Common Core Knowledge and Skills, as well as through the appropriate CEC Specialty Area(s) Knowledge and Skills for which the program is preparing candidates.

Standard 6: *Communication*

Special educators understand typical and atypical language development and the ways in which exceptional conditions can interact with an individual's experience with and use of language. Special educators use individualized strategies to enhance language development and teach communication skills to individuals with ELN. Special educators are familiar with augmentative, alternative, and assistive technologies to support and enhance communication of individuals with exceptional needs. Special educators match their communication methods to an individual's language proficiency and cultural and linguistic differences. Special educators provide effective language models, and they use communication strategies and resources to facilitate understanding of subject matter for individuals with ELN whose primary language is not English.

Principle 5

The teacher uses an understanding of individual and group motivation and behavior to create a learning environment that encourages positive social interaction, active engagement in learning, and self-motivation.

Implications for students with disabilities: Students' affiliation and acceptance within a community is an important basis for developing social responsibility, self-esteem, and positive peer relations. Students learn more effectively when they are valued members of a learning community in which everyone can grow and learn. Teachers welcome students with disabilities and take deliberate action to ensure that they are included as members of the learning community. Teachers may also need to structure activities that specifically foster engagement, self-motivation, and independent learning in students with disabilities.

Principle 6

The teacher uses knowledge of effective verbal, nonverbal, and media communication technologies to foster active inquiry, collaboration, and supportive interaction in the classroom.

Implications for students with disabilities: Students with disabilities often have communication or language delays or disorders associated with their disabilities. They may require multiple and alternative modes of communication. Teachers set a high priority on establishing a safe and comfortable environment in which students with disabilities are encouraged and supported to use language and contribute their ideas. They teach language and communication skills, make accommodations to promote effective communication, and

Beginning special educators demonstrate their mastery of this standard through the mastery of the CEC Common Core Knowledge and Skills, as well as through the appropriate CEC Specialty Area(s) Knowledge and Skills for which the program is preparing candidates.

Standard 7: *Instructional Planning*

Individualized decision making and instruction is at the center of special education practice. Special educators develop long-range individualized instructional plans anchored in both general and special curricula. In addition, special educators systematically translate these individualized plans into carefully selected shorter-range goals and objectives taking into consideration an individual's abilities and needs, the learning environment, and a myriad of cultural and linguistic factors. Individualized instructional plans emphasize explicit modeling and efficient guided practice to assure acquisition and fluency through maintenance and generalization. Understanding of these factors, as well as the implications of an individual's exceptional condition, guides the special educator's selection, adaptation, and creation of materials, and the use of powerful instructional variables. Instructional plans are modified based on ongoing analysis of the individual's learning progress. Moreover, special educators facilitate this instructional planning in a collaborative context including the individuals with exceptionalities, families, professional colleagues, and personnel from other agencies as appropriate. Special educators also develop a variety of individualized transition plans, such as transitions from preschool to elementary school and from secondary settings to a variety of postsecondary work and learning contexts. Special educators are comfortable using appropriate technologies to support instructional planning and individualized instruction.

Beginning special educators demonstrate their mastery of this standard through the mastery of the CEC Common Core Knowledge and Skills, as well as through the appropriate CEC Specialty Area(s) Knowledge and Skills for which the program is preparing candidates.

Standard 8: *Assessment*

Assessment is integral to the decision making and teaching of special educators, and special educators use multiple types of assessment information for a variety of educational decisions. Special educators use the results of assessments to help identify exceptional learning needs and to develop and implement individualized instructional programs, as well as to adjust instruction in response to ongoing learning progress. Special educators understand the legal policies and ethical principles of measurement and assessment

Principle 7

encourage and support the use of technology to promote learning and communication.

The teacher plans instruction based on knowledge of subject matter, students, the community, and curriculum goals.

Implications for students with disabilities: While students with disabilities often pursue the same learning goals within the general curriculum and benefit from instruction in a manner that is similar to that of their non-disabled peers, they may require adjustments in goals, teaching strategies, or supports. Some students with disabilities may require an expanded curriculum that may include areas such as functional life skills, communication skills, or behavior/social skills. Planning for students with disabilities requires an individualized plan of instruction and is a collaborative process that involves special and general educators, the student (when appropriate), families, and other professionals.

Principle 8

The teacher understands and uses formal and informal assessment strategies to evaluate and ensure the continuous intellectual, social, and physical development of the learner.

Implications for students with disabilities: Individualized comprehensive assessments are required for students with disabilities and are used to determine eligibility for special education services, to plan individualized instruction, and related to referral, eligibility, program planning, instruction, and placement for individuals with ELN, including those from culturally and linguistically diverse backgrounds. Special educators understand measurement theory and practices for addressing issues of validity, reliability, norms, bias, and interpretation of assessment results. In addition, special educators understand the appropriate use and limitations of various types of assessments. Special educators collaborate with families and other colleagues to assure nonbiased, meaningful assessments and decision making. Special educators conduct formal and informal assessments of behavior, learning, achievement, and environments to design learning experiences that support the growth and development of individuals with ELN. Special educators use assessment information to identify supports and adaptations required for individuals with ELN to access the general curriculum and to participate in school, system, and statewide assessment programs. Special educators regularly monitor the progress of individuals with ELN in general and special curricula. Special educators use appropriate technologies to support their assessments.

Beginning special educators demonstrate their mastery of this standard through the mastery of the CEC Common Core Knowledge and Skills, as well as through the appropriate CEC Specialty Area(s) Knowledge and Skills for which the program is preparing candidates.

Standard 9: *Professional and Ethical Practice*

Special educators are guided by the profession's ethical and professional practice standards. Special educators practice in multiple roles and complex situations across wide age and developmental ranges. Their practice requires ongoing attention to legal matters along with serious professional and ethical considerations. Special educators engage in professional activities and participate in learning communities that benefit individuals with ELN, their families, colleagues, and their own professional growth. Special educators view themselves as lifelong learners and regularly reflect on and adjust their practice. Special educators are aware of how their own and others' attitudes, behaviors, and ways of communicating can influence their practice. Special educators understand that culture and language can interact with exceptionalities, and are sensitive to the many aspects of diversity of individuals with ELN and their families. Special educators actively plan and engage in activities that foster their professional growth and keep them current with evidence-based best practices. Special educators know their own limits of practice and practice within them.

Beginning special educators demonstrate their mastery of this standard through the mastery of the CEC Common

to monitor and evaluate student performance. It is also expected that students with disabilities will participate in the overall assessment programs of the classroom, school district, and state, and that they may require accommodations to demonstrate their knowledge and skills. In addition, some students with disabilities may require assessments related to achievement in an expanded curriculum (i.e., alternate assessments).

Principle 9

The teacher is a reflective practitioner who continually evaluates the effects of his/her choices and actions on others (students, parents, and other professionals in the learning community) and who actively seeks out opportunities to grow professionally.

Implications for students with disabilities: Teacher reflection is essential for designing, monitoring, and adapting instruction for all students, including students with disabilities. Teachers reflect on their knowledge of the learning strengths and needs of individual students with disabilities, and question and evaluate the appropriateness and effectiveness of their instructional choices and practices for building on those strengths and meeting those needs. Based on their data-based reflections, teachers engage in actions that consistently support and promote the achievement of students with disabilities.

Core Knowledge and Skills, as well as through the appropriate CEC Specialty Area(s) Knowledge and Skills for which the program is preparing candidates.

Standard 10: *Collaboration*

Special educators routinely and effectively collaborate with families, other educators, related service providers, and personnel from community agencies in culturally responsive ways. This collaboration assures that the needs of individuals with ELN are addressed throughout schooling. Moreover, special educators embrace their special role as advocate for individuals with ELN. Special educators promote and advocate the learning and well being of individuals with ELN across a wide range of settings and a range of different learning experiences. Special educators are viewed as specialists by a myriad of people who actively seek their collaboration to effectively include and teach individuals with ELN. Special educators are a resource to their colleagues in understanding the laws and policies relevant to individuals with ELN. Special educators use collaboration to facilitate the successful transitions of individuals with ELN across settings and services.

Beginning special educators demonstrate their mastery of this standard through the mastery of the CEC Common Core Knowledge and Skills, as well as through the appropriate CEC Specialty Area(s) Knowledge and Skills for which the program is preparing candidates.

Principle 10

The teacher fosters relationships with school colleagues, families, and agencies in the larger community to support students' learning and well-being.

Implications for students with disabilities: Families, schools, and communities are important contexts for teaching, learning, and development. Teachers advocate for students with disabilities to receive the support they need to be successful in the general curriculum and to achieve the goals of their individual education plans. They collaborate with each other, with other professionals, and with families to ensure that students with disabilities are valued members of the classroom, school, and larger communities.

Sources: Council for Exceptional Children. (2003). *What every special educator must know: The international standards for the preparation and certification of special education* (5th ed.). Arlington, VA: Author; Council of Chief State School Officers. (1992). *Model standards for beginning teacher licensing, assessment, and development: A resource for state dialogue.* Washington, DC: Author. Available at www.ccsso.org/content/pdfs/corestrd.pdf. Reprinted with permission.

Glossary

ABC analysis Systematic recording of antecedents, behaviors, and consequences as a strategy for analyzing student behavior.

absence seizure Seizure that is brief and often characterized by momentary lapses of attention. Also called a *petit mal seizure*.

academic learning time The time students are meaningfully and successfully engaged in school.

academic survival skills Skills needed to succeed in school, including regular and punctual attendance, organization, task completion, independence, motivation, and appropriate social skills.

acceleration Approach for educating gifted and talented students based on allowing them to move through all or part of the curriculum at their own, accelerated pace.

accuracy The extent to which a student's academic performance is without errors.

acquired immune deficiency syndrome (AIDS) Disease that results when students are infected with the human immunodeficiency virus (HIV) and their bodies lose the ability to fight infection.

activity reinforcer Positive activity that causes a behavior to increase. An example of an activity reinforcer is a student being rewarded with extra time to work on the computer.

ADA *See* Americans with Disabilities Act.

adaptive physical educator Specialist with expertise in assessing students' motor needs and designing and delivering physical education programs that accommodate those needs.

ADD *See* attention deficit disorder.

adequate yearly progress (AYP) The minimum level of improvement, set by each state, that schools and districts must achieve toward reaching the goals of the No Child Left Behind Act of 2001.

ADHD *See* attention deficit–hyperactive disorder.

administrator Professional responsible for managing some aspect of schools; includes principals, assistant principals, department chairpersons, team leaders, special services coordinators, district administrators, and others.

advance organizer Information, often presented as organizational signals, that makes content more understandable by putting it within a more general framework.

advocate Individual who works to ensure that parents understand their rights and that school professionals provide an appropriate education for parents' children with disabilities.

AIDS *See* acquired immune deficiency syndrome.

alternate assessment A form of functional assessment for students with severe disabilities who are unable to participate in the standard state and district-wide assessment programs.

alternative forms of questions Testing adaptations that involve changing the construction of a test item or substituting one kind of test item for another. Examples of alternative forms of questions include reducing the choices on a multiple choice item from four to two or adding a word bank to fill-in-the-blank items.

alternatives to letter and number grades Ways to evaluate student test performance using pass-fail grades and/or checklists of student skills.

alternative teaching Co-teaching option in which students are divided into one large and one small group. The large group receives the planned instruction. The small group receives reteaching, preteaching, enrichment, or other special instruction.

alternative test site A type of testing accommodation that involves changing the location where a student with a disability is tested to make sure the results of the test are accurate. An example is testing a student with attention problems in a room having fewer distractions.

alternative ways of administering tests Testing adaptations that involve changing the ways students respond on tests and/or the ways teachers give tests. An example of changing the way students respond on tests is responding orally to written test items. An example of changing the way teachers give tests is giving a test orally.

American Sign Language (ASL) A sign language not based on the grammar or structures of English, used by some people with hearing impairments.

Americans with Disabilities Act (ADA) Civil rights law passed in 1990 that protects individuals with disabilities from discrimination and requires building and transportation accessibility and reasonable accommodations in the workplace.

anecdotal recording Strategy for recording behavior in which incidents before and after a behavior are recorded along with a description of the behavior.

annual goal Broad statement describing estimated yearly outcomes for a student with a disability. Annual goals address areas of identified needs.

annual review Yearly process of convening a team that includes a parent, teacher, administrator, and others as needed to review and update a student's IEP.

ANOTES Learning strategy for organizing lecture notes for test preparation. The steps are: ask yourself if you have a date and topic, name the main ideas and details, observe ideas also in text, try margin noting and use SAND strategy, examine for omissions or unclear ideas, and summarize key points.

anticipation guide Series of statements, some of which may not be true, related to material that is about to be presented during instruction, given to students as a way of activating their knowledge by making predictions about the topic.

anxiety Condition in which an individual experiences extraordinary worry in some situations or worries excessively about future situations.

articulation Production of speech sounds.

Asperger syndrome Mild form of autism in which an individual develops speech but has gross motor problems, intense interests in a narrow range of topics, and chronic difficulty in forming and sustaining social relationships.

assessment Process of gathering information to monitor progress and make educational decisions.

assistive technology (AT) Any of a wide variety of technology applications designed to help students with disabilities learn, communicate, and otherwise function more independently by bypassing their disabilities.

asthma Physical condition in which an individual experiences difficulty breathing, especially during physically or psychologically stressful activities.

at risk Term used to describe students who have characteristics, live in conditions, or have experiences that make them more likely than others to experience failure in schools.

attention deficit disorder (ADD) Term sometimes used as a synonym for attention deficit–hyperactivity disorder.

attention deficit–hyperactivity disorder (ADHD) Medical condition in which students have significant inability to attend, excessive motor activity, and/or impulsivity.

attribution retraining Teaching program that increases student task persistence and performance by convincing them that their failures are due to effort and can therefore be overcome.

augmentative and alternative communication (AAC) Ways other than speech to send a message to another individual, including nonaided communication such as using sign language or gestures and facial expressions and aided communication such as using computers or other simple or complex devices as communication tools.

authentic learning tasks Tasks used in performance-based assessment that are based on real-world contexts and lead to real-world outcomes.

autism Condition in which an individual lacks social responsiveness from a very early age, has a high need for structure and routines, and demonstrates significant language impairments. These characteristics interfere with learning.

autism spectrum disorder (ASD) Contemporary term used to convey the diversity of autism and related disorders, from classic autism that usually includes intellectual disabilities, to Asperger syndrome in which individuals may be intellectually gifted.

balanced grading A type of grading adaptation that considers effort and/or the performance of learning strategies along with products of performance when determining a student's grade.

basal textbook A book used for instruction in basic-skills areas that contains all key components of the curriculum to be taught for that subject. Often called a *basal*.

basic-skills instruction Instruction in the tool skills of reading, writing, and math.

behavior contract Agreement between a teacher (or other adult) and student that clearly specifies student performance expectations, rewards for meeting expectations, consequences of not meeting expectations, and the time frame for which the agreement is valid.

behavior intervention plan (BIP) A detailed strategy, developed on the basis of a functional behavior assessment, to address significant behavior problems being experienced by a student with a disability. The plan typically includes detailed descriptions of interventions, persons responsible, a timeline, and methods for data collection. This plan is required by federal law when a student with a disability has significant behavior problems.

big ideas Important principles that help learners understand the connections among facts and concepts they learn.

bilingual education program Education approach in which students with limited English skills learn core subjects in a separate setting in their native language and spend the remainder of their school day with English-speaking peers.

bilingual special education program Special education approach in which students with disabilities with limited English skills learn core subjects in a separate setting in their native language.

bilingual special education teacher Teacher who works with students with disabilities whose native language is not English.

bilingual teacher Teacher who teaches students whose native language is not English.

blind Condition in which an individual has little or no vision and relies on auditory and other input for learning.

Braille Writing system, used by individuals who have vision impairments, that uses various combinations of six raised dots punched on paper read with the fingertips.

brainstorming Strategy for generating solutions to problems in which participants call out ideas, building on one another's responses, deferring all evaluation.

Brown v. Board of Education Supreme Court decision in 1954 that established that it is unlawful and discriminatory to create separate schools for African American students. This "separate cannot be equal" concept was later applied to students with disabilities.

bypass strategies Ways of receiving or expressing information that allow students to gain access to or demonstrate mastery of the curriculum in alternate ways. For examples, a bypass strategy for a student with a reading disability would be a book on a CD-ROM.

CALL UP Learning strategy for taking lecture notes. The steps are: copy from board or transparency, add details, listen and write the question, listen and write the answer, utilize the text, and put in your words.

CAPS Four-step learning strategy for helping a student decide what is important in a story: ask who the characters are; identify the aim of the story; decide what problem happens; and determine how the problem is solved.

catch 'em being good Behavior management strategy in which a teacher notices appropriate student behavior and positively comments on it, either privately to the student or publicly to the class.

CBA *See* curriculum-based assessment.

CBM *See* cognitive behavior management.

cerebral palsy Most common type of orthopedic impairment among public school students, caused by brain injury before or during birth and resulting in poor motor coordination and abnormal motor patterns.

changing letter or number grades A way of clarifying letter and number grades by supplementing them with other ways of evaluating and reporting learner progress such as written or verbal comments, logs of student activities, and portfolios.

CHECK Learning strategy for using spell checkers more effectively. The steps are: check the beginning sound of the word; hunt for the correct consonants; examine the vowels; check changes in suggested word lists for hints; and keep repeating steps 1–4.

child abuse Situation in which a parent or other caregiver inflicts or allows others to inflict injury on a child, or permits a substantial risk of injury to exist.

child neglect Situation in which a parent or other caregiver fails to provide the necessary supports for a child's well-being.

CHROME Mnemonic for remembering the six methods of scientific investigation: categorization, hypothesis, reasoning, observation, measurement, and experimentation.

chunking Memorization strategy in which students are taught to remember five to seven key ideas at one time.

CIRC *See* Cooperative Integrated Reading and Composition.

Circle of Friends Program designed to help students without disabilities understand how important it is to have friends with disabilities and to encourage them to form friendships with classmates with disabilities.

classroom climate The overall atmosphere of a classroom, including whether it is friendly and pleasant, based on the expectations of teachers and their interactions with students.

classroom grouping Various grouping arrangements, such as teaching the whole class at once or in small groups, that modify the classroom environment. Classroom grouping may be teacher centered or peer mediated.

classroom instruction Strategies through which a teacher presents curriculum content to students.

classroom organization Strategies through which a teacher establishes and maintains order in a classroom.

classwide peer tutoring (CWPT) Peer-mediated instruction in which all students in a class are partnered. Both students serve as the tutor and tutee following a clear procedure, and they are rewarded for demonstrating appropriate social behaviors.

cluster programs Special education service delivery system in which students with similar needs from several schools or an entire district attend a single school to receive special education services.

cognitive behavior management (CBM) Behavior management strategy in which students learn to monitor and change their own behavior.

collaboration A style of interaction professionals use in order to accomplish a goal they share, often stressed in inclusive schools.

community-based education Approach to instruction in which what is learned in school is related to activities that occur in the community.

compensatory strategies *See* bypass strategies.

competency checklist Evaluation technique in which student learning is checked against a listing of key concepts or ideas being taught.

comprehension Reading skill involving understanding the meaning of what has been read.

concept diagram Specific type of graphic organizer used to present vocabulary words that includes definitions and characteristics.

concept map Graphic organizer showing relationships among concepts of instruction as well as essential characteristics of the concepts.

constructivistic teaching Type of teaching based on the belief that students are capable of constructing meaning on their own, in most cases, without explicit instruction.

consultant Specialist who provides particular expertise to teachers and others when an extraordinary student need arises.

consultation Specialized problem-solving process in which one professional with particular expertise assists another professional or parent who needs the benefit of that expertise; used as an instructional approach for some students with disabilities.

consulting teacher Special education teacher who meets with general education teachers to problem solve and monitor student progress but who typically has little or no direct contact with students.

content-area textbook A book used for instruction in science, social studies, or other content areas.

controlled materials Instructional materials at the student's reading level, of high interest and free of complex vocabulary and concepts, often used while teaching students a learning strategy.

cooperative integrated reading and composition (CIRC) Cooperative learning program for teaching reading, writing, and other language arts to students in upper elementary grades.

cooperative learning Student-centered instructional approach in which students work in small, mixed-ability groups with a shared learning goal.

COPS Learning strategy for proofreading papers with these steps: Have I capitalized the first word and proper nouns? How is the overall appearance of my paper; have I made any handwriting, margin, or messy errors? Have I used end punctuation, commas, and semicolons carefully? Do words look like they are spelled right; can I sound them out or use a dictionary?

co-teaching Instructional approach in which two or more teachers or other certified staff share instruction for a single group of students within a single classroom setting.

counselor Specialist with expertise in meeting students' social and affective needs.

credit/no credit grading system *See* pass/fail grading system.

cross-age tutoring Peer tutoring approach in which older students tutor younger ones.

cross-categorical approach Instructional approach in which the cognitive, learning, affective, and social and emotional needs of students, not their disability labels, form the basis for planning and delivering instruction.

cue words Words that make patterns of information more conspicuous for students, such as the words "similar" and "different," signalling the presence of a compare/contrast pattern.

curriculum-based assessment (CBA) Method of measuring the level of achievement of students in terms of what they are taught in the classroom.

curriculum placement Type of assessment decision concerning where to begin instruction for students.

CWPT *See* classwide peer tutoring.

cystic fibrosis Genetically transmitted disease in which the body produces excessive mucus that eventually damages the lungs and causes heart failure.

daily activity log Strategy for providing ongoing information for students and their parents about learning by noting daily observations of student work, effort, and outcomes.

DARE A strategy for writing persuasive essays that stresses four key steps: develop a topic sentence, add supporting details, reject counter-arguments, and end with a conclusion.

deaf Hearing impairment in which the individual cannot process linguistic information through hearing with or without the use of hearing aids and relies on visual and other input for learning.

deaf–blind Condition in which an individual has both significant visual and hearing impairments that interfere with learning.

decibel (dB) Unit for measuring the loudness of sounds.

decoding Reading skill involving accurately identifying words and fluently pronouncing them.

DEFENDS Learning strategy for writing a defense of a position with these steps: decide on an exact position; examine the reasons for the position; form a list of points to explain each reason; expose the position in the first sentence; note each reason and supporting points; drive home the position in the last sentence; and search for errors and correct.

depression Condition in which an individual is persistently and seriously unhappy, with a loss of interest or pleasure in all or almost all usual activities. Symptoms of depression include changes in appetite or weight, sleep disturbances, loss of energy, feelings of worthlessness, and thoughts of death or suicide.

developmental delay Significant delay in one or more of the following areas leading to the need for special education and related services: physical development, cognitive development, communication development, social or emotional development, or adaptive development. Applicable only for children ages 3–9.

developmental disability A significant, chronic condition, typically physical, cognitive, or a combination of both, that results in the need for special education and related services.

IDEA-97 permits the use of this term in lieu of a more specific disability label for children until age 9.

diabetes Disease in which the body does not produce enough insulin to process the carbohydrates eaten.

diagnosis Type of assessment decision concerning whether or not a student meets established federal guidelines for being classified as having a disability and, if so, the nature and extent of the disability.

diagnostic teaching Sample lessons and other instructional activities carried out with students experiencing extreme academic or behavioral difficulty as part of screening.

differential reinforcement of incompatible behaviors Reinforcing an appropriate behavior that is incompatible with another undesirable behavior in order to increase the positive behavior.

differentiated instruction A form of instruction that meets students' diverse needs by providing materials and tasks of varied levels of difficulty, with varying degrees of support, through multiple instructional groups and time variations.

differentiated report cards Report cards that have individualized provisions for students, including additional information to clarify grades and separate grades for different grading elements such as progress and effort.

direct instruction Research-based instructional approach in which the teacher presents subject matter using a review of previously taught information, presentation of new concepts or skills, guided practice, feedback and correction, independent student practice, and frequent review.

disability Condition characterized by a physical, cognitive, psychological, or social difficulty so severe that it negatively affects student learning. In the Americans with Disabilities Act, a disability is defined as a condition that limits some major life activity.

discipline Term to describe the set of classroom expectations, including rules for behavior, that serves as a means for facilitating student learning.

discovery learning *See* inquiry learning.

Down syndrome Most prevalent type of biologically caused cognitive disability, caused by the failure of one pair of chromosomes to separate at conception.

DRAW Strategy for teaching multiplication facts that are not yet committed to memory, consisting of these steps: discover the sign; read the problem; answer, or draw and check; and write the answer.

drill-and-practice programs A form of computer-assisted instruction in which students learn in small steps, are given systematic feedback, and engage in a lot of practice until mastery is attained.

due process Procedures outlined in IDEA for ensuring that parents' and children's rights are protected and for resolving disputes between parents and school district personnel concerning any aspect of special education.

duration recording Strategy for recording behavior in which the length of time a behavior occurs is recorded.

dyslexia A word used to refer to the condition of a severe reading disability.

echolalic speech Occurs when an individual communicates by repeating what others have said instead of producing original speech.

ED *See* emotional disturbance.

Education for All Handicapped Children Act (EHCA) *See* Public Law 94-142.

emotional disturbance (ED) Condition in which an individual has significant difficulty in the social and emotional domain, so much so that it interferes with learning.

English-language learners (ELLs) Students whose native language is not English and who are developing their English skills while in school.

enrichment Approach for educating gifted and talented students based on helping them elaborate on or extend concepts being presented to all students.

environmental inventory Assessment procedure, often used for students with moderate or severe disabilities, designed to find out what adaptations or supports are needed to increase student participation in classroom and community environments.

epilepsy Physical condition in which the brain experiences sudden but brief changes in its functioning leading to seizures.

evaluation Procedures used to determine whether teaching is effective, to provide feedback to students and their parents about student learning, and to inform school boards and communities about school effectiveness.

event recording Strategy for recording behavior in which each occurrence of the behavior is counted.

example selection Teacher choice of examples during instruction. Example selection directly affects student understanding of instruction.

example sequence Order of presentation of examples during instruction. Example sequence directly affects student understanding of instruction.

exemplar A sample student performance designed to specify a level of achievement in authentic learning evaluation. For example, a writing sample of an "average" seventh-grader is an exemplar against which other students' writing can be compared.

expressive language An individual's ability to communicate meaning clearly through speech.

extinction Strategy for decreasing negative behavior by no longer reinforcing it; most effective when the undesirable behavior has been inadvertently reinforced by the teacher.

facilitated communication Method of assisting individuals with autism and other disabilities to communicate by gently supporting the wrist, arm, or shoulder on a typewriter or computer keyboard. This method is controversial.

fading out Gradual process for decreasing the use of behavioral strategies to support appropriate student behavior.

FAE *See* fetal alcohol effects.

family-centered practices Approach for working with families based on the notion that outcomes are best for students when their families' perspectives are respected, family input is sincerely sought, and families gain information that can assist them to make the best decisions for their children.

FAS *See* fetal alcohol syndrome.

FASTDRAW Strategy for helping students make the transition from pictures to abstract numbers. The following steps are performed before beginning the DRAW strategy: find what you're solving for; ask yourself, "What are the parts of the problem?"; set up the numbers; and tie down the sign.

FBA *See* functional behavior assessment.

fetal alcohol effects (FAE) Mild form of fetal alcohol syndrome (FAS), often without physical characteristics. Students with FAE often experience a variety of learning and behavior problems in school.

fetal alcohol syndrome (FAS) Medical condition caused by prenatal maternal abuse of alcohol, often resulting in slight physical abnormalities and learning, cognitive, or emotional disabilities.

finger spelling Communication system in which each alphabet letter is assigned a specific hand position. Finger spelling is often used to communicate proper names or technical words for which no other sign language signs exist.

five R's of note taking Learning strategy for note taking with these steps: record the main ideas and important details; reduce to concise phrases; recite key information using your concise phrases as cues; reflect on your notes by adding your own ideas; and review all the key information.

fluency The rate at which a student performs an academic task such as calculating math problems or reading.

FOIL Four-step learning strategy for multiplying binomials in algebra: multiply the first terms; multiply the outermost terms; multiply the innermost terms; and multiply the last terms.

frame of reference An individual's predisposition to respond to a situation in a certain way based on his background, education, experiences, and work history.

functional behavior assessment (FBA) The process of gathering detailed data on a student's behavior and the context in which it occurs for the purpose of determining the reasons for it and creating a behavior intervention plan. This process is required by federal law when a student with a disability has significant behavior problems.

functional curriculum Instructional approach in which goals and objectives are based on real-life skills needed for adulthood. Examples of skills addressed in a functional curriculum include shopping and making purchases; reading common signs such as exit, stop, and sale; riding public transportation; and interacting with peers and adults.

general education teacher Elementary, middle school, junior high, or high school teacher whose primary responsibility is teaching one or more class groups.

generalized tonic-clonic seizure Seizure involving the entire body. Also called a *grand mal seizure.*

gifted and talented Demonstrated ability far above average in one or several areas including overall intellectual ability, leadership, specific academic subjects, creativity, athletics, or the visual or performing arts.

GIVE ME FIVE A learning strategy that focuses students' attention on five body parts to improve their listening skills: eyes on speaker, mouth quiet, body still, ears listening, and hands free.

Good Behavior Game Strategy for reducing disruptive behavior and promoting positive behavior in the classroom in which students work on teams to earn points for appropriate behavior toward a reward.

grading contract Agreement between a teacher and student that specifies the quantity, quality, and timeliness of work required to receive a specific grade.

grading criteria The standard on which a student's academic performance is evaluated and graded.

grand mal seizure *See* generalized tonic-clonic seizure.

graphic organizer Visual format that helps students to organize their understanding of information being presented or read and the relationships between various parts of the information.

group-administered standardized achievement test Standardized achievement test given to large groups of students at one time, usually administered by general education teachers, useful as a screening measure.

group roles Assigned roles for students in cooperative groups that help the group function effectively. Roles commonly assigned include encourager, monitor, leader, and recorder.

guided practice A teaching technique where students are given verbal cues when first attempting a skill.

handicap Term, generally no longer preferred, to describe disabilities.

hard of hearing Hearing impairment in which an individual has some hearing through which to process linguistic information, possibly with the assistance of hearing aids or other assistive devices.

hearing impairment Condition in which an individual has the inability or limited ability to receive information auditorily such that it interferes with learning.

hemophilia Genetically transmitted disease in which blood does not properly coagulate.

hertz (Hz) Unit for measuring the pitch or tone of sounds.

heterogeneous grouping *See* mixed-skill grouping.

high-incidence disability Any of the most common disabilities outlined in P.L. 105-17, including learning disabilities, speech or language impairments, mild mental retardation, and serious emotional disturbance.

highly qualified teacher Term from both NCLB and IDEA and defined by each state; specifies that a professional has met rigorous requirements documenting qualifications to teach in a specific academic area (e.g., math, English) or special education. Some teachers are highly qualified in both academic content areas and special education.

high-stakes tests Assessments designed to measure whether students have obtained state learning standards.

HIV *See* human immunodeficiency virus.

homework The most common form of student practice.

homogeneous grouping *See* same-skill grouping.

human immunodeficiency virus (HIV) Viral disease in which the body loses its ability to fight off infection. Individuals with HIV often become infected with AIDS.

hyperactive-impulsive disorder Type of ADHD characterized by excessive movement and other motor activity including fidgeting, a need to move around a room even when others are seated, and rapid changes in activities.

individualized grading Accommodations made for individual students that are included on students' IEPs. Individualized grading includes accommodations that involve changing either the elements being graded such as curriculum content, class participation, and homework, or the value or weights assigned to these elements.

Individuals with Disabilities Education Improvement Act (IDEA) Public Law 101-476. Current federal special education law.

IEP *See* individualized education program.

IFSP *See* Individualized Family Service Plan.

improvement grade Giving credit in evaluation of student performance for progress made, based on the student's level of learning prior to instruction.

impulsivity The extent to which an individual acts before thinking, often a characteristic of students with high-incidence disabilities or ADHD.

INCLUDE A strategy for accommodating students with special needs in the general education classroom.

inclusion *See* inclusive practices.

inclusion specialist Special education teacher responsible for providing a wide variety of supports to students with disabilities and general education teachers who teach them. Inclusion specialists most often work with students with low-incidence disabilities. Sometimes called a *support facilitator.*

inclusive practices Term to describe a professional belief that students with disabilities should be integrated into general education classrooms whether or not they can meet traditional curricular standards and should be full members of those classrooms.

independent learning skills Skills students need to manage their own learning, including note taking, textbook reading, test taking, written expression, and time management.

indirect instruction A type of teaching based on the belief that children are natually active learners and that given the appropriate instructional environment, they actively construct knowledge and solve problems in developmentally appropriate ways.

individualized education program (IEP) Document prepared by the multidisciplinary team or annual review team that specifies a student's level of functioning and needs, the instructional goals and objectives for the student and how they will be evaluated, the nature and extent of special education and related services to be received, and the initiation date and duration of the services. Each student's IEP is updated annually.

individualized family service plan (IFSP) Education plan for children receiving services through P.L. 99-457. Similar to an IEP.

individualized instruction Instruction designed to meet the specific needs of a student with a disability; a requirement of IDEA.

individually administered diagnostic test Diagnostic achievement test given to one student at a time, often administered by a special education teacher or school psychologist, useful as a diagnostic measure. These tests provide more specific information than group-administered achievement tests do.

Individuals with Disabilities Education Act (IDEA) Federal education law that updates the 1975 Education for All Handicapped Children Act and ensures that students with disabilities receive special education and related services through prescribed policies and procedures.

inquiry learning The most common method of nondirect instruction. *See also* nondirect instruction.

instructional accommodations Services or supports provided to help students gain full access to class content and instruction, and to help them demonstrate accurately what they know.

instructional adaptation Any strategy for adapting curriculum materials, teacher instruction, or student practice activities that increases the likelihood of success for students with special needs.

instructional assistance team (IAT) Team of teachers, specialists, and administrators that solves problems about students experiencing academic or behavior difficulty and decides whether students should be individually assessed for possible special education services.

instructional evaluation Type of assessment decision concerning whether to continue or change instructional procedures that have been initiated with students.

instructional materials The textbooks, manipulatives, models, and technology used as part of instruction.

instructional methods The ways in which teachers present content or skills to students and evaluate whether learning has occurred.

instructional modifications Changes in classroom instruction that involve altering student content expectations and performance outcomes.

integration The physical, social, and instructional assimilation of students with disabilities in general education settings.

intellectual disability Term sometimes used as a synonym for *mental retardation.*

intent The purpose or goal of a student's behavior, not always clear from the behavior itself. An example of an intent occurs when a student repeatedly calls out in class to gain the teacher's attention; that is, the intent is teacher attention.

interval recording Strategy for recording behavior in which observation occurs for brief segments of time and any occurrence of the behavior during the segment is noted.

intervention assisstance team Group of professionals, including general education teachers, that analyzes the strengths and problems of referred students to identify strategies to address the problems. If not successful this team may recommend that a student be assessed to determine special education eligibility.

itinerant teacher Special education teacher who provides services to students with disabilities and teaches in two or more schools.

Jigsaw Classroom Cooperative learning program in which work group team members are assigned to expert groups to master part of the assigned material to which no other group has access. In the work group, each team member has an opportunity to present his or her part of the material. Students are then assessed for mastery individually.

job coach A special education professional who accompanies students with disabilities to job sites and helps them master the skills needed to perform the job.

keyword method Mnemonic for remembering definitions and factual information in which visual imagery is used to enhance recall.

KWL Plus Three-step learning strategy for reading comprehension: what you already know; what you want to know; and what you learned.

LAMPS Learning strategy for remembering the steps for regrouping in addition with these steps: line up the numbers according to their decimal points; add the right column of

numbers; if more than nine continue to the next step; put the 1s below the column; and send the 10s to the top of the next column.

LD *See* learning disability.

learned helplessness Characteristic of some students with disabilities in which they see little relationship between their own efforts and school or social success, often resulting in a belief that they cannot perform challenging tasks.

learning and behavior disabilities Term used to describe collectively learning disabilities, serious emotional disturbance, and mild cognitive disabilities.

learning disability (LD) Condition in which a student has dysfunction in processing information typically found in language-based activities, resulting in interference with learning. Students with learning disabilities have average or above-average intelligence but experience significant problems in learning how to read, write, and/or use a computer.

learning outcomes Specific goals or outcomes students are expected to accomplish as a result of a unit of instruction.

learning strategies Techniques, principles, or rules that enable a student to solve problems and complete tasks independently.

Learning Together Cooperative learning program in which groups of two to six members learn specific skills for interacting with one another and then work together in various formal and informal group structures to learn material.

least restrictive environment (LRE) The setting as similar as possible to that for students without disabilities in which a student with a disability can be educated, with appropriate supports provided. For most students, the LRE is a general education classroom.

legal blindness Visual impairment in which an individual's best eye, with correction, has vision of 20/200 or less, or the visual field is 20 percent or less.

lesson organizer routine A teaching method that helps teachers convert content into understandable formats that meet the diverse needs of students. The method has three components: the lesson organizer device, linking steps, and cue-do-review sequence.

low demand request Behavior management strategy in which the teacher helps a student transition from one activity to another by making a series of simple requests of the student that are unrelated to the targeted task.

low-incidence disability Any of the less common disabilities outlined in P.L. 105-17, including multiple disabilities, hearing impairments, orthopedic impairments, other health impairments, visual impairments, deaf-blindness, autism, and traumatic brain injury.

LRE *See* least restrictive environment.

mainstreaming Term for placing students with disabilities in general education settings when they can meet traditional academic expectations with minimal assistance, or when those expectations are not relevant.

maintenance goal Type of goal teams set that describes what the team wants to accomplish in terms of its own effectiveness.

manipulatives Concrete objects or representational items used as part of instruction. Examples of commonly used manipulatives include blocks and counters.

MDT *See* multidisciplinary team.

mediation Process in which a neutral professional assists parents and school district personnel in resolving disputes concerning any aspect of a student's special education.

mental retardation Condition in which an individual has significant limitations in cognitive ability and adaptive behaviors that interfere with learning. Also referred to as a *cognitive disability.*

mild intellectual disabilities Condition in which students have some difficulty meeting the academic and social demands of general education classrooms due in large part to below-average intellectual functioning (55–70 on an IQ test).

minimum intervention Strategy for promoting positive behavior that is nonintrusive and often spontaneous instead of systematic and long term. Examples of minimum interventions include noticing positive student behavior and commenting on it and moving students from one activity to another by making unrelated but easily accomplished requests first.

mixed-skill grouping Classroom grouping arrangement in which students are clustered for instruction without focusing on specific skill needs. Also referred to as *heterogeneous grouping.*

mnemonic A device or code used to assist memory by imposing an order on the information to be remembered.

mobility specialist Specialist who helps students with visual impairments learn to be familiar with their environments and able to travel from place to place independently and safely.

model Concrete representation that can help students make connections between abstractions and real-life physical objects or processes.

modified test construction Individualized changes made to tests to make them more accessible for students with disabilities. For example, triple spacing a test for a student with a learning disability who has difficulty reading tests that have lots of clutter.

modified weights and scales A type of grading adaptation that involves changing the number of points or the percentages required to earn a specified grade or changing the weights assigned to different performance areas.

multicultural education Approaches to education that reflect the diversity of society.

multidisciplinary team (MDT) Team including teachers, specialists, administrators, and parents who assess a student's individual needs, determine eligibility for special education, and develop the IEP.

multimedia software Computer programs that combine written words, graphics, sound, and animation.

multiple disabilities Condition in which individuals have two or more of the disabilities outlined in P.L. 101-476, although no one can be determined to be predominant.

multiple intelligences Concept proposed by Howard Gardner (1993) that suggests there are seven types of intelligence, not just one.

multisensory approach Instructional approach that emphasizes the use of more than one modality for teaching and learning. For example, having a student read a vocabulary word, spell it out loud, and then write it on paper is a multisensory approach to teaching vocabulary.

muscular dystrophy Disease that weakens muscles, causing orthopedic impairments. This disease is progressive, often resulting in death during the late teenage years.

negative example Instructional stimulus that does not illustrate the concept being taught, used with examples to ensure that students understand the instruction. Also called *nonexample.*

negative reinforcement A potential negative consequence to a behavior that causes the behavior to increase.

No Child Left Behind Act of 2001 (NCLB) Reauthorization of the Elementary and Secondary Education Act of 1965; this law set high standards for student achievement and increased accountability for student learning and criteria by which teachers are considered highly qualified.

novelty Approach for educating gifted and talented students based on allowing students to learn traditional content using alternative or unusual strategies that might include working with an adult mentor, creating materials for other students to use, or using a problem-based learning approach.

Numbered Heads Together Cooperative learning program in which students number off. The teacher poses a question; the students work together to ensure all members know the answer, and then the teacher calls a number. Students with the number stand, and one is called upon to respond to the question, with correct responses scoring points for the team.

nurse Specialist who has expertise in understanding and responding to students' medical needs and who sometimes serves as a liaison between medical and school professionals.

occupational therapist Specialist with expertise in meeting students' needs in the area of fine motor skills, including self-help skills such as feeding and dressing.

one-to-one instruction Classroom grouping arrangement in which individual students work with either a teacher or computer in materials geared to their level and at their own pace.

organizational patterns Ways in which content area texts are written to reflect main ideas such as compare-contrast, cause-effect, and problem solution.

orthopedic impairments (OI) Physical conditions that seriously impair the ability to move about or to complete motor activities and interfere with learning.

other health impairments (OHI) Medical or health conditions such as AIDS, seizure disorders, cancer, juvenile diabetes, and asthma that are serious enough that they negatively affect a student's educational performance.

overcorrection Type of presentation punishment in which a student makes restitution for misbehavior. An example of overcorrection is a student cleaning all the desks in a room as a consequence for writing on one desk.

parallel teaching Co-teaching option in which students are divided into small groups and each group receives the same instruction from one of the teachers in the room.

paraprofessional Noncertified staff member employed to assist certified staff in carrying out education programs and otherwise help in the instruction of students with disabilities.

PARS Learning strategy for reading textbooks with these steps: preview the material, ask questions, read the chapter, and summarize the main ideas.

partially sighted Condition in which an individual has a significant visual impairment but is able to capitalize on residual sight using magnification devices and other adaptive materials.

passive learner Learner who does not believe in his or her own ability, has limited knowledge of problem-solving strategies, and is unable to determine when to use a strategy.

pattern guide A graphic organizer designed to help students organize their written papers.

peer-assisted learning strategies (PALS) Research-based form of reciprocal classwide peer tutoring designed to assist struggling students across all grade levels to learn key math and reading skills.

peer comparison A component of curriculum-based assessment in which a student's performance is compared to that of classmates as a means of determining whether a learning problem exists.

peer editing Component of student writing in which students review, evaluate, and provide feedback to each other about their written work.

peer tutoring Student-centered instructional approach in which pairs of students help one another and learn by teaching.

performance-based assessment Method of evaluation that measures what students can do with knowledge rather than measuring specific bits of knowledge the student possesses.

permanent product recording Strategy for recording behavior in which samples of student work and other permanent evidence of student behavior are collected and evaluated.

personal assistant Paraprofessional specially trained to monitor and assist a particular student with a disability.

personal role One of the roles individuals bring to a team, consisting of characteristics, knowledge, skills, and perceptions based on life experiences broader than those in the professional area.

petit mal seizure *See* absence seizure.

physical punishment Type of presentation punishment, not recommended for use by teachers, that involves a negative physical consequence for misbehavior.

physical therapist Specialist with expertise in meeting students' needs in the area of gross motor skills.

placement Location in which education will occur for a student with a disability.

planning think sheet Set of questions to which students respond as a strategy for assisting them to activate background knowledge in preparation for writing.

portfolio assessment Method of evaluation in which a purposeful collection of student work is used to determine student effort, progress, and achievement in one or more areas.

positive behavioral interventions and supports (PBIS) Strategies for preventing behavior challenges as well as techniques for addressing common and intensive behavior problems; PBIS is based on clearly defined outcomes, behavioral and biomedical science, research-validated practices, and systematic approaches.

positive reinforcement A consequence to a behavior that causes it to increase. Also called a *reward*.

POSSE Learning strategy for reading comprehension with these steps: predict ideas, organize the ideas, search for the structure, summarize the main ideas, and evaluate your understanding.

POWER Learning strategy for writing with these steps: planning, organizing, writing, editing, and revising.

practice test An adaptation used before students take tests. Students are given a test with the same format and content but different questions. Practice tests clarify test expectations and familiarize students with test content.

PReP (PreReading Plan) strategy Strategy for determining how much background information students have about a topic.

prereferral assistance team *See* instructional assistance team.

present level of functioning Information about a student's current level of academic achievement, social skills, behavior, communication skills, and other areas that is included on an IEP.

presentation punishment Presenting negative consequences as a strategy for decreasing behavior.

preskill Basic skill necessary for performing a more complex skill.

primary reinforcer Food or other items related to human needs that cause a behavior to increase, used only occasionally in schools. An example of a primary reinforcer is a piece of licorice earned for appropriate behavior.

prioritization of curriculum A type of grading adaptation in which a student's grade is based on specific content determined to be most important by the teacher.

probe Quick and easy measure of student performance (accuracy and fluency) in the basic-skill areas of reading, math, and written expression consisting of timed samples of academic behaviors.

probe of basic academic skills *See* probe.

probe of prerequisite skills Specific type of probe designed to assess whether a student has the prerequisite skills needed to succeed in the planned instruction.

professional role One of the roles individuals bring to a team, including knowledge, skills, and perceptions based on professional training and experience.

program evaluation Type of assessment decision concerning whether a special education program should be terminated, continued as is, or modified.

program placement Type of assessment decision concerning where a student's special education services will take place.

progress on IEP objectives A type of grading adaptation in which a student's grade is based on the measurable goals and objectives and progress monitoring components of the IEP.

psychological test Test designed to measure how efficiently students learn in an instructional situation; often used to assess intelligence and to determine whether learning disabilities exist.

psychologist *See* school psychologist.

psychometrist Specialist with expertise in assessment who in some states completes much of the individual assessment required to determine eligibility for special education services.

Public Law 94-142 Education for All Handicapped Children Act; first federal special education law that incorporated many of the rights captured today in the Individuals with Disabilities Education Improvement Act (IDEA).

pullout model Instructional approach in which students with disabilities leave the general education classroom once or more each day to receive special education services.

punishment Any response or consequence that has the effect of decreasing a behavior.

rate of skill introduction The pace at which new skills are introduced during instruction.

RAP Reading comprehension strategy consisting of three steps: read the paragraph; ask yourself "What was the main idea and what were two details?"; put the main idea and details in your own words.

READS Textbook-reading strategy consisting of five steps: review headings and subheadings; examine boldfaced words; ask, "What do I expect to learn?"; do it—read!; summarize in your own words.

reasoning A range of important learning skills, including comprehension, generalization, induction, and sequencing.

receptive language An individual's ability to understand what people mean when they speak.

reciprocal teaching Teaching students to comprehend reading material by providing them with teacher and peer models of thinking behavior and then allowing them to practice these thinking behaviors with their peers.

reciprocal tutoring Same-age tutoring approach in which students in the same class are randomly assigned and take turns teaching each other. *See also* reciprocal teaching.

regular class One placement for students with disabilities. Also referred to as a *general education class*.

rehearsal strategy Test-taking strategy that involves saying information out loud, repeating it, checking it for accuracy, and repeating it again as part of studying.

reinforcement Any response or consequence that causes a behavior to increase.

reinforcement menu List of rewards from which students may choose, often most effective if students participate in its development.

related services Services students with disabilities need to benefit from their educational experience. Examples of related services include transportation, speech therapy, physical therapy, and counseling.

removal punishment Taking away from a student something that is desired as a strategy for decreasing inappropriate behavior.

residential facility Placement for students with disabilities when their needs cannot be met at a school. Students attend school and live at a residential facility.

resource room Special education setting in which a special education teacher works with groups of students with disabilities for parts of the school day.

resource teacher Special education teacher who provides direct services to students with disabilities either in a special education or general education classroom and who also meets to solve problems with teachers. Resource teachers most often work with students with high-incidence disabilities.

response cost Type of removal punishment in which a student loses privileges or other rewards as a consequence of inappropriate behavior.

response to intervention (RtI) An approach for the identification of learning disabilities based on whether student learning progress improves or fails to improve after the student receives increasingly intense, research-based interventions; the latter may be an indication of a learning disability.

retention Ability to remember information after time has passed.

RICE Strategy for involving students in the portfolio process. Steps include: rationale—why are you keeping a portfolio?; identify goals—what do you want to improve?; contents—what will you include in your portfolio?; evaluation—how, and when, will you assess your portfolio?

Ritalin Psychostimulant medication commonly prescribed for individuals with ADHD.

RUDPC Learning strategy to help students derive important information from a webpage. The steps are read the title and headings, use the cursor to skim the page, decide whether you need the page, print the page, and copy the bibliographic information.

same-age tutoring Peer-tutoring approach in which students in the same class or grade level tutor one another, typically with higher-achieving students assisting lower-achieving students.

same-skill grouping Classroom grouping arrangement in which all students needing instruction on a particular skill are clustered for that instruction. Also referred to as *homogeneous grouping*.

SAND Learning strategy to visually organize lecture notes. The steps are: state important ideas; arrange arrows to connect ideas; number key points in order; and devise abbreviations.

satiation Situation in which a positive reinforcer, used repeatedly, loses its effectiveness.

scaffolding Instructional approach for teaching higher-order thinking skills in which the teacher supports student learning by reviewing the cognitive strategy to be addressed, regulating difficulty during practice, providing varying contexts for student practice, providing feedback, increasing student responsibility for learning, and creating opportunities for independent student practice.

school psychologist Specialist with expertise to give individual assessments of students in cognitive, academic, social, emotional, and behavioral domains. This professional also designs strategies to address students' academic and social behavior problems.

SCAN Self-questioning strategy for proofreading sentences. The questions are: Does it make sense? Is it connected to my belief? Can I add more? and Are there any errors to note?

screening Type of assessment decision concerning whether or not a student's academic or behavior performance is different enough from that of his or her peers to merit further, more in-depth assessment.

SCROL Learning strategy for teaching students to use text headings to aid their comprehension with these steps: survey the headings, connect, read the text, outline, and look back.

Section 504 The section of the Vocational Rehabilitation Act of 1973 that prohibits discrimination against all individuals with disabilities in programs that receive federal funds.

self-advocacy Extent to which a student can identify supports needed to succeed and communicate that information effectively to others, including teachers and employers.

self-awareness Extent to which a student has an accurate perception of his or her learning strengths, learning needs, and ability to use strategies to learn independently.

self-control training A strategy in which students who lack self-control are taught to redirect their actions by talking to themselves.

self-determination Providing meaningful opportunities for students with disabilities to express their needs and goals so that their wishes guide decision making.

self-image Individual's perception of his or her own abilities, appearance, and competence.

self-instruction Strategy in which students are taught to talk themselves through tasks.

self-monitoring Strategy in which students are taught to check whether they have performed targeted behaviors.

self-questioning Strategy in which students are taught to guide their performance by asking themselves relevant questions.

sensory impairment Disability related to vision or hearing.

separate class Classroom in which students with disabilities spend 50 percent or more of the school day.

separate grades Differentiating report cards by assigning grades for different grading elements such as effort and progress.

separate school School serving only students with disabilities.

shared problem solving Process used by groups of professionals, sometimes including parents, for identifying problems, generating potential solutions, selecting and implementing solutions, and evaluating the effectiveness of solutions.

short-term objective Description of a step followed in order to achieve an annual goal.

sickle-cell anemia Inherited disorder occurring most often in African Americans in which red blood cells are abnormally shaped and weakened.

sign language interpreter Specialist who listens to instruction and other communication and relays it to students with hearing impairments through sign language.

simulation Activity in which students experience what it might be like to have a disability; in a technology context, simulations are computer programs that teach problem solving, decision making, and risk taking by having students react to real-life and imaginary situations.

SLANT Learning strategy to help student stay engaged while the teacher is talking. The steps are: sit up straight, lean forward, ask questions, nod your head, and track the teacher with your eyes.

SLICK A learning strategy for helping students comprehend textbooks recorded on CD-ROM. The steps in using a text on CD-ROM include: set it up, look ahead through the chapter, comprehend, and keep it together.

SLOBS Learning strategy to help students with regrouping in subtraction with these steps: if smaller, follow the steps; if larger, leap to subtract; cross off the number in the next column; borrow by taking one 10 and adding to the next column; subtract.

slow learner Student whose educational progress is below average, but not so severe as to be considered a cognitive disability, and is consistent with the student's abilities.

social cues Verbal or nonverbal signals people give that communicate a social message.

social reinforcer Positive interpersonal interaction that causes a behavior to increase. An example of a social reinforcer is a teacher praising a student's appropriate behavior.

social skills Behaviors that help students interact successfully with their peers, teachers, and others and that help them win social acceptance.

social skills training Strategies for improving students' social interaction skills through modeling and guided and independent practice with feedback.

social worker Specialist with expertise in meeting students' social needs and fostering working relationships with families.

sophistication Approach for educating gifted and talented students based on helping students learn complex principles about subject matter being presented to the entire class.

SPACE A strategy for writing stories that emphasizes five key story elements: setting, problem, actions, consequence, and emotions.

special education Specially designed instruction provided by the school district or other local education agency that meets the unique needs of students identified as disabled.

special education teacher Teacher whose primary responsibility is delivering and managing the delivery of special education services to students with disabilities.

Special Friends Program designed to promote friendships between students with disabilities and those without disabilities.

special services coordinator Administrator responsible for interpreting guidelines related to educating students with disabilities and assisting other school district personnel in carrying out those guidelines.

speech articulation The ability to produce sounds correctly at the age where they would normally be expected to develop.

speech or language impairment Condition in which student has extraordinary difficulties in communicating with others due to causes other than maturation and that interferes with learning.

speech reading Strategy used by individuals with hearing impairments to gain information by watching a person's lips, mouth, and expression. Only a small proportion of a spoken message can typically be discerned through speech reading.

speech/language therapist Specialist with expertise in meeting students' communication needs, including articulation and language development.

spina bifida Birth defect in which there is an abnormal opening in the spinal column, often leading to partial paralysis.

spinal cord injury Condition in which the spinal cord is damaged or severed because of accident or injury, leading to orthopedic impairments.

STAD *See* Student Teams–Achievement Divisions.

standardized achievement test Norm-referenced test designed to measure academic progress, or what students have retained in the curriculum.

standards-based education Education that is based on meeting state expectations of what students should know or be able to do as a result of public education.

STAR Learning strategy that helps older students solve math problems, including algebra. The steps are: search the word problem, translate the word problem, answer the problem, and review the solution.

station teaching Co-teaching option in which students are divided into small groups and each group receives part of its instruction from each teacher.

stereotypic behavior An action or motion repeated over and over again. Examples of stereotypic behaviors include spinning an object, rocking the body, and twirling.

story grammar Description of the typical elements of stories, including theme, setting, character, initiating events, attempts at resolution, resolution, and reactions.

story map Graphic organizer for narrative material.

student evaluation Determination of the extent to which students have mastered academic skills or other instructional content, frequently communicated through grades.

student self-evaluation Assessment approach in which students are asked to perform a task, are given a checklist of strategy steps for the task, and then are asked to tell which of these steps they did or did not use.

study guide General term for outlines, abstracts, or questions that emphasize important information in texts.

stuttering Speech impairment in which an individual involuntarily repeats a sound or word, resulting in a loss of speech fluency.

supplementary aids and services Term in IDEA for a range of supports provided in general education classes and other education-related settings that enable students with disabilities to be educated with students who are not disabled to the maximum extent appropriate.

support facilitator *See* inclusion specialist.

surface behaviors Initial student behaviors that teachers could interpret as misbehavior. Responding appropriately to surface behaviors can prevent them from escalating into more serious discipline problems.

TAG Learning strategy for peer editing with these steps: tell what you like, ask questions, and give suggestions.

TALS A listening strategy that helps students prepare for the material to come and sift through all they hear for the most important information. The steps are: think, ask why, listen for what?, and say to self.

tangible reinforcer Prizes or other objects students want and can earn through appropriate behavior and that cause that behavior to increase. An example of a tangible reinforcer is a school pencil earned for appropriate behavior.

task analysis Six-step strategy for managing time: decide exactly what you must do; decide how many steps are needed to complete the task; decide how much time each step will take; set up a schedule; get started; finish the task.

task goal Type of goal teams set that describes the business the team was formed to accomplish.

TASSEL A learning strategy that helps students sustain their attention during longer lectures. The steps include: try not to doodle, arrive at class prepared, sit near the front, sit away from friends, end day dreaming, and look at the teacher.

TBI *See* traumatic brain injury.

teacher-centered instruction Classroom instructional arrangement in which the pattern of interaction is between teacher and student, with the teacher as the central figure.

team Formal work group that has clear goals, active and committed members, leaders, clear procedures followed in order to accomplish goals, and strategies for monitoring effectiveness.

team role One of the formal or informal roles individuals bring to a team, consisting of contributions made to help ensure effective team functioning. Examples of formal team roles include team facilitator, recorder, and timekeeper. Examples of informal team roles include compromiser, information seeker, and reality checker.

team teaching Co-teaching option in which students remain in one large group and teachers share leadership in the instructional activity of the classroom.

test administration The conditions under which a test is given to students.

test construction The way in which test items are worded, ordered on the test, and formatted.

test site The location in which a test is given.

test-taking skills Learning strategies taught to students to help them succeed in studying for and taking tests.

thinking reader An enhanced electronic version of a textbook designed to offer support for students in word identification, comprehension, and study skills.

three-year reevaluation Triannual process of reassessing the needs of a student with a disability, carried out by a multidisciplinary team.

time-out Type of removal punishment in which a student is removed from opportunities for reward. An example of time out is a "penalty box" for misbehavior on the playground.

time sampling Strategy for recording behavior in which a behavior is periodically observed and measured during a specified time period.

token economy Group behavior management procedure in which students earn a representative or token currency for appropriate behavior that can later be exchanged for rewards.

tracking Educational practice of grouping students for instruction by their perceived ability level.

transition plan Document for students with disabilities who are as young as 14 years old that describes strategies for assisting them to prepare to leave school for adult life.

transition specialist Special educator who helps prepare students with disabilities for postschool activities, including employment, vocational training, or higher education.

transition time The time it takes a group of students to change from one classroom activity to another.

traumatic brain injury (TBI) Condition in which an individual experiences a significant trauma to the head from an accident, illness, or injury and that affects learning.

tutorial Computer program designed to present new material to students in small sequential steps and/or to review concepts.

unison responding All students responding at once to teacher questions or other instruction.

universal design The design of instructional materials, methods, and assessments that are compatible with a diverse range of student needs and minimize the need for labor-intensive adaptations.

video self-modeling A form of instruction in which students learn by watching themselves successfully perform a behavior.

visual impairment Condition in which an individual has an inability or limited ability to receive information visually, so much so that it interferes with learning.

wait time Amount of time a teacher gives a student to respond to a question.

written language difficulties Problems that students with learning and behavior disabilities have with skills related to handwriting, spelling, and written expression.

References

Abell, M. M., Bauder, D. K., & Simmons, T. J. (2005). Access to the general curriculum: A curriculum and instruction perspective for educators. *Intervention in School and Clinic, 41,* 82–86.

Abedi, J., Hofstetter, C. H., & Lord, C. (2004). Assessment accommodations for English language learners: Implications for policy-based empirical research. *Review of Educational Research, 74*(1), 1–28.

Adreon, D., & Durocher, J. S. (2007). Evaluating the college transition needs of individuals with high-functioning autism spectrum disorders. *Intervention in School and Clinic, 42,* 271–279.

Affleck, J. Q., Lowenbraun, S., & Archer, A. (1980). *Teaching the mildly handicapped in the regular classroom.* Columbus, OH: Merrill.

Agran, M., Blanchard, C., Wehmeyer, M., & Hughes, C. (2002). Increasing the problem-solving skills of students with developmental disabilities participating in general education. *Remedial and Special Education, 23,* 279–288.

Agran, M., Cavin, M., Wehmeyer, M., & Palmer, S. (2006). Participation of students with moderate to severe disabilities in the general curriculum: The effects of the self-determined learning model of instruction. *Research and Practice for Persons with Severe Disabilities, 31,* 230–241.

Alberto, P. A., & Trautman, A. C. (2005). *Applied behavior analysis for teachers* (7th ed.). Upper Saddle River, NJ: Prentice Hall.

Albrecht, S., & Jones, C. (2003). Accountability and access to opportunity: Mutually exclusive tenets under a high-stakes testing mandate. *Preventing School Failure, 47,* 86–91.

Algozzine, B., Ysseldyke, J. E., & Campbell, P. (1994). Strategies and tactics for effective instruction. *Teaching Exceptional Children, 26*(3), 34–36.

Al-Hassan, S., & Gardner, R. (2002). Involving immigrant parents of students with disabilities in the educational process. *Teaching Exceptional Children, 34*(5), 52–59.

Alley, G. R. (1988). Effects of generalization instruction on the written language performance of adolescents with learning disabilities in the mainstream classroom. *Reading, Writing, and Learning Disabilities, 4,* 291–309.

Allinder, R. M., Bolling, R. M., Oats, R. G., & Gagnon, W. A. (2000). Effects of teacher self-monitoring on implementation of curriculum-based measurement and mathematics computation achievement of students with disabilities. *Remedial and Special Education, 21,* 219–226.

Allport, G. (1954). *The nature of prejudice.* Cambridge, MA: Addison-Wesley.

Al Otaiba, S., & Pappamihiel, N. E. (2005). Guidelines for using volunteer literacy tutors to support reading instruction for English language learners. *Teaching Exceptional Children, 37*(6), 6–11.

Ambrose, R. (2002). Are we overemphasizing manipulatives in the primary grades to the detriment of girls? *Teaching Children Mathematics, 9*(1), 16–22.

American Academy of Pediatrics. (2000). Clinical practice guideline: Diagnosis and evaluation of the child with attention-deficit/hyperactivity disorder. *Pediatrics, 105,* 1158–1170.

American Academy of Pediatrics. (1999). The treatment of neurologically impaired children using patterning. Retrieved November 6, 2007, from http://aappolicy.aappublications.org/cgi/reprint/pediatrics;104/5/1149.pdf

American Association on Mental Retardation. (2002). *Mental retardation: Definition, classification, and systems of supports* (10th ed.). Washington, DC: Author.

American Cancer Society. (2007). *Detailed guide: Cancer in children: What is childhood cancer?* Retrieved July 9, 2007, from www.cancer.org/docroot/CRI/content/CRI_2_4_1X_Introduction_7.asp?sitearea=

American Institutes for Research. (1999, February). *Voluntary national tests in reading and math: Background paper reviewing laws and regulations, current practice, and research relevant to inclusion and accommodation for students with limited English proficiency.* Palo Alto, CA: Author.

American Psychiatric Association. (2000). *Diagnostic and statistical manual of mental disorders* (4th ed., text rev.). Washington, DC: Author.

Anderson, J. A., Kutash, K., & Duchnowski, A. J. (2001). A comparison of the academic progress of students with EBD and students with LD. *Journal of Emotional and Behavioral Disorders, 9,* 106–115.

Anderson, K. M. (2007). Differentiating instruction to include all students. *Preventing School Failure, 51*(3), 49–54.

Anderson, L. B. (2007). A special kind of tutor. *Teaching PreK-8, 37*(5). Retrieved August 25, 2007, from www.teachingk-8.com/archives/articles/a_special_kind_of_tutor_by_linda_brown_anderson.html

Anderson, L. W., & Krathwohl, D. R. (Eds.). (2001). *A taxonomy for learning, teaching and assessing: A revision of Bloom's taxonomy of educational objectives: Complete edition.* New York: Longman.

Antshel, K. M., Faraone, S. V., Stallone, K., Nave, A., Kaufmann, F. A., Doyle, A., et al. (2007). Is attention deficit hyperactivity disorder a valid diagnosis in the presence of high IQ? Results from the MGH longitudinal family studies of ADHD. *Journal of Child Psychology and Psychiatry, 48,* 687–694.

Aprile, D., & Mistry, R. S. (2007). Congruence of mother and teacher educational expectations and low-income youth's academic competence. *Journal of Educational Psychology, 99,* 140–153.

Archer, A. L., Gleason, M. M., & Vachon, V. L. (2003). Decoding and fluency: Foundation skills for struggling older readers. *Learning Disability Quarterly, 26,* 89–101.

Archer, A., & Gleason, M. (2004). Direct instruction in content-area reading. In D. W. Carnine, J. Silbert, E. J. Kame'enui, & S. G. Tarver (Eds.), *Direct instruction reading* (4th ed., pp. 260–306). Upper Saddle River, NJ: Merrill/Prentice Hall.

535

Arends, R. I. (2004). *Learning to teach* (6th ed.). New York, NY: McGraw-Hill.

Arivett, D. L., Rust, J. O., Brissie, J. S., & Dansby, V. S. (2007). Special education teachers' perceptions of school psychologists in the context of individualized education program meetings. *Education, 127,* 378–388.

Armbruster, B. B. (1984). The problem of "inconsiderate text." In G. G. Duffy, L. R. Roehler, & J. Mason (Eds.), *Comprehensive instruction: Perspectives and suggestions* (pp. 202–217). New York: Longman.

Armbruster, B. B., & Anderson, T. H. (1988). On selecting "considerate" content area textbooks. *Remedial and Special Education, 9*(1), 47–52.

Armbruster, B., Lehr, F., & Osborn, J. (2001). *Put reading first: The research building blocks for teaching children to read.* Washington, DC: Partnership for Reading.

Arndt, S. A., Konrad, M., & Test, D. W. (2006). Effects of the self-directed IEP on student participation in planning meetings. *Remedial and Special Education, 27,* 194–207.

Aronson, E. (2005). *Jigsaw in 10 easy steps.* Middletown, CT: Social Psychology Network. Retrieved February 8, 2005, from www .jigsaw.org/index.html

Artiles, A. J., Harris-Murri, N., & Rostenberg, D. (2006). Inclusion as social justice: Critical notes on discourses, assumptions, and the road ahead. *Theory into Practice, 45,* 260–268.

Artiles, A. J., Rueda, R., Salazar, J. J., & Higareda, I. (2005). Within-group diversity in minority disproportionate representation: English language learners in urban school districts. *Exceptional Children, 71,* 283–300.

Ashton, T. M. (1999). Spell checking: Making writing meaningful in the inclusive classroom. *Teaching Exceptional Children, 32*(2), 24–27.

Asthma and Allergy Foundation of America. (2007). *Asthma facts and figures.* Retrieved July 8, 2007, from www.aafa.org/display .cfm?id=8&sub=42

August, D., & Shanahan, T. (Eds.). (2006). *Developing literacy in second-language learners: Report of the national literacy panel on language-minority children and youth.* Mahwah, NJ: Lawrence Erlbaum Associates.

Avcioğlu, H. (2007). Examining the effectiveness of a program developed to teach social skills to hearing impaired students based on cooperative learning. *Educational Sciences: Theory and Practice, 7,* 340–347.

AVERT. (2007). *United States statistics summary.* Retrieved July 8, 2007, from www.avert.org/statsum.htm

Babkie, A. A. (2006). Be proactive in managing classroom behavior. *Intervention in School and Clinic, 41,* 184–187.

Bahamonde, C., & Friend, M. (1999). Bilingual education: An alternative approach for collaborative service delivery. *Journal of Educational and Psychological Consultation, 10,* 1–24.

Bahr, M., & Kovaleski, J. (2006). The need for problem-solving teams. *Remedial and Special Education, 27*(1), 2–5.

Baker, J. M., & Zigmond, N. (1995). The meaning and practices of inclusion for students with learning disabilities: Implications from the five cases. *The Journal of Special Education, 29,* 163–180.

Baker, S., Gersten, R., Dimino, J. A., & Griffiths, R. (2004). The sustained use of research-based instructional practice: A case study of peer-assisted learning strategies in mathematics. *Remedial and Special Education, 25,* 5–24.

Banda, D. R., & Kubina, R. M. (2006). The effects of a high-probability request sequencing technique in enhancing transition behaviors. *Education and Treatment of Children, 29,* 507–515.

Bandura, A. (1969). *Principles of behavior modification.* New York: Holt, Rinehart, and Winston.

Banks, J. A. (2001). *Cultural diversity in education: Foundations, curriculum and teaching.* Boston: Allyn and Bacon.

Banks, J. A., & Banks, C. A. (2007). *Multicultural education: issues and perspectives,* (6th ed.). Hoboken, NJ: John Wiley & Sons, Inc.

Barkley, R. (1995). *Taking charge of ADHD: The complete authoritative guide for parents.* New York: Guilford Press.

Barkley, R. A. (2004). Adolescents with attention-deficit/hyperactivity disorder: An overview of empirically based treatments [Electronic version]. *Journal of Psychiatric Practice, 10,* 39–56.

Barkley, R. A. (2006). *Attention-deficit hyperactivity disorder: A handbook for diagnosis and treatment* (3rd ed.). New York: Guilford Press.

Barootchi, N., & Keshavarz, M. H. (2002). Assessment of achievement through portfolios and teacher-made tests. *Educational Research, 44,* 279–288.

Barrie, W., & McDonald, J. (2002). Administrative support for student-led individualized education programs. *Remedial and Special Education, 23,* 116–121.

Barron, A. M., & Foot, H. (1991). Peer tutoring and tutor training. *Educational Research, 33,* 174–185.

Barth, R. S. (2006). Improving relationships within the schoolhouse. *Educational Leadership, 63*(6), 8–13.

Barton-Arwood, S., Morrow, L., Lane, K., & Jolivette, K. (2005). Project IMPROVE: Improving teachers' ability to address students' social needs. *Education and Treatment of Children, 28,* 430–443.

Bateman, B. D., & Herr, C. M. (2006). *Writing measurable IEP goals and objectives.* Verona, WI: IEP Resources.

Bateman, B. D., & Linden, M. A. (2006). *Better IEPs: How to develop legally correct and educationally useful programs* (4th ed.). Verona, WI: IEP Resources.

Bateman, B. E. (2004). Achieving affective and behavioral outcomes in culture learning: The case for ethnographic interviews. *Foreign Language Annals, 37*(2), 240–253.

Bateman, B., Warner, J., Hutchinson, E., Dean, T., Rowlandson, P., Gant, C., Grundy, J., Fitzgerald, C., & Stevenson, J. (2004). The effects of a double blind, placebo controlled, artificial food colourings and benzoate preservative challenge on hyperactivity in a general population sample of preschool children. *Archives of Disease in Childhood, 89,* 506–511.

Bausch, M., & Hasselbring, T. (2004). Assistive technology: Are the necessary skills and knowledge being developed at the preservice and inservice levels? *Education and Special Education, 27*(2), 97–104.

Baxendell, B. W. (2003). Consistent, coherent, creative: The 3 C's graphic organizers. *Teaching Exceptional Children, 35*(3), 46–53.

Beck, I. L., & McKeown, M. G. (2002). *Bringing words to life.* New York: Guilford.

Behrmann, M., & Jerome, M. K. (2002). Assistive technology for students with mild disabilities: Update 2002 (ERIC Digest No. E623). Arlington, VA: ERIC Clearinghouse on Disabilities and Gifted Education. (ERIC Document Reproduction Service No. ED463595)

Beigel, A. R. (2000). Assistive technology assessment: More than the device. *Intervention in School and Clinic, 35,* 237–245.

Benner, A. D., & Mistry, R. S. (2007). Congruence of mother and teacher educational expectations and low-income youth's academic competence. *Journal of Educational Psychology, 99,* 140–153.

Bennett, A. (1932). *Subnormal children in elementary grades.* New York: Columbia University, Teacher's College, Bureau of Publications.

Bennett, C. I. (2003). *Comprehensive multicultural education: Theory and practice* (5th ed.). Boston: Allyn and Bacon.

Berger, K. S. (2007). Update on bullying at school: Science forgotten? *Developmental Review, 27,* 90–126.

Berliner, D. (1990). What's all the fuss about instructional time? In M. Ben-Peretz & R. Bromme (Eds.), *The nature of time in schools: Theoretical concepts, practitioner perceptions.* New York: Teachers College Press. Retrieved Date, from http://courses.ed.asu.edu/berliner/readings/fuss/fuss.htm

Berliner, D. C. (1984). The half-full glass: A review of research on teaching. In P. L. Hosford (Ed.), *Using what we know about teaching (1984 yearbook)* (pp. 69–83). Alexandria, VA: Association for Supervision and Curriculum Development.

Birdsall, P., & Correa, L. (2007, March/April). Gifted underachievers. *Leadership,* 21–23.

Bishop, V. E. (2004). *Teaching visually impaired children* (3rd ed.). Springfield, IL: Charles C. Thomas.

Blachman, B. A. (Ed.). (1997). *Foundations of reading acquisition and dyslexia: Implications for early intervention.* Mahwah, NJ: Lawrence Erlbaum Associates.

Blanchett, W. J., Brantlinger, E., & Shealey, M. W. (2005). Brown 50 years later—Exclusion, segregation, and inclusion. *Remedial and Special Education, 26,* 66–69.

Blankenship, C., & Lilly, M. (1981). *Mainstreaming students with learning and behavior problems.* New York: Holt, Rinehart & Winston.

Blatt, B. (1958). The physical, personality, and academic status of children who are mentally retarded attending special classes as compared with children who are mentally retarded attending regular class. *American Journal of Mental Deficiency, 62,* 810–818.

Blatt, B. (1987). *The conquest of mental retardation.* Austin, TX: PRO-ED.

Blue-Banning, M., Summers, J. A., Frankland, H. C., Nelson, L. L., & Beegle, G. (2004). Dimensions of family and professional partnerships: Constructive guidelines for collaboration. *Exceptional Children, 70,* 167–184.

Blue-Banning, M., Turnbull, A. P., & Pereira, L. (2002). Hispanic youth/young adults with disabilities: Parents' visions for the future. *Journal of the Association for Persons with Severe Handicaps (JASH), 27,* 204–219.

Boaler, J. (2006). Promoting respectful learning. *Educational Leadership, 63*(5), 74–78.

Bond, R., & Castagnera, E. (2006). Peer supports and inclusive education: An underutilized resource. *Theory into Practice, 45,* 224–229.

Bonner, F. A. (2003). To be young, gifted, African American, and male [Electronic version]. *Gifted Child Today, 26*(2), 26–34.

Bos, C. S., & Vaughn, S. (2005). *Strategies for teaching students with learning and behavior problems* (6th ed.). Boston: Allyn and Bacon.

Bouck, E. (2007). Co-teaching . . . Not just a textbook term: Implications for practice. *Preventing School Failure, 51*(2), 46–51.

Bovey, T., & Strain, P. (2003). *Promoting positive peer social interactions. What works briefs.* Champaign, IL: Center on the Social and Emotional Foundations for Early Learning, University of Illinois. (ERIC Document Reproduction Service No. ED481996)

Bowen, J. M. (2005). Classroom interventions for students with traumatic brain injuries. *Preventing School Failure, 49*(4), 34–41.

Bowen, S. (n.d.). *Daily story problem.* Retrieved November 23, 2004, from www.pacificnet.net/~mandel/math.html

Boyle, E. A., Washburn, S. G., Rosenberg, M. S., Connelly, V. J., Brinckerhoff, L. C., & Banerjee, M. (2002). Reading's SLiCK with new audio texts and strategies. *Teaching Exceptional Children, 35*(2), 50–55.

Boyle, J. R., & Weishaar, M. (2001). The effects of strategic notetaking on the recall and comprehension of lecture information for high school students with learning disabilities. *Learning Disabilities: Research and Practice, 16,* 133–141.

Bracken, B. A., & Brown, E. F. (2006). Behavioral identification and assessment of gifted and talented students. *Journal of Psychoeducational Assessment, 24,* 112–122.

Brady, K. P. (2004). Section 504 student eligibility for students with reading disabilities: A primer for advocates. *Reading & Writing Quarterly, 20,* 305–329.

Brain Injury Association of America. (2004). *Causes of brain injury.* McLean, VA: Author. Retrieved March 13, 2004, from www.biausa.org/Pages/causes_of_brain_injury.html

Brandwein, P. F., & Bauer, N. W. (1980). *The United States, living in our world: Research, evaluation, and writing.* Barton R. Clark et al., consulting social scientists. San Francisco and New York: Center for the Study of Instruction/Harcourt Brace Jovanovich.

Brigham, N., Morocco, C. C., Clay, K., & Zigmond, N. (2006). What makes a high school a good high school for students with disabilities. *Learning Disabilities Research & Practice, 21*(3), 184–190.

Brimijoin, K., Marquisse, E., & Tomlinson, C. A. (2003). Using data to differentiate Instruction, *Educational Leadership, 60*(5), 70–73.

Brinckerhoff, L. (1994). Developing effective self-advocacy skills in college-bound students with learning disabilities. *Intervention in School and Clinic, 29*(4), 229–237.

Broderick, A., Mehta-Parekh, H., & Reid, D. K. (2005). Differentiating instruction for disabled students in inclusive classrooms. *Theory into Practice, 44*(3), 194–202.

Brophy-Herb, H. E., Lee, R. E., Nievar, M. A., & Stollak, G. (2007). Preschoolers' social competence: Relations to family characteristics, teacher behaviors and classroom climate. *Journal of Applied Developmental Psychology, 28,* 134–148.

Browder, D. M., Wakeman, S. Y., & Flowers, C. (2006). Assessment of progress in the general curriculum for students with disabilities. *Theory into Practice, 45*(3), 249–259.

Browder, D. M., Wakeman, S. Y., Spooner, F., Ahlgrin-Delzell, L., & Algozzine, B. (2006). Research on reading instruction for individuals with significant cognitive disabilities. *Exceptional Children, 72,* 392–408.

Brown, G. M., Kerr, M. M., Zigmond, N., & Harris, A. L. (1984). What's important for student success in high school? "Successful" and "unsuccessful" students discuss school survival skills. *High School Journal, 68,* 10–17.

Brown, T. E. (2007, February). A new approach to attention deficit disorder. *Educational Leadership,* 22–27.

Brownell, M. T., Adams, A., Sindelar, P., & Waldron, N. (2006). Learning from collaboration: The role of teacher qualities. *Exceptional Children, 72*(2), 169–185.

Bruce, S. M. (2007). Teacher preparation for the education of students who are deafblind: A retrospective and prospective view. *Deaf-Blind Perspectives, 14*(2), 9–12.

Bruce, S., Godbold, E., & Naponelli-Gold, S. (2004). An analysis of communicative functions of teachers and their students who are congenitally deafblind. *RE:view: Rehabilitation Education for Blindness and Visual Impairment, 36,* 81–90.

Bryan, T. (2005). Science-based advances in the social domain of learning disabilities. *Learning Disability Quarterly, 28*(2), 119–121.

Bryan, T. H., & Bryan, J. H. (1986). *Understanding learning disabilities* (3rd ed.). Palo Alto, CA: Mayfield.

Bryan, T., Burstein, K., & Bryan, J. (2001). Students with learning disabilities: Homework problems and promising practices. *Educational Psychologist, 36*(3), 167–180.

Buchholtz, K., & Helming, M., (2005). Making history come alive through technology. *Phi Delta Kappan, 87*(2), 174.

Buck, G. H., Polloway, E. A., Smith-Thomas, A., & Cook, K. W. (2003). Prereferral intervention processes: A survey of state practices. *Exceptional Children, 69,* 349–360.

Bulgren, J. A., Schumaker, J. B., & Deshler, D. (1988). Effectiveness of a concept teaching routine in enhancing the performance of LD students in secondary-level mainstream classes. *Learning Disability Quarterly, 11,* 3–17.

Bullara, D. T. (1993). Classroom management strategies to reduce racially-biased treatment of students. *Journal of Educational and Psychological Consultation, 4*(4), 357–368.

Bullock, L. M., Gable, R. A., & Mohr, J. D. (2005). Traumatic brain injury: A challenge for educators. *Preventing School Failure, 49,* 6–10.

Burks, M. (2004). Effects of classwide peer tutoring on the number of words spelled correctly by students with LD. *Intervention in School and Clinic, 39,* 301–304.

Burns, M. K. (2004). Empirical analysis of drill ratio research: Refining the instructional level for drill tasks. *Remedial and special education,* 25(3), 167–173.

Burns, P. C., Roe, B. D., & Ross, E. P. (2001). *Teaching reading in today's elementary schools* (8th ed.). Boston: Houghton Mifflin.

Burris, C. C., Heubert, J. P., & Levin, H. M. (2006). Accelerating mathematics achievement using heterogeneous grouping. *American Educational Research Journal, 43,* 105–136.

Burstein, N., Sears, S., Wilcoxen, A., Cabello, B., & Spagna, M. (2004). Moving toward inclusive practices. *Remedial and Special Education, 25,* 104–116.

Bursuck, B., Damer, M., & Dickson, S. (2005, May). Translating reading research to practice in three urban schools: An account of successful school-wide change. Presented at Annual Convention of the Association for Behavioral Analysis, Chicago, IL.

Bursuck, W. D., & Damer, M. (2006). *Literacy instruction for special education/at risk students.* Boston: Allyn and Bacon.

Bursuck, W. D., & Damer, M. (2007). *Reading instruction for students who are at risk or have disabilities.* Boston: Allyn and Bacon.

Bursuck, W. D., & Lessen, E. (1987). A classroom-based model for assessing students with learning disabilities. *Learning Disabilities Focus, 3*(1), 17–29.

Bursuck, W. D., Harniss, M. K., Epstein, M. H., Polloway, E. A., Jayanthi, M., & Wissinger, L. M. (1999). Solving communication problems about homework: Recommendations of special education teachers. *Learning Disabilities Research and Practice, 14,* 149–158.

Bursuck, W. D., Polloway, E. A., Plante, L., Epstein, M. H., Jayanthi, M., & McConeghy, J. (1996). Report card grading and adaptations: A national survey of classroom practices. *Exceptional Children, 62,* 301–318.

Bursuck, W. D., Smith, T., Munk, D., Damer, M., Mehlig, L., & Perry, J. (2004). Evaluating the impact of a prevention-based model of reading on children who are at risk. *Remedial and Special Education, 25,* 303–313.

Byrnes, M. A., & Majors, M. (2004). No teacher left behind: Training teachers to meet the challenge of accessing the general curriculum for deafblind students. *Deaf-Blind Perspectives, 11*(3), 1–5.

Calderon, M. E. (1999). *Promoting language proficiency and academic achievement through cooperation.* Washington, DC: ERIC Clearinghouse on Languages and Linguistics. (ERIC Document Reproduction Service No. ED436983)

Calhoon, M. B. (2005). Effects of a peer-mediated phonological skill and reading comprehension program on reading skill acquisition for middle school students with reading disabilities. *Journal of Learning Disabilities, 38,* 424–433.

Calhoon, M. B., & Fuchs, L. S. (2003). The effects of peer-assisted learning strategies and curriculum-based measurement on the mathematics performance of secondary students with disabilities. *Remedial and Special Education, 24,* 235–245.

Callahan, C. M., (2005). Identifying gifted students from underrepresented populations. *Theory into Practice, 44,* 98–104.

Callins, T. (2006). Culturally responsive literacy instruction. *TEACHING Exceptional Children, 39*(2), 62–65.

Cameron, M. (2006). Managing school discipline and implications for school social workers: A review of the literature. *Children and Schools, 28,* 219–227.

Camp, B. W., & Bash, M. A. (1985). *Think aloud.* Champaign, IL: Research Press.

Canney, C., & Byrne, A. (2006). Evaluating circle time as a support to social skills development—reflections on a journey in school-based research. *British Journal of Special Education, 33,* 19–24.

Carey, T. A., & Bourbon, W. T. (2006). Is countercontrol the key to understanding chronic behavior problems? *Intervention in School and Clinic, 42,* 5–13.

Carlo, M. S., August, D., Mclaughlin, B., Snow, C. E., Dressler, C., Lippman, D. N., Lively, T. J., & White, C. E. (2004). Closing the gap: Addressing the vocabulary needs of English-language learners in bilingual and mainstream classrooms. *Reading Research Quarterly, 39,* 188–215.

Carlson, C., & Henning, M. (1993). *The TAG peer editing procedure.* Unpublished manuscript, Northern Illinois University.

Carlson, E., Chen, L., Schroll, K., & Klein, S. (2002). *SPeNSE: Study of Personnel Needs in Special Education* [final report of the paperwork substudy]. Gainesville: University of Florida. (ERIC Document Reproduction Service No. ED479674)

Carnes, S. L., & Quinn, W. H. (2005). Family adaptation for brain injury: Coping and psychological distress. *Families, Systems, and Health, 23,* 186–203.

Carney, R. N., Levin, M. E., & Levin, J. R. (1993). Mnemonic strategies: Instructional techniques worth remembering. *Teaching Exceptional Children, 25*(4), 24–30.

Carnine, D. W. (1981). High and low implementation of direct instruction teaching techniques. *Education and Treatment of Children, 4,* 42–51.

Carnine, D. W., Silbert, J., Kame'enui, E. J., & Tarver, S. G. (2004). *Direct instruction reading* (4th ed.). Upper Saddle River, NJ: Pearson/Merrill Prentice Hall.

Carolan, J., & Guinn, A. (2007). Differentiation: Lessons from master teachers. *Educational Leadership, 64*(5), 44–47.

Carr, E. G. (2007). The expanding vision of positive behavior support: Research perspectives on happiness, helpfulness, hopefulness. *Journal of Positive Behavior Interventions, 9,* 3–14.

Carr, M., & Jessup, D. L. (1997). Gender differences in first grade mathematics strategy use: Social and metacognitive influences. *Journal of Educational Psychology, 89,* 318–328.

Carter, E. W., & Kennedy, C. H. (2006). Promoting access to the general curriculum using peer support strategies. *Research and Practice for Persons with Severe Disabilities, 31,* 284–292.

Carter, E. W., & Wehby, J. H. (2003). Job performance of transition-age youth with emotional and behavioral disorders. *Exceptional Children, 69,* 449–465.

Casella, R. (2003). Zero tolerance policy in schools: Rationale, consequences, and alternatives [Electronic version]. *Teachers College Record, 105,* 872–892.

Cass, M., Cates, D., Smith, M., & Jackson, C. (2003). Effects of manipulative instruction on solving area and perimeter problems by students with learning disabilities. *Learning Disabilities Research & Practice, 18*(2), 112–120.

Cassidy, V. M., & Stanton, J. E. (1959). *An investigation of factors involved in the educational placement of mentally retarded children: A study of differences between children in special and regular classes in Ohio.* (U.S. Office of Education Cooperative Research Program, Project No. 43). Columbus: Ohio State University. (ERIC Document Reproduction Service No. ED002752)

Catts, H. W., & Kamhi, A. G. (2005). *Language and reading disabilities.* (2nd ed.). Boston: Allyn and Bacon (Pearson).

Causton-Theoharis, J., & Malmgren, K. (2005). Building bridges: Strategies to help paraprofessionals promote peer interaction. *Teaching Exceptional Children, 37*(6), 18–24.

Cawley, J. F., Miller, J., & School, B. (1987). A brief inquiry of arithmetic word problem solving among learning disabled secondary students. *Learning Disabilities Focus, 2*(2), 87–93.

Cawley, J., Hayden, S., Cade, E., & Baker-Kroczynski, S. (2002). Including students with disabilities into the general education science classroom. *Exceptional Children, 68*, 423–436.

Cawley, J., Parmar, R., Foley, T. E., Salmon, S., Roy, S. (2001). Arithmetic performance of students: Implications for standards and programming. *Exceptional Children, 67*, 311–328.

Celce-Murcia, M. *Discourse and context in language teaching: A guide for language teachers.* New York: Cambridge University Press.

Center for the Study of Reading. (1988). *A guide to selecting basal reading programs: Workbooks.* Cambridge, MA: Bolt, Beraneck, and Newman.

Centers for Disease Control and Prevention. (2002). *AIDS in the United States.* Retrieved November 15, 2004, from www.cchs.net/health/health-info/docs/1100/1171.asp?index=5905

Centers for Disease Control and Prevention. (2004a). Prevalence of overweight among children and adolescents: United States, 2003–2004. Retrieved May 15, 2007, from www.cdc.gov/nchs/products/pubs/pubd/hestats/overweight/overwght_child_03.htm

Centers for Disease Control and Prevention. (2004b). *Tourette syndrome.* Retrieved November 20, 2004, from www.cdc.gov/ncbddd/tourette/default.htm

Centers for Disease Control and Prevention. (2005, September). Mental health in the United States: Prevalence of diagnosis and medication treatment for attention-deficit/hyperactivity disorder—United States, 2003. *Morbidity and Mortality Weekly Report, 54*, 842–847. Retrieved August 2, 2007, from www.cdc.gov/mmwr/preview/mmwrhtml/mm5434a2.htm

Centers for Disease Control and Prevention. (2006). Youth risk behavior surveillance—United States, 2005. *Morbidity & Mortality Weekly Report 2006, 55*, 1–108. Retrieved October 18, 2007, from www.cdc.gov/mmwr/PDF/SS/SS5505.pdf

Centers for Disease Control and Prevention. (2007, Summer). *Youth violence: Facts at a glance.* Washington, DC: Author. Retrieved August 7, 2007, from www.cdc.gov/ncipc/dvp/YV_DataSheet.pdf

Centers for Disease Control and Prevention, U.S. Department of Health and Human Services. (2002, May). *MMR vaccine and autism (measles–mumps–rubella): Fact sheet.* Retrieved February 6, 2004, from www.cdc.gov/nip/vacsafe/concerns/autism/autism-mmr-facts.htm

Cermak, L. S. (1976). *Improving your memory.* New York: Norton.

Cesaroni, L., & Garber, M. (1991). Exploring the experience of autism through firsthand accounts. *Journal of Autism and Developmental Disorders, 21*, 303–313.

Chadsey, J., & Han, K. G. (2005). Friendship-facilitation strategies: What do students in middle school tell us? *Teaching Exceptional Children, 38*(2), 52–57.

Chaffin, J. (1975). Will the real "mainstreaming" program please stand up! (Or . . . should Dunn have done it?). In E. L. Meyen, G. A. Vergason, & R. J. Whelan (Eds.), *Alternatives for teaching exceptional children.* Denver, CO: Love.

Chambers, C. R., Wehmeyer, M. L., Saito, Y., Lida, K. M., Lee, Y., & Singh, V. (2007). Self-determination: What do we know? Where do we go? *Exceptionality, 15*(1), 3–15.

Chard, D., & Dickson, S. V. (1999). Phonological awareness: Instructional and assessment guidelines. *Intervention in School and Clinic, 5*, 261–270.

Cheek, E. H., Jr., & Cheek, M. C. (1983). *Reading instruction through content teaching.* Columbus, OH: Merrill.

Child abuse characteristics. (2000). Retrieved September 13, 2000, from www.angelfire.com/fl2/ChildAbuse/Characteristics.html

Children's Defense Fund. (2003). *2002 facts on child poverty in America.* Washington, DC: Author. Retrieved December 4, 2004 from www.childrensdefense.org/familyincome/childpoverty/basicfacts.asp

Choate, J. S., Enright, B. E., Miller, L. J., Poteet, J. A., & Rakes, T. A. (1995). *Curriculum-based assessment and programming.* Boston: Allyn and Bacon.

Chopra, R. V., Sandoval-Lucero, E., Aragon, L., Bernal, C., De Balderas, H. B., & Carroll, D. (2004). The paraprofessional role of connector. *Remedial and Special Education, 25*, 219–232.

Christopolos, F., & Renz, P. (1969). A critical examination of special education programs. *Journal of Special Education, 3*, 371–379.

Clayton, J., Burdge, M., Denham, A., Kleinert, H. L., & Kearns, J. (2006). A four-step process for accessing the general curriculum for students with significant cognitive disabilities. *Teaching Exceptional Children, 38*(5), 20–27.

Cohen, M., & Riel, M. M. (1989). The effect of distant audiences on students' writing. *American Educational Research Journal, 26*, 143–159.

Cohen, S. B. (1983). Assigning report card grades to the mainstreamed child. *Teaching Exceptional Children, 15*, 186–189.

Colangelo, N. (2002, Fall). Counseling gifted and talented students. *National Research Center on the Gifted and Talented Newsletter.* Storrs, CT: National Research Center on the Gifted and Talented. (ERIC Document Reproduction Service No. ED447662)

Colangelo, N., & Davis, G. A. (Eds.). (2003). *Handbook on gifted education* (3rd ed.). Boston: Allyn and Bacon.

Cole, C. M., Waldron, N., & Majd, M. (2004). Academic progress of students across inclusive and traditional settings [Electronic version]. *Mental Retardation, 42*, 136–144.

Coleman, M. C., & Webber, J. (2002). *Emotional and behavioral disorders: Theory and practice* (4th ed.). Boston: Allyn and Bacon.

Coleman, R. J. (2005). Academic strategies that work for gifted students with learning disabilities. *Teaching Exceptional Children, 38*(1), 28–32.

Conners, N. A., Bradley, R. H., Mansell, L. W., Liu, J. Y., Roberts, T. J., Burgdorf, K., et al. (2004). Children of mothers with serious substance abuse problems: An accumulation of risks. *American Journal of Drug & Alcohol Abuse, 30*, 85–100.

Connor, D. J. (2006). Michael's story: "I get into so much trouble just by walking": Narrative knowing and life at the intersctions of learning disability, race, and class. *Equity & Excellence in Education, 39*, 154–165.

Connor, D. J., & Ferri, B. A. (2007). The conflict within: Resistance to inclusion and other paradoxes in special education. *Disability & Society, 22*, 63–77.

Contrucci-Kuhn, S. A., Lerman, D. C., & Vondran, C. M. (2006). Analysis of factors that affect responding in a two-response chain in children with developmental disabilities. *Journal of Applied Behavior Analysis, 39*, 263–280.

Conyers, C., Miltenberger, R., Romaniuk, C., Kopp, B., & Himle, M. (2003). Evaluation of DRO schedules to reduce disruptive behavior in a preschool classroom [Electronic version]. *Child and Family Behavior Therapy, 25*, 1–6.

Cook, B. G., Semmel, M. I., & Gerber, M. M. (1999). Attitudes of principals and special education teachers toward the inclusion of students with mild disabilities. *Remedial and Special Education, 20*, 199–207, 243.

Cooper, H. (1989). Synthesis of research oh homework. *Educational Leadership, 47*(3).

Cooper, S. M. A. (2002). Classroom choices for enabling peer learning. [Electronic version]. *Theory into Practice, 41*(1), 53–57.

Copeland, S. R., Hughes, C., Carter, E. W., Guth, C., Presley, J. A., Williams, C. R., et al. (2004). Increasing access to general education: Perspectives of participants in a high school peer support program. *Remedial and Special Education, 25,* 342–352.

Correa-Torres, S. M., & Howell, J. J. (2004). Facing the challenges of itinerant teaching: Perspectives and suggestions from the field. *Journal of Visual Impairment & Blindness, 98,* 420–433.

Cott, A. (1977). *The orthomolecular approach to learning disabilities.* New York: Huxley Institute.

Cott, A. (1985). *Help for your learning disabled child: The orthomolecular treatment.* New York: Time Books.

Council for Exceptional Children. (2000). *Transition specialist competencies: Fact sheet.* Arlington, VA: Author.

Council of State Directors of Programs for the Gifted. (2001). *The 1999–2000 state of the states gifted and talented education report.* Longmont, CO: Author.

Coutinho, M. J., & Oswald, D. P. (2000). Disproportionate representation in special education: A synthesis and recommendations. *Journal of Child and Family Studies, 9*(2), 135–156.

Cowen, E. L., Pederson, A., Babijian, H., Izzo, L. D., & Trost, M. A. (1973). Long-term follow-up of early detected vulnerable children. *Journal of Consulting and Clinical Psychology, 41,* 438–446.

Coyne, M. D., Kame'enui, E. J., & Carnine, D. W. (2007). *Effective teaching strategies that accommodate diverse learners.* Upper Saddle River, NJ: Prentice Hall.

Crawford, C. G. (1980). *Math without fear.* New York: New Viewpoints/Vision Books.

Cullinan, D. (2007). *Students with emotional and behavioral disorders: An introduction for teachers and other helping professionals* (2nd ed.). Upper Saddle River NJ: Pearson Merrill/Prentice Hall.

Cullinan, D., Epstein, M. H., & Lloyd, J. (1983). *Behavior disorders of children and adolescents.* Englewood Cliffs, NJ: Prentice-Hall.

Cunningham, M. M., & Wodrich, D. L. (2006). The effect of sharing health information on teachers' production of classroom accommodations. *Psychology in the Schools, 43,* 553–564.

Curry, C. (2003). Universal design: Accessibility for all learners. *Educational Leadership, 61*(2), 55–60.

Curtin, D. F., Pisecco, S., & Hamilton, R. J. (2006). Teacher perceptions of classroom interventions for children with ADHD: A cross-cultural comparison of teachers in the United States and New Zealand. *School Psychology Quarterly, 21,* 171–196.

Czarnecki, E., Rosko, D., & Fine, F. (1998). How to CALL UP notetaking skills. *Teaching Exceptional Children, 30*(6), 14–19.

D'Angelo, A., Lutz, J. G., & Zirkel, P. A. (2004). Are published IDEA hearing officer decisions representative? *Journal of Disability Policy Studies, 14,* 241–252.

Dabkowski, D. M. (2004). Encouraging active parent participation in IEP team meetings. *Teaching Exceptional Children, 36*(3), 34–39.

Dalton, B., & Pisha, B. (2001). Developing strategic readers: A comparison of computer-suggested versus traditional strategy instruction on struggling readers' comprehension of quality children's literature. Paper presented at the 51st annual meeting of the National Reading Conference, San Antonio, TX.

Dalton, B., Sable, J., & Hoffman, L. (2006, September). Characteristics of the 100 largest public elementary and secondary school districts in the United States: 2003–2004 [statistical analysis report]. Washington, DC: National Center for Education Statistics. (ERIC Document Reproduction Service No. ED493585)

Daly, P. M., & Ranalli, P. (2003). Using countoons to teach self-monitoring skills. *Teaching Exceptional Children, 35*(5), 30–35.

Darch, C., & Gersten, R. (1985). The effects of teaching presentation and praise on LD students' oral reading performance. *British Journal of Educational Psychology, 55,* 295–303.

Dardig, J. C. (2005). The McClurg monthly magazine and 14 more practical ways to involve parents. *Teaching Exceptional Children, 38*(2), 46–51.

Davern, L. (2004). School-to-home notebooks. *Teaching Exceptional Children, 36*(5), 22–28.

Davies, D. M., Stock, S., & Wehmeyer, M. L. (2002). Enhancing independent time management and personal scheduling for individuals with mental retardation through use of a palmtop visual and audio prompting system. *Mental Retardation, 40,* 358–365.

Davis, L. J. (2007). Deafness and the riddle of identity. *Chronicle of Higher Education, 53*(19), B6.

Day-Vines, N. L., Patton, J. M., & Baytops, J. L. (2003). Counseling African American adolescents: The impact of face, culture, and middle class status [Electronic version]. *Professional School Counseling, 7,* 40–51.

DeBettencourt, L. U. (2002). Understanding the differences between IDEA and Section 504. *Teaching Exceptional Children, 34*(3), 16–23.

de Boo, G. M., & Prins, P. J. M. (2007). Social incompetence in children with ADHD: Possible moderators and mediators in social-skills training. *Clinical Psychology Review, 27,* 78–97.

Deidrick, K. K., & Farmer, J. E. (2005). School reentry following traumatic brain injury. *Preventing School Failure, 49*(4), 23–33.

Deitz, D. E. D., & Ormsby, D. (1992). A comparison of verbal social behavior of adolescents with behavioral disorders and regular class peers. *Behavioral Modification, 16,* 504–524.

DeLaPaz, S. (1999). Composing via dictation and speech recognition systems: Compensatory technology for students with learning disabilities. *Learning Disabilities Quarterly, 22,* 173–182.

Demchak, M. A. (n.d.). *Fact Sheet: Circles of friends.* Reno: Nevada Dual Sensory Impairment Project, University of Nevada, Reno. Retrieved February 9, 2005, from www.unr.edu/educ/ndsip/factsheets/circle.friends.pdf

Denham, A., Hatfield, S., Smethurst, N., Tan, E., & Tribe, C. (2006). The effect of social skills interventions in the primary school. *Educational Psychology in Practice, 22,* 33–51.

Denham, A., & Lahm, E. A. (2001). Using technology to construct alternate portfolios of students with moderate and severe disabilities. *Teaching Exceptional Children, 33*(5), 10–17.

Dennison, P. E., & Dennison, G. E. (1994). *Brain Gym™ teacher's edition: Revised.* Ventura, CA: Edu-Kinesthetics.

Denning, C. B. (2007). Social skills interventions for students with Asperger syndrome and high-functioning autism: Research findings and implications for teachers. *Beyond Behavior, 16*(3), 16–23.

Deno, S. L. (1985). Curriculum-based measurement: The emerging alternative. *Exceptional Children, 52,* 219–232.

Deno, S. L. (2003). Developments in curriculum-based measurement. *Journal of Special Education, 37,* 184–192.

Deno, S. L., Reschly-Anderson, A., Lembke, E., Zorka, H., & Callender, S. (2002). *A model for school wide implementation: A case example.* Paper presented at the annual meeting of the National Association of School Psychology, Chicago, IL.

DePaepe, P., Garrison-Kane, L., & Doelling, J. (2002). Supporting students with health needs in schools: An overview of selected health conditions. *Focus on Exceptional Children, 35*(1), 1–24.

DeRosier, M. E., & Marcus, S. R. (2005). Building friendships and combating bullying: Effectiveness of S.S. GRIN at one-year follow-up. *Journal of Clinical Child and Adolescent Psychology, 34,* 140–150.

Deshler, D., Ellis, E., & Lenz, B. (Eds.). (1996). *Teaching adolescents with learning disabilities: Strategies and methods* (2nd ed.). Denver: Love.

DeSimone, J. R., & Parmar, R. S. (2006). Middle school mathematics teachers' beliefs about inclusion of students with learning disabilities. *Learning Disabilities Research and Practice, 21,* 98–110.

Dettmer, P., Thurston, L. P., & Dyck, N. J. (2005). *Consultation, collaboration, and teamwork for students with special needs* (5th ed.). Englewood Cliffs, NJ: Prentice-Hall.

deValenzuela, J., Copeland, S., Huaquing Qi, C., & Park, M. (2006). Examining educational equity: Revisiting the disproportionate representation of minority students in special education. *Exceptional Children, 72,* 425–441.

DeVito, J. A. (2005). *Messages, building interpersonal communication skills* (6th ed). Boston: Allyn & Bacon.

DeVito, J. A. (2006). *The interpersonal communication book* (10th ed.). Boston: Allyn and Bacon.

Dickson, S. V., & Bursuck, W. D. (1999). Implementing a model for preventing reading failure. *Learning Disabilities Research and Practice, 14*(4), 191–202.

Dickson, S. V., & Bursuck, W. D. (2003). Implementing an outcomes-based collaborative partnership for preventing reading failure. In D. L. Wiseman & S. L. Knight (Eds.), *Linking school-university collaboration and K–12 student outcomes* (pp. 131–146). Washington, DC: AACTE.

Dieterich, C. A., Villani, C. J., & Bennett, P. T. (2003). Functional behavioral assessments: Beyond student behavior [Electronic version]. *Journal of Law and Education, 32,* 357–368.

Disability Films. (2007). *Films involving disabilities.* Retrieved August 20, 2007, from www.disabilityfilms.co.uk

Dole, R. L. (2004). Collaborating successfully with your school's physical therapist. *Teaching Exceptional Children, 36*(5), 28–35.

Doman, G., & Delacato, D. (1968). Doman–Delacato philosophy. *Human Potential, 1,* 113–116.

Dopp, J., & Block, T. (2004). High school peer mentoring that works? *Teaching Exceptional Children, 37*(1), 56–62.

Doré, R., Dion, E., Wagner, S., & Brunet, J. P. (2002). High school inclusion of adolescents with mental retardation: A multiple case study. *Education and Training in Mental Retardation and Developmental Disabilities, 37,* 253–261.

Dover, W. F. (2005). 20 ways to . . . Consult and support students with special needs in inclusive classrooms. *Intervention in School and Clinic, 41*(1), 32–35.

Downing, J. A. (2004). Related services for students with disabilities: Introduction to the special issue. *Intervention in School and Clinic, 39,* 195–208.

Downing, J. E. (2002). *Including students with severe and multiple disabilities in typical classrooms: Practical strategies for teachers* (2nd ed.). Baltimore: Brookes.

Downing, J. E. (2005). Inclusive education for high school students with severe intellectual disabilities: Supporting communication. *Alternative and Augmentative Communication, 21,* 132–148.

Downing, J. E., & Eichinger, J. (2003). Creating learning opportunities for students with severe disabilities in inclusive classrooms. *Teaching Exceptional Children, 36*(1), 26–31.

Dowrick, P. W., Kim-Rupnow, W.S., & Power, T. J. (2006). Video feedforward for reading. *The Journal of Special Education, 39*(4), 194–207.

Doyle, W. (1986). Classroom organization and management. In M. Wittrock (Ed.), *Handbook of research on teaching* (pp. 392–431). New York: Macmillan.

Doyle, W. (1990). Classroom management techniques. In O. C. Moles (Ed.), *Student discipline strategies* (pp. 83–105). Albany, NY: State University of New York Press.

Drasgow, E., Yell, M. L., & Robinson, T. R. (2001). Developing legally correct and educationally appropriate IEPs. *Remedial and Special Education, 22,* 359–373.

DuFour, R., DuFour, R., Eaker, R., & Many, T. (2006). *Learning by doing: A handbook for professional learning communities at work.* Bloomington, IN: Learning Tree.

Duhaney, L. M. G. (2003). A practical approach to managing the behaviors of students with ADD. *Intervention in School and Clinic, 38*(5), 267–279.

Duke, N. K. (2000). 36 minutes per day: The scarcity of informational texts in first grade. *Reading Research Quarterly, 35,* 202–224.

Dunn, C., Chambers, D., & Rabren, K. (2004). Variables affecting students' decisions to drop out of school. *Remedial and Special Education, 25,* 314–323.

Dunn, L. M. (1968). Special education for the mildly handicapped— Is much of it justifiable? *Exceptional Children, 35,* 5–22.

Dunst, C. J. (2002). Family-centered practices: Birth through high school. *Journal of Special Education, 36,* 139–147.

DuPaul, G. J., & Stoner, G. (2003). *ADHD in the schools: Assessment and intervention strategies* (2nd edition). New York: Guilford.

DuPaul, G. J., Jitendra, A. K., Volpe, R. J., Tresco, K. E., Lutz, J. G., & Vile Junod, R. E. (2006). Consultation-based academic interventions for children with ADHD: Effects on reading and mathematics achievement. *Journal of Abnormal Child Psychology, 34*(5), 633–646.

DuPaul, G. J., & Wyeandt, L. L. (2006). School-based intervention for children with attention deficit hyperactivity disorder: Effects on academic, social and behavioural functioning. *International Journal of Disability, Development and Education, 53,* 161–176.

Durlak, C. M., Rose, E., & Bursuck, W. (1994). Preparing high school students with learning disabilities for the transition to postsecondary education: Teaching the skills of self-determination. *Journal of Learning Disabilities, 27,* 51–59.

Dyson, B. (2002). The implementation of cooperative learning in an elementary physical education program [Electronic version]. *Journal of Teaching in Physical Education, 22,* 69–85.

Dyson, L. (2005). Kindergarten children's understanding of and attitudes toward people with disabilities. *Topics in Early Childhood Special Education, 25,* 95–104.

Easterbrooks, S. (1999). Improving practices for students with hearing impairments. *Exceptional Children, 65,* 537–554.

Echevarria, J. C. (1998). Preparing text and classroom materials for English-language learners: Curriculum adaptations in secondary school settings. In R. Gersten & R. Jimenez (Eds.), *Promoting learning for culturally and linguistically diverse students: Classroom applications from contemporary research.* Belmont, CA: Wadsworth.

Edgemon, E. A., Jablonski, B. R., & Lloyd, J. W. (2006). Large-scale assessments: A teacher's guide to making decisions about accommodations. *Teaching Exceptional Children, 38*(3), 6–11.

Egyed, C. J., & Short, R. J. (2006). Teacher self-efficacy, burnout, experience and decision to refer a disruptive student. *School Psychology International, 27,* 462–474.

Ehri, L. C. (2004). Teaching phonemic awareness and phonics: An explanation of the National Reading Panel meta-analyses. In P. McCardle & V. Chhabra (Eds.), *The voice of evidence in reading research* (pp. 153–186). Baltimore, MD: Brookes.

Eigenbrood, R. (2004). IDEA requirements for children with disabilities in faith-based schools: Implications for practice. *Journal of Disability Policy Studies, 15,* 2–8.

Elbaum, B., Moody, S. W., & Schumm, J. S. (1999). Mixed-ability grouping for reading: What students think. *Learning Disabilities Research and Practice, 14,* 61–66.

Elhoweris, H., & Alsheikh, N. (2006). Teachers' attitudes toward inclusion. *International Journal of Special Education, 21,* 115–118.

Eli Lilly. (2003). *The history of ADHD.* Retrieved June 28, 2003, from www.strattera.com/1_3_childhood_adhd/1_3_1_1_2_ history.jsp

Elliot, L. B., Stinson, M. S., McKee, B. G., Everhart, V.S., & Francis, P. J. (2001). College students' perceptions of the C-print speech-to-text transcription system. *Journal of Deaf Studies and Deaf Education, 6*, 285–298.

Elliott, S. N., & Roach, A. T. (2002). *The impact of providing testing accommodations to students with disabilities.* Retrieved from www.wcer.wisc.edu/testacc/Publications/aera2002.doc

Ellis, A., & Ryan, A. (2003). Race and cognitive ability test performance: The mediating effects of test preparation, test-taking strategy use and self efficacy. *Journal of Social Psychology, 33,* 2607–2629.

Ellis, E. (1996). Reading strategy instruction. In D. Deshler, E. Ellis, & K. Lenz (Eds.), *Teaching adolescents with learning disabilities: Strategies and methods* (2nd ed., pp. 61–125). Denver, CO: Love.

Ellis, E. S., & Colvert, G. (1996). Writing strategy instruction. In D. Deshler, E. Ellis, and B. Lenz (Eds.), *Teaching adolescents with learning disabilities: Strategies and methods* (2nd ed., pp. 127–207). Denver, CO: Love.

Ellis, E., & Lenz, B. K. (1996). Perspectives on instruction in learning strategies. In D. Deshler, E. Ellis, & B. K. Lenz (Eds.), *Teaching adolescents with learning disabilities: Strategies and methods* (2nd ed., pp. 9–60). Denver: Love.

Ellis, E. S., & Sabornie, E. S. (1990). Strategy-based adaptive instruction in content-area classes: Social validity of six options. *Teacher Education and Special Education, 13,* 133–144.

Ellis, E., Lenz, B. K., & Sabornie, E. (1987a). Generalization and adaptation of learning strategies to natural environments: Part 1: Critical agents. *Remedial and Special Education, 8*(2), 6–24.

Ellis, E., Lenz, B. K., & Sabornie, E. (1987b). Generalization and adaptation of learning strategies to natural environments: Part 2: Research into practice. *Remedial and Special Education, 8*(2), 6–23.

Emmer, E. T., & Gerwels, M. C. (2002). Cooperative learning in elementary classrooms: Teaching practices and lesson characteristics [Electronic version]. *Elementary School Journal, 103,* 76–91.

Emmer, E. T., Evertson, C. M., Sanford, J. P., Clements, B. S., & Worsham, M. E. (1983). *Organizing and managing the junior high classroom.* Austin: Research and Development Center for Teacher Education, University of Texas.

Engelmann, S., & Bruner, E. C. (2003). *Reading mastery classic.* Columbus, OH: SRA/McGraw-Hill.

Englert, C., & Mariage, T. (1991). Making students partners in the comprehension process: Organizing the reading "POSSE." *Learning Disability Quarterly, 14,* 123–138.

Englert, C. S., Raphael, T. E., Anderson, L. M., Anthony, H. M., Fear, K. L., & Gregg, S. L. (1988). A case for writing intervention: Strategies for writing informational text. *Learning Disabilities Focus, 3*(2), 98–113.

Englert, C. S., Zhao, Y., Dunsmore, K., Collings, N. Y., & Wolbers, K. (2007). Scaffolding the writing of students with disabilities through procedural facilitation: Using an internet-based technology to improve performance. *Learning Disability Quarterly, 30,* 9–29.

Epilepsy Foundation. (n.d.). *Understanding epilepsy: Epilepsy and seizure statistics.* Retrieved July 8, 2007, from www.epilepsyfoundation.org/about/statistics.cfm

Epstein, M. H. (2004). *Behavioral and emotional rating scale* (2nd ed.). Austin, TX: PRO-ED.

Epstein, M. H., Polloway, E. A., Buck, G. H., Bursuck, W. D., Wissinger, L., Whitehouse, F., & Jayanthi, M. (1997). Homework-related communication problems: Perspectives of general education teachers. *Learning Disabilities Research and Practices, 12,* 221–227.

Epstein, M. H., Rudolph, S., & Epstein, A. (2000). Using strength-based assessment in transition planning. *Teaching Exceptional Children, 32*(6), 50–55.

Erion, J. (2006). Parent tutoring: A meta-analysis. *Education and Treatment of Children, 29*(1), 79–106.

Ervin, R. A., Schaughency, E., Matthews, A., Goodman, S. D., & McGlinchey, M. T. (2007). Primary and secondary prevention of behavior difficulties: Developing a data-informed problem-solving model to guide decision making at a school-wide level. *Psychology in the Schools, 44,* 7–18.

Espin, C., Shin, J., & Busch, T. (2005). Curriculum-based measurement in the content areas: Vocabulary matching as an indicator of progress in social studies learning. *Journal of Learning Disabilities, 38*(4), 353–363.

Etscheidt, S. (2006). Behavioral intervention plans: Pedagogical and legal analysis of issues. *Behavioral Disorders, 31,* 223–243.

Etscheidt, S. K. (2006). Progress monitoring: Legal issues and recommendations for IEP teams. *Teaching Exceptional Children, 38*(3), 56–60.

Etzel-Wise, D., & Mears, B. (2004). Adapted physical education and therapeutic recreation in schools. *Intervention in School and Clinic, 39,* 223–232.

Evertson, C. M., Emmer, E. T., Clements, B. S., Sanford, J. P., Worsham, M. E., & Williams, E. L. (1983). *Organizing and managing the elementary school classroom.* Austin: Research and Development Center for Teacher Education, University of Texas.

Fairbanks, S., Sugai, G., Guardino, D., & Lathrop, M. (2007). Response to intervention: Examining classroom behavior support in second grade. *Exceptional Children, 73,* 288–310.

Farmer, T. W., Goforth, J. B., Clemmer, J. T., & Thompson, J. H. (2004). School discipline problems in rural African American early adolescents: Characteristics of students with major, minor, and no offenses. *Behavioral Disorders, 29,* 317–336.

Feingold, B. F. (1975). *Why your child is hyperactive.* New York: Random House.

Fennema, E., Carpenter, T. P., Jacobs, V. R., Franke, M. L., & Levi, L. (1998). A longitudinal study of gender differences in young children's mathematical thinking. *Educational Researcher, 27*(5), 6–11.

Ferguson, P. M. (2002). A place in the family: An historical interpretation of research on parental reactions to having a child with a disability. *Journal of Special Education, 36,* 124–130.

Ferrell, K. A. (2005). The effects of NCLB. *Journal of Visual Impairment & Blindness, 99,* 681–683.

Fiedorowicz, C. (2005). Neurobiological basis of learning disabilities: An overview. Retrieved from www.ldac-taac.ca/Research/neurobiological-e.asp

Field, S., Sarver, M. D., & Shaw, S. F. (2003). Self-determination: A key to success in postsecondary education for students with learning disabilities. *Remedial and Special Education, 24,* 339–349.

Fighting Autism. (2004, November). *U.S. and outlying areas public schools autism prevalence report school years, 1992–2003.* Gibsonia, PA: Author. Retrieved July 1, 2007, from www.fightingautism.org/idea/reports/US-Autism-Statistics-Prevalence-Incidence-Rates.pdf

Filter, K. J., McKenna, M. K., Benedict, E. A., Horner, R. H., Todd, A. W., & Watson, J. (2007). Check in/check out: A post-hoc evaluation of an efficient, secondary-level targeted intervention for reducing problem behaviors in schools. *Education and Treatment of Children, 30,* 69–84.

Finstein, R. F., Yang, F. Y., & Jones, R. (2007). Build organizational skills in students with learning disabilities. *Intervention in School and Clinic, 42*(3), 174–178.

Fitch, F. (2003). Inclusion, exclusion, and ideology: Special education students' changing sense of self [Electronic version]. *Urban Review, 35,* 233–252.

Fitzgerald, J. L., & Watkins, M. W. (2006). Parents' rights in special education: The readability of procedural safeguards. *Exceptional Children, 72,* 497–510.

Fleischer, D. Z., & Zames, F. (2001). *The disability rights movement: From charity to confrontation.* Philadelphia: Temple University Press.

Fleming, J. L., & Monda-Amaya, L. E. (2001). Process variables critical for team effectiveness: A Delphi study of wraparound team members. *Remedial and Special Education, 22,* 158–171.

Fombonne, E. (2003). The prevalence of autism. *Journal of the American Medical Association, 289,* 87–89.

Foorman, B. R. (Ed.). (2003). *Preventing and remediating reading difficulties: Bringing science to scale.* Baltimore, MD: York.

Foorman, B. R., Goldenberg, C., Carlson, C. D., Saunders, W. M., & Pollard-Durodola, S. D. (2004). How teachers allocate time during literacy instruction in primary-grade English language learner classrooms. In P. McCardle & V. Chhabra (Eds.), *The voice of evidence in reading research* (pp. 289–322). Baltimore, MD: Paul H. Brookes.

Fore, C., Riser, S., & Boon, R. (2006). Implications of cooperative learning and educational reform for students with mild disabilities. *Reading Improvement, 43*(1), 3–12.

Forest, M., Pierpoint, J., & O'Brien, J. (1996). MAPS, Circles of Friends, and PATH: Powerful tools to help build caring communities. In S. Stainback & W. Stainback (Eds.), *Inclusion: A guide for educators.* Baltimore, MD: Paul H. Brookes.

Forness, S. R., & Kavale, K. A. (2001). ADHD and a return to the medical model of special education. *Education and Treatment of Children, 24,* 224–247.

Foster, M. (1997). *Black teachers on teaching.* New York: New Press.

Foster, M. (1995) African American teachers and culturally-relevant pedagogy. In J. A. Banks & C. A. M. Banks (Eds.), *Handbook of research on multicultural education* (pp. 570–581). New York: Macmillan.

Frattura, E., & Capper, C. A. (2006). Segregated programs versus integrated comprehensive service delivery for all learners: Assessing the differences. *Remedial and Special Education, 27*(6), 355–364.

Frattura, E. M., & Capper, C. A. (2007). New teacher teams to support integrated comprehensive services. *Teaching Exceptional Children, 39*(4), 16–21.

Freeman, J. (2000). Teaching for talent: Lessons from the research. In C. M. F. van Lieshout & P. G. Heymans (Eds.), *Developing talent across the life span* (pp. 231–248). Philadelphia: Psychology Press.

Freeman, R., Eber, L., Anderson, C., Irvin, L., Horner, R., Bounds, M., et al. (2006). Building inclusive school cultures using school-wide positive behavior support: Designing effective individual support systems for students with significant disabilities. *Research & Practice for Persons with Severe Disabilities, 31,* 4–17.

Freeman, S. F. N., & Alkin, M. C. (2000). Academic and social attainments of children with mental retardation in general education and special education settings. *Remedial and Special Education, 21*(1), 3–18.

French, N. K. (2003). *Managing paraeducators in your school: How to hire, train, and supervise non-certified staff.* Thousand Oaks, CA: Corwin.

Frey, L. M., & Wilhite, K. (2005). Our five basic needs: Application for understanding the function of behavior. *Intervention in School and Clinic, 40,* 156–160.

Friedland, E. S., & Truesdell, K. S. (2006). "I can read to whoever wants to hear me read": Buddy readers speak out with confidence. *Teaching Exceptional Children, 38*(5), 36–42.

Friend, M. (2000). Perspective: Myths and misunderstandings about professional collaboration. *Remedial and Special Education, 21,* 130–132, 160.

Friend, M. (2008a). *Co-Teach! A manual for creating and sustaining effective classroom partnerships in inclusive schools.* Greensboro, NC: Marilyn Friend, Inc.

Friend, M. (2008b). *Special education: Contemporary perspectives for school professionals* (2nd ed.). Boston: Allyn and Bacon.

Friend, M., & Cook, L. (2007). *Interactions: Collaboration skills for school professionals* (5th ed.). Boston: Allyn and Bacon.

Friend, M., & Cook, L. (2004). Collaborating with professionals and parents without being overwhelmed: Building partnerships and teams. In J. Burnette, & C. Peters-Johnson (Eds.), *Thriving as a special educator: Balancing your practices and ideals* (pp. 29–39). Arlington, VA: Council for Exceptional Children.

Friend, M., & Cook, L. (2007). *Interactions: Collaboration skills for school professionals* (5th ed.). Boston: Allyn and Bacon.

Frye, H. (2005). How elementary school counselors can meet the needs of students with disabilities. *Professional School Counseling, 8,* 442–450.

Fuchs, D., & Deshler, D. D. (2007). What we need to know about responsiveness to intervention (and shouldn't be afraid to ask). *Learning Disabilities Research and Practice, 22,* 129–136.

Fuchs, L. S., & Fuchs, D. (2001). Helping teachers formulate sound test accommodation decisions for students with learning disabilities. *Learning Disabilities Research and Practice, 16,* 174–181.

Fuchs, L. S., & Fuchs, D. (2006). A framework for building capacity for responsiveness to intervention. *School Psychology Review, 35,* 621–626.

Fuchs, L. S., Fuchs, D., Hamlett, C., Philips, N., & Bentz, J. (1994). Classwide curriculum-based measurement: Helping general educators meet the challenge of student diversity. *Exceptional Children, 60,* 518–537.

Fuchs, L. S., Fuchs, D., Hamlett, C. L., Hope, S. K., Hollenbeck, K. N., Capizzi, A.M., Craddock, C.F., & Brothers, R.L. (2006). Extending responsiveness-to-intervention to math problem-solving at third grade. *TEACHING Exceptional Children, 38*(4), 59–63.

Fuchs, L. S., Fuchs, D., Hamlett, C. L., & Stecker, P. M. (1991). Effects of curriculum-based measurement and consultation on teacher planning and student achievement in mathematics operations. *American Educational Research Journal, 28,* 617–641.

Fuchs, L. S., Fuchs, D., Kazdan, S., Karns, K., Calhoon, M. B., Hamlett, C. L., & Hewlett, S. (2000). Effects of workgroup structure and size on student productivity during collaborative work on complex tasks. *Elementary School Journal, 100,* 201–210.

Fuchs, L. S., Hamlett, C. L., & Fuchs, D. (1997). *Monitoring basic skills progress: Basic reading* (2nd ed.) [Computer software, manual, and blackline masters]. Austin TX: PRO-ED.

Fuchs, L. S., Hamlett, C. L., & Fuchs, D. (1998). *Monitoring basic skills progress: Basic math computation* (2nd ed.) [Computer software, manual, and blackline masters]. Austin TX: PRO-ED.

Fuchs, L. S., Hamlett, C. L., & Fuchs, D. (1999). *Monitoring basic skills progress: Basic math concepts and applications* [Computer software, manual, and blackline masters]. Austin TX: PRO-ED.

Fulk, B. M. (1996). The effects of combined strategy and attribution training on LD adolescents' spelling performance. *Exceptionality, 6*(1), 13–27.

Furlong, M., & Morrison, G. (2000). The *school* in school violence: Definitions and facts. *Journal of Emotional and Behavioral Disorders, 8,* 71–82.

Fusell, J. J., Macias, M. M., & Saylor, C. F. (2005). Social skills and behavior problems in children with disabilities with and without siblings. *Child Psychiatry and Human Development, 36,* 227–241.

Gabe, J., Bury, M., & Ramsay, R. (2002). Living with asthma: The experiences of young people at home and at school [Electronic version]. *Social Science and Medicine, 55,* 1619–1633.

Gable, R. A., Mostert, M. P., & Tonelson, S. W. (2004). Assessing professional collaboration in schools: Knowing what works. *Preventing School Failure, 48*(3), 4–8.

Gagnon, J. C., & Maccini, P. (2001). Preparing students with disabilities for algebra. *Teaching Exceptional Children, 34*(1), 8–15.

Ganz, J. B., Cook, K. E., & Earles-Vollrath, T. L. (2007). A grab bag of strategies for children with mild communication deficits. *Intervention in School and Clinic, 42*(3), 179–187.

Garcia, S., & Ortiz, A. (2006). Preventing disproportionate representation: Culturally & linguistically prereferral interventions [Electronic version]. *Teaching Exceptional Children, 38*(4), 64–68.

Gardner, H. (1993). *Multiple intelligences: The theory in practice.* New York: Basic Books.

Gartin, B. C., & Murdick, N. L. (2005). IDEA 2004: The IEP. *Remedial and Special Education, 26,* 327–331.

Gay, G. (2002). Culturally responsive teaching in special education for ethnically diverse students: Setting the stage. *Qualitative Studies in Education, 15*(6), 613–629.

Gehrling, A. (2006). Classroom management and teaching strategies for students with attention deficit hyperactivity disorder. *Law & Disorder, 1,* 43–48.

Geisthardt, C. L., Brotherson, M. J., & Cook, C. C. (2002). Friendships of children with disabilities in the home environment. *Education and Training in Mental Retardation and Developmental Disabilities, 37,* 235–252.

Germinario, V., Cervalli, J., & Ogden, E. H. (1992). *All children successful: Real answers for helping at risk elementary students.* Lancaster, PA: Technomic.

George, M. P., White, G. P., & Schlaffer, J. J. (2007). Implementing school-wide behavior change: Lessons from the field. *Psychology in the Schools, 44*(1), 41–51.

Gersten, R., Baker, S. K., & Marks, S. U. (1998). *Teaching English language learners with learning difficulties.* Eugene, OR: Eugene Research Institute.

Gersten, R., Fuchs, L. S., Williams, J. P., & Baker, S. (2001). Teaching reading comprehension strategies to students with learning disabilities: A review of research. *Review of Educational Research, 71,* 279–320.

Gersten, R., Jordan, N. C., & Flojo, J. R. (2005). Early identification and interventions for students with mathematics difficulties. *Journal of Learning Disabilities, 38*(4), 293–304.

Gersten, R., Vaughn, S., & Brengelman, S. U. (1996). Grading and academic feedback for special education students and students with learning difficulties. In T. R. Guskey (Ed.), *Communicating student learning.* Alexandria, VA: Association for Supervision and Curriculum Development.

Gersti-Pepin, C. I. (2006). The paradox of poverty narratives: Educators struggling with children left behind. *Educational Policy, 20*(1), 143–162.

Getty, L. A., & Summy, S. E. (2004). The course of due process. *Teaching Exceptional Children, 36*(3), 40–43.

Ghere, G., & York-Barr, J. (2007). Paraprofessional turnover and retention in inclusive programs. *Remedial and Special Education, 28*(1), 21–32.

Giangreco, M. F. (2007). Extending inclusive opportunities. *Educational Leadership, 64*(5), 34–37.

Giangreco, M. F., & Broer, S. M. (2005). Questionable utilization of paraprofessionals in inclusive schools: Are we addressing symptoms or causes? *Focus on Autism and Other Developmental Disabilities, 20*(1), 10–26.

Giangreco, M. F., & Doyle, M. B. (2002). Students with disabilities and paraprofessional supports: Benefits, balance, and band-aids [Electronic version]. *Focus on Exceptional Children, 34*(7), 1–12.

Giangreco, M. F., Edelman, S. W., & Broer, S. M. (2003). Schoolwide planning to improve paraeducator supports. *Exceptional Children, 70,* 63–80.

Gibb, G. S., & Dyches, T. T. (2007). *Guide to writing quality individualized education programs* (2nd ed.). Boston: Allyn and Bacon.

Gillette, Y. (2006). Assistive technology and literacy partnerships. *Top Lang Disorders, 26*(1), 70–81.

Gillies, R. M. (2007). *Cooperative learning: Integrating theory and practice.* Thousand Oaks, CA: Sage.

Gillies, R. M., & Ashman, A. F. (2000). The effects of cooperative learning on students with learning difficulties in the lower elementary school. *Journal of Special Education, 34,* 19–27.

Ginsberg, M. B. (2005). Cultural diversity, motivation, and differentiation. *Theory into Practice, 44,* 218–225.

Giovacco-Johnson, T. (2007). Twice-exceptional children: Paradoxes and parenting. *Childhood Education, 83*(3), 175–176.

Goetz, L., & O'Farrell, N. (1999). Connections: Facilitating social supports for students with deaf-blindness in general education classrooms. *Journal of Visual Impairment and Blindness, 92,* 704–715.

Goldstein, A. P., Sprafkin, R. P., Gershaw, N. J., & Klein, P. (1980). *Skillstreaming the adolescent.* Champaign, IL: Research Press.

Goldstein, H., Moss, J. W., & Jordan, L. J. (1965). *The efficacy of special class training on the development of mentally retarded children* (U.S. Office of Education Cooperative Research Program Project No. 619). Urbana: University of Illinois Institute for Research on Exceptional Children. (ERIC Document Reproduction Service No. ED002907)

Gong, B., & Marion, S. (2006). *Dealing with flexibility in assessments for students with significant cognitive disabilities* (Synthesis Report 60). Minneapolis, MN: University of Minnesota, National Center on Educational Outcomes. Retrieved May 27, 2007, from http://cehd.umn.edu/nceo/OnlinePubs/Synthesis60.html

Good, R. (2002, April). *Catching kids before they fall: What schools can do.* Presentation at the Illinois branch of the International Dyslexia Association, Lincolnwood, IL.

Good, R. H., Gruba, J., & Kaminki, R. A. (2002). Best practices in using dynamic indicators of basic early literacy skills (DIBELS) in an outcomes-driven model. In A. Thomas & J. Grimes (Eds.), *Best practices in school psychology IV* (pp. 699–720). Bethesda, MD: National Association of School Psychologists.

Good, T. L., & Brophy, I. E. (1986). School effects. In M. C. Wittrock (Ed.), *Handbook of research on teaching* (3rd ed., pp. 570–602). Upper Saddle River, NJ: Prentice Hall.

Goodenow, C., Szalacha, L., & Westheimer, K. (2006). School support groups, other school factors, and the safety of sexual minority adolescents. *Psychology in the Schools, 43,* 573–589.

Goodman, H., Gottlieb, J., & Harrison, R. H. (1972). Social acceptance of EMR children integrated into a non-graded elementary school. *American Journal of Mental Deficiency, 76,* 412–417.

Graetz, J. E., Mastropieri, M. A., & Scruggs, T. E. (2006). Show time: Using video self-modeling to decrease inappropriate behavior. *Teaching Exceptional Children, 38*(5), 43–48.

Graham, S. (1999). Handwriting and spelling instruction for students with learning disabilities: A review. *Learning Disability Quarterly, 22,* 77–98.

Graham, S., & Freeman, S. (1986). Strategy training and teacher- vs. student-controlled study conditions: Effects on LD students' spelling performance. *Learning Disability Quarterly, 9,* 15–22.

Graham, S., & Harris, K. R. (1987). Improving composition skills of inefficient learners with self-instructional strategy training. *Topics in Language Disorders, 7*(4), 66–77.

Graham, S., & Harris, K. R. (2005). Improving the writing performance of young struggling writers. *The Journal of Special Education, 39*(1), 19–33.

Graham, S., Harris, K. R., & MacArthur, C. (2006). Explicitly teaching struggling writers: Strategies for mastering the writing process. *Intervention in School and Clinic, 41*(5), 290–294.

Grandin, T. (2002). *Teaching tips for children and adults with autism.* Salem, OR: Center for the Study of Autism. Retrieved November 22, 2004, from www.autism.org/temple/tips.html

Grandin, T. (2007). Autism from the inside. *Education Leadership, 64*(5), 29–32.

Grant, R. (1993). Strategic training for using text headings to improve students' processing of content. *Journal of Reading, 36*, 482–488.

Green, T. (2005). Using technology to help English language students develop language skills: A home and school connection. *Multicultural Education, 13*(2), 56–59.

Greenwood, C. R., Arreaga-Mayer, C., Utley, C. A., Gavin, K. M., & Terry, B. J. (2001). Classwide peer tutoring learning management system: Applications with elementary-level English language learners. *Remedial and Special Education, 22*, 34–47.

Gresham, F. M., Van, M. B., & Cook, C. R. (2006). Social skills training for teaching replacement behaviors: Remediating acquisition deficits in at-risk students. *Behavior Disorders, 31*(4), 363–377.

Gringel, M., Neubert, D. A., Moon, M. S., & Graham, S. (2003). Self-determination for students with disabilities: Views of parents and teachers. *Exceptional Children, 70*, 97–111.

Grossen, B. J. (2002). The BIG accommodation model: The direct instruction model for secondary schools. *Journal of Education for Students Placed At Risk, 7*, 241–263.

Grossman, H. (1995). *Special education in a diverse society.* Boston: Allyn and Bacon.

Gubbins, E. J. (Ed.). (2002, Fall). *National Research Center on the Gifted and Talented Newsletter.* Storrs: University of Connecticut, National Research Center on the Gifted and Talented. (ERIC Document Reproduction Service No. ED477662)

Gunter, P. L., Miller, K. A., Venn, M. L., Thomas, K., & House, S. (2002). Self-graphing to success. *Teaching Exceptional Children, 35*(2), 30–35.

Guskey, T. R. (2006). Making high school grades meaningful. *Phi Delta Kappan, 87*(9), 670–675.

Guskey, T. R., & Bailey, J. M. (2001). *Developing grading and reporting systems for student learning.* Thousand Oaks, CA: Corwin.

Haager, D., & Klinger, J. K. (2004). *Differentiating instruction in inclusive classrooms: The special educator's guide.* Boston: Allyn & Bacon.

Hallahan, D. P., Lloyd, J. W., Kauffman, J. M., Weiss, M. P., & Martinez, E. A. (2005). *Learning disabilities: Foundations, characteristics, and effective teaching* (3rd ed.). Boston: Allyn and Bacon.

Hammill, D. (1990). On defining learning disabilities: An emerging consensus. *Journal of Learning Disabilities, 23*(2), 74–84.

Handler, B. R. (2003, April). *Special education practices: An evaluation of educational environmental placement trends since the regular education initiative.* Paper presentation at the Annual meeting of the American Educational Research Association, Chicago. Retrieved October 4, 2004, from www.eric.ed.gov/contentdelivery/servlet/ERICServlet?accno=ED480184

Handler, M., W., Rey, J., Connell, J., Their, K., Feinberg, A., & Putman, R. (2007). Practical considerations in creating school-wide positive behavior support in public schools. *Psychology in the Schools, 44*(1), 29–39.

Hanline, M. F., & Daley, S. (2002). "Mom, will Kaelie always have possibilities?" The realities of early childhood inclusion. *Phi Delta Kappan, 84*, 73–76.

Hänze, M., & Berger, R. (2007). Cooperative learning, motivational effects, and student characteristics: An experimental study comparing cooperative learning and direct instruction in 12th grade physics classes. *Learning and Instruction, 17*, 29–41.

Hardman, M. L., Drew, C. J., & Egan, M. W. (2005). *Human exceptionality: School, community, and family, IDEA 2004 Update Edition* (8th ed.). Boston: Allyn and Bacon.

Harlacher, J. E., Roberts, N. E., & Merrell, K. W. (2006). Classwide interventions for students with ADHD: A summary of teacher options beneficial for the whole class. *Teaching Exceptional Children, 39*(2), 6–12.

Harley, D. A., Nowak, T. M., Gassway, L. J., & Savage, T. A. (2002). Lesbian, gay, bisexual, and transgender college students with disabilities: A look at multiple cultural minorities. *Psychology in the Schools, 39*, 525–538.

Harniss, M. K., Caros, J., & Gersten, R. (2007). Impact of the design of U.S. history textbooks on content acquisition and academic engagement of special education students: An experimental investigation. *Journal of Learning Disabilities, 40*(2), 100–110.

Harniss, M. K., Epstein, M. H., Bursuck, W. D., Nelson, J., & Jayanthi, M. (2001). Resolving homework-related communication problems: Recommendations of parents of children with and without disabilities. *Reading and Writing Quarterly, 17*, 205–225.

Harpin, V. A. (2005). The effect of ADHD on the life of an individual, their family, and community from preschool to adult life. *Archives of Disease in Childhood, 90*, i2-i7.

Harris, K. R., Graham, S., Mason, L. H. (2003). Self-regulated strategy development in the classroom: Part of a balanced approach to writing instruction for students with disabilities. *Focus on Exceptional Children, 35*(7), 1–16.

Harry, B. (2002). Trends and issues in serving culturally diverse families of children with disabilities. *Journal of Special Education, 36*, 131–138.

Harry, B., & Klingner, J. K. (2005). Why are so many minority students in special education?: Understanding race and disability in schools. New York: Teachers College Press.

Hartas, D. (2004). Teacher and speech-language therapist collaboration: Being equal and achieving a common goal? *Child Language Teaching and Therapy, 20*, 33–54.

Hartwig, E. P., & Ruesch, G. M. (2000). Disciplining students in special education. *Journal of Special Education, 33*, 240–247.

Hasbrouck, J. E., & Tindal, G. (2006). Oral reading fluency norms: A valuable assessment tool for reading teachers. *The Reading Teacher, 59*(7), 636–644.

Hauge, J. M., & Babkie, A. M. (2006). Develop collaborative special educator-paraprofessional teams: One para's view. *Intervention in School and Clinic, 42*(1), 51–53.

Heath, D. (1993). Using portfolio assessment with secondary LED students yields a cross-cultural advantage for all. *BeOutreach, 4*(1), 27.

Hehir, T. (2007). Confronting ableism. *Education Leadership, 64*(5), 8–14.

Hendley, S. L. (2007). Use positive behavior support for inclusion in the general education classroom. *Intervention in School and Clinic, 42*(4), 225–228.

Henley, M. (2003). *Teaching self-control: A curriculum for responsible behavior.* (2nd ed.). Bloomington, IN: National Education Service.

Heron, T. E., Villareal, D. M., & Yao, M. (2006). Peer tutoring systems: Applications in classroom and specialized environments. *Reading and Writing Quarterly, 22*, 27–45.

Hetzroni, O. E., & Shrieber, B. (2004). Word processing as an assistive technology tool for enhancing academic outcomes of students with writing disabilities in the general classroom. *Journal of Learning Disabilities, 37*, 143–154.

Hill, J., & Flynn, K. (2006). *Classroom instruction that works with English language learners.* Alexandria, VA: Association for Supervision and Curriculum Development.

Hinchey, P. H. (2003). Corporal punishment: Legalities, realities, and implications [Electronic version]. *Clearing House, 76*, 127–131.

Hitchcock, C. H., Dowrick, P. W., & Prater, M. A. (2003). Video self-modeling intervention in school-based settings. *Remedial and Special Education, 24*, 36–45.

Hitchcock, C., Meyer, A., Rose, D., & Jackson, R. (2002). Providing new access to the general curriculum: Universal Design for Learning. *Teaching Exceptional Children, 35*(2), 8–17.

Hitti, M. (2005, September). New numbers on ADHD in U.S. kids. *WebMD Medical News.* Retrieved July 25, 2007, from www.webmd.com/add-adhd/news/20050901/new-numbers-on-adhd-in-us-kids

Hobbs, N. (1975). *The futures of children*. San Francisco: Jossey-Bass.

Hodges, D., Mandlebaum, L. H., Boff, C., & Miller, M. (2007). Instructional strategies online database (ISOD). *Intervention in School and Clinic, 42*(4), 219–224.

Hodgkinson, H. (2000/2001). Educational demographics: What teachers should know. *Educational Leadership, 58*(4), 6–11.

Holliday, D. C. (2002). *Jigsaw IV: Using student/teacher concerns to improve Jigsaw III*. (ERIC Document Reproduction Service No. ED465687)

Holverstott, J. (2005). Promote self-determination in students. *Intervention in School and Clinic, 41*(1), 39–41.

Homme, L. (1970). *How to use contingency contracting in the classroom*. Champaign, IL: Research Press.

Hooper, S. R. (2006). Myths and misconceptions about traumatic brain injury: Endorsements by school psychologists. *Exceptionality, 14*, 171–182.

Hoover, J. J., & Patton, J. R. (2005). Differentiating curriculum and instruction for English-language learners with special needs. *Intervention in School and Clinic, 40*, 231–235.

Horton, S. V. (1987). *Study guides: A paper on curriculum modification*. Unpublished manuscript, University of Washington.

Hosp, J. L., & Reschly, D. J. (2002). Predictors of restrictiveness of placement for African-American and Caucasian students. *Exceptional Children, 68*, 225–238.

Hosp, J. L., & Reschly, D. J. (2003). Referral rates for intervention or assessment: A meta-analysis of racial differences. *Journal of Special Education, 37*, 67–80.

Hosp, J. L., & Reschly, D. J. (2004). Disproportionate representation of minority students in special education: Academic, demographic, and economic predictors. *Exceptional Children, 70*, 185–199.

Hosp, M. K., & Hosp, J. (2003). Curriculum-based measurement for reading, spelling, and math: How to do it and why. *Preventing School Failure, 48*(1), 10–17.

Howell, K. M., & Morehead, M. K. (1993). *Curriculum-based evaluation for special and remedial education* (2nd ed.). Columbus, OH: Merrill.

Huefner, D. S. (2000). The risks and opportunities of the IEP requirements under IDEA '97. *Journal of Special Education, 33*, 195–204.

Hughes, J, & Kwok, O. (2007). Influence of student-teacher and parent-teacher relationships on lower achieving readers' engagement and achievement in the primary grades. *Journal of Educational Psychology, 99*, 39–51.

Hughes, M., & Greenhough, P. (2006). Boxes, bags, and videotape: Enhancing home-school communication through knowledge exchange activities. *Educational Review, 58*, 471–487.

Hunt, P., Soto, G., Maier, J., & Doering, K. (2003). Collaborative teaming to support students at risk and students with severe disabilities in general education classrooms. *Exceptional Children, 69*, 315–332.

Hyatt, K. J. (2007). Brain Gym™ building stronger brains or wishful thinking? *Remedial and Special Education, 28*(2), 117–124.

Hyatt, K. J. (2007). The new IDEA: Changes, concerns, and questions. *Intervention in School and Clinic, 42*, 131–136.

Iano, R. P., Ayers, D., Heller, H. B., McGettigan, J. F., & Walker, V. S. (1974). Sociometric status of retarded children in an integrative program. *Exceptional Children, 40*, 267–271.

Idol, L. (2006). Toward the inclusion of special education students in general education: A program evaluation of eight schools. *Remedial and Special Education, 27*, 77–94.

Ingersoll, B., Dvortcsak, A., Whalen, C., & Sikora, D. (2005). The effects of a developmental, social-pragmatic language intervention on rate of expressive language production in young children with autistic spectrum disorders. *Focus on Autism and Other Developmental Disabilities, 20*, 213–222.

Institute of Education Sciences, National Center for Education Statistics (2007, July). *Percentage of high school dropouts (status dropouts) among persons 16 through 24 years old, by sex and race/ethnicity: Selected years, 1960 through 2005* [Table 104]. Retrieved July 31, 2007, from http://nces.ed.gov/programs/digest/d06/tables/dt06_104.asp?referrer=list

Ira, V. B. (2000). Safe and secure on the web: Pointers on determining a web site's credibility. *Exceptional Parent, 30*(1), 148.

Irlen, H. (1991). *Reading by the colors: Overcoming dyslexia and other reading disabilities through the Irlen method*. Garden City Park, NY: Avery.

Isaacson, S. (2001). Written language. In P. J. Schloss, M. A. Smith, & C. N. Schloss (Eds.), *Instructional methods for secondary students with learning and behavior problems* (3rd ed., pp. 222–245). Boston: Allyn and Bacon.

Ives, B., & Hoy, C. (2003). Graphic organizers applied to higher-level secondary mathematics. *Learning Disabilities: Research and Practice, 18*, 36–51.

Jackson, C. W., & Larkin, M. J. (2002). RUBRIC: Teaching students to use grading rubrics. *Teaching Exceptional Children, 35*(1), 40–45.

Jaffee, S. R., Caspi, A., & Moffitt, T. E. (2007). Individual, family, and neighborhood factors distinguish resilient from non-resilient maltreated children: A cumulative stressors model. *Child Abuse & Neglect: The International Journal, 31*, 231–253.

Jamie, K., & Knowlton, E. (2007). Visual supports for students with behavior and cognitive challenges. *Intervention in School and Clinic, 42*(5), 259–270.

Janiga, S. J., & Costenbader, V. (2002). The transition from high school to postsecondary education for students with learning disabilities: A survey of college service coordinators. *Journal of Learning Disabilities, 35*, 462–468.

Janisch, C., & Johnson, M. (2003). Effective literacy practices and challenging curriculum for at-risk learners: Great expectations [Electronic version]. *Journal of Education for Students Placed at Risk, 8*, 295–308.

Jarolimek, J., Foster, C. D., & Kellough, R. D. (2004). *Teaching and learning in the elementary school* (8th ed.). Upper Saddle River, NJ: Prentice Hall.

Jenkins, J. R., Antil, L. R., Wayne, S. K., & Vadasy, P. F. (2003). How cooperative learning works for special education and remedial students. *Exceptional Children, 69*, 279–292.

Jensen, R. J. (2004). Discipline preferences and styles among Latino families: Implications for special educators. *Multiple Voices, 7*(1), 60–73.

Jenson, W. R., Sheridan, S. M., Olympia, D., & Andrews, D. (1994). Homework and students with learning disabilities and behavior disorders: A practical, parent-based approach. *Journal of Learning Disabilities, 27*, 538–549.

Johns, B. H., Crowley, E. P., & Guetzloe, E. (2005). The central role of teaching social skills. *Focus on Exceptional Children, 37*(8), 1–8.

Johnson, D., Johnson, R., & Holubec, E. (1998). *Cooperation in the classroom*. Boston: Allyn and Bacon. Retrieved February 11, 2005, from www.intime.uni.edu/coop_learning/ch5/teaching.htm

Johnson, D. W., Johnson, R. T., & Maruyama, G. (1983). Interdependence and interpersonal attraction among heterogeneous and homogeneous individuals: A theoretical formulation and a meta-analysis of the research. *Review of Educational Research, 53*, 5–54.

Johnson, E. S. (2000). The effects of accommodations on performance assessments. *Remedial and Special Education, 21*, 261–267.

Johnson, E., & Arnold, N. (2004). Validating an alternate assessment. *Remedial and Special Education, 25,* 266–275.

Johnson, G. O., & Kirk, S. A. (1950). Are mentally handicapped children segregated in the regular grades? *Exceptional Children, 17,* 65–68, 87–88.

Johnson, J., & Duffett, A. (2002). *When it's your own child: A report on special education from the families who use it.* New York: Public Agenda Foundation. (ERIC Document Reproduction Service No. ED471033)

Johnson, L. R., & Johnson, C. E. (1999). Teaching students to regulate their own behavior. *Teaching Exceptional Children, 31*(4), 6–10.

Johnston, J., Knight, M., & Miller, L. (2007). Finding time for teams: Student achievement grows as district support boosts collaboration. *Journal of Staff Development, 28*(2), 14–18.

Jones, J. M. (2007). Exposure to chronic community violence: Resilience in African American children. *Journal of Black Psychology, 33,* 125–149.

Jones, V. F., & Jones, L. S. (1990). *Comprehensive classroom management.* Boston: Allyn and Bacon.

Jones, V. F., & Jones, L. S. (2004). *Comprehensive classroom management: Creating communities of support and solving problems* (7th ed.). Boston: Allyn and Bacon.

Juel, C. (1988). Learning to read and write: A longitudinal study of 54 children from first through fourth grades. *Journal of Educational Psychology, 80*(4), 437–447.

Kagan, S. (1990). A structural approach to cooperative learning. *Educational Leadership, 47*(4), 12–15.

Kalyva, E., & Avramidis, E. (2005). Improving communication between children with autism and their peers through the 'Circle of Friends': A small-scale intervention study. *Journal of Applied Research in Intellectual Disabilities, 18,* 253–261.

Kame'enui, E. J., Carnine, D. W., Dixon, R. C., Simmons, D. C., & Coyne, M. D. (2002). *Effective teaching strategies that accommodate diverse learners* (2nd ed.). Upper Saddle River, NJ: Merrill/Prentice Hall.

Kaminski, R. A., & Good, R. H. (1996). Toward a technology for assessing basic early literacy skills. *School Psychology Review, 25,* 215–227.

Kampfer, S. H., Horvath, L. S., Kleinert, H. L., & Kearns, J. F. (2001). Teachers' perceptions of one state's alternative assessment implications for practice and preparation. *Exceptional Children, 67,* 361–374.

Kamps, D., Wendland, M., & Culpepper, M. (2006). Active teacher participation in functional behavior assessment for students with emotional and behavioral disorders: Risks in general education classrooms. *Behavioral Disorders, 31*(2), 128–146.

Kampwirth, T. J. (2005). *Collaborative consultation in the schools* (3rd ed.). Upper Saddle River, NJ: Merrill.

Karger, J. (2004). *Access to the general curriculum for students with disabilities: The role of the IEP.* Washington, DC: National Center on Accessing the General Curriculum. Retrieved August 15, 2004, from www.cast.org/ncac/index.cfm?i=5312

Kauffman, J. M. (2005). *Cases in emotional and behavioral disorders of children and youth.* Upper Saddle River, NJ: Merrill/Prentice Hall.

Kauffman, J. M., Mostert, M. P., Trent, S. C., & Hallahan, D. P. (2002). *Managing classroom behavior: A reflective, case-based approach* (3rd ed.). Boston: Allyn and Bacon.

Kavale, K. (2002). Mainstreaming to full inclusion: From orthogenesis to pathogenesis of an idea [Electronic version]. *International Journal of Disability, Development, and Education, 49,* 201–214.

Kavale, K. A., & Forness, S. R. (2000). History, rhetoric, and reality: Analysis of inclusion debate. *Remedial and Special Education, 21,* 279–296.

Kavale, K.A., Hirshoren, A., & Forness, S.R. (1998). Meta-analytic validation of the Dunn and Dunn Model of learning-style preferences: A critique of what was Dunn. *Learning Disabilities Research and Practice, 13*(2), 75–80.

Kazdin, A. E. (1977). *The token economy: A review and evaluation.* New York: Plenum.

Kearns, J., Kleinert, H., Clayton, J., Burdge, M., & Williams, R. (1998). Inclusive educational assessments at the elementary school level: Perspectives from Kentucky. *Teaching Exceptional Children, 31*(2), 16–23.

Keefe, E. B., Moore, V., & Duff, F. (2004). The four "knows" of collaborative teaching. *Teaching Exceptional Children, 36*(5), 36–43.

Keefe, E. B., Moore, V. M., & Duff, F. R. (2006). *Listening to the experts: Students with disabilities speak out.* Baltimore: Paul H. Brookes.

Kern, L., & Clemens, N. H. (2007). Antecedent strategies to promote appropriate classroom behavior. *Psychology in the Schools, 44*(1), 65–75.

Kerr, M. M., & Nelson, C. M. (2006). *Strategies for addressing behavior problems in the classroom* (5th ed.). Upper Saddle River, NJ: Pearson/Merrill/Prentice Hall.

Kerr, M. M., & Nelson, C. M. (1998). *Strategies for managing behavior problems in the classroom* (3rd ed.). Columbus, OH: Merrill/Prentice Hall.

Kerschner, J. R. (1990). Self-concept and IQ as predictors of remedial success in children with learning disabilities. *Journal of Learning Disabilities, 23,* 368–374.

Khisty, L. L. (2002). Mathematics learning and the Latino student: Suggestions from research for classroom practice. *Teaching Children Mathematics, 9*(1), 32–36.

Khorsheed, K. (2007). Four places to dig deep: To find more time for teacher collaboration. *Journal of Staff Development, 28*(2), 43–45.

Kim, A., Vaughn, S., Klinger, J. K., Woodruff, A. L., Reutebuch, C. K., & Kouzekanani, K. (2006). Improving the reading comprehension of middle school students with disabilities through computer-assisted collaborative strategic reading. *Remedial and Special Education, 27*(4), 235–249.

Kinch, C., Lewis-Palmer, T., Hagan-Burke, S., & Sugai, G. (2001). A comparison of teacher and student functional behavior assessment interview information from low-risk and high-risk classrooms [Electronic version]. *Education and Treatment of Children, 24,* 480–494.

Kindler, A. L. (2002). *Survey of states' limited English proficient students and available educational programs and services 1999–2000 summary report.* Washington, DC: National Clearinghouse for English Acquisition and Language Instruction Educational Programs.

King, E. W. (2005). Addressing the social and emotional needs of twice-exceptional students. *Teaching Exceptional Children, 38*(1), 16–20.

King, M. A., Sims, A., & Osher, D. (2007). *How is cultural competence integrated in education?* Retrieved June 1, 2007, from www .mayoclinic.com/health/childhood-obesity/DS00698

King, M. B., & Youngs, P. (2003). *Classroom teachers' views on inclusion (Riser Brief No. 7).* Madison: University of Wisconsin-Madison, Research Institute on Secondary Education Reform for Youth with Disabilities (RISER). (ERIC Document Reproduction Service No. ED477878)

King-Sears, M. E. (2007). Designing and delivering learning center instruction. *Intervention in School and Clinic, 42*(3), 137–147.

King-Sears, M. E. (2001). Three steps for gaining access to the general education curriculum for learners with disabilities. *Intervention in School and Clinic, 37,* 67–76.

King-Sears, M. E., Burgess, M., & Lawson, T. L. (1999). Applying curriculum-based assessment in inclusive settings. *Teaching Exceptional Children, 32*(1), 30–38.

Kleinert, H., & Kearns, J. (2001). Accountability for all students: Kentucky's alternate portfolio system for students with moderate and severe cognitive disabilities. *Journal of the Association for Persons with Severe Handicaps (JASH), 22,* 88–101.

Kleinert, H. L., Miracle, S., & Sheppard-Jones, K. (2007). Including students with moderate and severe intellectual disabilities in school extracurricular and community recreation activities. *Intellectual and Developmental Disabilities, 45,* 46–55.

Klinger, J. K., & Harry, B. (2006). The special education referral and decision-making process for English language learners: Child study team meetings and placement conferences. *Teachers College Record, 108*(11), 2247–2281.

Klinger, J. K., & Vaughn, S. (2002). The changing roles and responsibilities of an LD specialist [Electronic version]. *Learning Disability Quarterly, 25,* 19–31.

Kluth, P. (2003). *"You're going to love this kid": Teaching students with autism in the inclusive classroom.* Baltimore: Brookes.

Knackendoffel, E. A. (2005). Collaborative teaming in the secondary school. *Focus on Exceptional Children, 37*(5), 1–16.

Knight, J. (2002). Crossing boundaries: What constructivists can teach intensive-explicit instructors and vice versa. *Focus on Exceptional Children, 35*(4), 1–15.

Knotek, S. (2003). Bias in problem solving and the social process of student study teams: A qualitative investigation of two SSTs. *Journal of Special Education, 37,* 2–14.

Kode, K. (2002). *Elizabeth Farrell and the history of special education.* Arlington, VA: Council for Exceptional Children.

Kohn, A. (2004). Challenging students . . . and how to have more of them. *Phi Delta Kappan, 86,* 184–193.

Kohn, A. (2006). *Beyond discipline: From compliance to community* (10th anniversary edition). Alexandria, VA: Association for Supervision and Curriculum Development.

Kolb, S. M., & Hanley-Maxwell, C. (2003). Critical social skills for adolescents with high incidence disabilities: Parental perspectives. *Exceptional Children, 69,* 163–180.

Kollins, S. H., Barkley, R. A., & DuPaul, G. J. (2001). Use and management of medications for children diagnosed with attention deficit disorder. *Focus on Exceptional Children, 33*(5), 1–24.

Kozen, A. A., Murray, R. K., & Windell, I. (2006). Increasing all students' chance to achieve: Using and adapting anticipation guides with middle school learners. *Intervention in School and Clinic, 41*(4), 195–200.

Kroesbergen, E. H., Van Luit, J. E. H., & Maas, C. J. M. (2004). Effectiveness of explicit and constructivist mathematics instruction for low-achieving students in the Netherlands. *The Elementary School Journal, 104*(3), 233–251.

Kuiper, E., Volman, M., & Terwel, J. (2005). The web as an information resource in K–12 education: Strategies for supporting students in searching and processing information. *Review of Educational Research, 75*(3), 285–328.

Kunsch, C. A., Jitendra, A. K., & Sood, S. (2007). The effects of peer-mediated instruction in mathematics for students with learning problems: A research synthesis. *Learning Disabilities Research & Practice, 22,* 1–12.

Ladson-Billings, G. (1994). *The dreamkeepers: Successful teachers for African American children.* San Francisco: Jossey-Bass.

Lambert, M. A., & Nowacek, J. (2006). Help high school students improve their study skills. *Intervention in School and Clinic, 41*(4), 241–243.

Lane, K. L., Givner, C. C., & Pierson, M. R. (2004). Teacher expectations of student behavior: Social skills necessary in elementary school classrooms. *Journal of Special Education, 38,* 104–110.

Lane, K. L., Mahdavi, J. N., & Borthwick-Duffy, S. (2003). Teacher perceptions of the prereferral intervention process: A call for assistance with school-based interventions. *Preventing School Failure, 47,* 148–155.

Lane, K. L., Pierson, M. R., & Givner, C. C. (2004). Secondary teachers' views on social competence: Skills essential for success. *Journal of Special Education, 38,* 174–187.

Lane, K. L., Wehby, J., & Barton-Arwood, S. M. (2005). Students with and at risk for emotional and behavioral disorders: Meeting their social and academic needs. *Preventing School Failure, 49*(2), 6–9.

Lane, K. L., Wehby, J. H., & Cooley, C. (2006). Teacher expectations of students' classroom behavior across the grade span: Which social skills are necessary for success? *Exceptional Children, 72*(2), 153–167.

Lange, A., Mulhern, G., Wylie, J., & McPhillips, M. (2006). Assistive software tools for secondary-level students with literacy difficulties. *Journal of Special Education Technology, 21*(3), 13–22.

Langer, J. (1984). Examining background knowledge and text comprehension. *Reading Research Quarterly, 19,* 468–481.

Larkin, M. J. (2001). Providing support for student independence through scaffolded instruction. *Teaching Exceptional Children, 34*(1), 30–34.

Lannie, A. L., & McCurdy, B. L. (2007). Preventing disruptive behavior in the urban classroom: Effects of the good behavior game on student and teacher behavior. *Education and Treatment of Children, 30*(1), 85–98.

Lasky, B., & Karge, B. D. (2006). Meeting the needs of students with disabilities: Experience and confidence of principals. *NASSP Bulletin, 90,* 9–36.

Lavoie, R. (1991). *How difficult can this be? Understanding learning disabilities* [Videotape]. Portland, OR: Educational Productions.

Lavoie, R. D. (1989). *Mainstreaming: A collection of field-tested strategies to help make the mainstreaming classroom more successful for learning disabled children, their classmates . . . and their teachers.* Norwalk: Connecticut Association for Children with Learning Disabilities.

Lawton, M. (1995, Nov. 8). Students post dismal results on history test. *Education Week, 1,* 12.

Lee, S. W., & Jamison, T. R. (2003). Including the FBA process in student assistance teams: An exploratory study of team communications and intervention selection. *Journal of Educational and Psychological Consultation, 14,* 209–239.

Lee-Tarver, A. (2006). A survey of teachers' perceptions of the function and purpose of student support teams. *Education, 126*(3), 525–533.

LeFever, G. B., Villers, M. S., Morrow, A. L., & Vaughn, E. S. (2002). Parental perceptions of adverse educational outcomes among children diagnosed and treated for ADHD: A call for improved school/provider collaboration. *Psychology in the Schools, 39,* 63–71.

Leinhardt, G., & Zigmond, N. (1988). The effects of self-questioning and story structure training on the reading comprehension of poor readers. *Learning Disabilities Research, 4*(1), 41–51.

Lemanek, K. L. (2004). Adherence. In R. T. Brown (Ed.)., *Handbook of pediatric psychology in school settings* (pp. 129–148). Mahwah, NJ: Erlbaum.

Lenz, B. K. (1983). Using the advance organizer. *Pointer, 27,* 11–13.

Lenz, B. K., Ellis, E. S., & Scanlon, D. (1996). *Teaching learning strategies to adolescents and adults with learning disabilities.* Austin, TX: PRO-ED.

Lenz, K. (2006). Creating school-wide conditions for high-quality learning strategy classroom instruction. *Intervention in School and Clinic, 41*(5), 261–266.

Lerner, J. (2006). *Learning disabilities: Theories, diagnosis, and teaching strategies* (10th ed.). Boston: Houghton Mifflin.

Lessen, E., Sommers, M., & Bursuck, W. (1987). *Curriculum-based assessment and instructional design.* DeKalb, IL: DeKalb County Special Education Association.

Levy, F., Hay, D. A., & Bennett, K. S. (2006). Genetics of attention deficit hyperactivity disorder: A current review and future prospects. *International Journal of Disability, Development & Education, 53,* 5–20.

Licht, B. G., Kistner, J. A., Ozkaragoz, T., Shapiro, S., & Clausen, L. (1985). Causal attributions of learning disabled children: Individual differences and their implications for persistence. *Journal of Educational Psychology, 77,* 208–216.

Lilly, M. S. (1971). A training model for special education. *Exceptional Children, 37,* 740–749.

Lindamood, P., & Lindamood, P. (1998). *LiPS: The Lindamood phoneme sequencing program for reading, spelling, and speech: LiPS teacher's manual for the classroom and clinic* (3rd ed.). Austin, TX: PRO-ED.

Lindstrom, L., Doren, B., Metheny, J., Johnson, P., & Zane, C. (2007). Transition to employment: Role of the family in career development. *Exceptional Children, 73,* 348–366.

Lindquist, T. (1995). *Seeing the whole through social studies.* Portsmouth, NH: Heinemann.

Lindstrom, L., Doren, B., & Metheny, J. (2007). Transition to employment: Role of the family in career development. *Exceptional Children, 73,* 348–366.

Lingo, A. S., Slaton, D. B., & Jolivette, K. (2006). Effects of corrective reading on the reading abilities and classroom behaviors of middle school students with reading deficits and challenging behavior. *Behavioral Disorders, 31*(3), 265–283.

Little, J. W. (1993). Teachers' professional development in a climate of educational reform. *Educational Evaluation and Policy Analysis, 15,* 129–151.

Lo, Y., & Cartledge, G. (2006). FBA and BIP: Increasing the behavior adjustment of African American boys in schools. *Behavioral Disorders, 31*(2), 147–161.

Lohmeier, K. L. (2005). Implementing the expanded core curriculum in specialized schools for the blind. *RE:view: Rehabilitation Education for Blindness and Visual Impairment, 37,* 126–133.

Long, N. J., & Newman, R. G. (1971). Managing surface behavior of children in school. In N. J. Long, W. C. Morse, & R. G. Newman (Eds.), *Conflict in the classroom: The education of children with problems* (2nd ed., pp. 442–452). Belmont, CA: Wadsworth.

Lorenzi, D. G., Horvat, M., & Pellegrini, A. D. (2000). Physical activity of children with and without mental retardation in inclusive recess settings. *Education and Training in Mental Retardation and Developmental Disabilities, 35,* 160–167.

Lortie, D. C. (1975). *Schoolteacher: A sociological study.* Chicago: University of Chicago Press.

Lott, B. (2003). Recognizing and welcoming the standpoint of low-income parents in the public schools. *Journal of Educational and Psychological Consultation, 14,* 91–104.

Love, A., & Kruger, A. C. (2005). Teacher beliefs and student achievement in urban schools serving African American students. *The Journal of Educational Research, 99*(2), 87–98.

Lovitt, T. C., Rudsit, J., Jenkins, J., Pious, C., & Benedetti, D. (1985). Two methods of adapting science materials for learning disabled and regular seventh graders. *Learning Disability Quarterly, 8,* 275–285.

Lowell-York, J., Doyle, M. E., & Kronberg, R. (1995). *Module 3. Curriculum as everything students learn in school: Individualizing learning opportunities.* Baltimore, MD: Paul H. Brookes.

LRP Publications. (1997). *Grading individuals with disabilities education law report, 25*(4), 381–391.

Luckner, J. L., & Muir, S. (2001). Successful students who are deaf in general education settings. *American Annals of the Deaf, 146,* 450–461.

Luecking, R. (2004). *In their own words: Employer perspectives on youth with disabilities in the workplace: Essential tools.* Minneapolis: National Center on Secondary Education and *Transition,* University of Minnesota (NCSET). (ERIC Document Reproduction No. ED484254)

Luster, J. N., & Durrett, J. (2003, November). *Does educational placement matter in the performance of students with disabilities?* Paper presented at the annual meeting of the Mid-South Educational Research Association, Biloxi, MS. (ERIC Document Reproduction Service No. ED482518)

Lytle, R. K., & Bordin, J. (2001). Enhancing the IEP team: Strategies for parents and professionals. *Teaching Exceptional Children, 33*(5), 40–45.

Maag, J. (2004). *Behavior management: From theoretical implications to practical applications* (2nd ed.). Belmont, CA: Wadsworth.

Maag, J. W. (2001). Management of surface behavior: A new look at an old approach. *Counseling and Human Development, 33*(9), 1–10.

Maag, J. W. (2005). Social skills training for youth with emotional and behavioral disorders and learning disabilities: Problems, conclusions, and suggestions. *Exceptionality, 13,* 155–172.

Maag, J. W., & Katsiyannis, A. (2006). Behavioral intervention plans: Legal and practical considerations for students with emotional and behavioral disorders. *Behavioral Disorders, 31*(4), 348–362.

Maag, J. W., & Reid, R. (2006). Depression among students with learning disabilities: Assessing the risk. *Journal of Learning Disabilities, 39*(1), 3–10.

MacArthur, C., Schwartz, S., Graham, S., Malloy, D., & Harris, K. R. (1996). Integration of strategy instruction into a whole language classroom: A case study. *Learning Disabilities Research and Practice, 11,* 168–176.

MacArthur, C. A., & Stoddard, B. (1990, April). *Teaching learning disabled students to revise: A peer editor strategy.* Paper presented at the Annual Meeting of the American Education Research Association, Boston.

Macy, M. G., & Bricker, D. D. (2007). Embedding individualized social goals into routine activities in inclusive early childhood classrooms. *Early Child Development and Care, 177,* 107–120.

Madden, J. A. (2000). Managing asthma at school. *Educational Leadership, 57*(6), 50–52.

Maheady, L., Mallette, B., and Harper, G. F. (2006). Four classwide peer tutoring models: Similarities, differences, and implications for research and practice. *Reading and Writing Quarterly, 22*(1), 65–89.

Maheady, L., Michielli-Pendl, J., Harper, G. F., & Mallette, B. (2006). The effects of Numbered Heads Together with and without an incentive package on the science test performance of a diverse group of sixth graders. *Journal of Behavioral Education, 15,* 25–39.

Mandlebaum, L. H., & Wilson, R. (1989). Teaching listening skills. *LD Forum, 15*(1), 7–9.

Margolis, H. (2005). Resolving struggling learners' homework difficulties: Working with elementary school learners and parents. *Preventing School Failure, 50*(1), 5–12.

Marino, M. T., Marino, E. C., & Shaw, S. F. (2006). Making informed assistive technology decisions for students with high incidence disabilities. *Teaching Exceptional Children, 38*(6), 18–25.

Maroney, S. A., Finson, K. D., Beaver, J. B., & Jensen, M. M. (2003). Preparing for successful inquiry in inclusive science classrooms. *Teaching Exceptional Children, 36*(1), 18–25.

Marschark, M., Convertino, C., & LaRock, D. (2006). Optimizing academic performance of deaf students: Access, opportunities, and outcomes. In D. F. Moores & D. S. Martin (Eds.), *Deaf learners: Developments in curriculum and instruction.* (pp. 179–200). Washington, DC: Gallaudet University Press.

Marsh, L. G., & Cooke, N. L. (1996). The effects of using manipulatives in teaching math problem solving to students with learning disabilities. *Learning Disabilities Research and Practice, 11,* 58–65.

Marston, D. B. (1989). A curriculum-based measurement approach to asessing academic performance: What it is and why do it. In M. R. Shinn (Ed.), *Curriculum-based measurement: Assessing special children* (pp. 18–78). New York: Guilford Press.

Marston, D. B. (1996). A comparison of inclusion only, pull-out only, and combined service models for students with mild disabilities. *Journal of Special Education, 30*(2), 121–132.

Marston, D. B., Tindal, G., & Deno, S. (1984). Eligibility for learning disability services: A direct and repeated measurement approach. *Exceptional Children, 50,* 554–556.

Marston, D., Muyskens, P., Lau, M., & Canter, A. (2003). Problem-solving model for decision making with high-incidence disabilities: The Minneapolis experience. *Learning Disabilities Research and Practice, 18*(3), 187–200.

Martin, B. N., Johnson, J. A., Ireland, H., & Claxton, K. (2003). Perceptions of teachers on inclusion in four rural Midwest school districts [Electronic version]. *Rural Educator, 24*(3), 3–10.

Martin, J. E., Marshall, L. H., & Sale, P. (2004). A 3-year study of middle, junior high, and high school IEP meetings. *Exceptional Children, 70,* 285–298.

Martin, J. E., Van Dycke, J. L., Christensen, W. R., Greene, B. A., Gardner, J. E., & Lovett, D. L. (2006). Increasing student participation in IEP meetings: Establishing the self-directed IEP as an evidenced-based practice. *Exceptional Children, 72,* 299–316.

Marzola, E. S. (1987). Using manipulatives in math instruction. *Reading, Writing, and Learning Disabilities, 3,* 9–20.

Marzano, R. J. (2004). *Building background knowledge for academic achievement.* Alexandria, VA: Association for Supervision and Curriculum Development.

Marzano, R. J. *Building background knowledge for academic achievement: Research on what works in schools.* Alexandria, VA: Association for Supervision and Curriculum Development Press.

Marzano, R. J., & Marzano, J. S. (2003). The key to classroom management. *Educational Leadership, 61*(1), 6–13.

Mason, C. Y., McGahee-Kovac, M., & Johnson, L. (2004). How to help students lead their IEP meetings. *Teaching Exceptional Children, 36*(3), 18–25.

Mason, L. H., Snyder, K. H., Sukhram, D. P., Kedem, Y. (2006). TWA + PLANS strategies for expository reading and writing: Effects for nine fourth-grade students. *Exceptional Children, 73*(1), 69–89.

Massat, C. R. (2006). The many faces of school social work [Letter]. *School Social Work, 30*(2), vii–viii.

Mastropieri, M. A. (1988). Using the keyword method. *Teaching Exceptional Children, 20*(4), 4–8.

Mastropieri, M. A., Scruggs, T. E., & Berkeley, S. L. (2007). Peers helping peers. *Educational Leadership, 64*(5), 54–58.

Mastropieri, M., Scruggs, T., Graetz, J., Norland, J., Gardizi, W., & McDuffie, K. (2005). Case studies in co-teaching in the content areas: Successes, failures, and challenges. *Intervention in School and Clinic, 40*(5), 260–270.

Mastropieri, M. A., Scruggs, T. E., Norland, J. J., Berkeley, S., McDuffie, K., Tornquist, E. H., & Connors, N. (2006). Differentiated curriculum enhancement in inclusive middle school science: Effects on classroom and high-stakes tests. *Journal of Special Education, 40,* 130–137.

Mastropieri, M. A., Scruggs, T. E., Spencer, V., & Fontana, J. (2003). Promoting success in high school world history: Peer tutoring versus guided notes. *Learning Disabilities: Research and Practice, 18,* 52–65.

Mathur, S., & Smith, R. M. (2003). 20 ways to collaborate with families of children with ADD. *Intervention in School and Clinic, 38*(5), 311–315.

Mattox, R., & Harder, J. (2007) Attention deficit hyperactivity disorder (ADHD) and diverse populations. *Child and Adolescent Social Work Journal, 24*(2), 195–207.

Matuszny, R. M., Banda, D. R., & Coleman, T. J. (2007). A progressive plan for building collaborative relationships with parents from diverse backgrounds. *Teaching Exceptional Children, 39*(4), 24–31.

McCardle, P., & Chhabra, V. (Eds.). (2004). *The voice of evidence in reading research.* Baltimore, MD: Brookes.

McCleary, L. (2002). Parenting adolescents with attention deficit hyperactivity disorder: Analysis of the literature for social work practice [Electronic version]. *Health and Social Work, 27,* 285–292.

McCollin, M., & O'Shea, D. (2005). Increasing reading achievement of students from culturally and linguistically diverse backgrounds. *Preventing School Failure, 50,* 41–46.

McDonnell, J., Thorson, N., Disher, S., Mathot-Buckner, C., Mendel, J., & Ray, L. (2003). The achievement of students with developmental disabilities and their peers without disabilities in inclusive settings: An exploratory study [Electronic version]. *Education and Treatment of Children, 26,* 224–236.

McDougall, D., & Brady, M. P. (1998). Initiating and fading self-management interventions to increase math fluency in general education classes. *Exceptional Children, 64,* 151–166.

McGinnis, E., & Goldstein, A. P. (2005). *Skills-streaming: Teaching prosocial skills to the elementary-school child.* Champaign, IL: Research Press.

McGrath, M. Z., Johns, B. H., & Mathur, S. R. (2004). Is history repeating itself? Services for children with disabilities endangered. *Teaching Exceptional Children, 37*(1), 70–71.

McGuire, J. M., Scott, S. S., & Shaw, S. F. (2006). Universal design and its applications in educational environments. *Remedial and Special Education, 27,* 166–175.

McLaughlin, M. J. (2002). Examining special and general education collaborative practices in exemplary schools. *Journal of Educational and Psychological Consultation, 13,* 279–284.

McLeskey, J., & Waldron, N. L. (2007a). Comprehensive school reform and inclusive schools. *Theory into Practice, 45,* 269–278.

McLeskey, J., & Waldron, N. L. (2007b). Making differences ordinary in inclusive classrooms. *Intervention in School and Clinic, 42,* 162–168.

McLeskey, J., Waldron, N. L., So, T. H., Swanson, K., & Loveland, T. (2001). Perspectives of teachers toward inclusive school programs. *Teacher Education and Special Education, 24,* 108–115.

McMaster, K. L., Fuchs, D., & Fuchs, L. S. (2006). Research on peer-assisted learning strategies: The promise and limitations of peer-mediated instruction. *Reading and Writing Quarterly, 22,* 5–25.

McMaster, K. N., & Fuchs, D. (2002). Effects of cooperative learning on the academic achievement of students with learning disabilities: An update of Tateyama-Sniezek's review. *Learning Disabilities: Research and Practice, 17,* 107–117.

McNeil, J. (2001). *Disability.* Retrieved October 24, 2007, from www.census.gov/population/www/pop-profile/disabil.html

Meichenbaum, D. (1977). *Cognitive behavior modification: An integrative approach.* New York: Plenum.

Mercer, C. D., & Mercer, A. R. (2001). *Teaching students with learning problems* (6th ed.). Upper Saddle River, OH: Merrill/Prentice Hall.

Mercer, C. D., & Pullen, P. C. (2005). *Students with learning disabilities* (6th ed.). Upper Saddle River, NJ: Pearson.

Miles-Bonart, S. (2002, March). A look at variables affecting parent satisfaction with IEP meetings. In *No Child Left Behind: The vital role of rural schools. Annual national conference proceedings of the American Council on Rural Special Education (ACRES)* (22nd, Reno, Nevada, March 7–9, 2002) (pp. 180–187). Logan, UT: ACRES. (ERIC Document Reproduction Service No. ED463119)

Miller, G., & Hall, T. (2005). *Classroom management*. Wakefield, MA: National Center on Accessing the General Curriculum. Retrieved from www.cast.org/publications/ncac/ncac_classroom.html

Miller, M. C., Cooke, N. L., Test, D. W., & White, R. (2003). Effects of friendship circles on the social interactions of elementary age students with mild disabilities [Electronic version]. *Journal of Behavioral Education, 12*, 167–184.

Miller, R. V. (1956). Social status of socioempathic differences. *Exceptional Children, 23*, 114–119.

Miller, S. P., & Hudson, P. J. (2007). Using evidence-based practices to build mathematics competence related to conceptual, procedural, and declarative knowledge. *Learning Disabilities Research & Practice, 22*(1), 47–57.

Miller, S. P. (1996), Perspectives on mathematics instruction. In D. D. Deshler, E. S. Ellis, & B. K. Lenz (Eds.), *Teaching adolescents with learning disabilities: Strategies and methods* (2nd ed., pp. 313–367). Denver, CO: Love.

Milsom, A., & Hartley, M. (2005). Assisting students with learning disabilities transitioning to college: What school counselors should know. *Professional School Counseling, 8*, 436–441.

Minskoff, E., & Allsopp, D. (2003). *Academic success strategies for adolescents with learning disabilities and ADHD*. Baltimore, MD: Paul H. Brookes.

Miranda, A., & Guerrero, M. (1986). The funny farola. In *Adventures* (pp. 42–53). Boston: Houghton Mifflin.

Miranda, A., Jarque, S., & Tárraga, R. (2006). Interventions in school settings for students with ADHD. *Exceptionality, 14*(1), 35–52.

Mittan, R. J. (2005). S.E.E. program parents manual: How to raise a child with epilepsy. Part two: Coping with stigma. *Exceptional Parent, 35*(11), 58–66.

Moats, L. (2007). Whole-language high-jinks: How to tell when "scientifically-based reading instruction" isn't. Thomas B. Fordham Institute. Retrieved from www.fordhaminstitute.org/doc/Moats2007.pdf

Mock, D. R., & Kauffman, J. M. (2002). Preparing teachers for full inclusion: Is it possible? [Electronic version]. *Teacher Educator, 37*, 202–215.

Montague, M., Warger, C. L., & Morgan, H. (2000). Solve It! Strategy instruction to improve mathematical problem solving. *Learning Disabilities Research and Practice, 15*, 110–116.

Montgomery, K. (2001). *Authentic assessment: A guide for elementary teachers*. New York: Longman.

Moody, J. D., & Gifford, V. D. (1990). *The effect of grouping by formal reasoning ability, formal reasoning ability levels, group size, and gender on achievement in laboratory chemistry*. (ERIC Document Reproduction Service No. ED326443)

Moore, J. L., Ford, D. Y., & Milner, H. R. (2005). Underachievement among gifted students of color: Implications for educators. *Theory into Practice, 44*, 167–177.

Moreno, R., & Duran, R. (2004). Do multiple representations need explanations? The role of verbal guidance and individual differences in multimedia mathematics learning. *Journal of Educational Psychology, 96*(3), 492–503.

Morgan, S. A. (2006). Introduction: Four classwide peer tutoring programs—research, recommendations for implementation, and future directions. *Reading and Writing Quarterly, 22*, 1–4.

Mortweet, S. L., Utley, C. A., Walker, D., Dawson, H. L., Delquadri, J. C., Reddy, S. S., et al. (1999). Classwide peer tutoring: Teaching students with mild mental retardation in inclusive classrooms. *Exceptional Children, 65*, 524–536.

Mosteller, F., Light, R., & Sachs, J. (1996). Sustained inquiry in education: Lessons from skill grouping and class size. *Harvard Educational Review, 66*, 797–828.

Mruzek, D. W., Cohen, C., & Smith, T. (2007). Contingency contracting with students with autism spectrum disorders in a public school setting. *Journal of Developmental and Physical Disabilities, 19*(2), 103–114.

MTA Cooperative Group. (2004). National Institute of Mental Health multimodal treatment study of ADHD follow-up: 24-month outcomes of treatment strategies for attention-deficit/hyperactivity disorder [Electronic version]. *Pediatrics, 113*, 754–761.

Munk, D. D. (2003). *Solving the grading puzzle for students with disabilities*. Whitefish Bay, WI: Knowledge by Design.

Munk, D. D. (2007). Equitable, effective, and meaningful grading practices for students with disabilities/exceptionalities. Retrieved September 14, 2007, from http://icdd.idaho.gov/pdf/Parent%20League/GradingWebinarMar07Handout.pdf

Munk, D. D., & Bursuck, W. D. (2001). Personalized grading plans: A systematic approach to making the grades of included students more accurate and meaningful. In L. Denti & P. Tefft-Cousin (Eds.), *Looking at learning disabilities in new ways: Connections to classroom practice* (pp. 111–127). Denver, CO: Love.

Munk, D. D., & Bursuck, W. D. (2003). Grading students with disabilities. *Educational Leadership, 61*(2), 38–43.

Munk, D. D., & Bursuck, W. D. (2005). *Personalized grading plans for students with disabilities*. [Manuscript in preparation.]

Munk, D. D., Bursuck, W. D., Epstein, M. H., Jayanthi, M., Nelson, J., & Polloway, E. A. (2001). Homework communication problems: Perspectives of special and general education parents. *Reading and Writing Quarterly, 17*(3), 189–203.

Munoz, M. A., Dossett, D., & Judy-Gullans, K. (2003). *Educating students placed at risk: Evaluating the impact of Success for All in urban settings*. (ERIC Document Reproduction Service No. ED480178)

Murray, C. (2004). Clarifying collaborative roles in urban high schools: General educators' perspectives. *Teaching Exceptional Children, 36*(5), 44–51.

Myles, B. S. (2005). *Children and youth with Asperger syndrome: Strategies for success in inclusive settings*. Thousand Oaks, CA: Corwin.

Myles, B. S., & Adreon, D. (2001). *Asperger syndrome and adolescence: Practical solutions for school success*. Shawnee Mission, KS: Autism Asperger Publishing.

Myles, B. S., Ferguson, H., & Hagiwara, T. (2007). Using a personal digital assistant to improve the recording of homework assignments by an adolescent with Asperger syndrome. *Focus on Autism and Other Developmental Disabilities, 22*, 96–99.

Myles, B. S., & Southwick, J. (1999). *Asperger syndrome and difficult moments: Practical solutions for tantrums, rage, and meltdowns*. Lawrence, KS: Autism Asperger Publishing.

Nansel, T., Overpeck, M., Pilla, R., Ruan, W., Simons-Morton, B., & Scheidt, P. (2001). Bullying behaviors among US youth: Prevalence and association with psychosocial adjustment. *Journal of the American Medical Association, 285*, 2094–2100.

Nash, J. M., & Bonesteel, A. (2002, May 6). The geek syndrome. *Time, 159* (18), 50–51.

National Association of School Psychologists. (2002). *Position statement on inclusive programs for students with disabilities*. Retrieved September 5, 2004, from www.nasponline.org/information/pospaper_ipsd.html

National Center for Children in Poverty. (2006, September). *Basic facts about low-income children: birth to age 18*. New York: Author. Retrieved August 3, 2007, from www.nccp.org/publications/pdf/text_678.pdf

National Center for Education Statistics. (2004). *Crime and safety in America's public schools: Selected findings from the school survey on crime and safety*. Retrieved December 30, 2004, the school survey on crime and safety website, from http://nces.ed.gov/surveys/ssocs

National Center for Education Statistics. (2007, June). *Dropout rates in the United States, 2005*. Retrieved October 18, 2007, from http://nces.ed.gov/Pubsearch/pubsinfo.asp?pubid=2007059

National Center for Education Statistics (NCES). (2007, June). *Dropout rates in the United States: 2005*. Washington, D.C.: Author. Retrieved August 3, 2007, from http://nces.ed.gov/pubSearch/pubsinfo.asp?pubid=2007059

National Center on Secondary Education and Transition. (2002). *Age of majority: Preparing your child for making good choices*. Minneapolis, MN: Author. (ERIC Document Reproduction Service No. ED467248)

National Clearinghouse for Professions in Special Education. (2003). *School counselor: Making a difference in the lives of students with special needs* [Brochure]. Arlington, VA: Author. Retrieved April 19, 2003, from www.special-ed-careers.org/pdf/schcoun.pdf

National Coalition for the Homeless. (2006, June). How many people experience homelessness? [NCH fact sheet #2]. Washington, DC: Author. Retrieved August 1, 2007, from www.nationalhomeless.org/publications/facts/How_Many.pdf

National Council of Teachers of Mathematics. (2000). *Principles and standards for school mathematics*. Reston, VA: Author.

National Council on Disability. (2006, November). *National disability policy: A progress report*. Washington, DC: Author.

National Dissemination Center for Children with Disabilities. (2006). *Traumatic brain injury fact sheet*. Retrieved July 9, 2007, from www.nichcy.org/pubs/factshe/fs18txt.htm

National Institute of Mental Health. (2003). *Attention deficit hyperactivity disorder*. Bethesda, MD: Author. Retrieved December 3, 2004, from www.nimh.nih.gov/publicat/adhd.cfm

National Institute of Mental Health (NIMH). (2006). *Attention deficit hyperactivity disorder: A detailed booklet that describes the symptoms, causes, and treatments, with information on getting help and coping*. Bethesda, MD: Author. Retrieved August 2, 2007, from www.nimh.nih.gov/publicat/adhd.cfm#intro

National Institute of Mental Health (NIMH). (2007). Autism spectrum disorders: Pervasive developmental disorders. Bethseda, MD: Author. Retrieved July 6, 2007, from www.eric.ed.gov/ERICDocs/data/ericdocs2sql/content_storage_01/0000019b/80/27/fe/bb.pdf

National Institute of Neurological Disorders and Stroke. (2007). *NINDS muscular dystrophy information page*. Retrieved July 8, 2007, from www.ninds.nih.gov/disorders/md/md.htm

National Institute on Deafness and Other Communication Disorders. (2006). *What are communication considerations for parents of deaf and hard-of-hearing children?* [NIDCD fact sheet]. Bethesda, MD: Author. Retrieved July 10, 2007, from www.eric.ed.gov/ERICDocs/data/ericdocs2sql/content_storage_01/0000019b/80/28/0c/98.pdf

National Institute on Drug Abuse. (2006, December). *NIDA infofacts: High school and youth trends*. Washington, DC: Department of Health and Human Services. Retrieved July 5, 2007, from www.nida.nih.gov/infofacts/HSYouthtrends.html

National Organization on Fetal Alcohol Syndrome. (2004). *What are the statistics and facts about FAS and FASD?* Washington, DC: Author. Retrieved December 4, 2004, from www.nofas.org/faqs.aspx?ID=1

National Reading Panel (2000). *Teaching children to read: An evidence-based assessment of the scientific research literature on reading and its implications for reading instruction*. Washington, DC: National Institute of Child Health and Human Development.

National Resource Center on ADHD. (2004). *Managing medication for children and adolescents with AD/HD*. Retrieved October 18, 2007, from www.help4adhd.org/en/treatment/medical/WWK3

National Spinal Cord Injury Association. (2004). *Factsheet on spinal cord injury*. Bethesda, MD: Author. Retrieved March 9, 2004, from www.spinalcord.org/html/factsheets/spinstat.php

Nazzal, A. (2002). Peer tutoring and at-risk students: An exploratory study. *Action in Teacher Education, 24,* 68–80.

Neal, J., Bigby, L., & Nicholson, R. (2004). Occupational therapy, physical therapy, and orientation and mobility services in public schools. *Intervention in School and Clinic, 39,* 218–222.

Neal, L. V. I., McCray, A. D., Webb-Johnson, G., & Bridgest, S. T. (2003). The effects of African American movement styles on teachers' perceptions and reactions. *Journal of Special Education, 37,* 49–57.

Nelson, B. (2005). Creating positive outcomes for deafblind youth and young adults: A personal futures planning transition model. *RE:view: Rehabilitation Education for Blindness and Visual Impairment, 36,* 173–177.

Nelson, J. S., Epstein, M. H., Bursuck, W. D., Jayanthi, M., & Sawyer, V. (1998). The preferences of middle school students for homework adaptations made by general education teachers. *Learning Disabilities: Research and Practice, 13,* 109–117.

Nelson, L. G. L., Summers, J. A., & Turnbull, A. P. (2004). Boundaries in family-professional relationships: Implications for special education. *Remedial and Special Education, 25,* 153–166.

Neuman, R. J., Sitdhiraksa, N., Reich, W., Ji, T. H-C., Joyner, C. A., & Todd, R. D, (2005). Estimation of prevalence of DSM-IV and latent class ADHD subtypes in a population based sample of child and adolescent twins. *Twin Research and Human Genetics, 8,* 392–401.

Newcomer, L. L., & Lewis, T. J. (2004). Functional behavioral assessment: An investigation of assessment reliability and effectiveness of function-based interventions. *Journal of Emotional and Behavioral Disorders, 12,* 168–181.

Nieto, S. M. (2002/2003). Profoundly multicultural questions. *Educational Leadership, 60*(4), 6–10.

Nolet, V., & McLaughlin, M. J. (2005). *Accessing the general curriculum: Including students with disabilities in standards-based reform* (2nd ed.). Thousand Oaks, CA: Corwin.

Núñez, R. G., González-Pienda, J. A., González-Pumariega, S., Roces, C., Alvarez, L., González, P., (2005). Subgroups of attributional profiles in students with learning difficulties and their relation to self-concept and academic goals. *Learning Disabilities Research and Practice, 20*(2), 86–97.

O'Connor, R. (2000). Increasing the intensity of intervention in kindergarten and first grade. *Learning Disabilities: Research and Practice, 15,* 43–54.

Oakes, J., & Lipton, M. (2003). *Teaching to change the world*. Boston: McGraw-Hill.

Oakland, T., Black, J. L., Stanford, G., Nussbaum, N. L., & Balise, R. R. (1998). An evaluation of the dyslexia training program: A multisensory method for promoting reading in students with reading disabilities. *Journal of Learning Disabilities, 31,* 140–147.

Obiakor, F. E. (2007). Multicultural special education: Effective intervention for today's schools. *Intervention in School and Clinic, 42*(3), 148–155.

Obiakor, F. E., Utley, C. A., Smith, R., & Harris-Obiakor, P. (2002). The comprehensive support model for culturally diverse exceptional learners: Intervention in an age of change. *Intervention in School and Clinic, 38,* 14–27.

Odom, S. L., Zercher, C., Li, S., Marquart, J. M., Sandall, S., & Brown, W. H. (2006). Social acceptance and rejection of preschool children with disabilities: A mixed-method analysis. *Journal of Educational Psychology, 98,* 807–823.

Ogle, D. M. (1986). K. W. L.: A teaching model that develops active reading of expository text. *Reading Teacher, 39,* 565.

Ohtake, T. (2004). Meaningful inclusion of all students in team sports. *Teaching Exceptional Children, 37*(2), 22–27.

Okolo, C. M. (2000). Features of effective instructional software. In J. Lindsey (Ed.), *Technology and exceptional individuals* (3rd ed.). Austin, TX: PRO-ED.

Okolo, C.M., Ferretti, R.P., & MacArthur, C.A. (2007). Talking about history: Discussions in a middle school inclusive classroom. *Journal of Learning Disabilities, 40*(2), 154–165.

Olmeda, R. E., & Trent, S. C. (2003). Social skills training research with minority students with learning disabilities [Electronic version]. *Learning Disabilities, 12*(1), 23–33.

Olson, J. L., Platt, J. C., & Dieker, L. (2007). *Teaching children and adolescents with special needs* (5th ed.). Upper Saddle River, NJ: Merrill/Prentice Hall.

Olson, R. K. (2006). Genes, environment, and dyslexia: The 2005 Norman Geschwind Memorial Lecture. *Annals of Dyslexia, 56*(2), 205–238.

Operation Sickle Cell. (2007). *Prevalence.* Retrieved July 8, 2007, from www.sicklecellnc.org/disease.php

Opitz, M. (2007). Back-to-school tips: Learning centers: The first week. Excerpted from Michael Opitz's book *Learning Centers: Getting Them Started, Keeping Them Going.* Retrieved from http://teacher.scholastic.com/professional/backtoschool/learning_center.htm

Orfield, G., & Lee, C. (2004). *Brown at 50: King's dream or Plessy's nightmare?* Cambridge, MA: Harvard Civil Rights Project. Retrieved December 5, 2004, from www.civilrightsproject.harvard.edu/research/reseg04/brown50.pdf

Organ, J., & Gonzalez-DeHass, A. (2004). How to infuse social skills training into literacy instruction. *Teaching Exceptional Children, 36*(6), 24–31.

Ornstein, A. C., & Lasley, T. J. II. (2004). *Strategies for effective teaching* (4th ed). New York, NY: McGraw-Hill.

Overton, T. (2005). *Assessing learners with special needs: An applied approach* (5th ed.). Upper Saddle River, NJ: Merrill/Prentice Hall.

Overton, T., Fielding, C., & Simeonsson, M. (2004). Decision making in determining eligibility of culturally and linguistically diverse learners: Reasons given by assessment personnel. *Journal of Learning Disabilities, 37*, 319–330.

Owens, R. E., Jr., Metz, D. E., & Haas, A. (2007). *Introduction to communication disorders: A lifespan perspective.* (3rd ed.). Boston: Pearson, Allyn and Bacon.

Paese, P. C. (2003). Impact of professional development schools: Preservice through induction. *Action in Teacher Education, 25*, 83–88.

Paine, S. C., Radicchi, J., Rosellini, L. C., Deutchman, L., & Darch, C. B. (1983). *Structuring your classroom for academic success.* Champaign, IL: Research Press.

Palincsar, A., & Brown, A. (1988). Teaching and practicing thinking skills to promote comprehension in the context of group problem solving. *Remedial and Special Education, 9*(1), 53–59.

Palley, E. (2006). Challenges of rights-based law: Implementing the least restrictive environment mandate. *Journal of Disability Policy Studies, 16*, 229–235.

Parette, H. P., Hourcade, J. J., & Huer, M. B. (2003). Using assistive technology focus groups with families across cultures. *Education and Training in Developmental Disabilities, 38*, 429–440.

Parmar, R. S., & Signer, B. R. (2005). Sources of error in constructing and interpreting graphs: A study of fourth- and fifth-grade students with LD. *Journal of Learning Disabilities, 38*(3), 250–261.

Parsons, L. D. (2006). Using video to teach social skills to secondary students with autism. *Teaching Exceptional Children, 39*(2), 32–38.

Patillo, J., & Vaughn, E. (1992). *Learning centers for child-centered classrooms.* Washington, DC: National Education Association.

Patton, B., Jolivette, K., & Ramsey, M. (2006). Students with emotional and behavioral disorders can manage their own behavior. *Teaching Exceptional Children, 39*(2), 14–21.

Patton, J. R. (1994). Practical recommendations for using homework with students with disabilities. *Journal of Learning Disabilities, 27*, 570–578.

Patton, J. R., Payne, J. S., & Beirne-Smith, M. (1986). *Mental retardation* (2nd ed.). Columbus, OH: Merrill.

Pavri, S., & Monda-Amaya, L. (2001). Social support in inclusive schools: Student and teacher perspectives. *Exceptional Children, 67*, 391–411.

Pearson, P. D., & Fielding, L. (1991). Comprehension instruction. In R. Barr, M. L. Kamil, P. Mosenthal, & P. D. Pearson (Eds.), *Handbook of reading research* (Vol. 2, pp. 815–860). White Plains, NY: Longman.

Peck-Peterson, S. M., Derby, K. M., Berg, W. K., & Horner, R. H. (2002). Collaboration with families in the functional behavior assessment of and intervention for severe behavior problems [Electronic version]. *Education and Treatment of Children, 25*, 5–25.

Pedrotty-Bryant, D., Bryant, B. R., & Raskind, M. H. (1998). Using assistive technology to enhance the skills of students with learning disabilities. *Intervention in School and Clinic, 34*, 53–58.

Pertsch, C. F. (1936). *A comparative study of the progress of subnormal pupils in the grades and in special classes.* New York: Teacher's College, Columbia University, Bureau of Publications.

Peterson, J. S., & Ray, K. E. (2006). Bullying and the gifted: victims, perpetrators, prevalence, and effects. *Gifted Child Quarterly, 50*, 148–168.

Peterson, L. D., Young, K. R., Salzberg, C. L., West, R. P., & Hill, M. (2006). Using self-management procedures to improve classroom social skills in multiple general education settings. *Education and Treatment of Children, 29*(1), 1–21.

Petscher, E. S., & Bailey, J. S. (2006). Effects of training, prompting, and self-monitoring on staff behavior in a classroom for students with disabilities. *Journal of Applied Behavior Analysis, 39*, 215–226.

Peverly, S.T., Ramaswamy, V., Brown, C., Sumowski, J., Alidoost, M., & Garner, J. (2007). What predicts skill in lecture note taking? *Journal of Educational Psychology, 99*(1), 167–180.

Piercy, M., Wilton, K., & Townsend, M. (2002). Promoting social acceptance of young children with moderate-severe intellectual disabilities using cooperative-learning techniques [Electronic version]. *American Journal on Mental Retardation, 107*, 352–360.

Pincus, A.R.H. (2005). What's a teacher to do? Navigating the worksheet curriculum. *The Reading Teacher, 59*(1), 75–79.

Pine, J., & Aschbacher, P. (2006). Students' learning of inquiry in 'inquiry' curricula. *Phi Delta Kappan, 88*(4), 308–313.

Pisha, B. (2003). Assistive technologies: Making a difference. *IDA Perspectives, 29*(4), 1, 4.

Pisha, B., & Coyne, P. (2001). Smart from the start: The promise of universal design for learning. *Remedial and Special Education, 22*(4), 197–203.

Pisha, B., & Stahl, S. (2005). The promise of new learning environments for students with disabilities. *Intervention in School and Clinic, 41*(2), 67–75.

Pittman, P., & Huefner, D. S. (2001). Will the courts go bi-bi? IDEA 1997, the courts, and deaf education. *Exceptional Children, 67*, 187–198.

Pivik, J., McComas, J., & Laflamme, M. (2002). Barriers and facilitators to inclusive education. *Exceptional Children, 69*, 97–108.

Pogrund, R. L, & Fazzi, D. L. (Eds.). (2002). *Early focus: Working with young blind and visually impaired children and their families* (2nd ed.). New York: American Foundation for the Blind.

Polloway, E. A., Bursuck, W. D., Jayanthi, M., Epstein, M. H., & Nelson, J. S. (1996). Treatment acceptability: Determining appropriate interventions within inclusive classrooms. *Intervention in School and Clinic, 31*, 133–144.

Polloway, E. A., Epstein, M. H., Bursuck, W. D., Jayanthi, M., & Cumblad, C. (1994). Homework practices of general education teachers. *Journal of Learning Disabilities, 27,* 100–109.

Popp, P. A., Stronge, J. H., & Hindman, J. L. (2003). *Students on the move: Reaching and teaching highly mobile children and youth* (Urban Diversity Series). Washington, DC: National Center for Homeless Education and ERIC Clearinghouse on Urban Education. (ERIC Document Reproduction Service No. ED482661)

Poston, D., & Turnbull, A. (2004). Role of spirituality and religion in family quality of life for families of children with disabilities. *Education and Training in Developmental Disabilities, 39,* 95–108.

Poteet, J. A., Choate, J. S., & Stewart, S. C. (1993). Performance assessment and special education: Practices and prospects. *Focus on Exceptional Children, 26*(1), 1–20.

Praisner, C. L. (2003). Attitudes of elementary school principals toward the inclusion of students with disabilities. *Exceptional Children, 69,* 135–145.

Pressley, M. (2000). What should comprehension instruction be the instruction of? In M. Kamil, P. B. Mosenthal, P. D. Pearson, & R. Barr (Eds.), *Handbook of Reading Research* (Vol. 3). Mahwah, NJ: Erlbaum.

Pressley, M., & Hilden, K.R. (2006). Cognitive strategies: Production deficiencies and successful strategy instruction everywhere. In D. Kuhn & R. Siegler (Eds.), W. Damon & R. Lerner (Series Eds.), *Handbook of Child Psychology: Vol. 2. Cognition, perception, and language* (6th ed.). Hoboken, NJ: Wiley.

Pugach, M. C., & Johnson, L. J. (2002). *Collaborative practitioners, collaborative schools* (2nd ed.). Denver, CO: Love.

Punch, R., Hyde, M., & Creed, P. A. (2004). Issues in the school-to-work transition of hard of hearing adolescents. *American Annals of the Deaf, 149,* 28–38.

Purcell, M. L., Turnbull, A., & Jackson, C. W. (2006). Linking early childhood inclusion and family quality of life: Current literature and future directions. *Young Exceptional Children, 9*(3), 10–19.

Quenemoen, R., Rigney, S., & Thurlow, M. (2002). *Use of alternate assessments results in reporting and accountability systems: Conditions for use based on research and practice* (Synthesis Report 43). Minneapolis: University of Minnesota, National Center on Educational Outcomes. Retrieved from http://education.umn.edu/NCEO/OnlinePubs/Synthesis43.html

Rafferty, Y., Piscitelli, V., & Boettcher, C. (2003). The impact of inclusion on language development and social competence among preschoolers with disabilities. *Exceptional Children, 69,* 467–480.

Raforth, M. A., & Foriska, T. (2006). Administrator participation in promoting effective problem-solving teams. *Remedial and Special Education, 27*(3), 130–135.

Ramirez, A. Y. (2005). Esperanza's lessons: Learning about education through the eyes of the innocent. *Multicultural Education, 13*(2), 47–51.

Ramsey, W. L., Gabriel, L. A., McGuirk, J. F., Phillips, C. R., & Watenpaugh, T. R. (1983). *General science.* New York: Holt, Rinehart, and Winston.

Raphael, T. E., Kirschner, B. W., & Englert, C. S. (1986). *Text structure instruction within process writing classrooms: A manual for instruction* (Occasional Paper No. 104). East Lansing: Michigan State University, Institute for Research on Teaching.

Rapp, W. H. (2005). Inquiry-based environments for the inclusion of students with exceptional learning needs. *Remedial and Special Education, 26*(5), 297–310.

Rappaport, J. (1982/1983). Effects of dietary substances in children. *Journal of Psychiatric Research, 17,* 187–191.

Rausch, K., & Skiba, R. (2006). *Discipline, disability, and race: Disproportionality in Indiana schools* (Education Policy Brief, vol. 4, no. 10). Bloomington, IN: Center for Evaluation and Education Policy. (ERIC Document Reproduction Service No. ED495751)

Rea, P. J. (2005). 20 ways to . . . Engage your administrator in your collaborative initiative. *Intervention in School and Clinic, 40*(5), 312–316.

Rea, P. J., McLaughlin, V. L., & Walther-Thomas, C. (2002). Outcomes for students with learning disabilities in inclusive and pull-out programs. *Exceptional Children, 68,* 203–224.

Readence, J. E., Moore, D. W., & Rickelman, R. (2000). *Prereading activities for content-area reading and learning* (3rd ed.). Newark, DE: International Reading Association.

Redl, F. (2007). Rethinking youthful defiance [Reprint]. *Reclaiming Children and Youth: The Journal of Strength-Based Interventions, 16*(1), 33–35.

Reetz, L., & Rasmussen, T. (1988). Arithmetic mind joggers. *Academic Therapy, 24*(1), 79–82.

Reeve, J. (2006). Teachers as facilitators: What autonomy-supportive teachers do and why their students benefit. *The Elementary School Journal, 106*(3), 231–236.

Reeves, J. R. (2006). Secondary teacher attitudes toward including English-language learners in mainstream classrooms. *Journal of Educational Research, 99,* 131–142.

Regan, K. S., Mastropieri, M. A., & Scruggs, T. E. (2005). Promoting expressive writing among students with emotional and behavioral disturbance via dialogue journals. *Behavioral Disorders, 31*(1), 33–50.

Reid, D. H., & Green, C. W. (2006). Preference-based teaching: Helping students with severe disabilities enjoy learning without problem behavior. *Teaching Exceptional Children Plus, 2*(3) Article 2. Retrieved August 10, 2007 from http://escholarship.bc.edu/education/tecplus/vol2/iss3/art2

Reid, R. (1996). Research in self-monitoring with students with learning disabilities: The present, the prospects, the pitfalls. *Journal of Learning Disabilities, 29,* 317–331.

Reid, R. (1999). Attention deficit hyperactivity disorder: Effective methods for the classroom. *Focus on Exceptional Children, 32,* 1–19.

Reid, R., Trout, A. L., & Schartz, M. (2005). Self-regulation interventions for children with attention deficit/hyperactivity disorder. *Exceptional Children, 71*(4), 361–377.

Reis, S. M. (2007). No child left bored: How to challenge gifted and talented students with a continuum of high-end learning opportunities. *School Administrator, 64*(2), 22–26.

Reis, S. M., & Renzulli, J. S. (2004a). Current research on the social and emotional development of gifted and talented students: Good news and future possibilities. *Psychology in the Schools, 41*(1), 119–130.

Reis, S. M., & Renzulli, J. S. (2004b). Curriculum compacting: A systematic procedure for modifying the curriculum for above average ability students. Storrs, CT: National Research Center on the Gifted and Talented. Retrieved April 1, 2004, from www.sp.uconn.edu/~nrcgt/sem/semart08.html

Renzulli, J. S. (2005). Applying gifted education pedagogy to total talent development for all students. *Theory Into Practice, 44*(2), 80–89.

Renzulli, J. S., & Park, S. (2002). *Giftedness and high school dropouts: Personal, family, and school-related factors* (Research Monograph Series). Storrs, CT: National Research Center on the Gifted and Talented. (ERIC Document Reproduction Service No. 480177)

Reys, B. J., & Reys, R. E. (2006). The development and publication of elementary textbooks: Let the buyer beware! *Phi Delta Kappan, 87*(5), 377–383.

Reyes, M. L., & Molner, L. A. (1991). Instructional strategies for second-language learners in the content areas. *Journal of Reading, 35,* 96–103.

Richards, H. V., Brown, A. F., & Forde, T. B. (2007). Addressing diversity in schools: Culturally responsive pedagogy. *Teaching Exceptional Children, 39*(3), 64–68.

Riggs, C. G. (2004). To teachers: What paraeducators want you to know. *Teaching Exceptional Children, 36*(5), 8–13.

Riley-Tillman, T. C., Chafouleas, S. M., & Briesch, A. M. (2007). A school practitioner's guide to using daily behavior report cards to monitor student behavior. *Psychology in the Schools, 44*(1), 77–89.

Rimm-Kaufman, S. E., & Chiu, Y. I. (2007). Promoting social and academic competence in the classroom: An intervention study examining the contribution of the responsive classroom approach. *Psychology in the Schools, 44*(4), 397–413.

Rimm-Kaufman, S. E., La Paro, K. M., Downer, J. T., & Pianta, R. C. (2005). The contribution of classroom setting and quality of instruction to children's behavior in kindergarten classrooms. *The Elementary School Journal, 105*(4), 377–394.

Roach, V., & Salisbury, C. (2006). Promoting systemic, statewide inclusion from the bottom up. *Theory into Practice, 45,* 279–286.

Robinson, B. L., & Lieberman, L. J. (2004). Effects of visual impairment, gender, and age on self-determination. *Journal of Visual Impairment and Blindness, 98,* 315–366.

Robinson, D. H., Katayama, A. D., DuBois, N. F., & DeVaney, T. (1998). Interactive effects of graphic organizers and delayed review in concept acquisition. *Journal of Experimental Education, 67,* 17–31.

Roblyer, M. D., Edwards, J., & Havriluk, M. A. (2004). *2004 Update: Integrating education technology into teaching* (3rd ed.). Upper Saddle River, NJ: Merrill/Prentice-Hall.

Roeber, E. D. (2002, November). *Appropriate inclusion of students with disabilities in state accountability systems.* Retrieved August 3, 2004, from Education Commission of the States website, www.ecs.org/clearinghouse/40/11/4011.htm

Rogers-Adkinson, D. L., Ochoa, T. A., & Delgado, B. (2003). Developing cross-cultural competence: Serving families of children with significant developmental needs [Electronic version]. *Focus on Autism and Other Developmental Disabilities, 19,* 4–8.

Rojas, N. L., & Chan, E. (2005). Old and new controversies in the alternative treatment of attention-deficit hyperactivity disorder. *Mental Retardation and Developmental Disabilities Research Reviews, 11*(2), 116–130.

Rose, L. C., & Gallup, A. M. (2006). The 38th annual Phi Delta Kappa/Gallup Poll of the public's attitudes. *Phi Delta Kappan, 88,* 41–53.

Rosenshine, B. (1997). Advances in research on instruction. In E. J. Lloyd, E. J. Kameanui, & D. Chard (Eds.), *Issues in educating students with disabilities* (pp. 197–221). Mahwah, NJ: Lawrence Erlbaum.

Rosenshine, B., & Meister, C. (1992). The use of scaffolds for teaching higher-level cognitive strategies. *Educational Leadership, 49,* 26–33.

Rosenshine, B., & Stevens, R. (1986). Teaching functions. In M. C. Wittrock (Ed.)., *Handbook of research on teaching* (pp. 376–391). New York: Macmillan.

Ross, R., & Kurtz, R. (1993). Making manipulatives work: A strategy for success. *Arithmetic Teacher, 40*(5), 254–257.

Rowland, A. S., Umbach, D. M., Stallone, L., Naftel, A. J., Bohlig, E. M., & Sandler, D. P. (2002). Prevalence of medication treatment for attention deficit-hyperactivity disorder among elementary school children in Johnston County, North Carolina [Electronic version]. *American Journal of Public Health, 92,* 231–234.

Rubin, R. (2005). A blueprint for a strengths-based level system in schools. *Reclaiming Children and Youth: The Journal of Strength-Based Interventions, 14,* 143–145.

Rubinson, F. (2002). Lessons learned from implementing problem-solving teams in urban high schools. *Journal of Educational and Psychological Consultation, 13,* 185–217.

Rudd, F. (2002). *Grasping the promise of inclusion.* (ERIC Document Reproduction Service No. ED471855)

Ruddell, R. B. (2006). *Teaching children to read and write: Becoming an effective literacy teacher* (4th ed.). Boston: Allyn and Bacon.

Ryan, A. L., Halsey, H. N., & Matthews, W. J. (2003). Using functional assessment to promote desirable student behavior in schools. *Teaching Exceptional Children, 35*(5), 8–15.

Ryan, J. B., Kats'yannis, A., Peterson, R., & Chmelar, R. (2007). IDEA 2004 and disciplining students with disabilities. *NASSP Bulletin, 91*(2), 130–140.

Ryan, J. B., Reid, R., & Epstein, M. H. (2004). Peer-mediated intervention studies on academic achievement for students with EBD: A review. *Remedial and Special Education, 25,* 330–341.

Ryan, J. B., Sanders, S., Katsiyannis, A., and Yell, M. L. (2007). Using time-out effectively in the classroom. *Teaching Exceptional Children, 39*(4), 60–67.

Ryndak, D. L., & Alper, S. (2003). *Curriculum and instruction for students with significant disabilities in inclusive settings* (2nd ed.). Boston: Allyn and Bacon.

Sabornie, E. J., & deBettencourt, L. U. (2004). *Teaching students with mild and high-incidence disabilities at the secondary level* (2nd ed.). Upper Saddle River, NJ: Pearson/Merrill/Prentice Hall.

Sabornie, E. J., Evans, C., & Cullinan, D. (2006). Comparing characteristics of high-incidence disability groups. *Remedial and Special Education, 27*(2), 95–104.

Sáenz, L. M., Fuchs, L. S., & Fuchs, D. (2005). Peer-assisted learning strategies for English language learners with learning disabilities. *Exceptional Children, 71,* 231–247.

Safran, S. P., & Oswald, K. (2003). Positive behavior supports: Can schools reshape disciplinary practices? *Exceptional Children, 69,* 361–373.

Sale, P., & Carey, D. M. (1995). The sociometric status of students with disabilities in a full-inclusion school. *Exceptional Children, 62,* 6–19.

Salend, S. J. (2005). Report card models that support communication and differentiation of instruction. *TEACHING Exceptional Children, 37*(4), 28–34.

Salend, S. J. (2006). Explaining your inclusion program to families. *Teaching Exceptional Children, 38*(4), 6–11.

Salend, S. J., & Duhaney, L. M. G., (2002). Grading students in inclusive settings. *Teaching Exceptional Children, 34*(3), 8–15.

Salend, S. J., & Duhaney, L. M. G. (2005). Understanding and addressing the disproportionate representation of students of color in special education. *Intervention in School and Clinic, 40,* 213–221.

Salend, S. J., & Rohena, E. (2003). Students with attention deficit disorders: An overview. *Intervention in School and Clinic, 38*(5), 259–266.

Salend, S. J., & Taylor, L. S. (2002). Cultural perspectives: Missing pieces in the functional assessment process. *Intervention in School and Clinic, 38,* 104–112.

Salend, S. J., Duhaney, D., Anderson, D. J., & Gottschalk, C. (2004). Using the internet to improve homework communication and completion. *Teaching Exceptional Children, 36*(3), 64–74.

Salisbury, C. L., & McGregor, G. (2002). The administrative climate and context of inclusive elementary schools. *Exceptional Children, 68,* 259–274.

Salvia, J., & Ysseldyke, J. E. (2007). *Assessment in special and inclusive education* (10th ed.). Boston: Houghton Mifflin.

Samuels, C. A. (2007, June). Team teaching key to turnaround: Classroom partnerships on behavior, instruction helped produce gains. *Education Week, 26*(42), 34–37. Retrieved July 2, 2007, from www.edweek.org/ew/articles/2007/06/20/42speceds1.h26.html

Sánchez, S. Y. (1999). Learning from the stories of culturally and linguistically diverse families and communities. *Remedial and Special Education, 20,* 351–359.

Saunders, W. M., Foorman, B. R., & Carlson, C. D. (2006). Is a separate block of time for oral English language development in programs for English language learners needed? *The Elementary School Journal, 107*(2), 181–198.

Scanlon, D., & Mellard, D. F. (2002). Academic and participation profiles of school-age dropouts with and without disabilities. *Exceptional Children, 68,* 239–258.

Scattone, D., Tingstrom, D. H., & Wilczynski, S. M. (2006). Increasing appropriate social interactions of children with autism spectrum disorders using social stories. *Focus on Autism and Other Developmental Disabilities, 21,* 211–222.

Scheerenberger, R. C. (1983). *A history of mental retardation.* Baltimore, MD: Paul H. Brookes.

Schifini, A. (1994). Language, literacy, and content instruction: Strategies for teachers. In K. Spangenberg-Unbschat & R. Pritchard (Eds.), *Kids come in all languages: Reading instruction for ESL students* (pp. 158–179). Newark, DE: International Reading Association.

Schmitz, M. F., & Velez, M. (2003). Latino cultural differences in maternal assessments of attention deficit/hyperactivity symptoms in children [Electronic version]. *Hispanic Journal of Behavior Sciences, 25*(1), 110–122.

Schoen, S. F., & Nolen, J. (2004). Action research: Decreasing acting-out behavior and increasing learning. *Teaching Exceptional Children, 37*(1), 26–31.

Schuler, P. (2002). Gifted kids at risk: Who's listening? New York: Advocacy for Gifted and Talented Education in New York. Retrieved March 3, 2004, from http://washougalhicap.virtualave.net/gifted.htm

Schulte, A. C., & Osborne, S. S. (2003). When assumptive worlds collide: A review of definitions of collaboration in consultation. *Journal of Educational and Psychological Consultation, 14*(2), 109–138.

Schumaker, J. B., Deshler, D. D., & Denton, P. (1984). *The learning strategies curriculum: The paraphrasing strategy.* Lawrence: University of Kansas.

Schunk, D. (1989). Self-efficacy and cognitive achievement: Implications for students with learning disabilities. *Journal of Learning Disabilities, 22,* 14–22.

Scott, P. B., & Raborn, D. T. (1996). Realizing the gifts of diversity among students with learning disabilities. *LD Forum, 21*(2), 10–18.

Scott, T. M., & Caron, D. B. (2005). Conceptualizing functional behavior assessment as prevention practice within positive behavior support systems. *Preventing School Failure, 50*(1), 13–20.

Scott, T. M., McIntyre, J., Liaupsin, C., Nelson, C. M., & Conroy, M. (2004). An examination of functional behavior assessment in public school settings: Collaborative teams, experts, and methodology. *Behavioral Disorders, 29,* 384–395.

Scott, T. M., Nelson, C. M., & Liaupsin, C. J. (2001). Effective instruction: The forgotten component in preventing school violence. *Education and Treatment of Children, 24,* 309–322.

Scott, V. G. (2006). Incorporating service learning into your special education classroom. *Intervention in School and Clinic, 42*(1), 25–29.

Scruggs, T., & Mastropieri. M. (1988). Are learning disabled students "test-wise"? A review of recent research. *Learning Disabilities Focus, 3*(2):87–97.

Seeley, K. I. (2004). Gifted and talented students at risk. *Focus on Exceptional Children, 37*(4), 1–8.

Seferian, R. (1999). *Design and implementation of a social-skills program for middle school students with learning and behavioral disabilities.* (ERIC Document Reproduction Service No. ED436863)

Selekman, J. (Ed.). (2006). *School nursing: A comprehensive text.* Philadelphia: F. A. Davis.

Sever, K., & Bowgren, L. (2007). Shaping the workday: District professional learning into the classroom. *Journal of Staff Development, 28*(2), 20–23.

Severson, H. H., Walker, H. M., & Hope-Doolittle, J. (2007). Proactive, early screening to detect behaviorally at-risk students: Issues, approaches, emerging innovations, and professional practices. *Journal of School Psychology, 45,* 193–223.

Shapiro, D. R., & Sayers, L. K. (2003). Who does what on the interdisciplinary team regarding physical education for students with disabilities? *Teaching Exceptional Children, 35*(6), 32–38.

Sharan, S., Kussell, P., Hertz-Lazarowitz, R., Bejarano, Y., Raviv, S., & Sharan, Y. (1984). *Cooperative learning in the classroom: Research in desegregated schools.* Hillsdale, NJ: Lawrence Erlbaum.

Shaywitz, S. (2003). *Overcoming dyslexia: A new and complete science-based program for reading problems at any level.* New York: Knopf.

Shaywitz, S. E., & Shaywitz, B.A. (2007). What neuroscience really tells us about reading instruction. *Educational Leadership, 64*(5), 74–76.

Sheets, R. H. (2002). "You're just a kid that's there"—Chicano perception of disciplinary events [Electronic version]. *Journal of Latinos and Education, 1,* 105–122.

Shepard, M. P., & Mahon, M. M. (2002). Family considerations. In L. L. Hayman, M. M. Mahon, & J. R. Turner (Eds.), *Chronic illness in children: An evidence-based approach* (pp. 143–170). New York: Springer.

Shin, J., Deno, S. L., & Espin, C. (2000). Technical adequacy of the maze task for curriculum-based measurement of reading growth. *Journal of Special Education, 34,* 164–172.

Shinn, M. R., Collins, V. L., & Gallagher, S. (1998). Curriculum-based measurement and problem solving assessment. In M. R. Shinn (Ed.), *Advanced applications of curriculum-based measurement* (pp. 143–174). New York: Guilford Press.

Shinn, M. R., & Hubbard, D. (1992). Curriculum-based measurement and problem-solving assessment: Basic procedures and outcomes. *Focus on Exceptional Children, 24,* 1–20.

Shippen, M. E., Simpson, R. G., & Crites, S. A. (2003). A practical guide to functional behavioral assessment. *Teaching Exceptional Children, 35*(5), 36–44.

Short, D., & Echevarria, J. (2004/2005). Teacher skills to support English language learners. *Educational Leadership, 62*(4), 8–13.

Sideridis, G. S., & Scanlon, D. (Eds.). (2006). Motivational issues in learning disabilities. *Learning Disability Quarterly, 29*(3), 131–135.

Siegal, L. S. (2005). IQ is irrelevant to the definition of learning disabilities. *Journal of Learning Disabilities, 22,* 469–486.

Siegle, D., & McCoach, D. B. (2005). Making a difference: Motivating students who are not achieving. *Teaching Exceptional Children, 38*(1), 22–27.

Sigafoos, J., & Littlewood, R. (1999). Communication intervention on the playground: A case study on teaching requesting to a young child with autism. *International Journal of Disability, Development, and Education, 46,* 421–429.

Silva, M., Munk, D. D., & Bursuck, W. D. (in press). Grading adaptation for students with disabilities. *Intervention in School and Clinic.*

Silver, L. B. (2006). *The misunderstood child: Understanding and coping with your child's learning disabilities.* (4th ed.). New York: Three Rivers Press.

Simmons, R., & Magiera, K. (2007). Evaluation of co-teaching in three high schools within one school district: How do you know when you are TRULY co-teaching? *Teaching Exceptional Children Plus, 3*(3), Article 4. Retrieved July 1, 2007, from http://escholarship.bc.edu/education/tecplus/vol3/iss3/art4

Simos, P. G., Fletcher, J. M., Sarkari, S., Billingsley-Marshall, R. L., Denton, C. A., & Papanicolaou, A. C. (2007). Intensive instruction affects brain magnetic activity associated with oral word reading in children with persistent reading disabilities. *Journal of Learning Disabilities, 40*(1), 37–48.

Simpson, R. L., de Boer-Ott, S., & Smith-Myles, B. (2003). Inclusion of learners with autism spectrum disorders in general education settings. *Topics in Language Disorders, 23,* 116–33.

Sindelar, P. T., Shearer, D. K., Yendol-Hoppey, D., & Liebert, T. W. (2006). The sustainability of inclusive school reform. *Exceptional Children, 72,* 317–331.

Sinha, D., & Efron, D. (2005). Complementary and alternative medicine use in children with attention deficit hyperactivity disorder. *Journal of Paediatrics and Child Health, 41*(1–2), 23–26.

Skiba, R. J., Michael, R. S., Nardo, A. B., & Peterson, R. L. (2002). The color of discipline: Sources of racial and gender disproportionality in school punishment [Electronic version]. *Urban Review, 34,* 317–342.

Skiba, R., Poloni-Staudinger, L., Gallini, S., Simmons, A., & Feggins-Azziz, R. (2006). Disparate access: The disproportionality of African American students with disabilities across educational environments [Electronic version]. *Exceptional Children, 72,* 411–424.

Skiba, R. J., Poloni-Staudinger, L. P., Simmons, A., Feggins-Assiz, L. R., & Chung, C. (2005). Unproven links: Can poverty explain ethnic disproportionality in special education? *Journal of Special Education, 39,* 130–144.

Slavin, R. E. (1994). *Cooperative learning* (2nd ed.). Boston: Allyn and Bacon.

Slavin, R. E. (1999). Comprehensive approaches to cooperative learning [Electronic version]. *Theory into Practice, 38,* 74–79.

Slonski-Fowler, K. E., & Truscott, S. D. (2004). General education teachers' perceptions of the prereferral intervention team process. *Journal of Educational and Psychological Consultation, 15,* 1–39.

Smith, C. R. (2004). *Learning disabilities: The interaction of students and their environments* (5th ed.). Boston: Allyn and Bacon.

Smith, K., & Weitz, M. (2003). Problem solving and gifted education: A differentiated fifth-grade fantasy unit [Electronic version]. *Gifted Child Today, 26*(3), 56–60.

Smith, S., Boone, R., & Higgins, K. (1998). Expanding the writing process to the web. *Teaching Exceptional Children, 30*(5), 22–26.

Smith, T. E. C. (2002). Section 504: What teachers need to know. *Intervention in School and Clinic, 37,* 259–266.

Smith-Arrezzo, W. M. (2003). Diversity in children's literature: Not just a black and white issue [Electronic version]. *Children's Literature in Education, 34,* 75–94.

Snider, V. E. (1997). Transfer of decoding skills to a literature basal. *Learning Disabilities Research and Practice, 12*(1), 54–62.

Snow, C. E., & Biancarosa, G. (2003). *Adolescent literacy and the achievement gap: What do we know about where do we go from here?* New York: Carnegie Corporation of New York.

Snow, C. E., Burns, M. S., & Griffin, P. C. (1998). *Preventing reading difficulties in young children.* Washington, DC: National Academy Press.

Sobel, D. M., & Taylor, S. V. (2006). Blueprint for the responsive classroom. *Teaching Exceptional Children, 38*(5), 28–35.

Spencer, V. G., & Balboni, G. (2003). Can students with mental retardation teach their peers? *Education and Training in Mental Retardation and Developmental Disabilities, 38,* 32–61.

Stainback, S., & Stainback, W. (1988). Educating students with severe disabilities in regular classes. *Teaching Exceptional Children, 21*(1), 16–19.

Stanovich, K., & Siegel, L. S. (1994). Phenotypic performance profile of children with reading disabilities: A regression-based test of the phonological-core variable-difference model. *Journal of Educational Psychology, 86,* 24–53.

Stanovich, P. J., & Jordan, A. (2002). Preparing general educators to teach in inclusive classrooms: Some food for thought [Electronic version]. *Teacher Education, 37,* 173–185.

Starr, E. M., Foy, J. B., Cramer, K. M., & Singh, H. (2006). How are schools doing? Parental perceptions of children with autism spectrum disorders, Down syndrome, and learning disabilities: A comparative analysis. *Training in Developmental Disabilities, 41,* 315–332.

Stein, M., Kinder, D., Silbert, J., & Carnine, D. G. (2005). *Designing effective mathematics instruction: A direct instruction approach.* (4th ed.). Upper Saddle River, NJ: Prentice Hall.

Steiner, H. H. (2006). A microgenetic analysis of strategic variability in gifted and average-ability children. *Gifted Child Quarterly, 50*(1), 62–75.

Stichter, J. P., Conroy, M. A., & Kauffman, J. M. (2007). *An introduction to students with high-incidence disabilities.* Upper Saddle River, NJ: Pearson.

Stipek, D. (2006). Relationships matter. *Educational Leadership, 64*(1), 46–49.

Strang, J. D., & Rourke, B. P. (1985). Arithmetic disability subtypes: The neuropsychological significance of specific arithmetical impairment in childhood. In B. P. Rourke (Ed.), *Neuropsychology of learning disabilities* (pp. 167–182). New York: Guilford Press.

Straus, M. A. (2001). New evidence for the benefits of never spanking [Electronic version]. *Society, 38*(6), 52–60.

Stronge, J. H. (2002). *Qualities of effective teachers.* Alexandria, VA: Association of Supervision and Curriculum Development.

Summers, J. A., Hoffman, L., Marquis, J., Turnbull, A., Poston, D., & Nelson, L. L. (2005). Measuring the quality of family-professional partnerships in special education services. *Exceptional Children, 72*(1), 65–81.

Swain, K. D., Friehe, M. M., & Harrington, J. M. (2004). Teaching listening strategies in the inclusive classroom. *Intervention in School and Clinic, 40,* 48–54.

Swanson, H. L. (2000). What instruction works for students with learning disabilities? Summarizing the results from a meta-analysis of intervention studies. In R. Gersten, E. Schiller, & S. Vaughn (Eds.), *Contemporary special education research: Syntheses of the knowledge based on critical instructional issues* (pp. 1–30). Mahwah, NJ: Lawrence Erlbaum Associates.

Swanson, H. L. (2001). Reading intervention research outcomes and students with learning disabilities: What are the major instructional ingredients for successful outcomes? *Perspectives, 27*(2), 18–20.

Swanson, H. L., & Deshler, D. (2003). Instructing adolescents with learning disabilities: Converting a meta-analysis to practice. *Journal of Learning Disabilities, 36,* 124–135.

Swanson, H. L., & Jerman, O. (2006). Math disabilities: A selective meta-analysis of literature. *Review of Educational Research, 76*(2), 249–274.

Taub, D. J. (2006). Understanding the concerns of parents of students with disabilities: Challenges and roles for school counselors. *Professional School Counseling, 10*(1).

Terman, L. (1925). *Genetic studies of genius: Vol. 1. Mental and physical traits of 1000 gifted children.* Stanford, CA: Stanford University Press.

Test, D. W., & Ellis, M. F. (2005). The effects of LAP fractions on addition and subtraction of fractions with mild disabilities. *Education and Treatment of Children, 28*(1), 11–24.

Test, D. W., Fowler, C. H., Brewer, D., & Wood, W. M. (2005). A content and methodological review of self-advocacy intervention studies. *Exceptional Children, 72*(1), 101–125.

Test, D. W., Mason, C., Hughes, C., Konrad, M., Neale, M., & Wood, W. M. (2004). Student involvement in individualized education program meetings. *Exceptional Children, 70,* 391–412.

Thompson, S., & Thurlow, M. (2003). *2003 state special education outcomes: Marching on.* Minneapolis, MN: University of Minnesota, National Center on Educational Outcomes. Retrieved January 31, 2005, from http://education.umn.edu/NCEO/OnlinePubs/2003StateReport.htm

Thurlow, M. L., Elliott, J. L., & Ysseldyke, J. F. (2003). *Testing students with disabilities: Practical strategies for complying with district and state regulations* (2nd ed.). Thousand Oaks, CA: Corwin Press, Inc.

Thurlow, M. L., Elliott, J. L., & Ysseldyke, J. F. (1998). *Testing students with disabilities: Practical strategies for complying with district and state requirements.* Thousand Oaks, CA: Corwin Press.

Tindal, G. A., & Marston, D. B. (1990). *Classroom-based assessment: Evaluating instructional outcomes.* Columbus, OH: Merrill.

Tindal, G., Mcdonald, M., Tedesco, M., Glasgow, A., Almond, P., Crawford, L., & Hollenbeck, K. (2003). Alternate assessments in reading and math: Development and validation for students with significant disabilities. *Exceptional Children, 69,* 481–494.

Titus, D. N. (2007). Strategies and resources for enhancing the achievement of mobile students. *NASSP Bulletin, 91*(1), 81–97.

Tomlinson, C. A. (2000). Reconcilable differences? Standards-based teaching and differentiation. *Educational Leadership, 58*(1), 6–11.

Tomlinson, C. A. (2001). *How to differentiate instruction in mixed-ability classrooms* (2nd ed.). Alexandria, VA: Association for Supervision and Curriculum Development.

Tomlinson, C. A. (2004). The Möbius effect: Addressing learner variance in schools. *Journal of Learning Disabilities, 37,* 516–524.

Tomlinson, C. A. (2005). Quality curriculum and instruction for highly able students. *Theory into Practice, 44,* 160–166.

Tomlinson, C. A., & Jarvis, J. (2006). Teaching beyond the book. *Educational Leadership, 64*(1), 16–21.

Toney, L. P., Kelley, M. L., & Lanclos, N. F. (2003). Self- and parental monitoring of homework in adolescents: Comparative effects on parents' perceptions of homework behavior problems [Electronic version]. *Child and Family Behavior Therapy, 25,* 35–51.

Topping, K. J. (2005). Trends in peer learning. *Educational Psychology, 25,* 631–645.

Torgesen, J. (1991). Learning disabilities: Historical and conceptual issues. In B. Wong (Ed.), *Learning about learning disabilities* (pp. 3–39). San Diego, CA: Academic Press.

Torgesen, J. K. (2000). Increasing the intensity of interventions in reading: The lingering problem of treatment resisters. *Learning Disabilities: Research and Practice, 15*(1), 55–64.

Toth, K., Munson, J., Meltzoff, A. N., & Dawson, G. (2006). Early predictors of communication development in young children with autism spectrum disorder: Joint attention, imitation, and toy play. *Journal of Autism and Developmental Disorders, 36,* 993–1005.

Tournaki, N. (2003). The differential effects of teaching addition through strategy instruction versus drill and practice to students with and without learning disabilities. *Journal of Learning Disabilities, 36,* 449–458.

Tournaki, N., & Criscitiello, E. (2003). Using peer tutoring as a successful part of behavior management. *Teaching Exceptional Children, 36*(2), 22–29.

Trautman, M. L. (2004). Preparing and managing paraprofessionals. *Intervention in School and Clinic, 39,* 131–138.

Trumbull, E., & Pacheco, M. (2005). Leading with diversity: Cultural competencies for teacher preparation and professional development. Providence, RI: Brown University. (ERIC Document Reproduction Service No. ED494221)

Tucker, J. A. (1985). Curriculum-based assessment: An introduction. *Exceptional Children, 52,* 199–204.

Turnbull, A. P., Blue-Banning, M., & Pereira, L. (2000). Successful friendships of Hispanic children and youth with disabilities: An exploratory study. *Mental Retardation, 38,* 138–153.

Turnbull, A. P., Pereira, L., & Blue-Banning, M. J. (2000). Teachers as friendship facilitators. *Teaching Exceptional Children, 32*(5), 66–70.

Turnbull, H. R., Turnbull, A. P., Wehmeyer, M. L., & Park, J. (2003). A quality of life framework for special education outcomes. *Remedial and Special Education, 24,* 67–74.

Turnbull, R., Huerta, N., & Stowe, M. (2006). *The Individuals with Disabilities Education Act as amended in 2004.* Upper Saddle River, NJ: Merrill.

U.S. Department of Education. (2004). PBIS goals. Retrieved December 19, 2004, from the U.S. Office of Special Education Programs, National Technical Assistance Center on Positive Behavioral Interventions and Supports (PBIS) website: www.pbis.org.

U.S. Department of Education. (2004a). PBIS goals. Retrieved December 19, 2004, from the U.S. Office of Special Education Programs, National Technical Assistance Center on Positive Behavioral Interventions and Supports (PBIS) website, www.pbis.org

U.S. Department of Education. (2004b). *26th annual report to Congress on the implementation of the Individuals with Disabilities Education Act.* Washington, DC: Author.

U.S. Department of Education. (2007, February). Bilingual cooperative integrated reading and composition (pp. 1–12). *What Works Clearinghouse Intervention Report.* (ERIC Document Reproduction Service No. ED495727). Retrieved August 31, 2007, from www.eric.ed.gov/ERICDocs/data/ericdocs2sql/content_storage_01/0000019b/80/29/e3/b6.pdf

U.S. Department of Education. (2007). *Final regulations on modified academic achievement standards.* Retrieved October 23, 2007, from Special Education and Rehabilitative Services website www.ed.gov/policy/speced/guid/modachieve-summary.html

U.S. Department of Health and Human Services. (2007, April). *Results from the 2005 national survey on drug use and health: National findings.* Washington, DC: Author. Retrieved August 2, 2007, from www.oas.samhsa.gov/NSDUH/2k5NSDUH/2k5results.htm#Ch2

U.S. Department of Health and Human Services, Children's Bureau. (2006, June). *Child maltreatment 2004.* Washington, DC: Author. Retrieved July 31, 2007, from www.acf.hhs.gov/programs/cb/pubs/cm04/index.htm

U.S. Department of Health and Human Services, Office of Civil Rights. (2006, June). *Fact sheet: Your rights under Section 504 of the Rehabilitation Act.* Retrieved October 18, 2007, from www.hhs.gov/ocr/504.pdf

U.S. Department of Justice, Bureau of Justice Statistics. (2005). *School crime supplement (SCS) to the National Crime Victimization Survey* [Table 17.1]. Retrieved August 10, 2007, from http://nces.ed.gov/pubs2006/2006001.pdf

Uberti, H. Z., Mastropieri, M. A., & Scruggs, T. E. (2004). Check it off: Individualizing a math algorithm for students with disabilities via self-monitoring checklists. *Intervention in School and Clinic, 39,* 269–275.

Uberti, H. Z., Scruggs, T. E., & Mastropieri, M. A. (2003). Keywords make the difference! Mnemonic instruction in inclusive classrooms. *Teaching Exceptional Children, 35*(3), 56–61.

Ulrich, M. E., & Bauer, A. M. (2003). Levels of awareness: A closer look at communication between parents and professionals. *Teaching Exceptional Children, 35*(6), 20–25.

United Cerebral Palsy (n.d.). *Cerebral palsy—facts and figures.* Retrieved November 26, 2004, from www.ucp.org/ucp_generaldoc.cfm/1/9/37/37–37/447

United Federation of Teachers. (2007, August). *Child abuse: Questions and answers for New York City's educators* (7th ed.). New York: Author. Retrieved August 2, 2007 from www.uft.org/member/education/development/brochure/article3

Vacca, R. T., & Vacca, J. L. (2004). *Content area reading: Literacy and learning across the curriculum* (8th ed.). Boston: Little, Brown.

Vandercook, T., York, J., & Forest, M. (1989). The McGill Action Planning System (MAPS): A strategy for building the vision. *Journal of the Association for Persons with Severe Handicaps (JASH), 14*(3), 205–218.

VanTassel-Baska, J. (2003). *Curriculum planning and instructional design for gifted learners.* Denver, CO: Love.

Vaughan, W. (2002). Effects of cooperative learning on achievement and attitudes among students of color. *Journal of Educational Research, 95,* 359–364.

Vaughn, S., & Haager, D. (1994). Social competence as a multifaceted construct: How do students with learning disabilities fare? *Learning Disability Quarterly, 2,* 253–266.

Vaughn, S., Linan-Thompson, S., Kouzekanani, K., Bryant, D. P., Dickson, S., & Blozis, S. A. (2003). Reading instruction grouping for students with reading difficulties. *Remedial and Special education, 24,* 301–315.

Verte, S., Geurts, H. M., & Roeyers, H. (2006). Executive functioning in children with an autism spectrum disorder: Can we differentiate within the spectrum? *Journal of Autism and Developmental Disorders, 36,* 351–372.

Villa, R. A., Thousand, J. S., Nevin, A., & Liston, A. (2005). Successful inclusive practices in middle and secondary schools. *American Secondary Education, 33*(3), 33–50.

Voix, R. G. (1968). *Evaluating reading and study skills in the secondary classroom: A guide for content teachers.* Newark, DE: International Reading Association.

Wade, S. L., Stancin, T., & Taylor, H. G. (2004). Interpersonal stressors and resources as predictors of parental adaptation following pediatric traumatic injury. *Journal of Consulting and Clinical Psychology, 72,* 776–784.

Wagner, M., Cadwallader, T. W., Garza, N., & Cameto, R. (2004, March). *Social activities of youth with disabilities* (NLTS2 Data Brief). Retrieved November 20, 2004, from www.ncset.org

Wakeman, S. Y., Browder, D. M., & Flowers, C. (2006). Principals' knowledge of fundamental and current issues in special education. *NASSP Bulletin, 90,* 153–174.

Walker, C. J. (2006). Adequate access or equal treatment: Looking beyond the IDEA to Section 504 in a post-Schaffer public school. *Stanford Law Review, 58,* 1563–1622.

Walker, H. M., & Rankin, R.J. (1983). Assessing the behavioral expectations and demands of less restrictive settings [SBS inventory of teacher social behavior standards and expectations and the SBS checklist of correlates of child handicapping conditions]. *The School Psychology Review, 12,* 274–284.

Walker, J. E., Shea, T. M., & Bauer, A. M. (2003). *Behavior management: A practical approach for educators* (8th ed.). Columbus, OH: Merrill/Prentice Hall.

Walker, L. (2006). Violence prevention through cooperative learning. *Reclaiming Children and Youth, 15*(1), 32–36.

Wallace, T., Anderson, A. R., & Bartholomay, T. (2002). Collaboration: An element associated with the success of four inclusive high schools. *Journal of Educational and Psychological Consultation, 13,* 349–382.

Wang, M. C., Reynolds, M. C., & Walberg, H. J. (1988). Integrating the children of the second system. *Phi Delta Kappan, 70,* 248–251.

Wanzek, J., Vaughn, S., Wexler, J., Swanson, E., Edmonds, M., & Kim, A. (2006). A synthesis of spelling and reading interventions and their effects on the spelling outcomes of students with LD. *Journal of Learning Disabilities, 39*(6), 528–543.

Warren, J. S., Bohanon-Edmonson, H. M., Turnbull, A. P., Sailor, W., Wickham. D., Griggs, P., et al. (2006). School-wide positive behavior support: Addressing behavior problems that impede student learning. *Educational Psychology Review, 18,* 187–198.

Wasburn-Moses, L. (2005). Roles and responsibilities of secondary special education teachers in an age of reform. *Remedial and Special Education, 26,* 151–158.

Wasburn-Moses, L. (2006). Obstacles to program effectiveness in secondary special education. *Preventing School Failure, 50*(3), 21–30.

Watson, S. (2004). Open the science doorway: Strategies and suggestions for incorporating English language learners in the science classroom. *Science Teacher, 71*(2), 32–35.

Wehmeyer, M. (2002). *Self-determination and the education of students with disabilities* (ERIC Digest). Reston, VA: ERIC Clearinghouse on Disabilities and Gifted Education. (ERIC Document Reproduction Service No. ED470036)

Wehmeyer, M. L. (2007). *Promoting self-determination in students with developmental disabilities: What works for special-needs learners.* New York: Guilford Publications.

Wehmeyer, M. L., Lattin, D. L., Lapp-Rincker, G., & Agran, M. (2003). Access to the general curriculum of middle school students with mental retardation: An observational study. *Remedial and Special Education, 24,* 262–272.

Welch, A. B. (2000). Responding to student concerns about fairness. *Teaching Exceptional Children, 33*(2), 36–40.

Welner, K. (2006). Legal rights: The overrepresentation of culturally and linguistically diverse students in special education. *Teaching Exceptional Children, 38*(6), 60–62.

Welton, E., Vakil, S., & Carasea, C. (2004). Strategies for increasing positive social interactions in children with autism: A case study. *Teaching Exceptional Children, 37*(1), 40–46.

Werts, M. G., Harris, S., Tillery, C. Y., & Roark, R. (2004). What parents tell us about paraeducators. *Remedial and Special Education, 25,* 232–239.

Whalen, C. K., Jamner, L. D., Henker, B., Delfino, R. J., & Lozano, J. (2002). The ADHD spectrum and everyday life: Experience sampling of moods, activities, smoking, and drinking. *Child Development, 73,* 209–227.

Wheeler, J. J., & Richey, D. D. (2005). *Behavior management: Principles and practices of positive behavior supports.* Upper Saddle River, NJ: Merrill/Prentice Hall.

Whitbread, K. M., Bruder, M. B., Fleming, G., & Park, H. J. (2007). Collaboration in special education parent-professional training. *Teaching Exceptional Children, 39*(4), 6–14.

Wiggins, R. A., Follow, E. J., & Eberly, M. B. (2007). The impact of a field immersion program on pre-service teachers' attitudes toward teaching in culturally diverse classrooms. *Teaching and Teacher Education, 23,* 653–663.

Wilen, W. W., Ishler, M., Hutchinson, J., & Kindsvatter, R. (1999). *Dynamics of effective teaching* (4th ed.). Boston: Allyn and Bacon.

Williams, G. J., & Reisberg, L. (2003). Successful inclusion: Teaching social skills through curriculum integration. *Intervention in School and Clinic, 38,* 205–210.

Willaimson, P., McLeskey, J., Hoppey, D., & Rentz, T. (2006). Educating students with mental retardation in general education classrooms. *Exceptional Children, 72*(3), 347–361.

Winn, J., & Blanton, L. (2005). The call for collaboration in teacher education. *Focus on Exceptional Children, 38*(2), 1–10.

Winnick, J. P. (Ed.). (2005). *Adapted physical education and sport* (4th ed.). Champaign, IL: Human Kinetics.

Winter-Messiers, M. A., Herr, C. M., Wood, C. E., Brooks, A. P., Gates, M. A. M., Houston, T. L., & Tingstad, K. I. (2007). How far can Brian ride the Daylight 4449 Express? A strength-based model of Asperger syndrome based on special interest areas. *Focus on Autism and Other Developmental Disabilities, 22,* 67–79.

Winzer, M. A. (1993). *The history of special education: From isolation to integration.* Washington, DC: Gallaudet University Press.

Wolf, P. S., & Hall, T. E. (2003). Making inclusion a reality for students with severe disabilities. *Teaching Exceptional Children, 35*(4), 56–61.

Wolfgang, C. H. (2001). The many views of "time-out": Teaching strategies [Electronic version]. *Journal of Early Education and Family Review, 8*(5), 18–28.

Wolraich, M. L., Wibbelsman, C. J., Brown, T. E., Evans, S. W., Gotlieb, E. M., Knight, J. R., et al. (2005). Attention-deficit/hyperactivity disorder among adolescents: A review of the diagnosis, treatment, and clinical implications. *Pediatrics, 115*(6), 1734–1746.

Wong, H. K., & Wong, R. T. (1998). *How to be an effective teacher: The first days of school.* Mountain View, CA: Harry K. Wong Publications.

Woods, J., & Poulson, C. L. (2006). The use of scripts to increase the verbal initiations of children with developmental disabilities to typically developing peers. *Education and Treatment of Children, 29,* 437–457.

Wormeli, R. (2006). *Fair isn't always equal: Assessing and grading in the differentiated classroom.* Portland, ME: Stenhouse Publishers.

Wright, J. (2007). *Behavior contracts.* Retrieved August 6, 2007, from www.interventioncentral.org/htmdocs/interventions/behavior/behcontr.php

Wright, P. W. D., & Wright, P. D. (2006). *IDEA 2004.* Hartfield, VA: Harbor House Law Press.

Wright-Gallo, G. L., Higbee, T. S., & Reagon, K. A. (2006). Classroom-based functional analysis and intervention for students with emotional/behavioral disorders. *Education and Treatment of Children, 29,* 421–434.

Wright-Gallo, G. L., Higbee, T. S., Reagon, K. A., & Davey, B. J. (2006). Classroom-based functional analysis and intervention for students with emotional/behavioral disorders. *Education and Treatment of Children, 29*(3), 421–436.

Yang, Y. F. (2002). Reassessing readers comprehension monitoring. *Reading in a Foreign Language, 14,* 18–42.

Yarger, C. C. (2001). Educational interpreting: Understanding the rural experience. *American Annals of the Deaf, 146,* 16–30.

Yell, M. L. (1990). The use of corporal punishment, suspension, expulsion, and timeout with behaviorally disordered students in public schools: Legal considerations. *Behavioral Disorders, 15,* 100–109.

Yell, M. L. (2005). *Law and special education* (2nd ed.). Upper Saddle River, NJ: Merrill.

Yell, M. L., Katisyannis, A., & Shiner, J. G. (2006). The *No Child Left Behind Act,* adequate yearly progress, and students with disabilities. *Teaching Exceptional Children, 38*(4), 32–39.

Yell, M. L., Rogers, D., & Rogers, E. L. (1998). The legal history of special education: What a long, strange trip it's been! *Remedial and Special Education, 19,* 219–228.

Yell, M., Clyde, K., & Puyallup, S. K. (1995). School district: The courts, inclusion, and students with behavioral disorders. *Behavioral Disorders, 20,* 179–189.

Youse, K. M., Le, K. N., Cannizzaro, M. S., & Coelho, C. A. (2002, June). Traumatic brain injury: A primer for professionals. *ASHA Leader Online.* Retrieved February 20, 2005, from www.asha.org/about/publications/leader-online/archives/2002/q2/020625a.htm

Ysseldyke, J., Algozzine, B., & Thurlow, M. L. (2000). *Critical issues in special education* (3rd ed.). Boston: Houghton Mifflin.

Zhang, C., & Bennett, T. (2003). Facilitating the meaningful participation of culturally and linguistically diverse families in the IFSP and IEP process [Electronic version]. *Focus on Autism and Other Developmental Disabilities, 18,* 51–59.

Zigmond, M. (2003). Where should students with disabilities receive special education services? Is one place better than another? *Journal of Special Education, 37,* 193–199.

Zilz, W. A. (2006). Manifestation determination: Rulings of the courts. *Education and the Law, 18*(2), 193–206.

Zirkel, P. A. (2004). The case law on gifted education: A new look. *Gifted Child Quarterly, 48,* 309–314.

Zuvekas, S. H., Vitiello, B., & Nordquist, G. S. (2006). Recent trends in stimulant medication use among U.S. children. *American Journal of Psychiatry, 163,* 586–593.

Name Index

Subject Index

characteristics and needs of students with, 280–282
controversial therapies for, 258–259
defined, 279
families of children with, 285–289
interventions for students with, 283–286, 287–288
students eligible for services under Section 504, 278–279
Attribution retraining, 267–268
Auditory processing training, 258
Augmentative and alternative communication (AAC), 212, 213
Authentic learning tasks, 430
Autism Society of America, 200
Autism spectrum disorders (ASD), 199–203
  Asperger syndrome, 19, 23, 201
  characteristics of students with, 200–201
  communicating with students with, 200, 202–203
  functional behavior assessment with, 456
  nature of, 22, 23, 197
  supporting appropriate behavior, 202
  teaching students with, 202, 204–205

Background knowledge, 173, 330–336
Balanced grading, 427–428
Basal textbooks, 172, 174–175
Basic skills instruction, 318–328
  adapting for students with special needs, 318–328
  asking for help, 323
  defined, 318
  direct instruction opportunities for practice and review, 323–328
  INCLUDE strategy in, 327, 328–329
  preskills, 319
  probes in, 129–136
  rate of introduction of new skills, 322
  selecting and sequencing examples, 319–321
Beach Center on Disability, 44
Behavior contracts, 264, 472–474
Behavior disabilities. See Emotional disturbance
Behavior intervention plan (BIP), 63, 166, 451, 461–464
  developing, 461
  implementing, 461
  monitoring, 461–464
  sample, 462–463
Behavior management
  classroom, 166–167, 474–475
  helping students manage own behavior, 474–475
Behavior Problem Checklist, 280
Big ideas, 172–173
Bilingual education programs, 302–303
Bilingual special education programs, 302–303
Bilingual special education teachers, 43
Bilingual teachers, 43
Blacks. See African Americans
Blending, in reading instruction, 298
Blindness, 214–215
Board of Education of Hendrick Hudson School District v. Rowley, 8
Braille, 220
Brain gym, 258
Brainstorming, 89
  INCLUDE strategy and, 158–161
Brown v. Board of Education, 8, 9, 294, 499
Bullying, functional behavior assessment with, 457
Bypass strategies, 158

CALL UP strategy, 383–385
Cancer, 230–231
CAPS strategy, 378
CAST (Center for Applied Special Technology), 153, 348
Catapress (clonidine), 288
Catch 'Em Being Good strategy, 450
Center for Applied Technology (CAST), 153, 348
Center for Collaborative Organization, University of North Texas, 94
Center for Effective Collaboration and Practice, 82, 264, 468
Center for Innovations, University of Missouri, 141
Centers for Disease Control and Prevention, 201, 286, 307, 308, 440
Cerebral palsy, 226
CHECK strategy, 391
Child abuse, 304–305, 306
Child neglect, 304–305
Children and Adults with Attention Deficit Disorder (CHADD), 279
Children's Defense Fund, 304
CHROME strategy, 408
Chunking, 408
Circle of Friends program, 46, 486
Civil rights movement, 8–10, 173, 294, 499
Clarity, 346–351
  in oral communication, 348–351
  in written communication, 347–348
Classroom climate, 165–166
Classroom groupings, 155, 168–170, 309
  large-group, 169–170
  one-to-one instruction, 170–171
  small-group, 170
  student behavior and, 450
  whole-class, 169–170
Classroom management, 155, 162–168
  behavior management in, 166–167, 474–475
  classroom climate, 165–166
  classroom rules, 166, 445
  instructional environments conducive to learning, 443–444
  monitoring, 166–167
  physical organization, 162–165
  routines for classroom business, 165
  use of time, 167–169
Classroom rules, 166, 445
Classroom tests, 406–418
  accommodations after test, 407, 414–418
  accommodations before test, 406–411, 412
  accommodations during test, 407, 411–414
  adaptations in construction of, 410, 412, 413–414
  adaptations of test administration, 414
  alternative grading procedures, 414–418
Classwide Peer Tutoring (CWPT), 494, 495
Clonidine (Catapress), 288
Cluster programs, 196
Cognitive and learning strategies, 156, 186. See also Learning strategies
Cognitive behavior management (CBM), 474–475
  nature of, 474–475
  teaching, 475
Collaboration, 77–110
  characteristics of, 79–86
  complexities of, 97–98
  consultation, 96–97
  co-teaching, 91–94, 160
  defined, 20, 79
  electronic, 87
  importance of, 20
  learning from others, 261

with other professionals, 310
with paraprofessionals, 108–109
with parents, 103–105, 210–212, 302, 311, 351–352, 356–357, 491
prerequisites for, 82–85
with related services personnel, 81
with school library media specialists, 88
for secondary teachers, 80, 106
shared problem solving, 86–91
to support students with significant disabilities, 211
team teaching, 92, 93–96
Communication
  augmentative and alternative (AAC), 212, 213
  barriers to effective, 84
  cross-cultural, 298–301
  effective classroom, 444
  home–school, 103
  improving clarity in, 346–351
  of observations, 48–49
  oral, 348–351
  with parents, 119, 421
  about peer tutoring, 498–499
  by school subject area, 351
  with students with autism spectrum disorders, 200, 202–203
  written. See Writing strategies; Written language skills
Communication disorders, 242–248
  accommodation for, 245–248
  language problems, 244–245
  speech problems, 243, 244–248
Community time, 68
Compensatory strategies, 158
Competency checklist, 417–418
Comprehension problems, 251
Computers. See also Assistive technology (AT); Technology
  collaboration with, 87
  collaboration with school library media specialists, 88
  in curriculum-based assessments (CBA), 142–143
  drill-and-practice software, 178
  electronic portfolios, 433–434
  hearing impairments and, 223, 225
  to improve student writing performance, 330–331, 332–333, 389–391
  for individualized education programs (IEPs), 60
  students with ADHD and, 285
  tutorials, 178
  visual impairments and, 221
Concept diagrams, 346
Concept maps, 330–331, 340
Concerta (methylphenidate), 287
Conferences, parent, 103–104
Connors Rating Scale, 280
Consequences, 166
Consultants, 43
Consultation, 96–97
Consulting teachers, 38
Content-area assessments, 136–140
  evaluating content-area textbook reading skills, 138–139
  measures of independent learning skills, 137–140
  probes of prerequisite skills, 136–137
Content-area textbooks, 138–139, 172–173
Contracts, behavior, 264, 472–474
Controlled materials, 373
Cooperative Integrated Reading and Composition (CIRC), 505

Photo Credits